COMPENDIUM

WRITTEN AND COMPILED BY

Salamat Ali (*Pakistan*)

Rowan Callick (*Papua Ne*

Su-ching Jean Chen (*T*

Neeraj Chowdhary (*In*

Don Cohn, Kari Huus (*China*)

Krzysztof Darewicz (*North Korea*)

Celine Fernandez (*Brunei, Malaysia*)

Veronica Garbutt (*Philippines*)

S. Kamaluddin (*Bangladesh*)

Neil Kelly (*Thailand*)

Lee Jung Hee (*South Korea*)

Mary Lee (*Singapore*)

Jeffrey Lilley (*Russian Far East*)

urma, Laos)

(*Sri Lanka*)

sian Republics)

Brian S

Manik de Silva (*Ma ves*)

Kedar Man Singh (*Nepal*)

Nate Thayer (*Cambodia*)

Vu Hong Anh (*Vietnam*)

Michael Westlake (*Hong Kong, Macau*)

Editor: Michael Westlake

Production Editor: Henry Chiu
Winnie Law (*Deputy*)
Leong Suk Bing (*Assistant*)

CATHAY PACIFIC
Swire Group
CONNECTIONS
From 43 cities around the world we offer you the most convenient connections around Asia and also on to 14 cities in China with our sister airline Dragonair. Cathay Pacific.
The Heart of Asia.

CONTENTS

COMPENDIUM EDITION

Review Publishing Co. Ltd., G.P.O. Box 160, Hong Kong

ISBN 962-701-060-X

Printed in Hong Kong

RUSSIA
KAZAKHSTAN
MONGOLIA
UZBEKISTAN
KIRGYZSTAN
N. KOREA
S. KOREA
TAJIKISTAN
PAKISTAN
CHINA
JAPAN
NEPAL
BHUTAN
BANGLADESH
LAOS
TAIWAN
BURMA
HONG KONG
MACAU
INDIA
VIETNAM
THAILAND
PHILIPPINES
CAMBODIA
BRUNEI
MALAYSIA
SRI LANKA
SINGAPORE
PAPUA
NEW
GUINEA
MALDIVES
INDONESIA

STANDARD TIME CONVERSION

Find your location, move across columns to current hour. Move up or down the vertical column to find the time in other zones. An asterisk (*) indicates that 30 minutes must be added to the hour.

Time in blue shaded area is yesterday. Time in grey shaded area is tomorrow. (Example: when it is 10 a.m. Tuesday in Hong Kong it is 9 p.m. Monday in New York.)

The chart below lists standard times only: Summer Time or Daylight Saving Time is observed in many countries, some with regional variations.

Tokyo, Fukuoka, Osaka, Seoul, Darwin*, Adelaide*	1	2	3	4	5	6	7	8	9	10	11	12	13	14	15	16	17	18	19	20	21	22	23	24
Sydney, Melbourne, Brisbane, Hobart, Port Moresby, Vladivostock	2	3	4	5	6	7	8	9	10	11	12	13	14	15	16	17	18	19	20	21	22	23	24	1
New Caledonia, Solomon Islands, New Hebrides	3	4	5	6	7	8	9	10	11	12	13	14	15	16	17	18	19	20	21	22	23	24	1	2
Auckland, Fiji, Wake Island, Kiribati	4	5	6	7	8	9	10	11	12	13	14	15	16	17	18	19	20	21	22	23	24	1	2	3
American Samoa, Western Samoa	5	6	7	8	9	10	11	12	13	14	15	16	17	18	19	20	21	22	23	24	1	2	3	4
Hawaiian Islands, Cook Islands	6	7	8	9	10	11	12	13	14	15	16	17	18	19	20	21	22	23	24	1	2	3	4	5
Anchorage, Tahiti	7	8	9	10	11	12	13	14	15	16	17	18	19	20	21	22	23	24	1	2	3	4	5	6
Los Angeles, San Francisco, Seattle, San Diego, Vancouver	8	9	10	11	12	13	14	15	16	17	18	19	20	21	22	23	24	1	2	3	4	5	6	7
Edmonton, Calgary, Denver, Salt Lake City, Albuquerque	9	10	11	12	13	14	15	16	17	18	19	20	21	22	23	24	1	2	3	4	5	6	7	8
Chicago, Detroit, Houston, Mexico City, San Jose, Managua	10	11	12	13	14	15	16	17	18	19	20	21	22	23	24	1	2	3	4	5	6	7	8	9
New York, Boston, Washington D.C., Atlanta, Miami, Toronto, Bogota	11	12	13	14	15	16	17	18	19	20	21	22	23	24	1	2	3	4	5	6	7	8	9	10
Halifax, Bermuda, San Juan, Caracas, La Paz, Santiago	12	13	14	15	16	17	18	19	20	21	22	23	24	1	2	3	4	5	6	7	8	9	10	11
Buenos Aires, Rio de Janeiro, Sao Paulo, Montevideo	13	14	15	16	17	18	19	20	21	22	23	24	1	2	3	4	5	6	7	8	9	10	11	12
Part of Greenland, South Georgia	14	15	16	17	18	19	20	21	22	23	24	1	2	3	4	5	6	7	8	9	10	11	12	13
The Azores, Cape Verde	15	16	17	18	19	20	21	22	23	24	1	2	3	4	5	6	7	8	9	10	11	12	13	14
London, Dublin, Iceland, Dakar, Accra	16	17	18	19	20	21	22	23	24	1	2	3	4	5	6	7	8	9	10	11	12	13	14	15
Stockholm, Amsterdam, Paris, Rome, Frankfurt, Zurich, Lagos	17	18	19	20	21	22	23	24	1	2	3	4	5	6	7	8	9	10	11	12	13	14	15	16
Helsinki, Athens, Bucharest, Cairo, Johannesburg	18	19	20	21	22	23	24	1	2	3	4	5	6	7	8	9	10	11	12	13	14	15	16	17
Moscow, Leningrad, Bahrain, Riyadh, Nairobi, Madagascar	19	20	21	22	23	24	1	2	3	4	5	6	7	8	9	10	11	12	13	14	15	16	17	18
Gorki, Baku, Dubai, Muscat, Seychelles Islands, Mauritius	20	21	22	23	24	1	2	3	4	5	6	7	8	9	10	11	12	13	14	15	16	17	18	19
Karachi, Bombay*, New Delhi*, Calcutta*, Colombo	21	22	23	24	1	2	3	4	5	6	7	8	9	10	11	12	13	14	15	16	17	18	19	20
Rangoon*, Tashkent	22	23	24	1	2	3	4	5	6	7	8	9	10	11	12	13	14	15	16	17	18	19	20	21
Bangkok, Jakarta, Hanoi, Medan	23	24	1	2	3	4	5	6	7	8	9	10	11	12	13	14	15	16	17	18	19	20	21	22
Hong Kong, China, Taipei, Manila, Singapore, Brunei, Malaysia, Perth	24	1	2	3	4	5	6	7	8	9	10	11	12	13	14	15	16	17	18	19	20	21	22	23

AMERICAN EXPRESS

INTRODUCTION

Humorist Nury Vittachi, author of the *Far Eastern Economic Review*'s popular Travellers' Tales column, takes a tongue-in-cheek look at travelling in Asia:

Mankind has always travelled. Scientists believe that early man originated in Africa. How did humans end up infesting the entire world? Obviously, they went on early package tours. I mean, you don't get from the cradle of civilization in Africa to the four corners of the globe without some kind of *logistics*. At some stage, our ancestors must have been standing around when one of them said: "I need a break. We've been in this jungle, what, a couple of million years?"

"Yeah," replies his buddy. "Let's go and see if there are any, like, ski slopes or something out there." They would then have headed to their nearest primitive hominid travel agency, where they would be told: "Sorry guys, Pterodactyl Airlines is fully booked for centuries yet. Best I can do is put you on a waiting list for four days and three nights in the Neanderthal Valley, if you don't mind the locals."

So off they went to buy tickets to ride the next available Velociraptor Overland Express **(Warning: Take lots to eat during your trip, or the 'raptor may eat *you*)**. Without any further ado or prehistoric humour, the rest — literally — is history.

Of course, you will notice that the people who stomped around at two miles an hour on their own two feet — Homo erectus, Australopithicus, Cro-Magnon man, the Neanderthals and so on — are all extinct. But Homo sapiens, who ultimately invented the Asian traffic jam, is alive and well, albeit only moving at about one mile an hour.

Travelling has become a major part of life for modern man. You have a big choice of transport systems in Asia. There are still man-drawn rickshaws in Hong Kong, though some of the elderly gentlemen who operate these appear to hail from the aforementioned Cro-Magnon period. In Ho Chi Minh City I was pedalled along in a bicycle-rickshaw by a man so thin and wiry that I felt obliged to offer to get out and change places with him. He declined, clearly suspecting me of planning to muscle in on his business.

But no one travels through Asia expecting — or wanting — the slick, impersonal service industries of the West. No, the challenges of moving around the region only add to the spirit of adventure that inspires people to trek around here. And your rewards are the unforgettable sights, sounds, smells and experiences of Asia — well documented in this comprehensive book.

Here are some practical pointers to help you on your way:

- Do not carry drugs. There is no surer way to put the dampeners on your Asian holiday than to find yourself having to undergo the death penalty in any of the several countries which apply it to those found carrying illegal substances. You may think

◄ *A Thai temple guardian typifies Asia's beauty and colour.* PHOTO: THE STOCK HOUSE

that's not funny. You're right, it's not.

- These days, no traveller needs to be reminded not to drink the water — but do take some stomach-settling pills, because sometimes you have no choice. In Vietnam, bottles of water are labelled "Free Bacteria" and it is a moot point whether this means "Bacteria-free" or what it actually says. I once opened a bottle of "mineral" water in a well-known Hong Kong restaurant only to find the last user's straw bobbing around inside. The restaurateur casually refills old bottles from the tap.
- Be nice to people in uniform, especially at airports. Remember that you have to have your sense of humour surgically removed to get a job as an airline official in Asia. Airport security is an arcane mystery, so be ready to accept new and ever more bizarre rules.

A friend of mine had his mangos confiscated "for security reasons" when boarding a domestic flight in India. He wondered whether this meant hijackers had once used the line: "Take me to Cuba or I'll squish this mango on your nice uniform."

- Travel light. The secret of this can be summed up in one word: layers. Don't carry an all-weather range of clothes. Take a lot of thin garments that can be worn on top of each other. In fiery Rajasthan, I wore a thin pair of short trousers. When I got to chilly Simla, I wore every garment in my bag.
- Take more money than you think you need. For decades, Westerners came to Asia and wrote postcards home saying: "Everything's so cheap here in the Third World. I bought a meal for four people for the equivalent of US$4." Now people from Singapore, Tokyo, Hong Kong and Beijing, write postcards back from London saying: "Everything's so cheap here in the Third World. I bought a meal for four people for the equivalent of 39 Singapore dollars."
- Be adventurous, within reason, especially in matters of food. Contrary to popular belief, Asians invented fast food, and still serve the tastiest, quickest meals in the world.

I wouldn't want you to think that swanning around the region is all sweetness and light. Here are my top bugbears about travelling in Asia:

- ▶ The ticket sales window you need to go to is the one with an impenetrable mass of bodies around it.
- ▶ The list of rules at your hotel appears to have been written by a surrealist.
- ▶ The person ahead of you at check-in thinks that if he spends enough time haranguing the staff, he can fly on an invalid ticket.
- ▶ The inflight audio tape is looped so that the track you want to hear is always omitted.
- ▶ The meal you didn't choose looks and smells edible, unlike what's on your tray.
- ▶ Any climactic moment in the inflight film is interrupted by a long announcement which has to be repeated in three languages.
- ▶ The person in front of you in the immigration queue has a passport from Belize with someone else's picture in it.
- ▶ The customs officer whose channel you choose is suffering from severe dyspepsia and has just been told his arrest quota is low.

The horror stories are often exaggerated, but when they are based on fact they can ruin your trip. They comprise one of the reasons that this book is updated. In each chapter you'll find a section warning you about the rip-offs which exist everywhere in one form or another. The edition you hold in your hands — the 17th — has been completely updated. These days, Asia really is a shoppers' paradise, with practically anything you can imagine on sale at streetside market stalls in every country. But the hardest thing to get in Asia remains reliable, good quality information — which is what we offer you in this book. Have a good trip.

The mosque and the Kampung Ayer. PHOTO: HILARY ANDREWS

ALL-ASIA TRAVEL GUIDE

SOUTHEAST ASIA

BRUNEI

Islam, gas and oil dominate the tiny sultanate of Brunei, socially, physically and economically. The capital, Bandar Seri Begawan, is built round the magnificent Omar Ali Saifuddin Mosque, which overlooks Kampung Ayer, a collection of villages perched on stilts over the Brunei River.

On shore, the capital is the centre of government and religion, though the economic heart of the state is 100 kilometres away at the oil and gas fields of Seria and Kuala Belait.

The state's wealth is entirely based on oil and natural gas, giving residents one of the highest standards of living in the world with a per capita income more than 30% higher than European Community residents. Moves to diversify the country's economic base are making slow progress — for instance, $4 billion was set aside for this purpose in the five years to 1990. With a limit on Brunei's oil reserves of around the year 2010 at recent extraction rates, these moves are likely to gather pace.

The objective is to provide alternative employment opportunities as oil reserves are depleted, supplying local demand rather than building a sizeable export market. Brunei's enormous cash reserves from oil sales will be more than enough to keep the country rich for generations.

Although a quiet, peaceful place, Brunei provides a few outlets for tourists and travellers prepared to exert themselves in a country not geared to the high-pressure tourism of the 1990s.

History

When Portuguese explorer Ferdinand Magellan's ships called at Brunei on their return from the Philippines in 1521, it was the centre of a powerful empire stretching from Sarawak as far north as Manila. Finely built cannon can still be seen and sometimes bought in Brunei. They are a reminder of the sea power the sultanate once wielded over countries bordering on the southern part of the South China Sea.

Brunei's power declined, however, and during the 19th century the much-reduced territory controlled by the state was further encroached on by the White Rajahs of Sarawak and the British North Borneo Co. in what is now the Malaysian state of Sabah. Towards the end of the 19th century Brunei became a British protectorate, and in 1906 the British Resident system was introduced. The discovery of the first Seria oilfield in 1929 in the western part of Brunei gave the state an economic stability that has continued to the present day as more and more oil and gas fields have been opened and developed.

The state was granted internal independence in 1959, though Britain remained responsible for defence and foreign relations and provided many senior officials in the Brunei Government. A rebellion nearly overturned the Sultan in 1962. Brunei gained its full independence on January 1, 1984. Sir Omar Ali Saifuddin abdicated in 1967 in favour of his eldest son, Sir Muda Hassanal Bolkiah Mu'izzaddin Waddaulah, who was crowned the following year with all the time-honoured pomp and ceremony of a Malay court.

There is a Legislative Assembly in Brunei, but it is purely a rubber-stamp parliament. The real power is in the Istana Nurul Imam (palace) in Bandar Seri Begawan. The sultan or members of his immediate family hold key government portfolios such as finance, foreign affairs and defence. The sultan has travelled extensively in recent years and takes a keen interest in foreign policy.

Brunei is a member of the British Commonwealth and in September 1984 became the 159th member of the United Nations, where it maintains a permanent mission. It is also a member of the Association of Southeast Asian Nations — along with Indonesia, Malaysia, Philippines, Singapore and Thailand. Brunei is also a member of the Organization of Islamic States. The country's official name is Negara (country) Brunei Darussalam (abode of peace).

Brunei's land area of 5,765 square kilometres is enclosed to the south by the Malaysian state of Sarawak and divided into two parts by a narrow strip of Malaysian land which reached the coast. Of the estimated 227,000 population about 25,000 are immigrant workers. Ethnically, Malays make up 65% of the population and the rest are mainly Chinese and indigenous ethnic groups related to those of neighbouring Sarawak and Sabah: the Iban, Murut, Duoun and Kedayan.

Entry

Air transport is the easiest and most convenient means of entry. Airlines serving Brunei include Royal Brunei Airlines, Singapore Airlines, Philippine Airlines, Malaysia Airlines, Cathay Pacific Airways and Thai Airways International with direct flights to Singapore, Hong Kong, Bangkok, Manila, Kuala Lumpur, Darwin, Jakarta, Kota Kinabalu (Sabah), Kuching (Sarawak) and the Middle East.

MAJOR AIRLINES
(all in Bandar Seri Begawan)

Cathay Pacific, c/o Royal Brunei Airlines RBA Plaza, Jalan Sultan Bandar Seri Begawan Tel: 240500.
Malaysia Airlines, 144 Jalan Pemancha Bandar Seri Begawan Tel: 224141, 223074.
Philippine Airlines, c/o Royal Brunei Airlines RBA Plaza, Jalan Sultan Bandar Seri Begawan Tel: 222970.
Royal Brunei Airlines, RBA Plaza, Jalan Sultan Bandar Seri Begawan Tel: 240500.
Singapore Airlines, 39/40 Jalan Sultan Bandar Seri Begawan Tel: 227253.
Thai Airways International, 93 Jalan Pemancha Bandar Seri Begawan Tel: 242991.

Entry or departure can also be made by launch via the Malaysian duty-free island of Labuan, from where there are direct flights to Kuala Lumpur and Zamboanga, which is also served by a few passenger ships. Overland there is a road linking Kuala Belait with the Malaysian oil town of Miri 22 kilometres inside

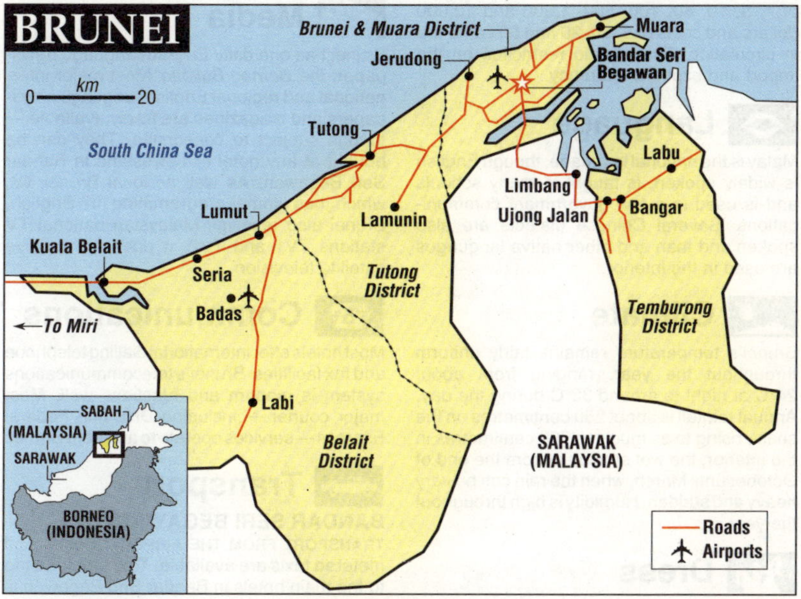

Sarawak. A bus service of dubious reliability operates daily between the two towns. An airport departure tax of B$5 is levied for journeys to Malaysia and Singapore and B$12 to all other destinations.

Immigration

A valid passport is required by all visitors and visas are also required for all purposes except for the following:

British, Malaysian and Singaporean arrivals for visits not exceeding 30 days. Citizens of Belgium, Canada, Denmark, Germany, Finland, France, Indonesia, Japan, Luxembourg, the Netherlands, Philippines, South Korea, Sweden, Switzerland and Thailand do not require a visa for visits not exceeding 14 days.

Nationals of all other countries require visas to visit Brunei. Visas are obtained from any Brunei diplomatic mission. Where there is none, they can be obtained at a British Consulate.

Health

Yellow fever inoculations are required for travellers of more than one year of age coming from infected areas. Malaria, cholera and smallpox have been eliminated from Brunei.

Customs

In addition to normal personal belongings, used portable items are exempt from duty if they accompany the traveller, though much is up to the discretion of individual customs officers. Two bottles of liquor or 12 cans of beer can be brought in duty free by non-Muslims only. Motor vehicles can be brought in from Sarawak provided the necessary exemption documents are completed and presented at the Kuala Baram customs post.

Currency

The unit of currency is the Brunei dollar (B$) which is divided into 100 cents and is on a par with the Singapore dollar. Both currencies circulate freely within the state. The Malaysian dollar is exchanged at a slightly lower rate, though some shopkeepers in Kuala Belait near the Sarawak border will accept it at almost par with the Brunei dollar. Notes in denominations of 1, 5, 10, 50, 100, 500, 1,000 and 10,000 dollars and coins of 5, 10, 20 and 50 cents are in circulation. There is no restriction on the import and export of currency.

Language

Malay is the national language, though English is widely spoken, is taught in many schools and is used in a few government communications. Several Chinese dialects are also spoken and Iban and other native languages are used in the interior.

Climate

Brunei's temperature remains fairly uniform throughout the year, ranging from about 24°C at night to around 32°C during the day. Annual rainfall is about 250 centimetres on the coast, rising to as much as 760 centimetres in the interior; the wet season is from the end of October until March, when the rain can be very heavy and sudden. Humidity is high throughout the year.

Dress

Light, easily washable clothing at all times of the year, but remember that brief or revealing clothing can offend citizens of this Islamic state.

Business Hours

Government offices are open from 7:45 a.m.-4:30 p.m. with a break between 12:15 p.m. and 1:30 p.m. for lunch and prayers; banks open from 9 a.m. until 3 p.m. and on Saturdays from 9 a.m.-11 a.m.

Government offices are closed on Friday and Sunday, but remain open all day Saturday. Private offices open from 9 a.m.-5 p.m. on weekdays and 9 a.m. to noon on Saturdays.

Most shopping centres are open daily from 10 a.m.-10 p.m.

Doing Business

Forcing the pace of business negotiations is likely to backfire. Brunei deals do not progress in the manner of some Western countries and patience and courtesy will get a lot further than aggressive negotiation. This is not a one-stop, sell and sign-the-deal society.

Media

Brunei has one daily English-language newspaper, the *Borneo Bulletin.* Most major international and regional English-language newspapers and magazines are freely available — though subject to censorship. They can be bought at any hotel or newsstand in Bandar Seri Begawan. As well as local Brunei TV, which has some programming in English, Brunei also receives Malaysian national TV stations TV1 and TV2. It does not receive satellite television.

Communications

Most hotels offer international dialling telephone and fax facilities. Brunei's telecommunications system is modern and functions well. Most major courier — including DHL and Federal Express — services operate to and from Brunei.

Transport

BANDAR SERI BEGAWAN

TRANSPORT FROM THE AIRPORT: Buses and metered taxis are available. Taxi fare for a trip to the main hotels in Bandar Seri Begawan is about B$25. Some hotels have courtesy bus services.

TAXIS: There are few cabs available in the capital. Taxis are metered and the flagfall fare is B$3.

HIRE CARS: There is a reasonable range of services. **Avis** has offices at the airport, the Sheraton Utama Hotel, in the capital itself and in Kuala Belait. The roads between towns are good, though parking can be a problem in Bandar Seri Begawan.

BUSES: A few bus services operate to urban and rural areas and are very cheap but infrequent and not too reliable.

WATER TAXIS: Water taxis or boats provide an efficient service to Kampung Ayer on the Brunei River and also upriver to Limbang in the neighbouring Malaysian state of Sarawak. Bargaining is in order if you hire a boat on a private basis.

Tours

Few organized tours are available, but the state is so small and road communications are so good that it is easy to organize your own outings with a little help from hotel staff. The tourist inquiry counter at the airport can provide

A view of the future. PHOTO: HILARY ANDREWS

information about what tour organizers are available.

Accommodation

The 154-room **Sheraton Utama Hotel** in Bandar Seri Begawan is the only genuine international hotel in the state, and even then its service may not be as crisp as other hotels in the Sheraton group around the world.

The hotel boasts a business centre offering a full range of services including advice on local business customs. **The Centre Point Hotel** is the newest in town and offers facilities on a par with those at the Sheraton.

Of the other bigger hotels, **Ang's** and the **Brunei Hotel** have improved considerably, though customers should not expect the standards of service they get in other capital cities in the region. The Brunei Hotel, which was given a face-lift in 1990, is pleasant and good value.

A few small Chinese hotels offer cheaper service but are difficult to find without the help of a local friend or guide. In Kuala Belait the choice is pretty much limited to the **Seaview** and **Sentosa** hotels.

Dining

The number of tourist-style restaurants and bars is fairly restricted. The Sheraton's **Deals Restaurant** and **Cempaka Cafe** at Ang's Hotel serve Western food. Try the Sheraton, Ang's or **Phongmun** in the Teck Guan Plaza for Chinese food; the **Aumrin** in Jalan Gadong for Thai food and the **Regent**'s **Rang Mahal** in the Warna complex for Indian cuisine.

No alcohol is sold at any hotel or restaurant in Brunei. Non-Muslims are permitted to consume alcohol in the privacy of their own homes. Muslim cooking is a speciality of several of the coffee shops in the capital, with curries being especially good. At night "foodstall gardens" serve cheap, local fare.

Entertainment

There is little or no entertainment for tourists, other than cinemas showing mainly Chinese martial arts epics and Malay love dramas (heavily censored).

Shopping

Brass cannon, ornamental *kris* (knives) and *kain songket* (hand-woven cloth patterned with silver or gold thread) are about the only locally produced handicrafts of interest to shoppers. A good selection and highest quality work is available at the **Arts and Handicrafts Centre** on Jalan Residency and at the airport, but prices are high. The **Serindipity** in Jalan Gadong is a good place to go for curios and handicrafts. Locally commissioned rattan furniture is of good quality and compares favourably in price with other parts of Asia. Most consumer products are available in Brunei.

Sports

The state has some fine beaches and scuba gear can be hired in Bandar Seri Begawan and Kuala Belait. Golf, rugby and sailing are also popular and every small community has a village *padang* (field or green) with a football pitch.

For windsurfing enthusiasts, the **Royal Brunei National Windsurfing Association** at Serasa Beach in Muara town has boards for hire.

Holidays

Brunei's holidays are largely in celebration of Muslim religious events. Dates vary from one year to the next according to the moon. Other holidays, celebrating birthdays and recent political events, have fixed dates.

January 1: New Year's Day (public holiday).
January-February: Chinese New Year is celebrated by the Chinese population. People dress in their new clothes, visit friends and enjoy fine meals (public holiday).
February 23: National Day (public holiday).
May 31: Anniversary of the Royal Brunei Armed Forces (public holiday).
June: Armed Forces Day (public holiday).
July 15: The Sultan's Birthday (public holiday).
September 29: Constitution Day (public holiday).
December 25-26: Christmas (public holiday, two days).
Variable: Awal Ramadhan — the first day of the Muslim month of fasting (public holiday).

Hari Raya Aidilfitri — the end of the Ramadhan fasting (public holiday, two days).

Hari Raya Aidiladha — also known as Hari Raya Korban, this marks the Muslim Haj celebration when goats and cows are sacrificed and the meat is distributed to friends, relatives and the less fortunate (public holiday).

Mauludun Nabi S.A.W. — birthday of the Prophet Muhammad (public holiday).

Me'raj — commemorates the ascension of the Prophet Muhammad (public holiday).

Anniversary of the Revelation of the Koran (public holiday).

MAJOR BANKS
All in Bandar Seri Begawan:

	Tel:
Citibank	243983
Hongkong Bank	227729
Malayan Banking Bhd	242494
Overseas Union Bank	225477
Standard Chartered Bank	24238
United Malayan Banking Bhd	222516
International Bank of Brunei	220686

DISCOVERING BRUNEI

BANDAR SERI BEGAWAN

Because of its small size, the capital is an easy place to explore, and with the aid of a car and a river boat you can also visit the several interesting sites just beyond the city limits. There is a relaxed atmosphere, making it a pleasant interlude for the traveller who may have just come from the bustle of Bangkok or Hong Kong.

The highlight of the town is the **Omar Ali Saifuddin Mosque** in the west; this is within easy walking distance from the town proper. It is partly bordered by a lagoon in which sits a replica of a 16th century barge, the **Mahligai**. **Kampung Ayer** (water village) was described by early European visitors as the "Venice of the East." These sprawling houses on stilts, spanning the greater part of the Brunei River, continue to attract visitors.

A short distance from the mosque is the **Churchill Memorial Building**. Its focal point is a bronze statue of Sir Winston Churchill giving his famous victory salute. Within the complex is the **Hassanal Bolkiah Aquarium**, which contains a large collection of tropical marine and freshwater fish. The **Lapau** or **Royal Ceremonial Hall** is another impressive building within Bandar Seri Begawan itself. Adjoining the Lapau is the **Parliament House**.

Also worth a visit is the **Brunei Museum**, on the Kota Batu road. An exhibition on Islamic art in Asia is a major feature of its displays. There is also a large collection of elaborately gilded Korans among treasured ceramics, jewellery and carpets.

One of the most pleasant excursions available is a boat trip on the Brunei River among the stilt-houses of the various parts of Kampung Ayer. While on the water, it is worth visiting the colourful **Royal Tomb**, a little more than a kilometre to the west on the north bank of the river.

Istana Nurul Iman, the impressive palace, also lies to the west of the city. Boasting 1,788 rooms, it is larger than the Vatican. Marble, 22-carat gold, Philippine mahogany and very rare Moroccan onyx have been incorporated in the richly decorated interiors. Although the palace is generally closed to the public, visitors may be able to arrange viewings through the tourism or information ministries.

UPCOUNTRY

Beyond the capital you can travel to **Seria** (100 kilometres to the southwest along the coast) and **Kuala Belait** (another 16 kilometres), the sites of Brunei's oil industry, where "nodding donkey" oil pumps dot the landscape. It is also possible to go by boat and then on foot into the interior and inspect

PHOTO: HILARY ANDREWS

Colourful dresses.

some of the few **Iban longhouses**, though such a trip is undertaken more rewardingly in neighbouring Sarawak.

The most spectacular scenery and wildlife in Bruneï can be seen in **Temburong**, the easternmost district, separated from the rest of the country by Sarawak. The main town of **Bangar** can be reached by a one-and-a-half-hour boat ride from Bandar Seri Begawan, but arrangements for visiting the interior must be made in advance.

HOTEL GUIDE

A: $150 and above

SHERATON UTAMA, Jalan Tasek, Bandar Seri Begawan. Tel: 244272, Fax: 221579, Tlx: 2308 UTAMA BU. *P, Gym, Biz. R: W & Chinese.*

THE CENTRE POINT HOTEL, Jalan Gadong, Bandar Seri Begawan. Tel.: 430430, Fax: 430200. *P, Gym, Biz. R: W & Chinese.*

B: $85-150

BRUNEI HOTEL, Jalan Pemancha, Bandar Seri Begawan. Tel: 242372, Fax: 226196, Tlx: BU 2287. *R: W & Chinese.*

RIVERVIEW INN, Jalan Kumbang Pasang, Bandar Seri Begawan. Tel: 238002, Fax: 237999. *P, Gym. R: W & Chinese.*

C: $60-85

ANG'S HOTEL, Jalan Tasek Lama, Bandar Seri Begawan. Tel: 243553, Fax: 227302. *P. R: W & Chinese.*

P — Swimming pool **Gym** — Health club **Biz** — Business centre **R** — Restaurant
W — Western food

CAMBODIA

Cambodia evokes images in most of a horribly suffering population, a series of brutal governments, and a dangerous and unpredictable environment inconducive to business or fun — in short, somewhere to avoid. But 1992 saw Cambodia emerge from more than two decades of war and devastation with the signing of a United Nations peace plan by the four warring factions. While the peace plan remains tenuous, the country has gone through a massive transformation as hundreds of new businesses, hotels, and restaurants have opened, scores of new diplomatic missions are present, and tourism has taken off. The timeless architectural wonders of Angkor Wat and other temples remain as extraordinary as ever, and the famous Cambodian gentleness obverse of a tendency to violence is still there to welcome tourists or business travellers alike.

After a US$2 billion UN peacekeeping effort that culminated in the democratic election of a monarchist government in May 1993, Cambodia has emerged from its dark years of warfare, harsh communism and suffering. The government, with the help of the international community, has created a vibrant — if somewhat anarchic — society that embraces free enterprise. It has gone to great lengths and invested hundreds of millions of dollars building up the kingdom's infrastructure to encourage visitors. A new airport has been built, numbers of flights to many points in Asia are growing and scores of new hotels and restaurants dot city and other major tourist sites. Cambodia is rapidly making up for its years lost in isolation.

History

Contemporary Cambodia is the remains of the once great Angkor empire, which 800 years ago extended into present day Vietnam, Laos, Thailand and the Malay peninsula.

The Cambodian monarchy is generally dated from when King Jayavarman II (802-50) founded his capital near Angkor near the present-day provincial capital of Siem Riep. The Angkor empire reached its zenith during the reigns of Suryavarman II (1113-50), builder of Angkor Wat, and King Jayavarman VII, builder of the Bayon temples and 100 hospitals throughout the kingdom. Angkor was abandoned in 1432 and the capital was moved south to near its present location.

After the 14th century, Cambodia's economic centre gradually moved down to Phnom Penh, and by the 18th century, Cambodia was caught between increasingly aggressive Thailand to the west and Vietnam to the east. Repeated incursions by Thailand resulted in Hinduism and Mahayana Buddhism being replaced by the Thai Therevada Buddhism. Vietnam took much of the fertile southern delta, including Saigon (Ho Chi Minh City), which the Cambodians still refer to as Kampuchea Krom (Lower Cambodia). By the mid-19th century, pressures from their neighbours threatened Cambodia with extinction, and it was the intervention of the French which, ironically, saved Cambodia from being swallowed altogether.

Cambodia became a French protectorate in 1864. The Japanese replaced the French during World War II, but in 1945, after the Japanese defeat, the French returned. The French had installed Norodom Sihanouk, then 19 years old, as king in 1941, assuming him to be a pliable playboy. After the French returned, Sihanouk joined others in demanding independence, which was granted in 1953.

◄ *One of Angkor's wonders.* PHOTO: GORDON FAIRCLOUGH

In 1955, Sihanouk abdicated the throne — taking the title of Prince — to enter politics and was replaced on the throne by his father. But Sihanouk remained head of state and sought to keep Cambodia neutral in the escalating war in neighbouring Laos and Vietnam, and the polarization of the region by the Cold War. In the process he suppressed opposition and his Royalist government depended on a sycophantic clique of corrupt elite that alienated both the left and the right. In March 1970, Sihanouk was ousted in a military-led coup launched by Marshal Lon Nol.

United States and South Vietnamese troops invaded Cambodia within weeks of the coup in an attempt to support Lon Nol and push the North Vietnamese out. Sihanouk announced from exile in Beijing that he was joining a coalition with the extreme hard-line communist Khmer Rouge. Fighting between the Khmer Rouge and the Lon Nol government ended when the Khmer Rouge seized the capital on April 17, 1975.

From then until the end of 1978, the Khmer Rouge made a bizarre attempt to create an agrarian utopia that left about a million people dead from starvation, disease and execution.

The Vietnamese invaded on Christmas Day 1978 and took the capital on January 7, 1979. Hanoi installed the communist regime of Heng Samrin in Phnom Penh, and another 13-year war began. The Khmer Rouge retreated to the Thai border where they joined in a coalition with two non-communist armies to fight the Vietnamese. The guerilla coalition was recognized and armed by China, Asean and the West as Cambodia again became a theatre of the Cold War, with the former Soviet Union backing its Vietnamese allies.

The Vietnamese-installed government, now led by reformist Prime Minister Hun Sen, instituted economic reforms in 1989 and began to move away from socialism.

A flurry of new diplomatic activity was launched to come to a political solution, with France, Australia, Asean, Thailand and Indonesia all playing a part. The four warring factions signed a UN peace agreement in Paris in October 1991.

The agreement provided for nearly 20,000 UN troops and civilian personnel to administer the country until elections for a new government. The UN was charged with disarming the four armies, repatriating nearly 350,000 refugees in camps along the Thai border and ensuring a neutral political environment. The May 1993 elections brought a stunning victory for the royalist, non-communist Funčinpec party which had fought for 12 years as a guerilla army from bases along the Thai border. The Vietnamese-installed, previously ruling Cambodian People's Party came second, but refused to hand over power.

After negotiations, the two formed a coalition government which is relatively stable and (as of March 1995) remains in power. The Khmer Rouge continue to wage low-level insurgency from the jungle, but while military battles remain a feature of Cambodian politics in the north and northwest of Cambodia, they have had limited impact on investment and tourism.

Phnom Penh has taken on a new life, with unrestrained economic activity. The city has a population of more than 1 million. Angkor Wat has returned to being a must for tourists.

Cambodia covers 181,000 square kilometres and has an estimated population of 9 million. The population is dominated by Khmers, but several hundred thousand ethnic Vietnamese also live in Cambodia. They are a source of political tension as many came after the 1978 invasion by Vietnam. There is also a significant ethnic Chinese population in the cities, and a variety of other small ethnic groups live in remote mountainous areas.

EMBASSIES

	Tel:
Australia	26000-1
Britain	27121
Bulgaria	23181
China	26271
Czech and **Slovak**	23781
Cuba	24181-2
France	26544, 26278
Germany	26381, 26193
Hungary	22781
India	22981
Indonesia	26148
Japan	27161
North Korea	26230
Laos	26441
Malaysia	26176-7
Poland	26250
Russia	22081
Thailand	01 881 0860
U.S.	26436-8
Vietnam	25481, 25681

Entry

In 1994 Phnom Penh's Poechentong airport was refurbished. Since the 1993 elections, Cambodia has become a major tourism and business destination. Cambodian airline Royal Air Cambodge is spreading its wings as numerous airlines negotiate for landing rights. Thai Airways International flies from Bangkok, Malaysia Airlines from Kuala Lumpur and Singapore, Silk Air from Singapore and Dragon Air from Hong Kong. Airport departure tax is US$10 for international flights and US$4 for domestic flights.

Land travel from Thailand is possible with special land visas, but is inadvisable because of the security situation along the Thai border. However, access by land from Vietnam is routine and the roads are adequate and secure.

Immigration

Visas are available upon arrival at Phnom Penh airport for US$20. No prior visa is necessary. Renewals and special visas are easily obtainable at the **Foreign Ministry**.

Health

No health certificates or vaccinations are required to visit Cambodia, but several are recommended. Visitors should receive vaccinations against both hepatitis A and B, and typhoid. For travel upcountry one should take preventives for malaria. Stomach ailments from poor hygienic practices and unclean water are common in Phnom Penh and visitors should come equipped with medicine for diarrhoea. Medicine is available in Phnom Penh, but the health care is rudimentary and there are limited facilities for serious illness.

Customs

Normal restrictions on currency, jewellery, and electronics exist, but are not strictly enforced.

Currency

The exchange rate for the Cambodian currency, the riel, has been stable since late 1993 and generally hovers at Riel 2,500-2,600:US$1. However, the dollar is the preferred currency in Cambodia, and should be used in almost all transactions. A small amount of riels is convenient for local transport and small transactions. The Thai baht is also generally accepted. The rate of exchange at hotels and government offices is generally lower than can be found in the market.

Language

The national language is Khmer, a non-tonal language from the Mon-Khmer family. It is the only language spoken by most. However, English is spoken in all the major businesses and government ministries and should be sufficient for most business and tourist activities. French is also common, but decreasing rapidly among younger Cambodians and is no longer the language of commerce. Thai is also quite commonly spoken.

Climate

Cambodia lies in the tropical monsoon belt and has an average annual rainfall of 150 centimetres, usually between late April and October. It becomes very hot with temperatures as high as 40°C prior to the onset of the monsoons. The coolest months are December and January. Air-conditioning is not usual except in the more upmarket hotels and restaurants.

Dress

Light tropical clothing is recommended throughout the year, with slightly warmer garments for December and January evenings.

Business Hours

Most government offices are open from 7-11 a.m. and from 2-5 p.m. Businesses generally remain open from before 8 a.m.-noon and from 2-5 p.m. or later.

Markets are open early and close in mid-afternoon. Banks also are closed between noon and 2 p.m. Most restaurants and entertainment establishments close relatively early, with restaurants generally closed by 11 p.m., with some exceptions.

Rip-Offs

There is a high incidence of fake U.S. dollar bills. Corruption is rampant, as is incompetence. Prices for such things as housing rental or property remain grossly inflated because of the massive sudden influx of UN personnel in 1992.

Government officials often are unavailable for impromptu appointments, many moonlighting in other jobs to supplement the meagre government salaries. Many businessmen remain perpetually exasperated by the level of corruption — in particular, by being shunted aside after a deal has been signed with government authorities, in favour of another company which has made a later but more lucrative offer to the officials responsible.

Communications

Communication with the outside world has improved tremendously since 1992, when there were only six external lines. Country code for Cambodia is 855, area code for Phnom Penh is 23; for Siem Riep it is 15. Telephone costs rank among the highest in the world, and collect calls from Cambodia are not yet possible. The Australian Overseas Telecommunications Co. (Telstra) has installed an entirely new telephone system to replace the old Soviet system. However, the remains a problem of congestion as supply is still way behind demand. Most businessmen and government officials rely on mobile telephones. Samart, a Thai company, has a network — the only one outside Phnom Penh — which links Phnom Penh to the key provinces of Kompong Som, Siem Riep, Battambang and Kompong Cham.

Major hotels have international direct dialling and facsimile services, but many hotels only have a telephone at the front desk. Message-taking is not well done, a cause of considerable frustration for visiting businessmen.

Mobile telephones are available for rent, but as the prices is generally US$50 a day it is often cheaper to buy one — the cheapest versions are about US$800. On top of this price, of course, come the charges for calls made, which are very high. All the major international courier services are available.

Transport

Cars can be hired at the airport (always with driver) and negotiated down to US$20 for a full day. A single ride from the airport to town will cost between US$5-10 by air-conditioned car.

There is no official public transport system in Phnom Penh. Cambodia has seen a large influx of new cars and motorcycles, but often the best (and cheapest) way to travel in Phnom Penh is by leisurely *cyclopousse*, a pedal trishaw, which can reach almost any part of the city within 15 minutes.

Any hotel can easily make arrangements for a hired car to go upcountry. They are relatively expensive, charging about US$1 per kilometre for a four-wheel drive or US$50 a day or more for an air-conditioned sedan. Permission is not required to travel anywhere in the country, but security in many areas is bad. With banditry a problem, travel after dark is not advised outside the capital. About 20% of the country remains outside government control and inaccessible to the foreign traveller.

TRANSPORT UPCOUNTRY

There are daily flights to **Siem Riep**, the town near Angkor Wat, and there are flights to other major provinces, including Battambang. Most tourists take the morning flight from Phnom Penh to Siem Riep, but a pleasant four-hour boat trip up the magnificent Tonle Sap lake can also be arranged by travel agents or hotels.

There are also twice-weekly flights to the remote mountainous northeastern province of Rattanakiri, where hilltribes dominate the areas along the old Ho Chi Minh trail. Accommodation is rudimentary at best, and should only be tackled by the most adventurous.

Except for the Phnom Penh-Siem Riep route, travel within Cambodia is not necessarily up to international safety standards. **Kompong Som**, Cambodia's premier beach resort, can be reached by road in less than four hours, or by train or helicopter. In 1994 six Westerners were murdered by Khmer Rouge bandits while travelling by road and/or train. While the road appears safe since the government destroyed Khmer Rouge enclaves in late 1994, embassies in March 1995 were still issuing strict warnings against such travel. Hotels in Kompong Som are not up to top standards, but the town and beaches remain charming.

Tours

The **Ministry of Tourism** is one of the government's most competent agencies. It is run largely by Khmer former expatriates who have returned since the fall of communism and who are professional and helpful in all respects. They can be reached at Tel: 26107, Fax: 26364.

There are scores of travel agents in Phnom Penh, and arrangements can also be made through major hotels. Among the larger agencies well-connected with other countries are: in Phnom Penh, **Diethelm Travel**, Tel: 26648, Fax: 26676; **East-West Group**, Tel/Fax: 26189; and in Siem Reap (area code 15), **Transair Cambodia Travel**, Tel: 911986, Fax (Phnom Penh): 26620.

Accommodation

Phnom Penh has undergone a boom in hotels. In mid-1989, there were only 400 rooms available in the whole city. Since then dozens of new hotels have opened with more than 10,000 rooms now being offered.

There are at least eight hotels in Phnom Penh which could be regarded as top quality. Heading the list is the **Cambodiana** (Tel: 26288, Fax: 26392). The first full-service, four-star hotel in Cambodia, it has all the amenities are is under French and Singaporean management. It has IDD telephones in each room, satellite TV, a business centre, conference rooms, several quality restaurants and stunning views around its site at the junction of the Mekong and Tonle Sap rivers. It is the only hotel in Phnom Penh with a full-size swimming pool and tennis courts. Rooms are about US$150 a night, but discounts can be arranged.

Also of top quality is the **Diamond Hotel**, on Phnom Penh's main Monivong Blvd, with 87 rooms, IDD in each room and satellite TV (Tel: 26635, 27221-2, Fax: 26636). Rates are US$50-120 a night.

Another in the top group is the **Juliana**, located downtown near major businesses. This hotel has communications and other amenities plus fine Thai and European cuisine at reasonable prices. Rates are set at US$120 a night but are negotiable (Tel: [18] 810209).

Upcountry, there are now guest-houses and hotels in every provincial capital, but most are very basic and have no communication with Phnom Penh. Arrangements cannot usually be made ahead of time, except (via a travel agent) for Kompong Som.

The major exception to this rule is Siem Riep, near the Ankor Wat temples, where there are plenty of pleasant bungalows with full services, as well as three-star hotels. There are many plans for five-star accommodation. The **Grand Hotel d'Angkor** is the oldest and most famous hotel here (Tel: 911292, Fax: 911291). Built in the 1920s, its colonial heritage and high ceilings give it an ambience unmatched in Siem Riep, but it has suffered from a lack of upkeep and does not have some of the modern facilities one would expect. It has restaurants, a business centre and IDD telephones. Rates are US$40-60 a night.

Also in Siem Reap is the **Banteay Srei** Hotel, with 55 air-conditioned rooms, satellite TV and a restaurant. Rates are around US$55 a night. Perhaps the most comfortable place is the **Taphrom Hotel** (Tel: 911783), along the river. It is Thai-managed, has good restaurants and satellite TV. Rates are US$70-120 a night.

Cheaper but pleasant are the bungalows which form the **Diamond Hotel** (Tel: 913130, Fax: 910020), with air-conditioning, hot water and an adjacent good Thai restaurant but little else. Rates are US$30-40 a night.

Dining

Phnom Penh has gone through a gastronomic revolution since the early 1990s, when UN peacekeepers from more than 100 countries arrived to stay until 1993. Hundreds of new restaurants have opened up to cater to almost any palate. In addition to the usual hundreds of street-corner restaurants found throughout Asia, there is Japanese, Thai, Indian, Chinese, Indonesian, Malay, Vietnamese, European (with a French accent) and American cuisine available. Khmer food is somewhat nondescript, generally without the bite of neighbouring Thailand or Vietnam.

Hygiene in Cambodia leaves much to be desired at street-corner restaurants, and one should be careful — even more so than in some other Asian cities — of where and what one eats. Stomach upsets are almost routine for most residents. Hotels and restaurants are generally safe.

Phnom Penh's best restaurants include **La Paillote**, in the hotel of the same name next to the central market. It offers very good European and French food with a good wine list. It serves breakfast, lunch and dinner at a reasonable price.

The **Deja Vu**, near the Royal Palace on St 242, offers continental cuisine and is a favourite among expatriate residents of Phnom Penh. Apart from its European dishes it also offers some Middle Eastern fare and a good wine selection, plus a pleasant upstairs cafe where food and drink can be had while listening to recorded jazz and reading daily newspapers. It also has backgammon and chess boards. Prices are reasonable.

For an after-dinner (or before-dinner) drink, the **Foreign Correspondents' Club of Cambodia** is one of Phnom Penh's most popular venues. It offers magnificent views of the Tonle Sap and Mekong rivers, and is the local spot for the somewhat rambunctious foreign press corps as well as development workers, businessmen and diplomats. It has a full menu but the food is mediocre. A pool table and satellite TV, plus weekly panel discussions and imported films, add to the charm. It is sited on the river a kilometre north of the Cambodiana.

Shopping

Phnom Penh offers half a dozen major markets where everything from fresh produce, antiques, rubies and electronics can be found. **Tual Thumpong, Central, New, Old,** and **Rassey** markets house scores of stalls under one roof. The **New Market (Psah Tmey)** is located in the heart of downtown and offers a little bit of everything, including silver and gold jewellery with local rubies at reasonable prices. Cambodia continues to mine some of the best rubies and sapphires in the world, but do not buy unless you have expertise because there are also fakes for sale.

The main strip of **Achar Mean Blvd** is chock full of shops selling everything from rattan furniture to antiques.

Sports

There are few sporting facilities in Phnom Penh. The best is the International Youth Club, with a full 50-metre Olympic pool, squash courts, a gym with an array of weights and machines, and 10 tennis courts. It also has a poolside restaurant that is reasonable in quality and price. It costs US$10 a day to use the club, though cheaper weekly and monthly passes are available. The **Cambodiana Hotel** has a swimming pool and tennis courts, also open to non-guests at a moderate price. The **Olympic Stadium** also has tennis courts and a running track. Running along the roads near the river is pleasant in the early morning before vehicular anarchy seizes control of the streets.

Holidays

Holiday dates vary slightly from year to year because of the Lunar calendar.

January 1: International New Year.

February: Chinese and Vietnamese (Tet) Lunar New Years are celebrated.

April 14-16: Cambodian New Year.

September/October: *Pachum Bon* — Bud-

dhist day of remembrance for the dead.
October 30: King's birthday.
October: Kahn, when families go to monasteries to offer respect to their ancestors by giving offerings to monks.
November 9: Independence Day.
November: The Mekong water festival.

DISCOVERING CAMBODIA

PHNOM PENH

Phnom Penh remains a pleasant sprawling city despite more than two decades of neglect and economic stagnation. The old colonial buildings and boulevards are tired but charming. One of the best ways to see the city is to hire a *cyclo* trishaw for the day for about US$5.

Everything is accessible within 15 minutes from anywhere, and it is a pleasant way to absorb the city.

The **Royal Palace** should be on the itinerary of any tour. On the grounds of the palace is the **Silver Pagoda**, with its silver tile floor, its 90-kilogram gold Buddha, and other religious relics.

The **National Museum** is near the palace, and houses a considerable exhibit of Khmer art and artifacts, even though some of the national heritage was stolen by the Vietnamese and Khmer Rouge during the wars of the 1970s and 1980s. **Wat Phnom** is a 200-year-old pagoda at the northern end of Tou Samouth Boulevard and is the temple after which Phnom Penh was named. A number of other Wat's are worth seeing, including **Wat Btum**, located immediately south of the Royal Palace.

Many people visit **Tuol Sleng**, the torture chamber in which more than 16,000 victims of the Khmer Rouge perished, though it is macabre and not to everybody's taste. Tour guides familiar with its history will answer your questions. Twelve kilometres south of Phnom Penh lie the Choueng Ek "killing fields," where the bones of the victims of Tuol Sleng and elsewhere are on display.

The **Bassac Theatre** offers irregular performances of traditional Khmer dance — the Apsara — and the **School of Fine Art**, behind the National Museum, also offers music, dance, and art presentations.

Visitors can also go to the **Tonle Bati** 11th century ruins, 40 kilometres south of Phnom Penh, as well as **Oudong**, the former capital, 30 kilometres northwest of the city.

Another very pleasant way to spend an afternoon is to hire a boat to cruise the Mekong. Tours can be arranged through hotels, but it is more pleasant to hire your own boat for about US$50 a day and cruise through the city and nearby rural agricultural areas.

UPCOUNTRY

Angkor Wat — the magnificent Hindu temple built by King Suryavarman II at the height of the Khmer empire in the 12th century — is easily accessible to visitors and is certainly one of the prime reasons for visiting Cambodia. Angkor, the world's largest temple complex, is spread over 228 square kilometres and consists of sandstone temples, chapels, causeways, terraces, and reservoirs. The walls of the temples are covered with thousands of carvings of battles between gods and demons from classical Hindu mythology, sensual dancing women, and royal processions with kings riding elephants.

Angkor was abandoned in the 15th century as Cambodia turned to Buddhism and the capital was moved to near its current location in Phnom Penh. It was "rediscovered" by a French explorer in the 1860s, and remains the symbol of Cambodia today. French experts worked to restore the temple until they were driven out by war in 1970, but Indian and UN restorers resumed work in the 1980s to preserve the massive complex. One of the more controversial aspects of the reconstruction involves pouring cement to fill gaps and recarving missing figures, which some archaeologists argue mars Angkor's ancient beauty.

Nature continues to threaten the complex, with moss, algae, and lichens disfiguring the stone, bat droppings and water eating away the bas-reliefs, and trees forcing a shift of the temples' foundations.

The 20th century wars have caused comparatively limited damage, but bandits have looted a number of carvings and whole statues. Only 15 of the Hindu deities in the "gallery of 100 statues" remain. Other pieces are believed to have been smuggled out by Vietnamese and other looters.

Angkor Wat is in fact only one of more than 70 temples and monuments in the area. The Bayon temple, known as **Angkor Thom**, features more than 200 magnificent, slightly smiling stone faces.

The temple complex near Angkor is best done in two or three days, but all can be viewed in one full day.

INDONESIA

The largest country in Southeast Asia, Indonesia is a sprawling archipelago of more than 13,600 islands straddling the equator south of the Asian mainland, north and west of Australia. With almost 185 million people, Indonesia is the fourth largest country in the world in terms of population.

Indonesia presents a tableau of cultures woven together by a colourful history of conquest, trade and empire. Travelling east from the capital, Jakarta, takes the visitor from a modern Muslim society to one steeped in tradition, a significant part of which still clings to the Hindu, Buddhist or animist past.

Jakarta is fast becoming a sprawl of modern high-rise buildings towering over a receding sea of red-tiled houses in urban villages, or *kampungs*. By day, the city screeches and groans with traffic sweltering in the brilliant sunshine and high humidity. Now a centre of government, business and industry, the city spreads over more than 670 square kilometres and has a population of more than 8.5 million. The city's rapid growth reflects Indonesia's remarkable economic development from the late 1980s.

To the east lies the historic city of Jogjakarta, regarded by many as the cultural heart of Java. With a still functioning court life and a sultan who acts as the city's governor, traditions are actively preserved. Nearby are the ancient Borobudur and Prambanan temples. Further east is Surabaya, the country's second-largest city, with its stately Dutch-built avenues and a charming rural hinterland. Off the eastern tip of Java lies Bali and beyond it the islands of Lombok, Sumba, Flores and others forming a chain all the way to Indonesia's eastern extremity, Irian Jaya, adjoining Papua New Guinea. To the west of Jakarta, lies the huge island of Sumatra.

To the northeast are Kalimantan (the Indonesian part of Borneo), Sulawesi and the Maluku islands (the Moluccas) — a vast area that the visitor cannot hope to explore fully. However, significant progress in transport throughout the country means that many of these areas are just a two-hour flight from Jakarta.

History

Although fossil remains of very early man have been discovered in Java, most of the present mixed population of Indonesia originated from relatively recent migrations — probably in several waves from the Asian mainland during the first and second millennia BC.

By the early centuries AD, several developed kingdoms throughout the archipelago were emerging as influential powers in the region. In the 7th century the Hindu kingdom of Sriwijaya around the contemporary town of Palembang on the eastern coast of Sumatra dominated sea-borne trade in the straits of Malacca.

Sriwijaya's golden era was later usurped by the kingdoms of Java, which were developing strength based on command over a rich rice-growing society governed by imported Hindu-Buddhist culture.

Intermarriage, wars of succession and shifts of capital cloud the picture hopelessly from this time until the last Hindu-Javanese kingdom of Majapahit succumbed to Islam in the 14th century. However, evidence of these pre-Islamic times in Indonesia is amply shown by the important status of the Ramayana and

◄ *Beautiful Sumatra.* PHOTO: PATRICK LUCERO

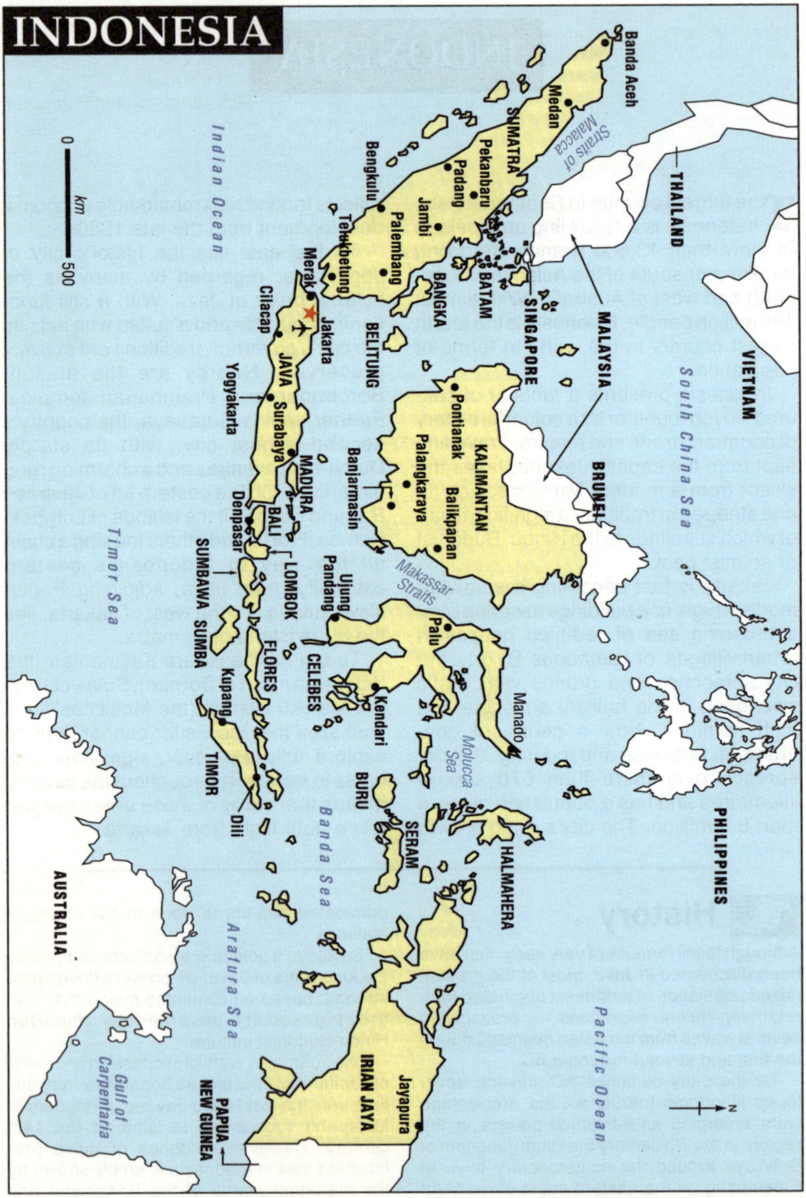
INDONESIA
Banda Aceh
Medan
SUMATRA
Straits of Malacca
Pekanbaru
Padang
Bengkulu
Jambi
Palembang
Telukbetung
Merak
BANGKA
BATAM
SINGAPORE
MALAYSIA
THAILAND
VIETNAM
Indian Ocean
0
km
500
Cilacap
Jakarta
BELITUNG
JAVA
Yogyakarta
Surabaya
Pontianak
KALIMANTAN
BRUNEI
Palangkaraya
Banjarmasin
Balikpapan
South China Sea
MADURA
BALI
Denpasar
LOMBOK
SUMBAWA
SUMBA
Timor Sea
Makassar Straits
Ujung Pandang
Palu
CELEBES
FLORES
Kupang
Kendari
Manado
Molucca Sea
TIMOR
Dili
BURU
SERAM
HALMAHERA
PHILIPPINES
Banda Sea
AUSTRALIA
Arafura Sea
Pacific Ocean
IRIAN JAYA
Jayapura
PAPUA NEW GUINEA
Gulf of Carpentaria
N

Mahabarata epic dramas in the cultural life of the contemporary Javanese people. The *wayang* leather puppet shows dramatizing the old Hindu epics reach down to the lowest level of Javanese village society.

The first European influences were imported by the Portuguese, who came in search of spices to the islands of Eastern Indonesia in the 16th century. Portuguese dominance was replaced 100 years later by the Dutch, who began a slow subjugation of Java and other islands. The process was not completed until the early years of this century with the conquest of Aceh and southern regions of Bali.

Dutch colonial efforts concentrated on Java, where they harnessed the population to produce sugar and coffee for export to Europe. The oppressive way in which the Javanese were forced to cultivate cash crops became a model of colonial exploitation. There were frequent rebellions, but no mass nationalist movement for independence until the early years of the 20th century.

By this time, the Dutch had introduced a school system and begun to send Indonesian graduates to Holland. As elsewhere in Southeast Asia, a new generation of indigenous intellectuals formed the core of the nascent independence movement. They might have been crushed by the Dutch had it not been for the Japanese occupation in 1942.

Under the Japanese, Indonesian nationalists were allowed to organize and on August 17, 1945, independence was declared. Sukarno became president of the new republic, which immediately had to contend with the returning Dutch. After a short war, during which British troops were also involved as Holland's allies, a UN-brokered agreement resulted in the formation of a unitary independent state in 1950.

Sukarno initially installed a full constitutional democracy, but the collapse in disunity of one government after another led him to impose what he called "Guided Democracy" in 1959. Parliament lost its power and the state began to intervene in the economy and the judiciary. Meanwhile, the army was facing rebellion in several outlying regions, including a move by Muslim communities in Sulawesi and west Java to establish an Islamic state.

With unity restored and Indonesia's area expanded to include West Irian after another war with the Dutch in 1962, Sukarno began to face opposition to his policies, particularly that of fostering close links with the communist party at home and abroad. Frustrated by Sukarno's belligerent policies towards the West and a pointless confrontation with Malaysia in 1963, the military became more and more opposed to Sukarno. An abortive communist uprising in 1965 proved to be their cue to topple him.

The new military government led by Gen. Suharto, who became president in 1968, set a more conservative political course for the country and launched economic policies which headed off the country's decline into poverty and bankruptcy. Relations with the West improved greatly while diplomatic ties with China were frozen and not resumed until 1990.

Suharto has ruled Indonesia for more than a quarter of a century, steering a course which has resulted in improvements in the welfare of the people. Shrewd policies of birth control and a drive to achieve self-sufficiency in rice have earned Suharto plaudits around the world. But recent years have seen Suharto and his government come under pressure to liberalize the economy after a disastrous fall in oil prices exposed the country's dangerous reliance on oil and the state sector.

Entry

Jakarta is served by most major international airlines. Many foreign carriers such as Qantas, Singapore Airlines, Malaysia Airlines and Cathay Pacific also have direct flights to Bali. Other cities served by international flights include Medan in North Sumatra, Kupang in West Timor, and Surabaya in East Java.

A limited number of passenger ships on regular trans-Pacific and round-the-world schedules call at Jakarta, with frequent connections from other Asian ports, especially Singapore. PELNI Lines (Pelayaran Nasional Indonesia), with offices at 50 Telok Blangah Rd, 02-02 Citiport Centre, Singapore (Tel: 272 6811, 271 5159) provide the most frequent services to Indonesian ports, including Jambi, Palembang, Panjang (all in Sumatra), Batam Island (off Sumatra), Pontianak (Kalimantan) and Jakarta.

An exit permit is required only for residents or visitors staying more than six months, with a tax of Rps 250,000 when leaving by air or Rps 100,000 leaving by sea being required from all residents. An airport tax of Rps 21,000 is levied on international departures. Tax for domestic flights depends on the airport. At Sukarno-Hatta, it is Rps 9,300. At some airports, there is no charge.

Immigration

All travellers to Indonesia must have a passport still valid for at least six months on arrival, with proof of onward or return passage. No visas for tourists are required for nationals of Australia, Austria, Argentina, Asean countries, Belgium, Brazil, Britain, Canada, Chile, Denmark, Egypt, Finland, France, Greece, Germany, Hungary, Iceland, Ireland, Italy, Japan, Kuwait, Lichtenstein, Luxembourg, Maldives, Malta, Mexico, Morocco, Monaco, New Zealand, the Netherlands, Norway, Saudi Arabia, South Korea, Spain, Sweden, Switzerland, Turkey, United Arab Emirates, United States, Venezuela, Yugoslavia, or for Taiwan nationals who hold MFA/M passports.

Visa-free entry is for a maximum of two months and is not extendable.

For nationals of countries not mentioned above, or for anyone making business trips, visas can be obtained from Indonesian embassies or consulates.

Citizens of South Africa and Israel must obtain special travel affidavits from Indonesian diplomatic missions. Taiwan passport holders are allowed visa-free entry only though Jakarta, Bali and Medan.

Holders of certificates of identity (CI) from Hong Kong can obtain 30-day visas for group travel comprising at least 10 people from the consulate-general in Hong Kong. Entry and departure must be in groups and travel and accommodation organized by a tour operator. Entry is allowed only through Jakarta, Bali and Medan.

Health

International certificates for smallpox and cholera are no longer required. However, typhoid, paratyphoid and cholera inoculations are strongly recommended. So are malaria pills, including those for choloroquin-resistant mosquito areas. Yellow fever inoculation is required of those arriving within six days of leaving or transiting an infected area. Vaccination against hepatitis B is also recommended.

Customs

Duty-free allowances for each visitor are: maximum one litre of alcoholic beverages; 200 cigarettes or 50 cigars or 100 grams of tobacco; a reasonable amount of perfume per adult. Photographic equipment, typewriters and recorders must be declared on entry and taken out on departure. TV sets, radios, narcotics, arms, ammunition, pornography, printed matter in Chinese characters and Chinese medicine are prohibited. Advance approval is necessary for transceivers and all movie films. Video cassettes must be censored by the Film Censor Board.

Currency

The rupiah is the unit of currency, exchanging about Rps 2,210:US$1. There are notes in denominations of 50,000, 20,000, 10,000, 5,000, 1,000, 500 and 100 and coins of 25, 50, 100 and 500 rupiah in circulation.

There is no restriction on the import or export of foreign currencies, but the export and import of Indonesian currency exceeding Rps 50,000 is prohibited. Most major foreign currencies can be readily exchanged in main city banks, money-changers and larger hotels. Some banks will not accept foreign notes, but these can be exchanged at a money changer. Cash is still the preferred transaction, although credit cards such as **American Express**, **Visa** and **MasterCard** are becoming more widely accepted.

In Jakarta, it is wise to carry a good amount of small notes for taxis and other small purchases. Not everyone will have change. Outside the capital, especially in areas that see few tourists, carry plenty of cash.

Language

The official language is Bahasa Indonesia, a version of Malay. Although it is spoken widely, there are still many areas — especially in the outlying islands — where regional languages and dialects are still spoken exclusively. On the main island of Java, the Javanese language coexists with Bahasa Indonesia, which does likewise with the Balinese language on Bali. English is the most common second language in the country, followed by Dutch. Among the Chinese population, one or more of the southern Chinese dialects are spoken and sometimes Mandarin. The Indonesian language uses the Roman script and alphabet, so reading signs is rarely a problem.

There is a wide selection of good local phrase books available at most books stores or department stores. Gramedia bookstores offer the largest variety of phrase books, particularly the *Kamus Lengkap* editions (in many languages) or *Short and Easy Conversation* and *How To Master the Indonesian Language.* Prices vary but they generally cost around Rps 5,000-10,000 each.

Climate

Straddling the equator, the country remains hot throughout the year, with day temperatures around 26-33°C. Temperatures at night vary considerably. While Jakarta remains warm, the temperature in Bandung can drop as low as 10°C. Jogjakarta, Bali and parts of east Java can be pleasantly cool in the evening. The humidity is usually high almost everywhere. Generally two seasons are well defined. The east monsoon from June to September brings dry weather while the west monsoon from December to March brings rain. Thunderstorms are frequent during the rainy season and the heaviest downfall is recorded in December and January. The average rainfall in the whole country is 102 centimetres.

Dress

Dress is normally informal in Indonesia. Light clothing with plenty of spares for changing during the day, is required for travel. In hilly regions a sweater is usually enough in the evening, though temperatures can reach freezing-point on slopes exceeding 3,000 metres. Day attire for men is shirt and trousers, with jacket and tie for formal occasions. Long-sleeved batik shirts are acceptable for evening functions. For women, dresses or blouses and shirt or trousers. Shorts, tank tops, mini skirts or low cut clothing should be worn only on the beach.

Business Hours

The Indonesian archipelago is spread over three time zones. Western Indonesia Standard Time is GMT plus seven hours, covering the islands of Sumatra, Java-Madura, West and Central Kalimantan. Central Indonesia Standard Time is GMT plus eight hours for East and South Kalimantan, Sulawesi, Bali and Nusatenggara. East Indonesia Standard Time is GMT plus nine hours for Maluku and Irian Jaya.

Government offices in Indonesia are open from 8 a.m.-4 p.m. Monday to Friday and some open from 8 a.m.-2 p.m. on Saturday.

Commercial offices and businesses are usually open from 8 a.m.-4:30 p.m. or from 9 a.m.-5 p.m., with a one-hour lunch break. Post offices open from 8 a.m.-3 p.m. Monday to Thursday, 8 a.m.-11.30 a.m. on Friday and 8 a.m.-2 p.m. on Saturday.

Local banks are open from 8 a.m.-4 p.m. Monday to Friday, and some are open from 8 a.m.-2 p.m. on Saturday.

In Jakarta, the Pasar Baru shopping centre, close to the Borobudur Hotel, is open from 9 a.m.-8 p.m. every day. Most of the shops in Block M at Kebayoran Baru are open from 9 a.m.-10 p.m. Sarinah, the large department store in Jalan Thamrin and Block M, is open from 9 a.m.-10 p.m. Monday to Saturday and from 10 a.m.-6 p.m. on Sunday. Smaller shops keep irregular hours, but usually open early in the morning and close late at night. In some provincial towns shops close in the afternoon and reopen at 5-6 p.m.

Restaurants are usually open until about 11 p.m. Smaller street stalls stay open later. Nightclubs stay open until 1-2 a.m. on weekdays, and until 3 a.m. on Saturday and Sunday. On religious and some public holidays night clubs are closed.

Doing Business

Business practice in Indonesia is pretty much standard, with a few alterations for local conditions and customs.

Most business people and senior government officials speak fluent English. However, it is worth checking before an appointment in case you need to take an interpreter. Jakarta is not an easy city to get around in. Do not make the mistake of scheduling too many appointments in one day — three to four should be enough, depending on where they are in relation to each other. Meetings also tend to last longer here.

Status is important in Indonesia. So, too, are social contacts. These cannot be divorced from business relationships and are very important to successful cooperation.

Bring plenty of business cards and hand them out freely. When receiving a card, read it and put it away carefully. Do not scribble or write notes on it. It is not necessary to have cards translated into Indonesian.

Punctuality is not as important to Indonesians as it is in the West. People will arrive late for appointments, miss deadlines, or events will start late. However, Westerners are expected to be on time, though some allowance is made for traffic and other such problems.

Likewise, do not make the mistake of thinking government offices open and close at the advertised hours. Many public servants arrive late and go home early.

When meeting people, and again when leaving, it is polite to shake hands, for both men and women. The visitor will often be served a drink (usually tea or coffee) and maybe a small snack. Wait until invited to do so before starting, and always at least sample whatever is offered.

The left hand is regarded as unclean, so avoid using it. Pointing with your forefinger or feet is rude. Most Indonesians are very polite and courteous people and value the same in others. Anger, shouting and aggression will not get you very far. Generally, Indonesians value harmony. This can sometimes mean they will agree with something to avoid disappointing you, rather than because they can deliver on their promise. It can also mean an inability to admit mistakes. High-pressure whirlwind business visits will accomplish nothing. Patience is a virtue.

Indonesia is proud of its religious tolerance, guaranteed in the Pancasila state ideology. Important religious holidays from all the main religions are observed. It is important visitors check they are not planning to arrive on such a day. Especially important is to avoid planning any business during Lebaran, the holiday which marks the end of the Ramadan fasting month. Many people return to their home villages or towns at this time and many businesses and shops close.

When it comes to business entertaining, business lunches are popular. Be careful about drinking alcohol and eating pork; your business contact may be a Muslim and take offence. Evening functions can also be useful. They tend to end early. It is best to avoid serving pork at such a function, though alcohol may be acceptable depending on your guest list.

Women are widely accepted, and successful, in business in Indonesia. Personal questions about your marriage, age and children are not intended to offend and are normal for both men and women.

Now that air-conditioning is widespread, western business suits are virtually standard business wear for meetings and appointments. However, business slacks and a shirt and tie are also acceptable in most circumstances. For women, fashionable short skirts are acceptable in Jakarta and the bigger cities. Do not wear skimpy tops anywhere. Invitations to functions will stipulate the dress requirements, usually batik or business suit. It is all right to wear a suit to a batik function. For women, wear a good business outfit. Casual means casual.

Courier services available include DHL (Tel: 830 6677-88); Skypax International (Tel: 520 1157-8, 525 2540) and Federal Express (Tel: 566 6944).

Car rental companies include:
Avis Tel: 314 2900, 315 0853
National Car Rental Tel: 314 3423, 314 3425
Blue Bird Tel: 794 4444, 794 1234
Jakarta International Taxi Tel: 314 3777

The leading hotels in Jakarta and major cities such as Surabaya and Bali have business centres which provide good secretarial services.

Rip-Offs

Like every country, Indonesia has its fair share of rip-offs. Most are fairly standard: problems with taxis, touts, people taking advantage of the visitor's unfamiliarity with the local currency, fake name brands being sold as the real thing.

When shopping, try to stick with authorized dealers. Beware: a sign bearing the logo of the brand does not mean the shop is an authorized dealer.

In Jakarta, most shops of any size are trustworthy. At Jakarta's Melawai Plaza, the place for gold, silver and watches, the shops clearly distinguish between genuine and fake watches and issue certificates for the weight of gold or silver bought. In Bali, ignore people selling "designer" items on the streets or beaches, unless you are more interested in getting a fake and a good story to tell your friends than a watch that works and perfume that does not cause people to give you dubious looks. The wrapping looks very genuine but the smell gives the game away.

One of the biggest potential problems is taxis. In Jakarta and several other major cities, they have meters and should use them. If not, get another; you do not have to wait long. At airports and train stations, only take a taxi from the marked stand. The touts who approach you are not offering a bargain.

If you are in a hire car, be wary of sudden flat tires or breakdowns. A popular trick, especially in Jakarta, is for gangs of three or four men to put spikes or tacks on the road at a busy intersection. When the car pulls over, they offer to change the tyre — then demand US$10 or so. Similarly, parked cars can be tampered with and once again the helpers who miraculously appear charge a hefty fee.

Whether in a car or taxi, always lock all the doors and keep the windows closed. Always keep a tight grip on your handbag, briefcase or carrycase; motorcycle-borne thieves can quickly relieve you of these and disappear through the traffic. Violent crime is not as big a problem as it is in other cities this size, but it does happen. Take the normal precautions.

Media

Three English language newspapers are published daily: the *Jakarta Post, Indonesian Observer* and *Indonesia Times*. These are available early in the morning in Jakarta. Outside the capital, they may be a day or two late. There are two weekly English language business magazines: *Business Indonesia Weekly* and *Economic and Business Review Indonesia*.

Major international and regional newspapers and magazines are relatively widely available in Jakarta and Bali. Newspapers such as the *Asian Wall Street Journal* and the *International Herald Tribune* can usually be bought the afternoon of publication. Some major newspapers from regional capitals, such as the *Singapore Straits Times*, can also be bought on the afternoon of publication. Some may take a day or two to arrive.

The best places to buy either local or international English language newspapers and magazines are bookshops in major hotels or shopping centres, such as the Times bookshop in the Sogo shopping centre in Jalan M.H. Thamrin.

Availability is limited outside Jakarta, Bali and major provincial cities.

Communications

International telephone, telex and fax connections are readily available in Jakarta, Bali and larger provincial cities in Java, though congestion is frequently a problem. The leading hotels provide all of these services.

Elsewhere, international communications can be difficult. Most hotels can arrange an operator-assisted international call, though delays are long — an hour or more. Many hotels outside the major cities do not yet have fax machines.

Public cardphones capable of making international calls are becoming increasingly available throughout the country. International communications from Indonesia are expensive. Depending on the country called, reverse charge or collect calls can be cheaper.

The line quality of telephone connections out of Indonesia is often poor, affecting data transmission.

Indonesia has a widespread and efficient network of public telephone offices, known as WARTEL. WARTEL offices are easy to find and the staff usually speak workable English. These offices all provide international phone call and fax facilities. Outside the main cities, these are the easiest and cheapest way of calling overseas.

Transport

Aircraft are the easiest and most comfortable means of travel in Indonesia. Regular services link all provincial cities to Jakarta daily. Flights are operated by **Garuda Indonesia**, **Merpati Nusantara Airlines**, **Sempati Air**, **Mandala** and **Bouraq**. Where possible, avoid Mandala and Bouraq.

SHIPS: Sea transport is the economic lifeline of the nation, both in the mass movement of people and trade. On Java, the main harbours are at Jakarta (Tanjung Priok) and Surabaya. From these two ports, ships ply to all corners of the archipelago.

PELNI, the state-owned shipping line at Jalan Gajah Mada 14, Jakarta (Tel: 384 4342, 385 4130) serves all the main Indonesian ports. The ships are by no means cruise vessels, though the fleet is being modernized. They can accommodate 1,000-1,500 passengers with air-conditioned cabins in all four classes. The first class cabins have private bathrooms. Sailing frequencies vary, but there is usually a service every week or two to most important ports.

TAXIS: Metered taxis are available in Jakarta, Surabaya, Bandung, Solo, Semarang and Medan. Fares are low — a 10-kilometre ride in Jakarta will cost about US$4. Transport from Sukarno-Hatta international airport to a hotel in the city centre will cost about US$12, including tolls and airport surcharge. At all major airports, taxis have fixed rates and vouchers are sold in terminal buildings. It is advisable to avoid touts offering taxi services.

Airport authorities operate buses to main points in Jakarta, leaving every half hour from outside the arrival terminal. Cost is Rps 3,000. In Jakarta, taxis are abundant, but passengers should insist they use their meter. A favourite ploy is to say the meter is broken. Get out and catch another taxi; you will not have to wait long. Flagfall is Rps 900.

Taxi rental by the hour is also available. **Blue Bird** (Tel: 794 1234) is one of the better operators. Knowledge of English among Indonesian taxi drivers is limited and, especially in Jakarta, knowledge of routes even worse.

MAJOR AIRLINES

Aeroflot, Tel: 570 2185
Air Canada, Tel: 570 1666
Air France, Tel: 520 2262
Air New Zealand, Tel: 571 1902
American Airlines, Tel: 231 1132
British Airways, Tel: 521 1500
Cathay Pacific, Tel: 380 6660
China Airlines, Tel: 570 6088, 570 4003
Continental Airlines, Tel: 334417, 334418
Delta Airlines, Tel: 521 2340
Eva Air, Tel: 520 5363
Finnair, Tel: 571 1911
Garuda Indonesia (head office), Tel: 231 1801; Reservations, 251 2259, 230 0892, 230 0308, 230 0568
Japan Airlines (JAL), Tel: 570 3883
KLM Royal Dutch Airlines, Tel: 310 7666
Korean Air, Tel: 521 2180
Lufthansa, Tel: 570 2005
Malaysia Airlines, Tel: 314 0909, 314 2102
Northwest Airlines, Tel: 520 3152
Pakistan International Airlines, Tel: 384 6264, 384 6256, 384 6141
Philippine Airlines, Tel: 384 2278, 384 2279
Qantas, Tel: 230 0277, 230 0655
Royal Brunei Airlines, Tel: 521 1842-6
Saudia Airlines, Tel: 571 0615, 522 4580-82
SAS, Tel: 252 4081, 252 4080
SilkAir, Tel: 520 8018
Singapore Airlines, Tel: 520 6881, 570 4422
Swissair, Tel: 378006, 373608
Thai Airways International, Tel: 314 0607
United Airlines, 570 7520

Where possible, have an address written in Bahasa Indonesia and a rough map or an idea of landmarks. It is not unusual for a taxi driver not to know even a major building or landmark.

BUSES IN JAKARTA: Non-air-conditioned buses in Jakarta cost Rps 250 regardless of the distance. More comfortable PATAS (blue and white) buses cost Rps 550 for non-air-conditioned and Rps 1,300 air-conditioned, again regardless of distance.

MICROLETS BEMOS: These are small buses which can carry 10 passengers and ply certain routes. Fares are cheap and depend on the distance.

BAJAJS: distinctive orange, small, three-wheeled motor-tricycles. Banned from major streets, but very useful in local areas.

BECAKS: Pedal trishaws are banned in Jakarta. They still operate in many other cities and towns and are an ideal way of taking a leisurely look around. Usually Rps 500-1,000 will be quite generous.

HIRE CARS: It is difficult to rent a car without a driver on a daily basis in Jakarta. Traffic congestion, unclear traffic signs and a confused street network make driving yourself a questionable proposition anyway. **Avis** (Tel: 314 2900) and **National** (Tel: 314 3423) are two companies that do hire. Cost is about Rps 200,000 a day for a small sedan. With driver, the cost is about Rps 230,000 a day. The locally produced Kijang is available at slightly cheaper rates.

Car hire is a much better proposition in Bali. Prices are quite reasonable, ranging from about Rps 75,000 without driver to around Rps 175,000 a day with driver. Most hotels will recommend a car hire firm, which will bring a car for you.

TRAINS: Train services are available throughout Java and in part of Sumatra, around Medan, in the north, and Lampung in the south. Several trains run between Jakarta and the main Javanese cities daily. The air-conditioned Bima and Mutiara night trains run from Jakarta to Surabaya. The Bima sleeper train travels south through Jogjakarta and Solo; the Mutiara north through Semarang. From Jakarta to Surabaya takes a little over 12 hours. Cost is about Rps 58,000 on either train for Executive A class.

There are also frequent services between Jakarta and Bandung.

Trains serving the west (to Sumatra) leave from Tanah Abang station, with connecting ferry services across the Sunda Straits. From Jakarta to Palembang can take about 30 hours.

Train timetables change frequently.

The low cost of train travel means the trains are usually full, and tickets can only be bought one or two days in advance. Buying tickets through a travel agent can save a lot of time and inconvenience.

COACHES: Express coaches linking the large towns and cities and local buses serving the surrounding countryside operate throughout Indonesia. Many of the long-distance buses offer video, toilets and air-conditioning. Others are more basic. Travelling by road through Indonesia can open up some beautiful scenery. However, bus drivers have a well-deserved reputation for very dangerous driving.

Tours

There are hundreds of reputable and reliable travel agencies operating in Indonesia, offering inbound, outbound and domestic travel services, documentation, hotel reservations, specialty tours, travel insurance and IATA agency protection. Most have offices in Jakarta, Bali and major cities.

They include: **Vayatour**, Jl Batutulis 38, Jakarta. Tel: 384 1601, 345 4457. Fax: 345 5252. **Tomaco**, Jakarta Theatre Bldg, Jl Thamrin. Tel: 390 8390, 230 0921. Fax: 314 0215. **Natrabu**, Jl Augus Salim 29A. Tel: 314 2876, 390 4689. Fax: 390 4690. **Anta Express**, G/F, Wisma Bumiputera, Jl Jend. Sudirman Kav. 75. Tel: 525 4625, 525 5450. Fax: 571 3007.

Accommodation

Optimism in the future of tourism in Indonesia has generated strong interest in hotel and resort development. In keeping with the government's desire to boost non-oil revenues, more hotels and resorts are being built and existing ones upgraded throughout the country. Jakarta, Bali, Jogjakarta, Surabaya and Bandung, in particular, offer first-class accommodation. Indonesia also abounds in pleasant and clean lower grade hotels to suit the budget traveller.

The top grade hotels in Jakarta include: **Borobudur Intercontinental**, **Grand Hyatt**, **Hyatt Aryaduta**, **Jakarta Hilton**, **Mandarin Oriental**, **Sahid Jaya**, **Sari Pan Pacific**, **Shangri-La**, **President Hotel**, **Le Meridien** and the state-owned **Hotel Indonesia**. All three and two-star hotels in the capital have air-conditioned rooms, private bathrooms with hot and cold water, telephones in the rooms, bars, restaurants and room service. Most three-star hotels have swimming pools, discos and shopping arcades. Top class hotels are frequently full, so book well in advance.

PHOTO: B.J. ADAMS

Fishing at Bali.

ACCOMMODATION UPCOUNTRY

Bali has experienced the highest rate of hotel growth, but other provinces such as West and Central Java are also experiencing a boom.

In Bandung (West Java) the most exciting development is the preservation of two old hotels in art deco style — **The Grand Hotel Preanger** and the **Savoy Homann**. **Hotel Papandayan** also offers top-rate accommodation. Further along the west coast there is the **Samudra Beach Hotel** at Pelabuhan Ratu.

In central Java, Jogjakarta has a number of fine hotels such as the **Ambarrukmo Palace**, **Garuda Hotel** and the **Mutiara**. Other tourist areas such as north and west Sumatra and north and south Sulawesi, now have all the comforts of star-rated hotels.

The choice of accommodation in Bali, whether at beach resorts or in the mountains, is almost inexhaustible and at the top end there are so many fine hotels it is impossible to single out a few for mention. Worthy of special note are the detached bungalow-style hotels which make up much of the accommodation on Bali. Most are set in pleasant garden surroundings on or near the beach, providing closer contact with the charm of Bali than would be possible in conventional-type hotels.

In towns where there are no first class hotels, most have air-conditioned rooms, but many are still equipped with Asian-style bathrooms, known in Indonesia as "Bak Mandi" — a tank of water and a plastic dipper for a "do-it-yourself" shower. Mosquitoes are a problem even in some of the better hotels and it is important to carry mosquito repellent and to take anti-malaria tablets.

Dining

Over the centuries, to the islands' rich abundance of fish, coconuts and spices, have been added culinary influences from India and, to a lesser extent, from China. There is plenty of tempting food on sale in the Jakarta streets, but eating from roadside stalls and carts can be risky, as well as delicious. Take a close look at the food and if in doubt don't eat. Also look around to see how the bowls and glasses are washed — sometimes the same bucket of murky water is used endlessly.

Fried rice in Indonesia rises above itself as **nasi goreng** to be virtually a national dish — rice is fried in coconut oil with eggs, meat, tomato, cucumber and chillies, usually with a fried egg on top. Try the spicy Padang food from Sumatra. Eaten with the fingers; different dishes are brought out on a dozen or so plates. At the end of the meal, what you have eaten is added up and your bill worked out. Also try the grilled fish from Makasar (South Sulawesi), the soto ayam (chicken soup) found everywhere and the Tapanuli specialties from North Sulawesi.

Most foreign cuisines are available, with Japanese one of the most popular. Regardless of the food chosen, eating out in Indonesia is very cheap, although imported wine is expensive.

One Indonesian experience not to be missed is the *rijstafel* — Dutch for "rice table." It is basically rice and lots of other Indonesian dishes, all with a Dutch interpretation. They are served all together on one table buffet-style, or brought individually to the diner's table by waiters and waitresses. One of the best in Jakarta is at the **Oasis Restaurant**, in Jalan Raden Saleh, where the dishes are brought to the table in an impressive procession.

Across the road is the **Raden Kuring**, which offers cheap, delicious Sundanese and Javanese food in an open-sided restaurant, accompanied by traditional dances from around the country.

As the food business expands to meet the growing demand, many restaurants around Jakarta are also specializing in Western food. **La Bastille** in Menteng, offering French dishes, is popular for its unique atmosphere and entertainment. **Cafe de Paris**, on Jalan Kapt. Tendean, is another good French restaurant. Try also **Le Maritime**, for French seafood, or **Le Rendezvous** for traditional French fare, both in **Le Meridien**.

For good, inexpensive Japanese food, go to **Sushi** on the fourth floor of the Ratu Plaza shopping centre, Jl Kebon Binatang III. Also in Jl Kebon Binatang III is **Art and Curio**, a popular place for Indonesian and European food. **Natrabu**, in Jl Augus Salim (most taxi drivers still know it as Jl Sabang), serves good Padang food. For those who fancy Italian food, **Il Punto** in the World Trade Centre, Jalan Sudirman, is one of the best, if a little pricey. Also good is **Pinocchio's**, nearby in Wisma Metropolitan I. **Hazara**, in Jl Wahid Hasyim, and **Eastern Promise**, in Jl Kemang Raya, are two of the better Indian restaurants.

For something different, try the **King Cobra**, Jl Mangga Besar, specializing in snake, cobra's blood and bat.

Bintang, Anker and San Miguel are the three locally brewed beers and can be recommended. But beer from all over the world is also available at reasonable prices.

In Denpasar, Kuta and Sanur in Bali there is also a good assortment of restaurants. One of the best known for seafood is **Poppies**, in Kuta. By the beachside market, try the seafood restaurant with stalls along the back offering a variety of tasty snacks. Also on the Sanur side, a few minutes' walk from the Bali Hyatt, the **Telaga Naga** serves excellent Sichuan and Cantonese food. The **Penjor**, also in Sanur, offers regional dishes. **Pertamina** Cottages, in Kuta, have a variety of good Japanese and European food.

Entertainment

Indonesian nightlife, even in Jakarta, is muted and very innocent compared with some Southeast Asian capitals.

As Indonesia's major tourist destination, Bali offers a constant parade of festivals and entertainment. Almost every day, in one village or another, there is a festival which visitors are welcome to attend. The elaborate cremation ceremonies can often be watched, as long as visitors do not rudely intrude and make their cameras too obtrusive.

Exhibitions of Balinese dancing can be seen on most evenings, either in the villages or at one of the hotel theatres. Some of the larger hotels will also have dinner music and other entertainment in the main dining room. Good jazz or cabaret are also performed by local entertainers in many restaurants.

Jogjakarta is also the home of some of Indonesia's traditional forms of entertainment. A performance of the *wayang kulit* shadow puppets, complete with *gamelan* accompaniment, can be seen most evenings at the outdoor theatre at the **Ambarrukmo Palace Hotel**.

The People's Amusement Park, open every evening, offers several performances for very little cost. The shows include drama, music and puppets. At the **Prambanan temple**, outside Jogjakarta, the Ramayana epic Hindu dance is performed during full moons.

Jakarta offers a complete range of entertainment from Western style, to traditional, to modern Indonesian dance and drama. **Taman Ismail Marzuk** is the capital's biggest arts centre. It has a 1,000-seat theatre, a smaller theatre, an open-air theatre and a theatre in the round. Two halls host fine arts exhibitions, and there is a planetarium and several movie theatres. There are always several shows, plays and exhibitions being staged.

Wayang Orang and *Ketoprak* (traditional Javanese performances) are staged at the Bharata Theatre in Jl Kalilio. The National Museum on Jl Merdeka Barat also has performances on Sunday at 8 p.m. and the puppet museum stages a play at 10 a.m. on Sunday. The large hotels all have discos and live bands. **Pitstop**, in the Sari Pan Pacific, and the Borobudur's **Music Room** are popular. Other nightspots worth a visit are the **Tanamur**, Jl Tanag Abang Timur, the **Jaya Pub**, in Jl Thamrin, the **Green Pub** in the Djakarta Theatre building, **Planet Hollywood** in Jl Gatot Subroto, **Jamz Jazz Club** in Jl Panglima Polim, **Sportsman's Bar & Grill** in Jl Palatehan I and **Hard Rock Cafe** in Jl M.H. Thamrin. Also, try the **Dynasty** nightclub, at the 8th floor, Glodok Plaza, in Jl Pinangsia Raya.

Shopping

With Indonesia's economic boom have come vast shopping centres and an increased variety of things to buy and places to buy them. Value for money is also improving and on many items the bigger shops offer prices competitive with other cities in the region.

An increasing number of products are being made here and finding their way into local shops at good prices. In addition to arts and crafts, products manufactured locally cover everything from electrical goods to sports gear. There are also porcelain and other pottery articles that have been imported into the country over the past centuries from China and other Asian countries. A number of antique shops in the capital sell such pieces. **Jalan Majapahit** has several such shops. In addition, to the traditional fabrics from different parts of Indonesia, there is also a wide range of garments which has been created and developed to meet the changing tastes of the fashion world.

Batik, *ikat* and *tenun* (hand-painted, hand-woven, tie-and-dye) have spread over different parts of the country and more are finding their way from remote areas to the bigger towns and cities. The Sumba blankets, the songkets of Sumatra, the silks of South Sulawesi and the *jumputan* (tie-dye) of Palembang are all available in Jakarta.

Traditional woodcarvings from Bali, the primitive arts of Irian Jaya, Nias and East Kalimantan, are all now in great demand.

Replicas of antique pieces can be made to suit any design. Rattan, bamboo and reed-weaving have long been on the international market. Some of the most unusual pieces are the rattan baskets from Lombok. Paintings and other works of art abound in Indonesia. Many galleries in Jogjakarta, Bali and Jakarta stock the works of internationally recognized Indonesian artists. **Neka Gallery**, in Ubud, Bali, is one. In Jakarta, look at **Djody**, **Oet's**, **Hadiprana**, **Mon Decor**, **Duta** and the **Pasar Seni** art market at Ancol.

Mass-produced canvasses and batik paintings are also widely available. Try **Jalan Suropati** in Jakarta, or **Jalan Malioboro** in Jogja.

Indonesian cultured and baroque pearls have also found their way on to the international market. Most of the cultured pearl farms are in the eastern part of the country. Gold is widely sold, at good prices. **Melawai Plaza**, near Blok M, is the best place for gold, silver and watches. The famed silverwork from Kota Gede can be found throughout Jakarta, Jogjakarta and in the village itself.

Other metals, such as bronze, brass and tin are widely available. The little shops along

Jalan Surabaya in Jakarta's Menteng suburb, and **Ancol's Pasar Seni** should not be missed.

Bandung is famous for its Indonesian-made jeans. The street where most of the jeans shops are, **Jalan Cihampelas**, shows just how imaginative shopkeepers can become to attract customers.

In Jakarta, the best places for a wide range of Indonesian handicrafts at reasonable, fixed, prices are the **Pasaraya department stores** in Blok M and Manggarai, **Plaza Indonesia**, attached to the Grand Hyatt hotel and **Sarinah's** on Jalan Thamrin.

Sports

Soccer, badminton, tennis and swimming are among the most popular sports in Indonesia. There are a number of public swimming pools and most of the better hotels have good pools. The larger hotels also have fitness centres. Among the best are the Borobudur and the Hilton, which also offer good facilities for tennis, squash and fitness workouts, and even have jogging tracks.

For tennis, try the **Senayan sports complex**, the **Kemayoran Tennis Centre** or the **Kemang Sport and Recreation Centre**.

Golf is booming in Indonesia and there are several good courses which allow visitors.

Holidays

Indonesia officially recognizes religious freedom and tolerance. Major holidays from the main religious are observed. Many of the religious holidays fall on different days each year. Muslim events slip about 10-11 days each year because they are decided by the lunar calendar.

Major holidays include:

January: January 1, New Year's Day.
Variable: Idhul Adha, the Muslim day of sacrifice.
January-February: Chinese New Year.
February: Maulid Nabi Muhammad, Muhammad's birthday. Isra' Mi'raj Nabi Muhammad, the ascension of Muhammad.
March-April: Wafat isa Almasih, the Christian Good Friday. Idul Fitri, two public holidays marking the end of the fasting month of Ramadan. Hari Raya Nyepi: The Hindu New Year, occurs at the spring equinox.
May: Kenaikan isa Almasih (the ascension of Christ). Hari Raya Waisak, commemorates Buddha's birth, death and enlightenment.
August: August 17, Hari Proklamasi Kemerdekaan, independence day. Tahun Baru Hijriyah, the Islamic New Year.
December: December 25, Natal Hari Pertama, Christmas Day.

ADDRESSES

The Director-General of Tourism (DGT) is in Jakarta and is administered under the Department of Tourism, Post and Telecommunications, which has offices in all the main tourist areas.

The offices are known as Kanwil PARPOSTEL, or Regional Office of Tourism, Post and Telecommunications. Each of the 27 provinces of Indonesia also has its own tourist offices, which can be identified by the abbreviation DIPARDA (regional tourist service). These offices can assist in providing the DGT's own publication, *Indonesia's Travel Planner*, other useful travel booklets and maps.

DISCOVERING INDONESIA

JAKARTA

The capital, Jakarta, seems at pains to hide itself in a maze of winding streets that pass through nondescript residential and shopping areas, with only here and there areas of dense high-rise buildings that suggest a major city. Wide expanses of parkland, such as the **Medan Merdeka** (Independence Park) with its towering **Monas monument** and **Banteng Square**, fragment the city and the visitor feels to be forever walking vast distances.

The city has expanded greatly since the days when it was called Batavia; the population is now more than 8.5 million, swollen with Indonesians from villages and islands all over the country attracted by work and the glitter of the capital. Very roughly, the city lies along a north-south axis, running from the old Dutch quarter near the sea, through the main centre of the newer part of town and further south to the modern detached residential suburbs.

Merdeka (independence) Square is the city's central landmark. The **Monas monument**, topped by a gilded flame, can be seen from miles around. It is an ideal spot from which to begin discovering the city. In Jalan Merdeka Utara, running along the north side of the park, is the presidential **Merdeka Palace**, the former official residence of the Dutch governors-general.

Several hundred yards away, on Jalan

Downtown Jakarta. PHOTO: PATRICK LUCERO

Merdeka Barat along the park's western edge, is the **National Museum** (Gedung Gajah). It contains an excellent collection of Indonesian and other Asian sculptures, ceramics, gold and jewellery, and a small prehistory collection. The museum closes at 2 p.m. on Tuesday, Wednesday and Thursday, 11 a.m. on Friday, 1 p.m. on Saturday and 3 p.m. on Sunday. Guided tours in English begin at 9:30 a.m. on Tuesday, Wednesday and Thursday, in French at 9 a.m. on Wednesday and Japanese at 9 a.m. on Tuesday.

From the northeast corner of Medan Merdeka, can be seen the massive bulk of the **Istiqlal Mosque**, the biggest in Southeast Asia. A short distance further on is the **Catholic Cathedral**, standing alongside Banteng Square, where the central statue depicts a West Irian man breaking the chain of colonial subjugation. Nearby, is the **Borobudur Intercontinental Hotel**, and a short walk from here north across Jalan Dr. Sutomo and its canal is **Pasar Baru**, one of the capital's interesting markets.

From the southwest corner of Medan Merdeka runs Jalan Thamrin, one of Jakarta's major streets. Most of the city's leading hotels, some embassies and some leading shops are along this street. There is a helpful **Visitor Information Centre** (Tel: 315 4094 or 314 2067) in the Djakarta Theatre building, across the road from McDonald's.

If you head west from the presidential palace along Jalan Merdeka Utara, you will come to Jalan Majapahit at the T-junction. A turn right will take you past several **antique shops**. Other antique shops in Jakarta can be found along Jalan Surabaya (worth a special visit), Jalan Kebon Sirih Timur, Blok M and Ciputat.

From Jalan Majapahit, northwards will take you to **Jalan Gajah Mada**, with **Jalan Hayam Wuruk** on the opposite side. These two main business streets, heavily congested during the day, are home to many discos, bars and other nightspots. Further north is the **Glodok "Chinatown"** area. The **National Archives** building on Jalan Gajah Mada, built in 1760, is a beautifully-preserved example of Dutch colonial architecture. Heading straight north will take you to the old Jakarta. Here is **Fatahillah Square**, once the centre of old Batavia. It contains three museums: **The Jakarta Museum**, in a 17th century building which was once the town hall; **the Puppet Museum**, with a collection from all over the country, on the west side of the square; and the **Art Gallery and Ceramics Museum** on the east side of the square.

At the port of **Sunda Kelapa**, not very far

from this area, there are vessels from the world's largest fleet of commercial sailing ships. These Buginese sailing ships are still sailing to and from Ujung Pandang (Makasar) just as they did in Joseph Conrad's time. Hire a water taxi and explore the waterfront. Also here is the **Maritime Museum** and the **fish market** (Pasar Ikan).

Towards the Bay of Jakarta and midway between old Jakarta and the Tanjung Priok port complex, is the **Taman Impian Jaya Ancol** entertainment park, which includes **Dunia Fantasi (Fantasy World)**, an arts and crafts market and the **Ancol Golf Course**. The complex also includes a drive-in theatre, night clubs, five swimming pools, an oceanarium, bowling alley and watersports.

Also worth visiting, is **Taman Mini Indonesia Indah** (Beautiful Indonesia in Miniature). This extensive park, south of the city centre, gives a glimpse of the diversity of Indonesia. Traditional houses, dresses and customs from all 27 provinces are displayed here.

As with the Ancol complex, **Taman Mini** is popular and is very crowded at weekends.

DAY TRIPS FROM JAKARTA

The small hill town of Bogor lies just 64 kilometres south of Jakarta. Here is the magnificent **Bogor Palace**, the country retreat for the Dutch colonial governors-general. Nearby, are the **Botanic Gardens**, conceived in 1827 and covering 111 hectares. The gardens contain more than 10,000 species of plants and trees, a herbarium, a zoological museum and a library of more than 60,000 scientific volumes. The orchid house contains more than 3,000 registered hybrids. In 1860, a branch of the gardens was established in **Cibodas**, to the southeast, for plants requiring a colder climate. This other garden stands on the slopes of the twin volcanoes **Pangrango** and **Gede** and is easily accessible from the main road running from Bogor to Bandung.

Beyond Bogor, on the south coast and 180 kilometres from Jakarta, is **Pelabuhan Ratu**, a popular coastal getaway.

Bandung, famous as the site of the first Afro-Asian conference in April, 1955, is 175 kilometres from Jakarta, via Bogor and the mountain resort of Cianjur. The town stands on a plateau 700 metres above sea level. From Bandung, you can make a trip to the top of the nearby **Tangkuban Prahu** volcano and descend into the crater. The town's zoological gardens are also worth visiting.

Just off the north shore of Jakarta is **Pulau Seribu** (Thousand Islands), which offer good snorkelling and diving. There are several resorts among the islands, which are reached by boat or aircraft. Trips can be arranged through any travel agent.

The **Carita-Sambolo** beach area on the west coast of Java offers an ideal place to escape the city for a day or two. It is about two hours by road from the capital and faces Sumatra, across the remains of the **Krakatau** volcano, which in 1883 erupted with one of the most devastating natural explosions ever recorded. The Krakatau Beach Hotel has an interesting collection of clippings and photographs about Krakatau.

DISCOVERING UPCOUNTRY JAVA

From Jakarta or Bandung, you can travel by road, rail or air to the central Javanese town of **Jogjakarta** — one of the most pleasant and quietly charming spots in Asia. The town is the cultural centre for the area and the seat of one of the remaining and most active sultans, Sultan Hamengku Buwono X. It was also the revolutionary capital of the Republic of Indonesia from 1946-50.

A long main street runs through the town, the central portion of which is a good shopping place for silverwork, batik and other local curios. At the southern end of the main street is the **kraton** (sultan's palace), which offers examples of traditional Javanese architecture and decoration. The pavilions in the kraton proper include the **Prabayeks**, in which the sacred weapons and gem-studded symbols of royalty are kept. Next to it is the **Golden Pavilion**, in which prominent guests were formerly received. The glass pavilion next door, called **Bangsai Manis**, was used for state banquets. Permits to visit the palace are available at the kraton entrance.

Nightly from 8 p.m. to 1 a.m. at the People's **Amusement Park** there is an interesting programme, including dance and drama performances. Most of the hotels also arrange a performance of the traditional *wayang kulit* (shadow puppets).

Also of interest nearby are the old fortress of **Diponegoro** at Tegalejo; the restored fortress of Hamengku Buwono I, built in 1761 and now called **Tamansari**; the village of **Kota Gede**, six kilometres east of Jogja, famous for its silverwork and the site of the tombs of the first kings of Mataram, from which the sultans are

Jogjakarta Palace. PHOTO: JOHN McBETH

descended; and the **royal tombs** of Imogiri, to the southeast.

The area around Jogjakarta is notable for its wealth of architectural remains of Java's classical period (eighth and ninth centuries), when the influence of Indian traditions, especially religious, was at its height. There are numerous sites from this and later periods spread widely over central Java; an interesting collection is located on the mystical **Dieng Plateau**, north of Jogjakarta, via Magelang and Wonosobo.

The most famous temples around Jogja are **Borobudur** and **Prambanan**. Borobudur, a Mahayana Buddhist stupe-temple, is a magnificent monument, dating from around AD 800 and rising 43 metres above the jungle.

The building, stone terraces mounted on an early mound, was probably built under the dynasty of the Sailendras (kings of the mountain) around 800. It was badly defaced by the Muslims and was in ruins until restored by the Dutch. The Indonesian Government, with aid from Unesco, undertook a major programme to restore and preserve the temple. This was completed in 1983.

Hotels and travel agents in Jogja can organize visits to Borobudur (generally a half day trip) for about Rps 30,000 per person.

About 16 kilometres northeast of Jogja on the Surakarta (Solo) road is the **Prambanan** group of temples — mainly Hindu, but featuring some Buddha images. The buildings were probably constructed in the second half of the 9th century under the Mataram dynasty. The compound has a square inner court enclosed by a wall. Within this court are eight stone shrines. From May-October each year, during the rainy season, the Ramayana Ballet Festival is held over four nights at each full moon at the Prambanan temple on a specially prepared stage. Not to be missed if you are in town at the right time.

From Prambanan, the road continues north to **Surakarta** (Solo) about 72 kilometres from Jogja. The kraton of the Susuhunan of Surokarta is larger than that of Jogjakarta. The first part of it is now an art gallery. The court dances, *bedoyo* and *serimpi*, are still taught and most of the dancers for the Ramayana Ballet Festival come from this area.

An interesting spot in the town is the **Sriwedani Amusement Park**, which has a zoological garden, a theatre for *wayang orang* (live classical dance), restaurants and curio shops. Free dance performances are held here on Sunday mornings.

About 120 kilometres north of Surakarta is the port of **Semarang**. The Pasar Johor mar-

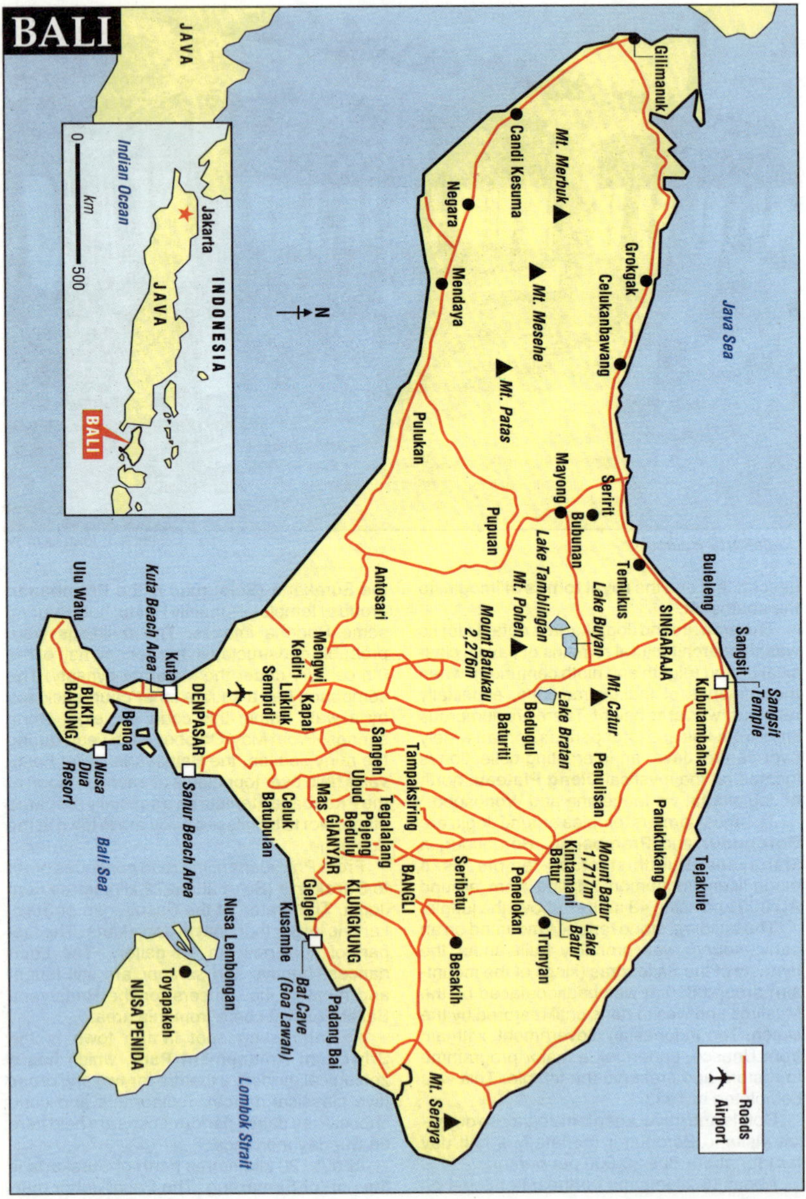
BALI
JAVA
Java Sea
Bali Sea
Lombok Strait
Gilimanuk
Candi Kesuma
Mt. Merbuk
Negara
Grokgak
Celukanbawang
Mendaya
Mt. Mesehe
Mt. Patas
Pulukan
Seririt
Mayong
Bubunan
Pupuan
Temukus
Lake Tamblingan
Lake Buyan
Mt. Pohen
Mount Batukau
2,276m
Antosari
Buleleng
SINGARAJA
Sangsit
Sangsit Temple
Kubutambahan
Mt. Catur
Lake Bratan
Bedugul
Baturiti
Penulisan
Panuktukang
Tejakule
Mount Batur
1,717m
Kintamani
Batur
Lake Batur
Penelokan
Trunyan
Besakih
Mt. Seraya
Seribatu
BANGLI
KLUNGKUNG
Gelgel
Kusambe
Bat Cave
(Goa Lawah)
Padang Bai
Tampaksiring
Tegalalang
Pejeng
Bedulu
GIANYAR
Mas
Ubud
Celuk
Batubulan
Sangeh
Kapal
Mengwi
Kediri
Lukluk
Sempidi
DENPASAR
Kuta
Kuta Beach Area
BUKIT BADUNG
Benoa
Nusa Dua Resort
Ulu Watu
Sanur Beach Area
Nusa Lembongan
Toyapakeh
NUSA PENIDA
N
Roads
Airport
INDONESIA
JAVA
Jakarta
BALI
Indian Ocean
0
km
500

ket is next to the public square and other places of interest include the great mosque and the main shopping street, Jalan Bojong.

Surabaya, to the east, is Indonesia's second-largest city. Home to Indonesia's eastern naval fleet, it is the country's second port and the centre of sea connections with the eastern islands.

Further southeast, via Pasuruan, is the still active volcano of **Mount Bromo**. You can ride a small pony across the sea of sand to the base of the mountain. Viewing the sunrise from the top is popular, but be sure to wear very warm clothes. **Mt Bromo Cottages**, below the summit, offers good accommodation, and balaclavas, pullovers, gloves and scarfs are on sale. You'll need them.

From Surabaya's Tanjung Perak port, a half-hour ferry ride brings you to the town of Kamal on **Madura Island**, famous for its bull races (karapan sapi). The rider stands on a large wooden pole slung between two yoked beasts. The races start at village level and culminate in the grand final in the local capital, Pemekasan, in October.

BALI

The singular character of Bali has always enchanted visitors. Alone of the Indonesian islands, Bali succeeded in preserving its Hindu culture against the advance of Islam. The island of 5,620 square kilometres has more than 20,000 temples. They are found everywhere — scattered in the terraced rice fields, in cemeteries, in markets, on the beaches, in caves and even among the roots of giant trees. It was said that the spirit world dominated the lives of the people of Bali more than anywhere on earth. Today modern commercialism has intruded, but there is still a spiritual quality to be found if it is looked for.

However, the majority of tourists these days come in package tours for the beaches — fast disappearing to erosion — the tropical weather (still intact) and Bali's reputation, especially in Australia, for a swinging, uninhibited lifestyle. Bali is the nearest part of Asia offering an easy holiday to Australians, for many of whom it constitutes their first and perhaps only contact with the region. Unfortunately they have attracted pedlars (the Balinese tend to say they are Javanese) who pester everybody with fake watches, "designer" perfume and other suspect goods.

One can fly direct to Bali from Jakarta or from outside Indonesia, but it can also be reached by ferry from Ketapang in eastern Java. The ferry crosses every hour to Gilimanuk, from where it's another three hours by bus to the capital **Denpasar**.

Sanur Beach, Bali's main tourist centre, lies 10 kilometres to the east of Denpasar. Most of the island's premier hotels are in this area. Others are in Denpasar itself or at **Nusa Dua** (a quieter area), and to the southwest at **Kuta Beach**, near the airport.

Denpasar has a good collection of cultural pieces from various periods in Balinese history. Bali's picturesque countryside and wealth of temples are beyond the town. The island's villagers are generally friendly and visitors can join in the crowds to watch the popular cock-fights or observe a ritual cremation.

From nearby villages, a number of interesting temples can be visited, some with distinctive scenic views. Many of these villages can be visited in a half-day by car, or better still, by four-wheel drive, since many roads are in poor condition. Vehicles are easily available and are brought to your hotel. It is worth asking the car-hire company for a list of bridges closed for repair. Road signs are few and primitive and a road map is essential. It is easy to misjudge distances, which are very short, and overshoot your destination.

Villages worth visiting include **Celuk** (for its silverware), **Mas** (woodcarving) and **Ubud**, 24 kilometres north of Denpasar, the cradle of the *legong*, the finest of Balinese dances and of Balinese dancing and music in general. It is also a centre of Balinese painting, with a large number of artists, both local and foreign. The town's small museum traces the development of the district's artists over recent decades. Close to the nearby village of **Bedulu** is the Goa Gaja (Elephant Cave), whose stone carvings date from the 11th century.

West of these villages (but one must take a separate road from Denpasar) is the Monkey Forest at Sangeh, home of hundreds of monkeys. Be careful. They are not averse to biting visitors and snatching cameras and bags and can be vicious.

To the northeast of Denpasar are the two holy volcanoes of **Gunung Agung** and **Mount Batur**. A very full day, by car, will allow you to visit both mountains and stop at the main sites along the way. **Mount Batur** (1,900 metres) can be reached via Celuk, Mas and Ubud. Visitors should also stop at **Gunung Kawi**, where there are ancient burial towers hewn from the rocky hillside, and also visit the holy

Tirta Empul Spring at Tampaksiring. The village of **Penelokan** stands on the edge of the **Batur** volcanic crater, offering a fine view of Lake Batur, in the crater. You can see where new lava has recently flowed from the small internal volcanic outlet.

Heading south from Penelokan by the more easterly of the two roads leading from the town, one reaches the town of **Bangli** and its temple of Pura Kehen. You must continue well south from Bangli to gain access to the road heading east through Klukung to make the ascent to the **Besakih**, the most holy of Bali's temples, more than 1,000 metres up the slopes of Gunung Agung.

LOMBOK

Just to the east of Bali lies Lombok. Often referred to as an unspoiled version of Bali, this small island with a Balinese Hindu culture offers clean beaches, rich tropical forests and, in some parts, dry country similar to outback Australia. Lombok's capital, Mataram, is also the capital of West Nusatengarra province. But the main tourist development is **Sengiggi Beach** on the west coast, near the capital. Lombok is well served by domestic flights and ferry service from Bali and Sumbawa, to the east.

SUMATRA

Medan, the island's chief city, lies far to the north on the east coast, almost opposite the Malaysian island of Penang. It is a centre for rubber production, but of no great tourist interest other than being a gateway to the pleasant highlands. Belawan Deli, 22 kilometres away, is the port for Medan. Berastagi, further south, a popular resort with several hotels, is noted for its volcano and hot springs. About 175 kilometres (six hours by road) from Medan is the strange and beautiful **Lake Toba**. The lake is more than 1,000 metres above sea-level and surrounds the densely populated island of Samosir. The cool upland countryside is covered with tobacco, rubber and palm-oil plantations. This is the region of the Bataks, whose architecture is distinguished by huge overhanging roofs, often with elaborately carved gables.

An adventurous traveller can continue almost right across Sumatra with a 28-hour bus journey from Toba to **Bukittinggi**, near the west coast of the island. Bukittinggi lies between a towering volcano and an equally grand mountain. From there it is only a few hours by bus or narrow-gauge train to the main port city of **Padang** — capital of the Minangkabau region. The Minangkabaus are famous for their houses and rice barns with high roofs rising to a peak at each end.

Palembang in the southeast now only a sad reminder of its past great days as capital of the Srivijaya Kingdom, is a centre for the great Sumatran oilfields across the Musi River at Plaju and Sungei Gerong. The old traditions manage to survive with the production of fine woven fabrics and unique local dances.

SULAWESI (CELEBES)

Ujung Pandang (once known as Makasar or Macassar) is the main southern city on the island and home of the seafaring Bugis. It is noted for crab, lobster and fish grilled over an open fire.

A road runs north for 280 kilometres to Rantepao, a region known for its splendid architectural woodcarving of the South Torajas and for the local burial sites.

The Minahasas of Manado, in the far north, are distinguished from the other peoples of Sulawesi by their light skins and almost universal adoption of Christianity. The seas off Manado are renowned for some of the best coral diving in the world.

FLORES

Flores is one of the world's most active earthquake and volcanic areas. The 375 kilometre-long island boasts 14 active volcanoes. The island is popular with tourists mainly for the famous three coloured lakes of the Kelimetu volcano, for snorkelling off the west coast and as a jumping off point for Komodo Island and its famous giant lizards, to the west.

The three lakes — each a different colour, which changes every few years — are one of the most photographed sites in Indonesia. According to local legend, the souls of the dead go to these lakes: one for the old, one for the young and one for murderers.

EAST TIMOR

Once under Portuguese rule, East Timor is now open to travellers. It had been a closed province since the bloody civil war and subsequent Indonesian invasion of 1975. It became Indonesia's 27th province in 1976.

The capital, Dili, has some charming Portuguese architecture and the Portuguese influence is everywhere. Although the province is open to foreign tourists, there are occasional reports of tourists being prevented from entering, or being told to leave.

RESTAURANT SELECTION

Average price for two

JAKARTA

DRAGON CITY, G/F, Lippo Plaza, Jl Sudirman. Tel: 522 1933. Sichuan and seafood. US$40.
DYNASTY, 8th Floor, Glodok Plaza, Jl Pinangsia Raya. Tel: 628 3888. Chinese. Music, dancing. US$40.
THE GREEN PUB, Jakarta Theatre Building, Jl Thamrin. Tel: 315 9332. Mexican. Music, dancing. US$40.
HAZARA, Jl Wahid Hasyim 112. Tel: 315 0424. Indian. US$40.
KUNINGAN SEAFOOD, Jl HOS. Cokroaminoto No. 122. Tel: 331601. Seafood. US$40.
LEMON GRASS, Le Meridien Hotel, Jl. Sudirman. Tel: 251 3131. Asian. US$70.
NATRABU, Jl Agus Salim 29A. Tel: 335668. Indonesian (Padang style). US$20.
OASIS, Jl Raden Saleh 47. Tel: 314 0646. Indonesian, European. Music. US$60.
ORLEANS, Jl Adityawarman 67. Tel: 720 2350. Western. Music. US$45.
PINOCCHIO, Wisma Metropolitan I, Jl Sudirman. Tel: 525 4736. Italian. US$45.
RADEN KURING, Jl Raden Saleh 62. Tel: 314 0744. Indonesian (Sundanese, Javanese). Music, traditional dance performances. US$20.
TOBA, Borobudur Hotel, Jl. Lapangan Banteng Selatan. Tel: 380 5555. European, French. US$80.
XIN, President Hotel, Jl Thamrin. Tel: 230 1122 ext. 2218. Chinese. US$30.

HOTEL GUIDE

BALI

A: US$120 and above

LEGIAN BEACH

BALI IMPERIAL HOTEL, Jl Dhyana Pura Seminyak. Tel: 730730, Fax: 730545. *P, tennis courts. R: L, W.*

KUTA BEACH

BALI OBEROI, Tel: 751061, Tlx: 35125 HOTEL DPR. *P. R: L, W.*
PERTAMINA COTTAGES, Jl Padma, Kuta. Tel: 751161, Fax: 752030, Tlx: 35131. *P. R: L, W.*

NUSA DUA

FOUR SEASONS RESORT, Kawasan Jimbasan. Tel: 701010, Fax: 701020. *P, tennis courts. R: L, W.*
GRAND HYATT BALI, Tel: 771234, Fax: 772038, Tlx: 35863 GHB IA. *P, tennis courts. R: L, W.*
NUSA DUA BEACH HOTEL, Tel: 771210, Tlx: 35206. *P. R: L, W.*

SANUR BEACH

BALI HYATT, Tel: 360315, Fax: 287826, Tlx: 35127 BALIHYATT. *P. R: L, W.*

UBUD

AMANDARI, Kodewataan. Tel: 975333, Fax: 975335. *P, tennis courts, SatTV. R: L, W.*

B: US$80-120

DENPASAR

BALI HOTEL, Jl Veteran. Tel: 235346, Fax: 235347, Tlx: 35166. *P. R: L, W.*
PAMECUTAN PALACE HOTEL, Jl Thamrin. Tel: 223491. *R: L, W.*
DENPASAR HOTEL, Jl Diponegoro. Tel: 226336. Tlx: 35125 HOTEL DPR. *P. R: L, W.*

KUTA BEACH

KARTIKA PLAZA BEACH HOTEL, Jl Kartika. Tel: 751067, Fax: 752475, Tlx: 35142 KAZADP IA. *P. R: L, W.*

LEGIAN BEACH

LEGIAN BEACH HOTEL, Jl Melasti, Legian. Tel: 751711, Fax: 752651, Tlx: 35351 LBHTL IA. *P. R: L, W.*

NUSA DUA

BALI SOL, Tel: 771510, Fax: 771360, Tlx: 35237. *P. R: L, W.*
PUTRI BALI, Tel: 771020, Fax: 771139, Tlx: 35247 NUSABALI. *P. R: L, W.*

SANUR BEACH

LA TAVERNA, Tel: 288497, Fax: 287126, Tlx: 35163. *P. R: L, W.*
BALI SANUR BUNGALOWS, Tel: 288421, Fax: 288426, Tlx: 35178 GHCBSB IA. *P. R: L, W.*

C: US$40-80

SURYA BEACH COTTAGE, Jl

P — Swimming pool **R** — Restaurant **L** — Local food **W** — Western food
SatTV — Satellite TV

HOTEL GUIDE

Mertasari. Tel: 288833, Fax: 287303, Tlx: 35810 SBC SNR. *P. R: L, W.*

SEGARA VILLAGE, Jl Segara Ayu. Tel: 288407, Tlx: 35143 SEGARA AYU. *P. R: L, W.*

NATOUR KUTA BEACH, Jl Pantai Kuta. Tel: 751361, Fax: 751362, Tlx: 35166 KUBEHOTT. *R: L, W.*

JAKARTA

A: US$120 and above

BOROBUDUR INTERCONTINENTAL, Jl Lapangan Banteng Selatan. Tel: 380 5555, Fax: 380 9595, Tlx: 44156 BDOIHC IA. *P, Gym, Biz, Ex, SatTV. R: L, W.*

CITRALAND, Jl Let. Jend S. Parman. Tel: 566 0640, Fax: 568 1616. *P, Biz, Ex, SatTV. R: L, W.*

GRAND HYATT, Jl M.H. Thamrin. Tel: 390 1234, Fax: 310 7300, Tlx: 61534 HYATT IA. *P, Gym, Biz, Ex, SatTV. R: L, W.*

HYATT ARYADUTA, Jl Prapatan 44-46. Tel: 386 1234, Fax: 380 4777, Tlx: 46295 JKT IA. *P, Gym, Biz, Ex, SatTV. R: L, W.*

HOTEL INDONESIA, Jl M.H. Thamrin. Tel: 390 6262, 230 1008, Fax: 230 1007, Tlx: 61347 HTL IND IA. *P, Gym, Biz, Ex, SatTV. R: L, W.*

JAKARTA HILTON, Jl Jend Gatot Subroto. Tel: 570 3600, Fax: 573 3089, Tlx: 65699 HILTON IA. *P, Gym, Biz, Ex, SatTV. R: L, W.*

LE MERIDIEN, Jl Jend Sudirman. Tel: 251 3131, Fax: 571 1633, Tlx: 65460 HOMER IA. *P, Gym, Biz, Ex, SatTV. R: L, W.*

MANDARIN ORIENTAL, Jl M.H. Thamrin. Tel: 314 1307, Fax: 314 8680, Tlx: 61755 MANDA IA. *P, Gym, Biz, Ex, SatTV. R: L, W.*

PRESIDENT HOTEL, Jl M.H. Thamrin. Tel: 230 1122, Fax: 314 3631, Tlx: 61401 PREHO IA. *P, Gym, Biz, Ex, SatTV. R: L, W.*

SARI PAN PACIFIC, Jl M.H. Thamrin. Tel: 390 2707, Fax: 323650, Tlx: 44514 HTLSARI IA. *P, Gym, Biz, Ex, SatTV. R: L, W.*

SAHID JAYA HOTEL, Jl Jend Sudirman. Tel: 570 4444, Fax: 573 3168, Tlx: 65635 SAHID IA. *P, Gym, Biz, Ex, SatTV. R: L, W.*

SHANGRI-LA, BNI City Complex, Jl Jend Sudirman. Tel: 570 7440, Fax: 570 3530. *P, Gym, Biz, Ex, SatTV. R: L, W.*

THE REGENT, Jl H.R. Rasuna Said. Tel: 252 3456, Fax: 252 4480. *P, Gym, Biz, Ex, SatTV. R: L, W.*

B: US$80-120

ATLET CENTURY PARK, Jl. Pintu Satu, Senayan. Tel: 571 2041, Fax 571 2094, Tlx: 65039 CENPAR IA. *P, Gym, Biz, Ex, SatTV. R: L, W.*

DAI-ICHI, Jl Senen Raya. Tel: 344 2828, Fax: 344 2929. *P, Gym, Biz, Ex, SatTV. R: L, W.*

KARTIKA CHANDRA, Jl Gatot Subroto. Tel: 520 5000, Fax: 520 4238, Tlx: 46470 KACHA IA. *P, Gym, Biz, Ex, SatTV. R: L, W.*

BANDUNG

B: US$80-120

GRAND HOTEL PREANGER, Jl Asia Afrika. Tel: 431631, Fax: 430034, Tlx: 28570 GHPBDO IA. *P, Gym, Biz, SatTV. R: L, W.*

PAPANDAYAN HOTEL, Jl Jend Gatot Subroto. Tel: 310799, Fax: 310988, Tlx: 28681 PADH IA. *P, Gym, Biz, SatTV. R: L, W.*

SAVOY HOMANN HOTEL, Jl Asia Afrika. Tel: 432244, Fax: 436187, Tlx: 28425 HOMANN IA. *P, Gym, Biz, SatTV. R: L, W.*

C: US$40-80

PANGHEGAR HOTEL, Jl Merdeka. Tel: 432286, 431583, Fax: 431583, Tlx: 28276 PANGHEGAR BDD. *P, Gym, Biz, SatTV. R: L, W.*

JOGJAKARTA

B: US$80-120

AMBARRUKMO PALACE, Jl Laksda Adisucipto. Tel: 566488, Fax: 563283, Tlx: 25111 APHYK IA. *P, Gym, Biz, SatTV. R: L, W.*

GARUDA HOTEL, Jl Maliaboro. Tel: 886457, Tlx: 25174. *P, Gym, Biz, SatTV. R: L, W.*

C: US$40-80

DWIPARI, Jl Pejaksaan. Tel: 562813, Fax: 565060. *R: L, W.*

MUTIARA HOTEL, Jl Maliaboro. Tel: 601585, Fax: 601288. *P, SatTV. R: L, W.*

JAVA WEST COAST

C: US$40-80

CARITA KRAKATAU BEACH HOTEL, Jl Labuan. Tel: (021) 314 0252, Fax: (021) 330846. *P. R: L, W.*

MARINA VILLAGE, Jl Raya Anyer. Tel: (021) 601585, Fax: 601288. *P. R: L, W.*

JAVA SOUTH COAST

PELABUHAN RATU SAMUDRA BEACH HOTEL, Tel: (021) 384 0601, 314 0581, Fax: (0268) 41203, Tlx:

P — Swimming pool
Gym — Health club
Biz — Business centre
Ex — Executive floor
SatTV — Satellite TV
R — Restaurant
L — Local food
W — Western food

HOTEL GUIDE

45237 HSB IA. *P. R: L, W.*

CENTRAL JAVA

SEMARANG

C: US$40-80

SANTIKA, Jl Jend Ahmad Yani. Tel: 412491, 414083. *R: L, W.*

SOLO

B: US$80-120

KUSUMA SAHID PRINCE, Jl Sugiyopranoto. Tel: 46356, Fax: 44788, Tlx: 25274 KSPH IA. *P. R: L, W.*

EAST JAVA

SURABAYA

A: US$120 and above

GARDEN PALACE HOTEL, Jl Yos Sudarso. Tel: 520951, Fax: 516111, Tlx: 34184 GPHSB IA. *P, Gym, Biz, SatTV. R: L, W.*

HYATT REGENCY, Jl Jenderal Basuki Rachmat. Tel: 521508, Fax: 521038, Tlx: 31391 HYATT BUMI. *P, Gym, Biz, Ex, SatTV. R: L, W.*

HILTON HOTEL, Jl Gunungsari. Tel: 582703-6, Fax: 574504. *P, Gym, Biz, Ex, SatTV. R: L, W.*

SHANGRI-LA HOTEL, Jl Mayjen Sungkono. Tel: 566 1550, Fax: 566 1570. *P, Gym, Biz, SatTV. R: L, W.*

B: US$80-120

ELMI, Jl Panglima Sudirmann. Tel: 522571, Fax: 515615, Tlx: 34131. *P, Gym, Biz, SatTV. R: L, W.*

KUPANG

C: US$40-80

ORCHID GARDEN HOTEL, Jl Gunung Fatelulu. Tel: 21707, Fax: 31399, Tlx: 35941 TELSAD. *P. R: L, W.*

HOTEL FLOBAMOR, Jl Jenderal Sudirmann. Tel: 21346. *P. R: L, W.*

LOMBOK

A: US$120 and above

SHERATON SENGGIGI BEACH, Jl Raya Senggigi. Tel: 93333, Fax: 93140, Tlx: 35761 IA SSBR. *P. R: L, W.*

C: US$40-80

GRAHA BEACH SENGGIGI, Jl Senggigi. Tel/Fax: 23782. *R: L, W.*

NORTH SUMATRA

MEDAN

C: US$40-80

DANAU TOBA INTERNATIONAL, Jl Imam Bonjol. Tel: 327000, Fax: 520653, Tlx: 51167. *P. R: L, W.*

TIARA HOTEL, Jl Cut Mutia. Tel: 516000, 523000, Fax: 510176, Tlx: 51721 GRYA IA. *P. R: L, W.*

WEST SUMATRA

BUKITTINGGI

C: US$40-80

DYMEN'S INTERNATIONAL, Jl Nawawi. Tel: 22781, Fax: 21613, Tlx: 55421. *P. R: L, W.*

SOUTH SUMATRA

PALEMBANG

BANDAR LAMPUNG

B: US$80-120

SHERATON INN LAMPUNG, Jl Wolter Monginsidi. Tel: 486666, Fax: 486690, Tlx: 26107 SHER LPG IA. *P. R: L, W.*

C: US$40-80

INDRA PALACE HOTEL, Jl Wolter Monginsidi. Tel: 62440, Fax: 62399, Tlx: 26286 IPH BDL IA. *P. R: L, W.*

NORTH SULAWESI

MANADO

C: US$40-80

KAWANUA CITY HOTEL, Jl Sam Ratulangi. Tel: 67777, Fax: 65220, Tlx: 74132 KCHMO IA. *P. R: L, W.*

GARDEN HOTEL, Jl WR Supratman. Tel: 51688. *P. R: L, W.*

SOUTH SULAWESI

UJUNG PANDANG

B: US$80-120

MARANNU CITY HOTEL, Jl Sultan Hasanudin. Tel: 315087, Fax: 321821. *P, Gym, Biz. R: L, W.*

C: US$40-80

MAKASSAR GOLDEN HOTEL, Jl Pasar Ikan. Tel: 325791, Fax: 316303, Tlx: 71290 MGH UP IA. *P, Biz. R: L, W.*

TANA TORAJA

C: US$40-80

MARANNU CITY HOTEL, Jl. Pongtiku, Makale. Tel: 22221, Fax: 22028. *P, tennis court. R: L, W.*

TORAJA COTTAGE, Desa Bolu, Paku. Tel: 84146, Tlx: 46621 HB IA. *P. R: L, W.*

P — Swimming pool **Gym** — Health club **Biz** — Business centre **Ex** — Executive floor
SatTV — Satellite TV **R** — Restaurant **L** — Local food **W** — Western food

LAOS

Once known as the land of a million elephants, Laos is a beautiful, friendly, slow-moving country with so much charm that it is a tragedy that more people have not been able to see it. The reason, of course, was the Indochina War, followed by the communist victory in December 1975. Tourism received low priority from the new government.

Laos is a traditional Buddhist, largely agrarian society with some of the most gentle and friendly people in Asia. From the late 1980s the government, in an attempt to attract hard currency, began allowing more tourists into the country, raising hopes that Laos was returning to the tourist trade, if only in a limited way.

History

The known history of Laos dates from the 13th century, when the Thai peoples (represented today by the Shan of northern Burma, the Thai of Thailand and the lowland Lao from Laos) came south from China's Yunnan province under pressure from the armies of Kublai Khan, who had conquered much of China.

Laos was first unified in 1353 by Fa Ngum, a Lao prince who had grown up in the Khmer court of Angkor and returned to his country with a contingent of Cambodian soldiers.

Internal dissension during the 17th century resulted in the kingdom being divided into three parts — the kingdom of Luang Prabang in the north, Vientiane in the centre, and Champassak in the south. Each state had its own royal rulers. So weakened, most of the country fell under Thai control in 1828, while the Vietnamese dominated the northeast.

The French took control of the country in 1893, incorporating it into French Indochina with Vietnam and Cambodia. Despite several armed revolts, Laos continued as a French colony until the Japanese occupation during World War II. On October 12, 1945, the nationalist Lao Issara (Free Lao) movement proclaimed the independence of Laos, but the French army again quickly seized control.

In response to nationalist pressures, France granted Laos formal independence within the French Union in July 1949.

The Geneva Accords in 1954, after the defeat of the French at Dien Bien Phu, granted full independence to Laos and called for free elections to establish a new Lao government. But when the pro-communist Lao Patriotic Front (Pathet Lao) gained 13 seats in the national assembly elections in 1958, the United States supported a rightwing faction in sabotaging the coalition government.

Fighting broke out and the Patriotic Front and neutralist forces quickly gained control of large portions of the mountainous countryside. Another attempt at a ceasefire and a coalition government of the Right, Centre, and Left failed after the Geneva Conference of 1962.

With the U.S. and Thailand supporting the Vientiane side and Vietnam, the Soviet Union, and China supporting the Patriotic Front, poor, underdeveloped Laos took on exaggerated geopolitical prominence.

Full-scale American bombing began in 1964 in the communist-held areas of the northeast and along the Ho Chi Minh Trail, which was used by North Vietnam to supply its war against U.S.-backed South Vietnam. The bombing eventually displaced a quarter of Laos' rural population.

The war continued until the signing of the Vientiane Accords in 1973 and the formation of a coalition government the following year. With the American withdrawal from Indochina in 1975, the communist Patriotic Front gained control of the government and proclaimed the formation of the Lao People's Democratic Republic on December 2.

◀ *The Mekong River.* PHOTO: HSENG NOUNG LINTNER

In 1986 the country's communist party abandoned its doctrinaire socialist goals, replacing cooperatives with family farms, offering unproductive industries to private entrepreneurs, and courting foreign capitalists and Western aid donors.

Landlocked Laos, with an area of 236,600 square kilometres, has borders with China, Vietnam, Cambodia, Thailand and Burma. More than two thirds of the country consists of mountains and dense jungles.

Laos' population is estimated at 4.5 million, about 90% of whom are engaged in subsistence agriculture. Lowland Lao culture reflects a deep Buddhist influence, while the other ethnic groups practise animism.

Entry

Vientiane, the capital, can be reached daily by air from Bangkok via either Thai Airways International or Lao Aviation. Vietnam Airlines and Lao Aviation connect Hanoi and Vientiane on Sundays, Tuesdays and Thursdays. The two airlines also fly to Ho Chi Minh City on Sundays and Fridays, while the Lao airline flies to Phnom Penh on Fridays. China Southern Airlines links Vientiane to Kunming and Guangzhou on Sundays.

Foreigners can also travel overland to Laos, but must use the Australian-built Friendship Bridge, not the Tha Deua ferry. Buses leave from the Thai side of the bridge (a few kilometres west of Nong Khai), cross the bridge and stop at the immigration and customs building on the Lao side. From there, take a Lao bus or taxi to Vientiane. The price of the taxi ride is about Baht 100-200, depending on your bargaining skills.

Trains to Nong Khai, across from the Lao border town of Tha Deua, leave Bangkok several times daily and take about 12 hours. The most comfortable way to travel is by first class sleeper. From the Nong Khai train station take a samlor (three-wheeled pedal trishaw).

Air-conditioned tour buses leave Bangkok

several times daily for Nong Khai, but the incidence of serious highway accidents is high.

It is also possible to cross by ferry from Chiang Khong in Thailand to Ban Houei Sai in Laos' Bo Kaeo province in the north. From Ban Houei Sai, speedboats runs to Luang Prabang.

EMBASSIES

Australia, Nehru St (near Independence Monument).
Tel: 413610, 413805, 413602.
Bulgaria, Sisangvonh area. Tel: 412110.
Burma, (Myanmar), Sokpaluang Rd. (off Tha Deua Rd). Tel: 312439, 314910.
Cambodia, Sophanethong Neua Rd.
Tel: 314952.
China, People's Republic, Sokpaluang Rd (off Tha Deua Rd).
Tel: 315103, 315100, 315101.
Cuba, Sophanethong Neua Rd.
Tel: 314902.
France, Sethathirat Rd (across from Mohosot Hospital). Tel: 215258.
Germany, Nehru Rd (near Independence Monument).
Tel: 312111, 312110.
India, That Luang Rd. Tel: 413802.
Indonesia, Phon Kheng Rd (near Independence Monument). Tel: 413910, 413909, 413907.
Japan, Si Sung Won Rd (near That Luang). Tel: 212623, 414400-2, 414406.
Korea, Democratic People's Republic, Wat Nak Village. Tel: 315261, 315260.
Malaysia, That Luang Rd (near That Luang). Tel: 414205.
Mongolia, Tha Deua Rd. Tel: 315220.
State of Palestine, Tel: 315252.
Poland, Nong Bone Rd (near That Luang). Tel: 313439, 312085.
Russia, Thaphalanxay area. Tel: 312219, 212222.
Sweden, Tel: 315018, 313772, 315000.
Thailand, Phon Kheng Rd (near Independence Monument). Tel: 214582, 214583, 241585.
United States, Near the Morning Market.
Tel: 212580, 212581, 312609.
Vietnam, That Luang Rd (near Independence Monument). Tel: 413400, 413409, 413403.

CHAMBER OF COMMERCE

Lao National Chamber of Commerce and Industry, P.O. Box 4596, Vientiane.
Tel: 414383, Fax: 414886, Tlx: 4346 CNML LS.

Immigration

A visa is required to enter Laos. This can be obtained from Lao embassies in Bangkok, Hanoi, Ho Chi Minh City, Phnom Penh, Rangoon, Jakarta, Kuala Lumpur, Tokyo, New Delhi, Beijing, Kunming, Ulan Bator, Havana, Moscow, Paris, Bonn, Stockholm, Warsaw, Canberra or Washington. Visa costs vary between embassies from about US$12-35 and are normally issued for a 15-day period.

It may take time to obtain a Lao visa outside the Asian region. Best option is to obtain one in Bangkok from the Embassy of the Lao People's Democratic Republic, 202/1-3 Soi Ramkhamhaeng 39, Bangkapi, Bangkok 10310 (Tel: 539 6667-9, Fax: 539 6678). There, visas are usually processed in a day or two.

Health

Vaccinations against cholera, typhoid, tetanus, rabies and hepatitis are advisable, while some health officials advise visitors travelling upcountry to take anti-malaria medicine. Avoid drinking unboiled water and uncooked vegetables.

Customs

Laos has no strict regulations at present on how much a traveller can bring into Laos duty-free, though an unusual quantity of cigarettes, alcohol, cameras or electronic equipment might raise the suspicions of customs officials. Currency declarations by visitors are not normally required.

Currency

The official exchange rate in early 1995 was Kips 720:US$1. Travellers' cheques are accepted at the state bank as well as by Lao Aviation and major hotels, but a 1% surcharge is levied. Credit cards, especially Visa and American Express, are slowly making an appearance in Laos. U.S. dollars and Thai baht are widely accepted in shops and restaurants, but the use of foreign currency is — at least on paper — an offence according to a September 1990 Council of Ministers' decree.

Language

The national language is Lao, a tonal language closely related to Thai, which is understood by

Lao along the Mekong River. English and French are used as second languages in most government offices. Russian is spoken by Lao who have been educated in the former Soviet Union. Minority tribal languages are spoken in the mountain regions.

Climate

Vientiane lies in the tropical monsoon belt and has about five months of heavy rainfall, from May to September, with an average of 25-30 centimetres per month. The remainder of the year is dry. A very hot period immediately precedes the monsoon, with temperatures rising as high as 38-40°C (100°F). The coolest months are November, December and January, when temperatures average around 21°C (70°F) but can drop as low as 5°C (41°F). In the mountains the temperatures may drop to near freezing during the winter months.

Dress

Light tropical clothing is best all year around, with some slightly warmer things for the nights of November to January. In the mountains woollens are required during the coldest months.

Business Hours

Government office hours are from about 8 a.m. to noon and from 2-5 p.m. Monday to Friday. Appointments should be scheduled early in the day. Many state employees leave early for "moonlighting" jobs because government salaries are too low to feed their families. On Saturdays government offices are open from about 8-11 a.m., with reduced staff.

Banks are open from 8:30 a.m.-4:30 p.m. Monday to Friday and 8:30 a.m. to noon on Saturdays.

Shops and markets are open from about 6:30 a.m. to sundown, while nightclubs as well as restaurants and bars catering to foreigners are open until about 11:30 p.m.

Doing Business

Economic reforms initiated in 1986 have given Laos what is now one of Asia's most liberal foreign investment laws, with 100% foreign ownership allowed in any enterprise. But the lack of personnel able to deal with foreign businessmen is a major problem, as is the small and largely unskilled Lao labour force.

Primary contact for foreign investors is the Foreign Investment Management Committee, Luang Prabang Rd (near the Apollo Hotel), Vientiane (Tel: 217020, 214591). While this is supposedly a one-stop shop, investors are recommended to keep all relevant ministries and other government institutions informed about their plans. This can lead to the development of personal contacts in a country in which the importance of such relationships remains strong.

Media

There are two daily newspapers in Lao, the party paper *Pasason* (The People) and the official *Vientiane Mai* (New Vientiane). In addition, there is the *Vientiane Times,* an English-language weekly which began publication in May 1994. The *Vientiane Times* is sold at major bookshops and supermarkets in Vientiane, and at its head office on the ground floor of the Pasason building opposite the Nam Phou fountain. (P.O. Box 5723, Vientiane. Tel: 216364, Fax: 216365.)

Communications

Long distance telephone service to Laos has improved since International Direct Dialling (IDD) equipment was installed several years ago. All telephones in Laos can receive IDD calls, though far from all are connected so as to make them.

Transport

VIENTIANE

FROM THE AIRPORT: Taxi fares for the five-kilometre trip to hotels in Vientiane cost about US$7-10, depending on the availability of cars and the number of arriving passengers. Passengers should negotiate the price with drivers, who usually request payment in Thai baht or U.S. dollars.

Newcomers to Laos may want to seek assistance from Lao Aviation ground service staff in obtaining transport from the airport. Sometimes Lao Aviation will provide a bus for groups from the airport, but this must be arranged in advance.

TAXIS: Taxis in Vientiane operate in much the same way as buses. They run along the main roads (making occasional detours for passengers), picking up and dropping off passengers as they go. A taxi can be rented for a whole day for about US$20. Ask your hotel staff to assist in bargaining for the price of taxi fares.

CAR HIRE: Cars with drivers can be rented for US$30-35 per day from several companies, including **Burapha Development Consultants** (Tel: 216708, 216600, Fax: 212981) at 14 Fa Ngum St, **Lane Xang Hotel** (Tel: 214102, 214106, Fax: 214108) on Fa Ngum St, **Vico Trading Co**. (Tel: 214810, Fax: 215444) and **Vientiane International Consultants** (Tel: 214182, Fax: 215797) at 234 Samsenthai St.

BUSES: Buses charging Kips 50-100 operate over set routes from the Morning Market to Vientiane's suburbs, but they are often crowded and pay little attention to schedules.

Buses depart from the market roughly every 45 minutes and travel west to Sii Khai market (near the airport), north to Done Noun (near Dong Dok) and east to Tha Deua.

TUK TUKS: Three-wheeled "tuk tuks," a motorcycle with a covered seating at the back, and pedal trishaws ply the streets of Vientiane and many other of Laos' towns. Be sure to bargain for your fare in advance.

UPCOUNTRY

Special permits, which were required by foreigners wanting to travel outside the Vientiane area, were abolished in 1994. Now the whole country is open to foreign visitors, barring a few areas which are restricted for security reasons. Foreigners can also travel by river, for instance from Ban Houei Sai to Luang Prabang.

Lao Aviation flies from Vientiane to Pakse, Salavan, Ban Houei Sai, Khong Island, Attapeu, Phongsaly, Oudomsay, Savannakhet, Thakhek, Luang Nam Tha, Xieng Khoung, Laksao, Luang Prabang, Sayaboury and Sam Neua.

MAJOR AIRLINES

Lao Aviation, 2 Pangkham Rd, Vientiane (Tel: 212051-4, 212057, Fax: 212056).

Thai Airways International, Pangkham Rd (Tel: 216143) or the airport (Tel: 521024).

Vietnam Airlines, c/o Air Lao Booking, 43/1 Sethathirath Rd (Tel: 216535, Fax: 216761).

Tours

Major tour operators are:

Diethelm Travel, Nam Phou Circle (P.O. Box 2675). Tel: 215920, 217243, Fax: 217151.

Inter Lao Tourism, Sethathirath Rd at Pangkham Rd (P.O. Box 2912). Tel: 214232, 214832, Fax: 216306.

Lane Xang Travel, Pangkham Rd (P.O. Box 4452). Tel: 212469, 215804, Fax: 215777.

Lao National Tourism (Lanatour), 8/2 Lane Xang Ave (P.O. Box 5122). Tel: 216671, Fax: 212013.

Lao Travel Service, 8/3 Lane Xang Ave (P.O. Box 2553). Tel: 216603, 216604, Fax: 216150.

Mixay Travel Service. Tel: 216213, 214620, Fax: 215445.

Phatana Khet Phoudoi Travel, 118/2 Luang Prabang Rd (P.O. Box 825). Tel: 214673, 216597, Fax: 216131.

Rajah Tours, 3 Heng Boun St (P.O. Box 3655). Tel: 213632, 213633, Fax: 213635.

Sode Tours, Fa Ngum St, Pakpassak. Tel: 216314, 215489, Fax: 216313.

That Luang Tours, 28 Kamkong Rd. Tel: 215809, Fax: 215346.

Vieng Champa Tours, Tha Deua Rd, Kilometre 3. Tel: 312489, Fax: 314412.

Accommodation

VIENTIANE

The **Belvedere** (Tel: 213573, Fax: 213572), refurbished by a Singaporean joint venture in 1992, was the first new modern hotel built in Vientiane since the end of the war. Rooms begin at US$120.

The hotel, which is part of the Best Western group, is located on the road to the airport, across the street from the country's only remaining three-headed elephant statue — the former symbol of the Lao monarchy which was abolished by the communists in 1975.

Rooms at the riverside **Lane Xang** (Tel: 214102, 214106, Fax: 214108), which has become run down in recent years, begin at US$42. Other centrally located hotels popular with foreign visitors are the **Asia Pavilion** (Tel: 213430-1, Fax: 213432) at 379-383 Samsentha which offer rooms beginning at US$26.

The **Tai-Pan Hotel** (Tel: 216906-9, Fax: 216233) is an old hotel which has been refurbished and redecorated and has become popular with foreign businessmen. **Le Parasol Blanc** (Tel: 216091, Fax: 215444) on Nahaidio St near the monument, is owned by famous

Lao entrepreneur Vinay Inthavong, and has a pleasant garden and swimming pool. There are also the **Samsenthai Hotel** at Manthathurath St (Tel: 216287, Fax: 212116) and the **Saysana** on Chao Anou St (Tel: 213581, 213580).

Several private guesthouses, offering rooms beginning at US$20, operate in the capital. Some of the more popular ones include the **Lani Guest House Number I** (Tel: 215639, Fax: 216103) at 281 Sethathirath St, which is a family-style house in a garden, with a limited number of rooms.

The same owner also runs the **Lani Guest House Number 2** (Tel: 213022, 216095, Fax: 216103) at 268 Saylom Rd. Also popular is the **Villa That Luang Guest House and Restaurant** (Tel: 413370, Fax: 412953) at 307 That Luang Rd.

LUANG PRABANG

Visitors can stay at the **Mitaphab** on a hill overlooking the city, or the **Phousi** near the city's pagodas and former royal palace. Rooms cost US$10-20 per night.

Or there is the Phou Vao Hotel (Tel/Fax: 212194), a new hotel with 52 air-conditioned rooms and the only swimming-pool in Luang Prabang (this hotel can also be booked in Bangkok — Tel: 2667867, Fax: 2381294).

PAKSE

Near the famous Wat Phou temple complex, guests can stay at the **Pakse Hotel**, **Souksamlane Hotel** or **Auberge de Pakse**, a small private guesthouse.

XIENG KHOUANG

Auberge de Plaine des Jarres, run by Frenchman Claude Claude, a long-time resident of Laos who also runs La Souriya Restaurant in Vientiane, is highly recommended.

Dining

Many new restaurants offering a wide variety of cuisines have opened in Vientiane in recent years thanks to the economic reforms which again allow private enterprise.

Uniquely Lao dishes are generally hard to find at restaurants in Vientiane. Adventurous visitors can find sticky rice, which you make into a ball with your fingers for dipping into chili sauce or eating with green papaya salad or barbecued chicken, at small street stalls in the vicinity of the theatres on Haeng Buon and Anou streets as well as along the Mekong River.

Pa Phao Restaurant (Tel: 413070), next to the State Bank's tennis courts off Nong Bone Rd, specializes in Lao and Thai food, as does the **Champa Lane Xang**, located on a small lake at Kilometre 2 on Tha Deua Rd.

Excellent French food is served at the **Nam Phou** (Tel: 216248), near the water fountain, and at **La Souriya** (Tel: 215887), opposite the Lao Aviation office. **L'Opera** (Tel: 215099), opened in 1992 opposite the water fountain, serves popular Italian dishes.

There are two less formal eating and drinking places in the same area as L'Opera: the **Swedish Bakery** serves pastries and coffee, while the outdoor cafe around the fountain offers snacks, Indian food and draught beer. Also, a very popular place for lunch, with good sandwiches, pasta and other Western food (and which does outside catering) is the **Deli Cafe** (Tel: 215651) around the corner on Sethathirath Rd.

Other restaurants serving Western food are the **Arawan** (Tel: 215373) at 474 Samsenthai Rd, **Ban Phim** on Luang Prabang Rd on the way to the airport, the **Mekong** (Tel: 312480) at Kilometre 4 on Tha Deua Rd and **Santisouk** (Tel: 215303) near the National Stadium.

The joint venture **New Asia Restaurant** at 276-286 Samsenthai Rd serves an extensive menu of Chinese dishes. **Dao Vieng** on Haeng Boun St also serves Chinese food, but the quality of its meals has never recovered since it was taken over by the state in 1975.

The Taj (Tel: 212890), near the water fountain, serves authentic North Indian cuisine.

The **Mekong night stalls** along the river from Pakpassak to the Russian Club offer a limited choice but are very cheap, and are good for unwinding with some spicy Lao good and a cold drink after a day's wandering or working.

The **Ban Haysok Restaurant** (Tel: 216103, 215639, 215417) offers Lao and southern Chinese food at 34 Heng Boun Rd, opposite the Anou Hotel. **Hong Kong Restaurant** (Tel: 213241) at 80/4 Samsenthai Rd, serves Cantonese and Sichuan food.

Lao vodka (*lao lao*), a rather potent variation of Japanese sake, can be found at many small stalls and in the local markets. Imported soft drinks, beer, wine and other alcoholic drinks are usually available at restaurants and bars catering to foreigners.

Entertainment

Most of the dozen nightclubs opened in Vientiane during the past few years offer drinks and simple Asian dishes along with live rock music. The most popular clubs among Lao patrons are the **Vieng Latri Mai** (operated by Vientiane municipality) on Lane Xang Ave near the Morning Market and **Nok Kaeo Latri Mai** on the road to the airport. There are three main nightclubs in Vientiane: **Dok Bouathong Club and Restaurant** (Tel: 216821) in Luang Prabang Rd, **Saysana Club** (Tel: 213581) on the ground floor of the Saysana Hotel and the **Lane Xang Hotel Snack Bar** (Tel: 214102).

Sporting activities in Vientiane are limited. Tennis is available at the **Vientiane Tennis Club** (Tel: 3370), and visitors introduced by members can play squash or swim at the **Australian Embassy Recreation Club** overlooking the Mekong River. In July 1994, a new golf and country club was opened 14 kilometres from the Friendship Bridge: **Santisuk Lane Xang Golf and Resort** (Tel/Fax: 213622) — nine holes, 2,800 metres, par 35.

Shopping

Thanks to economic reforms, more imported consumer goods and Lao handicraft items are again available in Lao markets. Beautiful hand-woven silk for a *sin* (Lao skirt) and elaborately embroidered skirt borders (often made with gold and silver thread) are available in the **Morning Market** on Lane Xang Ave.

A variety of Lao handicrafts such as silk and cotton fabrics, shirts, scarves, baskets and wood carving are available at **Kanchana Boutique**, opposite the That Dam monument. **Lao Antiques** at 072/08 Tha Deua Rd, **Lao Textiles** on Nokeo Khoumane and **Art of Silk** on Manh Thatourath St sell a variety of antique and modern Lao textile designs.

Somsri Handicraft at 18-20 Sethathirath Rd, **Lao Women's Textiles Centre Shop** in Bane Khounta and **Lao Cotton** near the water fountain display a variety of Lao dolls, wall hangings, purses, bed and table linen, and gift articles. **Artisant & Handicrafts** on Luang Prabang Rd and **Phonethip Handicrafts and Ceramics** on Saylom Rd sell Lao ceramic ware.

Various shops along Samsenthai Rd sell hill-tribe embroidered bed and cushion covers. Jewellery shops in the Morning Market and on Samsenthai Rd will produce almost any design of gold or silver necklace, bracelet or Lao skirt belt within a few days.

Holidays

Many Lao Buddhist festivals fall on different dates from one year to the next, depending on the lunar calendar. In the listing below, only the months are given for events with variable dates. Various ethnic groups celebrate other religious and cultural holidays.

January 1: International New Year

February: Wat Phou Festival held at the ancient Wat Phou Pagoda, near Champassak in southern Laos.

Makha Buja is observed in Lao pagodas in commemoration of the first sermon preached by Buddha.

April 13, 14, 15: Pee May (Lao New Year) is observed by pouring holy water on the Buddhist statues in pagodas. On the streets, people drench each other with water. Make sure to wear your old clothes and join in the fun.

May: International Labour Day (May 1). Visakha Buja. The most important of the annual Lao Buddhist celebrations commemorating the birth, enlightenment and the passing into Nirvana of Buddha. Candle processions in the evening make three clockwise circuits around the pagoda.

Boun Bang Fai, the traditional rocket festival, is held just before the rainy season.

June 1: International Children's Day.

July: Boun Khao Watsa. The Buddhist equivalent of Lent begins and lasts through the rainy season. Practising Buddhists are expected to lead a more devout life during this time.

September: Boun Khao Padabdin — a memorial day observed by the Lao people in memory of their departed relatives. Food is offered to their spirits at pagodas or their tombs.

Boun Khao Salak is a festival in which Buddhists take a basket filled with food and other gifts to monks, who "pass them on" to believers' departed parents or relatives.

Boun Ok Watsa: The end of Buddhist Lent is marked with a religious ceremony at each pagoda in the morning during which Buddhists offer food to the monks. In the evening, the people light candles in front of their houses, take part in candle processions and launch tiny boats made of banana leaves bearing flowers and burning candles.

Boun Song Hua: Boat races along the Mekong, sometimes with competition between Thai and Lao teams, mark the end of the rainy

Champasak Province village scene. PHOTO: RODNEY TASKER

season.

November: The That Luang Festival, which attracts tens of thousands of people, begins with religious ceremonies in which devout Buddhists give food to monks. During the first night of the festival a procession of people solemnly march around the stupa carrying candles and "money" trees, before monks end the evening with a fireworks display. The festival is accompanied by a fair which attracts exhibitions of traditional handicrafts and products from each province of the country.

Banks

Major local commercial banks:
Agricultural Promotion Bank, 58 Heng Boun Rd (Tel: 212024).
Banque pour le Commerce Exterieur Lao, 1 Pangkham Rd (Tel: 213200, 213201, Fax: 213202).
Nakhonluang Bank, Pangkham Rd (Tel: 213300-4).
Joint Development Bank, 31-33 Lane Xang Ave (Tel: 213530-2, Fax: 213530).
Vientiane Commercial Bank, Dong Palane Rd (Tel: 213510-2).
Thai banks:
Bangkok Bank, 38/13-15 Talat Sao Rd (Tel: 213561-2).
Bank of Ayudhya, 49-51 Lane Xang Ave (Tel: 213520-1).
Krung Thai Bank, 377 Samsenthai Rd (Tel: 213480, 213560).
Siam Commercial Bank, 062/4-5 Nong Bon Rd (Tel: 213501).
Thai Farmers Bank, 08/4 Lane Xang Ave (Tel: 213550, 213552).
Thai Military Bank, 69 Khounboulom Rd (Tel: 217174, 216486).

DISCOVERING LAOS

VIENTIANE

Vientiane, the city of sandalwood, has always been more of a rural Asian town than a bustling capital city. Traffic jams like those in Bangkok are unknown, and cows and chickens regularly roam the city's streets.

Sunsets on the Mekong River are beautiful. Except for the theatre areas, the streets of Vientiane are quiet and almost deserted by 8 p.m. and perfectly safe.

Buddhist pagodas (Wats) provide some of the most interesting sights in the city. **Wat Phra Keo** was built in 1563 to house the Emerald Buddha now possessed by the Thais, has been converted into a museum housing a collection of beautiful Buddhas.

Along the Mekong River 2 kilometres east of the Lane Xang Hotel, is **Wat That Khao**, built in traditional Vientiane style with thick masonry walls and a serpent along the edge of the roof. **Wat Sisaket**, built in the early 19th century at the corner of Lane Xang Ave and Sethathirat St, shows Burmese influence in its square compact design with a small stupa on top. Formerly, each new government was sworn in at this pagoda.

Among Vientiane's 30-odd pagodas, **Wat Ong Tu** (corner of Sethathirat and Anou st), **Wat Phiavat** (a kilometre east of the Lane Xang Hotel), and **Wat Sii Muang** (at the eastern junction of Sethathirat and Samsenthai streets) are some of the most interesting. The Lao always remove their shoes before entering a holy place and visitors should do likewise.

On the northeastern edge of Vientiane stands the **That Luang**, a golden stupa (domed Buddhist shrine) sitting on a pyramid surrounded by 30 smaller spires, built by King Sethathirat in 1566 and restored in 1929 and 1976. Before the communist takeover in 1975, the That Luang was a major focus of pilgrimages from all over Laos and northeastern Thailand.

In the centre of the city is the **That Dam**, a black stupa which, according to Lao legend, houses a sleeping dragon which will rise up in anger if Thailand, the traditional enemy, threatens Vientiane.

At the end of Lane Xang Ave stands **Independence Monument**, a massive arch sometimes called the "vertical runway" because it was built by the former regime with concrete provided by a U.S. aid project for Vientiane's airport.

A **revolutionary museum** detailing the Lao communist victories over France and the U.S., has been established on Samsenthai St near the National Stadium. A **war memorial** for soldiers from the communist side killed during both wars is near the That Luang.

UPCOUNTRY

Luang Prabang, the former royal and religious capital of Laos, is at the junction of the Nam Khan and Mekong Rivers, 350 kilometres north of Vientiane and 335 metres (1,099 feet) above sea level.

The city derives its name from the Pra Bang, or Gold Buddha which was brought to Fa Ngum, the first Lao king, by a priest from Angkor in Cambodia. The Pra Bang is believed to have originated in Sri Lanka and to have been, even at that time, at least 500 years old.

A hill called the **Phousi** rises in the centre of Luang Prabang and its peak, in clear weather, provides an outstanding view of the area. At the tip is the **That Chomsi** with a golden pyramid surrounded by nine ritual umbrellas, the former emblem of royalty. It is thought to have been built on the ruins of an old temple and was restored by King Sri Savang Vong in 1962.

The former **Royal Palace** lies between the Phousi and the Mekong, and next to it is **Wat May Souvanna Phoumakam**, founded in 1821 and completed in 1891. Its front walls are adorned with gilt reliefs showing the royal court and village life of Laos. Previously, this pagoda housed the Pra Bang.

Wat Xieng Thong, built in 1561, demonstrates northern Lao architectural style, with its steep roof sweeping down almost to the ground on either side. It is here that Lao kings were invested and crowned in the past.

Wat Pa Ke, which was restored in 1852, is sometimes known as the Dutch pagoda because of the gold frescoes on two doors depicting visitors from the Netherlands during the 17th and 18th centuries. Other interesting pagodas include **Wat Aphay**, **Wat May**, **Wat Manorom**, with its 12-tonne Buddha from the 14th century, **Wat Visoum** and the **That Mak Mo** which is adjacent.

Visitors can also arrange to take a 20-kilometre trip up the Mekong to the 400-year-old cave temples of **Tham Ting**, which house hundreds of carved wooden Buddhist statues.

Daily flights to **Xieng Khouang** province, best known for its **Plain of Jars**, have opened this area to growing numbers of visitors in recent years. Several hundred enormous jars, made of solid stone, are scattered over a small plateau about 10 kilometres from **Phonsevan**. Historians believe the jars could have been used as burial urns or to store water or rice, but no firm evidence as to their origin has emerged.

Xieng Khouang province is populated by many highland minority groups, particularly colourfully dressed Hmong. This strategically located province was heavily bombed by U.S. planes during the Vietnam War. As a result, the area still contains large quantities of unexploded ordnance.

Wat Pou, the crumbling ruins of an ancient temple built by Cambodian kings 800 years ago, is about two hours by road from the southern city of **Pakse**. Work on the temple was begun in the late 11th century by the Khmer king, Suryavarman II, who also started work on the more elaborate Angkor Wat complex in Cambodia.

From Pakse, which is well known for silk and cotton fabrics woven from tie-dyed threads, travellers can also visit the **Khone Falls**, near the Cambodian border.

BANK BUMIPUTRA

MALAYSIA

Rapid changes over the past two decades have made Malaysia an easy country in which to travel. Whatever few obstacles and pitfalls involving immigration, customs and the rest of officialdom there may be, there is still far less red tape in Malaysia than in many other countries in the region. It is best to tour the country at a gentle pace, choosing specific destinations in advance. High-standard accommodation outside Kuala Lumpur is limited exclusively to beach or highland resorts.

The relaxed and easy style of the country is in no small part due to the people — Malay, Chinese and Indians, Dayaks and Kadazans — who have evolved into a charming national identity. If the pace is slower than in Singapore, to the south, it is also softer. The people as a whole have forgotten hang-ups over the colonial past and welcome visitors quickly and easily. Although Bahasa Malaysia (Malay) is the national language, English is widely spoken and most business can easily be conducted in it.

The country's capital, Kuala Lumpur is a fascinating mixture of East and West styles, modern high-rise blocks interspersed with some fine surviving colonial architecture and the domes of mosques, an easily visible sign of the country's predominant Muslim religion.

The historical towns of Malaysia are on the west coast. North of Kuala Lumpur is the island of Penang, with old-fashioned streets, winding lanes and tree-lined-suburban avenues in Georgetown, the coastal road threading through villages and superb views from the top of Penang Hill.

To the south, Malacca is another charming old town steeped in history. Here the visitor can wander around ruins and remains of the settlements established by the several colonial masters the country has known — Portuguese, Dutch and English.

The east coast of Peninsular Malaysia is one of the great tourist attractions, with beautiful beaches and unspoilt countryside. Fishing boats will ferry tourists to some of the outlying islands, which boast idyllic scenery and clean beaches. On the east coast too, visitors can witness the annual visits of giant turtles, laying about 100 eggs at a time in the sand.

The states of Sabah and Sarawak lie in the South China Sea, on the western side of the island of Borneo, which is shared with Indonesia. Kota Kinabalu in Sabah is worth more than a passing look, for it is the starting point for a trip up Mount Kinabalu. In Sarawak, Kuching is unchanged enough to stir old colonial memories of Somerset Maugham's "Far East."

History

The early kingdom of Funan, based in the area of today's Cambodia, which flourished between the first and sixth centuries AD, extended its influence over the Malay Peninsula. Later, around the seventh century, the Sumatra-based Sri Vijayan Empire dominated many of the lands surrounding the South China Sea, including the Malay peninsula. Sri Vijaya's hegemony was replaced by that of Majapahit in the second half of the 13th century. It was the Sri Vijayan prince, Parameswara, fleeing from the forces of Majapahit around 1403, who was to establish a new kingdom at Malacca which was introduced to Islam in the early 15th

◄ *Kuala Lumpur's contrasts.* PHOTO: GERHARD JOREN

century and where, by 1498, the new faith was well-established and the kingdom counted much of the peninsula as well as certain parts of Sumatra in its domain.

The Portuguese came to Malacca in 1509 and by 1511 had taken over by force, and were to rule until displaced by the Dutch in 1641. The English became a power in the area in the late 18th century, establishing trading posts on Penang Island in 1786 and in Singapore in 1819. Malacca was ceded to the British in 1824.

The several other Malay states, each under their own sultan, signed agreements with the British and in 1895 Perak, Selangor, Negri Sembilan and Pahang states formed a loose union known as the Federated Malay States. Johor, along with the states transferred from Thai control in 1909 (Kelantan, Trengganu, Perlis and Kedah), existed under less direct British control and were known as the Unfederated Malay States. It was during the period of British rule that a good many Chinese and Indians migrated to Malaya to seek employment, establishing the present multicultural mixture.

The Japanese occupied the country from the time of their invasion in 1942 until September 1945. The states formed into the Malay Union after the war and then in 1948 into the Federation of Malaya.

In June 1948, a state of emergency was declared to cope with a communist insurgency and was not lifted until 1960. The first national elections, convincingly won by the Alliance, were held in 1955 and under the Alliance leader, Tunku Abdul Rahman, the country achieved independence on August 31, 1957.

Sabah was ruled by the British North Borneo Co. — which turned the territory into a substantial rubber producer — from 1882 until the Japanese occupation. Sarawak, as a result of successive concessions by the sultans of Brunei, came to be ruled by the "White Rajahs" of the Brooke family from the 1840s until 1942. Both were British colonies from the end of the war until 1963.

Malaya joined with Singapore, Sarawak and Sabah in 1963 to form the Federation of Malaysia but Singapore left the Federation in 1965.

Racial antagonism between the Malays and Chinese brought about serious clashes in 1969, and parliamentary rule was suspended until February 1971.

Rigorous efforts to redress the economic imbalance between the races followed and the Malays have now begun to acquire a larger share of the economy.

During 1972, Malaysia moved away from its previous close ties with the Western world. In 1981 Datuk Seri Mahathir Mohamad became Prime Minister, from which time Malaysia has played a role as a leading exponent of developing-world viewpoints.

Malaysia has a population of 18 million, with 75% of them living in Peninsula Malaysia.

Entry

Many international and Asian regional airlines operate into Kuala Lumpur. Apart from the national carrier, Malaysia Airlines (MAS), more than 30 international airlines have regular services to Malaysia.

There are regular direct flights to and from Europe every day of the week and to and from the U.S. five days a week. Domestic flights are available to the main cities of every Malaysian state. In the East Malaysian states of Sabah and Sarawak, Malaysian Airlines Rural Services serve many isolated towns and villages.

Another domestic air service within Peninsular Malaysia is Pelangi Air which operates a network covering Kuala Lumpur and Ipoh on the mainland as well as Langkawi, Pangkor and Tioman islands. Berjaya Air also flies to Tioman.

Malayan Railways operates two main lines, one from Singapore through Kuala Lumpur and Butterworth which meets the Thai railways at the border, and the other from the town of Gemas up to the northeastern part of the peninsula near Kota Baru, also meeting the Thai railways at the border. There is also a service from Singapore to Tumpat in Kota Baru. The daily Express Langkawi service runs from Kuala Lumpur to Haadyai in Thailand.

Tourists — but not Singaporeans — may buy Visit Malaysia Railpasses from Malayan Railways. The passes offer unlimited travel on any passenger train in the country.

Immigration

Visitors to Malaysia must be in possession of a valid passport/travel document with a minimum validity of six months beyond the period of intended stay. In the case of a national passport not recognized by the Malaysian Government, such as that of Taiwan, the holder must be in possession of a Document in Lieu of

MALAYSIA
THAILAND
Kangar
Changlun
Langkawi Island
Alor Star
Keruh
Georgetown
Butterworth
Penang Island
Taiping
Kuala Kangsar
Ipoh
Cameron Highlands
Lumut
Teluk Anson
Tapah
Fraser's Hill
Kuala Lipis
Bentong
Temerloh
Kuala Lumpur
Klang
Kajang
Seremban
Port Dickson
Cape Rachado
Malacca
Muar
Batu Pahat
Segamat
Kluang
Johor Bharu
SINGAPORE
Mersing
Tioman Island
Kuantan
Kuala Kemaman
Rantau Abang
Taman Negara
(National Park)
Kuala Trengganu
Kuala Besut
Kota Bharu
INDONESIA
East Malaysia
Roads
Railways
Airports
km
0
100
EAST MALAYSIA
km
0
200
Kudat
Kota Belud
Kota Kinabalu
Ranau
Sandakan
Beaufort
Penampang
Keningau
Limbang
Tenom
SABAH
Lahad Datu
Tawau
Miri
BRUNEI
Mukah
SARAWAK
Bintulu
Sibu
Belaga
Kuching
Sematan
Saratok
Kapit
Serian
Simanggang
INDONESIA

passport.

Only nationals of Bangladesh, Cuba, India, Pakistan, Sri Lanka, North Korea and all Certificate of Identity holders must obtain a visa before entering Malaysia. Chinese residents of Taiwan must have a Document in Lieu of passport, as well as a visa, since Malaysia does not recognize a Taiwan passport. Citizens of Israel are not allowed to enter Malaysia.

Citizens of other countries are allowed in for limited periods without visas. For exact details of permitted stay, consult your own immigration authorities or a Malaysian diplomatic mission.

Visas are issued by Malaysian Diplomatic Missions abroad or British Consulates acting for Malaysia in countries where no diplomatic representation of Malaysia is established.

Health

A valid vaccination certificate is required for visitors who, within the preceding 10 days, have been in any country in the yellow fever endemic zone such as countries in Central America and Central Africa. Any visitor who fails to have a valid vaccination certificate will be put under quarantine for a maximum period of six days upon arrival in Malaysia.

Customs

Travellers to Malaysia can bring into the country duty free one litre of wine or spirits, 200 cigarettes or 225 grams of tobacco, reasonable amounts of personal possessions including battery operated and other electrical appliances, and gifts worth up to M$200.

Visitors must declare any plant or parts of a plant or animals in their possession.

An export licence from the Director of Museums is necessary for the export of antiques and historical objects.

Currency

The Malaysian currency is the ringgit, commonly known as the Malaysian dollar. It comes in denominations of M$1,000, 500, 100, 50, 20, 10 and 1 notes. Coins of 1, 5, 10, 20 and 50 cents and M$1 denominations are also in circulation.

There is no restriction on much money in currency or travellers' cheques a tourist can bring into or take out of Malaysia or on the import or export of Malaysian currency notes.

Money and travellers' cheques may be freely exchanged at banks, authorized money changers and hotels, with money-changers offering the lowest rates. For visitors to the country it would be best to change your money and travellers' cheques at the money-changers in town rather than at the airport exchange counters.

Most international credit or charge cards such as American Express, Visa, MasterCard and Diners Club are accepted, but only by major establishments in the larger towns. Credit cards can be used for a wide range of goods and services in hotels, department stores and restaurants, but in the country cash is needed.

Language

The national language is Bahasa Malaysia or Malay but English is widely spoken and is also commonly used in business transactions. Mandarin is also widely spoken among the Chinese. Most Malaysians are bilingual. There are several local phrase books for those who wish to speak in Malay.

Climate

The climate on the lowland coastal areas is very warm throughout the year. Temperatures range from 21°C to 32°C with conditions in the hills cooler particularly in the evenings. The east coast of Peninsular Malaysia and Sabah and Sarawak experience heavy rainfalls during the months of November to February. For the west coast states of Peninsular Malaysia, the wet months are usually April, May and October.

Dress

Cool, lightweight summer clothing is ideal with only medium weight woollens required at night in cooler highland areas or if air-conditioning is too fierce, which it can be. For formal and semi-formal occasions, batik shirts or dresses are accepted. Jackets for men are only necessary for very formal occasions.

Women are not encouraged to wear shorts, miniskirts or off the shoulder or even sleeveless garments, as it offends Muslim practice, especially in rural areas. When entering a mosque or Hindu temple, visitors must remove their shoes. Women entering mosques are advised to cover their heads with a scarf.

Visitors to places of worship are reminded to be dressed modestly. Topless bathing or sunbathing is not allowed at Malaysian resorts.

Business Hours

In all states except Kedah, Kelantan and Trengganu, government offices open from Monday to Friday, plus Saturday morning. In the three exceptions, government offices open from Saturday to Wednesday plus Thursday morning — they are closed on Thursday afternoon and all day on Friday. In all states, the opening hours are 8 a.m.-4.15 p.m. on full days and 8.15 a.m.-12.45 p.m. on half days.

Banking hours are from 10 a.m.-3 p.m. on full days and 9.30 a.m.-11 a.m. on half days. Banks in each state observe the same working days as government offices.

Most private firms work 8:30-9 a.m.(some start at 8 a.m.) to 8:30-9 p.m. Monday to Friday and from 8:30-9 a.m. to 7610-4; p.m. on Saturdays.

In Kuala Lumpur and other major towns, shopping centres and department stores are open from 10 a.m.-10 p.m. Monday to Saturday and many remain open on Sunday.

Liquor can be purchased from sundry shops and supermarkets. However, there is a restriction on the time for purchase. At some shops, liquor cannot be purchased after 6 p.m. At others it is after 9 p.m. This depends on the locality of the shop. Liquor at pubs and bars can be purchased until midnight on weekdays and until 2 a.m. on weekends. Beer can be purchased at any time shops are open.

Doing Business

Punctuality is considered a sign of respect and good manners. If you know you are going to be late, it is common courtesy to inform the person's secretary. Remember to have your name cards on you and always present your card on introduction.

English is widely used both in business discussions as well as in everyday conversation. Women have made a mark in Malaysia business and occupy many leading positions. A handshake is the universal greeting, even with a Muslim woman, but wait for her to proffer her hand first. Casual touching of the opposite sex in public is very much frowned upon and touching of the head is taboo.

It is important to be dressed appropriately and neatly. You can never go wrong with a suit or a safari suit. A long sleeve batik shirt is well accepted as an evening attire. For women hemlines should ideally be knee length.

It is considered rude behaviour to point with your forefinger. Pointing, if necessary, is always done by the thumb over the fist. It is also rude to display the soles of your shoes to others.

Business entertaining is mostly done outside the home. When entertaining a Muslim, bear in mind that he or she is not allowed to eat pork or drink alcohol. It is always advisable to check that the venue at which you have chosen to entertain does not serve pork.

Generally no toast is made, but if you are called upon to do so, make a short polite toast and avoid touching on sensitive subjects such as religion and politics. If you must smoke, it is only polite to check with your host before lighting up. Some restaurants have no smoking signs which must be obeyed.

When giving a gift, always take into account the religious and cultural background of the recipient — obviously avoid giving a bottle of alcoholic drink or a pigskin wallet to a Muslim.

Forms of address are complex in Malaysia. While those of Chinese origin, unless they have adopted a Western style given name, put their family name first and given name (two words) second, Malays do not have surnames. Their first name is their name and their second name that of their father. It is important for foreigners to remember to call a Malay by the first name they hear, otherwise they might be calling this person by his father's name. The mysteries of Malay titles would require a whole book and are best picked up slowly. If a business colleague is to introduce you to such a person, the form of address will almost certainly be explained.

Indians originally from Southern India, similarly to Malays, only have one name, preceded by an initial which stands for their father's name. The initial should be ignored except when writing an Indian name. Northern Indians are likely to have a family name and with these one should use the Western way.

Translation services are available in Malay, English, French, Japanese, Mandarin and German, to name a few. Your hotel will be able to assist you with the names of a few good companies.

Secretarial services are available at hotels which have a business centre. A check with the yellow pages of the telephone directory will give you a list of other secretarial agencies.

Exploring Penang. PHOTO: MICHAEL VATIKIOTIS

Car-rental companies in Malaysia offer self-drive and chauffeur-driven services with competitive daily, weekly, monthly and corporate rates.

Rip-Offs

The setting up of a special unit of the police — the Tourist Police — to protect visitors from abuse has worked well and Malaysia is generally a safe place. It is sensible, however, not to visit isolated beaches wearing expensive jewellery or gold watches.

Occasionally hotel rooms are ransacked and guests should always deposit valuables — including passports — in the hotel's safety deposit boxes, which are found everywhere, including at holiday resorts.

Probably the most common complain is about overcharging by taxi drivers who either "forget" to put on their meters or claim they are broken. Refuse to ride in a taxi which does not have its meter on and report all abuses to the Road Transport Department or the police.

Media

The leading local English-language newspapers in the country are the *New Straits Times, The Star*, the *Business Times, The Sun, The Edge (weekly)* and the afternoon tabloid, the *Malay Mail*. Bookshops at leading hotels and in shopping complexes all carry major daily newspapers and weekly magazines from Britain, the United States and elsewhere, which all have free access to Malaysia.

Communications

Malaysia has a comprehensive communications system both internally and with the rest of the world. More than 170 countries can be dialled direct. Telekom Malaysia operates a highly developed telecoms network which covers all urban centres and a large part of rural areas.

The several courier companies operating in Malaysia all provide you with fast and reliable deliveries to virtually anywhere in Malaysia and to many other countries. The better-known courier companies are DHL, TNT Express Worldwide and Federal Express.

Transport

KUALA LUMPUR

TAXIS: Available at designated taxi-stands along major roads, outside shopping complexes and at hotels. Taxis are fitted with metres which start at M$1.50 for the first two kilometres and 10 M cents for each subsequent 200 metres, inclusive of air-conditioning charges. Between midnight and 6 a.m., a surcharge of 50% applies. For phone bookings, an extra M$1 is charged. For transfers from the airport or railway station, travel vouchers are available at the taxi counters. Rates are preset and depend on to which part of the city you are going.

Privately run companies operate bus services within the city as well as long inter-urban routes linking the city with neighbouring towns. Fares vary from as little as 30 M cents.

Minibuses charge a flat rate of 60 M cents irrespective of the distance travelled.

Several bus companies operate air-conditioned express services to other destinations in the country.

The Putra bus terminal opposite Putra World Trade Centre and the Pekeliling bus terminal in Jalan Pekeliling are for buses to the east coast of Malaysia. Pudu Raya bus terminal is for north and southbound buses including Singapore, and the MARA bus terminal at Jalan Tunku Abdul Rahman is also for buses to the south.

TRANSPORT UPCOUNTRY

SELF-DRIVE: Both self-drive and chauffeur-driven cars can be hired in Malaysia. **Avis**, **Hertz** and **Sintat** are among the many companies which offer a rent-it-here, leave-it-there service in Penang, Kuala Lumpur, Kuantan, Johor Baru and Singapore. Different car rental companies offer different rates.

Communications between states have improved tremendously with the construction of the 980-kilometre North-South Highway, which stretches from Kedah in the north to Johor Baru in the south. The Karak Highway links the east and west coasts of the peninsula.

TAXIS: Share-taxis (those taking a full load of four passengers) run between main Malaysian towns. The fares are higher than the bus fares, but the trips are quicker and more comfortable. The taxis leave from established depots in the towns. One can hire a taxi and not share it, but must pay the equivalent of a full load.

TRAINS: Rail services run on the main west coast line Singapore-Seremban-Kuala Lumpur-Ipoh-Butterworth, and on an east coast line that branches off the former at Gemas in the south and runs through the central mountain country via Kuala Lipis to Tumpat (a little north of Kota Baru). Both lines continue into Thailand in the north.

AIR: The national carrier, Malaysia Airlines, flies to the main towns of both Peninsular Malaysia and Sabah and Sarawak and also to a large number of smaller towns, especially in the two Borneo states.

Tours

A good many tour companies offer city tours in the comfort of air-conditioned buses, and hotels or travel agencies will provide plenty of brochures and make the necessary arrangements.

Accommodation

Hotel accommodation in Malaysia is of a high standard, especially as a result of the extensive expansion programme carried out over the past few years, notably in Kuala Lumpur and Penang. Kuala Lumpur has hotels of international standards such as the **Hilton**, **Shangri-La**, **Istana** and **Hyatt** to suit the more affluent. It also has the **Carcosa Seri Negara**, a magnificent conversion of two colonial era mansions into a luxurious hotel containing just 13 suites, suitable for visiting royalty, film stars and business tycoons — or anybody else who can afford up to US$351 a night. At the other end of the scale, the capital has a wide choice of moderate but good hotels for the budget traveller. Most of the larger hotels have business centres to cater to the needs of travelling businessmen. Most hotels have discotheques and bars with live entertainment shows. A government tax of 5% is levied on room rates plus a 10% service charge.

Upcountry there are luxury resorts in many places on the east and west coasts and in the central highlands. For the budget traveller there are old-fashioned guest houses which, if minimal in facilities, are clean and honestly run.

Dining

Malaysia is a paradise for food lovers. The different peoples that make up its multiracial community each have their individual foods and cooking styles, so one can eat with great variety around the country. You can eat in the comfort of well-decorated, air-conditioned restaurants or rub shoulders with the local people by trying out delicious local cuisine at street stalls. Restaurants cater for a wide variety of tastes and include Malay, Chinese, Indian, Japanese, Thai and Korean food. Cooking and eating at the open-air stalls is a distinctive Malaysian experience.

Malay food (along with that of Indonesia, which is closely related) is largely restricted to its home territory of Southeast Asia. The rich and spicy flavours vary from state to state. It makes ample use of seafood and meat (except pork), coconut and many other indigenous fruits and, of course, rice. Although a generous amount of chilli is used in some Malay cuisine, the food is rarely too spicy for even those unused to it.

Malay food varies according to the state from which it originates. In Kuala Lumpur, the most popular restaurant serving Malay food is the **Sri Melayu** in Jalan Conlay. Diners are entertained with cultural shows incorporating traditional Malaysian folk dances and music. Northern Malay food at moderate prices is available at the **Rasa Utara**, which has branches in Bukit Bintang Plaza, Central Market and Bangsar Shopping Complex.

For the ever-popular satay — skewered grilled meat eaten with a sweet but slightly spicy peanut sauce — try the **Satay Station** at the Holiday Inn On The Park. Also well worth a visit is the **Satay Anika** restaurant at Bukit Bintang Plaza.

For Nonya food — Straits Chinese cuisine (a cross between Malay and Chinese food) essentially from Penang and Malacca — the **Dondang Sayang** at the Weld Supermarket in Jalan Raja Chulan and in Bangsar is highly recommended, as are the **Bon Ton** and the **Kapitan's Club**, both in Jalan Ampang.

The large number of Indian restaurants in Kuala Lumpur is testimony to the popularity of this kind of food among all races in the country. The **Bombay Palace** in Jalan Tun Razak offers North Indian food, as do the **Taj** branches at the Crown Princess and Federal hotels. **Deepam House of Curries**, behind the Federal Hotel, serves both North and South Indian meals. The **Jewel In The Crown** serves North Indian food. Several coffee shops along Jalan Ampang serve Indian food on banana leaves instead of plates — a fun way to eat (with one's hands) for the adventurous.

Chinese restaurants, too, can be found in abundance in Kuala Lumpur. Not all Chinese restaurants serve pork. The ones which use neither pork nor pork fat for cooking show a "Halal" sign. Chinese food can mean anything from Cantonese to Sichuan (also spelled Szechuan or Sze Chuan).

Among the many popular restaurants in Kuala Lumpur is the **Tai Thong**, in Jalan Sultan Ismail, offering Cantonese food. **The Sze Chuan** restaurant in Jalan Sultan Ismail serves just what its name suggests, as does the **Hakka Seafood Restaurant** in Bangsar. Others worthy of mention are the **Kum Leng** in Jalan Pudu, the **Overseas** and the **Teochew**, both in Jalan Imbi. For vegetarians, the **Pure Mind** in Jalan Imbi is a good bet.

For Thai food, try the **Barn Thai** in Jalan Tun Razak, **Cili Padi** at The Mall, **D'Kalkatu** in Jalan Sultan Ismail and the **Thai Kitchen** in Central Market.

Japanese restaurants recommended are the **Munakata** in Menara Promet, **Chikuyo-tei** in Plaza See Hoy Chan, **Kampachi** at the Hotel Equitorial and the **Nadaman** at the Shangri-La Hotel. Any number of restaurants and pubs serve Western fare, and many of the international fast-food chains have outlets in Kuala Lumpur.

Entertainment

Night life is not as tame as it used to be, but there is still nothing to match the sort of raunchy entertainment — if that is the word — offered in neighbouring Bangkok. Kuala Lumpur offers a wide choice of places for entertainment ranging from venues for cultural shows to the most active Western-style pubs and discotheques. Hotels such as the **Shangri-La**, **Hilton**, **Istana**, **Holiday Inn**, **Parkroyal**, **Federal**, **Equatorial** and the **Hyatt** provide good bands and vocalists, local and foreign.

For those who want to dance, there are numerous discotheques complete with laser beams and the latest sound techniques at hotels. Other places with musical entertainment include the **Hard Rock Cafe** in Wisma Concorde, **The Pub** at the Shangri-La, **Pyramid Supper Club** in Pusat Bandar Damansarà, **The Jump** in Jalan Tun Razak and **The Monkey Bar** at the Legend Hotel. There is karaoke at **Life TV**, in the Life Centre on Jalan Sultan Ismail, **The Karaoke Kingdom** at the Hotel Istana and **Brannigan's** at Lorong Perak.

For those who prefer a slower evening, there are some good pubs and lounges which offer jazz, Country and Western and rock music. Try the **Blue Moon** at the Equatorial, **Stardust** at the Ming Court, the **Aviary Bar** at the Hilton and the **Taipan's Club** at the Hotel Istana.

Apart from discos and pubs, cultural shows and concerts are staged at various places in the city. Major hotels periodically stage dinner theatres featuring mostly Western plays. Contemporary plays by local theatre groups are staged regularly and a browse through the newspapers will tell you where to head for.

Shopping

From huge department stores to colourful bazaars to quaint little shops, shopping in Kuala Lumpur is a unique experience. Local handicraft items from the east coast and Sabah and Sarawak are all to be found in the capital.

For those with a hankering for branded goods and imported items, **Lot 10** in Jalan Sultan Ismail, the **Concorde** shopping arcade in Wisma Concorde, **Yow Chuan Plaza** on Jalan Tun Razak and **The Weld** on Jalan Raja Chulan are good places to look. For the less brand-conscious, try shopping complexes such as **Sungai Wan Plaza**, **The Mall** off Jalan Chow Kit, **Sogo** in Jalan Tuanku Abdul Rahman and **Bukit Bintang Plaza** in Jalan Bukit Bintang. For local handicrafts, souvenirs and curio items, and for clothes made from batik, try the **Central Market, Karyaneka, Infokraft and Batik Malaysia**.

For jewellery, **P.H. Hendry** in Jalan Tuanku Abdul Rahman has long been established as a leading jeweller as have **K.M. Oli** in Yow Chuan Plaza. and **The Jewel Mine** at The Weld. For Jade, try the **Dragon's Home** on Jalan Kabus, off Jalan Ulu Klang.

More adventurous shopping can be done in the smaller shops and stalls found in Petaling St and Jalan Tuanku Abdul Rahman, where bargaining is still very much in vogue.

Duty free outlets at the airport and in the city offer a wide variety of items. Hotels should be able to provide a list of duty free shops.

Sports

Spectator sports in Malaysia include soccer, rugby, hockey, cricket, badminton and horse-racing which is held throughout the year, with meetings on weekends and public holidays; race weekends rotate between Kuala Lumpur, Ipoh, Penang and neighbouring Singapore.

Game hunting is still permitted under certain limitations: details can be obtained by writing to the Director-General, Wild Life and National Park Department, Block K 20, Government Offices Bldg, Jalan Duta, Kuala Lumpur. Fresh water fishing requires a licence.

There are a number of golf courses across the country and permission to play (on the payment of green fees) is usually granted by the club secretary. Sets of clubs can be hired at the larger establishments.

Traditional Malay sports have been given a boost in the country since independence in 1957. One of them is *sepak raga,* which is elevated to an international level when Malaysia meets neighbouring Indonesia, Thailand, Singapore or the Philippines. Using what closely resembles a badminton court with a high net, youths lob, drive and smash a light rattan ball using their feet and body, excluding only the forearms and hands. Scoring rules resemble those of badminton. *Main gasing* (top spinning) is a popular pastime, even with adults, as is *man wau* (kite flying).

Silat — a Malay martial art — is a fighting technique with or without weapons. Unarmed demonstrations of the movements are a common sight at weddings and other celebrations. The sport is very popular in rural areas.

Holidays

Malaysia's crowded festival calendar reflects the multi-cultural character of the country: Malay, Chinese, Indian, Kadazan, Dayak and Western holiday (among others) are all celebrated.

Most occasions are determined by the lunar calendar and fall at different times each year. In Malaysia, when a holiday falls on a Sunday, the following Monday is a public holiday.

January 1: New Year's Day (a public holiday except in the states of Johor, Kedah, Kelantan, Perlis and Trengganu).

January-February: Chinese New Year. National Public holiday. On the eve of this festival, Chinese families hold reunion dinners followed by the firing of fireworks to ward off evil spirits.

Taipusam: Public holiday in Penang, Negri Sembilan, Perak, Johor and Selangor. Hindu celebration of Lord Subramaniam's birth, marked by rites of penitence. Devotees carry *kavadis*, or wooden frames decorated with flowers. Some have long needles stuck into their backs and chests, or skewers pushed through their tongues and cheeks.

Awal Ramadan. Public holiday in Johor and Malacca. The first day of the fasting month for Muslims.

March/April: Hari Raya Puasa. National public holiday. The end of the fasting month.

Good Friday: State holiday in Sabah and Sarawak.

May 1: Labour Day. Public holiday.

Wesak Day: National public holiday. Commemorate the birth, enlightenment and Nirvana of Lord Buddha.

Hari Raya Qurban (formerly known as Hari Raya Haji). National public holiday.
Maal Hijrah (formerly called Awal Muharram). National public holiday. Marks the beginning of the Muslim calendar.
First Saturday in June: National public holiday, Birthday of His Majesty the Yang di-Pertuan Agong, the King.
Turtle festival, held in Trengganu to celebrate the annual return of the giant leatherback turtles who come to lay their eggs on the beach. Not a holiday.
August 31: National Day marking the independence from British rule. National public holiday. Parades, concerts and firework displays are held.
Birthday of Prophet Muhammad (National public holiday).
October-November: Deepavali. Public holiday except in Sabah and Sarawak. The Hindu festival of lights.
December 25: Christmas Day. National public holiday.

DISCOVERING MALAYSIA

KUALA LUMPUR

Named after its site at the junction of the Kelang and Gombak rivers. Kuala Lumpur (muddy estuary) dates from 1857 as a settlement of Chinese tin miners. Today's cosmopolitan Kuala Lumpur, with its high-rise buildings creeping closer to the Lake Gardens, is not just the capital city but the heart and soul of the country. Its legacy of extraordinary colonial buildings, well preserved, and excellent modern architecture make it a major tourist destination in its own right.

The city centre lies astride the Kelang river. Situated at the junction of the Kelang and Gombak rivers is the **Masjid Jame (Jame Mosque)**. Built in traditional Arabian style, complete with intricately designed domes and minarets, the mosque nestles within a grove of coconut palms.

The old section of the city is in the south with its collection of Chinese-type shops spilling over on to the streets. It merges to the north with the newer section where there are many banks and commercial offices. But the growth is no longer confined to the central region. Many high-rise buildings are appearing further away from the centre.

From Masjid Jame, south and across the Gombak river is the **Sultan Abdul Samad Building**, which is elaborately Moorish in design. Built in 1894-97 this impressive structure stands with its 41-metre clock tower amid curving arches and domes. Across from this building is the **Merdeka Square** located on what used to be known as the Selangor Club Padang (field).

On the other side of the square is the very British Selangor Club itself. From the club, it is a pleasant walk of about 3.5 kilometres to the **Muzium Negara** on Jalan Damansara. The museum provides an excellent introduction to Malaysian culture. Two murals of Italian mosaic tiles flank the main entrance, depicting the history and customs of the Malaysians. Also in the south of the city is the extraordinary **Railway Station**. Built in 1911, the building with its domes, arches and pillars reflects a Moorish style of architecture.

The Malaysian Railways Headquarters Building opposite is also of Islamic design. Next to this is the old colonial building which was once the Majestic Hotel. It is now the **National Art Gallery** and contains a permanent collection by Malaysian artists. A short walk from the Railway Station will bring you to the **Masjid Negara** (National Mosque), one of the largest mosques in Southeast Asia. Surrounded by green lawns and ornamented with pools and fountains, it is built in traditional Muslim decorative style. A 73-metre-high minaret rises from the centre of the pool and the mosque is crowned by an unusual shell-shaped dome. Visitors may enter this mosque, though shoes must be removed and women must be covered — a covering garment is provided by the attendants.

Roughly a kilometre northeast from the mosque is the **Central Market**, a former wet-market and now an arts and crafts centre. It is renowned for its comprehensive array of traditional wares such as handicraft and batik.

From Masjid Jame, heading southeast will bring you to the old section of the town. At the junction of Jalan Maharajalela and Jalan Stadium is the interesting old **Chan See Shu Yuen Temple**. Erected in 1906 and of typical Chinese design, this temple is made up of courtyards and pavilions and surrounded by sculptures depicting the Taoist faith. Immediately behind this temple is the Chinwoo Stadium and up a small hill nearby is the Stadium Merdeka and the indoor Stadium Negara. In this old section of the town is also the **Sri Mahamariaman Temple**, a Hindu temple which

Traditional and modern styles coexist. PHOTO: RON McMILLAN ►

boasts a very elaborate decorative scheme which incorporates gold, precious stones and a mixture of clay and attractive tiles. Built in 1873, it is one of the largest and most ornate of such temples in Malaysia.

Kuala Lumpur's **Chinatown** is just around the corner in Jalan Petaling where one can buy almost anything from herbs and medicines to cheap designer watches and clothes. At night this stretch of the road is closed to traffic and becomes one long street market.

North of Masjid Jame is Jalan Tuanku Abdul Rahman, named after the first prime minister of independent Malaysia. This stretch of the road is a good place to hunt for antiques, curios, fabrics and Indian ethnic goods.

Parliament House, the **National Monument**, and the **Lake Gardens** are all situated west of Masjid Jame. Facilities for boating are also available here. Located on the fringe of the gardens is the Orchid Garden, full of different varieties, and close by the Bird Park and the Hibiscus Garden. Even more exotic is the butterfly sanctuary housing some 6,000 butterflies of over 120 species.

Perched on a hilltop overlooking the lake and surrounded by extensive lawns is the **Carcosa Seri Negara**. The buildings were once separate entities. The Carcosa was once the residence of the British Governor and after independence was occupied by a succession of British High Commissioners until it was formally returned to the Malaysian Government. The Seri Negara once served as a guest house for visiting foreign dignitaries. Today the Carcosa and Seri Negara together have been converted into a beautiful but exclusive hotel.

Proceeding east from Masjid Jame on Jalan Raja Chulan is the **Karyaneka Handicraft Village** — a cluster of wooden houses in traditional Malay architecture. Each house represents one of the 14 states in the country and feature the arts and culture of that particular state.

South of the city in the Sungei Besi area is **Mines Wonderland**, a recreational park created from what was the world's largest opencast tine mine. To the southwest of the city, in Petaling Jaya, is the **Sunway Lagoon** water park, which has the same origin.

About 12 kilometres out of the city centre, southeast of Masjid Jame, is the **Getsamani Catholic Church**. Perched on a slope, this church is surrounded by life-size statues depicting the crucifixion of Christ.

About 13 kilometres north of Kuala Lumpur, along the road to Ipoh, are the **Batu Caves** where, at the top of 272 steps, is a Hindu shrine within a huge limestone cave measuring 112 metres at its highest point. On the Hindu festival day of Taipusam the caves are crowded with thousands of devotees and tourists. Many tourists plan their holidays to witness some of the more spectacular ceremonies during the festival. These includes devotees in a deep hypnotic trance bearing a *kavadi* — a wooden cage supported by steel spikes pierced through the skin.

Along the same road about 23 kilometres from the city is the **Templer Park**, offering a natural sanctuary of jungle, waterfalls, picnic and camping areas and interesting jungle treks for the more adventurous. Another popular reserve 22 kilometres from Kuala Lumpur along the North-South Highway is the **Lipur Kanching** forest reserve, famous for its seven levels of waterfalls.

West of Kuala Lumpur is the state of Selangor, home to the largest port in the country, **Port Klang**. Shah Alam, the new state capital, which boasts the **Masjid Sultan Salahuddin Abdul Aziz Shah mosque**. The huge blue aluminium dome is reputed to be the largest of its kind in the world.

UPCOUNTRY — NORTH

About 50 kilometres inland by road from Kuala Lumpur are the **Genting Highlands**. Set in the finest mountain country at 1,700 metres, the Genting Highlands is the only resort in the country that has a gambling casino, which is very popular with people from the capital. Two other resorts — Fraser's Hill and Cameron Highlands — offer a more tranquil break from city life.

North of Kuala Lumpur — 65 kilometres from the town of Tapah, which is the turn-off point for Cameron Highlands on the main north-south highway — is the town of **Ipoh**, capital of Perak state. For centuries Perak was renowned for its rich tin deposits. It is believed that the state derived its name, which means silver in Malay, from the silvery tin ore. Ipoh, once an obscure *kampung* (village) with dilapidated buildings is now one of the most modern cities in Malaysia.

About six kilometres north of Ipoh are the huge limestone caves of Gunung Tasek. Within the caves is the Perak Tong Buddhist temple. Built in 1926, the temple houses over 40 Buddha statues including a 12.8 metre high sitting

Buddha. The railway station in Ipoh, popularly known as the Taj Mahal of Ipoh, is an impressive landmark of Moorish architecture.

About 30 minutes' drive from Ipoh is the curiosity of the ruins of **Kellie's Castle**. Built some 80 years ago by an English rubber tycoon, William Kellie Smith, the castle was never completed as Smith left for England in the middle of its construction and never returned.

Taiping, between Ipoh and Penang is the old capital of Perak. The two main attractions here are the Lake Gardens, one of the biggest and most beautiful parks in the country, and the Perak Museum, the oldest in the country. A short drive from Taiping brings you to Malaysia's oldest hill resort, **Bukit Larut** (formerly called Maxwell Hill).

Perak's royal town of **Kuala Kangsar**, 48 kilometres northwest of Ipoh, boasts one of the most beautiful mosques in the country. The **Perak Royal Museum** situated near the Istana (palace) Iskandariah, the Sultan's official palace, was built without any architectural plans and without using a single nail.

In the quaint village of **Pasir Salak** stands a memorial marking the incident in which J.W. Birch, the first British Resident in Perak, was killed. This village is also well known for its ancient Malay architecture and crafts.

Some 84 kilometres southwest of Ipoh is the seaport and naval base of **Lumut**. A 40-minute ferry ride from here is the popular island of **Pangkor**, where a wide range of activities such as scuba-diving, windsurfing, fishing and snorkelling can be enjoyed.

Further north on the west coast of the Malayan peninsula is Butterworth, linked across 1.6 kilometres of water spanned by the world's third-longest bridge with **Penang**. First established as a British trading post in 1786 this "Pearl of the Orient" — possibly the first of several places now claiming that title — is one of the major commercial and trading centres in Malaysia. The island bustles with all the activity of a metropolitan city and is famed for its picturesque beaches.

Fort Cornwallis marks the spot where Francis Light, the founder of Penang, landed in 1786. Originally a wooden fortress, it was later erected in stone by convict labour in 1804-05. A stone's throw from Farquhar St is **St George's Church** also built by convicts in 1818. This Anglican church is one of the oldest landmarks in the city.

Along Jalan Mesjid Kapital Keling is the **Kuan Yin (Goddess of Mercy) Temple**, built in 1800 by the first Chinese settlers on the island. **The Kapitan Kling Mosque** the oldest of the places of worship is also along this street. Built in the early nineteenth century by an Indian Muslim merchant, it is a fine example of Islamic architecture of Moorish influence.

In Lebuh Cannon a short walk from Jalan Mesjid Kapitan Keling is the **Khoo Kongsi** or clan temple. Master craftsmen from China created this magnificent building with intricate carvings. The **Leong San Tong (Dragon Hall)** of the kongsi is reputed to be the most picturesque temple in Penang.

In Lorong Burmah is the **Wat Chayamangkalaram**, a magnificent Buddhist temple which houses the world's third-largest reclining Buddha, measuring 33 metres.

For a panoramic view of the island, a visit to **Penang Hill** is recommended. The journey to the 821-metre summit by funicular railway is not to be missed. Ayer Hitam, at the foot of Penang Hill, is the site of the **Kek Lok Si Temple**, the largest Buddhist temple in Malaysia and one of the finest in Southeast Asia. Its seven storey pagoda is a mixture of Chinese, Thai and Burmese architecture.

Penang is not only famous for its religious houses but also for its palm-fringed beaches stretching from Tanjung Bungah and Batu Ferringhi to Teluk Bahang in the extreme north of Penang. Although these were among some of the first promoted in Asia, they have now become overshadowed by many competitors in more remote places which have become accessible through air travel.

Typical of this new freedom of access are the **Langkawi** group of islands, further north, off the coast of Kedah state. This formation of 99 islands, most of them uninhabited, offer attractions such as scuba-diving in the clear waters, rich with coral and marine life. Access to Langkawi is by air from Kuala Lumpur or Penang and by ferry from Kuala Kedah. It can also be reached from Singapore.

SOUTH

Just 150 kilometres south of Kuala Lumpur when heading towards Singapore is **Malacca**, one of the oldest towns in the country and a living museum of Portuguese, Dutch and British colonial rule.

One of the major tourist attractions is the old Portuguese fortress **A Farmosa**. This fort was built in 1511 to protect the Portuguese conquerors from other invaders. During the attack in which the Dutch defeated the Port-

A Sabah market. PHOTO: REVIEW

uguese, it was badly damaged and in 1670 the Dutch renamed it the "Voc." In 1807 the walls were demolished by the British when they occupied Malacca in their turn.

During Portuguese rule, Christianity became prevalent with the visit of St Francis Xavier. The leading Catholic church was built in 1521. Originally known as Duarte Coelho, the Dutch renamed the church **St Paul's**. In 1753 the Dutch started using St Paul's Hill as a cemetery, and huge tombstones with Latin and Portuguese inscriptions can still be found. St Paul's was where St Francis Xavier was buried before his body was moved to Goa.

The Church of **St Peter** dating from 1710 is now the Church of the Portuguese Mission. The other significant old church in the town, **Christ Church**, next to the **Stadthuys** (town hall), is a fine example of Dutch architecture. The handmade pews here are more than 200 years old. The brass bible rest dates from 1773. Still visible on the church floor are tombstones in Armenian script.

The **Stadthuys** is the oldest example of Dutch architecture in the East, dating from between 1641 and 1660. It once housed the Dutch governors and today houses the **Malacca Historical Museum**, which displays articles (clothing, weapons and coins, etc.) from the different periods of the town's history.

St John's Fort to the east of the town was constructed by the Dutch during the 18th century. It was once a private chapel. A visit to this fort on top of St John's Hill gives a good view of the surrounding area.

Before the Portuguese occupation, when the bride of the first ruler of Malacca arrived from China in 1459 together with her retinue, the sultan gave her **Bukit Cina** (Chinese Hill) for their residence. These Chinese women were the start of Chinese connections with Malaysia and are the origins of the mixed-race Straits-born Chinese, or Peranakan, people who live in Malaysia and Singapore today. Today Bukit Cina is said to be the largest Chinese cemetery outside China.

The architecture of mosques has always been in Moorish style — dome-shaped with minarets. But in Malacca you can find mosques with roofs rising like a pyramid and instead of minarets, pagodas. One such mosque is the **Kampung Kling** Mosque which has a three-tiered roof. Another pyramid-shaped mosque is **The Tranquerah Mosque**. The country's oldest mosque is also found in Malacca. Built in 1728, the **Kampong Hulu Mosque** has an architectural style which can only be found in Malacca.

Another place of worship that is a must to see is Malaysia's oldest Chinese temple — the **Cheng Hoon Teng temple**, built in 1646. Inside the temple are beautiful wood carvings and lacquer work, and the life of Buddha is depicted in the railings above the altars.

Jalan Hang Jebat (Jonker St) is the place for antiques. Its narrow, picturesque streets are full of treasures, some of which date back nearly 300 years.

Peranakan relics are housed in the **Baba Nonya Heritage** museum. This is the country's first private museum and is open to the public for a fee.

No visit to Malacca is complete without having tasted the local version of Portuguese food, offered by many local restaurants.

Examples of the arts and culture of the 14 states of Malaysia can be seen at the **Mini Malaysia Cultural Village**, 15 kilometres from Malacca. Here traditional houses of various designs display art and craft from each state.

For the nature lovers, a trip to the **Ayer Keroh** Recreational Forest is recommended.

South of Malacca, the road passes through pleasant coconut palm groves and traditional Malay houses. The towns of Muar and Batu Pahat are passed en route to **Johor Baru** on the southernmost tip of the Malay Peninsula, across the strait from Singapore. This is a thriving but not particularly attractive "border town," which offers little to the visitor.

There are several offshore tourist resort islands in Johor and the better known ones are Rawa, Sibu and Besar. These are almost unspoilt, with no modern developments as yet, and ideal for scuba-diving and other sea sports. Accommodation is available in chalets. They can be reached by sea from Mersing, on the East coast, and for more information contact the Tourist Centre in Mersing at 0779 1204.

EAST COAST

The east coast of Peninsular Malaysia is a Malay stronghold; the Chinese and Indians have encroached very little. Here the markets are effectively run by the Malay women while on the west coast business is a Chinese concern.

The people of the east coast are more conservative than those in the more outward looking states along the Straits of Malacca; the Muslim faith is stronger and the traditional Malay village customs are largely retained. The settled areas are mainly in the coastal regions, though there are pockets of settlements in the less rugged inland valley. In the north of Kelantan state, next to the Thai border, there is a noticeable Thai-Buddhist element.

There are beautiful unspoiled beaches along the whole coast, and there are some first class resorts. The whole coast is subject to the monsoon season from November to mid-January, and some resorts even close in this period.

At **Kuantan**, there are some good beaches close to the town. One such is the charming **Teluk Chempedak**, only five kilometres from town, and popular for sailing, surfing and skiing. Another beach which is popular especially among wind surfers is **Balok Beach**, 15 kilometres north of Kuantan.

If you are on the coast from early May to October then you must not miss the chance to watch turtles coming ashore to lay their eggs. One place to be is the **Chendor Beach** 1.5 kilometres from **Cherating** — site of Malaysia's **Club Med**. Turtle also come ashore further north in Trengganu state at Rantau Abang. Incidentally, Because of local sensitivities, at this Club Med there is no topless sun-worshipping.

Of all the fishing villages in Pahang, **Beserah** is almost certainly the only place where fishermen use water buffalo to take fish from their boats to the processing areas, rather than their more usual task of ploughing.

Tioman, one of the most beautiful islands in the world — and used for the setting of the film *South Pacific* — is in fact in the South China Sea off the coast. Accessible by boat from Mersing in Johor or by air from either Kuala Lumpur, Singapore or Kuantan, Tioman is rich in marine life and is an ideal place for skin-diving and snorkelling.

On the northeastern coast of Peninsular Malaysia is the state of **Kelantan**, known for its batik and silverware. It is home to traditional pastimes such as top-spinning, kite flying and *wayang kulit* (shadow plays). Fishing is the main livelihood of the rural people. In any of the many fishing villages can be seen traditional pastimes such as boat building, net-mending, treating of fish and so on.

Kelantan has its fair share of fine beaches, such as **Pantai Dasar Sabak beach** where in 1941 the Japanese troops landed in their successful invasion of Malaya and Singapore. North of **Kota Baru** is the beautiful **Pantai Cinta Berahi** (Beach of Moonlight). To the south is the perhaps even more attractive **Pantai Iramaeach** (Beach of Melody).

Trengganu the northeastern peninsular state, offers the visitor idyllic offshore islands and beautiful beaches. The enchanting beach resort of **Tanjung Jara**, 60 kilometres south of the state capital of Kuala Trengganu, is well known for its prizewinning hotel designed after an old Malay palace. A river safari up the **Dungun River** is organized for the adventurous at heart.

There are beautiful off-shore islands within reach of the fishing village of **Marang**. These include **Kapas**, renowned for its clear waters and corals, and **Perhentian** and **Redang**, tropical islands popular for scuba diving and windsurfing.

The **Kenyir Lake**, 55 kilometres away from Kuala Trengganu, is fast gaining reputation as an ideal place to fish for tropical freshwater fish.

SARAWAK

The east Malaysian state of Sarawak, with its mountainous landscape, tropical rainforests and rivers, is rugged but manageable for the adventurous.

Kuching, the state's capital, is a meeting place for the Ibans, Bidayuhs, Malays, Chinese, Melanaus, Kayans, Kenyah and other ethnic groups which made up Sarawak's population. As the entry point for visitors to Sarawak, Kuching has many attractions. The Court House, a splendid building facing the swift-flowing Sarawak River, was built in 1874.

Across the river from the courthouse is the Istana (palace), built in 1870 by the second "white rajah," Sir Charles Brooke (1870-1917). Downstream a little on the same side as the Istana is **Fort Margherita**, named after Sir Charles' wife, Ranee Margaret. Built in 1878, it is now a police museum. A reflection of Borneo's old head-hunting past, one of the fort's towers is known as **bilik antu pala**, or the chamber of laughing skulls. The skulls are said to be 200 years old and, according to legend, emit human laughter.

A major attraction in Sarawak is the **Iban longhouses** — community dwellings constructed of ironwood, roofed with palm leaves and standing on stilts, mainly along river-banks. They may be seen by taking a trip upstream along the Sarawak River.

Along the Kuching-Serian road are Sarawak's famous pepper plantations. A flight from Kuching to Miri, then by road to Batu Niah, followed by a boat trip will take a visitor to the **Niah National Park**, which has famous caves.

One of the important discoveries made here was evidence that man existed in Borneo more than 40,000 years ago. Also discovered here were remains from the so-called old and new stone ages. The Niah Caves are also famed for their bird's nests, a Chinese delicacy normally served as a soup.

The **Gunung Mulu National Park**, about 480 kilometres from Kuching, is also famous for its caves, which include the world's largest, the **Sarawak Chamber**.

Sarawak has several lovely beaches such as the one at the **Santaini resort**, about 28 kilometres from Kuching; **Siar Beach** in the fishing village of Santubong, 32 kilometres from Kuching; **Sematan beach**, which is two hours from Siar; and the **Penyok** and **Bandong** beaches, four kilometres north of Santubong.

SABAH

Sabah is known as the Land Below The Wind. It is endowed with jungle, rainforest and Southeast Asia's highest peak, Mt Kinabalu. Its colourful native culture and natural attractions have made tourism a major revenue earner for this state.

The state's capital, **Kota Kinabalu**, is a relatively new town equipped with the latest facilities and amenities of modern living. The city's gold-domed state mosque is about five kilometres from town in the direction of the airport. The **Sabah Museum** shows a rich collection of tools used by the early men of Borneo. Also displayed are some of Sabah's unique animals, birds, reptiles and fish.

At **Gaya St** on Sunday mornings there is what is called a *tamu* (open market), where locals gather to buy and sell their handicrafts, traditional wares and food items or barter their farm produce.

Less than two kilometres from the town centre is the **Tanjung Aru Beach**, lined with palm and casuarina trees along its soft fine sand. Half an hour's drive from Kota Kinabalu is the picturesque **Mengkabong Water Village**, where the houses are built on stilts over the sea.

One of the most popular marine parks in Malaysia is the **Tuanku Abdul Rahman National Park**, comprising five islands. The islands — Gaya, Sapi, Mamutik, Manken and Suluk — are 10-25 minutes away from Kota Kinabalu by speedboat. Coral formations and colourful marine life teem in the clear waters surrounding the islands, especially Mamutik and Suluk where rare corals can be found.

Just 77 kilometres from Kota Kinabalu lies **Kota Belud**, home of Bajau horsemen. On festive days Bajau cowboys — skilled horsemen noted for their flamboyant dress — parade on horses. One of the biggest and most colourful *tamus* is found here where the Bajaus and Kadazans gather to buy and sell their local goods.

The **Kinabalu National Park**, 93 kilometres from Kota Kinabalu, was conceived as a World War II memorial in honour of the men who died in what is known as the "death march." The march, which took 11 months, began in September 1944 when the Japanese moved 2,400 Allied prisoners-of-war to the foothills of Mt Kinabalu. The park is now a paradise for nature lovers and bird watchers. It is also the home of the world's largest flower, the Rafflesia, a reddish orange flower with huge petals.

Towering majestically 4,101 metres above the park, Mt Kinabalu, is regarded by the Kadazan people as the resting place of the dead. Its craggy, sawtooth summit jutting above the steaming jungle clouds is an awe-inspiring sight.

It is possible, with transport arranged to and from the base camp, to leave Kota Kinabalu, climb the mountain and be back in Kota Kinabalu in two hectic days. If, on the other hand, you are dependent on public transport to and from the mountain, you must allow four days for the excursion: day one, from Kota Kinabalu by Landrover to the National Park headquarters at the foot of the mountain where you can stay overnight; day two, climb to 3,600 metres and spend the night in one of the huts: day three, rise very early and make the final ascent to enjoy the best view and return to the park headquarters and stay overnight; day four, take the Landrover back to Kota Kinabalu.

Tambunan, 80 kilometres from Kota Kinabalu, is a hidden valley known for its green terraced paddy fields and rolling scrub-covered hills. The villages of Keranan, Tibabar and Sunsuron have concrete monuments containing human skulls — reminders of the area's head-hunting past.

In the southeast of Sabah is **Semporna**, where the famous giant Sabah pearls are found. The oyster farm here sells quality pearls and oyster shells at bargain prices. Semporna also boasts beautiful coral reefs and 30 kilometres off the coast is **Pulau Sipadan**, which has one of the best diving sites in Southeast Asia, offering sparkling blue waters which afford views of fascinating underwater scenery and marine life.

About 386 kilometres from Kota Kinabalu is **Sandakan,** and 24 kilometres from Sandakan is the **Sepilok Forest Reserve**, where rare plants, animals and birds have taken sanctuary. In this reserve is the world-famous **Sepilok Orang-Utan Sanctuary**. The orang-utans, rescued from captivity, are cared for here before being sent back to the forest.

RESTAURANT SELECTION

Average price for two

KUALA LUMPUR

BARN THAI, 370B Jalan Tun Razak. Tel: 244 6699. Thai. US$25.

BOMBAY PALACE, 388 Jalan Tun Razak. Tel: 245 7220. Indian. US$30.

CHIKUYO-TEI, G/F See Hoy Chan Plaza, Jalan Raja Chulan. Tel: 230 0729. Japanese. US$43.

CILI PADI, 2/F The Mall, Jalan Putra. Tel: 442 9543. Thai. US$25.

DONDANG SAYANG, The Weld, Jalan Raja Chulan. Tel: 261 3831. Nonya. US$20.

HAKKA, 231 Jalan Bukit Bintang. Tel: 985 8492. Chinese. US$30 (plus market price for seafood).

JEWEL IN THE CROWN, 34 & 36 Jalan Telawi Dua, Bangsar Baru. Tel: 282 7205. Indian. US$22.

KAPITAN'S CLUB, 35 Jalan Ampang. Tel: 201 0242. Chinese/Nonya. US$20.

MUNAKATA, 2/F Promet Building, Jalan Sultan Ismail. Tel: 241 7441. Japanese. US$43.

NADAMAN, Shangri-La Hotel, Jalan Sultan Ismail. Tel: 232 2388. Japanese. US$43.

OVERSEAS, G/F Central Market. Tel: 274 6407. Chinese. US$25.

PURE MIND, 102 Jalan Imbi. Tel: 241 0376. Chinese. US$25. (Veg.)

RASA UTARA, G/F Bangsar Shopping Centre, Jalan Maarof, Bangsar. Tel: 254 0226. Malay. US$23.

SRI MELAYU, 1 Jalan Conlay. Tel: 245 1833. Malay. Music. US$34.

SZE CHUAN, 42-3 Jalan Sultan Ismail. Tel: 248 2806. Chinese. US$20.

TAI THONG, 32 Jalan Sultan Ismail. Tel: 244 1939. Chinese. US$34.

TAJ, Federal Hotel, Jalan Imbi. Tel: 248 9166. Indian. US$30.

THAI KITCHEN, Central Market. Tel: 274 4303. Thai. US$17.

HOTEL GUIDE

CAMERON HIGHLANDS

B: US$75-115

YE OLD SMOKEHOUSE, Tanah Rata, 39000 Cameron Highlands, Pahang. Tel/Fax: 491 1214. *R: W.*

FRASER'S HILL

B: US$75-115

MERLIN, Jalan Guillemard, 49000 Fraser's Hill, Pahang. Tel: 382300, Fax: 382284. *R: L, W.*

JOHOR BAHRU

A: US$115 and above

HOLIDAY INN, Jalan Dato Sulaiman, Taman Century, 80250 Johor Bahru. Tel: 323800, Fax: 318884. *P, Gym, Biz. R: L, W.*

KOTA BAHRU

C: US$38-75

HOTEL PERDANA, Jalan Mahmud, 15720 Kota Bahru, Kelantan. Tel: 748 5000, Fax: 774 7621. *P, Gym, Biz. R: W, Malay, Asian, Italian.*

PERDANA HOTEL RESORT, (Chalet accommodation) Jalan Kuala Pa' Amat, Pantai Cinta Berahi, 15710 Kota Bahru, Kelantan. Tel: 774 4000, Fax: 774 9980, Tlx: MA 53143 HODANA. *P. R: L, W.*

KOTA KINABALU (SABAH)

A: US$115 and above

SHANGRI-LA'S TANJUNG ARU RESORT, Locked Bag 174, 88744 Kota Kinabalu, Sabah. Tel: 225800, Fax: 216585, Tlx: MA 80751 TABHOT. *P, Biz. R: Italian, Asian, L.*

HYATT KINABALU, Jalan Datuk Salleh Sulong, 88994 Kota Kinabalu, Sabah. Tel: 221234, Fax: 225972, Tlx: MA 80036 HYATKK. *P, Gym, Biz, Ex. R: L, W, Asian.*

KUALA LUMPUR

A: US$115 and above

CARCOSA SERI NEGARA, Tasik Perdana, 50480 Kuala Lumpur. Tel: 282 1888, Fax: 282 7888, Tlx: 30504 CACOSA. *P. Gym, Biz. R: L, W.*

THE REGENT, 160 Jalan Bukit Bintang, 551000 Kuala Lumpur. Tel: 241 8000, Fax: 242 1441, Tlx: MA 33912 REGKL. *P, Gym, Biz. R: W, Japanese, Asian, Malaysian.*

SHANGRI-LA, 1 Jalan Sultan Ismail, 50250 Kuala Lumpur. Tel: 232 2388, Fax: 230 1514, Tlx: MA 30021 SHNGKL. *P, Gym, Biz, Ex. R: L, W, Japanese.*

PAN PACIFIC, Jalan Putra, 50746 Kuala Lumpur. Tel: 442 5555, Fax: 441 7236, Tlx: MA 33706. *P, Gym, Biz, Ex. R: L, W, Japanese.*

THE CROWN PRINCESS, City Square Centre, Jalan Tun Razak, 50400 Kuala Lumpur. Tel: 262 5522, Fax: 262 4687, Tlx: MA 28190 TCPHL. *P, Gym, Biz, Ex. R: L, W, Indian, Asian.*

KUALA LUMPUR HILTON, Jalan Sultan Ismail, 50718 Kuala Lumpur. Tel: 242 2122, Fax: 244 2157, Tlx: MA 30495. *P, Gym, Biz, Ex. R: L, W, English, Italian, Asian.*

MICASA HOTEL APARTMENTS, 368B, Jalan Tun Razak, 50400 Kuala Lumpur. Tel: 261 8833, Fax: 261 1186, Tlx: MA 21362 MICASA. *P, Gym, Biz. R: Italian, L.*

PARKROYAL, Jalan Sultan Ismail, 50250 Kuala Lumpur. Tel: 242 5588, Fax: 241 5524, Tlx: MA 30486. *P, Gym, Biz. R: L, W, Asian.*

HOTEL ISTANA, 73 Jalan Raja Chulan, 50200 Kuala Lumpur. Tel: 241 9988, Fax: 244 0111, Tlx: MA 31110 ISTANA. *P, Gym, Biz, Ex. R: L, Italian, Asian, Japanese.*

MELIA KUALA LUMPUR, 16, Jalan Imbi, 55100 Kuala Lumpur. Tel: 242 8333, Fax: 242 6623, Tlx: MA 30987 PLAZA. *Biz. R: L, W.*

B: US$75-115

SWISS GARDEN HOTEL, 117 Jalan Puda, 55100 Kuala Lumpur. Tel: 241 3333, Fax: 241 5555, Tlx: 30819. *P, Gym, Biz, Ex. R: L, W.*

HOTEL EQUATORIAL, Jalan Sultan Ismail, 50250 Kuala Lumpur. Tel: 261 7777, Fax: 261 9020, Tlx: 30363 EQATOR. *P, Gym, Biz. R: L, W.*

C: US$38-75

GRAND CONTINENTAL, Jalan Belia/Raja Laut, 50350 Kuala Lumpur. Tel: 293 9333, Fax: 293 9732, Telex: MA 28200. *P, Gym, Biz, Ex. R: L, W.*

PLAZA HOTEL, Jalan Raja Laut, 50350 Kuala Lumpur. Tel: 298 2255, Fax: 292 0959, Tlx: MA 30987 PLAZA. *Biz. R: L, W.*

KUANTAN

B: US$75-115

HYATT KUANTAN, Telok Chempedak, 25050 Kuantan, Pahang. Tel: 513 1234, Fax: 513 7577, Tlx: MA 50252 HTTKN. *P, Biz. R: W, Asian.*

P — Swimming pool **Gym** — Health club **Biz** — Business centre **Ex** — Executive floor
R — Restaurant **L** — Local food **W** — Western food

HOTEL GUIDE

CLUB MEDITERANEE, 29th Mile, Kuantan-Kemaman Rd, 26080 Kuantan. Kuala Lumpur Tel: 261 4599, Fax: 261 7229, Tlx: MA 32840. *P. R: L, W.*

KUCHING (SARAWAK)

B: US$75-115

HILTON, Jalan Tuanku Abdul Rahman, 93748 Kuching, Sarawak. Tel: 248200, Fax: 428984, Tlx: MA 70184 HILKCH. *P, Gym, Biz, Ex. R: L, W, Asian.*

MALACCA

A: US$115 and above

MALACCA RENAISSANCE, Jalan Bendahara, 75720 Malacca. Tel: 284 8888, Fax: 284 9269, Tlx: RAMADA MA 62966. *P, Gym, Biz. R: L, W.*

B: US$75-115

MALACCA VILLAGE PARK PLAZA RESORT, Air Keroh, 75450 Malacca. Tel: 323600, Fax: 325955, Tlx: MA 62854 MVR. *P, Gym, Biz. R: L,W, Japanese, Asian.*

MIRI (SARAWAK)

B: US$76-115

HOLIDAY INN MIRI, Jalan Temenggong Datuk Oyong Lawai, 98008 Miri, Sarawak. Tel: 418888, Fax: 419999, Tlx: MA 74488. *P, Gym, Biz. R: L,W.*

PENANG

A: US$115 and above

HOTEL EQUATORIAL, 1, Jalan Bukit Jambul, 11900, Penang. Tel: 643 8111, Fax: 644 9111, Tlx: 40665 EQAPEN. *P, Gym, Biz, Ex. R: L, W.*

PENANG MUTIARA, Jalan Teluk Bahang, 11050 Penang. Tel: 881 2828, Fax: 881 2829, Tlx: MA 40768. *P, Gym, Biz. R: L, W. Japanese.*

GOLDEN SANDS RESORT, Batu Ferringhi Beach, 11100 Penang. Tel: 881 1911, Fax: 881 1880, Tlx: MA 40627 GOSAND. *P, Gym. R: L, W, Italian.*

SHANGRI-LA PENANG, Jalan Magazine, 10300 Penang. Tel: 262 2622, Fax: 262 6526, Tlx: 40878 SHNGPG MA. *P, Gym. R: L, W.*

SHANGRI-LA'S RASA SAYANG RESORT, Batu Feringgi Beach, 11100 Penang. Tel: 881 1811, Fax: 881 1984, Tlx: MA 40065. *P. R: L, W.*

B: US$75-115

BAYVIEW BEACH RESORT, Batu Feringghi Beach, 11100 Penang. Tel: 881 2123, Fax: 881 2140, Tlx: MA 41325. *P, Gym, secretarial services. R: L, W.*

THE FERRINGHI BEACH HOTEL, 12.5 km Batu Ferringhi, 11100 Batu Ferringhi, Penang. Tel: 890 5999, Fax: 890 5100, Tlx: MA 40634 FERTEL. *P. R: L, W.*

EASTERN & ORIENTAL, 10 Farquhar St, 10200 Penang. Tel: 263 0630, Fax: 263 4833, Tlx: MA 41325. *P, Gym, secretarial services. R: L, W.*

PORT DICKSON

C: US$38-75

REGENCY HOTEL AND RESORT, 5th Mile, Jalan Pantai, 71050 Port Dickson, Negeri Sembilan. Tel: 474090, Fax: 495016, Tlx: MA 31557. *P, Gym, Biz. R: L, W.*

PULAU PANGKOR

A: US$115 and above

PANGKOR LAUT RESORT, 32300 Pangkor, Perak. Tel: 685 2914, Fax: 685 1320. *Gym. R: L, W.*

SANDAKAN (SABAH)

A: US$115 and above

SANDAKAN RENAISSANCE, Jalan Utara, 90007 Sandakan, Sabah. Tel: 213299, Fax: 271271, Tlx: MA 82870. *P, Gym, Biz. R: L, W, Asian.*

SELANGOR

A: US$115 and above

HYATT SAUJANA, 3 kilometres off Subang International Airport Highway, 47200 Subang, Selangor. Tel: 746 1234, Fax: 746 2789, Tlx: MA 37903 HYTSJN. *P, Gym, Biz, R: L, W.*

PJ HILTON INTERNATIONAL, 2 Jalan Barat, 46200 Petaling Jaya. Tel: 755 9122, Fax: 755 3909, Tlx: PJHLTN MA 36008. *P, Gym, Biz, Ex. R: L, W.*

TIOMAN

B: US$75-115

BERJAYA TIOMAN BEACH RESORT, Tioman, 86807 Mersing, Johor. Tel: 445445, Fax: 445718, Tlx: MA 50279 TIOMAN. *P. R: L, W.*

P — Swimming pool **Gym** — Health club **Biz** — Business centre **Ex** — Executive floor
R — Restaurant **L** — Local food **W** — Western food

PAPUA NEW GUINEA

On one's arrival, Port Moresby, the capital of Papua New Guinea, looks very like any other developing modern city. But it sits at the edge of something very like a lost world. Although known from the sea by Portuguese explorers as early as the 14th century and subjected to various colonial rulers in its coastal areas, the interior mountains and jungle were not penetrated by outsiders until this century. Even now contact between the people and outsiders in many places is only peripheral. Much of the interior is absolutely inaccessible except by air, and even then only in the best weather conditions. The variety, traditions and lifestyle of its people — who speak more than 700 different languages — first strike the visitor; then the terrain makes a remarkable impression with its diversity, ranging from mountains, which reach 4,000 metres, coral reefs and palm-fringed, white-sand beaches.

Papua New Guineans see themselves as people more of the Pacific than Asia. About 80% of them live in villages, even though the towns offer comprehensive shopping facilities. The capital, Port Moresby, faces a fine bay and its national institutions — especially the imaginative new museum and parliament building — are eye-catching, but it is unlike the rest of the country, much of which can be reached only by sea or air. Papua New Guinea, or more familiarly simply PNG, is not a cheap country to visit or travel in. It is a country wealthy in natural resources, in oil, gas, copper, gold, coffee, cocoa, copra, oil-palm, timber and fish. Its people, though not rich, are far above the levels of poverty elsewhere, and are friendly, open and polite.

History

Virtually all Papua New Guineans are Melanesians whose forebears probably moved to New Guinea and its scattered outer islands about 50,000 years ago. The people lived largely unchanging lives in small autonomous tribal clans across much of the island until the Europeans arrived.

The first recorded European sighting of New Guinea island was by two Portuguese explorers. Another explorer, Jorge de Meneses, landed on the northwest coast and named the island Ilhas dos Papuas. In 1824 the Netherlands and Britain agreed to the Dutch claim on the western half of the island, now the Indonesian province of Irian Jaya. Later in the 19th century Britain made increasing landings in the eastern half — the present PNG — while the Germans entered the picture by claiming the north of the country. In 1906 the island's southern part — British New Guinea — was renamed Papua and Australia assumed responsibility for its administration. In 1920 the League of Nations handed German New Guinea, seized by British Imperial forces during World War I, to Australia as a mandated territory. The United Nations inherited this mandate until PNG became independent from Australia on September 16, 1975.

PNG was the scene of heavy fighting in the early stages of the Pacific War, when the allies successfully held and then began to beat back the Japanese advance towards Australia. Japanese ambitions in the region were finally crushed after intense fighting with Australian and American troops, notably along the Kokoda Trail that held the key to the defence of Port Moresby.

Sir Michael Somare, who was elected chief minister in 1972, led the country to independence from Australia in 1975 and remained

◄ *Highlands warrier.* PHOTO: MARK GRAHAM

PAPUA NEW GUINEA

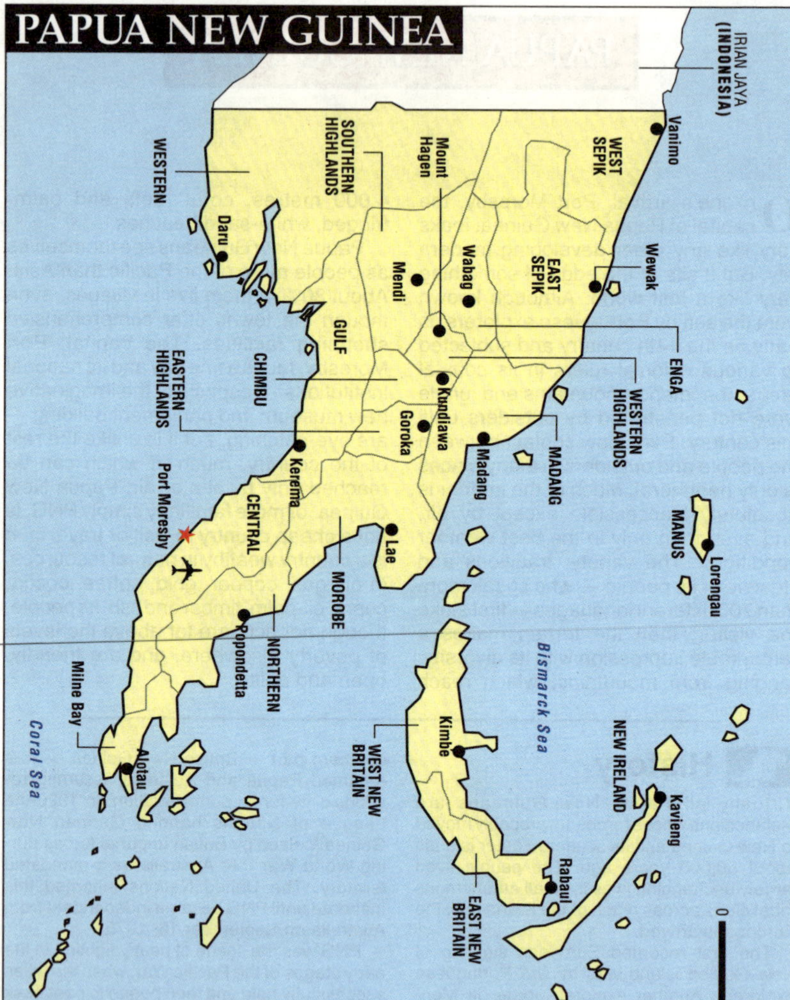

prime minister until losing his parliamentary majority to Sir Julius Chan in 1980. Somare regained the prime ministership at the next election in 1982, only to lose it again in parliament in 1985 — this time to highlander Paias Wingti. Wingti retained power following the 1987 election, but lost it the next year to Somare's successor as leader of the Pangu Party, Rabbie Namaliu. Namaliu immediately faced the country's greatest crisis — a rebellion on Bougainville Island that first closed the copper mine that produced 40% of PNG's export income, then in May 1990 led to a unilateral declaration of independence. Namaliu responded by blockading the island.

Wingti regained the prime ministership in July 1992 following a national election, and appointed Chan as his deputy, who in turn ousted Wingti in August 1994. PNG's currency (the kina) remains strong even after being floated in September 1994 when an economic crisis loomed, largely because of a fall in mining and oil exports. Despite a wealth of resources and prospects, living standards remain depressed as political complexities increase and government services decline. The country's land area is 461,700 square kilometres with territorial waters of a further 1.7 million square kilometres. Its population is about 4 million, plus a further 30,000 resident expatriates.

Entry

Apart from the occasional cruise ship, the inevitable form of arrival is by air.

The national carrier, Air Niugini, flies to Jackson's Airport, Port Moresby, from Sydney, Brisbane and Cairns in Australia, and from Singapore, Manila and Hong Kong. It also flies to Vanimo from Jayapura in Indonesia, and to Mount Hagen from Cairns.

Qantas flies from Sydney, Brisbane and Cairns. Solomon Airlines flies from Honiara in the Solomon Islands, offering access to further South Pacific destinations. There is no road link with neighbouring Irian Jaya, but there are some local connections from Vanimo for the adventurous. Airport departure tax is Kina 15.

Immigration

Passports and visas are required by all visitors, and business travellers must obtain business visas before travel. Tourist visas are usually granted for up to two months for Kina 10, and are available on arrival to citizens from Australia, Austria, Belgium, Britain (and its colonies), Canada, Cook Islands, Cyprus, Denmark, Fiji, France, Germany, Japan, Portugal, Sweden, Switzerland, Thailand, Tonga, Tuvalu, and the United States.

Visas for other nationalities can be obtained from PNG's diplomatic offices in Cairns, Brisbane, Sydney and Canberra in Australia; in Wellington, New Zealand; in Suva, Fiji; in Honiara in Solomon Islands; in Jayapura, Indonesia; and in Bonn, Brussels, London, Paris, Jakarta, Kuala Lumpur, Manila, Beijing, Seoul, Tokyo, New York and Washington. In countries without a PNG diplomatic office, Australian overseas posts issue visas. Visitors must have a return or onwards ticket and funds to maintain themselves, and must not engage in any form of employment.

EMBASSIES AND CONSULATES

	Tel:
Australia	259333
Britain	251677
China	259836
France	251323
Germany	252971
Indonesia	253544
Japan	211800
Malaysia	251506
New Zealand	259444
Philippines	256414
South Korea	254755
U.S.	211455
Vatican	256021

Health

Visitors entering from cholera and yellow fever infected areas require inoculation certificates. These vaccination certificates are not required for children younger than one year. The malaria-carrying anopheles mosquito is found in many parts of the country, so it is strongly recommended that visitors take a quinine-based anti-malarial pill for two weeks before arrival, during the entire stay and for four weeks after departure. It is unusual, however, for Malaria to be caught in Port Moresby.

Pharmacies in the major towns are open late in the evening according to a roster, which is published each day in the newspapers. Private doctors are available in all major centres, and are listed in the Yellow Pages of local telephone books as "medical practitioners."

Customs

In addition to the traveller's personal effects, new items worth no more than Kina 200, up to one litre of liquor and 250 grams of tobacco (200 cigarettes or 50 cigars) per person are exempt from duty. The import of most weapons is prohibited, as is that of videotapes or publications which could be deemed erotic — this includes magazines as mild as *Playboy*. There are stringent controls on the export of artifacts considered of national, historical or cultural significance — any made prior to 1960 require an export permit from the National Museum — or of flora and fauna. The export of Bird of Paradise plumes is forbidden.

Currency

The unit of currency is the kina, which is divided into 100 toea. In March 1995 the rate of exchange was Kina 1:85 U.S. cents. Notes in denominations of Kina 50, 20, 10, 5 and 2 and coins of Kina 1 (with a hole) and of 50, 20, 10, 5, 2 and 1 toea are in circulation. There are no restrictions on importing foreign currency, while the export of kina was relaxed in 1992 to allow up to Kina 500,000 to be taken out annually. Non-residents may take out the same amount of foreign currency they brought into the country.

Foreign currency is not normally accepted for the purchase of goods or services, but all banks and major hotels accept traveller's cheques and exchange currency. American Express is the most widely accepted credit card, with Visa and Diner's Club generally acceptable at major hotels, stores and artefact shops. However, the visitor should not depend on credit-card purchases beyond meeting hotel, air-ticket and car-hire bills.

PHOTO: MARK GRAHAM

Riverside church service.

Language

English, Pidgin and Hiri Motu are PNG's three official languages, though there are an additional 812 local languages. English is widely understood as it is the language of instruction in schools, though a Pidgin phrase-book is a useful aid to communication.

Climate

Temperatures vary little throughout the year, with the average daily coastal range fluctuating between 21°C and 32°C. In highland areas the temperature varies with altitude and it can be cool, or even cold, at night. Humidity is high, ranging on the coast between 70-88%. Average rainfall is 250 centimetres, but can be double that in some areas. Only Port Moresby, under the rainshadow of the Owen Stanley Mountains, has clearly distinct wet and dry seasons. There are two prevailing winds — the southeast or trade wind from May to October, and the northwest or monsoon from December to March.

Dress

Light, easily washable clothing with light jumpers is recommended if the traveller is visiting the highlands. Ties are rarely seen and never required, though many hotels and restaurants rule out sandals, shorts and T-shirts. While informality is otherwise fine, suggestive or revealing Western fashions are frowned upon, especially in rural areas.

Business Hours

Government offices are open from 7:45 a.m.-4 p.m. from Monday to Friday. Commercial firms work until 4:30 or 5 p.m. Stores normally open from 8:30 a.m.-5 p.m., Monday to Friday and 8 a.m.-noon on Saturday. Markets — selling mainly fresh foodstuffs — are open during daylight hours, normally 7 a.m.-6 p.m. Banks open from 9 a.m.-2 p.m. from Monday to Thursday and from 9 a.m.-5 p.m. on Friday. Liquor licensing is a function of the 19 provincial governments, so it differs from place to place. But it is generally possible to purchase liquor from 8 a.m.-5 p.m. on weekdays, and from 8 a.m.-noon on Saturday. Public bars tend to close at 8 p.m. and hotel cocktail bars at midnight.

Doing Business

PNG is a young and nationalistic country, and both Papua New Guineans and locally based foreign business and professional people expect visitors to share their largely positive outlook. People shake hands when meeting and business cards are usually exchanged. Business is almost always conducted in English; Papua New Guineans would only expect Pidgin to be used by long-term residents.

While punctuality is expected from visitors, Papua New Guineans — especially government officials — are frequently vague about timing, laughing it off as "PNG time." Usual business dress for a man is long trousers with short-sleeved shirt, occasionally with a tie but not a jacket. Women would be expected to wear a dress or blouse and skirt. Business entertaining is largely centred on the major hotels; an invitation to the home of a local business associate is a sign of some esteem. A bottle of wine, box of chocolates or flowers would be acceptable gifts for such an invitation.

Alcohol is the social norm, though a minority of Papua New Guineans — notably Seventh Day Adventists — do not drink at all. Although PNG is essentially an informal society it is best to follow the host's style rather than presume on such informality.

Since there is no stock exchange in PNG, bank financing is essential for most new projects, and final decisions will often need to await approvals elsewhere. When government agencies are involved, the best places to make first contact is the Investment Promotion Authority (Tel: 258777, Fax: 258770).

PNG's political and bureaucratic structures are complex and obstacles tend to obstruct apparently fast or smooth deals.

Secretarial services are offered only in Port Moresby, via **J.J. Executive Offices** (Tel: 256640) and **National Secretarial Services and Training** (Tel: 251038).

Rip-Offs

Although stories of crime in PNG have been exaggerated, travellers should take warnings seriously. Walking at night is risky in most urban centres, and drivers should stick to major roads. Taxis tend to be expensive and poorly maintained; hold out for hire cars or courtesy cars if possible. Business contacts often do not mind providing lifts.

Corruption and gift-giving to officials remains the exception and attempts to solicit bribes should and can be resisted. The business traveller may also be promised remarkable deals by an official or politician, but should not expect such promises to be bankable.

Media

There is a local TV station, and international satellite channels — including ABC and Channel 9 from Australia and CNN from the U.S. — are available. English-language local and Australian daily and weekly newspapers and international magazines are widely available.

Communications

International direct dial and fax are widely available in Port Moresby and upcountry. Mobile phone services are available in major centres.

Courier services throughout PNG include: **DHL** (Tel: 259866); **Fastapak** (Tel: 259788); **Express Mail Service** (Tel: 274937); **TNT** (Tel: 252411).

Transport

FROM PORT MORESBY AIRPORT (eight kilometres from the main two centres): Hotel buses and tour buses are available; taxis are metered.

HIRE CARS: Available at Port Moresby airport and at most large towns at about Kina 70-100 per day, with some franchisers adding a surcharge of up to 40 toea per kilometre. Car hire companies operating throughout PNG include **Hertz** (Tel: 254999); **Avis** (Tel: 258429); **Budget** (Tel: 254111). Only Avis offers a

Time for school. PHOTO: MARK GRAHAM

chauffeur service (Tel: 258299).

BUSES: Public motor vehicles ranging from medium-sized buses to open utility trucks, operate inside towns and between major centres. Fares inside towns are 50 toea or less, and long-distance fares in the highlands only a few kina. However, standards of comfort and maintenance vary. Foreigners should also be cautious about their security, and consider a hire car if making many calls during a short stay. Taxis are available in only a few centres.

BOATS: A large number of cargo boats operate in and around PNG and afford an adventurous, if slow and slightly uncomfortable, way of travelling. It is difficult to book far in advance.

AIR: Because of PNG's limited road network, air travel has become more common for ordinary people than perhaps anywhere else in the world. But flying is expensive. Air Niugini flies Fokker F28 jets and de Havilland Dash 7s between provincial centres; third-level operators serve the country's hundreds of smaller airstrips.

MAJOR AIRLINES

	Fax:	*Tel:*
Air Niugini	273482	273200
Islands Aviation		254055
Qantas	213073	211200
Singapore Airlines		213975
Philippine Airlines		211244
Solomon Airlines		255724

Tours

Increasing numbers of tours are now available, specializing in wildlife, traditional lifestyles, scuba-diving and so on. A number of provincial governments are also now establishing their own tourist bureaux, and further details can be obtained from the National Tourist Office.

The main tour operators are Melanesian Tourist Services, P.O. Box 707, Madang; Trans Niugini Tours, P.O. Box 371, Mount Hagen; Air Niugini Travel Service, P.O. Box 7186, Boroko. Other tour companies are Tribal World New Guinea, P.O. Box 86, Mount Hagen; Pacific Expeditions, P.O. Box 132, Port Moresby. The opportunity for reef diving is provided by Dive

Rabaul, P.O. Box 65, Rabaul; Diving Specialists of PNG, P.O. Box 337, Madang; Jais Aben Resort, P.O. Box 105, Madang; Niugini Diving Adventures, P.O. Box 707, Madang; Rabaul Dive Centre, P.O. Box 400, Rabaul; Telita Cruises, P.O. Box 303, Alotau; Tropical Diving Services, P.O. Box 1748, Port Moresby; Knight Dive Shop, P.O. Box 105, Lorengau; Walindi Diving, P.O. Box 4, Kimbe; and New Guinea Diving, P.O. Box 320, Lae.

Accommodation

Accommodation in PNG is comparatively expensive — on a par with similar but better-appointed hotels in Australia, despite the much cheaper labour costs. In most centres there are reasonably well-appointed hotels, and more intermediate-level accommodation is gradually becoming available.

Power is 240 volts, but most hotels have transformers for 110-volt appliances. Tipping is not expected or customary in hotels, but is acceptable for exceptional service. Deluxe tourist lodges include **Ambua Lodge** in the Southern Highlands and **Karawari Lodge** in the upper Sepik. The government is encouraging the establishment of clean, comfortable **village-style guesthouses** run by PNG nationals. The longest established of these is the Kofure Village Guesthouse, c/o Post Office, Tufi, Oro province. Others include the Kaiap Orchid Lodge at Wabag, Krangket Island Lodge off Madang and Kaibola Lodge on Kiriwina island.

Dining

Like a number of other towns in PNG, Port Moresby has several reasonably good Chinese restaurants. The **Kwangtung Village**, serving Cantonese and Szechuan food — and noted for its crab and fish — is the best. The **Daikoku** is the only Japanese restaurant, offering beef and seafood tepanyaki. The **Seoul House** provides traditional Korean cuisine, and the best European restaurant is the **Galley**, next to the Aviat Club. The **Kokoda Trail Motel** on the Sogeri plateau above Port Moresby serves tender kebabs of locally killed crocodile.

Licensing hours are strictly adhered to, both for take-away sales and in bars. The locally brewed South Pacific lager is a high quality beer, while a wide range of Australian and other wines and spirits are available. Drinkers may choose to specify the imported product in bars, instead of the reconstituted, locally bottled versions usually served. PNG-grown teas and its Arabica and Robusta coffees are also first rate.

Entertainment

There is virtually no nightlife entertainment outside the leading hotels in Port Moresby and Lae which usually provide live music in their restaurants.

Shopping

PNG offers a great variety of traditional artefacts, notably basketwork from the islands, carvings from the north coast, tapa cloth from the northern province, woven articles from the highlands and shells and pottery from the coast.

These are available in special shops, in most hotel foyers and occasionally from street sellers, particularly at Port Moresby's **Boroko** shopping centre on Saturday mornings. The country's attractively packaged Arabica coffee is also an ideal gift. While prices are fixed at stores and for market produce, street traders have begun to accept a degree of haggling.

INFORMATION

National Tourist Office, Tel: 251269; Fax: 259447. The industry's coordinating body, the Tourist Association of PNG, can be contacted c/o The Manager, Islander Hotel, P.O. Box 1981, Boroko.

Papua New Guinea, A Travel Survival Kit by Tony Wheeler (published by Lonely Planet Guides), is a helpful and down-to-earth guide. Air Niugini publishes a variety of useful brochures and *Paradise*, an award-winning inflight magazine. The National Tourist Office produces a Visitor's Guide.

Sports

Sport of all kinds is played in PNG. Soccer, rugby league, rugby union and Australian Rules football — the contact sports — are most popular. There are also bowls, cricket, tennis, basketball, softball, golf, squash and polo,

A friendly encounter. PHOTO: MARK GRAHAM

among others. Neither Port Moresby nor Lae offers good swimming beaches, though Moresby and Lae have public pools. There are opportunities for reef-diving, water-skiing, fishing, wind-surfing and sailing, mostly on the outer islands.

Holidays

January 1: New Year's Day.
March-April: Good Friday and Easter Monday.
June 18: Queen Elizabeth's (official) birthday.
July 23: Remembrance Day.
September 16: Independence Day.
December 25: Christmas Day.
December 26: Boxing Day.

The Highlands Show is usually held on alternate years at Goroka and Mount Hagen in August or September at variable dates. Other annual festivals include the Hiri Moale and the Agricultural Show (in Port Moresby, the former during the Independence anniversary, the latter over the Queen's Birthday weekend); the Frangipani and Warwagira Festivals (Rabaul); the Mabarosa Festival (Madang); the Malangan Show (Kavieng) and the Lae Agricultural Show. The Lunar New Year is most actively celebrated in Lae.

DISCOVERING PAPUA NEW GUINEA

PORT MORESBY

The capital is a sprawling city of 230,000 people with a ridge dividing the older town on the bay from the newer inland suburbs, including the government centre at **Waigani**, where the **National Museum** makes a good starting point for visitors (it is closed on Fridays and Saturdays).

Nearby is the new parliament, built in a style echoing that of the traditional Sepik *"haus tambaran"* or spirit-house; it is well worth observing a debate when the chamber is in session. The modern **university campus** is a few kilometres away, next to the **National Botanical Gardens** and its remarkable orchid collection.

The **Moitaka wildlife sanctuary**, including a crocodile farm, is on the road towards the hills and is open to the public on Friday afternoons. The **Varirata National Park**, on the cool **Sogeri plateau** 50 kilometres from Port Moresby, offers walks through tropical rainforest, barbecue sites and the occasional glimpse of Birds of Paradise, indigenous and a national symbol. However, visitors should seek and heed the advice from their hotel about the current security situation at the park, and if in doubt, stay away. The **Kokoda Trail Motel** is nearby. The ferry to the **Loloata Island** resort is only a few minutes' drive from Port Moresby.

DISCOVERING UPCOUNTRY

Lae — PNG's second city — is a major centre for secondary industry and the port for the newly prosperous highlands. The Highlands Highway winds through the **Markham Valley** up to the pleasant coffee town of **Goroka** and beyond to Mount Hagen, a fast-expanding frontier town some 2,600 metres above sea level. The highlands offer breathtaking views, a pleasant climate and the opportunity to meet an energetic and outgoing people whose contact with Western ways is recent. Local advice on security precautions needs to be heeded.

Madang, which can be reached by road from Lae or the highlands, offers the best example of relaxed Pacific style in PNG, with its lagoon, tiny islands and north coast drive through endless coconut plantations. The huge **Sepik** River, winding down to **Wewak** at its mouth, hosts one of the country's great cultures.

The islands region — stretching from **Milne May** in the south, up through **New Britain**, **New Ireland** to **Manus** — offers other experiences, with wonderful seascapes and engaging people. Tragically, **Rabaul** in East New Britain — considered by many to be the Pearl of the Pacific — suffered the latest in a series of volcanic eruptions in late 1994, and its future as a charming harbour town remains uncertain. But the nearby beautiful Duke of York Islands are seeking to attract visitors as a low-key alternative. Bougainville is still off-limits, though the violence of the rebellion that erupted in 1988 has considerably diminished.

HOTEL GUIDE

AMBOIN

A: US$130 and above

KARAWARI LODGE, P.O. Box 371, Mount Hagen. Tel: 521438, Fax: 522470, Tlx: 52012. *R: W.*

GOROKA

B: US$95-130

BIRD OF PARADISE, P.O. Box 12, Goroka. Tel: 721144, Fax: 721007, Tlx: 72628. *P, SatTV. R: W.*

LAE

B: US$95-130

LAE INTERNATIONAL, P.O. Box 2774, Lae. Tel: 422000, Fax: 422534, Tlx: 42473. *P, SatTV. R: W.*

MELANESIAN, P.O. Box 756, Lae. Tel: 423744, Fax: 423706, Tlx: 44187. *P, SatTV. R: W.*

MADANG

C: US$60-95

MADANG RESORT, P.O. Box 707. Tel: 822766/822655, Fax: 823543, Tlx: 82707. *P, SatTV. R: W.*

MOUNT HAGEN

B: US$95-130

HIGHLANDER, P.O. Box 34, Mount Hagen. Tel: 521355, Fax: 521216, Tlx: 55108. *P, SatTV. R: W.*

TRIBAL TOPS INN, P.O. Box 86 Mount Hagen. Tel: 565556, Fax: 551546, Tlx: 52070. *P, SatTV. R: W.*

PORT MORESBY

A: US$130 and above

GATEWAY, P.O. Box 1215, Boroko (Port Moresby). Tel: 253885, Fax: 254585, Tlx: 23082. *P, SatTV. R: W.*

ISLANDER, P.O. Box 1981, Boroko (Port Moresby). Tel: 255955, Fax: 213835, Tlx 22288. *P, Gym, Biz, SatTV. R: W.*

TRAVELODGE, P.O. Box 1661, Boroko (Port Moresby). Tel: 212266, Fax: 217534, Tlx: 22248. *P, Biz, SatTV. R: W.*

B: US$95-130

AIRWAYS, P.O. Box 1942, Boroko, (Port Moresby). Tel: 257033, Fax: 214759, Tlx: 23435. *P, SatTV. R: W.*

C: US$60-95

AMBER'S INN, P.O. 1139 Boroko, (Port Moresby). Tel: 255091, Fax: 259565. *P, SatTV. R: W.*

P — Swimming pool
Gym — Health club
Biz — Business centre
SatTV — Satellite TV
R — Restaurant
W — Western food

TUSA
TUSA
ODY GLOVE

PHILIPPINES

Despite political instability and some weak areas of the economy, the Philippines remains attractive — and a bargain — as a tourist destination. The country's assets include its round-the-year warm climate, comparatively low prices, breathtaking natural scenery and its people's hospitality, which remains charming, if tinged with hopes of financial gain.

The Philippine archipelago comprises 7,107 islands, of which only 11 main islands account for more than 95% of the country's total land area of 300,400 square kilometres. The islands abound with white-sand beaches, exotic tropical vegetation and beautiful lakes and rivers. The population is 65 million, of whom around 11 million are concentrated in Metro-Manila.

The Filipino people are basically Malay, but their characteristics have been shaped by Spanish, American and Chinese culture and influence. The English language is widely spoken — the Philippines has the third-largest English-speaking population in the world — the inheritance of 48 years as an American colony.

There is a vast array of local dialects — around 70. Some 85% of the population is Roman Catholic, as a result of the country's more than 300 years of Spanish colonization. The other significant religious groups are Muslims, mostly in the south, who make up 4.9% of the national population, with Protestants at 3.2% and Buddhists at 1%.

The capital is Manila, on the main island of Luzon, but this is now just the central area of the vast Metro-Manila, which covers a total of 12 municipalities and five cities. This vast conurbation, some of it depressing shanty towns squeezed on to any available open space, boasts 10,000 hotel rooms. Most of the modern hotels were built in the mid-1970s for a series of major international conferences that created a short-lived tourism boom. Most of the hotels offer big discounts on room rates of up to 50% at certain times of the year to boost occupancy.

Places in the Philippines worth visiting are so numerous that the tourist can only hope to see a few of them. They range from the fabled rice terraces of Banaue in the north to the pearl farms, guitar factories, tropical countryside and coral beaches in the south.

In Manila, even the traffic jams are enlivened by one of the Philippines' most colourful images — the gaily decorated jeepneys, or enlarged passenger jeeps.

In early 1993, the city authorities started a serious attempt to clean up the "girlie bars" in the Ermita district of the city, and as a result, most of the nightlife scene has moved to Makati.

History

The Philippines represents the northernmost extension of the Malay culture. Ferdinand Magellan, the Portuguese explorer, sailing in the service of Spain, discovered the Philippines for the Western world in 1521. He was killed soon afterwards when wading ashore at the island of Mactan off what is now the city of Cebu. The man who killed him and his troops was Lapu-lapu, the warrior king of Mactan, who has since become a legend. The archipelago was annexed for Spain by Miguel Lopez de Legazpi in 1565. Successive expeditions slowly strengthened Spanish influence over the northern Philippines.

Manila was captured in 1568. It had been

◄ *Practical diving class.* PHOTO: VERONICA GARBUTT

PHILIPPINES
To Batanes Islands (RP)
Babuyan Is.
N
km
0
200
Roads
Railway
Airport
Laoag
Aparri
Tuguegarao
Vigan
LUZON
South China Sea
San Fernando
Bontoc
Baguio
Banaue
Dagupan
Bagabag
Cabanatuan
Angeles
Manila
Philippine Sea
Lucena
Tagaytay
Daet
CATANDUANES
Lipa
Batangas
Boac
Naga
Virac
Mamburao
Camalig
Puerto Galera
Iriga
Legaspi
MINDORO
Sorsogon
Masbate
Matnog
Roxas
San Jose
Catarman
Allen
Calbayog
MASBATE
Boracay
SAMAR
CEBU
PANAY
Tacloban
El Nido
Iloilo
Ormoc
LEYTE
PALAWAN
Bacolod
Cebu
Surigao
Puerto Princesa
NEGROS
BOHOL
Tagbilaran
Dumaguete
Ozamis
Brooke's Point
Tubbataha Reefs
Dipolog
Iligan
Butuan
Cagayan de Oro
Malaybalay
Sulu Sea
Marawi
Cotabato
Davao
Zamboanga
Moro Gulf
JOLO
BASILAN
MINDANAO
SABAH (MALAYSIA)
Sulu Archipelago
Celebes Sea

ruled by the Muslim king Rajah Solaiman, who destroyed it in his retreat. The Muslims in the southern Philippines, comprising the large island of Mindanao and smaller islands of Sulu, Tawi-tawi and Basilan, held out against Spanish rule until the 19th century.

After the opening of the Suez Canal in 1869, ambitious Filipino youths went to Spain and elsewhere to study. They were to form the nucleus of the nationalist struggle. In 1872, some 200 soldiers of the Cavite Arsenal, just south of Manila, killed their officers and began a brief revolt. Behind the move were many educated and liberal Filipinos, but three priests (two locally born Spaniards and a part-Chinese Filipino) were the only leaders to receive the death penalty. They died martyrs to the cause, by garrotte. From that time, the struggle for independence grew rapidly. The national hero, Jose Rizal, drew much of his early inspiration from the events of 1872 and, notably through his writings, carried on the struggle against the domination of the friars and economic and administrative authoritarianism.

Rizal was executed by the Spanish in 1896, shortly after a general revolution had broken out. Independence was declared by Emilio Aguinaldo on June 12, 1898, after the back of the Spanish resistance had been broken by Spain's state of war with the United States. June 12 is now celebrated as Independence Day.

But the Filipinos were still far from real independence, for in December 1898 the Treaty of Paris provided for the cession of the Philippines to the U.S. Fighting broke out between the Americans and Filipinos early the following year and continued sporadically until 1946, with the exception of the period between 1942 and 1945, when the Japanese controlled the islands. After much lobbying, principally by the charismatic Manuel Quezon, who established a government-in-exile in Washington but died before the war ended, the Republic of the Philippines was proclaimed on July 4, 1946 with Manuel Roxas as the first president.

A communist-inspired peasant rebellion in central Luzon under the Hukbalahaps (Huks) raged during the 1940s and the early 1950s and sought to overthrow the government, but Ramon Magsaysay, who later became president, successfully crushed it with the help of the Americans.

Ferdinand Marcos, an ambitious lawyer, was elected president on November 9, 1965. He won a second term four years later. Marcos imposed martial law on September 21, 1972, declaring that the nation was threatened with a communist rebellion. Most of Marcos' political foes and critics in the media were jailed, some of them for years.

Marcos' closest political rival, former senator Benigno Aquino, who was freed from detention in May 1980 to undergo heart surgery in the U.S., was assassinated upon his return to Manila on August 21, 1983. The assassination outraged the vast majority of the populace, already disenchanted by corruption and the way Marcos favoured a few cronies in business and turned a blind eye to abuses of the military. Marcos' rule crumbled amid the resulting political and economic crisis.

A snap presidential election called for February 7, 1986 was characterized by widespread fraud. Marcos was declared the winner despite the irregularities. His opponent at the polls, the slain senator's widow Corazon Aquino, launched a non-violent civil-disobedience campaign to protest against Marcos' claim to victory. The movement was escalating when Marcos' own defence minister, Juan Ponce Enrile, and the armed forces' vice-chief of staff, Gen. Fidel Ramos, challenged the legitimacy of the Marcos government on February 22. They established their headquarters at two premier military installations, Camp Aguinaldo and Camp Crame, where they were joined within hours by thousands of civilian supporters. The putsch ended on the night of February 25 with Marcos, his close relatives (including his wife Imelda) and key military advisers fleeing to Clark Air Force Base, from where they were flown by the U.S. Air Force to Guam and subsequently Hawaii.

Aquino was quick to proclaim herself the rightfully elected president and champion of "people power," and the military leaders accepted this. In February 1987, the Filipinos ratified a new constitution providing for a democratic republican state and a presidential form of government.

Although under Aquino the economy showed modest signs of revival, this was desperately slow. The problems were exacerbated by a devastating earthquake in 1990 which caused widespread damage to the mountain resort town of Baguio. And the 1991 eruption of Mount Pinatubo finally persuaded the U.S. military to pull out from their huge bases at Clark and Subic Bay.

Despite seven military coup attempts, opposition from the traditional oligarchy and communist guerillas, Aquino served out her full six-year term and in 1992 Fidel Ramos was elected president in reasonably free and fair elections — at least by Philippine standards. Under Ramos the economy began to take off, with government reforms helping to attract private foreign investment into badly needed infrastructure.

Baguio, reconstructed with low-rise hotels, has regained its status as the country's leading non-beach resort. And the former Subic Bay naval base near Olongapo is being developed as a resort, ship-repair yard and industrial centre.

Luzon and the Visayas are Christian-dominated and exhibit a large degree of Western influence in their customs and traditions. Even here, however, there are interesting diversities: the Ifugaos of the northern Luzon mountains are famed for their woodcarvings, woven fabrics, dances and musical instruments, and their centuries-old rice terraces on the face of the mountains represent a crowning achievement in Filipino ingenuity.

Basically an agricultural country, though with expanding industrial development, much of the farmland is devoted to rice, corn, sugar and coconut plantations. There are substantial exports of sugar, coconut products, bananas and abaca (Manila hemp). Copper, iron, chromite and gold are among the mineral resources exploited.

Entry

Ninoy Aquino International Airport in Manila is served by no less than 40 airlines flying daily to cities throughout the world, as well as from other Asian countries. British Airways operates direct flights from Manila to London three times weekly; Lufthansa five times weekly to Frankfurt; Swissair once a week to Zurich; Northwest 13 times weekly to the U.S.; Philippine Airlines several times weekly to Europe and the U.S.

Departure tax is P500 per passenger.

Tourists can also arrive by cruise or passenger ship and there are many inter-island cruises from Manila.

Immigration

Passports are required, though in some cases other valid travel documents, complete with re-entry permits to ports of origin, are accepted. Most travellers are entitled to 21 days' stay, providing they have onward or return tickets. If they want to extend their stay up to 59 days they must apply to the **Commission of Immigration and Deportation** on arrival.

All visitors staying longer than 59 days must apply again for a visa extension and pay immigration fees at the Commission of Immigration and Deportation, Magallanes Drive, Intramuros, Metro-Manila (Tel: 407651).

Nationals of the following countries must obtain a visa from Philippine diplomatic missions overseas before travelling to the Philippines: Albania, Austria, Belgium, Cambodia, China, Cuba, Denmark, Finland, France, Germany, India, Italy, Iran, Laos, Libya, Luxembourg, Macau, the Netherlands, North Korea, Norway, Russia, South Africa, Spain, Sweden, Syria, Taiwan, Vietnam and stateless persons.

Health

Yellow fever inoculation is required of arrivals from infected areas, except children aged under 12 months who are subject to isolation or surveillance when deemed necessary.

Customs

Personal effects are allowed duty-free provided they are re-exported on departure.

Other duty-free allowances: 400 cigarettes or 100 cigars or 500 grams of tobacco and two bottles of alcohol.

It is prohibited to bring the following items into the Philippines:

Dynamite, gunpowder, ammunition and other explosives, firearms and weapons of war and parts thereof, except when authorized by law.

Written or printed articles, negatives or cinematographic films, photographic materials, engravings, objects, paintings and other representations of an obscene nature.

Written or printed articles in any form, containing any matter advocating or inciting treason, rebellion, insurrection, sedition or subversion against the government of the Philippines or forcible resistance to any law in the country.

Equipment, machines, and contrivances used in gambling.

Any article made of gold, silver or other precious metals, the brands or marks of which do not indicate the actual fineness of quality of the material.

Manila's Roxas Boulevard. PHOTO: VERONICA GARBUTT

Currency

The unit of currency is the peso (P). The exchange rate is liable to fluctuation, but in early 1995 was P24.50:US$1. Coins are of P1 and 2 and 25 and 50 centavo denominations, and notes of 5, 10, 20, 50, 100, 500 and 1,000 pesos.

Foreign currencies are allowed entry in unlimited volume but amounts exceeding US$3,000 must be declared on entry.

Exchange counters usually offer a better rate and swifter transactions than banks. Street money changers should be avoided as they invariably cheat the hapless tourist. The best foreign currency to hold is the U.S. dollar, which is widely acceptable outside Manila, though not at such good rates. Travellers' cheques can be cashed in major towns, but the transaction can prove time-consuming and sometimes frustrating. The rate for travellers' cheques is 5-10% lower than the rate for cash.

Purchase receipts for travellers' cheques and a passport are required. It is often difficult to encash travellers' cheques outside Manila.

Major credit cards such as **American Express**, **Visa**, **MasterCard** and **Diners Club** are accepted in Manila, in other cities and large towns and in many resort areas. Cash withdrawals by means of credit cards require the presentation of a passport. Holders of one of the major credit cards may obtain cash advances in pesos at the following addresses:

American Express: Philamlife Bldg, UN Ave/Orosa St, Ermita, Manila.

Visa and **MasterCard:** Equitable Bank, UN Ave/Bocobo St, Ermita, Manila.

Diner's Club: WIP Bldg, 349 Sen. Gil Puyat Ave, Makati.

Personal cheques are not usually accepted anywhere.

Language

The national language is Pilipino (Tagalog). English is spoken almost everywhere, being the medium of instruction in schools and often the language of administration. Spanish, though a considerable social asset, is now far less prevalent.

The widespread use of English in the Philippines allows the English-speaking visitor a chance to establish contact at many different social levels. The possibility of fluent conversation with the people is one of the great attractions for English-speaker visitors.

Climate

The climate is typically tropical: warm to hot with high humidity. The nights are often pleasantly cool and frequent sea breezes moderate the effects of the day's heat. There are two seasons: dry and rainy. The rains come between June and November, wet days interspersed with hot, sunny ones.

Before the heavy rains come, the temperature tends to be higher during the dry season from March to June, and people from Manila in particular (if they can afford it) like to get away to the beach or cool mountain resorts during this season. May to November invariably brings a few typhoons, often causing serious flooding and damage.

The average maximum daily temperature is a little above 30°C dropping to an average minimum of 22°C at night.

Dress

Light clothes of natural fibres are best for casual wear. Tropical conditions require frequent changes of clothing if you are moving around in the heat. Jackets are expected for men in some establishments in the evenings, though the Filipino *barong tagalog* (a light-weight, long-sleeved, embroidered shirt — traditionally made from woven banana leaf fibre — worn outside the trousers) is a sensible, acceptable substitute on such occasions. The short-sleeved *polo barong* is not considered formal.

Evening wear for women is much as it is in the West. When visiting churches and mosques, it is well to remember that shorts and scanty or provocative dress is inappropriate. Although no tourist is likely to be asked to leave, they would offend local feelings if these traditions are not observed.

Business Hours

Government and private offices are open on weekdays from 8 a.m.-5 p.m. Some private offices open on Saturdays from 8 a.m.-noon, but this is generally considered a day off.

The Post Office keeps government hours. The main one in Manila is situated at Liwasang Bonifacio by the MacArthur Bridge over the Pasig River. It offers a 24-hour cable service.

Commercial banks are open from 9 a.m.-3 p.m. on weekdays only.

Most savings banks remain open late, but also on weekdays only. Most of the department stores in Quiapo and Santa Cruz districts of Manila are open from 10 a.m.-9 p.m. The shops along Carriedo St in Quiapo stay open until 11 p.m. selling general goods. The shops of Escolta and Ermita districts close rather earlier, around 7 p.m. Some shops close between noon and 2 p.m. Fashionable commercial centres have sprouted in the plush shopping centres of Makati, Cubao, along EDSA and in Greenhills districts. They cater mostly to above-average-income residents but are convenient for tourists in a rush.

Most restaurants are open until midnight, at least. Most nightclubs swing all night. Some open as early as 2 p.m. for those who need a little something to help their lunch go down. Bars are normally open from mid-day or even mid-morning until the early hours.

Liquor can be purchased from liquor stores and supermarkets, generally open from 10 a.m.-8 p.m. Monday to Saturday. Some stores are open on Sunday with shorter hours. Beer and local spirits are also available at *sari-sari* stores, the Philippine equivalent of "Mom and Pop" stores, which are often open in the evening until 9 p.m. or 10 p.m.

Doing Business

Although the structure of multinational commerce in the Philippines is based on a Western model, this is merely a facade. The Filipino business style is laid back and leisurely. Although you are expected to be punctual for appointments, chances are that everyone else will either arrive late or not at all. A go-between is necessary to accomplish just about everything.

Do not try to rush meetings — to do so will only defer decision-making until the next one. Be prepared for long lunches and *merienda* (morning coffee or afternoon tea) meetings — during which the talk is mainly pleasantries. Note that the host pays. Learn about Filipino values and the importance of smooth interpersonal relations. And stock up on your repertoire of jokes and be prepared to smile a lot.

Among the advantages of doing business in the Philippines are English as the language of commerce and a surplus of low-cost labour. Some disadvantages are: traffic jams; inadequate telephone communications; slow mail delivery and complex customs procedures. The solutions to the last two are: 1. Use courier services and 2. Get a local colleague to arrange the *lagay* (bribe or "persuasive communication" money — unspoken, unwritten and officially illegal).

Business cards are necessary, as is business attire. A *barong* (local dress shirt) is always appropriate for men and cooler than a Western suit, shirt and tie. Women are widely accepted in business and should dress in executive style.

Business entertaining is done in restaurants, nightclubs and bars, and for residents, at home. Always call to confirm that your rendezvous will be kept, to reaffirm that it was not just a casual arrangement. It is polite to be a little late for a dinner or party at a private house. An acceptable gift is an imported quality brandy or whisky. There are no restrictions on alcohol or smoking. "*Mabuhay*" (literally, "Live!") is the traditional response to a toast.

Accept that to do business here you must provide generous margins for timetables, deadlines and work schedules. And don't even think of criticizing the Philippines.

First timers in the Philippines might consider hiring Manila-based international consultants to provide information research, analysis, conference and meeting organization, communications and other business services. Translation, interpreter, secretarial and typing services along with photocopying, typewriter and computer rentals are available at the business centres of major hotels.

Rip-Offs

Thieves abound in the Philippines, so watch out. Apart from taking the usual common-sense travel precautions, note the following:

Do not pay your taxi fare or alight from a cab until all your luggage has been unloaded; don't talk to or accept drinks from friendly strangers who might claim to know you. Chances are you might be drugged, robbed and abandoned; beware of fake policemen. Never get into an unmarked car with anyone; avoid unlicensed street money-changers.

The **Tourist Assistance Unit** is open 24 hours a day to assist visitors in trouble: Tel: 501728 or 599031 and ask for TAU. The **Department of Tourism** is at T.M. Kalaw St, Rizal Park, Manila. For **urgent police assistance** in Manila dial 166.

Media

Several morning and evening English-language daily newspapers are published in Manila. These include the *Inquirer, Philippine Star, Manila Bulletin, Manila Times, Malaya* and *Manila Chronicle*. There are also a number of local magazines published in English, including *What's on in Manila*.

A fairly large selection of international magazines and newspapers are available, including *Time, Newsweek, Far Eastern Economic Review*, and the *Asian Wall Street Journal*. All the above are sold either in major hotels or at bookstores, (**National Book Store** or **Alemar's**) or at supermarkets and newsstands throughout the city.

Communications

Direct international dialling is possible from Manila's best hotels but this does not apply to most provincial establishments. If a local operator is involved with getting your number, the experience will prove frustrating to anyone accustomed to Western-style efficiency. At major hotels cellular telephones are available for hire at reasonable rates, but a US$1,000 deposit is required.

The number of hotels with a fax facility is growing rapidly both in Manila and provincial towns.

LDC and **JRS** provide delivery to many domestic cities within 24 hours. The cheapest international courier service is provided by **LDC**, which also has the advantage over other internationally operating courier services that it has offices in many Philippine cities and towns. Other international courier companies include **DHL**, **Federal Express**, **TNT Skypack** and **United Parcel Service**. The business centres of major hotels will all arrange for courier delivery of documents and parcels.

Transport

MANILA

FROM THE AIRPORT: A limousine service offered by most tourist hotels costs approximately US$25 for the one-way journey. The taxi fare via Avis Coupon Taxi from the airport to hotels in Makati, Pasay and central Manila is approximately P300-350.

The Manila Hotel's airport transfer service requires 24 hours notice of arrival and costs US$35 per passenger one way.

TAXIS: Philippine taxi fares are among the cheapest in Asia — or the world for that matter. Non-air-conditioned cabs start their flagfall at P10 for the first 500 metres, with P1 for every 250 metres thereafter. For air-conditioned taxis the flagfall is P16, then P1 for each 125 metres thereafter. Tourists should be wary of the sharp taxi drivers who ask for a price — usually outrageous — for a journey and are reluctant to put their meters on.

JEEPNEYS: These are converted jeeps operating as mini-buses along set routes. To use

Manila Bay yacht race. PHOTO: JOSE REINARES

them, you must have some idea where you are going and its relation to the destination indicated on the front and at the sides of the jeepney. The jeepneys show the name of the suburb, or a particular place (such as a park or monument), and sometimes the name of the main road which they intend to use. Fares are low, starting at P1.50. Jeepneys are often equipped with stereo music (as are some taxis) and radio, and are lavishly decorated with coloured streamers, masses of wing-mirrors and other ornaments especially horses, a sign of power. Foreigners always receive a warm welcome from other passengers and riding jeepneys is an interesting way of travelling, and offers the chance of talking to average Filipinos. The vehicles can be stopped by simply waving them down.

BUSES: These operate along most of the main roads in Manila and its suburbs. Destinations are shown. Like the jeepneys, they are cheap, but you must know precisely where you are going. Many buses are being replaced by those of the government-run Metro-Manila Transit Co., some of which are air-conditioned, charging P10. Long-distance buses and coaches also can be caught in Manila for most parts of Luzon island.

LIGHT-RAIL TRANSIT (LRT): An elevated light-rail transit system in Metro-Manila, LRT charges a uniform rate of P6 between any points along its 15-kilometre line along Taft Ave from Baclaran in the south to Caloocan City in the north. There are 16 stations along the route. Tokens are required to pass through the turnstiles.

METRO TRAK: This commuter train operates from Paco Station to Mamatin, Laguna just south of Manila. It stops at Vito Cruz, Buendia, Pasay Rd, EDSA, FTI, Bicutan, Sucat, Alabang, Muntinglupa and San Pedro. Trains run every 30 minutes during morning and evening peak periods, otherwise hourly. Fares range from P1.25-10.25 according to distance.

HIRE CARS: You can rent cars, station wagons, buses, jeepneys and air-conditioned limousines. Cars may be rented with or without driver. Charges vary according to type of vehicle. Hourly rates are available, charged at one sixth the daily rate. In excess of six hours, daily rates apply. A valid foreign or international driver's licence is acceptable. Car-rental agencies normally want a deposit. Many car-rental companies have representatives in hotel lobbies. Sample hotel rates for limousine with driver are: First two hours US$60. Every succeeding hour US$25. Leading car hire companies include:

Avis Rent-A-Car, The Peninsula Manila, Makati. Tel: 854854.
Budget Rent-A-Car, The Peninsula Manila, Makati. Tel: 816 2211.
Dollar Rent-A-Car, Toyota Bel-Air Bldg, 325 Sen. Gil Puyat Ave, Makati. Tel: 883134.
Hertz, Carmen Apartments, M. Orosa St, Ermita. Tel: 583345.
Pacific Rent-A-Car, The Shangri-La Hotel Manila, Makati. Tel: 813 5037.
Thrifty Car Rental, 1430 A. Mabini St, Ermita. Tel: 521 0731.

TRICYCLES AND PEDICYCLES: A tricycle is a Filipino variation of a motorcycle and sidecar, with the sidecar covered on top and open on both sides. A pedicycle is a bicycle with a sidecar, and is often fitted with a ghettoblaster. In Manila, both types abound in the poorer parts of the metropolis, though they are not uncommon elsewhere and service sidestreets where jeepneys do not operate. Upcountry they operate just about everywhere. Expect to pay P10-20 for a short ride.

KALESAS: These horse-drawn rigs operate mainly in the older part of town, around the Manila City area, north of the Pasig River. Prices are subject to negotiation with the driver.

TRANSPORT UPCOUNTRY

TRAINS: Rail services in the country leave a lot to be desired. The Philippine National Railways (PNR) has closed its northern passenger line because commuters have better alternatives in bus services. A programme to update and reopen the line will take some time. The southern line runs to Naga City in Albay province. From there the brave tourist can take PNR buses to Legazpi City where the view of the Mayon Volcano is spectacular. Blumentritt serves as the railway's main station. The only other railway system in the country is on Panay island, linking Iloilo City with Roxas City. There are three services daily to Camalig at 5 a.m., 3 p.m. and 8 p.m. Fares are P100-200 and journey time is approximately 15 hours.

BUSES: The country has a fair system of roads, especially in the Central Luzon region surrounding Manila and near the provincial capitals on the more developed islands.

On Luzon, dozens of bus companies operate, providing good and frequent services. Philippine National Railways Bus Co. operates reasonably new buses at lower prices than many other lines. Pantranco-North Express (terminus in Quezon Boulevard) and Philippine Rabbit are two of the biggest bus operators on the northern routes. Batangas Laguna Tayabas Bus Co. (BLTB) operates from Manila as far southeast as Quezon province, while Pantranco-South Express and J.B.L. Transit Co. serve as far down as Bulan Town, near the southern tip of Luzon. BLTB is located on E. De los Santos Ave (usually known as EDSA), Pasay City. It has the largest network of buses comprising economy, air-conditioned and super deluxe classes. The latter, like tourist buses, sometimes offer video movies, stereo music and snacks for passengers on long journeys.

Fares are low, being under government control. Buses operate at fixed intervals on specific routes, with busy routes serviced more frequently. Also, air-conditioned buses (sometimes with added amenities such as TV and video) ply these busy routes. Sunshine Run (Tel: 584787) has regular services to Legazpi and some other cities. Fares are higher than on the regular bus service.

SHIPPING: For visitors who have lots of time and who do not mind roughing it, it is an experience to travel by ship between the islands. Many shipping companies ply the island routes from Manila. The yellow pages of the telephone directory provide a comprehensive guide to the shipping lines and services offered. But it is almost impossible to book a berth by telephone or to persuade a travel agency to take a booking. It is best to go to the port area and find the ship you want by perusing the notices outside the shipping offices. Then make your bookings on the spot.

Some of the coastal villages served by the steamers can hardly have changed since Conrad's day, and arriving at sunset with seemingly the entire local population on the wharf waiting to see who is aboard is well worth the effort involved.

Some ships have air-conditioned cabins, but where these are not available it is better to sleep on deck — using the camp bed and linen provided on request. Local food can be bought, though it is often of very poor quality. Take a bottle of water, chocolate and fruit.

Small boats serve the smaller islands. From Zamboanga in southern Mindanao, the Sin Hap Hing Agency, Governor Lim St, Zamboanga City (Tel: 3421), has ships sailing through the Sulu islands as far south as Sitangkai, near Sabah. Only deck accommodation is available. The ship calls at Jolo, Siasi, Bongao and sometimes Sibutu. Ships sail every four or five days, but the conflict with Muslim rebels in this area has also brought irregular services. Check with authorities.

Ferries run between such adjacent spots as Iloilo and Bacolod (between Panay and Negros islands) and Zamboanga City and Jolo. The Zamboanga-Basilan trip is P25 first class, P20 second class.

Information about these smaller boats is best obtained locally.

AIR: Air travel is the most convenient method of movement between the islands, with flights serving all important provincial cities. Most of the traffic is out of Manila, though Cebu's Mactan airport in the Visayas is an important centre. Examples of round-trip fares from Manila on Philippine Airlines (PAL) are Cebu P3,140; Davao P5,128; Zamboanga P4,058; Legazpi P1,814 and Baguio P1,136. There is an airport tax of P50 on domestic flights originating in Manila. Lower amounts are charged at some of the other local airports.

Although PAL is the major domestic (and international) carrier operating to over 40 domestic points, new airlines now compete with the flag carrier. These include Aerolift (to Daet, Cebu, Boracay, Bohol, Dipolog, Lubang and Busuanga), Pacific Airways Corp. (Lubang, Boracay and Busuanga) and Star Asia (Caticlan and San Jose). Charter flights can also be arranged to places which have airports but no regular air services — San Fernando in La Union on Luzon Island is just one example.

Tours

There are more than 200 licensed tour operators, many with offices in the main tourist hotels, which will arrange for any city or upcountry tours. Visitors may select from a variety of special interest tours lasting from one to 12 days. They include: camping, cruising, fishing, mountain-climbing, scuba-diving, bird- and wildlife-watching and special festivals. Most of the tour operators provide air-conditioned buses or cars for the tours. One of the out-of-town tours will give the visitor a look at rural life in the Philippines.

There are also tours of Malacanang Palace, the official residence of the Philippine president, where relics of the Marcos family's ostentatious lifestyle are on display.

English-language guides are available through **Guides, Inc.,** 1,300 Roxas Blvd, Pasay City, Metro-Manila. Tel: 522 1989. The rate is now approximately P1,000 per day for Metro-Manila.

Accommodation

The range of hotels in Manila allows travellers on various budgets to find accommodation to suit their needs. The best hotels match their counterparts in other parts of Asia; some of the cheaper hotels are very run down.

Service, though usually of a high standard, can be erratic. Filipinos are natural hosts and offer service with a genuine smile. From the excellence of the numerous top hotels to the cheap places in Santa Cruz and Quiapo, the traveller will generally find hotel staff helpful. The wide use of English helps and Filipinos will often volunteer all kinds of information even without being asked.

Most of the better hotels in Manila are scattered near the areas known as Ermita and Pasay, as well as in the business centre of Makati, though some have also opened further afield. In the provinces, there are many small beach resorts with adequate rooms, some with excellent seafood restaurants. In Baguio and at Subic Bay, former U.S. military recreation facilities have been converted for civilian use. Some of the modern resorts in the outer islands are outstanding, and their settings tend to compensate for any shortcomings.

A government tax of 13.7% and a service charge of 10% is added to all bills.

Better hotels provide transport to and from the airport. Most of the cheaper hotels, though lacking the gloss of luxury, are perfectly satisfactory for visitors who expect basic Western standards. Most rooms are air-conditioned, though many have only a shower rather than a bath.

Discounts ranging from 20-50% are available at many hotels, particularly in Manila, which often has more rooms than tourists. It is always worth asking when making a booking.

Outside Manila, except at modern resorts, accommodation is often basic and water and electricity may be rationed. Prices are lower, but not always as low as they might be given the standard of facilities.

Dining

At home under a sultry tropical sun, the Filipino has always enjoyed many kinds of fresh seafood and plump fruit. The people refer to their own dishes as "native" — in contrast to foreign. Typical Filipino food includes suckling pigs, banana flowers and hearts of palm. Although they may not be cooked in the traditional manner over open fires, today these very dishes, along with a great many more, are popular in some of the very best Manila restaurants.

One Filipino speciality is restaurants which specialize in food to be eaten with the hands — plenty of wash basins are always provided in the body of the restaurants for washing before, during and after a meal. A good example of this method — very enjoyable once one puts aside inhibitions — is the chain of Kamayan restaurants found around Metro-Manila.

Some of the best native dishes are *adobo,* in which chicken or pork — and sometimes both — is stewed in vinegar, garlic, spices and soy sauce; *kare-kare* — ox-tail prepared in a spicy peanut sauce and served with vegetables mixed in a sauce of shrimps cooked in pork lard; *lechon*, pork cooked so that the skin crisps, served with a liver sauce or one made from sweet and sour ingredients; *crispy pata* — pork knuckle boiled, dried and deep-fried in spices, again with crisp skin; *lumpia* — spring rolls prepared with shrimp, pork or chicken mixed with the tender heart of the young coconut plant; *afritada* — beef prepared in olive oil, tomato paste and served with olives and other vegetables; and the very fine soup known as *sinigang*, slightly sour and made from one of several meats or seafood, and vegetables. For dessert, *halo-halo* is a mixture of fruits, ice and coconut milk, not to mention a little sweetcorn and beans.

The Philippines' close association with first the Spanish and later the Americans, has led to a variety of dishes being modified in tastes peculiar to these two nations. Chinese cooking, too, has been an influence.

The traditional Filipino breakfast consists of fruit, followed by fried eggs with spicy beef and fried rice, then coffee or chocolate. Many of the tourist hotels serve it.

When ordering meals it is best to watch the Filipinos. Even before the food arrives, sauce dishes are brought in and people automatically reach for the vinegar bottle with hot chilli, or the soy sauce which they mix with the juice from *kalamansi* (small green citrus fruit). Grilled items are good with crushed garlic, vinegar and chili.

Manila, as an international city, also provides a wide range of restaurants offering other types of Asian, as well as Western, food.

Beer and mixed drinks are available throughout the Philippines, though they are expensive in certain establishments. Manila is home of one of Asia's best beers, San Miguel — though those versions of it brewed under licence elsewhere are not of such high quality. Locally made rums — some masquerading as "whisky" or "gin," — are cheap and will pass as a basis for a cocktail or punch, but except for the higher-grade (and more expensive) versions they are not recommended for taste or for after-effects. There are many local cocktails which, if judged by their names alone, endow one with all kinds of desirable traits. Imported wines and spirits are available at most liquor shops and supermarkets and in hotels, but they are comparatively expensive.

Entertainment

Music is the heart of Manila's night scene. Filipino musicians are famous throughout Asia, if not the world, and bands and singers are widely exported to other Asian capitals. The big hotels have cornered much of the best live music in town and you can enjoy top-rate bands and singers in just about all top-class hotels but notably at the **Calesa Bar** at the Hyatt Hotel and **Tap Room Bar** at the Manila Hotel. Those looking for dancing can head for the discos: **Euphoria** at the Inter-Continental Hotel; **Lost Horizon** at the Philippine Plaza Hotel; **Cats** at the New World Hotel; **Faces** on Makati Ave; **Cheek to Cheek** on Wilson St in Greenhills; and **Bistro RJ** in Makati, Quezon City and Manila. Popular with Filipinos, and well worth trying, are **Love City**, **Heartbeat** and **Miss Saigon** — but be prepared to make the long trek to Quezon City to get away from the tourist spots of Ermita.

For "girlie" shows, the higher-class ones are **Jools** on Makati Ave, Makati, and **Night Watch** on Kalayaan Ave, Makati, but there are dozens of others. The legitimate nightclubs will stay, but for many of the dozens of bars offering topless shows and "take away" girls, a 1993 crack-down by the city fathers closed the famous strips of M.H. del Pilar and Mabini St, which once sported 50-60 bars. A good many bars relocated to Makati. Beer costs P50-60, often two drinks for the price of one during Happy Hour. Drinks for the girls — who are normally not as aggressively mercenary as their counterparts in some other Asian capitals — cost P195. Ever-popular with foreign visitors are **Hang's N** and **The Pool**, on L. Guerrero St, just off the former Ermita strip.

The usual caution should be used in flashing money around and making sure what sort of charges one is involving oneself in.

Burgos St is now the epicentre of Makati's nightlife, and offers a more upmarket version of old Ermita. Head for the most flamboyant bars such as **Dimples**, **Papillon**, **Rogue**, **Jungle Room** and **Ritzy's**. For pool, check out the **Play House**, **Galleon** and **Cat House**. And if you are hungry, try the **Cafe Mogambo** or **Korea Garden**. There are also some less lively bars beyond those in or near Burgos St in Makati, notably the British-style **San Mig** pub in Legaspi St (and in Padre Faura, Ermita), the **Prince of Wales** in Greenbelt Park, **Strumms** on Makati Ave and **Kabooze** on Pasay Rd.

For other tastes, **Bodega Folk Theatre** on Quezon Ave offers excellent folk songs, while the so-called "Filipino Beatle," Freddie Aguilar, sings at **The Hobbit House** in Malate district.

Dinner theatre and fashion shows are presented at some of the best hotels in town. There was a time when fashion shows, with local film stars as models, were regular entertainment features during lunch at big hotels and restaurants, but the fad has somewhat faded.

Rather more serious entertainment can be enjoyed regularly at the impressive **Cultural Centre**, on the reclaimed land complex off Roxas Blvd. Concerts featuring local and visiting orchestras, jazz musicians and ballet are held in the grand main theatre. Plays are also staged here, as well as the nearby **Folk Arts Theatre** and sometimes at **Fort Santiago** and **Puerta Real**, Intramuros.

Free concerts are held at **Luneta Park** on Sundays and at **Paco Park** on Fridays from November to June.

Manila abounds in cinemas. Many are located along Quezon Blvd and Rizal Ave in Quiapo and Santa Cruz, and in the commercial centres of Makati and Greenhills. The city normally receives films from Hollywood soon after they are released. The local film industry also churns out movies in Tagalog, but many of these are of doubtful artistic merit. Filipino traditional dancing can be seen at several of the hotels and restaurants including the Manila Hotel's **Maynila**, the **Philippine Plaza** poolside, **Zamboanga** on Adriatico and **Pistang Pilipino** on M.H. del Pilar.

Shopping

By far the best buys both in Manila and upcountry are handicrafts, some of them unique to the Philippines. There is very little point in buying imported items with the exception of Chinese porcelain, some of which was shipped to the Philippines as export ware during the Chinese Sung, Yuan, Ming and Qing dynasties. Bargain in all places as a matter of principle. Even department stores can sometimes be persuaded to give a small discount. Look and compare prices before buying. The tourist shops will generally give a 10% discount without you trying too hard.

The transparent woven materials used for tablecloths, place-mats and the barong tagalog shirt are an interesting and inexpensive buy. They include *pina* (from pineapple fibre) and *jusi* (from banana tree fibre).

They are often heavily embroidered; this, of course, influences the price. Handmade lace, usually produced in country villages, is also a good buy. Try **Pistang Pilipino** or one of the many branches of **Tesoros** for such items.

For shoes, women can visit the outer suburb of Marikina, where there is a thriving shoe factory and prices are low.

Handbags as well as numerous household items — both of utility and for decoration — are available made from leather, *abaca* (Manila hemp), beads and snakeskin. Especially notable are objects made from *capiz* (mother-of-pearl) which, when polished, becomes beautifully transparent.

Manila is a town of dressmakers and this is a good place to have women's clothes made. Top designers are **Pitoy Moreno**, **Aureo Alonzo** and **Ben Farrales.** Also unusual are the knitted designs of **Lulu Tan Gan** and barongs by **Barge Ramos**.

The best work is of course expensive, but something inspired by the local tribal fashions would be excitingly different back home.

Some dining and kitchen household items in *kamagong* or acacia woods can be pleasing. Some of the wood is not kiln-dried and therefore subject to cracking or warping when taken out of the humid local climate. *Narra* (a teak-like hard wood) chests and furniture inlaid with bone or mother-of-pearl are local products of some character.

Antiques, especially Catholic religious figures and Chinese porcelains, are offered for sale. Many are probably recent copies. Most of the galleries exhibit mass-produced paintings.

Filipinas love to adorn themselves and spend much time buying and selling jewellery, which is also a popular investment. Gold, silver and diamonds are the traditional favourites but pearls are becoming very desirable. The best

Davao's Pearl Farm Beach Resort. PHOTO: PATRICK LUCERO

silver jewellery is to be found in Baguio where the guild-like training from St Louis University has resulted in fine craftsmanship. For antique jewellery try **Capricci** and for modern designs choose from **Diagem** and **Fe Panlilio**.

Cigars produced in the Philippines are of high quality — Alhambra and Tabacalera brands are among the best. Shops can arrange for the buyer's name to be printed on the cigar labels and inscribed on the box.

The city's main shopping areas, many being developed with air-conditioned shopping malls, are Ermita, Makati, Cubao (Araneta Centre), Escolta, Quaipo and Santa Cruz. Shoemart and Rustan's in Makati, Cubao, Harrison Plaza and EDSA in Greenhills are comprehensive department stores.

Sports

The Philippines is strong on both spectator and participatory sports. Basketball is the national sport and matches are played regularly at the **Ninoy Aquino Memorial Stadium** in Manila (mainly at amateur level) and at the **Cuneta Astrodome** sports complex (home of the only professional basketball league outside the U.S.) in Pasig. Baseball is played at Ninoy Aquino Memorial Stadium and at the **Rodriguez Sports Centre**. Soccer matches are also held at the Ninoy Aquino Memorial Stadium and ULTRA. Local newspapers carry useful guides to sporting activities.

Horse-racing is held on Saturdays and Sundays, alternating between the two tracks — the **Santa Ana** and the **San Lazaro**. There are also several golf courses. Some, like the **Muni** course that runs round the perimeter of Intramuros, are public, while others require an introduction from a member. Ask the manager of your hotel or ring the secretary of one of the clubs. Manila also has several golf driving ranges.

Cockfighting is legal and very popular in the Philippines, with many *barrio* (villages) having their own cockpit. In Manila cockfights are held on Sundays at the **Paranaque Cockpit** (near the airport), the **La Loma** (Quezon City) and the **Marikina** sports complex, in Marikina, Rizal. Fights are held between 9 a.m. and 7 p.m.

For the fisherman, the Philippines offers some excellent deep-sea sport. In the far north of Luzon, boats leave **Aparri** for the fishing grounds out among the **Babuyan Islands**. To the west of Luzon, off **Ilocos Sur** and **La Union** provinces, there are also fishing grounds. Fishing to the south is best in **Tayabas Bay**. The mouth of **Manila Bay** provides some fishing. Tuna, garoupa, snapper, marlin and sailfish are among those taken. Freshwater fishing can be had on **Santa Cruz Lake** and **Caliraya Lake**, where in season (May-September) duck may also be shot. Licences are required.

The Philippines' tropical waters teem with fish of many varieties as well as with coral reefs, so scuba-divers also enjoy activities such as underwater photography. There is a growing interest in water sports — such as hobie-cat sailing, windsurfing and water-skiing. Some local resorts offering scuba diving include: **Anilao Seasports Centre** in Batangas (Tel: Manila 801 1850); **Capt'n Greggs Dive Resort**, Puerto Galera (Tel: Manila 522 0248); **El Nido**, Palawan (Tel: 818 2623); **Badian Island**, Cebu (Tel: 581835) and **Dakak**, Dapitan, Mindanao (Tel: Manila 721 0426).

Sports facilities in the metropolis cover most types of games and exercises. Health clubs offer saunas, jacuzzis, and massage. The Manila Yacht Club has reciprocal arrangements with many other clubs round the world.

Jogging is quite popular, with Roxas Blvd and Rizal Park the favourite routes.

There are many golf and sports clubs in and around Manila:

Alabang Country Club, Ayala Alabang Village, Alabang, Muntinglupa, Metro-Manila (Tel: 842 3530-39). Championship swimming pool, 10-lane bowling concourse, 18-hole golf course, polo field, four indoor and four outdoor tennis courts, badminton court, squash court, softball field, basketball court, skating rink, recreation park and children's playground. Guests must be sponsored by members.

Canlubang Golf and Country Club, Canlubang, Laguna (Tel: 883402, 883458). Two 18-hole golf course, two swimming pools (one for adults, one for children), two tennis courts (covered and uncovered), courts for racquetball, squash and badminton. Golf package rates include green fees, lunch, drinks and use of locker room facilities.

Capitol Hills Golf Club, Old Balara Rd, Quezon City (Tel: 976691). Eighteen-hole championship golf course and driving range.

Makati Sports Club, Salcedo Village, Makati (Tel: 817 8731). Six-lane bowling alley, six covered tennis courts, swimming pool, pelota, squash, gym, sauna and massage. Guests must be sponsored by members.

Manila Golf and Country Club, Harvard Rd, Makati, (Tel: 817 4948). Eighteen-hole championship golf course. Guests must be sponsored by members.

Manila Polo Club, McKinley Rd, Makati (Tel: 817 0951). Polo fields, horse riding, tennis, racquetball, squash, bowling, swimming and soft-ball. Guests must be sponsored by members

Manila Yacht Club, 2351 Roxas Blvd, Manila (Tel: 521 4457, 502545 and 521 4458). Clubhouse with bar and restaurants, piers and moorings. Boats for rent. Guests must present membership cards from yacht clubs or must be sponsored by a member.

The Orchard Golf Club, Dasmarinas, Cavite (Tel: [090] 308 8134). Two championship 18-hole courses, swimming pool, tennis courts, basketball court, sauna and massage, beauty parlour. Guests must be sponsored by a member.

Tagaytay Highlands Golf and Country Club, Barangay Calabuso, Tagaytay (Tel: [090] 4672 3160. One 18-hole course, cable-cars, swimming pool, tennis courts. Guests must be sponsored by a member.

Wack-Wack Golf and Country Club, Shaw Blvd, Mandaluyong (Tel: 784021). Two 18-hole championship courses. Sponsorship by a club member is required and arrangements must be made a day before play.

Holidays

Filipinos always find an excuse to hold celebrations. Local festivals are held in honour of patron saints, mythical figures and historical events. The festivities are often a strange blend of native customs and Christian rites, topped up by the supreme ability of Filipinos to have fun and extend hospitality.

There are 11 national holidays during the year, and the president customarily declares special public holidays at national, provincial and municipal levels. The list of Philippine festivals and holidays is long and includes:

January 1: New Year's Day.

January (first Sunday): Feast of the Three Kings, official end of the Christmas festivities.

January 9: Feast of the Black Nazarene in Quiapo district in Manila.

January 10: Feast of the Santo Nino de Cebu, Cebu City.

January (third Sunday): Ati-Atihan in Kalibo, Aklan. A rowdy festival with much singing and street dancing.

January (third Sunday): Sinulog in Kabankalan, Negros Occidental. Similar to the Kalibo festival, which honours the birth of Christ.

January (fourth Sunday): Dinagyang, in Iloilo City. Another version of the Mardi-Gras-style of honouring the birth of Christ.
February 11: Lourdes Feast, in Quezon City.
February 22-25: People-Power Celebration. A fiesta commemorating the Corazon Aquino revolution.
February (movable): Hari Raya Hadji, in the Muslim provinces.
February 24-25: Bale Zamboanga Festival, in Zamboanga City.
March 10-16: Araw ng Dabaw, in Davao City. The week-long activities coincide with the city's founding anniversary.
March-April: Holy week (public holidays all week before Easter). On Good Friday, penitential rituals are seen best in suburbs of Manila where many people practise self-flagellation. In certain places, such as Cainta in Rizal province, heavy crosses are carried and thorns worn on the head. In San Ferdinand, Pampanga, north of Manila, penitents have themselves nailed to crosses.
April 24: Magellan's Landing, in Cebu City. Commemoration of the landing at Mactan of Portuguese explorer Ferdinand Magellan in 1521.
May 1: Labour Day (public holiday).
May 6: Araw ng Kagitingan (public holiday). The nation commemorates the fall of Bataan and Corregidor to the Japanese.
June 12: Philippine Independence Day (public holiday).
June 28-30: Feast of Saints Peter and Paul, in Apalit, Pampanga.
November 1: All Saints Day (public holiday).
November 30: National Heroes Day (public holiday). Leader of the revolution Andres Bonifacio gets most attention.
December 25: Christmas Day (public holiday).
December 30: Rizal Day commemorates the death of the national hero.

ADDRESSES
TOURIST AUTHORITIES
HEAD OFFICE

Department of Tourism Bldg, T.M. Kalaw St, Rizal Park, Manila, Philippines. Tlx: 401883 DEPTOUR PM, Cable: MINTOUR MANILA, Tel: 501969, Fax: 521 7374.

LUZON

Laoag Sub-office, Ilocandia Heroes Hall, Laoag City. Tel: 22098.
San Fernando, Paskuhan Village, San Fernando, Pampanga. Tel: 612665, Fax: 213361.
Baguio Regional Office, Department of Tourism Complex, Gov. Pack Rd, Baguio City. Tel: 6708.
La Union sub-office, DOT, Mabanag Bldg, San Fernando, La Union. Tel: 2098.
Legazpi Regional Office, Penaranda Park, Albay District, Legazpi City. Tel: 4492 4026.
Iloilo Regional Office, Sarabai Bldg, General Luna St, Iloilo City. Tel: 270245.
Tacloban Regional Office, Children's Park, Senator Enage St, Tacloban City. Tel: 321 2048.

CEBU

Cebu Regional Office, Fort San Pedro, Cebu City. Tel: 91530.

MINDANAO

Davao Regional Office, Apo View Hotel, S. Camus St, Davao City. Tel: 74866.
Zamboanga Regional Office, Lantaka Hotel, Valderossa St, Zamboanga City. Tel: 3931.
Cagayan de Oro Regional Office, A. Velez St, Cagayan de Oro City. Tel: 6394.

EUROPE

Frankfurt, Philippine Tourist Office, Kaiserstrasse 15, Frankfurt/M, Germany. Tlx: 413 9660, Cable: DOTFO D, Tel: (069) 20894, (069) 20895.
London, Embassy of the Philippines, 17 Albermarle St, London, W1X 7HA, Britain. Tlx: 265115, Cable: PTOEPL G, Tel: (071) 499 5443.

AUSTRALIA

Sydney, Highmount House, Level 6, 122 Castlereagh St, Sydney, NSW. Tel: (02) 267 2695.

ASIA

Tokyo, Embassy of the Philippines, 11-24 Nampeidai Machi, Shibuya-ku, Tokyo, Japan. Tlx: DPTOUR J J22105, Tel: 464 3630-35, Fax: 464 3690.
Osaka, Philippine Tourism Centre, 2nd Flr, Dainan Bldg, 2-19-23 Sinmachi, Nishi-ku, Osaka 550, Japan. Tlx: 522 2534, Cable: DIANAN J, Tel: 535 5071-72, Fax: 534 1780.
Hong Kong, Philippine Consulate General, Room 602, 6/F United Centre, 95 Queensway, Hong Kong. Tel: 2866 8738.

PUBLICATIONS

The Department of Tourism on the second floor, Department of Tourism building at Rizal Park (Tel: 501703) has the following publications available to visitors: *Road map of the Philippines, Philippine Travel Guide, Philippines — Diver's Paradise, Corregidor, The*

MANILA
SANTA CRUZ
Claro M. Recto Ave
Quezon Blvd
To Quezon City
SAMPALOC
SAN NICOLAS
San Sebastian Church
Quiapo Church
Chinatown
Carriedo Station
Mendiola
Chinatown BINONDO
To Guadalupe
QUIAPO
Malacanang Palace
Pasig River
Pasig River Ferry Boarding Point
SAN MIGUEL
Fort Santiago
Quezon Bridge
Malacanang Park
Pasig River
Central Terminal
Manila Cathedral
Ayala Bridge
INTRAMUROS
City Hall
Paz Mendoza Guazon
Bonifacio Drive
Port Area
Casa Manila Museum
Legislative Building
Intramuros Golf Club
PACO
Department of Tourism
Manila Hotel
UN Ave Station
Paco Park
T.M. Kalaw St
United Nations Ave
ERMITA
General Luna
Paco Railway Station
Taft Avenue
San Marcelino
Museo Pambata
Line to Makati and Carmona
Metro Trak Railway
M.H. Del Pilar
Pedro Gil
Pres. Quirino Ave
Pedro Gil Station
Manila Bay
Roxas Boulevard
A. Mabini
MALATE
Quirino Ave Station
km
0
0.1
Railways
Light Rail Transit Route
Manila Zoo
Vito Cruz Ave
Ninoy Aquino Memorial Stadium
Vito Cruz Station
Manila Yacht Club
Harrison Plaza Shopping Centre
Vito Cruz (Pablo Ocampo Sr.)
Cultural Centre Complex
Pasay City and International Airport
Taft Avenue
Philippine International Convention Centre
Coconut Palace
Corregidor Boat Quay
Gil Puyat Station
Gil J. Puyat Ave (Buendia)

Philippine (Quarterly magazine), *Incentive Travel Guide, Visitor's Guide to the Philippines, Fiesta Directory.*

Other useful publications: *What's on in Manila* magazine, available free of charge in the major hotels; *Ins and Outs*; and the *A-Z map book of Manila,* available at branches of National Bookstore. An addition, the following are available at hotel bookshops and National Bookstore which has several branches around town at Harrison Plaza; Greenbelt Arcade, Makati; Araneta Centre, Cubao; Virra Mall, Greenhills; North Edsa, Shoemart Centre and Quezon City:

Speak Filipino, Philippine Book Co., (P37).
English-Tagalog, Websters, (P39).
Bagong English-Pilipino Dictionary, Philippine Book Co., (P15).
English-Tagalog Visayan Vocabulary, Philippine Book Co., (P28).
English-Tagalog-Ilocano, Philippine Book Co., (P28).
Living in the Philippines, American Chamber of Commerce, (P200).

DISCOVERING PHILIPPINES

MANILA

Quezon City, adjacent to Manila, was formerly the capital of the Philippines, but now Manila has taken over, housing the political, social and economic life centres of the country. Metro-Manila, the great metropolis, is at times a confusing place to describe for so much of Manila in fact lies in other places: Pasay City, Makati. Caloocan City and Quezon City to name the main centres. In fact, Manila has sprawled beyond its original boundaries and now covers 12 municipalities and five cities.

The shoreline of Manila Bay runs approximately north-south and the city spreads along it, divided into northern and southern sections by the Pasig River. Ermita, on the southern side, is in the heart of the tourist belt, though that designated area runs southwards to include Malate and Pasay City. Within the area are the majority of the tourist hotels as well as much of the shopping. North of the river, Quiapo and Santa Cruz make up the nucleus of what one might call the Oriental part of Manila. Here shops, restaurants, theatres, apartments and churches jostle for room, while the swarming people jostle each other outside.

The conquering Spaniard Miguel de Legaspi founded the city in 1571 on the ruins left by the retreating Muslim ruler, Rajah Solaiman. It originally covered an area which the Spaniards enclosed with a broad, high wall and named Intramuros. This original area, only a few minutes' walk from the hotel district, is still being restored and is one of the best historical sites to see. It has cobbled streets, baroque churches and tile-roofed houses. It was reduced to a shambles in World War II.

Churches and convents became ruins, but one church, **San Augustin**, on General Luna St, the oldest stone church in the Philippines, survives, and warrants inspection. Of the churches destroyed, the cathedral alone has been rebuilt — for the sixth time since 1581. The new stained-glass window were designed by Filipino artists. Opposite San Augustin is **Casa Manila** — a museum and shops housed in an ornate building modelled on the style of a home from the rich Spanish era. It is also worth visiting **Silahis Arts and Artifacts** and **Illustrado** restaurant.

One of the seven gates to the city also serves as the entrance to **Fort Santiago**. Construction of the fort began in 1590, though the work remained incomplete for 150 years. The fort served as the seat of colonial power for both Spain and the Americans. During the Japanese occupation the fort was used as a prison and hundreds died there, most horrifyingly when the water from the nearby Pasig river flooded the dungeons. Today it is a park and contains a memorial museum to national hero Jose Rizal (who spent his last months imprisoned in the fort).

Immediately south of Intramuros is the vast **Rizal Park**, also known locally as Luneta. Rizal met his death here before a firing squad in 1896 and a monument now stands on the spot. The park is pleasant and swarms with people in the evenings and at weekends. Overlooking the park is the Museo Pambata (Children's Museum), housed in the colonial-style former Elks Club on Roxas Blvd. It is a boon for parents with children in tow, especially on a rainy day.

A pleasant outing is a Manila Bay cruise. Boats leave a pier at the south side of the park's waterfront, next to the Harbour View restaurant at the western end of T.M. Kalaw St. The best time to go is early morning or sunset, and it is very cheap.

Across the Quezon Bridge — one of the six that span the Pasig river — and very close to the shopping centres on Escolta and Rizal

Ave, lies the heart of Manila — Quiapo. Here, in **Plaza Miranda**, an unending parade of Filipinos of all types passes at all hours of the day and night. **Quiapo Church**, bordering the Plaza, is crowded with devotees every weekend from Friday evening onwards.

The official presidential residence, **Malacanang**, by the river, was originally the country house of a Spanish aristocrat. It became the official residence of the Spanish governor in 1863 and later of the American governor-general.

President Ramos, like his predecessor, Corazon Aquino, has chosen not to live in the palace, which is open to the public, who are able to see for themselves the lavish lifestyle enjoyed by Ferdinand and Imelda Marcos.

On the southeasterly fringe of Manila lies **Makati** district, which in the past few years has become the Philippines' richest municipality, housing the country's commercial centre and the exclusive suburb of **Forbes Park**. Makati is also home to the **American Memorial Cemetery**, where 17,186 American World War II dead are buried.

Mrs Imelda Marcos was the driving force behind two of Manila's civic projects. The majestic **Cultural Centre** stands off Roxas Blvd on land reclaimed from the bay, and contains a fine theatre in addition to a museum of Filipino and imported arts plus Imelda's party house, the **Coconut Palace**, which is now open to the public. Also of interest is the **Nayong Pilipino** park near Manila airport, where buildings representative of the country's principal regions sell handicrafts and other goods. For those not able to leave the capital it also gives an instant glimpse of the rural life of the Philippines.

UPCOUNTRY LUZON

A 90-minute drive south from Manila is **Taal** lake, lying in the crater of a vast volcano. Within the lake is a smaller volcano containing a small lake in its crater. This lake, in its turn, has a very small, and sporadically active, volcano projecting from it. In good weather the whole fantastic scene can be seen from Tagaytay City, on a ridge 600 metres above sea level.

Due east of Manila, less than an hour's drive away, is the pilgrimage town of **Antipolo**, containing a shrine to the image of Our Lady of Peace and Good Voyage, brought from Mexico in 1626.

The inland body of water known as **Laguna de Bay** lies immediately southeast of the capital and beyond it again is the province of Laguna. Here, the rivers have worn steep gorges in the land, and there are rapids and waterfalls along their courses. The most interesting of these rivers is the **Pagsanjan** with falls and rapids. The town of Pagsanjan lies just two hours away from Manila. The falls on the river are reached by a trip upstream through beautiful jungle. Local boatmen manhandle the boats up and steer them during the exciting trip down when visitors shoot the rapids. You will get wet on the river, so wear casual clothes, wrap your camera in plastic and take a towel.

Los Banos (The Baths) is a small town at the foot of **Mount Makiling** on the road to Pagsanjan. Hot springs flow in the area and their waters have been tapped for swimming pools and resort baths in the area.

The beaches at **Matabungkay** and **Nasugbu**, two to three hours drive from Manila, are the best within range of the capital for a day's visit. Nipa huts — small wood and thatch cottages — along the beaches provide facilities for a stay of a day or more. **Noveleta** and **Tanza** in Cavite have beaches closer to Manila but they are not as fine as at Matabungkay. **Puerto Azul** resort hotel complex overlooks the whole Manila Bay approach. Further south at Kilometre 72 in Nasugbu is the hill resort of Evercrest Balulao, which also boats a fine golf course.

Bataan, the peninsula forming the northern arm of Manila Bay, and **Corregidor**, the island near its tip, were the scenes of the stand by the Philippine-American forces against the Japanese invasion in 1942. These two famous battlefields have now been proclaimed national shrines. They may be visited from Manila on one of the special tours that run daily by boat from the ferry terminal near the Cultural Complex in Manila.

The many day trips from Manila include one to the mysterious **Hidden Valley Springs** in Laguna on the southern slope of the extinct volcano of Mount Makiling. A 90-minute drive gets you to where several springs — hot, cold and mineral — have been channelled into specially constructed swimming pools. A series of paths leads through the jungle of fruit trees, giant ferns and wild orchids to gurgling pools and a waterfall. After a native-style lunch you can go hiking to yet another waterfall for a swim in the waters, which are said to be therapeutic.

Mactan Island beach.

PHOTO: VERONICA GARBUTT

Deep in the heart of Quezon province, amid lush green fields and mountains, lies a coconut plantation which is one of the Philippines' more unusual experiences. **Villa Escudero** is a working coconut and rice farm situated just outside the town of Laguna, some 80 kilometres south of Manila.

The hacienda is home to an unusual museum crammed with artifacts from the Asia-Pacific region. The heart of the resort, however, is the river and a palm-fringed lake in which, on a clear day, Mount Banahaw is perfectly reflected. Jutting out into the fish-filled water is a restaurant and visitors can swim or ride narrow bamboo rafts.

Some 90 kilometres south of Manila, **Taal** in Batangas province is the base for the **Philippine Experience** (Tel: Manila 819 5495), a community-based tourism project on the idea that seasoned travellers' most savoured experiences occur when they can mingle with locals in their everyday environment.

Visitors ride by buffalo cart to the beach, see women embroider local cloth in intricate patterns and have a chance to buy embroidered dresses, tablecloths and napkins as well as barong materials. A trip across the Pansipit river on outrigger boats known as *bancas*, ends with lunch on banana leaves at an elegant Spanish-style house.

Northwest of Manila near the town of Olongapo the former U.S. naval base of **Subic Bay** is being developed as a resort, free port and industrial zone. Hotels and restaurants have been opened in former officers' quarters. The resort area's attractions include nature treks in a well-preserved forest, golfing, scuba-diving, swimming, tennis, squash and skeet shooting. And for nightlife **Olongapo** boasts a wide range of restaurants, discos and "girlie" bars.

North of Manila, 1,525 metres up in the mountains, lies the resort town of **Baguio**, which has made a rapid recovery from a devastating earthquake in 1990. This is a particularly picturesque spot, favoured by tourists and Filipinos alike for its tranquillity and respite from the lowland heat. The longer you stay here, the more you discover the pleasant walks through the pine woods as well as other recreation available. The summer capital of the Philippines and popular with officials, the town has its expensive areas where holiday homes are surrounded by gardens and dominated by the towering pines. The golf course at the former U.S. military camp, now a resort called **Club John Hay**, is of an excellent standard and is open to the public on the payment of green fees.

Woodwork, handwoven cloth in native designs and silverware are some of the local crafts available in Baguio either at the central market, or from one of a number of handicrafts shops. Baguio is a starting place for trips further afield into the mountains. Just 30 minutes ride away by bus or jeepney are the hot springs of **Asin**, where you can bathe. In the town itself, there are a number of faith healers, who attract many crippled or infirm foreigners looking for this unusual form of treatment. The government officially frowns upon such activities, but the trade goes on none the less.

About 100 kilometres north of Baguio at Banaue are the breathtaking rice terraces built on the mountain face by Ifugao tribespeople. The terraces are at least 2,000 years old.

The journey is rewarding in itself, taking you through attractive mountain scenery into a land where the locals still have very little contact with outsiders. The people in the barrio around Banaue and deeper into the mountain lead exceptionally primitive lives. Visits to these barrios can be arranged in Banaue. Walking through the town and in the surrounding hills, the traveller will meet near-naked tribespeople, the men carrying spears, as well as polite schoolchildren who greet you with "Good day, sir" in American-accented English. Elsewhere in the Philippines, the friendly call to foreigners is "Hey Joe," the American colonial-era refrain.

Even further north than Banaue is the **Batanes** archipelago (Home of the Winds) — the smallest and northernmost province in the Philippines. It consists of 10 main islands lying just 100 kilometres south of Taiwan. The best time for a visit is April or May, as the area is subject to typhoons for much of the year. Philippine Airlines operates five flights a week from Manila to **Basco**, the capital. With a population of just over 4,000 swelled by a few hundred visitors a year, Basco is one of the few "undiscovered" destinations in Asia. And it is likely to remain so as the locals do not welcome tourism development. The local architecture is unusual and one could almost be in rural Ireland, with the solid typhoon-proof structures built from grey rock with thatched roofs. The locals, called Ivatans, are a polite and hardy people, but not particularly outgoing in comparison with other Filipinos.

Luzon also offers good beaches in the north. Some of the best are in **La Union** province and at **Hundred Islands** in Lingayen Gulf, Pangasinan province. The best of the resorts along the great stretch of beach are found at **Bauang,** immediately to the south of San Fernando, La Union, which can be reached by bus or car from Manila.

Off the south of Luzon, **Mindoro** island can be reached by a two-hour ferry ride from Batangas to **Puerto Galera**. This has been developed — some would say overdeveloped — as a resort area. Although Sabang beach, only a decade ago a completely unspoilt area, has been described as "Little Ermita" owing to the proliferation of bars and "honky-tonks" as the locals call them, there are still a few peaceful, beautiful spots to be found. Try **Ensenada Beach, Coco Beach**, **Small Lalaguna Beach** (fine diving), **White Beach** and **Tamaraw Beach**.

CEBU ISLAND

Cebu City, Queen of the Visayas, the islands stretching over central Philippines, lies 560 kilometres southeast of Manila on the island of the same name. The flight — there is an excellent, frequent service — takes just one hour and 10 minutes from Manila and there are several flights a week direct from Hong Kong, Singapore and Tokyo.

Founded in 1565, Cebu is the oldest city in the Philippines and has many points of historical interest, though it has suffered the fate of many other Philippine cities and grown noisy, crowded and shabby in parts. There are many supermarkets and even drive-in theatres. A large hollow cross stands in its plaza, protecting an old inner cross, said to be the one planted by the explorer Magellan when he and his soldiers celebrated their first mass on the island. Nearby is the beautiful **San Augustin Church**, where rests the most ancient image in the Philippines — the *Santo Nino* (Holy Child) brought from Mexico more than 300 years ago.

One of the easiest and most popular excursions from Cebu City is to **Mactan** island where Magellan met his death. A monument marks the spot. Mactan, the site of Cebu's main airport, is connected to the mainland by a long bridge. Mactan is a lovely tropical island, with get-away-from-it-all white sand beaches and clear, coral sea.

Upmarket accommodation can be found at the Shangri-La's Mactan Island Resort, **Club Pacific Cebu, the Maribago Bluewater Bay** resort and the **Cebu Beach Club/Tambuli resort complex**.

For good seafood visit the town of **Talisay**, a short bus or taxi ride from Cebu City. Try also the food stalls at the nearby fishing village of **Tangki**, serving a range of fresh fish which you can eat while throwing the odd coin down to the group of young boys leaping around in the sea, waiting to dive for your money.

For sightseeing in Cebu, hire a public utility car, which with diver will cost about P150 per hour. For the romantic, the local horse and carriage (*tartanilla*) is a different way to see the town. Bargain over the price.

Taxis are cheaper than in Manila, as is just about everything else.

Guitars and ukeleles made in Mactan are a bargain. For those interested in jewellery, the aquamarine and pink Osmena pearls (from the chambered Nautilus) are available, as is a wide range of shells and coral. Black coral jewellery is much cheaper here than in Manila.

For good eating in town try either the revolving restaurant at the **Sundowner Centrepoint Hotel**, Cebu, the restaurant at the **Cebu Plaza Hotel** or **Alavar's** on Archbishop Reyes Ave. There are also a few good Chinese restaurants.

Cebuanos enjoy a reputation as being among the most beautiful women in the country.

Beyond Cebu City the province boasts many attractions. **Moalboal**, on the west coast, is a haven for scuba-diving enthusiasts and budget travellers while **Badian Island** is possibly the finest hideaway resort in the region. **Argao Beach Club** near Dalaguete, some 70 kilometres south of Cebu City, offers the full range of water sports, while **Alegre**, some 50 kilometres to the north, is currently the most fashionable resort.

Cebu City is a good point from which to set off to explore the other islands since it is a communications centre for the Visayas, with many aircraft and shipping routes either beginning or terminating here.

There are flights out of Mactan to all the important towns further south and several ships a day leave the harbour. No one can forecast sailing dates with any accuracy, however, and it is best to check at the jetty for exact information.

Across the strait from Cebu is the island of **Bohol**, celebrated for the unusual **Chocolate Hills** — so called because of their appearance in the dry season. The ferry ride to the island takes two hours, or there is a longer journey to the main town of **Tagbilaran** in the south of the island. The island shows off its brown hills to the best effect when seen from the air, as from flights heading for **Cagayan de Oro** and **Davao** in Mindanao. At present the most popular resort is **Bohol Beach Club**, but other resorts are also under construction on Panglao Island.

NEGROS ISLAND

Bacolod city in the province of Negros Occidental is the Philippines' sugar capital. From Manila the round-trip airfare is P3,100. The trip by boat, though much cheaper, takes 19 hours. Bacolod can be reached by air from Mactan and Iloilo.

Overland from Cebu City you take the bus to Toledo City on the west coast of Cebu Island, then use the ferry to cross to **San Carlos** on Negros island and from there again by bus on to Bacolod. The trip is hardly cheaper than going by air, but you see the countryside.

Bacolod has the **San Sebastian Cathedral**, and you can visit the neighbouring hot springs at **Mambucal** or travel down to the beach at **Santa Fe** — both about one hour from town. Another interesting trip from the city is to visit one of the many sugar plantations that surround it.

Taxis charge the usual cheap upcountry rates. From the jetty to the centre of town the jeepney fare is around P20. But if you take a taxi to your hotel, beware of the driver who will offer to carry your bag into the reception desk. He gets a commission for this service from the hotel — on your bill. The hotels are the best bet for good food in town. **Maxim's** combines eating facilities with its nightclub.

PANAY ISLAND

Two hours west of Bacolod by ferry or 15 minutes by air is Iloilo City on Panay island. The ferry crosses twice daily except on Sunday, when it makes only one journey. There are also regular flights from Manila and ships sail from the capital frequently.

Iloilo is a pleasant enough spot, though a little dilapidated. The town is noted for its fine local fabrics. The best barong tagalog shirts use such embroidered fabrics and the town is a good place to buy one. Ternos, the Spanish-inspired dress for Filipinas, with the butterfly sleeves, are also a good buy in Iloilo if you have time to have one made.

Iloilo has a museum with exhibits dating back to pre-Hispanic times. The baroque **Miagao Iloilo Church** is worth a visit. **Guimaras** island nearby boasts a handful of fine beach resorts.

Northwest of Panay, some three hours' drive by jeepney from **Kalibo**, followed by a 15-minute sea crossing by banca, lies **Boracay**. An island still of superlative beauty, it was previously a haunt of Manila cognoscenti and foreign backpackers. But the butterfly-shaped island is now moving upmarket, some fear too fast and putting its natural splendour severely at risk. Drugs have appeared on the scene, and assaults on visitors have brought Boracay's name down somewhat from its former heights. It boasts several resorts: **Friday's, Pearl of the Pacific**, **Lorenzo's**, **Sandcastles** and **Boracay Beach and Yacht Club** among them. A gentle sea, a slight breeze and tall coconut palms swaying in the wind can make this the almost perfect tropical paradise. By day there is boardsailing, scuba diving, tennis and horse riding. In the evenings there are gatherings at the **Beachcomber**, **Bazura** and **Sandbar** discos. Philippine Airways operates daily flights to **Kalibo**, but a faster way is to fly on **Star Asia, Pacific Airways** or **Aerolift to Caticlan**.

LEYTE AND SAMAR ISLAND

Leyte is best remembered as the scene of Gen. MacArthur's return to the Philippines in October 1944 to recapture the country from the Japanese.

The island is well served by sea, with services from Manila, Cebu, Samar and Mindanao. Air services connect it with Manila and Mactan.

Buses fan out from **Tacloban** to the outlying districts of the island, and a journey to **Ormoc City** on the west coast will prove rewarding to anyone prepared to sacrifice a little comfort for an excellent look at the countryside. The actual scene of MacArthur's landing is a red beach 16 kilometres south of Tacloban. In the city, a life-size mural immortalizes both Magellan and MacArthur.

MINDANAO ISLAND

The large southern island of Mindanao, or interest itself, also serves as gateway to the fascinating **Sulu** group of islands which stretch down to the southernmost **Tawi-tawi** islands, a few miles away from the north coast of the East Malaysian state of Sabah. However, travellers to Western Mindanao and the Sulu, Basilan and Tawi-tawi should check with their embassies in Manila first to find out if the sporadic conflict with Muslim rebels in the area allows for free movement.

A two-hour bus ride from the boom town of **Cagayan de Oro**, centre of the region's pineapple industry, on the north coast of Mindanao to **Balingoan**, followed by a one-hour ferry trip, takes you to **Camiguin**, a remote, unspoiled paradise island which has been described as "Boracay 10 years ago." For nature lovers, Camiguin's main attractions are **Hibok Hinok** volcano, **Katibasawan** waterfalls and **Salang** springs. Because accommodation is strictly Robinson Crusoe-style in simple nipa huts, Camiguin is a destination for adventure travellers who can enjoy a vacation without air-conditioning and mini-bars.

The city of **Davao**, on the east coast of Mindanao, boasts popular resorts such as **Pearl Farm** and **Davao Insular**. The area is the home of some of the most colourful tribal people in the Philippines, including the Bagobos, Manobos, Taga Kaolos, Mangguagan, Mandaya, Kulaman and Bilaan tribes. Some of these people are fast disappearing from their traditional lands as newcomers settle. Davao is a booming centre for the abaca industry. Its main attractions are the **Shrine of the Holy Infant Jesus of Prague**, **Magsaysay Park**, **Caroland Resort**, the **Buddhist Temple** and **Samal Island**. There is an 18-hole golf course and the swimming at **Talomo** and **White Beach** is good.

Mount Apo, the highest Philippine peak at 2,954 metres, presents a challenge for climbers. Of great interest to conservationists is the **Philippine Eagle Breeding Station** near Baracatan. This is isolated but can be reached by jeepney for Toril (from the Aldevinco Shopping Centre in Davao). From Toril to Baracatan is another jeepney ride. Alight at the terminus and walk 1.5 kilometres to the research station.

Zamboanga City is one of the most colourful, distinctly exotic places in the Philippines. It can be reached directly by air from Manila, as well as from other major provincial towns, and by sea. The air fare from Manila in early 1995 was P4,058. Zamboanga is a small, bustling port dating back to early Spanish times. The local dialect, Chabacano, is a corruption of Spanish. Unfortunately, the city was largely destroyed during World War II and its rebuilding has detracted a great deal from the old Spanish atmosphere. The tropical climate allows bougainvillaea and orchids to flower in profusion — Zamboanga is known as the city of flowers. The only relic of the Spanish occupation is **Fort Pilar**, which though small is quite a fine example of military architecture; it is now a barracks. The city also has the country's oldest nine-hole golf course.

Many Filipinos like to travel to Zamboanga simply to go shopping in the **barter market** at the wharf. Here, because of the legal barter

Muslim girl.

trade through neighbouring Sabah and elsewhere, you can buy batik cloth made in Malaysia and Indonesia, and nearly all kinds of imported goods — chocolates, TV sets, radios, perfumes and other goods which normally carry a high duty. There is also silk from Cotabato. Brassware in ornate style can be bought, both modern and supposedly antique. You might also be lucky and pick up a Ming or Qing piece of pottery at the antique market a few steps away from the **Lantaka Hotel**. But be careful because there is also a lot of fake porcelain.

There are one or two very good beaches, particularly on the nearby **Santa Cruz** island. Here you can dive among the fish and coral in crystal-clear water. The Lantaka Hotel is a charming place to stay or have a meal. You can have a drink or eat outdoors with a marvellous view of the harbour looking over to the island of Basilan. The local **Badjaos** (a water-gypsy tribe) float up to the edge of the hotel in their boats, offering shells and coral and beautiful eye-catching Sulu mats. Boats to Santa Cruz island can be arranged at the hotel.

For a look at the lush tropical countryside, you can take a hire car, taxi or tricycle cab to **Pasonanca Park**, which has a real tree-house, where you can stay for a night or two if you book well ahead. A letter to the Officer in Charge of the Tree-House Bookings, City Hall, Zamboanga, should do the trick. You may have to pay a few pesos for supplies. The tree-house is supposed to be for honeymooners, but as dozens of visitors pass through the house every day, serious honeymooners might be advised to look for other accommodation.

In Zamboanga City, for a night out, you might go to Justice R.T. Lim Boulevard, about 2 kilometres along the coast, where you can eat grilled chicken at the local stalls and have a beer to the accompaniment of some of the world's loudest jukeboxes. Then on to one of the few nightclubs in town — which include the **Fishnet Pub House** where they have hostesses and dancing to loud music.

North of Zamboanga City, some 40 minutes by air, is **Dipolog**, provincial capital of Zamboanga del Norte. Some 25 kilometres away lies the sleepy town of **Dapitan** where nationalist hero Jose Rizal was exiled from 1892 to 1896. It is said by some to be the prettiest town in the Philippines. A short boat ride will take you to the thatched-roof style **Dakak Beach Resort** with sandy beaches, swimming pools, jacuzzis, Spanish galleon-style bars, mango trees and air-conditioning.

Hundreds of wild animals roam free on **Calauit Island** on the northern tip of Palawan. Among their number are indigenous creatures such as parrots, bearcats, monkeys, wild boar and leopard cats.

In 1977 the island was declared a game reserve and wildlife sanctuary. There followed imports of exotic African species including zebra, eland, giraffe, impala and topi. To visit the sanctuary permission must be obtained from the Philippine Conservation and Resource Management Foundation (Tel: Manila 815 2451).

The underwater world around Palawan is equally rich in wildlife — perfect diving territory. Many wartime wrecks can be found to the northeast, around **Busuanga** and **Koron islands**. Puerto Princesa is the jumping-off point for these areas as well as for the famous dive areas around **Tubbataha Reefs,** in the middle of the Sulu Sea east of Palawan.

El Nido Ten Knots on **Miniloc island** is a diver's haven, complete with snorkelling, windsurfing and the whole gamut of aquatic sports — followed by shrimp and lobster dinners. Some 40 minutes by boat from El Nido village lies **Pangalusian Island Resort** on its own small island.

The luxury **Amanpulo** resort lies on the island of **Pamilican** in the Cuyo group of islands off eastern Palawan. As with other northern Palawan resorts, it is accessible by light aircraft.

THE SULU ARCHIPELAGO

Beyond Basilan what look like an infinite number of stepping stones — the far-flung islands of the Sulu archipelago — lead to Borneo. But note that travelling by sea is not recommended because of piracy and confrontations between insurgents and the Philippine military. Every day at 10 a.m. a Philippines Airlines flight leaves Zamboanga for Sanga Sanga, some 12 kilometres from the Tawi-tawi capital of Bongao. The sight which greets arriving passengers is pure Arabian Nights: a silver dome capping a mosque with graceful minarets towering above a water village on stilts; tall people with dazzling smiles feasting on *curachas* (coconut crabs) and children frolicking in the water.

Further out into the Celebes Sea is **Sibutu**, famous for its wild boar. Finally, almost at the border with Malaysia, is Sitangkai, one of several places dubbed "The Venice of the East"— a town built on stilts over a crystal-clear reef.

Other Sulu islands include **Siasi**, **Laparan**, **Simunul**, **Manuk Mankaw**, **Bubuan** and **Cagingaan**. Such journeys should only be tackled by adventurers with plenty of time to spare, as boat connections are infrequent and hotel accommodation almost non-existent.

RESTAURANT SELECTION

Average price for two

BACOLOD

CAFE NEGRENSE, Aquino Ave, Bacolod City. Filipino, Chinese. Music. US$25.

BAGUIO

HALFWAY HOUSE, Club John Hay, Baguio City. Tel: 442 7902. American, Mexican. Music, dancing. US$25.

CEBU

ALAVAR'S SEAFOOD HOUSE, 46 Gorordo Ave, Cebu City. Tel: 78126. Cebuano, Seafood. Music (tape), dancing. US$30.

DAVAO

LA PARILLA, Insular Century Hotel Davao. Tel: 76051. Filipino, Continental, Grill. Live music. US$30.

MANILA

BISTRO REMEDIOS, 1901 M. Adriatico St, Malate, Manila. Tel: 521 8097. Filipino. US$20.

CHAMPAGNE ROOM, Manila Hotel, Rizal Park, Manila. Tel: 470011. Continental. Music (string orchestra, piano). US$80.

EMERALD GARDEN, 1170 Roxas Blvd, Ermita, Manila. Tel: 501764, 504149. Chinese. US$20.

GINZA, Manila Hotel, Rizal Park, Manila. Tel: 470011. Japanese. US$40.

GUERNICA'S, 1326 M.H. del Pilar, Ermita, Manila. Tel: 500936, 582225, Filipino, Spanish, Vegetarian. Music (tape). US$40.

HARBOR VIEW, Luneta Terminal, Rizal Park, Manila. Tel: 501532. Filipino, American. Music (tape). US$25.

KASHMIR, Merchants Centre, Padre Faura St, Mabini, Manila and 7844 Makati Ave, Makati and 816 Pasay Rd, Makati. Tel: 506851, 816 0103, 882721. Mid-Eastern, Indian. Music (tape). US$30.

LA BELLE VUE, Diamond Hotel, Roxas Blvd cor. Dr. J. Quintos St, Ermita, Manila. Tel: 536 2211. French, Continental. Music (tape). US$110.

L'OPERA, Ground Flr, Anson's Arcade, Paseo de Roxas (corner Esperanza St), Makati. Tel: 844 3283. Italian. US$35.

LE SOUFFLE, 2/F Josephine Bldg, Greenbelt Drive cor. Makati Ave, Makati. Tel: 812 3287. Western. Music (tape). US$45.

MAYNILA, Manila Hotel, Rizal Park, Manila. Tel: 470011. Filipino. Live music. US$65.

NEW ORLEANS, La Tasca Bldg, Greenbelt Park, Makati or 1485 Quezon Ave, Quezon City. Tel: 817 2956. Cajun. Music (live jazz). US$30-55.

HANG'S N, 429 Arquiza St cor. Guerrero St, Ermita. Tel: 597147. British/pub food. Music (tape), Pool table. US$15.

TIA MARIA, Greenbelt, Makati/ Ortigas, Greenhills, Katipunan, Quezon City, Remedios, Malate, Manila. Tel: 854443, 722 2025, 996846, 522 0429. Tex/Mex. Music (tape). US$18.

ZAMBOANGA

THE LANAI, Lantaka Hotel by the Sea, Valderroza St, Zamboanga City. Tel: 3931, Filipino, Western. Music (tape). US$30.

HOTEL GUIDE

ALBAY

D: US$75 or below

LA TRINIDAD, Rizal St, Legaspi City. Tel: Manila 503306-09, Tlx: 2359 CS (PT&T). *P. R: L, W.*

AKLAN (For Boracay)

B: US$120-160

CLUB PANOLY, Boracay Island. Tel: Manila 812 0441, Fax: 816 0747. *P. R: L, W.*

D: US$75 or below

BORACAY BEACH & YACHT CLUB, Boracay Island. Tel: 588809. *R: L.*

BORACAY BEACH CLUB HOTEL, Boracay Island. Tel: 521 2751, Fax: 521 2762. *R: L, Spanish.*

FRIDAY'S, Boracay Island. Tel: Manila 521 2283, Fax: 521 1072. *R: L, W.*

LORENZO'S, Boracay Island. Tel: Manila 990719, Fax: 961726. *R: L, W.*

PEARL OF THE PACIFIC, Boracay Island. Tel: 990947, Fax: 987460. *R: L, W.*

SANDCASTLES, Boracay Island. Tel: Manila 500906, Fax: 817 1175. *R: L, W, Thai.*

BATANGAS

A: US$160 or above

EVERCREST GOLF CLUB & RESORT, Kilometre 72 Batulao, Nasugbu. Tel: Manila 473411-18, local 289/299, Fax: 497286. *P, Gym. R: L, W.*

BENGUET (For Baguio)

C: US$75-120

CLUB JOHN HAY, Lonkan Drive, Baguio City. Tel: 442 7902, Manila 810 4741, Fax: 442 6798, Manila 817 9566. *P. R: L, W, Mexican.*

VACATION HOTEL BAGUIO, 45 Leonard Wood Rd, Baguio City. Tel: 442 4545, 442 3144, Fax: 818 7756. *R: L, W.*

D: US$75 or below

SAFARI LODGE, 191 Leonard Wood Rd, Baguio City. Tel: 442 2419. *R: L, W.*

HOTEL SUPREME, 416 Magsaysay Ave, Baguio City. Tel: 442 2855. *R: L, W.*

SWAGMAN ATTIC HOTEL, 90 Abanao Rd, Baguio City. Tel: 442 5139, Manila 574951, Fax: 442 5139. *R: L, W.*

BOHOL

C: US$75-120

BOHOL BEACH CLUB, Panglao Island, Bohol. Tel: Manila 522 2301-4, Fax: Manila 522 2304. *P, SatTV. R: L, W.*

CAVITE

B: US$120-160

PUERTO AZUL BEACH HOTEL, Barrio Sapang, Ternate. Tel: Manila 571373, Fax: 597074, Tlx: 64915 AZUTEL PH. *Biz. R: L, W.*

C: US$75-120

CORREGIDOR INN, Corregidor. Tel: Manila 831194, 831 5741, Fax: Manila 831 2952. *R: L, W.*

TAAL VISTA HOTEL, Tagaytay City. Tel: Manila 817 2710, Fax: Manila 818 1208. *Biz. R: L, W.*

CEBU

A: US$160 and above

ALEGRE BEACH RESORT, Calumboyon, Sogod, Cebu. Tel: Manila 813 4083, Cebu 311231, Fax: Manila 815 6872, Cebu 214345. *P, SatTV. R: L, W.*

SHANGRI-LA'S MACTAN ISLAND RESORT, Mactan Cebu. Tel: (6332) 217707, Fax: (6332) 217709, 211701, Tlx: 62644 SHANGLA PN. *P, SatTV. R: L, W.*

B: US$120-160

BADIAN BEACH RESORT, Badian Island, Cebu. Tel: 61306, Fax: 213385, Tlx: 6288 BADUAN PU. *P. R: L, W.*

CEBU CLUB PACIFIC, Sagod, Cebu. Tel: 79417, Fax: 95343, Tlx: 24836 CLP PH. *P. R: L, W.*

CORAL REEF RESORT, Agus, Mactan Island, Cebu. Tel: 79203, Fax: 211192, Tlx: 48196 PM. *P, Gym, Biz. R: L, W.*

C: US$75-120

ARGAO BEACH CLUB, Dalaguete, Argao. Tel: Manila 522 2302. *P. R: L, W.*

CEBU MARINE BEACH RESORT, Subasbas, Lapu Lapu City. Tel: 501 0276, Fax: 54312. *P. R: L, W.*

CEBU MIDTOWN HOTEL, Osmena Blvd cor. General Maxilom, Cebu City.

P — Swimming pool
R — Restaurant
Gym — Health club
L — Local food
Biz — Business centre
W — Western food
SatTV — Satellite TV

HOTEL GUIDE

Tel: 219711, Fax: 219765, Tlx: 24663 CEBU MID PH. *R: L, W.*

CEBU PLAZA HOTEL, Nivel, Lahug, Cebu City. Tel: 311231, Fax: 312071, Tlx: 24861 CEPLA PH. *P. R: L, W.*

MAY Y CIELD BEACH RESORT, Mactan. Tel: 74613, Fax: 83934, Tlx: 22729 MIH PN. *P. R: L, W.*

MARIBAGO BLUE WATER BEACH RESORT, Buyong Beach, Mactan. Tel: 83863, Fax: 83934, Tlx: 48040. *P. R: L, W.*

TAMBULI BEACH RESORT/CEBU BEACH CLUB, Buyong Beach, Mactan. Tel: 70200, Fax: 53097, Tlx: 6272 PTCC PU. *P. R: L, W.*

DAVAO

B: US$120-160

PEARL FARM BEACH RESORT, Samal Island, Davao City. Tel: Manila 832 0893, Fax: Manila 832 0044. *R: L, W.*

C: US$75-120

INSULAR CENTURY HOTEL DAVAO, Lanang, Davao City. Tel: 234 3050, Fax: (82) 62959, Tlx: ITT 48209. *P. R: L, W.*

D: US$75 or below

APO VIEW HOTEL, J. Camus St, Davao City. Tel: 74861-69, Manila 857911, Tlx: 24853. *P. R: L, W.*

ILOILO

B: US$120-160

COSTA AGUADA, Inampulugan Is. Jordan, Guimaras. Tel: Manila 831 2261, Fax: (632) 833 0357. *R: L, W.*

ISLA NABUROT RESORT, c/o Philippine Air Lines, Iloilo City. Tel: 76112. *R: L, W.*

NAGARAO ISLAND, Jordan, Guimaras, Iloilo. Tel: 71057, Tlx: 5910 AISCPU. *R: L, W.*

LEYTE

D: US$75 or below

MAC ARTHUR PARK BEACH RESORT, Palo, Leyte. Tel: Manila 812-1984, Tlx: 63457 IPDC PN. *P. R: L, W.*

METRO MANILA

A: US$160 or above

CENTURY PARK SHERATON, Pablo Ocampo Sr. cor. M. Adriatico St, Manila. Tel: 522 1011, Fax: 521 3413, Tlx: 40489 CPH PN. *P, Gym, Biz, SatTV. R: L, W, Japanese ,Chinese.*

HOTEL INTERCONTINENTAL, No. 1 Ayala Ave, Makati. Tel: 894011/815 9711, Fax: 817 1330, Tlx: ITT 45005 PM. *P, Gym, Biz, Ex, SatTV. R: L, W. French.*

HYATT REGENCY, 2702 Roxas Blvd, Pasay City. Tel: 833 1234, Fax: 833 5913, Tlx: 45237 HATTMLA PM. *P, Biz, SatTV. R: L, W, Italian, Japanese.*

THE MANILA HOTEL, 1 Rizal Park, Manila. Tel: 247 0011, Fax: 530 0325, Tlx: 40537 MHOTEL PM. *P, Gym, Indoor Golf, Biz, Ex, SatTV. R: L, W, French, Italian, Japanese.*

MANILA DIAMOND HOTEL, Dr. J. Quintos St cor. Roxas Blvd, Ermita, Manila. Tel: 536 2211, Fax: 536 2255. *P, Gym, Biz, Ex, SatTV. R: L, W, Continental, Japanese.*

MANDARIN ORIENTAL HOTEL, Makati Ave, Makati. Tel: 816 3601, Fax: 817 2472, Tlx: 63756 MANDA PN. *P, Gym, Biz, Ex, SatTV. R: L, W, Asian, European.*

NEW WORLD HOTEL, Esperanza St cor., Makati Ave, Makati. Tel: 811 6888, Fax: 811 6777. *P, Gym, Biz, Ex, SatTV. R: L, W. Chinese, Italian.*

THE PENINSULA MANILA, Corner of Ayala and Makati Aves, Makati. Tel: 819 3456, Fax: 815 4825, Tlx: 22507 PEN PH. *P, Gym, Biz, SatTV. R: L, W, Asian.*

WESTIN PHILIPPINE PLAZA, Cultural Centre Complex, Roxas Blvd, Manila. Tel: 832 0701, Fax: 832 6923, Tlx: 40443 FILPLAZA PM. *P, Gym, Driving Range/Golf Park, Biz, Ex, SatTV. R: L, W. French.*

SHANGRI-LA'S EDSA PLAZA HOTEL, 1 Garden Way, Ortigas Centre, Mandaluyong, Metro Manila. Tel: 633 8888, Fax: 631 1063, Tlx: (075) 62616 EDSASL. *P, Gym, Biz, Ex, SatTV. R: L, W, Japanese, Chinese, Italian.*

SHANGRI-LA HOTEL MANILA, Ayala Ave cor. Makati Ave, Makati. Tel: 813 8888, Fax: 813 5499, Tlx: (075) 66898 SHAN MNL. *P, Gym, Biz, Ex, SatTV. R: L, W, French, Thai, Chinese.*

B: US$120-160

TRADER'S HOTEL, 300 Roxas Blvd, Pasay City. Tel: 521 7961-80, Fax: 581302, Tlx: 63487 PN. *P, Gym, Biz. R: L, W. French.*

THE HERITAGE HOTEL, Roxas Blvd cor. Edsa, Pasay. Tel: 891 8888, Fax: 891 8833. *P, Biz, SatTV. R: L, W, Chinese, Italian.*

P — Swimming pool | **Gym** — Health club | **Biz** — Business centre | **Ex** — Executive floor
SatTV — Satellite TV | **R** — Restaurant | **L** — Local food | **W** — Western food

HOTEL GUIDE

HOTEL NIKKO MANILA GARDEN, Ayala Centre, Makati. Tel: 810 4101, Fax: 817 1862, Tlx: 45883 GARDEN PM. *P, Gym. R: L, W, Japanese.*
HOLIDAY INN MANILA PAVILION, United Nations Ave, Manila. Tel: 522 2911, Fax: 522 3531. *P, Gym, Indoor Golf, Biz, Ex, SatTV. R: L, W, French, Chinese.*
MANILA MIDTOWN HOTEL, Pedro Gil St cor. Adriatico St, Ermita. Tel: 521 7001, Fax: 522 2629, Tlx: 27797 MNL. *P, Gym, Biz, Ex, SatTV. R: L, W, Chinese.*
GRAND BOULEVARD HOTEL, 1990 Roxas Blvd, Manila. Tel: 521 0004, Fax: 502526, Tlx: 40332 GBH BMC PM. *P, Biz, SatTV. R: L, W, Japanese, Chinese.*

C: US$75-120

ADMIRAL HOTEL, 2138 Roxas Blvd, Manila. Tel: 572081 to 94, Fax: 522 2018, Tlx: 742 0488 ADHOTEL. *P, Biz, Ex, SatTV. R: L, W.*
BAYVIEW PARK HOTEL, 1118 Roxas Blvd (cor. UN Ave), Ermita, Manila. Tel: 536 1526, Fax: 501953. *P, Biz, SatTV. R: L, W.*

D: US$75 or below

SUNDOWNER HOTEL, 1430 Mabini St, Ermita, Manila. Tel: 521 2751, Fax: 521 5331, Tlx: 63746 SUNDER PN. *Biz. R: L, W.*
CENTURY CITADEL INN MAKATI, 5007 P. Burgos St, Makati. Tel: 892 0149, Fax: 817 1658. *P, Biz, SatTV. R: L, W, Chinese.*
VACATION HOTEL MAKATI, Jacinta Bldg, 914 Pasay Rd, Makati. Tel: 867936 to 37, Fax: 818 7756. *R: L, W, Chinese.*

MINDORO

C: US$75-120

MAMBURAO BEACH RESORT, Mamburao c/o Cityland Condominium 3, Unit 4, Herrera cor. Esteban Sts, Legaspi Village, Makati. Tel: 815 2733 Manila, Fax: 819 1713 Manila, Tlx: 43105 MAXIMA PN. *R: L, W.*

D: US$75 or below

COCO BEACH, Puerta Galera c/o Ground Flr, Legaspi Towers, 300 Vito Cruz cor. Roxas Blvd, Manila. Tel: 521 4693, Fax: 522 2578. *P. R: L, W.*

MISAMIS ORIENTAL

C: US$75-120

PRYCE PLAZA CAGAYAN DE ORO HOTEL, Carmea Hill (c/o 8th Flr, BPI Condominium, Paseo de Roxas, Makati). Tel: 6464 Cagayan de Oro, 818 3421 Manila, Fax: 815 6954 Manila. *R: L,W.*
VACATION HOTEL DE ORO, Corrales Ave cor. R. Chavez, Cagayan de Oro. Tel: 723241 Cagayan de Oro, Fax: 818 7756 Manila. *R: L, W.*

NEGROS OCCIDENTAL (For Bacolod)

D: US$75 or below

BACOLOD CONVENTION PLAZA HOTEL, Magsaysay Ave, Bacolod City. Tel: 83551, Fax: 83392. *P, Biz. R: L, W, Chinese.*
GOLDENFIELD GARDEN HOTEL, Goldenfields Complex, Bacolod City. Tel: 83541, Fax: 22356. *P. R: L, W, Japanese.*

PALAWAN

A: US$160 or above

AMANPULO, Pamalican Island (Manila Sales Office). Tel: 804 0700, Fax: 832 7964. *P. R: L, W.*

B: US$120-160

CLUB NOAH EL NIDO RESORT, Miniloc Island. Tel: 810 7291-93 Manila, Fax: 815 4488 Manila. *R: L, W.*

ZAMBALES (For Subic)

C: US$75-120

SUBIC INTERNATIONAL HOTEL, Subic, Zambales (c/o Rajah Tours, 3/F Physician's Tower, 533 UN Ave, Manila). Tel: Manila 522 0541-48, Fax: Manila 521 2831, Tlx: 40329 RAJAH PM. *P, Ex, SatTV. R: L,W.*

ZAMBOANGA

C: US$75-120

DAKAK PARK AND BEACH RESORT, Dapitan City, Zamboanga del Norte. Tel: Manila 721 0426, Fax: 722 2463, Tlx: 29001 PXO PH. *P, SatTV. R: L, W.*

P — Swimming pool　**Gym** — Health club　**Biz** — Business centre　**Ex** — Executive floor
SatTV — Satellite TV　**R** — Restaurant　**L** — Local food　**W** — Western food

SINGAPORE

In many ways Singapore is the perfect place for the newcomer to Asia. It is like an Asian showhouse. It is tropical, colourful and multiracial. It is picturesque, verdant and striding confidently into the 21st century as a modern, prosperous city-state and fully computerized "smart" island.

Singapore is a showcase of Asia without the poverty, without the overcrowding, or space. It is certainly Asia without the dirt.

It is in every way admirable, but to many it is not quite real. And, to some at least, because every detail seems planned, it is without real character. But for the short-term visitor it has plenty to offer.

Conservation has won a hard-fought battle despite the unrelenting growth of high-rise buildings, new roads and air-conditioned shopping complexes. The ever-pragmatic authorities have come to see conservation as having a dual purpose: reminding Singaporeans of their heritage and also attracting the highly valued tourists. But even the "ethnic" aspects of the city and Singaporean life are carefully contrived.

Singapore — a crossroads for aviation (boasting one of the best modern airports in the world), shipping, business and commerce in much the same way as Hong Kong — has fashioned a new lifestyle for its people. The city-state owes much of its charm to the mixture of Chinese, Malays, Indians and Eurasians. It is still a place where the varied customs of different people are respected; where the East often lives in a very Western setting.

The lifeblood of Singapore is its harbour, and this has been changing considerably of late, in order to serve the types of ships typical of any modernized port, mostly tankers and container vessels, but also a growing number of cruise ships. Ships awaiting a berth stretch in their hundreds towards the islands of neighbouring Indonesia and Malaysia. The country in general enjoys a standard of living well above that of its neighbours, but only has a fraction of their populations and no rural poor.

With that high standard of living comes a strict determination not to let social standards drop. This has resulted in Singapore having rules which impose severe penalties for littering and outlaw chewing gum completely, for instance. Singapore is also one of the countries — referred to in this book's introduction — where the death penalty is applied to those found in possession of illegal drugs.

The republic consists of the island of Singapore, measuring 42 kilometres by 23 kilometres, and 57 smaller islands, the whole area being 626 square kilometres. Lying 136.8 kilometres north of the equator, Singapore is just across the Johor Straits from the southern tip of the Malay Peninsula, and is connected to it by a 1,056-metre causeway carrying a road, railway and water pipeline. A second causeway is being built from Tuas, on the southeastern corner of the island, to Malaysia.

In this multiracial state of just over 3 million (including foreigners on work permits or professional visit passes), Chinese account for 77% of the population, Malays 15%, Indians 6% and Eurasians 2%. This conglomeration makes race,

◄ *Tang Dynasty Village junggler.* PHOTO: PATRICK LUCERO

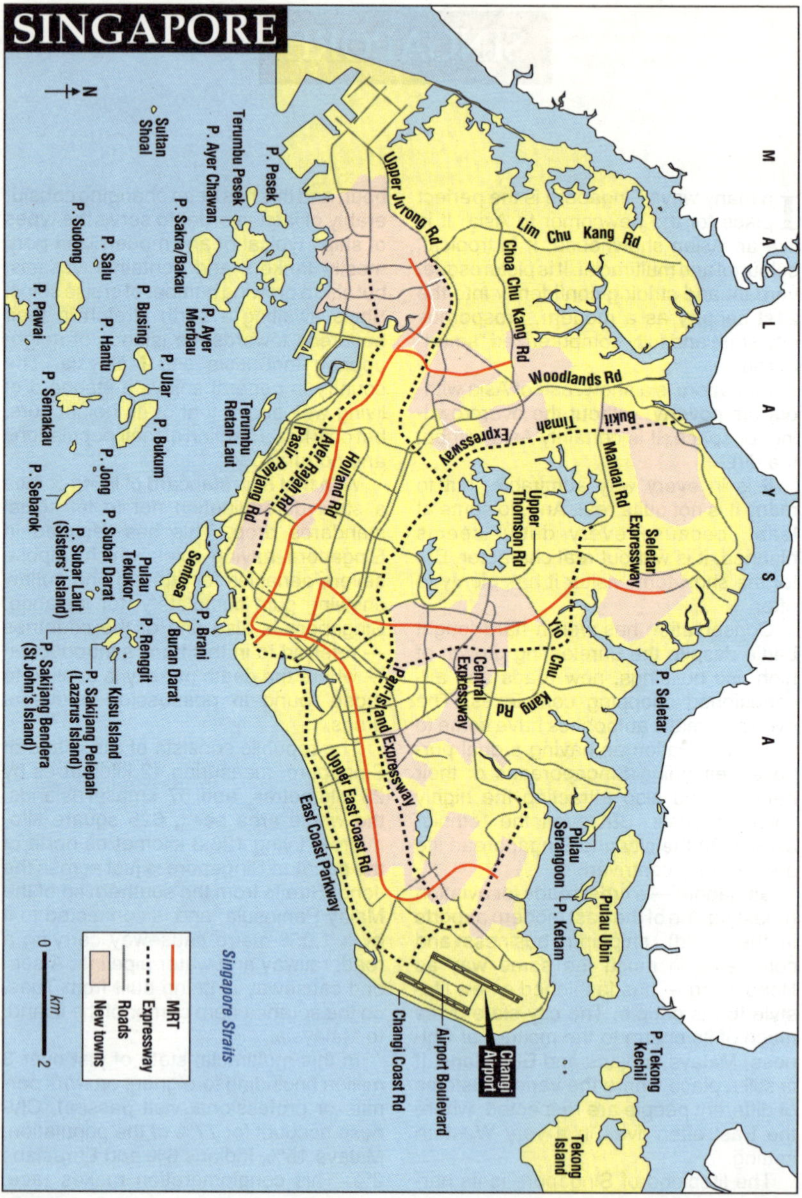
SINGAPORE
MALAYSIA
N
Lim Chu Kang Rd
Choa Chu Kang Rd
Woodlands Rd
Bukit Timah Expressway
Mandai Rd
Upper Thomson Rd
Seletar Expressway
Yio Chu Kang Rd
Central Expressway
Pan-Island Expressway
Upper Jurong Rd
Holland Rd
Ayer Rajah Rd
Pasir Panjang Rd
Upper East Coast Rd
East Coast Parkway
Changi Coast Rd
Airport Boulevard
Changi Airport
P. Seletar
Pulau Serangoon
P. Ketam
Pulau Ubin
P. Tekong Kechil
Tekong Island
P. Pesek
Terumbu Pesek
P. Ayer Chawan
Sultan Shoal
P. Sakra/Bakau
P. Sudong
P. Salu
P. Ayer Merbau
P. Busing
P. Hantu
P. Pawai
P. Ular
P. Semakau
Terumbu Retan Laut
P. Bukum
P. Jong
P. Sebarok
P. Subar Darat
P. Subar Laut (Sisters' Island)
Pulau Tekukor
Sentosa
P. Brani
Buran Darat
P. Renggit
Kusu Island
P. Sakijang Pelepah (Lazarus Island)
P. Sakijang Bendera (St John's Island)
Singapore Straits
0 km 2
MRT
Expressway
Roads
New towns

language and religion sensitive issues. English, widely spoken, is also an official language, serving as the common interracial tongue.

Multiracialism is one of the republic's great attractions. Singapore is an affluent society — the result of vigorous economic growth in the past 20 years. There was a brief but serious recession in 1985-86, but the economy has rebounded and a labour shortage is now inhibiting growth.

With no rural sector to complicate planning, the city-state has been able to push ahead rapidly into steel milling, shipbuilding and high technology, including the information technology and avionics industries.

History

The year 1819 saw the island's rebirth, but it was far from being Singapore's beginning, for its strategic site at the western entrance to the South China Sea made it a linchpin in the ambitions of the several earlier civilizations that have flourished in Southeast Asia. Indians and Chinese set foot in Singapore well before the Spanish and Portuguese.

The Malay name for the island in ancient Javanese chronicles was Temasek, meaning "sea town." Malay histories record that a Palembang prince, Sang Nila Utama, after being driven ashore during a storm, saw something "very swift and beautiful, its body bright red, its head jet black, its breast white, in size rather larger than a goat." Nila Utama was told it was a lion, which he considered to be a lucky sign, founded a city and called it Singapura — "the Lion city." This is almost certainly a myth, probably due to the Indian cultural influence, as it is believed there have never been any type of lions on the Malay peninsula — though there is an indigenous type of tiger in Sumatra, only just across the Malacca Strait.

Singapore was a Malay capital within the Sri Vijaya Empire until it was destroyed in the fighting that accompanied the rise of the Majapahit Kingdom. For a time, under the control of the Thais, Singapore eventually ran down to be little more than a fishing village.

Modern Singapore came into being when Sir Thomas Stamford Raffles, of the British East India Co. concluded a treaty on February 6, 1819, with Sultan Hussein Mohammed Shah and Temenggong Abdul Rahman, which allowed the company to establish a trading post at the mouth of the Singapore River. Full sovereignty over the island was ceded to Britain five years later. In 1826 Singapore was joined with Penang and Malacca to form the Straits Settlements, first administered from Penang but, after 1832, from Singapore. It grew to be the most important entrepot of Southeast Asia and a major British military base.

The Japanese occupation of Singapore in early 1942 brought an end to an extended period of profitable trading and, though entrepot trade resumed after World War II, the end of colonial rule and the changing political state of the whole area were to force Singapore itself to adopt a new outlook.

On June 3, 1959, Lee Kuan Yew became the first prime minister of the self-governing state of Singapore when the People's Action Party (PAP) won the general election. On September 16, 1963, Singapore gained independence from Britain as a member state of the Federation of Malaysia, but on August 9 two years later, Singapore separated from Malaysia and became an independent republic, joining the British Commonwealth on December 22, 1965. A PAP government has been elected by a wide margin ever since. In November 1990, Goh Chok Tong became the country's second prime minister, when Lee stepped down. Lee, however, remains a senior minister in the cabinet and is still a dominant figure.

Entry

Most visitors arrive in Singapore by air, and Changi airport serves 66 scheduled airlines which operate more than 2,800 scheduled flights each week to and from Europe, North America and Australasia and from many points within Asia. Airport tax charged on flights leaving Singapore is S$15.

Although a few people travelling to Singapore on the cheap, particularly from Australia, come by sea from the Indonesian ports of Jakarta or Palembang, these arrivals are not significant. But the country is aiming to be the cruise centre for Southeast Asia with a S$40 million passenger terminal at the **World Trade Centre**. A growing number of firms now offer fly/cruise packages that include a number of destinations in the region, including Japan, Thailand and Australia. All ferry services to Indonesia's Riau Islands leave from the cruise centre.

The Malaysian Railways network extends to Singapore with several trains daily, including an overnight train with sleeping berths, from Kuala Lumpur. It is possible to travel by train from Singapore all the way to Bangkok, Thailand (*see Transport*).

Immigration

Everyone entering or leaving Singapore must be in possession of valid passports or internationally recognized travel documents endorsed for Singapore when necessary.

Visas even for short social visits are required by nationals of Afghanistan, India, Cambodia, Laos, China, Russia, Vietnam, holders of refugee travel documents issued by the Middle East countries to Palestinian refugees and holders of Hong Kong certificates of identity. Stateless persons must in all cases be in possession of valid visas for Singapore.

Holders of valid Chinese passports may visit for a maximum of 24 hours without visas provided they hold confirmed onward/return bookings and tickets. Holders of Taiwan passports do not require visas as tourists but they must have visa cards, which can be obtained free from any Singapore overseas mission, airline or shipping company.

Health

Valid certificates of vaccination against yellow fever are required for any one above the age of one who has passed through any endemic zone in Africa or South America.

Customs

A 3% Goods and Services Tax (GST) has been in effect since April 1994. Tourists, however, can apply for a refund if they are taking purchases valued at S$500 or more home with them. To qualify for the refund, the purchases must be made in one outlet or separate outlets of the same company. They must first fill up a GST Claims Form available from participating retailers (not all shops provide GST refunds). The Claims Form is submitted together with purchases to the GST Refund Inspection Counter at Changi airport. Refunds will be made by the retailers, so it is best to agree to the form of the refund (credit card refund, cash or cheque).

Bona fide travellers other than those below 18 years of age or those coming from Malaysia may bring in duty-free one litre of wine, one litre of beer or stout or ale or port, and a litre of spirits; reasonable quantities of personal effects and household goods. These items are also granted GST relief provided travellers have spent more than 48 hours outside Singapore before their arrival. There are no duty-free concessions for cigarettes and tobacco.

Import permits are required for arms, ammunition, animals and birds and their by-products, live plants and seeds; poisons, vaccines, serum and controlled drugs, arms and explosives, bullet-proof clothing; toy guns, pistols, revolvers and walkie-talkies; weapons such as daggers, spears and swords; cartridges, cassettes and pre-recorded cine film, video tapes or discs, telecommunication and radio communication equipment.

The following are prohibited: controlled drugs, obscene publications, seditious and treasonable material, endangered species of wildlife and their by-products (including ivory) and reproductions of copyright publications, video tapes or discs, records or cassettes and chewing gum, chewing tobacco and imitation tobacco products.

The mandatory death sentence applies to people convicted of carrying more than 15 grams of heroin, 30 grams of morphine, 30 grams of cocaine, 200 grams of cannabis resin (hashish), 500 grams of cannabis or 1.2 kilograms of opium. This law is strictly enforced and many executions have been carried out. There is no exemption for foreigners.

Currency

There is no currency restriction in Singapore. The unit of currency is the Singapore dollar (S$) exchanging in early 1995 at approximately S$1.45:US$1. The Singapore dollar is divided into 100 cents, and S$10,000, 1,000, 500, 100, 50, 25, 10, 2 and 1 notes are in circulation, along with S$1 and 50 cent, 20, 10 and 5 cent coins. Money may be changed at banks or with official money-changers. Hotel exchange rates are always bad, so try the licensed money-changer located in almost every shopping complex.

Singapore is the best place in Southeast Asia for purchasing Asian currencies on the free market. Travellers' cheques denominated in Singapore dollars can be bought at any of the local banks.

Language

English is the language of business, administration and the law, and is widely understood. There are three other official languages: Mandarin (Chinese), Malay and Tamil. The main Chinese dialects are Hokkien, Cantonese, Teochew, Hainanese, Hakka and Foochow, though their use is being officially discouraged in favour of Mandarin. Indian languages such as Telegu, Urdu, Malayalam, Punjabi, Gujarah, Hindi and Bengali are also spoken. The lingual versatility of most Singaporeans is impressive.

Climate

Conditions are tropical. Daily temperatures are uniformly high, though rarely above 24°C at night. There is no distinct wet or dry season but from November to January during the northeast monsoon, it rains frequently. Showers are sudden and heavy, but in most cases brief.

Dress

Shirt and tie or blouse and skirt usually suffice for daytime office appointments. Some of the more up-market hotels and restaurants will require a man to wear a jacket at dinner. There is a need for frequent changes of clothing due to the heat and humidity. A jacket, shawl or light woollen cardigan is often required to combat intense air-conditioning in restaurants or office.

Business Hours

Government offices and commercial firms keep staggered hours, starting between 7:30 a.m. and 9 a.m. and closing between 4 p.m. and 5 p.m. Monday to Friday and between noon and 1 p.m. on Saturday. Bank hours are from 9:30 a.m.-3 p.m. Monday to Friday, and from 9:30-11:30 a.m. on Saturday. Two United Overseas Bank branches and three Oversea-Chinese Banking Corp. branches open on Sundays. Two of these are in the Orchard Rd tourist belt. Most post offices are open 8 a.m.-5 p.m. Monday to Friday and 8 a.m.-1 p.m. on Saturday. However, the General Post Offices at Fullerton Bldg and Comcentre at Somerset Rd are open 24 hours and the airport and Takashimaya Shopping Centre post offices are open seven days a week, including public holidays, from 8 a.m.-8 p.m. The post office at CK Tang's is open 10 a.m.-7 p.m. Monday to Friday and 10 a.m.-2 p.m. on Saturdays. Most shops open relatively late, at 10 a.m., but many stores catering to tourists stay open until 9:30 p.m. Shops in the big shopping malls and some small local shops are open on Sundays.

CHAMBERS OF COMMERCE

American Chamber of Commerce, Shaw Centre, 16-07, 1 Scotts Rd. Tel: 235 0077, Fax: 732 5517.

British Business Assoc., 41 Duxton Rd. Tel: 227 7861, Fax: 227 7021.

French Business Assoc., 89 Neil Rd, Tel: 226 6101, Fax: 226 6378.

Indonesian Business Assoc., 158 Cecil St, 07-03. Tel: 221 5063.

Japanese Chamber of Commerce & Industry, 10 Shenton Way, 12-04. Tel: 221 0541, Fax: 225 6197.

Singapore Chinese Chamber of Commerce & Industry, 47 Hill St. Tel: 337 8381, Fax: 339 0605.

Singapore Indian Chamber of Commerce & Industry, 23-01 Tong Eng Bldg. Tel: 222 2855, Fax: 223 1707.

Singapore International Chamber of Commerce, Denmark House 05-00, 6 Raffles Quay. Tel: 224 1255, Fax: 224 2758.

Singapore Malay Chamber of Commerce, 24-07 International Plaza, 10 Anson Rd. Tel: 221 1066, Fax: 223 5811.

Singapore Manufacturers' Assoc., 20 Orchard Rd. Tel: 338 8787, Fax: 338 3358.

Singapore Pakistan Chamber of Commerce, 171 Tras St, 07-177. Tel: 224 8562.

Doing Business

The standard business attire is shirt and tie or blouse and skirt. There are many women in senior positions in Singapore business. Woman generally do not wear trousers to work.

Singaporeans are fully conversant with Western practices such as shaking hands and, like the Japanese, seem to loosen up a little after business cards have been exchanged.

Singapore cityscape. PHOTO: VERONICA GARBUTT

Acquiring social graces is not high on Singaporeans' list of priorities, so at a first meeting get down to business and cut out any attempts at small talk.

Smoking is banned indoors (Singapore is determined to be a smoke-free island) and it is best to ask the host's permission when visiting people's homes if you must light up.

If you do not want to be taken to a nightclub or karaoke lounge, say so, or your host may feel obliged to do it. Many businessmen will be more than happy to play a round of golf with you instead. The younger businessmen drink a lot less alcohol than their fathers, although a glass of wine or beer at the end of the day is generally enjoyed. Very few women drink. There are stiff penalties for drunk driving.

If you have any critical views about the Singapore business or political scene, it is best to keep them to yourself, as Singaporeans do not accept criticism well. Sincere compliments are welcome. Any action which might hint at bribery is absolutely not acceptable. If invited to a Singaporean home, small gifts are appreciated but not necessary, but do not embarrass your host with something expensive. Exotic foods (your national specialities, for instance) are often a good choice, since virtually all Singaporeans are interested in food.

Car rentals are available in a full range to suit your budget, but it is always easier to rent big cars than small ones.

For courier or secretarial services, see the Yellow Pages of the telephone directory or simply ask your hotel.

Rip-Offs

As everywhere, the old adage about a fool and his money being soon parted is still true in Singapore despite official disapproval of people taking advantage of tourists.

The tourist who finds the friendly shop-owner transformed into an unpleasant bully who refuses to refund the cost of malfunctioning items should take the matter up immediately with the police. Action will be taken over any criminal offence, even if the tourist is home long before the shop-owner makes a court appearance. Bad publicity about such rip-off shops often follows as the newspapers take a dim view of such traders.

A tourist intent on buying any electrical appliances, including home entertainment, in Singapore in the belief that they will be cheaper, should bring along comparative prices of equipment on sale at home. Almost invariably, the service warranty will not apply back home, making repairs a costly business that could erode any savings from buying in Singapore.

While the problem of fakes is much reduced in Singapore because the government has cracked down on blatant trademark infringements, fakes can still be found, especially among cameras, watches and famous brands of leather goods. Buyers of brand-name leather accessories should insist on certificates of ownership that come with authentic makes.

Word of mouth (from friends and associates) about which shop to patronize is best; do not pay much attention to "recommendations" from hotel staff. Always keep receipts of purchases in case of trouble with the item purchased. Evidence of purchase is essential before any recourse can be sought.

And beware of travelling fortune tellers, whose persistence is always more remarkable than their clairvoyance.

Media

The local English-language daily newspapers are *The Straits Times*, *Business Times* and the afternoon tabloid, *The New Paper*. The *International Herald Tribune* is available on day of publication. The regional daily *Asian Wall Street Journal* is widely available on day of publication, though the Singapore Government currently allows only a limited number of copies to be sold. *Playboy*, *Penthouse* and *Cosmopolitan* are not allowed to circulate.

Communications

Singapore has arguably the best worldwide communications network in Asia and direct dialling to all parts of the world is available at all hotels. Mobile telephones can be rented from Singapore Telecom. For IDD enquiries, dial 104; for local numbers, dial 100. Calls made from hotel rooms now cost the same as from call boxes. For calls made outside, it is advisable to buy S$2 phone cards as there are more call boxes that take cards than coin-operated call boxes.

Transport

FROM THE AIRPORT: Taxis are metered, but there is a S$3 surcharge for journeys to and from Changi and Seletar Airports. A one-way trip should be around S$20, including surcharge. A bus service runs from the airport to hotels in the **Orchard Rd-Scotts Rd** area, while a number of others travel to various points on the island.

MRT: The fastest and most comfortable way to get around Singapore is by the **Mass Rapid Transit** which operates from 6 a.m. - midnight. There are two lines: north-south and east-west. S$10 stored value tickets (also valid on buses) are recommended if you want to spare yourself the effort of figuring out the local currency each time you take a trip. Fares of 60 cents-S$1.40 are cheap for the comfort and efficiency of the service.

TAXIS: In central Singapore they may stop only at designated ranks, where queues at rush hours are long. The charge is a standard S$2.40 for the first 1.5 kilometres and 10 cents for each additional 240 metres thereafter. There is an extra S$1 charge for trips originating in the central business district (CBD) at 4-7 p.m. weekdays and 12-3 p.m. on Saturday. Between midnight and 6 a.m. there is a surcharge of 50%. Multiple-loading taxis operate from the city to the Johor Baru, charging S$6-7 per passenger. These can be hired at Ban San St taxi stand. It is possible to dial a taxi but you should allow yourself plenty of time and be patient. A booking fee of S$3.20 is charged. For the 24-hour dial-a-taxi service, call 1 800 452 5555 or Fax: 1 800 456 6336.

BUSES: The Singapore Bus Service (SBS) fleet runs from 6 a.m.-11:30 p.m. and fares are low. Check the numbers in the very useful **Singapore Bus Guide**. However, a bus ride is recommended only for the adventurous as the bus service in Singapore is not on a par with modern development in the country. SBS operates a few air-conditioned services. **Singapore Explorer Tickets** costing S$5 for a one-day ticket and S$12 for a three-day ticket will take you to most of the tourist attractions. Bus services to **Malaysia** are readily available. Buses cross the causeway to the Malaysia's southern state capital, **Johor Baru**. Buses also run from Johor Baru and other towns in southern Malaysia to Singapore. Express buses to **Malacca** direct from Singapore leave seven times a day from the Lavender St depot and fares are S$11 for adults and S$5.50 for children. There is a twice-daily bus service to the Malaysian capital, **Kuala Lumpur**, costing S$17, and departing from Rochor Rd. Taxis to Kuala Lumpur cost S$40 per person or S$160 for individual hire.

TRAINS: Apart from a cheap rail link to **Malaysia**, there is a luxurious service, the Eastern & Oriental Express, that runs from Singapore to **Bangkok**, stopping at **Kuala Lumpur** and **Butterworth** in Malaysia, and **Hat Yai**, **Surat Thani** and **Hua Hin** in Thailand. Singapore-Bangkok one-way costs from S$1,920, with full board and shared compartments. (Tel: 323 4390)

TRISHAWS: A few pedal-driven trishaws remain on Singapore's streets. A group cluster in the shady nook around the Queen St/Bras Basah Rd junction. Prices are comparable to those of taxis. You should negotiate the price before you start the trip. They are increasingly becoming a tourist attraction. Trishaw drivers seem to think they have right of way anywhere and ignore vehicles, which can make for an exhilarating — and sometimes hair-raising — experience.

SELF-DRIVE CARS: Self-drive cars can be hired in Singapore and driven to **Malaysia**. To hire a car, all that is needed is a valid driver's licence from your own country or an international driving permit. Self-drive rates: from S$199 a day from major car hire firms plus S$20 a day for insurance. Chauffeur-driven air-conditioned cars are available from S$49-79 per hour. Traffic uses the left-hand side of the road in both countries.

Because of cheaper petrol prices in Malaysia and to prevent Singaporeans crossing the border merely to fill their tanks and return, no vehicle is allowed across the causeway from Singapore unless its tank is at least three-quarters full, and this is strictly enforced, with a S$500 fine, so make sure you conform.

BOATS: may be hired from **Clifford Pier** on **Collyer Quay**. Naturally the price depends on the size of the craft. A junk tour costs about S$20 for a two-and-a-half-hour run around the harbour. One can also cruise on a Chinese junk touring the harbour and island with buffet dinner on board, at a cost of about S$37; half-price for children. Motor boats for water skiing (with driver) rent for about S$65 per hour at **Sembawang Park** (**Bernatt Boating and Skiing**, Tel: 257 5859) on the island's northern side. Boat charters are available to **Malaysia** and **Indonesia**. Book two weeks ahead for weekend charters, but weekday cruises can be arranged at shorter notice.

Cruise operators on the second storey of the **World Trade Centre** (next to the **Cruise Centre**) offer a variety of trips to islands around Singapore, including Indonesian islands.

Tours

Many operators run package tours of the city, harbour or the island or across to Johor and up into Malaysia for trips lasting several days. See the classified ads in the local press, or enquire through travel agents or from the hotel lobby for information concerning various kinds of tours which operate almost daily. A simple city tour lasting three-and-a-half hours by coach costs S$23. For privately arranged tours, visitors are advised to use only **Singapore Tourist Promotion Board** licensed tourist guides who wear special badges and carry licences which must be shown on request. English-speaking guides charge S$50 for a half-day tour. Call the **Singapore Tourist Guides Association** for more information.

Accommodation

Hotel facilities are excellent though accommodation rates, like prices generally over the past several years, have risen to levels comparable with the most expensive cities in the world. Do not hesitate to ask for a discount, however. All hotels give "corporate" discounts.

The centre of gravity of the top-class hotels has shifted slightly away from Orchard Rd with the developments on or near the land reclaimed from the harbours, which include the twin towers of the **Westin Stamford** and **Westin Plaza** and the **Pan Pacific**, the **Marina Mandarin** and the **Oriental** all in **Marina Square**.

Most hotels have shopping arcades, several bars, business centres, health clubs, swimming pools and even art galleries. Some hotels have answering machines in rooms. Guests at other slightly less luxurious hotels are scarcely handicapped since the city offers any missing service within a reasonable distance.

For the romantics the "Grand Old Lady" — **Raffles Hotel** — is back after a major S$160 million restructuring, with a row of exclusive boutiques that now front North Bridge Rd. The enlarged hotel, still boasts its beautiful old Palm Court garden. Traditional Singapore Slings are served (now costing S$14.87) in the reconstructed Long Bar, now on the second and third storeys, the only place in Singapore where it is OK to litter (the floor with peanut shells).

Owing to personal taste and cultural preference, you will find certain nationalities tend to cluster in certain hotels. For instance, Americans tend to go for the known quantities — **Holiday Inn**, **Hilton** and **Westin**, whereas the French gather at the **Omni Marco Polo**, the **Meridien** or **Novotel Orchid** in Dunearn Rd. The Japanese tend to go to the **Harbour View Dai-Ichi** (located in the banking district), the **New Otani** and the **Crown Prince.** New hotels have opened: the five-star **Four Seasons** and the **Albert Court**. Boutique hotels offer a change from the huge facilities in Orchard Rd: in Chinatown there is the 49-room **Duxton**, while **Lloyds Inn** behind Orchard Rd is popular. Resort hotels on Sentosa (now linked to Singapore by causeway) are relaxing places for families — the **Beaufort**, a colonial-style rest-house, and the Shangri-la's **Rasa Sentosa**. All hotels impose a 10% service charge, a 3% government tax and 1% GST on room charges and on food, drink and other items.

Dining

For variety, quality and fair price, food is one of the main attractions of Singapore and eating is a national pastime. The island's mixed racial population, and the country's position on the sea/air routes between East and West over the past 170 years, have enabled its cooks to take wisely a little of this and a pinch of that to add to the collection of dishes that today constitute great Singapore food. Sometimes dishes have been modified under the influence of the new environment — as happened to southern Chinese cooking subjected to the spices of the Malay people and which is now known as *nonya* food. Nonya food is Straits-born (from Penang and Malacca) Chinese cooking which has become the indigenous cuisine. There are good Nonya specialist restaurants and the more popular nonya dishes, such as *laksa*, are available in most hotel coffee shops. **Violet Oon's Kitchen** in Bukit Pasoh Rd and the Apollo Hotel's **Luna Coffee House** are among those which offer nonya food of a consistently high standard, the latter in buffet form.

Some dishes, despite their names, are unique to Singapore. No one on China's Hainan island, for instance, has ever heard of a dish called Hainanese chicken rice. You will find Singapore's version of Cantonese, Peking, Sichuan, Shanghainese, Hunan, Hokkien, Teochew, Hakka and Hainanese food in a range of settings, from simple, cheap — and clean — hawker stalls to expensive restaurants. The stalls are regularly inspected for hygiene and nobody needs hesitate to use them. Most are in modern "food centres" where stalls serving Chinese, Malay and Indian food can all be found. Simply find a table (which is numbered), walk from stall to stall selecting the dishes you fancy, and they will be brought to you within minutes. Smoking is banned in all air-conditioned buildings, so coffee shops offer a rare opportunity for those who like to light up at meal times.

The Guide to Singapore Hawker Food by James Hooi (S$2.80 or US$2) is indispensable to food lovers who want to work their way through the virtually limitless range of hawker food. Armed with Hooi's guide, a visit to the **Satay Club** on Queen Elizabeth Walk and **Newton Circus** food stalls are a must, especially as these are scheduled to be torn down. Hawker food anywhere in Singapore is tasty, but where local patrons converge in large numbers is a good guide. Chilli crab is a famous Singapore dish. **The Seafood Centre** along the East Coast Parkway has a bewildering choice of restaurants. The supermarket-style restaurant at the **Big Splash** amusement centre in the East Coast Park — where you choose your raw seafood at a counter and it is then cooked for you — is another place which offers fresh seafood in an outdoor setting. The **No Name Seafood** stall at Farrer Park hawker centre is so popular in the evenings that long waits are commonplace.

As the Chinese represent nearly 80% of the republic's population, Chinese restaurants are more abundant than others. Although Hokkien-speakers predominate in the population, more Chinese restaurants serve Cantonese food than any other dialect group's cuisine.

Some of the better Cantonese restaurants in hotels include: **Shang Palace** in the Shangri-La Hotel; **Li Bai** at the Sheraton Towers; the **Summer Palace** at the Regent; **Inn of Happiness** at the Hilton; **Lei Garden** at the Boulevard; **Fragrant Blossom** at the Holiday Inn Park View; **Xin Cuisine** at the Concorde and **Tsui Hang Village** at the Hotel Asia. The **Wang Jiang Lou** at Clarke Quay has developed loyal patronage in a short time.

Many hotel Cantonese restaurants, such as the **Garden Seafood Restaurant** in the Goodwood Park, serve *dim sum* for lunch. Those who enjoy exotic food with health enhancing ingredients should try the **Imperial Herbal**

Restaurant in the Metropole Hotel on Seah St. **The Mouth** in Chinatown Point serves Chinese food at all hours.

For Peking food, try the **Jade Room** in Lucky Plaza shopping complex, **Pine Court** in the Mandarin Hotel, **Eastern Palace** in Supreme House and the revolving restaurant in **Prima Tower** in Keppel Rd.

After Cantonese, the hot and spicy Sichuan food is the next most popular cuisine. It is served in the following hotels: **Tai Pan Ramada**, **Novotel Orchid Inn**, **King's Hotel**, **Crown Prince Hotel**, **River View Hotel**, **Equatorial**, **Royal Holiday Inn**, **Grand Central**, **New Otani**, **Goodwood Park** and **Westin Plaza**.

Hokkien, Teochew, Hakka and Hainanese foods are found mostly in small coffee shops and food stalls plus such restaurants as the **Moi Kong** (Hakka) or **Beng Hiang** (Hokkien) in **Food Alley** on Murray St, or Teochew havens such as the **Ban Heng** on Boon Keng Rd, the **Ellenborough Market** stalls on Teochew St, or the **Guan Hin** on Whampoa West. The coffee shop along **Ophir Rd**, just before the Beach Rd junction, offers excellent Teochew dishes in the evening, when lighter traffic allows tables to be set up by the roadside. Occasionally, plush hotels pick some favourites from these types of food to add to their menus in the coffee shops under the heading of local dishes. The hawker stalls of **Rasa Sentosa Resort** in the evening offer a tasty and atmospheric variation to restaurant or fast-food meals on the resort island.

Malay food is best described as something between nonya (except that no pork is used) and mild Indian cooking. **Aziza's** in Emerald Hill Rd is about the most upmarket Malay restaurant. **Bintang Timur** in Far East Plaza is a more modest establishment. The most well-known Malay dish, satay, is served in nearly all hotel coffee shops and pool sides as well as at the development-doomed **Satay Club**. Tasting very similar to Malay food, but with more places serving it, is the Singapore version of Indonesian food. There are numerous Indonesian restaurants. They include the restaurant in the **Apollo Hotel**, **Jawa Timur** at Chiat Hong Bldg, **Tambuah Mas** in the Tanglin Shopping Centre, and **Sanur** in Centrepoint. The last two have branches all over Singapore, so check in the telephone directory for locations.

The Singapore penchant for adapting food also applies to Indian cuisine. Fish-head curry is one of the most popular local Indian dishes and can be found at several modestly priced restaurants in Race Course Rd. **Banana Leaf Apolo** — the spelling is correct if unconventional — is world famous for its curries, eaten with the fingers from, of course, banana leaves. A folk and spoon will be provided on request. The more humble eating establishments offer south Indian food, which tends to be hotter than its northern counterpart, including vegetarian dishes. Try the **Keralan Restaurant** in Food Alley on Murray St, or **Jubilee** on North Bridge Rd. For Indian vegetarian food, the **Komala Villas** and the **New Woodlands** on Serangoon Rd are recommended. The Indian *rojak* (deep-fried vegetable salad) stall on the second level of the **Farrer Park** hawker centre is tops with many foodies. The curry tiffin at **The Tiffin Room** at Raffles Hotel is pricey but good.

Singaporeans have adventurous taste-buds and so Korean, Japanese, Vietnamese and Thai food provide interesting Asian varieties. The **Han Do** in the Orchard Shopping Centre is well known for Korean food. The **Chao Phraya Thai Seafood Market & Restaurant** at Block 730, Ave 6, Ang Mo Kio is one of the oldest — and off the beaten track — of the Thai favourites, and well worth finding. **Saigon** in Cairnhill Place is a little hard to find but its Vietnamese food is excellent.

There are quite a few good Japanese restaurants, many in the Japanese-owned hotels. **Fujiya** in the multi-storey car park in Market St is one of the oldest and best. **Yamagen** in Yen San Bldg, **Sushi Nagawa** at the Crown Prince Hotel and **Kokishin** in the Boulevard Hotel are all popular. Japanese food in Singapore, as elsewhere, is expensive but supermarkets now sell take-away fresh sushi at 50 cents-S$2 a piece — the best fast-food development in years.

Western food is readily available. The **Hard Rock Cafe** just behind the Forum has good hamburgers and wickedly delicious brownies. **Royal Holiday Inn** has Austrian and German restaurants. The **Brasserie** in the Omni Marco Polo has a good atmosphere and simple but good French food. **Belvedere** in the Mandarin Hotel provides another variety. **Le Restaurant de France** in the Hotel Meridien is expensive, as is **Maxim's** in the Regent. **Nutmeg** in the Hyatt Regency has excellent food, a New York art deco atmosphere and (on Sunday until 3 p.m.) jazz. **Liana's** at The Oriental has different food themes throughout the year.

Of the Italian restaurants, **Prego** in the

Dancing fountains at Sentosa. PHOTO: PATRICK LUCERO

Westin Stamford, and **Pete's Place** in the Hyatt are the most popular. **Pasta Fresca** in Royalville, Upper Bt. Timah Rd and its branch on Boat Quay are small and trendy. **Seasons** at the Fours Seasons Hotel offers Italian/Californian cuisine and has an excellent wine list. Other restaurants serving French, Italian, Swiss and German-style dishes are **Latour** (Shangri-La), **Compass Rose** in the Westin Stamford, **Gordon Grill** in the Goodwood Park, **Liana's** at The Oriental and **Harbour Grill** in the Hilton. For Mexican food try **El Felipe's** at Holland Village or **Pancho V** in the Westin Stamford. After **Holland Village**, the trendiest and most cosmopolitan restaurant sectors are at **Boat Quay** and **Clarke Quay** on opposite sides of the Singapore River. Trendy carnivores are packing it in at **Brazil Churrascaria** on Sixth Ave, near the Bukit Timah Rd junction, where barbecued meats are served at your table.

Wines and other forms of alcoholic drinks are expensive. Anchor and Tiger beers are the local brews, but imported beers are widely available.

Entertainment

Hotels and cabarets provide ample opportunity for a good night out. The entertainment features excellent music from a number of imported bands and local groups. Once in a while international stars give performances in Singapore, (see the daily newspapers for entertainment news) but tickets can be hard to come by, especially during the biennial Arts Festival in June.

In general, the entertainment scene in Singapore is in keeping with the clean-cut mould into which the population has been eased. Perhaps because of government policy, the entertainment and arts scene lacks some of the excitement one would find in other less structured countries. Adult-rated films (a long way from hard-core pornography) have been spared censorship but can only be seen by over-21s. There are 91 air-conditioned cinemas, many with the latest digital sound systems, screening Western, Chinese, Indian, Malay or Indonesian films.

Singapore is building tourist entertainment in line with Western tastes, but Chinese cultural events are growing with the heightened consciousness of their cultural heritage among Chinese.

Piano bars are quite popular, but the rage is karaoke. **Java Jive** in Holland Village is one of many karaoke bars. But if you want professional musicians rather than often soused amateurs, go to **Fabrice's World Music Bar** for Latin rock. **Brannigan's** at the Hyatt Regency has jam sessions, while jazz is played at the **Saxophone** in Cuppage Terrace.

The Neptune Theatre Restaurant on Clifford Pier offers the big night out — dinner, dancing and a floorshow. These are top class with prices to match. There is no cover charge at the Neptune. **The Oasis** at Kallang Park offers a slightly less traditional evening out with girls available for chatting and dancing in addition to the food and music. For a raunchy yuppie Singaporean cabaret, the **Boom Boom Room** in Bugis St is great fun. Its star attraction is Kumar, an entertainer whose "confused" sexuality often brings the house down.

The best discos include: **Scandals** in Westin Plaza, Shangri-La's **Xanadu**, with girl bartenders, **Caesar's** in Orchard Towers, **Europa Ridley's** at the Ana Hotel, **Sparks** at Takashimaya Shopping Centre, **Studebaker's** at Pacific Plaza and **Zouk** by the Singapore River.

Another sort of entertainment is the occasional performances of Chinese *wayang* (Malay for performance). See the tourist publication *Singapore This Week* for places and times. Wayang is usually performed during festive occasions or for religious thanksgiving.

In keeping with the government's emphasis on a clean-living image and lack of corruption, there certainly is no equivalent to the raunchy girlie-bars of Bangkok or Manila, though there are a few vestiges of the old red-light districts, in Geylang and Desker Rd, which are orderly because they are policed. The notorious Bugis St, once famous for its transvestites, is gone. The transvestites have mostly dispersed, but some are still found around town late at night. They are sometimes seen at the new Bugis St, or in the Orchard Rd tourist area, but move their venue from place to place because they are subject to arrest for soliciting. Clusters of "sisters" hang out in Changi Village too. By far the best and safest way for a tired businessman to find female company is through the several escort agencies which advertise in the Yellow Pages of the telephone directory.

Shopping

Singapore enjoys much the same duty-free status as Hong Kong, but with the strong Singapore dollar and a 3% Goods and Services Tax, its prices for popular purchases (computers, electronics goods, shoes and handbags) are now similar to those in major cities. However, Singapore is the handicraft retail centre of the region. If you cannot visit other countries in the region, then buying in Singapore is an option. Although the range is never as wide or as cheap as you can get in the source countries, at least the prices are fair.

Things to look out for include silver, pewter, silk and batik. True handmade batik from Indonesia is far superior to the cheaper machine-printed batik on the market, but you need expert help in telling them apart. Indonesian wood-carvings from Bali are another excellent buy. **The Museum Shop** in Hill St is worth a visit for its excellent selection of ethnic handicrafts from the region.

It is best to buy at a shop displaying the lion-headed fish-bodied "Merlion" sign, marking retailers approved by the Consumers' Association of Singapore and the Singapore Tourist Promotion Board. For photographic and sound equipment, electrical goods and watches, buy at a store which is accredited to the manufacturer of the item you are buying and always get the manufacturer's guarantee rather than the shop's.

For those interested in paintings and art by locals, there are several art galleries in which to browse — usually in shopping centres and hotels. **Art Forum** in Cairnhill Rd, which specializes in art by Southeast Asians, is another place for browsing. In many of the shops selling Chinese artifacts, one can buy Chinese scroll paintings.

Gold and silverware, pearl, jade and other precious stones are sold at good prices, but should only be bought at recommended shops unless you are an expert. Goldsmiths along **North Bridge Rd** and the **People's Park Complex** offer competitive prices. Nothing is price-tagged, because gold items are sold by weight, set according to the day's gold price. While you cannot bargain over the gold price, feel free to get a good price for the workmanship.

Products from China are sold in Singapore, though in a very limited range compared with Hong Kong. Tianjin carpets and rosewood furniture in Chinese style are wonderful buys. The modern Chinese often have a sense of taste which is foreign to the discerning visitor, and thus some of their simple and elegant products are cheap while their garish items are expensive. If your taste runs to the simple, you can often pick up a real bargain.

Persian, Afghan and Baluchi carpets are sold in shops along **Orchard Rd** and **Tanglin Rd**. Carpets are duty-free items, both machine — and handmade. Taiping carpets are manufactured locally. Singapore-made cane furniture is sought after because of its low price.

Orchard Rd is the main shopping area for tourists and the shopping complexes along its one-kilometre length are served by one of three MRT stations — Dhoby Ghaut, Somerset and Orchard. But Orchard Rd is only the mecca for fashionable items. Look for spices in **Little India**, which leads off Serangoon Rd. For Chinese herbs and foodstuffs try **Chinatown** off South Bridge Rd.

Popular centres like the **People's Park Complex**, **Rochor Plaza** or **Sim Lim Towers** are not the cheapest places to shop (except for fabrics and haberdashery at People's Park). Often, however, after some hard bargaining, you see the same goods in a department store even cheaper. But such bargaining is fun and gets you into contact with local people, and the price differences do not amount to a rip-off. It is best to bargain only if you really want the item. A touch of humour is always helpful. Shopkeepers justifiably dislike people who waste their time haggling and walk away after the price has been lowered, but do not feel obliged to buy.

Sports

Apart from sports facilities such as tennis and squash offered by many of the bigger hotels, courts costing S$3-6 an hour are available at the **Clementi Recreation Centre** in West Coast Walk, the **East Coast Recreation Centre**, and at **Farrer Park**. One usually has to book a few days in advance for a court.

There are 17 golf courses (13 with 18 holes and three with nine). Visitors should contact the **Singapore Island Country Club** or one of the other clubs directly and request permission to play. Be prepared for high green fees (S$40-100) on weekdays. A cheaper alternative is **Green Fairways** (Tel: 468 7043) beside the Bukit Timah Turf Club on Eng Neo Ave. It has a driving range and a nine-hole course, and having a swing there is no hassle.

In the heart of the city, on the **Padang** (literally "field" in Malay) — stretching between the Singapore Cricket Club and the now demolished Singapore Recreation Club — passers-by can enjoy watching sports being played late on most afternoons, and at weekends there is often a cricket match in progress. Polo matches can be seen at the **Singapore Polo Club** in Thompson Rd, on Tuesdays, Thursdays, Saturdays (5:45 p.m.) and Sundays 5:30 p.m. during the season from mid-January to late October. Horse riding at S$50 for 45 minutes is offered at the polo club. Horse racing at the **Bukit Turf Club** is on most weekends. Race meetings alternate between Singapore and Malaysia.

PHOTO: SINGAPORE TOURIST PROMOTION BOARD

Festive charm.

Although Singapore is a tropical island and the sea can be seen from many places, it has no beach worthy of the name. There are some artificial beaches where sand has been deposited, such as at **Changi Beach**, **East Coast Park** and **Sentosa**. If you swim at one of these beaches check the tide information in the daily press — to avoid mud at low tide. For water-skiing go to **Sembawang Park** (turn right after the bus terminus) on the north of the island where there are speedboats and skis for hire. But the water there is not particularly clear.

Amateur pilots should contact the **Singapore Flying Club,** which offers Cessna, Piper or Twin Comanche aircraft. The club is near Seletar Air Base.

And then, there's jogging: Singapore's green surroundings and pavements make it a jogger's paradise, with tracks around the reservoirs, the **Botanical Gardens** and parks in the new towns.

Holidays

Singapore's calendar of festivals points up the multiracial nature of the republic's community. Chinese festivals are most common, though Indian festivals compete as intriguing spectacles and the Muslim community offers its solemn occasions of prayer and the beauty of its traditional wedding ceremonies. To offset the watering down of tradition behind such celebrations which have taken place, organizations have begun to put on events such as the *Chingay* procession down Orchard Rd during Chinese New Year. Visitors should take the opportunity to attend celebrations — which make for wonderful photographs.

Most festivals change their date of celebration from one year to the next because of the lunar calendar. Not all festivals are public holidays. Those dates listed below for celebration subject to the lunar calendar are the closest approximation for 1995. In Singapore as well as Malaysia, where a holiday falls on a Sunday, the day following is a public holiday.

January 1: New Year's Day (public holiday).

January: Ponggal, the southern Indians' thanksgiving, using rice in offerings to the gods. Go to the **Sri Srinivasa Perumal Temple** in Serangoon Rd to observe these rites.

February: Thaipusam. On this day Hindu devotees doing penance for their sins and those who have made pledges during serious illness carry *kavadis* (spiked frames) through the streets on their shoulders. The festival begins at dawn in the **Perumal Temple** in Serangoon Rd. Then follows a long journey to the **Chettiar Temple** in Tank Rd.

At the **Sri Mariamman Temple** in South Bridge Rd some devotees drive steel skewers through parts of their bodies. Fire-walking also takes place in this temple. There are **kavadi** processions, dancing and the beating of drums along **Serangoon Rd**, **Selegie Rd**, **Dhoby Ghaut**, **Orchard Rd** and **Clemenceau Ave**. In the evening processions go through **Maxwell Rd**, **Robinson Rd**, **Market St**, **Cecil** and **Cross streets**, **New Bridge Rd** and **River Valley Rd**.

Chinese New Year: The first two days are public holidays but the celebration lasts for 15 days. The Chinese walk about in new clothes visiting friends and relations. A week-long festival on the **Singapore River** has become a regular Chinese New Year event.

Birthday of the Monkey God: This celebrates one of the most famous Chinese mythological characters and the event is celebrated at the **Monkey God Temple** in Seng Poh Rd, with a procession of mediums in a trance who cut or pierce themselves and smear their blood on to paper charms which are then distributed to devotees. His birthday is also celebrated in October.

March-April: Hari Raya Puasa (public holiday). The major Muslim festival, to celebrate the end of Ramadan, the month of fasting which begins in March. **Bussorah St**, in the Arab St area, is full of stalls selling post-dusk meals to fasters.

Good Friday: (public holiday). A candlelight procession takes place in the grounds of St Joseph's Cathedral on Victoria St.

Qing Ming: Chinese families visit graves of relatives to sweep and clean up the ground.

May 1: Labour Day (public holiday).

Vesak Day: (public holiday) is celebrated by Buddhists to honour the birth, death and enlightenment of Lord Buddha by eating only vegetarian food or fasting and attending prayers. **The Temple of 1,000 Lights** on Race Course Rd and **Phor Kark See** on Bright Hill Drive are crowded with worshippers. It is a day of charity.

July: Hari Raya Haji (public holiday) has special significance to those who have completed their *haj* (pilgrimage) to Mecca. However, all Muslims celebrate by praying in the mosque and sacrificing goats and other animals.

August 9: National Day (public holiday). In the daytime there are processions and displays; in the evening fireworks light up the sky.

August: The seventh lunar month celebrates the festival of the **"hungry ghosts."** The Chinese believe that during this month, the souls of the dead are released from purgatory to roam the earth. Incense and joss sticks are burned and food is offered to appease them. Wayang and other street shows are performed.

September: Navarath. A festival which celebrates the consorts of the Hindu trinity of deities through music. At the **Chettiar Temple** in Tank Rd over nine nights.

Thimithi: At the **Sri Mariamman Temple** in South Bridge Rd, devotees walk over a four-metre pit of burning coals to show their faith (and courage).

Moon Cake Festival: According to the Chinese, the moon is at its roundest and brightest on the 15th night of the eighth moon, so they celebrate by eating moon cakes and persimmons. On the night of the festival, children light lanterns.

October: Festival of the Nine Emperor Gods

The view at Underwater World. PHOTO: SINGAPORE TOURIST PROMOTION BOARD

is celebrated in a similar fashion to the Monkey God's birthday.

Pilgrimage to Kusu Island: A month-long festival celebrated by both Malays and Chinese who visit shrines on the island said to have been a turtle which saved the lives of a Malay and a Chinese fisherman. The **Tua Pek Kong temple** and the **kramat** are where offerings are made.

November: Deepavali (public holiday) is also known as the Festival of Lights, and is celebrated by the Hindus to commemorate the slaying of the mythical tyrant Ravana by Lord Rama. This marks the victory of light over darkness, the triumph of good over evil. Hindus decorate their houses with oil lamps and visit friends.

December 25: Christmas Day (public holiday).

ADDRESSES

Singapore Tourist Promotion Board, Raffles City Tower, 37-00, 250 North Bridge Rd (0617). Tel: 339 6622.

Immigration Dept, Pidemco Bldg, 95 South Bridge Rd (0105). Tel: 339 6622.

PUBLICATIONS

The STPB produces many informative publications for distribution free to visitors. These can be obtained from the airport and from the board's office in Raffles City. Publications include *Tour It Yourself* and *101 Meals*. The *Singapore Street Directory* is worth buying for those who intend to stay some time.

The **Times Bookstore** is a huge bookstore chain (service is patchy). For more intelligent service, **MPH** on Stamford Rd or **Select Books**, on the third floor of Tanglin Shopping Centre, would offer greater joy. Select specializes in Asian subjects. *East Meets West* is a comprehensive summary of Singapore affairs and is well illustrated. *Singapore Reflections*, *Streets of Old Chinatown*, and *Singapore Mementoes* are very useful.

DISCOVERING SINGAPORE

Singapore is an easy place to explore on your own. It is small, transport is good and English is widely spoken. It is fairly safe to walk alone at night. The city has grown up around its harbour which remains the focus of much of its activity. Although most areas on the island have been developed, around the city centre and commercial areas you will be able to see preserved areas with early Singaporean traditional shophouses. Examples are in **Peranakan Place** off Orchard Rd, **Telok Ayer St** and **Tanjong Pagar**. In Chinatown, shophouses along **Smith St** and **Sago St** are thriving tourist shops.

To discover Singapore, start with the main artery, the **Singapore River**, which runs through the heart of the city. River-taxi rides at S$17 per adult are available at **Clarke Quay**. A S$5 ride through scenes of old Singapore offered by **Clarke Quay Adventure** in Clarke Quay is fun. The lighters that used to move up and down the narrow channel between the moored boats have been banished to an outlying industrial wharf in Pasir Panjang as part of Singapore's self-sanitization crusade. Nonetheless, a boat ride in the harbour at dusk is still a beautiful introduction to the city. One can take a small craft which may be hired at **Clifford Pier** on Collyer Quay.

Queen Elizabeth Walk is a wide pedestrian way near the pier facing the harbour. At its western end is the Merlion Statue — the symbol of Singapore — near the water. Its eastern end is connected to the massive **Marina Centre** (a shopping and hotel area) and **Marina Park**, all built in the 1980s on reclaimed land. Queen Elizabeth Walk in the morning is the venue for a number of Chinese who engage in the graceful exercise and discipline known as *tai chi chuan*. The area is inhabited throughout the day: in the evening it becomes crowded as the people come to take a little air by the water's edge and enjoy the good food to be bought at the **Satay Club**. This area, however, is earmarked for development — the Singapore Culture Centre will arise here in a few years.

Across **Connaught Drive** from Queen Elizabeth Walk is the green expanse of the **Padang**, the city's playing field, which has at one end the Singapore Cricket Club (the former British colonial club now mostly used by lawyers) and the Singapore Recreation Club (once reserved by the British for Eurasians) — currently being rebuilt. At the eastern end of the Padang rises the tall column of a war memorial to all those who lost their lives in World War II. Many of the city's public buildings stand round or near the Padang.

Along one side, the **Supreme Court** building is next to the **City Hall**, the core of which was built in 1827 as a private residence, but was later taken over by the government and altered extensively. Little of the original structure is now visible, though the present 1926-remodelled building retains much of the original dignity. A little further to the west is the **Victoria Theatre and Concert Hall**, with its distinctive clock tower. The statue of Sir Stamford Raffles has been moved about 100 metres from its original place near his landing site, to **Empress Place**, another preserved building now closed for wide-ranging repair work due to damage caused by rising damp.

East of City Hall across Coleman St is **St Andrew's Cathedral**, set in a wide and pleasant expanse of lawn. The cathedral was built between 1846 and 1861 to replace an earlier church, completed in 1837. The equally pleasant **Armenian Church**, a few hundred yards away to the west of Hill St, was constructed in 1835.

From the western end of Queen Elizabeth Walk you come to the "Wall Street of Singapore" — **Shenton Way**. Via the suspension bridge go past the sturdy grey banks and on into the bustle of **Raffles Place**. Here are shops, money-changers, restaurants and alleys showing much of what Singapore has to offer the tourist.

Stamford Rd runs northwest from the harbour past the northern end of the cathedral and leads to the **National Museum and Art Gallery** 500 metres away. The museum has a natural history collection and ethnographic rooms. The display of Malay artifacts is especially fine. Ceramics and Chinese pottery dating from as early as the Sung dynasty and textiles, sculpture and painting, which formed the former University of Singapore collection of art, are also on display. The museum is now also home to the jade pieces and Chinese art works formerly housed at the House of Jade, which has given way to Singapore's irrepressible progress. Interesting reproductions of paintings depicting the early colonial days are on sale at the museum, which is open from 9 a.m.-4:30 p.m. from Tuesday to Sunday and public holidays. Admission is free.

Rising behind the **National Library** and the museum is the small hill topped by **Fort Canning**, and the site of the original Government House — Singapore's only archaeological site.

Running parallel to Stamford Rd is Bras Basah Rd on which is **St Joseph's Institution**, an old Catholic establishment whose architectural style is beautiful. It is being restored and will reopen as a museum of fine art in late 1995. Turning to **Queen St**, **Victoria St**,

Middle Rd and **Waterloo St**, you will come across churches of many denominations as well as Chinese temples and Muslim or Hindu places of worship, all standing amid rundown shophouses and crowded residences.

North Bridge Rd runs roughly north from the Singapore River (south of the river it becomes South Bridge Rd), and is one of the main reference roads in the city. South Bridge Rd leads into **Chinatown**, where an ambitious restoration programme has been successfully undertaken.

At the northern end of North Bridge Rd is the **Arab St** area. The old Bugis St, the infamous night-time hang out of transvestites, is no more. A rebuilt, cleaned and spruced up **Bugis St** across from the old street now hosts food stalls that serve tasty but expensive fare. The **Boom Boom Room**, operated by people who were mere youngsters in the heyday of old Bugis St, does however provide some colour otherwise now missing in the new location.

The charming **Little India** area, smelling of jasmine flowers and spices, is enclosed by the lower end of Bukit Timah Rd, Sungei Rd, Jalan Besar and Race Course Rd, with Serangoon Rd running through it.

Around the **Orchard Rd** area, especially from the **Mandarin Hotel** to the **Omni Marco Polo**, is the main upmarket shopping area. For night owls, the Mandarin coffee shop is open 24 hours — one of the few such establishments in Singapore.

The restored **Raffles Hotel** — under whose palm trees Somerset Maugham is said to have penned "The Moon and Sixpence" — is a successful blend of colonial style and modern taste, and its museum on the third floor is definitely worth a visit.

For a scenic and refreshing view of the island, go to **Mount Faber**. On Mount Faber Ridge stands the **Alkaff** Mansion, once the home of a rich Arab trader and now preserved and refurbished as an "entertainment facility." From Mount Faber you can take a cable-car ride to the small island of **Sentosa**, which is also linked to the main Singapore island by causeway. Sentosa is given over to leisure activities basically aimed at Singaporeans, who suffer from a lack of such open-air facilities. It contains a swimming lagoon, camping ground, joggers' track, 18-hole golf course and two hotels, as well as an "Underwater World," "Asian Village", "Fantasy island" offering water-borne fun rides, "Volcano Land" and a museum dedicated to the surrender of Singapore to the

PHOTO: PATRICK LUCERO

Haw Par Village excitement.

Japanese in 1942. The five-minute ferry ride is packed on Sundays and public holidays but the bridge offers the more energetic a hassle-free 10-minute stroll across from the **Harbour Promenade**.

Several reservoirs outside the city make pleasant parks, such as **MacRitchie**, **Peirce** and **Seletar Reservoirs**. The **Botanic Gardens** are near the Tanglin road area, while the **Orchid Farm** and the **Zoological Garden** are both on Mandai Lake Rd. The zoo, build round Seletar Reservoir on the "open" concept, is well worth a visit as is the world's first night zoo, which opens at 7:30 p.m. daily, called **Night Safari**, next to the zoo. There is a **Crocodile Farm** on the East Coast Parkway. **Crocodile Paradise** is opposite the excellent **Jurong Bird Park**. Also worth a visit is the **Science Centre** in Jurong.

For older visitors there is a moving experience in a visit to the **Kranji War Memorial**, off Woodlands Rd, where the graves of 24,000 dead overlook the Straits of Johor. **Changi Prison** and the **Sembawang Naval Base** are other reminders of World War II. **Haw Par Villa** is a kind of Buddhist/Taoist/Confucian Disneyland teeming with gaudily daubed moral tableaux.

RESTAURANT SELECTION

Average price for two

BANANA LEAF APOLO, 66 Race Course Rd. Tel: 293 8682. South Indian. US$19-25.
BRASSERIE, Omni Marco Polo Hotel, 247 Tanglin Rd. Tel: 474 7141, Fax: 471 0521. French. US$60-80.
BRAZIL CHURRASCARIA, 14-16 Sixth Ave. Tel: 463 1923. From US$40.
EL FELIPE, 34 Lorong Mambong. Tel: 468 1520, Fax: 738 2119. Mexican. US$20-30.
EMPIRE CAFE, Raffles Hotel, 1 Beach Rd. Tel: 337 1886, Fax: 334 4550. Local & Western coffee shop cuisine. From US$10.
IMPERIAL HERBAL RESTAURANT, Metropole Hotel, 41 Seah St. Tel: 337 0491. Exotic Northern Chinese. US$40-50.
KOKISHIN, Boulevard Hotel, 200 Orchard Blvd. Tel: 737 2911, Fax: 737 8449. Japanese. US$50-70.
KOMALAS VILLAS, 78 Serangoon Rd. Tel: 292 4687. Indian, vegetarian. No reservations. US$10.
MOI KONG, 22 Murray St. Tel: 221 7758. Hakka. US$20-30.
LIANA'S, The Oriental, 5 Raffles Blvd, Tel: 338 0066. Continental. US$80-120.
PASTA FRESCA, Bik 833 Bt Timah Rd, Branch Boat Quay. Tel: 469 4920, 532 6283, Fax: 469 7986. Italian. US$20-30.
PREGO, Westin Stamford Hotel, 1 Stamford Rd. Tel: 338 8585, Fax: 337 1554. Italian. US$60-80.
TAMBUAH MAS, Tanglin Shopping Centre. Tel: 733 3333, Fax: 738 5152. Indonesian. US$15-20.
TIFFIN ROOM, Raffles Hotel, 1 Beach Rd. Tel: 337 1886, Fax: 334 4550. Indian curries buffet. From US$20.50 (lunch) and US$25.35 (dinner).

HOTEL GUIDE

A: US$200 and above

ANA HOTEL, 16 Nassim Rd. Tel: 732 1222, Fax: 732 1222, Tlx: RS21817. *P, Gym, Biz. R: L, W.*
APOLLO, 405-406 Havelock Rd. Tel: 733 2081, Fax: 733 1588, Tlx: RS21077. *P, Gym, Biz. R: L, W.*
DUXTON, 83 Duxton Rd. Tel: 227 7678, Fax: 227 1232. *P. R: L, W.*
FOUR SEASONS, 190 Orchard Boulevard, Tel: 734 1110, Fax: 733 0682. *P, Gym, Biz. R: L, W.*
GOODWOOD PARK, 22 Scotts Rd. Tel: 737 7411, Fax: 732 8558, Tlx: RS24377. *P, Gym, Biz. R: L, W.*
HARBOUR VIEW DAI-ICHI, 81 Anson Rd. Tel: 224 1133, Fax: 222 0749, Tlx: RS40163. *P, Gym, Biz. R: L, W.*
HILTON, 581 Orchard Rd. Tel: 737 2233, Fax: 732 2917, Tlx: RS21491. *P, Gym, Biz. R: L, W.*
HOLIDAY INN CROWNE PLAZA, 25 Scotts Rd. Tel: 737 7966, Fax: 737 6646, Tlx: RS21818. *P, Gym, Biz. R: L, W.*
HOLIDAY INN PARK VIEW, 11 Cavenagh Rd. Tel: 733 8333, Fax: 734 4593, Tlx: RS55420. *P, Gym, Biz. R: L, W.*
HOTEL IMPERIAL, 1 Jln Rumbia. Tel: 737 1666, Fax: 737 4761, Tlx: RS21654. *P, Gym, Biz. R: L, W.*
HYATT REGENCY, 10-12 Scotts Rd. Tel: 738 1234, Fax: 732 1696, Tlx: RS24415. *P, Gym, Biz. R: L, W.*
LE MERIDIEN, 100 Orchard Rd. Tel: 735 8855, Fax: 732 7886, Tlx: RS50163. *P, Gym, Biz. R: L, W.*
MANDARIN, 333 Orchard Rd. Tel: 737 4411, Fax: 732 2361, Tlx: RS21528. *P, Gym, Biz. R: L, W.*
MARINA MANDARIN, 6 Raffles Blvd. Tel: 338 3388, Fax: 339 4977, Tlx: RS22299. *P, Gym, Biz. R: L, W.*
MARRIOTT, 320 Orchard Rd. Tel: 735 5800, Fax: 735 9800. *P, Gym, Biz. R: L, W.*
PAN PACIFIC, 7 Raffles Blvd. Tel: 336 8111, Fax: 339 1861, Tlx: RS33821. *P, Gym, Biz. R: L, W.*
RAFFLES HOTEL, 1 Beach Rd. Tel: 337 1886, Fax: 339 7650, Tlx: RS39028. *P, Gym, Biz. R: L, W.*
REGENT, 1 Cuscaden Rd. Tel: 733 8888, Fax: 732 8838, Tlx: RS37248. *P, Gym, Biz. R: L, W.*
SHANGRI-LA, 22 Orange Grove Rd. Tel: 737 3644, Fax: 733 7220, Tlx: RS21505. *P, Gym, Biz. R: L, W.*
THE ORIENTAL, 5 Raffles Blvd. Tel: 338 0066, Fax: 339 9537, Tlx: RS29117. *P, Gym, Biz. R: L, W.*

P — Swimming pool **Gym** — Health club **Biz** — Business centre **R** — Restaurant
L — Local food **W** — Western
There is no Satellite TV in Singapore

HOTEL GUIDE

WESTIN PLAZA, 1 Stamford Rd. Tel: 338 8585, Fax: 338 2862, Tlx: RS22206. *P, Gym, Biz. R: L, W.*
WESTIN STAMFORD, 2 Stamford Rd. Tel: 338 8585, Fax: 338 2862, Tlx: RS22206. *P, Gym, Biz. R: L, W.*

B: US$130-200

ALBERT COURT, 180 Albert St. Tel: 339 3939, Fax: 339 3252, Tlx: RS24109. *Biz. R: L, W.*
ALLSON, 101 Victoria St. Tel: 336 0811, Fax: 339 7019, Tlx: RS21151. *P, Gym, Biz. R: L, W.*
AMARA, 165 Tanjong Pagar. Tel: 224 4488, Fax: 224 3910, Tlx: RS55887. *P, Gym, Biz. R: L, W.*
BAYVIEW INN, 30 Bencoolen Blvd. Tel: 337 2882, Fax: 337 2721, Tlx: RS26965. *P, Biz. R: L, W.*
BEAUFORT, 2 Bt Manis Rd, Sentosa. Tel: 275 0331, Fax: 275 0228. *P, Gym, Biz. R: L, W.*
BOULEVARD, 200 Orchard Blvd. Tel: 737 2911, Fax: 734 8449, Tlx: RS21771. *P, Gym, Biz. R: L, W.*
CAIRNHILL, 19 Cairnhill Rd. Tel: 734662, Fax: 235 5598, Tlx: RS26742. *P, Gym, Biz. R: L, W.*
CARLTON, 76 Bras Basah Rd. Tel: 338 8333, Fax: 337 3394, Tlx: RS42076. *P, Gym, Biz. R: L, W.*
COCKPIT, 115 Penang Rd. Tel: 737 9111, Fax: 737 3105, Tlx: RS21366. *P, Biz. R: L, W.*
CONCORDE, 317 Outram Rd. Tel: 733 0188, Fax: 733 0989, Tlx: RS50141. *P, Gym, Biz. R: L, W.*
CROWN PRINCE, 270 Orchard Rd. Tel: 732 1111, Fax: 732 7018, Tlx: RS22819. *P, Biz. R: L, W.*
EQUATORIAL, 429 Bt Timah Rd. Tel: 732 0431, Fax: 737 9426, Tlx: RS21578. *P, Biz. R: L, W.*
GOLDEN LANDMARK, 390 Victoria Blvd. Tel: 297 2828, Fax: 298 2038, Tlx: RS38291. *P, Gym, Biz. R: L, W.*
LADYHILL, 1 Ladyhill Rd. Tel: 737 2111, Fax: 737 4606, Tlx: RS23157. *P, Biz. R: L, W.*
LE MERIDIEN CHANGI, 1 Netheravon Rd. Tel: 542 7700, Fax: 542 5259, Tlx: RS36042. *P, Gym, Biz. R: L, W.*
MIRAMAR, 401 Havelock Rd. Tel: 733 0222, Fax: 733 4027, Tlx: RS24709. *P, Gym, Biz. R: L, W.*
NEW OTANI, 177A River Valley Rd. Tel: 338 3333, Fax: 339 2854, Tlx: RS20299. *P, Gym, Biz. R: L, W.*
NEW PARK, 181 Kitchener Rd. Tel: 291 5533, Fax: 297 2827, Tlx: RS33190. *P, Gym, Biz. R: L, W.*
NOVOTEL ORCHID SINGAPORE, 214 Dunearn Rd. Tel: 250 3322, Fax: 250 9292, Tlx: RS21756. *P, Gym, Biz. R: L, W.*
OMNI MARCO POLO, 247 Tanglin Rd. Tel: 474 7141, Fax: 471 0521, Tlx: RS21476. *P, Gym, Biz. R: L, W.*
ORCHARD, 422 Orchard Rd. Tel: 734 7766, Fax: 733 5482, Tlx: RS35228. *P, Gym, Biz. R: L, W.*
ORCHARD PARADE, 1 Tanglin Rd. Tel: 737 1133, Fax: 733 0242, Tlx: RS21488. *P, Gym, Biz. R: L, W.*
PARAMOUNT, Marine Parade Rd. Tel: 344 5577, Fax: 447 4131, Tlx: RS22234. *P, Gym, Biz. R: L, W.*
PENINSULA, 3 Coleman St. Tel: 337 2200, Fax: 339 3847, Tlx: RS21169. *P, Gym, Biz. R: L, W.*
PHOENIX, Somerset Rd. Tel: 737 8666, Fax: 732 2024, Tlx: RS23718. *P, Gym, Biz. R: L, W.*
PLAZA, 7500A Beach Rd. Tel: 298 0011, Fax: 296 3600, Tlx: RS22150. *P, Gym, Biz. R: L, W.*
RIVER VIEW, 382 Havelock Rd. Tel: 732 9922, Fax: 732 1034, Tlx: RS55454. *P, Gym, Biz. R: L, W.*
SEAVIEW, 26 Amber Close. Tel: 345 2222, Fax: 345 1741, Tlx: RS21555. *P, Biz. R: L, W.*
SHANGRI-LA's RASA SENTOSA RESORT, 101 Siloso Rd, Sentosa. Tel: 275 0100, Fax: 275 0355, Tlx: RS20817. *P, Gym, Biz. R: L, W.*
SHERATON TOWERS, 39 Scotts Rd. Tel: 737 6888, Fax: 737 1072, Tlx: RS37750. *P, Gym, Biz. R: L, W.*
TRADERS HOTEL, 1A Cuscaden Rd. Tel: 738 2222, Fax: 831 4314, Tlx: RS26104. *P, Gym, Biz. R: L, W.*

C: US$130 and below

ASIA, 37 Scotts Rd. Tel: 737 8388, Fax: 733 3563, Tlx: RS24313. *P, Biz. R: L, W.*
EXCELSIOR, 5 Coleman St. Tel: 338 7733, Fax: 339 3847, Tlx: RS20678. *P, Biz. R: L, W.*
GARDEN, 14 Balmoral Rd. Tel: 235 3344, Fax: 235 9730, Tlx: RS50999. *P, Gym, Biz. R: L, W.*
HOTEL GRAND CENTRAL, Orchard Rd/Cavenagh Rd. Tel: 737 9944, Fax: 733 3175, Tlx: RS24389. *P, Gym, Biz. R: L, W.*
INN OF THE SIXTH HAPPINESS, 9-37 Erskine Rd. Tel: 223 3266, Fax: 223 7951. *P. R: L, W.*
HOTEL ROYAL, 36 Newton Rd. Tel: 254 3311, Fax: 253 8668, Tlx: RS21644. *P, Gym, Biz. R: L, W.*

P — Swimming pool　**Gym** — Health club　**Biz** — Business centre　**R** — Restaurant
L — Local food　**W** — Western
There is no Satellite TV in Singapore

THAILAND

Thailand means "land of the free." Unlike many other Asian nations, it was never colonized by a foreign power, a fact that fills the Thais with pride. Although nominally ruled by a king, the government of Thailand has changed hands frequently through a remarkable succession of military coups and counter-coups, preventing the Thai people from enjoying full-fledged democracy. Even so, Thais have long enjoyed considerable personal freedom and a strident press has been allowed to flourish. General elections in September 1992 introduced a greater degree of democracy, though the military still carries considerable clout in the country's affairs.

Thailand's landscape, like its 59 million people, is remarkably varied and often beautiful. Thai people have a world reputation for being easy-going, courteous and hospitable. You can see at once why it is called "The Land of Smiles" and has become one of the most popular tourist destinations in the world. Tourism brings in 6 million visitors annually and more foreign exchange (about US$5.5 billion) than rice or any other export.

Tourism and economic development, though, are exacting a price. Traditional values and culture are disappearing and much natural beauty already has been lost. Beautiful beaches, historic ruins and temples, savoury food and friendly people still make Thailand one of the most attractive tourist destinations in all of Asia. But if you want to see the old Thailand, don't delay.

Bangkok's urban sprawl — with its traffic, noise and air pollution — is one of the horrors of the modern world. The capital is overcrowded — its population exceeds 8 million and may reach 12 million by 2000. Seasoned travellers now give themselves only two or three days in Bangkok before heading for delights that are still abundant upcountry and along the coast. Even in Bangkok, however, old Thai ways still exist behind the concrete towers and beyond the roar of the bulldozers and pile drivers.

Buddhism pervades Thai culture and signs of the religious tradition are everywhere. Soon after dawn, Buddhist monks in robes (these may vary in colour from dark saffron to bright orange) can be seen making their way across building sites, along the banks of the *khlongs* (canals) and down narrow streets. People wait to fill the monks' bowls with food and provide other essentials, a practice that Buddhist teaching says will reward the giver.

Many young men still become monks for a short time and older men spend time in a temple on retirement. Monks are forbidden to touch or be touched by a woman. If a woman has to give something to a monk or novice she must hand it to a man, who will pass it on. Otherwise the woman can place the item on the ground in front of the monk.

Every Thai house has its own "spirit house" to accommodate the spirits from the land on which the house stands. The custom owes more to animism than Buddhism but that does not bother the tolerant Thais, whose religion is the gentlest and most liberal form of Buddhism.

What is left of traditional Thai architecture is mainly visible in the glittering Buddhist temples and shrines and the simpler, wooden houses in which the monks live and study. Stylish domestic houses

◄ *Phi Phi Island.* PHOTO: B.J. ADAMS

of beauty and interest in Bangkok and other cities have all but gone. Thais now prefer to live in air-conditioned, concrete structures.

Some old ways and superstitions remain. Thai government and military leaders still commonly consult their astrologers before making important decisions. Astrologers nominate a propitious time for a new minister or general to take up his post or to make an important journey. On election day, politicians routinely make offerings of a pig's head at the popular Erawan Shrine in Bangkok. Buddhist shrines provide good luck numbers for buyers of lottery tickets and monks anoint the noses of new aircraft before they enter service.

History

Civilization was flourishing in northeastern Thailand more than 5,000 years ago. Recent discoveries at Ban Chieng, 500 kilometres northeast of Bangkok, yielded the first known human artifacts in Thailand and point to a civilization older than Middle East settlements, which have been regarded as mankind's first cradle of culture.

Some say the Ban Chieng people came from Vietnam, others contend they were indigenous to the region. They later were joined by people from what is now Malaysia, and later still by huge waves of people fleeing from southern China to escape the Mongols led by Kublai Khan.

The first independent Thai kingdom was established at Sukhothai in the 13th century after challenging the far-flung Khmer Empire based in Cambodia. The Thai success owed much to connections with China, which provided a big market for Thai rice and supplied Thailand with the latest implements and skills. By the early 1300s Thai authority extended west to the Bay of Bengal, south to include the entire Malay peninsula, and north to present-day Laos.

The great Sukhothai monarch, King Ramkamhaeng, known as the "father of Thailand," created a Thai alphabet, thereby uniting scattered tribes into a nation. After his death, decline began and a rival, Ayutthaya, became the dominant kingdom and remained supreme for 400 years.

Burma began to threaten Thailand in the early 1500s. A series of wars ended with the Burmese capture and destruction of Ayutthaya in 1767. This is still considered Thailand's darkest hour.

The Thais rallied under a new king, Taksin, who within 10 years had driven out the Burmese, reunited the shattered kingdom and established a new capital in Bangkok. Four years later, however, he was overthrown by an army coup and executed. Gen. Chakri became the first king of the Chakri dynasty, which still rules today.

The Chakris produced two outstanding monarchs in the 19th and early 20th centuries, Rama IV and Rama V, who led the country into the modern age and towards democracy. By skilful diplomacy they fended off threats to their independence from Britain and France, who were expanding their colonies on Thailand's borders.

Thailand remained independent, but watched with growing alarm wars between Britain and China and later between Japan and Russia. Thailand joined the allies in the war against Germany in 1917 and sent troops to fight in France in the last months of that conflict.

A bloodless revolution in 1932 overthrew the absolute monarchy, but the king was invited to be a constitutional monarch on the British model. What emerged, however, was a military dictatorship, rather than a parliamentary democracy.

Thailand has had few elected civilian governments over the past 60 years. Field marshals and generals have sustained their power with coups and counter-coups, many of them violent.

One of the most notable dictators was Field Marshal Sarit Thanarat, who made a name for himself by summarily executing arsonists and also by the mistresses and wealth he acquired during six years in power. His successor, Thanom Kittikachorn, who assumed power in 1963, declared martial law and annulled the constitution in 1971.

That led to a popular revolt in 1973, in which many hundreds of civilians were killed, and finally, to a short-lived democratic civilian government. Three years later, clashes between the military and democrats resulted in hundreds more civilian deaths and finally, a return to military rule under Gen. Kriangsak

THAILAND
LAOS
BURMA
VIETNAM
CAMBODIA
MALAYSIA
Chiang Rai
Chiang Mai
Lumphun
Lumpang
Vientiane
Uttaradit
Nong Khai
Sawankhalok
Udon Thani
Nakhon Phanom
Sukhothai
Sakon Nakhon
Tak
Phitsanulok
Maha Sarakham
Savannakhet
Khon Kaen
Roi Et
Phetchabun
Mukdahan
Korat Plateau
Korat
Sisaket
Ubon Ratchathani
Lop Buri
Surin
Nakhon Ratchasima
Ayutthaya
Sara Buri
Bang Pa In
BANGKOK
Nakhon Pathom
Aranvaprathet
Chon Buri
Pattaya
Ko Lan
Phet Chaburi
Sattahip
Hua Hin
Prachuap
Ranong
Ko Phangan
Ko Samui
Surat Thani
Nakhon Si Thammarat
Phuket
Phatthalung
Haadyai
Songkhla
Sungai-golok
Padang Besar
Kota Baru
Alor Star
Butterworth
Km
0
200
Railways
Roads

Chomanan.

Parliamentary politics slowly returned under the eight-year rule of Gen. Prem Tinsulanond, who assumed power in 1980. He lost an election to civilian Chatichai Choonhavan in 1988. But a bloodless military coup in February of 1991 easily overthrew the Chatichai administration, which had been weakened by corruption. Thus began the rule of Gen. Suchinda Kraprayoon and a step backward from the democratic process. Calls for the resignation of Suchinda and pro-democracy demonstrations in Bangkok ended in the notorious May 17-20 incident of 1992, in which troops slaughtered demonstrators.

King Bhumibol, who has had considerable influence over national affairs since the late 1970s, intervened, forcing Suchinda's resignation. General elections in September of 1992 brought a five-party coalition to power under the premiership of Chuan Leekpai, the leader of the Democrat Party.

Entry

AIR: Most visitors arrive by air at Thailand's five international airports. The major gateway is Bangkok's **Don Muang International Airport**, 25 kilometres from the city. More than 50 airlines from all parts of the world use the airport. Some also fly to domestic airports at **Phuket** and **Haadyai** in the south, **Chiang Mai** in the north and **U-Tapao**, southeast of Bangkok. Charter flights operate from Europe, North America and other parts of Asia.

There is a departure tax of Baht 200 for international flights and Baht 20 for domestic.

SEA: Travellers also can arrive by sea at Bangkok's **Khlong Toey** port just south of the city. A cruise ship, **Andaman Princess**, operates a regular passenger service between Singapore and Bangkok. For details, contact Siam Cruise Co. Ltd., (Bangkok, Tel: 255 8950-7; Fax: 255 8961).

ROAD: Travellers may enter Thailand over-

EMBASSIES IN BANGKOK

	Fax:	*Tel:*		*Fax:*	*Tel:*
Argentina	259 0402	259 0401	**Laos**	287 3968	213 1203
Austria	287 3925	287 3970	**Malaysia**	287 2348	286 1390
Australia	287 2029	287 2680	**Mexico**	236 8410	235 6367
Bangladesh	391 8070	392 9437	**Nepal**	381 2406	391 7240
Belgium	236 7619	236 0150	**Netherlands**	254 5579	254 7701
Brazil	254 2707	252 6023	**New Zealand**	253 9045	251 8165
Brunei	391 6017	391 6017	**Norway**	256 0477	253 0390
Bulgaria	513 9783	513 9781	**Pakistan**	253 0289	253 0288
Burma	236 6898	237 7744	**Philippines**	259 2809	259 0139
Canada	236 6463	237 4125	**Poland**	251 8895	251 8891
Chile	391 8380	391 4858	**Portugal**	238 4275	234 2123
China	246 8247	245 7032	**Romania**	279 7891	279 7902
Czech Republic	236 5843	266 7500	**Russia**	237 8488	234 2012
Denmark	213 1752	213 2021	**Saudi Arabia**	236 6442	237 1938
Egypt	254 9489	253 0161	**Singapore**	287 2578	286 1434
Finland	256 9310	256 9306	**Slovakia**	256 6141	256 6140
France	236 3511	266 8250	**South Africa**	253 8477	253 8473
Germany	287 1776	213 2331	**Spain**	255 2388	252 6112
Greece	254 2936	254 2937	**Sri Lanka**	255 3848	251 2788
Hungary	391 5250	391 2002	**Sweden**	254 4914	254 4954
India	258 4627	258 0300	**Switzerland**	255 4481	253 0156
Indonesia	255 1267	252 3135	**Taiwan**		
Iran	259 9111	259 0611	(Consulate)	254 9276	251 9274
Iraq	271 4218	278 5335	**Turkey**	275 9932	275 6173
Israel	254 5518	252 3131	**United Kingdom**	255 8619	253 0191
Italy	285 4793	285 4090	**United States**	254 2990	252 5040
Japan	253 4153	252 6151	**Vatican**	212 0932	212 5853
South Korea	318 6333	319 1442	**Vietnam**	251 7201	251 7202

land from Malaysia, Cambodia and Laos, but Burma is accessible only by air. Trains run daily both ways between **Butterworth**, in northern Malaysia, and Bangkok. The Bangkok-Butter-worth journey takes 21 hours. A second-class sleeper on this route will cost Baht 866 and a first-class sleeper (with air-conditioning), Baht 1,434. Overnight trains run both ways between Bangkok and Nong Khai on the border with Laos. Second-class sleepers cost Baht 496, first-class, Baht 730. A special land visa is needed between Thailand and Cambodia.

Malaysian trains run from Singapore and Kuala Lumpur to Butterworth. Those operating from the east coast also connect with Bangkok trains. Check the times carefully to ensure connections.

Provided strict customs regulations are observed, it is possible to drive between Thailand and Malaysia. The border is open daily only between 6 a.m.-6 p.m. (Thai time) and 7 a.m.-7 p.m. (Malaysian time) but these hours probably will soon be extended to 10 p.m. (Thai time).

Immigration

Many visitors may enter without a visa. Travellers from more than 40 countries in Western Europe, North America, Australasia, the Pacific and Southeast Asia may stay for up to 30 days without a visa. But travellers from most other Asian countries, from Africa and the Middle East need entry visas.

You must carry a passport or certificate of identity to enter Thailand. Hong Kong residents may travel with Hong Kong ID cards in lieu of a passport. Malaysians carrying a border pass may travel up to 50 kilometres into Thailand and stay for 15 days. Taiwanese residents can get an entry permit from the Taipei office of Thai Airways International or process their papers through the Thai Embassy in a third country.

If you wish to stay longer than 30 days, it is best to obtain a visa in your own country. Travellers from countries without a Thai embassy or consulate should apply to missions in neighbouring countries or apply with supporting evidence to the Immigration Division (Soi Suan Phlu, Sathorn Tai Rd, Bangkok 10120, Tel: 286 9176, 286 9230).

All visas must be used within 90 days of issue. Those on a tourist visa may stay 60 days, a transit visa, 30 days and a non-immigrant visa, 90 days. Non-immigrant visas may be extended at the Immigration Division in Bangkok. It is usually easier to extend a tourist visa by going to the Thai Consulate at Penang in northern Malaysia. If you are leaving Thailand and wish to return while your visa is still valid, you must obtain a re-entry visa at the Immigration Division (address above). Visa extensions and re-entry permits cost US$20.

Health

There is no requirement to be vaccinated unless you are travelling from or passing through a contaminated area.

Customs

THE DEATH PENALTY IS THE PUNISHMENT FOR THOSE ATTEMPTING TO SMUGGLE MORE THAN 50 GRAMS OF HEROIN OR OTHER NARCOTIC DRUG. THIS LAW IS ENFORCED RIGOROUSLY AGAINST ALL NATIONALITIES.

Thai courts have handed down death sentences to non-Asian foreigners, though none actually has been executed (as of March 1995). Hundreds of foreigners are serving long sentences in Thailand for drug possession. Be warned.

Customs authorities are generally liberal towards visitors. They will allow you to import personal effects and professional equipment duty-free. You may bring in duty-free one camera (and five rolls of film) and/or one movie or video camera (with three rolls of film). You may also bring in up to 250 grams of tobacco products, or 200 cigarettes, and one litre each of wine and spirits.

Thailand imposes stringent controls on the export of art objects. No Buddha image or fragment thereof, irrespective of its age, may be taken or sent out of the country. All other art objects, whether originals or reproductions, require export licences from the Fine Arts Department. Permission takes at least two weeks. The Bangkok National Museum, Bangkok, or reputable art dealers and shops will provide details.

Foreign visitors may bring in any amount of foreign currency, but must declare amounts in excess of US$10,000. You might be prevented from taking out more than US$10,000, though this restriction is rarely enforced. Regulations also say that a visitor should take out no more than Baht 50,000; in practice, however, currency imports and exports are rarely questioned.

Obscene literature and pictures are prohibited imports. Firearms and ammunition may be imported only if a permit is granted by the Police Department or Local Registration Office.

Currency

The Thai national currency is the baht. Thai baht come in Baht 1,000, 500, 100, 50, 20 and 10 notes and 10, 5, and 1 coins. The baht is divided into 100 satang; 50 and 25 satang coins (yellow in colour) are in circulation.

Major credit cards are acceptable almost everywhere, now that Thais use them widely.

When cashing travellers' cheques or foreign currency, avoid hotels or moneychangers who offer rates that are substantially less favourable than bank rates.

Language

Thai is spoken everywhere, with only minor differences from north to south. The ethnic Lao people, who are predominant in the northeast, speak their own language as well as Thai, but the two are closely related.

Some southerners speak a mixture of Thai and Malay. Those among Bangkok's large ethnic Chinese population speak various south China dialects, but mainly Teochew.

English is widely spoken in Bangkok and in the major tourist resorts.

Climate

Thailand's climate is tropical, with a mean annual temperature of 28°C. Temperatures as low as 11°C occur at night in rural areas during the November-February cool season. Daytime temperatures rarely reach 38°C, even in the hottest season, from March to June.

Humidity is high at most times. The annual average rainfall is 150 centimetres. The dry, hot season is from about late February to early June and the wet season runs from around June until late October. The relatively cool, dry, sunny season is early November until the end of February and is the best time of year to visit Thailand.

The weather in the far south is less predictable, as thunderstorms occur all year round.

Dress

Do not buy a new tropical wardrobe for the trip. Instead buy it in Bangkok, where light, casual garments are cheap but of good quality. Pullovers are useful in the cool season at night and early morning, particularly in rural areas, when temperatures drop to 11°C.

Thais are paragons of neatness and style, so some formality is advisable for business appointments and similar occasions. Shorts and T-shirts are frowned upon in government offices. Some hotels require jackets and ties. Dress discreetly at temples and national monuments. Wear slip-on shoes in temples — and socks without holes. Men should keep their shirts on at all times, except on the beach.

Business Hours

Government and most commercial offices are open from 8:30 a.m.-4:30 p.m. from Monday to Friday. Most government offices close for lunch between noon and 1 p.m.

Post offices keep government hours though many, including the General Post Office (GPO) in New Rd, Bangkok, are open on Saturday mornings. The GPO also provides telegraph, telex and international telephone services at all times.

Banks are open from 8:30 a.m.-3:30 p.m. from Monday to Friday. Banks in major centres operate automatic teller machines seven days a week.

Most shops open from 8 or 9 a.m.-9 p.m. or later and remain open during weekends. Department stores open at 10 a.m.-8 or 9 p.m. seven days a week.

Restaurants open early and generally stay open until business comes to an end. You may find eating places in hotels, most coffee shops and in markets in Bangkok and other big towns open 24 hours a day.

Doing Business

The younger generation in Thailand generally do business in the Western manner, but old ways die hard; the older person still expects deference from someone younger.

Punctuality is not a Thai trait, so a late arrival will be forgiven. But if you arrive on time, you will likely earn respect.

Language normally is no problem in the Bangkok business community where English is widely spoken. But you may need an interpreter for business negotiations when outside the capital. Personal business cards are essential.

Do not slap a Thai on the back or arm even in the friendliest manner. Physical contact of that kind is not welcomed. Do shake hands when meeting, with women as well as men. Women executives and directors have been prominent in Thai business for generations and neither expect nor receive special consideration.

A Thai always looks for a compromise before clinching a deal, even if one is unwarranted, and prefers to reach a conclusion indirectly.

Thais do not often give a blunt "no," but will veil a rejection in ways that can be misleading. They often laugh to conceal a mistake or confusion. Do not mistake this for derision.

Never raise your voice, thump the table, or express anger in other ways during a meeting, no matter how extreme the provocation. Thais feel contempt for such behaviour. It is impossible to be too polite.

Dress formally for business meetings — dark suit, tie for men, polished shoes. A polite body posture makes a good impression. Do not cross your legs . Never point the soles of your feet towards a Thai person or a portrait of the Royal Family or an image of the Buddha.

Smoking is more prevalent in Thailand than in many other countries, but it is forbidden on buses and in cinema and some other public places. In a social setting, the host always lights up first.

Business colleagues usually enjoy a drink outside the office and they often make a night of it. Informal toasts are not drunk to individuals but to "success, friendship" and so forth. Business entertaining is generally conducted in hotels or restaurants. Presents to a colleague could be flowers, a box of chocolates or basket of fruit delivered to home or office, but nothing over-expensive.

Thailand's King Bhumibol, who came to the throne in 1946, is deeply revered. There are heavy punishments, including imprisonment, for any insult to the throne. Offensive remarks about the monarchy can be dangerous.

It is best not to talk at all about the Thai Royal Family, religion or other national institutions unless they directly concern your business, and if it is necessary then be respectful.

Bangkok has several courier services for urgent deliveries. A few options are: **DHL Worldwide Express** Tel: 260 7600-9, 260 7610-4; **TNT Express Worldwide** Tel: 249 5702, 249 0242); and **CSS Couriers** Tel: 253 0098.

Major Bangkok hotels catering to foreigners have business centres, with fax facilities and translation services.

It is also possible to rent the services of secretaries and translators. Three options are: **Girl Friday Business** and **Secretarial Services** Tel: 233 9293, 237 6132; **International Translations Office** Tel: 233 7714; and **Conference and Office Secretariat** Tel: 251 5396.

Rip-Offs

When leaving the airport, avoid touts who will offer to guide you around or simply offer to supply you with "girl or boy." And ignore men with dilapidated vehicles offering taxi services.

Be wary of the friendly fellows in city streets who claim to know where you can buy jewellery at the best price or offer other "bargains."

Buy imported liquor only in the big supermarkets, not in sidestreet shops, where the drink may have been diluted or completely substituted for a local product.

Be careful when visiting upstairs bars that stage dancing and other spectacles. They may charge exorbitantly for the "entertainment." Men out for a night on the town should remember — some of the most attractive women may not be what they seem. Transvestites are numerous in Patpong and similar night-spot quarters.

Except for the fortnightly state lottery and horse racing, gambling is illegal. Reject invitations to play cards. Police even raid private homes and arrest gamblers playing for money.

Never accept food or drink from strangers on a long-distance bus. Many tourists have lost money and other valuables after being drugged in that way.

Foreigners are often charged higher entrance fees at museums, historic sites and other tourist spots. But this is difficult to prevent.

Take care when crossing streets with busy traffic. Cars often do not stop for people on pedestrian crossings. It is safer to wait for a break in the traffic.

Though politeness is paramount in Thai culture, a fierce anger exists beneath the smiles and gentleness, and many Thais can be quick to take offence.

Media

Thailand's two English-language dailies, *The Nation* and the *Bangkok Post*, are widely available. There are also two business weeklies published in English — *Business Review* and *Business in Thailand* — and the daily *Business Day*.

A limited selection of foreign newspapers and magazines is available at bookshops in major hotels and from **The Bookseller**, Patpong Rd.

Communications

Thailand has good but not the finest international communications. The problem is a shortage of international circuits, but this is being addressed. There is international direct dialling to and from Bangkok, Chiang Mai, Hua Hin, Pattaya, Phuket and Songkhla.

You may hire mobile phones in Bangkok in the arrivals terminal at Bangkok International Airport, or at **SC Telecom** (Vongvanit Bldg 12/F, 100/1 Rama 9 Rd, Tel: 246 9171) and **Telewiz** (2/F, Amarin Plaza, Ploenchit Rd, Tel: 256 9358).

Electricity: current throughout Thailand is 220 volts, 50 cycles.

Transport

BANGKOK

A limousine from the airport to a city hotel costs Baht 500. The airport bus that runs to the Asia Hotel costs Baht 100. Tickets are available at the desk inside the air terminal.

You can arrange for a taxi at the taxi desk in the terminal. Fares must be negotiated and should be about half the limousine fare.

TAXIS: There are few taxi stands, but cruisers are generally quickly available. Most taxis now have meters for fares. Tipping is not expected. Many drivers speak English, but it is wise to carry a hotel card to explain your destination.

SAMLORS: The increasing engine power of these three-wheeled vehicles has given them astonishing speed. Called "tuk tuks," because of their noise, you can rent them for Baht 20 and up. Expect to pay about two thirds of the cost of a taxi.

BUSES: There are extensive bus routes all over Bangkok. (The Tourist Authority of Thailand has route maps.) Services can be irregular with long delays and the vehicles are crowded at peak times. Fares range from Baht 2.5-3.5. You can travel in comfort in less crowded, air-conditioned buses for Baht 6.

BOATS: Regular boats on the river and khlongs (canals) cost only Baht 4 or Baht 5 for quite long journeys. Negotiate for hire of a personal boat.

CAR RENTAL: Bangkok has several internationally known car rental agencies, as well as local ones. Some options are: **Avis** (Tel: 255 5300-4); **Hertz** (Tel: 251 7575); **Winner Rent** (Tel: 252 4917); **Toyota** (Tel: 233 5490); **Highway Car Rent** (Tel: 235 5316).

TRANSPORT UPCOUNTRY

AIR: Thai Airways International flies from Bangkok to all the main centres, with connecting flights to remote areas. It flies from the capital to Chiang Mai (up to 12 flights daily, Baht 1,650 one-way); Phuket (more than 12 flights daily, Baht 2,000 one-way) and Haadyai (10 flights daily, Baht 2,280). Bangkok Airways flies to Koh Samui (nine flights daily, Baht 2,080).

BUSES: These are cheap and frequent to all parts of the country. You can pay slightly more to ride in air-conditioned comfort, but the accident rate is high for bus travel. Many roads are too narrow to cope with the heavy vehicle traffic and the authorities admit that drivers work overlong hours and take drugs to keep awake.

Bangkok has several special terminals where buses begin their journeys. There is a southern terminal, for example, for those going to the south, an eastern terminal and so on. To ride from Bangkok to Chiang Mai you will pay about Baht 304 for an air-conditioned coach, Baht 470 for a VIP coach. A bus trip to Phuket on an air-conditioned bus will cost about Baht 370, Baht 570 for a VIP coach. Buses without air-conditioning are much cheaper.

TRAINS: The trains in Thailand are comfortable and run on time. The extensive rail network covers most of the country. Trains are more expensive than buses, but are favoured by many because they are generally safer.

Daytime trains give visitors the most thorough view of Thailand. Most long-distance services run at night. There are some day services, however, so don't despair if you are hoping to go by daylight. Bookings can be made through travel agents or at the Bangkok main railway station, 8:30 a.m.-5:30 p.m. weekdays and 8:30 a.m.-noon at weekends and holidays.

The daily train from Bangkok to Butterworth in Malaysia takes 21 hours. Fares range from

Baht 876 for a second-class seat one-way, to Baht 1,434 for a one-way ticket on a first-class, air-conditioned sleeper. Lower-berth, second-class sleepers are good value and comfortable.

Trains from Bangkok to Haadyai (south) will cost around Baht 964, for a first-class, one-way ticket and Baht 313 for second class. You can ride from the capital to Ubon Ratchthani (north-east) for Baht 550 (air-conditioned sleeper) and Baht 300 for a second-class sleeper.

CAR RENTAL: Car rentals are available at some of the more popular tourist destinations. **Avis** has offices in Chiang Mai (Tel: 053 2220-13); Phuket (Tel: 076 3214-80); Pattaya (Tel: 038 4299-01); and Hua Hin and Cha-Am (Tel: 032 5200-08).

Tours

Most Bangkok hotels catering to foreigners have tour offices to arrange visits within the city area and beyond. **The Tourist Authority of Thailand** (TAT) offers information booklets and advice at their offices in Sydney, Singapore, New York, Los Angeles, London, Paris, Rome, Frankfurt, Kuala Lumpur, Hong Kong, Tokyo, Osaka, Seoul and Taipei.

TAT's head office is in Bangkok, Tel: 226 0060, 226 0072, Fax: 224 6221. TAT has branch offices in Chiang Mai, Tel: 248604, Fax: 248605; Pattaya, Tel: 428750, 429113; Phuket, Tel: 212213, Fax: 213582; and elsewhere.

Accommodation

BANGKOK

A hotel building boom in recent years has given the city a surplus of rooms, but it is still wise to book in advance, particularly at the peak of the tourist season (from November to January). There is an enormous choice of accommodation, from luxury five-star hotels to middle-range establishments and cheaper places (including agreeable guesthouses). Bear in mind that hotels levy a government tax of 7% on bills, plus another 10% service charge.

Male backpackers may stay in temples, where there is no set rate for accommodation but guests make a cash donation upon leaving.

Bangkok's top-class hotels provide the fullest range of facilities including swimming pool, tennis courts, gymnasium, massage, sauna, TV and video in rooms, shopping arcades, interpreters and business/secretarial services. Major hotels will send a representative to the airport to escort guests if you request it at the time of booking.

At the **Oriental**, Bangkok's most famous hotel, guests may even take lessons in Thai cooking. There is little to choose in terms of luxury among the top hotels. But if you are in Bangkok on business, you will want to make sure the hotel is conveniently located. The Oriental owes its popularity in part to its river location, and now there are other riverside hotels of similar distinction, notably the **Shangri-La** and the **Royal Orchid Sheraton**. Keep in mind, however, that travelling between the riverside and business and government centres in other parts of the city can be a nightmare during peak traffic periods and in the wet season.

The Regent, **Dusit Thani**, **Hilton International**, **Imperial**, **Montien**, **The Landmark** and the **Hyatt Erawan** are located more centrally. Close to the airport are the **Airport Hotel**, the **Rama Garden** and the **Central Plaza**.

Note that though tap water is now officially "potable," it is best not to drink it. Stick with bottled water, which is available everywhere.

Tipping: hotels and major restaurants add service but this is not the case in smaller Thai eating places. Baht 10-20 as a tip is adequate in those places. Taxi drivers are not tipped. Give hotel porters Baht 10.

ACCOMMODATION UPCOUNTRY

Outside the capital, hotels of international standard can be found only at major resorts. Expect to find them in Phuket, Pattaya, Jomtien, Chiang Mai, Hua Hin, Cha-am, Songkhla, Haadyai and Koh Samui. But many provincial capitals and big towns have Western-style hotels, often with swimming pools and tennis courts, and these offer some of the best accommodation bargains in Thailand. You can find these in Mae Sot, Chiang Rai, Surin, Ubon Ratchathani, Ayutthaya, Nakhon Pathom (**Rose Garden Country Resort**), Kanchanaburi, Bang Saen, Rayong, Chantaburi and Nong Khai.

Dining

Although it may appear to be similar, Thai food provides quite a different adventure from Chinese or Indian cuisine. It is a blend of five distinct tastes: sweet, sour, salty, bitter and hot. An extremely hot dish probably contains

Elephants on parade.

the yellowy-orange *phrik leung*, the hottest of all chillies. Thais say some chillies are mild, but few are safe to chew.

If you are not familiar with Thai food, try some first. If you find it unbearably hot, start asking for your food not too hot. Most first-class hotels tend to tone spices down for the Western palate. For those looking forward to the real Thai taste, you may have to ask for it hotter.

Thai cooking is simple compared with the complicated dishes of China, India and France. Dishes are prepared with fresh, local ingredients and fragrant and pungent spices and herbs, essentially lemon grass, basil, garlic, ginger, turmeric and coriander.

The best introduction to Thai food is *tom yum* soup, the nearest thing to a Thai national dish. It is a thin soup of prawn (shrimp), white fish or chicken, with vegetables, made sharp and hot with lemon grass, chillies and other herbs. If you like it, you will like Thai food.

A typical meal includes steamed rice (in the north it will be glutinous rice eaten with the fingers), five or six dishes of soup, fish, a curry blended with coconut milk, vegetables and perhaps grilled dried beef or an omelette stuffed with pork. Shrimp paste, fish sauce, tamarind sauce and other condiments are served on the side.

Thailand produces and exports huge quantities of seafood, but you cannot depend on Bangkok eating places, especially the huge establishments specializing in seafood, for fresh supplies. Near the coast, however, shrimps, prawns, crabs, lobster and mussels are fresh and sweet.

Thai desserts sometimes are too sweet and sticky for visitors, but mango (in season from March to May) with sticky rice blended with coconut milk is a treat for all. There are other desserts made from egg, mung beans, lotus seeds and palm sugar, and sticky rice mixed with peanuts and baked in a short length of bamboo.

The local fruit is some of the finest food to be had in Thailand. The mangosteen, which resemble a small purple tennis ball, pomelos (citrus), jackfruit, rambutan and durian are the best in the world. Durian is foul-smelling, but the Thais call it the King of Fruits and its rich, custardy flavour is unforgettable. It has become increasingly popular in the whole of Southeast Asia and now even in Hong Kong. Do not try to take one home with you; apart from any other restrictions on fresh produce, airlines do not usually permit passengers to carry durians aboard because of the pungent smell.

Enterprising growers in the northern mountains now produce temperate fruits, especially strawberries. Pineapples, bananas, papayas and oranges are available throughout the year.

Some of the best Thai food is served in open-front restaurants or in outdoor markets in Bangkok and other cities and towns. When there is a language problem, just point and you will almost certainly get what you want. Good areas for these places in Bangkok are: Pratunam Market (near the junction of Phetchaburi Rd and Rajprarop Rd); in the vicinity of the Ratchadamnoen Boxing Stadium (Ratchadamnoen Rd); along Silom and Sukhumvit roads and in the area between the Democracy Monument and the river.

Some of the riverside restaurants have boats which sail on the Chao Phraya river for dinner. Excellent Thai food is served during the two-hour voyage. One of the best floating restaurants sails from the **Yokyo Restaurant**, Visuthikasat Rd, near the Bank of Thailand, Tel: 282 7385.

The **Oriental Hotel** has vessels which make longer voyages up river but they are much grander and more expensive. On the Thonburi side of the river opposite the Oriental Hotel the **Sala Rim Nam** puts on a nightly show of classical Thai dancing with dinner.

There is also Thai music and dancing at **Tumpnakthai**, 131 Ratchadapisek Rd, Tel: 277 8833 or 277 8855. This claims to be the biggest restaurant in the world. It covers 10 acres and employs 1,000 waiters and waitresses bringing dishes to tables on roller skates.

Very few Bangkok restaurants provide live music or dancing, but they can be found in the restaurants of major hotels.

There is no point in coming to Thailand for European or American-style food because it is far better at home. There are a few French, Italian, German or Scandinavian restaurants which seem good to resident foreigners but visitors will not rate too highly. Western food in hotels, even five-star establishments, can be indifferent. Among the better places are **Ma Maison** (Hilton Hotel), **Normandie Grill** (Oriental Hotel) and **The Fireplace Grill** (Meridien President Hotel). The cooking is possibly better at smaller restaurants.

Entertainment

Bangkok's notorious nightlife is as male-oriented as ever, but fears about Aids have reduced the scale of business. There are hundreds of bars, discos, clubs and "massage parlours" open until the early hours of the morning. The main areas for these are: Patpong Rd (there are two parallel streets linking Silom and Suriwong roads) and the surrounding quarter; Soi 4, Sukhumvit Rd; and Soi Cowboy (off Soi 21, Sukhumvit Rd). Japanese bars can be found in Soi Thaniya, between Silom and Suriwong roads.

Some of the bars in the Patpong district feature "live shows" and other attractions upstairs. Some of these places charge you extra for the "entertainment," but do not announce that fact in advance. Customers often complain when the unexpected charge appears on the bar bill.

What might be called "real" bars, where customers may drink and talk without too much noise and hassle, are few and far between in these streets. **Crown Royal** (Patpong 2, near the car park) and the **Madrid** (on Patpong 1) are probably the best of these.

The proliferation of bars and other drinking places makes this section of the guide almost superfluous. Nobody will ever die for want of a drink in Bangkok, but it can be an expensive activity. A glass of local beer varies from US$1.20 in a noodle shop, to US$4 in a luxury hotel. Local "whisky" is the cheapest alcoholic drink. The most popular is Mekhong whisky at about US$2 for a half bottle. Try it with ice, soda and a squeeze of lemon. Foreigners find Kloster the best of the beers, though the big beer with Thais is Singha. Amarit Draught from the cask is not easy to find but it is palatable and the cheapest beer on the market.

Some bars are inclined to mix imported whisky and gin with local products. Imported wine in restaurants and liquor stores is expensive, as the government taxes it at the same rate as imported spirits.

Liquor is on sale at all times except religious holidays, when it is available only in hotels and Western-style restaurants. You pay more for drinks in hotels because they impose government tax and service charges on the bills.

Bangkok is not strong on other forms of entertainment, but you can find it. Those hoping to experience a bit of local culture can see Thai classical dancing, presented nightly at the **Sala Rim Nam restaurant** (opposite the

Oriental Hotel); a big, open-air establishment alongside **Florida Hotel** (Phyathai Rd) features interesting northeastern Thai music and dancing.

The relatively new **Thai Cultural Centre** (Ratchadapisek Rd) offers a fine variety of Thai, Asian and Western music, dance and drama.

Most big hotels have music bars where musicians, mostly from the Philippines, provide Western-style music. And Western jazz is popular in Bangkok. **Bobby's Arms** (Patpong 2) features jazz on Sunday nights. **Brown Sugar** (Soi Sarasin, opposite Lumpini Park), is a top spot every night of the week.

Massage parlours can be found all over Bangkok. The classified yellow pages of the telephone directory list more than 100 parlours. Depending on the service required and the plushness of the establishment, prices range from Baht 500-2,000.

Shopping

Bargaining is a way of life in Thailand and almost all shops (except department stores) will offer discounts, so join in. Do not forget to ask for receipts, especially for jewellery and antiques. Antiques and genuine works of art need export licences. Remember, you may not take a Thai Buddha image out of the country. Anyone with a complaint about a purchase should write to the Tourism Authority of Thailand (TAT, Ratchadamnoen Nok Ave, Bangkok 10100).

You generally can trust shops that display the TAT emblem. That means they have passed the scrutiny of the tourist authority and their performance is monitored regularly.

The main shopping centres in Bangkok are around Silom, Suriwong, Sukhumvit roads and Siam Square. For cut-price goods, the Banglumphu district near the Grand Palace and Pratunam Market are best. **Narai Phand**, the government shop on Ratchadamri Rd, offers Thai handicrafts. Shops in the **Oriental Plaza** near the hotel are also worth browsing through.

The really good buys in Bangkok are traditional Thai articles in silk, cotton, silver and nielloware, lacquer and bronzeware, celadon and woodwork. There are many "antique shops," but genuine articles are rare and very expensive. Some of the craftsmen making these articles ask dealers "do you want your pieces present-day or antique?" They can do them one way as easily as the other.

Genuine Thai silk is a good bargain. The pure stuff is bulky and rough (unfamiliar buyers may not even recognize it as silk), while that mixed with Japanese silk looks smoother and is softer to the touch. Most silk on sale in Bangkok is mixed and is good value for money.

The thing to avoid is rayon mixed with the silk. Many Indian merchants sell this type of fabric. Buy from well-established places such as the **Jim Thompson Thai Silk Company** (9 Suriwong Rd) or **Design Thai** (304 Silom Rd). You will pay more, but will get the real thing.

Thai tailors and dressmakers are outstanding for quick, made-to-measure suits, shirts and dresses.

Thailand is also a treasure trove of gems, gold and silver. Rubies and sapphires are mined here and also imported from Burma and Cambodia. Burma sends its jade to Thai workshops, renowned for their gem carving skills. You can buy every type of precious stone and metal in Bangkok, which has thousands of reputable retailers whose prices compare favourably with those in other countries.

Buyers should patronize only those shops that display the gem trade's official emblem — a gold ring mounted with a ruby — which guarantees the dealer's integrity. Make sure to get a detailed receipt and a certificate guaranteeing the authenticity of the gemstone or precious metal you have purchased. And try to determine whether the shop is a member of the **Thai Gems and Jewellery Traders Association** (Tel: 235 3039). **The Asian Institute of Gemological Science** (AIGS) (Tel: 221 6206-10) conducts tests to verify a stone's authenticity. Visitors with complains may also contact the Tourist Police (Tel: 221 6206-10 in Bangkok).

Upcountry, the night bazaar in Chiang Mai has some of Thailand's finest handicrafts. San Kamphaeng (13 kilometres outside the city) is noted for silk and Bo Sang village for parasols.

Outside Bangkok, the best place to buy gems is **Chantaburi**, 450 kilometres from the capital on the coast beyond Pattaya. Rubies and sapphires are mined nearby, and the town, which still has a French air about it, is famous for its gem cutters.

Sports

The Thais love sports and they love to gamble on the outcome of any contest (though organized gambling, aside from horse racing and the state lottery, is illegal). The traditional matches

— between Thai boxers, fighting fish, cocks, bulls and kites in the sky — still go on everywhere, but today there are also football, tennis, sailing and golf.

The English-language *The Nation* newspaper publishes sports details every Friday.

GOLF: The richer Thais have taken up golf with a passion scarcely equalled anywhere in the world. Golf courses and driving ranges are within easy reach and new ones open all the time. Entrance fees and membership in some cases exceed US$25,000. But more than 10 public courses in or near Bangkok are open to visitors. Fees for visitors range from Baht 500-1,000.

THAI BOXING: This unique sport combines orthodox punching with kicking and kneeing. Bouts are of five three-minute rounds with two minutes between rounds. Each fight begins with an elaborate dance and prayer ritual, in which the fighters invoke the aid of spirits, pay respect to their teachers and work themselves up to a high state of aggression. As the fight begins, so does frantic Thai music that sends the fighters and crowd into a frenzy. The fighting can be vicious and damaging because of the powerful kicking. Serious injuries, occasionally fatal, occur frequently. The top venues for boxing in Bangkok are **Lumpini Stadium** and the **Ratchadamnoen Stadium**. Bouts take place at one or the other every other week. Admission varies from Baht 30-200.

COCK AND FISH FIGHTING: These are traditional rural pastimes, but they are not easy to locate since they are officially illegal — not out of concern for the animals that are forced to duel, but because the gambling involved is against the law. In fish fighting, two large fighting fish are put into a tank together, and only one survives.

BULL FIGHTING: This sport, confined to the south of Thailand, radically differs from the Spanish tradition in that the bulls fight each other and humans are not directly involved.

TENNIS: Some major hotels have tennis courts. Public courts for hire are listed in the classified section of the Bangkok telephone directory.

HORSE RACING: Races take place on Saturday and Sunday, either at the **Royal Bangkok Sports Club** or **Royal Turf Club**.

Dec. 25 Holidays

The dates of many of the Thai festivals, particularly those connected with Buddhism, are determined by the lunar calendar and thus vary from year to year. The most interesting to visitors are the **Songkran** festival, which marks the traditional Thai New Year in April and **Loi Krathong** in November when Thais wash away their sins.

PHOTO: B.J. ADAMS

Sea and sun.

February 6: Makha Bucha Day, on full moon day — commemorates the occasion when 1,250 disciples spontaneously gathered to hear Lord Buddha preach. Public holiday.

April: Chakri Day — commemorates the founding in 1782 of the present ruling dynasty. This is the only day of the year when the Royal Pantheon, containing statues of the kings at the Temple of the Emerald Buddha, is open to the public. Public holiday.

April 13-15: Songkran Festival — the Thai new year, marked by religious merrymaking, beauty parades and nationwide water throwing. In Chiang Mai, the best place to experience the occasion, there is a procession of local beauties wearing Thai dress and carrying silver bowls of perfumed water. Westerners are favourite targets for the water throwers. Three public holidays.

May 1: Labour Day — the government provides free film shows and other public entertainment for the workers. Public holiday.

May 5: Coronation Day — the reigning monarch, King Bhumibol, was crowned on this day

in 1950. Public holiday.
May: Royal ploughing ceremony — this rite, near the beginning of the month, marks the official beginning of the rice-planting cycle and involves elaborate Brahma ritual to produce predictions about the forthcoming rice harvest. The King and Queen preside over the ceremony at Sanam Luang in Bangkok.
Rocket Festival: celebrated during the second weekend of the month at Yasothorn in the northeast. Villagers construct large rockets to fire into the sky to ensure plentiful rice season rains. Folk dancing and other revelry are part of the festival.
Wisaka Bucha Day: celebrated on the full moon in May, this is the holiest of all Buddhist days, marking Lord Buddha's birth, enlightenment and death. In the evening a procession of Buddhists, and tourists too, carries candles, incense and flowers three times around the temples. The Temple of the Emerald Buddha and the Marble Temple are among the best places to view the festival in Bangkok. Public holiday.
July: Asalaha Bucha Day — on the day of the full moon, this festival commemorates Lord Buddha's first sermon to his first five disciples and the beginning of Buddhist Lent, when monks retire to their monasteries to study and meditate. Public holiday. Candle festivals are also held on this day at Ubon Ratchathani in the northeast. Embellished beeswax candles are paraded before presentation to temples.
August 12: Queen's birthday — Queen Sirikit was born in 1932.
September: Vegetarian Festival — in late September-early October at Phuket, in the south, Chinese Buddhists commit themselves to a vegetarian diet for nine days (on both sides of the full moon). Some dress in white and inflict pain upon themselves by piercing their cheeks and tongues with metal skewers and walking on fire.
October: The end of the rainy season, near the full moon day, is celebrated with boat races wherever a suitable stretch of water is available. The illuminated boat procession on the Mekong river at Nakhon Phanom in the northeast is spectacular.
October 23: Chulalongkorn Day — honours King Chulalongkorn, who reigned from 1868-1910. He helped to lead feudal Siam towards the modern age by abolishing slavery, introducing railways and establishing personal contacts with foreign monarchs. Public holiday.
November: Phra Pathom Chedi Fair — during the first weekend of the month at Nakhon Pathom (80 kilometres from Bangkok) there is a colourful festival of drama, dancing, side-shows and popular entertainment.
Loi Krathong Festival: held on the night of the full moon, this is one of Thailand's loveliest festivals. Thais float small lotus-shaped banana-leaf boats, each containing a candle, incense and a small coin, to honour the water spirits and to wash away the previous year's sins. On this night all water places are crowded, so you must book ahead for organized events. It is often more rewarding to join the impromptu fun alongside a canal or stream.
Traditional Elephant Round-up: in the third week of November at Surin in the northeast, more than 100 elephants participate in this annual event, which includes wild elephant hunts, elephants at work and a spectacular medieval war-elephant parade.
December 5: The King's Birthday — King Bhumibol, Thailand's longest-ruling monarch (since 1946), was born on this day in 1927. Public holiday.
December 10: Constitution Day — a new constitution giving Thailand a parliamentary system and a constitutional monarchy came into force on this day in 1932. Public holiday.
December 31-January 1: New Year's Eve and New Year's Day — Thais celebrate these two Western calendar holidays with as much revelry as the Thai New Year.

PUBLICATIONS

Those interested in learning more about the language and culture may find some of the following books to be helpful:
Practical Thai, a communication guide for travellers and residents, Baht 100.
English-Thai Conversation, Baht 40.
A Pocket Guide to Spoken Thai, Baht 32.
Siam Guide, Baht 32.
A Guide to Thai Conversation, Baht 60.
Some of these are available at:
DK Books, Surawongse Rd, near Patpong Rd and at Siam Square, Rama I Rd.
Asia Book, four locations, at 221 Sukhumvit Rd, Peninsula Plaza, Ratchadamri Rd and Landmark Hotel, Sukhumvit Rd.
The Bookseller, Patpong Rd.

These shops have a wide range of guide books mainly in English but some too in French, German, Italian and Spanish. Prices range at around Baht 300.

Second-hand copies of guide and phrase books are available at **Elite Books**, 593

Bangkok's Democracy Monument. PHOTO: RON McMILLAN/ECHO

Sukhumvit Rd, Bangkok's best second-hand booksellers.

DISCOVERING THAILAND

BANGKOK

After a seemingly endless wait at Immigration, then dodging airport touts offering a taxi ride into town or a pretty girl (or boy), you may wonder if it is all a mistake. The run in from the airport through traffic jams and pollution will not dispel those early misgivings. Bangkok is an ugly city sprawling over low-lying land. The city has no obvious geographical centre, but it has a lot of heart. It is a friendly, vibrant place and, thus, visitors quickly brush aside the hassles and ugliness.

Bangkok scarcely possesses a building much more than 100 years old, but there are many older works of art brought in from earlier settlements. The city was founded more than two centuries ago on the site now occupied by the Grand Palace, an array of temples and shrines that has been called "a dazzling fairy tale of dreams." **Chakri Palace**, the Royal Family's original home, is also there, but the King now lives in the more modern **Chitlada Palace** nearby.

The Grand Palace complex houses Thailand's most famous and sacred Buddhist shrine — the **Temple of the Emerald Buddha**. It is so sacred that taking photos of the green image is prohibited. Only 76 centimetres high, the Buddha, which is made of jasper, is linked with the very survival of the Royal House. **The Temple of the Reclining Buddha**, an amazing figure measuring 48 metres long and 15 metres high, symbolizes the passing of the Lord Buddha from this life into Nirvana. Tickets costing Baht 100 each admit visitors to both temples. Mornings (from 8:30 a.m. on) are the best time for a visit. Shorts and sleeveless garments are forbidden in parts of the Grand Palace and in other holy places in Thailand. Discreet dress is essential; skirts for women, long trousers for men. A jacket may be required in some sections and may be rented on the spot.

The Temple of Dawn, on the banks of the river, is one of Bangkok's striking landmarks. Parts of it are 90 metres high and are covered with fragments of porcelain and pottery. Traditional Thai massage is available at the temple. Nearby, on the Thonburi side of the river, is the dock for the King's barges. For centuries, monarchs have travelled on the royal barges for state occasions. These 45-metre-long craft are brilliantly decorated in red, gold and black and on ceremonial occasions are manned by 60 oarsmen.

Wat Benchamabophit (Marble Temple), on Sri Ayutthaya Rd near the Dusit Zoo, is a perfect place to rest and enjoy the cool of Italian marble underfoot.

Wat Traimit (Temple of the Golden Buddha), near the Hualamphong railway station, contains a Buddha statue made from 5.5 tonnes of solid 18-carat gold. For nearly 200 years the image was encased in plaster, but the gold was revealed when it dropped from a crane 40 years ago.

If you want to know how Thailand became what it is today, do not miss the **National Museum** near the Grand Palace. The huge, grassy expanse outside the museum, known as **Sanam Luang**, is the stage for great occasions — state funerals, political meetings and even revolutions. In the breezy early months of the year, children and grown men fly colourful kites, a popular traditional pastime.

Journeys along the Chao Phraya river offer probably the most fascinating sightseeing in Bangkok. There are regular boat services and other craft are available for personal hire. Tourist offices in hotels and tour agents will organize trips, visits to floating markets and cruises along the *khlongs* (canals). Some of the riverside restaurants also have boats that sail on the Chao Phraya river for dinner. The Thai food served is excellent and the trip takes around two hours.

Jim Thompson's house (off Rama I Rd) is worth a detour for anyone interested in Asian art. The owner, who disappeared in Malaysia more than 20 years ago in circumstances never explained, revived the Thai silk industry after World War II, making Thai silk popular all over the world. His enchanting home, perhaps the most beautiful house in Bangkok, was built from six old teak houses brought from upcountry. It is filled with exquisite works of art from Thailand, Cambodia, Burma and China. The garden is an oasis of beauty and peace. Thompson's original silk factories are across the khlong. The house is open from 9 a.m.- 5 p.m. every day except Sunday (entrance fee, Baht 100).

Bangkok markets provide a panorama of city life, as well as good shopping and eating. **Pratunam** is the most central. Many restaurants and some shops stay open most of the night. **The Weekend Market** (Chatuchak Park, opposite the northern bus terminal), open from 7 a.m.-6 p.m. on Saturday and Sunday, is the biggest in the city. Here you can buy anything from live animals to old books. Chinatown is one bustling market specializing in imports from China, gold, festival decorations and Swiss watches — mostly fakes. For antiques try the so-called **Thieves' Market**, or Nakhon Kasem (bordered by Chakrawat, Yaowarat and Charoen Krung roads). **The Snake Farm** (Rama IV Rd) is open every weekday at 11 a.m. (entry Baht 40). You can watch keepers handle the snakes, including lethal cobras and pythons nearly six metres long. Tourists like to be photographed with pythons draped around their necks.

DAY TRIPS FROM BANGKOK

The Rose Garden Country Resort, only 30 kilometres from Bangkok on the road to Nakhon Pathom, has large and beautiful gardens, several restaurants and a hotel, as well as bungalows for rent. There is a Thai cultural show every afternoon, including dancing, boxing, sword fighting, cock fighting and a display of rural life. **The Crocodile Farm** and **Zoo** is nearby, housing the world's largest albino crocodile and other wild animals. The highlight is a wrestling match between a crocodile and a keeper.

Nakhon Pathom, 50 kilometres from Bangkok, is one of Thailand's oldest settlements and the site of the **Golden Chedi**, a bell-shaped shrine visible from afar. Rising 115 metres, it is the largest pagoda in Southeast Asia and the tallest Buddhist monument in the world.

Ayutthaya, only 80 kilometres from Bangkok, can be reached by road, rail or river. The capital of old Siam, Ayutthaya was razed by Burmese invaders in 1767. The city's canals were said to have run red with blood. Red-coloured ruins are just about all that is left now of the old capital, though a few buildings have been restored. The principal ruins lie around the former royal palace. There is a teak pavilion still standing, where the kings paid homage to their predecessors. The gardens are delightful, particularly in January and February when "flame of the forest" trees are in bloom. The newly opened Ayutthaya Historical Centre presents an exciting picture of Thailand's "Golden Age" and is a unique information and research centre. You may hire boats at the landing stage in the modern town, which will take you to some of the most interesting of the

Southern charms. PHOTO: VERONICA GARBUTT

ruins and to a number of good restaurants on large boats or floating rafts near the main bridge.

On the way back to Bangkok you can stop at the summer palace of **Bang Pa-In**. It was here that an early king met and fell in love with a beautiful girl called In. The place was therefore called the village (*bang*) where he met (*pa*) In. Now rarely used, the palace has a melancholy air, though the buildings and gardens have great beauty. One of the garden buildings is a Victorian observation tower built by King Chulalongkorn in memory of one of his wives, Queen Sunanta, and their child, who were drowned on their way to the palace in the 1870s.

The trip further north from Ayutthaya to **Lopburi** and Saraburi takes one long day, but it is worth it, as you leave the flat plain and enter scenic hilly country. At **Saraburi**, 130 kilometres from Bangkok, there is a shrine — **Phra Buddha Bhat** — said to contain the Buddha's footprint. The footprint was found, the local story goes, by a hunter who had wounded a deer which disappeared into the undergrowth and emerged completely healed. Nearby is the **Muak Lek** botanical park rich in plants and flowers.

Pattaya, dubbed "sin city," is still the most popular weekend resort for Bangkok residents. It is described as one of Asia's major beach resorts, yet the sea is officially classified as too polluted for safe swimming. Many hotel swimming pools are also dubious because freshwater supplies have not kept up with the enormous growth of hotels and high-rise apartments. But it is only 120 kilometres from Bangkok and the drive along the superhighway takes less than two hours. Pattaya has an enormous range of hotels guesthouses and restaurants at every price. The nightlife is a repeat of all that is available in Bangkok, plus transvestite shows.

Over the hill from Pattaya is the new resort of **Jomtien Beach**, which is less crowded and strident. The sea is also cleaner. Further down the coast is **Koh Samet**, which is less developed than many other resorts. Across the Gulf of Thailand from Pattaya are two popular weekend resorts on the coast, **Hua Hin** and **Cha-Am**. You can get to these places from Bangkok in about three hours by road, or by train.

UPCOUNTRY

Kanchanaburi, a prosperous town about 130 kilometres west of Bangkok, is the centre of the province of the same name. Good hotel accommodation is available here and further upriver. The area running up to the Burmese border at **Three Pagodas Pass** is worth a stay of two or three days. The road to the border is good all year round and limited accommodation is available at the pass.

Just outside Kanchanaburi stands the infamous **Bridge over the River Kwai**, built by prisoners of the Japanese army during World War II to carry the Thailand-Burma railway. The bridge was basically destroyed by Allied bombers in 1945; only the curved spans are part of the original structure. *Son et Lumiere* shows are held at the bridge every November. Cruises are available on the Kwai river, as are river rafts.

The present railway runs up to **Nam Tok**, where the line ends. This is a popular journey for tourists. The trains on this route are also used by farmers to bring their produce, mostly chillies, to market.

The **Kanchanaburi** war cemetery, in the centre of the town, holds the graves of almost 7,000 Prisoners of War (POWs), most of them British, Australian and Dutch, who died working on the railway. A smaller war cemetery, **Chungkai**, is on the other side of the river. A museum near the centre of town contains photographs, POWs' possessions and tools and tells the story of the railway. It is called the **Jeath** museum — made up of the first letters of the main nations involved (Japan, England, Australia, Thailand and Holland), since many people felt "death museum" was too stark a name.

Chiang Mai, called "the rose of the north" is well above sea level and lies in a valley ringed by mountains. Its fresh cool air, flowers, mountains, colourful festivals and beautiful women, have made Chiang Mai one of the most popular places in Thailand among Thais and foreigners alike. It is the home of Thai handicrafts — silk and cotton weaving, pottery, umbrella making, silverware, lacquerware and wood-carving. Artists and craftsmen can be seen at work everywhere. Varied groups of hilltribe people live in the nearby mountains and you can see them at work and in their villages and homes.

Chiang Mai means "city of a thousand temples." There are more than 1,100 in the city area, though many are now obscured by modern buildings. The oldest temple is **Wat Chiang Man**, built about AD 1300. The largest, **Phra Singh**, houses the most venerated Buddha image in the north. **Wat Koo Tao** has one of the strangest towers in Thailand; it was built in 1613 in the form of gourds in five tiers and was decorated with coloured porcelain.

The most famous structure in the north is **Wat Doi Suthep**, a 14th-century temple outside Chiang Mai. The nearby **Royal Winter Palace's** gardens are open on Fridays, weekends and public holidays, except when the Royal Family is there. There is a Thai saying that if you do not climb **Doi Suthep** or eat *kow soy*, you have not been to Chiang Mai. Kow soy is a savoury curry noodle dish, served widely in this area.

From Chiang Mai you can reach **Chiang Rai**, close to both Burma and Laos, by road and air. Just beyond it are the opium poppy fields of the infamous Golden Triangle, but it is an ideal spot to begin a jungle trek or a river rafting trip.

Mae Hong Son, a remote hill-town, has become more popular with improved access by road and air. Some of Thailand's last big, natural forests are in the vicinity. The town of wooden buildings is still unspoiled. Communist insurgents kept tourists away until recent years, though bandits occasionally make trouble.

Halfway between these northern resorts and Bangkok are **Sukhothai**, site of the first Thai capital, and **Phitsanuloke**, a convenient area for breaking the long journey. Two fine national parks and spectacular waterfalls are easily accessible.

Korat, a thriving commercial centre, is the gateway to the 17 provinces of the northeast. Attractions include the wild scenic beauty of the **Khao Yai National Park**. There are outstanding Khmer ruins at **Pimai**, 60 kilometres from the town.

Although the northeast is the poorest region of Thailand, there are many attractive places to visit. Among these are: **Nong Khai** and **Nakhon Phanom**, on the Mekong river, where Laotian and other outside influences are evident; and **Surin** and **Buri Ram**, where Khmer influence is strong. Surin stages the annual elephant round-up (third week in November), attended by people from all over the world. **Udorn Thani** province is famous for **Ban Chiang**, site of the birthplace of the Thai race 7,000 years ago (*see History*). The winters and mountains of northern Loei Province attract many people dried out by the tropics. It is the only place in Thailand to record frost.

THE SOUTH

Some of the most scenic country — and, therefore, increasingly popular with tourists — lies along the narrow peninsula that stretches down towards Malaysia. Most of Thailand's Muslim population live in these southernmost provinces. Tourism has now outpaced the traditional big businesses — rubber and tin — as the most valuable industry in this area.

The hub of the industry is the island of **Phuket**, off the coast in the Andaman Sea. The island is 800 square kilometres and is connected to the mainland by a causeway. It has magnificent coves and bays, sparkling sea and white beaches and hotels of the highest international standards, including some of the best in Southeast Asia. The best beaches are on the west coast. But building and other tourist developments are spoiling the ambience, polluting air and sea and destroying the coral reefs. **Patong** beach has become a mini-Pattaya; if you are not looking for a "good time in the old town tonight," look for the more remote resort hotels with private beaches.

Further east, **Krabi**, with its famous Phi Phi island offshore, remains unspoiled, but large-scale developments are already evident. **Satun**, on the edge of Malaysia, has a new marine national park with magnificent coral and crystal clear water. **Songkhla**, a seaside town with long, white beaches, has managed to escape the worst excesses of tourism. Not far away is **Haadyai**, a rip-roaring frontier town noted for its smuggling, cheap shopping and sex.

Koh Samui, a large island 40 kilometres off Surat Thani, is a popular resort for Thais and foreigners. Discovered by the hippies in the 1960s, it has gone upmarket with expensive hotels and restaurants. Boats from the mainland will take you there. There now are direct flights to Koh Samui from Bangkok, Hong Kong and other Asian cities. The two major beaches are among the most beautiful in Southeast Asia, but are crowded in high season.

Thailand has no fewer than 50 national parks all over the country. **Khao Yai National Park**, in the southeast, has more than 100 wild elephants and is one of the finest wildlife reserves in the country. There are also marine parks based on islands in the south. Two of these are **Ang Thong**, near Samui island, and **Tarutao** off the southwestern coast in the Andaman Sea. Limited accommodation is available in some of the parks. For details, contact the Tourist Authority of Thailand offices.

BANGKOK RESTAURANT SELECTION

Average price for two

ALL GAENGS, Suriwong Rd. Tel: 233 3301. Thai. US$28.

BEI OTTO, Soi 20, Sukhumvit Rd. Tel: 262 0892. German. US$40.

BOBBY'S ARMS, Patpong 2 Rd. Tel: 233 6828. English. Live dixieland jazz on Sunday evenings. US$36.

BUSSARACUM, Soi Pipat, Silom Rd. Tel: 235 8915. Thai. US$38.

CABBAGES AND CONDOMS, Soi 12, Sukhumvit Rd. Tel: 252 7349. Thai. US$18.

CAFE DE PARIS, Patpong 2 Rd. Tel: 237 2776. French. US$48.

LE DALAT, Soi 23, Sukhumvit Rd. Tel: 258 4192. Vietnamese. US$30.

CHINA HOUSE, Oriental Ave. Tel: 236 0430. Chinese. US$60.

LAICRAM, Soi 23, Sukhumvit Rd. Tel: 392 5864. Thai. US$32.

LE BISTRO, Soi Ruamrudee. Tel: 251 2523. French. US$75.

LE BORDEAUX, Soi 39, Sukhumvit Rd. Tel: 258 9766. French. US$58.

LEMON GRASS, Soi 24, Sukhumvit Rd. Tel: 258 8637. Thai. US$42.

L'OPERA, Soi 39, Sukhumvit Rd. Tel: 258 5606. Italian. US$50.

METRO, Soi Langsuan. Tel: 251 3058. French. US$52.

SALA RIM NAM, on riverside opposite Oriental Hotel. Tel: 236 0400. Thai. Thai show with dinner. US$48.

SILOM VILLAGE, 286 Silom Rd. Tel: 234 4581. Thai. Live music. US$28.

SPICE MARKET, Regent Hotel, Ratchadamri Rd. Tel: 251 6127. Thai. US$48.

THAI ROOM, Patpong 2 Rd. Tel: 233 7920. Thai/International. US$20.

THANYING, 10 Soi Pramual, Silom Rd. Tel: 236 4361. Thai. US$38.

WHITE ORCHID, 108 New Petchburi Rd. Tel: 253 7520. Chinese. US$42.

WHOLE EARTH, Soi Langsuan, Tel: 258 4900. Thai/Vegetarian. US$32.

WIT'S OYSTER BAR, Soi Ruamrudee. Tel: 251 9455. English. US$70.

HOTEL GUIDE

BANGKOK

A: US$180 and above

CENTRAL PLAZA, Phaholyothin Rd. Tel: 541 1234, Fax: 541 1087. *P, Gym, Biz, Ex, SatTV. R: L, W.*

DUSIT THANI, 946 Rama 4 Rd. Tel: 236 0450, Fax: 236 6400, Tlx: 81170 DUSITOTEL. *P, Gym, Biz, Ex, SatTV. R: L, W.*

GRAND HYATT ERAWAN, 494 Ratchadamri Rd. Tel: 254 1234, Fax: 253 5856, Tlx: 20975 HYATTBKK. *P, Gym, Biz, SatTV. R: L, W.*

MANSION KEMPINSKI, Soi 11, Sukhumvit Rd. Tel: 255 7200, Fax: 253 2329. *P, Biz, SatTV. R: L, W.*

ORIENTAL, Oriental Ave. Tel: 236 0400, Fax: 236 1937, Tlx: 82997 ORIENTL. *P, Gym, Biz, SatTV. R: L, W.*

REGENT, 155 Ratchadamri Rd. Tel: 251 6127, Fax: 253 9195, Tlx: 20004 REGBKK. *P, Gym, Biz, SatTV. R: L, W.*

ROYAL ORCHID SHERATON, Captain Bush Lane, Si Phraya Rd. Tel: 234 5599, Fax: 236 8320, Tlx: 84491 ROYORCH. *P, Gym, Biz, Ex. R: L, W.*

SHANGRI-LA, Soi Wat Suan Plu. Tel: 236 7777, Fax: 236 8579, Tlx: 84265 SHANGLA. *P, Gym, Biz, SatTV. R: L, W.*

SUKOTHAI, Sathorn Tai Rd. Tel: 287 0222, Fax: 278 4980. *P, Gym, Biz, SatTV. R: L, W.*

B: US$150-200

SWISSOTEL, Convent Rd. Tel: 233 5345, Fax: 236 9425. *P, SatTV. R: L, W.*

AMARI AIRPORT HOTEL, Opposite international airport. Tel: 566 1020, Fax: 566 1941. *P, Gym, Biz. R: L, W.*

BOULEVARD, Tel: 255 2930, Fax: 255 2950, Tlx: 84033 AMARIBV. *P, Gym, Biz, SatTV. R: L, W.*

HILTON HOTEL, Witt Hayu Rd. Tel: 253 0123, Fax: 255 7491, Tlx: 72206 HILBKK. *P, Gym, Biz, SatTV. R: L, W.*

HOLIDAY INN CROWNE PLAZA, Tel: 238 4300, Fax: 238 5289, Tlx: 82998 HIBKK. *P, Gym, Biz, Ex, SatTV. R: L, W.*

IMPALA, Tel: 258 8612-6, Fax: 258 8747, Tlx: 84056 IMPA. *P, Gym, Biz, SatTV. R: L, W.*

IMPERIAL, Wireless Rd. Tel: 254 0023, Fax: 253 3190, Tlx: 82301 IMPER. *P, Gym, Biz, SatTV. R: L, W.*

IMPERIAL QUEENS PARK, Soi 22, Sukhumvit Rd. Tel: 261 9000, Fax: 261 9530. *Gym, Biz, Ex, SatTV. R: L, W.*

LANDMARK HOTEL, Sukhumvit Rd. Tel: 254 0404, Fax: 253 4259, Tlx: 82072 CTYMARK. *P, Gym, Biz, SatTV. R: L, W.*

LE MERIDIEN PRESIDENT, Gaysorn Rd. Tel: 253 0444, Fax: 253 7565, Tlx: 81194 HOMRO. *P, Gym, Biz, SatTV. R: L, W.*

NOVOTEL, Siam Square. Tel: 255 6888, Fax: 255 1824, Tlx: 22780 NOVOTEL. *P, Gym, Biz, SatTV. R: L, W.*

SIAM INTERCONTINENTAL, Rama 1, Rd. Tel: 253 0355, Fax: 253 2275, Tlx: 81155 SIAMINT. *P, Gym, Biz, SatTV. R: L, W.*

TARA HOTEL, Soi 26, Sukhumvit Rd. Tel: 259 2900, Fax: 2259 2896. *P, Gym, Biz, SatTV. R: L, W.*

TAWANA RAMADA, Surawongse Rd. Tel: 236 0361, Fax: 236 3738. *P, Gym, Biz, SatTV. R: L, W.*

C: US$100-150

AMBASSADOR, Sukhumvit Rd. Tel: 254 0444, Fax: 253 4123, Tlx: 82910 AMTEL. *P, Gym, Biz, SatTV. R: L, W.*

BANGKOK PALACE, New Petchaburi Rd. Tel: 235 0570, Fax: 253 3359, Tlx: 84278 BANGHIL. *P, Gym, SatTV. R: L, W.*

SOMERSET, Soi 15, Sukhumvit Rd. Tel: 254 8500, Fax: 254 8534, Tlx: 72631 SOMRST. *P, Biz, SatTV. R: L, W.*

D: US$50-100

PLAZA HOTEL, Surawongse Rd. Tel: 235 1760, Fax: 237 0746. *P.*

MANHATTAN, Soi 15, Sukhumvit Rd. Tel: 255 0166, Fax: 255 3481. *P, R: L, W.*

CHA-AM

B: US$150-200

REGENT CHA-AM, Tel: 471480, Fax: 411492, Tlx: 72217 REGCHAM. *P, Gym. R: L, W.*

DUSIT RESORT AND POLO CLUB, Tel: 520008, Fax: 236 6400. *P, Gym. R: L, W.*

C: US$100-150

METHAVALAI, Ruamchit Rd. Tel: 471028, Fax: 471590. *P. R: L, W.*

CHIANG MAI

B: US$150-200

CHIANG MAI ORCHID, Huay Kaeo Rd. Tel: 222099, Fax: 221625, Tlx: 23537 CHIOR. *P. R: L, W.*

CHIANG MAI PLAZA, Sri Donchai Rd. Tel: 252050, Fax: 252230, Tlx: 49329. *P. R: L, W.*

P — Swimming pool **Gym** — Health club **Biz** — Business Centre **Ex** — Executive floor
SatTV — Satellite TV **R** — Restaurant **L** — Local food **W** — Western food

HOTEL GUIDE

RINCOME, Huay Keo Rd. Tel: 221044, Fax: 221915, Tlx: 49314. *P, Gym. R: L, W.*

C: US$100-150

CHIANG MAI HILLS, Huay Kaeo Rd. Tel: 221255, Tlx: 49316. *P. R: L, W.*
CHIANG DAO HILL RESORT, 28 MU, Amohoe Phiang Dao (100 kilometres from Chiang Mai). Tel: 236995, Tlx: 43573 HILLRES. *P. R: L, W.*
NOVOTEL SURIWONG, Chang Khlan Rd. Tel: 270051. *P. R: L, W.*

D: US$50-100

CHIANG MAI TRAVEL LODGE, Khamphemngdin Rd. Tel: 271572. *R: L, W.*

CHIANG RAI

C: US$100-150

DUSIT ISLAND RESORT, Kraisonrasit Rd. Tel: 715777, Fax: 715801. *P. R: L, W.*
WIANG COME, Pemawiphak Rd. Tel: 711800, Tlx: 41307 WANGCOM. *P. R: L, W.*

HAADYAI

C: US$100-150

J.B. HAADYAI, Shuti Anuson Rd. Tel: 234300, Fax: 23499. *P, Gym, Biz. R: L, W.*

HUA HIN

C: US$100-150

SOFITEL CENTRAL, Tel: 512021, Fax: 511014, Tlx: 78313. *P, Gym. R: L, W.*
ROYAL GARDEN RESORT, Phetkasem Rd. Tel: 511881, Fax: 512422, Tlx: 78309. *P, Gym. R: L, W.*
ROYAL GARDEN VILLAGE, Phetkasem Rd. Tel: 520050, Fax: 520259, Tlx: 78314. *P, Gym. R: L, W.*

KANCHANABURI

D: US$50-100

RIVER KWAI, Saeng Chuto Rd. Tel: 511184, Fax: 511269, Tlx: 78705 RAMARKH. *P. R: L, W.*
RIVER KWAI VILLAGE HOTEL, Saiyok (70 kilometres from Kanchanaburi town). Tel: Bangkok 215 7828, Fax: Bangkok 255 2350. *P. R: L,W.*
RIVER KWAI JUNGLE RAFTS, Tel: Bangkok 245 3069. *R: L, W.*

KOH SAMUI ISLAND

B: US$150-200

IMPERIAL SAMUI, Tel: 421390, Fax: 421397. *P, Gym. R: L, W.*
IMPERIAL TONGSAI BAY, Tel: 422020, Fax: 421397. *P, Gym. R: L, W.*

C: US$100-150

CHAWENG RESORT, Tel: 421378, Fax: 421378. *P, Gym. R: L, W.*
THE ISLAND, Chaweng Beach. Tel: 421026, Fax: 421178. *R: L, W.*
PANSEA SAMUI HOTEL, Chaweng Beach. Tel: 421384, Fax: 421385. *R: L, W.*

PATTAYA

B: US$150-200

ROYAL CLIFF, Mu 12 Cliff Rd. Tel: 421421, Fax: 428511, Tlx: 85907 CLIFFEX. *P, Gym, Biz, SatTV.*

C: US$100-150

ROYAL GARDEN, Mu 10 Beach Rd. Tel: 428126, Fax: 429926, Tlx: 85909 ROGADEN. *P, Gym, Biz, SatTV.*
ASIA PATTAYA, Cliff Rd. Tel: 428602, Fax: 423496. *P, Gym.*

PHUKET

A: US$200 and above

PACIFIC ISLAND CLUB, 323 Srisunthorn Rd. Tel: 324252, Fax: 311011. *P, Gym, SatTV. R: L, W.*
PHUKET YACHT CLUB, Vised Rd. Tel: 381156, Fax: 381164, Tlx: 69532 YACHT. *P, Gym, Biz. R: L, W.*
DUSIT LAGUNA, Chemgtalay. Tel: 324320, Fax: 324174. *P, Gym, R: L, W.*
AMANPURI RESORT, Amphoe Thalang. Tel: 311394, Fax: 311200. *P, Gym, Biz. R: L, W.*

B: US$150-200

LE MERIDIEN, Karon Beach. Tel: 321480. *P, Gym. R: L, W.*
KARON VILLA, Karon Beach. Tel: 381139, Fax: 381122. *P, Gym. R: L, W.*
THAVORN PALM BEACH, Karon Beach. Tel: 381034, Fax: 381555, Tlx: 69543 RELAX. *R: L, W.*
CLUB MEDITERRANEE, Kata Beach. Tel: 381455, Fax: 381462, Tlx: 69526 CLUBMED. *P, Gym, Biz. R: L, W.*
HOLIDAY INN, Patong Beach. Tel: 321020, Fax: 321435, Tlx: 69545 HIPHUKT. *P, Gym, Biz. R: L, W.*

P — Swimming pool **Gym** — Health club **Biz** — Business Centre **SatTV** — Satellite TV
R — Restaurant **L** — Local food **W** — Western food

VIETNAM

Stretching nearly 2,000 kilometres from the misty mountains on the Chinese border to the fertile Mekong delta, Vietnam is one of the most beautiful countries in Asia. Many of the scars of 30 years of war have disappeared, but economic development has been painfully slow. Obstacles have included years of rigid adherence to doctrinaire socialism — which is now being eased as the ruling Communist Party has introduced free-market reforms — and the United States trade embargo imposed on the country, which ended in 1994.

Vietnam began opening up rapidly to foreign visitors in the late 1980s as part of a drive to reinvigorate the economy. By 1992, some 450,000 tourists a year were visiting Vietnam, including growing numbers of overseas Vietnamese who had earlier fled the country as refugees.

Vietnam's desire to attract tourists, however, is offset by the lack of amenities in a country whose capital-starved economy is still several decades behind its more prosperous Southeast Asian neighbours. The main difficulties range from shortages of hotel rooms to the limited capacity of both internal transport and international flights to and from Vietnam. Access, however, has improved in recent years as more neighbouring countries have resumed flights to Ho Chi Minh City (formerly Saigon) and Hanoi.

History

The Vietnamese, who have their ethnic roots in southern China, began settling in the Red River delta some 4,000 years ago. In 111 BC, the Nam Viet kingdom fell under the authority of Han China and remained its province until AD 939. Even after Vietnam gained its independence, Chinese influence continued.

The country's scholars were imbued with Confucian values and Chinese characters were used for the written language. Many elements of government were borrowed from China, but the Vietnamese always retained their independent identity.

The country was ruled by several Vietnamese dynasties until the early 15th century, when the Chinese returned to power. They were driven out in 1428 and were replaced by the Le dynasty (1428-1776), begun by Le Loi.

The Vietnamese also began pushing south, capturing territory belonging to the kingdom of Champa in what is now central Vietnam. In 1471, the Vietnamese finally defeated the Cham and mounted their final march to the south. By 1765, they had captured the fertile Mekong River delta from the Cambodians, thereby gaining control of all of present-day Vietnam.

In the 18th century, an internal squabble erupted, with remnants of the Le dynasty controlling the north and a rival Nguyen family laying claim to the south. Eventually a civil war broke out and, in 1802, the Nguyen group won with help from French mercenaries and missionaries, and established the Nguyen dynasty, headed by Gia Long.

European traders and missionaries had begun arriving in Vietnam in 1511, but those from France gained particular influence after helping overthrow the Le dynasty. Later emperors opposed foreign intervention, but the killing of two Catholic missionaries gave the French a pretext to take Saigon by force in 1859. By 1886, northern and central Vietnam had been incorporated into French Indochina, along with neighbouring Laos and Cambodia.

Independence movements became increasingly active in the period prior to World War II. The Japanese occupied Indochina in 1941,

◄ *Riding a cycle to school.* PHOTO: CLARO CORTES/REUTER

but left the Vichy French in control. In March 1945, with defeat inevitable, Japan overthrew the French and granted independence to Vietnam with Bao Dai, the last Nguyen emperor, serving as head of state.

With the sudden surrender of the Japanese in August, the communists, under the leadership of Ho Chi Minh, seized control. Chinese and British forces soon handed the country back to France, which began a long struggle with the communists for control of the country.

The Geneva Agreements in 1954, following the defeat of the French at Dien Bien Phu, left the communists in control of the North and a pro-American, anti-communist regime ruling the South. National elections were to be organized to reunify the country, but they were never held.

In the early 1960s, the U.S. began sending military advisers to help South Vietnam fight a communist insurgency. The fighting gradually escalated into a full-scale war between southern Vietcong forces, backed by North Vietnamese troops infiltrated into the South, and southern soldiers supported by increasing numbers of U.S. combat troops. In 1965, U.S. President Lyndon Johnson swung the full weight of the U.S. military machine against the communists and began bombing North Vietnam.

While the fighting continued, a long drawn-out series of peace talks began in Paris in 1968. A peace accord was finally signed in Paris on January 27, 1973, which called for a ceasefire and allowed the remaining U.S. forces to withdraw.

The communist forces launched a new offensive in March 1975 and on April 30 their tanks crashed through the gates of the Presidential Palace in Saigon, ending the war and reunifying the country.

But real peace did not return. In December 1978, after brutal cross-border attacks by Cambodia's Khmer Rouge rulers, Vietnam's army invaded Cambodia, quickly capturing Phnom Penh and driving remnants of Pol Pot's forces to the mountains along Cambodia's border with Thailand. Hanoi then installed a friendly regime in Phnom Penh.

But China, Pol Pot's supporter, reacted by invading northern Vietnam to "teach it a lesson." Chinese troops withdrew after a few weeks, but cross-border artillery bombardments continued until the Vietnamese army completed its phased withdrawals from Cambodia in September 1989.

Most of the non-communist world apart from the U.S. ended its economic isolation of Vietnam after it signed the Paris peace agreement on Cambodia in October 1991. Economic liberalization since 1986 has produced modest improvements in living conditions and attracted some foreign investment.

Economic development, however, continued to be hobbled by a U.S. trade embargo and veto over IMF and World Bank funding for Vietnam.

Entry

A sharp rise in the number of businessmen and tourists visiting Vietnam has put flights under considerable pressure—particularly flights out of Ho Chi Minh City, which each year serve tens of thousands of visiting overseas Vietnamese and Vietnamese emigrating to the West.

Vietnam has responded by increasing the number of both international and domestic flights in cooperation with other airlines. Booking procedures and other passenger services have improved considerably with computerized reservations and more booking offices.

Bangkok, long the main point of departure for Vietnam, now faces increasing competition from Hong Kong, Singapore, Kuala Lumpur and Taipei. **Thai Airways International** operates three flights weekly between Bangkok and Hanoi, while **Vietnam Airlines** operates seven. Thai flies from Bangkok to Ho Chi Minh City seven times a week and Vietnam Airlines nine times. Three **Air France** flights from Paris to Ho Chi Minh City and two from Paris to Hanoi also stop in Bangkok.

Cathay Pacific and Vietnam Airlines jointly operate daily flights between Hong Kong and Ho Chi Minh City and fly between Hong Kong and Hanoi nine times each week. **Singapore Airlines** and its Vietnamese counterpart provide joint daily service between Singapore and Ho Chi Minh City and link the Vietnamese capital with Singapore twice a week. Two **Lufthansa** flights from Frankfurt to Ho Chi Minh City stop in Singapore.

China Airlines and **Eva Airways** of Taiwan have daily flights between Taipei and Ho Chi Minh City, and Vietnam's **Pacific Airlines** also flies the route daily. **Malaysia Airlines** provides daily service from Ho Chi Minh City to Kuala Lumpur, while Vietnam Airlines has three flights a week on the route. Malaysia Airlines serves Hanoi from Kuala Lumpur twice a week. Three flights a week link Manila with

VIETNAM
CHINA
Ha Giang
Cao Bang
Lai Chau
Lao Cai
Vinh Yen
Dien Bien Phu
Hanoi
Haiphong
Nam Dinh
LAOS
Thanh Hoa
Hainan Is.
Gulf of Tonkin
Vinh
Quang Tri
Hue
Da Nang
South China Sea
THAILAND
Quang Ngai
Kontum
Pleiku
Qui Nhon
CAMBODIA
Ban Me Thout
Nha Trang
Da Lat
Cam Ranh
Ho Chi Minh City
Phan Thiet
Gulf of Thailand
Mekong
Vinh Loi
km
0
100
Pte. de Ca Mau

Ho Chi Minh City.

Royal Air Cambodge and Vietnam Airlines operate two flights each week between Phnom Penh and Ho Chi Minh City, and one from the Cambodian capital to Hanoi. **Lao Aviation** and Vietnam Airlines link Hanoi and Vientiane twice a week, and also link Ho Chi Minh City with the Lao capital twice a week.

China Southern Airlines in 1992 began a twice-weekly service between Canton and Ho Chi Minh City and once-weekly Hanoi-Beijing flights. **Aeroflot** flies between Hanoi and Moscow twice a week. Six-to-eight flights daily operate between Hanoi and Ho Chi Minh City. The domestic aviation industry has 22 flights a day connecting major cities with various parts of the country.

Immigration

All visitors need visas. Businessmen require sponsorship by a government agency or a company which often acts as the visitors host. Tourists should apply through a travel agent whether they intend to travel independently or with a tour group. Embassies require applications at least a week in advance of the departure date, while travel agencies often need at least three weeks.

Vietnamese missions in Western capitals include Bonn, London, Ottawa, Paris, Rome and Stockholm. Other major embassies are located in Bangkok, Canberra, Jakarta, Kuala Lumpur, Manila, Tokyo and Vientiane. Hong Kong has a consulate and Taipei has a trade office which issue visas. Travel agencies in Bangkok, Hongkong, Taipei and Singapore offer tours to Ho Chi Minh City only, or longer trips including visits to Hanoi, Hue and Danang.

Visa fees range from US$15 for a single-entry, exit or transit visa to US$150 for a multiple-entry, six-month visa. Tourist visas are normally valid for two weeks or a month. If intending to use more than one exit point, this should be specified in the visa — a local tax may be levied. All registration procedures after arrival are performed by the visitor's hotel, guest-house or sponsor.

Health

Injections against cholera, hepatitis, Japanese encephalitis, tetanus and typhoid are recommended, but not required. Visitors may want to bring anti-mosquito lotion or coils and anti-diarrhoea tablets, and those travelling in highland regions should consider taking precautions against malaria. Tourists should drink only boiled or bottled water and should avoid raw vegetables. Avoid ice except in major hotels.

Currency

The Vietnamese currency is the dong, which since October 1, 1994, is required to be used in almost all transactions. Exchange counters can be found at hotels, guest-houses and many restaurants as well as in various parts of cities. The best exchange rate is obtained with larger denomination U.S. notes — and be warned that damaged U.S. notes are very difficult to exchange, though the local currency is accepted in even the most tattered condition. Since 1994, the rate has been stable at about Dong 11,000:US$1, and there is not much difference between official and free-market rates. Visitors should use only official exchange counters and avoid freelance changers, who often cheat their customers.

An increasing number of hotels, restaurants and shops accept credit cards (**Visa**, **MasterCard**, **American Express**, **JCB** and **Diners Club**). Banks and leading hotels will exchange travellers' cheques, and some banks will issue cash against credit cards.

Language

Vietnamese is the national language. A Roman script with added marks indicating tones and vowel changes is used in the written language. The spoken language differs slightly between the north, centre and south. English is spoken by many educated people. Some older people speak French, while those who studied in Moscow speak Russian.

Climate

It is best to visit the northern part of the country between September and December when the weather is sunny and mild. The winter from late December to February is usually chilly and cloudy. In spring, the north often suffers from almost continuous drizzly rain. Summers, especially June to August, can be unpleasantly hot and humid.

Conditions in the southern part of Vietnam are warm to hot throughout the year with the average daily maximum exceeding 31°C. At night temperatures drop to around 23°C. April and May are the hottest months when temperatures often reach 35°C and the humidity is very high. The most pleasant months in the south are November to January. The rainy season in Ho Chi Minh City is from about June to September. The rainy season around Danang and Hue in the centre is from about October to March.

Temperatures in the northern or central highlands are much lower than those in coastal areas. The average annual temperature in Dalat is 19.4°C.

Dress

Lightweight clothing is sufficient in Ho Chi Minh City all year around. Heavy sweaters and wind-resistant jackets are needed in the North during the winter months when temperatures often drop to 8°C or lower. Warmer clothing is also needed in the highlands, especially at night.

Business Hours

Working hours for government offices are from about 7:30-11:30 a.m. and 1-4:30 p.m. from Monday to Saturday. Banks are open from 7:30-11:30 a.m. and 1-3:30 p.m. Monday to Friday. Banks are also open on Saturday mornings. Private shops and restaurants open around 8:30 a.m. and close rather late in the evening. They are usually open seven days a week.

Doing Business

Few Vietnamese officials or businessmen speak English, but most of them have translators. It is important to ascertain politely but quickly how well the translator speaks English, because many of them pretend they understand even when they do not.

A visitor should carry plenty of business cards, because the Vietnamese are almost as fond of exchanging them as are the Japanese. Vietnamese men normally shake hands when greeting foreign visitors, but women traditionally do not shake hands with each other or with men. A visitor should only shake hands with a woman if she extends her hand first.

Vietnamese social relations are governed by politeness and modesty. The Vietnamese way is to talk around a sensitive point, assuming the listener will infer the meaning. Stressing the importance of harmonious relations, Vietnamese generally avoid direct confrontation. Westerners commonly associate a smile with pleasure and amusement, but in Vietnam it can also symbolize embarrassment, anxiety, frustration and anger.

Most Vietnamese officials and businessmen are punctual, but they often frustrate foreigners by appearing not to feel a lot of pressure to accomplish things quickly. A foreign businessman needs to make certain that the person he is talking to is in fact in a position to make a decision. Some of the most successful foreign firms in Vietnam are those which have found dynamic counterparts.

Touching someone on the head or pointing the sole of one's foot at another person is considered rude. It is also impolite to hail another person by waving a finger or hand in the upright position. Instead, Vietnamese summon each other by waving their hands in a cupped, downward position indicating "come to my side, sit with me." Nonetheless, the Vietnamese are hospitable people so as long as a visitor remains polite and calm, it is unlikely that he will seriously offend his hosts.

Business visitors will find that their business or government counterparts wear shirts and ties in Ho Chi Minh City and in Hanoi during the hot summer months. Suits are commonly worn for official functions and in Hanoi during the autumn, winter and spring. Vietnamese women, who play a significant role in business and government circles, commonly wear dress trousers or skirts and blouses.

Vietnamese businessmen often entertain their guests in restaurants. Most Vietnamese men love to drink beer and smoke cigarettes while partying. Vietnamese commonly toast each other with "*chuc suc khoe*," which translates as "wish you health." Vietnamese women rarely smoke or drink, at least in public.

Vietnamese usually begin a friendly conversation by asking about their guest's wife and children. They are open to discussing almost any subject, but a visitor should be cautious about raising overtly political questions until being well acquainted with his host.

A visitor wanting to give a gift to a Vietnamese male counterpart would rarely go wrong if he gave a carton of 555 or Marlboro cigarettes or a bottle of Johnnie Walker whisky.

Car rentals along with translation and secretarial services are available in many of the major hotels such as the Pullman Metropole in Hanoi and the Floating, Century Saigon, Continental and Rex in Ho Chi Minh City.

Rip-Offs

As in many other Asian countries, a visitor needs to bargain for almost everything, including taxis, food in markets, handicrafts and art works. One should beware of fakes. The Vietnamese are masterful at faking antiques and art pieces as well as brand-name alcohol and medicine.

Many shopkeepers also try to cheat their customers by giving short measure of almost anything being weighed.

One should only change money in banks or established shops. "Freelance bankers" on the street offer higher rates, but commonly swindle their customers.

Those walking the streets of Ho Chi Minh City should beware of young boys selling maps and post cards, heavily made-up transvestites and beggars, any of whom may be masterful at picking pockets for wallets and stealing watches, necklaces, pens or even glasses.

Media

A growing number of newspapers and magazines are being published in English. The Vietnam news agency publishes the daily *Vietnam News* and a daily bulletin. The Ho Chi Minh People's Committee publishes a weekly called *Saigon Times* and the Institute for Research on Market and Price in Hanoi puts out the weekly *Market & Price* bulletin, which gives weekly price information. *Vietnam Investment Review*, published by a joint venture between Vietnam's State Committee for Investment and Cooperation and an Australian firm, provides business and investment news. English-language magazines which have recently begun publishing in Vietnam include *Vietnam Economic Times* and *Vietnam Today*.

Magazines such as the *Far Eastern Economic Review*, *Time* and *Newsweek*, along with English-language dailies from Thailand, can be bought in many of the major hotels. Young boys also hustle foreign-language publications around the main hotels in Ho Chi Minh City.

Communications

International direct dial telephone services, fax and telex services are now available in most hotels in the major cities, but a visitor may have difficulty contacting the outside world from remote provinces. International calls cost at least twice as much as they cost in many neighbouring countries and are often charged from when the number you are calling starts ringing, not when it is answered. Many business centres charge by the page for faxes.

Collect calls can now be made from Vietnam at the post office, or ask your hotel operator to try for you. A charge of about Dong 11,000 will be levied for the service, but it is still far cheaper to do this and have your overseas party call you back.

A mobile phone service has been introduced in Hanoi, Ho Chi Minh City, Bien Hoa and Vung Tau.

Transport

Taxis are available at the Hanoi and Ho Chi Minh City airports, but the fare into the city (about US$25 and US$10, respectively) should be agreed in advance. For transport around Hanoi, cars with drivers can be hired from **Fujicab** (Tel: 255452), **Mansfield Toserco** (Tel: 269444), **Hanoi Car Service Corp.** (Tel: 254074) or **Hanoi Taxi** (Tel: 535252). Metered taxies in Hanoi include **PT Taxi** (Tel: 533171) and **Red Taxis** (353686).

In Ho Chi Minh City, cars and drivers can be hired from **Saigon Tourist Car Rental Co.** (Tel: 295925), **Saigon Auto Salon** (Tel: 291505) and **Fidi Tourist** (Tel: 296264). Metered taxis include **Vina Taxi** (Tel: 442170) and some **airport taxis** (Tel: 446666).

You may not yet rent a car to drive yourself.

In all cities and towns, visitors can hire three-wheeled pedicabs, or cyclos, for a modest fare, but they must be sure that the driver understands the destination.

Motorcycles and bicycles can be hired for within and outside city at many places. Motorcycles cost US$8 per day while bicycles cost less than US$1 per day.

The one-way air fare for foreigners between Hanoi and Ho Chi Minh City is US$170. Travel by train is now open to visitors and is cheaper than flying. But trains are often congested, the comforts minimal and the journey times quite variable. Buses also operate between major cities, but they are more rugged.

Accommodation

Hotel reservations can be made directly but it is more reliable for visitors to contact the travel agencies or individuals hosting their trip. The increasing number of visitors has put pressure on existing hotel accommodation, making it harder to find rooms and causing prices to rise. An increasing number of small guest-houses have begun operating in major cities.

In Hanoi, there are two four-star hotels: the **Sofitel Metropole** with rooms beginning at US$200 and the **Hanoi Hotel** offering rooms beginning at US$168. The **Thang Loi** hotel located on beautiful West Lake, is rather remote, but has rooms for US$76, while the **Saigon Hotel** has rooms beginning at US$79. The centrally located **Government, Military and Energy guest-houses** offer accommodation from US$45-80. Visitors can also stay at the newly renovated, former French hotels such as the **Dan Chu** and **Hoa Binh** for US$43-65 per night.

Ho Chi Minh City has four luxury hotels: the **Omni Saigon Hotel** and the **New World Hotel** offering rooms beginning at US$140 while the **Saigon Floating Hotel** and the **Century Saigon** have rooms beginning at US$100 and US$115 respectively. The comfortable **Continental and Rex** also have business centres and provide rooms from about US$80. Joint-venture hotels include the **Norfolk** and **Saigon Star** and have rooms from around US$85. Other popular, but slightly rundown, hotels include the **Caravelle**, **Mondial** and **Friendship** with rooms starting at US$50.

Major tourist spots at **Ha Long Bay** and **Do Son** sea resort in the north; **Hue**, **Danang**, **Nhatrang** and **Dalat** in the centre; **Vung Tau**, **Can Tho**, **My Tho** and **Ben Tre** in the south also have hotels, but the accommodation is often rather spartan.

Dining

Many Vietnamese restaurants are small, insignificant spots which serve delightful specialities, but visitors often have trouble making themselves understood and may be put off by the modest hygiene.

However, the recent economic liberalization has spawned a dramatic increase in the number of restaurants, some of which are of excellent quality.

Vietnamese cooking, comparable to Chinese but often more spicy, offers considerable variety. The best known seasoning is *nuoc mam*, Vietnamese fish sauce. Herbs and spices such as coriander, lemon grass, mint, pepper and a local variety of basil provide a light, subtle flavour. Many cooks use liberal quantities of monosodium glutamate in their cooking.

The long coastline means that excellent seafood is available. The French influence is apparent in the availability of excellent *baguettes*. Many visitors are attracted to *cha gio* or *nem Saigon*, deep fried spring rolls with pork or crab meat, egg, vermicelli and chopped vegetables. *Bo bay mon*, beef served seven ways, is popular, with each dish accompanied by its own traditional sauce and vegetables. *Cha tom* is ground seasoned shrimp grilled on sugarcane skewers which add a sweetness to the shrimp. *Banh hoi* is a thin noodle eaten with barbecued pork balls, fish sauce and fresh vegetables.

The southern *canh chua*, sour fish soup with pineapple and bean sprouts, is also tasty. *Pho*, the popular noodle soup, comes in many varieties, depending on the meat, noodles and other ingredients used.

All the hotels in Hanoi and Ho Chi Minh City serve some sort of Western food, but they are facing increasing competition from the burgeoning number of private restaurants.

In Hanoi the first class restaurant serving French and Asian food is the **Le Beaulieu** at the Sofitel Metropole Hotel while the **Chinese restaurant** at the Hanoi Hotel serves pricey Cantonese and Sichuan cuisine.

Other popular restaurants serving a variety of Western and Vietnamese cuisine include **202** (202 Hue St), **Lotus** (16 Ngo Quyen), **Mekki-Lan Anh** (9A Da Tuong), **Indochine** (16 Nam Ngu), **Club Opera** (59 Ly Thai To), **Sunset Pub** (Dong Do Hotel, 10 Giang Vo), **Piano Restaurant and Bar** (50 Hang Vai St) and **Bistrot** (34 Tran Hung Dao St). **La Vong** (14 Cha Ca St) has refined its popular fish speciality over five generations. Italian pizzas and spaghetti are available at **La Terrazza** (49 Nghi Tam) or **A Little Italian** (81 Tho Nhuom).

Restaurants in Ho Chi Minh City offer greater variety and better service. **Madam Dai's** (84A Nguyen Du, Dist 1), located in the library of the French-trained lawyer, Nguyen Phuoc Dai, serves both Vietnamese and French food, but advance reservations are a must. **Le Mekong** (159 Ky Con, Dist 1) offers delightful French fare, while **Chez Guido** located in the Continental Hotel, has the only broad selection of pasta and pizza in Vietnam.

Japanese food is served at the **Nihon Basi** (Rex Hotel) and **Kiku** (Caravelle Hotel).

Korean food is available at **Seoul House** (37 Ngo Duc Ke St, Dist 1) and **Angel** (34 Le Duan St, Dist 1).

Favourite bars for foreign businessmen include **Tiger Tavern** (225 Dong Khoi St, Dist 1) and **City Bar & Grill** (63 Dong Khoi St, Dist 1). **Apocalypse Now** and **B-4-75** (as in "Before 1975," the year the Vietnam War ended and Vietnam was reunified under communism), on Dong Du St in Dist 1, are popular with younger tourists and American war veterans because of their war memorabilia and music from the late 1960s and early 1970s.

Entertainment

Ho Chi Minh City remains the entertainment capital of Vietnam boasting a variety of discos and dancing establishments. Massage parlours and more risque bars known as *bia om* (literally "hugging bars") have reopened in recent years, though they are occasionally shut down for brief periods by the police.

Among the most fashionable dancing establishments are the **Super Star** (201/3 Hoang Viet St, Tan Binh Dist) and **Arc-en-ciel** (52-56 Tan Da St, Dist 5) as well as the discos in hotels such as the **Floating**, **Century Saigon**, **Rex**, **Friendship** and **Caravelle**. **Maxim's**, next to the Caravelle, offers a band and singing along with food of rather modest quality. Karaoke bars have also sprouted up throughout the city in recent years.

Hanoi, more austere and without Ho Chi Minh City's exposure to modern Western tastes, is just beginning to develop some semblance of nightlife. Apart from the burgeoning number of small cafes, where young locals sit in near darkness listening to Vietnamese and Western music, nightlife revolves almost entirely around a handful of dance halls where quick steps and foxtrots are still as popular as disco dancing. Most frequented by foreign residents are the **VIP Lounge**, 62 Nguyen Du St), **Saigon Pull** (217 Doi Can St) and the **Thanh Loi Hotel** (on Saturday nights).

Every Thursday night, visitors can attend Hanoi's unique **Water Puppet Theatre**, where hidden puppetmasters immersed in a pool of water, choreograph often hilarious scenes of peasant life.

Shopping

Traditional Vietnamese handicrafts include lacquerware, carved tortoiseshell, mother-of-pearl inlaid trays and boxes, along with jewellery, ceramics, baskets, bamboo and silk products. Lacquerware is ubiquitous but the quality is often uneven.

Handmade silver bracelets, pendants and earrings make attractive gifts and, if the silver content is not overestimated, the prices are still modest. Both Hanoi and Ho Chi Minh City have a growing number of art shops, selling paintings at rapidly rising prices.

In Hanoi, many arts and crafts shops are located in the old quarter around **Hoan Kiem Lake**. Ho Chi Minh City's shopping area is concentrated around **Dong Khoi** and **Le Loi** streets, **Nguyen Hue Blvd** and bustling **Ben Thanh** market.

Street hawkers in Ho Chi Minh City peddle T-shirts that say "Good Morning Vietnam" and war-era Zippo lighters once popular among American GIs. They are scratched and tarnished and bear inscriptions such as "1st Cav. Div.," but it is more likely that they were recently cloned rather than left behind by American soldiers.

Some items, such as lacquerware or household goods, may be purchased in local currency but most costlier items such as art work and antiques are priced in U.S. dollars.

Visitors should bear in mind that antiques may be confiscated by customs officers if the purchaser does not have a certificate from the Ministry of Culture allowing the item to be exported.

Holidays

January 1: New Year.

January-February: Tet, or Lunar New Year. The date depends on the lunar calendar and varies from year to year.

A traditional family ceremony is celebrated at midnight on New Year's eve, as the country erupts in an explosion of fireworks.

Over the next few days, gifts are exchanged, well-wishing visits are made to relatives and friends, and pagodas and temples are visited.

Tet is officially a three-day holiday in the cities, but at least a week in rural areas.

April 30: Reunification Day.

May 1: Labour Day.

September 2-3: National Day.

September-October: The Mid-Autumn Festival for children falls on the full-moon day of the eighth lunar month. Shops are filled with moon cakes and sell colourful lanterns.

DISCOVERING VIETNAM

HANOI

Under French rule, Hanoi became one of the most attractive cities in Asia and there is still charm in its broad, tree-lined boulevards and shady parks. Most of the visible scars of the wartime bombing have disappeared, but years of neglect and overcrowding have given Hanoi a rundown look. This is slowly being reversed by the construction boomlet which has erupted under the economic reforms launched in 1986.

Places to visit in Hanoi include **Hoan Kiem** (Returned Sword) Lake in the centre of the city, a charming lake with a small island on which stands **Turtle pagoda**. It marks the spot where, according to legend, a turtle rose from the water bearing a magic sword with which Le Loi, a 15th century Vietnamese hero, drove out the Chinese invaders.

North of the lake is the heart of ancient Hanoi, the so-called **36 Streets** area, with its low, narrow "tube houses" with curved, red-tiled roofs which have long captured the imagination of Vietnamese artists and foreign visitors. Today these houses are threatened, as merchants seek to replace them with the same kind of new shops popular in other Asian cities.

The 36 streets are still named after the craftsmen — silversmiths, leather workers and so on — who first settled in the area centuries ago. The bustling **Dong Xuan market**, built by the French but recently refurbished, is an adventure for a visitor interested in the wide variety of food and other products for sale.

South of Hoan Kiem Lake, one finds beautiful French colonial buildings dating back to the turn of the century. Among the most elegant are the **Government Guest-house**, **State Bank**, **Metropole Hotel** and the **Opera House** and the **Catholic cathedral**.

Hundreds of people line up each day outside the Russian-built, marble **Ho Chi Minh Mausoleum**, waiting for an opportunity to pay homage to the first president of independent, communist Vietnam. Nearby the Russians also built a museum which exhibits the still-widely venerated leader's personal belongings, including his famous sandals cut from a rubber tyre. Visitors are also welcome to visit the simple two-storey wooden house on stilts where Ho lived.

The **Chua Mot Cot** (or One-Pillar Pagoda), which many people believe looks like Buddha sitting on a lotus flower, was first built in the 11th century to honour Buddhist advisers who supported Ly Thai To, the founder of ancient Hanoi. Another popular Hanoi site is the **Dong Temple**, built by Ly in memory of a mythical three-year-old hero who brandished a sword and rode an iron horse to repel a Chinese invasion around 1,000 BC.

Visitors interested in the arts can visit the **Fine Arts Museum**, located near **Van Mieu** or "Temple of Literature," Hanoi's first university built in the 11th century to honour Confucius. Many of the country's early scholars passed examinations here and their achievements are recorded on stone stele.

Of interest are tours of the **History Museum**, including its bronze drums dating back some 3,000 years, and the **Revolutionary** and **War** museums, depicting Vietnam's almost continuous struggles against China, France, Japan and the U.S. Interested tourists can also visit the colourful flower villages on the north side of **West Lake**.

UPCOUNTRY

One of the most scenic spots in the country is **Ha Long Bay**, 164 kilometres east of Hanoi. The thousands of strangely shaped, lime rock mountains jutting out of the emerald sea resemble a Chinese silk painting. Two thirds of the way to Ha Long, lies **Haiphong**, northern Vietnam's major port. Visitors may also want to visit the popular nearby beach resort of **Do Son**.

Many Hanoi residents also frequent **Tam Dao** resort, famous for its beautiful **Thac Bac** (Silver) waterfalls, located in Vinh Phu province some 80 kilometres north of the capital at an elevation of 1,000 metres above sea level.

On the sixth day of the first lunar month, a growing number of people attend the colourful **Co Loa Festival**, celebrating King An Duong, who in the third century BC built the Co Loa citadel some 16 kilometres northeast of Hanoi. According to a popular legend, the fortress fell to invading Chinese forces after the king's daughter fell in love with the invading Chinese general's son and revealed to him the fortress' defence secrets. Three remaining earthen ramparts which once protected this ancient capital have survived.

Beginning on the 15th day of the Lunar New Year, tens of thousands of Vietnamese make a pilgrimage to attend the annual festival at the **Huong (Perfume) Pagoda**, located about 60 kilometres south of Hanoi. The pagoda is a complex of more than 30 temples, some of them in caves and grottoes, which can only be reached by taking an hour-long sampan trip on the Yen River and then walking about two kilometres up steep mountain trails.

From the ninth to the 11th day of the third lunar month, many Vietnamese trek to the **Hung Temple** in Vinh Phu province to attend a festival commemorating the founding of Vietnam by the Hung kings. According to a timeless legend, Vietnam originated from the union of a powerful sea god and a lovely mountain goddess. Half their 100 sons followed their father to the sea, while the other 50 went with their mother to the mountains, home of the Hung kings who later established Vietnam.

On the 10th day of the third lunar month, visitors can also travel southeast of Hanoi to attend a festival at **Hoa Lu**, the capital established after the Chinese were defeated in AD 939. Although the Vietnamese capital was moved to present-day Hanoi in the 11th century, a citadel, two temples and the tomb of Dinh Tien Hoang, the emperor who established Hoa Lu, still survive.

Driving north or west from Hanoi to the Lao or Chinese borders, the traveller sees some of the world's most beautiful scenery — sea-blue mountain ranges, lush, green hidden valleys and craggy outcrops. The mountains around **Son La** in the west are populated by Black Tai hill tribes, while **Lao Cai** and **Lai Chau** in the far north are inhabited by Hmong minorities, who still practise slash-and-burn farming on the mountain slopes, grow opium and wear colourful traditional costumes. At **Dien Bien Phu** in the far northwest, howitzers and tanks abandoned by the French in 1954 still litter rice fields in the valley, and a visitor can tour the famous hills where French positions were overrun by Vietnamese guerillas.

Cuc Huong National Park, a wildlife preserve 200 kilometres southwest of Hanoi, surprises its visitors with its narrow limestone canyons and the large, colourful butterflies that swarm into the area in April and May. Further south, near Vinh, once a major industrial centre levelled by U.S. bombers during the war, is the village of **Lang Sen**, Ho Chi Minh's home village.

Continuing south is **Hue**, the former imperial capital of Vietnam's last royal dynasty. On the banks of the Perfume River, Emperor Gia Long, the founder of the Nguyen dynasty, in 1802 began building a citadel, also known as the **Imperial City**, surrounded by 21-metre thick walls and a moat. By 1945, the dynasty's 13 emperors had built more than 300 palaces, temples, mausoleums, libraries and theatres in and around the fortress of the Imperial City.

The kings and their families lived in the **Forbidden Purple City**, which was built inside the old Imperial City, where most of the offices of the central government were housed. To the south is the **Ngo Mon**, or Noon Gate, a massive entrance formerly reserved for the use of the king on festive occasions.

From the Ngo Mon, a bridge over a small moat leads to the courtyards in front of the **Thai Hoa**, or Supreme Harmony, palace. Other buildings in the Citadel include the **Dien Tho** or **Everlasting Longevity Palace**, which was built as the Queen Mother's residence, and **The Mieu** and **Hung Mieu** ceremonial buildings. Nine huge bronze **Dynastic Urns** depict the achievements of the dynasty.

Seven of the Nguyen kings are buried in elaborate tombs located in parks near the tree-covered hills which surround **Hue**. The nearest, that of **Tu Duc** (1848-83) stands in a dense pine forest on the edge of a small lake. **Khai Dinh**'s (1916-25) memorial, the most elaborate of all the tombs, is a cement palace surrounded by stone mandarins, horses and elephants.

Only a third of these royal monuments survived the three decades of war against France and the U.S. which began in the mid-1940s. Since the war's end in 1975, the biggest threat to the monuments has come from the devastating typhoons which strike central Vietnam, tropical insects, thieves and neglect.

Five kilometres west of Hue on the north bank of the Perfume River is the seven-storey **Phuoc Duyen Tower**, which was built in 1844 on the grounds of the **Linh Mu** (Heavenly Lady) **Pagoda**. The original pagoda has disappeared but a huge two-tonne bell and a cylindrical stone stele remain.

Many visitors to Hue enjoy an excursion on the **Perfume River** in a small rented sampan, covered with a rounded palm roof. The town of Hue is unremarkable but it is interesting to walk around and note its more traditional atmosphere. The countryside is dotted with fascinating Buddhist temples.

From Hue, it is 112 kilometres by road — across the spectacular **Hai Van** pass or Pass of the Clouds, which geographically divides the country into north and south — to **Danang**. This city's **My Khe** beach, dubbed **China Beach** by American soldiers in the 1960s, is one of the country's most beautiful.

Nearby is the famous **Marble Mountain**,

which has a Buddhist monastery and a massive cave which is lit through a gap in the rock ceiling. Danang is also home to the **Cham Museum**, which displays some 300 stone art treasures from the Indian-influenced Champa state, which ruled the area until the 15th century.

Some 20 kilometres south of Danang, is **Hoi An**, once the Cham empire's busy trading port, which welcomed traders from Japan, India and China. Portuguese traders and Catholic missionaries settled here in the 17th century. Some of the original Chinese temples and the marvellous houses of wealthy merchants — with their curved ornamental tile roofs and intricate door panels — have been preserved.

HO CHI MINH CITY

Ho Chi Minh City, formerly called Saigon after the river on which it is located, is Vietnam's largest city and most dynamic business centre. Many people, even officials, still call the downtown area of the city "Saigon." In the 11th and 12th centuries, it was a seaport belonging to the Angkor kingdom, which had its capital at Angkor Wat in present day Cambodia. Vietnamese settlers and Chinese merchants only arrived at the beginning of the 17th century, so the city lacks the ancient charm of Hanoi.

One of the city's most prominent landmarks is **City Hall** built by the French between 1901-08 at the opposite end of bustling Nguyen Hue street from the Saigon River. The pastel yellow building with its ornate facade and elegant interior is now the headquarters for the city's People's Committee.

Other French buildings in the heart of the city's business district include the **Municipal Theatre**, which served as the National Assembly building for the U.S.-backed South Vietnamese government until the communist victory in 1975; the **Notre Dame Cathedral**, completed in 1883; and the central **Post Office**. The **History Museum** — which contains artifacts illustrating the evolution of the Vietnamese culture from the Dong Son Bronze Age to current civilization — and the **Revolutionary Museum** — the former French governor's mansion which now details the wars against France and the U.S. — are both housed in elegant French buildings.

Gia Long's Palace, another French-era building, now contains the **American War Crimes Museum**, which displays a collection of U.S. military equipment and has a model of the infamous "tiger cages" where many communist prisoners were held. Tourists can

Hue pagoda. PHOTO: JULIA WILKINSON

also visit **Reunification Hall**, which earlier served as the residence for former South Vietnamese president Nguyen Van Thieu.

Xa Loi Pagoda, a modern concrete structure and scene of agitation against the regime of former president Ngo Dinh Diem, is located about a kilometre southwest of Reunification Hall. The oldest pagoda in Ho Chi Minh City, **Giac Lam**, was completed at the end of the 17th century.

The city also has several temples honouring earlier national heroes. The **Tran Hung Dao Temple**, built in a T-shape with eight curved corners adorned with dragon and phoenix figures, commemorates Tran Hung Dao's victory over the Mongol invaders in the 13th century. The **Le Van Duyet Temple** in the suburb of **Gia Dinh** contains the tomb of the military hero who served the first Nguyen emperor.

Ho Chi Minh City's Chinatown, **Cholon**, or Big Market, dominated South Vietnam's foreign trade, rice market, foreign exchange and much of its industry during the war. The city almost ground to a halt after "socialist transformation" in 1978, but it has nearly regained its former bustle under the free market reforms introduced in 1986.

Cholon has many good restaurants, busy

markets and Chinese temples, including the 19th century **Thien Hau Temple**, dedicated to the Chinese goddess of the sea who protects sea travellers. The **An Quang Pagoda**, long known for the political activism of its monks, and the **Phu Tho Horse Race Track** are also located here.

UPCOUNTRY

Anyone interested in Vietnam's war with the U.S. should visit the **Cu Chi Tunnel Complex**, 70 kilometres northwest of the city. Communist guerillas hid from the Americans in an elaborate 200-kilometre network of tunnels, including smoke-tight kitchens, a field hospital, meeting rooms and living quarters. Most of the tunnels have now collapsed, but one section has been preserved for visitors.

Two hours southeast of Ho Chi Minh City is the beach resort of **Vung Tau**, nestled between hills and the South China Sea. Vung Tau has undergone something of a facelift since it served as a rather seedy rest-and-recuperation resort for Australian soldiers during the war, but the beach is no longer as clean and its water is no longer as unpolluted as it was in the past. The city today serves as a base for foreign oil companies exploring for oil off the coast of southern Vietnam.

The vast **Mekong delta**, a fertile area built up over the centuries with silt deposited as the nine branches of the Mekong River escape to the sea, begins south of Ho Chi Minh City. The delta is Vietnam's most important rice-producing region. Villages and individual houses lie along the irrigation and drainage canals which criss-cross the region.

Visitors can easily arrange day trips to **My Tho**, some 65 kilometres south of Ho Chi Minh City. Here they can rent a sampan for a short river cruise on one of the arms of the Mekong or cross the long ferry to **Ben Tre** and on to **Vinh Long** and **Can Tho**.

Vestiges of the ancient Oc Eo civilization, which actively traded with India, have been discovered in the southwestern province of **Kien Giang**. Scholars have found evidence that Oc Eo was a port city belonging to Funan kingdom, which flourished from the second to seventh centuries and predated Angkor. Archaeologists have concluded that the city contained large temples and palaces, and its artisans were skilled in working bronze, jade, silver and gold.

Tay Ninh, 96 kilometres northwest of Ho Chi Minh City, is the site of the **Cao Dai Temple**. The Cao Dai religion, a sect founded in the 1920s, is a synthesis of Buddhism, Confucianism, Islam and Christianity whose saints include Victor Hugo, Jesus Christ, Joan of Arc and Buddha. The elaborate temple contains pillars entwined with pink plaster dragons, and at one end is the eye of Cao Dai painted on a blue globe which represents the world.

The enchanting mountain resort of **Dalat** lies some 180 kilometres north of Ho Chi Minh City. A visitor arriving by road from the south passes through the breathtaking **Prenn** mountain pass and by the **Da Tan La** falls.

Dalat was founded in 1893 by a French doctor, Alexander Yersin, who recognized its therapeutic benefits. Some 1,200 metres above sea level, the town overlooks **Xuan Huong** lake and is surrounded by pine tree-covered hills. The average summer temperature is 20°C, and in winter 15°C.

The city's residential area is spread out, but the centre of town is at one end of the lake. Each of the many French-style villas, with their carefully tended lawns and delightful flower gardens, look like little parks.

Dalat is on the southern edge of the central highlands, so Montagnard hilltribes people — wearing their traditional garb and carrying baskets on their backs — can be seen in the market or walking along the roads. The central highlands, until recent years populated mainly by semi-nomadic minorities such as the Rhade and Jarai, has excellent soil for growing rubber, coffee and tea. Apart from Dalat, the area's other cities — **Ban Me Thuot**, **Pleiku** and **Kontum** — have been largely off-limits to foreign visitors.

Down from Dalat to the east lies **Phan Rang**, home of the Cham who ruled the central part of Vietnam until the end of the 15th century. Several of their brick towers, remnants of the Chams' much grander days, survive in the area. Some of the Cham surviving in the area are Hindus — eating no beef and cremating their dead — while others are Muslim — eating no pork and burying their dead.

One of the oldest Cham towers — the **Po Nagar**, built in 784 — can be found in **Nhatrang**, 100 kilometres north of Phan Rang. Nhatrang, set against a mountain backdrop, has some of the most beautiful beaches in Vietnam. The rock islands off the coast of Nhatrang are well known for the breeding of sea swallows. Sea swallow nest soup is considered a delicacy by many.

Kaliran mosque, Bukhara, Uzbekistan. PHOTO: AHMED RASHID

ALL-ASIA TRAVEL GUIDE

NORTHEAST ASIA

CENTRAL ASIAN REPUBLICS

The five republics of Central Asia — the vast Kazakhstan, with Turkmenistan, Uzbekistan, Tajikistan and Kirgyzstan ranged from west to east below it — together make up an area bigger than India and nearly half the size of China. But because of their basically inhospitable terrain, the lands are sparsely populated, with a total of only 51 million people — fewer than Thailand, for instance.

The five countries' ancient histories of colourful and at times powerful nomadic peoples came together in the 18th, 19th and 20th centuries when they were in turn subdued by the expanding Tsarist Russian empire and then subsumed — not without struggle and terrible loss — by the Soviet state which succeeded it. Then between 1990 and 1991 came their virtually simultaneous emergence into independent statehood, as the Soviet Union dissolved.

The republics are now open, in varying degrees, to travellers from the outside world, both for business and the hardier type of pleasure travel. Most of the region is backward, relying economically on agriculture and mining. Kazakhstan and Turkmenistan are both rich in oil and gas reserves, a lot of which still await exploitation.

Uzbekistan, with its fabled cities such as Samarkand and Bukhara, has already become a major tourist attraction, especially for Muslim visitors from Asia and the Middle East. For the others there are cities of varying interest and extraordinary and unusual terrain, from the stifling hot red sands of the Karakum desert in Turkmenistan in the east, through the expanses of windswept grassland steppes to the ice-clogged lakes and aromatic cypress forests of Kirgyzstan's mountains, near the Chinese border.

The following offers information on how to travel to these lands, so little known to the outside world. This information includes how you get there, visas and other requirements, what you should aim to take with you, what accommodation you can expect to find, how to travel once there and what communications you will have with the outside world.

After these general guidelines, there follows a country-by-country account of their geography and a pocket social and political history, invaluable for those planning an unusual business or tourist visit to these sometimes very different countries, not long ago lumped together as "Soviet Asia."

Climate

Temperatures are extreme in Central Asia, ranging from 43°C in summer in many places to -20°C in winter. Summers are very hot, dusty and dry. Winters are extremely cold, snow-swept or wet. In Tajikistan, Kirgyzstan and Kazakhstan where the Pamirs, the Tien Shan and other mountain ranges converge, the winters can last from October to April. But in Ashkhabad, the capital of Turkmenistan, which was the hottest place in the former Soviet Union, or Bukhara, in Uzbekistan, the summers can last for six months of the year.

The best times to visit Central Asia are in the spring (March and April) or autumn (September and October).

Dress

In spring and autumn it is best to take both winter and summer clothes to meet the varying climate. In winter a very warm coat, preferably fur, is advisable as well as a fur hat, gloves and thermal underwear. In summer the traveller should carry typical Asian summer gear, short sleeved shirts or blouses, cotton trousers or skirt and a summer jacket for the evenings. However it is always best to throw in a warm sweater as well for air-conditioning and especially if one is travelling in the mountains. Always take at least one very sturdy pair of walking shoes.

Immigration

Separate visas for each Central Asian republic are still only obtainable at Russian embassies abroad or through tour companies who arrange package tours to Central Asia. However, for travellers who plan to go to several destinations, it is best to acquire a visa for Moscow first and start your journey from there.

You can fly to Central Asia from Moscow with just a visa for Russia, getting a local visa when you arrive, but it is better to get the visas first. Some of the five republics have set up embassies in a few Asian countries which issue visas only for their own country. Uzbekistan requires a visa for every town you visit and these are also officially obtainable in other republics but not so efficiently as in Uzbekistan itself. Visas for each city are available from the foreign ministries in each country's capital. Hotels outside the capital normally require visas for that city before they allow a traveller to check in.

DIPLOMATIC REPRESENTATIVES

All five Central Asian capitals now have United States embassies and some representation from the European Common Market countries, but otherwise diplomatic representation is slim. The Europeans have tended to pool their resources and open one embassy to represent all of them. Pakistan, Turkey, China and Iran have possibly the best Asian representation in the region, followed by South Korea. Japan has been slow off the mark. The International Monetary Fund (IMF) has opened representative offices in Almaty (Kazakhstan) and Bishkek (Kirgyzstan), and the World Bank is opening offices in these capitals as well as in Tashkent.

Diplomats from some Asian countries are now returning to Dushanbe (Tajikistan) after pulling out because of the civil war. However, as of March 1995 the fighting had not ended and travel in Tajikistan is hazardous.

At this stage there are serious limits as to

CENTRAL ASIAN REPUBLICS

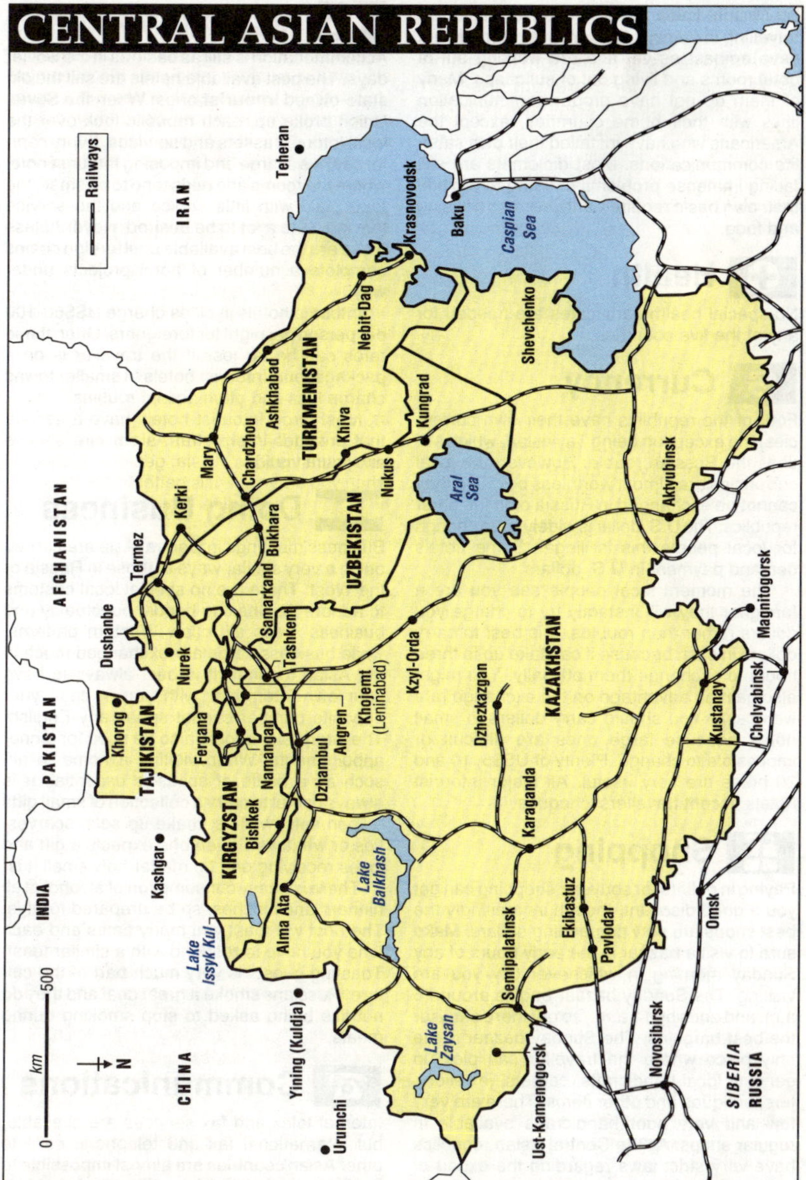

how much diplomats can help their nationals travelling in Central Asia. Most of them do not have embassies yet and are working out of hotel rooms and living out of suitcases. Many of them do not have proper communication links with their home countries, except the Americans who have installed their own satellite communications. Most diplomats are still facing immense problems in trying to provide their own basic requirements such as housing and food.

Health

No special health certificates are needed for any of the five countries.

Currency

Four of the republics have their own currencies, the exception being Tajikistan, which still uses the Russian rouble. However, the local currencies are almost worthless because they cannot be exchanged in Russia or in the other republics. The U.S. dollar is widely used, though for local people this is illegal. Some hotels demand payment in U.S. dollars.

The moment local people see you are a foreigner they will instantly try to charge you dollars rather than roubles. It is best to carry dollars in cash because it can take up to three hours to exchange them officially. You might also gain an advantage on the exchange rate with cash. You should carry dollars in small notes because large ones are difficult or impossible to change. Plenty of US$5, 10 and 20 notes are very useful. All major Intourist hotels accept travellers' cheques.

Shopping

Paying in dollars for souvenir shopping can get you a good discount, though increasingly the best shops are now demanding dollars. Make sure to visit a bazaar in the early hours of any Sunday morning in whichever city you are visiting. The Sunday bazaar begins around 6 a.m. and ends by 11 a.m., so get there early for the best bargains. The Sunday bazaar is the only place where the traveller can pick up genuine local handicrafts, carpets, jewellery, furs, antiques and other items. There are very few and very poor handicrafts available in regular shops. All the Central Asian republics have very strict laws regarding the export of antiques which must be obeyed.

Accommodation

Accommodation is still as basic as in the Soviet days. The best available hotels are still the old state-owned **Intourist** ones. When the Soviet Union broke up, each republic took over the local Intourist assets and services. Every capital city has a large and imposing Intourist hotel where the rooms and beds tend to be small, the food plain with little choice and the service leaving quite a lot to be desired. Nevertheless these are the best available until foreign chains complete a number of hotel projects under way.

Intourist hotels in cities charge US$60-100 per person per night for foreigners. Often these rates can be far less if the traveller is on a package tour. Intourist hotels in smaller towns charge less and often accept roubles.

Most large Intourist hotels have a service that provides interpreters, a car hire service and tourist guides.

Doing Business

Business meetings in Central Asia are carried out in a very similar ways to those in Russia or the West. There are no special local customs to adhere to. Shaking hands, punctuality and business dress all follow Western patterns, while business cards are exchanged much in the Asian manner. It is best always to have your own interpreter with you in case your opposite number cannot speak any English. The interpreter should also be used for dinner appointments. When visiting a home, a gift such as a bottle of spirits is essential. It is always useful to carry a collection of small gifts — pen sets, wallets, make-up sets, scarves, ties or whatever. Everyone expects a gift and loves receiving one no matter how small it is.

There is heavy consumption of alcohol at all dinners and lunches, so be prepared for this. The host will toast you many times and each time you have to respond with a similar toast. Toasting guests is very much part of the culture. Russians smoke a great deal and they do not like being asked to stop smoking during meals.

Communications

Internal telex and fax services are available, but international fax and telephone calls to other Asian countries are almost impossible to get because every call is still routed via Moscow. You may have to wait hours or even days for a call.

It is best to communicate to another country by telex, which is far more reliable than fax and it is unlikely you will be able to phone home or to your office while in Central Asia. If one is lucky enough to have an office or representative in Moscow, this is the best way of keeping in touch with the outside world, since Moscow has good outward communications and it is relatively easy to get through to Moscow from Central Asian capitals. However you must travel in Central Asia with the general assumption that your communications with the outside world will be minimal. Tashkent, in Uzbekistan, and Almaty, Kazakhstan, now have international satellite telephone connections, charged for in U.S. dollars.

Packing

Never drink local tap water anywhere in Central Asia because it is highly polluted, even in major cities. Local bottled mineral water is available for U.S. dollars from bars in most hotels. Western soft drinks and mineral waters are also available. It is advisable to carry water wherever you go, even for business meetings. If you are caught out without any bottled water, drink tea.

Travellers have to carry with them every possible item that they may need because most basic necessities are either not available or very difficult to find. Travellers should carry spare batteries for radios or recorders, films, cassettes, medicines, writing materials, shaving and washing requirements, shoe polish, any special dietary needs etc. Travellers should imagine they are going on a camping trip in the outback and be prepared for every need.

Transport

Uzbekistan and Kazakhstan are the two countries now becoming well connected with the international airline circuit. There are now direct flights at least once and sometimes twice a week to Tashkent (Uzbekistan) from **New Delhi**, **Islamabad**, **Teheran**, **Jeddah**, **Ankara** and other capitals. There are also direct flights to Almaty (Kazakhstan) from **Ankara**, **Hamburg** and other cities. There are frequent daily flights from Moscow to all Central Asian capitals including Dushanbe (Tajikistan), which is not connected to any other Central Asian city for the moment. **Tashkent** is the hub of Central Asian air travel and from Tashkent one can also catch flights to many smaller cities.

AIRLINES: Services inside the five countries are erratic, often late and offer poor service and food. Airports are poorly equipped for those waiting for flights. Foreigners have to buy all tickets in dollars, but this is actually an advantage, even if a little more expensive, because one always gets a seat if it is paid for in dollars. Buying a ticket on your own is a headache and can take hours. It is best to ask **Intourist** at your hotel to do it for you.

TRAINS: Services are regular, but remember that distances in Central Asia are huge and any journey can take many hours. The trains are reliable, even though seating is not very comfortable, and trains offer a superb view of the countryside. However there is no food or drink available on trains and very little at stations. Take everything you may need with you, including water.

TAXIS AND HIRE CARS: English-speaking drivers are available at Intourist hotels but if you have an interpreter it is advisable to ask the interpreter to negotiate a rate for the whole day, rather than by the hour. This will work out much cheaper.

KAZAKHSTAN

Kazakhstan is the largest of the Central Asian republics. Its area of 2.7 million square kilometres makes it the third-largest country in Asia, behind only China and India's 3.28 million square kilometres. The country stretches 3,000 kilometres from west to east and 2,000 kilometres north to south, and it takes nearly five hours to fly from Moscow to **Almaty**, the Kazakh capital.

Kazakhstan has a 5,000-kilometre northern and western border with Russia and a 1,700-kilometre eastern frontier with China. In the south it borders all the other Central Asian republics except Tajikistan. In the west it encompasses the northern shores of the **Caspian Sea**, the world's largest lake, and also much of the **Aral Sea**, the world's fourth largest.

Over the last 60 years, irrigation in an effort to increase cotton production has resulted in an ecological disaster as the Aral Sea has dried up alarmingly. The sea, also adjoining Uzbekistan, has reduced from 66,000 to 40,000 square kilometres and now contains only 31% of its original volume of water. Fishing villages on the old shoreline are now more than 30

Herdsmen on Kazakhstan's steppes. PHOTO: AHMED RASHID

kilometres away from the water and the hulks of abandoned boats are rusting on dry land.

Wind carries salt from the dried up sea hundreds of kilometres in all directions, polluting rivers and soil. Bird life as well as fish have been destroyed, while the shrinking of the sea has raised summer temperatures and shortened the frost-free season — results that have ironically badly affected the cotton crop in Uzbekistan, Turkmenistan and Kazakhstan. Drinking water in the whole area has been polluted.

Kazakhstan's landscape includes almost every type of terrain known to man except for tropical forests. In the south lie the great deserts and steppes of Central Asia, to the east and south are massive mountain ranges and in the north lie thick forests and vast tracks of steppe. In the far north lie the lowlands that form the southern part of the massive Siberian Plain.

Despite its arid surface, vast reservoirs of underground water and thousands of rivers and lakes enable the republic to account for 33% of the total agricultural land of the former Soviet Union. Across the seemingly endless steppes, where 70% of the ethnic Kazakhs live, nomads put up their *yurts* — felt tents — and race thoroughbred horses and camels as they did centuries ago.

The capital, **Almaty**, in the southeast corner of the country, is an entirely new city, with none of the traditional charm or the monuments of other Muslim cities. But it is one of the most beautiful in Central Asia because of its well-planned tree-lined streets and parks. Numerous fountains, lakes and small canals give it a distinctly European appearance. In winter the waterways become instant skating rings.

The People

Of the 17 million population of Kazakhstan, 41% are Russian while only 38% are Kazakh. The remainder of the population is comprised of minorities from 100 different nationalities. There are a million each of Ukrainians and ethnic Germans and nearly half a million each of Uzbeks, Tartars and Chinese. The Kazakhs themselves are scattered throughout Central Asia. Some 650,000 Kazakhs live in Xinjiang, the bordering province of China, largely as a result of mass migrations after the Bolshevik Revolution. Another 30,000 Kazakhs live in northern Afghanistan, while some 71,000 live in Mongolia. A quarter of a million Kazakhs live in other former Soviet republics.

The Kazakhs were converted to the Sunni sect of Islam in the 16th century.

History

From earliest times the Kazakh steppes were the grazing grounds for numerous nomadic empires which rose and fell in Central Asia. In 1218 the region was devastated by the Mongol hordes under Genghis Khan and it was not until the 15th century that the Kazakhs emerged as the distinct people known today.

In time the Kazakhs were divided into three *Ordas* or hordes. The Great Horde occupied eastern Turkestan, the Middle Horde lived in the central steppe region and the Little Horde occupied the west bordering the Urals.

The Russians had steadily extended their line of control southward from Siberia, at a time when the Kazakhs were facing numerous attacks from Uzbeks and Qirots. The Kazakhs finally asked for Russian protection and each Horde signed treaties with Russia between 1720-42. Between 1822 and 1848 the entire Kazakh territory was incorporated into the Tsarist empire.

After the 1917 Revolution, a small Kazakh nationalist party, Alash Orda, set up a provisional government in Kazakhstan but this was later crushed by the Bolsheviks. After the forced collectivization of their livestock in 1930-31, more tens of thousands of Kazakh nomads fled to China, while many Kazakh clans took up arms, only to be crushed by the Red Army cavalry. According to most estimates, in the 1930s, Kazakhstan lost 1.5 million people or a third of the entire indigenous population.

On December 5, 1936 the Kazakh Soviet Socialist Republic was established. In February 1954, in order to boost agricultural production, Soviet leader Nikita Khrushchev announced his Virgin Lands Scheme and tens of thousands more Russians arrived to farm the steppes. Massive anti-Russian protests erupted in Almaty in December 1986 after President Mikhail Gorbachov appointed a Russian, Gennady Kolbin, as First Secretary of the local communist party. He was replaced in March 1989 by a Kazakh, Nursultan Nazarbayev.

In the first direct elections on February 22, 1990, Nazarbayev was elected as First Secretary. On October 26, 1990, Kazakhstan declared its sovereignty. Nazarbayev supported the unity of the Soviet Union and backed Gorbachov during the August 1991 coup attempt. His efforts made him immensely popular not only amongst Kazakhs but also local Russians.

On December 1, 1991, Nazarbayev was elected president, winning 99.8% of the vote. On the same day Ukraine voted for independence, thereby ensuring the break-up of the Soviet Union.

Despite his popularity, Nazarbayev runs an authoritarian regime modelled on China, which does not allow serious political liberalization but instead argues for economic liberalization and development first. Kazakhstan has carried out the most ambitious privatization and economic liberalization programme in Central Asia. It replaced the rouble with the tenge in November 1993. In March 1994 Nazarbayev held parliamentary elections which he won by a large majority. Some opposition groups were allowed to take part, but there were charges of large-scale vote rigging.

There has been a spurt of Western interest in the region because of Kazakhstan's huge oil and gas reserves, mineral wealth and grain production. In fields along the Caspian Sea, Kazakhstan produced some 27 million tonnes of oil in 1992. Its oil reserves are 100 billion barrels, while gas reserves are 2.4 trillion cubic metres.

The break-up of the Soviet Union turned Kazakhstan into the first self-declared Muslim nuclear power. Kazakhstan has taken over from the Soviet state 104 SS18 ballistic missiles with more than 1,000 warheads, making it the fourth largest nuclear power in the world, but has since agreed to hand over its missiles to Russia in exchange for U.S. aid.

TURKMENISTAN

Turkmenistan, covering the territory of the former trans-Caspian region of Turkestan, is one of the poorest and most isolated of the former Soviet Union's 15 republics, though potentially very rich in oil and gas deposits, which still have to be fully exploited.

Lying between the Caspian Sea in the west, Iran and Afghanistan to the south and Uzbekistan in the east, about 350,000 square kilometres of the republic's 488,000 square kilometres are occupied by the waterless wastes of the **Karakum desert**, where only the hardy Turkmen nomads with their small flocks could survive the rigours of extreme temperatures. Rainfall in these regions is so rare that people remember single rainstorms that fell years ago.

Only 2.5% of Turkmenistan is arable and the only significant agriculture is along the banks of the **Amudarya river**, which runs along the eastern edge of the Karakum. Water is carried along the 1,100-kilometre **Lenin Canal** from the Amu river to the capital, **Ashkhabad**.

For the Turkmen nomads, borders were meaningless until the Bolshevik revolution, for they considered Iran and Afghanistan as much a part of their homeland as modern Turkmenistan is.

Ashkhabad, just 40 kilometres from the Iranian border, is set in some of the most desolate landscape in the world. The city sits on the bleak foothills of the **Kopet Dagh** mountains and beyond it lies the Karakum — a howling wilderness of red sand and shifting dunes.

With a population of 400,000 people, Ashkhabad is the hottest city in the former Soviet Union and is situated in an unstable seismic zone. First in 1929 and then again on October 6, 1948 Ashkhabad was struck by severe earthquakes. The latter measured nine on the Richter scale and destroyed the entire city, killing 110,000 people or two thirds of the entire population. Turkmen still relate the backwardness of their republic to that disaster, which wiped out virtually the entire educated class.

When it proclaimed its independence in 1991, Turkmenistan had one of the highest unemployment rates, the highest infant mortality rates, the lowest level of literacy and the most polluted agricultural land in the entire Soviet Union. Despite 70 years of communism, the majority of its 3.7 million people still define themselves according to their tribal loyalties.

Cardzhou, in the northeast, with a population of 162,000 people, has developed into the second largest city in the country, with the biggest industrial complex in the region, comprising cotton mills and sulphur, superphosphate and other chemical-processing plants.

The People

Of the 3.7 million population, 72% are Turkmen, 13% Uzbeks and 12.6% Russians who have settled in urban centres over the past 50 years. The republic shares its southern border with Iran, where some 313,000 Turkmen live, and its eastern border with Afghanistan where there are another 390,000 Turkmen.

The Turkmen language belongs to the southwestern or Oguz group of Turkic languages and is close to modern Turkish and Azeri.

History

For centuries Turkmenistan was a desolate no man's land, inhabited by the nomadic warrior Turkmen tribes who fiercely resisted but eventually succumbed to the Persians, the Turks and later the Russians. In the 18th and 19th centuries many Turkmen migrated into Mesopotamia and Anatolia.

The largest and most powerful of the Turkmen tribes, the **Tekkes**, led the resistance against the Russian intruders in the 19th century. In 1870 the Tekke chiefs began to attack Russian expeditions in a guerilla war that went on intermittently until the end of the century. The Russians suffered their worst defeat in 1881 when they tried to capture the Tekke fortress of **Geok Tepe** and an entire Russian army was decimated. In a retaliatory expedition, the Russians captured the fort and massacred 6,000 of its defenders. In the wake of the expedition, Russian administrators, soldiers and traders arrived in the territory to run it as a new protectorate.

After the 1917 revolution, Turkmen under their charismatic leader, Junaid Khan, resisted the Bolsheviks until 1927, when Junaid, then 70 years old, led his last attack on Bolshevik forces. He retreated into the desert and later crossed the border into Iran, finally settling in Afghanistan where he died in 1938. Today Junaid Khan's exploits are once again being revived and he is considered a national hero.

The intermittent revolts of the Turkmen nomads from 1870 to 1927 was the most sustained and bloody confrontation with Russian expansionism in Central Asia. No other Central Asian nationality fought so fiercely and suffered such retribution as the Turkmen. Stalin carried out numerous purges of the Communist Party of Turkmenistan (CPT) and tens of thousands of Russians moved in to run the republic.

The collapse of the Soviet Union came as a major shock to the government of President Saparmurad Niyazov. He had become First Secretary of the CPT in 1985 and consolidated his grip by proving loyal to Moscow and promoting those Turkmen communists who supported him. The government held elections on October 26, 1990, when 98% of the population cast their votes for Niyazov. After gaining independence, Niyazov ran again unopposed in June 1992 in Turkmenistan's first general elections, on a platform of nationalist rhetoric stating that with Turkmenistan's gas and oil wealth, his government would turn the republic into "another Kuwait." In November 1993 Turkmenistan introduced its own currency, the manat, to replace the rouble. In January 1994 Niyazov's hand-picked parliament decided to elect him as president until the year 2002. Elections for a new, smaller parliament were held in December 1994, with the opposition banned from taking part.

While Turkmenistan is famous for its carpets and *karakul* lamb pelts — Persian Lamb or Astrakhan — the only real money-earning export of the republic is the 85 billion cubic metres of natural gas produced a year at 28 gas fields. Turkmenistan has a phenomenal 10 trillion cubic metres of proven gas reserves and it is trying to draw in foreign companies who would be willing to exploit this. Turkey, Iran and Pakistan have expressed keen interest.

In November 1991, the border with Iran was opened for the first time since it was closed after the Iranian revolution.

UZBEKISTAN

Uzbekistan covers 447,400 square kilometres and its landlocked borders touch all four other Central Asian republics, as well as Afghanistan. To the north lies Kazakhstan, to the east Kirgyzstan and Tajikistan, to the west Turkmenistan and to the south Afghanistan.

Uzbekistan lies between the two fabled rivers of **Amudarya** and **Syrdarya** and some 70% of its territory forms part of the massive Central Asian steppes, the vast plains that have been seen so many nomadic invaders. In the eastern corner of the country are the **Tien Shan mountains**, while in the southwest lie the foothills of the **Pamirs** that rise to enormous heights near the Afghan border. In the Southeastern corner is the lush and heavily populated **Ferghana** valley.

In the centre of Uzbekistan, the steppes become one with the dry, lifeless deserts of Turkmenistan, while in the northeast lies the ecological disaster zone of the **Aral Sea**.

With a population of 20.5 million people, Uzbekistan is politically the most important of the Central Asian states. Over the centuries political and social movements in Uzbekistan have always affected the whole of Central Asia from the Ural to the Tien Shan mountains and beyond into China. The Uzbeks — the most numerous, aggressive and influential people of Central Asia — occupy the Islamic heartland, the political nerve centre and the economic hub of the region.

Tashkent has a 2,000-year history, though it was never a capital of the ancient world. Since the break-up of the Soviet Union, **Samarkand**, **Bukhara**, **Khiva** and **Kokand** have become major tourist attractions especially for Muslims from Pakistan, Iran and the Middle East. These are famous Islamic cities with ancient palaces, mosques and *madrassas* (religious colleges) as well as pre-Islamic remains. Uzbekistan is the only Central Asian republic with a viable tourist industry that has a great deal of sightseeing to offer. It introduced the sum currency to replace the rouble in 1994. In December 1994 there were parliamentary elections from which the opposition was banned.

The People

About 14 million people — 71% of the population — are ethnic Uzbeks. Another estimated 4 million Uzbeks live in the other Central Asian republics and they form substantial minorities in three of them — 23% of the population in Tajikistan, 13% in Turkmenistan and 12.9% in Kirgyzstan. In these republics, Uzbek aspirations have become important political factors that local governments cannot ignore and thus president Islam Karimov has emerged as the most important political actor on the Central Asian stage.

Bustling **Tashkent** is today the largest city in Central Asia with a population of 2.1 million people, the majority of whom are Russians.

History

For 2,500 years, the area now known as modern Uzbekistan has played host to a variety of nomadic conquerors who then created urban cultures. The Persians, Greeks, Arabs, Turks, Uzbeks and numerous other Central Asian tribes have passed through.

Despite the invasions of nomad tribes, the cities of Uzbekistan developed because they formed a crucial link in the chain of the all-important Silk Road from China to Europe. **Samarkand** — immortalized for so many English-readers in James Elroy Flecker's lines "for lust of knowing what should not be known, we take the Golden Road to Samarkand" — and Bukhara were major trading cities and caravan resting places en route.

The Mongol invasions destroyed both cities,

but they were rebuilt by the conqueror Tamerlane (Timur) whose empire stretched from Moscow to Delhi. He made Samarkand his capital in 1369. He imported architects and craftsmen from India, Arabia and Persia to create an Islamic architectural style that has in turn influenced Muslim society from North Africa to India.

The Uzbeks represented the last of the great nomadic movements in the region. The earliest Uzbek clans were a component of the Turko-Mongolian Golden Horde who trace their genealogy back to Uzbek Khan (1312-40), the grandson of the great Mongol conqueror, Genghis Khan. By the early 15th century the Uzbek tribes, ruled by the Shaybani clan, were made up of a fusion of Mongol, Turkic and Persian groups who established themselves between the Amudarya and Syrdarya. Uzbek consolidation took place under their ruler Mohammed Shaybani Khan, who ruled from 1500 to 1510. In 1500 he captured Bukhara and established his capital there.

Tsarist Russian involvement in Central Asia began with the capture of Tashkent in 1865 and Samarkand in 1868. Tashkent was made the capital for the new Russian Governor Generalship of Turkestan and in 1873 treaties with local rulers, the Khan of Khiva and the Amir of Bukhara, made their states Russian protectorates. As Russian repression increased, the Jadids or Muslim reformers played a major role in resurrecting Islamic and Pan-Turkic ideas amongst the intelligentsia. The Jadids were the first harbingers of political change in Muslim Central Asia for several centuries. Uzbeks under the Jadids carried out a number of anti-Russian rebellions in 1916.

The Bolshevik revolution began in Tashkent on September 12, 1917 when a Soviet was set up which was entirely led by ethnic Russians. Uzbek rebels called Basmachis began a revolt against the Bolsheviks, which was to continue until 1930. On October 27, 1924, the Khanates of Bukhara and Khiva were dissolved and the Soviet Socialist Republic of Uzbekistan was created. The Ferghana valley was divided between Uzbekistan, Tajikistan and Kirgyzstan while the Tajiks were divided between the newly created Tajikistan and their homeland in Uzbekistan.

Islam Karimov has led Uzbekistan since 1989 and he was elected unopposed as president on March 24, 1990. Ever since he has presented himself as the strongman of Central Asia, repressing his own opposition fiercely. He backed the failed August 1991 coup attempt against then President Gorbachov.

Karimov later banned the Communist Party of Uzbekistan, renaming it the People's Democratic Party of Uzbekistan. He held presidential elections on December 29, 1991, allowing another candidate — Mohammed Salikh of the Erk opposition party — to stand against him. Birlik, the main nationalist party, and the Islamic opposition remained banned. Karimov won 85.9% of the vote. The nationalist and Islamic fundamentalist opposition are the strongest of any Central Asian republic, but they are also opposed to each other, allowing the government room to manoeuvre between them.

TAJIKISTAN

Landlocked Tajikistan, covering 143,100 square kilometres, is the southern most republic of the former Soviet Union. To its south it shares a rugged, mountainous 1,030-kilometre border with Afghanistan, which in the east is separated from Pakistan by the thin wedge of the Wakhan corridor, in some places only 10 kilometre wide. In the east, Tajikistan shares a 430-kilometre border with China's Xinjiang province. Its northern border adjoins Kirgyzstan and its west Uzbekistan.

About 93% of Tajikistan's territory is covered in mountains — largely by the **Pamirs** which until recently were one of the most inaccessible mountain ranges in the world. Even in their deepest valleys the Pamirs are never lower than 3,500 metres above sea level.

Huge glaciers have created hundreds of river torrents that rush down the mountains and irrigate fields cut into the mountainside. The Pamirs are the crossroads of some of the highest ranges in the world. To the east and north of the Pamirs run the **Tien Shan** and the **Kun Lun** ranges, to the west run the **Himalayas** while southward into Afghanistan stretches the **Hindu Kush**.

Dushanbe, the capital, is surrounded by high peaks and lush orchards. Situated in the **Gissar valley** on the banks of the **Varzob** river, streams from nearby glaciers run into the city, providing water for parks and rows of trees. Before 1917, the village of Dushanbe was a small market town of 5,000 people where every Monday a lively bazaar was held. Dushanbe means Monday in Persian. In this century alone the city has suffered from 500

Harvesting cotton near Dzizak, Uzbekistan. PHOTO: AHMED RASHID

earthquakes. Possibly as a result, there are very few ancient monuments or buildings to be seen.

The Autonomous Region of Gorno-Badakshan, which shares its terrain, people and culture with northern Afghanistan, contains 44% of the total land area of Tajikistan but only 3% of the population.

In January 1994 Tajikistan the new Russian rouble. It is the only one of the five republics not to issue its own currency. After several rounds of United Nations-sponsored peace talks, a ceasefire was announced in November 1994, but fighting continued. In the same month, President Rakhmanov was elected for another term in polls boycotted by the opposition, which also boycotted parliamentary elections in January 1995.

The People

Tajikistan has a population of 5.4 million people, of whom only 58.8% are Tajiks, the original descendants of the Aryan population of Turkestan. Some 23% of the present population are Uzbeks while 11% are Russians who live mainly in the cities. More than 4 million Tajiks live in northern Afghanistan — at least 1.5 million more than in Tajikistan itself. Another 1 million Tajiks live in Uzbekistan and Tajiks are scattered throughout the other Central Asian republics. Some 20,000 live in China's Xinjiang province. There are more than a dozen other nationalities including Ismaelis, Kazakhs, Kirgyzs and Uighurs.

The Tajiks are Sunni Muslim and they are the only Central Asian people to speak Persian rather than Turkish based languages.

Many Tajiks consider their present homeland an afterthought carved out by the communists to divide and rule central Asia. For centuries Tajiks and Uzbeks lived together in the region. In the arbitrary divisions carried out by Stalin in the 1920s, these two ethnic groups were separated. The Ferghana valley — the home of political and Islamic movements in Central Asia — was divided. Tajiks also lost their major cultural and historical centres of Samarkand and Bukhara to Uzbekistan.

History

In ancient times, the forefathers of the modern Tajiks were a sedentary people who controlled a key section of the Silk Rd. They dominated the cities of Central Asia, even after they were ousted from political power, first by the Turkic tribes and later by the Mongols and Uzbeks.

The ancestors of the Tajiks were the Sogdians, who were one of the first ancient people to study the stars and compile calendars that were also used in neighbouring regions. The Sogdians inhabited the Pamirs when Alexander the Great, having defeated the Persians, left Kabul and crossed the Hindu Kush mountains to invade Central Asia in 329. Although Central Asia rapidly came under Turkic linguistic and political influence, the major cultural influence in the urban centres was still Tajik and Persian.

One of the earliest recorded crossings of the Pamir mountains was by Italian explorer Marco Polo in 1273, as he headed east into China. In the 19th Century, Russia annexed Tajikistan and began to exploit the mineral wealth of the Pamirs. When the communists took over in 1917, Tajik rebels, called Basmachis, fought a prolonged guerilla war against the Red army which did not end until the 1930s.

Tajikistan was one of the poorest of the 15 republics of the former Soviet Union with the lowest per capita income, 25% unemployment, a staggering 5% annual growth in population.

Stalin's division of Tajikistan created major ethnic and clan divisions. In the northern district of Leninabad, whose capital has now reverted to its former name of Khodjent, there is a strong separatist movement which it backed by local Uzbeks, with encouragement from some in Uzbekistan. Khodjent became the base of the communists and was developed as the economic powerhouse of Tajikistan. In the south there are long-standing economic and clan rivalries between the people of the Kuliab district in the south east — closely linked with the Khodjent communist elite — and those from Kurgan Tube in the south west, who are more overtly Islamic.

Rakhmon Nabiev became president of Tajikistan in September 1991 as a compromise candidate, after intense political unrest between communists and an opposition alliance of Islamic fundamentalists and democrats. The presidential elections on November 24, 1991 gave Nabiev a narrow and controversial victory with only 58% of the votes cast.

By the summer of 1992 factional rivalries, fuelled by the political polarization in the republic, erupted into civil war. The tragedy had been fuelled by the reluctance of the communists to share power or bring about economic reform and by the impatient Muslim fundamentalists who wanted power immediately. On September 7, 1992, Nabiev was forced to resign by Islamic fundamentalist gunmen. The civil war continued. About 20% of the population are now refugees from their homes because of the fighting and more than 100,000 people have been killed or injured. The economy and social structure has more or less collapsed. The communists recaptured Dushanbe in December 1992, but bloodshed continued.

KIRGYZSTAN

Kirgyzstan is bordered on the east by China and the vast Tien Shan range. To the west lies Uzbekistan and Kazakhstan, with its capital Almaty just a four-hour drive from Bishkek across the Central Asian plateau. To the south is Tajikistan and the Pamirs.

Kirgyzstan has always been one of the most inaccessible regions of the world. It is a vast cradle of snow-covered mountains, glaciers, forests and lakes. About 93% of the country's 198,500 square kilometres of territory is made up of mountains and nowhere does the land surface fall below 500 metres above sea level. The highest mountain is **Victory Peak** (7,429 metres) that stands in the immense **Mustag** massif, one of the world's largest areas of glaciers that covers 1,570 square kilometres.

The country has some 3,000 lakes, continuously filled by rivers flowing down from the mountain glaciers. Many of the lakes are more than 3,000 metres above sea level while others, such as **Lake Maerzbacker**, are so high that huge icebergs move from shore to shore within the lake. The great **Lake Issyk Kul**, in the eastern **Tien Shan** mountains, where the Kirgyz tribes built their earliest settlements, is a vast inland sea 182 kilometres long and 57 kilometres wide. It is a major tourist attraction today.

Those lakes below the tree-line are surrounded by magnificent aromatic juniper forests. The slow-growing juniper tree — a member of the cypress family — is revered by the nomads and called the queen of the forest.

Bishkek, formerly Frunze, the capital of Kirgyzstan, is surrounded by some of the highest mountain ranges in the world — the **Tien Shan** and the **Ala Ta** ranges. The mountains that are covered in snow even in June, encircle the city like a great bowl. The second-largest city, **Osh**, is predominantly an Uzbek town and is regarded as a holy city by Muslim pilgrims who visit it every year to pray at Islamic shrines.

The People

Kirgyz make up only 52.4% of the 4.4 million population. Some 21% of the people are Russian and 13% are Uzbek, while some 80 other ethnic groups from across the vast hinterland of Central Asia also make their home in Kirgyzstan. The Kirgyz are a Mongol people who speak a Turkic dialect called Kipchak. In all they number over 2 million people with 100,000 living in Chinese Xinjiang province and some 35,000 in the Wakhan corridor of Afghanistan. The Kirgyz are Sunni Muslims, but a strong streak of pre-Islamic shamanism is still evident in many of their traditions and daily life.

The population of Kirgyzstan has always been vastly outnumbered by its livestock. About 10 million sheep and goats, 2 million horses, yaks and cattle and half a million pigs feed on the lush grasslands of the high mountains, tended by shepherds and farmers whose lifestyle has changed little over the centuries. Nomadism is such an ingrained way of life that even the communist system proved incapable and eventually unwilling to break it down.

History

The first recorded evidence of the Kirgyz people comes from the Chinese chronicles dating back to the second millennium BC, which note the existence of some 40 Turkic-speaking clans in southern Siberia. One meaning of the word Kirgyz is 40 clans. During their migration south and in the Tien Shan mountains, the Kirgyz merged with other tribal clans. The Kirgyz were defeated by the Mongols under Genghis Khan in 1210 and later joined his Golden Horde or confederation of tribes.

As Russia extended its advance into Central Asia in the 19th century, Russian explorers reached the Tien Shan. Pyotr Semyonov, with an armed group of Cossacks, was the first to map Lake Issyk Kul in 1856. During the long and freezing winter of 1859-60, the Kirgyz suffered a catastrophe, losing 80% of their flocks. Thousands died in the snows of the Tien Shan as people tried to flee to Chinese Turkestan. In the next decade between 1860-70 the Kirgyz chiefs, depleted of resources and starving, had little choice but to accept Russian sovereignty. Little was known of the region until the 1917 Revolution.

With Russian control established, the Tsar ordered that 100 million acres of prime Kazakh-Kirgyz land should be given to Russian and Cossack settlers, who were to be exempted from taxes and military service. In 1916 these and other policies led to a large-scale revolt by the Kirgyz against the Russians, which was brutally repressed.

The Bolsheviks established a strong military presence to protect their fellow Russian settlers and created the Communist Party of Kirgyzstan (CPK), which was dominated by Russian settlers. On April 30, 1918, Kirgyzstan became part of the Turkestan Autonomous Soviet Socialist republic within the Russian Federation. A capital was established in the small market town of Bishkek in 1925. The next year it was renamed Frunze in honour of the conquering Russian Gen. Mikhail Frunze. In February 1926 the Kirgyz Autonomous Soviet Socialist republic was created and on December 5, 1936, Kirgyzstan joined the Soviet Union as a sovereign republic. There were large-scale purges within the CPK under Stalin.

In June 1990 the economic discontent and latent ethnic hostility between Uzbeks and Kirgyz in the city of Osh erupted and hundreds of people were killed. Askar Akaev, a non-communist academic, was elected president by the Supreme Soviet on October 28, 1990. Akaev declared full independence for Kirgyzstan on August 31, 1991 and he was the most strident Central Asian leader in opposing the August 1991 anti-Gorbachov coup attempt in Moscow. Also in 1991 Frunze once again reverted to its original name of Bishkek.

The most rapid programme of privatization in all Central Asia was put into effect in Kirgyzstan after August 1991. The first auction of state flats to individual owners in Bishkek took place in December 1991. However, the country still faced acute economic problems because of its lack of resources. The IMF expected to lend Kirgyzstan US$300 million in 1993. The communist era changed little of the nomadic lifestyle and the backbone of the economy remains the breeding of sheep and yaks for wool, milk, meat and fat.

The Russian rouble was replaced with the som in May 1993. In January 1994 Akaev won a referendum on his economic policies and extending his presidency to 1996. In July 1994 the IMF lent US$104 million for budgetary support, while the World Bank lent another US$60 million for agriculture. After a series of political and economic crises, a referendum in October 1994 permitted major changes to the constitution and gave the president more powers. In February 1995 there were parliamentary elections in which the opposition was allowed to take part.

CHINA

When you visit China its vastness is difficult to comprehend. It is as large as the United States, but with four times as many people. It covers an area the size of the whole of Europe from the Atlantic to Moscow, with peoples, cultures and languages almost as diverse.

It is many places, not just one. The "Middle Kingdom," a rough triangle with its points at Beijing, Xian and Shanghai; The Silk Road stretching west from Xian towards the Middle East and Europe; the landlocked, backward southwestern provinces of Yunnan, Guizhou and Sichuan; the mystical world of Tibet; the teeming, steaming coastal south of Fujian, Guangdong and Guangxi, at the leading edge of economic progress and looking towards the modernity of Hong Kong. In each area you encounter different landscapes, languages, cuisine, and lifestyles.

The policy of opening to the outside world, started in China in the late 1970s, has had a striking effect on the Chinese tourist industry. The loosening of the Chinese Communist Party's grip on the economy, encouragement of foreign investment and the rapid expansion of such things as air travel — with services to more than 100 cities — and facsimile transmission, have made it possible for more people to visit more of China more easily than at any time in history.

But modernization and openness have not eliminated the adventure, challenge and excitement. The Great Wall, the Forbidden City, the Grand Canal, the Silk Road, Tibet, Xian's Terracotta Warriors and the Three Gorges on the Yangtze all dazzle the visitor seeing these wonders for the first or the 10th time.

A shortage of hotel rooms is not a serious problem in major cities, though transport bottlenecks such as overbooked flights and trains and urban traffic jams are a common source of irritation to the tourist and local resident alike.

Group or individual travel on a full package basis (hotel, all meals, guides, sightseeing and transport) arranged by a Chinese or Hong Kong travel agent can eliminate most of the hassle involved in getting around this huge, overcrowded country, but restrict the visitor in terms of rigid daily timetables and being tied to probably mediocre restaurants and compulsory stops at designated shops.

Thanks to improvements in the tourist infrastructure, foreigners can do business and travel freely on their own in China without dealing with a Chinese host organization such as the ubiquitous China International Travel Service (CITS), their subsidiaries or competitors. The greatest obstacle to independent travel, however, is booking air or rail tickets for each sector of your itinerary along the way, something that can be frustrating and time consuming.

Now airlines and travel agents in Hong Kong and China offer mini-packages put together to your specifications — where to go and for how long at each stop — which include airline bookings, airport-hotel transfers, hotel accommodation and breakfast. But they leave the details — what you see and how you spend your time at each place — up to you. While not the cheapest way to go, mini-packages are ideal for both business people and tourists who want the freedom to choose but the support of experts.

The general organization of group tours is as it has been for years. A "national

◄ *China's new face.* PHOTO: GERHARD JOREN

CHINA
KAZAKHSTAN
UZBEKISTAN
KIRGHYZSTAN
TAJIKISTAN
AFGHANISTAN
PAKISTAN
INDIA
NEPAL
BHUTAN
BANGLADESH
BURMA
THAILAND
Bay of Bengal
Yining
Urumqi
Turfan
Aksu
Korla
Kashgar
XINJIANG
Dunhuang
GANSU
Yumen
Hotan
Golmud
QINGHAI
XIZANG
Shigatze
Lhasa
Gyantze
Zedang
YUNNAN
Xishuangbanna
Railway
Airports
0
km
500

RUSSIA
MONGOLIA
INNER MONGOLIA
HEILONGJIANG
Qiqihar
Jiamusi
Harbin
Mudanjiang
Changchun
JILIN
Shenyang
LIAONING
Erenhot
Chengde
Beijing
Hohhot
Yellow River
Datong
Yinchuan
Tianjin
Dalian
N. KOREA
S. KOREA
Shijiazhuang
Taiyuan
HEBEI
NINGXIA
Yanan
SHANXI
Jinan
Qingdao
Yellow Sea
SHANDONG
Xining
Lanzhou
Xuzhou
Xian
GANSU
Zhengzhou
JIANGSU
SHAANXI
HENAN
ANHUI
Nanjing
Wuxi
JAPAN
Hefei
Shanghai
Suzhou
SICHUAN
Yichang
HUBEI
Chengdu
Yangtze River
Wuhan
Hangzhou
Ningbo
East China Sea
Chongqing
Wanxian
Nanchang
ZHEJIANG
Changsha
HUNAN
JIANGXI
Fuzhou
Guiyang
FUJIAN
GUIZHOU
Guilin
Quanzhou
Taipei
Xiamen
TAIWAN
Pearl River
GUANGDONG
GUANGXI
Shenzhen
Shantou
Guangzhou
Nanning
VIETNAM
Hong Kong
Zhuhai
Macau
Haikou
South China Sea
HAINAN
PHILIPPINES
Sanya

guide" will accompany a group throughout the tour, while arrangements in each locality are left up to the local travel service office and local guides. The standards of travel-service guides vary enormously in terms of linguistic ability, professional knowledge and honesty. A good guide can make a trip a success and a poor guide can spoil it.

Tour groups today are run in a more commercial fashion than in the more easy-going, more amateur early 1980s.Requests for extra stops or overtime use of the bus can be met with instant demands for cash payment, and the system of restaurant kickbacks to travel agencies and shop commissions to guides has been refined to a high art.

Tourists, even if they are in a group, should find time in their itineraries to wander around on their own for a few hours in each destination. Do something just a little different, like hiring a bicycle (they are available everywhere) and taking a ride like a local. Tour guides have no objection to group members dropping out of part of a tour programme if they are confident the wanderers will find their way back to the hotel or next site on the itinerary.

Most guides are prepared to chat frankly about China. You may get officially approved replies at first, followed by more open discussions as the ice melts.

Photography is virtually unrestricted wherever tourists are allowed, but there is an infuriating rule banning or charging for photographs of certain cultural relics, such as cave-paintings and temple frescoes and even Xian's terracotta warriors. People in the streets may or may not object to being photographed, but it is always best to ask, if only with a gesture. Polaroid instant snapshots make popular gifts, and any visitor hoping to increase international goodwill by setting up as a street corner benefactor will soon draw a large crowd.

First time visitors usually suffer from a bout of culture shock. Spitting in public is common, even in hotels and restaurants. Due to generally low standards of public sanitation and hygiene, you should wash your hands frequently, especially before eating, and should always peel fruit.

Some 70% of men and a growing number of women in China smoke, and there is little or no regard for non-smokers' rights. Chinese can be seen smoking while eating; chopsticks in one hand, cigarette in the other (and a portable phone if they had a third). Non-smoking areas can only be found in a few modern joint-venture hotels.

Tipping is gradually becoming a way of life, particularly in the more modern hotels where porters are not reluctant to say "not enough." Tour guides (and bus drivers) have been spoiled by foreign tourists, to the point where they expect to receive a gratuity equal to half the annual average Chinese wage (US$150) for taking a group of people around for two weeks.

Newcomers also have to get used to the fact that rudeness is literally a way of life in China. People push and shove to get on a bus, force their way into queues (which are rare to begin with), and show amazing disregard for each other. It is all reciprocal and no hard feelings are meant. But if they discover you are a foreigner, scowls will turn to smiles and you will be made welcome.

History

Historically China, together with India, has been to East Asia what Greece and Rome have been to the West — teacher of the arts, exponent of political and social order and source of civilization. Over the centuries, China evolved a way of life which readily found its way into neighbouring lands. Peoples such as the Japanese, Vietnamese and Koreans — though developing their own cultures — have traditionally found inspiration in the Chinese way. Similarly, China has absorbed cultural influences from abroad, most significantly Buddhism from India and modern technology from the West, though China was already a highly developed civilization while the West was creeping out of the Middle Ages.

Ample evidence has been found in China of the neolithic cultures in the northwest of the country. The undocumented Xia Dynasty (c. 2200-1700 BC), is said to have existed in the latter part of the neolithic age. During the Shang Dynasty (1766-1112 BC), the Chinese written language was used for the first time — pre-dating the evolution of the Greek alphabet around 1000 BC.

The Shang were overthrown by the more vigorous peoples from further west and the Zhou Dynasty (1066-221 BC) was established, with its capital near present-day Xian. As Zhou civilization developed, the central government became weaker and the territory under Chinese control was divided into several kingdoms.

The period 722-481 BC is called the Spring and Autumn Period after a chronicle describing the time. Confucius was born in 551 BC and died in 479 BC. The discovery of iron at this time, among other factors, led to increased fighting between the many small and large kingdoms. The period from 481 BC to the founding of the Qin Dynasty is known as The Warring States.

The Qin Dynasty (221-206 BC), despite a brief life, was the beginning of the Chinese Empire, for never before had the country been brought under one leader and subjected to a single set of standards. "China" is considered to be derived from the name Qin. The first of many Great Walls was completed in the Qin Dynasty and served as a physical and psychological barrier against the war-like nomads of the northern steppes.

The authoritarian Qin Dynasty was overthrown and replaced by the Han Dynasty (202 BC-220 AD). Confucianism was established as the state ethic and the principles of government that evolved remained as models for future dynasties. On the collapse of the Han, China went through the chaotic Three Kingdoms period, and later the Northern and Southern Dynasties, until reunification was achieved under the short-lived Sui Dynasty (581-618 AD).

Under the Tang Dynasty (618-917 Chinese civilization blossomed (especially in literature, art, ceramics and architecture). The empire, with its capital at Chang'an became one of the world's great powers. But the empire collapsed during the Five Dynasties period (907-960) and was re-established by the Song Dynasty (960-1276), though for much of the time the Song held sway over only the southern half of the country with its capital at present-day Hangzhou.

Hangzhou fell to the invading Mongols under Khublai Khan in 1276, so beginning the Yuan Dynasty (1276-1368), though the Mongols (under Khublai's grandfather, Genghis Khan) had invaded North China earlier. The Yuan capital, Dadu (Khanbaliq), was built at the site of present-day Beijing. It was during the reign of Khublai Khan that Marco Polo made his epic journey to China from Italy, although no record of the Italian has been found in contemporary Chinese annals. However, *The Travels* of Marco Polo give a magical detailed account of the Mongol capital of the day, and make worthwhile travel reading.

The Mongols were eventually driven from China and the indigenous Ming Dynasty (1368-1644), replaced them. The capital, which had been moved to Nanjing, returned to Dadu/Beijing, where it was to remain throughout the Ming and the subsequent Qing Dynasty (1644-1911), under the Manchus. Chinese culture flourished during the Ming, but under the increasingly decadent rule of the alien Manchus the country was driven to the brink of collapse during the late 19th and the early 20th century.

During the second half of the 19th century, Europeans forcibly initiated trade with China and took over large tracts of the country as their own spheres of influence. Christian missionaries came in eager, evangelical hordes to convert the "pagans." Britain, the foremost foreign power, took Hong Kong for its own and opened five Chinese ports to foreign trade following the Opium War of 1839-42. Another 11 were opened and Kowloon, opposite Hong Kong Island, was ceded in perpetuity to the British after the Opium War of 1856-58.

China suffered further from its defeat in the Sino-Japanese War of 1894 and was forced to give up territory, including the island of Taiwan. By the turn of the century, under the triple burden of internal weakness, Manchu rule and foreign trade domination, China had weakened beyond repair. The Boxer Rebellion of 1900 led to demands for indemnity from the foreigners. But it was not until the Revolution of 1911, under the inspiration of the Cantonese leader Sun Yat-sen, that China set out on the way to recovery. The war that ended imperial rule began on October 10 in Wuhan.

With the Qing Dynasty removed, China became a republic on January 1, 1912, with Sun as the first president, but he soon yielded this office to the warlord Yuan Shikai in the interests of national unity. Yuan died in 1916, only to be replaced by a succession of equally brutal warlords who ravaged China until the success of Chiang Kai-shek's Northern Expedition in 1926, when the country again attained a semblance of unity.

The Chinese Communist Party (CCP) was founded in Shanghai on July 1, 1921. The warlord period also saw increasing nationalist sentiments among the people — especially students. One of the most famous popular demonstrations was the May Fourth Movement (1919) in Beijing, which began as a protest against the Versailles Peace Conference decision to hand territory previously held by Germany to Japan rather than back to China.

Chiang Kai-shek, as head of the Kuomintang (KMT or Republican) government, tried from 1926 until 1937 to bring order to the country. His continuing dependence on the West, however, weakened his position. Moreover, the regime was destructively corrupt, leaving the many provincial factions — notably the communists under Mao Zedong — unchecked. Repeated "search and destroy" campaigns against communist strongholds in the mountains of Jiangxi were unsuccessful until the fifth attempt in 1934. This sent the communists on their famous Long March of 9,650 kilometres to safety in Yanan in the northern province of Shaanxi.

The Japanese took control of Manchuria in the northeast in 1931-32 creating the puppet state of Manchukuo. During the Sino-Japanese War (1937-45) the Japanese forcibly assumed control of more Chinese territory, mainly in the north and along the coast.

After much bitter fighting among themselves, the communists and the KMT in 1937 joined in a strained alliance to fight the Japanese, who were expelled only at the end of World War II. With the Japanese gone, the communists proved far stronger than the divided and inefficient KMT forces and by October 1, 1949, the People's Republic of China was proclaimed with its capital in Beijing. Chiang and his followers fled to Taiwan.

Since coming to power, the communists have followed a rocky path in their attempts to bring China into the modern world. For the first decade, the Chinese relied heavily on Soviet aid and Soviet models. The movement launched in 1958 known as the Great Leap Forward was an attempt to modernize the economy at unprecedented speed, and the countryside was organized into a system of people's communes. The years 1959-61 were bitter ones owing to natural disasters and mistaken policies, with at least 30 million dying of starvation. These difficulties were compounded by the withdrawal of all Soviet aid and technicians at this time.

Progress was further disrupted in the decade-long Cultural Revolution (1966-76 in which the ageing Mao Zedong sought to abolish "bourgeois" tendencies that had begun to dampen revolutionary fervour. Red Guards, fired by thoughts of Mao in his "little red book," rampaged across China, and most of the members of the central committee of the CCP were swept from power. The People'sLiberation Army (PLA) took on increased authority and acted as a stabilizing influence. By late 1968 China was ruled by revolutionary committees in which party members and representatives of mass organizations joined with the army.

Millions suffered during the Cultural Revolution in "struggle sessions" as intellectuals, professionals, loyal party members and common citizens with overseas connections were jailed or sent to work on farms. So perverse was this "revolution" that in hospitals "bourgeois" surgeons were forced to clean the toilets while "proletarian" custodians performed operations on unanaesthetized patients shouting Mao's slogans.

Following the disgrace and death of the heir-apparent, Lin Biao, in 1971, and the country's admission to the United Nations in the same year, China began a rapid rapprochement with the West, crowned by the visits of then United States President Richard Nixon and Japanese Prime Minister Kakuei Tanaka in 1972.

In 1973, after seven years of political disgrace, Deng Xiaoping was rehabilitated and won recognition as the most active person in the leadership. In 1975 and early 1976, radicals surrounding the ailing Mao launched an all-out campaign to unseat Deng. Moderate Premier Zhou Enlai died in January 1976 and Hua Guofeng was named acting premier. Increasingly obvious press attacks on Deng continued until the Tiananmen Square riots on April 5. Deng was dismissed the next day.

Mao died on September 9 and a month later Hua Guofeng arrested Mao's widow Jiang Qing and other members of what came to be known as the Gang of Four.

After Deng's second reinstatement in 1977 China took an outward turn under the policy of the Four Modernizations. Mao, however, remained a revered figure, embalmed in a huge mausoleum in Tiananmen Square. In 1981, Hua Guofeng was ousted from the party and replaced by Hu Yaobang, a former leader of the Communist Youth League. Zhao Ziyang took over as premier and later party leader.

Deng's reforms permitting private enterprise in the agricultural and urban economies provided the basis for China's unprecedented growth rates and rising standards of living in the 1980s and early 1990s. Mao's cherished communes were abolished in 1985, leading to sharp increases in rural output and earnings. However, the reforms had less effect on antiquated state industries, and there was a sharp increase in corruption, smuggling and other "economic crimes." The PLA expanded its activities into producing goods for the civilian sector.

Increasing contacts with the outside world and a growing awareness of international events led to popular demands to step up the pace of reforms, ease ideological strictures and introduce greater democracy — Deng's unstated Fifth Modernization. These pressures developed into confrontation with the leadership in May and June of 1989 with massive pro-democracy demonstrations and hunger strikes in Beijing and other cities. Martial law was declared, and negotiations with the student leaders failed to quell the protests. With the world media recording events, the hardline political leaders called in the PLA which in the early hours of June 4 crushed the demonstrations in and around Tiananmen Square with tanks and bullets. The crackdown, which also brought about the downfall of Zhao Ziyang, continued with mass arrests, trials and executions or imprisonment throughout 1990, 1991 and 1992.

Since the crackdown, economic realities have prompted a papering over of the blemishes in China's international reputation caused by Tiananmen. Economic liberalization has continued apace, but with minimal loosening of the political reins. Consumerism — part of "Socialism with Chinese characteristics" — has replaced Mao Zedong Thought as the leading ideology, with government and military departments at all levels angling for a slice of the pie. Corruption also continues unbridled — it can be argued that China's near-universal corruption is "democracy with Chinese characteristics."

In 1993, China failed in its bid to host the Olympics in Beijing in the year 2000, and in 1994 it failed to gain entry into the World Trade Organization, the successor to the General Agreement on Tariffs and Trade (Gatt). In early 1995 Deng failed to make an appearance at Chinese New Year celebrations, the first year in many that this had happened, and his failing health highlighted the issue of the post-Deng succession. In February 1995, a trade war loomed with the U.S. over pirated intellectual property, with acrimonious statements and patched-up renewed talks apparently set to continue their cycle until or unless one side or the other lost its temper.

Entry

Most visitors enter China by air or by rail. The Civil Aviation Administration of China (CAAC) now oversees about 30 domestic airlines, including seven major regional carriers, several of them flying intercontinental routes. There are daily flights on these airlines between Hong Kong and Beijing, Tianjin, Shanghai, Guangzhou, Guilin, Haikou, Hangzhou, Nanjing, Shantou and Xiamen. There are also flights between Hong Kong and Changsha, Chengdu, Chongqing, Dalian, Fuzhou, Guiyang, Harbin, Hefei, Jinan, Kunming, Meixian, Nanchang, Nanning, Ningbo, Qingdao, Sanya, Shenyang, Xian, Zhenjiang and Zhengzhou. All can be booked by travel agents in Hong Kong.

However, for flights between Hong Kong and China, the airline of choice is Hong Kong-based Dragonair, which has taken over Cathay Pacific Airways' China routes and added many of its own. Dragonair flies between Hong Kong and Beijing, Changsha, Chengdu, Dalian, Guilin, Haikou, Hangzhou, Kunming, Nanjing, Tianjin, Xian and Xiamen.

More than other airlines operate in and out of one or more of China's international gateways (Beijing, Shanghai, Guangzhou, Kunming, Urumqi), including all the leading Asian airlines plus Aeroflot, Air France, British Airways, Lufthansa, Qantas, United Airlines and Northwest.

Inflight service on most Chinese domestic fights is unreliable and rudimentary and reservations procedures leave much to be desired, though it is now possible to book domestic flights to and from several major cities in advance.

The traveller who wishes to enter by rail from Hong Kong leaves from the Kowloon-Canton Railway (KCR) terminal at Hung Hom in Kowloon. Round trip tickets for the through express to Guangzhou are sold by the China Travel Service office at the station. The visitor can travel direct to Guangzhou or opt for cheaper trains, crossing the border bridge on foot at Shenzhen where health, customs and immigration formalities are necessary. There are often delays of up to one hour at the border due to the crowds.

There is a regular hovercraft service between Hong Kong and Guangzhou, Shekou and Zhuhai. Coach services from Hong Kong to Shantou (Swatow) and Xiamen (Amoy) are also available.

Immigration

Visas are essential for all visitors to China. In an effort to encourage foreign investment in China, some larger cities, including Beijing and Haikou, now grant visas on arrival for people travelling on business. In these cases, the traveller is expected to produce a letter or other documentation from a Chinese partner or ministry. Getting a visa in advance is still advisable when time permits.

Visas are issued by Chinese diplomatic missions in countries that have diplomatic relations with Beijing. Visas are also issued for a fee by the Hong Kong offices of China Travel Service at 77 Queen's Rd, Central, Hong Kong or 27-33 Nathan Rd, Kowloon, and at the People's Republic of China Visa Office, China Resources Bldg, 26 Harbour Rd, Wanchai, Hong Kong. Visa applications made in person in Hong Kong can be issued on the same or next day. Travel agencies arranging China tours, especially in Hong Kong, can obtain visas on your behalf.

Once in China, application for an extension of stay or permission to visit areas not normally open to overseas tourists must be made to the local Foreign Affairs Branch of the Public Security Bureau. Now that millions of Taiwanese have travelled to China, having a Taiwan visa in a passport has no influence on obtaining entry to China.

Health

Vaccinations are not required for entry except in the case of visitors arriving from or via Africa or Latin America, or any area in which yellow fever is prevalent, who must have certificates showing inoculation. Visitors from any country who arrive from or via a country in which there is an outbreak of cholera may also need certificates indicating inoculation against this disease. All visitors to China are required to fill in a simple health declaration form which is collected during entry procedures.

Many visitors to China contract minor respiratory infections, especially in the autumn and winter. Drinking a lot of fluids is recommended, and be sure to bring along your favourite cough-mixture. Food in Chinese hotels and restaurants is usually prepared hygienically, but in case of stomach-upsets it is useful to have some appropriate medicine. Be careful about cold dishes in the hotter months.

Never drink tap water or even brush your teeth with it. The cold water supplied in flasks in hotel rooms has been boiled. Bottled mineral water is readily available in every city in China.

Customs

A baggage declaration form is handed out to all travellers entering China, but customs officials tend to ignore them on both entry and exit unless you declare goods.

Duty-free import is allowed for two bottles of liquor (not exceeding 750 grams) and 400 cigarettes or their tobacco equivalent for personal use; up to 900 metres of movie film (not over eight millimetres) and up to 72 rolls of ordinary camera film (though the rule is flexibly enforced); cameras, tape-recorders, and movie and video cameras brought into the country are supposed to be taken out, though this is not strictly enforced.

The customs officers are most concerned with the import of goods and samples, recorded video tape, printed matter and antiques. Such things should be declared. Heavy fines can be levied for the illegal importation of arms, narcotics, pornographic videotapes and magazines, large amounts of cash, publications deemed detrimental to Chinese political, economic, cultural or moral interests, easily saleable items such as fax machines, portable computers, designer watches, etc. Customs officials tend to be more lenient with non-Asian travellers.

Antiques more than 100 years old and not authorized for export, and printed materials for internal or restricted circulation *(neibu)*, are

Beijing's Qianmen gate.

PHOTO: GERHARD JOREN

not allowed to be exported. State antique shops mark their goods with a wax seal, which must be left intact and shown, with the purchase receipt, to customs officials at time of departure. Most curios and 19th-century antiques sold in the free markets can be exported without the seal, but there is always a tiny risk of confiscation.

$ Currency

In 1994, as part of an attempt to join Gatt, China began to phase out Foreign Exchange Certificates (FEC). Since January 1, 1994, *renminbi* (people's currency) has been given out instead of FEC in exchange for foreign cash and travellers' cheques. This followed a major devaluation of the renminbi that brought the official exchange rate into line with the blackmarket rate. As of early 1995 there was still a blackmarket for foreign currency in China, but the rate was only about 5% higher than the official level. FECs continued to circulate during 1994, but they were becoming collectors' items by the end of the year.

The basic unit of currency is the *yuan*, which in April 1995 exchanged at Rmb 8.4:US$1. The yuan is divided into 10 *jiao*, in turn divided into 10 *fen*. The yuan is called *kuai* in everyday speech, while the jiao is always known as *mao*. There are three sizes of notes: the yuan, jiao, and fen grow progressively smaller, but it is easy to mistake one yuan for one jiao.

There are renminbi notes of 100, 50, 10, 5, 2 and 1 yuan; 5, 2 and 1 jiao; and 5, 2 and 1 fen. There are coins in the denominations of 1 yuan; 1 jiao; and 5, 2 and 1 fen. The coins and fen notes cannot be changed back to foreign currency when leaving the country. As of April 1995, Rmb 6,000 can be exported from and imported into China per trip.

Any amount of foreign currency may be imported, but no more than that declared upon entry may be taken out, though inspection upon departure is rare. Travellers' cheques fetch a slightly higher rate of exchange than cash. Dealers in the free markets trade (illegally) most major foreign currencies at rates slightly above the official levels. They do not accept travellers' cheques.

Money can be changed at airports, hotels, banks and some large shops. The exchange rate is the same everywhere in China on any given day. Keep the exchange slips to show to the bank when changing unspent renminbi back to foreign currency. In some places, you are only allowed to change back half of the amount shown on the slip. With the approach of Hong Kong's return to China in 1997, banks and money-changers in the territory have begun to accept renminbi from the mainland.

Major credit cards such as American Express, Visa, MasterCard, Diners Club, and JTB can be used to pay hotel bills and purchases in the major tourist cities. In some shops the credit-card commission is added to the purchase price.

Language

Guoyu — national language, or as it is better known in China, *putonghua* (common language) — is widely spoken throughout the country. It is known in the West as Mandarin. Putonghua is based on the language spoken in Hebei province, near Beijing.

Elsewhere Putonghua exists alongside the regional languages such as Cantonese, Fukienese and Hunanese, which are known as "dialects" but are incomprehensible to someone who speaks only Putonghua. Putonghua is replacing other Chinese languages in official usage, as the medium of instruction in schools and in most broadcasting. Most urban residents can speak and understand two dialects. They use their own at home and in the marketplace, but speak putonghua at school and in the workplace.

The various Chinese tongues are tonal; i.e. each sound unit has a fixed or changing pitch as an essential component.

The great genius of Chinese is that the written language is largely independent of regional variations in the spoken language. So two Chinese from different regions can read and understand the same text but would pronounce it quite differently. The characters in use at present in China have been simplified in many cases. The written language therefore differs somewhat from that in use in Hong Kong and Taiwan and by Overseas Chinese, who generally use unsimplified characters, but the differences are easily learned.

Romanized Chinese is only an approximation of the true sounds of Chinese, as certain Chinese sounds do not exist in Western alphabetic languages. Several systems of romanization are in use. The main ones are China's official *pinyin* system and the older Wade-Giles.

Even when used by the uninitiated, reading pinyin results in passable pronunciation of most consonants (though one should know that "zh" is read as the "j" in jug, "c" as the "ts" in its, "q" as the "ch" in cheap, and "x" at the start of the word as something between "see" and "she"). Some aural briefing on the system of vowels is very helpful.

In this guide, Chinese names are rendered in pinyin except in cases of established usage — for example, historical figures such as Sun Yat-sen and Chiang Kai-shek.

Chinese personal names always have the family name first, followed by the given name. Thus, in the name Mao Zedong (formerly rendered Mao Tse-tung), Mao is the family name, and Zedong the given name.

In China, the man in the street is unlikely to speak anything but Chinese. Taxi drivers generally do not speak English except for basic directions such as "airport," "train station" or "Great Wall Hotel." It is best to have directions written in Chinese or a bilingual map with you at all times to avoid misunderstandings.

The level of English spoken by telephone operators, front-desk staff or local managers in even the best hotels is often surprisingly low. Be sure to speak slowly and clearly and spell any names carefully. Have all messages and instructions repeated to you.

Climate

Conditions vary considerably from the north to the south of the country. In the north seasonal variation of temperature is particularly marked. The subtropical south has a climate similar to that of Hong Kong: hot and humid for six months (April-October), pleasant in the fleeting seasons of autumn and spring, and sometimes chilly in the winter.

The northern cities, including Beijing, experience cold, dry, windy winters. The average minimum temperature in Beijing throughout December, January and February is below -4°C and the average maximum temperature 0°C — but the wind-chill factor makes the cold more penetrating than the temperature suggests. There is a short snowy period and dust storms are frequent in March and April.

In June, July and August average minimum temperatures do not fall below -24°C while average maximums are around 26°C and often rise above 30°C July is usually hottest month of the year. Humidity stays high during much of the summer. Beijing has a rainy season during July and August. Spring and autumn are by far the best times of the year to visit the north. One can expect warm, pleasant weather, with clear skies and relatively little dust or rain from April to June and in September and October.

The towns along the Yangtze River are notorious for their summer heat. Nanjing, Wuhan and Chongqing are China's three furnaces. Shanghai, at the mouth of the river, has average maximum temperatures in excess of 24°C from May until mid-October. August is the hottest month with an average maximum of around 35°C December to March can be quite cool in Shanghai, with minimum average temperatures approaching freezing point; humidity remains very high during the whole year. The annual average rainfall is 114 centimetres.

Guangzhou, near the southern coast, has maximum temperatures in excess of 21°C for seven months of the year and above 30°C from May to September. Minimum average temperatures fall to around 10°C in January and February, but humidity remains high. The average annual rainfall is 160 centimetres.

Air pollution can be severe in the cities at certain times of the year. Unregulated industries, coal-burning stoves, increased vehicle use and demolition and construction fill the air with a variety of pollutants that makes walking in the streets — not to mention jogging — unpleasant and potentially unhealthy. Sensibly, Chinese wear face masks when they have a cold, as well as to keep out the dust.

Dress

Winter in the north demands really warm clothing, though central heating in hotels is such that lightweight suits can be worn indoors in comfort. Fleece-lined boots and long underwear are a good idea and one will also need gloves and headgear. Padded and fur garments, including overcoats and hats with ear-flaps can be bought at reasonable prices in China. Summer requires only light clothing. The south, with the exception of the months of December, January and February, when woollens will sometimes be advisable, demands very light clothing.

The Chinese are generally informal about dress, though the Western jacket and tie has nearly entirely replaced the Mao suit for men. Ties are generally worn for business meetings, particularly among China's up-and-coming entrepreneurial class. The Chinese generally dislike too much exposure of flesh. A foreign woman in scanty dress will be stared at, though young Chinese women have been experimenting with short skirts, high heels, heavy make-up and fashionable haircuts since the late 1980s.

Business Hours

The usual business hours for government offices are 8 a.m.-noon, and 2-5 p.m., Monday to Saturday, though appointments are usually not made on Saturday afternoons. Sunday is a holiday for most businesses, though shops, post offices and some banks stay open.

Opening hours of shops vary from 8 or 9 a.m. until 7 or 8 p.m., usually later in the south and in the big cities. Most stores, post offices and banks are open on Sundays.

State-run restaurants do not stay open too late, since most dinner parties finish before 9:30 p.m. Usual eating hours are between 5:30 p.m. and 7:30 p.m.

Doing Business

With the economic liberalization that began during the 1980s, China's state ideology has rapidly turned from socialism based on Mao Zedong Thought to "Capitalism with Chinese Characteristics." Capitalism needs little introduction here, but overseas businessmen should be acquainted with "Chinese characteristics" before embarking on a venture in China. The characteristics include, on the negative side, corruption, nepotism, xenophobia, inadequacy of legal protection, provinciality, blurred lines of authority, bureaucracy, reluctance to take responsibility and language barriers.

As China continues to open to the outside world, business relations have grown less formal and exotic. Chinese officials generally want to participate in the greater world outside and are increasingly willing to rely on outsiders to help them do this. It should be remembered that the Chinese economy is in a state of flux, and policies, personnel, laws, exchange rates, prices and nearly everything else involved in business transactions can change overnight.

Hierarchy is important and business cards are essential. They should be printed in Chinese on one side, and should state one's position. These can be printed quickly and cheaply in Hong Kong. As a matter of courtesy, Chinese usually hand their name card to others with two hands and they should be taken and given in the same way. Punctuality is important; hosts should arrive 10 minutes early; guests should arrive on time.

Shaking hands is the accepted form of greeting for a Westerner. Dress is usually formal, but follow the example of your Chinese hosts when it comes to removing jackets, ties, etc.

Exchanging cigarettes, going out of style in so many places, is still an ice-breaker in Chinese society.

Regardless of whether negotiations are conducted in Chinese or a foreign language, the foreign side should have a skilled Chinese speaker on the team to ensure accuracy. When speaking in English, make a concerted effort to speak slowly and avoid figures of speech, slang, sarcasm or irony, little of which will be understood by your Chinese counterparts.

During formal negotiations, it is rare to be invited to the home of someone on the Chinese side. Gifts of foreign whisky, cognac, fancy pens, ties or other high-status items are appreciated. The Chinese side will usually invite the foreign side to a banquet upon arrival; the foreign side will generally return the courtesy before departing, unless there has been a serious breakdown in relations.

Political and sexual jokes, critical references to the leadership and direct disagreement with Chinese state policies should be avoided.

The Chinese are extremely shrewd negotiators, and in China they take advantage of the fact that they are playing on their home ground. The sharpest negotiator on the team may appear superficially slow, ignorant or unresponsive. When dealing with Chinese, foreigners are advised to be frank, good-humoured but firm, patient and thorough. Tempers should be controlled and mistakes should not be exploited for advantage in an obvious way, nor laughed at. Remember that preserving "face" for both sides is an important element in business success.

Rip-Offs

China's paper currency can be confusing for the first-time visitor, as there is no English printed on it. The 1, 2 and 5 jiao notes (equal to Rmb 0.1, 0.2 and 0.5) can be mistaken for Rmb 1, 2 and 5 notes. The Rmb 1 coins can also be mistaken for 1 jiao coins. Visitors should also be aware that there is a relatively high percentage of counterfeit Rmb 100 and Rmb 50 notes circulating in China. Recent Rmb 100 notes have a metal strip sandwiched inside. Also check the watermark for the portrait of Chairman Mao.

Tour guides and bus drivers often offer to take tourists to overpriced shops where they receive commissions on your purchases. Some shops hand out numbered cards to tourists as they come off the bus to make it easier to pay the commission to the right guide or driver. Similarly, travel agents and drivers receive commissions from restaurants, taking the commissions out of the money paid for the meal.

Taxi drivers may not start the meter when you get in, and may have already run up a high fare before you. Meters on taxis in the major cities should begin at approximately Rmb 7-12, depending on the quality of the car. A taxi hotline system in Beijing, Shanghai and Guangzhou has reduced the number of taxi rip-offs, but they still occur.

Goods in tourist shops may be marked with absurdly high prices to trap the unwary, and curio and antique dealers may also quote ridiculous prices, as no prices are marked in most shops of this nature. Written prices should not be taken seriously in small or privately run shops. You will find salespeople quite prepared to spend hours arguing why you should pay 10 times the actual value of a piece. The best negotiation technique is to walk out of the shop if the price is not right and wait for the dealer to call you back. As in all antique trading, let the buyer beware. Bargaining, a way of life in China, is absolutely essential when shopping for curios or antiques and strongly recommended in all other free markets. Anyone who pays the first quoted price should consider himself/herself a fool.

Some restaurants may try adding unordered dishes to the bill or overcharge for items on or not on the menu. Check the bill carefully before paying, especially in restaurants where there are price discrepancies between the Chinese and English menus.

Tour guides may claim that a requested destination is not on the itinerary and demand immediate cash payment for "extra bus mileage" or admission charges. This may be hard to disprove without the tour contract in hand, and since the amount is usually nominal, guides often get away with it. Playing this scam several times a week can earn a guide a hefty sum by the end of the season.

Be wary of people — young or old — who approach you in the street with stories about needing foreign currency to buy a television set, study at an overseas university, travel abroad, pay for a parent's operation, etc. In China there is nothing new under the sun.

Transport

MAIN CITIES

TAXIS: Taxis are readily available in the main cities in the streets and at taxi stands at hotels. It is advisable to have the destination written down in Chinese or circled on a bilingual map for the driver's benefit. In most cities there are three or four different rates for taxis, depending on the type of vehicle. In general, flagfall ranges from Rmb 7-12. Pay only what is on the meter. In case of dispute, refuse to pay and telephone the hotline number listed in the cab. Receipts are given for each journey. Tipping is not expected. Taxis may be hired for the day, and the rate can be negotiated.

BUSES AND TROLLEYBUSES: All cities have frequent bus services, but destinations are indicated only in Chinese. However, route numbers and maps are available in most large cities. Fares vary with distance travelled but are very reasonable, generally costing no more than Rmb 1 for the longest journey.

PEDICABS: The pedicab has replaced the traditional rickshaws. Determine the fare before boarding. Foreigners tend to be overcharged. Rmb 10 should suffice for a 15-minute journey on level ground.

UPCOUNTRY TRANSPORT

TRAIN: The overburdened railway network covers much of the country. The standard of service offered is good on trains which carry foreigners and they are usually punctual. Tickets can be booked in advance in Hong Kong. There are different classes, but foreigners generally travel "soft" either on seats (for a short journey), or on convertible bunks — four to a pullman compartment — for a longer journey. Most Chinese take the "hard" seat or more crowded sleeper cars.

Air-conditioned trains run between Hong Kong, Guangzhou, Shanghai and Beijing. Heating in winter is usually adequate, though sometimes erratic. A knob — usually under the table in the sleeping compartments — turns down the volume of the irritating public-address loudspeaker. "Soft sleeper" cars have two toilets, one for squatting and the other Western-style, but they are rarely cleaned properly and can be quite disgusting at times.

All express trains have dining cars, which vary widely in terms of hygiene and the quality and variety of the cooking. Attendants will come to your compartment in advance to take your order. It is usually possible to get fried eggs and bread for breakfast. Coffee on trains is generally pre-sweetened. If this is not to your taste, carry your own instant coffee. The attendant will bring thermoses full of hot water to the compartments and sell packets of green tea. Cups are provided free of charge. There is beer as well as soft drinks and spirits.

The 2,300-kilometre journey by fast train between Beijing and Guangzhou takes about 36 hours. Beijing-Shanghai takes 22 hours; Shanghai-Guangzhou takes 36 hours. Services on these lines operate twice daily, but the soft sleeper ticket for tourists costs more than an air ticket.

Trains also leave Beijing for Moscow at least twice a week. There are two different trans-Siberian routes — one that passes through Mongolia and another that circumvents it. The trip takes five to five-and-a-half days. Tickets can be bought in Beijing up to five days in advance and should be bought as early as possible. Food on the Mongolian and Russian sections is poor and travellers are advised to take their own. Visas for Mongolia and Russia must be obtained before departure.

Overseas visitors can purchase train tickets in advance at ticket windows at the major train stations, through CITS and at many hotels. Last-minute tickets are difficult to obtain, but scalpers ply the stations. Check the date and destination carefully; tickets are printed in Chinese only but the date and train number can be read easily since numerals are universal.

AIR: China's around 30 airlines, some subsidiaries of the Civil Aviation Administration of China or of its now separate former major regional units and others independently run, operate all domestic services. Flights are sometimes delayed and service attitudes, inflight meals and safety procedures all leave much to be desired.

There are regular services to approximately 100 cities in China — certainly to somewhere near anywhere a visitor is likely to want to go. The free baggage allowance is 20 kilograms. Excess baggage is charged at 1% of the first-class or highest fare per kilogram. Check terms and conditions on the ticket, as Chinese airlines do not necessarily follow international practices with regard to cancellations and no-shows. If evening flights are cancelled, the airline will not necessarily provide overnight accommodation to stranded passengers, though this (like nearly everything else in China) is negotiable and may depend on how loudly you or your guide are prepared to shout.

Accommodation

International-style accommodation is available in all major cities in China. Prices have risen to world levels in spite of some overbuilding, much of it involving joint Chinese-foreign ventures. It can sometimes be difficult to find a decent hotel room in Beijing, Shanghai or Guangzhou, even if you are willing to pay the listed rate.

The better hotels have a complete range of amenities: complete business centres, health clubs, banquet and conference facilities, single rooms to presidential suites as well as Western, Chinese and other Asian restaurants and fleets of limousines.

Physically, joint-venture hotels built in the late 1980s and early 1990s meet international standards, though maintenance is a perennial problem. But the most significant factor explaining why potentially excellent hotels in China turn out too often to be mediocre is the local staff. The reasons for this are complex: cultural and economic differences, attitude towards work, linguistic gaps and poor training are a few of these. Major service mishaps take place in the five-star hotels, so it is wise to double check all instructions, information, etc., and if something goes wrong, go right to the top — the general manager — immediately and demand action. In more cases than one might expect, he or she is the only one who can solve your problem.

Cheap dormitory-style accommodation is available in most cities for the back-packing traveller. With such accommodation, washing and toilet facilities are extremely basic.

Dining

Chinese cuisine is one of the great glories of this ancient culture. The general theory of Chinese cooking is that ingredients are chopped finely and cooked briefly at high temperatures to preserve the natural flavour and nutrition. The meal should please the eye as well as the palate. Large pieces of meat are not usually presented at table and knives are rarely used in serving or eating — nearly all the cutting and chopping takes place before the food is cooked.

The common people eat simply most of the time — rice, steamed bread, millet, maize and other grains with some vegetables, egg, soup, fish, soybean curd (*doufu* or *tofu*) or a little meat to supply the protein and vitamins, and soy sauce, chili or vinegar for flavour.

At the other end of the spectrum, fine food exquisitely presented is available at reasonable prices at restaurants and hotels in the major cities. For around Rmb 100 per person, a memorable banquet can be arranged for groups of six or more. At some restaurants you can reserve ahead by telephone in English, but in general it is better to have a Chinese speaker, such as a hotel concierge, telephone or show up in person (especially for important occasions) to make the booking. Be sure to clarify the price: Some ordinary-looking restaurants, especially in the south, have minimum per-person prices of around Rmb 800.

One of the great pleasures in the major tourist cities — Beijing, Shanghai, Hangzhou, Guangzhou, Shenzhen — is eating in restaurants where levels of sanitation equal that of the best hotels.

In most other tourist cities — including Suzhou, Xian, Wuxi, Nanjing, Chengdu and the cities of the northeast — overseas visitors may find most of the restaurants outside of the hotels shabby, unclean and overcrowded, though the food can be excellent.

Regional variations in Chinese food make a fascinating study, though the principles of cookery are applied more or less uniformly throughout the country. In general northerners eat wheat as a staple food (in the form of steamed and baked bread and noodles) while southerners consume more rice.

The Chinese are said to eat everything with legs except tables and chairs, and that includes dog, cat, rat, giant salamander, turtle, camel, yak, bear's paw, cicada and snakes — highly prized in winter as a protection against ill health. Fear not; these will not be served to you unknowingly, since they are all delicacies and will be offered very much for what they are — and can be refused.

Guests at a Chinese meal are expected to help themselves from the dishes placed in the centre of the table, usually with a "public" spoon rather than one's own chopsticks. If no public spoon is available, health conscious people use the back ends of their chopsticks to serve themselves and others.

Steamed or fried rice, bread and noodles are usually served at the end of a banquet rather than during it, and soup is usually drunk at the end of the meal except in Guangzhou, when it often comes first.

Restaurants with private rooms (usually on the upstairs floors, with correspondingly higher prices) are more comfortable and the management will sometimes try to steer foreigners there. The hours of some state-run restaurants still follow austere socialist practice: lunch is served from 11:30 a.m. to 1:30 p.m., and dinner from 5:30 p.m. to 7:30 p.m. Don't be surprised if you are denied admission if you show up 30 minutes before closing. But there are thousands of private restaurants that have opened in the cities since the late 1980s that stay open longer hours and more readily accommodate guests' wishes.

Every city has at least one brewery, but quality varies widely. There are several joint-venture breweries. Most Chinese beer is of the lager or German pilsner type, and both bottled and draught beer is available. The famous Tsingtao (Qingdao) beer is sometimes hard to find. Coke, Pepsi, Sprite, Fanta and several other familiar fizzy drinks are readily available in the larger cities in cans and bottles, along with a host of local soft and health drinks.

Most Chinese grape wine is sweet, but there are a few dry varieties produced by joint-venture wineries: Great Wall, Dynasty, Huadong and Dragon Eye. Local vodka (*wodeke*) is good, but Russian vodka — and occasionally caviar — can be bought in the Beijing free markets. *Maotai*, made from sorghum, is a 120 proof spirit with a strong and, to many people, objectionable taste and smell. But it does not usually produce a serious hangover. There are numerous other types of grain liquor: beware of knocking them back. *Huang jiu*, a golden yeasty rice-wine (unrefined *sake*) made in Shaoxing, is a fine accompaniment to Chinese food, and is served warm; the best (driest) variety is called *Jiafan*. There are innumerable other types of Chinese liquors, some of them medicinal, flavoured with anything from crab apples and ginseng to lizards.

The Chinese have a formal concept of public drinking. At banquets, wait for the host's first toast before drinking, and later offer a toast of thanks. The Chinese may insist on standing up and clinking glasses, and drinking to friendship. There is no taboo against tipsiness as long as one does not become offensive or, worse still, amorous. Being called a big drinker is a compliment.

The most common Chinese toast is *ganbei* (bottoms up). There is no need to take it literally if you do not want to, but your hosts will be pleased if you can show, by tilting the empty glass towards them, that you have complied at least once. Touching the glass to your lips suffices to return the courtesy of a toast. If you do not drink alcohol, make sure you have a substitute drink to hand if you are likely to be involved in toasts, as you will look ungracious if you do not raise a glass.

Tea is served at meetings and is drunk before and after meals, rarely during. There are hundreds of varieties of teas in China: green, black, semi-fermented and flower tea with jasmine, rose, or chrysanthemum.

Scrupulously avoid tap water for drinking or brushing your teeth. Most hotel rooms are supplied with vacuum flasks of hot boiled water, and a second flask of cooled boiled water. Be cautious about ice except in the top hotels; many Chinese believe that freezing water "kills the germs" and therefore do not use boiled or bottled water to make it. There are many regional bottled mineral-spring waters packaged in plastic containers. The best-known is Laoshan, produced by the people who brew Tsingtao beer, and sold in glass bottles.

BEIJING RESTAURANTS

Beijing has the best range of restaurants in China, including regional Chinese fare, Asian and Western cuisines. Cantonese and Sichuan (sometime spelled Sze Chuan or Szechuan) restaurants greatly outnumber all other types in the capital, and the most expensive and lavishly appointed restaurants in town are joint-venture Cantonese restaurants. The top hotels have one or two regional Chinese restaurants.

Visitors to Beijing should try Peking duck at least once. A duck banquet consists almost entirely of the different parts of the force-fed duck, such as the liver, web, etc., culminating in the crisp outer skin with its underlying fat and meat. This is dipped in a dark-brown sauce made from fermented wheat and soybeans, garnished with fresh leek or spring onions and wrapped in thin, unleavened wheat pancakes. At the end, the tastiest parts of the duck are served — the halved head, strips of "tenderloin" from along the spine and the fatty triangle from near the tail, followed by duck broth, made from the remains of the carcass, with milk sometimes added. Peking duck is served at more than 75 restaurants in the capital. The best known is the **Quan Ju De Kao Ya Dian**, with six branches.

A popular autumn and winter speciality is mutton hot-pot (*shuan yang rou*). After cold and hot preliminary dishes a charcoal brazier with boiling water on the top is placed in the middle of the table. Guests plunge paper-thin strips of raw mutton into it, plus cabbage, *jiaozi* (mutton filled dumplings) and noodles. Chewy sesame rolls (*zhimabing*), are eaten as an accompaniment, with pickled garlic to cut the gaminess. Similar is barbecued mutton (*kao rou*) with egg and leeks or onions.

Food prepared according to recipes from the Qing Dynasty imperial kitchens is available at **Fang Shan** in Beihai Park. Book ahead for one of the upstairs rooms with a superb view of the lake.

Hunan and Sichuan cuisine are characterized by their hot, spicy sauces. Specialities include crisp-fried spiced beef, hot spiced soybean curd (*mapo doufu*) and camphor-smoked duck (*zhang cha ya*).

A popular snack is *jiaozi* (Chinese dumplings dipped in vinegar and crushed raw garlic) and *baozi* (steamed dumplings filled with meat and vegetables). These can be tried at the humblest restaurants and are an important component of meals at the Chinese New Year. Fine but expensive European food is available in Beijing at the better hotels, and there are more than a dozen upmarket Japanese restaurants.

For people tired of restaurants, Beijing offers a wide range of quality food shops, including **hotel gourmet shops**, local food emporiums (visually and gastronomically fascinating) and foreign-funded supermarkets such as those in the **China World** shopping arcade, the **Holiday Inn Lido** and **Yaohan** department store. It is possible to buy, at premium prices, fine imported cheeses, packaged condiments, fruits, pickles and wine.

Beijing has its own Chinese fast-food outlets. As well as six McDonald's, several Kentucky Fried Chicken, Pizza Hut and other brands' outlets have opened.

GUANGZHOU RESTAURANTS

In Guangzhou be sure to have a meal at one of the traditional vast garden restaurants, such as the **Ban xi**, **Bei yuan** or **Nan yuan**. Open from early morning — for *dim sum* or Cantonese dumplings and other snacks — to late at night, they are local social as well as gastronomic institutions. Roast suckling pig and seafood are among the specialities at **Da Tong**. At the **Da San Yuan**, *dim sum* is served most of the day. **Tao Tao Ju** serves traditional Cantonese cuisine and is famous for its autumn moon cakes. The **Snake Restaurant (She Can Guan)** offers some 30 snake dishes and is extremely popular among Cantonese during the winter. Many Guangzhou restaurants serve game, including endangered species, and display the living creatures in cages in front of the restaurants.

The **Garden Hotel** has a pizzeria and the **China Hotel**, **White Swan**, **Holiday Inn** and **Gitic Hotel** have restaurants serving European food.

SHANGHAI RESTAURANTS

October to December is the season for freshwater "hairy" crabs, extremely popular among locals. The females, filled with roe, demand the highest prices. Traditional Shanghainese food is served at the **Lao Fandian** near the Yu Garden in the old Chinese city, at the **Yangzhou Fandian** and at the two branches of **Mei Long Zhen**. The provincial cuisine of Zhejiang and Jiangsu is available at the **Mei Wei Zhai Fandian**, **Ningbo Fandian** and **Renmin Fandian**. There are a number of excellent bakeries, some with attached restaurants. These include the **De Da**, **Dong Hai**, **Kai Ge** and **Lao Da Chang**.

Entertainment

Cultural life in China is unrecognizable from that of only several years ago. Stage shows vary from traditional Chinese acrobatics and ancient Beijing operas to local pop music and bawdy cabaret. Most films shown in China are skilfully dubbed into Mandarin, with no foreign-language subtitles.

Western ballet, opera and classical music are also performed regularly. In the cities, live theatre is booming with new local plays and translations of foreign works, but foreigners unable to follow Chinese dialogue will probably find the melodramatic acting style off-putting. One visit to a Beijing opera is recommended. Martial themes provide the best entertainment with plenty of spectacular costumes and martial-arts displays. The **Li Yuan** (Pear Garden) theatre in the Qianmen Hotel in Beijing offers a nightly evening of excerpts from well-known operas, with superb costumes.

Tickets to various sports events can be obtained in advance at the venues, and sometimes through CITS. It is often possible to purchase tickets at the gate, usually at inflated prices; check the date on the ticket carefully.

Most big hotels have discos and/or karaoke rooms, where customers sing along to a video accompaniment in Mandarin, Cantonese, Japanese, English or Korean. There is almost always an entrance or cover charge which includes one drink.

Prostitution is widespread in the cities and girls often work out of leading hotels. Overseas visitors have been entrapped with Chinese prostitutes and fined heavily. Aids is a growing problem in the country, particularly in Yunnan, and there is little public education about safe sex.

Shopping

The consumer economy in China has developed to such a degree in the last decade that while state-owned Friendship Stores once sold only Chinese goods only to foreign visitors, they now sell mostly imported goods and name-brand products mainly to Chinese shoppers.

Souvenir shops selling cloisonne, cheap jewellery and figurines, stone carvings, hats, T-shirts, embroidered jackets and blouses have sprung up everywhere a visitor might conceivably go. Tour groups may be taken to jade-carving workshops, silk- and brocade-weaving mills, art stores, carpet factories and handicraft centres, complete with money changers and credit-card facilities. Hotels also have shops selling souvenirs.

But there is still very good value to be had for the serious shopper. Antique stores offer ceramics, brass and bronzeware, embroidery, paintings, wood carvings, and old household items. Officially, these should have a red wax seal affixed for export, but in practice there are many shops selling curios and antiques without the seal and there is usually no problem on leaving the country. Prices for antiques are negotiable, with the greatest flexibility to be found in the non-state shops. Excellent prices for fine objects are available to the knowledgeable collector. Some shops and outlets will arrange packaging and shipment of purchases such as antiques, carpets or furniture.

BEIJING now has a dozen large department stores, some of them managed by joint-venture concerns, thus breaking the monopoly once held by the **Friendship Store** as the only place to shop. Like the Friendship Stores, the larger department stores offer currency exchange, shipping, repair and tailoring services.

Wangfujing, the traditional heart of shopping for locals in Beijing, is quickly being transformed by construction of a massive joint-venture shopping complex, new subway stops and even an underground shopping complex. Some of the old shops selling furs, leather goods, paintings, watches, spectacles and books will remain, however. Similarly, **Xidan**, a north-south artery parallel to Wangfujing, features shops mainly targeting local residents, including boutiques with low prices on domestically made producers such as cashmere sweaters.

Liu Li Chang, famous since the 18th century for collections of books, antiques and art, has been restored in Qing Dynasty style. On the west side, the large, modern **Rong Bao Zhai** sells contemporary paintings and prints as well as writing and painting materials.

Additional curios and antiques markets can be found at **Chao Wai**, **Jin Song**, **Hong Qiao** (near the north entrance of the Temple of Heaven) and **Hou Hai**.

There is a new branch of the Friendship Store selling a wide range of goods at the Lufthansa Centre. **Hua Xia** arts and crafts shop on Dongdan Nandajie south of Chang'an Jie, known as the Theatre Shop, sells an odd assortment of old articles, including theatre costumes, carpets and furniture. There is a smaller branch in Wangfujing.

SHANGHAI's main shopping streets are crowded to the point of being overwhelming, yet strangely orderly. They are Nanjing Lu and Huaihai Lu (the heart of the former French Concession). The **Number One Department Store** on Nanjing Rd serves 150,000 customers a day. Fuzhou Rd has numerous specialized bookstores. The **Shanghai Exhibition Centre** sells an impressive array of Chinese handicrafts, jewellery, jade and ivory carvings, tapestries, carpets (a particularly good selection), silk, bamboo ware, screens and lacquer furniture.

A lively street curios bazaar takes place on the weekends at **Fu You Lu**, a 10-minute walk from the Yuyuan Garden. There is a more permanent market in Dong Tai Lu.

GUANGZHOU shopping opportunities have begun to rival those of nearby Hong Kong, and the prices are generally lower. There are several **Friendship Stores** — one on Huan Shi Dong Lu and another near the China Hotel. There is a department store attached to the **Guangzhou Trade Fair Exhibition Hall**, where interesting items can sometimes be found, especially during the spring and autumn fairs. The **Guangzhou Antique Store** is at 146 Wen De Bei Lu, but a more interesting street market for antiques operates at Dai He Lu.

In **XIAN**, there is a curios bazaar in the alley that leads up to the **Great Mosque**, and souvenir sellers at the **Terracotta Warriors and Soldiers Museum**, where attractive miniatures of the warriors can be bought.

Sports

Many forms of sport are actively promoted by the Chinese authorities and numerous sporting teams visit the country. The Chinese excel at table-tennis, badminton, women's volleyball, diving and gymnastics, and are making big strides in ice-hockey, soccer and fencing.

Sports facilities at hotels can include indoor and outdoor swimming pools, tennis and squash courts, fitness rooms, bowling alleys, steam rooms and saunas. Jogging is only recommended on those days when the air is not thick with pollution. For a taste of Chinese fitness techniques, join one of the many groups practising forms of *tai chi* (taiji), *qigong* breath energy exercises, tree-hugging, swordsmanship or a sort of geriatric disco dancing that gather in most urban parks and gardens at 6-8 a.m.

Holidays

With just three official celebrations per year, China has one of the shortest festival calendars in Asia. The Spring Festival (Chinese New Year) is dependent on the lunar calendar and so varies from one year to the next, falling in January or February. The Mid-Autumn festival (not officially observed as a holiday) is also dependent on the lunar calendar and may fall in either September or October. The other occasions are fixed in the Gregorian calendar.

January-February: The Spring Festival (Chinese New Year) is observed as a family occasion, though since 1949 it is celebrated rather less extravagantly than in the past. Those working away from home usually return for several days — there are public holidays for three days — and all transportation is strained to bursting.

May 1: May Day, International Labour Day, is a public holiday celebrated with various forms of entertainment in the parks of the large cities (public holiday).

October 1: China's National Day is celebrated in commemoration of the founding of the People's Republic in 1949. Entertainment is provided in public parks and in parades.

PUBLICATIONS

No single guidebook to China can be recommended as they go out of date within months of publication. *Nagels's China* remains the standard guide for most historical sites, though considerably outdated. The *Odyssey Series* consists of attractive and information-packed volumes for many cities and regions. Comprehensive guides to China include *The China Guidebook*, a bland publication mainly for group tourists, by F.M. Kaplan and A.J. de Keijzer; *China — A Travel Survival Kit* in the Lonely Planet series, the backpacker's bible, with much acerbic commentary; Fodor's *People's Republic of China*; *The Economist Business Traveller's Guide*: *China*, which contains excellent background information; and *Blue Guide: China*, by Francis Wood, which is good on history. *Peking Walks*, by Don J. Cohn and Zhang Jingqing, describes six strolls through Beijing's history.

There are plenty of excellent Chinese-language maps for tourists, but good English maps sell out quickly and are not reprinted. Ask for a local city map at your hotel desk. Many hotels distribute commercially produced tourist maps free. These contain plenty of useful tourist information.

In Beijing, *Beijing Weekly*, published every Friday by the official *China Daily*, is a source of information on cultural events taking place in the capital. It is available at the Friendship Store and some hotels. Consult also the What's On column of the *China Daily*.

The *Shanghai Star*, a twice-weekly paper, performs a similar function for Shanghai and the major cities of East China. It is distributed to the larger hotels.

TOUR SUGGESTIONS BY NUMBER OF DAYS

If you want to plan a short or medium-length stay in China, either as a side trip or complete in itself, here are some suggestions.

Two days: Starting from Hong Kong, take the train to Guangzhou and spend one night there.

Three days: Starting from Hong Kong, take the train to Guangzhou, spend one night. Fly to Guilin the second evening, take the cruise on the Li River the next day and fly back to Hong Kong that night.

Four days: Fly to Beiing; or spend two days in Shanghai, one day in Suzhou, and fly back to Hong Kong the fourth day.

Five days: Spend three full days in Beijing

and two in Shanghai.

Six days: Spend three full days in Beijing, two in Shanghai and one in Suzhou; or spend four days in Beijing and two in Xian.

Seven days: Spend three days in Beijing, two in Xian and two in Shanghai.

Eight days: Spend three days in Beijing, two in Xian, two in Shanghai and one in Suzhou.

Nine days: Spend three days in Beijing, two in Xian, two in Shanghai and two in Hangzhou.

DISCOVERING CHINA

BEIJING

Beijing or "Northern Capital" is one of the world's great historic cities. Visitors can hardly fail to be impressed by the vestiges of one of the world's best-preserved cultures. The earliest settlements date back 300,000-500,000 years, but it was not until around 1260 AD that a Chinese capital — that of the Mongol Yuan Dynasty found by Khublai Khan — was built there. It was first called Dadu, and the Italian explorer Marco Polo described its magnificence in glowing terms. In the early 15th century the Ming Dynasty rulers moved their capital from Nanjing to Beijing and redesigned the city. The basic design has survived until the present, though most of the old walls and gates were demolished in the early 1960s. The Ming design was that of two walled cities: a square in the north and a rectangle in the south separated by a common wall. During the Qing Dynasty the northern city became known as the Inner or Tartar City: it was the home of the ruling Manchus, while the southern part was the Chinese City. Within the Inner City was the Imperial City and within that the Forbidden City — the palace of the emperor, now a splendid museum.

Beijing, with its urban population of more than 7 million (Greater Beijing has around 11 million), spreads its residential and industrial suburbs far beyond the confines of the old walled areas. Once out of the centre, it is a city of generally uninspired architecture with countless new residential, commercial and hotel buildings punctuating the perfectly flat landscape.

Tiananmen Square is not only the heart of

DIPLOMATIC MISSIONS — BEIJING

Asia: Afghanistan 532 1582; Bangladesh 532 2521; Burma 532 1425; India 532 1908; Indonesia 532 5436; Iran 532 2040; Israel 505 2970; Japan 532 2361; Jordan 532 3906; Cambodia 532 1889; Kuwait 532 2216; Laos 532 1224; Lebanon 532 2197; Malaysia 532 2531; Mongolia 532 1203; Nepal 532 1795; North Korea 532 1186; Pakistan 532 2504; Philippines 532 2451; Singapore 532 3926; South Korea 505 3171; Sri Lanka 532 1861; Syria 532 1372; Thailand 532 1903; Turkey 532 2650; Vietnam 532 1125.

Africa: Algeria 532 1231; Benin 532 2741; Burundi 532 2328; Cameroon 532 1828; Chad 532 1925; Congo 532 1417; Egypt 532 1825; Equatorial Guinea 532 3697; Ethiopia 532 5258; Gabon 532 2810; Ghana 532 1319; Guinea 532 3649; Kenya 532 3381; Libya 532 3666; Madagascar 532 1353; Mali 532 1704; Mauritania 532 1396; Morocco 532 1796; Niger 532 2768; Nigeria 532 3631; Rwanda 532 2193; Senegal 532 2646; Sierre Leone 532 1222; Somalia 532 1752; Sudan 532 3715; Tanzania 532 1491; Togo 532 2202; Tunisia 532 2435; Uganda 532 1708; Zaire 532 1995; Zambia 532 1554; Zimbabwe 532 3795.

Europe: Albania 532 1120; Austria 532 2061; Belgium 532 1736; Britain 532 1961; Bulgaria 532 1946; Czechoslovakia 532 1531; Denmark 532 2431; Finland 532 1817; France 532 1331; Germany 532 2161; Greece 532 1391; Hungary 532 1431; Ireland 532 2691; Italy 532 2131; the Netherlands 523 1131; Norway 532 2261; Poland 532 1235; Portugal 532 3497; Romania 532 3315; Russia 532 2051; Spain 532 1986; Sweden 532 3331; Switzerland 532 2736; and Yugoslavia 532 1562.

Americas: Argentina 532 2090; Brazil 532 2881; Canada 532 3536; Chile 532 1641; Colombia 532 3377; Cuba 532 6656; Ecuador 532 3158; Guyana 532 1337; Mexico 532 2070; Peru 532 2913; U.S.A. 532 3831; Venezuela 532 2694.

Oceania: Australia 532 2331; New Zealand 532 2731.

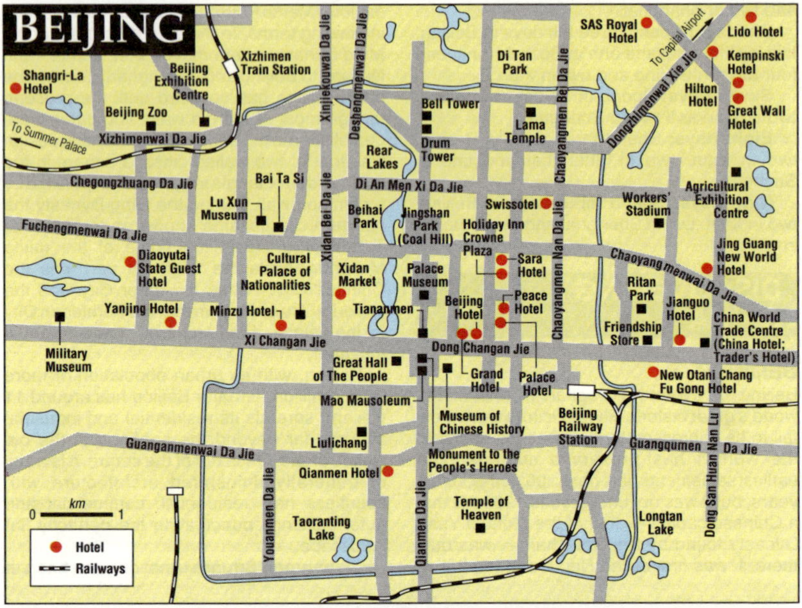

Beijing, it is also the symbolic heart of China. Here the country's leaders and masses come together for national celebrations — most notably National Day on October 1, commemorating the communist victory of 1949. The square is firmly in the present day, not only because of its worldwide association with the tragic events in China in 1989 but with other great historic events throughout the 20th century, while much of the rest of Beijing recalls China's long imperial past.

Tiananmen Square lies near the centre of the city's north-south axis, and extends over the better part of 40 hectares. On the north it is bounded by the southern wall of the old Imperial City with the impressively massive Tiananmen (Gate of Heavenly Peace), the official logo of the People's Republic of China.

At the southern extremity of the square stands the **Qianmen Gate** which once formed part of the now-demolished wall between the northern Tartar City and the southern Chinese City. Facing Tiananmen Square on the west is the **Great Hall of the People**, housing a huge banquet hall, auditorium and offices of the National People's Congress, which was built in 1958. Completed in the same year, the **Museum of Chinese History**, on the east side of the square, has displays of some of China's most spectacular artistic achievements.

In the centre of Tiananmen Square is the 45-metre-high **Monument to the People's Heroes**. Immediately south of the monument stands the **Mausoleum of Mao Zedong**, open to the public free of charge every morning for a look at Mao's embalmed remains.

Running east-west in front of Tiananmen is **Chang'an Jie**. West of Tiananmen is **Zhongshan Park**, named after Dr. Sun Yat-sen, which contains the **Altar of Land and Grain**. On the east side is the **Working People's Cultural Palace**, with the **Imperial Ancestral Temple**.

Passing through the Tiananmen and Duanmen gates one comes to the **Wu Men** (Meridian Gate), the main gate of the Forbidden City, where tickets are sold. Foreign visitors must purchase their tickets at the kiosk to the east; the Acoustaguide tape-recorded tour (available in several languages for an extra fee) that the ticket seller will try to sell as part of the entrance ticket is optional, but well worthwhile.

The Forbidden City — now called Gu Gong or Palace Museum — covers an area of 100 hectares and is surrounded by a moat. A palace was first established here in the Yuan Dynasty and the Ming Emperor Yongle rebuilt it between 1407 and 1420. Further rebuilding took place during the Qing Dynasty, and many of the existing buildings date from the late 19th century.

North of the Wu Men is a vast paved courtyard with five marble bridges spanning the **River of Golden Water**. On ceremonial occasions high officials entered the Forbidden City here — military officers passing through the west gate and civilian officials through the **Gate of Supreme Harmony (Taihe Men)** into the courtyard facing the **Hall of Supreme Harmony (Taihe Dian)**, which stands upon a three-tiered marble terrace. It is the first of the three main ceremonial halls. Here stands the emperor's throne. Behind the Hall of Supreme Harmony is the **Hall of Complete Harmony (Zhonghe Dian)**, where the emperor made final preparations for his appearances in the hall of Supreme Harmony, and where inspection of seed-grain for the new harvest took place. In the **Hall of Preserving Harmony (Baohe Dian)** the emperor entertained tributary missions and scholars who won the highest honours in examinations.

To the north of this hall is the **Gate of Heavenly Purity (Qianqing Men)** which leads into the inner courtyard of the Forbidden City. A turn eastward leads to the **Six Eastern Palaces** which were mostly occupied by the women of the imperial family. They include the **Palace of Abstinence (Zhai Gong)** and the Palace of **Peace and Longevity (Ningshou Gong)** built by Emperor Qianlong for his retirement.

The easternmost series of buildings begin at the south with the glazed tile **Nine Dragon Wall**. The corridor west of the Gate of Heavenly Purity leads to the **Hall of Mental Cultivation (Yangxin Dian)**, which served mainly as the emperor's private study and sitting room and now houses a display of palace treasures, and the **Six Western Palaces**, the apartments of the emperor's wives and concubines.

Directly north of the Qianqing Men are the **Three Rear Palaces (Hou San Gong)**: the **Palace of Heavenly Purity (Qianqing Gong)** served as the emperor's bed-chamber during the Ming and early Qing period and was later used for banquets and audiences. The last emperor, Puyi, was married in this hall in 1922. The **Hall of Union (Jiaotai Dian)**, built in 1420 and restored in 1655, was originally the empress' throne room and also housed the imperial seals. The **Palace of Earthly Tranquillity (Kunning Gong)** was the residence of the Ming empresses (the side-room to the east was the bridal chamber of three Qing emperors).

Further north, beyond the Kunning Gate, is the **Imperial Garden (Yu Hua Yuan)**, laid out in the Ming Dynasty. Through two small gates to the north of this garden one reaches the **Gate of Martial Prowess (Shen Wu Men)**, the north gate of the palace.

The many palace buildings, dominated by their huge yellow roofs, can be viewed from the top of **Coal Hill (Mei Shan)**, which lies north of the Shen Wu Gate. The hill, raised from soil dredged from the moat, is the highest point in a park that was the private domain of the court from the Yuan Dynasty onwards. The last emperor of the Ming Dynasty supposedly hanged himself from a tree on the east slope of the hill after learning of the success of the Manchu invasion. A legend tells that the emperors kept hidden supplies of coal within the hill, but there is no evidence of this.

Beihai (North Lake) is one of three interconnected lakes which lie to the east of the palace in the imperial city. The other two are the Central and South Lakes, or Zhongnanhai, closed to visitors because round them are the homes of many Chinese leaders and the offices of the Central Committee.

Qionghua Island, home of the **Fang Shan Restaurant**, lies in the southern reaches of Beihai, surmounted by the **White Dagoba** built in Tibetan style to commemorate the visit of the first Dalai Lama to Beijing in 1651. The island is dotted with halls, terraces and pavilions and on the north shore there is a covered passageway offering views of the **Wulong Ting (Five Dragon Pavilion)** across the lake.

In the Chinese City to the south of Tiananmen Square is **Temple of Heaven (Tiantan)**, one of the capital's most famous attractions. Most of the temple buildings were constructed in the 15th century, but the temple was not open to the public before 1912, and was used exclusively by the emperor for sacrificing to his only superior and ultimate ancestor — Heaven.

The Hall of Prayer for a Good Harvest was rebuilt soon after its destruction by fire in 1889 using huge wooden columns imported from Oregon. Standing on top of a triple marble terrace, the hall is round, with three splendid, blue-tiled roofs surmounted by a gold ball.

The round **Imperial Vault of Heaven**

(Huang Qiong Yu), is surrounded by the famous **Echo Wall. The Round Altar** consists of three round terraces of white marble, each with a decorated balustrade. The emperor prayed to heaven here, and sacrifices were offered.

The former **Legation Quarter (Dong Jiao Min Xiang)**, bound on the east by the Zinc Hotel, east of Tiananmen Square, was the main diplomatic quarter until the Kuomintang moved the capital to Nanjing in 1928. This district was besieged in the Boxer Rebellion in 1900. A few European-style buildings which served as foreign missions still stand; some are used as government guesthouses and offices of the police and Justice Ministry.

The **Lama Temple (Yonghe Gong)**, is in the northeast of the city. The birthplace of the Qing Emperor Yongzheng, the palace was converted into a temple upon his accession to the throne in 1723. Its five large halls contain Buddhist statues, and the side pavilions house outstanding Tibetan bronzes. Many of the gods are in sexual embraces — hence the shrouds. The **Pavilion of Ten Thousand Happinesses** houses the 25-metre-high wooden statue of Maitreya, the Buddha of the Future. Today as in the past the temple is staffed by monks from Inner Mongolia.

Close by is the **Confucius Temple**, which contains the Capital Museum, exhibiting archaeological finds from the Beijing area.

Sites in the northwestern suburbs of Beijing include the **Great Bell Temple (Da Zhong Si)** housing a famous Ming Dynasty bronze bell that weighs more than 46 tonnes. **Beijing Zoo** is worth a visit just to see the panda house. Behind the zoo is the **Five Pagoda Temple (Wuta Si)**, a copy of an Indian temple.

Other places of interest in Beijing include the **Altars of the Sun, Moon and Earth**, the **Lu Xun Museum**, the **Military Museum**, the **Nationalities Cultural Palace** and the **Ancient Observatory** near Jianguomen.

About 16 kilometres from the city centre to the northwest is the **Summer Palace (Yi He Yuan)**, which is well worth the journey. Spread over 266 hectares, the site includes a wooded hilly area, **Longevity Hill (Wan Shou Shan)** in the north and Kunming Lake in the south.

The first palace in the area was built by a lake in 1153 by a Jin Dynasty emperor. Later, under the Yuan Dynasty, the lake was enlarged. Under the Ming, several pavilions and a temple were built. Emperor Qianlong made significant improvements to the garden in the 18th century and gave the hill its present name in honour of his mother's 60th birthday. In 1860 the old Summer Palace was sacked by French and British troops, the latter under the command of Lord Elgin. In 1888 the Empress Dowager Cixi diverted funds earmarked for the modernization of China's navy and built the present palace, which in turn was sacked by the Europeans in the aftermath of the Boxer revolt. Cixi again restored it.

The main entrance gate is in the east. Beyond the second courtyard stands the **Hall of Benevolence and Longevity (Ren Shou Dian)** where the emperor held audiences.

On the east shore of the lake is the **Hall of Jade Ripples (Yu Lan Tang)** where Emperor Guangxu was imprisoned by Cixi for 10 years until his death in 1908. Cixi herself lived in the **Palace of Joy and Longevity (Le Shou Tang)**, to the west of which begins the **Long Corridor (Chang Lang)**, which runs some 800 metres along the lake's north shore. The pillars and crossbeams feature painted scenes of West Lake in Hangzhou, which served as a model for Kunming Lake.

Midway along the covered walk stands the handsome arch that leads by way of a compound to the buildings on **Longevity Hill**, which include Buddhist pagodas and temples. Down by the lake, at the western end of the Long Corridor, is the famous **Marble Boat**. The marble hull, built as a "ship of state" by Emperor Qianlong, had its superstructure and paddle wheels added by Cixi.

The northern slope of Longevity Hill is dotted with Tibetan-style temple buildings inspired by the Samye Monastery in Tibet. Further to the north is **Suzhou St**, a reconstructed commercial street where the Empress Dowager would come with her retinue to go shopping in shops staffed by her eunuchs. The **Rear Lakes** offer a prospect similar to that of South China, and are a wonderful place for a quiet walk. Here also is the glazed tiled **Pagoda of Many Treasures (Duo Bao Ta)**.

Excursion boats ply Kunming Lake, leaving from near the Marble Boat. Linking the island and the east shore of the lake is a fine **17-arched bridge**. The courtyard restaurant, the **Pavilion for Listening to the Orioles (Ting Li Guan)**, is popular for tourists.

THE GREAT WALL

A popular day's excursion from Beijing combines a visit to the **Great Wall** at **Badaling** and **The 13 Ming Tombs**, though there are several other places to visit the wall.

The Great Wall is one of the greatest feats of human engineering in the history of the world. The actual length of the wall is disputed, for in fact there is no single Great Wall of China. But in all there are some 20,000 kilometres of walls. The first "great wall" originated in the Qin Dynasty (221-206 BC), when Qin Shihuang, the megalomaniac First Emperor of the Qin linked together the defensive walls of several states that he had conquered. Subsequent dynasties carried out building and maintenance projects on the wall at various points in northern China, but in the end the wall provided the Chinese with more psychological than military protection, as attested by its failure to repel the Mongols and the Manchus who ruled China for more than three centuries. The several segments of the wall open to the public near Beijing are all restored versions of the Ming wall.

Badaling, about one hour from Beijing by a fine highway and the most popular and crowded point at which to climb the wall, has two cable cars (not always operating) that take all the pain, and most of the fun, out of the steep climb. Further from the city, the wall can be climbed at much less crowded **Mutianyu** (also with a cable car) and even further afield, at **Jinshanling**.

The Ming tombs lie in a natural amphitheatre formed by the hills, and are approached through a gateway and along a road lined with pairs of splendidly carved marble figures and animals. The most grandiose of the tombs is the Chang Ling of Emperor Yongle, who ruled from 1403 until 1425. The other noteworthy tomb is the **Ding Ling** of Emperor Wanli, who ruled from 1573 to 1620. Exhibition rooms display the possessions of the emperor and his two consorts, and visitors can descend into the underground mausoleum and examine the five interconnected chambers of the actual burial place, an architectural wonder.

Some 50 kilometres west of Beijing is the **Monastery of the Pool and the Wild Mulberry (Tan Zhe Si)**, one of the largest Buddhist monasteries in the Beijing area. Khublai Khan's daughter spent a number of years there as a nun, and some of the trees in its numerous courtyards are said to be 1,000 years old. The road to the monastery passes another important temple, the **Ordination Terrace Temple (Jie Tai Si)**. A visit to the two makes a wonderful day trip.

Another long excursion is the **Eastern Qing Tombs (Qing Dong Ling)**, 134 kilometres east of Beijing. One of two burial sites chosen by the Manchu imperial family, it contains the remains of emperors Shunzhi, Kangxi, Qianlong, Xianfeng and Tongzhi, the Dowager Empress Cixi and a number of other empresses, concubines and royal offspring. The **Western Qing Tombs (Qing Xi Ling)** in Yixian, Hebei province, 125 kilometres southwest of the city, are of less interest to the visitor.

An excursion from Beijing to **Chengde**, site of the summer residence of the Qing emperors, is a pleasant trip by fast train or hired car. Emperor Kangxi built this resort as a summer retreat and called it the Mountain Hamlet for Fleeing the Heat. Some of the most interesting features are the temples constructed in Tibetan style where the Manchus worshipped.

Beidaihe is a seaside resort on the shallow **Bohai Gulf**, due east of Beijing and about six hours by slow train via Tianjin. The former fishing settlement was developed in the 19th century, largely by foreign residents of Beijing and Tianjin, as a summer refuge. Most of the villas and guest houses are reserved for privileged Chinese, but the Beijing International Club has a spacious establishment for the use of foreigners. Hotel-style accommodation or separate bungalows are also available. **Kiessling's** once-famous Austrian restaurant serves ice-cream and other Western confections. A day-trip can be made from Beidaihe to the **Shan Hai Pass**, the point where the Great Wall meets the sea.

Tianjin, a municipal enclave in Hebei province 96 kilometres southeast of Beijing, is connected to the capital by a toll superhighway. From 1860 until the founding of the People's Republic in 1949, Tianjin had a cultural life second only to Shanghai, and a considerable foreign population, now attested by a number of European-style buildings. Tianjin was badly damaged in the 1976 earthquake which struck nearby Tangshan. It makes a worthwhile day trip from Beijing.

Five hours by train from Tianjin is the Shandong provincial capital of **Jinan**, best known for its 72 springs. On the railway line travelling east to Qingdao is the coal-mining centre of **Zibo**. In nearby **Linzi** visitors can see excavations of a fifth-century BC grave containing the skeletons of 600 warhorses. Further east is the small walled city of **Weifang**, famed for its traditional handicrafts, New Year wood-block prints and an annual kite festival held in April.

On the east coast of Shandong is the industrial city of **Qingdao**. Annexed in 1898 by the Germans, who built a handsome European-style city, mined coal and built railways, it was ceded to the Japanese at the Treaty of Versailles in 1919. China regained control of the territory in 1923. The famous Tsingtao beer is made here. **Laoshan**, home of Taoist temples and the source of China's best-known mineral water, is a short drive east of the city. Another seaside city, north of Qingdao on the Bohai Gulf is the fishing port of **Yantai** (Chefoo), a summer resort for foreigners and missionaries in the 19th century and still a pleasant city to visit.

Tourists may either take a cable-car or climb the 2,700-metre **Tai Shan**, once considered the most sacred of China's mountains. Further south is the small town of **Qufu**, birthplace of Confucius, where one can visit the vast Mansion of Confucius.

Some 10 hours by train from Beijing, and south of the Yellow River, is the large city of **Zhengzhou**, capital of Henan province. Near Zhengzhou are the excavated ruins of **Anyang**, a capital city during the Shang Dynasty (17th-12th century BC). East of Zhengzhou is the town of **Kaifeng**, capital of five Chinese dynasties, including the Northern Song. The 11th-century **Iron Pagoda** and the **Xiangguo Monastery** may be seen here.

Three hours west of Zhengzhou by rail is the ancient city of **Luoyang**. The site has been occupied since neolithic times, but first became important as the Zhou Dynasty capital in the eighth century BC. About 14 kilometres south of the town are the famous **Longmen Caves**, containing monumental Buddhist sculptures dating from as early as 494 AD. The nearby **White Horse Temple (Bai Ma Si)** is supposedly China's earliest -Buddhist temple. At **Gongxian**, 65 kilometres east of Luoyang, are the **Song Dynasty Tombs** and the **Gongxian Buddhist Caves** of the North Wei period, featuring some fine stone carvings. Near **Dengfeng**, 80 kilometres southeast of Luoyang, are two famous temples — the **Shaolin Monastery**, whose monks were renowned for the practice of the martial arts, and the Taoist **Zhongyue Miao**.

XIAN

West of Luoyang (seven hours by train) is Xian, the capital of Shaanxi province and the most important site of historical or archaeological interest in China after Beijing. Xian, with an urban population of 2.5 million, has many of the qualities of a Wild West frontier town, but at the same time it is a conservative and provincial industrial and military city with a reluctance to open to the outside world.

Xian was the capital of the Western Han Dynasty, and by the Tang Dynasty (when it was called Changan) had become one of the most prosperous cities in the world, lying at the easternmost extreme of the Silk Road. The city's fortunes declined rapidly after the fall of the Tang, when the capital was moved to present-day Hangzhou and Kaifeng. Thus it is said that Xian's greatest treasures are found underground, in the tombs of emperors and high officials. There are more archaeological wonders to be uncovered and perhaps more to be discovered.

Monumental **Qing Dynasty walls** still surround the city, and near the centre are bell and drum towers built in the Ming period. To the south stands the 13-storey **Small Wild Goose Pagoda (Xiao Yan Ta)** and the square seven-storey **Big Wild Goose Pagoda (Da Yan Ta)**, which has undergone several extensive renovations since its construction in 652 AD. The former **Confucian Temple** houses the **Forest of Steles (Bei Lin)**, a collection of paintings and texts inscribed on stone slabs, and other exhibits of early Chinese art. The new **Shaanxi Historical Museum**, the first major building in China to be designed by a woman, displays the treasures of Xian's ancient capitals and underground tombs in state-of-the-art galleries. It should not be missed.

The attraction which brings visitors from all round the world to Xian is about 30 kilometres to the east in Lintong. This is one of the most outstanding archaeological finds of modern times. Discovered accidentally by a peasant digging a well, is a horde of 6,000 life-size **terracotta warriors and horses** of China's first emperor, Qin Shihuang, buried to protect him in the afterlife. In trenches, some fully excavated, some still be to uncovered, the ghostly army stands in serried ranks, presenting one of the most extraordinary sights in the world, outdoing in scope even the tomb of Tutankhamen.

Also on display is an exquisite miniature bronze chariot and a second smaller pit where the terracotta command post was buried. A third pit was opened to the public in 1994. Taking photographs of the terracotta warriors in the pits is strictly forbidden.

A large neolithic village site of the Yangshao culture (approximately 6000 BC), and a

The Shanghai Bund's new boulevard. PHOTO: KEES

museum displaying painted pottery, stone tools and other finds unearthed during the excavations is located at **Banpo** on the road between Xian and Lintong.

The sprawling triple city of **Wuhan** (population 7 million), capital of Hubei province, lies on the Yangtze River at its confluence with the Han River and on the main north-south railway linking Beijing and Guangzhou. The three cities are **Hankou** (northwest of the confluence), **Hanyang** (southwest) and **Wuchang** on the south bank. It was in Wuhan that the revolution which overthrew the Manchu (Qing) Dynasty broke out with a military mutiny on October 10, 1911. Wuhan (along with Yichang) is a terminus for cruises through Yangtze gorges; otherwise, there are few compelling attractions to draw tourists to this city.

South of Wuhan is the Hunan provincial capital, **Changsha**, where Mao was a student. Three Han Dynasty tombs have been excavated at **Mawangdui**, where the perfectly preserved 2,000-year-old body of a woman was discovered inside four close-fitting coffins, with burial objects such as silks, brocades, lacquer ware and figurines. **Shaoshan**, Mao's birthplace, is 130 kilometres southwest of Changsha and still a minor pilgrimage site.

Near the Yangtze port of Jiujiang in Jiangxi province lies **Mt Lu (Lu Shan)**, famed for its dramatic scenery. **Nanchang**, the provincial capital, connects by road with **Jingdezhen**, which once supplied exquisite ceramics to the imperial court.

In southern Anhui province are two famous mountains: **Huang Shan** comprises a group of 72 peaks, the highest of which is 1,800 metres. Its scenic beauty has been eulogized in countless Chinese poems. **Jiuhua Shan** is one of China's sacred Buddhist mountains. Climbing these mountains takes great physical stamina and demands tolerance of simple accommodation and food.

Nanjing or "Southern Capital" is now the capital of Jiangsu province, and stands on the south bank of the Yangtze. It served as the capital of China for eight dynasties between the third and 14th centuries, when the capital was moved to Beijing. It was also the seat of government between 1927 and 1938 during the war with Japan. Nanjing was ravaged during the Japanese occupation of 1937-45.

Both the **Nanjing Museum** and the **Taiping Museum** are worth visiting. South of the city lies a mausoleum in memory of 100,000 revolutionaries executed by the KMT. Ancient sites within the city include the **Ming bell and drum towers**. **Xuanwu** and **Mochou lakes** are set in parks of the same name and make excellent quiet destinations.

East of the city are the **Purple and Gold Mountains (Zijin Shan)** where one can visit the tomb of the founder of the Ming Dynasty, Emperor Hongwu, and the vast **Sun Yat-sen Mausoleum** with the grounds designed in the shape of the American Liberty Bell. The beamless **Wuliang Hall** and the **ancient observatory** can also be seen. Numerous stone figures from royal tombs of the Liang Dynasty (502-557) may be seen along the 17-kilometre drive to the **Qixia Monastery** and Buddhist grottoes.

East of Nanjing, on the Nanjing-Shanghai railway, is **Zhenjiang**, historically important as a shipping port for the Yangtze and the Grand Canal. Zhenjiang's historical sites include **Small Jetty Street (Xiao Matou Jie)**; the **Golden Hill (Jin Shan)** with its famous monastery, **Pagoda and Dragon Cave**; **Beigu Hill**; and **Jiao Hill**, site of the **Dinghui Monastery**.

A vehicular ferry from Zhenjiang crosses the Yangtze, and a half-hour drive brings one to the delightful city of **Yangzhou**, during the Sui and Tang dynasties the main cultural and trading centre on the Grand Canal, where Marco Polo held an official post during the Yuan Dynasty. The **old town centre** near the canal has much charm, while the **Ge** and **He gardens** are in the tradition of Suzhou's famous private gardens. **Shouxi Lake**, **Wenfeng Pagoda**, **Daming Temple** and **Xianhe Mosque** can also be visited.

East of Zhenjiang is the old silk town of **Wuxi**, close to scenic **Tai Hu Lake**, dotted with more than 90 islands. Boat excursions can be arranged. Wuxi cuisine is excellent, and day trips can be made to **Yixing**, home of the red stoneware teapots popular all over China.

GRAND CANAL

Like the Great Wall, the Grand Canal is an ancient feat of Chinese engineering that has attained wonder-of-the-world status in the Western imagination. Built in the sixth-to-eighth centuries to transport grain and luxury goods about 1,000 kilometres from the south to the court in the north, it was maintained up until the 19th century. Today some sections of the Grand Canal and other man-made waterways continue to serve as an important form of short-distance transport in Jiangsu and Zhejiang provinces.

Tourists can take short rides on the heavily polluted and often malodorous canal at Suzhou and Wuxi, and it is possible to sail between the two cities on a four-hour jaunt that takes you through industrial backyards and rice paddies.

Known as the Venice of China, **Suzhou** is criss-crossed with canals spanned by hump-backed bridges. The town's most delightful features are its many exquisite landscape gardens, about a dozen of which are well preserved and open to the public. The best known are the **Forest of Lions (Shizilin)**, **Master of Nets Garden (Wangshi Yuan)**, **Lingering Garden (Liu Yuan)** and the large, oddly named **Humble Administrator's Garden (Zhuozheng Yuan)**. Suzhou women were traditionally considered the most beautiful in China.

The gardens of Suzhou were first built during the Song Dynasty and after, mainly by scholars and officials returning home to retire. Not merely places of amusement, the gardens were usually designed with philosophical principles (often Buddhist) in mind.

The nine-storey **Northern Temple Pagoda (Bei Si)**, stands to the north of the town. Built during the Song and rebuilt in the Qing Dynasty, it is a magnificent sight. **Tiger Mound (Hu Qiu)**, with its striking Five Dynasties period pagoda, is three kilometres to the northwest. Suzhou has long been famous for its silk and visitors are often taken to visit the Silk Museum and local embroidery and silk factories, where the entire process of silk manufacture, from cocoon to screen printing, can be observed. From Shanghai, Suzhou can be visited as a day trip, for the journey is only 80 minutes by train.

SHANGHAI

China's largest city, Shanghai, occupies its own administrative region at the mouth of the Yangtze River. The entire municipality covers 5,760 square kilometres and has a population of 14 million — though the city proper is smaller, located on the northern and eastern banks of the Huangpu River, where it is joined by the Wusong (Suzhou) Creek.

Although Shanghai existed as a small trading town before the arrival of foreigners, it was only after the founding of the various concessions following the First Opium War (1839-42) that it began to expand rapidly, especially after the Taiping rebels were driven away in 1854. Banks, clubs, hotels and a customs house (controlled by foreign interests) soon sprang up along the **Bund**.

In Shanghai the foreign presence has left an indelible mark on the city's architecture, and to a lesser extent culture and lifestyle. The Chinese Communist Party was founded in the

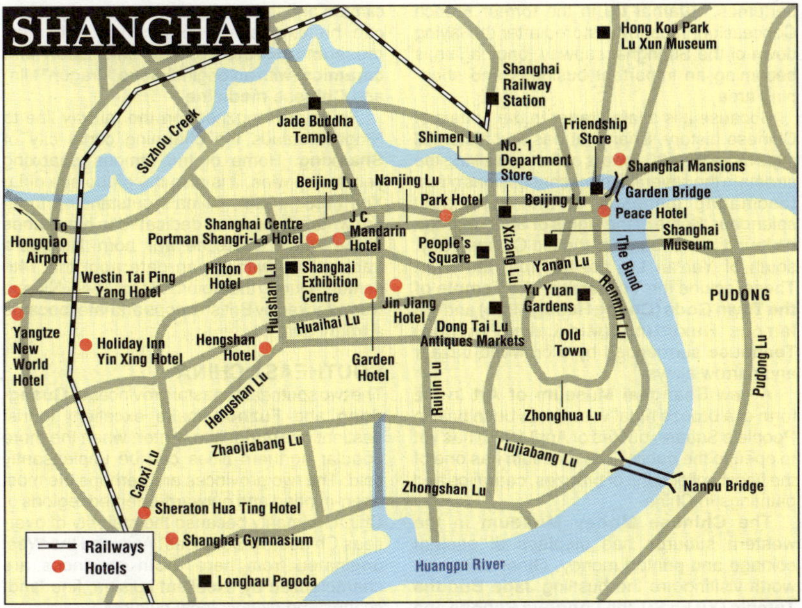

city on July 1, 1921. After the founding of the People's Republic in 1949, Chairman Mao discouraged the growth of Shanghai out of fear of a U.S. takeover launched from Taiwan. Despite this, Shanghai is an economic powerhouse. The **Pudong New Zone** — an area the size of the U.S. state of Rhode Island — on the east bank of the Huangpu River, is a key element in Shanghai's bid to become the reatest trading port and manufacturing base in the country in the 21st century. The first segment of the Shanghai subway began operating in 1994.

Shanghai is no longer the "paradise for adventurers" it was in the 1920s and 1930s, but it does retain certain qualities of the Paris of the East insofar as Shanghainese consider themselves, quite justifiably, the most fashionable and cosmopolitan people in the country. The city is one of China's most sophisticated entertainment centres, with fine restaurants and crowded nightclubs, discos and karaoke lounges, as well as that tourist standby, the Shanghai Acrobatics Troupe, with its own purpose-built theatre.

The main reason Chinese tourists come to Shanghai is to shop. The city offers the widest variety and highest quality of goods in eastern China, and Chinese come from hundreds of kilometres away to stock up on household appliances, hi-fi equipment, fashionable clothing and luxury items such as pens, lighters, watches, cosmetics and foreign cigarettes to meet the needs of a growing resurgence in consumption.

Everyone who comes to Shanghai visits the **Bund (Wai Tan)**, a two-kilometre strip along the west bank of the Huangpu River where the major Western-built bank buildings, hotels and government offices are concentrated. In 1992, the Bund was widened and raised to protect the city from possible flooding. The present version lacks the charm of the former Bund, but can accommodate more people and incorporates a parking lot.

Nanjing Lu (Nanjing Rd) is the city's most famous thoroughfare. It has many of the largest shops, including **Number One Department Store** and **Hualian Department Store**, and hundreds of well-decorated shops selling clothing, food, jewellery, medicine and works of art. From 1993, foreign retailers have rushed to set up shop on Nanjing Rd, selling everything from jeans to high-priced jewellery and perfumes. **Huaihai Lu** in the former French Concession, recently restored after the laying down of the Shanghai subway, once again is becoming an important business and shopping area.

Because it is a late starter in the annals of Chinese history, Shanghai has few historical sites more than 200 years old. Just walking the streets in the several former concessions offers fascinating glimpses of the city's past splendour. Some of the sights of Shanghai can be found in the region of the old Chinese City, south of Yan'an Lu, not far from the river. These include the **Yu Garden**, the **Temple of the Town Gods (Cheng Huang Miao)** and the famous **Huxinting (Mid-Lake Pavilion) Teahouse** surrounded by a crowded bazaar and narrow alleys.

A new **Shanghai Museum of Art** in the form of a bronze ritual vessel has been built in People's Square, but (as of April 1995) has yet to open to the public. The museum has one of the finest collections of bronzes, ceramics and paintings in China.

The **Chinese Money Museum** in the western suburbs has displays of ancient coinage and printed money. Other sites well worth visiting are the bustling **Jade Buddha Temple (Yu Fo Si)**, the **Longhua Pagoda** and **Temple** and the **San Shan Huiguan**, with its displays of private collections of everything from combs to birdcages to bus tickets.

Shanghai's older hotels retain some of the atmosphere of an earlier era, but are not the best places to stay, which are the modern hotels built recently. The vintage properties are the **Jinjiang**, **Park**, **Peace**, and **Hengshan** hotels and **Shanghai Mansions**. The art deco lobby of the Peace Hotel has been restored to a semblance of its former glory.

Some 160 kilometres south of Shanghai is **Hangzhou**, capital of Zhejiang province. The train ride between the two cities takes about five hours. Hangzhou lies between the Qiantang River and the beautiful **West Lake (Xi Hu)**, and enjoys one of the finest settings of any city in Asia. Two ancient causeways divide West Lake into three parts. Around it and on the islands are many gardens, temples and pagodas, reflected in the still waters.

To the west of the lake are the city's **botanical gardens**, and to the southwest the bustling **Lingyin Temple** complex, a veritable Buddhist circus. Excellent Buddhist stone carvings in the caves nearby date from the Yuan Dynasty. Hangzhou cuisine, as gentle and sweet as the climate and the character of the local people, can be exquisite. Hangzhou boasts new **museums devoted to tea, silk, Guan kiln ceramics** (with an original Song "dragon" kiln) and **Chinese medicine**.

South of Hangzhou, on the railway line to Ningbo, stands the charming canal city of **Shaoxing**. Home of the famous Shaoxing yellow rice wine, it is also the birthplace of Lu Xun (1881-1936), China's outstanding modern writer. A museum dedicated to him stands in the house where he was born. **Ningbo's** trading links with Japan date from the 14th century. During the Opium War of 1841, Ningbo was attacked by British troops and later became a treaty port.

SOUTHEAST CHINA

The two southeast coastal provinces of **Guangdong** and **Fuzhou** make excellent tourist destinations during the winter, when the more popular northern cities can be unpleasantly cold. The two provinces are perhaps the most open-minded and outward-oriented regions of China, primarily because the majority of overseas Chinese in Southeast Asia and the West originated from here. Both provinces are characterized by excellent cuisine, fine landscapes and distinct local cultures.

Fuzhou, capital of Fujian province, stands on the Min River. Many overseas Chinese who have returned to live in China have settled here. The impressive **Yongquan Monastery** on Drum Hill is just east of the city. Fuzhou plays an important role in the growing participation in the Chinese economy by the Taiwanese, many of whom trace their roots to this province. One of the loveliest spots in southeast China is the tea-growing area of **Wuyi Shan**, a half-day journey from Fuzhou.

In southern Fujian are the port cities of **Quanzhou** and **Xiamen**. The charming town of Quanzhou lies on the highway between Fuzhou and Xiamen, and the lack of rail communication has contributed to the preservation of many 19th century buildings. Xiamen (Amoy) has a long history of trading with foreigners, particularly the Portuguese, Spanish and Dutch. It became a treaty port in the 19th century. A harbour ferry takes the visitor to **Gulangyu Island**, which became a foreign settlement in 1903. Fine colonial-style buildings remain, and the local cuisine, little known outside China, is remarkable. There are regular sailings between Hong Kong and Xiamen.

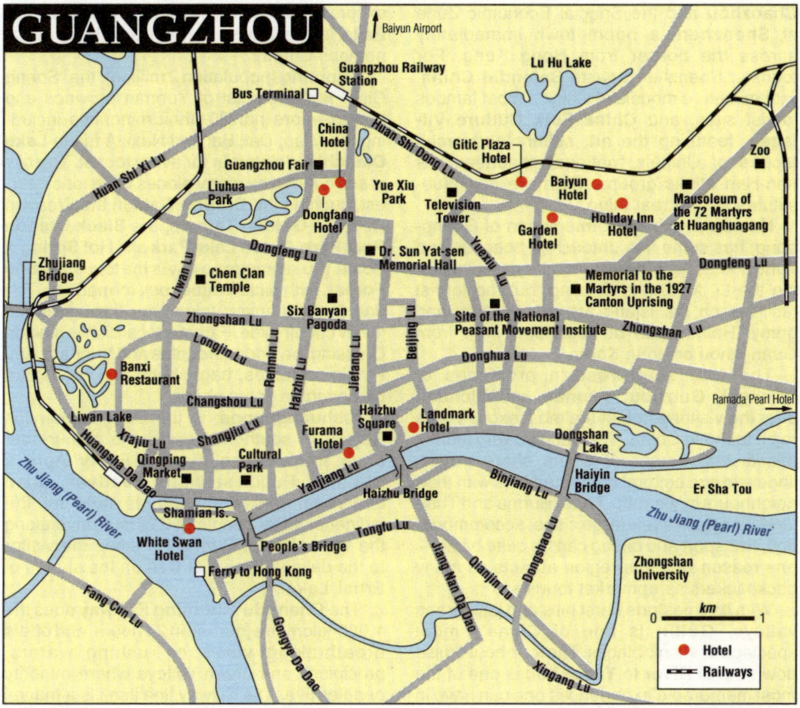

Guangzhou, a city of 5 million and the capital of Guangdong province, stands in the midst of the fertile Pearl River delta, one of China's great rice-growing basins. The famous **Guangzhou Trade Fair** is held here in April and October; tourists are warned to stay away at that time, as the cost of hotel accommodation doubles.

Guangzhou had trading contacts with the Arabs in the Tang Dynasty, which resulted in the building of the first mosque in China. In the mid-17th century European merchants established warehouses known as "factories" where they traded in tea and silk. The sale of British India's opium to China culminated in the Opium Wars of the mid-19th century. The Kuomintang (KMT, or Nationalist Party) was established by Dr. Sun Yat-sen in 1923, and the city became the base for the military campaign against the northern warlords in 1926-27.

There are a number of pleasant parks: **Yuexiu Park**, **Liuhua Lake**, **Liwan Lake**, **Dongshan Lake** and the fine **South China Botanical Gardens** in the northern suburbs. **The Temple of the Six Banyan Trees (Liurong Si)** and the **Guangxiao Temple** are among the city's ancient buildings. The recently excavated **Tomb of the Nan Yue King** is an archaeological wonder. **The Sun Yat-sen Memorial Hall**, the **National Peasant Movement Institute** and the **Mausoleum of the 72 Martyrs** reflect the city's revolutionary history. The **Chen Clan Temple** contains a museum of remarkable folk carvings. The foreign residences, embassies and churches on the former concession island of **Shamian** make an interesting destination for a walk. Suburban excursions include **Foshan**, famous for its Shiwan pottery and paper-cutting tradition and Song Dynasty **Temple of the Ancestors**, and the **White Cloud Mountain (Bai Yun Shan)** resort.

Other tourist sites in Guangdong province include **Zhaoqing**, **Shantou (Swatow)**,

Chaozhou and the Special Economic Zone of **Shenzhen**, a boom town immediately across the border from Hong Kong. For tourists, Shenzhen boasts **Splendid China**, with miniature models of China's most famous tourist sites, and **China Folk Culture Villages**, featuring the art, culture and architecture of China's "national minorities," or non-Han ethnic groups. Both are poor substitutes for the real thing.

Hainan province, formerly part of Guangdong, has some fine untouched beaches and is the home of several ethnic minorities, including the Li, Miao and Zhuang, but the tourist facilities on the island are mostly grim and grimy. Hainan can be reached by air from Guangzhou or Hong Kong.

The four southwestern provinces of **Guangxi**, **Guizhou**, **Yunnan** and **Sichuan** offer the visitor some of the most exotic vistas to be found in China. The peoples who inhabit this distant corner of China share ethnic, linguistic and cultural characteristics with their neighbours in Vietnam, Laos, Burma and Thailand. Except in a few large cities, accommodation, transport and dining can be quite basic — one reason why this region attracts as many backpackers as upmarket tourists.

With its limestone karst hills and lush green valleys, **Guilin** is one of China's most spectacular scenic places. The four-hour cruise down the **Li River** to **Yangshuo** is one of the most memorable experiences one can have in China. In the **Reed Flute Caves** in the outskirts of the town, the stalactites and stalagmites have been enhanced with multi-coloured lights. Guilin itself is a highly commercialized tourist town. It is recommended to leave as soon as possible after the boat ride, for everything else is anti-climactic.

Nanning is the capital of the Guangxi Zhuang Autonomous Region. About two hours' drive from Nanning are the deep caves where large sections of the population hid from the occupying Japanese troops during World War II. The **Provincial Museum** in town is the most worthwhile place to visit.

The mountainous province of Guizhou lies north of Guangxi and, like Yunnan, is the home of many minorities — the Buyi, Tong, Shui, Yi and various tribes of Miao. The capital, **Guiyang**, has little of historical interest, but the Huaxi Guesthouse, some 20 kilometres to the southwest, is situated on the pretty **Huaxi River** near an ancient water mill and close to several handsome Buyi stone villages. A day's excursion can be made to the **Huangguoshu Falls** in the Zhenning Buyi and Miao Autonomous County.

Kunming (population 2 million), the "Spring City," is the capital of Yunnan province and home of more than 20 ethnic minorities, including the Miao, Dai, Bai and Naxi. A trip to **Lake Dianchi** is de rigueur for every tourist. The city is surrounded by many places of historic interest, such as the **Dragon Gate** in the Western Hills, the **Golden Temple**, the **Black Dragon Pool Park**, **Green Lake Park** and **Hot Springs**. Some 120 kilometres away is the touristy **Stone Forest**, with picturesque rock formations. The ride from Kunming takes you through some lovely countryside. Famous local dishes include Crossing the Bridge Noodles and Yunnan ham. Ethnic costumes, bags, belts and shoes can be bought in some shops.

Xishuangbanna, in the Dai Autonomous Region in southern Yunnan, is a four-hour drive from Simao airport. Every April a colourful Buddhist **water festival**, when everyone gets drenched, is held by the indigenous Dai people. A 12-hour drive along the World War II Burma Rd takes the visitor to the delightful town of **Dali** on the shores of **Erhai Lake**.

The **Chengdu-Kunming Railway** does the 1,085-kilometre journey in 24 hours, and offers breathtaking views of rushing waters, precipices and green valleys where minority peoples live. The railway line itself is a marvel of engineering, running through 170 tunnels.

Sichuan province supports 10% of the nation's population, more than 100 million people. A mountainous region, its climate is oppressive much of the year, and spring and autumn are the best seasons to visit. Sichuan cuisine is renowned for its hot and spicy dishes, though some of the finest dishes are, in fact, bland. The capital **Chengdu** (population 4 million), is noted for its two-storey structures with carved wooden balconies. Chengdu is famed for its many teahouses, and the street markets are fascinating.

Leshan, 165 kilometres south of Chengdu, boasts the largest stone Buddha in China (71 metres tall), carved into the rock at the confluence of two rivers. **Mt Emei**, 192 kilometres south of Chengdu, is one of the sacred Buddhist mountains of China. Comfortable accommodation is available at the base of the mountain. Special permission is required to visit the **Wulong Panda Reserve** in western Sichuan.

Pearl River countryside. PHOTO: XINHUA

YANGTZE GORGES

Chongqing (Chungking) is perched upon rocky outcrops above the confluence of the Jialing and Yangtze rivers. It is best avoided in summer due to the heat. Chongqing was the capital of Nationalist China during World War II. Chongqing's main attraction is as the departure point for the **Three Gorges** cruise which takes three full days to reach **Wuhan**, depending on the type of boat. There are more than 10 ships exclusively for foreign tourists, with air-conditioning and hot showers in every cabin, that make stops at **Wanxian**, **Fengdu** and **Shibaozhai**, and offer a half-day small-boat excursion up the **Daning River** where the "Little Three Gorges" are located. In 1994 a number of luxurious joint-venture liners came on stream, including one managed by Holiday Inn. The local passenger ships, which can accommodate foreigners in second class cabins (the best available), make more stops, but only to pick up or let off passengers, and do not offer the Daning River trip.

Between Chongqing and Yichang the Yangtze River flows through three spectacular gorges in the course of about two hours: the Qutang, Wushan and Xiling. For those who have seen the fjords of Norway, the Yangtze Gorges may seem overrated, and for many the boat trip will be "something to tell the grandchildren about," as the gorges may be submerged in a few years as part of a highly controversial hydroelectric dam project, the world's biggest, which was going ahead at the time of publication.

Passengers can disembark at **Yichang** and take the overnight train to Wuhan, shortening the downstream journey by a day. It is also possible to take the boat upstream from Wuhan or Yichang, but this adds a day to the itinerary. The upstream overseas tourist ships tend to be less crowded than the downstream ships.

Lanzhou, capital of Gansu province, is the main industrial city for the upper reaches of the Yellow River. It is a long, narrow, heavily polluted place, stretching along both sides of the river and surrounded by hills. The **museum**, Lanzhou's main redeeming feature, has an outstanding collection of neolithic Yangshao pottery and Silk Road treasures, including the famous bronze flying horse. The splendid **Bingling Si Caves** contain Buddhist carvings and frescoes dating from the Northern Wei period up to the Ming Dynasty. The caves are accessed by river and are open seasonally. The one-day trip from Lanzhou takes about 12 hours.

Travelling northwest through Gansu province on the Lanzhou-Urumqi railway, the journey may be broken at historically important stops along the Silk Road. **Jiayuguan**, a stop on flights between Lanzhou and Dunhuang, was one of the strategic passes at the western end of the **Great Wall** and was built in the Han Dynasty, while the present fortress there dates from the early Ming. The setting, in the middle of the desert, is remarkable.

Visitors can fly to Dunhuang from Lanzhou or Xian. The **Thousand Buddha Mogao Caves** at **Dunhuang** comprise more than 460 grottoes of varying sizes, cut out of the cliff-face on five levels connected by external wooden balconies. The caves contain some of the finest Buddhist sculpture and wall paintings in the world. The earliest date from the Wei Dynasty, while others are from the Sui, Tang, Five Dynasties, Song and Yuan periods. It was in these caves that Aurel Stein and Paul Pelliot discovered thousands of manuscripts and artifacts and acquired them for a pittance from Abbot Wang, the sacristan, whose desire for funds to restore the caves overrode his fear of imperial reprisal for the sale. Reproductions of the finest caves have been built — courtesy of the Japanese Government — to accommodate tourists as a way of protecting the originals.

Marco Polo described the apparent sound of thunder — the wind rippling across the tall sand dunes beside the tiny **Lake of the Crescent Moon** — a few kilometres from Dunhuang, where one can rent a camel for a memorable ride into the sunset.

Xining, capital of Qinghai province, has historically been an important centre for trade between China and Tibet. The famous Tibetan monastery **Ta'er Si** is 25 kilometres from Xining; it was built in 1577 at the birthplace of Zongkapa, founder of the Yellow Hat Sect. The bird sanctuary at salty **Lake Qinghai (Kokonor)** is 300 kilometres west of the capital. A railway links the provincial capitals of Xining and Lanzhou.

The **Ningxia Hui Autonomous Region** has a population of almost 4 million, of whom one third are Hui (Chinese Muslims). It is a poor, semi-desert region irrigated with water from the Yellow River. **Yinchuan**, the capital of the Western Xia empire more than 1,000 years ago, is the principal city. To the south of Yinchuan, near the **Qingtong Gorge**, stand 108 pagodas. At **Shapotou**, in the Tengger Desert, trips on inflated sheepskin rafts can be made on the Yellow River.

The grasslands of the **Inner Mongolian Autonomous Region** also beckon. **Hohhot (Hu he hao te)**, the provincial capital, is the setting-off point for visits to Mongol encampments in the **Da Mao Banner**. Tourists can stay in gentrified yurts overnight, watch the herding of camels, horses, cattle and sheep, and a colourful local rodeo — though they may find the Mongol diet of boiled mutton and millet tea daunting. There are interesting but neglected Lama Buddhist monasteries in the area. **Baotou** is the industrial centre of the region.

Remote **Xinjiang (Sinkiang)**, largely peopled by the Muslim Uighurs, Kazakhs and Tajiks, is an exotic destination for the adventurous. Transport, accommodation — except for a Holiday Inn that opened in Urumqi in 1992 — and the mutton-based cuisine are basic at best. The best periods to visit are in the spring during the melon season or in the autumn during the grape harvest. Pay extra attention to food and water here; avoid all cold dishes, and drink bottled water only.

The provincial capital of **Wulumuqi (Urumqi)** is not one of China's most attractive cities, but the **Provincial Museum** is excellent. Visits can be made to the beautiful **Tian Shan Mountains** and **Heavenly Lake (Tianchi)**, or to the southern pastures to see Kazakh herdsmen.

Turfan (Tulufan), a grape-growing oasis watered by ancient underground irrigation channels from the **Flaming Hills**, is half a day's journey from Urumqi by car. The population is almost entirely Uighur. The town boasts a small bazaar, and the favoured form of local transport is the donkey cart. The most fascinating sites here are the stark, rammed-earth ruins of two ancient cities — **Gaochang and Jiaohe** — which have been partly excavated. They date from the first century BC when they were garrisoned by Chinese troops, after which they were successively occupied by forces of the Chinese empire and Uighur khanates. The **Imin Pagoda (Su Gong Ta)** dates from the 1770s and the **Astana Graves** site contains well-preserved 1,500-year-old corpses. The **Thousand Buddha Caves** at **Bezeklik**, badly plundered in the early part of this century, are dramatically situated in the Flaming Hills. The Turfan Depression is an inhospitable basin which sinks to 200 metres below sea level, and boasts some of the highest temperatures in China (50°C).

Kashgar stood on the great Silk Road. Much has been written of this fabled oasis city by early Western explorers, and it was one of the centres of the "Great Game" during the 19th and early 20th centuries, when Russia and Britain vied for domination of Central Asia. Its central bazaar is fascinating; favourite purchases are hats, knives and old carpets. The **Id Kah Mosque** is the centre of the city's religious activities. Outside the city is the **Tomb of Xiang Fei**, the Uighur concubine of Emperor Qianlong. Kashgar is reached by air from Urumqi. Most tourists like to visit the **Sunday Bazaar**, where urban and rural residents meet to trade everything from goats to old shoes.

It is possible to make the journey down the **Karakorum Highway** into Pakistan. However tourist facilities are minimal.

Visitors to **Tibet (Xizang) Autonomous Region** should be in good health because of the high altitude. The 4,000-metre elevation of **Lhasa**, the regional capital, can cause discomfort to people not accustomed to such thin air, and it is essential to rest for the first day after arrival. The altitude, plus the exotic surroundings and palpable warmth of the Tibetan people, justifies the fictionalization of Tibet as Shangri-La, despite the heavy Chinese military presence and tragic recent history. The normal route to Tibet is by air, via Chengdu, which has several daily flights.

Tibet is the home of Lama Buddhism, a blend of Indian Buddhism and local animistic and magical traditions. The 13-storey fortress-temple, the **Potala**, which dominates Lhasa, was built in the 17th century by the fifth Dalai Lama and was his palace and place of worship. Tourists may walk (slowly) up its 120-odd steps or be driven up by a side road. Part of the **Red Palace**, in the centre, was the Dalai Lama's private quarters and is now a museum. The **White Palace** — on either side of the Red Palace — once contained offices and apartments. Altogether there are 1,000 rooms containing chapels, altars, statues and wall-paintings. Most of the rooms are ill-lit and smell of a combination of incense and yak butter.

The **Jokhang Temple**, in the heart of the old Tibetan city, contains a number of treasures, including the statue of Sakyamuni Buddha presented by the Tang Dynasty Chinese princess Wen Cheng on her marriage to a local king. Around its walls one may see daily processions of pilgrims prostrating in prayer. The **Barkhor** a street that forms a ring around the temple complex, is the scene of a lively bazaar.

The **Jewel Park**, known as the **Norbulingka**, was the summer palace of the Dalai Lama and contains many trees and pavilions. This is a favourite summer spot for picnic-loving Tibetans.

PHOTO: MARK GRAHAM

The Great Wall.

The **Drepung Monastery**, eight kilometres west of Lhasa, dates from the 15th century and once housed 10,000 lamas. Built on a high cliff, it is a superb example of Tibetan architecture. Drepung ("Rice Heap") was the centre of power of the Yellow Hat Sect and was a stronghold of Tibetan resistance during the fighting with the Chinese army in 1959.

Sera Monastery on the northern outskirts of Lhasa, was founded in 1419, and is the third largest of the three great monasteries of Lhasa (the other two being **Ganden** — destroyed, with only a few halls rebuilt but worth a visit — and **Drepung**).

On the road between Lhasa and Zedang, the **Samye monastery** can be visited by taking a boat across the lake-like Brahmaputra River. The provincial towns of **Shigatse (Tashilunpo Monastery)** and **Gyantse** are also open to foreign visitors. The ride to these cities by bus takes you over some of the highest highways in the world, where every turn is fraught with danger. With the opening of the China-Nepal border, it is possible to go by road from Lhasa to Kathmandu.

RESTAURANT SELECTION

Average price for two

BEIJING

BRASSERIE, Shangri-La Hotel, 29 Zi Zhu Yuan Lu. Tel: 841 2211, ext. 2719. Continental. US$50.

CAFE KRANZLER, Kempinski Hotel, West Wing, 50 Liang Ma Qiao Lu. Tel: 465 3388, ext. 5700. German cafe. US$30.

CHIU CHOW GARDEN, Palace Hotel, Jin Yu Hutong, Wangfujing. Tel: 512 8899. Chiu Chow (Chaozhou). US$40.

DYNASTY, Jing Guang Centre, Hu Jia Lou. Tel: 501 8888, ext. 2599. Cantonese. US$40.

THE FAN, Great Wall Sheraton Hotel, Dong Huan Bei Lu. Tel: 5005 5667, ext. 2237. Shanghai, Huaiyang. US$40.

FANG SHAN, Beihai Park. Tel: 441184. Imperial. US$40.

FRANK'S PLACE, Gong Ti Dong Lu. Tel: 507 2617. American bar. US$15.

HARDROCK CAFE, Landmark Towers, 8 North Tower, Dongsanhuan Rd. Tel: 501 6688, ext. 2571, 2574. US$30.

HONGBINLOU, 82 Xi Chang'an Jie. Tel: 601 4832. Muslim. US$30.

HONGKONG FOOD CITY, 18 Dong An Men Da Jie. Tel: 513 6668. Cantonese. US$50.

KAMAGOWA, China World Hotel, 1 Jian Guo Men Wai Da Jie. Tel: 505 2266. Japanese. US$50.

LAXENOXEN, SAS Royal Hotel, 6A Dong Bei San Huan Lu. Tel: 466 3388. Scandinavian. US$40.

LI JIA CAI, 11 Yangfang Hutong. Tel: 601 1915. Imperial. US$40.

NAKABACHI, Jianguo Hotel, Jian Guo Men Wai Da Jie. Tel: 500 2233, ext. 21976. Japanese. US$50.

OMAR KHAYYAM, Asia-Pacific Bldg. Tel: 513 9988, ext. 20188. Indian. US$30.

PALACE RESTAURANT, Palace Hotel, Jin Yu Hutong, Wangfujing. Tel: 512 8899, ext. 7900. Sichuan. US$40.

PAULANER BRAUHAUS, Kempinski Hotel, West Wing, 50 Liang Ma Qiao Lu. Tel: 465 3388, ext. 5734. German pub. US$30.

QIANMEN PEKING DUCK RESTAURANT, 32 Qianmen Dajie. Tel: 511 2418. US$30.

ROMA RISTORANTE, Palace Hotel, Jin Yu Hutong, Wangfujing. Tel: 512 8899, ext. 7492. Italian. US$60.

SICHUAN RESTAURANT, 51 Xi Rong Xian Hutong. Tel: 656348. Sichuan. US$30.

TINGLIGUAN (Pavilion of Listening to the Orioles), Summer Palace. Tel: 258 1955. Imperial. US$20.

TSUI HANG VILLAGE, Jian Guo Men Wai Da Jie. Tel: 515 8833. Cantonese. US$40.

GUANGZHOU

BEI YUAN (Northern Garden), 318 Xiao Bei Lu. Tel: 333 3365. Cantonese. US$30.

CAFE LA, Gitic Plaza Hotel, 339 Huan Shi Dong Lu. Tel: 331 1888. Continental. US$40.

CALIFORNIA CAFE, Ramada Pearl Hotel, 9 Ming Yue Yi Lu, Dong Shan. Tel: 777 2988. American. US$30.

DONG JIANG, 337 Zhong Shan Si Lu. Tel: 333 5568. Cantonese. US$30.

GAME RESTAURANT (Ye Wei Xiang), Beijing Lu. Tel: 333 0997. US$30.

GRILL ROOM, White Swan Hotel, Shamian Island. Tel: 888 6968. Continental. US$60.

GUANGZHOU, 2 Wen Chang Lu. Tel: 888 7840. Cantonese. US$30.

NAN YUAN (Southern Garden), 120 Qian Jin Lu. Tel: 444 0532. Cantonese. US$30.

PAN XI, 151 Long Jin Xi Lu. Tel: 888 5655. Cantonese. US$30.

THE ROOF, China Hotel, Liu Hua Lu. Tel: 666 6888. Continental. US$60.

SHA HE RESTAURANT, Sha He Da Jie. Tel: 777 5639. Cantonese, noodles. US$20.

SNAKE RESTAURANT (She Can Ting), 4 Jiang Lan Lu. Tel: 888 3811. Snake. US$30.

TAO TAO JU, 20 Di Shi Fu. Tel: 888 5769. Cantonese. US$30.

HANGZHOU

HANGZHOU JIU JIA, 52 Yan An Lu. Tel: 766414. Hangzhou. US$25.

LOU WAI LOU, 30 Wai Xi Hu. Tel: 729023. Hangzhou. US$25.

OCEANIC RESTAURANT, Dragon Hotel, Shu Guang Lu. Tel: 554488. Cantonese. US$40.

SHAN WAI SHAN, 8 Yu Quan Lu. Tel: 726621. Hangzhou. US$25.

SHANG PALACE, Shangri-La Hotel, 78 Bei Shan Lu. Tel: 777951. Hangzhou. US$50.

TIAN XIANG LOU, 166 Jie Fang Lu. Tel: 762038. Hangzhou. US$25.

SHANGHAI

BRASSERIE TATLER, Shanghai J.C. Mandarin, 1225 Nanjing Xi Lu. Tel: 2791888. Continental. US$45.

CHEERS, Holiday Inn Yin Xing, 388 Pan Yu Lu. Tel: 252 8888. Continental. US$40.

CONTINENTAL ROOM, Garden Hotel, 58 Mao Ming Nan Lu. Tel: 433 1234. Continental. US$50.

DREAMLAND SPICE GARDEN, Yangtze New World Hotel, 2099 Yan An Xi Lu. Tel: 275 0000. Southeast Asian. US$25.

RESTAURANT SELECTION

FU RONG ZHEN, Holiday Inn Yin Xing, 388 Pan Yu Lu. Tel: 252 8888. Sichuan. US$40.
GIOVANNI'S, Westin Tai Ping Yang Hotel, 5 Zun Yi Nan Lu. Tel: 275 8888. Italian. US$45.
GUAN YUE TAI, Sheraton Hua Ting Hotel, 1200 Cao Xi Bei Lu. Tel: 439 1000. Cantonese. US$50.
INAJIKU, Westin Tai Ping Yang Hotel, 5 Zun Yi Nan Lu. Tel: 275 8888. Japanese. US$50.
MEI LONG ZHEN, 22, 1081 Long, Nanjing Xi Lu. Tel: 253 5353. Shanghai, Huaiyang. US$25.
OLD TOWN RESTAURANT, 242 Fu You Lu. Tel: 328 2782. Shanghai, Huaiyang. US$25.
SAKURA, Garden Hotel, 58 Mao Ming Nan Lu. Tel: 433 1111. Japanese. US$50.
SHANGHAI JAX, Portman Shangri-La, 1376 Nanjing Xi Lu. Tel: 279 8888. Continental. US$35.
SICHUAN COURT, Shanghai Hilton Hotel, 250 Hua Shan Lu. Tel: 255 0000. Sichuan. US$50.
TAPPAN GRILL, Shanghai Hilton, 250 Hua Shan Lu. Tel: 255 0000. Continental and Japanese. US$50.
TEA GARDEN, Portman Shangri-La Hotel, 1376 Nanjing Xi Lu. Tel: 279 8888. Southeast Asian. US$35.
YANGZHOU, 308 Nanjing Dong Lu. Tel: 233 5826. Shanghai, Huaiyang. US$20.
YINDO, 350 Yu Yuan Lu. Tel: 252 0909, ext. 52. Cantonese. US$40.

TIANJIN

GOUBULI BAOZI (steamed dumplings), Nanshi Food St. Tel: 223277. US$20.
PINES CAFE, Hyatt Palace Hotel, Jie Fang Bei Lu. Tel: 318888. Continental. US$30.
SHI HU, Sheraton Hotel, Zi Jin Shan Lu. Tel: 343388. Cantonese. US$40.

XIAN

FOOD STREET, Grand New World Hotel, 48 Lian Hu Lu. Tel: 716868. Chinese regional. US$40.
GOLDEN POND CAFE, Golden Flower Hotel, 8 Chang Le Lu. Tel: 332981. Continental, buffet. US$50.
JIE FANG LU DUMPLINGS RESTAURANT, 229 Jiefang Lu. Tel: 23185. Dumplings banquets. US$30.
PAVILION, Hyatt Xi'an Hotel, Dong Da Jie. Tel: 712020. Cantonese, Sichuan. US$40.
TANG DYNASTY THEATRE RESTAURANT, 39 Chang An Lu. Tel: 711633. Cantonese. US$70 (with show).

HOTEL GUIDE

BEIJING

A: US$150 and above

CHINA WORLD, Jianguomenwai Dajie. Tel: 505 2266, Fax: 505 0828. *P, Gym, Biz, SatTV. R: C, W, J.*
GRAND HOTEL, 35 Dong Chang'an Jie. Tel: 513 7788, Fax: 513 0048. *P, Gym, Biz, SatTV. R: C, W.*
GREAT WALL SHERATON, Donghuan Bei Lu. Tel: 500 5566, Fax: 5001 919. *P, Gym, Biz, SatTV. R: C, W.*
HILTON, 1 Dongfang Lu. Tel: 466 2288, Fax: 465 3052. *P, Gym, Biz, SatTV. R: C, W.*
KEMPINSKI, Lufthansa Center, 50 Liangmaqiao Lu. Tel: 465 3388, Fax: 465 3366. *P, Gym, Biz, SatTV. R: C, German, Middle Eastern.*
NEW OTANI CHANG FU GONG, 26 Jianguomenwai Dajie. Tel: 512 5555, Fax: 513 9813. *P, Gym, Biz, SatTV. R: C, W, J.*
PALACE, 8 Jinyu Hutong, Wangfujing. Tel: 512 8899, Fax: 512 9050. *P, Gym, Biz, SatTV. R: C, Italian, J.*
GUANGDONG REGENCY, 2 Wangfujing Dajie. Tel: 513 6666, Fax: 513 4248. *P, Gym, Biz, SatTV. R: C, W.*
SHANGRI-LA, 29 Zizhuyuan Lu. Tel: 841 2211, Fax: 841 8002-04, 841 8006. *P, Gym, Biz, SatTV. R: C, W.*
TRADERS, 1 Jianguomenwai Dajie. Tel: 505 2277, Fax: 505 0818, 505 0838. *Biz, SatTV. R: C, W.*

B: US$100-150

BEIJING, 33 Dong Chang'an Jie. Tel: 513 7766, Fax: 513 7703. *Gym, Biz, SatTV. R: C, W, J.*
BEIJING TORONTO, 3 Jianguomenwai Dajie. Tel: 500 2266, Fax: 500 2022. *P, Gym, Biz, SatTV. R: C, W.*

P — Swimming pool | **Gym** — Health club | **Biz** — Business centre | **SatTV** — Satellite TV
R — Restaurant | **C** — Chinese food | **W** — Western food | **J** — Japanese food

HOTEL GUIDE

HOLIDAY INN CROWNE PLAZA, 48 Wangfujing Dajie. Tel: 513 3388, Fax: 513 2513. *P, Gym, Biz, SatTV. R: C, W.*
HOLIDAY INN LIDO, Jichang Lu, Jiangtai Lu. Tel: 500 6688, Fax: 500 6237. *P, Gym, Biz, SatTV. R: C, W.*
JIANGUO, 5 Jianguomenwai Dajie. Tel: 500 2233, Fax: 500 2871. *P, Biz, SatTV. R: C, W, J.*
JING GUANG NEW WORLD, Hu Jia Lou. Tel: 501 8888, Fax: 501 3333. *P, Gym, Biz, SatTV. R: C, W.*
RADISSON SAS ROYAL HOTEL, 6A Dong Beisanhuan Lu. Tel: 466 3388, Fax: 465 3186. *P, Gym, Biz, SatTV. R: C, Scandinavian.*
SWISSOTEL, Dongsi Shitiao Lijiao Qiao. Tel: 501 2288, Fax: 501 2501. *P, Gym, Biz, SatTV, handicapped facilities. R: C, W.*

GUANGZHOU

A: US$150 and above

GITIC PLAZA, 339 Huanshi Dong Lu. Tel: 331 1888, Fax: 331 1666. *P, Gym, Biz, SatTV. R: C, W, J.*
WHITE SWAN, Shamian. Tel: 888 6968, Fax: 886 1188. *P, Gym, Biz, SatTV. R: C, W.*

B: US$100-150

CHINA HOTEL, Liuhua Lu. Tel: 666 6888, Fax: 667 7014. *P, Gym, Biz, SatTV. R: C, W.*
GARDEN, 368 Huanshi Dong Lu. Tel: 333 8989, Fax: 335 0467. *P, Gym, Biz, SatTV. R: C, W, pizzeria.*
HOLIDAY INN CITY CENTRE, 28 Guangming Lu, Huanshi Dong Lu. Tel: 776 6999, Fax: 775 3126. *P, Gym, Biz, SatTV, cinema. R: C, W.*
RAMADA PEARL, 9 Mingyue Yi Lu. Tel: 777 2988, Fax: 776 7481. *P, Gym, Biz, SatTV. R: C, W.*

C: US$50-100

EQUATORIAL, 913 Renmin Lu. Tel: 667 2888, Fax: 667 2583. Tlx: 441168. *P, Gym, Biz, SatTV. R: C, W, J.*
FURAMA, 316 Chang Di Lu. Tel: 886 3288, Fax: 886 3388. *Biz, SatTV. R: C.*

CHENGDU

B: US$100-150

DYNASTY HOTEL CHENGDU, 3 Sanguiqian Jie, 610016. Tel: 667 8888, Fax: 662 4313. *P, Gym, Biz, SatTV. R: C, W.*

CHONGQING

B: US$100-150

HOLIDAY INN YANGZI, 15 Nan Ping Bei Lu. Tel: 203830, Fax: 200884. *P, Gym, Biz, SatTV. R: C, W.*

DALIAN

B: US$100-150

FURAMA, 74 Stalin Lu. Tel: 230888, Fax: 204455, Tlx: 86441. *P, Gym, Biz, SatTV. R: C, W, J.*
HOLIDAY INN, 18 Sheng Li Guang Chang, Zhongshan. Tel: 808888, Fax: 809704. *P, Gym, Biz, SatTV. R: C, W, J.*

C: US$50-100

INTERNATIONAL, 9 Stalin Lu. Tel: 238238, Fax: 230008. *Gym, Biz, SatTV. R: C, W.*

GUILIN

B: US$100-150

HOLIDAY INN, 14 Ronghu Nan Lu. Tel: 223950, Fax: 222101. *P, Gym, Biz, SatTV. R: C, W.*
PLAZA, 20 Lijiang Lu. Tel: 442488, Fax: 223323. *P, Gym, SatTV. R: C, W.*
ROYAL GARDEN, Yuan Jiang Lu. Tel: 442411, Fax: 445051. *P, Gym, Biz, SatTV. R: C, W, J.*
SHERATON, Binjiang Nan Lu. Tel: 225588, Fax: 225598. *P, Gym, Biz, SatTV. R: C, W.*

HANGZHOU

B: US$100-150

DRAGON, Shu Guang Lu. Tel: 554488, Fax: 558090. *P, Gym, Biz, SatTV. R: C, W.*
SHANGRI-LA, 78 Bei Shan Lu. Tel: 777951, Fax: 773545. *Gym, Biz, SatTV. R: C, W.*

LHASA

B: US$100-150

HOLIDAY INN, 1 Mu Zu Lu. Tel: 22221, Fax: 25796. *Biz, SatTV. R: C, W, Himalayan.*

NANJING

A: US$150 and above

JINLING, 2 Hanzhong Lu. Tel: 742888, 741999, Fax: 714695. *P, Gym, Biz, SatTV. R: C, W.*

SHANGHAI

A: US$150 and above

EQUATORIAL, 65 Yan An Xi Lu. Tel:

P — Swimming pool
R — Restaurant
Gym — Health club
C — Chinese food
Biz — Business centre
W — Western food
SatTV — Satellite TV
J — Japanese food

HOTEL GUIDE

279 1688, Fax: 248 4033. *P, Gym, Biz, SatTV. R: C, W, J, Thai.*
GARDEN, 58 Mao Ming Nan Lu. Tel: 433 1111, Fax: 433 8866. *P, Gym, Biz, SatTV. R: C, W, J.*
HILTON, 250 Hua Shan Lu. Tel: 248 0000, Fax: 248 3834. *P, Gym, Biz, SatTV. R: C, W, J.*
HOTEL SOFITEL HYLAND, 505 Nanjing Rd (East), Shanghai 200001. *Gym, Biz. Executive club. R: C, W.*
JC MANDARIN, 1225 Nan Jing Xi Lu. Tel: 279 1822, Fax: 279 2341. *P, Gym, Biz, SatTV. R: C, W.*
PORTMAN SHANGRI-LA, 1376 Nan Jing Xi Lu. Tel: 279 8888, Fax: 279 8999, Tlx: 33272. *P, Gym, Biz, SatTV. R: C, W, J.*
WESTIN TAI PING YANG, 5 Zun Yi Nan Lu. Tel: 275 8888, Fax: 275 0643. *P, Gym, Biz, SatTV. R: C, W, J.*

B: US$100-150

HOLIDAY INN CROWNE PLAZA, 388 Pan Yu Lu. Tel: 252 8888, Fax: 252 8545. *P, Gym, Biz, SatTV. R: C, W.*
NIKKO LONGBAI, 2451 Hong Qiao Lu. Tel: 255 9111, Fax: 255 9333. *P, Gym, Biz, SatTV. R: C, W, J.*
REGAL (F.T.), 1000 Qu Yang Lu. Tel: 542 8000, Fax: 544 8447. *Gym, Biz, SatTV. R: C, W.*
SHERATON HUA TING, 1200 Cao Xi Bei Lu. Tel: 439 1000, 439 6000, Fax: 255 0830, 255 0719. *P, Gym, Biz, SatTV. R: C, W, Italian.*

C: US$50-100

PEACE, 20 Nanjing Dong Lu. Tel: 321 1244, Fax: 329 0300. *Gym, Biz, SatTV. R: C, W.*

SHENZHEN

B: US$100-150

SHANGRI-LA, East of Shenzhen Railway Station. Tel: 223 0888, Fax: 223 9878. *P, Gym, Biz, SatTV. R: C, W.*
SUNSHINE HOTEL, 1, Jia Bin Rd, Shenzhen 518001. Tel: 223 3888, Fax: 222 6719 (Hong Kong Tel: 2735 7272, Fax: 2736 9100). *Biz. R: C, W. (P, Gym mid-1994).*

C: US$50-100

CENTURY PLAZA, Kin Chit Rd. Tel: 222 0888, Fax: 223 4060. *P, Gym, Biz, SatTV. R: C, W, J.*

SUZHOU

B: US$100-150

BAMBOO GROVE HOTEL, Zhuhai Lu. Tel: 225 601, 227601, Fax: 778778. *Gym, Biz, SatTV. R: C, W.*

TIANJIN

B: US$100-150

CRYSTAL PALACE, 28 You Yi Lu, He Xi. Tel: 310567, Fax: 310591. *P, Gym, Biz, SatTV. R: C, W.*
HYATT, Jie Fang Bei Lu. Tel: 318888, Fax: 310021. *Gym, Biz, SatTV. R: C, W, J.*
SHERATON, Zi Jin Shan Lu, He Xi. Tel: 343388, Fax: 318740. *P, Gym, Biz, SatTV. R: C, W.*

URUMCHI

B: US$80-120

HOLIDAY INN, 53 Bei Xin Hua Lu. Tel: 217077, Fax: 217422. *Gym, Biz, SatTV. R: C, W, Muslim.*

XIAN

A: US$150 and above

GRAND CASTLE, 12 Xidyan, Huancheng Nan Lu. Tel: 723 1800, Fax: 723 1500. *Biz, SatTV. R: C, W.*

B: US$100-150

GARDEN, 4 Dong Yan Yin Lu. Tel: 711111, Fax: 711998. *Gym, Biz, SatTV. R: C, W.*
HYATT REGENCY, Dong Da Jie. Tel: 712020, Fax: 716799. *Gym, Biz, SatTV. R: C, W.*

C: US$50-100

GRAND NEW WORLD, 48 Lian Hu Lu. Tel: 716868, Fax: 714222. *P, Gym, Biz, SatTV. R: C, W.*
GOLDEN FLOWER, 8 Xi Chang Le Lu. Tel: 332981, Fax: 335477. *P, Gym, Biz, SatTV. R: C, W.*
SHERATON, 12 Feng Gao Lu. Tel: 741888, Fax: 742983. *P, Gym, Biz, SatTV. R: C, W.*
BELL TOWER, Zhong Lou Xi Nan Jiao. Tel: 29201, Fax: 718767. *Gym, Biz, SatTV. R: C, W.*
HOLIDAY INN, 8 Nan Huan Cheng Dong Lu. Tel: 333888, Fax: 335962. *Gym, Biz, SatTV. R: C, W.*

P — Swimming pool
R — Restaurant
Gym — Health club
C — Chinese food
Biz — Business centre
W — Western food
SatTV — Satellite TV
J — Japanese food

HONG KONG

Hong Kong rates as one of the great cities of the late 20th century. Great cities are built when society is prepared to put massive resources into them, for one reason or another. Some have come about at different stages in human history to celebrate political or religious dominance. Hong Kong, as is fitting for a place devoted to commerce, has come about almost entirely from a confluence of market forces under political pressures.

Through the late 1970s and the entire decade of the 1980s, property prices boomed. Given the restricted land space and the limited life of British rule — to end on July 1, 1997 when Hong Kong reverts to Chinese control — Hong Kong could only go up — and fast. The result is that the skyline of the city centre, round its spectacular harbour site, now rivals New York.

Affluence allowed the building of not purely utilitarian but architecturally worthy buildings, such as British architect Norman Foster's Hongkong and Shanghai Bank headquarters. Then commerce was joined by politics to spur the future masters to put the final touch, with the magnificent Bank of China Tower, by American-Chinese architect I.M. Pei, now forming a superb and worthy centrepiece for the rest of the city.

If Singapore — Asia's other city state — is the ideal introduction to Asia, Hong Kong is very much the advanced and intensive course. So much so that getting into the hustle and bustle of the city and its jostling, hurrying masses too quickly can lead to an overdose of impressions, resulting in confusion and sometimes dislike.

Because of its concern with day-to-day living and a fever relating to making as much money as possible before 1997, Hong Kong often fails to establish any form of rapport with visitors. Its initial impact is tremendous and, for the first-time visitor, overwhelming — shops crammed with every conceivable artifact, glitzy boutiques, superb restaurants serving some of the world's best Chinese food, a harbour crammed with ships, sampans and junks, and a feeling of tremendous dynamism and purpose.

But it is a place of contrasts as well. The dazzling Central area and the packed frenzy of the tourist shopping mecca in Kowloon across the harbour can be left behind in a matter of minutes (traffic permitting) and a new world of quiet hills, seascapes and beaches is revealed to the visitor. But you may need to hurry. Such is the pace of development that anything that resembles a flat surface — and a lot that does not — is being built on.

Hong Kong has been legendary for the rudeness of its inhabitants. It is much less the case now. While there are those determined to maintain a tradition for surly manners, the general affluence and self-assurance of its people is manifest in more courteous behaviour these days. Because it is a very crowded environment there is, inevitably, still a great deal of pushing and shoving in the narrow streets, getting on to buses, in and out of lifts and almost anywhere else. The best advice is to do as everyone else does and join the scramble. The people are not unfriendly, though they may be a bit preoccupied. If they can assist they will. Lack of knowledge and confidence in the English language can be misinterpreted as rudeness.

◄ *Hong Kong Island's Causeway Bay by night.* PHOTO: GREG GIRARD

Despite a preoccupation with dollars and cents, Hong Kong still has very beautiful, peaceful and almost untouched places of interest. The New Territories and the many outlying islands still contain havens of tranquillity, not just for visitors but for many Hong Kong people. Although they too are threatened by developers, they still provide alternatives for visitors not interested in shopping.

For the visitor just passing through there is plenty to fascinate, to bewitch and to entertain. A passing affair with Hong Kong is unlikely to bring you into contact with any of its problems, except one: Hong Kong is no longer cheap. The territory's commercial success has spawned an affluent middle class which demands the best in goods and services — and is prepared to pay for it. Some of Hong Kong's leading retailers charge more for name-brand goods than their counterparts in Paris, Rome, New York or London. In virtually all sectors, the city has become a lot more expensive than it used to be, but it does give value for money.

Hong Kong has one of the highest average standards of living in Asia outside Japan. It contains examples of poverty and affluence, security and lawlessness, honesty and corruption, dedication and self-indulgence. It is a cocktail of human types and nationalities. For the visitor, Hong Kong can perhaps offer more in a small area than anywhere else in Asia.

History

By the 18th century, the trading arm of Britain had reached out to touch China. Using the Portuguese settlement of Macau as a base, British traders spent part of the year up the Pearl River in Guangzhou. The British sought to reverse the balance of trade, which favoured the Chinese, by stepping up the import of opium, which was ineffectually banned by the Chinese emperor in 1799.

The trade continued and increased until the Chinese took steps to stamp it out again in 1839. The Chinese seized British traders and representatives until they surrendered opium supplies. In retaliation the British sent an expeditionary force in 1840 seeking a trade treaty on favourable terms or the cession of land where British traders could live under their own flag, thus starting the first of the so-called Opium Wars.

Hong Kong Island was ceded by the Chinese under the Nanking Treaty of 1842, confirming the occupation that had taken place during the First Opium War (1839-41). The additional 3.75 square kilometres of Kowloon Peninsula and Stonecutters Island were ceded under the First Convention of Beijing in 1860 after the Second (or Arrow) Opium War (1856-58).

Much later, in 1898, to match the territorial acquisitions of its rival trading nations on the China coast and to secure the better defence of the territory, Britain obtained the 99-year lease of the New Territories on the mainland and 235 islands — 976 square kilometres in all.

The whole of the territory — with promised political autonomy — is to revert to China in 1997, when the New Territories lease expires, under an agreement reached between London and Beijing in 1984.

From the 1840s until the 1950s, apart from the Japanese occupation of 1941-45, Hong Kong served as a staging post and transshipment centre for trade between China and the Western world. With the Korean War and the United States embargo on export of strategic goods to China, much of this trade was cut off, and Hong Kong turned to manufacturing for a livelihood, also becoming a considerable financial centre.

By the mid-1970s, Hong Kong seemed once again to have reached calm waters. Turmoil inspired by China's Cultural Revolution, which began in mid-1966, fizzled out in the second half of 1968. Hong Kong returned to the more congenial task of making money, aided by a booming economy.

It was in the 1980s that Hong Kong came of age as a sophisticated financial centre, as well as acting as the world's staging area for the commercial march on the opening Chinese market. With the Chinese obsession for edu-

cation, more and more Hong Kong families saved to send at least one of their children overseas for a Western education. As the decade wore on, graduates flooded back to the territory with a combination of Western qualifications, Chinese pragmatism and Hong Kong-imbued commercial drive. They gave an international flavour to family wealth which had been derived almost solely from hard work in the manufacturing sector.

But though the territory has been promised a high degree of autonomy after British rule ends, the uncertainty over the future has led to a massive drain of educated Chinese to settle in the U.S., Canada, Australia and elsewhere. The sudden realization of the impending change also has sparked a remarkable and uncharacteristic interest in political development and the British are rushing to introduce some form of democratic process which they had neglected for 150 years.

Hand in hand with this neglect has been the minimum of government interference, leaving exceptionally low taxes and no import duties except on liquor, tobacco and some petroleum products. There are no currency restrictions. These things have made the territory particularly attractive to investors and financiers as a centre for their operations. Though the commercial risk has changed little, some companies are now understandably nervous about the political risk component of their investments.

Hong Kong's future remains bound by the whims of other countries, particularly China. The whole dramatic situation has led to increased worldwide interest in Hong Kong and, indeed, it could be argued that anyone wishing to experience this unique mix of Sino-British culture in all its freebooting fascination had better do so soon.

Entry

Hong Kong is the hub of Asia's civil aviation and sea transport network, but traffic shuts down at Hong Kong's Kai Tak airport from midnight to 6 a.m. Entry into Kai Tak by air is an attraction in itself. Aircraft skim low over the rooftops of Kowloon and drop frighteningly on to the finger of airstrip stretching into the harbour. Aircraft coming in to land from the western end give passengers the disquieting feeling that they are about to land in either the city or the sea. Views are spectacular and it is well worth securing a window seat just for this experience.

There is an airport departure tax of HK$50 on all those over 12 years of age.

Immigration

A valid passport is required for entry into Hong Kong. Visa requirements vary as listed below: they are not needed by many foreign nationals, depending upon length of stay. Some foreign passport holders must have a visa before entry is allowed.

Holders of most types of British passport issued in Britain do not require visas for a stay up to 12 months. However, on arrival in Hong Kong you may have to satisfy an immigration officer that you have sufficient means of support, or a valid return ticket, or evidence of employment in Hong Kong.

Nationals of the following countries do not require visas for a visit not exceeding three months: certain British Overseas citizens and Commonwealth citizens (e.g. Australia, Canada, Malaysia, Singapore, Malawi, etc.), Andorra, Austria, Belgium, Brazil, Chile, Colombia, Denmark, Ecuador, France, Irish Republic, Israel, Italy, Liechtenstein, Luxembourg, Monaco, the Netherlands, Norway, Portugal, San Marino, Spain, Sweden, Switzerland and Turkey.

Nationals of the following countries do not require visas for a visit not exceeding one month: Argentina, Bolivia, Costa Rica, Dominican Republic, El Salvador, Finland, Germany, Greece, Guatemala, Honduras, Iceland, Japan, Mexico, Morocco, Nepal, Nicaragua,

MAJOR AIRLINE OFFICES

	Reservations	Flight Information
ON-LINE		
Aeroflot	2537 2611	2769 6031
Air France	2524 8145	2769 6662
Air-India	2522 1176	2769 6558
Air Lanka	2529 9708	2769 8571
Air Mauritius	2523 1114	2769 6048
Air New Zealand	2524 9041	2769 6046
Air Niugini	2524 2151	2769 6038
Alitalia	2523 7047	2769 6032
All Nippon Airways	2810 7100	2769 8609
Anselt Australia	2537 9088	2769 6046
Asiana	2523 8585	2523 1358
British Airways	2868 0303	2868 0768
Canadian	2868 3123	2769 7113
Cathay Pacific	2747 1888	2747 1234
China Airlines	2868 2299	2769 8391
China National Aviation	2861 0322	2769 8571
Delta	2526 5875	2769 6032
Dragonair	2590 1188	2769 7727
Emirates	2526 7171	2769 8571
Garuda	2840 0000	2769 6681
Gulf Air	2882 2892	2769 8337
Japan Airlines	2523 0081	2769 6524
Japan Asia Airways	2521 8102	2769 6534
KLM Royal Dutch Airlines	2808 2111	2382 7272
Korean Air	2368 6221	2769 7511
Lauda Air	2525 5222	2769 7107
Lufthansa	2868 2313	2769 6048
Malaysian Airlines	2521 8181	2769 7967
Northwest Airlines	2810 4288	2769 7345
Philippine Airlines	2369 4521	2769 6031
Qantas	2524 2101	2525 6206
Royal Brunei Airlines	27471888	2747 7888
Royal Nepal Airlines	2869 8608	2769 6031
S.A.S	2865 1370	2769 6048
Singapore Airlines	2520 2233	2769 6387
South African Airways	2877 3277	2868 0768
Swissair	2529 3670	2769 6031
Thai Int.	2529 5601	2769 6038
United	2810 4888	2769 7279
Varig	2511 1234	2769 6048
Vietnam	2810 6680	2769 6046
Virgin	2532 6060	2769 7155
OFF-LINE		
American Airlines	2826 9111	
Kenya Airways	2846 7911	
Pakistan Int.	2366 4770	
T.W.A.	2851 1411	

Panama, Paraguay, Peru, South Africa, Tunisia, U.S.A., Uruguay and Venezuela.

Nationals of the following countries do not require visas for a visit not exceeding one-and-a-half days: Algeria, Angola, Bahrain, Benin, Bhutan, Bosnia, Burkina Faso, Burundi, Cameroon, Cape Verde Republic, Central African Republic, Chad, Comoros, Congo, Croatia, Egypt, Equatorial Guinea, Estonia, Ethiopia, Federated States of Micronesia, Gabon, Guinea, Guinea-Bissau, Haiti, Indonesia, Ivory Coast, Jibuti, Jordan, Kuwait, Latvia, Liberia, Lithuania, Madagascar, Mali, Mauritania, Mozambique, Niger, Oman, Philippines, Poland, Qatar, Republic of the Marshall Island, Republic of Yemen, Rwanda, Sao Tome and Principle, Saudi Arabia, Senegal, Slovenia, South Korea, Surinam, Thailand, Togo, United Arab Emirates, Vatican City, Yugoslavia (the former states of), Zaire and various U.S. Trust Territories.

Nationals of almost every other country are allowed entry into Hong Kong for periods not exceeding seven days, with the exception of the following — nationals of which always require a valid visa for entry into Hong Kong: Afghanistan, Albania, Bulgaria, Cambodia, People's Republic of China, CIS (the former USSR), Cuba, Laos, Mongolia, North Korea, Romania and Vietnam. This applies also to passport holders from the Czech and Slovak republics, Hungary, Iran, Lebanon, Libya, Somalia, Sudan, Syria, Burma and Taiwan. Nationals of Iraq are required to hold a valid visa for Hong Kong even if only in airport transit.

For visa extensions, or queries relating to continued stay in Hong Kong, contact the Hong Kong Immigration Department, 7 Gloucester Rd, Wanchai, Hong Kong. Tel: 2824 6111, Fax: 2824 1133, Tlx: 69996.

Health

The only certificates of vaccination now required are those against yellow fever for those travelling from infected areas in Africa and South America.

Customs

Visitors are allowed duty-free import of 200 cigarettes, 50 cigars or 250 grams of tobacco and one litre of alcoholic beverages. There is no duty on perfumes and cosmetics. Most items are allowed duty-free entry since Hong Kong is a free trading centre.

Firearms must be declared and handed into custody until departure. The strictures against carrying firearms are severe, as they are with the possession of most other weapons.

Currency

The Hong Kong dollar (HK$) is the legal currency. Since 1983 it has been pegged to the U.S. dollar at an exchange rate of US$1:HK$7.8.

Notes in denominations of HK$10, HK$20, HK$50, HK$100, HK$500 and HK$1,000 and coins of 10, 20 and 50 cents (bronze colour) and HK$1, HK$2, HK$5 (silver colour) and HK$10 (silver and bronze) are in circulation.

There are no restrictions on the amount of foreign or Hong Kong currency which may be imported or exported. Currency can be exchanged at banks or local money-changers. There are money-changers at the airport, though better exchange rates can be obtained from city exchange offices. Banks offer good exchange rates, and it pays to shop around.

All major credit cards are accepted in Hong Kong by most restaurants and retail establishments. In addition there are a number of automated-teller installations that offer local currency against credit cards. American Express card-holders can withdraw local currency at an auto-teller machine located at New World Tower (opposite the Landmark in Queen's Rd, Central). Visa card holders can get local currency at Hongkong Bank machines at the airport and a number of other locations.

Language

Despite having been ruled by Britain for 150 years the use of English is far from universal. Be prepared to have difficulties making taxi drivers (especially) and even shop assistants in many places understand you. Although English and Chinese are both official languages of Hong Kong, Cantonese (a south China dialect) is the mother tongue of most of the population, and is widely used on radio, TV and in films. Mandarin and a number of other Chinese dialects are understood by a limited number of people.

Other languages are not widely understood, though many shop assistants in the tourist areas have a smattering of Japanese. Trained interpreters for almost all languages are available for hire. Hotels, business centres and the

Hong Kong Tourist Association (HKTA) can advise.

Climate

The climate is subtropical with the year more or less equally divided between a hot, humid summer and a cool — sometimes chilly but generally dry and sunny — winter. There are short autumn and spring seasons. The rain falls mainly in spring and summer: falls can be very heavy. The difference between day and night temperature is around 5.5°C on average.

From late May to mid-September, Hong Kong's summer takes its toll on residents and visitors alike with temperatures up to 35°C and 90%-plus humidity. Life becomes more pleasant in late September to early December. It can get decidedly cool from mid-December to the end of February with temperatures averaging 15°C and the humidity at 75%. The temperature can, however, dip below double digits at times and visitors should include an overcoat in their luggage in winter.

Most years, typhoons affect Hong Kong between May and October. But the early warning systems are most efficient. Visitors, especially if unfamiliar with the city, should not stray too far from base if a typhoon signal appears imminent. Radio and TV stations broadcast reports regularly and hotels post the signals. If you are caught out, it is best to retire to the nearest hotel, restaurant or bar and see out the worst of the storm. The atmosphere in some bars is definitely party-like.

The greatest danger to life and limb during typhoons comes from flying debris, and only fools venture out after the number eight signal is hoisted. Even if safely ensconced inside, common sense suggests you should stay away from windows and take reasonable precautions.

Dress

If coming solely as a visitor, in the summer dress is informal, lightweight and cool. Shorts and T-shirt, slacks and polo-shirt are pretty much the norm for both sexes. More formal attire might consist of a light shirt and slacks for men, or a dress or light skirt and blouse for women. Except during mid-summer it is advisable to pack a sweater. For winter months warmer clothing is required, though there are only a few days each year when the temperature drops to near freezing.

Business visitors will need to dress more formally. Although not as rigorous as it use to be, the Hong Kong business dress code is still formal. Suits for men and formal attire for women are expected (though it has become acceptable to carry the jacket).

Air-conditioning is universal in hotels, restaurants and better class tourist shops and malls. These are usually turned up to maximum setting with the result that outside temperatures of 30°C plus outside can suddenly become closer to 10°C inside. It is advisable to take a jacket or wrap if dining out.

Business Hours

Government offices are open 9 a.m-1 p.m. and 2-5 p.m. Monday to Friday, and 9 a.m.-1 p.m. on Saturdays. Most banks are open to the public 10 a.m.-4 p.m. Monday to Friday, and 9.30 a.m.-noon on Saturdays. Some have longer hours. Many commercial firms work 10 a.m.-7 p.m. Sunday is a holiday though most shops are open. A five-day week is becoming more common in Hong Kong business life, though it is not yet the norm.

The main Post Office by the Star Ferry in Central, is open 8 a.m.-6 p.m. Monday-Saturday.

Doing Business

Hong Kong has prospered through international trade. Local businesspeople are generally used to dealing with customers and sales people from all over the world. By and large the customs and protocols in business are the same as in any Western city. The dress code is still rather formal, but even this is changing. Chinese businesspeople would expect to shake your hand on meeting. The exchange of business cards is normally done by presenting the card with both hands. You will not gravely offend anyone if you tender it in one hand, but the more formal gesture would be noted and appreciated. There are no particular conventions that apply solely to women. Gift giving is not expected — the only real caveat being that if you must offer a gift it should not be a clock, which has connotations of death for Chinese.

The Chinese take meals seriously. An invitation to join them for a meal is no formality. If you refuse they will probably be more concerned about your health than take offence, however. English is widely spoken, though there are none the less a fair number especially among smaller businesses where English is either non-existent or very limited. The rules on smoking are as in the West — ask your host whether it is acceptable.

All hotels are used to dealing with business people and their requirements. Hotel lobbies are the best place to seek advice on things such as courier services, car rentals, translation services, secretarial services, etc. Indeed, many hotels offer these services themselves. Be sure to have medical insurance cover for a stay in Hong Kong, since medical and dental bills are frighteningly high.

Rip-Offs

Despite Hong Kong's efforts to clean up its act — which have been largely successful — horror stories of tourists being ripped-off persist.

In Tsimshatsui, in Kowloon, especially in and around Nathan Rd, are the camera, hi-fi and video shops waiting to trap the unwary. (*See Shopping*). Shop around and establish price guidelines first. If the salesperson even starts to act in a hostile manner, or you feel is pressuring you, be prepared to walk out then and there. The same goods can be purchased at any number of other outlets. Do not assume you can get the better of such techniques. Even if you bargain a good price do not assume that the goods placed in the box are those you thought you had bought. Do not assume all the guarantees are provided. There are plenty of honest, friendly traders who will be happy to discuss your requirements and will not take offence if you ask to see the goods being packaged and will allow you to inspect the guarantees.

Media

Hong Kong has three English-language dailies. *The South China Morning Post* and *Hongkong Standard* are published seven days a week, while the *Eastern Express* is appears Monday-Saturday. In addition there are a host of English-language periodicals, both weekly and monthly, the majority of which are business related. The *Far Eastern Economic Review, Asiaweek, Asian Business, Window* and *Asia Inc.* are just a few. *The Asian Wall Street Journal* and the *International Herald Tribune* print daily. Most major British, U.S., European and Australian newspapers are available a few days after publication, and international magazines such as *Time, Newsweek* and *The Economist* are all available at most hotels or the many newsstands throughout Central and Tsimshatsui. Newsstands outside the Star Ferry on both sides of the harbour tend to be especially well stocked.

Local English-language radio and TV is available as well as satellite TV.

Communications

Hong Kong has one of the most modern telecommunications systems available. Telephone and facsimile calls within Hong Kong are free of charge (though nominal charges are made for coin-operated machines). Mobile phones are more widely used than anywhere else on earth. IDD is available to all countries, including parts of mainland China. Operators speak fluent English. Line quality is superb and digital data sent over the phone should not be a problem.

Note: All telephone numbers now have eight digits and start with a "2."

Transport

FROM THE AIRPORT: Taxis are available (though there is usually a queue) at Kai Tak airport. A fare chart indicator is displayed prominently immediately outside the airport en route to the taxi stand. Taxis to Hong Kong Island via the Cross-Harbour Tunnel charge HK$20 in addition to the fare shown on the meter (for most hotels, a total of around HK$90. Many taxis may try to take you via the Eastern Harbour Tunnel, which increases the fares by about 70% but is often faster because the approach roads are less crowded. They may ask you first, claiming that the older tunnel is crowded. More likely they will just do it. It is best to make clear to the driver, if at all possible, whether you want to go via the shortest or the fastest route.

Fares to Tsimshatsui, in Kowloon where many tourist hotels are located should be about HK$35. An extra HK$5 per piece of luggage may be charged if you have large suitcases.

Unless you have mountains of luggage it may be just as quick, and certainly much cheaper, to take an air-conditioned airport bus. There are four main routes with departures every 10-20 minutes. Operating hours are from 7 a.m. to midnight, with costs about one fifth of a taxi. Exact change is required. Departure is from the same area as the taxi ranks and is clearly marked. Buses stop a short walk from

SUBWAYS (MTR) IN HONG KONG

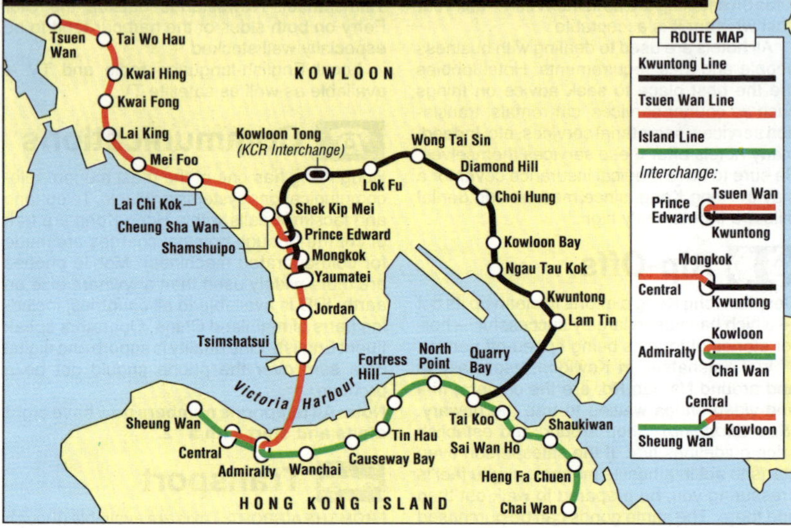

some of the hotels served and luggage has to be carried. For airport bus information telephone 2745 4466.

Most first-class hotels in Hong Kong arrange transfer with their own vehicles. On arrival you can contact the uniformed representative of your hotel as you leave the customs area. The cost of transport to the hotel is added to your hotel bill, though some Kowloon hotels make no charge for this service.

TAXIS: Taxis are the most convenient means of transport for the visitor. In April 1995, the flag fall on all urban (red) taxis was HK$13 for the first two kilometres and HK$1.10 per 0.2 kilometres thereafter. Waiting time was HK$1.10 per minute. Taxis are all metered, and — people arriving at the airport for the first time please note — all meters show only Hong Kong dollars and cents and no other currency, despite what the driver may try to claim. Make sure the meter is turned on at the beginning of your journey. Be careful what notes you pay with and what change you get. Drivers are not above giving change from HK$100 when a HK$500 or HK$1,000 note has been given, and beware of possible "confusion" over HK$10 and HK$20 notes.

Many drivers speak enough English to get you to well-known spots, but some speak none, and some speak very little Cantonese either, having arrived in Hong Kong recently. If you are going out of the way it is best to have the address written in Chinese. It is also a good idea to have the address of wherever you are staying written in Chinese — as on a hotel matchbox or a piece of letterhead paper, for instance. Not all drivers know the whole of Hong Kong or of Kowloon very well, depending on where they live. Hotels or business associates will assist with this.

Taxis are scarce during peak periods, when it is raining, and on horse-racing days (Wednesday and Saturday from September to June). There are more taxi stops being introduced as main roads become more clogged. There are ranks on both sides of the harbour at the Star Ferry piers and other points. One of the surest ways to get a cab is to join the queue at the nearest hotel. Hotel guests may get priority but there is usually a doorman on duty to assist with any language problem.

Cabs may be hailed in the street, though there are many stopping restrictions and taxis cannot stop except in designated areas. This applies to dropping you off as well as picking you up. A yellow line drawn close to the kerb indicates no stopping at certain times of the day, usually morning and evening rush hours. A double yellow line indicates no stopping at any time.

MASS TRANSIT RAILWAY (MTR): A 43.2-kilometre underground system which extends along the northern side of Hong Kong Island, from west to east, and in two lines across the harbour into Kowloon. It covers all the urban areas tourists are likely to want to reach, but does not go to the south of Hong Kong Island. Fares for the air-conditioned system are HK$3-10.

Avoid rush hours — the underground is used by up to 1 million commuters each day. The system is clean, fast and efficient. Tickets are bought for each journey, or there are stored value tickets for those expecting to travel extensively on the network.

BUSES: Double-decker buses serve most parts of the territory, fares ranging from a minimum of HK$1.50 for some journeys in the city to a maximum of HK$27 to the New Territories. Buses are very crowded at peak hours, but otherwise provide a reasonable means of getting around. There are major terminals under Exchange Square in Central, at Admiralty, and just in front of the Star Ferry in Kowloon. Get a leaflet from the **HKTA** for information on bus routes.

MINIBUSES (public light buses): colour-coded with either red or green bands, operate over many routes in the territory, providing a quick, convenient way of getting about. Most are air-conditioned. Fares range from HK$2.70 to HK$14, depending on route and time of day. Drivers of the red-banded buses appear to set their own fares according to market forces. Green-banded mini-buses usually have a fixed fare.

Destinations are displayed on the front, along with the price — sometimes only in Chinese. Once you get into the idea they are a good way to travel, but you have to know the city. If the driver understands where you are going, he will tell you when to get off. Fares are paid on leaving red minibuses — on the green ones, pay as you board.

TRAMS: On Hong Kong Island only, quaint double-decker trams run from Kennedy Town in the west, through Central District to Causeway Bay, North Point and Shaukiwan in the east. Trams on another route head off a short way inland to Happy Valley. There is a single HK$1.20 fare, regardless of distance: pay the exact fare on your way out. From the upper deck, the journey offers an excellent picture of bustling Hong Kong life, and is a good place from which to photograph the city. Avoid travel at crowded peak periods. One of the best shorter journeys is to take a tram from Central to North Point (destination written on the front), a trip which ambles through Wanchai, Causeway Bay, past Victoria Park and down the back-street market at North Point. Get off at North Point and shop or simply pay your fare and get on again for the return journey. Not the fastest way around town.

PEAK TRAM: The lower terminus is located on Garden Rd, a short walk up the hill from the Hilton Hotel and opposite the U.S. Consulate. The journey costs HK$10 each way or HK$16 return (children under 12 pay HK$4 or HK$6 return). This funicular railway provides a unique view of the city — to be avoided by anyone suffering from vertigo. A free shuttle-bus service to the Peak tram station operates from the Star Ferry pier from 9 a.m. to 8 p.m. daily.

TRAINS: Overground trains operate over two routes in Hong Kong. From Kowloon (the station, Hunghom, is near the exit of the Cross Harbour Tunnel) to the market town of Sheungshui in the New Territories, not far from the border with China. The train passes through Shatin, the Chinese University, Taipokau, Taipo and Fanling. The return class fare is HK$28. On Sundays, holidays and race days at Shatin, the train is unbearably crowded. Two through-train services to Guangzhou operate daily. In addition, a Light Rapid Transit rail service operates from Tuen Mun to Yuen Long in the New Territories.

FERRIES: In addition to the famous green and white Star Ferry, which crosses between Kowloon and Hong Kong Island every few minutes (top deck HK$1.70, bottom deck HK$1.40), the Hong Kong and Yaumatei ferries operate across the harbour to outlying districts. They leave from Hong Kong Island piers in Central (Star Ferry pier area or 400 metres to the west of the piers), from Wanchai, North Point and Shaukiwan, and cross the harbour to points in Kowloon and the New Territories such as Yaumatei, Shamshuipo, Kwuntong, Tuen Mun, Tsing Yi, Hunghom (train station for China) and Tsimshatsui East. At the Outlying Districts Piers, between the Star Ferry and Macau Ferry terminals, ferries run every 30 or 60 minutes to islands such as Lantau, Lamma and Cheung Chau. A very relaxing 45-70 minute trip, except on hectic weekends and holidays, when such journeys should be avoided. The ferries stop running around 10 p.m. to midnight. Timetables are available at the piers. Massive redevelopment of Hong Kong Island's harbour front means that the map on page 234 is somewhat speculative as to ferry pier locations. All temporary piers are clearly signposted — if in doubt, check with the HKTA.

HIRE CARS: Hire cars are available, but roads are very congested in Hong Kong and the visitor is advised against hiring a car in the inner areas. For trips to the New Territories or the southern side of Hong Kong Island, they may be worthwhile for a group of several people. Self-drive cars cost from HK$400 upwards daily, while a chauffeur-driven car will cost considerably more. Several car-hire companies are listed in HKTA publications.

RICKSHAWS: For photo-opportunities only. There are a few around the Star Ferry in Central. If you want a trip — only a few yards round the block — negotiate the price first.

Tours

There is no shortage of tour operators in Hong Kong. It is easy to make arrangements at any hotel for trips to different places of interest. Tours include a Heritage Tour, taking in local historical sights: the **Land Between Tour** around the surprisingly tranquil parts of the New territories: the **Come Horse-Racing Tour** and **Sports and Recreation tours** which con-

CONSULATES AND COMMISSIONS

	Tel:		*Tel:*		*Tel:*
Argentina	2523 3208	**Greece**	2774 1682	**Pakistan**	2827 1966
Australia	2827 8881	**Grenada**	2517 2827	**Panama**	2545 2166
Austria	2522 8086	**Guinea**	2744 5211	**Papua New Guinea**	2499 3611
Bangladesh	2827 4278	**Guinea-Bissan**	2832 9866	**Paraguay**	2987 6687
Barbados	2526 6911	**Iceland**	2528 3911	**Peru**	2868 2622
Belgium	2524 3111	**India**	2528 4028	**Philippines**	2866 8738
Belize	2838 2331	**Indonesia**	2890 4421	**Poland**	2840 0779
Benin	2525 7011	**Ireland**	2826 2798	**Portugal**	2802 2584
Bhutan	2376 2112	**Israel**	2529 6091	**Russia**	2877 7188
Botswana	2525 6088	**Italy**	2522 0033	**St Lucia**	2866 9023
Brazil	2525 7002	**Jamaica**	2579 8216	**Seychelles**	2549 5337
Camaroon	2868 3362	**Japan**	2522 1184	**Singapore**	2527 2212
Canada	2810 4321	**Jordan**	2311 9203	**Slovenia**	2545 2107
Cape Verde	2375 3728	**S. Korea**	2529 4141	**South Africa**	2577 3279
Central Africa	2311 8828	**Liberia**	2865 2132	**Spain**	2525 3041
Chile	2827 1826	**Luxembourg**	2877 1018	**Sri Lanka**	2866 2321
Colombia	2545 8547	**Malaysia**	2527 0921	**Suriname**	2573 3077
Commonwealth of Dominica	2598 6899	**Maldives**	2376 2114	**Sweden**	2521 1212
Costa Rica	2566 5181	**Malta**	2739 1515	**Switzerland**	2522 7147
Cote D'Ivoire	2802 2411	**Mauritius**	2368 9882	**Thailand**	2521 6481
Cuba	2525 6320	**Mexico**	2511 3318	**Togo**	2340 0285
Cyprus	2820 1100	**Monaco**	2893 0669	**Tonga**	2522 1321
Denmark	2827 8101	**Mongolia**	2338 9033	**Trinidad & Tobago**	2368 0918
Djibouti	2771 7622	**Morocco**	2736 7286	**Tunisia**	2959 3123
Dominican Republic	2521 2801	**Mozambique**	2738 4400	**Turkey**	2527 1331
Egypt	2827 0668	**Burma**	2827 7929	**United States of America**	2523 9011
Fiji	2375 1618	**Namibia**	2586 1339	**Uruguay**	2868 0330
Finland	2525 5385	**Netherlands**	2522 5127	**Venezuela**	2730 8099
France	2529 4351	**New Zealand**	2525 5044	**Vietnam**	2591 4510
Gabon	2890 2771	**Nicaragua**	2698 0909	**Western Samoa**	2521 5621
Germany	2529 8855	**Nigeria**	2827 8813		
Great Britain	2523 0176	**Norway**	2574 9253		
		Oman	2873 0888		

tain pretty much what you'd expect from their titles. There are trips around Hong Kong Island by land or by sea. There are trips to the Chinese border, and others across the border (for which one requires separate documents and a visa, except for Shenzhen). There are plenty of water tours — some of which are very scenic. Macau is only about an hour away by means of a choice of extremely fast ferries. Macau is sufficiently different from Hong Kong to be worth the visit; cheap to get there and inexpensive (unless you gamble). You will need to check on visa requirements first. Prices of tours vary, but many offer good value.

For information on visa applications for the People's Republic of China contact your travel agent or hotel tour desk; for Taiwan call **Chung Wah Travel Service** on 2525 8315.

Accommodation

The standard of accommodation available in Hong Kong is second to none anywhere in the world. Several of the territory's hotels rank as deluxe and the majority of others catering to the tourist trade are well up to international levels. Almost all are air-conditioned, have private bathrooms, telephones and TV, and in most cases, refrigerators and minibars. The majority are located in the tourist shopping areas of Tsimshatsui (in Kowloon), or Causeway Bay, Central and Wanchai on Hong Kong Island. (See *Hotel Guide* at end of this chapter).

Hong Kong receives about 9.3 million tourists a year and even with some 31,000 rooms available the hotels are sometimes fully booked. Hotel reservations should be made before arrival. The **Hong Kong Hotels Association** does have a service at Kai Tak airport for those who have not made bookings. If you are booking one of the higher grade hotels, it will almost always be cheaper for you to book before you arrive in Hong Kong. Hotels offer a number of very good packages for intending tourists provided bookings are made before arrival.

The **HKTA** will be able to advise if your travel agent has difficulty. There are HKTA offices in Auckland, Barcelona, Chicago, Frankfurt, London, Los Angeles, Milan, New York, Osaka, Paris, Rome, San Francisco, Seoul, Singapore, Stockholm, Sydney, Tokyo and Toronto.

Outside the luxury and family hotels, the YMCA and YWCA have several good hostels which are almost up to hotel standard. There are also a number of reasonable, simple hostels and guesthouses where rates range from US$30 to US$50 for a single room. Chungking Mansions, 40 Nathan Rd, Kowloon, has guesthouses of various classes (unprepossessing would be the best adjective). A variety of cheap accommodation is published in the local newspapers, some offering discount rates for weekly or monthly stays. Many hotels, too, offer discounts for periods of as little as one week, depending upon the time of year. For visitors staying a month or more, serviced apartments are available for around HK$13,000 for bedroom, lounge and small kitchen.

Dining

Chinese food in Hong Kong is available in greater variety and of a generally higher standard than probably anywhere else in the world. The Cantonese (southern Chinese) food is certainly unrivalled anywhere, and many other types of regional Chinese cuisine can be found. There are a large number of Japanese, Thai, Indian, Vietnamese and Western-style restaurants, plus a generous serving of restaurants covering every cuisine the world has to offer. For a comprehensive guide to the range of food and restaurants available in Hong Kong, the HKTA publication *Dining and Entertainment* is hard to beat.

Chinese meals are better taken by a group. Cantonese food centres on chicken, pork, fish and other seafood plus rice and vegetables. It tends to be juicy rather than dry and sometimes includes ingredients that many Westerners tend to consider unappetizing. Anyone can enjoy crab and green vegetables, fried rice with eggs, pork and shrimps, salt-baked chicken, shark's fin and mushroom soup (with a dash of Chinese vinegar to enhance the flavour), leaving such bizarre (to the uninitiated) items as ducks' feet, snake soup and sea slug to the real connoisseur.

It is best to order one dish per person in the party (stick to small dishes if your party is fewer than four), accompanied by plain or fried rice and a soup. The usual condiments — soy sauce, vinegar, chili sauce and mustard — will be provided automatically. Tea is always served and beer, wine or spirits are available at most Hong Kong restaurants.

A favourite way to enjoy lunch in Hong Kong is to partake of *dim sum* — Chinese snacks — washed down with plenty of tea. Trolleys of hot and cold food pass by tables at regular intervals and diners indicate which dishes they would like as the trolley ambles by. A tally is kept either by staff filling in a "scorecard" on the table or, in some restaurants, simply totting up the number of empty plates. Costs will typically be HK$8-20. per item.

If you have a local Chinese friend to accompany you, so much the better. But you can manage alone: just about all types of *dim sum* are to Western taste. Spring rolls (*chun gun*), barbecued pork dumplings (*cha siu bao*), small dumplings of shrimp (*ha gau*) and pork (*siu mai*) are among the best known. Try water-chestnut jelly (*ma tai go*) or sweet rice pudding (*sa mai bo din*) for dessert.

Cantonese food is good almost anywhere — few restaurants last more than five minutes if the food is not up to scratch. Peking food, characteristic of north China, is also available in Hong Kong, though there are far fewer restaurants than those serving Cantonese food. Peking food tends to be crisp and light. One of the great specialities of the north is Peking duck — eaten rolled up in thin wafers of unleavened bread known as *bao bing*, with strips of cucumber, leek and plum sauce. If you are having Peking duck, do not order too much else as it is very filling, especially if you have soup made from the remains of the duck as a final course.

Yellow fish in wine sauce, prawns in chili sauce and beggar's chicken (a whole chicken wrapped in lotus leaves and baked in ashes until tender — order well in advance), bamboo shoots fried with green vegetables and for dessert, *ba sal* (candied apple cooled on the spot in iced water), are all excellent, characteristically northern dishes. Peking cuisine also boasts *jiao zi* (ravioli-like morsels containing meat that can be had either steamed or fried) and delicious onion bread.

What is known as Mongolian hot pot is also offered at Peking — as well as other — restaurants during the winter months: fish, squid, beef, kidney, liver, vegetables and other ingredients are prepared at your table. Dip them into boiling broth for a minute or so before eating and at the end of the meal there is a nourishing soup left for a final course.

Shanghainese dishes are also available in abundance in Hong Kong. The food, often diced into small fragments and cooked in rather more oil than is the case with either Cantonese or Peking-style dishes, is rather more spicy than either northern or southern food.

Sichuan (sometime spelled Szechuan or Sze Chuan) cooking is becoming more common in Hong Kong and is worth trying since its rich, spicy flavours readily become a favourite of those who really enjoy Chinese food.

Restaurants in Hong Kong are often crowded during the lunch period and 7-9:30 p.m. and reservations are recommended. English language menus are generally available.

Wandering in the streets of Hong Kong you will notice a good many small restaurants with chickens, ducks, chunks of pork and various other items displayed in the window. The chances are no one will speak English, but you can get a long way by simply pointing.

Prices in Hong Kong for Chinese food generally average around US$15-30 per person at most middle-grade restaurants. A meal of steamed rice (*pak fan*), pork and green vegetables will only cost around US$3.50-4.50 in the smaller restaurants. Noodles work out cheapest for the budget traveller, a good meal of noodles with meat and vegetables usually costs no more than US$3.50. Meals available at the many foodstalls in Hong Kong are even cheaper — but hygiene is not necessarily their strongest quality.

Most Chinese will only drink tea with their meals, but those who do drink alcohol will favour beer, whisky, brandy or Chinese *shao xing* or *mao tai* (rice wines similar to Japanese sake, which are best consumed warm). Hua Diao is the most common type of *shao xing*, while Jia Fan is the best and a little more expensive. Those who do not mind a little adventure when it comes to drinking might care to try a bottle of the liqueur-like Mooikwai Lo after their meal.

In the past few years, a number of Vietnamese restaurants have opened, serving variations of prawns and spring rolls among other dishes.

For Western food, the standard of food in the restaurants of first-class hotels can rarely be faulted but is not cheap. All first-class hotels have at least one showpiece European-type restaurant.

All the world's beers and liquor can be obtained in Hong Kong. The beers most enjoyed locally include San Miguel (brewed in Hong Kong), and Carlsberg. A beer will usually cost about US$5 (supermarket prices about 50-60 U.S. cents) and Scotch whisky US$5-7 a shot, except in the large hotels and hostess bars where the charge is considerably higher. Excellent Chinese beer, especially the lager-like Tsingtao, is also available and cheaper.

Martial arts training session. PHOTO: GERHARD JOREN

Entertainment

During January and February, the **Hong Kong Arts Festival** schedules several first-rate events, and there is an **International Film Festival**, usually in April. The biennial Asian Arts festival generally occurs in the fourth quarter of the year.

Chinese opera can be seen at any number of venues ranging from concert halls to local playgrounds. There are performances of Chinese art forms twice a week in such places as large shopping malls or local district town halls. The shows are free. These are well worth seeking out to get a taste of everything Chinese from martial arts to puppet theatre.

The city's offerings of Western films are usually badly cut, not only by the censors — who cut all explicit or even semi-explicit sex but leave in all the violence — but also by managements to fit in an extra performance. The screen is dominated by Chinese martial arts films, comedies or a combination of both, though leading Western films are shown soon after release.

The **Hong Kong Cultural Centre** on the waterfront near the Star Ferry in Tsimshatsui, came in for a good share of criticism because of its architecture, but at last has provided Hong Kong with a world-standard concert hall and two theatres, which are drawing higher quality performers than the territory has previously seen.

The Hong Kong **Academy for Performing Arts** in Wanchai is an impressive training centre and has within it six fairly good venues for performances. Its next door neighbour, the **Hong Kong Arts Centre**, concentrates on providing an outlet for local amateur and professional performances.

The City Hall, near the Star Ferry on Hong Kong Island, which has a concert hall capable of holding 1,500 people and a theatre for drama and chamber music, is a convenient place to call in to get information about what is happening at other venues in the city.

The Fringe Club is housed in an old warehouse in the Central District, a 10-minute climb up the hill via Ice House St or Wyndham St. It is worth paying the HK$10 one-night membership fee for a relaxed and informal evening.

The **Hong Kong Coliseum** (which looks like an inverted pyramid) near the Hunghom railway station in Kowloon has enormous capacity and is best suited for big-name pop concerts or sporting events.

Hong Kong's **nightlife** falls into four main categories: drinking spots of various grades with or without music; discos, nightclubs and girlie bars. In addition, the ubiquitous Japanese karaoke "do-it-yourself" singing bars are mushrooming all over the city. Major hotels have supper clubs offering floor shows and sometimes a singer or dance band.

The Lan Kwai Fong area of Central District, at the top of D'Aguilar St, a block uphill from Queen's Rd, was spawned in the 1980s yuppie era. It has matured into a nightlife area offering the gamut of options from an excellent jazz club for serious buffs of the genre to a disco/restaurant offering some of the best hamburgers in town — with music. The area includes the well-established **California Bar and Grill**, an up-market cocktail lounge with West Coast cuisine and dining and dancing until 4 a.m. The **Post 97** group comprises a restaurant on the first floor, and the Club 1997 disco immediately below. There are also a number of smaller restaurants, and music bars which give the area a chic-quarter aura.

Discos are very popular. In Tsimshatsui, **Apollo 18** is in the basement of the Silvercord building across from Ocean Centre. **The Tropical** disco in Tsimshatsui East is popular with locals. Cover charges run around the HK$100 mark and usually include a couple of drinks. The upmarket **Downstairs** at Duddell's Discotheque has a pretty good restaurant service to accompany its elaborate sound and light systems.

In Kowloon, there is a loose collection of seven bars and clubs in the New World Centre (Salisbury Rd, Tsimshatsui) called **Bar City**. It includes a disco, and a country-and-western tavern, live bands and cabaret. The **Godown** (in the basement of the Furama Hotel Kempinski) is popular, and has good food and a pleasant informal atmosphere. The **Dicken's Bar** at the Excelsior Hotel is a favourite haunt for jazz on Sunday afternoons. The **Gallery Lounge** at the Park Lane has show-band style music. Among pubs and taverns on Hong Kong Island, look for traditional pub fare from **Mad Dogs** in D'Aguilar St near Lan Kwai Fong, and the **Bull and Bear** on the ground floor of Hutchison House in Central. In Kowloon, try **Ned Kelly's Last Stand**, best after 10.30 p.m., and the **Blacksmith's Arms** in Tsimshatsui. **The China Coast Pub** at the Regal Airport Hotel has excellent fish and chips and a boisterous pub atmosphere. **Bonker's Bar** is not a bad spot despite its name and you should not go home without calling for at least one drink at **Bottoms Up** — a lot of good, clean, naughty fun. Bottoms Up welcomes couples, lonely bar-hoppers and others looking for a good time with equal enthusiasm.

More exclusive bars include the **Noon Gun Bar** in the Excelsior (very good); **Browns' Wine Bar** in Exchange Square has an excellent range of good and vintage wines and the **Champagne Bar** at the Grand Hyatt serves champagne by the glass, a variety of caviar and live music in the evening. In Kowloon try **Nathan's** in the Hyatt or the **Tiara Lounge** at the Shangri-La.

Visitors should be warned that the famous Wanchai and Kowloon topless bars — not quite like they were in the days of Suzie Wong — can be tempting but also very very expensive, with their sleazy habit of assuming that any Western or Japanese customer is buying drinks for all the hostesses.

Although they may well be sipping cold tea, the customer will be charged for brandy — and there is no arguing against the management when the bill is presented. Be warned. The "bar fine" for taking one of the hostesses out also is way above the going rate in Asia and does not include any favours negotiated for later.

There are also several up-market clubs, designed for the expense-account executive and almost unbelievably lavish (or garish depending on your taste). Emulating the Japanese "super-club," they are huge. **Club Bboss** and its sister operation, the **Metropolitan** in Tsimshatsui East cover 13,000 square metres and have about 1,500 hostesses on duty. These clubs usually have large dance floors, a number of bands (usually Filipino) plus female singers. Decor includes upholstered ceilings, Italian marble statuary, gushing fountains and partitions of etched glass around the many VIP rooms, where groups of businessmen may settle in a cosy atmosphere with their hostesses while a clock — like a taxi meter — ticks up the cost for their company. These places are expensive, yet fully patronized even on week nights.

Other examples are the **New Tonnochy Nightclub**, which displays its charges (and its charms) clearly and the **Club Celebrity** both in

Wanchai. In Tsimshatsui are the **Club Deluxe**, the **Club de Hong Kong, Club Cabaret** and the **China City**. None of them is for the faint-hearted without a credit card, but if one wants to be parted from one's money, these up-market establishments probably offer better value than the sleazy ones.

Shopping

Shopping is still one of Hong Kong's prime attractions, though you should not assume that Hong Kong prices are always necessarily lower than elsewhere. Some are good in comparison with other places and some are not. A lot of knowledge and a lot of hunting for the best prices is required if your only object is to get extra value for money. On the other hand, there is probably more, especially as regard to garments, on sale in Hong Kong than anywhere on earth.

Hong Kong no longer deals exclusively in the bargain basement, having found a market for luxury goods for which better off visitors are pleased to pay high prices.

With some 9.3 million visitors annually passing through Hong Kong, there are sure to be a few fools and some shopkeepers still operate on the basis that you are one of them.

Until recently a hard and fast rule for shopping in Hong Kong was to visit several shops and try to knock the price down progressively until you reach what was fairly obviously the market price. This hardly applies these days. Most large shops, department stores and chains have fixed prices. So have an increasing number of smaller shops, although these may allow a small discount to be negotiated.

Shops which do not display prices may reasonably be assumed to start quoting prices well above the selling price. One good way is to price items in the fixed-price department stores — you ultimately may find the prices cheaper and a greater variety there than in the "bargain" shops, together with the peace of mind from knowing the guarantee is valid. Do not expect a "no quibble" exchange of faulty goods, except once again from the larger, established outlets.

Less reputable shops in Hong Kong still occasionally sell falsely represented goods — fake name-brand goods, for instance — though the practice is now much more rare. Shops carrying the emblem of the HKTA can usually be expected to carry on their business in a proper manner.

With goods such as watches, cameras and hi-fi equipment, one should always buy from a shop properly certified as an agent for a particular brand of equipment and get the manufacturer's international guarantee, not the shop's guarantee. The HKTA's guide *Shopping* is available free of charge and includes a list of the agents for many leading brand name goods. Be warned that prices at duty-free shops at the airport are sometimes higher than in town.

An invaluable aid to shopping in Hong Kong is a small pocket-book entitled *Complete Guide to Hong Kong Factory Bargains* published by Delta Dragon Publications, which gives details on how to find these bargain vendors. The same publishers also produced a guide to gems and jewellery.

The usual shopping hours are 10 a.m.-7 p.m. or even 11 p.m. for European-type shops and department stores. Almost all are open on Sundays and the majority of public holidays, even over the Christmas holiday.

Main items visitors find alluring are table linen, embroidery, silk (especially the new washable varieties), brocades, pewter, copper, jewellery, jade, camphor-wood chests, carpets, rugs, furniture, rattan ware, porcelain, pottery, curios, watches, cameras and electronic goods. The export of carved ivory — once a major attraction — is now barred under an international agreement to try to save the African elephant from extinction and there are penalties for attempting to export ivory illegally.

Hong Kong tailors have a worldwide reputation for speed, and suits can be made in 48 hours, but you will get a much better product if you give them a week.

Prices are not as competitive as was once the case. Made-to-order women's garments usually take longer to make (especially at the better shops). Off-the-peg women's wear is very fashionable and there is a good range of garments. Again, be warned. If at all possible, patronize a tailor who has been recommended. There are some unscrupulous traders known to make up garments from cheaper material than that chosen and paid for.

The principal tourist shopping areas in both Kowloon and Hong Kong Island radiate out from the Star Ferry piers on each side of the harbour. **Causeway Bay** has both great variety and good prices. **Tsimshatsui East** is worth exploring and is much favoured by Japanese tourists. In **Central District** on Hong Kong Island, Connaught Rd, Des Voeux Rd, Queen's

Rd, and the streets that run between them are devoted to shopping malls, arcades, shops, restaurants and offices. Many excellent shops are found in arcades, especially in hotels and on the second or third levels. Hong Kong shopping should never be confined to the ground floor — prices on higher floor shops can be cheaper because rents are lower. Wyndham, D'Aguilar and Wellington Streets also of interest, especially for Chinese curios.

State-owned Chinese mainland department stores are a novel feature of the Hong Kong shopping scene. They can be found on both sides of the harbour, selling a wide range of items including clothes, linen, household goods, silk, pottery and Chinese crafts. They offer excellent value especially for those none-branded goods made on the mainland. Prices are fixed. Service is efficient if far from gracious. **Chinese Emporium and China Arts and Crafts** each have several branches in Hong Kong and Kowloon and should not be missed.

Fixed prices are also the case in such non-communist department stores as the Japanese-owned **Daimaru** and **Sogo** in Causeway Bay; the up-market **Lane Crawford**; the clothing groups such as **Bossini**, **Giordano**, **G2000** and **U2**; electrical group **Fortress**, and watch retailer **City Chain**, among many others.

Market-style shopping is everywhere. The best known is the "designer" market in **Stanley**, on the south side of the Island, which sells mainly name-brand casual and sports clothes, as well as silk goods and bed linen.

Stanley market has become rather expensive and other markets sometimes offer the same goods at almost half the price. But a visit can be combined with a trip on a double decker bus from Central which winds along the spectacular coast road and there are some excellent pubs and bistro type restaurants in Stanley, facing the sea.

Bargains can be found at the Sunday clothes market one street back towards the harbour from the main street in **North Point**. Take a tram from Central to North Point (experience the Hong Kong crush). The Ladies' Market in Tung Choi St in **Mongkok**, Kowloon, is worth visiting. It is open 1-11 p.m. daily — go after 7 p.m. when the trolley vendors have finished their regular jobs and take to the streets with a range of "over-runs."

The Temple St market in **Kowloon** runs 8-11 p.m. specializing in menswear, watches and electronic gadgetry. The markets can be extremely crowded and, while they are well policed, visitors should keep wallets secure against pickpockets. Do not flash around large quantities of notes when buying goods.

Market stallholders deal exclusively in cash but almost all shops will take some form of credit card. Visa, MasterCard and American Express are the most popular, though sellers may insist on a 3-5% surcharge for accepting a card.

Sports

Clubs catering for several kinds of sporting activities can be found in Hong Kong, and visitors may either be granted temporary membership on the payment of a small fee or be allowed to use the facilities, again for a fee. Most golf courses are open Monday to Friday, with the exception of public holidays. The **Royal Hong Kong Golf Club** has three 18-hole courses at Fanling in the New Territories. Contact the club secretary by telephone, confirm that the course is available and check details of transport to this course or the nine-hole courses at Deep Water Bay. Or you can use the new Sports and Recreation Tour offered by the HKTA. Packages include pick-up from hotels, lunch at a club and return to hotel. Golf clubs, badminton and squash rackets can be hired, but you must supply your own sportswear and appropriate shoes.

Squash, basketball and tennis are very popular and there are many courts in the territory, including public ones as well as private clubs. Soccer, too, has a big following and there is a professional league which plays in the winter months. Amateur cricket can be seen each weekend at the **Hong Kong Cricket Club** in Wongneichong Gap Rd during the cooler months.

The Hong Kong international seven-a-side rugby tournament is held on the last weekend in March and offers a weekend of non-stop rugby attracting world-class teams. Book early with your travel agent as seats sell out long before the event. Tickets are often more easily obtained abroad than in Hong Kong.

In the summer, Hong Kong's plentiful sea comes into its own, with sailing, water-skiing, scuba-diving — all have their supporters. Details of clubs can be obtained from the HKTA. Most hotels have swimming pools and there are 42 public beaches throughout the territory. They tend to be crowded on weekends and often the water is far from free of pollution.

Gold, gold and more gold. PHOTO: CHRIS GAY

Cleaner beaches can be found on the outlying islands. A rating system for the cleanliness of beaches is published at regular intervals throughout the summer in the press.

Joggers, even in summer, will find companionship in **Kowloon Park**, **Victoria Park** (in Tsimshatsui and Causeway Bay respectively) and Bowen Rd — one of the few flat roads in Hong Kong.

For hikers, Hong Kong still has many trails to take one's mind off the urban congestion. Despite its congestion, some 80% of the territory is classified as a rural or country park. For the truly adventurous, the **MacLehose Trail** offers 100 kilometres of hiking through some of the most scenic sections of the New Territories. It passes through eight country parks.

Bus stops intersect the trail periodically so the hiker can choose easy or difficult routes, or plan to walk for one or several days. There are plenty of shorter walks available for the casual stroller. Be sure to take a water bottle as the heat can become severe as the day progresses.

By far the most popular "sport" in Hong Kong is horse racing — or rather betting. Hong Kong's racing season at Happy Valley and Shatin is from September to June. Turnover has topped US$153 million a day. Racing is held most Saturday afternoons, some Sundays and on Wednesday evenings during the season. One should reach the course well before the first race to be sure of getting in. Guest tickets for admission to the members' enclosure (HK$50 and passport proof that you are a bona fide visitor) can be obtained from the **Off-Course Betting Centre**, near Star Ferry, or at the club itself on the day. The HKTA has horse-racing tours that will pick you up from the hotel, take you to the course, feed you and bring you home again. It will not, however, guarantee you a winner.

Holidays

Hong Kong's festivities very much revolve around the traditional Chinese lunar calendar, which means that particular events will fall on different dates from one year to the next. A number of Western events are celebrated and fall on set dates (with the exception of Easter).

January 1: New Year's Day (public holiday).

January-February: Chinese New Year. The Chinese community celebrates in a carnival atmosphere. Everyone wears new clothes, debts are paid, families visit one another. Traditional firecrackers are banned in urban areas but on the outer islands and rural areas police "look the other way" and at midnight on New Year's Eve there are barrages of exploding firecrackers which continue sporadically most of the night (three-day public holiday).

The Lantern Festival marks the end of the Chinese New Year on the 15th day after the first moon. Lanterns are hung in homes and at restaurants. In Victoria and Kowloon parks thousands of children go out with their families waving lanterns to celebrate the event.

March-April: *Ching Ming* festival (fourth or fifth day of the third moon) is a family festival when visits are made to the graves of relatives to perform "spring cleaning" and other traditional rites (public holiday).

Easter: Three-day public holiday.

April-May: *Tin Hau* festival is the greatest festival of the year for Hong Kong's fishing community and others connected with the sea, when they celebrate the birthday of Tin Hau (the Goddess of Heaven). There are many Tin Hau temples in Hong Kong and on the surrounding islands. On the festival day the most striking celebrations are held at the Tai Miu (great temple) at Joss House Bay. Very picturesque and good for photographers. At dawn the fishermen and boat people set out for the temple in gaily bedecked junks, sampans, motor boats and a special ferry which runs to the temple. Lion dances are performed outside the temple.

April or May: The Bun Festival on Cheung Chau island lasts a week during which there are religious observances, processions, Chinese opera and a fiesta atmosphere on the island. The main procession is held on the fourth day. This festival has lost some of its interest for tourists, as the giant bun towers have been scaled down since two fell over in 1978 while villagers were climbing them to get the lucky buns at the top. Climbing the towers is now prohibited.

May: Birthday of Lord Buddha is celebrated most notably at Po Lin Monastery on Lantau Island.

May-June: *Tuen Ng* (Dragon Boat) Festival on the fifth day of the fifth moon is one of the territory's most famous occasions. It is traditionally associated with the drowning by suicide of the poet-statesman Chu Yuan (332-296 BC), who died in protest against the social conditions of the time.

The dragon boat races held on this day perhaps symbolize attempts to rescue him. The principal race is held at Taipo (the town can be reached by the Kowloon-Sheungshui train): others are held at Aberdeen, Stanley, Tuen Mun, Shatin and Cheung Chau. The boats used are long, thin shells with a dragon's head at the bow and they carry as many as 50 rowers. Amidships a huge drum is beaten to give time. The races are a most exciting occasion (public holiday).

In recent years international races, held in Hong Kong harbour off Kowloon, usually on the weekend following the actual festival, has been introduced and attracts entries from all over the world.

August: Liberation Day (last Monday of August) commemorates the territory's liberation from the Japanese in 1945 (public holiday).

August-September: *Yue Lan* (hungry ghost) festival on the 15th day of the seventh moon marks the day that hungry ghosts wander the world and paper money, fruit and other offerings are made to appease them.

September-October: The Mid-Autumn (moon) festival on the 15th day of the eighth moon is one of the major events of the year. Moon cakes (sweet and not particularly appealing to most foreigners) are eaten and children carry beautiful lanterns made in the shape of birds and fish. People flock to the peaks of Hong Kong to view the full moon.

September-October: The Birthday of Confucius (27th day of the eighth moon) is commemorated at the Confucian temple in Causeway Bay.

October: *Chung Yeung* Festival on the ninth day of the ninth moon. People flock to the high places on the Island following the advice of a Han Dynasty sage that this is the way to avoid disaster.

December 25, 26: Christmas Day and Boxing Day (public holiday).

PUBLICATIONS

A number of excellent publications on Hong Kong, available free or for a small charge are available from **HKTA** offices.

Titles may change but they are extremely comprehensive and include guides to shopping, eating out, walking tours, hotels, Chinese festivals and special events, sightseeing, arts and crafts and museums, public transport and the outlying islands.

Also available from the HKTA centres are facts sheets on factory outlets, hostels, campsites and other accommodation in Hong Kong.

The head office of the HKTA is on the 11 Flr of the Citicorp Centre, 18 Whitfield Rd, North Point (Tel: 2807 6543). Information and souvenir outlets for the HKTA are located at the Star Ferry concourse in Kowloon and Shop 8 in the basement of Jardine House, Central. They are open from 8 a.m. or 9 a.m. to 6 p.m. weekdays and 8 a.m. or 9 a.m. to 1 p.m. on Saturdays. Telephone information is available by calling 2807 6177 (multilingual), 2807 7133 (Mandarin) or 2807 6188 (Japanese).

For a deeper read on what makes Hong Kong tick and some excellent maps, try the **Government Information Services** shop on the ground floor of the main Post Office in Central.

The South China Morning Post Family Book Stores are located on both sides of the harbour. Handy for visitors are the ones located in the Star Ferry concourse in Central and the Ocean Centre in Harbour City, Tsimshatsui.

The **Swindon Book Co.** has three outlets in Kowloon: 13-15 Lock Rd (Tel: 2366 8001); 3249 Ocean Terminal and 64 Nathan Rd. The **Hong Kong Book Centre** has stores in the basement at the Landmark and another in Des Voeux Rd.

DISCOVERING HONG KONG

HONG KONG ISLAND

The first, almost essential, excursion is to the **Peak**, reached either by taxi or minibus from the Central District of Hong Kong Island or — much better — by the **Peak Tram**, whose lower terminal is just a little way up Garden Rd (200 metres up the hill from the Hilton Hotel). Free shuttle bus from the **Star Ferry**. The view from the Peak, 397 metres above sea level, is one of the great sights of the world. Unfortunately, the weather has to be clear to see it, and this happens on probably less than half the days of the year. If you can see the peak from central Hong Kong, go up it immediately, as there may not be another opportunity during your stay.

To ride up in the late afternoon and down again after dark enables you to enjoy views of the city both by day and when lit at night. From the top, you can look down on the astonishing high-rise city, as if from a low-flying plane, taking in the whole span of the harbour, packed with busy traffic. The panorama extends right across to Kowloon's hills.

From the Peak tram top station there is a spectacular 45-minute circular flat walk round the Peak on the narrow Lugard Rd, which gives a full view of Hong Kong and the harbour, and also — visibility permitting — over the islands of the South China Sea out towards Macau. Alight from the tram, walk down the 30-metre corridor, turn right and take the level road to the right — not the one up the hill — to reach Lugard Rd, which is really only a path for much of the way.

If you are feeling energetic you might walk up to the gardens at the top of the Peak, from which there is a view almost all round the island. For those unable to make the walk, which is steep, there are taxis at the Peak Tram station which will make the trip to the top. From the Peak, one can also walk through Hong Kong's undisturbed countryside by taking the Pokfulam Reservoir Rd running southwest some three kilometres down to Pokfulam Rd from where buses and taxis run either back to Central district or in the opposite direction to Aberdeen, Deepwater Bay and the south coast.

Buy a copy of the Hong Kong Island map available at the HKTA information offices, which clearly shows **Lugard** and **Pokfulam Reservoir** roads and a great many other enjoyable walks.

The Peak tram funicular cable car has been recently modernized (still with old-style carriages) and fully automated and computerized. The tram is often crowded on the ascent, but not so busy on the descent. If you find it busy at the bottom consider taking a taxi to the top and riding the tram down.

To relieve the congestion on the pavements in **Central District**, a network of elevated walkways links the whole area, and most access and exit points are by escalator. There is also a giant "ladder" of escalators linking Central with the Mid-Levels. From Jardine House the walkways take you towards the Macau Ferry Terminal via the Outlying Island ferry terminals in one direction or across the road and through Swire House, Prince's Bldg, The Landmark and the Mandarin Hotel and nearby buildings without having to touch ground to cross a road — often a hazard in Hong Kong.

Two of the most impressive of Hong Kong's skyscrapers are both relatively new — the Hongkong and Shanghai Bank building and the Bank of China Tower, built in very contrasting but equally impressive styles.

But the title of "Tallest Building in Asia" is claimed by Central Plaza in Wanchai. At today's rate of development throughout the re-

51
紅雙喜
高級 名煙
高級名煙
紅雙喜

gion it is a title it may not hold for long.

On Sundays, some of the streets in Central are closed off to traffic and given over to strollers, who include thousands of Filipino maids having their day off. **Government House**, the residence of the British governor of Hong Kong — source of executive power and representative of Queen Elizabeth II — is located on Upper Albert Rd, a right-hand turn from Garden Rd. Across the road are the **Zoological and Botanical Gardens** (with good aviaries) from which one has a better view of Government House. In the early morning Chinese enthusiasts come to practise their graceful art of *tai chi chuan* (shadow-boxing).

Virtually all the 19th century buildings in Hong Kong have made way for modern blocks, with the old **Supreme Court** building (now used by the Legislative Council) opposite the war memorial, and **St John's Cathedral** two of the few old buildings still remaining.

Along Queen's Rd in a westerly direction (to the left as you face the harbour) the streets soon assume a much more Chinese character, and the many open-fronted shops offer an exciting picture of Chinese exotica. Climbing any of the steep, narrow, staircase streets that lead up the hillside from Queen's Rd will lead you to tiny stalls and shops selling a jumble of merchandise.

Of special interest are the curio shops to be found in **Ladder St** and **Hollywood Rd**, which lie up the hill from Queen's Rd. The HKTA has an excellent publication called **Central and Western District Walking Tour** which takes about three-and-a-half hours.

Beginning about 1 kilometres to the east of Central District is **Wanchai**, once the home of the fictional Suzie Wong (at the now modernized Luk Kwok Hotel).

There are still "girlie" bars, but there is little romance about them. Indeed, Wanchai has turned itself into a commercial area. New skyscrapers abound, many "business class" hotels are opening, and the massive Central Plaza does not look that out of place among its towering neighbours.

Nearer the harbour is the **Arts Centre**, which presents hundreds of recitals and shows each year and the Academy for the Performing Arts. On the opposite side of the road to the Arts Centre, the Grand Hyatt and New World Harbour View hotels stand watch at either end of Hong Kong's very impressive **Convention and Exhibition Centre**.

Go into the **Exhibition Centre** and take the escalators up a few floors. The views across the harbour are superb, and there are a couple of very good restaurants in the centre with the view.

Behind the impressive Pacific Place Shopping Centre opposite Admiralty is the **Hong Kong Park**: it is small, but imaginatively laid out, with a large aviary, waterfall, small art gallery and a very pleasant restaurant.

A little way inland from Wanchai is **Happy Valley**, where race meetings are held on alternate Saturday afternoons and Wednesday evenings with Shatin Racecourse from September to June.

Causeway Bay, a little further to the east is an excellent shopping/restaurant area. The **Royal Hong Kong Yacht Club** is located here, opposite the Excelsior Hotel and World Trade Centre. Further to the east is densely-populated North Point.

To reach these areas by tram (ride on the upper deck), you travel along a main road lined almost all the way with shops and restaurants bustling with crowds from early morning to late at night.

Hong Kong is not well provided with museums, but the **Flagstaff House Museum of Tea Ware** in Hong Kong Park offers a rare opportunity to view one of the few specialized collections of its kind in the world. Formed mainly of tea wares of Chinese origin, this impressive collection features pieces from the Six Dynasties to contemporary work.

Flagstaff House itself is an interesting setting for the Museum, and has its own distinct place in the history of Hong Kong. Dating from 1844, it was the home of the Commander of the British Forces. It has been restored as much as possible to its former 19th century glory and is the oldest domestic Western-style building in the territory. Opening hours are 10 a.m.-5 p.m. daily except Wednesdays. Admission is free.

On the far (south) side of Hong Kong Island, and rapidly disappearing under the weight of new high-rise apartment blocks, is the fishing centre of **Aberdeen** (20 minutes by taxi, double the time by minibus or bus from Central District), which is worth a visit for its picturesque harbour jammed with fishing junks and luxury cruisers. A Chinese lunch on board the famous Jumbo floating restaurant is a feature of most organized tours.

Apleichau Island, which forms the outer barrier of the harbour, is worth visiting to see junks being made. A bridge leads to the island.

Ocean Park, an aquatic theme park, is

◄ *Rush-hour in the city.* PHOTO: GERHARD JOREN

located on a picturesque site at **Brick Hill** near Aberdeen. Its attractions including a rather fearsome roller coaster ride called the Dragon which includes a complete loop-the-loop. Rather impressive is an attraction called the **Middle Kingdom**, a collection of recreated temples, shrines and pavilions covering 13 dynasties of Chinese history. The attraction is brought alive by demonstrations of ancient crafts, traditional dancing, lion dances and acrobatics.

Admission to the park is HK$140 for adults, HK$70 for children under 11. There is an Ocean Park Citybus which leaves from the Admiralty MTR station to the park, which is open 10 a.m.-6 p.m. on weekdays and 9:30 a.m.-6 p.m. Sundays and public holidays. Admission to the adjoining **Water World**, a swimming experience with giant slides, winding rivers and assorted swimming pools, is HK$60 for adults, HK$30 for children.

Strung out along Hong Kong Island's southern side are a number of beaches. The water quality varies but most of those listed below are safe for bathing. However, check first. **Repulse Bay** is the largest and most crowded beach (HK$50-60 by taxi from Central District), and there are adequate refreshment facilities in the area. South Bay lies a little further on and has a smaller, quieter beach which can be reached by minibus from Repulse Bay. Immediately to the west of Repulse Bay at **Deepwater Bay** is another good beach.

Further east is Stanley, and following the circuitous coastal road are the beaches of **Shek O** and **Big Wave Bay** on the east coast of Hong Kong Island. You can do a little modest surf-riding at Big Wave Bay when conditions are right. There is lifeguard supervision. At most of the other frequented beaches the sea is usually very calm.

Hong Kong's hills and reservoir areas are an escape from the trauma of downtown; you wander in such fresh and green countryside that you begin to doubt that you are in Hong Kong at all. Roads and trails lead beside streams and lakes where you can enjoy the fine views. Large butterflies are common throughout much of the year, including some quite exotic species.

The Island's centre for walking is **Tai Tam Reservoir**. A copy of the Hong Kong Island map from one of the information offices will be a handy precaution against getting lost. Coming from **Shaukiwan**, on the bus bound for Stanley, you will pass along the shore of the reservoir for about 1 kilometre. Alight at the bus stop at the far end of the reservoir. You enter the park area on the reservoir side of the road.

Immediately to the left is a path leading up some steep steps by the side of a water culvert; this leads for some three kilometres to the southwest, eventually coming out on the main road a short way past Stanley.

Going straight on into the park you cross an embankment, Then proceed through pleasant wooded country into the catchment area. You may choose any of several pathways and even cross over the north side of the Island to reach Happy Valley.

KOWLOON AND THE NEW TERRITORIES

Nathan Rd, which runs up the centre of the Kowloon Peninsular, beginning 200 metres east of the Star Ferry piers, is lined in Tsimshatsui by shops, arcades and hotels. The areas on both sides of the road are crowded with shops and restaurants making up the start of the **Golden Mile** (actually five eighths of a mile) which extends all the way to Boundary Street, via Jordan and Mongkok — all worth a visit. The back streets around Mongkok show Hong Kong street life at its most vibrant.

A good many "girlie" bars can be found in this area. **Temple St** night market in Yaumatei, starting at 6 p.m., is fascinatingly Chinese. The **Jade Market**, a popular attraction and local trading venue, is in Kansu St in Yaumatei. In Hong Lok St hundreds of songbirds are on sale in the aptly named **Bird Market**.

On the waterfront, near the beginning of Nathan Rd is the **Space Museum**, with its dramatic shows in a planetarium — one of the world's most advanced. There is also a Hall of Solar Sciences, and Exhibition Hall and, nearby, the Tsimshatsui **Cultural Centre**.

The promenade from the Star Ferry following the waters' edge past Tsimshatsui East should be walked. This is a half-hour stroll when you are likely to be joined by many of Hong Kong's inhabitants, especially at weekends and in the evenings.

Shatin, in the New Territories, is worth a visit to get some idea of the speed with which Hong Kong is developing. Not long ago it was a simple village on the edge of mud flats.

Now it has some of the territory's latest buildings and is a bustling city in its own right. But Shatin retains a certain charm, not least because it is laid out in a more leisurely fashion than elsewhere. It can be reached easily on the KCR railway line. The HKTA has an *Explorer's Guide to Sai Kung*.

Shatin is also the site of Hong Kong's second racecourse, built on about 250 acres of reclaimed land of a shallow bay at **Tide Cove**. The complex can accommodate nearly 50,000 spectators.

A landscaped bird sanctuary and parkland, **Penfold Park**, is situated in the centre of the racecourse. Adjoining the racecourse is the **Jubilee Sports Centre**. A special station, appropriately named Racecourse, on the KCR line, is opened on race days.

From Shatin you can see the **Amah Rock** — shaped like a woman with a baby on her back. On top of one of the hills above Shatin is the **Ten Thousand Buddhas monastery** (actually 12,800 Buddhas).

Except near the Lok Ma Chau "view of China" hillock, the Chinese frontier is separated from the New Territories by a border area for which — except for those on the train or bus to China — a special permit is needed. Tourists can get a visa to visit China within one or two days. The border crossing facilities are invariably very crowded, but the formalities are otherwise straightforward and uneventful.

Those peering over the border into **Shenzhen** may wonder where Hong Kong ends and China begins. The Shenzhen skyline is just like Hong Kong's, full of skyscrapers and pollution. Those doing business in Asia might want to cross to Shenzhen — no visa is required — just to get a feel of the place. Shenzhen is not typical of China, but the vibrancy of the city does provide an insight into the changes taking place in China.

Impressive in a different way is the **Sung Dynasty** Village, with tours leaving from all major hotels. The 60,000 square-metre village follows the plan of the Sung Dynasty (960-1279 AD), perhaps the greatest epoch for the arts in China. The tours include shows, food and a vivid reconstruction of the era. Tickets cost between HK$210-290 (children HK$165-190).

THE OUTLYING ISLANDS

Much of the New Territories is made up of islands — some 235 in all, many uninhabited — and a visit to one allows a glimpse of the

Kai Tak airport's dramatic approach. PHOTO: RON McMILLAN

more traditional side of Chinese life. A launch or junk picnic to the islands is an ideal way to spend a day, but for the average visitor to Hong Kong it will be more convenient to go by one of the regular ferries.

Ferries to the outer islands leave from the piers marked Outlying Districts on Connaught Rd waterfront, Hong Kong Island, 500 metres west of the Star Ferry piers, in the direction of the Macau Ferry Terminal. Timetables are posted at the piers. Generally avoid travelling on Sundays when the ferries are very crowded.

Peng Chau and **Cheung Chau** are both small islands but densely populated. **Lantau Island**, on the other hand is huge — almost twice the size of Hong Kong Island — and sparsely populated. A hilly ridge runs the length of the island making much of it uninhabitable. Lantau abounds in fascinating walks and uncluttered (and unpolluted) beaches. There is a country parks information booth outside the ferry pier entrance. Most settlements are along the southern coast of the island.

The ferry from Central docks at **Silvermine Bay** (Mui Wo) at the eastern end of Lantau. A bus service meets the ferries and routes serve the several points of interest on the island.

The **Po Lin (Precious Lotus) Monastery** is perhaps the most popular attraction. It stands on a plateau dotted with small pagodas that house the remains of former abbots. A large and ornate temple has been overshadowed by the world's largest outdoor seated bronze Bhudda, perched on the crest of the hills that split the island. It is 34 metres high and weighs some 250 tonnes.

Tai O, the so-called capital of Lantau, is at the far western tip of the island. It is grubby and noisy but still thoroughly authentic. A small boat crosses the creek that divides the town.

Hong Kong's new airport, **Chek Lap Kok**, is being built adjoining Lantau's northern shore, and will probably open in 1998. The effect on other parts of the island may be some years off, but now is the time to see this beautiful island while it is still unspoiled.

Off the west coast of Hong Kong is **Lamma Island**, a favourite place for visitors and Hong Kongers alike to spend an evening at one of the many fish restaurants at **Sok Yu Wan**, reached by regular ferry from Central. The island has no roads and much of it is unspoiled.

The bulk of the population are at the northern end which they share with a massive three-stack power station, which rather spoils the idyllic vistas.

RESTAURANT SELECTION

Average price for two

AMIGO, 79A Wongneichung Rd, Happy Valley. Tel: 2577 2202, 2577 8993. French. US$100.

BEIJING, 34-36 Granville Rd, Kowloon. Tel: 2366 9968. Peking. US$60.

BENKAY JAPANESE, 1st Basement, Gloucester Tower, The Landmark, Central. Tel: 2521 3344. Japanese. US$90.

BLUE OCEAN, 9 Flr, Aberdeen Marina Tower, 8 Shum Wan Rd, Aberdeen. Tel: 2555 9415. Cantonese, *dim sum.* US$35.

CASA MEXICANA, Victoria Centre, Watson's Estate, Hong Kong. Tel: 2566 5560. Tex, Mex. US$40.

CHILI CLUB, 88 Lockhart Rd. Tel: 2527 2872, 2520 2318. Thai. US$45.

DAN RYAN'S CHICAGO GRILL, Pacific Place, Central. Tel: 2845 4600. At Ocean Terminal, Kowloon. Tel: 2735 6111. American. US$60.

DIAMOND, 273 Des Voeux Rd, Central. Tel: 2544 4708. Cantonese, *dim sum.* US$35.

GAYLORD (INDIA), 1 Flr, Ashley Centre, 23-25 Ashley Rd, Kowloon. Tel: 2376 1001. Indian. US$50.

GOLDEN UNICORN, 6 Flr, The Hong Kong Omni Hotel, 3 Canton Rd, Kowloon. Tel: 2730 6565. Cantonese, *dim sum.* US$80.

GRAND CHINESE, 5 Flr, Grand Tower Hotel, 627-641 Nathan Rd, Mongkok. Tel: 2789 0011. *Chiuchow.* US$50.

GREAT SHANGHAI, 26 Prat Ave, Kowloon. Tel: 2366 8158. Shanghai. US$35.

GUANGZHOU GARDEN, 4 Flr, 2 Exchange Square, 8 Connaught Place, Central. Tel: 2525 1163. Cantonese. US$80.

KING HEUNG, G Flr, Riviera Mansions, 59-65 Paterson St, Causeway Bay. Tel: 2577 1035. Peking. US$55.

LANDAU'S, 2 Flr, Sun Hung Kai Centre, Harbour Rd, Wanchai. Tel: 2827 7901. European. US$90.

LA PLACITA, 1301 Times Square, Causeway Bay. Tel: 2506 3308. Mexican. US$45.

MIRAGE THAI SEAFOOD MARKET, 24 Tai She Wan, Leung Shuen, Wan Chau (High Island), Sai Kung. Tel: 2792 2808. Thai. US$40.

SHANGHAI GRAND, 4 Flr, Island Shopping Centre, 1 Great George St, Causeway Bay. Tel: 2890 6828. Shanghai, *dim sum.* US$55.

SZE CHUEN LAU, 466 Lockhart Rd, Wanchai. Tel: 2891 9027. Sichuan. US$50.

W's ENTRECOTE, 1303 Times Square, Causeway Bay. Tel: 2506 0133. French. US$50.

HOTEL GUIDE

HONG KONG ISLAND

A: US$200 and above

CONRAD, Pacific Place, 88 Queensway. Tel: 2521 3838, Fax: 2521 3888, Tlx: 69678. *P, Gym, Biz. R: C, W.*

FURAMA KEMPINSKI, 1 Connaught Rd, Central. Tel: 2525 5111, Fax: 2845 9339, Tlx: 73081. *Gym, Biz. R: C, W, J.*

GRAND HYATT, 1 Harbour Rd, Wanchai. Tel: 2588 1234, Fax: 2802 0677, Tlx: 68434. *P, Gym, Biz. R: C, W.*

HOTEL VICTORIA, Shun Tak Centre, 200 Connaught Rd, Central. Tel: 2540 7228, Fax: 2858 3398, Tlx: 86608. *P, Gym, Biz. R: C, W, Cantonese.*

ISLAND SHANGRI-LA, Pacific Place, Supreme Court Rd. Tel: 2877 3838, Fax: 2521 8742, Tlx: 70373. *P, Gym, Biz. R: C, W, J.*

J.W. MARRIOTT, Pacific Place, 88 Queensway. Tel: 2810 8366, Fax: 2845 0737, Tlx: 66899. *P, Gym, Biz. R: C, W.*

MANDARIN ORIENTAL, 5 Connaught Rd, Central. Tel: 2522 0111, Fax: 2810 6190, Tlx: 73653. *P, Gym, Biz. R: C, W.*

NEW WORLD HARBOUR VIEW, 1 Harbour Rd, Wanchai. Tel: 2802 8888, Fax: 2802 8833, Tlx: 68967. *P, Gym, Biz. R: C, W.*

REGAL HONG KONG, 68 Yee Wo St, Causeway Bay. Tel: 2890 6633, Fax: 2881 0777, Tlx: 62932. *P, Gym. Biz. R: C, W.*

RITZ-CARLTON, 3 Connaught Rd, Central. Tel: 2877 6666, Fax: 2877 6778. *P, Gym, Biz. R: C, W, J.*

P — Swimming pool **Gym** — Health club **Biz** — Business centre **J** — Japanese food
R — Restaurant **C** — Chinese food **W** — Western food

HOTEL GUIDE

B: US$125-200

CENTURY, 238 Jaffe Rd, Wanchai. Tel: 2598 8888, Fax: 2598 8866. *P, Gym, Biz. R: C, W.*

CITY GARDEN, 231 Electric Rd, North Point. Tel: 2887 2888, Fax: 2887 1111, Tlx: 69128. *P, Gym, Biz. R: C, W,*

EVERGREEN PLAZA, 33 Hennessy Rd, Wanchai. Tel: 2866 9111, Fax: 2861 3121, Tlx: 70727. *P, Gym, Biz. R: C, W, J.*

EXCELSIOR, 281 Gloucester Rd, Causeway Bay. Tel: 2894 8888, Fax: 2895 6459, Tlx: 74550. *Biz. R: W.*

LUK KWOK, 72 Gloucester Rd, Wanchai. Tel: 2866 2166, Fax: 2866 2622, Tlx: 69628. *Biz. R: C, W.*

PARK LANE, 310 Gloucester Rd, Causeway Bay. Tel: 2890 3355, Fax: 2576 7853, Tlx: 75343. Gym, *Biz. R: C, W.*

RICHMOND, 1A Wang Tak St, Happy Valley. Tel: 2574 9922, Fax: 2838 1622. *P, Gym, Biz. R: C, W.*

WHARNEY, 57-73 Lockhart Rd, Wanchai. Tel: 2861 1000, Fax: 2865 6023, Tlx: 82590. *P, Gym, Biz. R: W.*

C: US$100-125

CHARTERHOUSE, 209-219 Wanchai Rd, Wanchai. Tel: 2833 5566, Fax: 2833 5888. *Biz. R: C, W.*

GRAND PLAZA, 2 Kornhill Rd, Quarry Bay. Tel: 2886 0011, Fax: 2886 1738, Tlx: 67645. *P, Gym, Biz. R: C.*

NEWTON, 218 Electric Rd, North Point. Tel: 2807 2333, Fax: 2807 1221. *P, Biz. R: C, W.*

SOUTH CHINA, 23 Morrison Hill Rd, Wanchai. Tel: 2572 3838, Fax: 2893 7773. *Biz. R: C, W.*

D: US$60-100

HARBOUR VIEW INTERNATIONAL HOUSE, 4 Harbour Rd, Wanchai. Tel: 2802 0111, Fax: 2802 9063, Tlx: 61073. *R: W.*

NEW CATHAY, 17 Tung Lo Wan Rd, Causeway Bay. Tel: 2577 8211, Fax: 2576 9365, Tlx: 72089. *R: C.*

NEW HARBOUR, 41-49 Hennessy Rd, Wanchai. Tel: 2861 1166, Fax: 2865 6111, Tlx: 65641.

WESLEY, 22 Hennessy Rd, Wanchai. Tel: 2866 6688, Fax: 2866 6633, Tlx: 47666. *Biz. R: C, W.*

KOWLOON/NEW TERRITORIES

A: US$200 and above

HOLIDAY INN CROWNE PLAZA HARBOUR VIEW, 70 Mody Rd, Tsimshatsui East. Tel: 2721 5161, Fax: 2369 5672, Tlx: 38670. *P, Gym, Biz. R: C, W, J.*

HONG KONG RENAISSANCE, 8 Peking Rd, Tsimshatsui. Tel: 2375 1133, Fax: 2375 1066, Tlx: 45243. *P, Gym, Biz, squash courts. R: C, W.*

HYATT REGENCY, 67 Nathan Rd, Tsimshatsui. Tel: 2311 1234, Fax: 2739 8701, Tlx: 43127. *Biz. R: C, W.*

KOWLOON SHANGRI-LA, 64 Mody Rd, Tsimshatsui. Tel: 2721 2111, Fax: 2723 8686, Tlx: 36718. *P, Gym, Biz. R: C, W, J.*

NEW WORLD, 22 Salisbury Rd, Tsimshatsui. Tel: 2369 4111, Fax: 2369 9387, Tlx: 35860. *P, Gym, Biz. R: C, W.*

NIKKO, 72 Mody Rd, Tsimshatsui East. Tel: 2739 1111, Fax: 2311 3122, Tlx: 31302. *P, Gym, Biz. R: C, W, J.*

OMNI MARCO POLO, Harbour City, Canton Rd, Tsimshatsui. Tel: 2736 0888, Fax: 2736 0022, Tlx: 40077. *Biz. R: W.*

OMNI HONG KONG, Harbour City, 3 Canton Rd, Tsimshatsui. Tel: 2736 0088, Fax: 2736 0011, Tlx: 43838. *P. R: C, W, J.*

OMNI PRINCE, Harbour City, Canton Rd, Tsimshatsui. Tel: 2736 1888, Fax: 2736 0066, Tlx: 50950. *P, Biz. R: Asian.*

THE PENINSULA, Salisbury Rd, Tsimshatsui. Tel: 2366 6251, Fax: 2722 4170, Tlx: 43821. *Biz. R: C, W.*

THE REGENT, Salisbury Rd, Tsimshatsui. Tel: 2721 1211, Fax: 2739 4546, Tlx: 37134. *P, Gym, Biz. R: C, W.*

ROYAL GARDEN, 69 Mody Rd, Tsimshatsui East. Tel: 2721 5215, Fax: 2369 9976, Tlx: 39539. *Biz. R: C, W, J.*

SHERATON, 20 Nathan Rd, Tsimshatsui. Tel: 2369 1111, Fax: 2739 8707, Tlx: 45813. *P, Gym, Biz. R: C, W, J.*

B: US$125-200

HOLIDAY INN GOLDEN MILE, 50 Nathan Rd, Tsimshatsui. Tel: 2369 3111, Fax: 2369 8016, Tlx: 56332. *P, Gym, Biz. R: C, W.*

MIRAMAR, 118 Nathan Rd, Tsimshatsui. Tel: 2368 1111, Fax: 2369 1788, Tlx: 44661. *P, Gym, Biz. R: C, W, Vietnamese.*

PARK, 61-65 Chatham Rd South, Tsimshatsui. Tel: 2366 1371, Fax: 2739 7259, Tlx: 45740. *Biz. R: C, W.*

P — Swimming pool
R — Restaurant
Gym — Health club
C— Chinese food
Biz — Business centre
W — Western food
J—Japanese food

HOTEL GUIDE

RAMADA, 73-75 Chatham Rd South, Tsimshatsui. Tel: 2311 1100, Fax: 2311 6000. *Biz. R: W, J.*

REGAL KOWLOON, 71 Mody Rd, Tsimshatsui East. Tel: 2722 1818, Fax: 2369 6950, Tlx: 40955. *Gym, Biz. R: C, W, J.*

ROYAL PACIFIC, China Hong Kong City, 33 Canton Rd, Tsimshatsui. Tel: 2736 1188, Fax: 2736 1212, Tlx: 44111. *Gym, Biz. R: Swiss.*

C: US$100-125

CONCOURSE, 22 Lai Chi Kok Rd, Mongkok. Tel: 2397 6683, Fax: 2381 3768, Tlx: 46841. *R: C, Korean.*

EATON, 380 Nathan Rd, Yaumatei. Tel: 2782 1818, Fax: 2782 5563, Tlx: 42862. *R: C, Thai.*

GRAND TOWER, 627 Nathan Rd, Mongkok. Tel: 2789 0011, Fax: 2789 0945, Tlx: 31602. *R: C, J, Asian.*

GUANGDONG, 18 Prat Ave, Tsimshatsui. Tel: 2739 3311, Fax: 2721 1137, Tlx: 49067. *R: C, W.*

HILLVIEW, 13-17 Observatory Rd, Tsimshatsui. Tel: 2722 7822, Fax: 2723 3718, Tlx: 45051. *R: C, W.*

KIMBERLEY, 28 Kimberley Rd, Tsimshatsui. Tel: 2723 3888, Fax: 2723 1318, Tlx: 43198. *Gym. R: C, J.*

KOWLOON, 19-21 Nathan Rd, Tsimshatsui. Tel: 2369 8698, Fax: 2369 9811, Tlx: 47604. *R: C, W.*

KOWLOON PANDA, 3 Tsuen Wah St, Tsuen Wan, N.T. Tel: 2409 1111, Fax: 2409 1818. *P, Gym. R: C, W.*

METROPOLE, 75 Waterloo Rd. Tel: 2761 1711, Fax: 2761 0769, Tlx: 45063. *P. R: C, W.*

NEW ASTOR, 11 Carnavon Rd, Tsimshatsui. Tel: 2366 7261, Fax: 2722 7122, Tlx: 52222.

REGAL AIRPORT, Sa Po Rd, Kowloon City. Tel: 2718 0333, Fax: 2718 4111, Tlx: 40950. *R: C, W, J.*

REGAL RIVERSIDE, Tai Chung Kiu Rd, Shatin, N.T. Tel: 2649 7878, Fax: 2637 4748, Tlx: 30013. *P, Gym. R: C, W, Asian.*

ROYAL PARK, 8 Pak Hok Ting St, Shatin, N.T. Tel: 2601 2111, Fax: 2601 3666, Tlx: 45776. *P, Gym, Biz, tennis courts. R: C, J.*

WARWICK, East Bay, Cheung Chau Island, N.T. Tel: 2981 0081, Fax: 2981 9174, Tlx: 67790. *P. R: C, W.*

WINDSOR, 39 Kimberley Rd, Tsimshatsui. Tel: 2739 5665, Fax: 2311 5101, Tlx: 44419. *R: C.*

D: US$60-100

BANGKOK ROYAL, 2-12 Pilkem St, Yaumatei. Tel: 2735 9181, Fax: 2730 2209, Tlx: 52999. *R: C, W, Thai.*

IMPERIAL, 30-34 Nathan Rd, Tsimshatsui. Tel: 2366 2201, Fax: 2311 2360, Tlx: 55893.

INTERNATIONAL, 33 Cameron Rd, Tsimshatsui. Tel: 2366 3381, Fax: 2369 5381, Tlx: 34749. *R: C, W.*

KING'S, 473 Nathan Rd, Yaumatei. Tel: 2780 1281, Fax: 2782 1833. *R: C, W, Thai.*

NATHAN, 378 Nathan Rd, Yaumatei. Tel: 2388 5141, Fax: 2770 4262, Tlx: 31037. *R: C.*

PRUDENTIAL, 222 Nathan Rd, Jordan. Tel: 2311 8222, Fax: 2311 4760, Tlx: 46752. *P. Biz.*

SHAMROCK, 223 Nathan Rd, Yaumatei. Tel: 2735 2271, Fax: 2736 7354, Tlx: 50561. *R: W, Malaysian.*

STANFORD, 118 Soy St, Mongkok. Tel: 2781 1881, Fax: 2388 3733. *R: C, W.*

HOSTELS & GUEST HOUSES

US$40 and above

CARITAS BIANCHI LODGE, 4 Cliff Rd, Yaumatei. Tel: 2388 1111, Fax: 2770 6669. *R: C, W.*

CARITAS LODGE (BOUNDARY STREET), 134 Boundary St, Kowloon. Tel: 2339 3777, Fax: 2338 2864.

GARDEN VIEW INT. HOUSE (YWCA), 1 Macdonnell Rd, Mid-Levels. Tel: 2877 3737, Fax: 2845 6263. *P, Gym.*

S. T. B. HOSTEL, 2 Flr Great Eastern Mansion, 255-261 Reclamation St, Mongkok. Tel: 2710 9199, Fax: 2385 0153.

Y.M.C.A. of HONG KONG (English-speaking), 41 Salisbury Rd, Tsimshatsui. Tel: 2369 2211, Fax: 2739 9315. *P, Gym, squash courts. R: W, Asian.*

Y.M.C.A. INTERNATIONAL HOUSE, 23 Waterloo Rd, Yaumatei. Tel: 2771 9111, Fax: 2388 5926.

Y.W.C.A. GUESTHOUSE, 5 Man Fuk Rd, Waterloo Hill Rd, Kowloon. Tel: 2713 9211, Fax: 2761 1269.

P — Swimming pool
R — Restaurant
Gym — Health club
C— Chinese food
Biz — Business centre
W — Western food
J—Japanese food

MEGURO

JAPAN

Japan is such a complex place with so many layers of society and activity that it is not surprising that Japanese customs and civilization can be exceedingly difficult for foreigners to take in. Yet it is surprising that the average visitor will find in the strange mixture of old and new, subtle and brash, expensive and cheap, much that overlaps with his or her own way of life, so that there is much to be enjoyed amid the apparent confusion.

The capital, Tokyo, is an enormous sprawling city with a population of about 15 million. Only from the air at night can one get a clear idea of just how large it really is, with lights stretching into the far distance in almost every direction. Tokyo manages to be frantic, energetic and automated, yet often personal. Happily, next to its modern aspects, traditional cultural forms such as sumo wrestling, kabuki and wonderful seasonal cuisine still thrive, and with a little help from local friends, you can have a splendid evening out which will cost you far less than an evening in (say) Hong Kong. On the other hand, the pace of life in this fantastic place leaves little margin for error. It takes only a visit to a bar in the Ginza or Roppongi to spend a fortune.

Traditional Japan has a stronger and more obvious hold outside the major cities, and in the countryside the visitor in search of Japanese culture can find more than enough to satisfy the most avid curiosity. Kyoto, with its magnificent temples, inns and natural surroundings, is an essential stop for many foreigners, and a dream for those interested in photography. Nara, Nikko and the former seaside capital of Kamakura also attract thousands of visitors each year.

Despite widespread industrial pollution in Japan, which has been recognized as a serious problem (and which has prompted efforts to avoid spoiling the environment further), there is much visual beauty. And just as you must leave New York or London to see the real America or Britain, your visit to Japan will be a much richer experience if you venture off the well-trodden tourist track. Most visitors confine their stay in Japan to Honshu, the main island. Although there are plenty of worthwhile sights and scenes on Honshu, the other main islands of Hokkaido, Kyushu and Shikoku all offer a range of experiences that will significantly deepen the Japanese experience.

Hokkaido, for example, has scenery to rival that of the western United States wide-open spaces, while its climate resembles that of Scandinavia. Although most tourists flock to Japan in spring and autumn, a summer trip to Hokkaido provides much cooler temperatures than the sauna conditions prevalent on the other Japanese islands. And Hokkaido's long winter season offers skiers and other outdoor sports fans many months to choose from.

Kyushu — as well as boasting of the strongest men and the most beautiful women in Japan — also has rolling green hills, tea plantations, possibly the best hot-spring baths in Japan and several active volcanoes, including the magnificent Mt Aso, and the recently reawakened Mt Unzen.

Separated from the main island by the Inland Sea, the island of Shikoku — least Westernized by the post-World War II allied occupation forces — is often perceived as having been left out of

◄ *Girls in traditional dress.* PHOTO: GREG GIRARD

Japan's "economic miracle". But Shikoku is shedding its backward image, as seen by major projects aimed at opening up its economic potential. Its seafood, as well as its *mikan* (Japanese oranges) are deservedly famous throughout Japan.

Throughout the lesser-known parts of Japan, prices are lower and people often more receptive to foreigners. They have more time, and their natural curiosity remains much less jaded than dwellers in Japan's urban canyons. So, whether you are paying your first or one of many trips to Japan, try to get outside Tokyo.

History

The Japanese people are considered as being chiefly of Mongoloid stock, having come originally from the Asian mainland via the Korean peninsula. There is also thought to be an ethnic element introduced from Southeast Asia.

Although ancestors of the Japanese were making primitive pottery as early as 10,000 BC, it was not until around AD 300 that the various clan groupings scattered in the relatively isolated river valleys of Honshu Island were brought into loose confederacy under the rule of the state of Yamatai. Beginning with this rise to ascendancy of the people based near the present-day town of Nara, Japan could reasonably be called a nation.

Much of the early development of the nation was along Chinese lines. The written language at first utilized Chinese characters while elements of Confucianism — and later during the sixth century, Buddhism — were introduced as supplements to the indigenous Shinto beliefs. During the sixth and seventh centuries, ambitious and progressive rulers gradually brought about a structuring of the society along the lines of the contemporary Chinese state of T'ang and in AD 710 the first permanent Japanese capital, Nara, was founded.

The capital was shifted to Kyoto in 794. Kyoto remained nominally the capital, though for centuries far from the real centre of power, up to 1868. After a period of stability, imperial power began to be eclipsed by the rich landowning families, chief among whom were the Fujiwaras, who went on virtually to rule the country up to the early 11th century. What is called the Heian Period lasted until 1185 and saw the flowering of Japanese culture, including the adoption of the Japanese kana syllabaries — Japan's "alphabet" — as something increasingly independent from China.

Following a period of bitter fighting between the Minamoto and Taira clans in the late 12th century, imperial power collapsed completely, to be replaced by that of the newly titled shoguns, first of whom was the eventual victor in the clan wars, Minamoto Yoritomo, who came to power in 1192. The line of emperors continued, though with little more than ceremonial purpose. The Minamoto ruled from their power base in the town of Kamakura, located about 50 kilometres southeast of Tokyo.

In the late 13th century, Kublai Khan's Mongol Dynasty in China, which had overpowered Korea, attempted to repeat the conquest in Japan but its armada was defeated (once in 1274 and again in 1281) with the aid of typhoons which the Japanese gratefully named *kamikaze* — divine wind.

The second of the great shogunal families, the Ashikaga, came to power in 1338 and was to rule from Kyoto over what is known as the Muromachi Period until 1573. It was during the later years of the period that the first Europeans, including Francis Xavier, visited Japan.

Much of the 16th century was marked by fighting in the independent domains within the country, each under the rule of a local aristocratic lord known as the *daimyo*. It was only with the advent of Toyotomi Hideyoshi — and his successor Tokugawa Ieyasu — that the country was reunified. Ieyasu's victory at the battle of Sekigahara marked the beginning of the Tokugawa Period — also known as Edo (the name of the town from which the Tokugawas ruled and which was destined to be renamed Tokyo). From its beginning in 1603 this, the third great shogunate, governed until the restoration of the emperor in 1868.

After some 80 years of contact with Europeans — chiefly the Portuguese, Spanish and Dutch — the Tokugawas resolved to have no more to do with the outsiders, chiefly it seems from fears that their domestic adversaries might profit from foreign support. So Japan embarked on a period of isolation from the outside world. Nevertheless, it was a period marked by consolidation of the national social structure into what was to become a springboard for the amazing progress that followed during the second half of the 19th century.

JAPAN
CHINA
RUSSIA
HOKKAIDO ISLAND
Daisetsuzan National Park
Abashiri
Sounkyo Gorge
Asahikawa
Sapporo
Otaru
Kushiro
Noboribetsu
Akan National Park
Hakodate
Railways
Aomori
Sea of Japan
Akita
Morioka
N
Yamagata
Sendai
Fukushima
HONSHU ISLAND
Niigata
Toyama
Kanazawa
Himeji
Fukui
Tokyo
Choshi
Matsumoto
Chiba
Matsue
Tottori
Yokohama
Izumo
Kyoto
Nagoya
Hakone
Iwakuni
Okayama
Kobe
Shimoda
Hiroshima
Osaka
Toba
Mt. Fuji
Kitakyushu
Ise
Imabari
Fukuoka
Saga
Beppu
Wakayama
Tokushima
SHIKOKU ISLAND
Takamatsu
Kotohira
Pacific Ocean
Oita
Matsuyama
Uwajima
Kumamoto
Miyazaki
Nagasaki
Hinagu
KYUSHU ISLAND
Kagoshima
km
0
400

Japan's isolation was finally broken by the arrival of an American, Commodore Perry, at Uraga in 1853. Thereafter, Japan modernized its administrative and economic structure and started out on its quest for world power; this was to include conquests in Korea, Manchuria, China and finally Southeast Asia. Defeat in World War II put an end to the country's aspirations in that direction. Today, as Asia's dominant economic power, Japan has emerged from the protective wing of the U.S. to challenge it as a world financial power. A severe earthquake centred near Kobe on January 17, 1995 killed 5,000 people and did trillions of yen worth of damage to buildings, roads, ports and other infrastructure in Japan's Kansai region surrounding Osaka and Kobe, disrupting transport between eastern and western sections of the country.

The country's recent moves towards more involvement in world politics seem to have gained impetus following the death in January 1989 of Emperor Hirohito, and the ascension of the crown prince, now Emperor Akihito.

While the imperial family religion is Shinto, which with vigorous government support remains a formidable influence in the lives of most Japanese, Buddhism and residual Confucianism are also major cultural forces. Japanese Christians, about half Catholic and half Protestant, number around 1.5 million.

Entry

Japan's air transport facilities are becoming increasingly strained by rising international traffic. Around 50 airlines currently operate into Tokyo (Narita Terminals 1 & 2) and Osaka (Kansai, opened in 1994) international airports from Asia as well as Europe, North and South America and Australia. A departure tax of ¥2,000 (¥1,000 for children two to 11 years old) is levied at Narita airport, and ¥2,500 (¥1,300 for children) at Kansai.

Passenger ships sail several times weekly between the South Korean port of Pusan and the Japanese port of Shimonoseki. There are also cruise services between Yokohama and Nakhodka in Russia and between Naha in Okinawa and Keelung in Taiwan.

Immigration

Apart from the exemptions listed, foreign visitors require a valid passport with a visa issued by a Japanese consular officer abroad or by the head of the Japanese Embassy or legation. Visas are valid for 90 days or less for travellers in transit and for tourists. Commercial visas, for those visiting Japan on business, are issued on a case-by-case basis for varying periods.

Multiple-entry visas are issued to some foreign nationals, with the duration of validity dependent on the reciprocal arrangement reached with each country. Validity of a visa indicates only the time period within which the visa may be used, not the period of stay actually allowed in Japan.

Citizens of the following countries are exempted from obtaining visas, providing they do not engage in business while in the country: For a stay of six months or less: Austria, Germany, Ireland, Liechtenstein, Mexico, Switzerland, and the United Kingdom except when the passport is originally issued in British colonial territories.

For a stay of three months or less: Argentina, Bahamas, Bangladesh, Barbados, Belgium, Canada, Chile, Colombia, Costa Rica, Cyprus, Denmark, Dominica, El Salvador, Finland, France, Greece, Guatemala, Honduras, Iceland, Iran, Israel, Italy, Lesotho, Luxembourg, Malaysia, Malta, Mauritius, Netherlands, New Zealand, Norway, Pakistan, Peru, Portugal (except when the passport is originally issued in present or former Portuguese colonial territories), San Marino, Singapore, Spain, Surinam, Sweden, Tunisia, Turkey, Uruguay, the U.S.: for a stay of up to 14 days, Brunei.

Special permits instead of visas are issued in the cases of passengers on commercial carriers for maximum 72-hour layovers ashore at a Japanese port while the vessel or aircraft remains at the point of entry, or for a maximum of 15 days to allow an in-transit overland tour between two ports, as long as the passengers depart Japan on the same vessel.

For an extension of the period of stay, application must be made to the appropriate immigration office on any date prior to expiry of the original permission. Extensions are not granted automatically.

Exit Formalities: passports must be stamped by the immigration inspector.

Health

No inoculations are needed to enter Japan. Travellers' medical insurance is recommended, as medical services are costly.

Customs

On arrival, air passengers are required to give only an oral declaration of contents of baggage, though passengers arriving by ship and those with unaccompanied baggage must complete declaration documents. Customs duty will not be levied on personal effects or on dutiable goods if they are for personal use and the customs officer considers them of a reasonable quantity. Portable professional equipment is allowed duty-free entry. Duty-free entry of tobacco products is limited to 400 cigarettes, or 100 cigars, or 500 grams of tobacco; three bottles of liquor (each 760 millilitres); 60 millilitres of perfume; goods other than the above with a total market value not exceeding ¥200,000. Narcotics, obscene materials, weapons and ammunition are all prohibited imports.

Currency

The yen is the unit of currency in Japan, in April 1995 exchanging at a rate of about ¥90:US$1, though the yen is floating and so varies in exchange value from day to day, and rose sharply from about ¥120 against the U.S. dollar over only a few months. Currency notes in denominations of ¥10,000, 5,000, and 1,000 are in circulation, with coins of ¥500, 100, 50, 10, 5 and 1. No limit exists on import and export of foreign currency. Import of Japanese currency is unlimited, but export is limited to ¥5 million. Approximately equal exchange rates are given by banks, authorized moneychangers and by hotels (though the latter in many cases will show a ¥2-3 spread). Both the Tokyo and Osaka international airports have 24-hour banking services to facilitate currency exchange.

Language

Japanese is the national language, and the only one spoken universally throughout the country. Many visitors are surprised that despite the plethora of signboards and advertising in English, relatively few Japanese are comfortable speaking it. English is, however, spoken extensively in hotels and shops catering to foreign tourists, but only minimally beyond such places. Japanese inns (*ryokan*) rarely have any staff able to communicate in English, but some Japanese patrons may wish to practise their conversation. English is taught as a second language in schools, so when asking for directions it is best to ask a young person who will be more likely to understand a little simple English.

Train stations and major roads have their names displayed in English, as well as Japanese, but most other transport facilities use Japanese only. Written Japanese uses a combination of syllabic symbols (*kana*) and characters borrowed from the Chinese (*kanji*), so it is impossible for a visitor unfamiliar with the system to read signs of any kind in Japanese.

But with some determination, you can learn some principal Japanese characters before you arrive in Japan. The effort is worth it. It also helps a lot to learn how to pronounce Japanese written in Romanized form, so you will be able to use place names with some hope of being understood by the Japanese. It may help to remember that consonants are always separated by vowels, with the only exception of "n." It is easier to get the hang of it by pronouncing English loan-words in their Japanese form e.g. restaurant = resutoranto. There are thousands of examples like this; you may be surprised how far a little guesswork and "Japlish" can go. In general, it is advisable to get directions written in Japanese for any place you may wish to visit. This is virtually essential when you travel by taxi in the large cities.

Climate

Although Japan is in the temperate zone it experiences markedly variable conditions of climate throughout the year. Apart from the temperature differences between Hokkaido in the north and Okinawa in the south, the fluctuations between summer and winter are extreme, ranging from above 30°C to well below zero. Cold winds from Siberia in winter and hot, humid winds from the Pacific in summer are largely responsible for the variation. These two factors also explain the differences in climate between the Japan Sea coast and the Pacific coast. Summer along the Pacific coast is hot and humid, while winter is usually cold and dry. Summer on the Japan Sea coast is relatively dry while in winter the moisture-laden wind from the sea brings heavy snowfalls to the western slopes of the mountain ranges.

With the exception of Hokkaido there is a wet season lasting through late June and early July.

Tokyo's average winter temperatures are -1°C-9°C; spring, 8.5-18°C; summer, 22-30°C; autumn, 13-21°C.

Hokkaido, the northern island, has an almost six-month-long winter and is snow-bound for at least four months of the year. In the main city of Sapporo the average minimum temperature in winter is -10°C.

Dress

Light clothing is all that is necessary for summer months in the hot and often humid main cities along the Honshu Pacific coast. Spring and autumn often get quite chilly and woollens will be required, especially in the evenings. Mountain areas are cooler. Winter gets cold and there are snowfalls all over Honshu Island. Heavy winter clothing is required and particularly heavy if travelling in Hokkaido.

A wide range of good quality Western-style clothing can be bought in Japan, but sizes tend to be small, especially for women's clothing and all kinds of shoes.

Business Hours

Government and private company offices are open from 9 a.m. until 5 p.m. Mondays to Fridays. Post offices are open 9 a.m.-5 p.m. weekdays. A few central branches keep longer daily hours and are open seven days a week. Commercial and savings banks are open 9 a.m.-3 p.m. Mondays to Fridays, closed on weekends. Automatic teller machines are open weekdays 8.45 a.m.-7 p.m. and Saturdays and Sundays 9 a.m.-5 p.m., but do not operate on public holidays. Large city shops usually open at around 10 a.m. and remain open until around 8 p.m., with regular business hours each day of the week in most cases.

Department stores open 10 a.m-6 or 7 p.m. six days a week: the various stores stagger their one-day holiday so that you can always find several department stores open any day. Convenience stores such as 7-Eleven are found throughout Japan. Restaurants in the main cities open in time for lunch, and close around 10 p.m. or 11 p.m. Lunch is taken at mid-day by most Japanese, resulting in a frantic rush in the business districts, easily avoidable if you eat an hour later. The traditional Japanese places close early, usually around 9 p.m. or 10 p.m.

Doing Business

Much has been written about Japan's long period of isolation, its racial homogeneity and the effects of these upon the national psyche. And while the Japanese do have some customs which may be considered uniquely peculiar (not least by the Japanese themselves), foreigners on business visits here cannot go far wrong behaving in much the same way as anywhere else where courtesy is called for. Few Japanese expect the intricacies of their social behaviour to be grasped instantly — many would prefer they never were. A few points however are worth keeping in mind.

Meeting people is likely to take up much of any business trip to Japan. Namecards (*meishi*) are essential — in Japan they determine more than anything else (by company name, size and status) the way business people regard each other on first meeting. This is perhaps less true for foreigners, but a name card should be regarded respectfully and studied carefully when received and not put quickly away without study. If you are meeting around a table it is common practice to leave the cards face up on the table until the end of discussion.

The Japanese do not shake hands between themselves, but you may find that the people you meet expect that you would like to. Letting them make the first move is usually wise. If bowing does not make you feel awkward, bow.

Meetings and conferences both short, long, productive and inefficient are a staple activity of corporate life in Japan. Foreign visitors may be left wondering what else there is to talk about, but patience is advisable — just when everything looks settled is when it is all most likely to change again, necessitating of course, more meetings. A book once published on doing business here was aptly subtitled *Never Take Yes for an Answer*. On the other hand, many Japanese people do not take kindly to what they view as "pushy" behaviour, and a little discretion will go a long way.

Nevertheless, one advantage of a Japanese-style meeting is that all grievances and doubts can usually be aired, and while open confrontation is definitely not recommended, foreign visitors can get away with being a little more direct in stating their opinions than their Japanese counterparts. A good interpreter is invaluable for rephrasing the visitor's requests more euphemistically.

Little English is spoken in Japan although international companies tend to have a fair number of English speakers. If possible arrange your own interpreter. Jokes and the use of irony and sarcasm in business discussions are not on the whole appreciated — sometimes even the most innocent-seeming humour can give the impression that you are not serious.

While there are few women in powerful positions in Japan, women in business are generally accepted, though Japan certainly lags behind the West in this respect. Smoking is common with some 60% of male adults being smokers. Some companies have made moves to restrict smoking in the workplace — smoke only if there is an ashtray.

As might be expected, the Japanese in general place importance on punctuality. If running late for a meeting, think twice before jumping into a taxi when a subway is nearby.

The Japanese love to drink, and going for a drink after work is the norm. Alcohol not only relaxes the tired worker; it allows people to convey their true feelings (or furnishes an excuse for doing so) on any number of matters. Something which may not be acceptable at work — especially with the constraints of the seniority-by-age hierarchy — can be said over a drink. Such gatherings are worth attending for the insight they provide. When drinking it is customary not to serve yourself — there is the saying "he who fills his own glass is an alcoholic" — though most Japanese regard it as simply good manners to pour each other drinks (or have an office junior do it). When your host offers, raise your glass so that he or she may fill it. You can then reciprocate. Drinks at lunch are very rare and mostly frowned upon.

Going to lunch in any of Japan's business centres is typically a hurried affair. Most people seem to decide what they wish to eat before even entering the restaurant. Eating is carried out at an equally fast pace. Noodles of all sorts are slurped loudly.

Given the cramped living quarters of most Japanese, it is unlikely that you will be invited to a dinner party at your host's home. More probably you will be taken to a restaurant and then on to a bar or even for karaoke if things progress that far. Do not hesitate to make a fool of yourself — this is highly appropriate when drinking and will endear you to your hosts no end. Events of the night before are not usually brought up the next day.

In the event that you are invited to someone's house or apartment, you will probably be given some slippers to wear after you have removed your shoes in the entrance. A small gift will be well appreciated — indeed this holds true for any time you have enjoyed somebody's hospitality, though often a clearly conveyed "thank you" the following day is enough. And as with most any other people, the Japanese will be delighted if you try and use simple greetings in their own language.

Courier, car-rental and secretarial services: Tokyo (Area Code 03): Courier: **Sagawa Kyubin**, 3699 3333. Car rental: **Nippon Rent-a-Car**, 3845 7196. Limousine: **Hinomaru Limousine**, 3505 0707. Translation: **Simul International**, 3586 8911. Secretarial: **Pasona Inc.**, 3508 1431.

Osaka (Area Code 06): Courier: **Sagawa Kyubin**, 647 5101. Limousine: **Hinomaru Hire**, 853 6221. Translation: **Simul International**, 231 2441. Secretarial: **Pasona Inc.**, 363 8404.

Nagoya (Area Code 052): Courier: **Sagawa Kyubin** 652 2121. Car rental & translation — contact Tokyo or Osaka offices. Secretarial: **Pasona Inc.**, 951 1421.

Fukuoka (Area Code 092): Courier: **Sagawa Kyubin**, 574 1111. Car rental & translation — call Tokyo or Osaka offices. Secretarial: **Pasona Inc.**, 711 1600.

Sapporo (Area Code 011): Courier: **Sagawa Kyubin**, 865 3333. Car rental & translation — call Tokyo or Osaka offices. Secretarial: **Pasona Inc.**, 241 2171.

Rip-Offs

Virtually everything in Japan and especially Tokyo (except perhaps the subway) is expensive. This is true of local food, anything imported, cosmetics, coffee shops, medical care and taxi fares. However apart from these institutionalized "rip-offs," there are few traps for the visitor unless you stray into the realm of gangster-run entertainment, which can cost a great deal of money. Anybody planning to reside in Japan will be shocked by the common requirement of paying six months' rent in advance for a house or apartment, of which only two months are refundable. One month's rent is given to the agent as a fee, and another two months goes to the landlord as a gift. For a very average dwelling in Tokyo, the six months can easily come to US$10,000.

Ask prices anywhere they are not advertised. Most central Tokyo restaurants print their menus with prices in Japanese only. The amount you are charged will often be presented as a lump sum, sometimes only verbally, but almost without exception this will be correct, as will your change. The stereotype image of the Japanese as being scrupulously honest is in this instance basically true. One exception is the upmarket sushi shops and bars which do not display prices. Here, the head waiter or waitress will quote you a price which may sometimes appear to be determined by his or her subjective feelings towards you — and do not confuse this price with the basic cover charge of many bars.

Street crime is rare though drunks can be a nuisance. There have been some reports of foreign women being molested so a degree of caution is advisable. Unfortunately, if you are in trouble in Japan, few bystanders are likely to rush to your aid. With the economic slowdown, newspapers are emphasizing supermarket robberies and pickpocketing, but in fact you can enjoy Japan safely with about a tenth of the street sense necessary to survive in almost any other country.

Communications

Japan has very good communications links with the outside world and it is easy to make international calls from public telephones in all the major cities. Pre-paid telephone cards are readily available at railway kiosks and often from vending machines inside telephone booths themselves. And since the mammoth KDD corporation lost its monopoly on overseas calls, rates have come down significantly.

International fax is available from all good hotels.

Transport

FROM TOKYO AIRPORT: Travel to and from Tokyo International Airport at Narita, 60 kilometres east of downtown Tokyo, can be either a breeze or a nightmare, depending on your time of arrival or departure and the day of the week.

There are five main means of transport to and from Narita airport: the easiest is perhaps the new Narita Express train which makes 23 round trips a day. A trip to central Tokyo takes about an hour, and costs ¥2,890. Then there is the Limousine Bus service running from the downtown Tokyo City Air Terminal (TCAT), which is especially convenient for those leaving the country. If your airline happens to be one of those utilizing check-in facilities at TCAT, you can check your baggage there and go through security checks and immigration, thus avoiding a repeat performance at Narita (those arriving in Japan who wish to ride the bus into Tokyo can buy tickets at the counter in the lobby just outside customs.) The buses leave every five to 20 minutes — different buses connect the airport with all parts of Tokyo and directly with most major hotels. The trip usually takes about 70 minutes (it can take as little as 55 minutes or as long as two-and-a-half hours — important for departing passengers to remember). The cost is ¥2,800-2,900.

Another means of transport, if you either know your way around Tokyo or are adventurous, is the Keisei Railway Skyliner express train that travels between Narita and Tokyo's Ueno station. The trip takes an hour (with trains leaving every 30 minutes) and the price is ¥1,740. The drawbacks are that you must carry your own baggage (space for which is limited on the train) and seats on the Skyliner are reserved, so if you hit a busy period you may have to wait for the next express. A slower express is also available on the same railway (75 minutes' travelling time to or from the airport) at only ¥940 per one-way ticket, but this means you must ride with daily commuters as well as air passengers — not recommended.

Japan Railways (JR) also has a Tokyo-Narita link but it is a bit more primitive and time-consuming. JR runs 16 rapid express round-trips per day between Tokyo Station and Narita Airport Terminals 1 & 2. Cost: ¥1,260 one-way. If expense does not matter, a taxi is the obvious means for travelling between the airport and the city. Clear roads and a fast driver could allow you to cover the distance in an hour. Price: ¥25,000, or higher. International passengers who seek to meet connecting domestic flights also have transport. A limousine bus offers passengers direct service to and from Narita and Haneda airports which takes from one-and-a-half hours upwards; Price: ¥2,900. Haneda Airport is easily reached from central Tokyo by a monorail link from JR Hamamatsucho Station. Note: Taiwan's China Airlines is the only international carrier to use Haneda.

TRAINS AND SUBWAYS: Travelling by train and subway is the key to getting about cheaply and rapidly in Tokyo. There are dozens of lines serving the inner city area, as well as running into the sprawling outer suburbs and neighbouring districts from suburban terminals such as Shinjuku and Ueno as well as Tokyo Central. Taken as a whole it is a vast network, but the newcomer can very quickly become familiar with the inner area transport. For travelling further afield get specific instructions from your

Tokyo 'Salarymen' rush to work. PHOTO: LIAU CHUNG REN

hotel or the Japan National Tourist Organization (JNTO) or at the railway stations.

The most useful train line in Tokyo for the visitor is the JR Yamanote line on which green-striped trains operate in a loop which encircles Tokyo's inner metropolitan area, running both clockwise and anticlockwise from Tokyo Station. From early in the morning until late at night — the service stops only in the early hours of the morning — the trains run as frequently as one every two minutes, with fares ranging from ¥120 minimum to a maximum of ¥190. Tokyo Station and Yurakucho (for the Ginza area) are the two most central stations, but the train makes 29 stops, including the important stations of Shinjuku and Ueno, which as well as being places of great tourist interest are also stations from which a great many upcountry trains leave.

The several subway lines are the other really important links in the inner city network and, used in conjunction with the Yamanote line, will enable you to reach the great majority of interesting places in the city with but a short walk to be taken from the terminal station. The most important element in making inquiries is that you are able to pronounce reasonably correctly the name of your destination. But you should not need to inquire too often if you read the signs carefully and make frequent and intelligent use of your map. The best map to use — covering both the subways as well as the main JR lines — is that issued by the JNTO.

TAXIS: Taxis are usually plentiful in Tokyo, though at busy periods a vacant one may be hard to come by. They are convenient for the visitor who is in town for only one or two days and has no time to become familiar with the railway system: and for those journeys (for example from Akasaka to Roppongi) where to use the subways would involve a very roundabout trip. In most situations however, the subway is by far the fastest and most convenient route, even for novices. Traffic is often heavy in Tokyo, so if you are using a taxi allow plenty of time. You may hail a taxi in the street and most large hotels usually have a number waiting close by. If you are leaving from your hotel, get the doorman to give specific instructions to the driver as to your destination and take a hotel card or matchbox — with the hotel's name and address in Japanese on it — with you. This is a useful tactic also for find restaurants and clubs or bars that you have already been to. The taxi driver will usually not speak English and in Tokyo they have a reputation for being unhelpful to foreigners.

With few street names and an entirely haphazard system of house numbering, Tokyo addresses are not easy to find, even for locals, so do not get upset at your driver's apparent ignorance when he has to ask for guidance from one of the police boxes or at a shop.

Tokyo fares are ¥650 flagfall, which includes the first two kilometres, and then ¥80 for each additional 280 metres, plus a time charge when the car slows to less than 10 kilometres per hour. Between 11 p.m. and 5 a.m., a 30% surcharge applies. Tipping is not the usual practice, though you may choose to do so if the driver has been especially helpful.

BUSES: Unless you are introduced to the mysteries of bus travel in Tokyo by a local friend you will be well advised to use other means. Most Japanese buses have their destinations marked only in Japanese characters. The fare is generally ¥200 per ride, be it one stop or to the end of the line within the 23 wards of the city.

HIRECARS: Cars with a chauffeur cost about twice as much as taxis, though daily, weekly or monthly fees can be arranged. Hotels and the various leading travel agencies will be your best source of chauffeured vehicles. Drive-yourself rates run out per day are anything from ¥8,800 for a sub-compact to around ¥28,000 for a big car. Insurance is included in the rental rate but the customer pays for fuel. Details vary a great deal from one operator to the next and many have special plans for extended periods of hire. Some companies arrange for cars to be hired in one city and returned in another. An international driving licence is required to drive in Japan.

The following are among the major car-rental companies:

Nissan Rent-A-Car, 3-2-10 Shirokanedai, Minato-ku, Tokyo. Tel: 5424 4043.

Nippon Rent-A-Car, 55 Kamiyamacho, Shibuya-ku, Tokyo. Tel: 3845 7196 (over 850 branch offices nationwide).

TRANSPORT IN OTHER CITIES

TRAINS AND SUBWAYS: Japan's major cities are all served by extensive rail networks, and in the large urban centres of Osaka, Yoko-

MAJOR AIRLINES

	Tel:
Japan Air Lines (JAL) (Information and Reservation)	5489 1111
Aeroflot	3434 9671
Air Canada	3585 5082
Air France	3475 1511
Air-India	3214 1981
Air New Zealand	3287 1641
Alitalia	3580 2181
All Nippon Airways	3272 1212
American Airlines	3248 2011
Ansett Australia	3214 6876
Asiana Airlines	3582 6600
Austrian Airlines	3582 2231
British Airways	3593 8811
Air China	5251 0711
Canadian Airlines Int'l	3281 7426
Cathay Pacific	3504 1531
China Airlines	3436 1661
China Eastern	3506 1166
Continental	3592 1631
Delta Air Lines	5275 7000
Egypt Air	3211 4521
Finnair	3222 6801
Garuda	3593 1181
Iberia Airlines	3582 3631

	Tel:
Japan Air System	3438 1155
Japan Asia Airways	5489 5411
KLM Royal Dutch	3216 0771
Korean Air	5443 3311
Lufthansa	3580 2111
Malaysia Airlines	3503 5961
Northwest Airlines	3533 6000
Pakistan Int'l	3216 6511
Philippine Airlines	3593 2421
Qantas	3593 7000
Sabena (Belgian)	3585 6151
Scandinavian (SAS)	3503 8101
Singapore Airlines	3213 3431
Swissair	3212 1016
Thai Airways Int'l	3503 3311
United Airlines	3817 4411
Varig Airlines	3211 6751
Virgin Atlantic	3499 8811

NOTE: The Tokyo area code is 03. This has to be dialled from anywhere in Japan outside Tokyo before the above numbers. From within Tokyo this area code is omitted. Similarly, 06 denotes Osaka; 092 denotes Fukuoka and 052 denotes Nagoya.

hama, Nagoya and Kyoto especially there are extensive JR and private railways serving the suburban areas. Osaka, Nagoya and Kyoto also have subways. A single subway line also operates south from the Central railway station in the city of Sapporo in Hokkaido.

Osaka is almost as complex as Tokyo in its layout of above-ground lines and subways, and has no equal at all when it comes to the huge underground and above-ground railway and shopping complex where the Umeda and the Osaka stations meet. JR, private and subway lines all meet on three or four different levels. Osaka has a JR loop similar to that in Tokyo. Advice on how to get around is as mentioned for the Tokyo section; the map to use is the *Buyer's Map of Osaka* published by the Osaka Municipal Trade Centre and available at the Osaka Tourist Information Office in the JR Osaka Station. Without maps you will just not be able to move around the city with any freedom.

Nagoya is a little less complicated, having just two subways which run at right angles to each other, crossing beneath the TV tower in the centre of the city. Most of the above-surface railways radiate from the Central station. Again use a map; this time the *Tourist Map Nagoya*, available from the Nagoya City Tourist Information Office in the JR section of the Central station.

In Kyoto, you can obtain maps of the city from the JNTO office on the first floor of the Kyoto Tower Building just opposite the Central railway station. The best is JNTO's Kyoto and Nara map.

TRAMS: Trams or streetcars have disappeared from Japan's largest cities but can still be found in regional centres such as Hiroshima, Nagasaki and Kagoshima. As the cars usually run in straight lines, they may be easier to use than buses, providing you have a city map.

BUSES: The use of buses in cities other than Tokyo and Osaka is a manageable proposition for the visitor. The routes are usually numbered and maps of the bus routes are available from information offices. Getting special instructions from your hotel, including a note written in Japanese as to what bus you wish to take, is a practical idea. Fares are very reasonable, ranging from around a minimum of ¥140 up, depending on the length of the journey.

TRANSPORT UPCOUNTRY

PRIVATE VEHICLES: Japan's major roads are toll highways. There are three special toll expressways: the Tomei, 326 kilometres between Tokyo and Nagoya (¥6,500); the Meishin, 204 kilometres between Nagoya and Kobe (¥4,500); and the Chuo, 94 kilometres between Tokyo and Lake Kawaguchi in the vicinity of Mt Fuji (¥2,100). Accommodation and refreshment facilities are becoming common along the major highways as the Japanese take to the roads in ever-increasing numbers. Driving anywhere during peak holiday periods is not recommended. Highways have some signs in English, but generally you will be dependent on maps which you may buy in the cities.

The under-sea Kammon Tunnels link Honshu and Kyushu islands between Shimonoseki and Kitakyushu cities. Between Honshu and the other main islands, Shikoku and Hokkaido, other mammoth transport projects have recently been completed. The Seikan rail tunnel, longest undersea tunnel in the world, has linked Aomori and Hokkaido, while the 12.3-kilometre Seto Ohashi bridge (9.4 kilometres of it over water) now links Okayama prefecture on the mainland with Kagawa prefecture in Shikoku near the town of Sakaide.

BUSES: Modern, comfortable highway buses operate over the expressways and along the main highways in Japan, serving not only as feeder links from the railway to resorts and small towns, but also as a means of connecting large towns and cities. JR runs its own large fleet of buses on the Tokaido route, charging ¥8,030 for the eight-hour trip to Kyoto and ¥8,450 through to Osaka, about 15 minutes shorter. Buses operate at night, usually from Shinjuku station. Travel by bus can present a language problem since drivers rarely speak English.

RAILWAYS: Rail transport is highly developed in Japan. The JR system comprises more than 21,000 kilometres of track and runs about 20,000 trains daily. An additional 7,000 kilometres of track are privately electrified. Railways literally run to all corners of the country.

The *piece de resistance* is the New Tokaido Line between Tokyo and Osaka, which now reaches to Hakata in Kyushu via Okayama another 630 kilometres further west called the New Sanyo Line. The whole line is also referred to as Shinkansen, literally new trunk line. On this stretch of railway line running through the most densely populated portion of Japan, the 200-kilometres-per-hour-plus super express Bullet Trains, Nozomi and Hikari, operate. Nozomi, Hikari and the limited express Kodama, each leave every five to 10

SUBWAYS IN TOKYO

Tobu-Dobutsu-Koen
Kita-Ayase
Tobu Isesaki Line
Toride
MACHIYA
KITA-SENJU
AYASE
Keisei Line
Tabata
NISH-NIPPORI
Aoto
Narita-Airport
OSHIAGE
Thru trains run on Keisei Line
Minami-Senju
Minowa
Sendagi
Nezu
Nippori
Honjoazumabashi
Iriya
Uguisudani
Yushima
Inaricho
Tawaramachi
UENO
ASAKUSA
Nakaokachimachi
Uenohirokoji
Oka Chi-Machi
Kuramae
Suehirocho
AKIHABARA
ASAKUSABASHI
AWAJICHO
Iwamo-Tocho
OGAWA-MACHI
KANDA
MOTOYAWATA
Shin-Nihombashi
BAKUROCHO
NISHI-FUNABASHI
Tsudanuma
OTEMACHI
MITSUKOSHIMAE
BAKUROYOKOYAMA
HIGASHI-NIHOMBASHI
Kodemmacho
Shino-Zaki
Barakinakayama
TOKYO
NIHOMBASHI
NINGYOCHO
Hamacho
Morishita
Mizue
Gyotoku
Kikukawa
Ichinoe
Minami-Gyotoku
Sumiyoshi
Ginza Itchome
Kyobashi
Nishi-Ojima
Funabori
Urayasu
KAYABACHO
Takaracho
Suitengu-Mae
Ojima
Kasai
GINZA
HIGASHI-GINZA
HATCHOBORI
Monzen-Nakacho
Higashi-Ojima
Shintomicho
Nishi-Kasai
Kiba
Toyocho
Minami-Sunamachi
Tsukiji
SHIN-KIBA
Tsukishima
Toyosu
Tatsumi
Maihama
Chiyoda Line
Yurakucho Line
Hanzomon Line
Namboku Line
Toei Asakusa Line
Toei Mita Line
Toei Shinjuku Line
Toei No.12 Line
XXXX Junction connecting to subways
XXXX Junction connecting to subways, East Japan Railway and Private Railway Lines
East Japan Railway Line
Private Railways
Street Car
Stations with a Pass Office

minutes (between the hours of 6 a.m. and 8:30 p.m.) from Tokyo and Osaka, and a little less frequently on the New Sanyo section. The Hikari takes just three hours 10 minutes for the 552-kilometre trip from Tokyo to Osaka, stopping at Nagoya and Kyoto: travel time to Nagoya is two hours, and to Kyoto two hours 50 minutes. The Kodama makes 11 stops along the way, completing the journey in four hours 14 minutes. The fastest Nozomi from Tokyo to Hakata takes five hours.

The train ride on the Shinkansen is one of the highlights of a visit to Japan. Running on "seamless" rails, the trains are incredibly smooth; seats are aircraft type, carriages are air-conditioned and there is a dining car. There is a telephone system on the train enabling you to call major cities or receive calls. Every Shinkansen train now has a non-smoking car at one end.

Two classes of car exist on the Shinkansen trains — ordinary and Green Car, the latter being equivalent to first class. Most seats on both Hikari and Kodama are reservable but several cars are available on a free seating basis. Sample ordinary class fares on the Shinkansen are as follows: Tokyo-Nagoya ¥10,380; Tokyo-Kyoto ¥12,970; Tokyo-Shin Osaka ¥13,480; Tokyo-Hiroshima ¥17,700. A sample Green Car fare is: Tokyo-Nagoya ¥14,000. Frequencies and timing may be subject to changes due to repairs being made after the Kobe-area earthquake — check with your travel agent or your hotel.

In the opposite direction from Tokyo, the Tohoku Shinkansen connects Ueno in Tokyo and Morioka in the northeast, travelling 535 kilometres in three hours 21 minutes. The Joetsu links Ueno and Niigata on the Japan Sea side, covering 334 kilometres in two hours seven minutes.

Shinkansen trains bound for Kyoto and points west depart from Tokyo Station. Joetsu and Tohoku Shinkansen trains, however, leave from underground platforms in Ueno, the major terminus four stops north of Tokyo Station on the Yamanote line. The Shinkansen station in Osaka is called Shin (i.e. new) Osaka and is some five kilometres from the main Osaka railway station. Similarly in Kobe the station is Shin-Kobe and in Yokohama it is Shin-Yokohama.

Tickets for all JR trains may be purchased at JR stations and at principal offices of the Japan Travel Bureau (JTB). Advance reservation tickets can be bought from one week ahead of the journey and JTB makes available a limited number from three weeks in advance. Simple English is spoken at the major city booking office, but it would be a good idea to have your exact trip details written out in Japanese by someone at your hotel. Visitors may wish to take advantage of the Japan Rail Pass which is only available through overseas travel agents. Savings can be remarkable, as rail travel in Japan is not cheap.

In addition to the excellent service offered by JR, the private lines have many services, especially from the main cities to popular resort areas. Some of these lines carry deluxe excursion trains on which there are snack booths serving coffee, sandwiches, etc.

JNTO publishes excellent maps giving comprehensive coverage of the rail networks. A condensed timetable for JR trains, available from JTB offices, is a valuable source of general information about train travel.

SHIPS: A great many regular steamship services are available, linking various points on the Japanese coast. Ferry services between Honshu and the other three main islands are frequent. JR operate some, though most are private-company services.

In the vicinity of the many coastal national parks, hydrofoils and hovercraft operate. Many small and interesting ferries service the tiny island villages scattered along the coastal regions.

AIR: Three airline companies operate over the domestic routes in Japan. Japan Air Lines flies almost exclusively between the major cities of Tokyo, Osaka, Nagoya, Fukuoka, Sapporo and to Naha in Okinawa. All Nippon Airways (ANA) and Japan Air System fly to many provincial centres in addition to serving the large cities. Fares are much the same from one airline to another.

Between such major cities as Tokyo and Osaka flights are very frequent, and those to major centres such as Sapporo and Fukuoka only slightly less so. Advance bookings are usually required in every case as domestic traffic in Japan is extremely heavy.

Tours

The tourist industry in Asia is nowhere better developed than in Japan. The Japanese themselves have a long-standing love affair with sightseeing, both domestic and abroad. And a steady increase in visitors to Japan has encouraged a willingness in most Japanese to help you enjoy their homeland. Taking a tour is certainly going to give you a standardized view of the sights, and Japan is such a fascinating place that over a week or two it is difficult for the tour operator to go wrong. The bigger organizations like the JTB can also plan itineraries for more independent travellers and make booking arrangements for transport, accommodation and other special matters. If you are an independent traveller, you will be wise to use the tourist services as much as possible.

Details of tour agencies are available from hotels.

Among the leading tour operators in Japan are:

JTB, 1-13-1 Nihombashi, Chuo-ku, Tokyo. Tel: 3276 7777, Fax: 5620 9495.

Nippon Travel Agency, 2-20-25 Shimbashi, Minato-ku, Tokyo. Tel: 3572 8741; Fax: 3587 0563.

Tobu Travel, 3-4-12 Nihombashi, Chuo-ku, Tokyo. Tel: 3278 1251, Fax: 3272 1818.

Hankyu Express, 2-18-2 Nishi-Shimbashi, Minato-ku, Tokyo. Tel: 3459 9080, Fax: 3459 9090.

Japan Gray Line, 3-4-2 SS Bldg 6/Flr, Nishi-Shimbashi, Minato-ku, Tokyo. Tel: 3433 4801, Fax: 3436 5189.

Kinki Nippon Tourist Co., 19-2 Kanda-Matsunagacho, Chiyoda-ku, Tokyo. Tel: 3255 7111, Fax: 3255 7128.

Accommodation

Viewed on the national level, Japan's accommodation is among the best available in Asia. Prices are to match, being on average the highest in the area.

Western-style hotels add a tax of 3-6% nightly per person for rooms that charge under ¥10,000 and over ¥10,000 respectively. In addition, a 10-15% service charge is tacked on at better hotels. Hotel rates may vary according to the season. Bookings at most places of interest are heavy throughout most of the year and advance reservations are advisable.

Most deluxe and first-class hotels in the country's major cities offer limousine bus connections direct to the airport, and a few deluxe hotels in Tokyo now provide business centres and executive floors — the latter give you complimentary secretarial services, which include access to facsimile and computer facilities.

However, business travellers should also consider the virtues of business hotels, which have become more popular since the mid-1980s as prices in Japan have shot up. These hotels give you no-frills treatment, geared to a typical Japanese businessman in transit. While services are distinctly limited, business hotels are usually clean, with Western styling and individual baths and are typically close to train stations. English is not usually spoken, but checking in and out is simple. Rooms are commonly singles and total charges come to around ¥9,000 per person.

But for those after a taste of old Japan at prices that commonly range from ¥10,000 to ¥20,000 per person, including two meals, a local ryokan is your best bet. About 80,000 of them are scattered around Japan.

If the ryokan personnel speak English then you are of course more easily introduced the system, but usually they do not.

There you will be greeted with much smiling and bowing, to which you should respond. Take off your shoes on the lower level and step up to the upper level where you will be provided with slip-on sandals: these are to be worn at all times in the ryokan except in your room on the tatami straw floor, where you go in your bare or stockinged feet, and in the toilet where you change to the other slippers you will find there.

Kerosene or gas heaters are often used in winter; the ryokan maid will normally show you how to use it. But be very careful. Japanese dwellings are readily combustible.

Clothing is provided by way of a light *yukata* robe and a heavier **tanzen**. The pockets of the tanzen are hidden in its billowing sleeves. The yukata is used as an undergarment for the tanzen and also worn to bed. It is acceptable to wear the one or the other in the public corridors.

At night the bedding — consisting of *futon* quilts and a small pillow (the pillow filled with unhusked rice) — will be laid out by the maid. In the morning the maid returns to put your bedding back into the wall cupboards.

Ryokan usually serve two meals daily — breakfast and dinner which are included in the normal rate. If you want lunch as well you must specifically request the management to provide this, usually in advance. A so-called Western breakfast, which can consist of anything from a slice of toast and a hard-boiled egg to cold spaghetti and chopped cabbage, can be had in many ryokan if an arrangement is made; otherwise meals are usually Japanese type.

The ryokan bath, or *o-furo,* is one of the delights (or tortures) of living *à la Japonaise.* Indicate to the maid when you wish to have your bath and she will put you on the list of those waiting for the bath. The more expensive rooms have private baths. Soap yourself outside the tub, and only enter after rinsing off all the suds. The tub is for restful soaking, not for washing in.

Many ryokan only have Japanese-style squat-type toilets. Most ryokan tack on a 10-20% service charge. Tipping is not expected, but if you wish, it is acceptable to tip the maid, provided this is done privately.

JNTO publishes the very useful *Japan Ryokan Guide.* It is obtainable at JNTO information offices in Tokyo, Osaka and Kyoto which also have other information at hand concerning hotels and ryokan throughout the country. JTB and travel agent offices found in most main centres across Japan can also recommend ryokan. They will also telephone and make a reservation for you.

Of special interest to budget travellers are the 344 **Kokumin Shukusha** or People's Lodges throughout Japan. Although primarily designed for the Japanese public they are also made available to visitors. The per-person charge is about ¥6,500, including two meals. If space is available, accommodation can be obtained without prior reservations. However, it is recommended that foreign visitors have reservations made at JTB offices for those People's Lodges which have a Green Coupon agreement with JTB. When reservation is secured, a Green Coupon — the reservation voucher — is issued to the applicant. People's Lodges are usually located in national parks, at hot springs resorts or in the mountains.

Dining

There was a time when nothing escaped the aesthetic shaping by which the Japanese converted matter into form. Even food was transformed and became art. Mere eating, on the other hand, was a crude follow-up to the far more rewarding act of contemplating the likes of two prawns poised with *ikebana* grace upon a shroud of rice. While the higher mysticism surrounding food continues to flourish amongst some Japanese, times have changed.

Nowhere is that more clear than in Tokyo, where you can have delivered in 30 minutes a pizza comparable to those in New York. Fast-food restaurants are everywhere, and international cuisine has largely upstaged Japanese food amid Japan's new affluence and the trend towards *kokusai-ka* (internationalization).

But putting foreign food aside for the moment, dishes available in Japan fall into roughly three types. First the special, characteristically Japanese dishes such as *tempura, sushi, sukiyaki* and *shabu-shabu,* the latter two being available only in the better and more expensive restaurants; next the everyday Japanese dishes such as *soba* and *yakitori* which are generally cheaper and widely available; and lastly, hybrid dishes which are a mixture of Japanese and Western styles.

Of the special dishes, sukiyaki and shabu-shabu are undoubtedly the best known and most popular. Appetizingly prepared at the table, the simple ingredients of meat (thinly sliced beef most commonly), vegetables, bean curd and vermicelli lightly stewed, in the case of sukiyaki, in a broth of soy-sauce, rice wine and sugar, are ideal for small groups. With sukiyaki, a beaten egg is used as a cooling sauce into which you dip each morsel. With shabu-shabu, the ingredients are very briefly cooked in a lighter, clear broth, and are accompanied by a variety of sauces, often combining lemon-juice and soy-sauce. As beef is expensive in Japan, expect to pay accordingly — a good meal based around such delicacies as grain-fed Kobe or Matsuzaka beef could easily run out at ¥20,000 per head, though perfectly acceptable sukiyaki and shabu-shabu can be had for between ¥2,500-6,000 at a reasonable restaurant.

Tempura and sushi shops can be found everywhere in Japan. Good tempura is delightfully crisp and light, and the cooking relies on extremely hot, fresh vegetable oil in which fresh fish, prawns and a variety of vegetables, all coated with a flour and egg batter, are deep-fried as you order and served with a special sauce which you make yourself by mixing in the grated radish to the soy sauce already provided. Rice, pickles and soup usually come together with tempura.

A basic set tempura meal with soup and rice will cost around ¥1,200, but once you move into the speciality shops and order *a la carte,* prices will range from ¥3,000-6,000 plus. (Simple tempura with just a couple of prawns on rice — called *tendon* — will cost as little as ¥400 in street-level shops where you stand and eat at the counter; while tasty enough, when compared with the "real thing" as served

Sakurajima Volcano, Kagoshima. PHOTO: MARTIN MOOS

in more expensive places, this is roughly on a par with McDonald's compared with a fine steak).

Traditional Japanese cuisine is known as *kaiseki-ryori.* Its roots are in *Zen* and the tea ceremony, and it is made up of a array of dishes, including soup, several kinds of raw, boiled and steamed fish and vegetables; the whole served in examples of the art of pottery-making on lacquer trays. In the best places this type of meal will be rather expensive (¥8,000-20,000 plus) and is only recommended to those more than a little familiar with the delicate tastes of Japanese food.

On the other hand, yakitori, for example, is a cheap meal but in its usual forms — chicken, pork, chicken liver, balls of minced chicken meat, garnished with portions of green pepper and onion — delicious. If you want to check out plenty of noodle or yakitori shops with old-time ambience and consistent quality, spend a night or two roving under and around the JR tracks near Tokyo's centrally located Yurakucho station. These establishments flourish in an area that runs roughly several blocks from the station to the Imperial Hotel.

Noodles of various kinds are popular with the Japanese. Many of the small, pavement shops sell soba (buckwheat noodles) and udon (thick white noodles) for ¥400 or so. Soba and udon are served hot in soup, while soba is also served cold on a bamboo platter with a separate dipping sauce — *zaru-soba* — available. Udon is rarely served cold. Some hot varieties are; fried tofu (*kitsune-soba/udon*), seaweed (*wakame-soba*), tempura (*tempura-soba*), and marinated vegetables such as carrot and potato (*kenchin-soba*). A delicious udon dish is *nabe-yaki udon*, in which egg, vegetables, mushrooms and tempura prawns are cooked together with udon in a clay pot which is brought bubbling to your table.

Ramen is the name for the Chinese noodles which are popular throughout Japan, and especially good in Sapporo and Kyushu. *Shio* (salt) ramen, *batah* (butter) ramen, *miso* (bean-paste) ramen and *shoyu* (soy sauce) ramen are all good and filling, as are the fried meat dumplings — *gyoza* — which have become a fundamental part of the Japanese diet.

In addition to the standing five-minute bowl of soba just off the pavement, Japan's most efficient indigenous fast food experience is the *guru, guru* (round and round) sushi shops, where customers sit around plates of sushi rotating on a belt, grabbing whatever looks good and paying per plate. A good meal for someone with an average appetite comprises about five to seven plates. You can see clearly whatever the chefs are preparing. A cup of green tea is included in the price, regardless of the number of plates consumed.

Basic-fare Western-style restaurants serving spaghetti, pizza, and hamburgers are popular, and the fast-food chains do phenomenal business, as do the many pizza delivery operations. Average price of a hot pizza delivered to your hotel, home or office ranges from around ¥1,500 to ¥3,000.

One thing lacking anywhere outside the big hotels and a couple of Western chain restaurants is a good, hearty American-style breakfast of eggs, ham or bacon, hashed potatoes and coffee with toast or muffins. However, many small coffee-shop style restaurants do serve dainty "morning set" — sandwich, toast, hard-boiled egg, fruit or salad with coffee. Average price for a cup of coffee is about ¥350 in coffee shops.

The so-called beer halls, sometimes with pleasant outdoor beer gardens, are good-value eating places. Big breweries operate chains of these halls where you can get good Western-style food as well as a limited number of basic Japanese dishes.

Prices for Western liquors have dropped considerably since the late 1980s, in the wake of vigorous foreign efforts to break Japanese trade barriers. But the local alcoholic products are good. The 17% proof rice wine, sake, makes excellent drinking once you settle into the taste. It is usually taken hot, but may also be drunk with ice. Japanese-made beers are delicious, and available in a bewildering number of malts, lagers and "drys." Kirin, Asahi and Sapporo (which also makes the premium, sharp-tasting Yebisu beer) are favoured brands. Japanese whisky, Suntory and Nikka especially, can be compared with Scotch.

Most of the better Japanese restaurants do not stay open very late at night, so plan to eat no later than 8 p.m. Most hotels and large restaurants have a service charge and tax that, combined, comes to about 13%. Tips are almost never required. While Chinese cuisine has long been popular in Japan, lately the number of French and Italian establishments has exploded, and competition to produce authentic, top-class dishes has heated up among international restaurants in general.

Entertainment

Japan's entertainment scene is almost overwhelming. In the big cities there is too much to do, so finding what will interest you most becomes a problem. Almost all hotels have a range of free pamphlets listing events and movies, though the best information plus interesting behind-the-scenes city stories can be found in the monthly *Tokyo Journal* magazine (¥600 at English-language bookstores and some major hotels).

Theatre is popular, though with the chronic shortage of space in centres such as Tokyo, plays, opera and dance performances tend to have very short runs, often of only a few days. Broadway musicals such as *Miss Saigon* and what others there are, of course, are performed in Japanese. Traditional *Kabuki* has great appeal to the visitor. The plays are usually based on legends and stories from Japanese history and are presented with much colour, music and drama. Main Tokyo centres for kabuki are the **Kabukiza Theatre** (on the eastern edge of the Ginza district, close to the fishmarkets of Tsukiji) and the **National Theatre** (opposite the southwest corner of the Imperial palace grounds). Performances begin at 11 a.m. and 4:30 p.m. at the Kabukiza, and at noon and 5 p.m. at the National Theatre. Tickets are usually in high demand and good seats are expensive.

There are variations in programming however, and it is essential to check. Osaka's Shin Kabukiza Theatre and Kyoto's **Minamiza Theatre** each present a single, 25-day-long season of kabuki annually. The highly stylized *noh* drama is a totally different art form. It has changed little over the past three centuries and is much more solemn and slow-moving than kabuki and is likely to become quite boring to those without a deep interest in it. Main actors wear the characteristic masks of noh and chant their lines to the accompaniment of drums and flute. Only the Japanese language is used. Tokyo, Kyoto and Osaka have several theatres which present noh drama. Check with your hotel, JNTO or JTB offices for details of performances during your stay.

Bunraku is a fascinating dramatic form utilizing large puppets, the largest operated by three men. Traditional stories are enacted to the accompaniment of *shamisen* music and recitation of ballads. It is marvellous how the puppeteers, constantly in full view, seem virtually to disappear as one is drawn into the action. Osaka is considered the home of bunraku. The National Theatre in Tokyo presents four seasons of bunraku annually.

In a more modern yet conventional vein are the musical reviews featuring gorgeously costumed dance groups. Performances are often on a seasonal theme — the springtime Tokyo Odori and Kyoto Miyako Odori Cherry Dances, for example — though there are usually performances of one kind or another throughout the year.

Western and Japanese films are widely shown in the cities. In Tokyo theatres showing newly released Western films can be found in the vicinity of the Imperial Hotel, between Hibiya Park and the Ginza, as well as in Shinjuku and Shibuya districts. Cinemas showing revivals of older films and first runs of films with less than mass appeal are dotted around the city. Some cinemas show Japanese films with English subtitles one day a week, usually Friday, though this is not common.

Shinjuku is probably the most rewarding section of Tokyo at night for the visitor who likes to stroll around, have a meal and a beer, listen to some hi-fi jazz, watch a film, check out the boutiques and mingle in the crowds. Shinjuku can be reached most conveniently from the Ginza by the Marunouchi-line subway.

Tokyo's night-club, cabaret and bar scene is most highly developed in Ginza and Akasaka districts and the upscale "foreigners' ghetto" of Roppongi. Akasaka is some three kilometres to the west of the Ginza (best reached by either Ginza or Marunouchi-line subways to Akasaka-Mitsuke subway station), and Roppongi lies about 1.6 kilometres to the south of Akasaka in the vicinity of the Roppongi road junction. Roppongi can be reached on the Hibiya-line subway, though from Akasaka it is quicker to take a taxi.

But be warned that Tokyo is one of Asia's most expensive nightlife cities. For example, at the best of the cabarets your first drink for the night will run out at around US$30 — made up of the cover charge to the cabaret, hostess charge, price of your drink and hers, then the 15% tax and 15% service charge on top. And that is not counting tips.

Japan also has many saunas, and many major hotels offer luxurious (legitimate) bathing facilities. On the shadier side, almost any kind of pleasure can be had in Tokyo, for a price. Many of Tokyo's "Turkish baths" were not what the name implied, having adopted the name in the wake of the 1956 anti-prostitution laws. Turkish diplomatic indignation later forced a name change to "Soapland." These days, an experience at a "Soapland" costs upwards of ¥20,000, and the attentive staff are more likely to be Southeast Asian than Japanese (let alone Turkish).

The cheapest places for a drink in the Japanese cities are the very good beerhalls (e.g. **Suntory**, **Sapporo**, etc.), the beer gardens on the rooftops of big department stores in the summer and at any of the smaller restaurants, snack bars and coffee shops. At a beerhall, a large beer will cost around ¥800.

In a different class are the hostess bars. Prices vary tremendously from place to place; some have cover charges, others do not; some have a hostess charge, while others have highly priced hostess drinks (some have both). Japanese hostesses certainly have a great reputation for beauty, elegance, charmingly demure female behaviour and flattering conversation. But unless money is no object, if you are planning something more than polite conversation you will find it cheaper (even including the air fare) to fly to Taiwan.

Shopping

Shopping in Japan is one of the great pleasures of a trip to this country. The goods are generally of a high quality — but so are the prices. The huge department stores in all the main cities are a cultural experience in themselves, even if you do not buy a thing. Certainly one learns a great deal about contemporary Japan. Main department stores can be found in the Ginza, Nihonbashi and Shinjuku districts of Tokyo.

There is also a wide range of small, specialist stores in all the cities. For art lovers the best place to look for pictures are a number of shops in the main road which lies immediately to the south of the Nezu Art Museum in Aoyama district. Reasonable copies of *ukiyo-e* woodblock prints can be found in the traditional bookshop district of Kanda. For a huge selection of ski wear and equipment, as well as summer sporting gear, **Kanda's** Ogawamachi district can be reached easily on either the Shinjuku subway line to Ogawamachi station or on the Chiyoda line to Shin-Ochanomizu station.

There are bargains to be had in **Akihabara**, Tokyo's frenetic central electronics goods shopping district, but it can be an exhausting experience, though in the end often satisfying. Be prepared to allow yourself at least half a day comparing prices and bargaining. Shopping effectively in Akihabara requires determination and a clear idea of what you want.

Traditional works of Japanese art are a good, but expensive buy. Japanese craftsmanship in pottery, wood, modern prints, etc. is unsurpassed in Asia. Bargaining is acceptable in many art shops, though one should apply rather more finesse in the game than elsewhere. Silk goods are of exquisite quality and the major department stores regularly hold sales of kimono and accessories. Japanese lacquerware is excellent. Japanese dolls of all kinds are a unique buy.

For souvenir shopping and a delightful taste of old Edo's "working class" area, do not miss Asakusa, on the northeast fringes of the city near the Sumida River. The enormous wooden **Kannon Temple** is a magnificent attraction for out-of-town visitors both foreign and Japanese, and the surrounding narrow lanes and shopping streets are full of stalls and shops selling food and souvenirs. Asakusa, like the market district under the tracks at Ueno, is a bustling traditional centre quite different from other modern parts of Tokyo; both are great places to encounter the Japanese at their most relaxed — humorous, loud and earthy.

Shopping in **Kyoto** offers special delights. The old capital still retains its leadership in several crafts, including those of silk production, lacquerware (in the black and gold and red and gold characteristic of the art development under the Tokugawas), pottery-ware (in the Kiyomizu style) and also dolls. Shops spread out from the intersection of Kawaramachi and Shijo streets, and many can be found nearby on the well-known **Shinmonzen St**. The north side of **Gojo St** east of the Kamo River has many shops selling kiyomizu ware, as has the small street leading up to the entrance of **Kiyomizu Temple**. Antiques, painted scrolls, woodblock prints, screens, paper lanterns and many other items are available around the city. You will buy at better prices in the odd little shops, though there will be a language difficulty.

Sports

Japan offers a great many interesting sporting activities. You can participate in swimming, mountaineering, skiing, skating, fishing and golf, or watch any of the special national sports such as sumo, judo, kendo, karate, aikido, baseball and the now enormously popular soccer. Golf courses and ski areas tend to be overcrowded, especially at weekends.

With its long, indented coastline, the country is well endowed with beaches, many of which can be found along the south coast of Honshu island to the west of Tokyo. They are crowded in summer and, owing to the huge pollution in the vicinity of the industrial centres, a day at the beach is no great attraction for visitors to Japan.

Beaches along the Izu Peninsula, well south of Tokyo, are among the cleanest. Windsurfing and scuba-diving have exploded in popularity since the mid-1980s. Shops and schools for both sports have multiplied to offer anyone a chance to get into the water. Scuba lessons, which involve two days in a swimming pool and two more in the ocean, cost about ¥70-100,000; windsurfing lessons cost ¥19,000 or so for a two-day course. Renting a windsurfing board (with sail) costs ¥1,000 per hour, plus ¥1,000 for a wetsuit, regardless of how long you use it; hiring a board and sail for the day costs around ¥6,000.

Moutaineering in summer (including the ascent of Mt Fuji) and skiing in winter make the Japan Alps and other ranges in northern Honshu and Hokkaido popular destinations for holidaymakers. Equipment can be hired at most ski resorts (charges being in the order of ¥4,000 per day and more for skis and boots) and facilities are generally of excellent standard, including even night flood-lighting of the slopes in certain places. Late December to mid-April is the usual Japan Alps skiing season, though one may ski from November to May at some of the Hokkaido ski areas.

Skating is available on frozen lakes and ponds in winter at many resorts and in the cities at indoor rinks.

Freshwater fishing is a rapidly growing sport in Japan and many inland waters are now being freshly stocked annually. The trout season extends from March to September; licences are necessary. Sea fishing is increasingly popular, with urban fishermen flocking to the shores on weekends to cast from concrete sea walls and breakwaters. South of Tokyo around the Sagami Bay numerous fishing tour boats take parties out for a day of fishing and may even provide lodging (about ¥3,000 per night) in dormitories. The cost for a one-day outing offshore is around ¥7,000 per person, plus ¥1,000 if you rent the fishing gear.

With some 1,700 courses now open in Japan, golf has become the great status symbol, following trends in the West. Especially in the

Tokyo's dramatic skyline. PHOTO: GERHARD JOREN

many resort areas, visitors are allowed to use the courses. In Tokyo and other centres it is hard to get a game unless you are the guest of a club member. Golf driving-ranges are common in the cities.

Of spectator sports, Sumo wrestling has a great fascination for visitors. With several Hawaiian wrestlers now in the top ranks, sumo is increasingly attracting international attention. A series of 15-day tournaments are held across the country: January, May and September at the Ryogoku Kokugikan in Tokyo, March in Osaka, July in Nagoya and in November at Fukuoka. The sport gets wide TV coverage. Matches begin at about 10:30 a.m., though the top division wrestlers start their bouts at about 4:30 p.m. Judo, kendo, karate, aikido and Thai kick-boxing can be seen at several places in main cities.

Baseball games are held regularly during summer. The best teams are divided into two leagues (Central and Pacific) with the Japan Series games held in the middle of October each year. The games are televised.

Limited opportunities for hunting exist in Japan, mainly for game birds and deer.

Holidays

Now almost totally aligned to the Western calendar, the annual festivals and public holidays in Japan fall on set dates so that one can conveniently plan ahead and arrange to be in Japan during occasions of special note. Certain festivals attract large crowds and if you wish to arrange accommodation it should be done many months in advance.

The country's famous cherry trees begin to bloom around April 5 (though this is variable depending on the climate) in the Kyoto and Tokyo areas. In the warmer south they will be a little earlier. Lasting only a week or two in any one area, the blossoming moves gradually northward until May 10.

JNTO publishes a useful pamphlet, *Annual Events in Japan*, describing the major festivals and holidays throughout the country.

January 1: New Year's Day (Public holiday). The gates of houses are decorated with pine twigs, plum branches, bamboo stalks and ropes with paper festoons. People pay homage at shrines and visit friends and relatives to exchange greetings.

January 15: Coming of Age Day (Public holiday). People congratulate young men and women who have become 20 years of age. Young women dress in kimonos.
February 3: Lantern Festivals of Kasuga Shrine, Nara. More than 3,000 lanterns are lit in and around the shrine.
February 3-4: Setsubun Bean-Throwing Festival marks the last day of winter when people throng temple grounds to participate in the traditional throwing of beans to drive away imaginary devils, shouting: "Fortune in, devils out!"
February 5-11: Snow Festival at Sapporo, Hokkaido. Elaborate giant sculptures in snow are built along the city's main thoroughfare.
February 11: National Foundation Day (Public holiday). Commemoration of the Founding of the Nation.
March: Mid-late March: Fire Festival, Mt Aso, Kumamoto Pref. (Kyushu). Ceremonial grass-fires and torchlight Noh performance.
March 21: Vernal Equinox Day (Public holiday).
April: Cherry dances at Tokyo and Kyoto theatres are special spring attractions. Also the International Festival of Osaka.
April 8: Buddha's Birthday. The festival is commonly called *Hana Matsuri* (Flower Festival) and is celebrated at temples.
April 29: Greenery Day (Public holiday).
May 3-4: Constitution Memorial Day on May 3 (Public holiday for two days).
May 5: Children's Day (Public holiday). Originally the Boy's Festival, now both boys and girls are celebrated and the wish expressed that they grow to be good citizens. Giant carp banners fly from homes, as symbols of strength and determination.
May 15: Aoi Matsuri Hollyhock Festival of Shimogamo and Kamigamo shrines in Kyoto. The festival features a magnificent pageant.
May (Third Sunday): Mifune Matsuri Boat Festival at Arashiyama in Kyoto. This charming festival is held on the Ohi River in the suburbs of Kyoto.
June 10-16: Sanno Festival of Tokyo's Hie Shrine in Akasaka. One of the capital's big events, with a parade of portable shrines through the streets.
July 13-15 (August in some regions): Bon Festival or Feast of Lanterns. Religious rites are held throughout the country in memory of the dead who, according to Buddhist belief, revisit the earth during this period. Lanterns are lit for their souls.
July 17: Gion Matsuri of Yasaka Shrine, Kyoto. This most famous of Kyoto festivals dates from the ninth century when the head priest of the Yasaka Shrine authorized a huge procession hoping to rid the city of the pestilence then afflicting it. This is a unique opportunity to see old Kyoto's usually closed inner life in an atmosphere of gaiety and spontaneous friendliness.
Last Saturday in July: Fireworks display above Sumida River, Asakusa, Tokyo: The most spectacular show of its kind.
August 6: Peace Ceremony, Hiroshima: Held at Peace Memorial Park for atom-bomb victims. Somewhat commercialized these days, though in the evening thousands of lighted lanterns set adrift on Ota River make a powerfully memorable sight.
August 6-8: Tanabata Festival at Sendai, Miyagi Pref. An offering to the stars. Thousands of brightly coloured paper streamers and strips adorn the entire town.
August 16: Daimonji Bonfire, Kyoto. The most spectacular display for the Bon Festival in Kyoto, an enormous bonfire in the shape of a Chinese character is ignited on the side of Mt Nyoigadake.
September 15: Respect for the Aged Day (Public holiday).
September 23: Autumnal Equinox Day (Public holiday). People attend the temples to pray for the souls of the departed.
October 10: Health-Sports Day (Public holiday).
October 22: Jidai Matsuri Festival of Eras, Heian Shrine, Kyoto. The festival and parades commemorate the founding of the old capital in 794.
November 3: Culture Day (Public holiday). Daimyo Procession, Hakone. A long procession passes along the old Tokaido Highway in the vicinity of the resort area.
November 23: Labour Thanksgiving Day (Public holiday).
December 17-19: "Hagoita Ichi," or Battledore Fair, Asakusa, Tokyo. A host of stalls open all night selling a huge range of gaily decorated ornamental bats, traditionally used in an ancient ball game.
December 23: Emperor's Birthday (Public holiday).

ADDRESSES

JNTO has three offices: at Narita Airport, in central Tokyo, and in Kyoto. Addresses are as follows:

Airport: Airport Terminal Bldg, Narita. Chiba Pref. Tel: (0476) 328711.
Tokyo: Kotani Bldg, 1-6-6 Yurakucho, Chiyoda-ku, Tokyo. Tel: (03) 3502 1461.
Kyoto: Kyoto Tower Bldg, Higashi-shiokojicho-ku, Kyoto. Tel: (075) 371 5649.
Tourist Information Centre (TIC) offices are open 9 a.m.-5 p.m. on weekdays, 9 a.m.-12 noon on Saturdays, closed for lunch from 12 noon to 1 p.m. There is also a TIC office in each of the terminal buildings at Narita, with the office in Terminal 2 staying open 9 a.m.-8 p.m. everyday. The office in Terminal 1 is open 9 a.m.-8 p.m. weekdays, 9 a.m.-12:30 p.m. Saturdays only. Tel: (0476) 322960 (Terminal 1), (0476) 346250 (Terminal 2). Even when you are away from Tokyo and Kyoto you can avail yourself of TIC's services by means of the Japan Travel-Phone. This is free outside Tokyo and Kyoto. Dial 0120 222800 to ask questions about eastern Japan (Kanto) or 0120 444800 for western Japan (Kansai). You will be put through to an English-speaking expert who's job it is to assist you. Inside Tokyo and Kyoto the same service is available by dialling a local number: for Tokyo TIC is 3502 1461; Kyoto TIC is 271 5649. It costs ¥10 for three minutes for local calls.

JNTO head office is at 10-1, Yurakucho 2-chome, Tokyo. Normal tourist inquiries should not, however, be directed to the head office.

There are JNTO overseas offices in New York, Chicago, Dallas, San Francisco, Los Angeles, Toronto, London, Sydney, Hong Kong, Seoul, Bangkok, Paris, Geneva, Frankfurt, Mexico and Sao Paulo and tourist information and maps, etc., can be obtained at these centres.

Other main tourist information offices (non-JNTO) include: Osaka Tourist Information Office, JR Osaka Station East Gate, Umeda-cho, Kita-ku, Osaka. Tel: 345 2189. Nagoya International Centre, 4/Flr, Nagoya Kokusai Centre Bldg, Nagono 1-chome, Nakamura-ku, Nagoya. Tel: (052) 581 5678.

PUBLICATIONS

JNTO makes available an excellent range of maps and booklets (through their Japan and overseas information offices). So valuable are these that anyone planning a tour of Japan would be advised to obtain them in advance and use them in planning the tour. The Tokyo map, which shows train and subway routes, as well as main places of interest, is an indispensable tool for any traveller moving about Tokyo. Guides to hotels and ryokan across the country are also available, and you may refer to the listings of reasonably cheap accommodation in the main cities.

Buyer's Map of Osaka is published by the Osaka Municipal Trade Centre and available from the Osaka Information Office.

Tourist Map of Nagoya is published by the Nagoya international Centre.

Kyoto Monthly Guide is an excellent booklet providing a general guide and calendar of events in the city. It is a available from the JNTO office and some hotels.

(All of the above publications are available free of charge.)

DISCOVERING JAPAN

There is so much to see and do in this fabulous country that one is very tempted to stay on for the necessary several months or even years to complete the scene. Even that may not be long enough, so it at once becomes obvious that the visitor spending a few days or even a week or two must be selective in choosing the highlights.

Exploring Tokyo requires the constant use of a good map and fortunately they are widely available (usually at no cost) from such places as hotels, travel agencies and the Japan National Tourist Organization (JNTO). The JNTO map is especially recommended, as is JNTO itself. Drop into the office at Narita Airport or visit the city office, right by Yurakucho railway station, on Harumi Dori Ave, the street that runs through the middle of the Ginza district. Tel: 3502 1461 (if dialling from outside Tokyo prefix with 03, the Tokyo area code; better still, take advantage of the Japan Travel-Phone service).

JNTO offers **Teletourist Service**, a 24-hour taped information service that gives the latest goings-on in Tokyo or Kyoto. In Tokyo, call 3503 2911 (3503 2926 for French); Kyoto (075) 361 2911. The city office has a supply of excellent brochures and maps; the staff are extremely helpful and you can check up-to-the-minute details on such things as Kabuki theatre performances. The JNTO office is an essential initial reference for the traveller exploring Tokyo alone.

Getting about in Tokyo, or any other Japanese city, is complicated. Streets are rarely named and though buildings are numbered, until 1955 this was done in chronological order of their being constructed — which is not much use to a visitor.

The Japanese use what is simply called the *kumachi-cho-chome-banchi* system of addresses (otherwise known as blindman's bluff). Tokyo, for example, is divided up into 23 municipal wards known as *ku* (Chuo-ku, Chiyoda-ku and Minato-ku, to name but three), each of which is covers several hectares. Within a ku are found several so-called towns or *machi* and within each of these, several villages or *cho*; Yurakucho, Nagatacho and Hirakawacho, for example. Within cho or machi are found *chome* which are in fact blocks or clusters of blocks. These are numbered. Within each chome, buildings then have another number.

The address of the Imperial Hotel, for example, is 1-1-1, Uchisaiwaicho, Chiyoda-ku, Tokyo. The first numeral refers to the chome within Uchisaiwaicho, the next to the block within the chome and the last to the building's number. The new Otani Hotel is located at 4, Kioicho, Chiyoda-ku, Tokyo. It is an extensive property and in itself constitutes chome No. 4 of Kioicho.

There are many tricky variations in the scheme, but above you have the fundamentals. Although it may make sense on paper, it is next to useless on the ground; so much so that restaurants and bars print maps on their business cards for the guidance of customers.

Kyoto does name its streets, which adds further complication to the system, since it also uses ku and cho. Osaka operates pretty much on the Tokyo system. The term gun appears quite often in upcountry addresses. It means a county, the first subdivision of a prefecture.

Travelling by rail and then on foot you can visit all the sights of the city. Alternatively you may go by taxi, but you should be well prepared with directions written out in Japanese to show the driver.

TOKYO

Lying at the city's centre, and a good place to begin your sightseeing, is the magnificent **Imperial Palace**. From ground level one sees little else but huge stone walls and a moat set in pleasant strips of parkland, but if you start your city tour from the Palace Hotel on the east side of the palace you can go up to its roof and look over into the grounds before walking around.

The palace grounds are open to the general public only twice annually — on January 2 and on December 23 (the emperor's birthday) — but foreign visitors are allowed to visit at other times by requesting permission from the Imperial Household Agency. For details of this inquire at the JNTO city office.

Almost directly opposite the Palace Hotel is the eastern gate to the lovely **Imperial Palace Eastern Garden** (there are also north and west gates). The garden may be visited between 9 a.m. and 4:30 p.m. (no admission after 3 p.m.) on Tuesdays, Wednesdays, Thursdays, Saturdays, Sundays and public holidays. Imperial functions sometimes make the garden unavailable to the public. No charge is made for admission.

From the north gate of the Eastern Garden one can head northeast to explore the interesting bookshop district of **Kanda**, not quite a kilometre away near the **Meiji University**.

Continuing in an anticlockwise direction from the Eastern Garden one reaches **Kitanomaru Park**, next to the northern end of the palace. Besides being a pleasant place in which to stroll, the park houses the **National Museum of Modern Art**, the **Science Museum** and the **Nippon Budokan Hall**; the latter is an interesting specimen of modern Japanese architecture. The stretch of water to the east of the park (part of the moat system surrounding the palace), known as **Chidorigafuchi**, is used for pleasure boating.

Two-and-a-half kilometres to the north of the palace is the **Korakuen Garden**, one of the few great classical gardens extant in the capital. (The Korakuen can also be reached conveniently from Ginza subway station, taking the train to Korakuen station.) Near the garden is the **Kodokan Judo Hall**. Just a little under a kilometre from the northwest corner of the palace is the **Yasukuni Shrine** — an impressive and controversial Shinto memorial to the Japanese war dead. It enshrines, amongst others, former Class A war criminals, and is annually visited by a handful of high-profile politicians. Two massive *torii* gateways guard the entrance, one of bronze and another of granite (the largest in Japan).

Along the western side of the palace stretches the great moat with its inner bank surmounted by a massive, impregnable wall. Near the southwest corner is the splendidly modern **National Theatre**; while rather more to the south, the **Diet building** — home of the nation's government — stands with solid

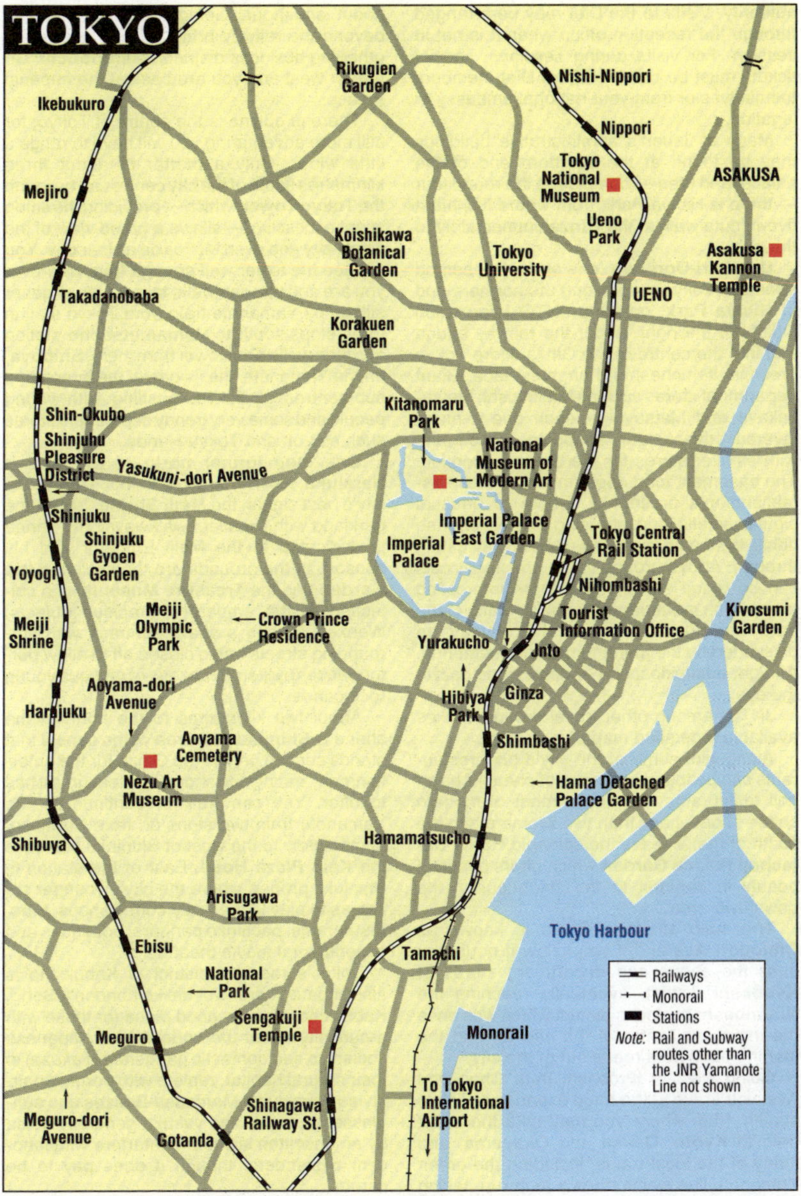
TOKYO
Ikebukuro
Rikugien Garden
Nishi-Nippori
Nippori
Tokyo National Museum
ASAKUSA
Mejiro
Ueno Park
Koishikawa Botanical Garden
Tokyo University
Asakusa Kannon Temple
UENO
Takadanobaba
Korakuen Garden
Kitanomaru Park
Shin-Okubo
Shinjuhu Pleasure District
Yasukuni-dori Avenue
National Museum of Modern Art
Shinjuku
Imperial Palace East Garden
Tokyo Central Rail Station
Shinjuku Gyoen Garden
Imperial Palace
Yoyogi
Nihombashi
Meiji Shrine
Meiji Olympic Park
Crown Prince Residence
Tourist Information Office
Kivosumi Garden
Yurakucho
Jnto
Aoyama-dori Avenue
Hibiya Park
Ginza
Harajuku
Aoyama Cemetery
Shimbashi
Nezu Art Museum
Hama Detached Palace Garden
Shibuya
Hamamatsucho
Arisugawa Park
Tokyo Harbour
Ebisu
Tamachi
National Park
Railways
Monorail
Stations
Note: Rail and Subway routes other than the JNR Yamanote Line not shown
Sengakuji Temple
Monorail
Meguro
To Tokyo International Airport
Meguro-dori Avenue
Shinagawa Railway St.
Gotanda

authority. Visits to the Diet may be arranged through the reception office when it is not in session. For visits during sessions, special tickets must be obtained from Diet members themselves or from your national embassy or legation.

Many of Japan's administrative buildings may be found at the southern end of the palace, and then — completing the round tour — there is Hibiya Park, from where it is but a five-minute walk to the **Ginza**, immediately to the east.

Uchibori-Dori Ave (one of the few named streets in Tokyo) runs along the northern end of **Hibiya Park**, past the JNTO Information Office on the right, under the railway bridge and into the centre of the Ginza. Here Tokyo presents its richest and brightest face. Giant department stores such as Mitsukoshi, Matsuzakaya and Matsuya — each one a multi-layered adventure in shopping — compete with smaller stores for the buyer's attention. The basement food departments of these establishments present a babble of unusual sights, smells and shouting voices offering tidbits to sample, and are well worth navigating through. Above ground in the smaller streets can be found some of the more interesting shops, with restaurants and bars. Many of the bars are private clubs and you may be dissuaded by the management from entering. At night a kaleidoscope of neon signs dazzle the eye.

JNTO, among other travel groups, makes available a detailed map of the Ginza.

Along with some of the city's best restaurants can be found a number of cheaper beer-hall restaurants and any number of modern coffee shops. Less than two kilometres to the south of the Ginza is the splendid **Hama Detached Palace Garden** which offers peaceful beauty in contrast to the splendour of the downtown area.

The main street in Ginza is known as **Chuodori Ave** and if you follow it north you pass the shops and department stores of **Kyobashi** district, eventually reaching the **Nihonbashi** business district which was once the merchant centre of the capital, and the starting point from roads out of the city.

Going west in Kyobashi from Chuo-Dori Ave, you arrive at the huge expanse of Tokyo station, from where you may take the bullet train to **Kyoto**, **Osaka** and **Okayama**, and many of the local trains, including the green Yamanote line which does a loop run, taking about one hour. Going further west again beyond the railway brings you to one of the other big business districts, **Marunouchi**. Go further west and you are back at the Imperial Palace.

There in outline is the centre of Tokyo; for still more adventuring you will have to range a little wider. Only a matter of about three kilometres south of the city centre can be found the **Tokyo Tower**, which — providing the smog is not excessive — allows a grand view of the whole city and even Mt Fuji on a clear day. You will see the tower well enough from wherever you are and you can walk, take a cab, or better still go by Yamanote train from Tokyo station three stops south to **Hamamatsucho** station and then walk to the tower from there. **Shibuya**, on the Yamanote line, is one of the interesting sub-centres of Tokyo, bustling with young people and some very trendy department stores such as Loft and Tokyu Hands.

One stop further north of Shibuya is **Harajuku**, where you alight to reach one of the city's best sights, the **Meiji Shrine**. Set in fine parkland with excellent walkways. The shrine is dedicated to the Meiji Emperor and his consort. In the grounds are the secluded **Iris Garden** and the **Treasure Museum** — a collection of the emperor's precious objects. Weekends bring a sharp contrast, with surrounding streets being closed off to allow performances by literally dozens of raucous young rock bands.

About two kilometres to the north of the shrine is **Shinjuku**, an area of the capital that stands second only to the Ginza for the entertainment, eating and shopping pleasures it has to offer. You can walk or continue by the Yamanote train two stops on from Harajuku. Immediately to the west of Shinjuku station is the **Keio Plaza Hotel**. East of the station is Shinjuku proper, where the city's younger set comes to play in the jazzy coffee shops, bars, restaurants, pachinko parlours, boutiques and experimental movie theatres.

Tokyo's red-light district of Kabukicho is also situated here. Not unlike London's Soho, Kabukicho is also a good place for those with a curiosity about the underside of Japanese society to see domestic gangsters (*yakuza*) in their natural habitat, replete with permed hairstyles, loud suits, Mercedes-Benzes and sunglasses at night. The yakuza generally abide by an unwritten law not to interfere with innocent bystanders, though it does pay to be careful.

The Inland Sea near Innoshima. PHOTO: MARTIN MOOS

Like the Ginza, Shinjuku is at its best in the early evening, though it stays open far later than the Ginza does with a lot going on throughout the night, or at least until the first trains start running again. Shinjuku is generally rougher and faster paced than the Ginza and has more of a "big city" feel. Food is cheaper than in the Ginza, especially in Japanese-style places. Shinjuku's 2-chome district to the east is well known for its gay nightlife, though some establishments try to maintain privacy for their Japanese clientele by denying foreigners entry.

Shinjuku is also a centre for the big department stores: Keio and Odakyu right at the station's western entrance, and Mitsukoshi and Isetan in the main eastern shopping area. If you wish to continue for a view of the inner Tokyo area, go on the Yamanote train via Takadanobaba (which is a more peaceful suburban spot with good little restaurants), Ikebukuro (a large shopping and restaurant complex) and Ueno (fascinating markets on weekends). Otherwise you may take the subway from Shinjuku, heading back into the centre of town. Shinjuku Gyoenmae station is the second stop back towards central Tokyo on the Marunouchi Line and allows access to the **Shinjuku Gyoen Garden** which is best at cherry-blossom time.

Taking the subway nearly all the way back brings you to Akasaka-Mitsuke station in the midst of the nightlife district of **Akasaka**. Some of the big cabarets are here and there are a number of small and usually expensive hostess bars. Doormen in the street will invite you to their clubs where men can meet lovely English-speaking girls and it will cost them a great deal of money. There are cheaper bars but they take a lot of finding.

To the northeast of the city centre is Ueno (take the Yamanote train to Ueno station) with its large railway station for country, local and subway trains and its interesting shopping areas; it is here also that the city's best museums (both Western and Japanese traditional and contemporary art) may be found in the precincts of Ueno Park. The park itself is unspectacular except in cherry-blossom season, though nevertheless a good place to see the Japanese family at leisure on a weekend.

On Sundays in the shopping area traffic is banned from the streets (as also happens on Sundays in the Ginza, Shinjuku and Shibuya areas), and Tokyo's people walk about the streets and sit at the sidewalk tables under colourful umbrellas in the middle of the road.

The **Tokyo National Museum** at the northern end of the park houses in several buildings one of the finest collections of Japanese and Asian art anywhere in the world. Also in the area are the **Tokyo Metropolitan Fine Art Gallery**, the **National Museum of Western Art**, the **National Science Museum** and the **Tokyo Metropolitan Festival Hall**. A big zoo and the Toshogu Shrine are also in the grounds, while less than one kilometre to the west is **Tokyo University** with its ecclesiastical architecture, ancient carved Red Gate and rock-girdled Sanshiro's pond.

Located near the Sumida River, just south of Asakusa, is the **Kokugikan Sumo Stadium and Museum** where several Japanese wrestling tournaments are held annually. Some 10 kilometres east of central Tokyo is **Tokyo Disneyland**, the theme park which has precipitated Japan's biggest boom in tourism for years. Laid out on 46 hectares of reclaimed land in Chiba prefecture, the park is modelled very closely on the Disney parks in California and Florida. There are several ways of getting to the park. From **Tokyo station** the JR Keio Line gets you to **Maihama station** next to Disneyland in around 15 minutes for ¥210; the Tozai subway line gets you from Tokyo's Nihonbashi station to Urayasu station in 15 minutes, and from there a shuttle bus gets you to the park in another 20 minutes. Alternatively, a special limousine bus service to Disneyland operates between Tokyo (about 35 minutes), Ueno and Yokohama (about 70 minutes) stations. Buses are fairly infrequent however, about one or two an hour. There is also service from Narita and Haneda airports (both about 50 minutes). Advance tickets to Disneyland can be purchased at the TDL Ticket Centre at Tokyo station (Yaesu Exit) for ¥4,400/ ¥3,000. For information on Disneyland call (0473) 540001.

UPCOUNTRY

THE MIURA AND BOSO PENINSULAS

The main port entrance to Japan is Yokohama, 25 kilometres south of Tokyo on the western shore of Tokyo Bay. The cities have now grown so tremendously that their boundaries have merged and they form one huge conurbation. Yokohama itself has a population of more than 3 million. The city centre is beginning to show the effects of some unusually enlightened city planning, and close by are remnants of the major 19th-century foreign settlement. Places of interest include the foreigners' cemetery, **Yamashita Park** (commanding a view of the harbour), **Sankeien Garden** (with fine landscaping and historic buildings) and isezaki-cho (the main shopping street). The **Yokohama Museum of Art** (reached via Sakuragicho Station) is worth a visit, and there is also an amusement park nearby with a huge ferris wheel. Restaurants in Yokohama's Chinatown are more authentic than most in Tokyo, which surprisingly has no such district.

Yokohama can be reached by taking the JR Yokosuka-line train from Tokyo station. The Yokosuka line proceeds from Yokohama to **Kamakura**. About 50 kilometres from Tokyo and overlooking the Sagami Bay, Kamakura is quiet for a few months in winter, but otherwise packed with Japanese and foreign tourists, especially on weekends. Its beaches, stretching westward to the neighbouring island-town of **Enoshima**, are popular in summer and usually packed. The principal objects of interest in Kamakura include the **Daibutsu** (a massive bronze image of the Buddha 12.8 metres high); the **Hase Kannon Temple** nearby; the **Tsurugaoka Hachimangu Shrine**; the **Enkakuji**, **Kenchoji**, **Gokurakuji** and other Buddhist temples. The Daibutsu is extraordinarily beautiful — don't miss it.

Reaching south from Yokohama and Kamakura is the **Miura Peninsula**, served by both the Yoksuka Line and the Keihin Kyuko railway, which runs from Shinagawa station. At the end of the JR line is the town of Kurihama, a fishing port with good bathing beaches. On the other side of Tokyo Bay is the far larger Boso Peninsula. The area is noted for its sea produce which supplies much of the capital's needs. The excellent beaches to be found along the Pacific coast are usually not too crowded, mainly because it takes two to three hours in a crowded train to reach them. To the north of Tokyo, **Nikko National Park** spreads over a large area of beautiful mountain country, including the Nikko region itself as well as the **Nasu** and **Shinobara** spas. The region is noted for its lakes, waterfalls and forests, and particularly for the splendour of the shrines and temples surrounding the tomb of the founder of the Tokugawa Shogunate, Ieyasu.

Nikko City, the park's main jump-off point, is 150 kilometres from Tokyo and is most conveniently reached by rail: either JR from Tokyo station or by the very comfortable privately operated Tobu trains from Asakusa — the journey taking about two hours. The sloping street leading from Nikko station to the celebrated Toshogu Shrine is lined with hotels and souvenir shops. Spanning the Daiya River is the red-lacquered **Sacred Bridge**, from which one passes through a forest of giant Japanese cedars, past the Buddhist **Rinnoji Temple** to the shrine. Completed in 1636, the **Toshogu Shrine** was built by the Shogun Iemitsu for his grandfather Ieyasu. It is an elaborately decorated set of buildings with gilded and coloured carvings of birds and animals, including the proverbial **Three Monkeys** and the **Nikko Sleeping Cat**. Its chief glory is the **Yomeimon Gate**. The Inner Shrine has fine paintings on its screens and doors. Other excellent examples of architecture in the area are the **Five-Storey Pagoda**, the **Yakushido**, the **Futarasan Shrine** (built in 1617 and the oldest building in the district) and the **Daiyuin Mausoleum** (containing Iemitsu's tomb).

Chuzenji, a beautiful oval lake surrounded by hills, lies 1,280 metres above sea-level, 18 kilometres above Nikko. An interesting way to reach the lake is to go by bus or tram to Umagaeshi and from there to take the electric tramway which runs up the steep hillside to **Akachidaira**, where the view is fabulous. An even better view of the countryside is obtained from the point reached by the cable car operating from Akachidaira. From Akachidaira a bus continues on to the village of Chuzenji. The **Kegon Waterfall** can be reached just a short distance from Chuzenji and at the other end of the lake are the **Ryuzu Falls** and a trout hatchery. Further on, the **Nikko Yumoto spa**, near Lake Yunoko (a 45-minute bus ride from Chuzenji village), has hot springs and one may also fish. There is a picturesque walk taking some two to three hours back to Chuzenji by the **Yudaki Falls** and along the **Yugawa River**.

Mashiko, one hour by bus from Utsunomiya station on the way to Nikko, is a centre of folk pottery. More than 150 kilns turn out various kinds of Mashiko-yaki, as the pottery is called. The earthenware is admired for its durability, simple beauty and usefulness. Visitors can take a turn at the potter's wheel and make a teacup or a tray. The **Mashiko Sankokan Museum**, founded by the late Shoji Hamada, Japan's world famous potter, who in his lifetime was designated a "living national treasure," displays pottery, crystal ware, metal work and other objects from around the world.

FUJI-HAKONE-IZU NATIONAL PARK

Located to the southwest of Tokyo, the park spreads over a substantial area of south central Honshu and comprises four regions: **Mt Fuji** — including the sacred mountain area of the Five Lakes to its north; **Hakone** — a volcanic mountain area with hot springs, a lake and pleasant scenery; the Izu Peninsula — noted for its scenery, beaches and hot springs, and the **Seven Islands of Izu**, scattered in the Pacific to the south of the peninsula. The three mainland regions of the park are all interconnected by rail or road and the islands may be reached by boat from the Izu Peninsula.

The Hakone region is the most readily accessible of the four. The town of **Odawara** can be reached by Odakyu Line from Shinjuku station, JR super-express bullet train from Tokyo station (40 minutes), or by bus. From Odawara to Hakone proper one has a choice of frequent services to **Hakone-machi** on the southern shore of Lake Ashi — also called Lake Hakone — via many of the other resort sites; by the Odakyu limited express train to Yumoto (15 minutes); or by the Hakone Tozan railway to Gora (40 minutes). The private-line Odakyu limited express train runs directly from Shinjuku railway station in Tokyo to Yumoto.

The town of Yumoto is the first spa resort as one enters the Hakone mountains from Odawara. About four kilometres on from there is the thriving spa of **Miyanoshita**, a conveniently central place for exploring the surrounding country. Buses and cable cars provide transport to the several sulphurous and bubbling hot springs at Kowaki-dani and Owakudani lakes: Ashi (where one may cruise, fish or simply meditate on the reflection of Mt Fuji, **Mt Koma** (whose peak offers splendid views), **Sengokuhara Spa** (which has several golf courses) and **Kojiri** (at the far end of Lake Ashi and reached via the scenic Ashinoko Skyline Driveway).

Mt Fuji (3,776 metres) is the highest and most celebrated mountain in Japan. The Fuji-Five Lakes region is easily reached by JR express from Tokyo's Shinjuku station via Otsuki, where one changes to the private-line Fuji Express train to **Lake Kawaguchi**. Several JR trains also make the journey without the need for changing trains. JR trains departing from Tokyo and Shinjuku railway stations run to the town of Gotemba, between the Hakone and Mt Fuji regions, and from there one takes the bus to **Lake Yamanaka**. Journey time by rail to the Five Lakes region from Tokyo is some two-and-a-half hours. The Five Lakes (from east to west, Yamanaka, Kawaguchi, Saiko, Shoji and Motosu) region is one of Japan's favourite recreation centres, providing facilities for leisure and sport in all seasons amid splendid scenery. Camping, swimming, boating and fishing are popular in summer, while in autumn the surrounding forests are a mass of gold and red leaves. Winter brings skating, wakasagi fishing and duck hunting among other popular pursuits.

From Kawaguchiko one may take the bus up to the 2,514-metre level on the slopes of Mt Fuji. The mountain is officially open to climbers from July 1 to August 31. One may reach the summit after a climb of five-and-a-half hours from the bus terminus. Many, of course, for reasons of honour, climb the whole mountain using any one of the five trails leading up the mountain from **Kawaguchiko**, **Fuji-Yoshida**, **Lake Shoji**, **Gotemba** and **Fujinomiya**. The routes from Kawaguchiko and Gotemba are by far the most popular. Stone huts provide accommodation at almost all stages on the ascent of the mountain: with an evening meal the cost is approximately ¥4,500. If Japanese food is unacceptable to your taste you will need to bring your own provisions. Average temperatures on the summit are 4.9°C in July and 5.9°C in August. Appropriately warm clothing should be taken for the climb, including a light raincoat.

The Ochudo-meguri is a trip on foot around the waist of Mt Fuji, about half-way up (2,514 metres). The distance is some 19 kilometres and takes eight to 10 hours to complete. It makes a pleasant summer excursion.

The **Izu Peninsula**, to the south, is popular with Japanese and foreigners alike for its mild weather, beautiful coastal and island scenery, hot springs and beaches. The area is particularly enjoyable early in the year with its gentle winter climate and early flowering plum blossoms. Atami (which can be reached by way of Shinkansen Kodama bullet train as well as normal express from Tokyo station) is the northeastern entrance to the peninsula, and a commercial sort of coastal resort centre featuring hot springs. Rather more pleasant is the southern coastal town of **Shimoda**, rich in historical remains, old houses, museums and coastal scenery. There is good bathing at **Shirahama** beach, five kilometres to the east, and pleasant walks along the coast. Izu is a good area to take advantage of a chance to stay in Kokumin Shukusha (People's Lodges).

Forming a chain running southeast from near the entrance to Tokyo Bay are the Seven Isles of Izu, noted for the distinctive manners and customs of their peoples. **Oshima**, the largest and nearest to Tokyo, can be reached by air from Tokyo (ANA) or sea (seven hours overnight by Tokai Kisen Co. steamer from Takeshiba Pier, Tokyo), and also by sea from Atami and Shimoda. The island's indented shoreline is ideal for fishing and there is a conical, active volcano, **Mt Mihara**. Further out to sea lies **Hachijojima** (one hour by air or 13 by sea), with its two extinct volcanoes. The island is especially noted for the beautiful silk fabric called *kihachijo*.

THE JAPAN ALPS

Mountains dominate the greater part of Japan's land surface and it is the Japan Alps, northwest of Tokyo, which offers the greatest concentration of high country suitable for the winter sports of skiing and skating, as well as climbing in summer and winter.

The most convenient access to the ski areas is by train and then by bus. Trains on the Joetsu line from Tokyo's Ueno station serve the **Naeba**, **Yuzawa** and **Iwappara** ski areas. For Naeba you take the train to Gokan (two hours and 15 minutes) and then the bus (one hour). For Yuzawa you take the train to Yuzawa (two hours and 40 minutes). The slopes are just a 15-minute walk from the station. For Iwappara also alight at Yuzawa but then take the bus (10 minutes). Buses serve the Akakura and Shiga Heights ski areas.

For Akakura take the train to Myoko-kogen (four-and-a-half hours) and from there the bus (20 minutes). For Shiga Heights take the train to Nagano (four hours), change to the private-line train that travels up to Yudanaka and from there go by bus. JR trains also run directly from Ueno to Yudanaka. Trains on the Chuo line leave from Tokyo's Shinjuku station and serve the Happone ski area. Take the train on the Chuo and then the Oito line (changing at Matsumoto — direct train service also available), six hours 40 minutes to Hakuba and then by bus (10 minutes).

The skiing season normally extends from

Giant Buddha statue and pagoda on Awaji Island. PHOTO: MARTIN MOOS

late December to early April. Accommodation, all the way from luxury resorts to minshuku, is available and equipment can be rented. Especially on weekends bookings should be made from Tokyo to ensure accommodation. Many of the ski resorts are located at hot springs.

Matsumoto (three-and-a-half hours from Tokyo or three hours from Nagoya) is a gateway to much of the alps. The railway journey (Chuo line) from Tokyo is through some of the most picturesque rural country in Japan. The town itself is a pleasant, slightly old-fashioned place in a wide, peaceful valley dominated by mountains and possesses an interesting museum and historic castle. From Matsumoto, branch rail lines and buses take mountaineers to the best climbing locations. Shirouma, Otenji, Harinoki and Tateyama mountains have the greatest number of rest huts and the best paths.

Mt Yari (Spear Peak), the highest in the northern range, is approached from Matsumoto via the Jonen Range. The beautiful Kamikochi Valley can be reached from Mt Yari or directly (one-and-a-half hours by bus) from Matsumoto. The valley, 16 kilometres long by 1.6 kilometres across, is at an altitude of 1,524 metres and is surrounded by high, snow-clad peaks. The clear River Azusa runs through the valley and with its lakes, hot springs, alpine flora and cool bracing air, it is perfect in summer for camping, fishing and boating. Another summer mountain resort of note is Karuizawa on the Shin-etsu train line three hours from Tokyo.

NORTHEASTERN JAPAN

The northern region of Honshu Island (known as Northeastern Japan or Tohoku) gives the visitor an opportunity to see a quieter and, some think, friendlier side of Japanese life than in the more crowded south. **Sendai**, the most important city of the region, is the capital of a land of traditional crafts (unique lacquerware, copper and iron utensils, textiles and *kokeshi* dolls), of hard winters and excellent ski areas (the Zao ski areas), and of national parks and hot springs. On the four-hour journey from Tokyo, the traveller sees many northern-style thatched farmhouses, though Sendai itself is rapidly becoming an industrial city.

Matsushima, a fishing village and seaside resort just half an hour from Sendai, is famous for its fascinating scenery. Some 250 oddly shaped rock islets, helmeted with ancient pines, lie scattered over the bay: ferries and other boats convey sightseers among these natural grotesques. Matsushima also offers hillside walks with views in abundance. Near the shore of Matsushima, the ancient **Temple of Zuiganji** (founded in 828, though the present building dates from 1609) contains many historical memorials and art treasures. A fine avenue of Japanese cedars leads past cave after cave in the rocky cliff face where once priests spent long hours in meditation.

Aomori is the main town in the very north of Honshu and the departure point for ferries making the crossing to Hokkaido. (Since the winter of 1988, the Seikan Tunnel, which runs under the Tsugaru Strait, has been in commercial operation to allow rail passage on the Tsugaru Kaikyo line between Aomori and the northern island of Hokkaido.) South of Aomori is the **Towada National Park** where forested mountains surround Lake Towada, the largest mountain lake in Japan. The lake can be reached in one-and-a-half hours by road from the railway station at Towada-Minami on the Hanawa line. Almost circular, it is studded with pine-clad islands and offers trout fishing in June and July. There are agreeable ryokan on the shores and places of historic interest. In the north of the park and just 35 kilometres from Aomori can be found the **Hakkoda Mountains**, a volcanic range where one may camp and climb in summer and ski in winter.

NAGOYA AND SURROUNDS

The city of Nagoya, with a population of more than 2 million, lies 350 kilometres west of Tokyo. It ranks among Japan's leading industrial cities and forms, with Tokyo and Osaka, the heart of the country's economic activities. Its history dates from the 17th century when Ieyasu Tokugawa built an imposing castle there which is now the city's symbol. Largely destroyed in the course of the war, Nagoya has been rebuilt and is now noted for its wide boulevards. Being a centre of industry, Nagoya has little to offer the visitor compared with Japan's more historical towns and cities, but places of interest to the visitor include the Nagoya Castle (rebuilt in 1959 in the original design), the **Atsuta Shrine** (the most sacred of Shinto shrines after Ise and containing the sacred imperial sword), **Higashiyama Botanical Gardens** and **Zook**, the Noritake China Factory and the underground shopping arcades near the railway station. Nagoya is most easily reached by the Shinkansen bullet trains from Kobe, Osaka, Kyoto and Tokyo. Travel time from Tokyo is two hours, and from Osaka, one hour.

One hour by bus north of Nagoya is the town of **Gifu**, site of the famous night-time cormorant fishing on the Nagara River. The season is from May 11 until October 15, and fishing takes place on all nights except during the full moon and after heavy rains. One hires a boat and joins in the carnival atmosphere in the vicinity of the fishing boats. Nagoya is one of the most convenient points from which to visit the most sacred Shinto shrines at Ise. The Mikimoto pearl farms are in the vicinity of Ise. (Ise may also be reached from Osaka.) Ise can be reached by the private-line Kintetsu (also called Kinki-Nippon) railway from Nagoya station to Uji-Yamada station (one-and-a-half hours). It takes two hours from Osaka or Kyoto. At the town of Toba, 14.5 kilometres further on from Ise, one can take a boat to inspect the cultured-pearl farms.

The Ise shrines are Japan's great link with the past. The **Naiku** (Inner Shrine) is consecrated to Amaterasu-Omikami, the Sun Goddess and supposed ancestor of the Japanese royal line. The **Geku** (Outer Shrine) is dedicated to Toyouke-Omikami, Goddess of the Harvest. Both utterly simple in design and execution, the shrines are constructed of plain cypress beams and are completely rebuilt every 20 years, as has been the custom for something like the past 1,500 years. The Naiku contains one of the three greatest Shinto treasures: the **Yata-no-Kagami** (mirror). The peaceful natural surroundings of the shrines are most evocative of the Shinto belief in the divinity that pervades all nature; rock, tree and people alike. The Naiku can be reached by bus from Uji-Yamada in 15 minutes. Geku is just a 10-minute walk from the railway station. The Ise-Shima Skyline Rd runs between Ise and Toba, commanding a panoramic view of the Ise and Toba Bays, the Ise Plain and the neighbouring mountains.

The beach resort of Futamiga-Ura is nearby and offers excellent bathing. Due north of Nagoya, on the northern side of Honshu on the Japan Sea, is Kanazawa, famous as the former castle town of the Maeda Clan, the second-largest clan in feudal Japan. During the three centuries of the town's prosperity the citizens acquired the taste for noh drama, tea ceremony and flower arrangement-cultural aspects that are still very evident in life there today. In the heart of the city can be found the famous

Kenroku park, dating from 1643, one of the country's most celebrated gardens.

Meijimura, 25 minutes from Inuyama Rhine Park or one hour by bus from Nagoya, is a museum village that seeks to preserve monuments from the early days of Japan's modernization. More than 50 genuine historic buildings, brought to the village from throughout Japan, are on display. Included are the imperial carriage of the Meiji Emperor, the main entrance hall and lobby of the old Imperial Hotel designed by Frank Lloyd Wright, and other unique attractions. Open 10 a.m.-5 p.m. March 1-October 31, and 10 a.m.-4 p.m. November-February. Admission ¥1,240. Buses leave every 15 minutes from Inuyama station.

KYOTO

Kyoto is among the world's loveliest cities. Spared from the bombs of World War II, the city is graced by elegant timber buildings — both religious and domestic — as a stroll down any of the smaller streets will reveal. Wood is the material with which the artisans and artists of Japan are most at ease. The people love it in life, adoring its reflection of the passing seasons in blossom and fading leaf, and they cherish it nonetheless as timber which they work into Buddha or flooring with just about the same care and sensitivity. At the same time however, and as Japan's fifth-largest city, Kyoto possesses an inevitable amount of the ugly commercial and industrial clutter so necessary to contemporary viability, and one has to go searching for much of the traditional beauty.

Old Kyoto is very much a place of wood. Burned to the ground many times in part or whole, the city possesses a resilience which has enabled it always to spring back into life. Begun in 793 to replace the short-lived capital at Nagaokakyo, Kyoto was to remain the capital of Japan until the Meiji Restoration brought about the shift in 1868 to Tokyo. Along with that of the emperor, the city's power has fluctuated from time to time depending on the degree to which the military leadership of the period was allied with the court. But just as the emperor has always been the spiritual leader of the Japanese people — their link with the Sun Goddess and so with the very mystery of their creation — so too has Kyoto been the cultural fountainhead of the nation. Today it still retains much of that privileged glory.

A great deal that is special is known only to residents. Still, what is publicly available is experience enough for most visitors — several hundred Shinto shrines and well over a thousand Buddhist temples, many of them officially designated national treasures or housing national treasures. Superficially they are a splendid collection of beautiful buildings, sculptures, paintings and gardens and nonetheless enjoyable for being merely that, though all these things of course developed within the framework of Japanese cultural life (especially the religious aspect) and it is with an appreciation of this that one best relates to the artistic riches of Kyoto.

Accessible from Tokyo by the Hikari superexpress train in less than three hours, from Osaka by express train in 40 minutes and from Kobe in little over an hour, Kyoto is within easy reach of the main international entry points to Japan. Bus transport at approximately halfhourly intervals operates from Osaka International Airport to Miyako, Kyoto, New Hankyu, International and Grand hotels in Kyoto. JNTO has an excellent office in Kyoto on the ground floor of the Kyoto Tower Bldg with its entrance on Karasuma St. A great deal of printed information is available from the office and the staff there speak excellent English and will be glad to advise you. They have a comprehensive listing of the cheaper accommodation offered, so it is a good place to telephone from and arrange something if you arrive in town without having booked a hotel. They also have a monthly listing of the festivals, concerts and other special entertainment offered in the city.

If you need help to communicate with a Japanese person who speaks no English ring the JNTO office on 371 5649. The office is open 9 a.m.-5 p.m. It is closed on Saturday afternoons, Sundays and public holidays. They will also arrange for a home visit in the Kyoto area for those wishing to meet the Japanese in their home surroundings. In addition to maps and transport guides, the monthly guide *Kyoto* is worth obtaining along with the smaller *Kyoto Monthly Guide* published by the Department of Cultural Affairs. These will give you reliable calendars of the city's events for the time of your stay. As elsewhere, a map is an indispensable aid to moving about the city and surroundings. The JNTO map obtainable at the JNTO Information Office is satisfactory and you should also ask for their guides to bus and subway routes. The several companies operating tours in the city can show you Kyoto in a series of half-day tours including arts and crafts visits costing less than ¥5,000 per tour. Kyoto operators offer around a dozen different tours.

Sunset in Kagoshima. PHOTO: MARTIN MOOS

You can also schedule a trip to see cormorants fishing on the **Oi River**. The price range is roughly the same as for the regular tours. One should always take off one's shoes before entering a temple or shrine, and you are expected to be respectfully quiet in the buildings.

The old **Imperial Palace**, though repeatedly destroyed by fire and then rebuilt, has been the home of 26 emperors from the time of its original construction by the Emperor Kammu in 794 up to the Meiji Restoration of 1868. Built in classically simple style in 1855, the present palace lies behind high walls set in an outer public garden of 80 hectares. Its inner Shishinden Hall is used for imperial ceremonies, including the emperor's enthronement. The palace buildings contain some excellent paintings, and in the grounds can be found a notable garden. The palace lies just to the north of the centre of town.

To visit the palace, permission must be obtained 30 minutes in advance of the visiting times (between 10 a.m. and 2 p.m. on weekdays and 10 a.m. on Saturdays — it is closed on the second and fourth Saturdays of each month, Sundays and National Holidays) from the Imperial Household Agency office (open 9 a.m.-noon and 1-4 p.m. on weekdays; 9 a.m.-noon on the first and third Saturdays) in the northwest corner of the outer palace grounds.

Just a few minutes walk to the west from the city centre is the **Nijo Castle**, built in 1608 by Tokugawa Ieyasu, the founder of the last of Japan's shogunal dynasties. The castle was Ieyasu's residence when he visited from Edo, and remained a glorious symbol of his power for the notice of Kyoto in his absence. Many of the original inner buildings have been destroyed by fire, but the remaining Nino-maru Halls are so excellent, especially as regards their wall paintings, as to be well worth a visit.

Kyoto has several excellent museums. Of special note is the **Kyoto National Museum** to the southeast. Its exhibitions include pieces from Japan's pre-history as well as other examples of Japan's religious and secular arts.

To the near east can be found the Municipal **Art Gallery** which, in addition to its collection of painted scrolls and screens, also holds periodic exhibitions of modern art and photography; and directly across the road the **National Museum of Modern Art** holds a number of exhibitions, largely of contemporary Japanese work.

But it is the Buddhist temples, and to a lesser extent the Shinto shrines of Kyoto, which make the city justly famous; many of them are treasure houses of religious sculpture, paintings and sacred texts.

Kyoto is principally a Buddhist city — certainly as regards its architecture — and the great remains of the past are largely of that belief. Shinto shrines there are, but in far less imposing array.

Conspicuous by their central position are the **Yasaka Shrine** and the **Chion-in Temple**. The shrine, with its brilliant red torii, stands at the eastern end of Shijo St and marks the entrance to Maruyama Park, a favourite strolling place for the townsfolk, especially when the cherry trees are in blossom. Up the hill and to the north a little way is Chion-in. First built in 1211 as the headquarters of the Jodo sect, the temple has been repeatedly destroyed by fire, and the present building dates from 1639. The main hall is decorated in gold and dedicated to the sect's founder, Honen Shonin.

Only several hundred metres to the north of the two art galleries already mentioned is the **Heian Shrine**, erected in 1895 to commemorate the 1,100th anniversary of the founding of Kyoto as the capital. The buildings, spread around a vast courtyard, are a replica on a reduced scale of the first Imperial palace in Kyoto. The shrine has a fine landscape garden with cherry tress (April) and irises (June). The excellent **Kyoto Kaikan Bldg** is nearby.

Southeast of the Heian Shrine, on the edge of the forested hills that extend along the whole eastern aspect of the city, is **Nazen-ji Temple**. Of the Zen Rinzai sect, the temple's main building is finely decorated with paintings on the sliding doors and there is an excellent sand garden.

Kamigamo and **Shimogamo** shrines (3.2 kilometres apart) lie not far from the eastern bank of the Kamo River, before it joins the Takano River. The May 15 Aoi Matsuri (Hollyhock) Festival is held jointly by the shrines, representative of the imperial processions that once came to pay homage to the local deities. The prefectural Botanical Garden lies between the shrines.

Going west one reaches **Daitokuji Temple**. This is a well-known Zen centre with powerfully impressive buildings, some dating from the 15th century, though most are from the 16th and 17th. The two-storeyed Sanmon gateway was built in the 16th century under the direction of Senno Rikyu, a noted master of the tea ceremony.

Temples of interest in the west of the city include three of special note. **Koryu-ji Temple's** Preaching Hall is the oldest wooden structure in Kyoto, dating from 1165. The **Reihokan Bldg** is used as a museum and contains, among other fine works of sculpture, the delightful Miroku Bosatsu **seated Bodhisattva**. This wooden carving of great elegance and delicacy dates from the period 552-645. **Tenryu-ji Temple**, further west, has a celebrated 14th-century garden. Across the river to the south of Tenryu-ji is **Saiho-ji** (The Moss-Garden Temple) where the entire wooded garden is covered with more than 120 species of moss. Seen on a rainy day it has its own special mystery.

Lake Biwa (15 minutes by train from Kyoto) beyond Mt Hiei is the largest freshwater lake in Japan. It is famous for the eight views of the neighbouring countryside it offers. Regular sightseeing steamers cruise the lake.

Another interesting trip is to shoot the rapids of the Hozu River from Kameoka to Arashiyama, taking about one-and-a-half hours. Kameoka is about 16 kilometres from Kyoto and can be reached by the San-in line from Kyoto station or Nijo station. The return journey to Kyoto from Arashiyama can be made on the Keifuku Electric Railway Ranzan line.

Nara, 40 kilometres from Kyoto to the south, is the site of Japan's first permanent capital during the years 710 to 784. Previously, the ruling clan had moved their capital each time a new ruler came to power. Now quite a substantial provincial town. Nara still retains much of the past: temples from as early as the seventh century and museums and treasure houses bearing the artistic masterpieces of Japanese Buddhism. The more recent past is everywhere on display as you walk in the peaceful lanes surrounded by traditional houses.

Nara is reached by rail from Kyoto in about an hour and from Osaka in about 40 minutes. Best access is by the private-line Kintetsu (Kinki Nippon) trains. The one from Kyoto leaves from the station immediately to the south of the main Kyoto station: that from Osaka leaves from Namba station. The Nara Kintetsu station is the centre of the modern section of the town. The town's famous Nara (Deer) Park lies the best part of a mile to the east and here visitors can wander and hand-feed the tame, sacred deer. Right in the town, only a short distance to the southeast of the railway station, is the **Kofuku-ji Temple**. Along to the east from the Kofuku-ji Temple, and near the entrance to Nara Park, is the **Nara National**

Museum housing a valuable collection of Buddhist art — much of it from neighbouring temples — dating from as early as the Nara period (645-794). The museum offers a good opportunity to see some of the country's finest treasures, better displayed than in their scattered and often gloomy original settings.

On the east side of Nara Park lies the **Kasuga Shrine**. The 3,000 bronze and stone lanterns on and around the shrine are lit each year on February 2, 3 and 4 and on August 15 to celebrate the end and start of winter. An impressive historic procession is held at the shrine on March 13. The buildings are simple and dignified, their lines and colour in harmony with the peaceful grove in which they are set.

About five kilometres southwest of the town are the temples of **Toshodai-ji** and **Yakushi-ji**; Nishinokyo station on the Kintetsu Kashiwara-line provides access to them.

About 13 kilometres to the southwest is **Horyu-ji Temple**, one of Japan's most valuable repositories of ancient art. It is the second-oldest existing temple in the country, having been founded in 607, and is considered the most perfect group of Buddhist buildings in Japan. It is also a supreme example of seventh-century Chinese architectural style. Remarkably preserved throughout the ages (though many times rebuilt and repaired), it shows the ability of the Japanese to preserve their most respected historical monuments. Horyu-ji can be reached by bus (40 minutes) from the square outside the JR Nara railway station. Alternatively, one can go by JR train on the Kansai line from Nara JR station to Horyu-ji station. The temple is less than two kilometres to the north of the station.

OSAKA

Osaka, 500 kilometres to the west of Tokyo and 40 kilometres southwest of Kyoto, is Japan's second city. The population is now well in excess of 3 million. A great business centre and port, Osaka is famous as the place where people use as a greeting: "Are you making any money?" But it is noted not only for its exuberant industrial and commercial life but also for its interest in the arts. Home of the *Bunraku* puppet drama, Osaka also hosts a splendid extravaganza of the arts — Japanese and Western alike — at its annual **International Trade Fair** held in April.

Travel time by shinkansen Nozomi bullet train between Tokyo and Osaka is usually just on two-and-a-half hours: almost as quick and more convenient than air travel. A great many international airlines call at Osaka, and the large port of Kobe is only just over 30 kilometres away to the west. Rail and road travel schedules are likely to be disupted for some time as infrastructure damaged in the January 1995 Kobe area earthquake is repaired, including railway tracks, roads, electrical and water supplies, houses and other buildings. As of April 1995, Kobe's hotels were closed. Check with the JNTO, your hotel or travel agent before planning a trip to the Osaka-Kobe area. The bullet trains arrive at Shin-Osaka station in the north, beyond the Yodo River from the city proper. Trains and subways run from there throughout the city, but it might be just as well to take a taxi to your hotel if you are a newcomer to the city.

THE INLAND SEA AND SHIKOKU ISLANDS

The Inland Sea of Seto stretches from Osaka, between the islands of Honshu and Shikoku to the resort town of **Beppu** on the east coast of Kyushu island, a distance of some 480 kilometres. Really a chain of five seas linked by channels, it is one of the most picturesque expanses of water in the world. The numerous islands, beaches and coastal plateaux along with the sea itself go to make up the Inland Sea National Park. The park's small ports, fishing villages, salt fields and coastal farms are all part of the picture. Regular cruise boats run from Osaka (leaving from the Benten Pier Terminal) to Beppu, stopping at Kobe (Naka Pier), Takamatsu, Imabari and Takahama.

The trip takes 15 hours and the fare runs from about ¥6,000-19,000, depending on choice of berth. Perhaps more interesting is to combine sea and train travel through the region, stopping for a day or more at places of interest. Ferries link Honshu and Shikoku at many points and railways run along the length of both coasts of the Inland Sea. The Honshu coast (known as the Sanyo Coast) has various points of interest. **Iwakuni** is famous for its Kintai (Brocade Sash) Bridge, its five wooden spans stretching 228 metres. **Miyajima (Shrine Island)** is the gem of the area, about an hour by train and ferry from Hiroshima. Its **Itsukushima Shrine** is said to have been founded by the Empress Suiko (554-628) and then enlarged to its present grandeur some 600 years later. It has galleries built over the sea, so that at high tide the whole edifice seems to be floating. The 16-metre-high O-torii shrine gate of red-painted camphor-wood rises from the sea, but can be reached on foot at low tide. Mt Misen (530 metres) near the centre of the island is covered with forest inhabited by monkeys and deer. A temple founded in the ninth century stands near the summit.

HIROSHIMA

Hiroshima, with a population of about 1.1 million, is the capital of Hiroshima prefecture, as well as western Honshu's biggest city. A bustling commercial and industrial centre, levelled by the first atomic bomb dropped by U.S. forces on August 6, 1945, near the end of World War II, resulting in casualties estimated at 130,000. Now almost entirely rebuilt, the city acts as a magnet for reasons quite different than most other tourist centres. Hiroshima comprises six islands connected by over 80 bridges spanning the Ota River. Near the eastern edge of the Aioi Bridge stands the **Atomic Bomb Dome**, which was close to the centre of the explosion. It is the only atomic-bombed building that has been preserved in the city. The dome is just 15 minutes from Hiroshima station.

Peace Memorial Park is also about 15 minutes by bus or tram from the station, or 15 minutes' walk from **Hiroshima Castle**. Laid out after the war, the park includes the modern **Peace Memorial Hall**, a cenotaph for the A-bomb victims and the **Peace Memorial Museum**, which while presenting a harrowing and deeply moving display of the destructive power of nuclear weapons, offers little historical perspective on the war itself.

Further east of Hiroshima is **Okayama**. Here can be found the famous **Korakuen Garden**, one of the most celebrated in the country (another being the Kenrokuen at Kanazawa). The garden was completed in 1700 by the *daimyo* (warlord) of the province. Kurashiki, west of Okayama, has a fine museum of Japanese folk art (*mingei*). While there are other mingei museums in Tokyo, Osaka and Tottori, Kurashiki's is best known for being housed in four of the traditional rice granaries (*kura*) which give the town its name and distinctive atmosphere.

Shikoku, the smallest of Japan's four main islands, has its own distinctive charm. Traditional customs have survived rather better in Shikoku's rural atmosphere than in bustling central and western Honshu. The island is also a favourite destination for Japanese pilgrims visiting the 88 holy temples to be found there. The city of **Takamatsu** is the main gateway to the island and can be reached by both JR and private-company ferries from Uno, south of Okayama, by steamer and hydrofoil from Osaka and Kobe. The town's attractions include the fine landscape garden of **Ritsurin Park**, and there is an excellent view of the Inland Sea from the Yashima Plateau (30 minutes by bus or train from the city.)

An hour by train to the southwest of Takamatsu is **Kotohira**, site of the Kompira Shrine, which ranks with those of Ise and Izumo in importance as a centre of Shinto. In front of the Kotohaira railway station is a lantern 27-metre-tall built in 1965 as a landmark for pilgrims to the shrine. **Tokushima**, on the east coast of Shikoku, is noted for its exciting annual Awa Odori summer dance festival. Naruto Strait to the north, is famous for its tidal whirlpools which may be observed from a special tower. **Shodo Island**, in the Inland Sea (one hour 30 minutes by regular steamer from Takamatsu), is a particular attraction for its Kankakei Valley which features grotesque rock formations and an abundance of wild monkeys.

Matsuyama lies on the west coast of Shikoku and possesses one of the best preserved castles in Japan. The three-storeyed keep, remodelled in 1784, contains a museum of armour and weapons of the era. Uwajima, two hours to the south by rail, has a castle (built in 1602) and the Warei Shrine and Tenshaen Gardens are worth a visit. The special fights between oxen are a distinctive feature of the area. The animals tussle with one another, head to head, with the first to step back the loser. The southwest corner of Shikoku is much subjected to typhoons, and the villages along the coast have characteristic protective stone walls.

KYUSHU

Nagasaki

Kyushu is the most southern of the main Japanese islands, known for its subtropical scenery, hot springs, volcanoes and numerous historical sites which serve as reminders of the former cultural flow between this area and the European and Asian continents. One may fly directly to either Fukuoka, Kumamoto, Nagasaki or Miyazaki from Tokyo. Train services link the island with such centres as Osaka and Tokyo; travel time from Tokyo by bullet train and then limited express to Nagasaki is about eight hours. Nagasaki — target of the second U.S.

atomic bomb in 1945 — can also be reached from Osaka and Kobe by Inland Sea steamer to the east coast resort of Beppu and then overland by train or by bus. A bustling port town built on steep hills around its harbour, Nagasaki is vaguely reminiscent of Hong Kong. Fukuoka (the old section of the town is known as Hakata, as is the railway station) in the north, is the main commercial and industrial centre.

Just over 50 kilometres to the west is **Karatsu**, with its splendid white, sandy beach at Nijino-matsubara. Further west, just north of Sasebo, is the small island town of Hirado, with its castle museum bequeathed to the town by the Matsuura clan containing numerous remains and relics from early British and Dutch trade expeditions to Japan.

But for visitors, the main destination is Nagasaki, reached by train in about three hours from Fukuoka. The chief sites in Nagasaki include the **Peace Park** and **Atomic Bomb Memorial**; the **Chinese Sofuku-ji Temple** and nearby Meganebashi Bridge; **Glover House** for its fine view of the harbour and for its association with the story of Madame Butterfly; and such mementoes of early Japanese Christianity as Oura Catholic Church, Urakami Catholic Cathedral and the Site of Martyrdom of the Twenty-six Saints of Japan. The city has a distinctive air of leisured sophistication.

Three hours' drive from Nagasaki is **Unzen**, a popular hot springs resort in the Unzen-Amakusa National Park, famous for its lovely azaleas and maples. Due east of Nagasaki towards central Kyushu is the town of Kumamoto, gateway to **Mt Aso Volcano** in the centre of the island. Kumamoto's castle was originally built by Kato Kiyomasa (1562-1611), one of Hideyoshi's generals during the invasion of Korea, who was lord of this district. Most of the structure was destroyed in the Satsuma rebellion of 1877; the keep was restored in 1960.

At the centre of the Aso National Park is Mount Aso (1,600 metres), noted for its crater basin, 77 kilometres in circumference and the largest of its kind in the world. South of Kumamoto, Yatsushiro Bay is famous for its **Shiranui** (Fire of Mysterious Origin), which every year on the nights of early August appears far out in the bay as a red light, soon becoming a stretch of flickering illumination across the dark water. No convincing explanation is available for the phenomenon. At this time of year the popular **Hinagu Spa**, which provides charming views of the Amakusa Islands opposite, is crowded with people who come to witness the event. Amakusa was the scene of the martyrdom of tens of thousands of Japanese Christians in the 17th century — their heads were buried in Amakusa, Nagasaki and Shimabara at the foot of Mt Unzen.

Beppu, on the east coast, is a popular hot springs resort where may be found boiling ponds, hot sand baths and, for those so inclined, a thriving nightlife. The town is, to say the least, rather commercialized.

HOKKAIDO

Sapporo

Japan's northernmost main island, Hokkaido, presents a marked contrast to the more developed and heavily settled south. Often compared to Scandinavia or Canada, Hokkaido is a rugged land marked with great mountains, sites of volcanic activity and extensive pasture lands. Winter lasts for six months and much of the island is snow-covered for at least four months. Once the exclusive domain of the Ainu people, the island has for many centuries been under Japanese control. Certainly as a culture, and perhaps even as a people, the Ainu are a dying race. With them, on a windswept peninsula, a small colony of Snow Monkeys — found north than any other primates except man — are also fighting against the harsh elements. Hokkaido is most conveniently reached by air from Tokyo: flight time is just one hour 10 minutes though the bus journey from Chitose Airport to the capital city of **Sapporo** takes another hour, on average.

The train journey to Sapporo, via the new Seikan tunnel, takes a little under 17 hours by direct night train (with several classes of sleeping accommodation) from Ueno Station, leaving at 9:24 p.m. daily and arriving next day at 2:15 p.m., allowing one to take in the almost Siberian landscape during daylight hours. JR ferry service ceased with the opening of the new tunnel, but ferry service from Aomori to Hakodate on another line continues to make about 10 round trips a day. Sapporo is a pleasant modern city: Founded in 1871, its wide boulevards, intersecting at right angles, are the result of American planning advice. The University of Hokkaido, a 10-minute walk from Sapporo station, and founded a year after the city itself, possesses a noteworthy museum and botanical gardens. The centrally located Odori Park is the site of the annual **Snow Festival** (held in early February), which features huge carvings in snow. Ski areas abound within easy reach of the city and one can even ski on suburban Mount Moiwa, which is equipped with tows and night lighting.

Noboribetsu Spa (in the extensive **Shikotsu-Toya National Park**), one of the many startling natural wonders of Hokkaido, is located to the southwest of the capital (one-and-a-half hours by express train and then 10 minutes by bus from the railway station).

It lies in a wooded ravine, and the eight different varieties of therapeutic water available are piped into the many hotels and the two enormous public bathing halls in the middle of the town. Public bathing, though mixed, is very decorous.

Around a bend in the road the so-called **Valley of Hell** can be found — a huge, desolate depression 1.6 kilometres in circumference and 120 metres deep filled with hillocks, crevices issuing steam and encrustations formed by the springs. A short distance away is an immense chasm with a lake of hot mud and boiling water, pouring out steam and sulphurous smoke.

There are slopes nearby which are used for skiing in the winter. **Lake Toya**, two hours by road from Noboribetsu, is more than 43 kilometres around the circumference, with a wooded island in the middle. Salmon and freshwater crabs can be caught in the lake. **Toyako Spa** stands on the southern shore.

Daisetsuzan National Park lies east of Sapporo in the very centre of Hokkaido. The park is largely mountainous, the lofty peaks covered with conifer forests, while gorges and ravines abound. The numerous, well-equipped spas include Sounkyo, Tenninkyo, Shirogane, Yukomambetsu and Shikaribetsu.

The splendid **Sounkyo Gorge** can be reached by train from Sapporo to the sizable town of Asahikawa, and then by bus which leaves from the front of the railway station. Its dramatic and varied scenery, with towering wooded cliffs sometimes rising sheer from the river, and waterfalls can be seen by road and footpath.

The spa itself, beneath the 1,800-metre Daisetsuzan (Great Snow Mountain), is a pleasant and restful spot with excellent accommodation available amid forests of silver and white fir.

THE RYUKYU ISLANDS (OKINAWA)

The Ryukyu Archipelago, comprising in all 73 islands of which Okinawa is by far the largest, lies well to the south of the rest of Japan, the capital **Naha** being 1,560 kilometres from Tokyo (and only 630 kilometres from Taipei). Under U.S. rule after World War II, the Ryukyus were only returned to Japanese control in May 1972.

A mixed race of Chinese, Korean, Japanese and Malay ethnic origins, the Okinawans came under Chinese rule in the 14th century. In the early part of the 17th century, the Japanese wrested control of the island from the Chinese, and the new invaders gradually increased their hold until in 1871 it was incorporated as part of Kagoshima and then became a separate prefecture.

Naha is a modern city and the economic heart of the islands. Kokusai Street, in the central area, is lined with department stores and other shops, offices and banks.

The alleys of **Tsuboya** — called "Black-market Alley" from the period after the war when the only goods on sale had to be "liberated" from the U.S. Army — are near Kokusai Street, many of them too narrow for cars. Pottery and lacquerware are the main attractions on sale.

The remains of **Sogen-ji Temple** — burial place of the Luchu kings of old and built more than 450 years ago can be visited. The gates to the temple still stand as part of the high wall along Matayoshi Street and other parts of the temple have been restored. Naminoue Shrine, on the rugged coral cliffs overlooking the sea to the north of the city, is dedicated to the three gods believed to be ancestral deities of the once-ruling family. In the south, beyond the Kokuba River, are the other Shinto shrines of Gokoku and Yamoti.

One hour and 20 minutes by road from Naha is **Moon Beach**, on the west coast to the north of Koza. One can swim or ride in the glass-bottom boats for hire. About 10 kilometres north of Moon Beach is Manzamo, offering a fine view of the coastline.

Further north again is the underwater observatory in Nago Bay. The fishing village of **Nago** — so-called "capital of the north" — remained relatively undisturbed by the American presence.

About 30 kilometres to the east of Naha are the **Kerama Islands** — good fishing grounds, readily accessible by boat from Okinawa. Ishigaki Island, a two-hour flight to the south from Naha, preserves its pre-war appearance, and the traditional customs are to a large degree retained.

RESTAURANT SELECTION

Average price for two

TOKYO

AKIMOTO, 3-4, Kojimachi, Chiyoda-ku. Tel: 3261 6762. Japanese eel restaurant. US$60.

ANGKOR WAT, Juken Bldg, 1-38-13 Yoyogi, Shibuya-ku. Tel: 3370 3019. Cambodian. US$40.

BAN THAI, 1-23-14 Kabukicho, Shinjuku-ku. Tel: 3207 0068. Thai. Music. US$40.

BENGAWAN SOLO, 7-8-13, Roppongi, Minato-ku. Tel: 3403 3031. Indonesian. US$100.

BISTRO SABIATINI AND TRATTORIA SABATINI, 2-13-5, Suncrest Bldg, B1, Kita-Aoyama, Minato-ku. Tel: 3402 3782. Italian. US$150 and US$100 respectively.

EL MOCAMBO, 1-4-38, Chitose Bldg, B2, Nishi-Azabu, Minato-ku. Tel: 5410 0468. Latin American. Music. US$80.

ERAWAN, Top floor, Roi Bldg, 5-5-1, Roppongi, Minato-ku. Tel: 3404 5741. Thai. US$80.

ICHO, 4-10-3, Nishi-Azabu, Minato-ku. Tel: 3409 9646. Contemporary Japanese. US$50.

LUNCHAN AOYAMA, 1-2-5 Shibuya, Shibuya-ku. Tel: 5466 1398. American bistro style international food. US$75.

ORIZURU TEI, Nishi-Shinjuku, 2, Shinjuku, NS Bldg, 30 Flr. Tel: 3348 1770. Japanese (Kaiseki). US$100.

SABATINI DI FIRENZE, 7 Flr, Sony Bldg, Ginza. Tel: 3573 0013. Italian. US$200.

SPAGO, 5-7-8 Roppongi, Minato-ku. Tel: 3423 4025. Californian/European. US$75.

TEMPURA TENICHI, Ginza and eight other branches. Tel: 3571 1949. Japanese (tempura). US$200.

ZAKURO, 5-3-3, TBS Kaikan Bldg, B1, Akasaka, Minato-ku. Tel: 3582 6841. Japanese (shabu-shabu). US$180.

HOTEL GUIDE

Note: Japanese hotel rates are quotes as single occupancy. A surcharge is made for double occupancy.

AKITA

D: US$50-100

AKITA NEW GRAND HOTEL, 5-2-1, Nakadori, Akita. Tel: (0188) 345211, Fax: 345365. *R: J, W.*

AOMORI

D: US$50-100

HOTEL NEW CASTLE, 24-1, Kamisayashi-machi, Hirosaki-shi, Aomori-ken 036. Tel: (0172) 361211, Fax: 361210, Tlx: 818334. *SatTV. R: J, W.*

HAKONE

A: US$200 and above

HAKONE PRINCE HOTEL, 144, Moto Hakone, Hakone-machi, Ashigarashimo-gun, Kanagawa, 250-05. Tel: (0460) 37111, Fax: 37616, Tlx: 389 2609. *P, Biz, SatTV. R: J, W.*

HOTEL DE YAMA, 80, Moto Hakone, Hakone-machi, Kanagawa. Tel: (0460) 36321, Fax: 37419, Tlx: 389 2734. *Biz. R: J, W.*

HAKONE HOTEL, 65, Hakone, Hakone-machi, Ashigarashimo-gun, Kanagawa. Tel: (0460) 36311, Fax: 36314, Tlx: 389 2765. *SatTV. R: J, W.*

B: US$150-200

HAKONE HOTEL KOWAKI-EN, 1297, Ninotaira, Hakone-machi, Ashigarashimo-gun, Kanagawa, 250-04. Tel: (0460) 24111, Fax: 24137, Tlx: 389 2730. *P, SatTV. R: J, W.*

PALACE HOTEL HAKONE, 1245, Sengokuhara, Hakone-machi, Ashigarashimo-gun, Kanagawa, 250-06. Tel: (0460) 48501, Fax: 48500, Tlx: 389 2601. *P, SatTV. R: J, W.*

FUJIYA HOTEL, 359, Miyanoshita Hakone, Ashigarashimo-gun, Kanagawa, 250-04. Tel: (0460) 22211, Fax: 22210, Tlx: 389 2718. *P. R: J, W.*

ODAKYU HAKONE HIGHLAND HOTEL, 940, Shinanoki, Sengokuhara, Hakone-machi, Ashigarashimo-gun, Kanagawa. Tel: (0460) 48541, Fax: 49592, Tlx: 389 2730. *Ex. R: J, W.*

P — Swimming pool
Biz — Business centre
SatTV — Satellite TV
R — Restaurant
J — Japanese food
W — Western food

HOTEL GUIDE

YUMOTO FUJIYA HOTEL, 256, Yumoto, Hakone-machi, Ashigara-shimo-gun, Kanagawa. Tel: (0460) 56111, Fax: 56142, Tlx: 389 2631. *P. R: J, W.*

HIROSHIMA

C: US$100-150

ANA HOTEL HIROSHIMA, 7-20, Naka-machi, Naka-ku, Hiroshima, 730. Tel: (082) 241 1111, Fax: 241 9123, Tlx: 652751. *P, Gym, SatTV. R: J, W.*

HIROSHIMA TERMINAL HOTEL, 1-5, Matsubara-cho, Minami-ku, Hiroshima. Tel: (082) 262 1111, Fax: (082) 262 4050, Tlx: 053717 HTHJ. *SatTV. R: J, W.*

D: US$50-100

HIROSHIMA RIVERSIDE HOTEL, 7-14, Kaminobori-cho, Naka-ku, Hiroshima. Tel: (082) 228 1251, Fax: 228 1250, Tlx: 652554. *SatTV. R: J, W.*

HOTEL NEW HIRODEN, 14-9, Osuga-cho, Minami-ku, Hiroshima, 732. Tel: (082) 263 3456, Fax: 263 3784, Tlx: 653884. *Biz, Ex, SatTV. R: W.*

HOKKAIDO

ASAHIKAWA

C: US$100-150

NEW HOKKAI, 6-5 Asahikawa-shi, Hokkaido. Tel: (0166) 243111, Fax: 223510, Tlx: 922520. *SatTV. R: J, W.*

D: US$50-100

ASAHIKAWA TERMINAL HOTEL, 7, Miyashita-dori, Asahikawa, Hokkaido 078. Tel: (0166) 240111, Fax: 212133, Tlx: 922455. *SatTV. R: J, W.*

ASAHIKAWA PALACE HOTEL, 6, Shichijo-dori, Asahikawa, Hokkaido 070. Tel: (0166) 258811, Fax: 258200, Tlx: 922424. *P, SatTV. R: J, W.*

TOYA-KO

B: US$150-200

TOUYAKU MANSEIKAKU, 21, Touyaku Onsen-machi, Abuta-gun, Hokkaido. Tel: (0142) 752171, Fax: 752271, Tlx: 987803. *P. R: J, W.*

HAKODATE

C: US$100-150

HAKODATE KOKUSAI HOTEL, 5-10, Ohtemachi, Hakodate, Hokkaido, 040. Tel: (0138) 235151, Fax: 230239, Tlx: 992604. *R: J, W.*

KUSHIRO

D: US$50-100

KUSHIRO PACIFIC HOTEL, 2-6, Sakaemachi, Kushiro-shi, Hokkaido, 085. Tel: (0154) 248811, Fax: 239191, Tlx: 962605. *R: W.*

SAPPORO

B: US$150-200

HOTEL ALPHA SAPPORO, Minami-1, Nishi-5, Chuo-ku, Sapporo. Tel: (011) 221 2333, Fax: 221 0819, Tlx: 935345. *P. R: J, W.*

C: US$100-150

SAPPORO GRAND HOTEL, Kita-1, Nishi-4, Chuo-ku, Sapporo, 060. Tel: (011) 261 3311, Fax: 231 0388, Tlx: 932613. *Ex, SatTV. R: J, W.*

HOTEL NEW OTANI SAPPORO, 1-1 Nishi, Kita-2, Chuo-ku, Sapporo, 060. Tel: (011) 222 1111, Fax: 222 5521, Tlx: 933650. *Ex, SatTV. R: J, W.*

SAPPORO TOKYU HOTEL, Nishi-4, Kita-4, Chuo-ku, Sapporo, 060. Tel: (011) 231 5611, Fax: 251 3515, Tlx: 934510. *SatTV. R: J, W.*

KEIO PLAZA HOTEL SAPPORO, 2-1, Kita 5-Jo, Nishi 7-chome, Sapporo, 060. Tel: (011) 271 0111, Fax: 221 5450, Tlx: 933271. *P, Gym, SatTV. R: J, W.*

IZU PENINSULA (SHIZUOKA PREFECTURE)

ATAMI

A: US$200 and above

KAWANA HOTEL, 1459, Kawana, Ito, Shizuoka-ken. Tel: (0557) 451111, Fax: 453834, Tlx: 392 7565. *P. R: J, W.*

C: US$100-150

NEW FUJIYA HOTEL, 1-16, Ginza-cho, Atami, Shizuoka-ken, 413. Tel: (0557) 810111, Fax: 818052, Tlx: 392 7682. *R: J, W.*

SHIMODA

B: US$150-200

SHIMODA TOKYU HOTEL, 5-12-1, Shimoda City, Shizuoka-ken. Tel: (0558) 222411, Fax: 224970, Tlx: 392 9732. *P (summer only), Ex, SatTV. R: J, W.*

P — Swimming pool **Gym** — Health club **Biz** — Business centre **Ex** — Executive floor
SatTV — Satellite TV **R** — Restaurant **J** — Japanese food **W** — Western food

HOTEL GUIDE

KANAZAWA (ISHIKAWA PREFECTURE)

C: US$100-150

KANAZAWA NEW GRAND HOTEL, Takaoka-machi, 1-50, Kanazawa City. Tel: (0762) 331311, Fax: 331591, Tlx: 512 2357. *Ex, SatTV. R: J, W.*

KANAZAWA MIYAKO HOTEL, 6-10, Konohana-cho, Kanazawa City. Tel: (0762) 612111, Fax: 612113, Tlx: 512 2203. *SatTV. R: J, W.*

KARUIZAWA

A: US$200 and above

KARUIZAWA PRINCE HOTEL, Karuizawa, Karuizawa-machi, Kitasaku-gun, Nagano-ken. Tel: (0267) 428111, Fax: 427139, Tlx: 332 8660. *P, SatTV. R: J, W.*

B: US$150-200

KARUIZAWA MANPEI HOTEL, 925, Karuizawa, Nagano-ken, 389-01. Tel: (0267) 421234, Fax: 427766, Tlx: 332 8661. *R: J, W.*

KOBE

C: US$100-150

KOBE PORTOPIA HOTEL, 10-1, 6-chome, Minatojima, Nakamachi, Chuo-ku, Kobe City, 650. Tel: (078) 302 1111, Fax: 302 6877, Tlx: 562 2112. *P, Gym, SatTV. R: J, W.*

ROKKOSAN HOTEL, 1034, Minami Rokko, Rokkosancho, Nada-ku, Kobe, 657-01. Tel: (078) 891 0301, Fax: 891 0736, Tlx: 562 2739. *SatTV. R: J, W.*

D: US$50-100

SEISHIN ORIENTAL HOTEL, 6-3, 5-chome Kojidai, Nishi-Ku, Kobe, 651-22. Tel: (078) 992 8111, Fax: (078) 992 8108, Tlx: 992 8105. *SatTV. R: J, W.*

KOFU (YAMANASHI PREFECTURE)

C: US$100-150

KONAYA HOTEL, 1-7-15, Chuo Kofu, Yamanashi-ken, 400. Tel: (0552) 351122, Fax: 330878. *R: W.*

KUSATSU (GUNMA PREFECTURE)

A: US$200 and above

HOTEL VILLAGE, 618, Kusatsu-machi, Agatsuma-gun, Gunma, 377-17. Tel: (0279) 883232, Fax: 884513, Tlx: 349 5267. *P, Gym. R: J, W.*

KYOTO

B: US$150-200

KYOTO CENTURY HOTEL, 680, Higashi Shiokoji-cho, Shiokoji-sagaru, Higashinotoin-dori, Shimogyo-ku, Kyoto, 600. Tel: (075) 351 0111, Fax: 343 3721, Tlx: 542 2380. *P, Ex, SatTV. R: J, W.*

THE MIYAKO, Sanjo Keage, Higashiyama-ku, Kyoto, 605. Tel: (075) 771 7111, Fax: 751 2490, Tlx: 542 2132. *P, Biz, SatTV. R: J, W.*

C: US$100-150

INTERNATIONAL HOTEL KYOTO, Facing Nijo Castle, Kyoto, 604. Tel: (075) 222 1111, Fax: 231 9381, Tlx: 542 2158. *SatTV. R: J, W.*

KARASUMA KYOTO HOTEL, Shijokarasuma, Shimogyo-ku, Kyoto, 600. Tel: (075) 371 0111, Fax: 371 2424, Tlx: 542 2126. *P, SatTV. R: J, W.*

HOTEL PALACE-SIDE KYOTO, Shimodachiuri, Karasuma Kamikyoku, Kyoto, 602. Tel: (075) 431 8171, Fax: 414 2018, Tlx: 542 3236. *R: W.*

KYOTO GRAND HOTEL, Shiokoji-Horikawa, Shimogyo-ku, Kyoto, 600. Tel: (075) 341 2311, Fax: 341 3073, Tlx: 542 2551. *P, SatTV. R: J, W.*

KYOTO ROYAL HOTEL, Kawaramachi-sanjo, Nakagyo-ku, Kyoto, 604. Tel: (075) 223 1234, Fax: 223 1702, Tlx: 552 2888. *SatTV. R: J, W.*

KYOTO PARK HOTEL, 644-2, Mawari-cho, Sanjyu Sangendo Side, Higashiyama-ku, Kyoto, 605. Tel: (075) 525 3111, Fax: 551 4350, Tlx: 542 2777. *R: J, W.*

D: US$50-100

NEW MIYAKO HOTEL, 17, Nishi-Kujoincho, Minami-ku, Kyoto, 601. Tel: (075) 661 7111, Fax: 662 3235, Tlx: 542 3211. *R: J, W.*

KYOTO DAI-NI TOWER HOTEL, Higashinotoin-dori, Shichigo-sagaru, Shimogyo-ku, Kyoto, 600. Tel: (075) 361 3261, Fax: 351 6281, Tlx: 542 2715. *R: W.*

KYOTO TOWER HOTEL, Shiokoji, Nanajo-sagaru, Shimogyo-ku, Kyoto, 520-02. Tel: (075) 361 3211, Fax: 343 5645, Tlx: 542 3423. *R: W.*

HOTEL NEW KYOTO, Horikawa, Marutamachi-kado, Kamigyo-ku, Kyoto. Tel: (075) 801 2111, Fax: 801 4519, Tlx: 542 2326. *SatTV. R: J, W.*

P — Swimming pool
SatTV — Satellite TV
Gym — Health club
R — Restaurant
Biz — Business centre
J — Japanese food
Ex — Executive floor
W — Western food

HOTEL GUIDE

KYUSHU

BEPPU

A: US$200 and above

SUGINOI HOTEL, Kankaiji, Beppu, Oita. Tel: (0977) 241141, Fax: 210010, Tlx: 773467. *P, SatTV. R: J, W.*

D: US$50-100

KAMENOI HOTEL, 5-17, Chuo-machi, Beppu, Oita, 874. Tel: (0977) 223301, Fax: 211232, Tlx: 773475. *P. R: J, W.*

FUKUOKA

C: US$100-150

HOTEL STATION PLAZA, 2-1-1, Hakata Ekimae, Hakata-ku, Fukuoka City, 812. Tel: (092) 431 1211, Fax: 431 8015, Tlx: 723536. *SatTV. R: J, W.*

HAKATA MIYAKO HOTEL, 2-1-1, Hakataeki, Higashi, Hakata-ku, Fukuoka City, 812. Tel: (092) 441 3111, Fax: 481 1306, Tlx: 724585. *R: J, W.*

ANA HOTEL HAKATA, 3-3-3, Hakata Ekimae, Hakata-ku, Fukuoka City, 812. Tel: (092) 411 2111, Fax: 472 7707, Tlx: 722288. *P, SatTV. R: J, W.*

NISHITETSU GRAND HOTEL, 6-60, Daimiyo 2-chome, Chuo-ku, Fukuoka City, 812. Tel: (092) 771 7171, Fax: 751 8224, Tlx: 723351. *SatTV. R: J, W.*

HAKATA TOKYU HOTEL, 1-16-1, Tenjin, Chuo-ku, Fukuoka City, 810. Tel: (092) 781 7111, Fax: 781 7198, Tlx: 723295. *SatTV. R: J, W.*

TOKYO DAICHI HOTEL FUKUOKA, 5-2-18, Nakasu, Hakata-ku, Fukuoka City, 810. Tel: (092) 281 3311, Fax: 281 3938, Tlx: 726342. *Biz, SatTV. R: J, W.*

KAGOSHIMA

A: US$200 and above

IBUSUKI IWASAKI HOTEL, 3755, Juni-cho, Ibusuki, Kagoshima City, 891-04. Tel: (0993) 222131, Fax: 243215, Tlx: 786711. *P, SatTV. R: J, W.*

D: US$50-100

KAGOSHIMA HAYASHIDA HOTEL, 12-22, Higashi Sengoku-cho, Kagoshima City. Tel: (0992) 244111, Fax: 244553, Tlx: 782707. *R: J, W.*

KAGOSHIMA SUN ROYAL HOTEL, 8-10, Yojiro, Kagoshima City, 890. Tel: (0992) 532020, Fax: (0992) 550186, Tlx: 782291. *SatTV. R: J, W.*

KUMAMOTO

C: US$100-150

ANA NEW SKY HOTEL, 2, Higashiamidajicho, Kumamoto City. Tel: (096) 354 2111, Fax: 354 8973, Tlx: 762254. *P, Gym. R: J, W.*

MIYAZAKI

B: US$150-200

SUN HOTEL PHOENIX, 3083, Hamayama Shioji, Miyazaki City. Tel: (0985) 393131, Fax: 396496, Tlx: 777859. *P, Ex, SatTV. R: J, W.*

SEASIDE HOTEL PHOENIX, 3083, Hamayama Shioji, Ohaza, Miyazaki City, 880-01. Tel: (0985) 391111, Fax: 391639, Tlx: 777859. *P, SatTV. R: J, W.*

D: US$50-100

HOTEL PLAZA MIYAZAKI, 1-1, Kawahachio, Miyazaki City. Tel: (0985) 271111, Fax: 272729, Tlx: 777977. *P, Biz, Ex, SatTV. R: J, W.*

NAGASAKI

C: US$100-150

NAGASAKI PARKSIDE HOTEL, 14-1, Heiwa-machi, Nagasaki City. Tel: (0958) 453191, Fax: 465550, Tlx: 752381. *SatTV. R: J, W.*

NAGASAKI GRAND HOTEL, 5-3, Manzai-machi, Nagasaki City. Tel: (0958) 231234, Fax: 221793, Tlx: 752343. *Ex, SatTV. R: J, W.*

OITA CITY

C: US$100-150

OITA NISHITETSU GRAND HOTEL, 1-4-35, Maizuru-machi, Oita City, 870. Tel: (0975) 361181, Fax: 324125, Tlx: 772286. *Ex. R: J, W.*

D: US$50-100

OITA DAI-ICHI HOTEL, 1-1-1, Funaicho, Oita City, 870. Tel: (0975) 361388, Fax: 381901, Tlx: 772480. *R: J, W.*

SAGA

C: US$100-150

HOTEL NEW OTANI SAGA, 1-2, Yokamachi, Saga City, 840. Tel: (0952) 231111, Fax: 231122, Tlx: 746476. *SatTV. R: J, W.*

P — Swimming pool
SatTV — Satellite TV
Gym — Health club
R — Restaurant
Biz — Business centre
J — Japanese food
Ex — Executive floor
W — Western food

HOTEL GUIDE

MAEBASHI (GUNMA PREFECTURE)

D: US$50-100

MERCURY HOTEL, 3-24-1, Odomo-machi, Maebashi, Gunma-ken. Tel: (0272) 520111, Fax: 515523. *R: J, W.*

NAGANO

C: US$100-150

NAGANO KOKUSAI KAIKAN, 576, Agata-machi, Nagano, 380. Tel: (0262) 341111, Fax: 342365, Tlx: 332 2546. *SatTV. R: J, W.*

D: US$50-100

NAGANO HOTEL SAIHOKUKAN, 528-1, Agata-machi, Nagano City, 380. Tel: (0262) 353333, Fax: 353365, Tlx: 332 2316. *Ex, SatTV. R: J, W.*

NAGOYA

B: US$150-200

NAGOYA KANKO HOTEL, 19-30, Nishiki, 1-chome, Naka-ku, Nagoya, 460. Tel: (052) 231 7711, Fax: 231 7719, Tlx: J59946. *Biz, SatTV. R: J, W.*

C: US$100-150

HOTEL NAGOYA CASTLE, 3-19, Hinokuchi-cho, Nishi-ku, Nagoya, 451. Tel: (052) 521 2121, Fax: 531 3313, Tlx: J59787. *P, Gym, Biz, SatTV. R: J, W.*

NAGOYA TERMINAL HOTEL, 1-2, Meieki, 1-chome, Nakamura-ku, Nagoya, 450. Tel: (052) 561 3751, Fax: 581 3236, Tlx: 445 7623. *SatTV. R: J, W.*

MEITETSU GRAND HOTEL, 2-4, 1-chome, Nakamura-ku, Nagoya, 450. Tel: (052) 582 2211, Fax: 582 2230, Tlx: 442 2031. *R: J, W.*

NARITA

B: US$150-200

HOTEL NIKKO NARITA, 500, Tokko, Narita City, Chiba, 286-01. Tel: (0476) 320032, Fax: 323993, Tlx: 376 2165. *SatTV. R: J, W.*

HOLIDAY INN TOBU NARITA, 320-01 Tokko, Narita City, Chiba, 286-01. Tel: (0476) 321234, Fax: 320617, Tlx: 376 2133. *P, Gym. R: J, W.*

D: US$50-100

NARITA VIEW HOTEL, 700, Kosuge, Narita City, Chiba, 286-01. Tel: (0476) 321111, Fax: 321078, Tlx: 376 2123. *P, Gym, SatTV. R: J, W.*

NIIGATA

C: US$100-150

HOTEL NIIGATA, 11-20, Bandai, 5-chome, Niigata City, 950. Tel: (025) 245 3331, Fax: 243 0493, Tlx: 312 2219. *SatTV. R: J.*

OKURA HOTEL NIIGATA, 53, Kawabata-cho, 6-chome, Niigata, Niigata City, 951. Tel: (025) 224 6111, Fax: 224 7060, Tlx: 312 2815. *SatTV. R: J, W.*

D: US$50-100

BANDAI SILVER HOTEL, 1-3-30, Bandai, Niigata City, 950. Tel: (025) 243 3711, Fax: 243 3720, Tlx: 312 2653. *SatTV. R: J, W.*

NIKKO

A: US$200 and above

CHUZENJI KANAYA HOTEL, 2482, Chugushi, Nikko, 321-16. Tel: (0288) 510001, Fax: 510011. *SatTV. R: W.*

NIKKO LAKESIDE HOTEL, 2482, Chugushi, Nikko, Tochigi-ken, 321-16. Tel: (0288) 550321, Fax: 550771, Tlx: 354 4462. *R: W.*

OKAYAMA CITY

C: US$100-150

OKAYAMA ROYAL HOTEL, 2-4, Ezu-cho, Okayama City, 700. Tel: (086) 254 1155, Fax: 254 0777. *R: J, W.*

HOTEL NEW OKAYAMA, 1-1-25, Ekimae-cho, Okayama City, 700. Tel: (086) 223 8211, Fax: 223 1172. *Biz. R: J.*

D: US$50-100

OKAYAMA PLAZA HOTEL, 2-3-12, Hama, Okayama City, 703. Tel: (086) 272 1201, Fax: 731557. *Biz. R: J, W.*

OKAYAMA PREFECTURE (KURASHIKI)

D: US$50-100

KURASHIKI KOKUSAI HOTEL, 1-44, 1-chome, Chuo, Kurashiki City, Okayama-ken, 710. Tel: (086) 422 5141, Fax: 422 5192, Tlx: 593 3158. *Biz. R: J, W.*

OKINAWA

B: US$150-200

OKINAWA GRAND CASTLE HOTEL, 1-132-1, Yamakawa-cho, Shuri, Naha City, Okinawa, 903. Tel: (098)

P — Swimming pool | **Gym** — Health club | **Biz** — Business centre | **Ex** — Executive floor
SatTV — Satellite TV | **R** — Restaurant | **J** — Japanese food | **W** — Western food

HOTEL GUIDE

886 5454, Fax: 887 0070, Tlx: 795375. *P, SatTV. R: J, W.*

OKINAWA HARBORVIEW HOTEL, 2-46, Izumizaki, Naha City, Okinawa, 900. Tel: (098) 853 2111, Fax: 346043, Tlx: 795236. *P, Ex, SatTV. R: J, W.*

C: US$100-150

OKINAWA OCEANVIEW HOTEL, 2-1-5, Kume, Naha City, Okinawa. Tel: (098) 853 2112, Fax: 862 6112, Tlx: 795236. *Ex, SatTV. R: J, W.*

OKINAWA MIYAKO HOTEL, 40, Matsukawa, Naha City, Okinawa. Tel: (098) 887 1111, Fax: 886 5591, Tlx: 795363. *P, SatTV. R: J, W.*

OSAKA

A: US$200 and above

HOTEL NEW OTANI OSAKA, 1-4-1, Shiromi, Chuo-ku, Osaka 540. Tel: (06) 941 1111, Fax: 941 9769, Tlx: 529 3330. *P, Gym, Biz, SatTV. R: J, W.*

OSAKA HILTON, 8-8 Umeda 1-chome, Kita-ku, Osaka 530. Tel: (60) 347 7111, Fax: (06) 347 7001, Tlx: 524 2201. *P, Gym, Biz, Ex, SatTV. R: J, W.*

B: US$150-200

HOTEL NIKKO OSAKA, 1-3-3, Nishi Shinsaibashi, Chuo-ku, Osaka, 542. Tel: (06) 244 1111, Fax: 245 2432, Tlx: 522 7575. *Biz, Ex, SatTV. R: J, W.*

NANKAI SOUTH TOWER HOTEL, 5-1-60, Namba, chuo-ku, Osaka 542. Tel: (06) 646 1111, Fax: (06) 648 0331, Tlx: 526 7717. *P, Gym, Biz, Ex, SatTV. R: J, W.*

C: US$100-150

TENNOJI MIYAKO HOTEL, 10-48, Hidenin-cho, Tennoji-ku, Osaka, 543. Tel: (06) 779 1501, Fax: 779 8800, Tlx: 527 8930. *R: W.*

HOTEL NEW HANKYU, 1-35, Shibata, 1-chome, Kita-ku, Osaka, 530. Tel: (06) 372 5101, Fax: 374 6885, Tlx: 523 3830. *SatTV. R: J, W.*

INTERNATIONAL HOTEL, 2-33, Honmachibashi, Chuo-ku, Osaka, 540. Tel: (06) 941 2661, Fax: 941 5362, Tlx: 529 3415. *SatTV. R: J, W.*

OSAKA DAI-ICHI HOTEL, 1-9-20, Umeda, Kita-ku, Osaka. Tel: (06) 341 4411, Fax: 341 4930, Tlx: 523 4423. *R: J, W.*

ROYAL HOTEL, 5-3-68, Nakanoshima, Kita-ku, Osaka, 530. Tel: (06) 448 1121, Fax: 448 4414, Tlx: J63350. *P, Gym, Biz, Ex, SatTV. R: J, W.*

HOTEL OSAKA GRAND, 2-3-18, Nakanoshima, Kita-ku, Osaka, 530. Tel: (06) 202 1212, Fax: 227 5054, Tlx: 522 2301. *Biz, SatTV. R: J, W.*

OSAKA TOKYU HOTEL, 7-20, Chayamachi, Kita-ku, Osaka. Tel: (06) 373 2411, Fax: 376 0343, Tlx: 523 6751. *P, SatTV. R: J, W.*

OTSU (NEAR KYOTO ON LAKE BIWA)

D: US$50-100

BIWAKO HOTEL, 5-35 Yanagasaki, Otsu City, Shiga-ken, 520. Tel: (0775) 241511, Fax: 241214, Tlx: 546 4868. *P, Ex, SatTV. R: J, W.*

SENDAI

C: US$100-150

HOTEL SENDAI PLAZA, 2-20-1, Honcho, Aoba-ku, Sendai, 980. Tel: (022) 262 7111, Fax: 262 8169, Tlx: 852965. *SatTV. R: J, W.*

D: US$50-100

HOTEL RICH SENDAI, 2-2-2, Kokubuncho, Aoba-ku, Sendai, 980. Tel: (022) 262 8811, Fax: 262 8822, Tlx: 853483. *Biz, SatTV. R: J, W.*

SHIKOKU ISLAND

EHIME

D: US$50-100

HOTEL LADYBIRD, 1-7-7 Kubota-cho, Nihama, Ehime, 792. Tel: (0897) 331000, Fax: 345151. *Biz. R: W.*

MATSUYAMA

D: US$50-100

ANA HOTEL MATSUYAMA, 3-2-1, Ichibancho, Matsuyama City, Ehime-ken, 690. Tel: (0899) 335511, Fax: 216053, Tlx: 584 2013. *SatTV. R: J, W.*

TOKUSHIMA

D: US$50-100

TOKSUSHIMA PARK HOTEL, 2-32-1, Tokushima-cho, Tokushima City, 770. Tel: (0886) 253311, Fax: 253319, Tlx: 586 2345. *SatTV. R: J, W.*

HOTEL ASTORIA, 2-26-1, Ichibancho, Tokushima City, 770. Tel: (0886) 536151, Fax: 536151. *Biz, Ex. R: W.*

P — Swimming pool
SatTV — Satellite TV
Gym — Health club
R — Restaurant
Biz — Business centre
J — Japanese food
Ex — Executive floor
W — Western food

HOTEL GUIDE

SHIZUOKA

C: US$100-150

ASSOCIA TERMINAL HOTEL, 56, Kurogane-cho, Shizuoka City, 420. Tel: (054) 254 4141, Fax: 255 3721, Tlx: 396 2111. *SatTV. R: J, W.*

TAKAMATSU

C: US$100-150

KEIO PLAZA HOTEL, Takamatsu, 11-5, Chuo-cho, Takamatsu, Kagawa-ken, 760. Tel: (0878) 345511, Fax: 340800, Tlx: 582 2725. *SatTV. R: W.*

D: US$50-100

RIHGA HOTEL ZEST, 9-1, Furushinmachi, Takamatsu City. Tel: (0878) 223555, Fax: 227516, Tlx: 582 2141. *Ex. R: J, W.*

TOKYO

A: US$200 and above

DAI-ICHI HOTEL TOKYO, 1-2-6, Shimbashi, Minato-ku, Tokyo, 105. Tel: (03) 3501 4411, Fax: 3501 7290, Tlx: 222 2233. *Ex, SatTV. R: J, W.*

TOKYO HILTON, 6-2, Nishi-Shinjuku, 6-chome, Shinjuku-ku, Tokyo. Tel: (03) 3344 5111, Fax: 3342 6094, Tlx: 232 4515. *P, Gym, Biz, Ex. R: J, W.*

PALACE HOTEL, 1-1-1, Marunouchi, Chiyoda-ku, Tokyo, 100. Tel: (03) 3211 5211, Fax: 3211 6987, Tlx: 222 2580. *Biz, SatTV. R: J, W.*

HOTEL OKURA, 2-10-4, Toranomon, Minato-ku, Tokyo, 105. Tel: (03) 3582 0111, Fax: 3582 3707, Tlx: J22790. *P, Gym, Biz, Ex, SatTV. R: J, W.*

TAKANAWA PRINCE HOTEL, 13-1, Takanawa, 3-chome, Minato-ku, Tokyo, 108. Tel: (03) 3447 1111, Fax: 3446 0849, Tlx: 242 3232. *P, Biz, Ex, SatTV. R: J, W.*

NEW TAKANAWA PRINCE HOTEL, 13-1, Takanawa, 3-chome, Minato-ku, Tokyo, 108. Tel: (03) 3442 1111, Fax: 3444 1234, Tlx: 242 7418. *P, Biz, SatTV. R: J, W.*

CAPITOL TOKYU HOTEL, 2-10-3, Nagatacho, Chiyoda-ku, Tokyo, 100. Tel: (03) 3581 4511, Fax: 3581 5822, Tlx: J2429. *P, Biz, SatTV. R: J, W.*

IMPERIAL HOTEL TOKYO, 1-1-1, Uchisaiwai-cho, Chiyoda-ku, Tokyo, 100. Tel: (03) 3504 1111, Fax: 3504 1288, Tlx: 222 4141. *P, Gym, Biz, Ex, SatTV. R: J, W.*

HOTEL NEW OTANI, 4-1, Kioicho, Chiyoda-ku, Tokyo, 102. Tel: (03) 3265 1111, Fax: 3221 2619, Tlx: J24719. *P, Gym, Biz, Ex, SatTV. R: J, W.*

CENTURY HYATT TOKYO, 2-7-2, Nishi Shinjuku, Shinjuku-ku, Tokyo, 160. Tel: (03) 3348 1234, Fax: 3344 5575, Tlx: J29411. *P, Gym, Biz, Ex, SatTV. R: J, W.*

KEIO PLAZA INTERCONTINENTAL HOTEL, 2-1, Nishi Shinjuku, 2-chome, Shinjuku-ku, Tokyo, 160. Tel: (03) 3344 0111, Fax: 3345 8269, Tlx: J26874. *P, Biz, Ex, SatTV. R: J, W.*

AKASAKA TOKYU HOTEL, 2-14-3, Nagatacho, Chiyoda-ku, Tokyo, 100. Tel: (03) 3580 2311, Fax: 3580 6066, Tlx: 222 4310. *Biz, SatTV. R: J, W.*

HOTEL PACIFIC MERIDIEN, 2, Takanawa, Minato-ku, Tokyo, 108. Tel: (03) 3445 6711, Fax: 3445 5733, Tlx: J22861. *P, Biz.*

B: US$150-200

GINZA DAI-ICHI HOTEL, 8-chome, 13-1, Ginza, Chuo-ku, Tokyo, 104. Tel: (03) 3542 5311, Fax: 3542 3030, Tlx: 252 3714. *SatTV. R: J, W.*

HOLIDAY INN TOKYO COMMERCIAL CENTRE, 1-13-7, Hatchobori, Chuo-ku, Tokyo, 104. Tel: (03) 3553 6161, Fax: 3553 6040, Tlx: 252 3748. *P. R: W.*

HILLTOP HOTEL, 1-1, Kanda, Surugadai, Chiyoda-ku, Tokyo, 101. Tel: (03) 3293 2311, Fax: 3233 4567, Tlx: 222 6712. *SatTV. R: J, W.*

GINZA NIKKO HOTEL, 4-21, Ginza 8-chome, Chuo-ku, Tokyo, 104. Tel: (03) 3571 4911, Fax: 3571 8379, Tlx: 252 2812. *SatTV. R: W.*

HANEDA TOKYU HOTEL, 2-8-6, Haneda Airport, Ota-ku, Tokyo, 144. Tel: (03) 3747 0311, Fax: 3747 0366, Tlx: 246 6560. *P, SatTV. R: J, W.*

MIYAKO HOTEL TOKYO, 1-50, Shiroganedai, 1-chome, Minato-ku, Tokyo, 108. Tel: (03) 3447 3111, Fax: 3447 3133, Tlx: 242 3111. *P, Gym, SatTV. R: J, W.*

GINZA TOKYU HOTEL, 15-9, Ginza, 5-chome, Chuo-ku, Tokyo. Tel: (03) 3541 2411, Fax: (03) 3541 6622, Tlx: 252 2601. *Biz, SatTV. R: J, W.*

HOTEL GRAND PALACE, 1-1, Iidabashi, 1-chome, Chiyoda-ku, Tokyo, 102. Tel: (03) 3264 1111, Fax: 3222 6600, Tlx: 232 2981. *SatTV. R: J, W.*

HOTEL TAKANAWA, 1-17, Takanawa, 2-chome, Minato-ku, Tokyo, 108. Tel: (03) 5488 1000, Fax: 5488 1005, Tlx: 242 2553. *P, SatTV. R: J, W.*

P — Swimming pool | **Gym** — Health club | **Biz** — Business centre | **Ex** — Executive floor
SatTV — Satellite TV | **R** — Restaurant | **J** — Japanese food | **W** — Western food

HOTEL GUIDE

C: US$100-150

HOTEL SUNROUTE TOKYO, 2-3-1, Yoyogi, Shibuya-ku, Tokyo, 151. Tel: (03) 3375 3211, Fax: 3379 3040, Tlx: 232 2288. *SatTV. R: J, W.*

FAIRMOUNT HOTEL, 1-17, Kudan-Minami, 2-chome, Chiyoda-ku, Tokyo, 102. Tel: (03) 3262 1151, Fax: 3264 2476, Tlx: 232 2883. *R: W.*

DIAMOND HOTEL, 25, Ichiban-cho, Chiyoda-ku, Tokyo, 102. Tel: (03) 3263 2211, Fax: 3263 2222, Tlx: 3232 2764. *SatTV. R: J, W.*

TAKANAWA TOBU HOTEL, 7-6, 4-chome, Minato-ku, Tokyo, 108. Tel: (03) 3447 0111, Fax: 3447 0117, Tlx: 242 5252. *SatTV.*

TOKYO STATION HOTEL, 1-9-1, Marunouchi, Chiyoda-ku, Tokyo, 100. Tel: (03) 3231 2511, Fax: 3231 3513. *R: W.*

GAJOEN KANKO HOTEL, 1-8-1, Shimomeguro, Meguro-ku, Tokyo. Tel: (03) 3491 0111, Fax: 3495 2450, Tlx: 246 6006. *Ex, SatTV. R: W.*

HOTEL TOKYO, 2-17-8, Takanawa, Minato-ku, Tokyo, 108. Tel: (03) 3447 5771, Fax: 3447 5250, Tlx: 242 5095. *R: J, W.*

D: US$50-100

ASIA CENTRE OF JAPAN, 10-32, Akasaka, 8-chome, Minato-ku, Tokyo, 112. Tel: (03) 3402 6111, Fax: 3402 0738. *R: W.*

TOMAKOMAI

D: US$50-100

TOMAKOMAI HOTEL NEW OJI, 2-1-30, Omotemachi, Tomakomai, 053. Tel: (0144) 336121, Fax: 366502, Tlx: 984215. *SatTV. R: J, W.*

TOTTORI

D: US$50-100

YONAGO KOKUSAI HOTEL, Kamo-cho, 2-180, Yonago City, Tottori. Tel: (0859) 336611, Fax: 338729, Tlx: 579 7491. *R: J, W.*

HOTEL NEW OTANI TOTTORI, 2-153, Ima-machi, Tottori City, Tottori, 680. Tel: (0857) 231111, Fax: 230979, Tlx: 579 2225. *SatTV. R: J, W.*

TOYAMA

D: US$50-100

MEITETSU TOYAMA HOTEL, 2-28, Sakurabashi-dori, Toyama City, Toyama, 930. Tel: (0764) 312211, Fax: 410867, Tlx: 515 2952. *Ex, SatTV. R: J, W.*

URAYASU (CHIBA PREFECTURE NEAR TOKYO)

A: US$200 and above

DAI-ICHI HOTEL TOKYO BAY, 1-8, Maihama, Urayasu City, Chiba, 279. Tel: (0473) 553333, Fax: 553366, Tlx: 299 3123. *P, Gym, Biz, SatTV. R: J, W.*

TOKYO BAY HILTON, 1-8, Maihama, Urayasu City, Chiba, 279. Tel: (0473) 555000, Fax: 555019, Tlx: 299 3108. *P, Gym, Biz, Ex, SatTV. R: J, W.*

HOTEL SUNROUTE PLAZA TOKYO, 1-6, Maihama, Urayasu City, 279. Tel: (0473) 551111, Fax: 547871. *P. R: J, W.*

SHERATON GRANDE TOKYO BAY HOTEL AND TOWERS, 9-1, Maihama, Urayasu City, 279. Tel: (0473) 555555, Fax: 555566, Tlx: 299 3155. *P, Gym, Biz, Ex, SatTV. R: J, W.*

YOKOHAMA

A: US$200 and above

YOKOHAMA GRAND INTERCONTINENTAL, 1-1-1 Minato-mirai, Nishi-ku, Yokohama-shi, Yokohama 220. Tel: (045) 223 2222, Fax: 221 0650, Tlx: 382 2752 YGIHTL. *P, Gym, Biz, Ex. R: J, W.*

P — Swimming pool
SatTV — Satellite TV
Gym — Health club
R — Restaurant
Biz — Business centre
J — Japanese food
Ex — Executive floor
W — Western food

열성

NORTH KOREA

North Korea was founded in 1945 when the Soviet Union accepted the Japanese surrender in Korea north of the 38th parallel. Three years later, the Soviet occupation ended when the Democratic People's Republic of Korea was proclaimed on September 9, 1948. The country has had a communist government since then, and only one head of state until July 8, 1994, when Kim Il Sung died. North Korea then became the world's first communist dynasty as his son, Kim Jong Il, took over.

History

Since its devastation in the course of the 1950-53 Korean War, North Korea has developed a unique communistic society in almost total — and largely self-imposed — isolation from the outside world. Under the *Juche* (self-reliance) ideology it achieved a degree of independence from the two communist giants, China and the former Soviet Union, and has a respectable record of basic post-war reconstruction and a broad range of social welfare provisions. Since the late 1950s, however, the total domination of Kim Il Sung — always referred to as "The Great Leader" — has led to the development of a rigid police state whose degree of control over the individual lives of its people is unmatched. Virtually unaffected by the collapse of communism and the dissolution of the Soviet Union, this interned "workers' paradise" looks more and more anachronistic as time passes. Even Kim Il Sung's death brought no obvious changes.

It is a ruggedly beautiful country, with its west coast's lowlands slowly rising into steep mountain ranges, culminating in the grandeur of the remote Changbaek Range on the Chinese border, which has the huge extinct volcano and crater lake of Paekdu as its crown.

Entry

Most visitors to North Korea travel by air from Beijing by national carrier Air Koryo, which flies from Pyongyang to Beijing and back on Tuesday and Saturday. A one-way ticket costs US$130.

China Northern Airlines is scheduled to fly to Pyongyang and back to Beijing every Wednesday, but in practice these flights are often cancelled because of the lack of passengers. Air Koryo also flies to Moscow and Berlin, but the flights are irregular and travellers should check in advance with the airline. Another way of travelling to North Korea is by rail, on Chinese or North Korean trains from Beijing. A one-way ticket costs US$70-100 and the trip, via Shenyang, takes 24 hours. Trains leave Beijing and Pyongyang on Monday, Wednesday, Thursday and Saturday. There are also trains linking Moscow with Pyongyang; they leave Moscow on Thursday, Friday and Saturday and Pyongyang on Monday, Wednesday and Saturday. The journey takes seven days.

Immigration

Tourists and businessmen who want to obtain entry visa must submit an application at least 10 days before the planned trip. An invitation is not required, as it was in the past, except for citizens of the United States, Israel, South Africa, South Korea — and journalists. Group tours are available through travel agents in Tokyo, Hong Kong and Macau or are directly arranged by one of three North Korean tourist companies. Their tours are usually for four to eight days but they also offer special longer tours for those interested in mountaineering, the martial art *taek won-do*, Korean folk customs, hiking, hunting or flora and fauna.

Health

There are no special health requirements for tourists but on arriving in North Korea, visit-

◄ *This way to the workers' paradise.* PHOTO: RON McMILLAN

Pyongyang's Kim Il Sung Square. PHOTO: HANS VRIENS

ors may be asked to show vaccination cards or medical certificates if they come from regions where typhoid fever, cholera, measles or Aids are prevalent. Because of the acute shortage of medicines in North Korea, especially Western varieties, travellers who need systematic medication are advised to take all the medicines they will need for the entire trip, and some to spare in case of delays.

Currency

The currency is the North Korean won (divided into 100 chon), import and export of which is prohibited. Foreigners are allowed to use only foreign-exchange certificates, which are reconvertible.

The exchange rate in early 1995 was Won 2.12:US$1.

Major Western currencies and travellers' cheques are acceptable, except U.S. dollar banknotes issued before 1953. Credit cards are dealt with only at the Trade Bank of the DPRK, which is in Pyongyang's Sungri St, near Kim Il Sung Square. A foreign visitor will discover that Pyongyang is a very expensive city with most prices in hotels, restaurants and dollar shops as high as in Seoul. In some cases prices are exorbitant, so one should be prepared, for example, to pay Won 30 a page to send a fax to Europe.

Language

Korean is the national language. Japanese, Chinese, Russian and English are the most widely understood foreign languages. Interpreters who speak other languages are also available. Few ordinary North Koreans, including hotel and restaurant staff and taxi drivers, are able to speak foreign languages.

Climate

Climatic conditions are similar to those in South Korea, though the North's proximity to the Chinese landmass brings colder weather in winter. In summer it is less humid than in the South. The four seasons are distinct, with average temperatures in January being -8°C, in August 21°C, and average annual rainfall 100-120 centimetres.

Transport

Visitors will usually have all essential transport provided. There is also a taxi service available at hotels or cabs may be ordered by phone, on 813160-1 or 817684-5. A sample fare from the **Koryo Hotel** to the diplomatic district is Won 8 for a 10-minute drive. Pyongyang has two underground railway lines stretching from east to west and north to south. The Pyongyang metro is a unique tourist attraction itself for its

architectural style and interior design, which is different in each station. The fare is 10 chon. There are also extensive trolley-bus and tramway networks in Pyongyang.

Accommodation

There are nine hotels now available in Pyongyang, with the deluxe **Koryo Hotel** in the heart of the city, the most favoured by foreign visitors.

Opened in 1985, the 45-storey twin towered Koryo has 500 rooms, restaurants, bars, meeting rooms, shops, post office, swimming pool, sauna and billiard room, among other attractions (Tel: 817600).

Other first-class hotels are the **Potonggang**, **Ryanggang**, **Sosan**, and **Chongnyon**. Second-class hotels include **Taedonggang**, **Pyongyang**, **Changgwangsan** and **Haebangsan**.

The only traditional Korean-style hotel, where one can sleep on a heated floor and dine on a low table as Koreans do, is the **Minsok (Folk) Hotel** in **Kaesong City**.

First-class hotel rooms range from Won 450, second-class rooms start at Won 300 and third class from Won 160 in March 1995. The first- and second-class hotels offer cheaper second- and even third-class rooms.

If an individual trip is arranged by the North Korean Travel Co., a minimum daily charge for one person is US$160, which includes hotel accommodation, three meals, transport and guide/interpreter.

Dining

People in Pyongyang regard the restaurant in the **Teadonggang Hotel** as very good, as it serves tasty combinations of Korean and Chinese dishes. Another option for a good meal is the **Diplomatic Club** on the east bank of the Taedong River. The **Ongnyu** and **Chongnyu** restaurants are also prestigious but it is necessary to book in advance. **Koryo Hotel** and **Ansan Club** (opposite the **Potonggang Hotel**) have authentic Japanese restaurants. Except for the above-mentioned and hotel restaurants, it is generally impossible for a foreign visitor to eat at an ordinary restaurant among the local people.

Entertainment

The place to meet for all local foreign residents and visitors is the coffee shop in the lobby of the **Koryo Hotel** or the **Diplomatic Club** billiard room (closed on Wednesday). Every Saturday night foreigners have an extra chance to meet and have fun in the disco on the 18th floor of the **Changgwangsan Hotel**. **Sosan Hotel** has — mini-golf and the **Pyongyang Golf Course** is located around the **Taesong Reservoir**. Neighbouring **Taesong Mountain** and **Mangyongdae** have fun fairs.

In the sphere of official culture, there is the **Pyongyang Circus** in Kwangbok St and tickets are freely available. For "revolutionary operas" such as *Flower Girl, Sea of Blood* and *A True Daughter of the Party* ask a guide or interpreter to arrange an evening in the **Pyongyang Grand Theatre** or the **East Pyongyang Grand Theatre**. The **National Restaurant** has performances of Korean folk songs by a female band and beautiful female vocalists every evening. Pyongyang's new **Karaoke Bar** is hidden behind a high-rise building for foreign residents on **Changgwang St** opposite the Koryo Hotel.

Shopping

There are some dollar shops in Pyongyang — **Ragwon**, **Taesong**, **Taedong**, **Diplomatic** — where food, souvenirs and luxury items may be bought. There are also dollar shops in most hotels, but other shops except **Pyongyang Department Store No. 1** will usually refuse to serve foreigners. Among things to buy in North Korea are Korean ginseng products, snake liquor and other local liquors, postage stamps, embroidery, ceramics and traditional Korean paintings.

The widest choice of folk souvenirs and art pieces is offered by the shop in the east wing of **Changgwangsan Hotel** (entrance from Chollima St) and **Taesong** store.

Holidays

January 1: New Year's Day.
February 16: Birthday of Kim Jong Il.
May 1: May Day.
August 15: Anniversary of liberation from Japanese rule.
September 9: Anniversary of founding of the state.
October 10: Anniversary of founding of Workers' Party of Korea.
December 27: Constitution Day.

USEFUL ADDRESS

The Korea International Travel Co., Central District, Pyongyang, DPRK. Tel: 850-2-817201, Fax: 850-2-817607, Tlx: 5998 RHS KP.

MAJOR AIRLINE

Air Koryo, Pyongyang. Tel: 43076-7. In Beijing the airline's representative office is at the Swiss Hotel (Tel: 501 1557, 501 1559).

DISCOVERING NORTH KOREA

Visitors cannot discover North Korea on their own but must be shown the country by the ever-present guide-interpreters. So visitors interested in seeing a particular site or activity should advise the North Koreans in advance or immediately on arrival. The usual itinerary includes visits to museums, parks, historic monuments, theatres and, if requested, industrial plants, farms, schools, institutes or homes of Korean families. Most sightseeing is centred in Pyongyang, but it is also possible to travel to scenic mountains as well as some cities and the truce village of Panmunjom at the centre of the Demilitarized Zone which separates the two Koreas.

PYONGYANG

The capital is one of the oldest continually settled sites in Korea, with a recorded history back to 37 BC. It occupies a superb natural position on a bend of the Taedong River, at the foot of a hill called **Moranbong** (Magnolia Peak) and its tree-lined quays, wide streets and many parks provide a pleasant vista. During the three years of the Korean War the city was completely razed to the ground, so the history of modern Pyongyang began just 40 years ago.

The heart of the city is **Kim Il Sung Square**. Important political and cultural functions, celebration soirees, mass rallies and parades are held in the square. The traditional Korean-style building behind the podium in the square is **The Grand People's Study House**. The **Korean Central History Museum** and **The Korean Art Gallery** stand across the square,

Rush-hour in Pyongyang.

PHOTO: GREG GIRARD

which also affords a fine view of the **Tower of Juche** on the opposite bank of the river. The 170-metre-high tower was unveiled in 1982 on the 70th birthday of Kim Il Sung.

One of the musts on any trip to North Korea is a visit to **Mangyongdae**, the birthplace of Kim Il Sung. This once humble farm, 12 kilometres west of the heart of the city, has been transformed into a national shrine. The small hut in which Kim was born has become a centre of pilgrimage for the communist faithful.

For those in search of glimpses of the traditional culture of Pyongyang and Korea, the best approach is to take a long walk through **Moranbong Hill** in the city centre, where there are historic relics of the Koguryo dynasty. **Teasong Mountains**, 10 kilometres northeast of the city, also has some historic structures. Visitors may soon be able to see Kim Il Sing's preserved body on display in the **Kumsusan Palace**, his former residence now turned into a mausoleum.

UPCOUNTRY

Even the simplest forms of individual travel are still prohibited, but organized groups can go outside the capital. The **International Friendship Exhibition** in the scenic **Myohyang Mountains** is a must for visitors and it takes three hours' drive north of the capital to get there. The Exhibition is housed in a six-storey building in traditional Korean style where tens of thousands of gifts sent to Kim Il Sung and Kim Jong Il — his son and heir known as "The Dear Leader" — from all over the world are on display in more than 50 rooms. The tour of the building takes at least four hours but the mountain scenery and the nearby ancient **Pohyon Temple** make the outing worthwhile.

Nampo is the port city for Pyongyang and has a reasonable beach resort area. Tours to **Kaesong**, capital of the Koryo dynasty, and to the truce village of **Panmunjom** on the border with the South, are also conducted.

Preserved here are the barracks where the Korean armistice talks were held and the armistice agreement was signed. On the Demarcation Line there are meeting halls for the Military Armistice Commission and one for the Neutral Nations Supervisory Commission.

Undoubtedly the two most spectacular trips outside Pyongyang are those to **Kumgang (Diamond) Mountains** in the southwest of the country and to **Paekdu (White-topped) Mountain** on the Chinese border. The **Kumgang Mountains** are a remote and spectacular stretch of granite pinnacles ranging over tens of kilometres along the **Taebak** mountain range and the Japanese Sea coast. Fabled in literature and art, they also contain a number of now-empty Buddhist temples and many waterfalls, pools and caves.

지하철
Subway
2
을지로입구
Ulchiro 1-ga
지하철
2
을지로입구

SOUTH KOREA

South Korea is a land of climatic, geographic and visual extremes. There are extremes of humid heat and biting cold, and the countryside changes abruptly from the central plains and plateaux, which form the country's granary area, to the stark mountains. The visual extremes are obvious to the visitor. New high-rise towers jostle with old buildings, open spaces created for smooth traffic flow seem oddly placed against crowded central city office blocks and, though the city of Seoul in particular has an open look about it, it is always teeming with people.

A bridge, a battlefield and a wartime staging post for China and Japan, South Korea is a land with a proud history and a proud people, who are used to hard work — though increasingly assertive about being well rewarded for their labours — and who enjoy showing their country to visitors.

History

Despite a heavy cultural infusion from China and 36 years of Japanese colonial rule, modern South Korea has managed to preserve its customs in dress, food, music, dance, art and language. The country's recorded history begins with the period of the Three Kingdoms, which continually waged war on one another for about 700 years. Between AD 660 and 670, the Kingdom of Silla — with considerable help from China — succeeded in unifying the country from its capital at Kyongju. Silla's dominance was replaced in 935 by the Kingdom of Koryo, from which the country's present name is derived. After Koryo crumbled, the Mongols occupied the country for 130 years until driven out by Gen. Yi Song Gye, who in 1392 moved the national capital to Seoul and founded the dynasty that was to rule Korea until 1910.

For six years from 1592 the country was ravaged by a number of Japanese invasions under the Japanese *shogun* Hideyoshi. Although the Japanese were eventually driven off, again with the help of the Chinese, the battle exhausted Korea and the country remained weakened for centuries. During the Manchu period in China, Korea acknowledged Chinese sovereignty but in practice remained independent. From the 1880s Korea was finally compelled to open its doors to foreigners. It was also at this time that the Japanese began the encroachment that finally led to formal annexation in 1910. Under the Japanese, who renamed the country Chosen, the country was run as a police state that ruthlessly suppressed any nationalist or revolutionary movements.

At the end of World War II Soviet troops occupied the northern half of the peninsula and United States troops the south. In 1948 rival governments were set up in each region. After abortive attempts at unifying the country by negotiation, North Korea attacked the South on June 25, 1950. Despite the arrival of U.S. troops, the North's armies occupied most of the country with the exception of the far southeast within five weeks. The Inchon landing in September restored the situation, but China entered the war when the allies approached its border with Korea on the Yalu River. Seoul fell again on January 4, 1951, but was recaptured on March 14. The armistice of July 27, 1953 left the boundary between the two zones more or less where it had been before hostilities.

Syngman Rhee was president of South Korea from 1948 until he was overthrown in April 1960. The democratically elected government that succeeded him was toppled a year later in military coup led by Gen. Park Chung Hee, who went on to narrowly win a presidential election in October 1963. Park was re-elected for a third term in April 1971, winning against the New Democratic Party's Kim Dae Jung. The ruling Democratic Republican Party was also successful in the National

◄ *Wall art in Seoul.* PHOTO: KEES

SOUTH KOREA
NORTH KOREA
km
0
100
Sea of Japan
Panmunjom
Mt. Sorak
Kangnung
Chunchon
Seoul
Inchon
Suwon
Samchok
Wonju
Chungju
Chonan
Yongju
Chongju
Andong
Mt. Songni
Sangju
Taechon
Taejon
Pohang
Kunsan
Taegu
Kyongju
Chonju
Yellow Sea
Masan
Tongnae
Chinju
Pusan
Kwangju
Chungmu
Mokpo
Sunchon
Yosu
Cheju
Cheju Island
Mt. Halla
Sogwuipo
km
0
25
Roads
Highways
Railways
Airport
To Cheju Island

Assembly elections held in May 1971, though its power was considerably reduced.

Opposition to Park swelled in the late 1970s, culminating in riots in the southern cities of Pusan and Masan in October 1979. On October 26, 1979, Park was assassinated by his intelligence chief, Kim Jae Kyu, ostensibly because Kim thought Park had become too dictatorial. Kim was convicted along with six accomplices and executed. A brief period of liberalization followed Park's death, when an emergency decree that banned criticism of the government was lifted. The military, however, continued to jockey for power, and a young group of generals led by Chun Doo Hwan made their first move on December 12, 1979, by arresting some of their superiors.

In early 1980, just as a presidential campaign contested by three major contenders — including Kim Dae Jung, an outspoken critic of the Park regime — was under way, the military halted the country's move towards democracy. Martial law was declared on May 16, sparking demonstrations across the country — but particularly in Kim's home town, Kwangju — which escalated in to one of South Korea's most bloody internal insurrections. The army was called in to quell the riots and, according to official figures, more than 200 casualties resulted. Hundreds of politicians were banned from public life as Chun steadily tightened his grip over the country. On August 16, 1980, President Choi resigned and Chun assumed formal authority as South Korea's leader on August 27 when he was named president by the electoral college. The country's economic performance throughout most of the 1980s was extraordinary. From 1986 to 1988 the economy expanded more than 12% annually, leading to the country's first trade surpluses and allowing it to pay off much of its foreign debt. The country has moved into the ranks of the world's top dozen traders thanks to a quadrupling of exports during the 1980s.

Under the Chun government many of the outward appearances of the authoritarian past were dispensed with, but criticism of the government was still not tolerated for most of his eight-year rule. But huge demonstrations in June 1987 forced the government to ease political controls. A direct presidential election in December 1987 saw the election of Chun's fellow 1979 coup-maker, Roh Tae Woo, as the opposition split between Kim Dae Jung and Kim Young Sam. In January 1990 Kim Young Sam dramatically altered the political constellation by joining Roh in a grand political coalition, one that effectively neutered Kim Dae Jung as a political force. This was confirmed in a general election in December 1992 when Kim Young Sam's Democratic Liberal Party swept to victory. Kim was subsequently inaugurated as president on February 25, 1993.

Seoul's successful hosting of the 1988 Olympic Games gave South Korea a chance to show the world what it had accomplished in its three decades of rapid industrialization. Coupled with changes in the communist world, the new face of South Korea allowed it to establish relations with most of its former adversaries, including the then ailing Soviet Union and China.

Talks with North Korea have so far made little progress towards reunification. High-level talks between the two countries, which were represented by their prime ministers, took place in 1990. Several more rounds followed, but with little result. The death of North Korean President Kim Il Sung in 1994, and the accession of his son, Kim Jong Il, led to hopes that a new approach might be forthcoming from the North. But in early 1995, tentative steps towards formal relations were becoming mired in disputes by both sides over a U.S.-brokered deal intended to swap North Korean nuclear arms production for South Korean-made power reactors and U.S. oil.

Entry

The most common means of access to South Korea is by air. Two Korean carriers, Korean Air and Asiana Airlines, and some 29 other airlines serve the country's three international airports: Kimpo in Seoul, Kimhae just outside Pusan and Cheju Island. An airport tax of Won 8,000 is required on leaving South Korea.

There are also regular passenger shipping services between South Korea and Japan. The Pukwan (Pusan-Shimonoseki) Ferry travels between Pusan and Shimonoseki, Japan, daily, departing from Pusan at 6 p.m. and Shimonoseki at 5 p.m. on the seven-hour journey. The ship also carries vehicles, and South Korean regulations allow cars to be brought in for extendable 30-day periods. The Kukje Ferry between Osaka and Pusan leaves Osaka on Wednesday and Saturday at noon and Pusan on Monday and Thursday at 5 p.m. The voyage takes 22 hours.

There is also a ferry service between Inchon and Weihai, on China's Shandong peninsula.

The ferry leaves Inchon at 4 p.m. on Wednesday and Saturday and leaves Weihai on Monday and Thursday at 5 p.m. The trip takes 17 hours.

Immigration

Entry visas are generally required and may be obtained from South Korean diplomatic missions. Those not requiring visas include holders of re-entry visas and nationals of the following countries, provided they do not take up employment: Austria, Bangladesh, Belgium, Britain, Chile, Colombia, Costa Rica, Denmark, Dominican Republic, Finland, France, Germany, Greece, Iceland, Italy, Lesotho, Liberia, Liechtenstein, Luxembourg, Malaysia, Mexico, the Netherlands, Norway, Pakistan, Peru, Portugal, Singapore, Spain, Surinam, Sweden, Switzerland, Thailand and Turkey. Those wishing to visit for business purposes should make special application to a South Korean diplomatic mission.

Visas are also not required by those who desire to land in transit for sightseeing only. If the visitor is a national of a country maintaining diplomatic relations with South Korea, has confirmed reservations for an outbound destination and has enough money to stay, the immigration inspector at the port of entry can issue a 15-day landing permit. Japanese may only obtain a five-day landing permit: permits can be extended only in case of an emergency. Extensions for tourist visas for periods of 15, 30 and 60 days are available.

Health

Vaccination against cholera is required only of those arriving from infected areas. Inoculation against hepatitis and typhoid is recommended for those travelling or working outside the usual areas visited by tourists. Cats and dogs must be left in quarantine for 10 days for observation to check for possible diseases before being released to their owners.

Customs

Incoming visitors may import duty-free up to one carton of cigarettes and one bottle of liquor. Luggage is usually examined on entry. Export of South Korean antiques, or curios which have been designated cultural treasures, is illegal. If you are considering the purchase of an antique take it to the Art and Antiques Assessment Office. For further information on customs call Customs Administration (Tel: 512 3100) or Kimpo Customs House (Tel: 660 5555).

Currency

The unit of currency is the won, exchanging in April 1995 at the rate of Won 795:US$1. The currency is issued in Won 1,000, 5,000 and 10,000 denomination notes. Coins are issued in Won 10, 50, 100 and 500 denominations. All foreign currencies are allowed into the country, but it is forbidden to import local currency. An unlimited amount of foreign currencies can be brought in, but US$5,000 or more must be declared on arrival. Unused local currency may be reconverted into foreign currency up to the amount originally exchanged provided a proper exchange receipt is shown. Currency is freely exchanged at all banks and at major hotels.

Language

Korean is the national language. Although English is taught in school and college students have a working knowledge of it, their reading ability is far better than their comprehension of the spoken language, so it is often advisable to write requests if you are having trouble communicating. Little English is spoken in the countryside.

Japanese is widely understood, especially among the older generation as it was compulsory during the pre-1945 colonial period. Chinese characters are still used widely to supplement the Korean alphabet in writing and many Koreans will understand basic written Chinese.

Climate

There are four distinct seasons. Spring and autumn are pleasantly warm and dry. Summer is hot and relatively humid. Winter is dry and cold. Autumn and spring are generally considered the best times to visit, but the many temples look especially beautiful in the snow. Temperature extremes are from -20°C in winter to 35°C in summer. In Seoul the average temperature in January (the coldest month) is -3°C, while in August (the warmest month) it is 25°C. The rainy season generally begins about the end of June and lasts into early September.

Dress

In July and August the temperature is often high enough to justify only the lightest clothing. For most of the year conditions are moderate and one should have a range of clothing, including heavier items for the cool evenings. Winter, especially December and January, gets very cold and heavy clothing is required.

Business Hours

Government office hours are normally 9 a.m.-6 p.m. However, in winter (November-February) office hours are 9 a.m.-5 p.m. Offices are generally open on Saturday until 1 p.m. Commercial firms normally begin at the same time as the government offices but may stay open later, especially in the case of smaller businesses. Commercial banking hours are 9:30 a.m.-4:30 p.m. on weekdays and 9:30 a.m.-1:30 p.m. on Saturday.

The Seoul International Post Office opens 9 a.m.-6 p.m., but only until 1 p.m. on Saturday, as are most branch offices. The central Seoul post office, across from the Shinsegae department store, has extended evening (until 10 p.m.) and weekend and holiday hours (both until 6 p.m.) for ordinary mail services only. Larger shops such as department stores are open 10:30 a.m.-7:30 p.m. Smaller shops usually open on Sunday and take one day off during the week or month.

Doing Business

Acceptable, indeed mandatory, behaviour requires that a visitor always offers a business card. South Korea is a generally conservative, male dominated society that retains many of the Confucian codes of behaviour. Respect, therefore, is expected for those who have gained a position of authority and the elderly even from outsiders, or these figures lose dignity. It is impolite to address strangers by their first name, to show undue familiarity — like patting anybody on the shoulder — to speak too loudly during a business meeting or talking too much during a meal. When being introduced to a woman do not shake hands or address her by her first name. When sitting, do not stretch your leg out in front of elderly people or women.

During a meal pour your host or colleague a drink before you help yourself, and always reciprocate when offered a drink. If invited to visit an associate at home, always take a present for your host, and remember to take off your shoes when entering the house.

PHOTO: RON McMILLAN

Colourful Itaewon.

Rip-Offs

Apart from the usual precautions any visitor should take when in a big city, there are a few local twists worth bearing in mind. Never enter a restaurant or bar offering private rooms unless a local colleague invites you; they are incredibly expensive. Also, avoid cars without official taxi licence plates and always bargain when buying at street markets such as Itaewon. Initial prices, especially when asked of visitors, will always be reduced if you are persistent.

Communications

South Korea has drastically upgraded its communications and now has one of the best networks in Asia. International direct dialling and fax are available in hotels all over the country — in fact everywhere except the most remote areas.

Media

The English-language *Korea Times* and *Korea Herald* are available in most hotels. Copies of leading international newspapers also are avail-

SUBWAYS IN SEOUL

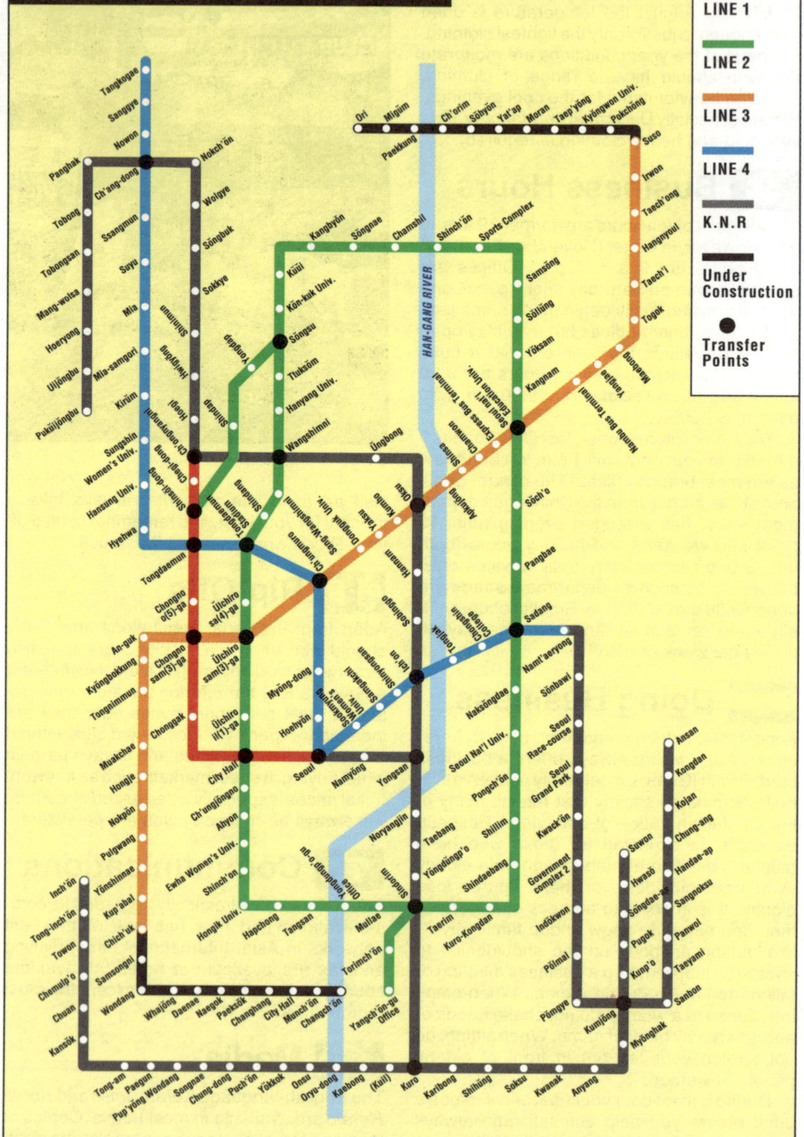

able in Seoul. Reception of satellite television has been actively discouraged by governments, but is provided by leading hotels for their guests. The U.S. forces television service, AFKN, is also available and carries news.

Transport

SEOUL

FROM THE AIRPORT: Taxis are available at Kimpo International Airport and the fare into the city where most of the hotels may be found is about Won 12,000. However, unscrupulous drivers often try to take advantage of visitors, regularly refusing to use the meter and demanding three or four times as much as the official fare. It is best to ensure the cab driver will use the meter before placing any luggage in the vehicle.

A cheaper and easier way to reach the city is to take the airport bus, which leaves every seven minutes and costs Won 600 to the major tourist hotels. The major hotels also operate infrequent shuttle buses from the airport.

TAXIS: Taxis are not always easy for the visitor to find unless one is starting from a hotel. The normal system used with the ubiquitous small taxis is for passengers travelling the same route to share the cab. If you are confident enough of your Korean, find a street corner where you see others trying to hail a cab and shout your destination or a nearby landmark to the driver as he swerves towards you at a high speed. Joining a queue, or what passes for one at a taxi-stand in Seoul, is often more successful. Otherwise, you can have your hotel doorman hail a taxi for you. The rate for the standard taxis is Won 1,000 for the first two kilometres and Won 100 for each additional 381 metres. Larger cars charge slightly higher fares.

The recently introduced **Deluxe Taxis** — whose drivers wear black uniform — are far more comfortable, and expensive, than normal taxies. The basic rate is Won 3,000 and Won 200 for each additional 250 metres.

BUSES: There are two grades of city bus: the standard lavender or green vehicle, with a fare of Won 300 paid with a token purchased in advance at one of the well-marked token stalls, and the olive-green express mini-buses, which cost Won 600 but are more likely to have a vacant seat. The standard network is extensive, though most buses are unpleasantly crowded. In addition, destination signs are only in Korean.

TRAINS: There is a suburban rail system in the capital and an extensive subway system, which is in the process of being extended. Existing lines run past the Toksu Palace in the centre of town eastwards to Tongdaemun (Great East Gate) and south past Namdaemun (Great West Gate) out of the city to Suwon and Inchon, as well as to the north. There is also a loop railway that runs through the outer areas of the city and then into the countryside to the north.

HIRE CARS: Daily rental charges range from Won 115,000-281,000, including chauffeur service, which is strongly recommended in Seoul's chaotic traffic. There is also a mileage charge.

TRANSPORT UPCOUNTRY

TRAINS: An extensive railway network allows access to most parts of the country, either by ordinary, express, deluxe or Saemaul express trains. Express trains run almost hourly in both directions on the Seoul-Pusan line. A night train with seating and sleeping accommodation also operates between Seoul and Pusan. A journey on the ordinary trains enables a visitor, sitting amid baskets of fish and bags of grain, to get a feel for the countryside. If the train is crowded — and it often is — the passengers sit three to a seat. Tickets for the Saemaul train can be purchased up to three months before the journey. Stations' names are displayed in both Korean and English on the platforms.

BUSES: Excellent highway bus services operate on the several expressways throughout the country. The Seoul-Pusan bus takes six hours over the almost 480-kilometre trip. Freeways also link Seoul and Inchon, Seoul and the east coast town of Kangnung via Wonju and also Taejon and Chonju. Air-conditioned buses run on the main routes. Once off the freeways, however, bus transport can become something of a challenge as there are still many badly paved roads across the country. There are several terminals for inter-city express buses, including **Kangnam Terminal**, just south of the Han River, which is served by the underground. Seats can be reserved for journeys between major points.

BOATS: Ferries ply the southern waters between Pusan and Cheju Island (about 11-1/2 hours) and Mokpo and Cheju (five-and-a-half hours). There is also a hydrofoil that runs between Pusan and Yosu, calling at Chungmu on the way.

AIR: **Korean Air** flies to 14 cities and **Asiana**

Seoul's Great South Gate. PHOTO: RON McMILLAN

Airlines to 12 cities in South Korea, including Pusan and Cheju City.

Tours

Almost every major hotel in Seoul has its own tour programmes and is willing to book pre-arranged group tours in and out of Seoul. The best place to check is the **Korea Tourist Bureau** which has offices at the following hotels: Chosun, Lotte, Hyatt Regency, Shilla, Koreana.

Accommodation

SEOUL

The hotel situation in Seoul is generally adequate, even in September-October high tourist season, with a growing number of international-standard rooms now available. For the adventurous, accommodation is also available in traditional Korean *yokwan* (inn), though for Western visitors a number of adjustments may have to be made. For example, the inns do not have showers as many Koreans bathe at public bath-houses.

ACCOMMODATION UPCOUNTRY

The main resorts and large towns throughout the country have Western-style accommodation. Pusan, Cheju Island and the Bomun Lake Resort, near Kyongju, boast top-class international standard hotels. Yokwans may be found at most of these places, while off the beaten track in the smaller towns and villages they will be the only available accommodation.

Dining

Korean foods and cooking styles are highly distinctive. Wandering in the country towns one may find a tiny restaurant where great chunks of beef or pork are displayed, ready to be mixed with hot, stew-like soup and perhaps noodles. In all the large towns, rather more established local dishes acceptable to unconditioned foreign tastes can be found. The best known dish is *bulgogi*, strips of marinated and seasoned beef broiled on a convex cooker. *Kalbi* is steamed or broiled ribs of beef. *Sinsollo* — meat, fish, eggs and vegetables, sometimes including ginkgo nuts — is cooked in a special brazier pierced by a small chimney, and Genghis Khan is thin slices of beef cooked in broth mixed with herbs, spices and vegetables. These dishes and many more are all cooked at your table.

Broiled *to-mi* (red snapper fish served with sweet and sour vegetables), *takmokam* (stewed chicken) and *sojum kui* (beef pieces barbecued on an iron hot-plate and then dipped in mixed salt and pepper) are other common dishes. The normal Korean meal includes steamed rice and a multitude of vegetable side-dishes, including several kinds of *kimchi* (pickled cabbage), pickled spinach, sweet spiced cucumber, radish and *mool-kimchi* (watery kimchi served in a bowl of weak brine).

For the less adventurous, all the four-star hotels have restaurants with Korean, Chinese, Japanese or Western cuisine. These hotels are about the only places in Seoul offering good Western food, though recent years have seen the arrival of a number of Western fast-food chains. There are also many Chinese restaurants in Seoul.

Entertainment

All businesses are supposed to close at midnight under a government edict issued in January 1990 intended to cut down on extravagant living. There are many beer halls and informal eateries throughout the city, especially in the **Myong-dong** area. These beer halls can be identified by the noisy character at the door who invites you in, or by the omnipresent OB Beer signs. Bottled, draught and black beer is available at reasonable prices.

Itaewon is next to the main U.S. Army base in Seoul, from which it draws its distinctive character. However, for the footloose male in search of English-speaking female company, Itaewon's tangle of bars, restaurants and discos may provide an answer. The eastern end of the Itaewon strip is increasingly Korean. The **Taehak-no** area (**Hyehwa** subway stop), is the largest entertainment area for Korean students and has a more festive atmosphere than many of the more traditional entertainment spots.

Classic Korean entertainment — Korean equivalent of the Japanese *geisha* — may be enjoyed at the *kisaeng* houses, but an evening in one can be incredibly expensive. A visitor in Seoul would be most unwise to visit a kisaeng house without a Korean friend.

Shopping

Korean handicrafts in some variety are available, though Seoul is not the bargain for shopping it was until the late 1980s. Mother-of-pearl, brassware, amber, gold and silver jewellery, local amethyst and topaz stones, leather goods, silk fabrics and dolls are all local specialities. Goods of dependable quality can be bought at the large stores such as **Midopa**, **Shinsegae** or **Lotte** department stores, but prices will be higher than in the smaller shops. There are special areas for foreign shoppers in the department stores.

Seoul is rapidly catching up with Hong Kong and other Southeast Asian cities as the place for ordering good, hand-tailored suits. Prices can be steep, and the range of fabrics is often limited, however. Lower prices can be found at the many small tailor shops in the suburban Itaewon area, which is used to dealing with customers from the nearby U.S. Army base. Quality can vary, so try for a recommendation, if you know a local resident. Leather goods are one of Seoul's best buys. Leather jackets and bags are found in abundance in Itaewon. Handmade shoes can be a good buy but, quality varies widely, so make certain you have time for several fittings. Ski suits and other outdoor and sportswear are among the best values.

For the serious shopper or lover of markets, the East Gate Market (**Dongdaemun**) and the South Gate Market (**Namdaemun**) are fascinating. The huge **Noryangjin** fish market, near Yoido, is one of the largest seafood markets in Asia.

Sports

Golf has taken on almost a cult quality among businessmen and government officials in South Korea, with a man's power measured by his ability to get a good tee time. There are now about five dozen golf courses in the country, including the Seoul Country Club and the Taenung Country Club. The clubs sometimes allow visiting players to use their facilities, especially on weekdays when no scheduled matches are being played. Inquire through your hotel so that a check can be made with the club secretary for permission for you to play.

Tennis is increasingly popular and there are many courts around the city open to visitors. Other sports include horse-racing, *taekwondo* (the Korean art of unarmed combat), fishing and hunting. Special hunting licences are re-

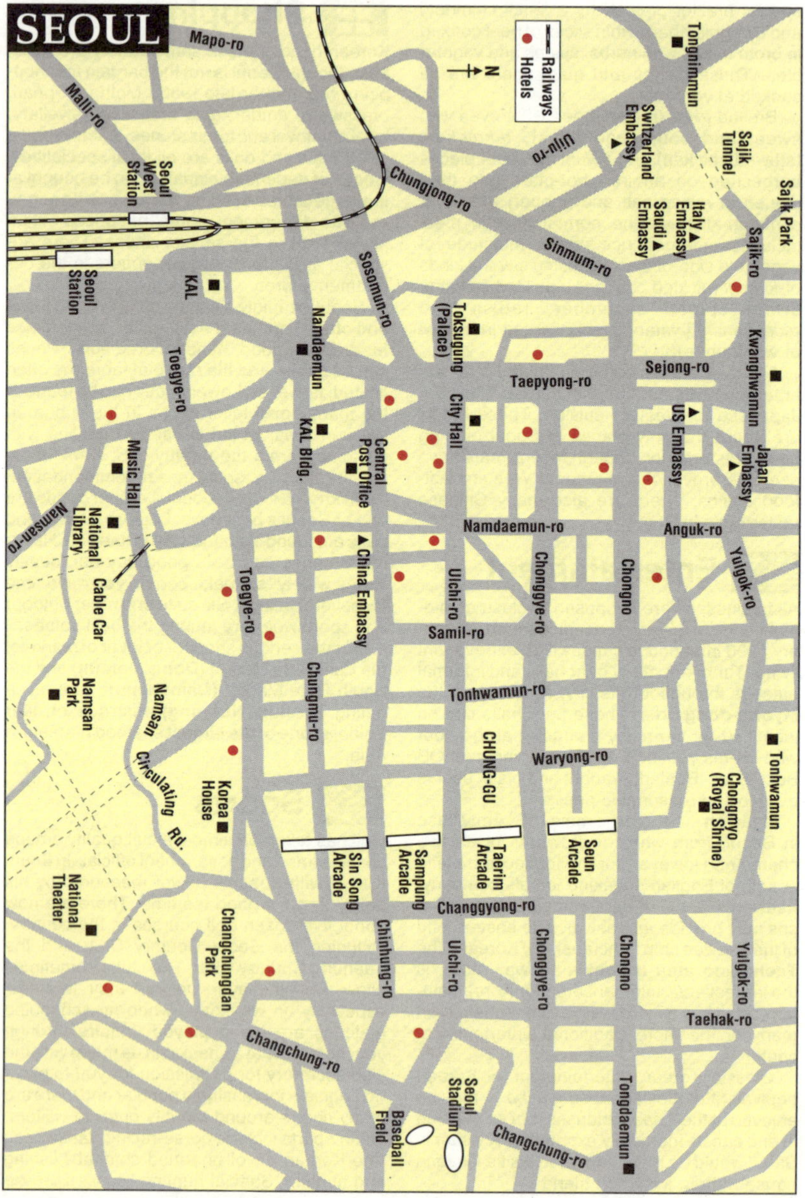
SEOUL
Railways
Hotels
N
Mapo-ro
Malli-ro
Seoul West Station
Seoul Station
KAL
Chungjong-ro
Uiju-ro
Tongnimmun
Switzerland Embassy
Sajik Tunnel
Sajik Park
Sajik-ro
Italy Embassy
Saudi Embassy
Sinmum-ro
Sosomun-ro
Toksugung (Palace)
Namdaemun
Toegye-ro
Kwanghwamun
Sejong-ro
Taepyong-ro
City Hall
KAL Bldg.
Central Post Office
US Embassy
Japan Embassy
Music Hall
National Library
Namsan-ro
Namdaemun-ro
Anguk-ro
China Embassy
Cable Car
Ulchi-ro
Chonggye-ro
Chongno
Yulgok-ro
Samil-ro
Chungmu-ro
Namsan Park
Namsan Circulating Rd.
Tonhwamun-ro
CHUNG-GU
Waryong-ro
Tonhwamun
Chongmyo (Royal Shrine)
Korea House
Sin Song Arcade
Sampung Arcade
Taerim Arcade
Seun Arcade
National Theater
Changchungdan Park
Changgyong-ro
Chinhung-ro
Taehak-ro
Changchung-ro
Seoul Stadium
Baseball Field
Tongdaemun

quired, and there are closed seasons. Baseball and soccer games are held in the main stadiums throughout the country according to season.

Holidays

As in many other Asian countries, many of South Korea's festivals and holidays dependent on the lunar calendar — though some have been standardized with the Western calendar and so fall on the same date each year. Most such days are public holidays.

January 1-2: New Year's Day.
January-February: Lunar New Year.
March 1: Independence Day.
April 5: Arbor Day (tree-planting day).
May 5: Children's Day.
May: Buddha's Birthday.
June: Tano Festival (marks end of spring planting).
July 17: Constitutional Day.
August 15: Liberation Day.
August-September: Confucius' Birthday (August 27 in lunar calendar).
September: Chusok (three-day moon festival).
October 1: Armed Forces Day.
October 3: National foundation Day.
October 8-10: Silla festival.
October 9: Hangul Day.
December 25: Christmas Day.

ADDRESSES

Seoul City Tourist Information Centre, rear annex of the Seoul City Hall, Tel: 731 6337. In addition, it maintains information centres at Kimpo Airport, the Seoul Express Bus Terminal, the Seoul Railway Station and five other prominent locations in the central part of town. Open 9 a.m.-6 p.m. daily, with maps and brochures available from English speaking staff.

Kimpo International Airport Information Desk, general information, maps and help with hotel reservations. The staff are most friendly and speak good English.

DISCOVERING SOUTH KOREA

SEOUL

Seoul, with its population of more than 10 million people, is South Korea's political, cultural, commercial and industrial centre. Despite the city's somewhat drab facade, there are many surprises hidden in the back alleys of downtown Seoul. Much of the city, however, simply sprawls into the surrounding foothills. Here and there the splendid remains — sometimes original, though more commonly reconstructed after the ravages of fire and late 16th-century Japanese invaders — of the palaces and temples of the Yi Dynasty.

The **Kyongbok (Great Happiness) Palace** was built by Yi Tae Jo as his main residence in 1395. During the Japanese invasion of 1592 it was burned down by Korean slaves anxious to destroy the records of their serfdom. The palace was rebuilt in the original style in 1867 as a symbol of Korea's intention to reassert its independence. It was here that Queen Min, wife of King Kojong and mother of the last king, Sunjong, was murdered by Japanese soldiers on October 8, 1896. It now forms a spacious backyard to the Japanese colonial-era Capitol Building.

The palace's soaring Throne Hall, set in a paved courtyard and partly ringed by remnants of Buddha images and steles, and the lovely Kyonghweru Banquet Hall — raised on 48 granite pillars over a lotus pond — are national showplaces.

The **Capitol Building**, built by the Japanese governor-general in 1927, deliberately disrupted the plan and view of the Kyongbok Palace, much of which was actually torn down at the time. It now houses the **National Museum**, which has an excellent collection of Korean art treasures. Behind the Capitol Building is the **National Folklore Museum**, which houses a fine collection of traditional arts, crafts and everyday objects.

Some two kilometres east of the Capitol Building is the entrance gate to the 32-hectare park known as **Piwon (Secret Garden)**. In the park's southwest corner is the **Changdok (Illustrious Virtue) Palace**, which was built in 1405 and later restored in 1611 when it replaced the ruined Kyongbok as the seat of government. Also within the park is the complex known as **Naksonjae**, the residence of the Yi crown prince where the Dowager Queen Eun died in 1966. It is the best preserved monument of the Yi Dynasty.

The **Tonhwa Mun** main entrance gate is one of the oldest wood structures in Seoul, dating from the end of the 14th century. The gate, the **Throne Hall** and blue-roofed **Audience Hall** are the most imposing structures, but the tree-shaded, pink-walled inner courtyards have an atmosphere of delicacy and charm, and the rambling irregularity of the complex reveals unexpected views and pleasant corners.

The Piwon serves as a refuge from the bustle of Seoul, with its springs, ponds and pleasure pavilions. Its largest structure, the **Yun Kyung Dang**, is a replica of an upper-class country house of the Yi period and displays the interior of a traditional Korean residence. The Changdok Palace and the Piwon are best visited on a weekday when there are fewer visitors. However, it is difficult to enjoy the sights at leisure as visitors must join an organized tour of the gardens and palace. The tours are not that illuminating, so there is little to be lost by joining a Japanese or Korean-language group.

Beyond the Piwon's eastern wall are the grounds of the **Changyong-won (Garden of Bright Happiness)**. The buildings are relatively small, few and modest, but they are mostly the original structures of 1488 and the only ones to survive the disasters of 1592.

In the Changyong-won's southwest corner are the grounds of the Chong Myo Royal Shrine, where two long, pillared halls contain the memorial tablets of the Yi kings. A small house beyond the memorial buildings holds the kings' signatory seals and other mementoes.

Seoul, when founded by Yi Song Gye, was surrounded by a 19-kilometre-or-so stone wall — however today only small sections remain. One section in **Namsan (South Mountain) Park** is easily accessible, while another stretch over Mount Inwang to the west offers a pleasant and occasionally challenging half-day's hiking. But the best sections are those from the **North Gate** over **Bukaksan (North Mountain)** that reach down to the northeast part of the city. Although hiking is not allowed in this area for security reasons — the area overlooks Chung Wa Dae, the Presidential Mansion — it is possible to drive up to the wall. Photography is forbidden, but the view is excellent with villages visible in the mountains to the north and Seoul to the south. Just to the north across a steep valley is **Pukansan National Park**, which offers what must be some of the world's best hiking in a metropolitan area.

Five of the city's original eight gates remain. **Nam Dae Mun**, the **Great South Gate**, is in the centre of the main street from Seoul railway station and remains the city's principal entrance — though traffic now flows around rather than through it. Constructed in 1398 and rebuilt in 1447, its curving roofs and massive granite walls have become a familiar image of Korea. The **Great East Gate**, somewhat smaller, is protected by a semi-circular forecourt and the present work dates from 1869. The **North Gate**, rebuilt in 1741, is much smaller but a good place from which to view portions of the wall. The other two gates are only of minor interest and one is now off-limits.

Further along Chong-ro is **Pagoda Park**, where on March 1, 1919 a group of 33 Korean patriots read a Declaration of Independence for Korea that triggered a wave of peaceful demonstrations. The Japanese responded with executions, torture and mass imprisonment — scenes of which are depicted on some rather sensational bas-reliefs in the park.

In the northeast part of the city, just beyond the Piwon, is **Sungkyunkwan University**, founded in 1397 as the country's highest educational institution and training school for the Confucian bureaucracy. It is still a centre for Confucian scholarship, though the shrines, study halls, dormitories and libraries where ambitious young men once prepared for the national civil service are now surrounded by a large modern university.

The South Gate Market area is an excellent place to experience the bustling atmosphere of a typical Asian market place. By contrast, the area between Myong-dong and Chong-ro boasts many small hotels, bars, nightclubs, cinemas, teashops and restaurants and serves as the city's main night-time entertainment district.

The Great East Market, once entirely housed in a concrete structure, has since spilled out into surrounding streets. The second floor of the building is a brilliant sight — a great silk bazaar with vendors wearing traditional dress matching the bright colours of the many materials they sell.

Yoido Island in the **Han River** is the site of a new government complex and the **National Assembly** building. The **Korea Stock Exchange** and many securities firms are also located on the island, as is one of the world's largest churches, the **Yoido Full Gospel Church**, which holds 17,000 people.

DAY TRIPS FROM SEOUL

One-day excursions around Seoul can give the visitor some idea of the Korean countryside and its traditional small-town and village life. The easiest and most rewarding is a trip to the walled city of **Suwon**, 40 kilometres south of Seoul and a 30-minute train ride away or an

Seoul by night. PHOTO: RON McMILLAN

hour on the subway. Suwon's recently restored eight-metre-high walls date from 1795 and run for more than five kilometres around the town. Built when the kingdom was prosperous and at peace, Suwon's fortifications are the most artistic in Korea and the most diversified and advanced in their design. The entire circuit can be easily made in three or four hours, and there are few better combinations of scenery and historic remains anywhere in Korea.

Just south of Suwon at Yongjo is an important monastery that justifies a side-trip. Also nearby is the **Korean Folk Village** — not, as the name would suggest, an instant-culture tourist attraction, but a real village community with the traditional thatch-roofed houses of farmers and the tiled roofs of country gentlemen's homes. Families living in this village follow the ways of old Korea, wearing traditional dress and observing old customs. The instant culture is, however, present in one respect — folk entertainment is presented daily, with mask dramas, lion dances and slightly bawdy puppet plays.

Southeast from Seoul lies the mountain fortress of **Namhansan Castle**, whose present walls date from 1625. It is about eight kilometres in circumference, with well-preserved east and south gates. The valley inside contains farmland, a village and several historic buildings. There are magnificent views from the walls and peaks, especially from the highest crest, **Sojangdae**, where there is a royal pavilion. Bus services run from Seoul to this popular spot.

Inchon, 39 kilometres west of Seoul, is South Korea's second port after Pusan, and part of a fast-growing industrial zone that forms metropolitan Seoul. It was here that Gen. Douglas MacArthur ordered the United Nations forces' landing on September 15, 1950: visitors can walk on Green Beach where the North Korean invaders were outflanked. Offshore are some beautiful islands, such as **Songdo** and **Palmido**, which have excellent sandy beaches. **Wolmido Island**, which has a strip of fine seafood restaurants, has now been joined to the mainland by a causeway. There is little sightseeing in the town itself, but buses connect directly from Seoul to the beaches and the **Olympos Hotel**, a casino resort. On the eastern fringe of Seoul itself is another casino at the **Sheraton Walker Hill Hotel**.

To the east of the capital and spread over much of **Kyonggido province** are many of the Yi royal tombs. The most elaborate are those of the last two kings, Kojong and Sunjong, at **Kumkoknung**. The largest group is at **Tonggunung**, where some 15-20 tombs in nine groups lie in a vast wooded park. Both areas are accessible by local bus but, as with all the areas surrounding the capital, it is wise to have directions written in Korean to aid you when on the buses and moving around on foot. On weekends many Koreans picnic in the area and it is often crowded and noisy.

Panmunjom, an hour's drive to the north of Seoul, is a reminder of the divided state of the country and its continuing tensions. Tourists can observe the meeting room of the Military Armistice Commission, composed of North Korean and UN Command representatives, where communist and U.S. troops stand guard virtually next to each other. The trip to the site, in the middle of the four-kilometre Demilitarized Zone, is made under U.S. military police escort.

UPCOUNTRY

The hot spring resort town of **Onyang** is a two-and-a-half hours train ride south from Seoul. Famed for the supposed therapeutic value of the waters, the resort lies in an area noted for its scenery and its historical associations. It is here that the tomb, shrine and museum of Adm. Yi Sun Shin are found. Yi is Korea's greatest naval hero, inventor of the turtle-shaped ironclad warships that were instrumental in defeating the invading Japanese in 1592 and 1598.

Further south in the same province (**Chung-chongnamdo**, also called **Chungnam**), and only nine kilometres from the provincial capital Taejon, is the resort town of **Yusong** — which also has hot springs. In the neighbouring province of **Chung-chongpukdo** (also called **Chungpuk**) is **Mt Songnisan**, famous for its scenic beauty and the **Popjusa Temple**, which stands at its foot. Built by the priest Uisin of the Silla Dynasty, the temple has one of the largest Buddha statues in the world — the 23-metre-high **Maitreya Buddha**, completed in 1964.

Pusan, South Korea's main seaport and second business, industrial and population centre, is a sprawling city in the southeast corner of the country.

Although of no great tourist interest, Pusan is the gateway for those coming by sea from Japan. About 16 kilometres north of the city is the beach and hot-spring resort of **Haeundae**, while further inland is the hot-spring resort town of **Tongnae**. Beyond Tongnae is the important monastery of **Pomosa**. The present buildings date from the 16th century and are arranged in rising tiers up the mountain. This is probably the most accessible of the country's major temples.

Also near Pusan north is **Tongdosa**, an elaborate monastery complex with about 45 outlying hermitages and nunneries scattered about a wide, forested valley beside a small river. Visits can be made by local bus from Pusan.

Kyongju, capital of the Silla Kingdom from AD 313 until 939, is the country's prime tourist attraction. The town itself is quiet and sleepy, but all around lie the remains of what was once a city of a million people, with palaces, monasteries, a wall with 20 gates and a brilliant flowering of art, literature and technology. Kyongju is accessible from both Pusan and Taegu: express buses from each town leave for Kyongju every 30 minutes. From Seoul the Saemaul train leaves twice daily for Kyongju and takes four-and-a-half hours. The local branch of the Korean Tourist Bureau is a useful source of information.

Pukguksa Temple lies about eight kilometres southeast of Kyongju on the lower slopes of **Mount Toham**. The cave of **Sokkuram**, with its renowned Buddha and bas-relief stone work dating from 751, is three kilometres from Pulguksa up a steep path offering excellent views between scruffy souvenir and drink shops. The alternative is to take a taxi up and walk down.

About four kilometres from Kyongju city, midway between the residential area and Pulguksa Temple, is **Bomun Lake Resort**, a tourist development opened in 1979. The 10-square-kilometre resort complex, which was partly financed by the World Bank, centres on a man-made lake set between wooded hills and includes several international-class hotels and a wide range of sports and recreation facilities.

Near the hotels on the lake front is a sprawling amenity centre which houses dozens of specialty shops and snack bars. Boating, water skiing, tennis an 18-hole golf course and swimming are available.

Haeinsa Temple, up in the mountains about

Cheju's Mt Halla volcano. PHOTO: KOREA NATIONAL TOURISM CORP.

80 kilometres west of Taegu (three hours by direct bus), is an excellent example of the classic Korean monastery. However, its chief glory is its great library, notably the **Palmandae-jang-gyung** — a complete set of the Buddhist scriptures in Chinese characters carved in 1251.

In the southwest of Korea are monasteries at **Kumsansa** and **Hwaomsa**. **Cheju Island**, about 96 kilometres off the southwest tip of South Korea, is famous for its women divers who gather abalone and seaweed and the extinct **Mount Halla** volcano — the country's highest peak. The visitor will find the climate rather warmer than the mainland and the pace of life markedly slower. Specialty products of the island include woollens from the mountain sheep, black coral, mushrooms and lobster.

Chungmun Beach on the island's southern coast is the site of the second of South Korea's international tourist resort developments. As with the Bomun Lake resort, the emphasis of development is on sports and leisure.

The east coast of the mainland is an area also noted for its natural beauty. **Mount Sorak**, just south of the 38th parallel is an excellent example. Its slopes, brilliant with multicoloured leaves in the autumn and covered with snow in winter, draw serious mountain climbers and skiers.

The main ski resort is south of Kangnung at **Taekwallyong**. Further down along the coast are many fine beaches. The area includes the important **Sinhungsa Monastery** and the **Eight Famous Views of Kwandong** — a series of scenic spots, temples and pavilions at intervals along the coast.

Kangnung, the air terminal for the northeast coast, has magnificent beaches at **Kyongpodae** a few kilometres to the north, which can be reached by bus, train or taxi. Fine oysters and abalone can be bought locally at reasonable prices.

From Kangnung south along the coast to **Kyongju**, the road winds along precipitous mountainsides, past fishing villages and narrow beaches. The scenery is memorable, but facilities along the way are still rudimentary. It is wise to make careful inquiries about accommodation and transport before travelling in this region.

RESTAURANT SELECTION

Average price for two

ASHOKA, 119-25, Itaewon-dong. Tel: 792 0117. Indian. US$50.
ATHENE, 1362-26, Socho-dong. Tel: 554 3200. French. Music. US$120.
CHALET SWISS, 104-4, Itaewon-dong. Tel: 795 1723. Swiss. Music. Thur-Fri. US$70.
CHINA CITY, 563-33, Shinsa-dong. Tel: 548 2222. Chinese. US$88.
DAEWONGAK, 323, Songbuk-dong. Tel: 762 0161. Korean. US$170.
KOREA HOUSE, 80-2, Pil-dong 2-ka. Tel: 267 8752. Korean. Music. US$140.
L'ABRI, 1, Jongno 1-ka. Tel: 739 8830. French. US$100.
LA CANTINA, 50, Ulchiro 1-ka. Tel: 777 2579. Italian. US$50.
LONDON PUB, 16-2, Yoido-dong. Tel: 783 7701, English-style. US$43.
MOGHUL, 116-2, Itaewon-dong. Tel: 796 5501. Pakistani. US$63.
PANGNI-HYANG, DHL 63 Bldg, Yoido-dong. Tel: 789 5742. Chinese. US$100.
WA KO, DHL 63 Bldg, Yoido-dong. Tel: 789 5751. Japanese. US$158.
WOORAEOAK, 2-32-8, Myung-dong. Tel: 265 0152. Korean. US$55.
YONGSUSAN, 118-3, Samchong-dong. Tel: 732 3019. Korean. US$90.

HOTEL GUIDE

All room rates quoted in South Korea are for double occupancy.

CHEJUDO

A: US$265 and above

CHEJU GRAND, 263-15, Yondong. Tel: (064) 475000, Fax: (064) 423150. *P, Gym. R: W, K.*
HYATT REGENCY CHEJU, 3039-1, Saekdal-dong. Tel: (064) 331234, Fax: (064) 322039, Tlx: NAMJU K66749. *P, Gym. R: W, K.*
SHILLA CHEJU, 3060, Saekdal-dong. Tel: (064) 355114, Fax: (064) 355415. *P, Gym. R: W, K.*

B: US$111-174

CHEJU PRINCE, 731-3, Sohong-dong. Tel: (064) 329911, Fax: (064) 329900. *R: W, K.*
CHEJU WASHINGTON, 291-30, Yon-dong. Tel: (064) 424111, Fax: (064) 464111. *P. R: W, K.*
SOGWIPO KAL, 486-3, Topyong-dong. Tel: (064) 329851, Fax: (064) 339377, Tlx: SKALHTL K66717. *P. R: W, K.*

C: US$101-114

CHEJU ROYAL, 272-34, Yon-dong. Tel: (064) 432222, Fax: (064) 420424. *R: W, K.*
HOLIDAY CHEJU, 1192-20, 863, Kosong-ri. Tel: (064) 993111, Fax: (064) 992920. *R: W, K.*

CHOLLABUK-DO

B: US$138-202

CORE, 627-3, Sonosong-dong, Chonjushi. Tel: (0652) 851100, Fax: (0652) 855707, Tlx: HANSHIN K66613. *R: W, K.*

C: US$118-140

NAEJANGSAN TOURIST, 71-14, Naejang-dong, Jongjushi. Tel: (0681) 535 4131. *R: W, K.*

D: US$38-60

KUNSAN TOURIST, 461-1, Kyong-jang-dong, Kunsanshi. Tel: (0654) 430811. *R: W, K.*

CHOLLANAM-DO

C: US$88-140

CHIRISAN PLAZA, 27-1, Hwangsari, Masanmyon, Kurye-kun. Tel: (0664) 782 2171, Fax: (0664) 782 3675. *R: W, K.*
SHINAN BEACH, 440-40, Chukgyo-dong, Mokposhi. Tel: (0631) 433399, Fax: (0631) 430030. *R: W, K.*

D: US$50-88

SUNCHON KUMKANG TOURIST, 22-20, Namnae-dong, Sunchon. Tel: (0661) 528301, Fax: (0661) 529193. *R: W, K.*
YOSU SEJONG TOURIST, 1054-1, Songhwa-dong, Yosu. Tel: (0662) 626111, Fax: (0662) 621929. *R: W, K.*

CHUNGCHONGBUK-DO

C: US$88-140

FRIENDLY, 102-1, Hoam-dong,

P — Swimming pool **Gym** — Health club **R** — Restaurant **K** — Korean food
W — Western food

HOTEL GUIDE

Chongjushi. Tel: (0441) 848 9900, Fax: (0441) 429403. *R: W, K.*
SUANBO WAIKIKI TOURIST, 806-1, Onchonri, Sangmomyon, Chungwonkun. Tel: (0441) 846 3333, Fax: (0441) 846 0500. *R: W, K.*

CHUNGCHONGNAM-DO

C: US$88-140

ONYANG GRAND PARK, 300-28, Onchong-dong, Onyangshi. Tel: (0418) 439711, Fax: 439727. *R: W, K.*
TOGO ROYAL TOURIST, 174-13, Kigokri, Togomyon, Asankun. Tel: (0418) 435511, Fax: (0418) 435520. *R: W, K.*

INCHON

B: US$100-160

SONGDO BEACH, 812, Tongchon-dong. Tel: (032) 865 1311, Fax: (032) 865 1325. *Gym. R: W, K.*

C: US$95-140

NEW INCHON, 746-8, Soongui-dong. Tel: (032) 887 5635, Fax: (032) 884 8703. *R: W, K.*
ROYAL TOURIST, 173-432, Kansok-dong. Tel: (032) 435 2318, Fax: (032) 421 0473. *R: W, K.*

KANGWON-DO

B: US$100-150

HOTEL SORAK PARK, 74-3, Sorak-dong, Sokchoshi. Tel: (0392) 347711, Fax: (0392) 347732, Tlx: SPHOTEL K24142. *R: W, K.*
YONGPYONG RESORT DRAGON VALLEY, 130, Yongsanri, Toam-myon, Pyongchangkun. Tel: (0374) 355168, Fax: (0374) 350160. *P, Gym. R: W, K.*

C: US$82-100

CHUNCHON SEJONG, 1, Pongui-dong, Chunchonshi. Tel: (0361) 521191, Fax: (0361) 543347. *R: W, K.*
KANGNUNG TOURIST, 1117, Ponam-dong, Kangnumgshi. Tel: (0391) 413771, Fax: (0391) 417712. *R: W, K.*

KWANGJU

B: US$125-150

MUDUNGSAN ONCHON, 9-2, Chisan-dong. Tel: (062) 226 0026, Fax: (062) 226 0020. *R: W, K.*

C: US$75-108

KWANGJU GRAND, 121, Pullo-dong. Tel: (062) 224 6111, Fax: (062) 224 8933. *R: W, K.*
KWANGJU PALACE, 11-4, Hwang-kum-dong. Tel: (062) 222 2525, Fax: (062) 224 9723. *R: W, K.*
SHINYANG PARK, 40, Chisan-dong. Tel: (062) 228 8000, Fax: (062) 232 3731. *R: W, K.*

KYONGGI-DO

C: US$70-106

BOOLIM, 560, Shimgok-dong, Puchonshi. Tel: (032) 611 5500, Fax: (032) 611 5509. *R: W, K.*
SEOUL HOF, 1-15, Pyollyang-dong, Kwachonshi. Tel: (02) 504 2211, Fax: (02) 503 8035. *R: W, K.*

D: US$60-88

DONGSUWON, 144-4, Uman-dong, Suwonshi. Tel: (0331) 211 6666, Fax: 212 8811. *R: W, K.*
HOT SPRING SOLBONG, 313-5, Anhungri, Ichonup, Ichonkun. Tel: (0336) 635 5701, Fax: (0336) 336305. *R: W, K.*
NEW KOREA, 674-251, Anyang-dong, Anyangshi. Tel: (0343) 486671, Fax: (0343) 486687. *R: W, K.*

KYONGSANGBUK-DO

A: US$152 and above

CONCORDE, 410, shinpyong-dong, Kyongjushi. Tel: (0561) 745 7000, Fax: (0561) 745 7010, Tlx: CCDJK K54328. *P, Biz. R: W, K.*
KOLON, 111-1, Ma-dong, Kyongjushi. Tel: (0561) 746 9001, Fax: (0561) 746 6331, Tlx: KOLHTL K54469. *P. R: W, K.*
KYONGJU CHOSUN, 410, Shinpyong-dong, Kyongjushi. Tel: (0561) 745 7701, Fax: (0561) 408349. *P, Gym, Biz. R: W, K.*
KYONGJU HILTON, 370, Shinpyong-dong, Kyongjushi. Tel: (0561) 745 7788, Fax: (0561) 745 7799, Tlx: KHILTON K54512. *P, Gym, Biz, SatTV. R: W, K.*

C: US$76-92

ANDONG PARK, 324, Unhung-dong, Andongshi. Tel: (0571) 859 1500, Fax: (0571) 575445. *R: W, K.*
KUMI, 1032-5, Wonpyong-dong, Kumishi. Tel: (0546) 512000, Fax: (0546) 512002. *R: W, K.*
KYONGJU HOT SPRING, 145-1, Kujong-dong, Kyongjushi. Tel: (0561) 746 6661, Fax: (0561) 746 6665. *R: W, K.*
PAEKAM RESORT, 964, Onjongri,

P — Swimming pool | **Gym** — Health club | **Biz** — Business centre | **SatTV** — Satellite TV
R — Restaurant | **K** — Korean food | **W** — Western food

HOTEL GUIDE

Ulchinkun. Tel: (0565) 787 3500, Fax: (0565) 787 4233. *R: W, K.*
POHANG BEACH, 311-2, Songdo-dong, Pohang. Tel: (0562) 411401, Fax: (0562) 427534. *R: W, K.*
SAEJAE, 159-4, Chomchon-dong, Chomchonshi. Tel: (0581) 538000, Fax: (0581) 522983. *R: W, K.*

KYONGSANGNAM-DO

B: US$87-150

CHUNGMU, 1 Tonam-dong, Chungmushi. Tel: (0557) 645 2091, Fax: (0557) 428877, Tlx: HANRYEO K53850. *R: W, K.*
DIAMOND, 283, Chongha-dong, Ulsan. Tel: (0522) 327171, Fax: (0522) 327170, Tlx: DIAMNT K52224. *P, Gym. R: W, K.*
HAEINSA, 16-1, Chalinri, Hapchonkun. Tel: (0599) 332000, Fax: (0599) 332989. *R: W, K.*
ULSAN KOREANA, 255-3, Songnam-dong, Ulsan. Tel: (0522) 449911, Fax: (0522) 441665, Tlx: KOTEL K52550. *R: W, K.*

PUSAN

A: US$185 and above

HYATT REGENCY PUSAN, 1405-16, Chung-dong. Tel: (051) 743 1234, Fax: (051) 743 1250. *P, Gym, Biz, Ex, SatTV. R: W, K.*
PARADISE BEACH, 1408-5, Chung-dong. Tel: (051) 742 2121, Fax: (051) 742 2100, Tlx: PARABH K52145. *P, Gym, Biz, Ex, SatTV. R: W, K.*
WESTIN CHOSUN BEACH, 737, U 1-dong. Tel: (051) 742 7411, Fax: (051) 742 1313, Tlx: K53718. *P, Gym, Biz, Ex, SatTV. R: W, K.*

B: US$110-150

COMMODORE, 743-80, Yonju-dong. Tel: (051) 466 9101, Fax: (051) 462 9101. *P, Gym, Biz. R: W, K.*
KUKJE, 830-62, Pomil 2-dong. Tel: (051) 642 1330, Fax: (051) 642 6595. *R: W, K.*
SORABOL, 37-1, 1-ka, Taechong-dong. Tel: (051) 463 3511, Fax: (051) 463 3510, Tlx: SOHOTEL K53827. *R: W, K.*

C: US$82-126

MIRABO, 1124-25, Yonsan-dong. Tel: (051) 866 7400, Fax: (051) 866 8770. *R: W, K.*
SAPPHIRE, 302-2, Dangri-dong. Tel: (051) 207 1300, Fax: (051) 207 1400. *R: W, K.*

D: US$47-70

PUSAN ARIRANG, 1204-1, Choryang-dong. Tel: (051) 463 5001, Fax: (051) 463 2800. *R: W, K.*
SHIN SHIN, 263-11, Pujon 1-dong. Tel: (051) 816 0360, Fax: (051) 802 5847. *R: W, K.*

SEOUL

A: US$228 and above

HILTON, 395, 5-ka, Namdaemunno. Tel: (02) 753 7788, Fax: (02) 754 2510, Tlx: KHILTON K26695. *P, Gym, Biz, Ex, SatTV. R: W, K.*
HYATT REGENCY, 747-7, Hannam-dong. Tel: (02) 797 1234, Fax: (02) 798 6953, Tlx: HYATT K24136. *P, Gym, Biz, Ex. R: W, K.*
INTER-CONTINENTAL, 159-8, Samsong-dong. Tel: (02) 555 5656, Fax: (02) 559 7990, Tlx: IHCSEL K33970. *P, Gym, Biz, Ex, SatTV. R: W, K.*
LOTTE, 1, Sogong-dong. Tel: (02) 771 1000, Fax: 752 3758, Tlx: LOTTEHO K23533. *P, Gym, Biz, Ex. R: W, K.*
LOTTE WORLD, 40-1, Chamshil-dong. Tel: (02) 419 7000, Fax: (02) 417 3655, Tlx: LOTTEHW K33728. *P, Gym, Biz, Ex. R: W, K.*
PLAZA, 23, 2-ka, Taepyongno. Tel: (02) 771 2200, Fax: (02) 755 8897, Tlx: PLAZAHL K24424. *Biz, SatTV. R: W, K.*
RAMADA RENAISSANCE, 676, Yoksam-dong. Tel: (02) 555 0501, Fax: (02) 553 8118, Tlx: RAMDAS K34392. *P, Gym, Biz, Ex, SatTV. R: W, K.*
RITZCARLTON, 602-4, Yoksam-dong. Tel: (02) 3451 8000, Fax: (02) 556 8855. *P, Gym, Biz, SatTV. R: W, K.*
SHERATON WALKER HILL, 21, Kwangjang-dong. Tel: (02) 453 0121, Fax: (02) 452 6867, Tlx: WALKHTL K28517. *P, Gym, Biz. R: W, K.*
SHILLA, 202, Changchun-dong. Tel: (02) 233 3131, Fax: (02) 233 5073, Tlx: SHILLA K24160. *P, Gym, Biz, Ex, SatTV. R: W, K.*
SWISS GRAND, 201-1, Hongun-dong. Tel: (02) 356 5656, Fax: (02) 356 7799, Tlx: SGHSEL K34322. *P, Gym, Biz, Ex, SatTV. R: W, K.*
WESTIN CHOSUN, 87, Sogong-dong. Tel: (02) 771 0500, Fax: (02) 752 1443, Tlx: CHOSUN K24256. *P, Gym, Ex, Biz, SatTV. R: W, K.*

B: US$110-170

CAPITAL, 22-76, Itaewon-dong. Tel: (02) 792 1122, Fax: (02) 796 0918, Tlx: HCAPITL K23502. *P, Gym, Biz.*

P — Swimming pool **Gym** — Health club **Biz** — Business centre **Ex** — Executive floor
SatTV — Satellite TV **R** — Restaurant **K** — Korean food **W** — Western food

HOTEL GUIDE

R: W, K.
EMERALD, 129, Chongdam-dong. Tel: (02) 514 3535, Fax: (02) 516 3098. *P, Gym, Biz. R: W, K.*
KING SEJONG, 611-3, 2-ka, Chungmuro. Tel: (02) 776 1811, Fax: (02) 755 4906, Tlx: SEJONG K27265. *Gym, Biz, SatTV. R: W, K.*
KOREANA, 61, 1-ka, Taepyongno. Tel: (02) 730 9911, Fax: (02) 734 0665, Tlx: KOTEL K26241. *SatTV. R: W, K.*
NEW WORLD, 112-5, Samsung-dong. Tel: (02) 557 0111, Fax: (02) 557 0141, Tlx: NWORLD K33226. *P, Gym, SatTV. R: W, K.*
PALACE, 63-1, Panpo-dong. Tel: (02) 532 0101, Fax: (02) 532 0399. *Gym, Biz, SatTV. R: W, K.*
PRESIDENT, 188-3, 5-ka, Ulchiro. Tel: (02) 753 3133, Fax: (02) 752 7417, Tlx: PRETEL K27521. *Biz. R: W, K.*
RAMADA OLYMPIA, 108-2, Pyongchang-dong. Tel: (02) 287 6000, Fax: (02) 396 6633, Tlx: RAMADA K23171. *P, Gym, Biz. R: W, K.*
RIVERIA, 53-7, Chongdam-dong. Tel: (02) 541 3111, Fax: (02) 546 6111, Tlx: RIVIERA K32465. *P, Gym. R: W, K.*
RIVERSIDE, 6-1, Chamwon-dong. Tel: (02) 543 1001, Fax: (02) 543 5310. *Gym. R: W, K.*
ROYAL, 6, 1-ka, Myong-dong. Tel: (02) 756 1112, Fax: (02) 756 1119, Tlx: SLROYAL K27239. *Biz. R: W, K.*
SEOUL GARDEN, 169-1, Tohwa-dong. Tel: (02) 717 9441, Fax: (02) 715 9441, Tlx: SGARDEN, K24742. *Biz. R: W, K.*
SOFITEL AMBASSADOR, 186-54, 2-ka, Changchung-dong. Tel: (02) 275 1101, Fax: (02) 272 0773, Tlx: AMHOSK K23269. *Gym, Biz, Ex. R: W, K.*
TOWER, 5-5, 2-ka, Changchung-dong. Tel: (02) 236 2121, Fax: (02) 235 0276, Tlx: TOWER K28246. *Gym. R: W, K.*

C: US$69-100

AROMA, 505-23, Dunchon-dong. Tel: (02) 653 1999, Fax: (02) 651 1389. *Gym. R: W, K.*
CROWN, 34-69, Itaewon-dong. Tel: (02) 797 4111, Fax: (02) 796 1010, Tlx: CROWNTH K25951. *R: W, K.*
NEW KUKJE, 29-1, 1-ka, Taepyongno. Tel: (02) 732 0160, Fax: (02) 732 1774. *R: W, K.*
PUKAK PARK, 113-1, Pyongchang-dong. Tel: (02) 395 7107, Fax: (02) 391 5559. *R: W, K.*
SOKYO, 354-5, Sokyo-dong. Tel: (02) 333 7771, Fax: (02) 333 3388. *P, Gym. R: W, K.*
VICTORIA, 42-8, Mia 4-dong. Tel: (02) 986 2000, Fax: (02) 984 3679. *P, Gym, Biz. R: W, K.*

D: US$57-72

ASTORIA, 13-2, Namhak-dong. Tel: (02) 267 7111, Fax: (02) 274 3187. *R: W, K.*
CLOVER, 129-7, Chongdam-dong. Tel: (02) 546 1411, Fax: (02) 544 1340. *R: W, K.*
GREEN PARK, 14, Ui-dong. Tel: (02) 900 8186, Fax: (02) 902 0030. *P. R: W, K.*

TAEGU

B: US$137-164

KUMHO, 28, Haso-dong. Tel: (053) 252 6001, Fax: (053) 253 4121. *R: W, K.*
TAEGU PRINCE, 1824-2, Taemyong-dong. Tel: (053) 628 1001, Fax: (053) 628 2833. *R: W, K.*

C: US$70-88

CRYSTAL, 1196-1, Turyu 1-dong. Tel: (053) 252 7799, Fax: (053) 253 0323. *R: W, K.*
HWANGKUM, 847-1, Hwangkum-dong. Tel: (053) 765 6006, Fax: 766 8004. *R: W, K.*

TAEJON

B: US$122-153

RIVIERA YUSONG, 478, Pongmyong-dong. Tel: (042) 823 2111, Fax: 822 5250. *P, Gym. R: W, K.*

C: US$65-122

ADRIA, 442-5, Pongmyong-dong. Tel: (042) 824 0210, Fax: (042) 823 5805. *R: W, K.*
DAELIM, 230-6, Sonhwa-dong. Tel: (042) 255 2161, Fax: 255 2166. *R: W, K.*
HONGIN, 536-8, Pongmyong-dong. Tel: (042) 822 2000, Fax: (042) 822 9410. *R: W, K.*
PICASSO, 63-31, Yongchong-dong. Tel: (042) 627 3001, Fax: (042) 627 3011. *R: W, K.*

P — Swimming pool
SatTV — Satellite TV
Gym — Health club
R — Restaurant
Biz — Business centre
K — Korean food
Ex — Executive floor
W — Western food

MACAU

Macau, consisting of a total of 19.3 square kilometres (including the islands of Taipa and Coloane), is a Portuguese colonial outpost built on a peninsula on the South China coast. It is a "living museum," traditionally a leisurely place steeped in memories of great days when East met West and fought for territory amid its fortresses and chapels.

Much of the sleepy image engendered by the old Macau is being shaken off as modernization continues apace, and most of the charm of the waterfront area of Macau has been lost to a reclamation project. But in the city's back streets and in large parts of Taipa and Coloane, it retains an old-world charm and tranquillity in contrast with nearby Hong Kong.

Now, gearing up to take its place in modern Asia — and due to be handed back to China in 1999 — the enclave is transforming itself into a vibrant, go-ahead tourist venue in its own right. While huge investments in deluxe hotels and other attractions are already providing competition to Hong Kong, the Macanese are determined to preserve the cobbled streets, terraced houses and old churches that create its air of graciousness.

For weary travellers seeking complete peace, Macau is arguably as near ideal as can be found anywhere in Asia, though the two annual bursts of noise, the Macau Grand Prix motor race and Chinese New Year, might drive visitors over to Taipa and Coloane.

These are accessible via two bridges and causeway. A new 3,900-metre bridge between Macau and Taipa connects to a road system linked with a new airport and port on this island. With Macau's romantic atmosphere of the past retained, it is still possible for the visitor to relax, to stroll without playing life-or-death games with the traffic, to study the territory's event-packed history or to test a private gambling system in the famed casinos.

History

Officially styled City of The Name of God, There Is None Other More Loyal, Macau is the oldest European outpost in Asia. It was founded in 1557, apparently by agreement with the neighbouring Guangdong (China) province's authorities. But no official treaty has ever been found. Macau was an early centre of missionary activity, becoming the seat of a bishopric of China and Japan created in 1575.

In its first century, Macau grew rich on trade with China and Japan, but later went into a long decline, mainly because Japan closed its doors to foreign merchants. The Portuguese also had to deal with commercial and piratical competition from Dutch and other European adventurers.

As more and more Westerners were attracted to the lucrative China trade, Macau became the summer residence for the British (and sometimes United States) *taipans* (big traders) who retreated from their factories in Guangzhou to wait for the next trading season.

In 1845 Macau was declared a free port. Tonnage dues, import duties and ground rent previously paid to the Chinese authorities in Guangdong province were abolished. This situation was consolidated by Governor Joao Ferreira do Amaral when he arrived in 1846. He expelled the Chinese customs officials from the city and declared it a free port — a status which is still maintained today. (Governor Amaral was later set upon by angry local

◀ *From backwater to big city.* PHOTO: ANDREW SHERRY

farmers near the border because of his harsh rule. He was dragged from his horse and beheaded.)

On December 1, 1887, a Treaty of Amity and Commerce was signed between Portugal and China, and Macau acquired official Chinese recognition under Portuguese rule. Portugal undertook in return "never to alienate Macau and its dependencies without agreement with China."

Like Portugal, in World War II Macau was neutral. In 1951 it was proclaimed an overseas province of Portugal. In the winter of 1966-67 riots triggered by the Cultural Revolution in China badly shook the Portuguese authorities, but calm later returned.

The change of government in Portugal following the bloodless military coup on April 25, 1974 and its subsequent decolonization programme for the Portuguese African territories did not at first affect the status quo of Macau — a Chinese territory with a Portuguese administration and a community at that time of 400,000, of which 97% were Chinese. (The present population is about 460,000.)

However, in 1984 the Legislative Assembly was dissolved by Portugal at the request of the governor, Vasco Almeida-e-Costa, and new electoral laws were introduced with a view to making the assembly more democratically representative.

In June 1986 Beijing and Lisbon opened talks on returning Macau to Chinese sovereignty. Macau's future administration is expected to be similar to that of Hong Kong, which will revert to Chinese sovereignty in 1997 but retain a large degree of autonomy.

Macau lies some 64 kilometres west-southwest of the British territory of Hong Kong, across the mouth of the Pearl River. Tourism, gambling and export trade (principally textile goods) provide a large part of Macau's revenue.

Entry

Macau can be reached in a variety of ways: by river ferry or road from adjacent Guangdong province, by ferry or helicopter from Hong Kong, or — according to the schedule — from late 1995 by aircraft landing at the new international airport. Most people arrive from Hong Kong, by ferry.

Jetfoils make the trip in an hour, while the various types of catamaran take 50-70 minutes; helicopters take 20 minutes. Faster new surface craft (tri-cats and foil-cats) were due to enter service in late 1995. Most vessels and the helicopters leave Hong Kong from the **Macau Ferry Terminal** at Shun Tak Centre, 200 Connaught Rd Central. Hong Kong Ferries sail from the **China Hong Kong Ferry Terminal in** Canton Rd, Tsimshatsui, Kowloon.

Buying tickets is a simple process. Except at weekends and during public holidays, you can usually obtain them on the spot at the terminals. Jetfoil tickets are also available at Hong Kong's **Mass-Transit Railway** service centres in some MTR stations, or can be booked 28 days in advance by telephone (2859 5696) using Visa, Diners Club, MasterCard or American Express cards. CTS-Parkview turbo-cats and jumbo-cats can be booked in **China Travel Service** offices and by telephone (2789 5421-3) up to 30 days in advance. Hong Kong Ferries' catamarans can be booked at Hong Kong and **Yaumati Ferry Co.** offices up to 30 days in advance.

The fare structure is complex, with one, two or three classes having different fares on various craft, and higher fares on weekends and holidays and for night services. Prices were expected to change by mid-1995, but in the early part of the year daytime, weekday, one-way fares on jetfoils were HK$90 and HK$105; for turbo-cats they were HK$85, HK$185 and HK$1,240 (for the VIP cabin). Other catamarans were similarly priced. Departure taxes (HK$26 from Hong Kong and HK$22 from Macau) are usually added to the ticket prices. Helicopters cost HK$1,206 one way on weekdays.

Immigration

Visitors need a passport or other valid travel document. Nationals of the following countries do not require a visa:

Australia, Austria, Belgium, Brazil, Britain, Canada, Denmark, Finland, France, Germany, Greece, India, Italy, Japan, Luxembourg, Malaysia, Mexico, the Netherlands, New Zealand, Norway, Philippines, Republic of Ireland, Singapore, South Africa, South Korea, Spain, Sweden, Switzerland, Thailand, the United States and Hong Kong residents and other British Commonwealth subjects.

All visas are now valid for up to 20 days, except Brazil where the validity extends to six months. Nationals of countries that do not have diplomatic relations with Portugal must

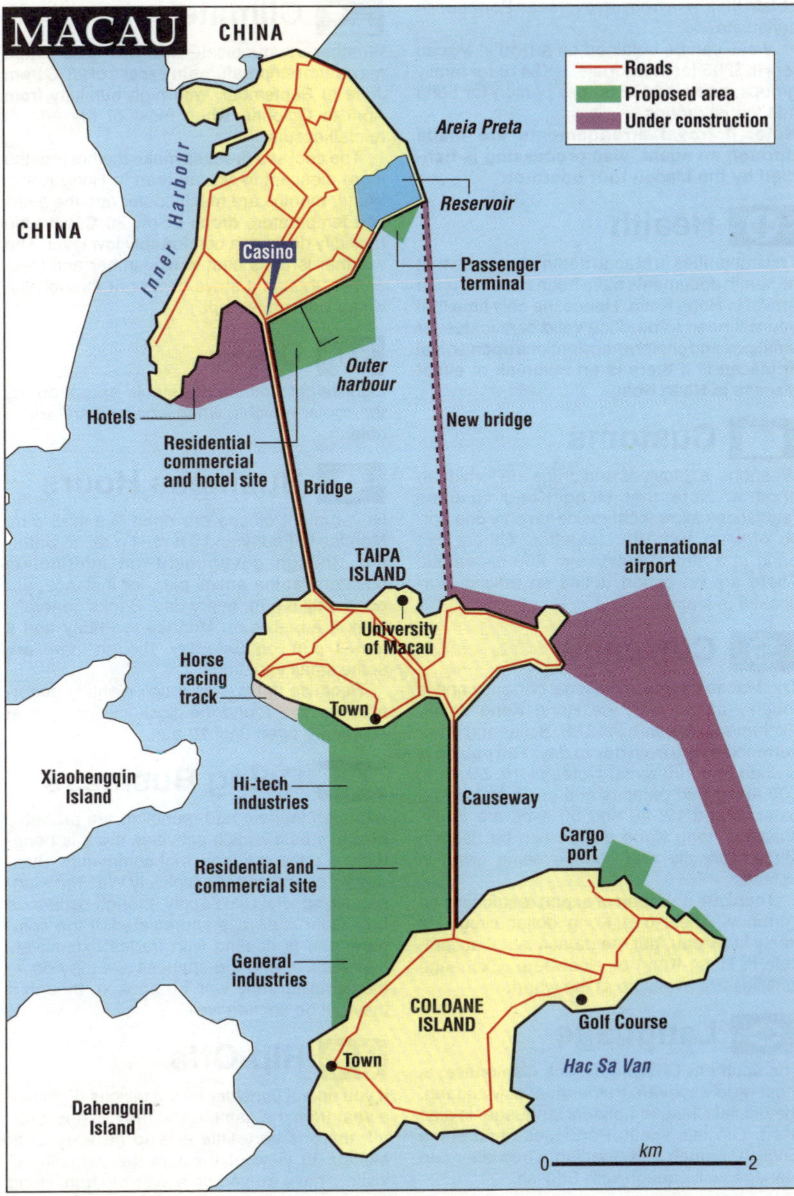
MACAU
CHINA
Roads
Proposed area
Under construction
Areia Preta
Inner Harbour
Reservoir
CHINA
Casino
Passenger terminal
Outer harbour
Hotels
New bridge
Residential commercial and hotel site
Bridge
International airport
TAIPA ISLAND
University of Macau
Horse racing track
Town
Xiaohengqin Island
Hi-tech industries
Causeway
Cargo port
Residential and commercial site
General industries
COLOANE ISLAND
Golf Course
Town
Hac Sa Van
Dahengqin Island
km
0
2

obtain their visa from an overseas Portuguese consulate.

Visas can be obtained on arrival in Macau for HK$205 for individuals, HK$410 for family groups, and HK$102.50 per person for bona fide tourist groups.

Note: If travel arrangements are made through an agent, visa processing is handled by the Macau tour operator.

Health

The authorities in Macau seem to assume that all health documents have been checked upon arrival in Hong Kong. Hence the only time that you will need to produce valid certificates for smallpox and cholera vaccinations upon arrival in Macau is if there is an outbreak of either disease in Hong Kong.

Customs

Weapons, explosives and drugs are forbidden imports. Note that Hong Kong customs regulations allow local residents only one bottle of wine and 100 cigarettes. Others can bring in a litre of liquor and 200 cigarettes. There are no export duties on articles purchased in Macau.

Currency

The Macau pataca is the legal currency and is roughly at par with the Hong Kong dollar. Exchange rates with the U.S. dollar and other currencies vary from day to day. The pataca is divided into 100 avos. Notes of 10, 50, 100, 500 and 1,000 patacas and coins of 1 and 5 patacas and 10, 20 and 50 avos are in circulation. Hong Kong dollars can be used in Macau, usually with change being given in patacas.

There are no import or export restrictions on currency. The Hong Kong dollar circulates freely in Macau, but the pataca is not acceptable in Hong Kong or elsewhere. Exchange facilities are available at the wharf.

Language

The southern Chinese dialect, Cantonese, is most widely spoken. Putonghua, or Mandarin, the official Chinese national language, is also used. Officials speak Portuguese and some English, French and Spanish. The visitor can manage well enough with English.

Climate

Weather is subtropical — warm to hot, average maximum temperatures in excess of 28°C from June to September, with high humidity from April to October, when most of the annual rainfall occurs.

The cool sea breezes make the hot months more pleasant in Macau than in Hong Kong. Winter months are much cooler and the average temperature drops below 20°C, with the humidity down to a comfortably low level. The weather is at its best in November and December, though it stays cool right through the winter until early April.

Dress

Lightweight clothing is suitable except during the cooler months, when woollens are advisable.

Business Hours

Government offices are open 9 a.m.-5 p.m. Monday to Friday and 9 a.m.-1 p.m. on Saturday, though government-run information counters, at the arrival pier, for instance, are open until 6 p.m. every day. Banks generally work 9 a.m.-5 p.m. Monday to Friday and 9 a.m.-1 p.m. on Saturday, though there are some small variations.

Because there is so much nightlife generated by the round-the-clock casinos, most shops are open until 10 p.m.

Doing Business

Although tourism and gambling are probably Macau's best-known activities there is nonetheless a thriving industrial community. Business is conducted in a typically Western manner. No special rules apply, though courteous behaviour is always appreciated. If the company one is dealing with trades extensively overseas — and the chances are they do — then English may well be spoken, though it may not be spoken well.

Rip-Offs

If you do not consider taking billions of dollars a year from the gamblers in the casinos a rip-off, there is very little else to be wary of in Macau. In view of the fact that virtually all visitors have arrived on a side-trip from Hong

Kong, and assuming they have read the advice in this book on the British colony, there is nothing to be frightened of in the Portuguese enclave — except for being very careful about making purchases of gold jewellery.

Media

English-language newspapers and publications from Hong Kong are readily available in central Macau and at major hotels. Those hotels equipped to receive satellite have access to English language TV channels as well.

Communications

Public payphones are IDD equipped and can access some 180 countries. Local calls cost Pataca 1 (HK$1). Other telecommunications services are available through the local telephone company's service counters. Express mailing facilities can be had at the **Central Post Office**, and many major express carriers have branch offices in Macau.

Transport

TAXIS: Macau has almost 600 taxis. Flagfall is Patacas 8 for the first 1,500 metres, then Pataca 1 for every subsequent 250 metres. There is a Patacas 5 surcharge to Taipa, and Patacas 10 to Coloane (no surcharge on the return trip). If you want to negotiate your own rate for special purposes — such as hiring the vehicle to explore Macau — bargain with the driver. When doing this, make sure that the driver understands that the price agreed is in patacas and includes all passengers in the taxi. Not all taxi drivers speak English, so carry with you a trilingual map available from the **Department of Tourism**. Taxi fares on the islands of Taipa and Coloane are the same as in Macau.

PEDICABS: A gentle way to see the Macau sights. You should negotiate the fare before setting off. The average is Patacas 20 for a short trip and Patacas 80-100 for about one hour's sightseeing. Pedicab men understand some English and know what the tourist usually wants to see.

BUSES: Public buses run from 7 a.m. until midnight, and the fare on all city routes is Patacas 2. Bus service No. 3 runs between the ferry pier and the centre of the city. Several buses serve the islands, including open-top double-deckers in summer. Fares are Patacas 2.50 to Taipa, Patacas 3.20 to Coloane and Patacas 4 to Hac Sa beach. A convenient pick-up point in Macau is outside the Hotel Lisboa.

MINI-MOKES: These open-topped jeep-like vehicles are one of the most popular forms of tourist transport (**Happy Mokes Ltd.**, **Avis Mokes Ltd.** — both have sales offices in Hong Kong and Macau). Saloon cars can also be hired. Mini-mokes can be hired from about HK$430-450. There are also special whole-weekend prices and a mid-week special deal. You need a valid international driver's licence.

BICYCLES: On Taipa island the village has two or three bicycle-renting establishments. Pedalling down the causeway to Coloane is a delightful experience. Bicycles are not permitted across the bridge linking Macau with Taipa.

Tours

A wide variety of tours are available, run by several operators. These include **Able** (Tel: Macau 975109, HK 2545 9993); **Asia** (Macau 593844, HK 2548 8806); **China Travel Service** (Macau 782331, HK 2540 6333), especially for one-day trips to China; **Estoril** (Macau 573614, HK 2559 1028); **F. Rodrigues** (Macau 581777); **Guangdong** (Macau) (Macau 588807, HK 2832 9118); **Hi-No-De Caravela** (Macau 338338, HK 2368 6181-2); **International** (Macau 975183, HK 2541 2100), the pioneers in one-to-five-day trips to China; **Lotus** (Macau 972977); **Macau Star** (Macau 558855, HK 2366 2262); **Macau Tours** (Macau 385555, HK 2542 2338); **Sintra** (Macau 710111, HK 2540 8028); **South China** (Macau 781811, HK 2815 0208); **TKW** (Macau 591122, HK 2723 7771). All these agencies can arrange overnight or day tours of Macau and, if the tour is booked in Hong Kong, will arrange your transfers from the hotel to the ferry wharf in Hong Kong as well as tickets and visas.

Accommodation

Macau now has a good range of hotels, and the current over-capacity means that healthy discounts are available mid-week; advance bookings are still required for weekends. The new airport's opening, scheduled for late 1995, is likely to spur further hotel developments.

The big change in recent years has been the number of international hotels that have entered the Macau market — **Mandarin Oriental**, **Hyatt Regency**, **Westin**, **Holiday Inn** and **New World**. These have brought new

PHOTO: PATRICK LUCERO

Food, glorious food.

standards of comfort, facilities and service to the territory.

The top two hotels are the smallest ones: the Portuguese-style **Pousada de Sao Tiago**, built into them foundations of a 17th century fort; and the **Hotel Bela Vista**, renovated and restored to its original cream and white colours and converted into an eight-suite property managed by Mandarin Oriental.

With the four- and five-star properties, Macau now has a variety of top dining rooms featuring Chinese and Western cuisines, health centres and meeting facilities. The middle range of accommodation has been expanded to cater to family visitors, while there are also some one- and two-star properties to accommodate the more budget-conscious traveller. For those who prefer atmosphere to luxury, some of the older accommodation (the **Grand** or **Central** hotels or the **Pousada de Coloane** on Cheoc Van beach) may be preferable.

Several hotels have swimming pools, and five have casinos (**Lisboa, Hyatt**, **Mandarin Oriental**, **Holiday Inn** and **Kingsway**). Many of the newer hotels are clustered in the Outer Harbour area, but the **Westin Resort** has a unique location on a hillside overlooking Hac Sa beach, with a championship 18-hole golf course on the landscaped hills above it.

Most of the major hotels can be booked in Hong Kong through the hotels' offices or through the **Macau Tourist Information Bureau** (2540 6513). Mid-week, the hotels in Macau are cheaper than in Hong Kong. Information is readily available.

Dining

To the traveller who has become a little jaded by a surfeit of Chinese food in Hong Kong, Macau beckons as an oasis. Most of the Western food available is Macanese or Portuguese in the simple country style. Typical ingredients to accompany meats, poultry and fish are tomatoes, potatoes and tiny, delicious black olives. Many dishes are stewed. Even lobster can be prepared this way and is surprisingly good. Seafood is excellent and generally cheaper than in Hong Kong restaurants. Some specialities such as "African chicken" — grilled and coated with an exotic blend of spices — have an intriguing influence that can be traced to the Portuguese colonies in Africa. Preserved cod and fresh sardines, both imported from Portugal, are other outstanding local dishes. The cod comes in many forms, including deep-fried fish cakes which make an excellent starter, or fish stew with vegetables. The sardines — most of the year frozen but in season flown out fresh — are grilled and three or four with plenty of lemon juice can hardly be bettered for fish-lovers. Roast quail are another local standard.

A favourite is **Henri's Gallery** at 4 Ave da Republica, with tables by the roadside where you can order huge spicy prawns, African chicken and a delicious fondue. Sunday lunch at the **Solmar**, 11 Rua da Praia Grande, is popular, though the food is good any time of the week. For pure Portuguese food, one must try the Sunday lunch buffet at **Pousada de Coloane**.

At 69 Ave Sidonio Pais is **Riquexo**, a strange little place on a balcony in a building basement, overlooking Park'n Shop grocery store. Open 11 a.m.-3 p.m. only, it is worth sampling, though you are advised to get there early. The home cooking is Macanese style and the atmosphere informal. You can go to **Belo's** afterwards for an almond souffle (45 Ave Almeida Ribiero).

On the outer islands, one should visit **Pinocchio's**, 4 Rua do Sol, Taipa, for its roast quail and chili crab, as well as the fine wines. Though the food is still good, Pinocchio's has lost its open-air charm and has become perhaps too popular — booking a table ahead is essential at weekends.

The hotel restaurants vary. The Lisboa's **A Galera** has Portuguese food in an elegant setting. While the Pousada de Sao Tiago's **Grill Fortaleza** cuisine might be considered high-priced, it can be enjoyed in a priceless setting. Its coffee shop food, meanwhile, is superbly prepared and inexpensive.

The Mandarin Oriental has a good Italian restaurant, **Mezzaluna**, and the more locally inspired **Cafe Girassol**, while the Hyatt Regency has the excellent **Afonso** and **Flamingo** restaurants. The Pousada de Coloane has, besides its Sunday buffet, excellent lunches and dinners, and good wines. The **Presidente** has a fine Korean restaurant and the **Royal** a first-class Cantonese dining room.

Non-European or non-Chinese restaurants tend to have a short life in Macau, though there are a number of Thai, Burmese and Italian and Japanese restaurants around. By the Leal Senado in the Largo do Senado is the **Long Kei** Chinese restaurant. Birds' nest soup or pigeon in a great many styles, and dozens of other delights, give the place a good reputation.

Roast pigeon is the house speciality at the **Fat Siu Lau** restaurant on Rua da Felicidade, one of the town's oldest eating houses. Here the styles of South China and Portugal have blended in a way typical of Macau itself. The **Lee Hong Kee**, 35 Rua da Caldeira, and the popular **Pun Kai**, 44 Rua da Praia Grande, are other excellent Chinese restaurants. Chinese food prices are moderate. Also noted for their good food are **A Lorcha**, **Praia Grande** and the **O Porto Interior**. Popular on Taipa island are the **Galo** and **Mocambique**, and on Coloane island **Fernando's** and **Balichao** eateries.

Portuguese wines, both red and white, are very good and, by Hong Kong standards, very cheap. Table wines range from the light, slightly fizzy, white vino verde, through the rich, heavy Dao red, to many varieties of Port (including the unusual white Port). Prices range from as little as HK$20 up to HK$50 for a top vintage Portuguese wine. All are free of import duty.

On the whole, with wine, a meal will cost 40% less in Macau than in Hong Kong.

Entertainment

Evening entertainment operates around the nine casinos. The **Casino do Lisboa**, taking up two floors of the Lisboa Hotel, is a gambling extravaganza, offering such international games as roulette, blackjack, boule, chemin-de-fer, craps and keno, row upon row of slot machines and the Chinese games — *fan tan* and *dai sui* (the big and the small). The casino in the Mandarin Oriental is elegant and less hectic, open from noon to 4 a.m.

The **Macau Palace**, like a Mississippi steamer gone Oriental, is moored in the inner harbour near the opposite end of the Avenida de Almeida Ribeiro from the Lisboa. It has a casino over two of its floors, as well as a restaurant, nightclub and bar. It is open 24 hours a day.

The **Crazy Paris Show** at the Lisboa features a dozen or so girls from Europe in a pretty classy, revue-style show once described as "a little naughty, a little nice." There are two shows on weekdays at 8 p.m. and 9:30 p.m. On Saturdays and public holidays the shows are at 8 p.m., 9:30 p.m. and 11 p.m. Tickets are Patacas 200. No one under 18 is allowed in. Tickets are available at the wharf in Macau, the Hotel Lisboa and Hotel Sintra, and at the theatre itself one hour before show time.

For those who want something a little raunchier, there are several Bangkok-style nightclubs. There are also Thai and Filipina masseuses available in many of the hotels.

The Hotel Presidente has the **Skylight Discotheque** (and a cabaret) which is open 9:30 p.m.-4 a.m. A modest, minimum charge is levied. The **Royal Discotheque** at the Royal, open 10 p.m.-3 a.m., also has a minimum charge. Over at the Jai Alai Palace, the Ritz Night Club on the top floor is open 11 a.m.-midnight, and becomes a nightclub on Tuesdays, Thursdays and Saturdays.

The casinos in Macau are strictly controlled under a government franchise. Minimum tables stakes are normally around HK$10 but, not surprisingly, can go a lot higher. There is no entry fee, but those under 18 years of age may be refused admission. Dress code is informal. The peculiarities of Macau gambling are explained in *The Macau Gambling Guide*, published by A-O-A Ltd., (2389 0352).

Shopping

Away in the back streets of the town (Travessa Armazen Velho, for example) are charming antique shops selling the cultural remains of a China that no longer exists, as well as historical curios from a colonial period dying but not quite dead. And if you are prepared to search the general merchandise shops, Macau is still enough of a real Chinese city to have available the interesting chinaware and carved wooden furniture that local people use in their daily lives. Many such objects retain the characteristics of the great artistic tradition of old China.

Sports

The Macau Grand Prix is the highlight of the sporting calendar. It is held in late November and the event attracts the world's Formula 3 drivers and several of Europe's racing teams.

Greyhound-racing is highly popular in the town, with events held four nights a week at the canidrome. Horse-racing on Taipa is also popular, though it has yet to achieve the scale and quality of its Hong Kong counterpart.

Holidays

Chinese and many Western (Christian) festivals are linked to the lunar and church calendars. Consequently their dates vary from one year to the next. Other religious occasions and events marking Portuguese political events fall on fixed dates.

January-February: New Year's Day (public holiday); Chinese New Year's Day (public holiday); Lantern Festival.

March-April: Procession of Our Lord of Passos; Feast of the God Toutei; Easter (public holiday); Ching Ming Festival (public holiday); Anniversary of the Portuguese Revolution (public holiday); A-Ma Festival.

May-June: Labourers' Day (public holiday); Procession of Our Lady of Fatima; Feast of the Bathing of Lord Buddha; Corpus Christi (public holiday); Camoes Day and Portuguese Communities Day (public holiday); Dragon Boat Festival (public holiday); Feast of St Anthony of Lisbon; Feast of St John the Baptist, Patron Saint (public holiday).

July-August: Feast of Battle of July 13 (holiday only on the islands); Feast of Maidens; Feast of the Assumption of Our Lady (public holiday); Festival of the Hungry Ghosts.

September-October: Mid-Autumn Festival (public holiday); Confucius Day; Republic Day (public holiday); Festival of Ancestors — Chung Yeung (public holiday); International Fireworks Display Contest; International Music Festival.

November-December: All Saints Day/All Souls Day (public holiday); Macau Grand Prix; Restoration of Independence (public holiday); Feast of the Immaculate Conception (public holiday); Winter Solstice; Christmas (public holiday).

ADDRESSES

The **Department of Tourism** is at 11 Largo do Senado, Macau. Tel: 315566. A number of useful publications is available. There is also an information office in the arrival terminal.

The **Macau Tourist Information Bureau** in Hong Kong is in Room 3704, Shun Tak Centre, 200 Connaught Rd Central, Tel: 2540 8180. Hotel and tour bookings can be arranged through the office and general information can be obtained. Information about Macau can also be obtained from the following offices:

Australia: Macau Tourist Information Bureau, 449 Darling St, Balmain, Sydney, NSW 2041. Tel: (02) 555 7548, Toll Free (008) 252 488, Fax: (02) 555 7559.

Britain: Macau Tourist Information Bureau, 6 Sherlock Mews, Paddington St, London W1M 3RH. Tel: (071) 224 3390, Fax: (071) 224 0601.

France: Portuguese National Tourist Office, 7 Rue Scribe, 75009 Paris. Tel: (01) 742 5557.

Germany: Portuguese National Tourist Office, Kaiserstr 66-IV, 6000 Frankfurt-Main. Tel: 0611 234094-97, Fax: (069) 231433.

Japan: Macau Tourist Information Bureau, 4 Flr, Toho Twin Tower Bldg, 5-2 Yurakucho 1-chome, Chiyoda-ku, Tokyo 100. Tel: (03) 3501 5022-3, Fax: (03) 3502 1248.

North America: Macau Tourist Information Bureau, 3133 Lake Hollywood Drive, P.O. Box 1860, Los Angeles, California 90078. Tel: (213) 851 3402, (800) 331 7150, Fax: (213) 851 3684. Macau Tourist Information Bureau, Suite 2R, 77 Seventh Ave, New York, NY 10011. Tel: (212) 206 6828, Fax (212) 924 0882. Macau Tourist Information Bureau, 630 Green Bay Rd, P.O. Box 350, Kenilworth, Illinois 60043-0350. Tel: (708) 251 6421, Fax: (708) 256 5601. Macau Tourist Information Bureau, Suite 1103, 999 Wilder Ave, Honolulu, Hawaii 96822. Tel: (808) 588 7613. Macau Tourist Information Bureau, Suite 157, 10551 Shellbridge Way, Richmond, B.C., Canada V6X 2W9. Tel: (604) 231 9040, Fax: (604) 231 9031. Macau Tourist Information Bureau, 13 Mountalan Ave, Toronto, Ontario, Canada M4J 1H3. Tel/Fax: (416) 466 6552.

Portugal: Macau Tourism Representative, Avendia 5 de Outubro 115-5th Flr, 1000 Lisbon. Tel: 793 6542, Fax: 797 9328.

Malaysia: Macau Tourist Information Bureau, 10.03 Amoda, 22 Jalan Imbi, 55100 Kuala Lumpur. Tel: 245 1418, 243 3922, Fax: 248 6851.

New Zealand: Macau Tourist Information

Bureau, P.O. Box 42-165, Orakei, Auckland 5. Tel: (649) 520 3317, Fax: (649) 520 3327.
Singapore: Macau Tourist Information Bureau, 11-01A PIL Bldg, 140 Cecil St, Singapore 0106. Tel: 225 0022, Fax: 223 8585.
Thailand: Macau Tourist Information Bureau, 150/5 Sukhumvit 20, Bangkok 10110, or G.P.O. Box 1534, Bangkok 10501. Tel: 258 1975, 484 3208, Fax: 258 1975.

PUBLICATIONS

Maps and various brochures are available from either the information office in Hong Kong at Shun Tak Centre, or from the Tourism Department and main hotels in Macau. This literature is free. The Macau Tourism Department publishes brochures on restaurants and places of interest, either free or at nominal prices.

Books to look out for include: *Macau (a guidebook)*, *Macau Miscellany* and *More Macau Miscellany*, by Shann Davies; *Macau Narrative* and *Macau and the British*, by Austin Coates (as well as his novel, *City of Broken Promises*); *Fidalgos in the Far East* and *Seventeenth Century Macau*, by Prof. C.R. Boxer; *Macau on a Plate*, by Annabel Doling; *Falstaff in Macau*, by Bradley Winterton; *Historic Macao*, by C.A. Montalto de Jesus; any of the books by Msgr Manuel Teixeira; *Colour and Noise*, by Philip Newsome (the definitive Macau Grand Prix history); and *Macau*, by Cesar Guillen-Nunes.

Specialists will find plenty of Macau material in *An American in Canton (1825-44)* by William C. Hunter, and in any of the books about the artist George Chinnery.

DISCOVERING MACAU

From the wharf on the outer harbour you can take a taxi or a bus to the central area where most of the hotels are. First, you will see the **Mandarin Oriental Hotel** and the pits for the **Macau Grand Prix**, and later the odd wedding cake-looking **Lisboa Hotel**. Outside the hotel, where a statue of an assassinated Portuguese governor, Ferreira do Amaral, used to stand, there is part of a development scheme including an underground car park. Amaral and his horse have been shipped home to Portugal.

Around the corner from the harbour is the Rua da Praia Grande, which runs as a broad and pleasant tree-lined avenue along the

PHOTO: MACAU TOURIST INFORMATION BUREAU

A little peace and quiet.

water's edge — though the water is fast disappearing in a reclamation scheme to make more land for offices. Macau's main commercial street, the **Avenida Almeida Ribeiro**, cuts across the peninsula from the Praia Grande to the inner harbour, right by the **Macau Palace** casino and fishing port.

In the centre of town a square, the **Largo do Leal Senado**, adjoins the Avenida Almeida Ribeiro and here may be found the imposing **Leal Senado** (Loyal Senate) **Bldg** — the town hall. The square is also the location of the **Macau Government's Tourist Office**. The Senado acquired its epithet in 1809, having sent a warship to the aid of the Portuguese court that had fled to Brazil from the armies of Napoleon.

The present building is said to have been built in 1784 on the site of a previous Senate building. The facade was added in the 1870s and a complete restoration effected a few years ago. Inside is a beautiful courtyard and art gallery. A staircase leads up to the **Council Chamber** and library, which boasts some splendidly carved woodwork. The library has an interesting collection of old books, some dating from around the 16th century.

At the northeastern end of the Largo do Leal Senado stands the fine **Church of St Dominic**, most of which probably dates from the 17th century. In early 1995, it was closed for two years of renovation. The streets behind the church are especially picturesque and along them can be found a number of shops selling antiques and other items of historic and cultural interest, along with a great deal of fascinating old junk. The morning market here is quite picturesque. On the Largo also stands the **Santa Casa da Misericordia** (Holy House of Mercy), a branch of a charitable institution founded in 1498. The Macau branch owes its origin to Dom Belchior Carneiro, first Bishop of China and Japan. His skull is preserved in a glass case in a council room on the first floor.

From beside the Leal Senado, the **Rua Central** leads to the **Church of St Augustine**, the largest in the territory and an excellent example of the baroque style. The present building dates from 1814 and the facade from 1873. The restrained plaster-work of the interior is particularly fine. Across the lane is the **Teatro Dom Pedro V**, which is part of the premises of the **Club de Macau**. If you ring the bell of the club's door, one of the staff will be happy to show you the delightful little theatre. A few yards along the same way is the **Church of St Lawrence**, with its baroque interior and crystal chandeliers. Down the slope beyond is an old residential district, the most typical and photogenic in town.

Immediately behind St Lawrence's is the **Seminary of St Joseph**, which possesses a church built in 1746-58, with a facade situated at the top of a flight of stairs. From St Lawrence's a narrow street descends to the **Praia Grande**, emerging beside the pink stuccoed **Government House**. From the Praia Grande, along towards the end of the peninsula, a road leads up to **Penha Hill**, where stands a chapel and the Bishop's residence. The Penha provides a view of the town and the inner harbour.

A walk around the end of the peninsula — past the walls of the **old Fortress of Barra**, now the hotel **Pousada de Sao Tiago**, and the area of the naval dockyard storage sheds — brings one to the **Ma Kok Miu Chinese Temple**, sacred to a sea-goddess known as A-Ma, from whom the province's name seems to have been derived. The shrine, said to be more than 600 years old, is built of rock quarried from the outcrop nearby, where you can see a brightly painted carving of the ship said to have carried the goddess. The oldest section is the lower pavilion to the right of the entrance. Close to the fortress is a small but comprehensively stocked **Maritime Museum**.

On the western side of the peninsula (the area north of the Avenida Almeida Ribeiro) are the **Camoes Gardens**, overlooking the inner harbour and the hills of China beyond, with clusters of simple village houses, watchtowers and fields. The view of China from the gardens is far more revealing than that obtained from Hong Kong's New Territories. The gardens contain the grotto dedicated to Portugal's great national poet, Camoes, who is supposed — on fairly flimsy evidence — to have lived in Macau about the year of its foundation. The nearby **old Protestant Cemetery** with its weather-beaten grave stones also provides extremely interesting testimony to the past.

Macau's most celebrated attraction is the great facade of **Sao Paulo**, which is all that remains of **St Paul's collegiate church**. It was built between 1601 and 1673 by Catholic-Japanese artisans under the direction of Italian Jesuits. The church, which originally stood behind the facade, burned down in 1835, but what remains is an impressive example of Italian-influenced baroque architecture, and the carvings show a fascinating combination of Western and Oriental motifs. You will need binoculars to study the fine details at the top of the facade.

Overlooking Sao Paulo from the hill nearby is the **fort of Sao Paulo do Monte**, built about 1620 and displaying many old cannons. There is a good view from the fort.

High upon **Guia Hill** are a fort — built about 1637 — a chapel and the **Guia lighthouse**, first lit in 1865 and the oldest of its kind on the China coast.

The **Porta do Cerco** (Barrier Gate), separating Macau from China, stands in the very north of the town. However, the Barrier Gate no longer has the mystery of the past. More and more day-trippers to Macau extend their journey by an extra day with a side trip through the Barrier Gate into China. Most travel agents can arrange this, though it costs a few hundred patacas. The trip includes visits to a commune or school, a market town, the home of Sun Yat-sen (founder of modern China), a few museums and lunch. Or one can continue the trip to embrace Canton, returning to Macau down through Hong Kong. A Hong Kong travel agent for this is **International Tourism**, Tel: Macau 86522, HK 2541 2100.)

Some distance south of the gate is the

interesting, labyrinthine temple of **Kun Iam Tong**, dedicated to the goddess Kwan Yin. There are fine Buddha statues in the temple and the main hall possesses a carving of the Goddess of Mercy herself. In the temple grounds is the stone table on which was signed the first treaty between China and the U.S. in 1844. This temple is also popularly supposed to have been sacred to Marco Polo. On the way back to the Leal Senado are the monuments that commemorate a remarkable victory over the Dutch fleet, which attacked Macau in 1622, and Vasco da Gama, discoverer of the sea route to India.

In two of the colonial-style mansions in **Avenida de Conselheiro Ferreira de Almeida** are the **Archives**, and **new National Library** containing letters, books and manuscripts pertaining to Portugal's exploration and Macau's relations with Europe, China, Japan and South-east Asia.

Across the picturesque bridges from Macau is Taipa, whose best-known attractions are the race-track and the **University of East Asia**. Also on Taipa is a delightful old church (**Our Lady of Carmel**); a folk museum; some wooded areas worth exploration and two temples.

Across the causeway is the island of Coloane, which has junk-building yards, two pine-shaded beaches of middling quality and an interesting old church built early in the 20th century.

In the church are some bones of martyrs who died in the 17th century and a (bone) relic of St Francis Xavier. Nearby is an old temple with a large model boat carved from whale-bone. The Pousada de Coloane on the way to **Hac Sa beach** is a pleasant small hotel.

HOTEL GUIDE

Note: A 10% service charge and 5% government tax are added to all bills.

A: US$100 and above

BELA VISTA, Rua Comendador Kou Ho Neng. Tel: 965333, Fax: 965588 (HK booking: 2881 1688). *R: W.*

GRANDEUR, Rua Pequim. Tel: 780610, Fax: 780622. *P, Gym, Biz. R: C, W.*

FORTUNA, Rua da Cantao. Tel: 786333, Fax: 786363. *R: C, W.*

HOLIDAY INN, Rua Pequim. Tel: 783333, Fax: 782321. *R: C, W.*

HYATT REGENCY, Taipa Island. Tel: 321234, Fax: 320595, Tlx: 88512. *P, Gym, Biz, casino, tennis/squash courts. R: W.*

MANDARIN ORIENTAL, Avenida de Amizade. Tel: 567888, Fax: 594589, Tlx: 88588 OMA OM. *P, Gym, Biz, Casino. R: C, W.*

POUSADA DE SAO TIAGO, Fortaleza de S. Tiago da Barra. Tel: 378111, Fax: 552170, Tlx: 88376. *P, conference facility. R: W.*

RITZ, Rua Boa Vista. Tel: 339955, Fax: 317826, Tlx 88316. *P, Gym. R: C, W.*

WESTIN RESORT, Estrada de Hac Sa, Coloane. Tel: 871111, Fax: 871122. *P, Gym, Biz, golf course. R: C, W.*

B: US$75-100

BEVERLY PLAZA, Ave. Do Dr Rodrigo Rodrigues. Tel: 782288, Fax: 780684, Tlx: 88345.

KINGSWAY, Rua de Luis Gonzaga Gomes. Tel: 702888, Fax: 702828.

LISBOA, Avenida da Amizade. Tel: 577666, Fax: 567193, Tlx: 88203. *P, casino, nightclub. R: C, W. 24-hour food.*

NEW CENTURY, Estrada Almirante Marques Esparteiro, Taipa. Tel: 831111, Fax: 832222. *P, Gym, Biz. R: W.*

NEW WORLD EMPEROR, Rua de Xangai. Tel: 781888, Fax: 782287. *R: C, W.*

PRESIDENTE, 355 Avenida da Amizade. Tel: 55388, Fax: 552735, Tlx: 88440. *Disco. R: C, W.*

ROYAL, Estrada da Vitoria. Tel: 552222, Fax: 563008, Tlx: 88514. *P, Gym. R: C, W, Japanese.*

C: US$50-75

GUIA, 1-5 Estrada do Engenheiro Trigo. Tel: 513888, Fax: 559822. *Disco.*

MASTERS, 162 Rua das Lorchas. Tel: 937575, Fax: 937565.

POUSADA DE COLOANE, Praia de Cheok Van, Coloane Island. Tel: 328143, Fax: 328251. *P. R: W.*

D: US$35-50

CENTRAL, Avenida Almeida Ribeiro. Tel: 373888, Fax: 332275.

METROPOLE, 63 Rua de Praia Grande. Tel: 388166, Fax: 330890. *Nightclub. R: C, W.*

P — Swimming pool **Gym** — Health club **Biz** — Business centre **R**—Restaurant
C — Chinese food **W** — Western food

199
198

MONGOLIA

Geographically Mongolia is one of the world's most remote places, but it is no longer inaccessible from Asia's main travel routes and tourist centres. Until recently it could only be reached with difficulty by air or rail through Russia, but the development of routes from China, following the end of the Soviet Union's local dominance, has greatly improved access. Direct flights to Beijing from many European and Asian capitals now connect with regular air services to the Mongolian capital Ulan Bator. Mongolia is a place for the rugged traveller and not for the faint hearted or those who expect Western standards of luxury.

If you do not fancy long bus or jeep rides across hundreds of kilometres of unique and beautiful country, or riding with reindeer herders, then spending the night in a *yurt* (a local felt tent) Mongolia is not worth the effort of getting there. Mountaineering, riding (camels or yaks as well as horses) and even hunting are offered for the specialists. There is little scope for an unplanned business trip.

The collapse of communist rule and birth of multiparty democracy in Mongolia in the 1990s brought about a fundamental change of national attitude. Yet despite the country's need for hard currency, mass tourism has not been encouraged. Because of the continuing shortage of hotel rooms and other facilities, the number of tourists (8,000 in 1993) is still limited by visa control and relatively high prices, with group package travel being favoured. However tourism is no longer a government monopoly and several private companies are competing in the market. Foreign visitors can now tour parts of the country far from the capital, which were previously out of bounds, and stay at private hotels or with Mongolian families.

With an area of 1,565,000 square kilometres and a population of only 2.2 million, Mongolia is a land of contrasts and great natural beauty with much to offer the visitor, from mountain forests and rolling steppe to great lakes and desert sands, as well as a wide variety of wildlife. This crossroad of empires has seen nations and civilizations come and go, and their traces are still to be found in the runic monuments of the Turks, the fortresses of the Uighurs, the Mongol imperial capital Karakorum, and the monasteries of Tibetan Lamaism. Above all Mongolia offers a welcome from its friendly people, many of whom still live a simple but colourful nomadic life virtually unchanged since the times of their illustrious ancestor, Genghis Khan.

History

In the 13th century, united under Genghis Khan, the Mongol people began the conquest of a huge empire which eventually extended from Korea to Hungary and from Lake Baikal to Java. Following its collapse, the Mongols accepted Manchu rule in 1691. When the Qing dynasty fell in 1911 the Mongol princes declared their independence. Unrecognized by China or Russia, however, autonomous Outer Mongolia, as it was then called, was invaded by Chinese troops and then by units of the Russian tsarist army evading the Bolshevik seizure of Siberia. In 1921 a revolutionary government took power in Mongolia with Bolshevik assistance, and in 1924 the Mongolian People's Republic was proclaimed, establishing the Soviet Union's first communist satellite.

For nearly 70 years Mongolia was virtually

◄ *Children compete in the summer's Naadam.* PHOTO: ROBYN BECK/AFP

ruled from Moscow. In 1946 the Republic of China (the Nationalists) recognized Mongolia's independence, but in 1949 Mongolia established diplomatic relations with the communist People's Republic of China. Wider international recognition of Mongolia came after it joined the United Nations in 1961. Mongolia had a mutual defence treaty with the Soviet Union and until 1992 Russian troops were stationed there. It was also a member of the old communist economic grouping Comecon, on which it depended for economic aid, which was mainly used to develop the country's mining and processing industries. However, the economy is still largely based on the products of its 26 million head of livestock — sheep, goats, cattle, horses and camels.

The collapse of communism in Eastern Europe encouraged the birth in Mongolia of the democracy movement which in 1990 forced the leaders of the ruling communist party out of office. The party abandoned Soviet-style socialism in favour of reform. The country's first free elections put non-communist deputies into the new legislature, which set about the transition to a market economy. When Mongolia's main trading partner, Russia, followed suit, the ensuing turmoil disrupted economic ties and Mongolia faced increasing hardship. Adoption of a new constitution in 1992 paved the way to fresh elections in which the reformed communists won an overwhelming victory.

Entry

Land-locked Mongolia can be reached only from Russia or China. There are no scheduled direct flights to Ulan Bator from elsewhere because the capital's Buyant-Uhaa airport is too small to take long-haul aircraft. But now that international airlines fly large jets regularly across Siberia from European capitals direct to Beijing in eight or nine hours, access is improving. Since Beijing is easily reached from other Asian capitals and there are daily flights in summer from Beijing to Ulan Bator direct in two hours and a quarter, or via Hohhot in Inner Mongolia, most visitors to Mongolia fly via China. Flights are made by Air China BAe 146s or Mongolian Airlines Antonov An24s, and the fare is US$200 one way.

Aeroflot (Tupolev Tu154) and Mongolian (Boeing 727) flights from Moscow via Novosibirsk or Omsk and Irkutsk once a week in the summer are still relatively cheap (US$600), but they take longer (eight hours from Moscow). Mongolian has An24 flights on some days to Irkutsk, China and Ulan-Ude, all on the Trans-Siberian Railway route.

Instead of flying, one can make the 36-hour journey from Beijing to Ulan Bator on the Trans-Mongolian Railway, and see something of the Gobi desert, but the service is not daily and comfortable berths are limited. Those making the trip would be wise to stock up on food for the Mongolian section of the journey. The Trans-Siberian was once a comfortable if slow alternative way of reaching Mongolia from the west (five days from Moscow, three from Khabarovsk, with air connections to Japan), but the service has been reduced and the trains are overcrowded.

It is generally cheaper to pay for air and rail tickets, except for intercontinental travel, as part of a tour package. Whichever route is chosen, early booking is essential because demand far exceeds supply, especially in the summer months.

Immigration

A valid passport and visa are necessary for visiting Mongolia. It is best to apply for a Mongolian visa first and then for a Russian or Chinese visa (plus any visas necessary for other countries being crossed during the journey). Applications for visas can be made to Mongolian embassies in London, Tokyo, New Delhi, Jakarta, Beijing, or Moscow. Visas should be applied for well in advance of the planned visit.

Accommodation vouchers purchased in advance through travel agents usually set out the length of the stay permitted, though visas may be extended in Ulan Bator. Group tours are still the most practical way of seeing the country. Individual accommodation can be cheap, but internal travel is expensive.

Health

No vaccinations are now required for Mongolia, Russia or China.

Customs

Visitors are required to enter passport and visa details and to declare all their currency and valuables on the forms provided on entry and exit. No antiques, religious relics, old paintings, etc., are allowed to be taken from Mongolia.

Currency

The tughrik (Tugs 450:US$1 in April 1995) is the official currency. Importing and exporting Mongolian currency is forbidden. U.S. dollars and sterling (in cash or travellers' cheques) are accepted for exchange. Foreign currency may be exchanged at Ulan Bator hotels. Visitors must keep currency receipts for customs inspection on departure.

Language

Mongolian is considered to be a member of the Altaic group of languages, loosely related to the various forms of Turkish, Manchu and perhaps Korean. Everyday writing is in a modified form of the Russian (Cyrillic) alphabet. The traditional script (descended from ancient Sogdian) is used mainly for decorative purposes, but is receiving official encouragement again.

Climate

The spring is windy and dusty. July and August are warm but can be rainy. September is dry and sunny. Frost begins to form on the hills around Ulan Bator in early September and during winter (November to March) temperatures as low as -45°C are common. Summer temperatures rise to around 15°C during the day.

Dress

In summer, light clothing is usually sufficient, but woollens may be needed at higher altitudes or for cool evenings. Heavy clothing is obviously required during the winter. Long, woollen underwear; thick woollen socks (two pairs); thick-soled, waterproof boots; thick trousers and sweater; a long windproof, fleecy-lined overcoat; inner gloves and outer mittens; and a fur hat with ear flaps make up an adequate winter attire. Good clothing is expensive in Mongolia so it is best to go prepared.

Business Hours

Government offices work approximately from 8 a.m. to 5 p.m. Monday to Friday with a half day on Saturday. Sunday is a holiday. Food shops, general stores and supermarkets stay open later.

Transport

All transport is best arranged in advance. Visitors will be met at the railway station and the airport (16 kilometres from the centre of Ulan Bator) and necessary motor transport is provided in the capital. Depending on prior arrangements, transport will be either by road or air. Visits to outlying areas such as Hovd (in the far west), Hujirt (in the mid-west) and the South Gobi are by air. The round-trip fare to Hujirt (from where you can go overland to the ruins of the ancient capital, Karakorum, and Erdenedzuu Monastery) is US$200. The town of Darhan in the north is also accessible by rail from Ulan Bator, lying on the line linking Irkutsk and Ulan Bator. Jeeps with drivers may be hired for unscheduled trips once in the country but costs are very high — 60 U.S. cents a mile for in-town travel and 30 U.S. cents a mile for country journeys.

Accommodation

Foreign visitors invariably stay at the modern **Ulan Bator Hotel** or the **Bayangol Hotel** in the capital. The beds are comfortable but the bathroom fittings poor. The 300-seat dining rooms (mainly fixed menu) serve some Western-style food. No room service is available. A new hotel, the Genghis Khan (240 rooms), had still not been completed in early 1995. It is intended to have two restaurants and a conference centre. Elsewhere the accommodation is poor (which partly explains the Mongolians' reluctance to allow many visitors into the country). At the spa town of Hujirt, there are 50 *ger* (yurts), the local round felt tents, with 180 beds and a communal sanitary block; dining is in a large ger. Tourists may sleep in comfortable yurts during excursions to the Gobi (156 beds, restaurant, communal sanitary block). Otherwise there will usually be neither shower nor bath available and the food will be strictly Mongolian.

Dining

The Ulan Bator and Bayangol hotels offer schnitzel and *bifsteks* (hamburger) but elsewhere Mongolian mutton stews or meat dumplings are the rule. Rice and potatoes are the standard staple. Other vegetables are usually pickled.

Foreign beers and soft drinks are available for hard currency in the capital, but out of town you will probably find only vodka and *koumiss* (fermented mare's milk). For good koumiss you will probably have to visit the encampments where it is made. Wines and spirits may be bought from duty-free shops for hard currency.

Entertainment

The State Opera and Ballet Theatre offers *Tosca*, *Swan Lake* and *The Barber of Seville*, as well as Mongolian operas of which *Three Sad Hills* is highly recommended. Likewise, the State Drama Theatre puts on Mongolian plays, besides Shakespeare and Brecht. Other entertainments include the State Circus, a folk song-and-dance ensemble, and a puppet theatre as well as several cinemas, usually showing Russian films. At the Ulan Bator Hotel there is ballroom dancing to small dance bands or a jukebox. Russian and Mongolian TV channels and United States TV news and current affairs programmes are available at the hotels.

Shopping

Silver articles (koumiss bowls), ivory and wood carvings, jewellery, paintings, Mongolian costumes and recordings of Mongolian music are among the most interesting buys. Prices are high. The state department store sells a number of these items, as well as a limited range of consumer goods. Some articles are available for hard currency only at the special shops at the Ulan Bator Hotel and Bayangol hotel.

Sports

Wrestling, archery and horse-racing, the traditional sports of Mongolia, are best seen at the *Naadam* (National Sports) in Ulan Bator starting on July 11, National Day. In winter, wrestling matches are held at the Palace of Sport.

Holidays

January 1: New Year's Day.
January-February: Lunar New Year *(Tsagaan Sar)*.
July 11, 12 and 13: Anniversary of the 1921 Revolution.

ADDRESS

Mongolian Tourism (Zhuulchin) can be reached by letter in Ulan Bator, but normally arrangements are made through accredited agents who can at the same time handle travel

PHOTO: PETER HANNAM

Suhbaatar Square, Ulan Bator.

through Russia and China. British agents of Zhuulchin are **Regent Holidays**, 15 John St, Bristol, BS1, 2HR. Tel: 01179 211711, Fax: 01179 254866.

DISCOVERING MONGOLIA

ULAN BATOR (ULAANBAATAR)

Ulan Bator (Red Hero) is a city of multi-storey office blocks and housing and broad main streets built since World War II. **Peace Ave**, the main street with the heaviest traffic, including trolley buses, runs east-west, dividing the city in two. An equestrian statue of the national revolutionary hero, **Suhbaatar**, occupies the centre of the huge main square named after him. On the north side of the square, in front of the **State Palace (Grey House)**, is a smaller version of Moscow's Lenin mausoleum, but the remains of Suhbaatar and the Stalin-like dictator Choybalsan inside are not on display. Choybalsan's statue still stands in front of the national university, but there is only an empty space where the infamous Stalin statue once stood outside the State Library. In the suburbs, people still live mostly in gers inside fenced compounds; they have electricity and telephones, but no piped water. The visitor will see passers-by in their colourful *deel* or Mongolian national costume, and livestock grazing on the grass verges.

The capital's most obvious tourist attraction is the **Gandan Lamasery** on the edge of town, which is said once to have had 10,000 Buddhist monks. People come there to pray, stretching out on the inclined boards. Services are held on Sundays to the clashing of cymbals and the sounds of five-metre-long trumpets. You can usually see the monastery's treasures, including statues, paintings and ancient manuscripts in Mongol, Tibetan and Manchu, and perhaps take refreshments with the abbot in his ceremonial yurt close by.

The former **Palace of the Bogdo Gegen** (the Hutukhtu or Living Buddha) who once ruled Mongolia — the last one died in 1924, and no further incarnations were permitted — is now a museum. The adjoining temple is full of art treasures.

Near the vast Suhbaatar Square, the Choyjin Lamyn Sum — another former monastery — has a large collection of dance masks and other ceremonial objects.

The **National Museum** has a section devoted to Mongolian history; and in another part reside collections of animal and plant life — including the complete skeletons of dinosaurs discovered in the Gobi Desert. There is also a **Fine Arts Museum**, with examples of religious paintings and sculpture. Museums are closed on Tuesdays.

Starting on July 11, the anniversary of the

1921 Revolution, the **Naadam** (National Sports) are held for three days in Ulan Bator. Wrestling, archery and horse-racing are the main attractions. The wrestling contests are fiercely fought, with hardly any holds barred, by young men in richly embroidered but scanty costumes.

From Ulan Bator excursions can sometimes be made to a large livestock farm, where you may see traditional horse-racing with even small children riding, and also a demonstration by mounted horsemen. They show the Mongolian method of catching horses with a lasso on the end of a long, flexible pole.

UPCOUNTRY

Group **countryside tours** of seven to 10 days provide sightseeing in Ulan Bator as well as a close look at rural life. There are few roads and cross-country travel by bus or jeep is slow and can be uncomfortable, and long hikes can also be tiring, but the country's natural beauty and diversity and its colourful and friendly people more than compensate for this. Some tours:

DELUUN BOLDOG (Genghis Khan's birthplace)**:** Fly northeast from Ulan Bator to **Dadal** (375 kilometres) in Hentiy province and camp near the Onon river; visit **Gurvan Nuur** (Three Lakes) holiday resort and **Deluun Boldog** to see the Genghis Khan monument; bus back to Dadal to tour local museum; visits to **craftsman's family and Buural caves** for picnic and folk music.

HORGO: Fly west from Ulan Bator to **Tsetserleg** (400 kilometres), centre of Arhangay province, and bus northwest to **Chuluut Gol** riverside campsite (100 kilometres, overnight in gers); bus to Horgo tourists camp (35 kilometres, gers); walks to **Mt Horgo** and **Terhiyn Tsagaan**, lake formed by a volcanic lava dam; return via **Tayhar Chuluu**, a volcanic "plug" with ancient inscriptions, in Ih Tamir district; excursions to the eighth century Turkish monuments to **Bilge Kagan** and **Kultegin** at Hoshoo Tsaydam (Hashaat district) and ruins of the ninth century Uighur capital **Har Balgas** (Hotont district).

SHARGALJUUT: Fly southwest from Ulan Bator to **Bayanhongor** (528 kilometres), centre of Bayanhongor province, and bus 130 kilometres northwest to tent camp at **Galuut**; excursions to monastery at **Erdenetsogt** and to view rock drawings and stone figures at **Doromt**; return to Bayanhongor and continue 16 kilometres east to stay at **Shargaljuut** mineral springs; then bus south to **Bayanlig** (223 kilometres) to view rock drawings via **Bogd** or **Horiult** (overnight in tents) and **Lake Orog**.

TSOGT TAYJ: Fly northwest from Ulan Bator to **Bulgan** (265 kilometres), centre of Bulgan province, and bus 110 kilometres west to **Sayhan** for stay at local hotel, viewing Uighur and Turkish monuments en route; return to Bulgan and bus 103 kilometres south to **Mogod** to see "deer stones," drive 93 kilometres to **Dashinchilen** then 45 kilometres east to the 17th century palace of Tsogt Tayj; return by bus direct to Ulan Bator; excursions to 10th century Uighur town **Har Bahyn Balgas**.

LAKE HOVSGOL: Fly northwest from Ulan Bator to **Moron** (525 kilometres), and bus 50 kilometres north to lakeside town of **Hatgal**, camping in tents on the **Egiyn Gol** river; walks along shores of this beautiful deep freshwater lake; bus back to Moron, with visit to Bronze Age "deer stones" (May to August); if the weather is good, fly from Moron to **Dood Tsagaan Nuur** and ride out to meet the **Tsaatan reindeer herders**.

DARIGANGA: Fly southeast from Ulan Bator to **Baruun Urt** (515 kilometres), centre of Suhbaatar province, for an overnight stay in hotel before flying 180 kilometres south to **Dariganga** and taking a bus 17 kilometres to the camp site; walks to see 13th century stone tablets and birds at **Lake Ganga**; bus 45 kilometres to **Mt Shiliyn Bogd** (1,778 metres) and walk to nearby caves, **Ereen Tolgoy** mineral springs and extinct volcanoes; see prehistoric stone figures at **Altan Ovoo** and **Hoogiyn Hondiy** and steppe deer at **Lhachinvandad** reserve.

GOBI OASIS: Fly west from Ulan Bator to **Altay** (826 kilometres), and stay at local hotel; jeep 85 kilometres south to **Tsagaan Gol** river, 50 kilometres southeast to **Tsogt**, and 65 kilometres to **Mt Eej Hayrhan**, viewing oasis, to visit experimental farm; return via **Tsogt** and **Biger**; see desert, wild sheep and antelope (overnight in tents).

HALHYN GOL: Fly east from Ulan Bator to **Choybalsan** (600 kilometres), centre of Dornod province, stay at local hotel; visit nearby ruins of Turkish and Mongol town **Herlen Bars**; fly 200 kilometres east to Halhyn Gol settlement, bus to hotel in **Sumber**, 60 kilometres southeast of Halhyn Gol; see giant Buddha picked out in stones beside **Lake Buyr** at Ih Burhant, Battle of Halhyn Gol (1939) monument, local state farm.

GUNJIN SUM: Bus northeast from Ulan Bator to **Terelj** resort (40 kilometres) for stay in gers with local walks to **Turtle Rock**; bus to

River Tuul, then three days of walking (some 40 kilometres a day) north to **Gunjin Sum** (temple) and back through fine mountain and forest scenery, camping in tents.

AMARBAYASGALANT: Bus north from Ulan Bator to **Darhan** (250 kilometres), Mongolia's second-largest town, in Selenge province for overnight stay in hotel; bus via town of Hotol 170 kilometres west to 18th century **Amarbayasgalant monastery** for two-day camp and local excursions; this beautiful monastery has been restored and some lamas now live there again.

Several week-long tours offer visitors horse or camel riding as an alternative to buses or jeeps for reaching the most popular attractions:

ERDENE DZUU: Fly west from Ulan Bator to **Hujirt** (320 kilometres), spa town in Ovorhangay province, overnight in gers; ride in two stages via **Shanh monastery** to **Erdene Dzuu** (16th century, Mongolia's oldest Buddhist monastery) and the site of the Mongolian imperial capital **Karakorum** (Harhorin); trips to the **Orhon river waterfall** (24 metres) at Ulaan Tsutgalan. Horses are also available for riding to **Har Balgas** and **Hoshoo Tsaydam** in neighbouring Arhangay province (see Horgo).

SOUTH GOBI: Fly south from Ulan Bator to South Gobi camp (520 kilometres), situated northwest of **Dalandzadgad**, centre of Omnogov province; accommodation in gers; camelback tours (40 kilometres) to herders' camp and dinosaurs' graveyard at **Bayandzag**; excursions to **Yolyn Am** (Lammergayer Valley) reserve in the **Dzuun Sayhan Mountains**, south of the camp, to a river gorge usually icebound even in summer.

BOGD UUL: In the Ulan Bator area a three-day horse riding tour (170-200 kilometres) takes riders from the 18th century **Mandshir monastery** on the southern side of Mt Bogd Uul round the mountain and back to **Dzuun Mod**, centre of Tov province. Horse riding instruction and day tours to **Gachuurt farm**, east of the Ulan Bator, are available from Mt Dzaysan on the northern side of Mt Bogd Uul, across the Tuul river from the city centre. Also, bus excursions are available to **Mandshir** and eighth century Turkish monument to Tonyukuk near the coal town of **Nalayh**, 40 kilometres southeast of Ulan Bator.

Some of Mongolia's highest mountains may now be tackled by experienced climbers in the course of week-long mountaineering expeditions in May to August, with professional guides; conditions are often difficult:

TAVAN BOGD (4,082 metres)**:** fly west from Ulan Bator to **Olgiy** (1,385 kilometres), centre of Bayan-Olgiy province, and jeep 120 kilometres northwest via **Ulaanhus** (overnight stay) to base camp; walk 40 kilometres along the **Tsagaan Gol** river to tented campsite for acclimatization before the main ascent, completed in one day; return by the same route.

OTGON TENGER (4,021 metres)**:** fly west from Ulan Bator to **Uliastay** (851 kilometres), centre of Dzavhan province, and bus 70 kilometres east to **Otgontenger** mineral spring resort hotel; walk or ride (horses) 20 kilometres with equipment to base camp (tents); following a day's acclimatization, ascent completed in one day; return by the same route. The province is partly wooded mountains and partly desert and specializes in sheep raising.

MONH HAYRHAN (4,204 metres)**:** fly west from Ulan Bator to **Hovd** (1,175 kilometres), centre of Hovd province, and jeep 200 kilometres south via **Tsenher** to base camp (tents); after acclimatization, complete the ascent in one day; mountain walks in the locality before return by the same route. South of Hovd there are cave drawings (15,000-20,000 years old) at **Hoyt Tsenher** and a Hun burial ground (3 BC-AD 99) at **Tahilt Hotgor**.

TURGEN (3,965 metres)**:** fly west from Ulan Bator to **Ulaangom** (1,145 kilometres), centre of Uvs province, and jeep 60 kilometres southwest to **Delgermoron** (overnight in gers); ride (horses or yaks) to first camp, then walk to base camp (tents); following acclimatization, make ascent in one day; return by the same route (or partly down river by raft), viewing stone figures and ninth century Turkish and Uighur inscriptions at **Doloodoyn Bulsh**.

A fortnight's **hunting safari**, including travel to and from Ulan Bator, camping, catering, provision of horses, guides, etc., hunting licence and one trophy, costs in the region of US$25,000 per hunter. Wild sheep (argali) are hunted at Baatar Hayrhan and other parts of the **Mongol Altai Mountains** in Hovd province and at **Baruun Sayhan** in the **Gobi Altai** Mountains west of the South Gobi tourist camp, and wild goats at **Myangan Yamaat** in Bayanhongor province; wildfowling at **Sangiyn Dalay**, Dornod (Eastern) province. Hunting is controlled to protect rare wildlife, but in recent years snow leopards have increased in number and are now also hunted under licence. Safaris may also be arranged for visitors wishing to photograph, video or film Mongolian flora and fauna.

ВЛАДИВОСТОК

RUSSIAN FAR EAST

Siberia and the Russian Far East represent one of Asia's last great wildernesses, where tigers and bears still roam and hunters and ice bathers brave the cold. The catch is that it's not all easy to get to. But for travellers with a healthy constitution and sense of adventure, there is much to see and experience. Visitors here will find fishing and hiking, virgin forests, volcanoes and lagoons as well as getting a look at Russia's growing links with Asia.

On the Pacific frontier, signs of Asia — Japanese cars in Vladivostok, Korean merchants in Sakhalin and Chinese traders along the border — signify the region's look towards its neighbours.

Eastern Siberia offers a multitude of sightseeing opportunities, from reindeer farms in northern Sakha Republic, to the scenic vistas of Lake Baikal and the steppes of Buryatia, home of Asia's northernmost Buddhists.

Siberia is a flat land stretching 7,000 kilometres between the Ural mountains in the west and the Pacific Ocean in the east. With a population of 30 million, it is home to one in five Russians. Some 90% of its people are Slavic, but there are 26 indigenous nationalities in the region, including Yakuts and Evenks, who have preserved their nomadic way of life.

Russian influence is strongest in southern Siberia. Irkutsk contains beautiful Russian orthodox churches and 300-year-old wooden houses with ornate window carvings.

The Pacific Coast provinces of Russia, are a land of rugged mountains and untouched ocean coves, seemingly endless forests and surging rivers. For the adventurous traveller, there are many interesting natural sights, from active volcanoes in the northern peninsula of Kamchatka to the lagoons of the southern Kurile Islands. In between, there is a wealth of unexplored territory, a welcome change from the hustle and bustle of Asian cities.

Changes are beginning in the form of Western-style hotels and tourist services, but things are still a long way from the more usual Asian standards of service and hospitality. Visitors to the Russian Far East must still expect lazy waiters, delayed flights and rustic accommodation outside the main cities.

History

The people of Novgorod reached the Ob River in western Siberia as early as the 11th century. But the conquest of Siberia did not really begin in earnest until the 16th century, after Cossack mercenaries, under the order of the powerful Stroganov family (the same family for which the beef dish was named), ventured into western Siberia. Russian Cossacks, loyal to the tsar, built a series of fortified settlements there and it became the centre of a lucrative fur trade. By 1640, the Cossacks had reached the island of Sakhalin from their base in Yakutsk.

The Russians began to settle the Amur River Valley, ceded by China under the Treaty of Aigun in 1858, just as the Qing dynasty was weakening. In 1860, Russia was given the territory east of the Ussuri River, what is now the Maritime Region, where the port of Vladivostok became a major naval base.

The legacy of the free-spirited Cossacks (Cossack means "free man" in Tatar) stayed on in Siberia even after the October Revolution. Siberia was the last stand for the Mensheviks before they retreated into northern

◄ *Lenin points to Vladivostok's railway station.* PHOTO: ADRIAN BRADSHAW

China in the early 1920s. During the Soviet period, the difficulties caused by great distances and harsh climate were lessened by development, but Sibiryaki (as Siberians call themselves) still maintained their close ties to nature.

Siberians are a hardy lot, known for cultivating vegetables in their country plots, picking wild berries in the forests and ice-fishing. Russian patriotic writers such as Solzhenitsyn, who returned to Russia in 1994 after 20 years in exile in the United States, have lauded the Siberian way of life and point to a return to nature as a solution to the problems caused by modernization.

The "Russianization" of Siberia was achieved relatively effortlessly. Local tribes, whose descendants remain today in the peoples of the 26 indigenous nationalities, swore their allegiance to St Petersburg. But the tsars became tired of administering distant provinces.

Starting in the 19th century, Siberia became a backwater, best known as a place of exile for political prisoners. This grim tradition continued when Joseph Stalin set up labour camps in the 1930s and 1940s.

In the 1990s, Siberians are exercising their freedom in a new Russia liberated from the restrictions of the former Soviet Union's command economy. Vladivostok has become home to consulates from Australia, Japan, South Korea and the U.S. Chinese, Korean and Japanese restaurants can be found in most Far Eastern cities. There is already an Australian restaurant/bar in the Vladivostok suburbs, and the first American-style grocery store in the region is scheduled to open in 1995.

Entry

Flights to and from the Russian Far East are increasing. Closed off from the world until the early 1990s, Vladivostok now has weekly flights to and from Anchorage in the U.S., Niigata in Japan, South Korea's Seoul and cities in northern China. Khabarovsk's upgraded international airport has similar connections except for Seoul — it has flights to and from Singapore instead.

Rail connections link Irkutsk with China on the famous Trans-Siberian Railway. From Irkutsk, it is a three-day train trip to Khabarovsk, around Lake Baikal and through the rolling valleys above the Amur river. Detailed railway information can be obtained from **Intourist**.

Immigration

All travellers to Russia must have a visa, which can be obtained from Russian diplomatic missions abroad in about seven to 10 days. However, a businessman with an invitation from a Russian enterprise can get a visa within 72 hours. Visa charges depend on intergovernmental agreements, but are usually in the range of US$25. You can also arrange visas through travel agents. If you are interested in visiting other former Soviet republics after a trip to Russia, it is best to play it safe and get a separate visa for each country.

Health

No inoculations are required for those arriving from Europe. Drink bottled water when travelling throughout Russia. Mineral water and bottled water are available in most big cities. If you are headed far off the beaten track, take your own.

Customs

Intourist advises that you register any valuables you bring into the country for personal use such as jewellery, furs, personal computers and cameras on the customs declaration when you arrive so that "nothing will hamper their smooth clearance on departure." Limited quantities of cigarettes' tobacco and liquor are also permitted. All cash and travellers' cheques must be registered on the customs declaration.

Currency

Unlike the old days, when the then Soviet government artificially set the rate of the rouble, commercial banks in Russia now establish their own rates. The Russian Central Bank sets the rouble conversion rate daily, based on transactions in Moscow's hard-currency auction. Commercial banks then add a margin. The black-market, so famous in the Soviet Union, is now defunct. Roubles are used for payments virtually everywhere, but beware of its volatility. It has been sliding since 1992, and in one day's trading in 1994 it lost 40% of its value.

The number of foreign-exchange centres has increased dramatically in big cities. Either change your money at these places or use hotel exchange offices.

The dollar fetches more roubles in Vladivostok than perhaps anywhere else in Russia,

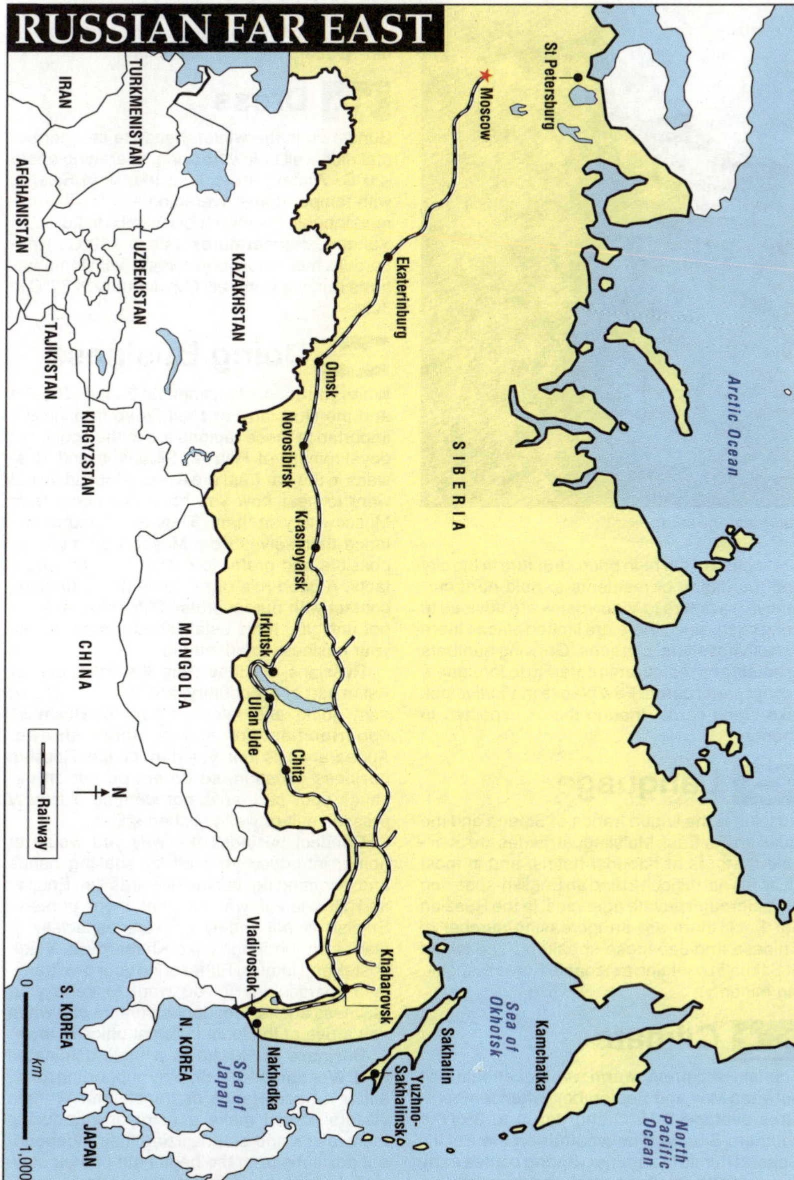
RUSSIAN FAR EAST
IRAN
TURKMENISTAN
AFGHANISTAN
UZBEKISTAN
TAJIKISTAN
KAZAKHSTAN
KIRGYZSTAN
CHINA
MONGOLIA
SIBERIA
St Petersburg
Moscow
Ekaterinburg
Omsk
Novosibirsk
Krasnoyarsk
Irkutsk
Ulan Ude
Chita
Khabarovsk
Vladivostok
Nakhodka
Sakhalin
Yuzhno-Sakhalinsk
Kamchatka
Arctic Ocean
Sea of Okhotsk
Sea of Japan
North Pacific Ocean
N. KOREA
S. KOREA
JAPAN
N
Railway
0
km
1,000

Sakhalin museum.

a reflection of the high price structure in the city and the desire of residents to hold hard currency. Travellers to Vladivostok are advised to bring cash, since there are limited places there to cash travellers' cheques. Growing numbers of hotels and restaurants catering to foreigners accept credit cards. Few places in Vladivostok take credit cards, though this is expected to change.

Language

Russian is the lingua franca of Siberia and the Russian Far East. Multilingual guides are available for tours at Intourist hotels, and in most cities it is not difficult to find an English-speaking guide through private agencies. In the Russian Far East, there are an increasing number of Chinese and Japanese speakers. The island of Sakhalin contains a sizeable Korean-speaking minority.

Climate

Tourists who prefer warm weather should visit between May and September, when temperatures average 7-18°C and go up to 35°C in southern Siberia. The weather on the Pacific Coast is humid in summer. Spring comes early to the port city of Vladivostok and the summers are foggy with lots of rain. The best months to visit the Pacific Coast are August and September. Winters are very cold inland.

Dress

Bundle up in the winter, because the thermostat dips well below freezing, averaging about -20°C. Winters are cold in Irkutsk in Siberia, with temperatures averaging -21°C. (In summer, though, the thermostat climbs to 20°C.) In Yakutsk, temperatures fall to -50°C. Khabarovsk has a monsoon climate, with temperatures ranging from -26°C in January to 20°C in July.

Doing Business

When you conduct business in Eastern Siberia and the Russian Far East, keep in mind the importance these regions are to the economic development of Russia. Siberians and Russians in the Far East are a proud lot and do not want to hear how you have just come from Moscow to visit them. They are trying to distance themselves from Moscow as much as possible and prefer to set up their own contacts. A good rule of thumb is not to mention contact with bureaucrats in Moscow, at least not until you have established a rapport with your business interlocutors.

Russians, be they from the European or Asian part of the country, are for the most part easy-going and informal people. Business opportunities are making them shrewd. Appearance is not yet part of the Russian business equation, so do not be put off because your partner is not wearing a freshly pressed suit or well-polished shoes.

Conduct business the way you would at home; introduce yourself by shaking hands and exchanging business cards (in English and Russian if you can get them printed). English is not widely spoken, especially in places on the fringes like Khabarovsk, Vladivostok and Irkutsk. Either bring your own translator (particularly if you want to keep your business affairs confidential) or hire one when you arrive at the local Intourist office in town.

Business in Russia is a male-dominated field. Women still usually play supporting roles, either as secretaries or translators. Women visitors should make a point of introducing themselves and emphasizing their independent positions from the beginning of their stay.

Take gifts, but do not distribute them immediately. Wait until the appropriate moment when you have made some progress on the deal or are about to leave. Russians do not like to be patronized. Establish a relationship, get to know your partner and then give a token of friendship. Scotch or even American whisky, perfume and useful things such as office supplies are well received. A quick way to a Russian's heart is to bring a gift for a child; the Russian can receive it without embarrassment.

Russians are not used to entertaining business partners from abroad. At official receptions the spread probably will not be lavish, but try to eat something if you plan to partake in the long, ritual vodka toasts. If you are not a big drinker, refuse politely but firmly. It does help to do a few toasts — they can loosen up a first gathering and lead to friendly exchanges. Russians are an eloquent people, and their toasts are long-winded. Listen carefully and you may learn something about your partner.

Russians are most comfortable entertaining in their homes. If you are invited to a Russian's apartment, consider it an honour as well as an opportunity to see Russians at ease.

Rip-Offs

The Russian Far East is, in many ways, the "last frontier." There is much opportunity, but also a good deal of swindling. As a foreigner in Russia, you wield *blat* — influence gained by the fact that you can dole out hard currency for services. The special arrival and departure lounges for foreigners at the airports are one remainder of the privileged position once bestowed on foreigners (most often to isolate them).

But do not be fooled; during the current rough-and-tumble transition to a market economy, "foreigner" status also marks a visitor as a crime target. To make your visit as pleasant as possible, be wise about what you do and be aware of what is going on around you. Be careful walking at night and stay in a group if you can. Crime, especially in Vladivostok, is on the rise. Do not carry huge sums of cash and do not show it off in public places, such as restaurants and shops. Try not to bring attention to yourself. A rowdy table of foreigners is an identifiable target.

When you change money, be particularly attentive. It is probably best to use officially sanctioned foreign exchange centres in hotels or banks. But when you leave these places, be wary of anybody who may have seen you changing money. Pickpockets are a problem in the Russian Far East.

Taxi drivers in big cities are a crafty lot and will try to dupe foreigners by charging high prices, usually in dollars. Learn some Russian and bargain them down in roubles. Allow yourself plenty of time and let a few cars go by before you settle on a price.

In Russia, many cars moonlight as taxis. Often a motorist driving by can give you a better rate, but be careful. If you are in town for a few days, to avoid hassles you might consider renting a car and driver. For personal security, decline rides in cars with two people in front.

Communications

Local Siberian telephone networks still present a challenge to a businessman trying to call out of the country. You can order international calls ahead of time through local Russian operators, but this can be a time-consuming process. It's best to use direct international lines at major joint-venture hotels in Vladivostok, Khabarovsk and Yuzhno-Sakhalinsk. Usually the hotels have business centres.

As more businesses come in, telecommunication links with the outside world are increasing. In Nahodka and on Sakhalin Island, Cable & Wireless has set up joint ventures which offer long-distance service. The ventures, called **Nahodka Telecom** and **Sakhintelecom**, are staffed by expatriates. **Sprint** also has long-distance service in major Russian Far East cities. **US West** has won the right to install a mobile phone network in Khabarovsk, Kamchatka and Vladivostok, but the system will not be up and running for another year or so. Also, **AT&T** reportedly is upgrading Vladivostok's city network.

Transport

Flying in and out of the Russian Far East is more or less a smooth experience, given the opening up of services by foreign carriers and improved international services by Aeroflot. Should you choose to continue to travel by air inside Russia, be warned: air safety deteriorated sharply in 1994 from a level that was far from inspiring in the first place. Also, in the Russian Far East, the Vladivostok and Yuzhno-Sakhalinsk airports are particularly prone to fuel shortages and are periodically closed down.

If you must fly inside Russia, check at your hotel about the status of flights.

Foreigners are charged premium prices, but price rises have decreased demand and there are usually seats available on domestic flights. Payment is made in roubles at local Aeroflot counters, so sometimes it is possible to buy tickets through hotels.

On domestic flights, be sure to arrive at the airport at least an hour before take-off or you will risk having your ticket sold to stand-by passengers. Bring your own food.

Vladivostok is becoming the main international hub on the Pacific coast. Its airport has greatly expanded service. Khabarovsk is also more accessible these days. It is a 14-hour train trip from Vladivostok to Khabarovsk. A round-trip ticket costs about US$50 and can be bought at the Vladivostok railway station or through a travel service.

Irkutsk is the major airline junction in Siberia. Its international airport handles regular flights from Shenyang, Ulan Bator and Niigata as well as from the European parts of Russia.

Sakhalin is an eight-hour flight away from Moscow. There is a charter air service from Sakhalin to Japan.

Tours

Tour operators in Siberia and the Russian Far East are catering to foreign tourists with new activities, such as hiking, fishing, biking and bird watching in the Lake Baikal area. More cities along the Trans-Siberian Railway are now open to visitors.

The foreign-travel company **Intourist** now has taken over many tourist services in Russia from its all-union predecessor. Intourist (which has 57 branch offices throughout Russia) remains in a pre-eminent position to provide services. It will arrange for translators, transportation, tours and wilderness expeditions. If you do not have travel plans set up by a travel agent or by a Russian host, you should work through Intourist.

You can either go through the company's head office in Moscow or arrange accommodation directly with regional Intourist bureaux in Siberia and the Far East. Intourist Moscow has a chain of representative offices overseas, including Australia and Thailand, which can help set up a visit to the Asian parts of Russia.

Addresses of Intourist offices in Asia: in Thailand, Intourist Asia Ltd. (21/4 Thai Wah Tower, 3/F, South Sathorn Rd, Bangkok 10120, Thailand); and in Australia, Intourist Australia Ltd. (Underwood House 37-49 Pitt St, Sydney, NSW 2000, Australia).

Intourist offices in Russia: Intourist Vladivostok (Tel: 4210 258666); Intourist Khabarovsk (Tel: 4210 399370); Intourist Irkutsk (Tel: 3952 244686).

But in the transition to the free market there are also options to Intourist. Throughout the Russian Far East private tour operators are popping up. Some run legitimate operations. If you are interested in exploring the hot geysers and volcanoes of Kamchatka, call **Alpha-Tour** (Tel: 50901 640081) or **Kamchib** (Tel: 41522 74988 or 41522 74977). In Khabarovsk, try **Michael Travel Agency** (Tel: 4210 334992) or **Khabarovsktourist Tourism Co.** (Tel: 4210 339390). In Vladivostok, call **ACFES-Tour Centre** (Tel: 4232 319492) or **Primorsk Tourist Co.** (Tel: 4232 251987). On Sakhalin, there's **Tunaicha Tourism Co.** (Tel: 42422 33661).

REI Adventures out of Seattle, Washington (U.S. Tel: 206 395 8111, Fax: 206 395 4744) has made a name for itself by offering adventure tours in exotic parts of eastern Siberia and the Russian Far East. REI offers two tours of Kamchatka's volcanoes and geysers and a train trip through the Russian Far East and around Lake Baikal.

Accommodation

All major cities in the Russian Far East and Eastern Siberia have Intourist hotels, which vary in service. The Khabarovsk Intourist, overlooking the Amur River, is well-run and clean. Most other Intourists are below average and dingy, still clinging to old ways. A double room in an Intourist Hotel runs from US$60-100.

Fortunately for the traveller, there are better choices: Several Western and Japanese-run hotels have opened. In Vladivostok, it is better to search out the newly opened **Vlad Motor Inn**, a Canadian venture built in the state dacha compound at Sanatornaya (19 kilometres outside town). An added bonus is the Australian restaurant and bar, **Captain Cook's** (Tel: 215341) around the corner from the hotel in the same compound. Captain Cook's serves breakfast, lunch and dinner, and the bar is a gathering place for expatriates.

Opened by a couple of first-generation Russians from Australia, Captain Cook's is modelled like the inside of a ship. It has wines from Australia and offers seafood. In the same compound is the residence of the Governor of the

Vladivostok street scene. PHOTO: SOPHIE QUINN-JUDGE

Maritime Region, as well as the House of Negotiations built specially for then U.S. President Gerald Ford's visit in the mid-1970s. If you are going to stay at the Vlad Motor Inn or frequent Captain Cook's, it's best to rent a car to go to and from town — but the cost is high, at US$8-9 per hour.

More convenient is the recently built **Versailles Hotel** in downtown Vladivostok (Tel: 4232 264201-301). Japanese-financed, Chinese-built and with a casino run by Finns, the Versailles is the most luxurious hotel in the Russian Pacific region. Expect to pay about US$160-200 for a double room.

In Khabarovsk, a city where you cannot always depend on heat and hot water, the **Hotel Intourist** (Tel: 4212 399313) stays warm. There is also a Japanese hotel and restaurant complex called **Sapporo** in downtown Khabarovsk. Price for a room is about US$200 a night. Lower-priced and sited in the centre of town is the **Amethyst Hotel** (Tel: 4212 334699), a three-story, corner inn minutes from the city's central square. Cost of a large double room is about US$100.

On Sakhalin, there's the box-like but warm **Sakhalin Sapporo** at 181 Lenin St (Tel: 42422 32634) or the more secluded and expensive **Santa Resort Hotel** (Tel: 42422 59265). Alternatively, you can try the island's (and perhaps the Russian Far East's) first bed-and-breakfast establishment. Set up with assistance from a small-business programme run by a U.S. university, **Address Bed & Breakfast** (call Luba Lee, Tel: 50441 62226) offers good, clean accommodation and a hearty breakfast.

Dining

Siberian cuisine is hearty and filling. There are pelmeni, tasty meat dumplings served with sour cream or butter, pastries and, of course, tea from a steamy Russian samovar. Fresh fish dishes are popular and widely available, due to the region's many rivers and long coastline. There is not much choice of fresh vegetables in Siberia and the Far East, especially in winter.

In downtown Vladivostok there are a good number of privately owned Japanese, Chinese and Korean restaurants. Overlooking the Amur Bay is the **Okean Restaurant**, which serves an array of fried seafood dishes. For Korean food, try the **Moranbon** at 6 Pervaya Morskaya. For American fast-food aficionados, there's **Magic Burger**. Ask at the Vlad Motor Inn about the **American supermarket** scheduled to open in 1995.

In Khabarovsk, **Sapporo's Japanese** restaurant has some of the finest Japanese food in the Russian Far East. The island of Sakhalin has a number of Asian restaurants catering to Japanese and Korean tourists.

DISCOVERING RUSSIAN FAR EAST

VLADIVOSTOK

Vladivostok, founded in the 19th century by Russian sailors, was built on a series of hills overlooking **Golden Horn Bay**. The city has generously been nicknamed "The San Francisco of the Far East" because of its hilly topography. What it lacks in charm it makes up in hustle and bustle. The city is fast becoming the administrative and business capital of the Russian Far East.

Vladivostok boasts one of the oldest museums in the country — the **Arseniev Folklore Museum** — which has exhibits on the exploration of the Maritime region and on the area's indigenous populations. Chekhov even worked there for a time. Be sure to ask about the museum's resident folk-dance troupe, which performs traditional Russian songs and dances. The Far Eastern University is one of the nation's leading schools of maritime studies. There is also a museum of the Russian Pacific Fleet, an art museum and botanical garden with a showcase of the Russian Far East's exotic fauna.

NAKHODKA

About a three-and-a-half-hour drive from Vladivostok is the port city of Nakhodka. This area is home to the **Ussurisk tiger**. Nakhodka's harbour is among the world's most beautiful and its coastal areas resemble the headlands of northern California in the U.S. Nakhodka has been declared a free economic zone, and there is much international shipping in the port.

KHABAROVSK

Khabarovsk was founded as a military trading post in the 19th century. Situated on the banks of the **Amur River** not far from the border with China, the city these days is the centre of a bustling border trade.

The city occupies a series of rolling hills and bluffs along the river and, with its 19th century wood houses, has a simplicity and grace rare in a country where cement-block buildings have made many cities monotonously similar.

Since it is difficult to get a cab in Khabarovsk, you may want to hire a car and driver to get around. In town there is a fine art museum with a wide variety of icons and works of the famous Russian itinerant painters Repin, Shishkin and Levitan. The more adventurous traveller can take an overland helicopter ride to the village of **Sikachi-Alin** and visit prehistoric rock paintings. The Khabarovsk region contains villages of various ethnic groups native to the region. A river-boat tour along the Amur is worth it, especially in summer.

IRKUTSK

Irkutsk, on the banks of the Angara River, is the administrative and cultural centre of eastern Siberia. This city of 500,000 people is one of the oldest in Siberia. It was the starting point for caravans heading for China and Mongolia in the 17th century.

Irkutsk is famous for its wooden houses with carved windows. Visitors can stroll past the 18th and 19th century homes just a few minutes from Lenin St, the main thoroughfare. Outside of Irkutsk, there is a museum of wooden architecture in the form of a well-preserved 18th century Siberian village. Visitors to Irkutsk from December 25-January 5 can catch the city's winter festival and take a troika ride straight out of *Dr. Zhivago*.

Irkutsk is only 70 kilometres from **Lake Baikal**, one of nature's true wonders, and you can get there from the city by bus or hydrofoil (in summer). Baikal is the world's deepest lake — at more than 1,600 metres. It contains 20% of the fresh water on the earth's surface.

Outdoors lovers should join one of the many recreational activities that Irkutsk Intourist now offers, which allow tourists to enjoy the beautiful nature surrounding the lake. There are fishing trips for pike and Siberian salmon, camping and hiking through the cedar forests, biking along old spurs of the Trans-Siberian Railway and bird-watching. And to freshen up, enjoy a real Siberian bath with birch boughs to clean out your pores.

REI offers a 17-day train and boar trip around Baikal. The excursion includes a three-day stint on the Trans-Siberian Railway from Khabarovsk to Lake Baikal and a look at the lake's native seal population.

SAKHALIN ISLAND

Sakhalin Island, which stretches 948 kilometres from north to south, was opened to tourists in 1992. The island is a veritable botanical gar-

Yuzhno-Sakhalinsk's river. PHOTO: JEFFREY LILLEY

den of birch, yew, fir and acacia trees. Wild grapes also grow there.

Sakhalin has deep-sea and river fishing, as well as sulphur baths for the health-conscious tourist. Like other spots in Siberia and the Russian Pacific coast, Sakhalin has a dark past; it was a former penal colony for Tsarist prisoners.

The island has an Asian heritage as well. It was home to the Japanese when they occupied the island for 40 years after the Russo-Japanese War. The Japanese governor's house still stands in **Yuzhno-Sakhalinsk**, and there is a Japanese war cemetery. The island's strongest link with Asia today is its population of 43,000 ethnic Koreans, many of whom were brought to the island as labourers by the Japanese before World War II.

To attract both Korean and Japanese tourists, the most frequent visitors to the island, there are a number of Asian restaurants scattered throughout Sakhalin. Two popular restaurants in Yuzhno-Sakhalinsk are the **Arirang**, which serves Korean food, and the Japanese restaurant **Sakura**.

ULAN UDE

Ulan Ude is the capital of Buryatia, the home of Russian Buddhism. The largest **Buddhist temple**, or *datsan*, in Russia is located 25 kilometres from Ulan Ude. Buddhism has undergone a revival since the advent of *perestroika*. Travellers can take tours of the monastery and visit the open-air **Ethnography Museum of the Trans-Baikal Peoples** outside Ulan Ude. In the centre of town, Ulan Ude boats what was the biggest bust of Lenin in the former Soviet Union.

KAMCHATKA PENINSULA

Kamchatka Peninsula is one of the world's last wildernesses. More than 200 volcanoes dot the peninsula, 29 of which are active. The highest — **Klyuchevskaya Sopka** — is the Fuji of Kamchatka Peninsula. The **Kronotsky Nature Preserve** contains the second-largest geyser field in the world, with more than 200 hot geysers. For 50 years (from the time of its discovery in 1941 until 1991) Kronotsky's **Valley of the Geysers** was closed to foreigners and to most Russian visitors. In 1991, however, the Kronotsky management began to issue permits to a limited number of foreign visitors. If you are interested in joining a group to scale volcanoes or explore geysers in the summer, contact REI Adventures.

TAIWAN

Legend has it that aeons ago dragons, cavorting off the coast of China, stirred up the seabed and created an island. When Portuguese sailors came upon the island's lush west coast in 1517, they exclaimed: "Ilha Formosa [beautiful island]!" Now called Taiwan, or "terraced bay," the island is still beautiful, especially along the central mountain range that runs the length of the country.

On the east coast the mountains drop sharply into the sea. But in the west the peaks slope gently through terraced tablelands into a coastal plain. The highest mountain is Yushan, or Jade Mountain (formerly known as Mt Morrison), which approaches 4,000 metres. Because of the rocky terrain, little more than one third of the land is arable. Most of the farm cultivation — mainly rice, fruit and vegetables — and the bulk of Taiwan's 20.6 million inhabitants thrive on the western plain.

The main island of Taiwan is separated from the Chinese mainland by the Taiwan Strait, which ranges in width from 130 to 220 kilometres. The island of Taiwan, shaped roughly like a tobacco leaf, is 377 kilometres long and 142 kilometres wide at the broadest point. Peripheral territories include the Pescadores (Penghu) islands halfway to the mainland in the Taiwan Strait, Lanyu (Orchid Island) and Green Island off the southeast coast. The offshore island chains of Quemoy and Matsu both lie within sight of Chinese mainland territory. The total land area of Taiwan is 36,000 square kilometres. Taiwan's economic boom and high population density have spawned several smoggy urban centres, but rugged forests and unspoiled beaches are usually not far from the beaten path.

The capital, Taipei (population 2.7 million), is a teeming city caught halfway between East and West. Ancient Chinese temples and makeshift food stalls stand alongside high-rise buildings and boutiques. The Chinese cuisine is magnificent, reasonably priced and endlessly varied. Taipei night-life is also diverse, ranging from traditional Chinese opera to English-style "pubs."

Gift shops are everywhere and they overflow with Chinese antiques, crafts and curios. Taiwan's marble products are highly coveted and local jade is fairly inexpensive. But antique jade, and even antique copies, cost a mint. Small stores and out-of-the-way markets are most likely to have that "special something" unavailable anywhere else in the world.

History

Before the Chinese settled in Taiwan, a people thought to be of proto-Malayan origin populated the island's coastal plains; their descendants are Taiwan's aborigines, who now number 336,000. The Chinese claim that records dating before the **Han Dynasty** (206 BC-AD 220) identify Taiwan as part of the Chinese empire. But the large-scale migration from China, mostly from Fujian province directly across the Taiwan Strait, did not reach its peak until the 1600s. These travellers were the ancestors of the present-day native Taiwanese, who make up 85% of the population. The rest of the population are referred to as "mainlanders." They or their parents came to Taiwan from the mainland around and after 1949. Before then the island was host to a succession of non-Chinese colonists and invaders, including the Portuguese, Dutch, Spanish, French and Japanese.

◄ *Ami tribal girls in Hualien.* PHOTO: BOB REECE

TAIWAN
Tanshui
Keelung
Taipei
Taoyuan
Hsinchu
Ilan
Lotung
Suao
Miaoli
Taiwan Strait (Formosa Strait)
Tachien
Tienhsiang
Tungshih
Lishan
Kukuan
Tayuiling
Taroko
Taichung
Changhua
Wushe
Hualien
Nantou
Sun Moon Lake
Makung
Touliu
Penghu
Alishan
Chiayi
Pacific Ocean
Kuanshan
Hsinying
Haituan
Paolai
Chengkung
Yuching
Tainan
Santimen
Taitung
Pingtung
Chihpen
Lutao
Kaohsiung
Fangliao
km
0
50
Orchid Island
Highway
Chungshan Freeway
Railways
Airports
Checheng
Hengchun
Oluanpi
Kenting

The Dutch invaded Taiwan in 1624, meeting little resistance from the 30,000 or so Chinese farmers living there, and set up a capital in the south on the site of what is now Tainan. Two years later the Spanish set up a stronghold in northern Taiwan, only to be expelled by the Dutch in 1641. The Dutch, in turn, were ousted in 1662 by **Ming Dynasty** loyalist Cheng Cheng-kung, known to the West as Koxinga, who had fled the victorious Manchu forces of the **Qing Dynasty** (1644-1911). Koxinga's followers managed to maintain a Ming stronghold on Taiwan until 1683, when the island was finally captured by the Manchu empire. The following year, Emperor Kanghsi made Taiwan a prefecture of Fujian province, with the idea of turning it into a strong base to protect China from menacing Dutch warships.

This marked the beginning of more than 200 years of nominal Chinese rule. Further Chinese migration was to be strictly limited. The failure to enforce this rule, however, led to Taiwan's development as a rowdy dependency, a rough frontier society. During most of this period, the Manchu officials assigned to the island were inefficient and corrupt, leading to numerous uprisings and social and political instability. "Every three years a rebellion, every five a revolution," it was said of Taiwan at this time.

In the mid-19th century the Western powers began to show renewed interest in the island. Under the treaties of Tianjin (Tientsin) secured by the British and French in 1858, two ports in Taiwan were opened to foreign trade. Several countries set up trading posts. The arrival of Christian missionaries followed.

Liu Ming-chuan, a capable official and a reformer, was sent to administer the island in 1885. One year later Taiwan was made a separate province of China, with Liu as its first governor.

Taiwan was ceded to Japan in 1895 by the Treaty of Shimonoseki, the pact that ended the first Sino-Japanese War of 1894-95. But the inhabitants objected and declared a republic — the first in Asia. This uprising was quickly put down by the Japanese, who went on to govern the island for the next 50 years. Taiwan became an important military base and source of foodstuffs and raw materials for Japan. At the same time, the Japanese endowed the island with economic and educational standards much more advanced than those on the Chinese mainland at the time. Even today the Japanese influence can be seen in many parts of the country.

With Japan's defeat in 1945, Taiwan was returned to Chinese rule. In February 1947 yet another revolt by native Taiwanese inhabitants was suppressed, this time by Nationalist Chinese soldiers. An estimated 18,000-28,000 Taiwanese were massacred.

In December 1949, as Chinese communists took control of the mainland, Generalissimo Chiang Kai-shek's Nationalist Government moved to Taiwan. On March 1, 1950, Chiang "resumed" the presidency of China in Taipei, vowing to use the island as a base for the eventual recovery of the mainland.

U.S. President Harry Truman, no admirer of Chiang and his government, had announced a policy of non-involvement in China's affairs in January 1950, saying the United States would not supply military aid to the Kuomintang (KMT) forces on Taiwan. With the Nationalists' fate apparently sealed, the State Department drafted the statement they would make once Taiwan had been overrun by the People's Republic of China (PRC). But as Taiwan waited nervously, history stepped in to save the KMT.

On June 25, 1950, a massive North Korean force crossed the 38th Parallel and invaded South Korea. A nervous Truman ordered the Seventh Fleet to patrol the Taiwan Strait, giving the island a new important role in U.S. defence strategy. U.S. military guarantees and economic aid engendered public confidence and allowed the KMT government time to carry out economic and political changes.

U.S. aid to a prospering Taiwan was phased out in 1964, forcing the island to become more self-reliant. Foreign investment from overseas Chinese, the U.S., Japan and Western Europe helped introduce modern, labour-intensive technology in the 1960s. The island's economy began to take off, paving the way for what would become one of the fastest-growing economies in the world over the next two decades.

Taiwan's diplomatic standing declined sharply with the forced withdrawal of Nationalist China from the United Nations in 1971, and the admission of Beijing. The worst blow came on December 15, 1978 when Washington announced it would establish diplomatic ties with the PRC. As part of this new foreign policy, U.S. relations with Taiwan were severed on January 1, 1979. The U.S. Government also announced that the 1954 mutual defence treaty with Taiwan would be allowed to lapse at the end of 1979.

The U.S. Congress later passed the Taiwan Relations Act, which replaced the embassy in Taiwan with the American Institute in Taiwan, which now functions as a U.S. interests section. At the same time, Washington gave assurances that it remained deeply concerned about the security of the island.

Chiang Kai-shek effectively ruled the country as president and director-general of the KMT until his death in April 1975. Vice-President C.K. Yen succeeded to the presidency to serve out the term. Chiang Ching-kuo, Chiang Kai-shek's son, was elected president in 1978. He had served as premier for six years and had been chairman of the KMT since 1975. Chiang Ching-kuo was re-elected president in 1984, and continued his policy of economic and political liberalization, bringing many younger Taiwanese officials into positions of influence.

Chiang Ching-kuo allowed the island's first opposition political party to form in 1986, despite a long-standing ban on new parties. In July 1987 he announced both the lifting of martial law, which his father had imposed nearly 40 years earlier, and of foreign-exchange controls. In November 1987 he allowed Taiwan residents to visit relatives on the mainland for the first time since 1949. Chiang Ching-kuo died on January 13, 1988, ending 60 years of Chiang rule.

After Chiang's death, Lee Teng-hui succeeded to the presidency, becoming the first native-born Taiwanese to become head of state and head of the ruling KMT. Lee carried on Chiang's liberalization programme and continued the policy of opening up to the mainland. Lee was elected the eighth president of the Republic of China in May 1990, despite efforts by the increasingly weakened mainlander old guard to promote Gen. Chiang Wei-kuo, the brother of Chiang Ching-kuo, to the post.

One year later, Lee declared an end to the "period of communist rebellion" and lifted the "temporary provisions" under which the presidency had enjoyed extra-constitutional powers since 1948. Lee's decree restored constitutional rule and cleared the way for full elections to Taiwan's legislative bodies, ending the mainland officials' long-held monopoly over the posts to which they were elected in China in the late 1940s.

Although the number of nations which maintain diplomatic relations with Taiwan is declining, other countries are now willing to establish unofficial organizations to deal with Taiwan's economic juggernaut, which has brought its people one of the highest living standards in Asia. Leading European and Asian countries have opened trade offices in Taipei.

Entry

The **Chiang Kai-shek (CKS) International Airport** is located in Taoyuan, 40 kilometres from Taipei. **Kaohsiung Airport** in southern Taiwan, seven kilometres from Kaohsiung City, also handles daily China Airlines flights to and from Hong Kong. Passengers leaving from the Taoyuan and Kaohsiung airports on international flights must pay a NT$300 airport tax. Pay this tax before checking in at counters located at the head of each check-in counter.

Taiwan straddles several East Asian air routes and is served by some 20 airlines, so it is easily accessible.

A special taxi service is available at controlled rates: from CKS Airport to Taipei passengers pay according to the meter, plus a 50% service charge. Expect to pay about NT$1,200. Taxis are available in front of the arrivals building. From Taipei to CKS Airport, negotiate with the driver before entering the taxi — NT$800-1,000 is the going rate (as of April 1995). Some drivers want more because they can't pick up passengers at the airport for the trip back to town. No tip is required.

Buses run between the airport and Taipei every 15 minutes from 6:15 a.m. to 10:30 p.m. Purchase tickets inside the arrival area or outside near the bus stop. There are two routes: one bus travels to the domestic Sungshan Airport in Taipei; the other goes to Taipei Railway Station. The fare is NT$85. There is sufficient luggage space. For passengers heading south, buses also go to the major cities of Taichung, Tainan and Kaohsiung. Both EVA Airways and China Airlines offer transfer flights from CKS to Kaohsiung.

A taxi-ride from Taipei's domestic **Sungshan Airport** to most hotels in town costs about NT$100. Many hotels provide transport from the Taoyuan Airport for little or no charge. Ask about transport when you make your reservation. Transport to the airport is usually available from most hotels at reasonable rates.

The **Taiwan Visitors' Association** has a desk at the Taoyuan Airport to help visitors and to make hotel bookings by telephone. It also gives out free copies of hotel listings, travel guides and a monthly publication on Taiwan. All contain useful telephone numbers and addresses. Although more than 2,000 new hotel rooms have become available since 1990, the most popular hotels are often booked during peak periods, so make your reservations early.

Kaohsiung Airport is close to town and is serviced by city buses. These are inconvenient, however, if you have a lot of baggage. A taxi to downtown Kaohsiung costs about NT$200.

The Japanese Arimura Line sails weekly between Keelung and Okinawa, with connections to and from Japan. The trip costs NT$2,420 one-way. For more information, contact Yung An Maritime Co. (11 Jenai Rd, Section 3, Taipei. Tel: [02] 771 5911).

MAJOR AIRLINES

	Tel:
China Air Lines (Int'l)	715 1212
China Air Lines (Local)	715 1122
Cathay Pacific Airways	715 2333
Delta	551 3656
EVA Airways	501 1999
Far Eastern Air Transport	712 1555
Formosa Airlines	514 9811
Great China Airlines	775 2450
Japan Asia Airways	776 5151
KLM	717 1000
Korean Air	521 4242
Malaysia Airlines	716 8388
Northwest Airlines	716 1555
Philippine Airlines	505 1255
Singapore Airlines	551 6655
South African Airways	713 6363
Thai Airways International	717 5200
TransAsia Airlines (formerly Foshing Airlines)	557 5767
United Airlines	325 8868

Immigration

Nationals of Australia, Austria, Belgium, Britain (United Kingdom), Canada, France, Germany, Holland, Japan, Luxembourg, New Zealand and the U.S. may stay for up to 14 days without visas, providing their passports and more than six month's validity remaining. For others, visas may be obtained from Taiwan diplomatic and designated representative offices abroad. Tourist-visa holders may stay in Taiwan for 14-60 days. Unless restricted to two weeks, visa-holders may apply for a maximum of two extensions of 60 days each, for a total of six months. For visa extensions and alien-resident certificates in Taipei, call the **Municipal Police Headquarters** at the **Foreign Affairs Dept** (Tel: 321 9011). Visas may be single- or multiple-entry. Holders of tourist visas are not permitted to accept employment without authorization.

Health

Travellers who have stayed more than five days in cholera-infected areas must have valid inoculation certificates before arrival in Taiwan.

Customs

Personal belongings may be brought into Taiwan duty-free, but stereo sets, TVs and video recorders must be declared. Each person is allowed to bring in one litre of alcoholic beverages, 25 cigars, 200 cigarettes or one pound of other tobacco products.

Passengers may not bring in, or leave with, local currency amounting to more than NT$40,000 in cash without a permit from the Central Bank of China. You may not leave the country with more than US$5,000 in cash (or an equal amount of other currencies) unless it has been declared upon arrival.

Currency

Taiwan's legal currency, the New Taiwan Dollar (NT$), is pegged loosely to the U.S. dollar at around 26.5 to 1, though it fluctuates slightly from time to time. The smallest practical denomination is the NT$1 coin and the largest is the NT$1,000 note.

Major foreign currencies may be exchanged at most commercial banks and at hotels in major cities. Credit cards are now widely accepted in most restaurants and stores in the cities. Many rural areas, however, will not accept foreign currency, so be sure to bring enough NT dollars with you when travelling to out-of-the-way places. Unused NT dollars can be converted into U.S. currency at banks in the airport upon departure, provided you can produce official exchange receipts less than six months old. If you have lost your receipt, however, and the amount is not significant, you can still convert your money.

Language

Mandarin Chinese, the national language in both Taiwan and China, is a derivative of the Chinese dialect spoken in Beijing. But most residents speak Taiwanese, a derivative of the Fujian dialect. Several Hakka dialects are also spoken in Taiwan. None of these three language groups are mutually intelligible. Some older Taiwanese do not speak Mandarin at all, but can speak Japanese, owing to the Japanese occupation (1895-1945). Most mainlanders speak Mandarin, and many also speak the dialect of their home province. The younger generation is more familiar with English. There are also several aborigine dialects, resembling Malay, but most aborigines speak Mandarin and Taiwanese as well.

Few taxi drivers understand English. Since most street names and other signs are written in Chinese characters (though many are now written in Roman characters as well), ask your hotel reception clerk to write down any destinations or instructions in Chinese. Bilingual business cards are also helpful for finding well-known locations.

If the street names and place names spelled out in English letters do not look quite like the Chinese words you are used to seeing in newspapers or in mainland China, it is because Taiwan uses the old Wade-Giles system of romanization, rather than the widely accepted pinyin system. The proper names you see in this chapter are given in Wade-Giles, as in Taiwan.

Climate

Taiwan's best months are during the brief spring and autumn. The island's subtropical climate has an average annual temperature of 22°C in the north and 24.5°C in the south. Summer months (May-October) are hot and humid, punctuated by sudden showers. The winter is short but January and February are often cold enough to bring snow to the higher mountains for a brief ski season. Summer temperatures hover around 30°C and winter temperatures can drop to as low as 10°C.

The island's mean annual rainfall is about 2,500 millimetres, with marked regional variations. May to October is typhoon season. If a typhoon warning has been announced, it would be wise to avoid travelling to outlying areas, which are sometimes cut off for several days after severe storms.

Dress

Casual clothing is de rigueur for travellers to Taiwan. Light-weight clothing is best from April to the end of October and humid weather may require frequent changes. Air-conditioning in restaurants is often turned up full blast, so women may like to carry a light sweater. Handbags or shoes that are not used constantly during the winter may get mouldy. Umbrellas are a must all year round.

Cooler months call for medium-weight clothing, including sweaters and light jackets. Mountain areas are cool throughout the year. Warm clothes are essential at the Hohuanshan ski resort during the winter season.

Business Hours

Government and private offices are open 8:30 a.m. or 9 a.m.-noon and 1:30 p.m.-5:30 p.m. on weekdays. Saturday hours are 8:30 a.m. or 9 a.m.-noon. Sunday is a holiday.

In the heart of Taipei, the Central Post Office (opposite the train station on Chung Hsiao W. Rd near the Old North Gate) is open daily 8 a.m.-9 p.m. (but is closed on Sunday), and maintains a 24-hour telephone and telegram service. Smaller branch offices operate 8 a.m.-6 p.m. Monday-Saturday. Banks are open 9 a.m.-3:30 p.m. on weekdays and 9 a.m.-noon or 1 p.m. on Saturdays. Sunday is a holiday.

Shops have variable hours but are generally open 9 a.m.- 9 p.m. Most big department stores are open 10 a.m.-10 p.m., but check before going. Most shops and department stores are open on Saturdays and Sundays. Restaurants are open from about 11 a.m. to 9 p.m., so it is wise to begin dinner before 8 p.m. at any of the larger restaurants.

Buses normally start operation at 6 a.m. and stop around 11:30 p.m., but taxis have no set hours.

Doing Business

Body language is extremely important when dealing with Chinese, and name cards are a must when doing business in Taiwan. When giving or accepting a name card, remember to do so with both hands. Handshaking is customary, but body contact should be avoided. It is considered impolite to turn the sole of one's foot towards a Chinese person, as is pointing to a person with the index finger.

Business is often done around a dinner table. The best rule when eating out is to watch your hosts and act accordingly. Chinese usually do not drink alone when eating a meal, but wait for someone else at the table to make a toast before taking a drink.

It is perfectly correct for the guest to toast the host or another person at the table. Simply raise your glass with two hands and nod towards the recipient of the toast. After taking a drink, raise the glass once again in the direction of your fellow drinker. You may be repeatedly entreated to *ganbei* (literally "dry glass"), but if you are not a serious drinker you can usually beg off with a sip. If invited to someone's house for a meal, take along a gift such as fruit, chocolates or a bottle of alcohol.

Rip-Offs

Taiwan is relatively free of rip-offs, but there are a few things the traveller should keep in mind. Be careful when buying antiques, as there are quite a few authentic-looking "Ming" and "Qing" pieces floating around the island's antique markets.

Posh clubs that provide hostesses can be quite expensive, with the bill rising to as much as US$500 for a small group of drinkers in just a couple of hours, without any "special services." Make sure you know what the prices are before sitting down.

Media

Two English-language dailies, the *China Post* and *China News*, cost NT$12. *Business Taiwan*, a business weekly, is available only through subscription to the *United Daily News*. *The International Herald Tribune, Asian Wall Street Journal*, and leading international magazines such as *Time*, *Newsweek* and the *Far Eastern Economic Review* are available.

ICRT, the island's only English-language radio station, broadcasts news and music on FM (100 megahertz) and AM (576 kilohertz), 24 hours a day. The island's three TV stations broadcast primarily in Chinese, but a number of popular programmes are aired in English each week. The reach of cable TV is expanding rapidly. Most hotels and many households are hooking up to more than 50 channels, including CNN, Asia Business News, StarTV, CBS Hour, Discovery, TNT Cartoon, HBO Asia and NHK.

For reading on Taiwan and China in general, Caves, an English-language bookshop (103 Chungshan North Rd, Section 2), offers a broad range of publications.

Communications

Local calls are NT$1 for three minutes. Calls are automatically cut off after three minutes, but you can continue your call by inserting more coins. Telephone cards of NT$100 are available from most convenience stores. International direct dialling is available in most good hotels. For directory assistance in English, call (02) 311 6796. International cables, faxes and telexes may be sent from hotels and **International Telecommunications Administration** offices. The main ITA office, at 28 Hangchow South Rd, Section 1, Taipei, is open 24 hours a day.

Electricity supply is 110 volts AC, 60 cycles.

Transport

The language barrier is the biggest obstacle to getting around in Taiwan. Still, transport facilities are excellent and non-Mandarin speakers can manage to get around by planning ahead and by taking advantage of the English-speaking staff of regular tourist establishments (hotels, travel agencies, railway and bus information services). Hotels will arrange ticket bookings at a small service charge.

The key to travelling in Taiwan is preparing enough material — including transport bookings and directions in Chinese — at one English-speaking centre to get you through to the next.

TRANSPORT IN TAIPEI

TAXIS: Taxis are metered and cost NT$50 for the first 1.5 kilometres and NT$5 for each additional 400 metres, plus an additional NT$5 for every five minutes the cab is standing still or moving below five kilometres an hour. There is a 20% surcharge between 11 p.m. and 5 a.m. and during rush hour. It can be difficult to get a taxi during rush hours (8-10 a.m. and 5-7 p.m.), so give yourself extra time to get to important appointments.

Since few taxi drivers speak English, you will need your destination written in Chinese. Take along your hotel's business card with its name and address in Chinese to help your return. If you plan to take a taxi out of the city, it is possible to negotiate a round-trip price with the driver for less than the meter fare. Ask your hotel reception desk to handle this. Women should avoid taking taxis alone late at night.

BUSES: Taipei is criss-crossed by a comprehensive network of urban bus routes. If you

A Taoist festival in progress. PHOTO: HILARY ANDREWS

cannot read or speak Chinese, however, negotiating the bus routes can be difficult, as the signs are all in Chinese characters.

Buses also run to many nearby suburban areas, mainly from the highway bus stations near the **Taipei Railway Station**. Simple English is spoken at the information counters and there are English signs above the ticket windows, so you should have no trouble buying the right ticket and getting on the right bus. Your best chance, of course, is to carry instructions written in Chinese. If your destination is not the last stop on the bus line, tell the bus driver or conductress your destination as you board so that he or she can let you know where to get off. Otherwise you may end up miles from your intended goal.

TRAINS: The new **Taipei Railway Station** on Chung Hsiao West Rd has English signs above the ticket windows and a service centre desk. Each railway station is named in English as well as Chinese, but English probably will not get you far in the smaller stations.

CAR RENTAL: To rent a car you need an international or Taiwan driver's licence. There are a few agencies that allow self-drive rentals at short-term rates. But Taiwan's traffic is often so horrendous, and the Chinese-language street signs so incomprehensible, that most visitors prefer to rent cars with chauffeurs at NT$4,200 for eight hours a day, with a surcharge of NT$400 per extra hour. This includes unlimited mileage. Information is available at the **Taiwan Visitors' Association** booth at the CKS International Airport. The association also maintains service centres at Taipei's Sungshan Airport and the railway station, and at the airports in Taichung, Tainan and Kaohsiung. Its tourist hotline is (080) 211734. A leading local agency catering to foreign tourists is the **Central Auto Service** (Taipei, Tel: 882 1000). Weekly rental for a standard compact is around NT$2,000 per day.

TRANSPORT UPCOUNTRY

Down-island transport is of two general kinds: that which operates for local residents and is slow, cheap and crowded; and that which operates for tourists — Chinese and Western — which is semi-express, sometimes air-conditioned and with reserved seats. If you have the time, local buses and trains can be fascinating, but be prepared to be packed in like a sardine.

BUSES: Taiwan's comprehensive bus network includes round-island, cross-island, coastal, internal and connecting highway routes. There is also an air-conditioned, non-stop bus service, the Kuokuang, operating between Taipei and points south on the superhighway that opened in 1978. Reserved-seat tickets may be purchased two days in advance. Another air-conditioned express bus — the Chunghsin — runs from Taipei to major cities in central and southern Taiwan. It is cheaper than the Kuokuang, but does not have restrooms. The Chunghsin line also operates on the superhighway. Seats may be reserved on highway buses up to 24 hours before departure. This is best done through your hotel or travel agent. In towns along the railway, the bus stations are always within convenient walking distance of the station. Apart from during holiday seasons, reservations are not essential. Most highway bus lines operating between Taipei and nearby satellite towns or other big cities run services at least hourly.

Coaches out of Taipei leave from the bus stations by the central railway station — southbound from the west station and northbound from the east. The two main bus routes from Taipei extend to Kaohsiung in the south via the main cities of Taichung, Chiayi and Tainan, and to Hualien on the east coast via Lotung on the northeast tip of Taiwan.

Highway buses run from the central Taiwan city of Taichung to the famous Sun Moon Lake resort and via the East-West Cross-Island Highway to Lishan, Tienhsiang and Hualien. From Hualien, highway buses manoeuvre the spectacular east coast road that winds precariously along the cliff face to the fishing town of Suao. Further south, buses make the trip around the island's extremity, connecting Taitung and Kaohsiung and including a side spur to Oluanpi on the southernmost tip.

Timetables are readily available in Taipei for the island-wide highway coach services. Information on the numerous local bus services is best obtained from local hotels or bus stations.

TAXIS: Taxis in Taipei, Taichung, Tainan, and Kaohsiung must have meters. Taxis in smaller towns and cities do not have meters and so you must agree on the price before getting into the taxi. The fare is usually NT$50-70 for any destination within a town or city.

Taxis can be hired for country trips. Some, also known as wild chicken taxis, specialize in certain runs — Taichung to Sun Moon Lake, for example — and lower the individual traveller's cost by loading up with four passengers. These specialized taxis usually load up near the train or bus stations. Their drivers will solicit passengers by calling out the name of the destination. Determine a price before beginning the journey. Taxis are obviously faster than buses, but many travel at breakneck speeds, so nervous travellers should beware.

TRAINS: Train travel in Taiwan is inexpensive, convenient and comfortable — and the trains run on time. A trunk line with sea and mountain routes runs the length of the island through the low country of the western plain, linking Keelung in the north with Kaohsiung in the south via Taipei, Taichung and Tainan. From Taipei, another line runs around the island's northeast corner through Fulung, Ilan and Suao to the east-central city of Hualien. Hualien and Taitung in the south are linked by another line.

The main west coast line has several express trains and each one is a single class. Categories range from the high-speed Tzuchiang and the luxury Chukuang, the Kuankuang and Kuanghua to the limited expresses. The fastest of these trains is the Tzuchiang, which runs from Taipei to Kaohsiung in a little more than four hours.

All express trains are excellent, varying only in service, speed and plushness. Most of them, except the Kuanghua, are air-conditioned. Hostesses provide tea, magazines and newspapers (mostly Chinese language). Snacks and lunchboxes are often sold on the train and some Chukuang runs include a dining car. Non-express trains operate on the same lines, but they often do not have reserved seats and stop more frequently. Both express and standard trains run on the Taipei-Suao and Hualien-Taitung lines. From Chiayi in the south, a quaint mountain train runs to the resort of Alishan.

Advance tickets for express-class trains can be bought for the following day or the day after in the train station (business hours 8 a.m.-10 p.m.). Tickets for same-day expresses may be purchased up to just before departure time, but often are unavailable because of heavy advance booking.

BOAT: Travel agencies can arrange boat reservations for travel between Kaohsiung and Makung in the Pescadores islands and between Taitung and Green Island and Lanyu (Orchid Island).

AIR: Regular domestic flights link Taipei with most other major cities, including Tainan, Kaohsiung, Taichung, Hualien, Taitung and offshore islands.

The **Tourism Bureau** (Tel: 349 1635 or 349-6) hands out free copies of a guide to walking around historical buildings in Taipei.

Tours

A number of tour companies arrange Taipei city and down-island tours. The more orthodox range from a half-day whiz through the capital's major sights (from around NT$500) to a three-day excursion to Taroko Gorge and Sun Moon Lake (NT$7,000 — including shared accommodation, not including meals). Popular tours in the Taipei vicinity include: a night tour of Taipei for NT$750, which includes a Mongolian barbecue dinner, visits to the Lungshan Temple, Hwashi night market and Chinese opera; a half-day tour of the Wulai aboriginal village for NT$750; and a half-day north coast tour of Yehliu Park and Chinshan beach for NT$650.

A one-day tour of Taroko Gorge (NT$3,300, including airfare and lunch) involves flying to Hualien and driving by air-conditioned coach through the breathtaking gorge. A two-day tour of Sun Moon Lake the Formosa Aboriginal Culture Village by bus costs NT$4,200 (including shared accommodation but not meals); a four-day round-the-island tour, excluding meals, costs NT$9,700. Single accommodation for the above overnight trips is priced slightly higher. Special tours focusing on tea, cuisine, art, hot springs, golf and nature also can be arranged.

Taipei is overflowing with tour and travel agencies. Stick to the ones recommended by your hotel or by the Taiwan Visitors' Association. Some tour operators: **South East Travel Service** (60 Chungshan North Rd, Section 2, Tel: 571 3001); **China Express Transportation Co.** (70 Chungshan North Rd, Section 2, Tel: 522 1956); **Pinho Travel Service Co.** (3/F, 142-1 Chihlin Rd, Tel: 551 4136); and **Taiwan Coach Tours** (Rm 802, 27 Chungshan North Rd, Section 3, Tel: 595 5321).

Accommodation

TAIPEI

Like many Asian countries, Taiwan has seen a hotel building boom over the past few years, which has led to an oversupply of rooms. Even so, rates are rising and some of the better hotels are full during the peak season.

Among the new hotels in the luxury class and charging top rates are the **Grand Hyatt Taipei**, the **Sherwood**, the **Far Eastern Plaza** and the **Grand Formosa Regent**. The smaller and quieter **Ritz Taipei Hotel** and **Hotel Royal Taipei** (the latter under Japanese management) have excellent reputations.

This does not mean that the older hotels have been left out in the cold. The **Hilton**, **Lai Lai Sheraton**, **Howard**, **Ambassador**, **Gloria**, **Fortuna**, **President** and **Imperial** have all been renovated and are still popular. Cheaper hotels in the middle-class range are the **Brother**, **Golden China**, **Majestic**, **Mandarin** and **Miramar**. There also are numerous small hotels for the budget traveller.

The doyen of Taiwan hotels, however, is the palace-style **Grand Hotel** in Taipei's northern suburbs, which dominates the landscape of northern Taipei and is often used as a symbol for the city. The splendour of the architecture is not matched by the food and service, though some find the old fashioned, run-down atmosphere entirely fitting. Since the hotel has strong government connections, prices are moderate.

Suites are considerably more expensive than basic twin rooms. Some single rooms are equipped with double beds and there is a flat charge, no matter how many persons occupying the room. Some hotels provide TV sets and refrigerators in all their rooms, while others feature them only in the more expensive twin and suite units. Hotels automatically levy a 10% service charge on room charges, food, drink and other items, so tipping is not required.

Do not drink unboiled or tap water in Taiwan. Hotels and restaurants serve either boiled, distilled or bottled mineral water.

The main road for tourists to remember is Chungshan North Rd. Many major hotels are within walking distance of sections 1, 2 and 3 of this road, and so are many bookstores, boutiques, gift shops and restaurants. As the city's commercial centre has moved gradually eastward, many top class hotels, shops and restaurants have sprung up on that side of the city as well.

Remember to make use of restrooms in hotels and Western fast-food restaurants before setting out. The toilets in public places and smaller restaurants and stores are usually the squat type. Always carry some toilet paper because many restrooms do not provide it.

Information on hotels and rates can be obtained at the Information Bureau run by the Taiwan Visitors' Association at the CKS International Airport and in free tourist guides available everywhere.

ACCOMMODATION UPCOUNTRY

There are hot springs resorts all over the island, some with lovely Japanese-style inns with *tatami* (sleeping mats) and sliding screen doors. Smaller hotels down-island charge half price for day rooms, for travellers who just want a place to wash up and rest for a few hours.

Youth hostels are still uncommon in Taiwan and they are often fully booked by visiting Overseas Chinese or other large tour groups. There are a few hostels along the East-West Cross-Island Highway — and comfortable lodges at Tienhsiang and Lishan — and along other hiking routes.

Plan ahead, since hotel reservations in more remote regions, such as Alishan, Orchid Island or Makung, may be in high demand for weekends and holidays. Many down-country hotels have reservation offices in Taipei, so inquire at your own hotel before making a long-distance call; where possible the Taipei numbers have been included in the hotel list at the end of this chapter.

Dining

The Chinese love to eat. Eating in Taiwan is an important social and cultural activity and almost every meal can be considered, as one visitor put it, "a theatre of the stomach." For those to whom Chinese food means Cantonese fried rice, eating in Taiwan is an eye-opening, mouth-watering adventure.

When refugees from all over China migrated to Taiwan more than four decades ago, they brought the unique culinary styles of every mainland province. Here, these regional cuisines were continued and perfected. Taipei undoubtedly offers the world's widest range of superb Chinese food accessible to Western tourists in one city. Within blocks of one another are clusters of excellent restaurants offering the fiery cuisine of Sichuan province, mouth-watering Peking duck, delicately prepared Shanghai-style seafood, Cantonese delicacies, Mongolian barbecue and hotpot and native Taiwanese and Hakka food.

If possible, dine in the company of Chinese friends during your stay in Taiwan. Insist that they order what they like — or you may end up with sweet-and-sour pork and fried rice selected by polite acquaintances trying to anticipate the taste of foreigners. If you think you can handle it, taste a dish first before asking what it is: pig stomach and duck blood taste much better than they sound. And the quality of the service and the trappings do not always reflect the quality of the food. A shoddy-looking restaurant may serve excellent fare, so taste before passing judgment.

Chinese meals are perfect for this kind of exploratory dining because dishes are ordered communally and guests help themselves from the collection placed in the centre of the table. Take only as much from each dish as you can eat immediately; it is considered impolite to amass a great pile of food on your side plate. In fact, side plates are absent in some restaurants and you are expected to use your rice bowl (filled with rice) as only the temporary resting place for food morsels on their way from dish to mouth.

A general rule of thumb for table manners is to watch your Chinese friends and act accordingly. Even in some of the classiest-looking restaurants, sipping soup straight from the soup bowl, spitting bones on to the table-cloth and loud, random belching are not uncommon. On the other hand, after-dinner toothpick manoeuvres must be discreetly shielded from view by the free hand.

If you cannot dine with Chinese acquaintances, do not be afraid to venture out on your own. After deciding what type of regional cuisine you want, order what seems to be a fair sampling of the menu — perhaps one meat dish, one fish dish, one vegetable dish, a soup and so on. Chinese menus usually are arranged under these headings and all well-known restaurants in Taipei have English translations. When deciding on quantity for a group of up to six, it's best to order small portions of as many dishes as there are diners, plus one soup. For larger groups, order several dishes in medium or large portions. You may want to ask the waiter for suggestions, especially about specialities of the house. Large restaurants automatically add a 10% service charge to the bill, so tipping is not required. Make reservations before going to the more popular restaurants.

The most popular regional cuisine is from Sichuan (sometimes spelled Szechuan), a huge, mountainous province in the southwest of China. Spicy and richly flavoured, this cuisine makes liberal use of hot peppers and may prove fiery to the uninitiated. Popular specialities include *gong bao ji ding* (boneless chicken chunks sauteed with chillies), duck smoked with camphor and tea (delicious and not hot), egg-plant with fragrant sauce (garlicky and hot), and *mapo doufu* (diced beancurd sauteed with ground pork, garlic, scallions, ginger and lots of chili peppers). Rice is offered, but you might try *yin si juan* (silver silk rolls), a type of bread-roll either steamed or deep-fried.

Cuisine from Beijing in northern China is mild but hearty. Wheat, rather than rice, is the staple and dumplings, breads and noodles feature prominently. The most famous dish — justifiably so — is Peking duck. The meat and crisp skin of the duck is wrapped in thin crepes of lightly fried, unleavened dough dabbed with sweet plum sauce and garnished with scallion. Soup made from the duck bones is also delicious.

Hunan cuisine, like that of Sichuan, is known for its liberal use of chilli peppers.

Seafood is the highlight of subtle Shanghai cooking: Taipei's abundant supplies of fresh seafood superbly complement this highly refined style of cuisine. Braised fish, sauteed eel and sauteed whole prawns are especially good.

Cantonese cooking from southeast China is the best-known provincial cuisine in most Overseas Chinese communities around the world. It is perhaps most famous for the brunchtime snack-and-tea morsels known in Cantonese as *dim sum* and in Mandarin as *tian-hsin*. Waitresses push trolleys holding endless varieties of Cantonese delicacies through the restaurant and diners simply choose from the parade of dumplings, sweet pastries, roasted meats and steamed treats.

Taiwanese cooking includes some very tasty fare, especially seafood. Most establishments serving native Taiwanese food also feature great local colour. Open-air stalls along **Huahsi St** in Taipei, also nicknamed "Snake Alley," offer seafood, fruit and fruit drinks, noodles, sausages, stews and, for the non-squeamish, an array of snake delicacies. A stroll down Snake Alley, which is essentially a night market complete with fortune tellers and brothels off to the side, is a good way to observe the local Taiwanese scene as well as sample the native cooking.

Hakka cooking is very earthy, representing this people's agricultural heritage. Popular dishes include tripe, pig's knuckles, pig's tongue, pig's kidney, *gou rou* (fatty pork cooked with dried salted vegetable), pickled vegetables as well as the more standard Chinese dishes.

Sucai, or vegetarian cuisine, has long been a part of Chinese cooking and, contrary to popular opinion, it is anything but bland. It is served at **Buddhist temples** and vegetarian restaurants around the island.

Taiwan also has a wide range of Japanese restaurants, a vestige of its 50-year occupation by Japan. These range from hole-in-the-wall places frequented by locals to palatial affairs in the major hotels.

Entertainment

The capital city offers an increasing number of places where couples and groups can enjoy a night out. Classical Beijing opera is performed almost nightly at the **Armed Forces Cultural Activities Centre** (69 Chunghua Rd). The programmes are all in Chinese and one play can last for hours; but tickets are inexpensive and even half-an-hour's viewing can give some idea of the extravagant pageantry of this colourful art form.

The **National Theatre** and **National Concert Hall**, located in the Chiang Kai-shek Memorial Hall complex, are the venues for big name international and Chinese performers. Well-known international orchestras, musicians and dance companies perform here regularly. Here you may also enjoy Chinese music, opera, dance and other traditional Chinese performing arts. Check the community page of the *China Post* and the *China News* for the latest information.

Dozens of pubs have opened around the city in the past decade, offering food, music, darts and a convivial atmosphere. An imported beer in a simple pub costs around NT$110, and as much as NT$200 in a larger place with a band. Most expatriates frequent the pubs around **Shuangcheng St**, between Chungshan North Rd and Linsen North Rd, behind the Ambassador Hotel, an area once popular with American GIs and affectionately dubbed the "combat zone." The most popular establishment is the **Farmhouse**, with live music most nights beginning at 9:30 p.m. and jazz on Sunday afternoons at 3:30 p.m. If the music is too loud, head to the downstairs bar, which has pool tables and a quieter atmosphere.

The Ploughman group of pubs, with traditional English atmosphere, has outlets conveniently located around the city: **The Farmhouse** (5, Lane 32, Shuangcheng St); the **Ploughman's Inn** (8, Lane 460, Tunhua North Rd); the **Ploughman's Cottage** (305 Nanking East Rd, Section 3); and **Pig and Whistle** (78 Tienmou East Rd).

Catering to Western businessmen and tourists are a handful of so-called "clubs" which date from the GI era, all in the **President Hotel** area. In these places, customers can order drinks (at about US$5 for a beer) and the company of hostesses, who will also require drinks (at about double the beer price).

The city has numerous piano bars, some with small combos and dancing, either attached to the big hotels or run separately. Taipei's best discotheques are in the leading hotels, including the **Asiaworld Plaza Hotel**, **Ambassador**, **Hilton**, and **Howard Plaza**.

Teahouses, once the reserve of old men, have made a comeback in recent years. The **Wisteria Teahouse** (No. 1, Alley 16, Shinsheng South Rd, Section 3), an old Japanese-style house with hundreds of potted plants in its yards, is popular with students, artists and intellectuals. Wisteria has both tables and tatami rooms where visitors can enjoy Chinese tea while they sit on the mats at small tables.

Shopping

Taipei's main shopping districts are: **Chungshan North Rd** and its side streets; the **West Gate** area of downtown near Chunghua Rd; and **Section 4 of Chunghsiao East Rd**, on the city's newly developed east side, which has taken over as the main centre for fashion shoppers. Prices in large establishments, especially department stores, are usually fixed and rather high. When shopping in smaller stores, especially for antiques and curios, you should bargain. The rule of thumb in the curio markets is to offer half the original price and then work towards a compromise. When antique shopping, beware of sales pitches for "genuine" Ming-period jade. The **National Palace Museum** sells authentic reproductions of the treasures in its possession and other gift items based on traditional Chinese designs.

Taiwan produces a lot of pottery with traditional designs, which are sold in stores specializing in ceramic ware and handicrafts. The **Chinese Handicraft Mart** at the corner of Chungshan South Rd and Hsuchow Rd offers this ceramic ware, as well as furniture, painting reproductions, jewellery made of coral and other semi-precious stones and marble products from the quarries in Hualien on the east coast. Jewellery made of Taiwan jade also is popular, but remember — the quality does not equal that of genuine antique jade. Handicrafts also can be found at the **Taiwan Crafts Centre** (7/Flr, 110 Yenping South Rd).

Many visitors have clothes and shoes custom-made in Taiwan. Tailors are especially numerous in the Chungshan North Rd area and most hotel arcades have tailor shops as well. Women may want to order a made-to-measure *chipao* (*cheongsam*, in Cantonese), the form-fitting Chinese-style dress that rarely fits when bought ready-made.

Western-style ready-made clothes can be found in any large department store, such as the Japanese-run **Sogo** (45 Chunghsiao East Rd, Section 4) or **Far Eastern** (32 Paoching Rd).

The **Kwanghwa Market**, under the Kwanghwa Bridge at the intersection of Shinsheng South Rd and Pateh Rd, has inexpensive computer and electronic items, antiques, and old Chinese and foreign-language books and magazines.

Sports

HIKING AND MOUNTAIN CLIMBING: There are many beautiful places around the island for pleasant hikes. However, special permits are required for climbs to many of the high mountains. The "Class A" mountain pass, for highly restricted areas, can be obtained only through the ROC Alpine Association in Taipei, which can arrange trips with accredited English-speaking guides for groups of four or more. The Alpine Association is at 10/F, 185 Chungshan North Rd Section 2, Taipei, Tel: (02) 594 2108. Access to other, less restricted mountains will be granted immediately after an identity check at a local police station upon entry to the area.

GOLF: Taiwan has 42 golf courses open to visitors and about 20 are within easy reach of Taipei. Major hotels can make arrangements for regular members to sponsor visitors; all of the courses rent equipment and caddies. Three clubs in Taoyuan, near Taipei, have special golf days for non-members (rates are around NT$2,470-2,900). They are the Taoyuan Golf Club, Tel: (03) 471 1616; Taipei Golf Club, Tel: (03) 324 4856; and Marshall Golf & Country Club, Tel: (03) 322 1786.

DIVING: The coastal waters of Taiwan offer snorkellers and scuba-divers a chance to explore a fascinating underwater world of strange coral formations and bioluminescent tropical fish. The north shore, from Tamsui to Suao, is one of Taiwan's most popular summer diving areas. In winter, divers move to Kenting Na-

A Double Tenth fan dance. PHOTO: GOVERNMENT INFORMATION OFFICE

tional Park in southern Taiwan, the island's best diving area. Diving is also popular around Green and Orchid islands, off Taiwan's southeast coast. A day of scuba-diving, including an experienced guide and rental equipment, costs about NT$7,000. Certification from a major national or international diving organization is required; some local diving companies have certified diving courses lasting from one to three weeks. For information and equipment rentals, call the ROC Diving Association in Taipei, Tel: (02) 567 0256.

MARTIAL ARTS: Chinese martial arts, known in the West as *kung fu*, and Chinese shadow boxing, or *taijiquan*, are widely pursued here. Every morning in parks and courtyards around the island, enthusiasts practise their graceful movements.

Holidays

A rich folk heritage of festivals and celebrations is still kept alive on Taiwan today. Traditional celebrations, especially *paipais*, religious observances, follow the lunar calendar and thus vary from year to year, sometimes by as much as a month. In addition, some festivals and government holidays do not occur every year. Information on the dates of the festivals is best obtained in Taiwan at the time of your visit.

January 1: Founding Day of the Republic of China: commemorates the birth of the republic in 1912. Public holiday.

January 2: Public holiday.

January-February: Chinese Lunar New Year: the first day of the Lunar New Year is an important festival that the Chinese observe with their families. Public holiday for three or more days, starting with Lunar New Year's Eve.

February-March: Lantern Festival: this marks the end of the traditional new year holiday. The Chinese used to believe they could see celestial spirits by the light of the first moon of the new year and lit torches in order to see them better. Lanterns are now used to symbolize this belief. The National Chiang Kai-shek Memorial has an impressive display of lanterns and holds a contest with prizes for the most fancifully fashioned lanterns.

March-April: Birthday of Kuan Yin, Goddess of Mercy: celebrated on a large scale in Taipei's Lungshan Temple.

March 8: Women's Day.

March 29: Youth Day: commemorates the 72 young revolutionary martyrs who sacrificed their lives on this day in 1911 in an abortive Canton uprising against the Qing dynasty. Public holiday.

April 5: Ching Ming Tomb-Sweeping Festival and the anniversary of the 1975 death of President Chiang Kai-shek: families visit cemeteries to pay respects to the deceased. Public holiday.

April-May: Birthday of Matsu, Goddess of the Sea: celebrated in hundreds of temples dedicated to Matsu, the most popular deity on Taiwan. The biggest observance is at the Matsu temple in Peikang, which attracts pilgrims from many other Matsu temples around the island.

The Flying Fish Festival: celebrated by Orchid Island's Yami tribe. This festival is based on an ancient myth about a talking fish named Blackfin who laid down strict rules governing the catching of fish. All males put on their most beautiful clothing and jewellery and their silver helmets and sail out to sea in their colourful boats to entice fish to appear.

June: Dragon-boat Festival. Dragon-boat races are held to commemorate the death in 299 BC of the poet-statesman Chu Yuan, who drowned himself to call attention to unheeded demands for government reform. This festival is also observed as Poet's Day. Public holiday.

August-September: Ghost Month begins. The Chinese believe the gates of Hades open on this day to allow spirits to return to the living world for a month-long holiday. As in all Chinese societies, locals burn symbolic money and incense and offer festival food to the ghosts, especially to the ones who have no living relatives or friends to take care of them.

The Ami Harvest Festival in Hualien: possibly the largest aborigine gathering of the year, this festival features seven days of traditional aborigine singing and dancing.

September-October: Mid-Autumn Moon Festival: one of the major events of the year, when moon-gazing celebrations are held. The Chinese believe the moon to be at its brightest and most radiant on this night. Public holiday.

September 28: Teachers' Day: commemorates the birth in 551 BC of Confucius, revered by the Chinese as the Teacher of all Generations. Special services are held at Confucian temples around Taiwan. Public holiday.

October 10: National Day or Double Tenth: commemorates the Wuchang Uprising on October 10, 1911, which led to the overthrow of the Manchu dynasty and the establishment of the Republic of China on January 1, 1912. The celebration is marked with huge rallies and a parade in the Presidential Square. Public holiday.

October 25: Taiwan Retrocession Day: commemorates the formal return of the island province of Taiwan to China in 1945 after 50 years of Japanese occupation. Public holiday.

October 31: Anniversary of the late president Chiang Kai-shek's birthday. Public holiday.

November-December: The Festival of the Little People: This is one of the most interesting aborigine festivals in Taiwan. This week-long celebration, including, worship, songs, dancing and drinking, is held every year to atone for the slaughter of a neighbouring pygmy tribe several hundred years ago.

November 12: Dr. Sun Yat-sen's Birthday: commemorates the Chinese leader's birth in 1866. Public holiday.

December 25: Constitution Day: commemorates the adoption of the Constitution of the Republic of China in 1946. Public holiday.

ADDRESSES

Taiwan Visitors' Association, 9 Minchuan East Rd, Section 2, 5/F, Taipei, Taiwan. Tel: 594 3261; Good for general inquiries and free pamphlets.

Tourism Bureau, Ministry of Communications, 280 Chunghsiao East Rd, Section 4, 9/F, Taipei, Taiwan. Tel: 349 1635, Fax: 773 5487. Or write to: The Travel Information Service Centre, Tourism Bureau, P.O. Box 45-99, Taipei, Taiwan. This office does not usually handle everyday inquiries, but offers maps and information brochures form free of charge. The bureau maintains information desks at airports to assist travellers.

The **Tourist Information Hotline** provides information on every aspect of travel in Taiwan, as well as emergency assistance, lost and found services and help with language problems. The line is open 8 a.m.-8 p.m. daily. Tel: 717 3737.

The **Government Information Office**, 2, Tientsin St, Taipei, Taiwan. Tel: 322 8888.

PUBLICATIONS

Tourist maps can be obtained free from the **Tourism Bureau**, Taiwan Visitors' Association, and at a small charge from bookshops. Other good sources of maps and information are the numerous tourist guides, including *This Month in Taiwan* and *Travel in Taiwan*, which are offered free of charge in hotels, restaurants, shops and bars.

DISCOVERING TAIWAN

TAIPEI

The best way to discover Taipei is on foot. Guided tours will cover the more well-known historical sights, but many visitors enjoy strolling through the area called Wanhua, the oldest district in Taipei. Here a profusion of noisy markets, shops selling temple accoutrements, herbal medicine stalls and houses built in the old architectural style, hint at the roots underlying Taipei's increasingly modern exterior.

Wanhua is between Chunghua Rd and the Tamsui River and includes **Lungshan Temple**, the oldest and most famous Buddhist temple in Taipei, and numerous other temples several hundred years old. Built in 1738 and almost totally rebuilt after World War II, Lungshan Temple is an ornate structure dedicated to Kuan Yin, the Goddess of Mercy. On festival days, devotees flock to this temple to make offerings and ask for divine guidance. The temple is surrounded by markets and bazaars.

In the night market along **Huahsi St**, open-air food stalls, hawkers, fortune-tellers and snake vendors compete for attention in a sideshow-like atmosphere that caters to strong-stomached adventurers. The Chinese believe that consuming snake soup of blood-and-bile mixtures will improve eyesight and general health. Little or no English is spoken here as Huahsi St is well off the beaten tourist path; if people object to your photographing them, it is best to stop.

Those to whom this does not appeal can take a tour of the area around the **Presidential Office Bldg**. This Renaissance-style building took seven years to build and was opened in 1919 as the Japanese governor-general's office. During the Japanese occupation it became a symbol of Japanese colonial authority. Allied bombers damaged the structure during World War II, but it was later renovated. The square in front of the building is the site of mammoth rallies on Double Tenth (October 10), celebrated as National Day.

The **National Chiang Kai-shek Memorial complex** includes **Chiang kai-shek Memorial Hall and Park**. The hall contains a museum as well as a pictorial history of his life. The honour guard on the main floor where the statue sits changes every hour on the hour, and puts on an impressive precision drill. The state-of-the-art **National Theatre** and **National Concert Hall** at the front of the park are among the finest in Asia.

Nearby is **New Park**, a green oasis in the middle of the city. A three-tiered pagoda, pavilions and a small lake contribute to the ambience. Fortune-tellers, artists and traditional craftsmen often set up shop on the pavements. The park has several Qing dynasty cannons and memorial arches and is also the retirement home of the island's first locomotives, imported from Europe in the late 1800s. New Park is also known to locals as a place where homosexuals seek each other out. The **Taiwan Provincial Museum**, with its collection of natural history and anthropological exhibits, is also located here. The building, a neo-Greek structure with fluted Doric columns, was built in 1915 by the Japanese.

Even more charming than New Park is the **Botanical Garden**, complete with lotus pool and 700 species of plants (Nanhai Rd, south of the downtown area). There you can find the **Hsunfu Yamen**, an important historical site that has colourful door gods and a Chinese garden. It served as the office of the civil affairs department in the provincial government of the Qing dynasty. Originally erected in 1893 near the Taipei Police Station, it was later torn down and reassembled on its present site.

The nearby **National Museum of History** (49 Nanhai Rd) houses an impressive collection of Chinese artifacts, including embroidery and imperial robes, oracle bones, religious implements, bronzes and earthenware and occasional special exhibits of contemporary Chinese master painters. Clear, but brief descriptions in English are provided.

The cultural complex on Nanhai Rd also includes the **National Science Hall** and the **National Arts Hall**, which features concerts, dance performances and regional opera originating from far-flung mainland provinces.

The **Postal Museum**, a short walk from the Botanical Gardens, is a must for stamp collectors. It displays the history of ancient China's postal system.

Traditional Beijing opera is performed at the **Armed Forces Cultural Activities Centre** (69 Chunghua Rd). Those interested in military history may want to visit the nearby **Armed Forces Museum** on Kuiyang St.

Since Taipei is not an exceptionally large city, many sights are easily reached on foot. Once you have mastered the main roads, take exploratory jaunts down side-streets and alleys where quaint restaurants and temples are tucked away. Chungshan Rd is the main north-south thoroughfare. It crosses the city from the Grand Hotel to the downtown area and is subdivided into sections 1, 2, 3, 4 and so on, with the higher numbers further north. Taipei's major east-west streets — such as Minchuan Rd and Nanking Rd — have eastern and western segments beginning at Chungshan North Rd. The west section of Chunghsiao Rd, another important thoroughfare, runs past the railway and bus stations downtown. Chunghua Rd runs the length of the major downtown area from north to south. Even though the many pedestrian subways and overpasses can be bothersome, it is worthwhile to cover this road by foot.

Despite Taipei's increasingly urban appearance, the city's temples retain their traditional style. Religious followers who flock to these structures attest to the strength of the Chinese Buddhist and Taoist traditions.

Confucianism is at least as compelling a concept. Taipei's **Confucius Temple** (275 Talung St) is unlike Buddhist temples in that it is not technically a place of worship and does not contain idols or images. Confucius is Taiwan's most revered philosopher and teacher and his code of ethics is still highly respected. The grounds of the Taipei temple are peaceful, dignified and appropriately reminiscent of the sage's teachings. On his birthday (September 28), a colourful dawn memorial service, complete with Ming-style court dances and ancient music, is held in the island's Confucian temples. Tickets are hard to get, so request them as far in advance as possible. Contact the Tourism Bureau.

By contrast, most Taiwanese religious ceremonies take place in the midst of social hubbub. Almost next door to the Confucius Temple is the **Pao An Taoist Temple** (61 Hami St). Built in 1805 by immigrants from Fujian province, it is considered one of the island's outstanding temples. The bustling **Hsing Tien Temple** (261 Minchuan East Rd) is dedicated to Kuan Kung, or Kuan Yu, worshipped as the God of War, the patron of businessmen. He figures prominently in the Chinese classic The Romance of the Three Kingdoms.

Tihua St, one of Taipei's oldest districts, remains nestled in a time warp. Here old world businesses survive in buildings that date back to the early 1900s. They sell traditional Chinese goods, such as bolts of colourful cloth, bamboo crafts, Chinese cooking utensils, dried foods and herbal medicines and other traditional remedies. Many shops continue to turn out handmade goods, from quilted blankets to coffins. This extremely narrow street is noted for its Gulangyu-style architecture, a hybrid of traditional southern Chinese architecture and rococo. The narrow red brick buildings are surprisingly deep, with a store in front and a living area at the back. Some have courtyards and a small garden in the centre.

For those with a serious interest in Chinese art, Taiwan is an unmissable experience, making it as vital as a visit to the Chinese mainland. **The National Palace Museum** is the great prize for visitors to Taipei. Not far from the city — 15 minutes by taxi from most parts of town — the museum is ensconced in the thickly wooded hills of Waishuanghsi. The building itself is imposing, with glazed tile roofs and moon gates. The collection of Chinese art within is unique both for its aesthetic excellence and magnitude. The museum holds more than 620,000 *objets d'art*, including Tang and Sung paintings, carved jade, exquisite Ming porcelain, calligraphy, bronzes up to 3,000 years old, rare books and documents, tapestries and the toys of Manchu emperors.

Publicized as the world's largest collection of Chinese art, these priceless treasures were spirited from the mainland in 1949. Most of the pieces come from the Chinese imperial collection begun more than 1,000 years ago. The museum changes its regular exhibits once every three months, a pace which will require 20 years to display all the items in storage. If you plan to take in everything on display at the museum, set aside time for more than one trip, as the sheer quantity tends to impart a dulling numbness after only an hour or two of viewing.

Leaving art aside, of the many attractions around Taipei, some are justifiably popular with the Taiwanese and others seem to be undeservedly so. The highly recommended **Yangmingshan Park** is a mountainous playground with waterfalls, lakes, hot springs, hiking trails and picnic areas. It is most beautiful from February to April when the traditional Chinese landscape is ablaze with cherry blossoms and azaleas. Unfortunately, tens of thousands of local tourists also know Yangmingshan is gorgeous at that time, and they mob the place until the rock gardens and pondside pavilions are crawling with people.

Only 30 minutes away by taxi or bus, Yangmingshan has several hotels offering hot spring baths. The residential area of Yangmingshan, also called Green Grass Mountain, is dotted with the sumptuous homes and suburban villas of Taipei's elite.

On the highway between Taipei and the northern suburb of Peitou are several pottery and stoneware factories. One of the most popular is the **China Pottery Arts Co.** (14 Chungyang South Rd, Section 2, Peitou) where visitors can watch craftsmen at work at every stage of ceramic production.

The Taiwan Folk Arts Museum (32 Yuya Rd, Peitou) exhibits and sells Taiwanese and aborigine crafts, and has a Chinese tea house and Mongolian barbecue restaurant.

Beyond Peitou is **Tamsui**, once the site of a flourishing port and now a lazy fishing town with the added attraction of an excellent golf course where visitors are welcome to play. Tamsui's old red-brick storefronts fit in well with the quaint atmosphere and seafood restaurants.

Across the Tamsui River is the unusually shaped **Mt Kuan Yin**, named after the Goddess of Mercy, whose profile is believed to be outlined on the mountain. The ancient Tamsui fort of **San Domingo**, built first by the Spanish in 1629 and later taken over by the Dutch, used to be called Hung Mao Cheng (the fort of the red-haired barbarians). Used until 1972 by the British Consulate, the red-walled fort has been reopened as a museum containing British memorabilia.

Yehliu Seaside Park, north of Taipei, features interesting seaside rock formations and a quaint fishing village. Yehliu is 80 minutes from Taipei via the large port of Keelung. It can also be reached by driving straight over scenic Yangmingshan. Visitors can take in **Ocean World**, an aquatic zoo featuring dolphin performances. Yehliu park's rustic atmosphere belies outrageous prices in seafood restaurants near the parking lots, but Yehliu's geological configurations are fantastic. The nearby beaches of Chinshan are popular with the Taiwanese, as is the resort of **Fulung** on the northeast coast. Compared with most other beaches, Fulung is better equipped to handle both overnight and day visitors.

South of Taipei are the hill resorts of **Pitan**, or Green Lake, which the Chinese consider one of the best attractions in the greater Taipei area. Pi Tan features swimming and boating, but many Western visitors cannot fathom why it is so popular. Further on in the same direction is the touristy **Wulai**, the most accessible aborigine area to Taipei. An hour's drive from the capital city, Wulai has a suspension bridge, an amusement park, a lake, cable cars and a scenic railway leading to an aboriginal village featuring song and dance shows for tourists. The Atayal tribe of Taiwan aborigines lives in this area. Look sharply! The woman dressed in her native finery standing seemingly by chance near the scenic waterfall is in fact waiting for some photographer to take her picture — and pay her a small fee for posing.

On the way to or from Pitan and Wulai you might visit **Chihnan Temple** — right outside Taipei in Mucha. Also called the Temple of the Eight Immortals, it stands on a beautiful hillside and is dedicated to Lu Tung-pin, one of the legendary Chinese Eight Immortals. The Chinese believe that devotees who stay overnight here receive divine revelations from Lu Tung-pin in the form of dreams. A temple annex with hostel facilities was built in the traditional Chinese palace style to accommodate these dream-wishers.

The **Shihmen Dam**, described as a beautiful recreation area, 55 kilometres southwest of Taipei, has little more to offer the Western visitor than a pleasant view over the Shihmen Reservoir and the appreciation of an impressive dam project.

Peaceful **Lake Tzuhu** is on the way to the dam. The lake is important for more than just scenic reasons: a mausoleum there holds the sleek black sarcophagus of President Chiang Kai-shek, who died in 1975. Formerly a meditation retreat of Chiang, Tzuhu is called the generalissimo's temporary resting place by Chinese who believe his remains will be laid to rest permanently in the KMT capital of Nanjing after the Nationalist Chinese return to the mainland. Visitors to the Tzuhu mausoleum should maintain a solemn demeanour.

UPCOUNTRY

Buddhist temples, shrines and monasteries, evoking the flavour of ancient China, dot the cool hills of **Lion's Head Mountain**, which straddles Hsinchu and Miaoli counties, about two hours south of Taipei. This mountain has some dozen temples, the oldest of which is about 70 years old. Many are set into shallow caves on the slopes. The hike begins at a stone arch at the foot of the mountain. The path leads up to the Moon Viewing Pavilion at the summit, then leads down through flower-scented forests and bamboo groves. The walk takes about three hours. Several of the temples offer food (vegetarian dinner and break-

Taipei's Grand Hotel. PHOTO: GOVERNMENT INFORMATION OFFICE

fast) and spartan, but clean lodging (a tatami room with quilts) for a suggested donation of NT$200 per person. Men and women, even if married, may not sleep in the same rooms. This does not apply to children. Yuan Kuang Temple, at the peak of the mountain, is the best place to stay.

Central Taiwan's main city is **Taichung** (population 762,000), site of the man-made harbour, one of Taiwan's Ten Great Construction Projects. Taichung is only two hours by bus or train from Taipei. The city is a convenient stepping-off point for trips to the **East-West Cross Island Highway**, **Sun Moon Lake**, **Hsitou Forest Recreation Area** and other locations in west-central Taiwan.

The most popular scenic attraction in central Taiwan is **Sun Moon Lake**, 72 kilometres from Taichung. A quiet spot ideal for hiking, the resort has satisfactory tourist accommodation and the two-hour bus ride from Taichung is both inexpensive and scenic. The resort includes an aboriginal Ami settlement that is somewhat commercial. Across the lake is the **Hsuan Tsang Temple** where a shard of the skull of Hsuan Tsang is enshrined. He was the Tang dynasty monk who carried Buddhist scriptures from India back to his homeland and is credited with the spread of the religion to China. On a cool misty day, the view of this temple and the pagoda on a peak above it is romantically picturesque, which is one reason Sun Moon Lake is Taiwan's foremost honeymoon resort.

On the outskirts of Taichung itself is the **Pao Chueh Temple** with a memorial bell tower and a 33-metre Buddha. The city of **Changhua**, not far from Taichung, is home to another large Buddha, this one 24 metres tall. Other sights nearby include the **Christian Tunghai University** with its numerous Oriental-style buildings and the notable Luce chapel designed by I.M. Pei.

Lukang, a small town just southwest of Taichung, was one of Taiwan's three earliest ports, along with Tainan in the south and Mengchia in the north. When restrictions on emigration were relaxed during the reign of Emperor Kanghsi (1662-1722), waves of Chinese immigrants from Fujian poured across the Taiwan Strait, the majority passing through Lukang. By the mid-1700s, Lukang was a major centre of commerce and shipping. Junks brought Taiwan's produce to the mainland through trade with Fujian province and returned with manufactured goods, new immigrants and artisans. The junks also carried as ballast shaped stone that later was used as construction material and is still in evidence in some of the town's buildings and pavements.

Visit the **Lukang Folk Arts Museum** (152 Chungshan Rd), housed in two buildings dating back to the Qing dynasty. The 18th century Koo Feng Lou was the original home of the Koo family and shows how people lived 200 years ago in Taiwan. **Yang Lou**, literally "foreign building," was built by a Japanese architect in the early 1900s and displays some 6,000 items, including historical documents and photographs, musical instruments, clothing and furniture.

Other points of interest in Lukang are: the **Lungshan Temple** (San Min Rd) a classic of temple architecture, built by early settlers in 1786. All the key materials were imported from the mainland; **Matsu Temple** (on the north end of Chungshan Rd) is named after the Goddess of the Sea, a popular Taoist deity. The temple was built along the coast in 1647, but later moved here and expanded. Take time to explore the back alleys of this small town, where you will find charming old structures and shops selling carved wooden furniture, oiled paper and bamboo fans, Buddhist religious effects, wood carvings, incense, kites and more.

Of Taiwan's 16 counties, **Nantou** is the only landlocked county and is perhaps the island's most scenic, containing not only Sun Moon Lake but also the **Hsitou Bamboo Forest Recreation Area**, a secluded mountain resort surrounded by ancient trees and dozens of varieties of bamboo.

Alishan is another mountain resort, perhaps Taiwan's most famous. Alishan is the name of both a range of mountain peaks flanking the rugged north-south Central Mountain Range and an aboriginal village linked by rail to the city of Chiayi in central Taiwan. The zigzag trip from Chiayi to Alishan, 2,220 metres high, takes almost four hours, during which the scenery changes from Chiayi's rice paddies and palm trees to the peak's cypresses and cedars. There are leisurely walks, a small museum of Taiwan flora and fauna and a few coal-burning locomotives still used to carry lumber and shunt cars around the Alishan station. From Alishan, visitors have a magnificent view of the sea of clouds over **Jade Mountain** (Yushan), at more than 3,997 metres the highest peak in Northeast Asia, and of the panoramic sunrise over the mountains. There is now a broad highway going to Alishan from Chiayi and continuing to the Yushan area.

East of Taichung, high in the central mountain range, is the 3,416-metre **Hohuanshan**, or Mt Hohuan, the island's only ski resort. Winter activities are normally possible in January and February and the area is good for year-round hiking. Hohuanshan is on a 42-kilometre spur of the **East-West Cross-Island Highway** that runs from Tayuling southwest to Wushe, just past the mountain spa of **Lushan**, which has hot springs and lodging. The main trunk of the East-West Highway runs from Taichung over the central mountain range to the east coast city of Hualien, via the magnificent Taroko Gorge. Visitors who take this scenic route often stop at the resort of Lishan, a half-way point that has good overnight accommodation.

An engineering marvel completed in 1960, the **East-West Highway** winds through rugged countryside, clinging to the steep mountain face and burrowing through hundreds of tunnels on its way across the island. Some 10,000 veterans of China's civil war worked more than 46 months to complete the highway at a cost of US$11 million and 460 lives. The scenery is breathtaking. Descending to Hualien, the road cuts almost vertically through heavy forest and levels out in the 19-kilometre stretch that passes through the **Taroko Gorge**. This is by far the most-travelled portion of the 192-kilometre highway and can be covered by car, bus, motorcycle or on foot. If you are pressed for time, it is possible to do a trip to Taroko within one day if you travel by plane via Hualien, the biggest city on the east coast.

The jagged mountains that separate the relatively undeveloped east coast from Taiwan's western plain are responsible for the abundant marble deposits for which Hualien is famous. They also form the breathtaking ravine at **Taroko**, considered by many to be the island's most worthwhile scenic attraction. Hualien has a village of Ami tribespeople who perform dances and songs at the **Ami Cultural Village**. A one-day tour to Hualien — including a visit to Taroko, an aboriginal performance, a tour of a marble-processing factory and showroom, and lunch — is offered daily.

If you cannot fly to Hualien, you can travel by land over the Ilan-Hualien spur of the East-West Highway on the east coast — but it's a hair-raising journey over precarious cliff faces. That trip begins at the fishing port of **Suao**, accessible from Taipei by bus or train. If you are travelling through Taroko from Hualien, taxis and buses make the four-hour trip to the **Tienhsiang Lodge**, at the western end of the gorge, and back. Taxis for this purpose are usually waiting at the airport when you arrive.

Traditional dresses and traditional dishes. PHOTO: TAO-CHUAN YEH/AFP

Fix a price with the driver before setting out.

The drive takes you north through the narrow coastal plain with the Pacific Ocean stretching out to the east and the mountains immediately inland. In some places the cliffs have fallen, leaving huge slides of marble suspended like glaciers. The road through the ravine has 38 tunnels, some with windows gouged out to provide light and ventilation. Indicate to your driver where you want to stop, though he will usually halt at the scenic points, such as the **marble bridge** and the **Eternal Spring Shrine**. The gorge winds up at **Tienhsiang**, where you can stroll over a suspension bridge to a temple and pagoda in the hills. The lodge here has overnight accommodation.

It is also possible to leave Hualien by a narrow-gauge railway, which runs down the east coast to **Taitung**. From there a bus runs around the southern coast. The entire trip can be done in one well-timed and exhausting day.

About 48 kilometres south of Taitung is **Chihpen**, a hot springs resort, an old Japanese spa popular with local tourists. There are several small hotels here offering soothing hot springs and simple accommodation.

From Taitung you can head south to **Kenting**. The sea is an attraction here and there are many good beaches dotting the coast. Since the weather is usually warm, swimming is possible throughout the year. The beautiful waters and coral reefs off the west coast are home to a multitude of colourful and exotic sea life and snorkelling and scuba-diving are popular here.

Kenting National Park, designated Taiwan's first national park in 1984, is famous for its tropical beaches and secluded coves, exotic plants, wildlife and unusual scenery.

Kenting has a variety of small hotels, bungalows, hostels and seafood restaurants. The luxury **Caesar Park Hotel** has enhanced the resort's status, though the prices are high. The best time to come to Kenting is during the week, since it is extremely crowded on weekends and holidays.

Oluanpi, the southernmost point of Taiwan, is eight kilometres south of Kenting. Marked by a lighthouse built in 1882, Oluanpi has excellent beaches for shell collecting, snorkelling and swimming — but watch out for sea snakes. On a clear day it is said that you can see across the Bashi Channel to the Philippines.

Kaohsiung (population 1.5 million) is Taiwan's second-largest city and biggest harbour. It is also the island's busiest industrial centre, encompassing a sprawling export-processing zone, aluminium-processing plants, oil and sugar refineries, the China Shipbuilding

Corp. and China Steel Corp.

Of scenic interest is **Cheng Ching Lake**, actually a man-made reservoir 10 kilometres northeast of Kaohsiung. Visitors staying at the **Kaohsiung Grand Hotel** adjoining the Cheng Ching resort can enjoy its pavilions, nine-turn bridge, tree-lined walks and famous seven-storey pagoda. Patterned after its parent hotel in Taipei, the Kaohsiung Grand is serene, removed from Kaohsiung's bustle and not far from an 18-hole golf course that hotel guests may use. The Kaohsiung area has other attractions such as **Longevity Mountain Park**, which offers a panoramic view of the city, the Buddhist **Temple to the Kings of Three Mountains** (54 Yenhuang St), the Taoist **Wen Wu shrine** (114 Fuyeh St), the **Three Phoenix Palace** (134 Hopei Rd, Section 2), where amateur folk musicians perform at intervals, and the **Spring and Autumn Towers** near the Chinese naval base of Tsoying.

If you are looking for an historical milieu, however, travel on to Tainan (population 655,000) just a short distance north of Kaohsiung. The oldest city in **Taiwan**, Tainan was the capital of the island for 203 years, from 1684 to 1887. The city is best known both for its colourful history, kept alive by the many historical sites that dot its maze of tiny lanes and streets, and for the many cultural and religious traditions that continue to thrive here.

Tainan is linked closely with the memory of Koxinga, the Ming loyalist who ousted the Dutch colonists in 1662. Koxinga landed in Tainan in 1661 and established his administrative and military centre in **Fort Provintia** (212 Mintsu Rd) after ousting the Dutch. Relics of the Dutch occupation include the site of Fort Provintia, now called **Chihkan Tower**, and Fort Zeelandia (28 Kuoshen Rd, Anping District). Built originally in 1632 with bricks imported from Holland, Zeelandia has been completely restored and the only authentic original relics left are remnants of an ancient wall. The fort is connected by an underground passage to the site of Provintia, which houses nine carved stone turtles with stele inscribed in the old Manchu script by order of Qing dynasty Emperor Chien Lung in 1786. A short distance from Zeelandia is Yi Tsai Chin Cheng, a fort built in 1875 to beef up Taiwan's coastal defences.

Tainan's **Confucius Temple** (2 Nanmen Rd), built in 1665 by the son of Koxinga, is the oldest of its kind on the island. Its grounds have traditionally offered a timeless sense of peace to visitors.

Tainan is called "The City of 100 Temples" (though there actually are some 300). Among them are: the **Koxinga Shrine** (152 Kaishan Rd), where Koxinga is worshipped as a deity; the bustling **Tien Tan Temple** (No. 16, Lane 90, Chungyi Rd) dedicated to the Jade Emperor; the **Kai Yuan Temple** (Kai Yuan Rd), reportedly built in 1685 as a home for one of Koxinga's concubines; and the charming **Shrine of the Five Concubines**, the site of the tomb of five female loyalists who committed suicide when the last Ming stronghold on Taiwan surrendered to the Qing dynasty in 1683.

Just off the main island of Taiwan are several smaller islands of interest. Penghu, also known as the **Pescadores**, is an archipelago in the Taiwan Strait, half-way between Taiwan and the Chinese mainland. Daily flights land in the major city of Makung, which has a bustling fish market, ancient temples, picturesque farms, fishing villages and delicious seafood. The sights include a sacred banyan tree with roots stretching over a one-acre temple courtyard, the long inter-island **Penghu Bay Bridge** and a temple dedicated to Matsu, Goddess of the Sea. Built during the Ming dynasty (1368-1644), this structure is the oldest Matsu temple in Taiwan and its unspoiled appearance is a refreshing change from some of the gaudier Taipei temples. Do not travel to Penghu from October to March because the winds at that time are uncomfortably fierce.

Off the southeast coast of Taiwan is **Lanyu**, or **Orchid Island**, inhabited by less than 3,000 members of the Yami aboriginal tribe. The Yami — not to be confused with the Ami aborigine tribe — are just starting to adopt the trappings of modern civilization. Even so, you may still see them wearing their traditional loincloths, going out in their traditional black-and-white canoes and living in stone houses built in pits to protect them from periodic typhoons. The beaches, orchids and butterflies are notable. A word of caution. The Yami do not like to have their photographs taken, so ask permission before using a camera. A modern hotel and one or two guesthouses on the island offer acceptable accommodation. To the north of Lanyu, and just off the eastern coast, is **Green Island**, known for its attractive coastal scenery and prison that once held the island's political offenders. Light aircraft make numerous runs from Taitung to both of these islands each day. The trip takes 15-30 minutes.

RESTAURANT SELECTION

Average price for two

TAIPEI

AN LO YUAN, 232 Tunhua North Rd. Tel: 715 4929. Cantonese. US$60.
CASA MIA, 628 Linsen North Rd. Tel: 596 4636. Italian. US$50.
CELESTIAL KITCHEN, 3/F, 1 Nanking West Rd. Tel: 563 2171. Beijing. US$60.
CHALET SWISS, 47 Nanking East Rd, Section 4. Tel: 715 2051. Swiss-German. US$80.
CHI-CHIA CHUANG, 45 Changchun Rd. Tel: 581 4360. Taiwanese. US$30.
KING JAIN, 21, Lane 107, Fuhsing South Rd, Section 1. Tel: 721 8653. Beijing. US$45.
HAKKA CUISINE, 58 Tungteng St. Tel: 704 7459. Hakka. US$30.
SHOULAN GOURMET, 118 Minsheng East Rd, Section 3. Tel: 712 5775. Jiangsu and Zhejiang. US$60.
MEI LIN, 14 Peiping East Rd. Tel: 391 0833. Chinese vegetarian. US$20.
PENGYUAN, 63 Nanking East Rd, Section 4. Tel: 541 9102. Hunan. US$80.
PONDOK MUTIARA, 292 Fuhsing North Rd. Tel: 508 1466. Indonesian. US$30.
TO-IT-TRUE, 506 Jenai Rd, Section 4. Tel: 729 7853. Beijing. US$35.

KAOHSIUNG

BEAUTIFUL GARDEN, 169 Chungcheng Rd. Tel: 224 6321. Taiwanese. US$65.
HAI PA WANG, 2 Hsingchung 2nd Rd. Tel: 333 4486. Taiwanese seafood. US$25.

TAICHUNG

BAMBOO GARDEN, 379 Wuchuang Rd. Tel: 201 3670. Taiwanese *dim sum*, seafood. US$28.
CHUANG-YUAN LOU, 10/F, 87 Mingchuan Rd. Tel: 223 0806. Jiangsu/Zhejiang. US$30.
PIG & WHISTLE, 394 Ying Tsai Rd. Tel: 322 6555. English. US$40.

TAINAN

BEIPING YIMU YUAN, 135 Tungning Rd. Tel: 238 8720. Beijing. US$15.
RONGHSING, 56 Chungcheng Rd. Tel: 221 3134. Sichuan. US$45.

HOTEL GUIDE

ALISHAN

D: US$75 and below

ALISHAN HOTEL, 2 West Alishan, Hsiang-lin Village. Tel: (05) 267 9811, Fax: 267 9596. *R: C, W.*

CHIAYI

D: US$75 and below

GALLANT HOTEL, 257 Wenhua Rd. Tel: (05) 223 5366, Fax: 223 9522, Tlx: 72789. *R: C, W.*

HUALIEN

B: US$100-175

CHINATRUST HUALIEN, 2 Yunghsing Rd. Tel: (038) 221171, Fax: 221185, Tlx: 11144. *P, SatTV. R: C, W.*

KAOHSIUNG

B: US$100-175

AMBASSADOR, 202 Minsheng Second Rd. Tel: (07) 211 5211, Fax: 281 1115, Tlx: 72105. *P, Gym, Biz, SatTV. R: C, W.*
GRAND HOTEL, 2 Yuanshan Rd, Tahwa Chuen, Niew Soong Shian. Tel: (07) 383 5911, Fax: 381 4889, Tlx: 7123. *P, Gym, SatTV. R: C, W.*
HOLIDAY GARDEN, 279 Liuho Second Rd. Tel: (07) 241 0121, Fax: 251 2000, Tlx: 81948. *P, Biz, SatTV. R: C, W.*

C: US$75-100

BUCKINGHAM, 394 Chihsian Rd. Tel: (07) 282 2151, Fax: 281 4540, Tlx: 71500. *R: W.*
SUMMIT HOTEL, 426 Chiuju First Rd. Tel: (07) 384 5526, Fax: 384 4739, Tlx: 72423. *R: C, W.*

KENTING

A: US$175 and above

P — Swimming pool | **Gym** — Health club | **Biz** — Business centre | **SatTV** — Satellite TV
R — Restaurant | **C** — Chinese food | **W** — Western food

HOTEL GUIDE

CAESAR PARK, 6 Kenting Rd, Hengchun Township. Tel: (08) 886 1888, Fax: 886 1818, Tlx: 28029. *P, Gym, Biz, SatTV. R: C, W.*

D: US$75 and below

KENTING HOUSE, 451 Kenting Rd, Hengchun Township. Tel: (08) 888 1301, Fax: 886 1377. *R: C, W.*

PESCADORES (PENGHU ISLAND)

D: US$75 and below

HOTEL CHANG CHUN, 6, Chungcheng Rd, Makung. Tel: (06) 927 3336, Fax: 926 2112. *R: C, W.*

PAO HWA HOTEL, 2 Chungcheng Rd, Makung. Tel: (06) 927 4881, Fax: 927 4889. *R: C, W.*

SUN MOON LAKE

D: US$75 and below

EVERGREEN HOTEL, 142 Chung Hsing Rd. Tel: (049) 855311, Fax: 855314. *R: C, W.*

CHINATRUST HOTEL (SUN MOON LAKE), 23 Chungcheng Rd. Tel: (049) 855911, Fax: 855268. *P. R: C.*

TAICHUNG

B: US$100-175

EVERGREEN LAUREL HOTEL, 6, Chung Kang Rd, Section 2. Tel: (04) 382 9988, Fax: 328 6642. *P, Gym, Biz, Ex, SatTV. R: C, W.*

C: US$75-100

TAICHUNG HOTEL, 87 Minchuan Rd. Tel: (04) 242121, Fax: 224 9946, Tlx: 51134. *R: C, W.*

TAINAN

D: US$75 and below

HOTEL TAINAN, 1 Chengkung Rd. Tel: (06) 228 9101, Fax: 226 8502, Tlx: 71365. *P, SatTV. R: C, W.*

REDHILL HOTEL, 46 Chengkung Rd. Tel: (06) 225 8121, Fax: 221 6711, Tlx: 73591. *SatTV. R: C, W.*

TAIPEI

A: US$175 and above

ASIAWORLD PLAZA, 100 Tunhwa N. Rd. Tel: (02) 715 0077, Fax: 713 4148, Tlx: 26299. *P, Gym, Biz, SatTV. R: C, W.*

FAR EASTERN PLAZA HOTEL, 201 Tunhwa S. Rd, Section 2. Tel: (02)378 8888, Fax: 377 7777, Tlx: 26376. *P, Gym, Biz, Ex, SatTV. R: C, W.*

GRAND HYATT, 2 Sungshou Rd. Tel: (02) 720 1234, Fax: 720 1111. *P, Gym, Biz, Ex. SatTV. R: C, W.*

HILTON, 38 Chunghsiao W. Rd, Section 1. Tel: (02) 311 5151, Fax: 331 9944, Tlx: 11699. *P, Gym, Biz, Ex, SatTV. R: C, W.*

HOTEL ROYAL, 37-1 Chungshan N. Rd, Section 2. Tel: (02) 542 3266, Fax: 543 4897, Tlx: 23915. *P, Gym, Biz, Ex, SatTV. R: C, W.*

HOWARD PLAZA, 160 Jenai Rd, Section 3. Tel: (02) 700 2323, Fax: 700 0729, Tlx: 10702. *P, Gym, Biz, Ex, SatTV. R: C, W.*

LAI LAI SHERATON, 12 Chunghsiao E. Rd, Section 1. Tel: (02) 321 5511, Fax: 394 4240, Tlx: 23939. *P, Gym, Biz, Ex, SatTV. R: C, W.*

GRAND FORMOSA REGENT, 41 Chungshan N. Rd, Section 2. Tel: (02) 523 8000, Fax: 523 2828, Tlx: 20385. *P, Gym, Biz, Ex, SatTV. R: C, W.*

RITZ HOTEL, 41 Minchuan E. Rd, Section 2. Tel: (02) 597 1234, Fax: 596 9223, Tlx: 27345. *Gym, Biz, SatTV. R: C, W.*

SHERWOOD HOTEL, 110, Section 3, Minsheng E. Rd. Tel: (02) 718 1188, Fax: 713 0707. *P, Gym, Biz, SatTV. R: C, W.*

B: US$100-175

AMBASSADOR, 63 Chungshan N. Rd, Section 2. Tel: (02) 551 1111, Fax: 531 5215, Tlx: 11255. *P, Biz, SatTV. R: C, W.*

GRAND HOTEL, 1 Chungshan N. Rd, Section 4. Tel: (02) 596 5565, Fax: 594 8243, Tlx: 11646. *P, Gym, Biz, SatTV. R: C, W.*

REBAR HOLIDAY INN CROWNE PLAZA HOTEL, 32 Nanking E. Rd, Section 5. Tel: (02) 763 5656, Fax: 767 9347, Tlx: 14207. *Gym, Biz, SatTV. R: C, W.*

C: US$75-100

CHINA HOTEL, 14 Kuanchien Rd. Tel: (02) 331 9521, Fax: 381 2349, Tlx: 21757. *SatTV. R: C, W.*

TAIPEI FORTUNA HOTEL, 122 Chungshan N. Rd, Section 2. Tel: (02) 563 1111, Fax: 561 9777, Tlx: 21578. *Gym, Biz, SatTV. R: C, W.*

D: US$75 and below

BAGUIO, 367 Pateh Rd, Section 2. Tel: (02) 781 3121, Fax: 771 8796. *R: W.*

P — Swimming pool
Gym — Health club
Biz — Business centre
Ex — Executive floor
SatTV — Satellite TV
R — Restaurant
C — Chinese food
W — Western food

Bengali New Year festival in Dhaka. PHOTO: MUFTY MUNIR/AFP

ALL-ASIA TRAVEL GUIDE

SOUTH ASIA

BANGLADESH

Situated at the confluence of the mighty Ganges and Brahmaputra rivers, occupying the huge delta that they form, much of Bangladesh lies at most only a few metres above sea level, subject to the vagaries of monsoon and cyclone. But the capital, Dhaka, boasts many Moghul buildings and the port city Chittagong some fine mosques, while at Cox's Bazar there are 100 kilometres of beaches.

A bitter and bloody nine-month war of independence in 1971 resulted in the birth of Bangladesh, one of Asia's youngest nations. Originally part of Pakistan, the Bengali-speaking people rose in revolt following a Pakistani army crackdown at midnight on March 25, 1971 and declared their independence on December 16.

Independence, however, failed to resolve most of the country's problems. About a seventh of the country's 55,000 square kilometres are under water. Regular flooding and other natural calamities, such as cyclones and drought, wipe out crops and livestock on a virtually annual basis. Although vast amounts of foreign aid have been pumped into Bangladesh, it has not yet fully negated the massive damage wrought during the war of independence.

For nearly four years after independence, Bangladesh had a stable though indifferent political life. However, in August 1975 the nation's leader, Sheikh Mujibur Rahman, was assassinated in a coup that ended the Awami League's rule. Khandker Mushtaq Ahmed, a member of Mujib's cabinet, took over but only lasted 11 weeks in power until he was removed by another putsch on November

BANGLADESH
NEPAL
Chilhat
Kurigram
Rangpur
Biral
Brahmaputra R.
INDIA
Phulchari
Bahadurabad Ghat
Mahasthan
Chhatak
Sylhet
Mohanganj
Amnura
Bogra
Mymensingh
Rajshahi
Madhupur
Sirajganj
Ganges R.
Ishurdi
Bhairab Bazar
Dhaka
Brahman Baria
Narayanganj
Meghna R.
Mainamati
INDIA
Comilla
Jessore
Benapol
Maijdi
Khulna
Chalna
Rangamati
Sundarbans
Kaptai
Chittagong
Bay of Bengal
Ramu
Cox's Bazar
Roads
Railways
Airport
km
0
100
Nhile
Teknaf
BURMA

4, 1975. Three days later Maj.-Gen. Ziaur Rahman was installed in office with the backing of the armed forces. Although Justice A.M. Sayem held the title of president, the country was under the de facto rule of a three-man martial law administration made up of the three armed forces chiefs.

In late 1976, Zia became the chief martial-law administrator. In April 1977 he took over the presidency from Sayem, who retired on health grounds. In May 1977, Zia held a referendum on his appointment as president and promised to hold a general election by the end of 1978. Zia was elected president in June 1978 for a five-year term under free elections. He also kept his promise by holding a general election for a 300-seat parliament in February 1979. Zia subsequently withdrew martial law rule following the first session of the newly elected parliament in March 1979.

However, another group of army officers attempted a coup and murdered Zia while he was visiting Chittagong on May 30, 1981. The attempt ended in failure, and the rebel leader was killed by a loyal officer.

Vice-president Abdus Sattar took over and was elected president in November 1981, but on March 24, 1982 the chief of the army staff, Lieut.-Gen. H.M. Ershad, seized power.

Ershad held parliamentary polls to elect a 300-seat house on May 7, 1986, which the government-backed Jatiya Party won with a simple majority. Ershad resigned from the army and was elected president on October 15, 1986. Following violent anti-government agitation in November 1987 by the mainstream opposition parties, a state of emergency was proclaimed at the end of that month and parliament was dissolved soon afterwards.

The March 1988 parliamentary elections were boycotted by the main opposition parties and the ruling Jatiya Party gained a two-thirds majority. Ershad was forced to stand down in the face of widespread unrest in late 1990. In a general election held on February 27, 1991 Khaleda Zia, a long-standing opponent of Ershad, led her Bangladesh Nationalist Party to power. In September 1994 the country's constitution was amended to end 16 years of executive presidential rule, returning Bangladesh to a Westminster-style of governance.

History

The region's history dates from the early Gupta period (fourth century AD) when there were already established kingdoms, notably the Samatata in the delta of the Brahmaputra River. Excavations at the two important sites of Mainamati and Paharpur have revealed significant Buddhist structures dating from at least as early as the seventh century.

The region was linked with the other Bengali-speaking people of eastern India from the 18th century until the creation of the eastern wing of Pakistan on August 14, 1947. Muslim influence dates from around the 13th century, when the Turks, under the suzerainty of the Delhi Emperor Ghori, captured Bengal. The Muslim faith of eastern Bengal was to continue under the Moghuls and the British, and provided the rationale for this ethnically distinct people to join those from the other side of the Subcontinent to make up the state of Pakistan.

The union, however, was not to last. The economically neglected people of East Pakistan had demanded a measure of autonomy from the earliest stages of independence from the British *raj*. Events leading to the dismemberment of Pakistan began in December 1970, when President Yahya Khan held the first free election in the country's history. The Awami League won a landslide victory in East Pakistan and, partly because of the numerical supremacy of the eastern over the western wing, became qualified to form a new government of Pakistan.

Bangladesh dates its independence from March 26, 1971 when Maj.-Gen. Ziaur Rahman announced the country's independence over a clandestine radio operating from the Chittagong area. Zia made the announcement in the name of Sheik Mujibur Rahman, then the undisputed leader of the country. Just over a decade later, rebel army officers assassinated him in Chittagong on May 30, 1981.

Entry

Dhaka can be reached by air from almost anywhere in the world. It is served by Biman Bangladesh Airlines, the national flag carrier. International airlines serving Dhaka include Air-India, Indian Airlines, Pakistan International Airlines, Royal Nepal Airlines, Singapore Airlines, Thai International, Gulf Air, Emirates, Kuwait Airways, Saudia and British Airways.

Overland routes are generally confined to road and rail links from the Indian state of West Bengal, and by road only from Assam and Tripura states — though the land route from Assam is often difficult to negotiate. There is no overland route to Burma from Bangladesh. Entry by sea is normally confined to the country's major port city of Chittagong and through Chalna near the Sundarbans.

Immigration

Passports are required of all visitors, and must be valid for three months beyond the intended length of stay. Nationals of India must have their passports specially endorsed for Bangladesh at any Indian regional passport office.

All foreign visitors should obtain a visa unless otherwise exempted. The list of exemptions is long, but complex because of difference lengths of stay permitted — this information can be obtained by contacting the nearest Bangladesh Embassy or diplomatic mission. For nationals of countries without any Bangladesh representation, 15-day visas may be obtained at Dhaka and Chittagong airports. Further extensions may be subsequently granted for up to three months.

Health

Travellers coming from yellow fever infected areas must possess a certificate showing inoculation against the disease.

Customs

Visitors may bring in duty-free 200 cigarettes, 50 cigars or 227 grams of tobacco, one small bottle of perfume, two bottles of liquor or wine and reasonable quantities of personal belongings. Items such as cameras, portable typewriters and radios will usually be recorded at the point of entry to ensure their re-export. Those wishing to bring motor vehicles into Bangladesh via India should be in possession of the usual international carnet de passage.

Currency

The taka is the unit of currency. In March 1995 the official exchange rate was Taka 40.10:US$1. The taka is divided into 100 poisha. Notes of Taka 5, 10, 20, 50, 100 and 500 denomination and coins of 5, 10, 25 and 50 poisha are in circulation.

Any amount of foreign currency may be brought into the country, but local currency is restricted to Taka 100 only. Foreign currency not exceeding US$1,000 does not have to be declared. Foreign currency up to the amount declared on arrival may be taken out of the country.

Currency declaration forms will be collected on departure and should tally with the amount of cash held by the traveller. When leaving the country, a visitor may reconvert up to Taka 500 — or 25% of the total amount of foreign exchange changed during a stay — into a convertible currency.

Language

While Bangla (Bengali) is the official language, English is widely used by officials. An English-speaking visitor will have no problem finding someone speaking English, even in the villages.

Climate

The climate is semi-tropical, with an average annual rainfall in Dhaka of 190 centimetres, most of which falls during the mid-May to early October monsoon season. April and September are the hottest months in the capital, when the temperatures may exceed 38°C with high humidity, though in recent years the humidity seems to have reduced somewhat.

The weather is quite pleasant from November through March, with daytime temperature maximums in the range of 20-26°C. Evenings are cool in this period and temperatures may fall to 10°C or even lower.

Dress

Except for the winter November-March months, easily laundered clothing is suitable throughout the country. Light woollens are

Dhaka street stall. PHOTO: KEES

required for the winter months, especially in the evening.

Business Hours

Government offices are open 8:30 a.m.-2:30 p.m. Saturday to Thursday. They are closed on Friday, as are the offices of international firms and embassies — most of which remain closed on Saturday as well.

Commercial offices are open 9 a.m.-5 p.m. with a 1 p.m.-2 p.m. lunch break. All firms are closed on Friday, and most firms work only to 1 p.m. on Thursday.

Banks are open 9 a.m.-3 p.m. Saturday to Wednesday and up to noon on Thursday. Post offices work government hours, though major post offices stay open until 8 p.m. and some telegraph offices in Dhaka and Chittagong never close.

Most shops in Dhaka and the main towns are open 9 a.m.-8 p.m., work a half-day on Thursday and remain closed on Friday. However, some markets, such as Dhaka Government New Market, are open on Fridays and closed on Tuesdays. Restaurants, with the exception of larger hotels, close by 9 p.m. The few bars are open 11 a.m.-3 p.m. and 6-11 p.m. All bars are closed on Friday, but hotel guests can order drinks in their rooms.

Doing Business

Bangladesh blends the old ways with the modern and any business people you are likely to come into contact with will be well-educated with knowledge of Western ways.

There will be a handshake as a greeting — yours should be firm for a man but a mere touch for a woman. There are few women in Bangladeshi business but visiting businesswomen will be greeted courteously.

Light suits should be worn for first meetings but something less formal such as a safari suit can be worn later.

The pace of life and business is leisurely and there is no point in trying to rush anything, partly because of the local culture and partly because of the poor infrastructure which makes communications and travel slow.

Hospitality will be warm, usually at a hotel, but no alcohol will be served and public drinking should be avoided.

Rip-Offs

There is very little tourism of an organized kind in Bangladesh, and as yet taxi drivers and traders at all levels have not adopted the outlook and practices of those in other Asian places where fleecing the visitor is a way of life. However, visitors would do well to reject unsolicited offers of help at the airport on arrival.

Since Bangladesh is a poor country, obviously large amounts of money can be a temptation and bundles of notes should not be displayed. Also, care should be taken against the opportunist pickpocket. As long as visitors are not fools, there is no reason to assume they will be cheated.

Communications

International communications to and from Bangladesh have developed considerably, though there is still a lot of room for improvement, with a shortage of international lines causing congestion. Sometimes it takes repeated efforts to get a telephone or fax line out even from Dhaka. The situation is much worse from elsewhere in the country.

Transport

Transport facilities, both surface and air, have improved tremendously over the past few years. It is now possible to travel virtually anywhere in the country by car from Dhaka, a major achievement considering the country's topography.

Biman Bangladesh Airlines, with DC10s and other modern aircraft, operates two daily flights between Dhaka and Calcutta — a third is operated Indian Airlines. These two carriers also run two flights a week between Chittagong and Calcutta, while Biman and Air-India each fly twice weekly between Dhaka and New Delhi. Biman's international network includes regular flights to London, Rome, Athens, Amsterdam, Paris, Frankfurt, New York, Tripoli, several Middle Eastern destinations, Rangoon, Kuala Lumpur, Karachi, Singapore, Bangkok, Hong Kong and Kathmandu.

An airport tax of Taka 300 is charged on all passengers leaving Dhaka by an international flight.

TRANSPORT IN DHAKA

FROM THE AIRPORT: A taxi is the usual means of transportation from the airport, though minibuses are also available. Taxis normally charge Taka 250 from the Zia International Airport to the city hotels. Bangladesh Parjatan Corp. (BPC, the government tourist organization) runs cheaper pick-up services between the city's main hotels and the airport. A number of small private hire-car firms are also available, but though they are cheaper than the BPC, they are not as reliable.

TAXIS: Taxi stands are located in Dhaka at the Sheraton, Sonargaon, Purbani and Sundarbans hotels and the airport. Check the fare for the journey with the hotel reception desk and bargain with the taxi driver before setting out.

HIRE CARS: BPC runs regular car rental services, including transfers from airport to hotels. The charge is Taka 100 (air-conditioned) and Taka 80 (non-air-conditioned) an hour, plus Taka 12 and Taka 9 per kilometre with a minimum charge of Taka 594 and Taka 462 respectively. BPC charges Taka 145 and Taka 110 per hour and Taka 25 per kilometre and Taka 15 per kilometre respectively for its air-conditioned and non-air-conditioned microbuses.

RICKSHAWS: Pedal trishaws are the most convenient way to travel in the city for short distances and are readily available. Fares are Taka 4-5 per kilometre, to be negotiated before the journey starts to avoid disputes at the end. It is always better to ask your hotel reception desk for advice on such fares. In any event, rickshaws are not very expensive.

MOTOR RICKSHAWS (SCOOTERS/BABY TAXIS): Fares are about Taka 4-5 per kilometre and should be negotiated beforehand — the minimum fare is Taka 20. Although they are faster than trishaws, motor rickshaws are not easily available and are extremely noisy.

BUSES: City buses are always crowded, though the slightly more expensive minibuses are a viable option to rickshaws outside peak travel times. The bus fare is 47 poisha per kilometre while minibuses charge a little more.

RIVER BOATS: Non-motorized boats can be hired at about Taka 30-35 per hour, but motor boats are not easily available for hire except through the BPC at Dhaka and Rangamati.

TRANSPORT UPCOUNTRY

Although Bangladesh is criss-crossed with numerous waterways, one can now travel either by rail or road from Dhaka to any part of the country. Despite a number of ferry crossings on certain routes, no place in the country is more than 12 hours by car from Dhaka. Only during

Country boy market-bound. PHOTO: KEES ▶

the height of he monsoon season and because of sudden floods are road links disrupted.

BUSES: The government-owned **Bangladesh Road Transport Corp.** runs regular bus services between the main cities and towns and into outlying areas. These buses are reasonably comfortable and give the visitor a chance to see more of the countryside. Fares are extremely low, but in some cases seats must be booked in advance. A large number of private operators also run dependable bus services between Dhaka and other parts of the country. Express buses, some of them air-conditioned, are perhaps the best alternative for the visitor as they do not carry more passengers than seats available.

TRAINS: A fairly well-organized railway system provides a cheap and relatively comfortable service. There are now several express services between Dhaka and other major cities, with air-conditioned coaches available during the summer season.

WATER TRANSPORT: Boats of all kinds operate throughout the country and local inquiries are necessary for routes and prices. Of special note, however, is the 18-hour Rocket steamer service which runs daily between Dhaka and the southern Sundarbans town of Khulna. All first-class bookings, which cost about Taka 2,000 for the round trip, must be made in advance. The food available on board is excellent.

AIR: Biman provides domestic air services from Dhaka to Chittagong, Sylhet, Jessore, Saidpur, Rajshahi and Cox's Bazar. Internal airfares in Bangladesh are exceptionally low, so advance bookings are essential.

Tours

BPC offers sightseeing tours around Dhaka and Chittagong. Upcountry tours can be arranged by BPC, which also provides bilingual guides for tourist groups. BPC has offices in Chittagong, Cox's Bazar, Kaptai, Rangamati, Bogra, Sylhet, Rajshahi and Khulna.

Accommodation

The **Sheraton**, **Sonargaon** and **Purbani** hotels in Dhaka and the hotel **Agrabad** in Chittagong, offer international-class accommodation. Also at the top of the range, a new 450-bed **Hyatt Regency** was being built in early 1995, and should be open in 1997.

A number of inexpensive but clean hotels have been built in Dhaka and Chittagong to meet the increased number of budget-conscious travellers, while government and semi-government corporation resthouses all over Bangladesh offer reasonable — if simple — accommodation. BPC-owned motels at Cox's Bazar, Rangamati, Chittagong, Khulna, Bogra and Rajshahi offer air-conditioned rooms and suites. Bookings can be made in advance in Dhaka.

Dining

Western food is available in all major hotels and most of the big restaurants in the main cities, but local dishes are normally far more interesting. The local cuisine in based around chicken, mutton, beef, seafood and vegetable curries accompanied by rice or breads in myriad forms. There are also numerous Chinese restaurants in Dhaka, and a new one seems to open each month. Imported alcoholic beverages are expensive. Scotch whisky, for example, will cost around US$4.50 for a small measure and a can of imported beer almost the same in big hotels — though they are considerably cheaper outside the hotels, at the few bars in the city. Although there is no locally brewed beer, Bangladesh produces good-quality gin, vodka, rum and whisky.

Entertainment

There is very little in terms of regular nightlife in Bangladesh. Several top hotels have a band and vocalists in the bar and in the dining room and also put on weekly or bi-weekly special shows. A few dozen theatrical groups perform in Dhaka daily, including the occasional play in English. There are more than 300 cinemas throughout the country showing mostly Bengali films, though English-language films are screened. December and January are good months for entertainment with folk music, dances and country fairs. In Dhaka, a month-long national theatre festival is held each year from mid-January. Similar festivals are also organized in most important cities and towns.

On Thursday evenings (Friday being a day off) a few privately organized disco parties are arranged in Dhaka and Chittagong, with alcoholic drinks at half the hotel bar prices. Hotels can arrange admission. These are reckoned to be fairly safe events, frequented by younger people.

PHOTO: KEES

Just messing about on the river.

Shopping

Browsing in the bazaars for local items is the best way to shop in Bangladesh. The famous Dhaka muslin is worth looking for, while Rajshahi silk and homespun *khadi*-cotton textiles are good buys.

Those who are prepared to spend a little more can purchase pink pearls. Unusual jute goods, cottage industry and handicraft products, also attract visitors. Ready-made shirts and *kurtas* of raw silk and khadi products are available in many shops.

Sports

A trip by launch through the waterways that lattice the densely forested Sundarbans may allow a visitor to see the famous Royal Bengal Tigers, spotted deer and crocodiles. More conventionally, golfers can choose between the **Dhaka Club's course** (only nine holes) and the **Kurmitola Golf Club** (18 holes). The Bhatiary Golf Club in Chittagong can be used by visitors by appointment.

For tennis, contact the **Bangladesh Lawn Tennis Federation**, about 100 metres from Dhaka's Sheraton Hotel.

The Dhaka Club, next to the Lawn Tennis Federation, also provides playing facilities for tennis and squash. Many of the bigger hotels also have sporting facilities.

Holidays

Festivals and holidays combine observance of religious occasions and significant events in the nation's history. The former are dependent on the lunar calendar and vary, while the latter fall on fixed dates.

Variables: Eidul Fitr; Eidul Azha; Eid-i-Mila-dun-nabi; Birthday of the Prophet Mohammad.
February 21: Shaheed (Martyr's) Day.
March 26: Independence Day.
Bengali New Year: variable but usually around April 15-16.
May 1: May Day.
October: Durga Puja.
December 16: Victory Day.
December 25: Christmas Day.

ADDRESSES

BPC's head office is at 233 Airport Rd, Tejgaon, Dhaka 1215. Tel: (8802) 817855-9, 325155-9, Fax: 817235, Cable: PARJATAN, DHAKA, Tlx: 642206 TOUR BJ.

Tourist information centres in **Dhaka**: Airport, Tel: 894416. Dhaka Sheraton Hotel, Tel: 509479, 863391. Hotel Sonargaon, Tel: 811641-9.

Regional BPC offices are at **Chittagong**: Motel Shaikat, Station Rd, Tel: 209514, 209845, 220181-5. **Cox's Bazar**: Hotel Shaibul, Motel Rd, Tel: 3274-5. **Bogra:** Parjatan Motel, Tel: 6733. **Rangamati**: Deer Park, Tel: 3126. **Sylhet**: Parjatan Motel, Tel: 2426. **Rangpur:** Parjatan Motel, Tel: 3681, 2111, 3900 and 2911. **Moulvi Bazar:** Parjatan Motel, Tel: 350. **Khulna**: Parjatan Motel, Banani, Tel: 5044. **Rajshahi**: Parjatan Motel, Tel: 5492.

DISCOVERING BANGLADESH

DHAKA

While what is known as the city of Dhaka was founded in 1608 by the Moghuls, there are records suggesting a thriving town existed in the same place as early as the 11th century. It is said that nothing of that period survived because of a great fire. However, many interesting structures built by the Moghuls have survived, notably in the Old City.

In the west of the old city is the **Lalbagh (Red Garden) Fort**, which was built by Prince Mohammad Azam, son of the Moghul Emperor Aurangzeb in 1678. Next to the fort is the **Pari Bibi's Mazar** (Tomb of the Fair Lady), daughter of the Moghul governor at that time. The **Chawk**, or Old Market Place, is a large square from which four bazaars lead off in different directions. Shops and houses crowd all around and the area has a good many mosques, including the **Chawk Masjid** built in 1676.

There are as many as 700 mosques in regular use in Dhaka. The most significant are the **Baitul Mokarram**, the **University Mosque**, the **Kar Talab** (built in 1709), the **Star Mosque** and the Saat Gambuz (Seven Domes) Mosque.

Dhaka University's **Curzon Hall**, a blend of Western and Moghul architecture, is worth a visit, as is the nearby **Dhaka Museum** with its collection of stone, metal and wood sculptures, paintings and coins.

UPCOUNTRY

About 16 kilometres south of Dhaka on the banks of the Sitalakhya River is the town of **Narayanganj**, the largest inland river port in the country whose harbour swarms with hundreds of small boats bringing jute to the town's mills. Just a few miles away is the ancient town of **Sonargaon**, the seat of the first Pala Dynasty, which ruled from the seventh to 10th centuries. A number of monuments and shrines from that time are still intact. Bangladesh's only **Museum of Folk Art and Culture** has been set up at Sonargaon.

Approximately 80 kilometres to the east is the township of **Comilla**, lying almost on the eastern border with India. Some eight kilometres outside the town are the important archaeological sites of **Mainamati** and **Lalmai**. Believed to be the remains of the then political and cultural centre of the region, the structures run for about 17 kilometres along a ridge. Most are unexcavated, but the sites known as **Salban Vihara**, with a museum (closed on Thursdays), are fully accessible.

Chittagong, on the shores of the Bay of Bengal in southeastern Bangladesh, is the country's biggest port and second-largest city. The **Chandanpura**, **Shah Jame** and **Kadam Mubarak** mosques are of particular interest — Kadam Mubarak contains a slab bearing what is claimed to be the footprint of the Prophet Mohammad.

The **Chittagong Hill Tracts** start north of the city. Kaptai (56 kilometres from Chittagong) and **Rangamati** (72 kilometres) are both located on the shores of the 663-square-kilometre Kaptai Lake. A dam on the reaches of the Karnaphuly River has created the largest man-made lake in the Subcontinent. There are modern air-conditioned resthouses and bungalows, and yachting, boating, fishing and water-skiing on the lake. Inquire in Chittagong at the tourist office for information regarding renting accommodation. Several hill tribes, some of whom are Buddhists, live in this area. The **Murong** and **Mogh** people are particularly worth visiting.

About 150 kilometres south of Chittagong is **Cox's Bazar** with its 100-kilometre-long natural beach. The inhabitants of the area are a mixture of Muslims, Hindus and Buddhists, the latter migrants of Burmese and Arakanese origin. Colourful and architecturally interesting Buddhist temples, known as *kyangs*, are found in Cox's Bazar and in the villages of **Ramu**, **Teknaf** and **Nhila** to the south. Cox's Bazar has a modern complex of hotels and motels run by BPC. Resthouses also provide reasonable accommodation.

Sylhet, nestling among the tea estates in the picturesque **Surma Valley**, is the main town of the country's northeast. Access is easiest by air or rail. About 130 kilometres northwest of Dhaka is the **Modhupur National Park and Forest Area**, where there are hunting lodges and resthouses for overnight stays.

DHAKA RESTAURANT SELECTION

Average price for two

ABAKASH, Mohakhali Commercial Area, Mohakhali, Dhaka. Tel: 607085-9. Bangladeshi, North Indian. Taka 700.
CAFE JHEEL, Mitijheel Commercial Area. Tel: 230617. Bangladeshi, North Indian. Taka 400.
COCKPIT, Hotel Pritom Bldg, Topkhana Rd, Dhaka. Tel: 233057. Bangladeshi, European. Taka 500.
GRILL HOUSE, 18, Kemal Ataturk Ave, Banani, Dhaka. Tel: 804015. European. Taka 800.
MOGHUL ROOM, 18 Kemal Ata Turk Ave. Tel: 884015. Subcontinental dishes. Taka 600.
PANDA GARDEN, Abbas Garden, Mahakhali, Dhaka. Tel: 608458. Sichuan, Peking cuisine. Taka 800.
ROYAL ORCHID, Gulshan Ave, Gulshan, Dhaka. Tel: 605373. Thai, Chinese. Taka 900.
SEA FOOD RESTAURANT, 76/A Gulshan Ave, Gulshan, Dhaka. Tel: 606175. Thai, Chinese. Taka 900.
SHANGRI-LA ABEDIN TOWER, 35, Kemal Ataturk Ave, Banani, Dhaka. Tel: 882025. Thai, Chinese. Taka 1,000.
SKY ROOM RESTAURANT, 8, Kemal Ataturk Ave, Banani, Dhaka. Tel: 882648. Indonesian, Bokhara. Taka 800.
WAKANA, 116 Gulshan Ave, Gulshan, Dhaka. Tel: 886189. Japanese. Taka 2,000.

HOTEL GUIDE

BOGRA

D: US$5-20

HOTEL AKBARI, Nazrul Islam Rd. Tel: 6994.
HOTEL PARK, Borgola Rd. Tel: 5329.
PARJATAN HOTEL, Station Rd. Tel: 6753.

CHITTAGONG

A: US$130 and above

HOTEL AGRABAD, Agradabad. Tel: (031) 500111-20. *P, Gym, Biz. R: L, W.*

D: US$5-20

GOLDEN INN, 336 Station Rd. Tel: (031) 207803-4, 207835-7, Fax: (031) 225683.
HOTEL SAINT MARTIN, Agrabad Rd, Chittagong.
HOTEL SHAIKAT, Station Rd. Tel: (031) 209845, 220181-5.

COX'S BAZAR

C: US$20-40

HOTEL SHAIBAL, Motel Rd. Tel: (0341) 3274-5. *P. Golf course, tennis and squash courts. R: L.*

D: US$5-20

HOTEL SAIMON, Saimon Rd. Tel: (0341) 3272, 3235.

DHAKA

A: US$130 and above

HOTEL SONARGAON, 107, Kazi Nazrul Islam Ave, Dhaka. Tel: 811005, 812927-9. *P, Gym, Biz, Bar. R: L, W.*
HOTEL SHERATON, 1, Minto Rd, Dhaka. Tel: 863391, 861191, Fax: 832915. *P, Gym, Biz, Bar. R: L, W.*

B: US$40-85

PURBANI INTERNATIONAL, Motijheel Commercial Area, Dhaka. Tel: 864926-30. *Gym, Bar. R: L, W.*

C: US$20-40

ABAKASH, Mahakhali Commercial Area, Dhaka. Tel: 607085-9, Fax: 817235, Tlx: 642206 TOUR BJ.
HOTEL MIDTOWN, Gulshan Ave, Dhaka. Tel: 610437, 610959, Fax: 883132.
SUNDARBAN HOTEL, Sonargaon Rd, Dhaka. Tel: 505055-9, Fax: 863 3341.
ZAKARIA INTERNATIONAL, 35 Gulshan Rd, Mahakhali, Dhaka. Tel: 885003-4, Fax: 886407 *Bar.*

D: US$5-20

PRITOM HOTEL, 42 Topkhana Rd, Dhaka. Tel: 244339, 250380, 238010, 232475.

P — Swimming pool
L — Local
Gym — Health club
W — Western food
Biz — Business centre
R — Restaurant

BHUTAN

For most of this century, the kingdom of Bhutan has pursued an isolationist policy and discouraged foreign visitors. Over the past 20 years, however, it has grown increasingly outward looking.

Tourism began on a limited basis in the early 1970s, but the number of tourists remains low (1993's all-time peak was 2,997) mostly due to a substantial daily tariff — from US$80 a head in the lowest season to US$220 a head at peak festival times. Limited facilities at peak times (at the Paro festival in March-April, for example) also discourage tourism.

Those who persevere, however, find it is well worth the trip. Bhutan is graced with a rare beauty — striking mountain and forest scenery, an abundance of bird life and flowers. The architecture of the homes and monasteries, the pageantry of the religious festivals and the gracious people are unforgettable.

The Bhutanese are known for their hospitality and generosity of spirit. Most are still largely untouched by change, which is most noticeable in the capital, Thimphu, and in the market towns. The population (1990 estimate: 600,000) is concentrated in pockets in the south and east. The farming community lives in the broad, fertile valleys of the inner Himalayas, at altitudes of 1,200-3,500 metres. The rural economy is largely based on barter, though cash crops are being developed, mainly in the south. Rice, wheat, maize, buckwheat and fruit are grown.

The state religion is a form of Mahayana Buddhism — the Drukpa sect of the Kagyud school. Religious sentiment is strong in Bhutan, especially in the centre and the east of the country, and still plays a vital role in the culture and national institutions. Since other communities of Tibetan culture have been absorbed by surrounding countries, Bhutan remains, as one expert writes, "the one resolute and self-contained representative of a fast-disappearing civilization."

Even non-trekking visitors will reach altitudes of 3,500 metres and should have a medical check-up before journeying to Bhutan.

History

Little is known for certain about the peoples of Bhutan before the introduction of Buddhism in the seventh century AD. The Tibetan Buddhist king Srongtsen Gampo is recorded as having built the first *lhakhangs* (shrines) in old Bhutan, that of Jampe in Bumthang (central Bhutan) and of Kyichu in Paro. At the end of the eighth century, the Indian Buddhist saint Padmasambhava (Guru Rimpoche) came to Bumthang from Tibet and established several monasteries (including the Taktsang, or Tiger's Nest, in Paro valley).

The Kagyud school of Mahayana Buddhism came along in the 11th century, but the Drukpa sub-sect was not established as orthodoxy until the time of the scholar Padmalingpa (1450-1521) This laid the basis for the independent theocracy of Druk-yul (land of the thunder-dragon), which Shabdrung Ngawang Namgyal (who came to Bhutan from Tibet in 1616) firmly institutionalized.

The Shabdrung is widely venerated today as the one who unified the country, established law and built most of the remarkable administrative temple-fortresses known as *dzongs*. He also established a dual system of spiritual and temporal rulers, which continued — uneasily at times — until the election of Sir Ugyen Wangchuck (governor of Trongsa from 1883) as the first hereditary king of Bhutan.

The hereditary monarchy evolved into the

◄ *A colourful festival in Trashigang.* PHOTO: FELICITY SHAW

present "proto-constitutional monarchy" form of rule. Sir Ugyen ruled until he was succeeded in 1926 by his son, Jigme Wangchuck, who in turn ruled until March 1952. The third monarch, Jigme Dorji Wangchuck, ruled until his sudden death in July 1972 at the age of 43. He is venerated as "the father of modern Bhutan," since major developments (such as a major road-construction programme) occurred during his reign. His son, the present king, Jigme Singye Wangchuck, became the fourth monarch in 1974.

In practice, though the king is supreme, his policies are framed around the resolutions of the National Assembly, to which he considers himself accountable. Instituted in 1953, the National Assembly (Tshogdu) now has 151 members of whom 106 are directly or indirectly-elected representatives of the people. Twelve are elected by the Monk Body and 33 are nominated officials. The assembly usually meets twice a year, and is, in principle, the supreme authority for law within the country.

There is also a Royal Advisory Council of 10 members that meets in permanent session and functions virtually as a government department. The king chairs a cabinet, consisting of ministers and deputy ministers, secretaries of departments, members of the advisory council and others, but it meets infrequently.

Bhutan's foreign affairs have been shaped largely by its close relationship with India. The Indian Government, as part of an attempt to pre-empt a Chinese move southward beyond Tibet, struck a treaty with Bhutan in 1910. It provided, among other things, that the Indian Government would advise Bhutan on external relations, while refraining from interference in Bhutan's internal affairs. An independent India renewed this agreement in 1949. In the wake of China's annexation of Tibet in 1959, Bhutan aligned itself with India and began a massive process of modernization (primarily funded by India) to escape Tibet's fate.

Bhutan joined the United Nations in 1971 with India's sponsorship. Following the relaxation of many policies in China since 1978, Bhutan has moved cautiously to assert its own position on regional and world affairs — one that takes account of (but is not always identical with) that of India.

Entry

AIR: Most travellers to Bhutan fly by Druk-Air to Paro airport from either Bangkok, Calcutta, Dhaka, Kathmandu or New Delhi. Flights are offered twice a week to Calcutta and once to Dhaka, linking en route to or from Bangkok. Extra flights are sometimes scheduled to meet demand (to accommodate groups of 15 or so). The fare from Paro to either Calcutta, Dhaka or Kathmandu is US$165 each way; to New Delhi, US$286; to Bangkok, US$329.

OVERLAND: From Bagdogra in West Bengal (India), it is possible to drive the 175 kilometres to the Bhutan border at Phuentsholing for an overnight stop. The drive from Phuentsholing to Thimphu (179 kilometres) takes about six hours. It is rather long and tiring, but it is still the best way to appreciate the country's strategic situation and observe the changing living conditions at different altitudes. There are several privately operated buses and minibuses that run daily from Shiliguri (West Bengal) to Phuentsholing and vice-versa; others run from Kalimpong, also in West Bengal, to Phuentsholing.

You can travel to Phuentsholing direct from Calcutta by de luxe coach service. A subsidiary of the **Royal Bhutan Insurance Corp.** offers this service three times a week.

Immigration

To travel to Bhutan, you must be either a privately invited guest, a sponsored expert or a member of a tour group paying (except for South Asian nationals) in hard currency. You need a valid passport and also a visa (or appropriate clearance or entry permit) in advance of travel. Applications (in triplicate on the prescribed form) take at least one month to process, though foreign nationals sponsored by departments or agencies may be processed in a minimum of two weeks. Tourist arrangements are made through travel agencies.

Visas will be stamped into your passport on arrival. You must pay the visa fee (US$20 per person) directly to a representative of the **Ministry of Foreign Affairs** (visa section) at the entry point. Visas are initially granted for two weeks, extendable according to circumstances (and on payment of the prescribed fees) through the Visa Section, Protocol Division, Ministry of Foreign Affairs, Thimphu. All private visitors are normally permitted to visit Bhutan for a maximum of one month.

Unless the Ministry of Foreign Affairs has notified Druk-Air's head office of your visa clearance in advance of your flight, you will not be allowed to board the aircraft at foreign

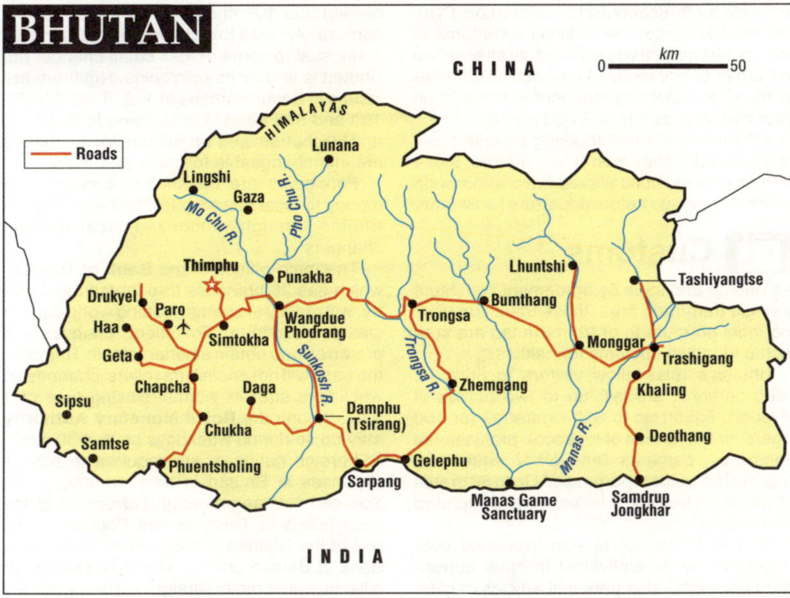

ports, even if you hold a confirmed ticket.

To travel beyond the immigration checkpoints (at Chuzom, Dochula, Gelephu, Kharbandi, Chukha, Samdrup Jongkhar, Wamrong or Chazam [Trashigang]), you need a prior permit from the **Department of Immigration and Census** in Thimphu.

If you are passing through Indian ports to reach Bhutan (by land or by air), you must also comply with Indian visa and other immigration requirements. Information concerning travel to Bhutan can be obtained from any of the following:

New Delhi: The Royal Bhutan Embassy (Chandragupta Marg, Chanakyepuri, New Delhi 110021, India. Tel: 609213, 609217-8, Fax: 687 6710).

New York: The Permanent Mission of the Kingdom of Bhutan to the United Nations, 866 Second Ave, New York NY 10017, U.S.A. Tel: (212) 826 1919, 826 1990-1, Fax: (212) 926 2998.

Geneva: The Permanent Mission of the Kingdom of Bhutan to the UN in Geneva 17-19 Chemin du Champ d'Amier, 1209 Geneva, Switzerland. Tel: (022) 798 7871, 798 7972-3, Fax: (022) 788 2593. There is an airport departure tax of Nu 300 per person.

Health

Health certificates are not required, except for those travellers coming directly from an area infected with yellow fever.

It would be wise, especially in the summer and at lower altitudes, to take precautions against malaria, which is endemic in southern Bhutan. The main illnesses among the local population are influenza, dysentery and respiratory ailments. You should carry appropriate remedies. Other health dangers include rabies and hepatitis. In the spring especially, lip salve will be helpful against the very dry air. And do not forget mosquito repellent, especially during summer nights.

The government provides free medical service — diagnosis and emergency treatment — to all visitors. Medical facilities are available in the main towns and civil administrative centres, but they are not geared to treat serious or complex illnesses.

It may take a day or so to acclimatize to the altitude properly. If you feel short of breath after you arrive by air, take it easy to begin with and avoid both alcohol and over-exertion. Even the most fit person can display symptoms of altitude sickness; if you sleep badly after arrival in Paro or in Thimphu, take advice on whether to travel to Taktsang monastery if this is on your itinerary, as it is at 3,000 metres.

Although most non-trekking travellers will rarely travel higher than 3,500 metres, those with heart conditions should have a thorough medical check-up before departure for Bhutan.

Customs

As Bhutan and India by agreement constitute a single free-trade area, those travellers visiting India en route to or from Bhutan are subjected to Indian customs formalities.

Bhutan's rules allow visitors to bring in: used personal articles; up to two bottles of alcoholic liquor; up to 600 cigarettes (or 150 cigars, or 500 grams of tobacco), professional apparatus, cameras "and other equipment required for tourism purposes." Up to 50 grams of gold and 1 kilogram of silver may be imported free of duty.

You must declare foreign exchange over US$2,000 (or its equivalent in other currencies) and high-value personal articles or gifts. It is forbidden to bring in: any unlicensed firearms, explosives, dangerous weapons, narcotics, goods subject to quarantine, indecent or obscene works or articles.

Restrictions on exports are vigorously enforced; bags are searched thoroughly. Travellers may not take out: antiques, icons, idols, *thangkhas*, musk, and bear bile; arms, ammunition, military stores and explosives; all kinds of narcotics; gold ingots, bars and biscuits. Any item which appears to be a cultural artifact might be confiscated, unless you bought the item at the Government Emporium at Thimphu and can produce a receipt.

You may bring out an artifact, idol or statue, if you obtain a certificate from the Department of Antiques Preservation (under the Special Commission for Cultural Affairs). Allow at least three full working days for the paperwork. Indian customs conduct baggage checks on passengers arriving at Calcutta or New Delhi airports from Bhutan.

Currency

The Bhutanese currency unit is the ngultrum, which is on a par with the Indian rupee at round Nu 31:US$1 (as of April 1995). The ngultrum is divided into 100 chetrum (the current coins, confusingly, spell this chhertum). As in India it is unusual to come across small change, but Bhutan is to mint its own coins. Ngultrum are issued in denominations of 1, 2, 5, 10, 20, 50, 100 and 500 notes. Coins come in 5, 10, 25 and 50 chetrum and 1 ngultrum. Indian rupees are interchangeable for trade purposes.

Foreigners are required to convert their money to local currency for their expenses in Bhutan through authorized local money-changers.

The main offices of the **Bank of Bhutan**, which has 26 branches throughout the country, will readily exchange leading world currencies for ngultrum. Travellers' cheques are preferred and obtain a better rate. In Thimphu, the bank will not encash travellers' cheques on weekdays after its normal closing time of 1 p.m., though the **Royal Monetary Authority** may do so during weekdays up to 4:30 p.m.

Foreign nationals are required to pay all expenses in Bhutan in local currency only. You can exchange foreign currencies at the main hotels in Thimphu and Phuentsholing, and at the Olathang hotel in Paro, or at major Bank of Bhutan offices. You may settle your bills in convertible foreign currency at the above hotels and also at travel agencies, Druk-Air and the Handicrafts Emporium. A foreign exchange counter at the Paro airport terminal building handles passengers' exchange requirements.

You can use the **American Express** credit card in Bhutan, but no other cards are yet valid there. The Thimphu American Express agent is **Chhundu Travels** (39-40 Norzin Lam. Tel: 22592), which can arrange travellers' cheque refunds, emergency cheque cashing, and other services. You can use the card: in Thimphu, at Hotel Druk, Hotel Jumolhari, Motithang Hotel, Etho Metho Tshongkhang, Pel Jorkhang Tshongkhang, Gyeltshen Tshongkhang, Handicrafts Development Corp., Yu-Druk Travels, Chhundu Travels; in Paro: at the Olathang Hotel and in Phuentsholing at Hotel Druk.

It will be impossible to change unused ngultrum outside Bhutan.

Language

Bhutan's official language is Dzongkha, a dialect similar to Tibetan but with many distinctive national characteristics (especially in pronunciation). Choekay (pronounced "chokey") is the written form used in traditional and monastic schools. Sharchopkha is an important dialect of the area around Trashigang in the east. Nepali is spoken in the south. Since the early 1960s, English has been the medium of instruction in the schools and is widely understood by all those who have regular dealings with visitors.

There is no phrasebook widely available yet, but you may be lucky enough to find an old copy of *Introduction to Dzongkha*, a school textbook from 1977. You may find a smaller, pocket-sized booklet — *Dzongkha Handbook* by Dorji Choden (1986) — at Etho Metho in the BTC complex downtown (near Lugar cinema), or at the nearby Pelkhang bookstore, or at Yangchengma bookstore.

Climate

On the whole, there are four distinct seasons in Bhutan: spring (between March and May), summer (June, July and August), when most of the country's rain falls, autumn (early September until mid-December) and winter (late December, January and early February).

But there are regional variations. In the southern foothills the climate is tropical, with an average rainfall of around 250 centimetres a year. Misty, cold hills — some up to 4,000 metres — enclose hot, sultry valleys. Sudden brief showers occur frequently in Phuentsholing during July and August.

In the higher, temperate regions of the Paro and Thimphu valleys, the winters are cold, the springs and autumns mild, and the summers warm. Rainfall is light, most days are sunny and clear, and nights are cool. The somewhat lower regions of Punakha and Wangduephodrang have mild winters and warm summers.

Dress

For tourists, only casual clothing is required. Foreign officials, experts or businessmen should wear formal clothes to meetings. Bhutanese (both men and women) are very smartly dressed in their national dress for formal events, but very much at ease in informal situations.

Daytime temperatures during most of the year (around 30°C in the sun; 20°C in the shade) call for light woollens. Cottons are better in the humid summer. You will need warmer clothes for the evenings.

The winter months call for heavy woollen clothing or down jackets, adequate headgear and warm gloves to protect against the icy winter wind.

In the mountain regions, temperatures can differ greatly (from -10°C to 30°C) between night and day and at varying altitudes You should wear layered clothing to allow yourself to adapt easily to changing conditions. Pack a comfortable, sturdy pair of walking shoes (preferably boots for ankle support on slopes). Trekkers should bring their own sleeping bags and warm clothes; the rest will be provided by the private trekking agencies.

Business Hours

Most government offices are open Monday through Friday and closed on Saturday and Sunday. The official working hours for the 11,000-strong civil service (based mainly at Thimphu) are: in summer, 9 a.m.-5 p.m.; during winter months (November 1-March 31), 9 a.m.-4 p.m.

The General Post Office is open 9 a.m.-5 p.m. daily during the week, but only 9 a.m.-1 p.m. on Saturdays (*see Shopping*).

Bank of Bhutan branches are open 9 a.m.-1 p.m. on weekdays and 9-11 a.m. on Saturdays; closed on Sundays and public holidays.

Communications

Since the March 1990 inauguration of a satellite earth station and switching system (financed by the Bhutan Government and built by Japanese companies for Bhutan Telecom), Bhutan has two-way IDD links with a score of countries. Outward calls from Thimphu are now either dialled direct or operator-assisted. The newly built internal microwave system has enabled telephone and fax communications between most major centres as well as internationally (through Thimphu). The country code for Bhutan is 975.

Electricity is 220-240 volts AC, 50-60 cycles in western Bhutan.

Transport

The main highway between Phuentsholing and Samdrup Jongkhar, and the side roads to Paro, Thimphu, Punakha and Tashiyangtse are all paved, so that the fleets of cars and minibuses of the many travel agencies are able to get tourists comfortably to places of interest.

Local farmers rent horses to carry travellers

up to (but not down from) the cliff-side Taktsang monastery (in accordance with an old proverb that "a horse is not a horse if it cannot carry a man up a mountain; a man is not a man if he cannot descend a mountain without a horse"). Local herdsmen also rent out yaks to accompany trekking parties in the higher places. These horses and yaks are pack animals, however, not riding animals, as their imperviousness to commands makes clear.

BUSES: Buses run most frequently from Phuentsholing to Thimphu and are often crowded, though there is a no-standing rule on minibus services. There are also buses from Thimphu to Bumthang, from Bumthang to Trashigang (via Monggar, whence there is a feeder service to Lhuntshi), from Trashigang to Samdrup Jongkhar, from Trongsa to Gelephu, and Phuentsholing to Gelephu (and vice-versa).

CAR RENTALS: Vehicles can be hired — always with driver — from a number of places (for instance, in Thimphu: **Tee Dee Car Rent**, 1 Flr, TCC Bldg [opposite clock tower]. Tel: 23010). The tourism companies may hire private vehicles (with their owners driving) to convoy smaller groups of foreign tourists to the most popular religious festivals.

Tours

Visitors can join a trekking or packaged tour. Groups are limited to no more than 30 and, in theory, no less than four. Independent travellers in small groups of up to three people may be accepted if guide arrangements can be made, subject to an additional payment of US$20 (three persons), US$30 (two persons), or US$40 (one person) per head per night.

Children up to three years old are not charged, but those aged from four to seven years or from eight to 12 years (and accompanied by their parents) will receive 50% and 25% discounts respectively on the seasonal rates. Full-time students below 25 years old and holding valid academic identity cards will also receive a 25% discount.

All international tourists booked through travel agencies will be charged for a shared double room; single occupancy rooms, when available, are an additional US$15 a night. For stays beyond seven or 14 nights respectively, the published rates (but not for those already enjoying reductions) are further discounted, by 15% or 25%.

The **Tourism Authority of Bhutan** (Ministry of Communications, Thimphu. Tel: 23251, Fax: 23695) is the regulatory authority for tourism policy and tourist visa approvals. It acts as a conduit for foreign-exchange payments, oversees all foreign tourism activities in the country, and subcontracts tour arrangements for Indian clients and for trekking companies (including the training of guides).

Independent tourism within Bhutan is not permitted, nor is it feasible, because of the limited infrastructure. All tours are escorted by guides who operate according to rules laid down by the Tourism Authority. The government's tourism policy continues to be based on group tourism, and it reserves the right to fix rates in convertible currencies from time to time, as this system automatically acts as a market control on the number of tourists coming to Bhutan.

In principle, tourists are not allowed access to religious sites, including temples, monasteries, meditation centres, and centres of Buddhist studies. Tourists are also barred from climbing sacred mountains. These rules came into effect in 1988, after the National Assembly argued (in July 1987) that these places should not be commercialized.

In practice, the rules have not greatly affected trekking, though cultural tours have relied on access to religious art in monasteries for much of their appeal. Some blame what they consider a commercialization of religion and culture on the growing number of foreign experts and volunteers residing in Bhutan, who since early 1985 have been allowed to invite friends and relatives to visit the country. Selected groups have been allowed to mountaineer on payment of royalties; other groups (Buddhist devotees, for example) have visited holy places such as Taktsang, which would otherwise be off limits to foreigners. Cases are decided on their merits.

You can take packaged tours which include sightseeing programmes for anywhere from three to 12 days or longer. The daily rates cover board, lodging, sightseeing, transport, guide charges, entertainment and all local taxes, but exclude laundry and bar charges. These tours cover the main points of interest in Paro, Thimphu, Punakha, Trongsa and Bumthang valleys and surrounding countryside (and Phuentsholing for those entering by road). They also include scenic excursions across high mountain passes, from which you can see the perpetual snow of the north. Visitors can also take cultural tours involving mini-treks to

Kurte (Lhuntshi) and Monggar, both in eastern Bhutan. Travel to Merak-Sakteng and Manas was prohibited by the **Home Ministry** in late 1992.

Various trekking tours are offered, ranging from 13 to 30 days. They include: two 13-day cultural treks to Dagala (mid-Himalayan range) or Samtegang; a 17-day trek to Chomolhari (7,316 metres), though the group will only go to the base camp; an 18-day Phubjikha cultural trek; and (but only for the very fit) a 26-day trek through Lunana, crossing high passes and reaching 5,140 metres.

Limited mountaineering expeditions have been allowed since April 1983, beginning with the opening of the 7,000-metre peak Jitchu Drake in the Lingshi area. The 7,200-metre Mt Masagang was opened in 1985.

Tourists are requested not to tip, and not to give sweets, pens, etc. to children, or to distribute medicine, however much it might seem to be wanted, to villagers.

The former government tour agency, Bhutan Tourism Corp., privatized and reorganized in 1991, is also Bhutan's general sales agent for Lufthansa. Up to 30 smaller companies also have been offered competing travel and trekking licences, though this number will diminish with competition. The smaller companies operate with varying degrees of efficiency.

The following are the names and addresses of some of Bhutan's tour agencies:

Bhutan Tourism Corp. Ltd. (BTCL) (Head Office, P.O. Box 159, Thimphu. Tel: 22045, 22647, Fax: 22479, 23392, Tlx: 890 217 BTCTPU BT, Cable: BHUTRISM); **Bhutan Mandala Tours and Treks** (P.O. Box 397, Thimphu. Tel: 23676, 22107, Fax: 23875); **Bhutan Tours and Travels** (P.O. Box 224, Thimphu. Tel: 22594, Fax: 23515); **Chhundu Travels** (39-40 Norzin Lam, Thimphu); **Etho Metho Tours and Travels** (P.O. Box 360, Thimphu. Tel: 23162, 23085, Fax: 22884, Tlx: 890213 EM TPU BT); **Kinga Tours and Treks** (P.O. Box 635, Thimphu. Tel: 23468, Fax: 22088, Tlx: 890 2340); **Takin Travels & Trekking Co.** (P.O. Box 454, Thimphu. Tel: 23129, Fax: 23130); **Taktsang Tours** (P.O. Box 199, Thimphu, Hotel Taktsang Bldg, Doibom Lam, Thimphu. Tel: 22102, Fax: 23284); **Tashi Tours and Travel** (c/o Tashi Commercial Corp., Thimphu), handles airline bookings; **Yangphel Travels** (Gatoen Lam, opposite Benez. Tel: 22897, Tlx: 224 YANENTTPU BT); offers air ticketing and reservations out of Bangkok; **Yu-Druk Travel and Tours** (P.O. Box 140, Thimphu. Tel: 23400, 22914, 23461, Fax: 22116).

Official Tourism Rates

US$ per night	*HTL*	*LDGE*	*CAMP*	*TREK*
Peak season (Apr., Oct.)	**220**	**150**	**130**	**120**
Middle season (Mar., May, July-Sept., Nov.)	**175**	**130**	**120**	**100**
Low season (Jan.-Feb., June, Dec.)	**130**	**100**	**90**	**80**

Accommodation

Bhutan has comfortable hotels, cottages and guesthouses, many of which were constructed for the present king's coronation in 1974 and have since been extended, and are well appointed. There are a number of private hotels and guesthouses for local people and tourists from neighbouring countries.

The rates range from Nu 285 (for a single at the Hotel Namgay in Phuentsholing) to Nu 1,200 (for suites at the Motithang Hotel in Thimphu). Expect to pay about Nu 700-800 for an air-conditioned double room. All international tourists booked through travel agencies are charged for a shared double room. If you ask for a single, you will be charged US$15 a night extra. Room rates vary subject to inflation. Hotels add an additional 10% service charge and 20% sales tax to the base rates.

THIMPHU

The **Motithang Hotel** (Tel: 22434-5, 23517, Fax: 23392), three kilometres from town, is the main accommodation for tourists. It is an imposing hillside building that was formerly a royal guesthouse. It has 36 twin rooms, efficient central heating and reasonably good cuisine (usually provided in the form of buffets) if you are with a tourist group. Service for individuals, however, leaves much to be desired in timeliness and quality. Businessmen will do better to stay downtown at any of a growing number of modest but adequate hotels that have come up in the past few years.

The privately owned **Jumolhari Hotel** (Tel: 22747, 22787, Tlx: 210 JUMOTPU BT), which opened its doors in March 1983, is centrally located.

Hotel Druk, which opened in September 1985 (Tel: 22966, Fax: 22677, Tlx: 207 DRUKTPU BT), is owned by the Tashi Corp. Normal restaurant hours are 11 a.m.-3 p.m. and 6-10:30 p.m.

The **Druk Sherig Guesthouse** (Tel: 22598, Tlx: 231 SHERIG TPU), in the centre of Thimphu's main street opened in mid-1988. It has 12 well-appointed rooms and two suites.

Hotel 89 in Chorten Lam (Tel: 22931) offers good food. The privately owned and well-constructed **Taktsang Hotel** (Tel: 22102, Fax: 23282), located in the middle of town near the Swiss Bakery, has the popular Orchid Restaurant and a 35-seat boardroom.

ACCOMMODATION UPCOUNTRY

Phuentsholing: The **Hotel Druk** (formerly the Motel Druk, now completely renovated and refurbished, Tel: 2426-8) is operated by the Welcom Group. Located in the middle of town, right next to the upcountry bus station (which springs noisily to life at a remarkably early hour), the hotel is well managed and offers good Continental, Indian, Chinese and Bhutanese meals.

Hotel Namgay (Tel: 2374), with 16 rooms on three floors, is well appointed.

Hotel Kuenga (Tel: 2293) is central, with a good kitchen, which serves good, medium-priced *biryani*.

Elsewhere: The main towns have tourist lodges and government guesthouses: in Paro, the **Olathang Hotel** (Tel: 58 and 99); in Wangduephodrang, the **PWD Guesthouse** (Tel: 214); and in Trongsa, the **Sherubling Tourist Lodge** (Tel: 26), formerly the Trongsa Guesthouse). In Bumthang, the **Chhokhar Guesthouse** for VVIPs has five rooms and two suites; but most groups are accommodated in **Wangdichholing Tourist Lodge**, a complex of four separate buildings. The **Helvetas Guesthouse** can accommodate a limited number of guests; make bookings one week in advance via civil radio.

Dining

Tourists will usually be restricted by circumstances to food in the hotels, generally in the form of a buffet. These are mainly vegetarian. *Dartsi* (cow's-milk cheese) is a favourite food. It is not usually eaten on its own but is added to cooked vegetables, to make a sauce, or served as a pungent dressing on salads. *Ema dartsi* (red chilies cooked in melted cheese) is a popular dish.

The local red rice is by far the preferred staple, but you may also care to try *desi* (sweetened or saffron rice). Bhutanese soup is a nutritious mixture of gruel (*thukpa*) and rice.

Fresh yak cheese is agreeable, and you may also find some of the Tilsitter-style cheese made in Bumthang by the **Department of Agriculture**. *Churpi* (cubes of dried yak cheese strung like beads on a string or a yak hair) are sustaining to have on a trek. Millet is the staple in the Bumthang area; the local millet noodles are tasty.

Souza or Bhutanese tea (brick tea, a pinch of soda, some butter and salt) is refreshing but not immediately to everyone's taste. Outside the hotels and private homes, the quality of food is quite depressing and the presentation uninteresting. The red chilies, used liberally by the local people, are quite hot and can be provided on request at hotels. It is also worth making an effort to sample the large Bhutanese apples when they are in season.

Distilleries at Samtse and Gelephu produce a variety of liquors, which are all sweet and taste similar. Bhutan Mist (a malt whisky) is perhaps the most famous, but Bhutanese consider Special Courier (a blended whisky) is the best local product. Apple brandy from Bumthang is a fine brew. You can sample *chang*, which is made from fermented wheat and tastes like a rough cider, at the many liquor shops in towns. *Arra* (or arrak), distilled from fermented rice or barley is popular in the east.

Entertainment

There is no public nightlife in Bhutan to speak of; people go to bed early and rise early during the working week. Bhutanese like to party in their homes on holiday eves, and put on splendid provisions of drinks and cooked foods.

Indian films (mostly with Hindi soundtracks) show regularly to packed houses at the two rather scruffy cinemas in Thimphu. All of the hotels have bars which are reasonably well stocked with local and some imported drinks.

Dances at the local festivals are based broadly on Tibetan tradition but reflect substantial changes and creativity from local custom. The **Royal Bhutan Dance Troupe** may give short open-air performances of both southern and western Bhutanese dances and songs on the grounds of one of the hotels, but these are no substitute for the real communal gatherings.

Shopping

In the towns there are small bazaars where you can find some interesting local items, including antique silverware and old Tibetan or Bhutanese coins. (You will need a certificate to be allowed to export the antiques, however.) In the larger towns, most shopkeepers speak some English. Shop stalls close around 7 p.m.

The **Handicrafts Emporium** in the centre of Thimphu is open 9 a.m.-noon and 1-4 p.m., Monday to Friday (and 9 a.m.-1 p.m. on Saturdays). It offers a growing range of Bhutanese handicrafts at prices somewhat higher than in the market. Here you can buy papier-mache masks (in miniature sizes to suit air travellers), woven cloth of wool or silk, prayer wheels, decorative motifs silk-screened on handmade paper, rings and ornaments for clothing.

The hand-woven cloth (of wool or of *endi* silk) used for making up the national dress is of excellent quality and a good buy. You can also purchase fossil coral beads from Tibet, though these are very dear. Himalayan "fossil" stones, which are a blotchy greenish-blue hue, are also expensive. But the polished bright blue turquoise, brought from Iran via India, are very cheap. All other stones are brought in from India: tiny freshwater pearls are beginning to appear, but are somewhat overpriced in relation to their size. Dolkar's shop, opposite the Lugar Commercial Bldg, probably has the best selection in Thimphu.

Bhutan produces attractive postage stamps on both international and local themes; the latter make lightweight souvenirs, but they are not always available at hotels. They can be found at Thimphu's **General Post Office** (open until 3 p.m. daily).

Sports

Archery is the national sport — national teams were coached for the last three Olympics and also for recent Asian regional competitions. It is well worth seeing the Sunday practice session to appreciate the keen eyes and sturdy hands of the archers, and the victory dance performed after a successful hit.

A swimming-pool complex in Thimphu is open during summer months; temporary membership is available. Soccer, volleyball, golf, badminton, basketball, tennis and table tennis are other popular sports.

Holidays

Most national public holidays in Bhutan are religious holidays, which vary according to the Bhutanese calendar (similar to the Chinese lunar calendar). Secular holidays are related to the institutions of monarchy and state.

January-February: Losar, Bhutanese New Year. Public holiday for two days.

May 2: Birthday of the late king.

May-June: Buddha Parinirvana, also birthday of Guru Padmasambhava.

June 2: Coronation anniversary (1974) of the fourth hereditary king.

June-July: First sermon of the Lord Buddha. Yar Nyidlok, the summer solstice, also falls during this period.

July 21: Anniversary of the death of the late king.

September-October: Blessed Rainy Day; Thimphu Domchey; Thimphu Tsechhu (three days' holiday for the latter).

October-November: Dussehra (Southern Bhutanese New Year).

November 11-13: Celebrations of the king's birthday.

December 17: National Day.

December-January: Nine Evils' Day. Guen Nyidlok, the winter solstice, is also celebrated during this period.

DISCOVERING BHUTAN

THIMPHU

Capital of Bhutan since 1960, Thimphu lies in a broad west-central river valley at an altitude of 2,435 metres. The town (population 60,000) is dominated by the **Tashichho dzong** ("fortress of the glorious religion"). The dzong retains the central keep of the original structure built in 1641, but otherwise was entirely reconstructed in 1961-62.

Today it houses the main government departments, the meeting room of the National Assembly, the throne room of the king and the summer headquarters of the Central Monastic Body. Women are forbidden to remain in the dzong after sunset, a rule dating back several centuries.

A short way uphill from the dzong you will find the new **National Library**, the **High Court**, and the **Royal Bhutan Golf Club**. The splendid new **Convention Centre** faces the dzong from across the river. The bazaar consists of

PHOTO: VISHWANATH

Thimpu's dzong.

several lines of shops in the traditional style, run by Bhutanese and Tibetans. At the "Sunday market" (actually at its best on Saturdays), held below the bazaar, vendors offer fruits, vegetables, meat, fish and sundries.

The entrance to Thimphu valley, about eight kilometres from the town, is guarded by Bhutan's oldest dzong, **Simtokha** (built in 1627); there are fine frescoes and slate carvings here. Simtokha houses the Rigney School for Dzongkha and monastic studies.

From here, you can reach the **Phajoding monastery** by way of a trail that offers fine views overlooking the town. The path, which dates from 1748, climbs 700 metres to the monastery and continues on to Paro valley. There are many other monasteries and forts on the hilltops surrounding the valley.

As you enter the valley you can see the prominent **memorial** *chorten* to the late king and to world peace. It contains wall paintings and religious representations of high quality. There will nearly always be the sight of devout pilgrims circling the chorten clockwise as they tell their beads.

The queen mother resides at the Royal Palace at Dechenchholing, about 15 minutes by car up the valley from the town centre. **Dechenphodrang lhakhang** is on the western slopes of the valley near the Indian Embassy. From here, one can walk up or around the ridge to **Wangditse**, where there are fine examples of sculptured stupas.

UPCOUNTRY

If you are entering Bhutan from **Phuentsholing**, you will see much countryside during the 179-kilometre drive to Thimphu. The black-topped road, built by recruits doing national service in the early 1960s, rises sharply from the plains to around 1,800 metres. It eventually climbs to 2,526 metres at the Chapcha pass before descending to Paro, Thimphu and on to the east.

You can see traces of the old track used before the highway was constructed (when it took an arduous five or six days to travel by pony or mule from Thimphu to Phuentsholing). A little more than three hours after leaving Phuentsholing, one comes to the **Chukha** hydroelectric works. India began this as a goodwill project in 1976, offering very favourable terms for Bhutan.

Some 45 minutes on, the **Khujoog Jakhang** (cafeteria) at Bunakha comes into view for a welcome meal halt. From here it is 40 minutes to **Chapcha pass** from where you can get an excellent view of some of the road you have travelled.

Chuzom, where the Paro and Wang rivers meet (2,102 metres above sea level), is about another half-hour down the road. Thimphu is roughly two hours further along the main road.

Paro (altitude 2,250 metres) is about 45 minutes away. The Paro river meanders gently through a patchwork of rice paddies and wheat fields dotted with houses. Many people consider this the most beautiful of Bhutan's valleys, especially in spring when peach and apple trees blossom.

On a hillside above the river, not far from the airfield, stands **Rimpung dzong** (or Paro dzong), built on foundations dating back to 1645. Burnt down in 1907, it was rebuilt and now houses the state monastery. The inner court is brilliantly carved and painted; the towering central keep is an impressive example of Bhutanese architecture. It also contains a collection of sacred masks, ritual objects and ornaments, some dating back several centuries.

On a steep ridge above the dzong is **Ta dzong**, an ancient watchtower, where the **National Museum** has been housed since 1967 (photography not permitted). Thangkhas, gold and silverwork and other artistic treasures are on display here.

Just down the road from the museum you will see the distinctive hat-shaped **Duntse lhakhang**. This was originally constructed by Thangton Gyalpo, known as "The iron-bridge builder," from Tibet.

Kyichu lhakhang, one of the holiest temples of Bhutan, lies about eight kilometres west of Paro bridge on the left. Like Jampe lhakhang of Bumthang, it dates from the seventh century AD.

Further west the **Taktsang (Tiger's Nest)** monastery, on the right, clings to the sheer cliffside at 3,000 metres. Legend asserts that Guru Rimpoche travelled from Tibet on the back of a flying tigress, which landed at the exact spot where the monastery stands today. It is a place of pilgrimage that all Bhutanese seek to visit once in a lifetime. Even higher than Taktsang, 15 minutes further on, is the **Santog Pelri monastery** (Monastery of Heaven), a 300-year-old retreat.

From Thimphu, a 45-minute drive east through the Dochu-la (3,114 metres) plus a further two hours' descent, brings you to **Punakha** (1,200 metres), the former capital. An outstanding example of Bhutanese architecture, the majestic Punakha dzong (built in 1637) stands guarding the confluence of the **Mo Chu** and the **Po Chu**, where they become the **Sunkosh River**. The climate of this valley is temperate, and the Central Monastic Body goes there from Thimphu to spend the duration of the winter.

The **Wangduephodrang dzong**, perched on a hilltop above the confluence of the Sunkosh and the **Tang Chu**, commands the road to central and eastern Bhutan. This dzong was also built by the first Shabdrung in 1638; for many centuries the administrative leaders of the district centred around this dzong were among the country's most powerful.

From Wangduephodrang it takes about six hours by black-topped road to **Trongsa** (2,080 metres) in central Bhutan, crossing the Pele-la (3,350 metres). The **"eye-chorten" of Chendebji**, with fine slate carvings, appears on the right after about three-and-a-half hours of driving. The **Trongsa dzong** (Chhokhor Rabtse dzong) is in many ways the most impressive in Bhutan, and commands a superb view of the **Mangde Chu** and of the east-west passage.

From Trongsa to **Bumthang** bazaar (2,650 metres), 66 kilometres to the east, normally takes two hours, but to that time you must be prepared to add delays in case of rock falls, especially in the wet season. The road crosses the Yatu-la (3,536 metres). **Jakar dzong ("the castle of the white bird")** was (like Trongsa dzong) built in the 16th century.

From Bumthang, the road to Monggar goes through the picturesque village of Ura (at 3,091 metres) after about an hour's drive. Here, unusually, the houses are close together, rather than spread out. The road continues through Black Mountain's **Thrungselma pass** (3,758 metres), and down a landslide-prone road to Monggar.

Monggar dzong was built in 1930. The settlement is the second largest in eastern Bhutan. Basically it is a way-station (typically a night-stop) for travel between Samdrup Jongkhar and Thimphu (which normally takes three days). A road goes north from here to Lhuntshi dzong. From Monggar it is a short but demanding drive of two and a half hours to Trashigang (descending the Yadi loop, then following the Manas river for an hour or so).

Trashigang (altitude 1,120 metres) lies at the junction of the east-west road and the road from the southern market town of Samdrup Jongkhar. The people of this populous region are known for the vivid colours and complex designs of their textiles. Endi silk, spun in the households from dry cocoons from Assam, is also a specialty. The dzong (1667) is on a steep ridge overlooking the Manas river bridge.

Across the **Manas bridge** from the dzong's hill, the road continues north for 44 kilometres to **Chorten Kora**, part of Bhutan's "chorten path," and nearby **Tashiyangtse** village. Two days' walk northeast from Trashigang, on from Radi, is the Brokpa village of Sakteng and its twin across the valley, Mera (Mera-Sakteng) at an elevation of around 3,000 metres.

The journey south from Trashigang to Samdrup Jongkhar (180 kilometres) is pleasant. Kanglung (about 20 kilometres from Trashigang, one hour by car) is the site of Sherubtse Degree College. Khaling, home to a School for the Blind and an experimental weaving centre, is more than an hour further on. **Samdrup Jongkhar** is a typical small frontier town with no special features, apart from a fruit and produce-auction yard lying along a river, where in past years woven and other goods from the north (especially Mera Sakteng) were displayed in a colourful annual *mela* (bazaar), revived for a month in mid-December 1994.

BURMA

Burma (Myanmar) is a land of almost unparalleled scenic variety and ethnic diversity. The Burman-dominated rice-lands in the central plains are surrounded by a horseshoe-shaped ring of wild and remote mountain ranges and high plateaux where an abundance of ethnic minorities live.

All peoples of Burma are naturally friendly and hospitable, English is widely spoken and a foreign visitor will encounter few problems when dealing with the ordinary people in the street or in the countryside.

The Burmese capital, Rangoon (Yangon), is devoid of tall residential blocks, fuming industrial complexes and noisy traffic jams. Towering above Rangoon is the famous Shwedagon pagoda, magnificently gilded and symbolic of a country rich in religion and resources. Seen from the height of the pagoda precincts, the city presents a view of broad expanses of green woodland and parks interspersed with small white villas.

The city centre is still dominated by colonial-style buildings and tree-lined streets which run east-west and north-south. Government offices, law courts, commercial houses, shopping centres, hotels, restaurants and cinemas are mostly concentrated in this area. There is, however, a total absence of the garish nightlife that is to be found in many Southeast Asian cities.

Outside the confines of Rangoon, Burma is a country of enchanting scenic beauty, pleasant towns and historical sites which are unique even in an Asian context. The northern city of Mandalay, the royal capital prior to the British conquest in 1885, is well worth a visit, as is nearby Pagan, though some of its famous ruins were damaged by an earthquake in 1975. The more important edifices have since been restored, to become once again marvels of ancient architecture and a source of fascination for visitors. The hill stations of Maymyo and Taunggyi enjoy a purity of air rarely found anywhere else in Asia.

Burma is a place in which to meet friendly and sophisticated people, to relax and absorb the atmosphere without having to go out and chase it. It is ideal for those who want to shake off the concerns of life for a while and escape from familiar surroundings.

So long as you do not expect all the modern conveniences of Western life, a holiday in Burma can provide a rewarding experience. It is particularly rewarding for those looking for unusual and striking images to photograph.

On May 27, 1989, it was decided by the government to use the traditional Burmese name for Burma, Myanmar. Shortly afterwards, the military government decided to Burmanize local place names as well. Thus, Rangoon has officially become Yangon, Moulmein is now referred to as Mawlamyine, Maymyo is now Pyin Oo Lwin and the Irrawaddy River has become the Ayeyarwady.

However, for reasons of simplicity, the *All-Asia Travel Guide* will continue to use the English names since even English-speaking Burmese use these in daily conversations and these place names are found on most maps. Whenever deemed necessary, the new spellings will be added in brackets.

◄ *Village children in ceremonial dress at Pagan.* PHOTO: ELLEN RUDOLPH

BURMA
BHUTAN
INDIA
CHINA
BANGLADESH
LAOS
THAILAND
Chindwin R.
Irrawaddy R.
Sittang R.
Salween R.
Mekong R.
Myitkyina
Tamu
Bhamo
Tiddim
Lashio
Mogok
Ye-u
Haka
Mandalay
Monywa
Maymyo
Sagaing
Amarapura
Myingyan
Ava
Kengtung
Nyaung U
Meiktila
Pagan
Chiauk
Taunggyi
Kyaukpadaung
Akyab
Magwe
Loikaw
Pyumana
Toungoo
Prome
Sandoway
Myanaung
Bay of Bengal
Pegu
Kyaikto
Wakema
Rangoon
Pyapon
Moulmein
Ye
km
0
200
Andaman Sea
Roads
Railways
Airport
Tavoy
Andaman Islands
Mergui
Gulf of Thailand
Kawthaung

History

By the fifth century BC, a Burmese kingdom was in existence at Tagaung, a place about 160 kilometres up the Irrawaddy River from the present site of Mandalay. A dynasty of 50 kings ruled Tagaung until it fell to Tartar invaders from the north. A scion of the last king then fled south and founded a new dynasty at Sri Khettara (near the present site of Prome, 320 kilometres north of Rangoon), which was peopled by the Pyus, the forefathers of the modern Burmese.

By about this time, a Mon-Khmer group of early immigrants from India had also settled in the Irrawaddy delta and south Burma. Called Mons or Talaings (derived from the Indian word Telegana), these immigrants were the first to come under the influence of Buddhism spreading from India.

In about the first century AD, the Pyu kingdom of Sri Khettara fell apart, wrecked by internal dissension and threats from the Mons in the south. A nephew of the 27th and the last Pyu king regrouped his scattered countrymen and led them in a 12-year-long march to the Pagan site in central Burma where another group of Pyus had settled. There, he founded the famous Pagan Dynasty, of which Anawrahta, the 42nd and most noted king in Burmese history, inaugurated, in the 11th century, the country's first golden age.

But the Pagan Dynasty ended with its 50th king following a Mongol invasion in the 13th century. The kingdom broke up into small principalities until national unity was restored under the Ava Dynasty (1364-1555), with the imperial capital at Ava (near the present site of Mandalay). After about 200 years the dynasty was succeeded by another, the Toungoo Dynasty (1486-1752). The most eminent member of this dynasty was King Bayinnaung who forged Burma into a strong, united and respected nation. The dynasty did not get on well with neighbouring Thailand; wars between the two nations culminated in the Burmese sacking of the Thai capital of Ayudhia (now styled Ayutthaya) in 1767.

Meanwhile, the Mons of south Burma had restored their kingdom at Pegu, ending the Burmese Toungoo Dynasty, but Burmese supremacy was re-established with the coming of a new dynasty under King Alaungpaya at Shwebo (north of Mandalay) in 1752. Pursuing a policy of expansionism, the dynasty conquered Arakan in the west in 1785 and Manipur and Assam in 1819. But in operations against rebels in these regions, it came into conflict with the British in India. This led to three Anglo-Burmese Wars — in 1824, 1852 and 1885 — ending with Burmese defeats and piecemeal British annexation of Burma. In 1886 the British deported Thibaw, the 11th and the last king of the dynasty, to India (where he lived until 1916) and turned Burma into a province of India.

In 1937 Burma became a separate colony with its own constitution. Five years later the Japanese occupied Burma and the British retreated to India. Shortly before the Japanese occupation a group of 30 young Burmese nationalists (known as the Thirty Comrades) had received military training in Japan and followed the Japanese army when it invaded Burma for Thailand. The Thirty Comrades formed the nucleus of the Burmese army which in March 1945 broke with the Japanese and contacted the Allies. When the Japanese eventually had been driven out, the leader of the Thirty Comrades, Aung San, headed a provisional government and began to negotiate Burma's independence from Britain.

On July 19, 1947, Aung San and several of his cabinet ministers were assassinated in Rangoon. U Nu, an old colleague of Aung San, took over and became Burma's first prime minister when it was declared an independent republic on January 4, 1948. But the young nation almost immediately faced rebellions launched by communist groups and various ethnic minorities. The insurgency was brought under control after a few years but even so, the military, led by Gen. Ne Win, seized power on March 2, 1962, claiming that the rebels were threatening to break up the country.

Ne Win's coup ended Burma's 14-year-long experiment with parliamentary democracy. The ideology of the military government was "the Burmese Way to Socialism" and the Burma Socialist Programme Party (BSPP) became the country's only legally permitted political organization. The economy declined, the insurgencies flared anew and Burma went into a state of self-imposed isolation which has lasted more than 30 years and is showing little sign of ending properly even now.

Ne Win resigned as president in 1981 but remained chairman of the BSPP. He was succeeded as head of state by one of his most trusted proteges, San Yu. Both Ne Win and San Yu resigned from their respective posts in July 1988, amid mounting opposition against the one-party rule of the BSPP.

The new president and BSPP chairman, Sein Lwin, was forced to resign after only 18 days in office as hundreds of thousands of people all over Burma demonstrated against his government. Sein Lwin's successor, Dr. Maung Maung, remained at the helm for a month, marked by daily mass demonstrations. On September 18, 1988, the country's army chief, Gen. Saw Maung, assumed power and violently suppressed the pro-democracy movement. It is estimated that several thousand people were shot by the army in Rangoon and other cities and towns all over Burma in the wake of Saw Maung's coup.

Since then Burma has been under martial law and all opposition strictly controlled. Most leading opponents of the regime remain in jail or under house arrest, among them Aung San's popular daughter, Aung San Suu Kyi, who had come to the fore of the 1988 pro-democracy movement. She emerged as the most prominent leader of Burma's main opposition party, the National League for Democracy (NLD) which was formed shortly after the military takeover in September 1988.

General elections were held on May 28, 1990 and the NLD won a landslide victory, winning 80% of the seats in the National Assembly. But even so, the military has shown no sign of relinquishing power and in early 1995 Aung San Suu Kyi remained under house arrest. Although few political changes have happened, the economy over the past few years has begun to show signs of both recovery and growth.

Entry

Most foreign visitors enter Burma by air, but in late 1992 the Mae Sai-Tachilek border crossing from Thailand was opened for tourists. Special visit passes can be obtained in Mae Sai for a three-day tour by car to Kengtung and back again. However, it is not possible to continue from Kengtung to Rangoon or any other points beyond: visitors to Burma proper still have to enter and leave the country by air via Rangoon. Return-same-day visits across the Thai-Burmese border are possible at Myawaddy (opposite Mae Sot in Thailand), at Three Pagodas Pass (opposite Kanchanaburi province) and at Kawthaung (Victoria Point) across the estuary from Ranong in southern Thailand.

Chinese tourists may cross the border from Yunnan at Lweje in Kachin State and at Namkham, Muse and Kyohkok in northern Shan State (all places near Ruili in northwest Yunnan).

The following airlines fly to Rangoon:

Myanmar Airways International: the national flag carrier, flies from Bangkok, Kuala Lumpur, Singapore and Hong Kong;

Thai Airways International: flies from Bangkok;

Biman Bangladesh: flies from Dhaka and Bangkok;

SilkAir: flies from Singapore;

Air China (formerly CAAC)**:** flies from Kunming on Wednesdays.

There is a US$6 airport tax per passenger on departure from Rangoon.

Immigration

Passports and visas are required for visits to Burma. Tourist visa are valid for 28 days. Business visas are usually valid for 14 days and can be extended for up to three months. Visas should be obtained from Burmese embassies. Tourist visas are given to groups as well as to independent travellers. Sponsorship is not usually required for business visas.

Health

Yellow fever certification is required if arriving within nine days after leaving or transiting affected areas. Other vaccinations are not needed though doctors recommend travellers to Burma to be inoculated against cholera. Malaria is rampant in all forested areas of Burma; prophylactic medicine is recommended and should start before arrival on the recommendation of a doctor.

Customs

There is duty-free shopping for passengers on arrival at Rangoon's Mingaladon airport. Visitors are allowed to bring 400 cigarettes, 100 cigars or half-a-pound of tobacco, two litres of liquor, half a litre of perfume or *eau de Cologne* into the country without duty. Personal effects in reasonable quantities are allowed, as are jewellery and professional instruments such as typewriters, still and movie cameras, radios and tape-recorders on condition that they are re-exported. Baggage is usually examined on entry and departure.

Export of Burmese antiques is prohibited. Only jewellery and gems bought from the government diplomatic shop in central Rangoon or at the duty-free store at the airport can be exported.

There is no restriction on export of other articles, but export permits may be required for certain items and one should inquire on purchasing expensive souvenirs whether such a permit is required.

People arriving and declaring more than US$2,000 must obtain receipts for all purchases in Burma, and the total for these purchases must tally with the amount of foreign currency exchanged for Foreign Exchange Certificates (FECs).

Currency

The currency unit is the kyat (pronounced "chat") which is divided into 100 pyas. In April 1995, the official exchange rate was US$1:Kyats 5.41. Notes in denominations of 50 pyas and Kyats 1, 5, 10, 15, 20, 45, 50, 90, 100, 200 and 500 (market with Arabic and Burmese numerals) and coins in denominations of 1, 5, 10, 25 and 50 pyas and Kyat 1 (in different shapes and sizes but marked only with Burmese numerals) are in circulation.

The Burmese Government issues Foreign Exchange Certificates (FECs) for visitors to use in the country. These exchange at FEC 1:US$1. They are commonly accepted by hotels and major restaurants, but their acceptance by merchants varies. There is a flourishing black-market, with the rate for FECs slightly lower than that for U.S. dollars. Dealing in the black-market is against the law. Visitors must change US$300 into FEC 298 on arrival at the airport, before claiming their baggage. Visitors can use travellers' cheques or American Express, MasterCard or Visa credit cards to obtain FECs, but cannot obtain hard currency with them. It is very difficult to change personal cheques in Burma.

Language

The main language of Burma is Burmese, which is also the official language. But there are also regional tongues of minority races spoken in their respective areas, the most important being Arakanese (in Arakan State, west Burma), Shan (in Shan State, east Burma), Kachin (in Kachin State, north Burma) and Karen and Mon (in Karen and Mon States, south Burma). Hindi, Bengali and several Chinese dialects are also spoken among Indian, Bangladeshi and Chinese communities, found mostly in the large towns and border areas adjoining India, Bangladesh and China.

Signboards of shops, restaurants, banks, government offices etc., are written in Burmese though some are written in English as well. Written Burmese is based on a modified version of the old Mon alphabet which, in turn, is derived from South Indian alphabets.

Street names are written only in Burmese, as are the names of railway stations. But a visitor will have no difficulty in finding someone who understands English and is willing to help him find places.

Climate

The greater part of Burma lies in the tropics. The Tropic of Cancer runs about 160 kilometres north of Mandalay in central Burma, leaving only northern Burma outside the zone.

There are three general seasons: winter from November to February; the hot seasons from March to May and the rainy seasons from the end of May to the end of October. Climatic conditions, however, vary with the regions. The heat of the hot season, for instance, will not be as intense in the mountain regions of the Shan State (where the hill stations of Maymyo and Taunggyi are situated) as in what is known as the dry zone in central Burma (which contains Mandalay) where temperatures may rise above 38°C.

In the rainy season the annual rainfall may vary from 86 centimetres in the dry zone to around 250 centimetres in the Rangoon delta region and 500 centimetres in the Arakan and Tennasserim coastal regions and the hilly areas of the far north.

The arrival of the monsoons in May usually means welcome relief from the intense heat, though it results in rather humid conditions. Rain falls mostly in the afternoon and evenings. But it is wise to carry an umbrella at all times.

Winter (November-February) is the most pleasant time of the year in which to visit Burma. The temperature in Rangoon and Mandalay can fall to as low as 16°C. It is much cooler in the hill areas such as Maymyo and Taunggyi where temperatures hover around 4.5°C.

Dress

Tourists are asked to dress to conform with local customs. To be properly dressed for women means to avoid bra-less T-shirts or singlets, shorts, miniskirts or anything too revealing.

Note: Wearing shoes, slippers, footwear or socks within the precincts of Buddhist pagodas, temples and monasteries is strictly forbidden.

Light tropical clothing is enough for most of the year in Burma, though heavier or warmer clothing is needed if you plan to visit the hill stations of Maymyo and Taunggyi.

Business Hours

Government offices are open 9:30 a.m.-4:30 p.m. Monday-Friday without a break. Usual working hours for the military administration are 8 a.m.-3 p.m. Saturdays and Sundays are holidays for all offices.

The Post Office also keeps government hours though the Central Telegraph Office remains open 8 a.m.-9 p.m. on weekdays and 8 a.m.-8 p.m. on Saturdays and Sundays and other holidays. Banks are open to the public 10 a.m.-2:30 p.m. on weekdays only.

Government and cooperative shops follow government hours, though on certain occasions such as the approach of an important anniversary or a religious festival, they may be open extra hours. They close on Saturdays and Sundays but shops dealing in medicines and drugs have their respective weekend holidays on different days of the week, so that some of them are open on Saturdays and Sundays.

Small private shops keep longer hours than government ones. Private restaurants stay open until around 9:30 p.m.

Doing Business

The Burmese have inherited the handshake from the British. To be extra polite, hold your right wrist lightly with your left hand as you shake hands. Business cards are expected. Punctuality is appreciated but not always possible in Burma (the Burmese themselves are notoriously unpunctual).

Women are accepted in business (in Burmese families, women hold the economic power, and the men are little more than powerless "constitutional monarchs" or figureheads).

English is widely spoken among the urban elite (which is surprisingly Westernized), but many are learning Japanese. There is a lot of private tuition going on in Rangoon and Mandalay.

Alcohol is always appreciated (especially Johnnie Walker whisky) and the Burmese use the English "cheers" when they toast. The Burmese are also heavy smokers: they prefer their own cheroots but appreciate foreign cigars as well. State Express 555 is the most popular brand of foreign cigarettes.

Shoes should be removed before entering Burmese homes. Burmese like to talk about their cultural heritage, religion and music, while visitors should avoid bringing up the subjects of politics, the role of the military and of the retired strongman Gen. Ne Win. If these subjects are brought up by a host or Burmese business partner, appropriate comments are expected. The Burmese can be surprisingly outspoken.

Burmese expect small gifts from visitors (whisky, cigarettes, souvenirs, perfume and so on) and usually present visitors with their own gifts (Burmese harps, precious stones, puppets). Government officials are almost invariably corrupt but sometimes in a very subtle way.

Contact: **U Myo Nyunt**, **Joint Secretary**, **Union of Myanmar Chamber of Commerce and Industry**, Ruby House, 74-86 Bo Sun Pat St, Pabedan Township, Yangon (P.O. Box 1557 Tel: 70749, 82208).

All foreign transactions are channelled through the **Myanmar Foreign Trade Bank**, 80-86 Maha Bandoola Garden St, Rangoon. (Tel: 84911, Fax: 89585).

Media

There is one daily newspaper in English, the state-run *The New Light of Myanmar*. In addition, *The Guardian* magazine is published monthly. They are sold almost everywhere: pavements, newsstands, markets and so on. Foreign magazines are restricted, but copies of publications such as *Time*, *Newsweek* and the *Far Eastern Economic Review* are usually available.

Communications

Communications from Burma to the outside world have greatly improved, but inward access is still bad. A new telephone system has been installed with Israeli help and it is now possible to make international calls from all major tourist centres. Incoming calls (especially from Bangladesh) are hampered by a shortage of lines.

Facsimile and telex services are available at major hotels and at the Central Post Office in Rangoon.

L.M. Ericson Australia signed an agreement with the Myanmar Post and Telecommunications in 1992 to install a cellular mobile telephone system which will include two radio stations, one mobile telephone exchange and two microwave stations. However, it is uncertain when this will begin to operate.

DHL is the only courier service operating in Burma so far. Its office is at 5248 Merchant St, Rangoon. Tel: 85473.

Transport

FROM THE AIRPORT: If travelling in a group, transfer from the airport to your hotel is arranged by your travel agent. Individual travellers may hire government or private taxis at the taxi-stand outside the airport. The fare has to be negotiated, and most drivers ask for payment in U.S. dollars. Local transport should be included in the cost of group package tours — the vast majority of tourists visiting Burma.

RANGOON TRANSPORT

TAXIS: The government provides a taxi service with a small fleet of cars distinguished by a red stripe over a blue-painted body. A far larger number of small private cars of various colours with red number-plates, cruise around the city's main streets as taxis seeking custom. Both government and private taxis are unmetered and fares are negotiated. Seek advice at your hotel as to how much to pay.

The government maintains a taxi stand at the Inya Lake Hotel with daily or hourly rates payable in U.S. dollars. Private tour agencies are licensed to rent vehicles (with drivers) to visitors with rates payable in FECs or U.S. dollars.

Some private cars are also registered for hire with driver by tourists both in Rangoon and other tourist centres. These vehicles can be identified by a sticker on the left side of the windscreen. Payment of fares to these cars will have to be made in "transfer service coupons" available at **Myanmar Travel and Tours** offices and at the counters of government hotels.

Most drivers of these cars speak English, but in case you meet one who does not, it is advisable to have a note from your hotel with directions in Burmese.

BUSES: Privately owned buses operate over most roads in Burma though most of them are in the Rangoon area. The fares are reasonable. Old private buses are primitive World War II machines kept going only by the amazing ingenuity of Burmese mechanics. New private buses are Nissan and Toyota Hilux. All the buses are crowded throughout the day and a good deal of pushing and pulling is necessary to get in and out of them.

TRISHAWS: These tricycles can be found everywhere in town except in a few busy streets where they are banned for reasons of road safety. Trishaw-men are usually polite and obliging, but to guard against inflated charges you should check with your hotel as to what is a fair price.

TRAINS: Commuter trains run shuttle services between Rangoon town and the suburbs in the north, east and west. Trains leave the central Rangoon station every half hour or so in the mornings and evenings, and about hourly at other times of the day. There are also circular-line trains running from Rangoon station between 5 a.m. and 8 p.m., returning about three hours later. Ten of these trains run in a clockwise and 13 in an anti-clockwise direction. Passing through the town area and the countryside, the trains provide a chance to see the ordinary lifestyle of the Burmese people. Although they are cheap, the trains tend to be overcrowded, especially in the morning and evening rush hours and provide little by way of luxury.

RIVER BOATS: Triple-decked catamarans and double-decker motor launches ply between Rangoon and Syriam town on the opposite side of the river. Leaving every half hour from the jetty about a mile to the east of the **Strand Hotel**, they take about half-an-hour for the crossing. The fare is Kyats 1-2 per person. There are also river sampans for hire at the riverfront below the Strand which can be taken out for a mid-river cruise. Some of them are fitted with outboard motors. The charges range from Kyats 5 upwards and can be negotiated with the operator. Boatmen speak little or no English, but gestures usually make them understand your requirements.

UPCOUNTRY TRANSPORT

TRAINS: Rangoon is the hub of a railway network linking all major destinations and traversing wide areas of the Burmese countryside with its kaleidoscopic scenery. One line runs for 620 kilometres to the old royal capital of **Mandalay**.

Rangoon's magnificent Shwedagon pagoda. PHOTO: PATRICK LUCERO

There are only two classes for passengers — upper and ordinary. Upper-class fares are roughly three times those of the ordinary. Fares vary and are usually included in the price of a package tour. Outside packages, travellers have to pay for train fares in foreign exchange, which also varies, so it is impossible to state what current fares are.

To go from Rangoon to **Mandalay**, almost due north of Rangoon in central Burma, the best train to take is the 6 a.m. express. Its neat and clean Japanese-made carriages carry efficient and courteous attendants recruited from among retired military personnel, and they look after the needs of passengers throughout the journey. Tickets are available 24 hours in advance. The trip takes 11 hours, with brief stops only at four intermediate stations.

As separate luggage vans are provided and seats in carriages are numbered and reserved, there is no congestion as in other trains. Another express train which leaves Rangoon at 6:15 p.m., reaching Mandalay the next morning, provides sleeping berths. A private contractor has been allowed to attach a carriage to the Rangoon-Mandalay train. This is more expensive but much more comfortable than the rest of the train.

To get to **Pagan**, to the south west of Mandalay and not on the railway line, it is best to go to **Thazi** by train and from there by bus. Myanmar Travel and Tours now operates a shuttle bus service between the two towns and bookings can be made at its office in Rangoon.

For a train journey up into the beautiful Shan hills to **Taunggyi**, take the Rangoon-Mandalay train, changing at Thazi, from where you proceed by train to **Shwenyaung**, the terminal town. From there you take a bus or taxi for the 18-kilometre road journey up a steep hill to Taunggyi — Burmese for "big hill."

For those bound for Shwenyaung on their way to Taunggyi, a special train leaves Rangoon at 6:15 p.m. running via Thazi. Special carriages with sleeping berths are marked for Shwenyaung, and are detached from the main train at Thazi, where it arrives at 5:30 a.m. the next day.

Information about train times, connections, etc., can be obtained from the English-speaking duty officer at the inquiry counter of the Rangoon railway station.

The trains have no restaurant car and only light refreshments and soft drinks are obtainable, so it is advisable to take your own food and drink. Burmese food (rice and chicken, beef or pork curry, as well as fruits — bananas, pineapples, guavas, oranges, watermelons or mangoes in season) can be had from vendors at the stations at each stop. But if your stomach is particularly sensitive to unaccustomed foods, carry tablets for diarrhoea or other intestinal ailments. A container of tea or water is strongly recommended for journeys during the hot months (March, April and May).

TAXIS: Jeep taxis are often a most convenient means of travel in Burma. A good number of them, as well as Nissan and Toyota pickups, can be found in Mandalay and can be hired for visits to places of interest in and out of town. The charges are negotiable but it is wise to inquire from your hotel about standard rates. There are no fixed rates for taxis but everything is negotiable in Burma.

You can hire a whole vehicle for the 67-kilometre trip from Mandalay to the hill station of **Maymyo**, but it is cheaper if you are prepared to share the taxi with other passengers and their luggage.

PONY CARTS: These horse-drawn conveyances can be found in most upcountry towns and provide a leisurely means of transport for short-distance travel. The rate is negotiable, depending on the length of the trip, and must be set before leaving. If you are unsure about what is a reasonable price, ask for help from local people.

BUSES: In general, long-distance buses in Burma are uncomfortable and unreliable and it is better to travel by train or air, unless one is on a very limited budget. Privately owned buses operate over most roads in Burma though most of them are not of a high standard. Lately, the state-owned **Road Transport Corp.** and some cooperative societies have also introduced long-distance bus services using 30-passenger buses between Rangoon and some main towns such as **Meiktila**, **Magwe** (in central Burma) and **Prome** (at the northern tip of the Irrawaddy delta). You can travel comfortably without fear of breakdown on these buses. Routes include Rangoon-Pegu, Rangoon-Meiktila, Rangoon-Magwe and Rangoon-Prome. The bus for **Magwe** leaves Rangoon at 3 a.m. and reaches Magwe in the evening. This service can be used for trips to Pagan or nearby **Nyaung-U**.

SHIPPING: Government, cooperative and privately owned ships of various sizes ply the rivers and you can pick and choose from among them to suit your convenience. Fares are generally higher if you travel in boats of the government-run **Inland Water Transport Corp.**, but they are comparatively more reliable for safety and punctuality. The delta town of **Bassein** is best reached by one of these boats. If you want a cruise down the placid **Irrawaddy**, you might take the boat from Mandalay to **Nyaung-U** near Pagan — 190 kilometres with ordinary and upper class accommodation. The double-decker boat sails from Mandalay at dawn and reaches Nyaung-U at about 7 a.m. or 8 a.m. the next day.

You may spend the night on board before sailing at no extra charge, but to get sleeping space you must spread out your own bedding or buy a woven sleeping mat. The same applies even if you are travelling upper class. All that is provided for upper-class passengers is a communal cabin on the upper deck at the bow of the vessel separated from the much more crowded lower and upper decks. Buddhist monks often travel in this cabin and as their religion forbids physical contact with women, female travellers should take care to observe this rule. There is no rule preventing them from talking with women or accepting alms or food offered by women. As only poor-quality Burmese rice and curry, tea and soft drinks are available on board, you would do well to take your own food. Visitors to Pagan should disembark at Nyaung-U and take the horse-cart or bus from there to Pagan. But do not go in March, April or May, when low water levels in the river cause navigation hazards.

Burma's coastal and overseas shipping is run by the state-owned **Myanmar Five Star Corp.** (132-136 Theinbyu St, Rangoon). The corporation is the agent for all foreign shipping lines calling at Burmese ports.

There may be restrictions on foreigners taking certain river trips, but these will be made clear when one applies for tickets.

AIR: The state-owned **Myanmar Airways Corp.** (Tel: 80710, 84566), operates domestic services linking many towns. There is also a private domestic carrier, **Air Mandalay** (Tel: 82561, 30144), which uses modern aircraft and flies between Rangoon and Mandalay.

Myanmar Airways has daily scheduled flights from Rangoon to most places of interest such as Mandalay, Pagan, Taunggyi and Sandoway (noted for its beautiful beach). You may also take flights from Mandalay to northern towns such as **Myitkyina** and **Lashio**.

Propeller-driven Fokker Friendships and jet Fokker F28s are used on most routes, though for short shuttle flights between Mandalay and northern towns 20-passenger turboprop de Havilland Twin Otters are used. There is a surcharge for the F28 Rangoon-Mandalay and

Nyaung-U flights over the slower Friendship.

The U.S. Government has warned visitors against using Myanmar Airways on safety grounds.

Air tickets must be purchased in foreign currency or exchange certificates produced to prove legal exchange if you are paying in local currency. The fares are cheaper if the flight is booked in advance and paid for overseas because of the favourable exchange rates given by some government agencies. Internal air fares are included in the price of most package tours.

Tours

By far the easiest way to visit Burma is in groups organized by authorized travel agents. Several travel agencies in Thailand offer tours to Burma with two of them being able to offer better service and facilities than the others: **Diethelm Travel**, 140-1 Wireless Rd, Bangkok. Tel: 255 9150-70 255 9115, Fax: 256 0248-9, and **Mandalay Myanmar Tours** which is a joint venture between the state-owned Myanmar Hotels and Tourism Services and Skyline Travel Service, and can be reached **c/o Skyline Travel Service**, 491/33 G Flr, Silom Plaza Bldg, Silom Rd, Bangkok 10500. Tel: 233 1864, 233 3440, 235 9115-8, Fax: 236 6585, 237 3292, Cable: SKYLIPS, Tlx: 82243 SKYLIPS TH.

A typical eight days/seven nights tour costs US$1,000-1,500. A 15 days/14 nights (economy) tour costs about US$1,650. A typical 15 days/14 nights programme includes Rangoon, Mandalay, Maymyo, Pagan, Taunggyi and Pegu. The price includes accommodation and internal travel in Burma — but not the Bangkok-Rangoon-Bangkok airfare, visa fee or departure tax.

Within Burma, the state-owned **Myanmar Travels and Tours** (Tel: 92800-1) now faces competition from many private tour agencies.

Accommodation

The hotels in Burma are of modest standard compared to those in some neighbouring countries, though they are almost as expensive. The cost of hotel rooms is usually included in packages arranged by travel agents.

The Strand, facing Rangoon port, is a relic of pre-World War II British days and was once rated one of the best in Asia. It still retains a tradition of homely atmosphere with a hint of the aristocratic breeding of the old days, and has been renovated over the past few years.

Others at the top of the range are the **Jade Pavilion Myanmar**, the **Narawat Hotel**, **Best Inn/Best Executive Suite** and the **Baiyoke Kandawgyi Hotel**. Another 12 or so top-grade hotels are due to open over the next few years.

There is also the **Thamada,** which overlooks the central railway station, and has less atmosphere than the Strand though its service is better. The **Inya Lake** is the biggest hotel, built by the Soviets as a gift in the early 1950s. It is located 11 kilometres north of the city centre. **The Kandawgyi** is a converted boat-club building on the southern shore of the Royal Lake near the zoological gardens. **The Dagon** is in the midst of the city's cinemas and is the least expensive of the state-run hotels.

There are also hundreds of small, clean and comfortable private hotels which have opened in 1993-94 and which can accept foreign guests.

Upcountry, accommodation is available in both state and privately owned hotels in Mandalay, Taunggyi, Kalaw, Maymyo, Pagan and Sandoway. Private hotels have also opened in Bassein, Prome and other smaller towns. The standard is adequate and prices are reasonable.

Dining

The staple Burmese food is boiled rice which is eaten with dishes of curry, fish, beef, mutton, chicken or pork, cooked with potatoes or green vegetables. The most favoured dish is *sibyan*, in which the fish or meat is stewed in a generous dose of groundnut oil mixed with condiments to give it a soft, sweet and soothing taste. Burmese food is usually accompanied by *ngapi*, a kind of fish sauce mixed with ground baked chilis. It is eaten with fresh vegetables such as slices of cucumber, green mango, cabbage or lettuce, or with boiled vegetables or bamboo shoots. A side dish called *pagigyaw* or *balachaung* is also often taken with the main dishes. The former is rather hot and is made of salted fish or shrimp paste fried in groundnut oil with chili, garlic and onions. The latter is much milder, as it contains less chili and the strong taste of the paste is softened by a mixture of sweet dry prawns. It is less liable to upset your stomach.

Hotels offer a limited choice of local dishes among their Western, Indian and Chinese food. But Burmese food is readily available at food-stalls scattered throughout the city, especially

Bargaining in the market. PHOTO: IRA CHAPLAIN

near market places. Stalls selling *mohinga* — a popular soup of rice noodles, fish, eggs, onion and banana — can be found in virtually every market in Burma. The soup is served sprinkled with coriander leaves and leeks. *Khaoswes* is another popular soup. It is based on a Shan dish (*khao soi*) and contains rice noodles and meat boiled in a thick gravy of coconut milk.

There are several Chinese restaurants in Rangoon. The most famous are the **Yankin Restaurant**, No. 1 (Kanbe Rd, Yankin township. Tel: 58925. **Mya Kan Tha**, 70 Natmauk Lanthwe. Tel: 52712. **Nagani** in Koemaing and the **Yin Swe** (Tel: 30361) at 137 University Ave.

In the airport park there is the **Penguin** (Tel: 64587), also specializing in Chinese food. The **Dolphin Restaurant** (Tel: 85084) in Kan Yeiktha Rd serves Chinese food and seafood, as do the **White House Restaurant** (Tel: 64235) at 6A Thukhawadi Rd and the **Panda Restaurant** (Tel: 21152) at 205 Warden St.

There is a Japanese restaurant on Shwegondaing Rd, called **Furusato**, which serves mediocre Japanese dishes but excellent sake.

Indian food can be found in the area west of the Sule Pagoda. The **Karaweik Restaurant** (Tel: 92800) on the royal lakes (houses in a copy of a royal barge of the ancient Burmese kings) serves good Burmese, Chinese and Western food.

Nan Yu Swe, 81 Pansodan St (Tel: 77796) in central Rangoon is clean and offers enormous servings of delicious noodles at reasonable prices. For Western food, the **Inya Lake** and **The Strand** are the best. Most restaurants serve imported European and Chinese beer, as well as the local brew, called Mandalay, when available.

Entertainment

Rangoon is virtually without nightlife. Everything is closed by about 9 p.m. but for a few teashops and a few music bars and one night club (**The Dynasty**). There is also **traditional Burmese dancing** nightly in the Karaweik Hall, a 50-minute performance arranged by **Myanmar Travels and Tours**.

But Burma is a land of festivals (each month having a particular festival) and Rangoon has a hefty share of them. In the cool dry season (November to April) — the most pleasant period in which to visit Burma — these festivals are held in the open air at night at one or more places in the city. The festivals are carnival-like affairs, boasting rows of brilliantly lit shops, cafes and amusement centres. But the main attraction is the *pwe*, a concert of dance and music given on a mobile stage and lasting from about 9 p.m. to midnight. After that the entertainment resumes with classical and dramatic performances called *zat*, with themes drawn from Buddhist lore or the life stories of ancient kings.

The performance opens with the famous Burmese duet dance in which the actor and actress sing and dance together in resplendent costumes to the accompaniment of exotic music. The theme of the drama is tacked on to the duet performance and then developed. The dancing does not end until about dawn.

These festivals will give you a chance to look at Burmese life and culture at close quarters. The music may sound strange as it is on the septitonic scale and has no chromatic scale. But modern Burmese music is beginning to show evidence of its contacts with the West. A good many musical pieces are adaptations of Western tunes, and Western musical instruments such as the piano, saxophone, guitar, clarinet and electronic organ now form part of the musical equipment of the better-known *pwe* troupes. You should ask at your hotel for information about these festivals.

Burmese, Western, Indian and often Japanese films show at the cinemas in Rangoon, Mandalay and other towns. Despite the language barrier, Burmese movies give a good insight into Burmese life and culture at various levels.

Shopping

Although Burma does not offer as wide a range of goods as in the past, it still has many attractive things to buy. In Rangoon, the **Bogyoke market** (formerly known as Scott Market), is one of the best shopping centres, where Burmese handicrafts can be found. Mandalay silk *longyis* (skirt-like pieces of cloth) of distinctive designs, beautiful Shan woven bags, Burmese slippers, wood and ivory carvings, lacquerware, silverware, Bassein parasols (women's sunshades made in the delta town of Bassein), paintings, Burmese cigarettes and cheroots, etc., can be bought here. Some curio and antique dealers have set up shop here, providing opportunities for bargain-hunters.

As trade in gems, rubies, sapphires, jade, pearls, etc., for which Burma is famous, is officially a government monopoly, they are best bought at the government-run **Diplomatic Shop** on Sule Pagoda Rd. There are good selections of stones set in jewellery of attractive local designs. It is safer to make gem and jewellery purchases there as their quality is guaranteed officially and export permitted. Silverware, lacquerware and mother-of-pearl items are also available at the shop.

The entrance to the **Shwedagon pagoda** is another big shopping centre. There you will find Burmese drums of different sizes, wooden puppets and horses for children, papier-mache toys and masks, brassware, Burmese swords and wood and ivory carvings. For lovers of curios and antiques, the place to go is **Curio da City** at 35 Bahan Rd on the eastern environs of the Shwedagon pagoda.

For book lovers there is the government-run **special bookshop** at 221 Sule Pagoda Rd and the **Sarpay Beikman** bookshop at 529-531 Merchant St.

At the latter shop you can buy books on Burma such as the *Pagan Guide* and *Historic Sites of Burma*. Those with a fascination for old or rare English-language books on a wide variety of subjects should find it rewarding to visit the well-stocked **Pagan Book Shop** in 31st St.

For art works, the places to visit are the **Burma Art Centre** at 187 Bogyoke market and **Lokanath Art Shop** at Phayre St. For shopping generally, new department stores and shopping centres are being built all over Rangoon.

In Mandalay, the old Zegyo market has gone — there is now a shopping centre there instead. Shops in the town offer a wide variety of Shan bags, jewellery, lacquerware, slippers, parasols, pottery and other handicraft items. Mandalay night bazaar, which opens at sundown near the railway station, is an excellent place to visit. Brilliantly lit with electric lights and lanterns and thronged with shoppers, it has the lively atmosphere of a carnival.

Sports

Soccer is the most popular sport, and **Aung San Stadium** in Rangoon near the Thamada Hotel is the venue of the major soccer events of the season which runs from June to February. Tennis, hockey, cricket, golf, volleyball and basketball are also played in the larger towns. There are many private golf courses near Rangoon — for instance, there is an 18-hole course at the **Yangon Golf Club** (Tel: 45563) at Danyingone, Mingaladon (near the airport), and another at **Myanmar Golf Club** (Tel: 61702), 9th Mile, Pyay Rd.

Boxing, both Western and Burmese style, is popular. The Burmese style is not governed by the Queensberry rules and allows the use of legs, elbows and head, and the bout ends as soon as one of the fighters gets a bleeding wound, however slight. The fight takes place to the accompaniment of Burmese martial music which rises to a crescendo as the tempo of the fight increases.

The most widely played national sport is the game of *chin-lone* or cane-ball. Similar to other variations played in most of Southeast Asia, it consists of keeping a small ball woven of thin strips of cane up in the air with the use only of the feet, head or shoulder, but not the hands. Played alone, or by a team of two to seven players of either sex, standing in a circle of about 3.5 metres in diameter, the game is most interesting to watch. It needs no special area on which to play, and is seen in progress in parks or even on the streets.

There is swimming at the **Kikine Swimming Club** (Tel: 50034), 23 Saya San Rd and at the Inya Lake Hotel. Yachtsmen may care to contact the **Yangon Sailing Club** (Tel: 31218) at 132 Inya Rd.

Dec. 25 Holidays

There are festivals and celebrations throughout the year in Burma. Many of these are centred on famous pagodas in cities such as Rangoon and Mandalay, but some are associated with pagodas which, though in jungles far outside the cities, are highly revered for their romantic legends. Other festivals are national affairs derived from Buddhist practices or related to the varying seasons. All these are linked to the lunar calendar and so vary in date from one year to the next. But there are also holidays marking political events and these occur on the same dates each year. In addition to national festivals, others are celebrated in the homelands of the various ethnic groups.

January 4: Independence Day — marking independence from the British in 1948 — is celebrated with public sports and festivities nationwide. Theatrical plays and dancing are presented in the evenings.

February 12: Union Day — marking nationalist leader Bogyoke Aung San's achievement in forming a union of the country's racial groups in 1947, which led to independence — is the biggest political festival. It features a grand, week-long government exhibition and carnival in Rangoon and fairs, dancing and theatrical performances in other towns.

February-March: The Full Moon of Tabaung Lunar Month marks the occasion of the rice harvest and also the enshrinement of eight sacred hair-relics of Buddha in the Shwedagon pagoda of Rangoon more than 2,500 years ago. Offerings are placed before Buddhist images and presented to monks. Among the offerings is the special food made of glutinous rice known as *htamane* which is shared by all.

March: Peasants' Day. (Public holiday).

March 27: Defence Services' Day. This marks the occasion in 1945 when the Burmese began organized resistance against the Japanese. There are military parades and an evening fireworks display. (Public holiday).

April: *Thingyan* (the Water Festival) welcomes the Burmese New Year. It lasts three to four days — determined by astrological requirements varying from year to year — and begins with ceremonial washing of Buddhist images in scented water and offering of a morning meal to monks. Then follows a period of rowdy merry-making for all; the throwing of water over one another is the most notable part of the fun and is the customary way of wishing good luck in the new year. Young men and women wearing colourful (often outlandish) costumes enjoy themselves a great deal, dancing and singing and attending the many shows in town. This period of revelry is followed by the calm solemnity of the New Year Day, which is observed by performing charitable deeds at pagodas and monasteries. (Four-day public holiday).

April-May: The Full Moon of Kason Lunar Month is in triple celebration of the Buddha's birth, enlightenment and attainment of Nirvana on his death. The sacred banyan trees are blessed with holy water and rituals are enacted at the Shwedagon and other pagodas. (Public holiday).

May 1: May Day (World Workers' Day — public holiday).

June-July: The Waso Festival marks the beginning of the three-month period of the Buddhist Lent and monks are presented with robes and gifts of everyday necessities. Over the Lenten period, monks observe a period of spiritual retreat and stricter religious duties, and it is the most common period for young men to enter the monkhood temporarily. The

Burmese children give a warm welcome. PHOTO: JONATHAN FRIEDLAND

general populace is also expected to heighten its religious observances during the period. Weddings are banned during Lent, as are festivities of most kinds. (Public holiday).

July 19: Martyrs' Day commemorates the assassination on July 19, 1947, of Bogyoke Aung San and members of his cabinet. Religious customs are observed and wreaths laid at the Martyrs' Mausoleum near the north entrance to the Shwedagon pagoda. (Public holiday).

August-September: The Festival of Nats (spirits) is held at Taungbyone village near Mandalay.

October: The Festival of Thadingyut (also called the Festival of Lights) marks the full moon in Thadingyut Lunar Month, the end of Lent. During a three-day period, lights — candles, oil lamps and electric lights — illuminate the night, especially at pagodas, and masses of fire-balloons are released into the air. There is dancing and other entertainment. The occasion commemorates the Buddha's return from a non-human world when angel-like beings illuminated his way. (Public holiday).

November: The Tazaungdaing Festival is another occasion for lights, again on the full-moon. There are celebrations in the towns with dancing and shows, and at the Shwedagon pagoda there is an all-night robe-weaving competition, the results of which are donated to the monks. (Public holiday).

December 25: Christmas Day. (Public holiday).

DISCOVERING BURMA

RANGOON

The present pattern of the city — which is home to well over 3.3 million people — was laid out by the British colonial administration. The main government and commercial centre is the neighbourhood of the **Sule Pagoda**, with broad streets running east to west parallel to the river and north to south ending at the river.

The main streets have names (Burmese now replacing the previous English names) and the side-streets have numbers, beginning with the north-south streets in the west, and then progressing to the east of the city and finishing with the less carefully laid-out streets north of the railway line. The more than 2,500-year-old **Shwedagon pagoda**, a richly gilded Buddhist stupa, rises almost 100 metres from the top of **Singuttara Hill**, the last of the Pegu range, about 6.5 kilometres north of the city centre. Shwedagon Pagoda Rd runs north from the riverside, past the city's main shopping centre to the base of the pagoda hill. Buses and taxis ply the route and a 15-minute bus ride will take you to the pagoda. Admission costs US$5.

At the base you can either take the lift up to the pagoda platform or walk up the stone steps which are flanked by stalls selling gilded Buddhist images and shrines of all shapes and sizes, flowers and incense to be offered at the pagoda, wooden and papier-mache toys for children, etc. You should go barefoot once you reach the pagoda precincts, which start from the base of the hill right up to the pagoda platform.

The treasure vault of the pagoda is believed to contain the sacred relics of the Buddha. Legend has it that, apart from the relics, it contains a fabulous collection of gold, jewellery and precious stones which successive kings and nobles of Burma donated to the pagoda for more than 2,500 years. (The original, a much smaller one, is believed to have been built in 524 BC.)

Once on the pagoda platform, you will experience the serene tranquillity of a Buddhist place of worship. The soft tinkling of the bells from the diamond bud at the pinnacle of the pagoda helps to soothe away worldly worries. Described by Sir Edwin Arnold, a British scholar on Buddhism, as "the great pyramid of fire" and by the poet Rudyard Kipling as the "waking, winking, tinkling wonder," the pagoda has 68 smaller pagodas and numerous shrines and prayer halls on its 432-metre base platform. The stupa has a plantain-bud-shaped pinnacle which since 1900 has been sheathed in gold plates, each 30 centimetres square.

The latest layer of gold plates, numbering 2,562, was affixed in a picturesque 13-day ceremony in March 1986. The pagoda now has a total of 20,912 plates weighing about 1.9 tonnes. At the top of the bud is the crown called *hti* (meaning umbrella) fitted with a vane studded with 5,448 diamonds and more than 2,000 other precious and semi-precious stones. In the pagoda precincts packets of gold leaf (25-100 leaves per packet) are sold to pilgrims wishing to have them pasted on to the pagoda or to the many Buddhist images in the surrounding shrines.

On the northwest corner of the platform is a giant bronze bell with an interesting history. Just over two metres high and weighing about 16 tonnes, it was donated to the pagoda by a Burmese king in 1778. After the second Anglo-Burmese War in 1824, which ended in British annexation of lower Burma, the victorious British troops tried to carry the bell away to Calcutta as a war trophy. But the great bell fell into the Rangoon river and defied all attempts by British military engineers to salvage it. Subsequently, the Burmese are said to have rescued it from the bottom of the river by the simple device of diving and tying bamboo poles to the bell until it floated. The bell was thus restored to the pagoda. Describing this incident, an English civil servant named H. Fielding Hall remarked: "The river gave back to them [the Burmese] what it had refused to us."

Another notable stupa is the **Sule pagoda**, a few minutes' walk northwest from the Strand Hotel. Some 48 metres high, the pagoda is said to have been built about 2,250 years ago. In its vault is believed to be enshrined the sacred hair of the Buddha. Apart from being a holy place, the pagoda and its surrounding

The following are some of the names which have been changed by the present government from their previous colonial spelling, in line with changing the name of the country from Burma to Myanmar.

TOWNS		
Rangoon	to	Yangon
Pagan	to	Bagan
Pegu	to	Bago
Boulmein	to	Mawlamyine
Akyab	to	Sittwe
Bassein	to	Pathein
Prome	to	Pyi (or Pyay)
Maymyo	to	Pyin Oo Lwin
Syriam	to	Tanyin
RIVERS		
Irrawaddy	to	Ayeyarwady
Salween	to	Thanlwin
Sittang	to	Sittoung
Chindwin	to	Chindwinn
ETHNIC GROUPS		
Karen	to	Kayin
Burman	to	Bamar
Arakanese	to	Rakhine

structures now form a picturesque traffic island.

The city has other important pagodas worthy of a visit. The **Kaba Aye** (meaning world peace) pagoda about 11 kilometres north from the city centre, was built under the orders of the former Prime Minister U Nu as the venue of the Sixth Buddhist Synod (1954-56) to be held on the occasion of the 2,500th anniversary of Buddha's enlightenment. Near the pagoda is the great **Sacred Cave**, designed and built by Burmese engineers specifically for holding the synod. It was here that the text of the *Tripitakas* (the three basic Buddhist canons) was recited, interpreted and wherever necessary revised by eminent Burmese Buddhist scholars during the synod. Near the cave is another building housing the **International Institute of Buddhist Studies**.

The **Mae La Mu pagoda** is about 13 kilometres from the city centre to the northeast at the edge of open fields. Around the main pagoda are a number of beautiful images showing scenes from Buddha's previous lives. Said to have been built by Mae La Mu, so-called because she was believed to have been born of a La Mu tree, the pagoda remained neglected until recent years. Mae La Mu later became queen by marrying the Rangoon king, and the pagoda was built in memory of her grandson who died in childhood. An elderly woman of Rangoon started to repair the pagoda a few years ago, reportedly in response to a dream in which the long-dead queen requested her to do so.

Besides pagodas and shrines, Rangoon has several places of worship of different faiths such as Hindu temples, Chinese temples, mosques, synagogues and churches of different Christian denominations, which testify to the country's freedom of religion.

The Rangoon Zoo, not far from the Shwedagon pagoda, houses rare species of birds, reptiles, apes, crocodiles, etc. **The National Museum** in Pansodan (Phyre St) has on display the Mandalay regalia, once belonging to the last two Burmese kings, that was returned to Burma by the British in 1964 as a gesture of goodwill. Price of admission: US$4.

For orchid lovers, the place to visit is the 20-acre **horticultural garden at Mingaladon**, 16 kilometres north of the city centre. Maintained by the state Agricultural Corp., the garden has more than 88,000 native, 23,000 foreign and 5,500 hybrid orchids. The garden forms part of a more ambitious 120-acre National Park being set up in Rangoon's northern environs.

DISCOVERING UPCOUNTRY

Starting in the southwest, the Irrawaddy delta town of **Bassein**, is a 30-minute flight from Rangoon, but a better approach is by river, offering a fine view of the region and its people. The town is most noted for the beautiful decorated umbrellas made there. Mentioned in sixth-century writings, subsequently it was the scene of frequent battles between the Mons and the Burmese.

To the southeast of Rangoon, **Moulmein**, on the Tennasserim coast at the mouth of the Salween river, can be reached by rail, road or air — the flight taking only 40 minutes. Once an important port, it has been superseded by Rangoon and Bassein owing to the difficulties of navigation on entry. The views from the pagoda-topped hills overlooking the town from the east are superb. **The Uzina pagoda** has beautifully carved life-size figures depicting the story of how the Buddha-to-be, while still a young unenlightened prince, saw the four visions which made him realize the futility of his life and sent him off to the jungle in search of the truth.

At one time Moulmein was Burma's great teak port, and at the timber yard will still see elephants at work moving the great logs.

Some 64 kilometres south is a large **war cemetery**, resting place of many prisoners-of-war forced by the Japanese to build the Burma-Thailand railway during World War II.

The rest of this route through Burma moves gradually north. Directly north of Moulmein and about 177 kilometres northeast of Rangoon, on top of a 1,066-metre-high cliff, lies one of Burma's most famous pagodas, the **Kyaiktiyo or Golden Rock** pagoda. The 5.4 metre-high pagoda stands on a big gilded boulder, which rests precariously on a downward-sloping, narrow ledge, separated from the main cliff by a six-metre gap. When pushed by pilgrims, the heavy boulder gives a mild shake, but hundreds of years of pushing by generations of pilgrims have not yet toppled the boulder. Burmese Buddhists regard this phenomenon as a miracle induced by a lock of Buddha's hair believed to be enshrined in the pagoda.

A visit to the pagoda involves a 160-kilometre bus ride to **Kyaikto**, another bus to a base-camp at Kinpun Skhan and then an 11-kilometre trek through wooded hills, lasting three to five hours: For the serious pilgrim, scholar or photographer only.

Pegu, 83 kilometres to the north of Rangoon, can be reached by road or rail and makes a good day-trip since the journey by car takes only two hours. It is said to have been founded in 573 AD and was at one time the capital of the Talaing (Mon) kingdom. It used to be Burma's greatest seaport and its magnificence was recorded by many 16th and 17th-century travellers. Since a change in the course of the river, Pegu has never regained its greatness.

En route from Rangoon to Pegu is the **Kyaikpun pagoda**, a favourite picnic spot for residents of the capital. The pagoda was erected by King Dhamazedi in 1476 AD and is distinguished by a sitting image of Buddha. The images, built of brick and stucco, are 30 metres high and lean back against a square pillar. One of the images facing west was destroyed in an earthquake in 1930.

Shwemawdaw (Great Golden God) pagoda lies to the east of the railway station in Pegu. It, too, is believed to contain relics of the Buddha and so is among the most venerated shrines in the country. Tradition has it that Lord Buddha, in his lifetime, bestowed on two devout Buddhist brothers two of his hairs. The brothers took them back to Pegu and enshrined them on a hill, where they built a pagoda, which has been added to through the ages. It was almost destroyed by the 1930 earthquake but was rebuilt in the early 1950s. Murals along the main entrance steps depict the destruction and the stages of reconstruction.

The **Hinthagone hill** behind the Shwemawdaw has a high-roofed platform over the remains of a pagoda and offers a good view. With their backs to the pagoda, there are four images of the standing Buddha facing north, south, east and west. It is an ideal spot for a picnic lunch and for photography, but remember to take off any footwear since these are considered to be the grounds of a pagoda named after the mythical Hintha bird. According to mythology, male and female Hintha birds flying over the sea could not find land to rest. Eventually they saw a mound but there was only room for one bird to land. The male landed and the female settled on top of him. Hence you will find the statue of two birds, one on top of the other, in front of the pagoda. A local joke is that men do not dare marry girls from Pegu or they will live the lives of henpecked husbands.

The Shwethalyaung (reclining golden Buddha) is another sight for tourists and reputed to be the most symmetrical and lifelike of all the reclining statues. It is 1.6 kilometres west of the railway station. The reclining Buddha was forgotten after the 1757 destruction but was rediscovered much later by a railway contractor. Now fully restored, it is an important landmark in the area.

Nearby is the **Kalyani Thein (Ordination Hall)** built in 1476 by the Talaing King Dhamazedi for the ordination of monks of absolute integrity and for the cultivation and development of true Buddhism. About 400 metres to the east of the Shwethalyaung pagoda is **Mahaceti (Grand Pagoda)**. It lay in ruins for four centuries until being rebuilt in 1979.

LAKE INLE

The people of the Shan state are fiercely independent of the central government, which sends troops to the area to combat local insurgency forces and attempts to curb widespread smuggling operations with bordering Thailand. The Shan area is the only place in Burma where Coca-Cola is available, and the powerful motors for the fishermen's boats are mostly smuggled in from across the border.

The chief attraction to visitors in this often-troubled region is the beautiful lake; an enormous, tranquil expanse of water surrounded by mountains, and home of the famous Shan leg-rowers who paddle and steer their long boats with one leg wrapped round the oar, releasing their arms to cast their fishing nets. Fast boats can be hired in the lakeside village of **Yaunghwe**; at least four hours are required to make a round trip.

At Kyats 350, hiring is expensive; but since each boat accommodates at least five people, the cost can be shared. From the boat you will be able to see the rowers and stops can be made at lake villages and pagodas resting on stilts. A normal part of the trip should be a visit to a government-managed hand-weaving workshop, but most of the materials, as well as the hand-woven Shan shoulder-bags, can be bought much cheaper elsewhere.

Open trucks (Burmese term them buses) and Toyota vans run the 32 kilometres from Yaunghwe up precipitous mountain roads to **Taunggyi**, the old British hill station and Shan capital, whose museum deserves a visit for its interesting relics and a good natural history section. Get there by daily flight from Rangoon or Mandalay to **He Ho**, then by bus to Yaunghwe/Taunggyi.

PAGAN (BAGAN)

A visit to Burma would not be complete without seeing **Pagan**, the 11th-century capital and cradle of Burmese civilization, northwest of Rangoon on the east bank of the Irrawaddy. There are daily flights from Rangoon to the nearby airport at **Nyaung-U** and from Mandalay.

Pagan covers a tract of about 25 kilometres of what is now cultivated land, yet within this small area there are the remains of over 5,000 temples — some scarcely more than rubble, others still able in size and beauty to give a vivid impression of a highly developed culture, mostly unknown to Westerners. Most of the monuments were erected between the 11th and 13th centuries AD when Pagan was the seat of the Burmese dynasty. In 1057 King Anawrahta conquered Thaton (believe to be Wakhon Pathom in Thailand) and brought back a large number of Buddhist monks, artists and craftsmen as well as more than 30 elephant-loads of Pali scriptures. From these Mon monks, the Burmese derived their alphabet and scriptures. In 1058 Anawrahta built the **Pitakat Taik** (library) near the middle of the present village to house the 30 loads of Buddhist scriptures.

During the next two centuries an incredible number of magnificent buildings were erected until the fall of the dynasty in 1287, when Kublai Khan sacked the city and the fleeing king dismantled several of the buildings for military purposes, starting the period of decay.

For the visitor arriving from the airport, the 20-minute bus ride to Pagan through the nearby town of **Nyaung-U** (itself worth seeing for its market) gives an unforgettable first glimpse of Pagan's bizarre arid flatland, dotted by countless spires, temples and pagodas, many crumbling or overgrown and some reduced to heaps of rubble.

Pagan village is little more than a collection of wooden houses lined along the main road linking it to Nyaung U. The **Sarabha Gateway** still serves as the market for the present village perimeter. It is the only structure remaining of the old city built in the ninth century AD, and was originally the main gate of the east wall. The entrance is guarded by two *nat* or spirit sculptures, representing a brother and sister.

The best way to see Pagan is to hire a local guide and one of the many horse buggies. Next to the gateway is the huge white **Ananda temple**. Built in 1091, it is highly venerated for the relics of the Buddha it supposedly contains. The ground-plan of the building is that of a Greek cross. Inside is a maze of corridors studded with inset statues of the Buddha and plaques inscribed in Mon script. The overall effect is not unlike that of some catacombs. In the centre lies a stone block with its sides facing directly north, south, east and west, and housing four colossal standing Buddhas. The centre corridor contains 80 statues in the lower niches showing the stages from birth to Nirvana of the Boddisatva. In the west-facing porch are two Buddha footprints on pedestals. The local museum is nearby.

Just south of the main street is **Thatbyinnyu temple**. Surrounded by the remains of red-brick stupas, the temple is easily recognized by its soaring white exterior, resembling a multi-storey wedding cake. Thatbyinnyu (omniscience) contains two main storeys connected by dark, perilously steep stairs on the inside to the passage on the first floor, and an external flight of stone stairs to the Buddha image on the upper storey. Further climbing on the outside to the narrow ledges on the top reveals magnificent panoramas.

The **Manuha temple** is named after the captured king of Thaton and its cramped style, including uncomfortably seated Buddhas, reflects the claustrophobia and stress suffered by the king.

Mingalazedi pagoda was constructed a few years before the Mongol invasion and in many ways is the most developed in style of the buildings in Pagan. The terraces have beautiful inscribed terracotta tiles.

When sightseeing becomes too tiring, visitors to Pagan are usually welcome to a free bowl of tea at any of the eating houses along the main streets. Accommodation is a problem in Pagan. If one is looking for Western-style luxury, then the **Thiripyitsaya** is the only place available. Built at great expense by the government, some way out of the village on the banks of the Irrawaddy for a captive market, it is an ugly imitation of a modern resort hotel and, by Burmese standards, extremely expensive. Other privately run resthouses offering lodging facilities at moderate rates are spartan by comparison, but much better value.

Pagan still has good-quality lacquerware for sale: but be sure to bargain over the price, and beware of buying gemstones; the stones are most likely fakes.

MANDALAY

Mandalay lies in the dry zone on the east bank of the Irrawaddy about 690 kilometres north of

Exploring Kentung. PHOTO: IRA CHAPLAIN

Rangoon. Founded in 1857, it was the capital of Burma for only 28 years but has great sentimental value for the Burmese, being the home of the last two Burmese kings, Mindon and his son Thibaw. It is the country's second-largest city with a population of 600,000.

Mandalay is the cultural heart of Burma and in the city the best in Buddhist carving can be found, as well as superb examples of timber-frame architecture. There are a number of notable pagodas and temples, but if you go searching you will find many small but splendid monasteries with their excellent Buddha images (**Tahat Htaw Kyaung** on 35th St, 90 metres west from 84th St, is a good example).

Luckily, the city's cultural and historic buildings remained unaffected by the big fires which swept through the southwest and northeast sectors of the city in March 1984.

Mandalay Hill, 235 metres above the surrounding plains just to the northeast of the palace walls, is covered with pagodas and monasteries and so footwear is forbidden. Near the top of the hill is a colossal standing image of the Buddha, with the right hand outstretched and a finger pointing to where the former palace grounds lie below.

Local legend says that while on a visit to this place accompanied by his disciple Ananda, the Buddha prophesied that in the 2,400th year of the propagation of the faith, a city which would be hailed as an outstanding centre of Buddhism would rise on the indicated spot. It was actually in that year, synchronizing with the Christian year 1857, that King Mindon started building a new capital at Mandalay.

At the bottom of the hill to the south is **Kyauktawgyi** built by King Mindon. The Buddha figure inside was carved from a single block of marble. The 90 figures around the pagoda represent the Buddha's disciples. The marble block was taken from Sagyin, a few kilometres to the north, and it was said to have been so large that 10,000 men were employed for 13 days to transport it from the canal to the site of the pagoda.

A few hundred metres to the northeast of the Kyauktawgyi pagoda lies the **Kuthodaw (Royal Bounty)** pagoda, (modelled after the Shwezigon pagoda of Pagan). Built by King Mindon in 1857, the Kuthodaw is also known as the Maha Lawka Marazein pagoda. Here stand 728 white marble tablets carrying, carved on their faces, the definitive edition of the Buddhist canon determined by the fifth Buddhist Synod held during Mindon's reign.

To the south of the Kuthodaw are the imposing ruins of the **Atumashi Kyaung** ("incomparable monastery"). All that remains of this great monument, which drew ecstatic accounts from Western travellers who saw it whole, indicate that the wooden building which previously stood there was mounted on five rectangular terraces. The monastery was known for the Buddha image made of silken garments of the king, with a lacquer exterior and a big diamond on the forehead which was stolen in the confusion following the annexation of Upper Burma in 1885 by the British.

The Mandalay Royal Palace was once a royal city within the city. Now, because of British bombing (of which the Burmese have long been resentful) during World War II, the palace grounds offer little more than a walk in the hot sun. The walls form a square with each side 1.6 kilometres long, punctuated by fine watchtowers and gates. A 77-metre-wide moat surrounds the whole shell. In the palace grounds is a small museum exhibiting models of the original palace buildings. The palace is being rebuilt, with the target for completion being "Visit Myanmar Year" in 1996.

Mandalay's famed **Zegyo bazaar**, designed in 1903 by an Italian named Count Caldrari, the first secretary of the Mandalay municipality, is now a shopping centre built on the same area.

In the heart of Mandalay stands the **Shwe Kyi Myint** pagoda built by King Monshinsaw (1114-67) of Pagan. This shrine on 24th St between 82nd and 83rd streets, predates Mandalay by many centuries. It is noted for two things: The image is the original one consecrated by the builder himself and it has now become the repository of many images made of gold and silver, salvaged from the palace and adorned with invaluable precious stones representing the collection of successive monarchs. There is also a small golden palanquin used by a lesser queen. Many Buddha images can also be seen in the quadrangle of the pagoda.

The **Mahamuni** or Arakan pagoda is the town's best-known and lies about three kilometres south of the market just off to the east from 84th St. The main Buddha figure is believed to be of great antiquity and was brought from Mrohaung — once the capital of Arakan — by King Bodawpaya (1782-1819). in 1784. The road the king built from his capital (nearby at Amarapura) to the pagoda can still be seen.

The Buddha image is enshrined in the pagoda and became the object of fervent devotion for his people and is still paid homage to by Buddhists throughout the world. It was originally cast out of metal but the body of it has for long been so lavishly gilded that it has assumed an irregular outline. The image, which is in the usual sitting posture of Buddha, is 3.8 metres high. The original pagoda was damaged by fire in 1884. The present pagoda, which has a terraced roof of gilded stucco, is therefore of late construction.

In the inner courtyard are hundreds of stone slabs bearing inscriptions recording religious endowments. Not far from the western entrance is a group of six bronze figures — two of men, three of lions and one of a three-headed elephant. Local legend has it that, by rubbing the appropriate anatomical part of the two bronze figures of men, one can be cured of similarly located diseases.

The **Eindawya pagoda** was built by the Pagan Min (Pagan Prince) in 1847 on the site of the palace he lived in before ascending the throne. It lies in the centre of the city. Heavily gilded, this beautifully proportioned shrine houses an image of the Buddha made of chalcedony (a type of quartz mineral with an admixture of opal) said to have been brought back from Buddha Gaya (India) in 1839.

In east Mandalay lies the **Sandamuni pagoda** built on the ground on which the temporary palace of King Mindon stood while the new palace was being erected. This pagoda is also known to have been raised over the graves of the Crown Prince and some members of the royal family who lost their lives in a palace rebellion of 1866 when an attempt was made on the life of King Mindon.

The manufacture of gold leaf flourishes in the southeastern part of the city. It is a hereditary occupation carried on as a cottage industry. Small bits of gold are laboriously beaten for days to get the required film-like thinness. The beating is done by men while the piecing together of the film is done by women. Packets of gold leaf are sold to devotees for gilding pagodas and images. Buses run to the outskirts of the town where many of the previously mentioned sites are located.

Surrounding Mandalay are three towns (or ruins of towns) which were in their time capitals of Burma. These are the towns of **Amarapura**, **Ava** and **Sagaing**. The town of **Mingun**, though never a capital, is also of note.

Maymyo (now officially called **Pyin Oo Lwin**) is a curiosity. A remote hill station, once a favourite refuge for the British during the wet season and hunting ground for expatriate spinsters, this incredible anachronism can be reached by a taxi service which leaves from near Mandalay bazaar. The trip takes about two hours. The views are breathtaking and a night at the former **Canda Craig Hotel**, now renamed the **Maymyo Inn**, will not be forgotten.

The altitude — as in Taunggyi — makes Maymyo very cold, so warm clothing should be taken. Transport in the town is by primitive horse-carriage and the town itself is a curious mixture of Burma and the English Home Counties. The Government Botanical Garden is worth a visit. Established in 1914 by the then British colonial government, the garden has 170 acres of land and 70 acres of well-maintained lakes.

Amarapura (Immortal City) lies a few kilometres to the south of Mandalay and can be reached cheaply by bus or by shared taxi. Founded by King Bodawpaya in 1781, it was the capital from 1782 to 1882. Ava became the capital for some years until Amarapura was restored to favour from 1837 to the founding of Mandalay in 1857.

Today the villages in the vicinity are centres for silk weaving and practically every house has its loom. The Kathe villages are famous for weaving of chequered longyi — the intricately patterned open skirt worn by Burmese women on ceremonial occasions.

Behind the town is a chain of lakes bordered by trees. **U Pein's bridge**, named after its builder, the Lord Mayor of Amarapura, was built of teak taken from the deserted palace of Ava. More than 250 years old, it is now the oldest bridge in Burma.

HOTEL GUIDE

RANGOON

A: US$90 and above

BAIYOKE KANDAWGYI HOTEL, Kandawgyi. Tel: 86521, Fax: 80412. *R: L, W.*

BEST INN/BEST EXECUTIVE SUITE, 96-98 Pansodan St. Tel: 72835, 86058. *R: L, W.*

INYA LAKE HOTEL, Kaba Aye Pagoda Rd. Tel: 62857-8, Tlx: 21502 INYAHOBM. *P. R: L, W.*

JADE PAVILION MYANMAR, 126 A Dhamma Zedi Rd, Bahan. Tel: 53062, 86021. *R: L, W.*

NARAWAT HOTEL, 257 Insein Rd. Tel: 67888, Fax: 67777. *R: L, W.*

STRAND HOTEL, 92 Strand Rd. Tel: 81530, 81533. *R: L, W.*

THAMADA HOTEL, 5 Signal Pagoda Rd. Tel: 71477, 71499, Tlx: 21339 TAMAHOBM. *R: L.*

All others B: US$30-90

DAGON HOTEL, 256-260 Sule Pagoda Rd. Tel: 71140. *R: L.*

KANDAWGYL HOTEL, Kan Yelktha Rd. Tel: 82255, 82327, 83925. *R: L.*

SAKANTHA HOTEL, Central Railway Station. Tel: 82975, 83292. *R: L.*

PAGAN (BAGAN)

AYEYAR INN (IRRA INN), Bagan-Nyaung Oo. Tel: 25. *R: L.*

THIRIPYITSAYA HOTEL, Bagan-Nyaung Oo. Tel: 89000. *P. R: L.*

MANDALAY

INWA HOTEL, Between 24th and 25th Streets. Tel: 27028-9. *R: L.*

MANDALAY HOTEL, Corner of 26th and 68th Streets. Tel: 22500, 22499. *R: L.*

MANNMYO HOTEL, 78th St. Tel: 26889.

MYAMANDALA HOTEL, Corner of 27th and 69th Streets. Tel: 21283. *P. R: L.*

PYIN OO LWIN (MAYMYO)

NANMYAING HOTEL, Tel: 2118. *R: L.*

THRIMYAING HOTEL, Tel: 2047. *R: L, W.*

TAUNGGYI

TAUNGGYI HOTEL, Shu-hum-yawhkin Rd. Tel: 21611, 21302. *R: L.*

KALAW

KALAW HOTEL, Tel: 47. *R: L.*

NGAPALI (SANDOWAY)

NGAPALI BEACH HOTEL, Tel: 28. *R: L.*

PYAY (PROME)

PYAY GUEST HOUSE, Tel: 21819. *R: L.*

PATHEIN (BASSEIN)

PATHEIN HOTEL, Tel: 21162. *R: L.*

P — Swimming pool **R** — Restaurant **L** — Local food **W** — Western food

INDIA

India is truly a country where the past and the present live side-by-side, even if the present sometimes seems stuck in the 1950s or earlier. In a few islands of modern technology such as Bangalore, it is up with the latest advances. But in most urban centres, the workforce toils in turn-of-the-century conditions. In vast stretches of rural India, tractors and biotechnology are at work along with almost medieval relationships between landowners and their labourers. The fast-disappearing forests are home to millions of tribal people who live by shifting cultivation.

India has an area of 3.2 million square kilometres and a population of 900 million (as of early 1995) spread across 24 states and many small union territories, each with its own state or territorial assembly. Its electorate of almost 500 million makes India the world's largest democracy.

But whether India is really one nation or a commonwealth of several is debatable. It encompasses peoples akin to those of the Middle East and Central Asia, Tibet and Burma, as well as a wide diversity of cultures rooted in the Subcontinent. One could spend a lifetime visiting India to explore each aspect, as well as the layers of relics from the Dravidian prehistory to the British Raj.

Visitors new to the Third World will be shocked by the abject poverty and neglect — as close as the grubby urchins and lepers who tap on the taxi window for *baksheesh* (alms). But Indian society is changing, if slowly. It has a steadily expanding middle class, perhaps 100 million people, though their incomes are still low and their housing and goods shoddy by the standards of the West or East Asia.

For the even greater number of poor people flooding to the cities, this middle-class living standard is a goal rather than a target of resentment. Squatters hope that by staying long enough, they may gain official sanction for their patch of ground and then gradually improve their *jhuggi* (shack) into a small, permanent house. The first inclination of visitors from prosperous countries is to give, or to recoil. Perhaps it is best to follow the example of better-off Indians: to give a little each day to at least one or two of the genuinely distressed or helpless, and ignore the obvious cadgers.

India is a country of crowds. Even in the forests, the deserts of Rajasthan, or the majestic valleys of the Himalayas, it will be hard to find a landscape without human figures. Being part of a vast ocean of humanity in the cities, at festivals and public ceremonies is one of the experiences of India: belittling, sometimes alarming, sometimes comforting. India is already the second-largest nation in the world, and is likely to overtake China in 30 years with a population of 1.3 billion or more. Whether India can provide for these numbers, economically and ecologically, is a great question yet to be answered, but today it presents an endlessly fascinating panorama for the traveller.

History

The exact origin of Indian civilization is still hotly disputed. Most historians accept that the dark-skinned Dravidians, of whom the southern peoples like the Tamils are survivors, es-

◄ *Hindu deities Ram and Sita.* PHOTO: RAKESH SAHAI

INDIA
Railways
Airports
CHINA
AFGHANISTAN
Line of control
Srinagar
Lea
Amritsar
Simla
Chandigarh
PAKISTAN
New Delhi
NEPAL
Gangtok
BHUTAN
Darjeeling
Bikaner
Lucknow
Jaisalmer
Jaipur
Agra
Patna
BANGLADESH
Jodhpur
Allahabad
Varanasi
Ahmedabad
Udaipur
Bhopal
Indore
Mhow
Calcutta
Bhubaneswar
BURMA
Bassein
Ellora
Puri
Bombay
Chalika Lake
Pune (Poona)
Bay of Bengal
Hyderabad
Goa
Bangalore
Madras
Kanchipuram
Mysore
Pondicherry
Andaman Is.
Nilgiri Hills
Tiruchirapalli
Indian Ocean
Trivandrum
Kany Kumari
SRI LANKA
km
0
500

tablished the first civilization in India, before being subdued by the light-skinned Aryan invaders from Iran around 1500 BC. Hindu nationalists object to the idea that their culture and religion developed from conquest; when in government, they try to have the history textbooks rewritten accordingly.

The Indo-Aryan civilization evolved into stable, agrarian states, with a hierarchical social order (a caste system based on colour, headed by Brahmin priests) and a pantheon of gods that formed the basis of the socio-religious philosophy that is now called Hinduism. Buddhism and Jainism emerged in the sixth century BC as attempts to reform and rationalize Hinduism by eliminating superstition, idolatry and intrinsic social inequality.

Alexander the Great's Greek armies came to northwest India in 327 BC and advanced to the present-day Punjab, but turned back at the Beas River when his exhausted troops refused to go further. The first Indian empire to extend its authority across the whole of North India, the Maurya Empire, rose in the fourth century BC under Chandragupta Maurya. Its capital was at the site of present-day Patna, capital of Bihar state. The empire reached its peak under Chandragupta's grandson Ashoka (273-232 BC). Ashoka, a convert to Buddhism, spread this faith across the Subcontinent. A great traveller, Ashoka left evidence of his wise rule in columns bearing his edicts.

Political power dispersed among numerous small kingdoms, and more invaders, including a second wave of Greeks, came from the northwest. Between 300 AD and 650 AD, the Hindu tradition was fully restored, with Brahminical states, notably the Gupta Dynasty, ruling much of northern India. Dravidian southern India developed differently from the Aryanized north: It had its own dynasties and its own maritime trade relations with countries as far east as Indonesia and even perhaps the Philippines.

Islam appeared in the 11th century, when Muslim armies pushed in from the west despite dogged resistance by the Rajput warriors of Rajasthan. The Delhi Sultanate was established in 1206, and from then on Muslim rule was to spread over most of India, except the far south.

Trade contact between India and Europe existed intermittently in the Greek and Roman eras, but the European Age of Discovery brought Portuguese explorer Vasco da Gama to Calicut (Kozhikode) in the present-day state of Kerala, in 1498. The Portuguese had possession of Goa on the west coast in 1510. The British East India Co. arrived in 1613, setting up precarious trading "factories" (warehouses) at Surat (in present day Gujarat) and the east coast at Madras. Until the next century, the Europeans remained dependent on the goodwill of the Moghul emperors in Delhi, who exercised their power through regional deputies called *nawabs*.

The British eventually began moving north. In the Battle of Plassy in 1757, Robert Clive defeated the Nawab of Bengal, while the French were expelled from their Bengal trading forts. Calcutta became the centre of British power, which now began to expand northwest along what became the Grand Trunk Rd, from Calcutta to Lahore. The East India Co. handed over control to the British crown following the Indian Mutiny of 1857. In 1876, Queen Victoria was crowned Empress of an empire comprising British India and a patchwork of smaller states. For the first time, a single authority ruled over all India which, at that time, included the present Pakistan and Bangladesh.

There was significant nationalist opposition to British rule as early as 1885. The movement, which crystallized under the leadership of Mahatma Gandhi and the Indian National Congress, brought independence to India on August 15, 1947. But India was partitioned along religious lines, creating Muslim-majority Pakistan out of Sindh, Western Punjab, Baluchistan, and the North West Frontier on one side of India, and eastern Bengal on the other.

Jawaharlal Nehru was India's first prime minister and held office until his death in 1964. He was followed briefly by Lal Bahadur Shastri. When Shastri died suddenly in 1966, Indira Gandhi — Nehru's daughter — was chosen to succeed him. In December 1971, India went to the aid of the struggling independence movement in East Pakistan, which became Bangladesh.

In June 1975, a court found Mrs. Gandhi guilty of technical malpractices while campaigning for her seat during the 1971 election. The court unseated her from parliament but, while an appeal was pending in the Supreme Court, she declared a state of emergency. Up to 100,000 people were detained, including many political foes. There were many abuses of power under the emergency, including an aggressive family planning programme launched by Indira's son Sanjay. This included many forcible sterilizations, which had lasting detrimental effects on India's population-control efforts.

Mrs. Gandhi risked elections for the lower house of parliament in 1977. This proved a major miscalculation. A combination of opposition groups under the banner of the Janata party won most of the seats in northern India, the crucible of Indian politics, and 82-year-old Morarji Desai became prime minister.

The new government fell apart within two years, however, and Mrs. Gandhi swept back to power. Her leadership was soured following the death of her son Sanjay in a flying accident in 1980, and Congress became bogged down in corruption. Communal relations deteriorated steadily in the Punjab, where Mrs. Gandhi attempted to use a faction of Sikh extremists to weaken political opponents. When she turned on these dubious proteges, the method was disastrous. Their leader, Jarnail Singh Bhindranwale, and his followers had holed up in an annexe of the Golden Temple at Amritsar. Instead of a long siege, Mrs. Gandhi opted for a direct army assault with tanks and massive fire-power. The desecration of the Golden Temple outraged many Sikhs in India and in emigre communities throughout the world. Mrs. Gandhi was assassinated by two Sikh bodyguards on October 31, 1984.

Her remaining son, Rajiv, had entered parliament a few years earlier and, despite his inexperience, most Indians accepted him as a rallying figure. Elections in December 1984 delivered the largest majority (401 out of 543 seats) that the Congress Party, or any other Indian party, had ever achieved.

Rajiv Gandhi began with brave intentions: he promised fair treatment for the Punjab and a liberalization of India's creaking, state-dominated economy. But promises to settle grievances in Punjab and elsewhere were not followed through, and Gandhi became increasingly hampered by scandals, some involving alleged commissions to his friends from foreign arms makers. Meanwhile, Indian troops became involved in a war with Tamil insurgents in Sri Lanka as a result of a July 1987 Indo-Sri Lankan accord that allowed New Delhi to dispatch a so-called peacekeeping force to help end ethnic civil war there.

The economy boomed during this period, with growth rates reaching 6-9% a year after 1985. However, that expansion was fuelled by widening budget and external account deficits, covered by foreign debt.

In a November 1989 election, the Congress Party was defeated for the second time in 42 years of Indian independence. A minority coalition government — formed from Janata Dal, the left and several regional parties — took power, led by Gandhi's former finance and defence minister, V.P. Singh. This government fell in November 1990, when the Hindu-national Bharatiya Janata Party (BJP) withdrew support over two issues: Singh had decided to carry out recommendations that government jobs and institutional places be reserved for more of the lower castes; and the authorities had also resisted attempts by BJP affiliates to demolish a 16th century mosque at Ayodhya, Uttar Pradesh, which was claimed to stand on the birthplace of the Hindu deity Ram.

Rajiv Gandhi's Congress backed an even weaker minority government, under Janata Dal breakaway Chandra Shekhar. This government fell in March 1991. While campaigning in new elections, Rajiv Gandhi was assassinated in a bomb blast in the southern state of Tamil Nadu on May 12, 1991. Congress emerged as the largest party in parliament, but without a majority, and no natural heir to Gandhi.

India was meanwhile on the brink of default on its foreign debt, as additional external payments due to the Gulf War, and political instability, led commercial banks to withdraw credit lines. Veteran Minister P.V. Narasimha Rao was plucked from imminent retirement to head a minority government. To the surprise of all, his government instituted sweeping market-oriented reforms, while accepting emergency finance from the International Monetary Fund. Rao skilfully built up Congress towards a majority, but faced a profound challenge when Hindu groups demolished the Ayodhya Mosque on December 6, 1992. Rao dismissed BJP governments in four northern states, and banned three big Hindu organizations. State elections in November 1994 brought mixed results but at least enabled Congress to keep its reform platform moving. By early 1995, the pressure was on for Rao to show that the reforms were not hurting poorer people, with a view to the 1996 general elections.

Entry

AIR: Access to India is not getting easier. The longer range of new airliners, plus the inconvenience and cost of dealing with Indian airport authorities, give many international airlines cause to fly over, rather than stop, in

Tradition and traffic in Bombay. PHOTO: HAMISH McDONALD

India. Since it is located in the middle of Europe-to-Asia air routes, the international flights that do stop tend to arrive and leave in the early hours of the morning. Red eyes are a mark of the air traveller here.

The four major cities — New Delhi, Bombay, Calcutta and Madras — have direct international air connections. In addition, there are some flights to Kathmandu from Calicut and Trivandrum. One of the great inconveniences, a result of India's poor relations with its neighbours, is the lack of direct flights from New Delhi to the capitals of Pakistan and Bangladesh, though Air Lanka opened a connection to Colombo in January 1993.

The largest domestic carrier, Indian Airlines, flies to neighbouring Sri Lanka, Nepal, Bangladesh, Afghanistan, Thailand and the Maldives. Air-India carries the Indian flag further afield.

SEA: Bombay, which used to be the main entry point from Europe by sea, still receives a few sea travellers, mostly aboard passenger/freighters operated by East European lines.

ROAD: Overland, there are several access points: Attari, which lies between Pakistan's city of Lahore and India's Amritsar; and Haridaspur, on India's border with Bangladesh to the east. For up-to-date information on border crossing-points, contact Indian overseas missions or government tourist information offices.

Immigration

All foreigners entering India, except for citizens of Bhutan and Nepal, must have a valid passport and a visa. Indian consular offices around the world issue visas for fees of around US$5 (British citizens pay an exceptionally high fee of £23).

Tourist visas are normally available for a maximum period of 180 days, including extensions, which are granted at no extra charge. Group tours of no less than four can apply for a collective visa, which is good for 30 days. The tour members may split into smaller groups while travelling, but must reassemble and depart the country as the original group.

Business travellers should apply for multiple-entry business visas, which are valid for one year, with a cumulative maximum stay of no more than 120 days. Special visas are also issued for trekking, botanical expeditions, sports and journalism.

If you wish to spend 120 days or more continuously in India, you may be required to obtain a tax clearance before leaving. You must also register at the Foreigners' Regional Registration Offices (FRROs), maintained by the Home Affairs Ministry in all major cities.

The FRROs in New Delhi, Bombay and Calcutta, and the Chief Immigration Officer in Madras, handle visa renewals. Visas can also be renewed in all state capitals and district centres through the police headquarters.

Visitors may move about freely throughout

AIRLINE OFFICES

Name, Telephone, C=City, A=Airport.

Aeroflot: Bombay C: 221682, 221743. A: 632 0178, 632 0700. New Delhi C: 331 2843, 331 0426. A: 548 2331. Calcutta C: 229831, 223765, 221617. A: 569611, ext. 342.
Afghan Airlines: New Delhi C: 331 1432.
Air Canada: New Delhi C: 372 0014-15, 372 0017. Bombay C: 202111, 202 9730. Madras C: 825 0884, 825 0882. Calcutta C: 247 7783, 247 5576.
Air France: New Delhi C: 331 7054, 331 2853. A: 545 2099. Bombay C: 202 5021, 202 5067. A: 832 8070, 832 3072. Bangalore C: 526 0548. A: 527 9083, 527 9088. Madras C: 825 0326, 825 0295. A: 852 1780. Calcutta C: 296161-2, 296169.
Air-India: New Delhi C: 331 1225, 331 3091. A: 545 2050, 545 2054. Bombay C: 202 4142, 287 6464. A: 836 6767. Calcutta C: 242 2356-59. A: 552 8787. Madras C: 827 4488. A: 234 0551.
Air Lanka: New Delhi C: 332 4789, 371 3768. Bombay C: 218 1440, 2185 4941. Calcutta C: 294464, 295967, 292092.
Air Mauritius: Bombay C: 202 8386, 202 6430. New Delhi: GSA Air-India. Calcutta: Do. Madras: Do.
Alitalia: New Delhi C: 335 4666, 331 3777. Bombay C: 204 5023. A: 832 8083.
Alyemda: Bombay C: 202 4343, 204 2743.
American Airlines: New Delhi C: 331 6284, 332 5876. Bombay C: 282 3275, 287 5091. Calcutta C: 475 1272, 475 9263. Madras C: 825 0882, 825 0884.
Biman Bangladesh: New Delhi C: 335 4403-4. Calcutta C: 293709, 292844. A: 552 8772. Bombay C: 224580, 224871. Madras C: 825 0882, 825 0884.
British Airways: New Delhi C: 332 7428, 332 8298. A: 545 2007, 545 2076. Bombay C: 282 0888. A: 832 9061, 832 9063-4. Calcutta C: 299161, 293453. A: 552 8424, 552 8262. Madras C: 827 7559, 827 7388. A: 234 4921, 234 4931.
Canadian: New Delhi C: 332 5262. Bombay C: 202 7083, 202 3284. Calcutta C: 747622-3. Madras C: 826 2315, 826 2294.
Cathay Pacific: New Delhi C: 332 3332, 332 1286. Bombay C: 202 9112. A: 836 6205, 836 6207. Madras C: 852 2418, 852 2519. Calcutta C: 403211, 403312.
Continental: New Delhi C: 372 2160-1. Madras C: 443212, 443215. Bombay C: 218 1431, 218 5494. Calcutta C: 295734. Bangalore C: 226 7613.
CSA Czechoslovak Airlines: New Delhi C: 331 1833. Bombay C: 282 0736, 282 0765, 284 4790.
Delta Airlines: New Delhi C: 332 5222. A: 545 2093. Bombay C: 202 9020. Calcutta C: 247 5008, 247 8140. Madras C: 852 5655, 852 5755.
Egypt Air: New Delhi C: 373 1896, 335 4493. Madras C: 849913, 840323.
Emirates: New Delhi C: 332 4803, 332 4665. A: 548 2861, 548 2851. Bombay C: 287 1645-8. A: 836 5730-1, 836 6700, ext. 3509, 3553.
Ethiopian Airlines: New Delhi C: 332 9235. Bombay C: 202 9378, 202 4525, 283 4482. A: 838 5618, 836 6700, ext. 3514.
Finnair: New Delhi C: 331 5454.
Garuda Indonesian Airways: Air-India is the agent.
Gulf Air: New Delhi C: 332 4293. A: 545 2065. Bombay C: 202 1626. A: 832 5226, 832 7588. Madras C: 827 2092. Calcutta C: 247 7783, 247 2526. Trivandrum C: 61129. A: 451205.
Iberia Airlines: New Delhi C: 332 4789, 371 3765. Bombay C: 218 1440, 218 1431. Calcutta C: 294464, 295967.
Indian Airlines: New Delhi C: 462 0566, 462 4332. A: 548 3535. Bombay C: 202 3131, 287 6161. A: 611 6633. Madras C: 825 1677, 827 7888. A: 234 3131, 234 3140, 825 1677. Bangalore C: 221 1914. A: 564433, 566233.

the country, except to restricted and/or protected areas or prohibited places. These include: the northeast frontier states of Arunachal Pradesh, Nagaland, Manipur, Meghalya, Mizoram and Tripura, plus parts of Assam and the Andaman Islands. Special permits are also required for Maziranga and Jaldapara, in West Bengal. Travellers may obtain permits for these areas (for a maximum of 15 days) from the FRROs in New Delhi, Bombay and Madras, from the Chief Immigration Officer in Madras, or when applying for a visa. Applications for group permits should be made at least two weeks in advance. Travellers bound for the Himalayan state of Sikkim should apply for a permit at least eight weeks

Iraqi Airways: New Delhi C: 331 8742, 331 8632. Bombay C: 202 0597, 221217. Madras C: 826 1740, 826 5616.
Iran Air: New Delhi C: 600121, 606471. Bombay C: 204 7070.
Japan Airlines: New Delhi C: 332 4922, 332 7606, 332 7608. Bombay C: 287 0611, 287 4936. Madras C: 852 4832, 852 3957. Calcutta C: 298370, 298363. Bangalore C: 227 5091, 227 5416.
Kenya Airways: New Delhi C: 331 8502, 331 4796. Bombay C: 282 0064, 282 0047. Calcutta C: 298370-1. Madras C: 852 2688.
KLM Royal Dutch Airlines: New Delhi C: 331 1747, 331 5833. A: 548 2874, 548 2894. Bombay C: 838 0773, 838077, 8380 7754. Calcutta C: 552 8420-2. Madras C: 234 0551, 234 4363.
Korean Air: New Delhi C: 372 1913-4. Bombay C: 208 8915, 200 4756. Calcutta C: 247 2550, 247 1230. Madras C: 852 3427, 852 2688.
Kuwait Airways: New Delhi C: 331 4221, 331 4223.
LOT Polish Airlines: New Delhi C: 332 4482, 373 1473-4. Bombay C: 218 1440, 218 1431. Madras C: 453211. Calcutta C: 295734.
Lufthansa: New Delhi C: 332 3310. A: 545 2064, 545 2328. Bombay C: 202 3430. A: 832 0827. Calcutta C: 299365-7. Madras C: 852 5095, 852 5197. A: 234 8757. Bangalore C; 558 8791, 558 7740.
Malaysia Airlines: New Delhi C: 371 3768, 371 3765. Madras C: 826 0550, 827 4882. Bombay C: 218 1440, 218 1431, 2185 4941. Calcutta C: 294464, 292092.
Northwest Airlines: New Delhi C: 371 6006,335 0920. Madras C: 852 0089, 852 3103. Calcutta C: 293986, 299218. Bombay C: 261 4743, 261 8385. Bangalore C: 560001, 268509.
Pakistan International Airlines: New Delhi C: 331 3161-2. A: 545 2011. Bombay C: 202 1225, 202 1373, 202 1455.
Philippine Airlines: New Delhi C: 331 3221, 331 2119.
Qantas: New Delhi C: 332 9027, 332 1434. Bombay C: 202 9297, 204 4931. Calcutta C: 247 0718. Madras C: 827 8649, 827 8680. Bangalore C: 226 6611, 226 4719.
Royal Jordanian Airlines: New Delhi C: 332 0635, 372 1787-8. A: 545 2478. Bombay A: 836 6681. Calcutta C: 475 1261, 475 1272. Madras C: 825 0884, 825 0882.
Royal Nepal Airlines: New Delhi C: 372 2989, 332 1164. A: 548 3876, 545 2021, ext. 2215. Calcutta C: 298534, 298549. A: 569611, ext. 388. Bombay C: 283 5489, 283 2438.
Saudia: New Delhi C: 331 0464. A: 548 1279. Madras C: 826 1583. A: 832 6084. Bombay C: 202 8177.
Scandinavian Airlines System (SAS): New Delhi C: 332 5262. Bombay C: 202 7083. Madras C: 826 2315, 826 2294. Calcutta C: 747622-3.
Singapore Airlines: New Delhi C: 332 6373, 332 0145. Bombay C: 202 3316, 202 2747. A: 832 7861, 832 7024. Calcutta C: 292632, 291037, 290740. A: 552917. Madras C: 852 2871. A: 234 3860.
Swissair: New Delhi C: 332 5511, 372 2993. A: 545 2535, 545 2531. Bombay C: 287 2210. A: 832 6084. Calcutta C: 242 4643-4. Madras C: 826 1583.
Syrian Arab Airlines: New Delhi C: 332 5262. Bombay C: 202 7083. Calcutta C: 747622-3. Madras C: 826 2315, 826 2294.
Thai Airways International: New Delhi C: 332 3638, 332 3608. A: 548 2526. Calcutta C: 299846-8.
Trans World Airlines: New Delhi C: 331 3221, 331 2119.
THY Turkish Airlines: Bombay C: 204 3605.
United Airlines: New Delhi C: 371 5550, 335 5588. Bombay C: 202 3284, 287 5944. Madras C: 826 2315, 826 2294. Calcutta C: 747622-3.

in advance.

Under military security rules, photography is prohibited at airports, railway stations, bridges and other installations.

Health

Apart from yellow fever vaccinations for those coming from infected areas (Africa and South America), there are no vaccination requirements. Those coming from yellow fever infected areas without a vaccination certificate are liable to be detained in quarantine for up to six days.

Cholera and hepatitis still present the great health hazards, so remember two rules: **DO NOT DRINK WATER THAT HAS NOT BEEN BOILED OR STERILIZED; AND PAY STRICT ATTENTION TO SANITATION.**

Vaccination against cholera is now regarded by international health authorities as only partially effective. But there is a reliable, multiple vaccination against typhoid, paratyphoid A and B, and against tetanus. The first two diseases result from poor sanitation, while the last normally results from a skin puncture. Visitors to India should also ensure that they have had a recent anti-polio booster, which lasts for five years.

There is only one way to reduce the risk of infectious hepatitis and that is to avoid eating uncooked foods or unboiled water. A gamma-globulin injection boosts immunity against hepatitis for up to six months, but it is not immunization.

Avoid all drinking water that does not arrive in a sealed bottle. Several brands of sterile drinking water are available in most places. Otherwise, tea made with freshly boiled water is sensible. Travellers to remote areas should take water purification tablets or a liquid water purifier. A drop of iodine solution also will sterilize water.

If possible, protect yourself from malaria by taking a daily or weekly tablet, as advised by a doctor. If you suffer from severe fever, see a doctor immediately — there is a potentially fatal strain of malaria in the region. Dengue fever is another common mosquito-carried illness, usually causing a week of fever and lassitude. The only protection from it is to guard against insect bites.

Rabies is widespread, so dogs, monkeys, squirrels and other mammals should be avoided. If you are bitten by an animal, seek immediate medical attention.

Customs

Visitors possessing more than US$10,000 (or the equivalent in travellers' cheques or bank notes) must fill in a currency declaration form.

Visitors may bring in duty-free up to 200 cigarettes or 50 cigars, and one litre of alcohol. Non-sporting firearms are prohibited. So, too, are gold bullion or coins (except by Indian nationals returning from working abroad, who may bring in a maximum of five kilograms) or dangerous drugs. The penalties for violations are heavy.

If you plan to bring in your own videotape recorder or portable computer to use while in India, ask for a re-export permit from Customs officials when you arrive. The permit will be written into the back of your passport. Unless you can present the item to Customs on leaving India, full duty will be levied. If the item has been lost or stolen, make a prompt report to the nearest police station and get a copy of the "first information report" (FIR) taken down by the police. When you leave India, show this report to the Assistant Collector of Customs, who will decide whether or not to levy duty.

India restricts the export of antiques, including foreign-made artifacts and items more than 100 years old. The Archaeological Survey of India is the authority that determines whether items are restricted. Visitors may not bring in or take out of India anything made from endangered animal species.

Currency

The national currency is the Indian rupee, which is divided into 100 paise. Coins are available in the following units: 5, 10, 20, 25 and 50 paise; and 1 and 2 rupees. Notes come in Rs 1, 2, 5, 10, 20, 50, 100 and 500.

The rupee is convertible for importers and exporters, with the rate set daily by the foreign-exchange market run by leading banks. In April 1995 the rate floated around Rs 31.43:US$1. Visitors can change their foreign currency at this rate, but should keep their copy of the transaction record to get any surplus rupees reconverted at the end of their trip.

Visitors may not bring in or take out any Indian currency, except in the form of travellers' cheques. There are no limits on foreign currency, but you will need receipts (encashment certificates) from all your currency exchanges in order to convert rupees when leaving the country.

Foreigners are required to pay domestic and international airfares, and often hotel bills, in foreign currency or with foreign credit cards. Rupees will be accepted, however, if you can show (with an encashment certificate) that they originated as foreign exchange.

Exchanging foreign currency with unauthorized money-changers is an offence. One also risks receiving forged rupees, or being cheated.

You can generally find foreign-exchange facilities at airports and docks. Authorized money-changers usually display the rates of exchange. Nevertheless, dealing with any bank or foreign-exchange office provides a frustrating taste of Indian bureaucracy. Visitors even to specialist money-changers such as Thomas Cook should set aside at least half an hour for queuing and laborious clerical work.

Major credit cards are now widely accepted in India. The American Express offices in India's major cities have the usual facility to provide cash. The major hotel chains (Taj, Oberoi, Sheraton) accept all major international credit cards, as do many big restaurants and shops catering to tourists.

Language

English is the *lingua franca* between Indians of different regions, and it is spoken by service staff in national institutions such as airlines, railways and telecommunications authorities. Most direction signs have an English version. Visitors may wish to read the excellent book *Words in Indian English* by S. Muthiah to interpret local additions to vocabulary and grammar.

Hindi, the official and most widely spoken language, is concentrated in the northern states of the Ganges plain. Dravidian languages such as Telugu, Malayalam, Tamil and Kannada prevail in the south.

Climate

India has three major seasons: winter, summer and the monsoon. The winter months (November to March) are pleasant in most of India, with bright sunny days and cool nights. In the northern plains, the minimum temperature at times drops steeply and there is snowfall in the Himalayas and their foothills, sometimes as late as early April. In Maharashtra, further south and in eastern India, however, December and January are pleasantly cool but never really cold.

During the summer months (April-August) northern India becomes the country of heat and dust, with daytime temperatures of 45°C common around New Delhi. Hill resorts such as Simla, Mussourie and Nainital are packed at this time; the burgeoning Indian middle class has been gradually taking over from the pith-helmeted sahibs who, in the days of the Raj, shifted government en masse to the hills.

The southwest monsoon usually hits the southern tip of India in early June, and tracks north over the next two months. Most of India receives the major share of its rainfall between June and September, but southeastern areas get the northeast monsoon rains between mid-October and the end of December.

Dress

Light and loose, easily laundered clothing is best for the south and the northern plains from April to September. You will need warmer clothes, however, including woollens, for the north during winter. Travellers to New Delhi during December and January may even need an overcoat. Warm clothing is a must for the hill stations all year round.

India is not very formal about dress. Indians, themselves, adopt widely differing garbs: men can wear *dhotis*, pyjamas, *lunghis* or Western-style trousers. Some hotels and clubs will insist on a minimum formality in dining rooms, usually long trousers and a conventional shirt. Businessmen should wear a jacket and tie or tailored safari suit when meeting counterparts or senior officials. Women should follow the same principle and, when touring, avoid revealing tops, short skirts and all but the baggiest shorts, to minimize harassment. A set of loose-fitting *salwar-kameez* — providing neck to ankle (and wrist) coverage — is a good investment for travelling on and off the beaten track.

Business Hours

Business hours vary from one part of India to another, but 10 a.m.-5 p.m. (with 1-2 p.m. for lunch) is the norm. Businesses are closed on Saturday afternoons and Sundays.

Central government offices in New Delhi and their branches in the states normally work 9 a.m.-6 p.m. (with 1-2 p.m. for lunch) Monday-Friday. But it is rare to find anyone at middle to senior levels functioning before 10 a.m.

State government hours may differ from

those of central government. In Calcutta, for example, state government offices work 10:30 a.m.-5:30 p.m. Monday-Friday, and 10:30 a.m.-2 p.m. on Saturdays. Some other state government offices work a five-day week.

Banks are open to the public 10 a.m.-2 p.m. weekdays, and 10 a.m.-noon on Saturdays. In New Delhi, a bank branch is open 24 hours a day at the Ashoka Hotel, including holidays, for purposes of money exchange.

Larger shops in New Delhi are open 9:30 a.m.-1:30 p.m. and 3:30-7:30 p.m. Smaller stores stay open longer. Most restaurants close around 11 p.m., except for a few upmarket hotels with 24-hour restaurant service.

Doing Business

Businessmen will find their Indian counterparts follow conservative, English-style ways. Initial approaches should be made in writing, or at least by fax, with plenty of background about personnel, companies and projects involved. Follow these up with a telephone call to the personal assistant of the executive or official involved, usually a senior male clerk.

Take plenty of business cards, as Indian companies field squads of executives. Westerners should bring a suit for meetings with senior counterparts in their offices, but may switch to shirtsleeves or tailored safari-suit for working sessions, site visits and the like. The handshake is the accepted greeting, firm with men and a quick clasp with women. Some Indians may put their palms together for a traditional greeting: a nod and a smile is the best response.

Control is very much at the top, so meetings with chairman and chief executives will not be mere formalities. Although most big Indian corporations are listed in the country's highly active stock exchanges, control by the founding family is still the order of the day. Sons, brothers, and uncles will occupy senior positions. Discussions will be preceded by some jocular small talk, but soon get down to business.

When making a deal in India, be prepared for a delay in the follow-up. Indians, especially in government, tend to expect that once a plan is agreed, it is as good as carried out. Although licensing requirements have been greatly reduced since 1991, governments require myriad approvals and clearances. Decisions might be reopened with a change of ministers or senior personnel. In competitive tenders, losers frequently resort to the courts to have selections overturned.

Although it is a conservative society whose upper orders still tend to see married women in a home-maker's role, India generally accepts the principle of female equality in the workforce. Women occupy senior ranks in politics and the civil service, and female business visitors will be no rarity. The same is true in industries such as banking, computers, travel and fashion.

Indians usually entertain business clients in the evening, most often with drinks and dinner at a leading hotel.

Most businessmen and officials enjoy alcoholic drinks in the evening, but some are teetotallers for religious reasons, especially in the south, so do not insist on alcohol when mixing with them. Whisky and beer are the preferred drinks; wine is rarely appreciated.

Indian cities have little in the way of risque nightlife and what is there would not be part of the business entertainment scene. You might be invited home to dinner, more likely when a deal is nearly clinched. Be prepared for a long wait before dinner, which is usually an Indian buffet. Since the prelude may involve many stiff whiskies, it is a good idea to have a sandwich or other snack before going. Once dinner is over, guests depart quickly.

The big hotels usually offer executive services, including translation, communications and secretarial service.

Rip-Offs

At the top end of the market, foreign visitors find they pay a lot for comparatively shoddy services. Only one or two of the leading hotels merit the five-star prices they charge. The cost of staff, who tend to be poorly trained, cannot justify them either. On top of this expensive scale, the central government levies a 20% luxury tax and state governments usually another 10% tax. New Delhi claims that foreigners are more than compensated by the rupee's tumble in recent years, but leading hotels set their rates for foreigners in U.S. dollars, and the government requires such bills to be paid in foreign currency.

One glaring rip-off run by nearly all leading hotels is the loading of trunk and international telephone charges. "Service charges" can be as much as 100% of the public telecoms rates. When a 30% combined tax is applied, the charge is 260% of the telecoms rate. Indian hotels are highly secretive about their policy on this; demand details when you check in. You can avoid prohibitive surcharges charges by using any of the numerous IDD/STD booths springing up in cities. In the backstreets behind Bombay's Taj Mahal Hotel, for example, there are several.

Media

India has a thriving English-language press and some newspapers are well into their second century. Some newspapers circulate nationally, but their regional editions may differ widely in substance and topicality. *The Times of India*, *The Hindustan Times* and the *Hindu* (based in Madras) reflect the views of the English-speaking educated elite, who are generally upper-caste. The *Indian Express* tries to break stories that discomfort government officials and ministers. *The Pioneer*, for which both Rudyard Kipling and Winston Churchill once worked, some time ago shifted its base from Lucknow to New Delhi and has gained a reputation for clear writing and lively stories. The *Economic Times* provides good coverage of economic and business news and succinct write-ups of politics events. Calcutta has two good English papers, *The Statesman* and the *Telegraph*.

There are also several good Indian news magazines. The best are *India Today, Sunday, Frontline, Business India* and *Business Today*.

Some foreign newspapers and magazines are available in bigger cities. You can buy *The International Herald Tribune* and *The Asian Wall Street Journal* in Bombay and New Delhi. Bookshops and hotel newsstands in the two cities also sell some London papers. News magazines such as *Time* and the *Far Eastern Economic Review* are available.

The state TV monopoly, Doordarshan, is under pressure from satellite TV (often fed via cable) because of its technical ineptitude, dull programming and compliance with the government of the day. Satellite programming is widely available. Nearly all big hotels and many medium-bracket ones are hooked up to the Hong Kong-based StarTV service, including the BBC World Service TV. CNN also is widely available.

Communications

International telephone connections vary in quality and availability. Lines are readily available to Europe and North America, but inadequate to East Asia.

Major international courier firms operate in India, either on their own account or through local partners. But be warned: delivery times are generally scarcely better than the Speedpost service offered by the Indian postal service at major post offices (three days to most big overseas cities).

Voltage in most places is 220 volts AC, 50 hertz, though a few areas have DC supply as well. Check the voltage before using any electrical appliance.

Transport

MAIN CITIES

FROM THE AIRPORT: All international airports have coach and taxi services to town.

To avoid taxi rip-offs on arrival at airports, make arrangements through the "pre-paid taxi" counter, usually located just outside customs. This is run by local traffic police, and issues a coupon for a taxi ride into town according to the number of bags carried. Participating drivers accept the coupon, and usually hope for a moderate tip of Rs 30-50. Where meters are not used, ask a local person for an approximate estimate of the taxi fare to your destination before getting down to bargaining with the driver.

TAXIS: Taxis are easy to find in India's main cities, though the vehicles themselves — the Hindustan Ambassador (modelled on the early 1950s Morris Oxford) or Premier Padmini (a copy of an early Fiat) — leave much to be desired, especially in summer, when air-conditioning would be appreciated. Cabs do not have radios, but operate from roadside shacks equipped with a telephone.

Taxis have meters (the driver or hotel doorman will set it going). In some cities, including Bombay, drivers may produce a printed card from the transport authority, which scales up the fees from out-of-date prices shown on the meter. Drivers are usually happy to wait, but expect an extra charge for the waiting time. Try to get the most detailed directions possible before setting off, since city maps are rudimentary and outdated.

BUSES: Buses run along many suburban routes in the main cities, but are usually too crowded for all but the most dedicated budget-travellers. Fares are very cheap, at less than Rs 1.50-2 for most trips within the city area. English may or may not be spoken and some destination boards are in Indian script only. In some cities, such as Bombay, and a few states, such as

Road users of a different kind in New Delhi. PHOTO: RAVEENDRAN/AFP

Tamil Nadu and Kerala, the bus service is more efficient and comfortable.

TRAINS: Bombay has an extensive suburban railway system, which is jam-packed during the morning and evening rush hours. Some carriages in Bombay are reserved for women only. Madras has steadily expanded its own, much smaller system. Calcutta now has a limited, but efficient and clean underground railway line, which opened in 1984. Its above-ground trains, much grubbier, make a number of suburban stops.

AUTO-RICKSHAWS: Based on Italian-style scooters and also known as "three-wheelers," these are a convenient, surprisingly fast and cheap means of getting around cities. They are metered, and can carry up to four passengers in a squeeze.

CAR RENTALS or "DLY taxis": These chauffeur-driven cars, carrying a licence plate beginning with the letters "DLY," may carry four passengers. They are best used for touring cities or country excursions, and are hired on an hourly basis. An air-conditioned DLY taxi in New Delhi typically costs Rs 550 for eight hours, including up to 80 kilometres, plus Rs 5.50 for each additional kilometre. Since traffic is anarchic, few newcomers trust themselves behind the wheel. A few operators in major cities hire out self-drive cars at comparatively steep rates.

TRANSPORT UPCOUNTRY

AIR: Domestic air services are dominated by **Indian Airlines**, a government corporation, but a growing number of private "air-taxi" companies, including **East-West Airlines** and **ModiLuft** offer flights between major cities. These smaller operators are pushing Indian Airlines on quality of service, such as inflight refreshments and attention to passengers' needs.

The Indian Airlines network connects more than 50 cities and tourist centres, with international connections to South Asian neighbours, the Gulf and Thailand. It is hard to make bookings by phone and air services are far from reliable. Try to check take-off times before setting off for the airport and bring plenty of reading material. Air terminals are usually run down and overcrowded.

Indian Airlines expects foreigners to pay in

foreign currency (by credit card), at fares set in U.S. dollars that are much higher than the rupee equivalent. But tickets are still relatively cheap and, unlike rupee-paying passengers, those who pay in foreign exchange may cancel or change their reservations without forfeiting their money.

Indian Airlines offers several special fares, including an unlimited-distance **Discover India** ticket (valid for 21 days) for US$400, payable in foreign currency. You can buy this at Air-India offices abroad or at Indian Airlines offices in India. **The India Wonder** fare plan offers a week of unlimited travel in any one region for US$200. **Youth Fare India**, gives those between 12 and 30 years old a discount of 25% on U.S.-dollar air fares on domestic and Indo-Nepal routes. There is also the South India Excursion, which offers 30% discounts on selected sectors in southern India. Anyone living permanently outside India (including anyone of Indian origin) is eligible for these fares year-round. Foreign residents in India are also eligible, provided they pay in foreign currency.

The free baggage allowance is 20 kilograms per adult passenger. First-class ticketholders on international flights are allowed 30 kilograms, with certain conditions.

TRAINS: Train travel is a great part of the romance of touring India. Everyone should try to include at least one rail segment in their trip. Although trunk lines have been extensively modernized, there is still a flavour of *Bhowani Junction* about the 62,000-kilometre rail network, and steam engines are still at work on narrow-gauge country lines. Station platforms are always busy and crowded with families squatting among cloth bales, soldiers stretched out on their bedrolls, railway officials, red-jacketed porters and vendors of tea, snacks and magazines.

Indian Railways has a system of classes and fares almost as intricate as the caste system: First Air-conditioned (1AC), Second Air-conditioned (2AC), air-conditioned chair cars and second-class sitters. Fares in the top classes on trunk routes include meals, snacks and that great leftover of the British Raj, a cup of "bed tea" to wake you up in the morning. Sleeper compartments normally have four bunks, so sharing with strangers is part of the routine. However, each first-class carriage has one two-berth compartment in the middle: this is always in great demand, but couples seeking privacy might as well try for it when booking. Bedding is provided in the air-conditioned sleeper classes.

The booking offices in major cities are linked to a computerized reservation system, which allocates berth numbers. Sometimes, however, you may find seat assignments listed on printouts pasted up on the platform or by the carriage doors.

Fares are low. The premier New Delhi-Bombay express, the all air-conditioned Rajdhani, has two trains in each direction nightly. The 1,388-kilometre trip takes 16 hours. First sleepers cost Rs 2,260 one-way, second sleepers Rs 1,287 and armchair places Rs 640. Fares are similar for the New Delhi-Calcutta express (the 1,450-kilometre trip takes 17 hours).

Trips between north and south are cheaper and slower. Bombay-Cochin trains take about 36 hours to cover 1,852 kilometres, and Calcutta-Madras trains take 27 hours for the 1,663-kilometre trip. If you are willing to sit long days and nights in cramped and hot carriages (and friends to keep an eye on the baggage while you fight your way to the toilet), the ordinary second class is a cheap option. The second-class fare from Bombay to Cochin, for example, is Rs 197.

Indian Railways offers **Indrail** passes for unlimited travel on any route for as long as the ticket is valid (and provided you have a reservation). Prices vary. A seven-day, First AC pass costs US$165, for example, while a 90-day First AC pass costs US$800. (The tickets are half-price for children between five and 12 and those below five ride for free.) Foreigners are required to pay for rail passes in convertible currencies. The passes are non-transferable; be prepared to show your passport on demand. You may apply for an extension in case of travel delays or transport breakdowns, illness, etc. Indrail passes are neither refundable nor replaceable when lost, stolen or mutilated. Detailed rules cover refunds in other cases.

Within India, you can buy Indrail passes at any of the following offices: New Delhi, **Railway Tourist Guide** (Northern Railway, Baroda House); Bombay, **Central Reservation Office** (Northern Railway, Churchgate) and **Railway Tourist Guide** (Central Railway, Victoria Terminus); Calcutta, **Central Reservation Office** (South-Eastern Railway, Esplanade Mansions); Madras, **Central Reservation Office** (Southern Railway, Madras Central).

You can buy passes outside India at certain

leading travel agents, but be sure to do so at least one month before travel. The rail office or travel agency from which you buy the rail pass will arrange reservations for your entire itinerary, if you ask.

Weary rail travellers seeking a cheap and convenient alternative to a hotel can bed down in a "retiring room," available at the major rail stations for up to 72 hours. These may be booked ahead of time. Travellers with their own sleeping bags or air mattresses may also stretch out in waiting rooms, which have bathrooms attached.

During the cooler winter months (October to March), Indian Railways and the Rajasthan state tourist authority run the **Palace on Wheels**, a special tourist train, which stops at Agra — for the Taj Mahal — and the palace-towns of Rajasthan. The original train of vintage coaches, used by rulers of India's princely states, was replaced in 1991 with a modern train with suitably luxurious compartments and bathrooms, dining cars and a lounge car. The week-long round-trip from New Delhi stops at Jaipur, Chittaurgarh, Udaipur, Jaisalmer, Jodhpur, Bharatpur, Fatehpur Sikri and Agra, with side-excursions to forts, palaces, monuments and artefact markets. For reservations in India contact the Rajasthan Tourism Development Corp.: in New Delhi (Central Reservation Office, Chanderlok Bldg, 36 Janpath, Tel: 332 1820, 332 2332); in Bombay (Tel: 267162); and in Calcutta (2 Ganesh Chandra Ave, Tel: 234261).

HILL TRAINS: The small mountain railways of India are an attraction in themselves, running up to Darjeeling, Simla, Ootacamund, and Matheran (near Bombay). The blue-and-cream train to Ootacamund or "Ooti" (featured in the film of *A Passage to India*) starts at Mettupalayam and runs through the Nilgiri Hills tea-growing area, gaining traction on steep climbs from a gear that engages a toothed rail on the track.

BUSES: Long-distance bus services are generally improving in terms of comfort and convenience, but speeding and dangerous overtaking provide many heart-stopping moments. Rail is a safer and more enjoyable way to travel, but in some places, especially in the mountain districts of the north, there is no alternative to buses for those who cannot hire a driver and car. Beware the "Video-Buses," plying intercity routes such as Chandigarh to New Delhi: the video monitor just above the driver's seat plays Indian movies at ear-blasting volumes — you might need earplugs to prevent hearing damage.

SHIPS: Ships operate on a number of coastal runs. A ship runs daily between Bombay and Goa (and back), except during the bad weather in the June-September monsoon.

CAR RENTAL: Chauffeur-driven cars may be hired in all the main cities for trips upcountry, and are a cost-effective way of sightseeing, especially for small parties.

Think twice before deciding to drive yourself, however. Driving in India is not for the faint-hearted. The inadequate network of dilapidated roads is dominated by trucks and buses driven at reckless speed. There is also an incredible range of other traffic on major highways, including camel-drawn carts, ox-wagons, tractors and donkey-trains. The veteran Hindustan Motors Ambassador car (the make of many taxis) may be hot and uncomfortable, but its wraparound heavy steel provides a reassuring protection.

For information on road conditions, driving regulations and licences, contact:

New Delhi: **Automobile Association of Upper India** (Lilaram Bldg, 14 Flr, Connaught Place, New Delhi 110001, Tel: 331 2323);

Bombay: **Western India Automobile Association** (Lalji Narainji Memorial Bldg, 76 Veer Nariman Rd, Bombay 400020, Tel: 204 1085);

Madras: **Automobile Association of Southern India** (187 Anna Salai, Madras 600005, Tel: 442705);

Calcutta: **Automobile Association of Eastern India** (13 Promothesh Barua Sarani, Calcutta 700019, Tel: 759012).

Third-party insurance for cars is compulsory and must be paid to a company registered in India or to a foreign insurer who has a guarantor in India.

Tours

Leading travel agencies and government tourism corporations offer tours in cities and upcountry areas. City tours, in particular, are very cheap and on the whole of good standard. They cover the major temples, monuments, museums and gardens. The **Indian Tourism Development Corp. (ITDC)** offers half-day tours of the sights of New Delhi. You can take a day-and-a-half tour of Bombay led by government or private company tours, as well as half-day tours to the **Elephanta Caves**, seven caves containing ancient religious sculptures and paintings, located on Gharapuri island near Bombay. The West Bengal state tourist office offers a full-day tour of Calcutta.

Upcountry tours out of New Delhi include one to Agra, site of the **Taj Mahal**. The tour begins with a train trip from New Delhi (departing at 7:15 a.m.) to Agra and a bus trip to the Taj Mahal and **Agra Fort**, among other places. The return train leaves Agra at 7 p.m. and arrives back in New Delhi at 10 p.m. Car tours to Agra are also available.

English-speaking guides are available at fixed charges at all important tourist sites through the government tourist offices. Unregistered guides are not permitted to enter protected monuments. Tourists are advised to use guides who carry a certificate issued by the **Department of Tourism**.

India abounds in opportunities for close-up photography of animals and birds. Most big travel agencies will arrange visits to well-known wildlife sanctuaries such as **Corbett Park** (Uttar Pradesh), **Kipling Camp** (Madhya Pradesh) and **Ranthambhore** (Rajasthan). Sightings of tigers require increasing patience, as poaching for skins and bones (used in Chinese medicines) is rapidly reducing the tiger population.

GOVERNMENT OF INDIA TOURIST OFFICES

	Tel:
Agra	363377, 363 3959
Aurangabad	31217
Bangalore	558 5417
Bhubaneswar	54203
Bombay	203 2932, 203 3144
Calcutta	242 1402, 242 1475
Cochin (Kochi)	682009
Guwahati	547407
Hyderabad	660037
Imphal	21131
Jaipur	372200
Khajuraho	2047, 2048
Madras	826 9685, 826 9695
Naharlagun	328
New Delhi	332 0342, 332005, 332008, 332 0109, 332 0266
Panaji	43412
Patna	225295, 226721
Port Blair	21006
Shillong	25632
Trivandrum	451498
Varanasi	43744

Accommodation

The large cities have modern Western-style hotels, usually offering Indian, European and Chinese cuisine. Few are truly of five-star quality in terms of rooms or service, though many pretend to this level. Central and state "luxury" taxes and sales taxes bump up the charges. Many tourist centres have travellers' lodges or tourist bungalows, which offer meals and comfortable rooms. These are run by the ITDC, or state government tourist agencies. In Srinagar, fully furnished and staffed houseboats are moored to the banks of the city's lakes and waterways.

The **Government of India Tourist Offices** in New Delhi, Bombay, Calcutta and Madras arrange for tourists to stay with an Indian family as a paying guest. Some government tourist offices in other areas may also offer this service.

Larger towns often have **YWCA**s and **YMCA**s, and youth hostels exist all over the country. Details can be obtained from the **National Council of YWCA or YMCA**, New Delhi, and the **Youth Hostels Association of India**. The National Council of YMCAs of India is located in New Delhi at Massey Hall, Jaisingh Rd, (Tel: 310769).

Dining

One of the supreme pleasures of India is to discover the immense variety of Indian food and to learn the more sophisticated and delicate dishes. The Indians, above all others in Asia, are masters of the art of spicing food. This is due, in large part, to the Indian technique of grinding or rolling ingredients immediately prior to use.

Not every dish in India is in the form of a curry. And many dishes, especially in the north, are not hot, though they may be richly garnished to provide exciting flavours to complement the meat or vegetable of the dish.

Each region has its own cuisine, some enriched by the influence of foreign cuisines. Bombay's Parsee food, for instance, is the contribution of the Zoroastrians, who fled religious persecution in Persia 1,300 years ago. "Goanese food" is Indo-Portuguese cooking, a legacy of five centuries of Portuguese rule over Goa. Outside Goa, the best Goanese food is to be found in Bombay.

Northern Indian food is usually served with varieties of flat breads such as *naan*, *chappati*, or *paratha*. Tandoori-style dishes are becoming increasingly popular throughout India and are immediately popular with visitors, since they are not too spicy hot. Tandoori refers to a method of cooking that was brought to India by the Moghuls from the northwestern areas beyond India. The food (usually chicken, but lamb, mutton and seafood are also cooked this way) is marinated for up to 48 hours in yoghurt, together with a blend of Himalayan herbs and spices. Then it is cooked in the tandoor — a special charcoal-fired clay oven kept at a very high temperature — which gives the food a slightly smoked taste. The food may be served whole, in tasty chunks on a *shaslik* or as a *seekh* (minced and moulded into long thin patties).

India has long been swayed by contradictory thinking about alcohol, the abstemious Brahminical ideal clashing with worldly gusto for enjoyment. Urban elites have taken to whisky in a big way, so much so that India is said to consume more Scotch than Scotland produces.

Prohibition has been applied at various times in the past, and invariably resulted in massive bootlegging and corruption. Today, the only state with total prohibition is Gujarat. Many states, however, still try to have it both ways — by making it hard to buy and consume alcohol, while collecting a hefty share of revenue from liquor taxes.

Where genuine stocks are not available (from duty-free imports or smuggling), bootleggers skilfully seal local blends inside empty name-brand Scotch bottles. Mass poisonings from "spurious liquor" sometimes occur when low-income groups cannot get normal supplies.

Bombay has the most European attitude to drink and bars and shops freely serve beer and spirits. New Delhi has a system of "semi-prohibition" — an irregular supply of odd domestic brands from all over India are sold by surly staff in a limited number of rundown outlets, risibly known as "tourist shops." Several states observe certain "dry days" — usually coinciding with animal slaughtering days, and the first and last days of the month — but major hotels, restaurants and clubs are exempt.

Entertainment

India has little in the way of organized night life — a result of prudishness and tight cash. A few hotel restaurants have Western-style popular music bands and dancing, while some of the elite British-style clubs such as the **Delhi Gymkhana** have dance nights that would appeal to nostalgia buffs.

Bangalore, the centre of India's computer industry, has a network of pubs serving draft beer, but even in this yuppie haven the clientele is almost entirely young men. The pub habit is spreading to other cities, along with draft beer. In New Delhi, the Broadway Hotel runs **Thugs Pub**. The Maurya Sheraton also has a jazz bar on Friday evenings off the main lobby: be prepared for chaos, as the staff are too overwhelmed with paperwork to have much time for serving drinks.

Each major city has one or two ambitious discotheques, invariably in major hotels, such as **My Kind of Place** at New Delhi's Taj Palace or the **Pink Elephant** at Calcutta's Oberoi Grand. They tend to be expensive and deserted.

Traditional performing arts — dancing, plays and music — are available. Performances normally are early in evening, so patrons tend to dine afterwards. English-language newspapers carry programmes of cultural events, as do the regular tourist guide-magazines such as *Delhi Diary*. Hotel information desks should also be able to help. Some hotels put on traditional entertainments.

Indian and a limited number of foreign films are shown at a great many theatres in the main centres. The Indian film industry (using Hindi, Bengali, Tamil, Telugu, Marathi) produces more feature films than Hollywood every year.

Shopping

The best buys in India are traditional products made from natural materials: cottons, silks, woollen carpets, carvings and furniture. There are many regional specialities to look for during your travels: Kashmir's hand-loomed rugs, furs, papier-mache utensils and paisley shawls; Jaipur's tie-dyed shawls, jewellery and brassware; Varanasi's silks. Carpets from the Northwest Frontiers, miniature paintings, jewellery, and artifacts such as southern Indian bronzes are also valuable buys.

All the big cities will have selections from all over India, but New Delhi's Connaught Circus area is perhaps the best concentration. The **Central Cottage Industries Emporium**, on Janpath, has a broad selection at reasonable fixed prices and is certainly worth visiting for price comparison at least. You can find various state emporiums along Baba Kharak Singh

Marg, and specialized shops along the inner circle of Connaught Circus. The underground **Palika Bazaar**, at the end of Janpath, has several tiers of shops selling handicrafts, cottons, garments and novelties. Other big cities also have government-run stores for cottage industries.

Forgeries and reproductions are widespread. If you are not an expert, buy from the larger established dealers with good reputations, even if the price is somewhat stiff. Shops pay commissions to middlemen, so take "special introductions" by hotel staff, drivers, and so on, with scepticism. They are not helping you. Remember also that genuine antiques may require a special permit from the Archaeological Survey of India for export.

Exploring the specialized bazaars of Indian cities is a great pleasure. For antiques and curiosities, try **Sunda Nagar Market** in New Delhi or **Mutton St** in Bombay's Chor Bazaar. Bargaining is in order. Sample several shops to get an idea of the typical asking range, and then work your way reluctantly up from an opening offer of about halfway. Abandoning negotiations and walking away is an acid test: If you are close to an acceptable price, the vendor will not let you go.

Gems and jewellery are India's biggest export items and Bombay is the centre of the industry. Only a tiny fraction of the estimated 200 tonnes of gold consumed each year is mined in India. The rest is smuggled in either by small operators attempting to carry concealed gold bars (known as "biscuits") through Customs, or large rings based in Dubai who run dhows into small ports and creeks along the west coast.

Gold and jewellery shops can be found throughout India. Although banking has spread down to the smallest villages, gold is still a preferred method of saving, and elaborate gold ornaments are part of bridal costumes. Almost every precious and semi-precious stone you can think of — diamonds, emeralds, amethysts, blue sapphires, star rubies, lapis lazuli, garnet and tourmaline, among others — are available. But only rubies, sapphires and cat's-eyes are still mined within India. Even the famed "pearls of Golconda," said to come from the oysters of the Hyderabad lakes, most often originate now in China and Japan. The "diamonds of Surat," equally famous, no longer originate there, while the Kashmir sapphire mines have been closed since early this century. But the skills of cutting, processing and setting remain. Many shops will readily reproduce designs at short notice.

If the purchase is large and you have doubts, you can have a gem certified in New Delhi at the **Gem Testing Laboratories** of the Indian Gemology Institute before making a purchase. The Institute, affiliated with the Ministry of Commerce, is located at F-32, Flatted Factories Complex, Rani Jhansi Rd, New Delhi 110055 (Tel: 779732). It is open 11 a.m.-3 p.m., but visitors should phone ahead for an appointment.

Sports

HUNTING: India is no longer the land of big game hunting. *Shikar* (safari-style hunting) is now forbidden, though small game hunting (for duck, for example) is permitted. Hunting is normally managed by one of the registered agencies in India, a list of which can be obtained by writing to the Government of India Tourist Office in New Delhi.

FISHING: Fishermen may go after the masheer that swim the upper reaches of some of India's larger rivers — this is reputedly better sport than even salmon fishing. There you can also fish for fresh-water goonch, which can reach a weight of 150 kilograms. Kashmir and Himachal Pradesh have trout-fishing (for which a licence is required) during the April 1-September 30 season. Trout are also found in the Nilgiri Hills of Tamil Nadu. You can arrange to go deep-sea fishing off Kerala's coast. Fishing gear, both inland and sea fishing, is available locally.

SNORKELLING: Snorkellers will find good reefs off Kovalam Beach in Kerala, the Lakshadweep Islands, and the Andaman Islands. At Kovalum, local fishermen will take you out to the reef on their canoes, made of three logs lashed together. You can rent masks, snorkels and flippers from stalls on the beach.

GOLF: There are many golf courses scattered around the country, especially in the hill stations. To request permission to play, contact the club secretaries directly. In most cases, you will have to pay a small fee.

SKIING: Skiing is the up-and-coming sport in north India. With Kashmir a security risk, newer resorts in Himachal Pradesh and Uttar Pradesh are being promoted. The season usually runs from December until February.

RAFTING: Air-India has a special section that deals with adventure sports, including white-water rafting in the headwaters of the Ganges.

The most popular rivers are: the **Zanskar**, **Indus**, **Chenab** and **Lidder** (all in Kashmir); the **Sutlej** in Himachal Pradesh; the **Bhagirathi** and **Alaknanda** in Uttar Pradesh and the Rangit in Sikkim.

OTHERS: Indians also enjoy hockey, cricket, polo, football, volleyball and basketball. Riding is a passion with the military and landowning classes of the north. Inquire with club secretaries about temporary arrangements, and make sure you meet dress requirements. The venerable Devi Chand outfitters in Connaught Circus (close to the American Express office) sells pith helmets and other riding gear at reasonable prices. In many hill stations ponies may be hired for excursions.

Motor rallyists find climatic and topographical diversity in India: deserts, forests, mountain passes, swamps and wasteland. Gliding and ballooning have also become popular, with leading clubs located at **Safdarjung** airport, New Delhi. Other adventure sports include camel safaris, heli-skiing and hang-gliding in the Himalayas.

Holidays

As the home of numerous religions, the Indian calendar is replete with religious festivals, as well as secular commemorations. Many Hindu festivals are linked to seasonal changes and farming cycles. These often fall on dates fixed by the lunar calendar or astrological calculations. Muslim holidays also move around the year. The major ones are Idu'l Fitr, marking the end of the month-long Ramadan Fast (public holiday); Muharram, commemorating the martyrdom of Imam Hussain, the grandson of the holy prophet Muhammad (public holiday); and Id-Uz-Zuha, celebrating the sacrifice of Abraham (public holiday).

Mid-January: *Pongal/Sankranti* — this holiday, which celebrates harvests and venerates cattle, is observed in many areas of the South and Bengal.

January 26: Republic Day — marks the day in 1929 when the Indian National Congress pledged to strive for a sovereign democratic republic in India. This was achieved on January 26, 1950, when independent India's new constitution came into force. The day is marked with a magnificent parade of military machines, soldiers, camels, elephants, and display floats along New Delhi's Raj Path. Two or three days later, the pageantry continues with a poignant beating-the-retreat ceremony at dusk. Public holiday.

February-March: *Holi* — Indians celebrate spring by throwing water and coloured powder over all and sundry. Do not be caught out in your best clothes. Public holiday.

March-April: *Ramanavami* — the birthday of the Hindu god, Lord Rama, celebrated in temples throughout India. Public holiday. *Mahavir Jayanti* — A Jain commemoration of the birthday of the 24th Vardhamana Mahavira in 599 BC. Public holiday. *Good Friday* — This public holiday is observed by the Christian community.

May-June: Buddha Purnima — celebrates the Lord Buddha's birth, enlightenment and attainment of Nirvana. (Each of these events took place on the same date in different years of Buddha's life.) Public holiday.

June-July: Car festival of Lord Jagannath — takes place in Puri in Orissa state and several other places. Idols are paraded by frenzied devotees on huge wooden chariots.

August 15: Independence Day — marks the end of the British Raj and India's independence on this day in 1947. The prime minister speaks from the ramparts of Delhi's Red Fort. Public holiday.

August-September: *Janmastami* — the birth anniversary of Lord Krishna (one of the incarnations of the god Vishnu), mainly celebrated in Mathura, Bombay and Agra. Public holiday. *Onam Harvest Festival* — This is celebrated in Kerala state, with long "snake-boat" races on the backwaters in Aranmulal and other towns. *Ganesh Chaturhi* — A popular festival dedicated to the elephant-headed god Ganesh. Bombay, Pune and Madras are the main centres of observance.

September-October: *Dussehra* — the most popular of all Indian festivals, this occasion celebrates the slaying of the demon-king Ravana by Rama (hero of the Ramayana epic). The festival runs for 10 days and is observed in New Delhi (where it is known as Ram Lila) by enactments of the Ramayana and fireworks; in Mysore by a splendid procession; in West Bengal (where it is known as Durga Puja) by music, dance and drama, and also in the south. Kulu, in Himachal Pradesh, celebrates later with colourful processions. Public holiday for two days.

October 2: Mahatma Gandhi's Birthday — the day is solemnly observed with prayer meetings at the Raj Ghat in New Delhi, where Gandhi's body was cremated. Public holiday.

October-November: *Diwali* — the gayest of

all the country's festivals, celebrated with lights and fireworks. It originally marked Rama's return from exile, but now Indians in Bombay and many other places venerate the Lakshmi, the Goddess of Wealth. In Calcutta, Kali, the Goddess of Destruction, is the focus. Public holiday.

November: *Govardhana Puja* — a Hindu festival celebrated by the public veneration of cattle. Public holiday. *Pushkar Fair* — This colourful celebration, including a huge camel market and camel races, is held in the town of the same name near Ajmer, Rajasthan. Government and private tour agencies arrange packages, which can include accommodation in elaborate tents. *Nanak Jayanti* — The birthday of Guru Nanak (1469-1539) the founder of the Sikh religion. Public holiday.

December: The Feast of St Francis Xavier (December 3) and The feast of Our Lady of Immaculate Conception (December 8) are richly celebrated in Goa.

December 25: Christmas Day. Public holiday.

PUBLICATIONS

India has a flourishing English-language book industry, which turns out nearly 100 new titles a month. Bookshops in the main cities offer local publications and Indian editions of major overseas works, often at a fraction of the overseas price. In New Delhi, the best concentration of bookshops is at Khan Market, not far from the Taj Mahal and Ambassador hotels. Elsewhere, bookshops in major hotel lobbies are the best place to look.

DISCOVERING INDIA

NEW DELHI

India's capital, New Delhi (really a kind of twin city with New and Old sections), lies in the plains of northern India, on the main invasion route into India. With the exception of the Europeans, who came by sea, most of India's new blood — Aryans, Greeks, Kushans, Huns and finally the Muslims — arrived from the northwest. Delhi is built upon and around ruins (some of which can still be seen today) of the cities built at this strategic location by successive emperors.

Delhi was the centre of Hindu monarchies until 1192, when the last reigning king in Delhi, Prithvi Raj, was killed while battling to keep out the armies of Muhammad of Ghor. From then on it became the capital of Muslim empires in India. The capital was moved under Muslim rule: the Tughluq Shah founded a new capital Tughluqabad (six kilometres from Delhi) in 1324; a ruler of the same dynasty, Feroze Shah Tughluq (1351-88), founded yet another at Ferozabad (some 12 kilometres to the north). The early Moghuls (who swept to power in 1526, ending 75 years of Afghan rule) preferred to rule from Agra or Lahore, but Shah Jahan (1627-58) eventually restored Delhi as the capital. It remained the centre of the Moghul empire until Moghul rule ended in 1857.

The British Raj built Calcutta as the capital, but returned the central government to the old site with the foundation of New Delhi in 1911 (though it was not formally inaugurated until 1931). The designer, Sir Edwin Lutyens, laid out a spacious city of avenues radiating from the **Rajpath**, the principle avenue, which runs from the ceremonial **India Gate** (a memorial to India's war dead) to the pink and yellow sandstone majesty of **Rashtrapati Bhavan**, the presidential residence (once home to the Viceroy). Rashtrapati Bhavan is flanked by two matching administrative buildings. The circular Parliament House lies to the north of these buildings.

The commercial centre of New Delhi lies approximately two kilometres to the north of Rajpath. Around its nucleus — **Connaught Circus** — you will find shops, airline offices, restaurants and the **Government of India Tourist Information Office**. South and southwest of Rajpath, avenues lined with shady Neem trees and white neo-classical bungalows spread out to the **Race Course** and **Jaipur Polo Ground**, and the **Chanakyapuri** diplomatic area.

Old Delhi adjoins the New to the north of Connaught Circus. The transition from the spacious garden-like atmosphere of New Delhi to the teeming traffic and bazaars of Old Delhi is abrupt.

The turgid, polluted River Yamuna runs along the eastern boundary of the city proper. Close to the walls of the **Red Fort** are the *ghats* — steps down the embankment — where India's leaders are cremated. Memorials mark the precise spots of the pyres of Mahatma Gandhi, and prime ministers Jawaharlal Nehru, Lal Bahadur Shastri and Indira Gandhi (Nehru's daughter) and Rajiv Gandhi (Indira's son). The Mahatma, Indira Gandhi and Rajiv Gandhi were all killed by assassins.

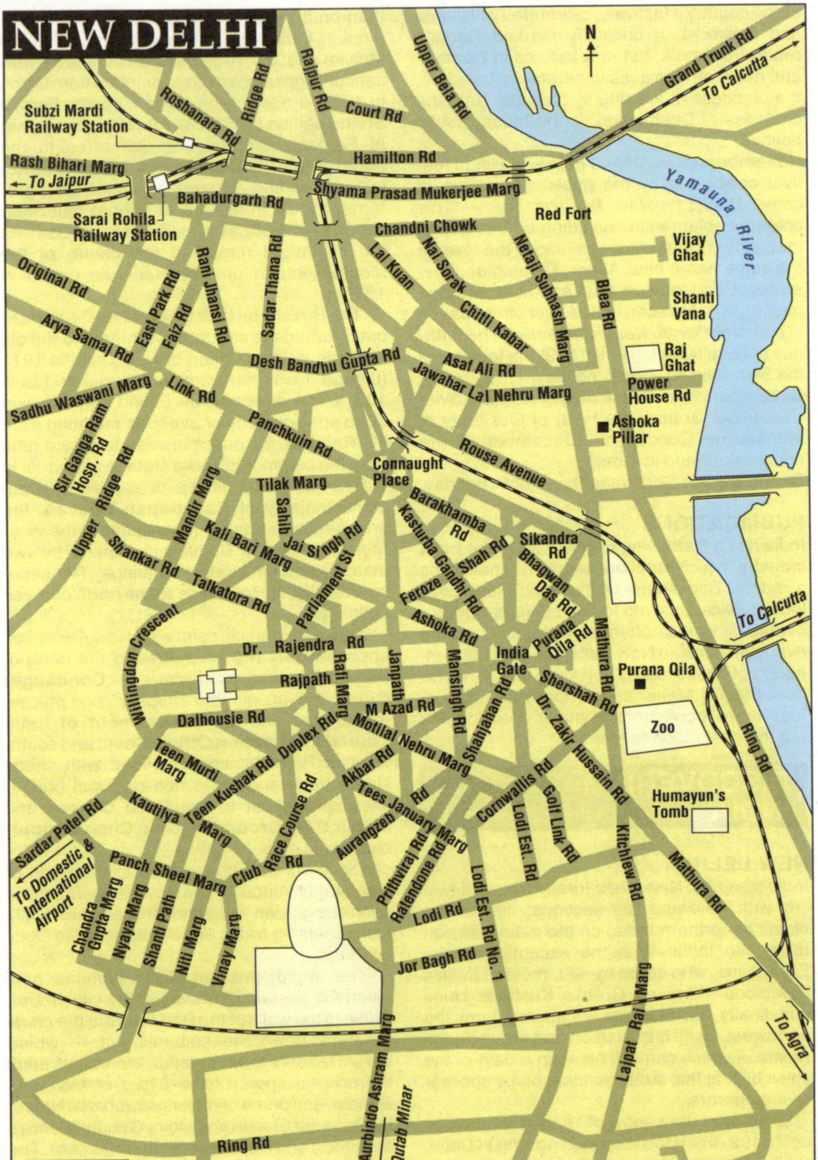
NEW DELHI
N
Subzi Mardi Railway Station
Rash Bihari Marg
← To Jaipur
Sarai Rohila Railway Station
Roshanara Rd
Ridge Rd
Rajpur Rd
Court Rd
Upper Bela Rd
Grand Trunk Rd
To Calcutta
Hamilton Rd
Shyama Prasad Mukerjee Marg
Bahadurgarh Rd
Yamauna River
Red Fort
Chandni Chowk
Vijay Ghat
Shanti Vana
Original Rd
Rani Jhansi Rd
Sadar Thana Rd
Lal Kuan
Nai Sorak
Netaji Subhash Marg
Blea Rd
Chilli Kabar
Arya Samaj Rd
East Park Rd
Faiz Rd
Desh Bandhu Gupta Rd
Asaf Ali Rd
Raj Ghat
Jawahar Lal Nehru Marg
Power House Rd
Sadhu Waswani Marg
Link Rd
Panchkuin Rd
Ashoka Pillar
Sir Ganga Ram Hosp. Rd
Upper Ridge Rd
Mandir Marg
Connaught Place
Rouse Avenue
Tilak Marg
Barakhamba Rd
Sahib
Jai Singh Rd
Kali Bari Marg
Kasturba Gandhi Rd
Sikandra Rd
Shankar Rd
Talkatora Rd
Parliament St
Feroze Shah Rd
Bhagwan Das Rd
Willingdon Crescent
To Calcutta
Ashoka Rd
Mathura Rd
Dr. Rajendra Rd
Purana Qila Rd
India Gate
Purana Qila
Rajpath
Rafi Marg
Janpath
Mansingh Rd
Shershah Rd
Dalhousie Rd
M Azad Rd
Shahjahan Rd
Zoo
Duplex Rd
Motilal Nehru Marg
Dr. Zakir Hussain Rd
Ring Rd
Teen Murti Marg
Teen Kushak Rd
Akbar Rd
Cornwallis Rd
Kautilya Marg
Race Course Rd
Tees January Marg
Golf Link Rd
Humayun's Tomb
Sardar Patel Rd
Aurangzeb Rd
Lodi Est. Rd
Kitchlew Rd
To Domestic & International Airport
Panch Sheel Marg
Club Rd
Prithviraj Rd
Ratendone Rd
Mathura Rd
Chandra Gupta Marg
Nyaya Marg
Shanti Path
Niti Marg
Vinay Marg
Lodi Rd
Lodi Est. Rd No. 1
Jor Bagh Rd
Lajpat Rai Marg
To Agra
Sri Aurbindo Ashram Marg
To Qutab Minar
Ring Rd
Railways

The old section contains many historical relics, including the Ajmeri and Delhi gates and other parts of the old city wall. The Red Fort of the Emperor Shah Jahan, built in 1638-45 originally overlooked the Yamuna River, but the watercourse has shifted some way to the east since. The entrance to the fort is through the **Lahore Gate** at the eastern end of Chandni Chowk (Silver St), which leads into a long vaulted hall lined with small shops selling postcards and souvenirs. The Dewan-i-Am (the Hall of Public Audience), with 60 pillars of red sandstone supporting a flat roof, is on the far side of the central gardens. This and other courtly buildings are lined with white marble inlaid with coloured stones in floral designs. *Son et lumiere* (sound and light) displays, relating the Red Fort's history, are held in the evenings (the time varies with the sunset).

Near the fort, old city mansions, approachable only through narrow alleys, are still standing. Visitors fortunate enough to be invited inside are astonished by the grace and coolness of these old buildings, which are surrounded by crowded and grubby bazaars. **Dariba Kalan**, a lane off Chandni Chowk, is lined with shops offering jewellery, antique and modern. **Jama Masjid** (Mosque), just south of Chandni Chowk, is another monumental creation of Shah Jahan, built between 1650 and 1656.

The **Ferozeshah Kotia**, all that remains of the former capital city of Ferozabad, stands near the river bank, between the walled city and New Delhi proper. It is famous for its **Ashoka Pillar** (dating from the third century BC), one of the many marking the travels of the great Emperor Ashoka, which Feroze Shah brought in to enrich his city. The **Purana Qila** (Old Fort) in New Delhi, also near the river bank, rises above Mathura Rd. It dates from the reign of the second Moghul emperor, Humayan, in the early 16th century.

Humayun's tomb (about two kilometres further south at Nazamuddin East) is one of New Delhi's most impressive Moghul structures. In terms of architecture, the tomb, which is set in pleasant gardens where water once flowed down many channels, is a precursor of the Taj Mahal. At the other end of Lodhi Rd from Humayun's tomb is the tomb of **Safdar Jang**, a ruler of the Oudh principality. Built in 1753, this has been called "the last flicker of the lamp of Moghul architecture." Close by is the fine tomb of **Sikander Lodhi** (1489-1517), adjoining the delightful **Lodhi Gardens**, where one can see retired generals and civil servants taking their constitutionals.

Other highlights of the city include: **The Jantar Mantar** (a massive observatory) on Parliament St in the city centre; the **National Museum** on Janpath (just to the south of Rajpath); the **National Gallery of Modern Art**, Jaipur House, where some of the finest Indian paintings can be seen; the **Delhi Zoo** (right by the Purana Qila), which is run down but has some white tigers; and the exuberant **Lakshmi Narayan Temple** (two kilometres due west of Connaught Place).

Qutab Minar (some 11 kilometres south of New Delhi) is a red sandstone minaret, surrounded by interesting ruins in parkland. The minaret, built between 1206 and 1236, has been closed to prevent suicides.

Tughluqabad, about eight kilometres east of Qutab, has a ruined citadel on a ledge of rock, which provides a fine view of New Delhi. On the other side of the road is the white-domed and massive tomb of **Ghias-ud-Din Tughluq**. The 11th century amphitheatre of Suraj Kund, just to the south, is said to be Delhi's earliest architectural remains. The Haryana state government has developed this as a tourist centre and people from New Delhi often go there for picnic weekends.

UPCOUNTRY FROM NEW DELHI

Mathura, on the main road south from New Delhi, was once a great Buddhist centre; as the legendary scene of Lord Krishna's frolicsome exploits, it is also one of the seven sacred centres for Hindus. There are two notable sights here: the **Masjid**; and the **Katra**, a great mosque built by Emperor Aurangazab on the ruins of a Buddhist monastery dating probably from the first years of the Christian era.

Agra, site of the **Taj Mahal**, is along the same road, 200 kilometres from New Delhi. Trips to Agra from New Delhi by air, rail or road can be done in a single day. The great Moghul Emperor Akbar made Agra his capital and built a huge fort. His grandson, Shah Jahan, built the incomparable Taj Mahal in 1630-52 as a memorial to his favourite wife Mumtaz Mahal. Skilled craftsmen were brought from as far away as Italy, Turkey and Persia to work on the stone carving. Both Shah Jahan and Mumtaz Mahal now lie in sarcophagi alongside one another beneath the central dome, in light that filters through a double screen of perforated marble. The Taj Mahal is stunning at any time, but sublime in the full moon or dawn.

The city is also the site of **Agra Fort**, comprising the **Dewan-i-Khas**, the palace known as the **Jahangiri** and the **Moti Masjid** built by Shah Jahan. There are two other worthwhile sights nearby: **Itmadud-Daulah** across the River Yamuna; and the impressively simple tomb of **Akbar** at Sikandra (about eight kilometres away along the road back to New Delhi). **The Bharatpur Bird Sanctuary**, 50 kilometres away, is best visited between October and March.

Gwalior (some 160 kilometres to the south of Agra) is an ancient city, with a magnificent fort. Inside are the **Man Mandir Palace**, built by the ruler Man Singh (1486-1516), and the **Karan Palace** of about the same date. For picturesque beauty, the palaces are unequalled in central India. Some fine Jain sculptures are carved from the solid rock under the fort.

Khajuraho is a day's drive from Gwalior via the town of Jhansi. Once the capital of the Chandela kings, the village is now famous for its temple ruins, including some of the masterpieces of India's erotic sculpture. The temples fall into three main groups of which the western is the best.

The oldest of this western group is the **Chausat Yogini**, the only one built of granite, dating from 900 AD, and dedicated to the Goddess Kali. The largest of the temples in the western group is the **Kandariya Mahadev**, dedicated to Shiva. This is decorated with sculptures and carvings of lovers, flying nymphs, musicians and crocodiles. The third part of the group centres on the **Chitragupta** (Bharatji) **Temple**, decorated with a depiction of the Sun God, Surya, who is driving a seven-horse chariot. The carvings on the outside depict hunting scenes, elephant fights, royal processions and dancers.

Three Hindu and three Jain shrines make up the eastern temple group. The southern group consists of the **Duladeo** and **Chaturbhuj** temples, which lie about three kilometres from Khajuraho village.

A daily flight links Khajuraho, Delhi, Agra and Varanasi.

Allahabad is an old city at the confluence of the Yamuna, the Ganga (Ganges) and the mythical river Saraswati (believed to have gone underground). This spot, called Triveni, or "the confluence of three rivers," is sacred to all devout Hindus. A fort overlooking the river junction contains an Ashoka Pillar, a palace erected by Akbar and an extensive arsenal. Boats take pilgrims and onlookers out to centre stream, where devotees immerse themselves and collect vials of holy water. Allahabad also has the tomb and gardens of **Khusrau**, son of the Emperor Jahangir (1605-27). The bathing festival known as the *Magh* (January-February) becomes the Kumbh Mela every 12th year, when as many as 2 million devotees arrive from all over India.

Lucknow, on the Gomti River, is the present-day capital of Uttar Pradesh, India's most populous state. It was capital of the former Kingdom of Oudh. Vestiges of the sophisticated lifestyle of its Muslim rulers live on in the subtly spiced Lucknow cuisine. Oudh buildings have not worn well, but there are a few notable exceptions. The **Great Imambara** (mausoleum) built by the Nawab Asaf-ud-Daula in 1784 is one of the world's largest halls with an arched roof. At the **Husainabad Imambara**, built by Mohammed Ali Shah in 1837, a small building on the grounds contains portraits of the nawabs and kings of Oudh. The most poignant relic in Lucknow is the old British residency, left as it was after the epic siege of 1857 by mutinous sepoys. Devotees of Rudyard Kipling will also be interested in the grotesque Indo-Gothic architecture of **La Martiniere School**, the boys boarding school where the waif Kim was sent for his English education in preparation for "the Great Game."

Varanasi (known as Benares in British times) is the most holy Hindu city in the country, standing at an especially sacred sweep of the Ganges. The city is very old: Hsuan Tsang, the celebrated Chinese pilgrim, visited it in the seventh century and reported 30 Buddhist monasteries and about 100 Hindu temples. By

Lucknow's La Martiniere school. PHOTO: HAMISH McDONALD

the 12th century it was occupied by the Muslim Sultan of Delhi, who destroyed all the temples.

Every Hindu hopes to visit Varanasi once in his life and bathe in the sacred waters. The sick come to be healed. Elderly people come to Varanasi to die, believing it will ensure the soul's immediate salvation. The bathing ghats are the magnet for all visitors. The dead are also washed in the river before they are placed on wood pyres. The softness of the light is renowned, especially in the early morning.

Varanasi has about 2,000 temples, mostly very small. The most important temple — the holiest spot in the holy city — is the **Viswanath** (Golden Temple), dedicated to Shiva, Lord of the Universe. It was built in about 1750. Monkeys populate the **Durga monkey temple**, located in the southern suburbs. Two mosques are prominent, the **Alamgir mosque**, in the northern quarter, and the **Aurangazeb mosque**, in the middle of the Hindu town.

Varanasi is a place for quiet observation: photography of cremations is not allowed, and non-Hindus are not supposed to enter temples. On a more earthly level, the city's Muslim weavers turn out brilliant fabric woven on handlooms, with borders of gold and silver thread. Benares silk is world-renowned. The city has one of the best universities in India, the **Varanasi Hindu University**.

Sarnath (some eight kilometres north of Varanasi) is where the Gautama Buddha delivered his first sermon after attaining enlightenment at Bodhgaya. The town has foundations of monasteries built more than 2,000 years ago and several shrines and stupas that attract Buddhists from all over the world. The Mahabodhi Society of India has built a new shrine here. The three-lion crest of the famous **Ashoka Pillar** at Sarnath has been adopted as the Indian national emblem. A fine museum houses finds from the excavation of Sarnath, started with Viceroy Lord Curzon's encouragement in 1904.

RAJASTHAN

The vast, half-desert state of Rajasthan is perhaps the most romantic part of India, with handsome people, colourful costumes, splendid forts and palaces, and a tawny landscape of rugged hills and broad plains.

The former princely city of **Alwar** is nestled in a valley 165 kilometres almost due south of New Delhi. A fortress, surrounded by a rampart and a moat with five gates, overlooks the valley from some 300 metres above. The

Sariska Wildlife Sanctuary (35 kilometres away) has lodging at the Tourist Bungalow, Forest Rest House and Sariska Palace Hotel.

Jaipur, "the Pink City" (300 kilometres by rail southwest of New Delhi) was founded in 1728 by the warrior-astronomer Maharaja Jai Singh. The people of Jaipur are noted for their colourful clothing and fine handicrafts, including tie-dyed material and jewellery. Houses have latticed windows and at sunset the buildings glow rose-pink. Crenellated walls surround the city and forts crown nearby rugged hills. The most famous of the buildings are the **Hawa Mahal** (Palace of the Winds) and the observatory. The huge stone instruments of the observatory, constructed by Jai Singh II, are even more fascinating than the ones he built at New Delhi and Varanasi.

Udaipur, called "the city of sunrise," lies in a valley by the **Pichola Lake**. The maharajah's palace, which crowns the city, was begun around 1570 but has since become a patchwork of architectural styles. It is noted for its walls inlaid with mosaic peacocks, tiled floors and roof gardens. In the lake are two islands with palaces (one a hotel) of the 17th and 18th centuries. The village of Ahar (two kilometres away) has cenotaphs of the Udaipur maharajas and their wives who committed *sati* (self-immolation on the funeral pyres of their husbands).

Further west is **Jodhpur** (founded in 1459), another walled town with a fort and several palaces. The ruins of **Mandor**, capital of the Marwar (Jodhpur rulers) lie about eight kilometres north of Jodhpur.

Jaisalmer, close to the Pakistan border in the far west, has buildings of yellow stone that shines golden above the desert sands in the morning and evening sun. The town, which dates from 1156, suffers from water shortages. Women draw water from the rain-fed lake in the middle of town throughout the day, carrying it home in shining brass vessels on their heads.

Dominating the town is a great fort, the second oldest in Rajasthan. Inside the formidable entrance are many beautiful temples of carved stone, and an old palace. Many of the Jain temples house ancient manuscripts and paintings on palm leaf and paper, some of which date back to the 12th century.

The town itself is a fascinating maze of bazaars and elaborate stone houses. Jaisalmer is also the home of India's finest breed of camel, the Jaisalmer Risala. The annual three-day Desert Festival held at Jaisalmer at full moon over January and February features music and dancing from the region.

Bikaner, northwest of Jaipur, can be reached by a branch line of the railway from Jaipur to Jodhpur. The city, with forts and palaces, is enclosed by a 5.5-kilometre wall. This region is the ancestral home of the astute Marwari merchants and industrialists who have thrived in business all over India.

Amritsar, the holy city of the Sikh religion, is 500 kilometres northwest of New Delhi by rail in the state of Punjab. It is also the jumping-off point for Attari, the only land-border crossing to Pakistan (30 minutes away by car). **Lahore** is similarly close on the other side. Porters will carry your baggage as far as a demarcation line on the tarmac road, where it will be picked up by porters from the other side of the border.

The focus of religious activity in Amritsar is the **Golden Temple**, which sits in a vast water tank surrounded by marble outbuildings. Visitors may deposit their shoes for safe keeping and borrow the required head covering before entering. Few will fail to be moved by the atmosphere of tranquil devotion in the temple, where priests read from holy texts and keep up a soft and melodic singing of hymns around the clock. The public relations office has guides and literature to explain.

Halfway between New Delhi and Amritsar is **Chandigarh**, the new town designed by the 20th century French architect Le Corbusier. It is the shared capital of both Punjab and Haryana states.

From **Kalka**, just north of Chandigarh, a

small mountain railway makes a fascinating ascent in about three hours to the hill station of **Simla**, where the former British Government of India migrated every summer.

Northwest of Simla are the twin valleys of Kulu and Kangra, noted for sweeping vistas, green orchards, forests, ancient forts and houses of a distinctive mix of timber and stone. From **Kangra** you can reach the hill station of **Dharamsala**, where the Dalai Lama has his residence. To the northwest, via Pathankot, is the hill station of **Dalhousie**, which has a famous golf course. The well-known summer resorts of **Mussoorie**, **Nainital** and **Ranikhet** are located in the region northeast of New Delhi. The latter two possess golf courses.

JAMMU AND KASHMIR

The predominantly Muslim state of **Jammu and Kashmir** (often known simply as Kashmir) is the scenic showplace of India. The region is graced by fast-running mountain streams, limpid lakes fed by Himalayan snows and forests ringed by snow-clad peaks. Kashmir is also noted for carpets, woollen goods, wood carvings and furniture, papier-mache and leather work. Kashmir has much to offer, but since an uprising against Indian rule began in 1989, it has become an increasingly grim war zone. Seek advice from your embassy before making travel arrangements.

Srinagar, the capital, which dates from the sixth century, straddles the River Jhelum and a canal network. Its eastern side is bounded by the Dal Lake. The famous houseboats that visitors can rent are moored along the waterways. The local version of the gondola, the *shikara*, is both transport and platform for traders.

Further from the city is the Nagin Lake, where the houseboats are more isolated and quiet. The **Sankaracharya Temple**, built in the eighth century, stands on a hill rising 300 metres above the valley floor. Srinagar's abandoned hilltop fort outside the city is also well worth the climb, but you will need a permit from the local tourist office. The **Jama Masjid** in Srinagar is a superb example of medieval Muslim architecture using timber beams. The building, which was originally built between 1389 and 1413, has been razed by fire three times. The present structure was restored on the original plan by the Moghul Emperor Aurangazeb in 1674.

A few kilometres out of Srinagar are the **Moghul Gardens of Shalimar** (Abode of Love), **Nishat** (Garden of Pleasure) and **Chashma Shahi** (Royal Spring). Some 40 kilometres from Srinagar is **Gulmarg** (Meadow of Flowers), at an altitude of 2,600 metres. It has a fine golf course (one of the highest in the world) and offers winter skiing. **Pahalgam** (about 100 kilometres from Srinagar at 2,134 metres), the meeting point of two snow-fed rivers, is famed for its scenic beauty; blue forests of pine and fir crowd the mountainsides. About 50 kilometres from Pahalgam in a hinterland of rock and ice is the sacred cave of **Amarnath**, a centre for pilgrimage.

Indian authorities have opened up the formerly closed **Ladakh** region in the east of the state, in part because of the virtual shutdown of the Kashmir Valley tourist industry. Peopled by Buddhists of Tibetan stock, Ladakh is a high, desolate, windswept plateau, separated from the lush Kashmir Valley by the Zojila pass, 3,529 metres above sea level on the Himalayan range.

The capital, **Leh**, offers a glimpse of Tibetan culture and architecture and is a good base for visits to the Mahayana Buddhist monasteries of **Hemis Gumpa**, **Spituk** and others. You can reach Leh by air on hair-raising (and heavily booked) Indian Airlines flights from Srinagar and Delhi. From mid-May to mid-November there is a daily bus service from Srinagar, with an overnight stop at Kargil. You can also hire a car at Srinagar for the journey. Leh is accessible by road in the summer from Manali. But either road can be closed due to bad weather at any time. Visitors, especially trekkers, should allow time for acclimatization to the altitude and possible transport delays.

THE WESTERN REGION

BOMBAY

The king of Portugal gave Bombay to Charles II of England upon his marriage to Catherine of Braganza in 1661. In 300 years, it has grown from a region of swamps and tiny islands into a metropolis of 10 million people. It is India's biggest port and commercial centre. Piratical trading, a freewheeling stockmarket followed by millions of small and large investors, and a glitzy film industry known as "Bollywood" make Bombay the most exciting city in the Subcontinent.

The **Gateway of India**, the city's most famous landmark, was erected on the Apollo Bunder to commemorate the landing of the King-Emperor George V and Queen Mary in 1911. Immediately northwest is the Fort area

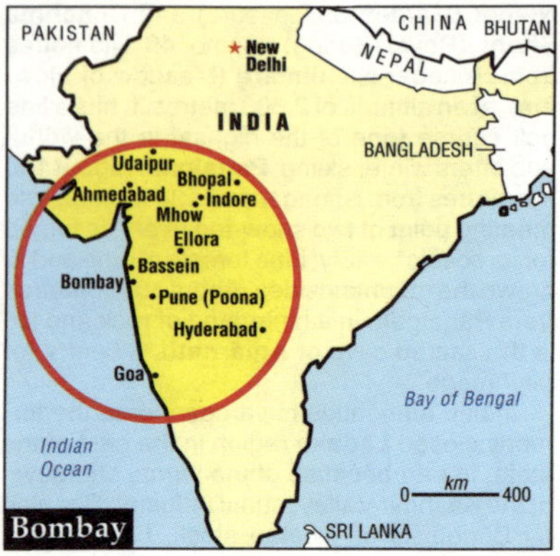

and the main commercial centre, though business areas exist all over this thriving city. Northwards is the main base of the Indian navy and then Ballard Pier, the general dock area.

On the other side of the peninsula is **Back Bay**, skirted by the sweeping Marine Drive, where Bombay residents like to take evening walks. **Chowpatty Beach**, studded with snack stalls, lies at the north end of Marine Drive. The coast sweeps westward to Malabar Hill, a well-to-do residential area. The **Ferozeshah Mehta Gardens** (popularly called the Hanging Gardens) give a good hilltop view of the ocean and city. Immediately beyond the gardens are the **Towers of Silence**, where the Parsees (followers of the Zoroastrian religion) expose their dead to be consumed by vultures; entry is not allowed.

The **Veermata Jijabai Bhonsle Udyan** (still better known by its original name of Victoria Gardens) is another notable sight. Laid out in 1861, it contains a zoo and the Victoria and Albert Museum, with natural history, geology and agriculture sections.

The principal museum in Bombay is the **Prince of Wales Museum**, a short distance inland from the Gateway of India. It houses the collection of the Natural History Society of Bombay as well as the Tata collection of rare paintings of the Moghul school and fine examples of Chinese jade and porcelain. In the grounds of the museum stands the **Jehangir Art Gallery**, completed in 1952, where art and photographic exhibitions are frequently mounted.

The **Elephanta Caves** are 10 kilometres to the southeast across the harbour on a small island locally known as Gharapuri. These are seven caves which contain huge sculptures of deities and panels in relief dating back to the eighth century. You can get there in a half-day trip by boat. Motor launches depart frequently from the steps at the Gateway of India.

UPCOUNTRY FROM BOMBAY

Bassein, some 50 kilometres north of Bombay, was a 16th century stronghold of the Portuguese. The ruins of churches, convents, manors and fortifications make it an interesting excursion from Bombay.

Karla, eight kilometres from Lonavala Station on the Bombay-Poona line, has fine cave-temples, notably the second-century Great Cave of Karla, which has ornamental columns rising to the ribbed, teak roof.

Pune (or **Poona**), 190 kilometres from Bombay (three hours away by the Deccan Queen railway express) was the capital of the Maratha empire (1750-1817). It was also the abode of the British governors of Bombay during the coast's sweltering mid-year monsoon. The city has extensive gardens, and temples and palaces of the 16th-19th centuries. It is an important industrial centre.

Ellora and Ajanta, the most famous of all the rock temples, are northeast of Bombay. Limited accommodation is available near both temples. At Ellora, caves extend along the face of the hill for two kilometres and are divided into three distinct series — Buddhist, Brahminical (Hindu) and Jain. The **Kailasa** is a copy of a complete Dravidian Temple, carved from the rock in 760-783 AD. Ajanta's 30 caves, all Buddhist, are excavated in the side of a ravine and, like Ellora, contain both temples and monastic living quarters. **Daulatabad Fort** is a magnificent 13th century citadel, with a moat, scarp and spiral passage hewn out of the solid rock. The fort is a good stop for tea.

Mandu, a ruined city that thrived in the 15th century, is off the main Bombay-New Delhi highway southwest of the towns of Indore and Mhow. It extends 13 kilometres along the crest of the Vindhya mountains. The battlemented wall is nearly 37 kilometres, enclosing many fine palaces, tombs and mosques.

Sanchi, near the Madhya Pradesh state capital Bhopal, has probably the oldest buildings still standing in India. Buddhist buildings were first erected here not long after the time of the Buddha himself. The Buddhist emperor Ashoka designed Sanchi as a centre for the religion. Stupas (memorial mounds) still stand

Festival in Tamil Nadu. PHOTO: HAMISH McDONALD ▶

on the level top of a small sandstone hill about 90 metres high on a bank of the River Betwa.

Ahmedabad, capital of Gujarat state and a textile industry centre, was founded in 1411 on the site of earlier Hindu towns. It became a meeting place of Hindu, Muslim and Jain architecture, with mosques built from the materials of Hindu temples. One example is the **Jama Masjid** (completed in 1424) with its 300 elaborately carved pillars. Two of the filigree marble windows in Sidi Said's mosque are marvels of artistic delicacy and grace rivalling any examples in Agra or New Delhi.

Mount Abu, on the railway north from Ahmedabad, is a steep granite island in the surrounding plains of Marwar. The peaks and shelves of the mountain are covered with shrines, temples and tombs. On the very top is a small round platform containing a chamber with a block of granite bearing the impression of the feet of Data Bhrigu (an incarnation of Vishnu). The two principal temples at **Dilwara**, at the middle of the mountain, are of white marble. One was built by a local governor, apparently about 1032. Simple and bold in style, it is one of the oldest and most complete examples of Jain architecture. The other was built by two rich merchant brothers between 1197 and 1247.

The **Gir Forest Sanctuary**, on Gujarat's Kathiawar Peninsula, is renowned for its Indian lions, and has a small guesthouse close by. The sanctuary is open from mid-October to mid-June, closing for the mid-year monsoon.

GOA

When Goa was captured by the Portuguese Alfonso de Albuquerque in 1510 it became the capital of Portuguese India (the former capital was Cochin). The territory remained in Portuguese hands until forcibly taken by India in 1961. Some 40% of the population is Christian and the culture is strongly Europeanized. The capital, Panaji or New Goa (previously called Panjim), can be reached daily by air, road or sea transport, though the ferry from Bombay is suspended during the monsoon months (June to October usually). Goa, with its fine beaches, sleepy towns and villages and hybrid cuisine, is the most relaxing place for a purely recreational holiday in the whole of India.

Old Goa reached the height of its prosperity between 1575 and 1625; it is now for the most part a city of ruins, but some splendid buildings have survived, among them the Basilica of the Bom Jesus (built between 1594 and 1603). This contains the tomb of St Francis Xavier, who lies in a silver coffin atop an elaborate monument in a side chapel. Next to the Bom Jesus is the **Convent of the Jesuits** (1590), which sent missionaries out in an attempt to convert the East. Across the square is the **Cathedral of St Catherine**, founded by Albuquerque in 1511 and rebuilt in 1623, still used for public services. **The Church of St Cajetan** (1665), a little north of Bom Jesus, is one of the best preserved buildings of old Goa.

THE EASTERN REGION
CALCUTTA

Calcutta is a byword for Third World poverty, but nearly all visitors are impressed with the sophistication of its culture and spirit of its citizens, from pavement-dwellers on up. Once India's largest metropolis (it was overtaken by Bombay in the 1991 census), Calcutta, the centre of Bengali culture, has 10 million people who manage to disavow materialism while struggling for their very existence. The disputatious Bengali intellectual is renowned across India.

An East India Co. writer (clerk), Job Charnock, founded Calcutta over 300 years ago on a high embankment of the Hooghly River in the Ganges delta. Calcutta became the capital of British India until the founding of New Delhi this century. Its *boxwallahs* (businessmen) kept it the country's biggest commercial centre until Bombay's faster expansion after World War II. Calcutta's port handles nearly half of India's seaborne trade.

Visitors should find any excuse to enter the

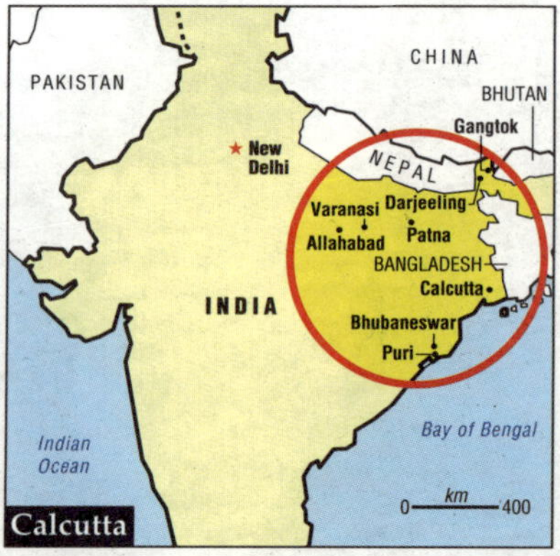

Patna women carry Ganges water in the Ashwamedh Yajna ritual. PHOTO: K.M. KISHAN/REUTER

splendid red brick **Writers' Bldg**, formerly the East India Co. offices. The building now houses most of the ministries of West Bengal's state government. The halls of clerks, nearly submerged by mouldering paper files, form the ultimate vision of bureaucratic inertia. Also around **Dalhousie Square** are the **Scotch Kirk of St Andrew** (opened in 1818), and the magnificent **General Post Office**, which stands on the site of the infamous "Black Hole" dungeon in which British captives perished in 1757.

Just off Council House St, near Dalhousie Square, is **St John's Church**, built in 1784, which has a monument to Charnock in the graveyard. Charnock is remembered not just for founding Calcutta, but for his gallantry in rescuing a lovely Brahmin widow from committing *sati* (ceremonial suicide) at the funeral pyre of her husband — and then marrying her himself.

Netaji Subhas Rd leads to the huge **Howrah Bridge** across the Hooghly River. The city's major rail terminus, Howrah Station, is on the opposite side. (Calcutta's other railway station is Sealdah). The **Oberoi Grand** and the **Ritz** hotels can be found on the eastern side of Nehru Rd. Stretching for several blocks behind them is the interesting bazaar area known as the New (or Hogg) Market. Off Nehru Rd is Park St, which has several of the city's best restaurants. The grand **Victoria Memorial** is a white marble building housing Raj memorabilia. All the great figures, Indian and British, are remembered in print, portrait or stone.

Across the river are the **Botanical Gardens**, noted for a huge banyan tree. The **Ashutosh Museum** has an excellent collection of regional arts and crafts, including some of the finest Bengali textiles. Calcutta's brightly modern underground railway — too expensive for most of its citizens to use — is in odd contrast to the city's decay at street level.

UPCOUNTRY FROM CALCUTTA

Some good excursions can be made by train or bus into Calcutta's neighbouring villages for a view of Bengali peasant life. **Serampore**, reached by launch up the Hooghly River, is a former Danish settlement with a church built in 1805. You can also take a boat to Chandernagore, which was French until 1951. The French influence only lingers in the names of several hotels. Another boat trip is to **Chinsura**, an old Dutch settlement with a church built in 1678. The terracotta temples at **Bishnupur**, 146 kilometres from Calcutta, are famous. **Santiniketan (Abode of Peace)**, some 160 kilometres to the north, is where Rabindranath Tagore (the famous Bengali poet and Nobel laureate whose songs became the national anthems of India and Bangladesh) founded the non-conformist Visva Bharati University as a centre for the study of Indian art and culture. Tagore's personal belongings, manuscripts and paintings may be seen at the Uttarayan complex. Santiniketan has a 20-room tourist bungalow run by the West Bengal Tourism Development Corp.

Calcutta is also one of the take-off points for Kathmandu, capital of Nepal, Gangtok, capital of Sikkim, and, within India, Darjeeling and Kalimpong in the northern mountains of West Bengal, with a view of the Himalayas.

Patna, the capital of Bihar state is 480 kilometres by rail from Calcutta. It stands on the site of the ancient city of Pataliputra, the capital of Emperor Ashoka's empire, which extended from the Bay of Bengal to the Hindu Kush (in present-day Afghanistan). After some centuries of fame as a great Buddhist centre, it fell into decline. But Patna recovered in the mid-16th century when it became the capital of the province of Bihar. It has several noteworthy mosques and a Sikh temple that marks the birthplace of the Govind Singh, 10th and last guru of the Sikhs, who was assassinated in 1708; his cradle and shoes are preserved in the temples.

The city's **Khudabuksh Oriental Library**, famous for its rare collection of Arabic and Persian manuscripts, possesses the only volumes saved from the sacking of the Moorish University of Cordoba, Spain.

Gaya district, some 80 kilometres to the south, contains the small town of **Bodhgaya** where Gautama Buddha attained enlightenment 2,500 years ago. A succession of temples have stood on the spot, the current one with its 50-metre tower restored under British archaeologists in 1882. A pipul tree outside the temple is believed to be a lineal descendant of the tree under which Buddha was meditating when he obtained enlightenment. Many Buddhist nations, including Thailand and Japan, have built ashrams in Bodhgaya for their monks.

The **Barabar Hills**, 25 kilometres north of Gaya, have cave shrines of the time of Ashoka, the most ancient excavated in India. Some 100 kilometres southeast of Patna by road lie the ruins of the great Buddhist monastery of **Nalanda**, where the Chinese pilgrim Hsuan Tsang studied for five years in the seventh century.

Puri, on the coast of Orissa state, is almost 500 kilometres southwest of Calcutta by rail (an overnight run). It has a wide and almost deserted beach stretching for miles. At daybreak people stand to worship in the water, facing east with heads bowed and hands folded.

Puri is above all the town of the great 12th-century temple of the god Jagannath. Only Hindus are admitted to the temple, but locally available guides may take non-Hindus to look from surrounding balconies. The famous **Rathyatra Car Festival** takes place in June or July (depending on the lunar calendar), when enormous idols are brought out through the Lion Gate and placed on wooden chariots. Thousands of pilgrims drag the cars to the Gundicha Bari (Garden House). Unfortunately, non-Hindus are barred at the time of the festival.

Bhubaneswar, capital of Orissa (100 kilometres from Puri), has eighth to 13th-century temples. The town is dominated by the 40-metre-high tower of the great **Lingaraj Temple** (built about 1050). To the west of Bhubaneswar, the twin Udayagiri and Khandagiri hills are honeycombed with decorated caves, both natural and artificial.

The **Sun Temple of Konarak**, also known as the Black Pagoda, is 65 kilometres from Bhubaneswar, accessible by car or bus. Built about 1250, it stands within a vast compound in a desolate stretch of sand about five kilometres from the sea. The temple is regarded as the peak of Orissan architecture.

Chilka Lake, south of Puri, is India's largest fresh-water lake, famous for its migrating duck in winter. Bungalows front the lake at Balugaon and Brakul.

Darjeeling, in the northernmost part of West Bengal, derives its name from the Tibetan *Dorje Ling* (Place of Thunderbolts). It commands sweeping mountain views to Mt Kanchenjunga and Mt Everest. From May to October, however, Darjeeling and the surrounding high country is veiled in mist. If you go by air to Darjeeling, there is no need to get a special pass (the town and environs are considered a restricted area by the Indian Government) as long as your stay is less than 15 days. Passes for overland travellers are a mere formality. To get them, contact the Ministry of Home Affairs. The town of Darjeeling is located on a series of hillside terraces and has many resort hotels. Surrounding hills have many interesting walks. Tiger Hill, accessible by car 11 kilometres from Darjeeling, has breathtaking views at sunrise.

You can reach **Guwahati**, the capital of Assam, by air and rail. Assam is a land of rice paddies, tea estates and forests, intersected by the massive Brahmaputra River. On its fringes are the border states of Arunyachal Pradesh, Tripura, Manipur, Nagaland, and Meghalaya, some of which were battlegrounds in World War II. Local insurgencies flare in nearly all the states, and much of Arunyachal Pradesh is disputed with China. Travel is not always open in this area.

Permits may be of limited validity, and may allow only trips by air to the state capital. Requirements vary from time to time, so seek up-to-date advice from Indian missions and official tourist agencies well before travelling.

The state of Sikkim, a former Himalayan kingdom annexed by India in 1975, occupies the gap in the border with Tibet between Bhutan and Nepal. It is often called the "land of mountains and orchids." Sikkim has the third-highest mountain in the world, the 8,585-metre Kanchenjunga, and dense tropical forest in its valleys. **Gangtok**, the Sikkim capital, can be reached by road from Darjeeling and Siliguri. Permits are required; you can get them in New Delhi (valid for 15 days) from the Sikkim Tourist Office (14 Panchsheel Marg, Chanakyapuri, Tel: 301 4236).

THE SOUTHERN REGION
MADRAS

When an official of the East India Co. chose Madras as the capital of Tamil Nadu statwe in 1639, it was a sleepy stretch of surf beach. **Fort St George** grew and survived against land and sea attacks by the French, based at Pondicherry further south. The fort was the chief British base in India until overtaken by Calcutta in the late 18th century. The old fort remains in the northern part of the city near the harbour, with old British buildings now used by the state government. Both Robert Clive, who later drove the French from Bengal, and Arthur

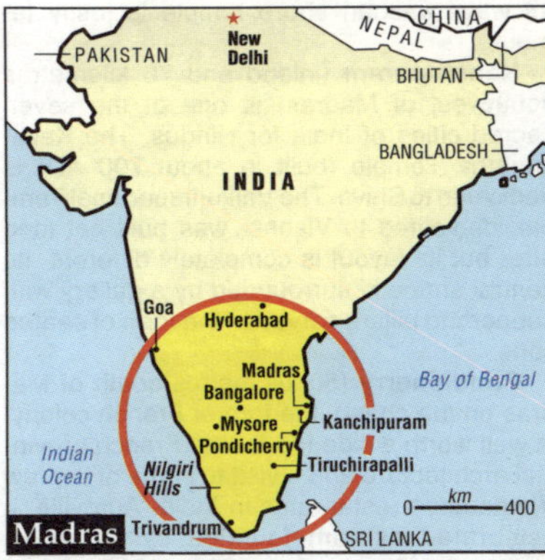

Wellesley (later the Duke of Wellington) lived within the fort. It also contains the **Church of St Mary**, consecrated in 1680 and the oldest Anglican church in India. **The Fort Museum** has many old documents on display, including the marriage certificate of Elihu Yale, who stayed in Madras before going on to found Yale University.

The **Marina Beach** is a broad strip of sand that runs for miles. Fisherman camp there around their raft-canoes. The beach is a favourite spot for meditation, exercise and relaxation.

The **National Art Gallery** on Pantheon Rd has a fine display of South Indian bronzes, including the famous Shiva dancing the Nataraj. The enormous Government Museum next door has an extensive archaeological collection.

San Thome, three kilometres south, was a trading fort of the Portuguese from 1504 until 1749. It has a cathedral dedicated to St Thomas the Apostle, who is reputed to have visited southern India and to have been killed by a hunter's arrow just outside Madras. The cathedral supposedly contains his tomb.

The modern centre of Madras has an agreeably slow pace. While the buildings are shabby, glittering colour comes from the giant outdoor portraits called "cut-outs." The five-storey high hoardings advertise the latest films from the vigorous Tamil movie industry and also the state's politicians — many of whom graduated from film acting and directing.

South of Madras (60 kilometres by road) are the ruins of **Mahabalipuram**, built by the Pallavas between 500 AD and 750 AD. The beautiful wave-washed shore temple is justly famous.

Kanchipuram (inland and 70 kilometres southwest of Madras) is one of the seven sacred cities of India for Hindus. The Kailasanatha Temple (built in about 700 AD) is dedicated to Shiva. The Vaikuntaperumal Temple, dedicated to Vishnu, was built not long after but its layout is completely different. Its central shrine is surrounded by a gallery with supporting pillars carved in the form of seated lions.

Pondicherry (50 kilometres south of Madras on the coast), the former French colony, is well worth a side trip for the French provincial architecture and a visit to some of the few Vietnamese restaurants in India. Auroville, a celebrated ashram founded by the poet-philosopher Aurobindo in 1910 is 10 kilometres to the north.

Tiruchirapalli (eight hours from Madras by rail) has a noted rock fort and Shiva Temple built between 1660 and 1670. The rock also has excavated cave temples of the Pallava kings, about 1,000 years earlier. The great 17th century temple at Srirangam (three kilometres away) is remarkable for its **Hall of One Thousand Pillars**. One row of pillars represents an entire colonnade of rearing horsemen, three metres high. The elaborate carving is typical of the great Hindu empire of Vijay Nagar, which broke up in 1565.

Thanjavur (also known as Tanjore) has the great Rajarajesvara Temple, built by Rajaraja Chola the Great (985-1081). It has a beautiful tower 60 metres high, capped by a single stone weighing 80 tonnes. A ramp six kilometres long was necessary for its erection.

Kanya Kumari (Cape Comorin) is at the southernmost tip of India. It is a sacred spot because the waters of the Bay of Bengal, Indian Ocean and Arabian Sea intermingle here. Bathing ghats go down to the water. Some of the ashes of Mahatma Gandhi were scattered on the water here. So many pilgrims have visited the Gandhi memorial that, after less than 50 years, the steps are already deeply worn. A memorial to Swami Vivekananda, an important figure in awakening respect in the west for Indian religion and culture in the 1890s, is also located on outlying rocks that you can reach by ferry-boat.

Kerala (Land of Coconut Palms) is the green lush state along the western coast of southern India, bordered inland by the Western Ghat hills. Although poverty stricken, it is noted in India for achieving almost total literacy (against a national average of just over 50% in the 1991 census) and the dramatic fall in its birthrate (which is linked to the high female literacy).

Trivandrum, the capital, lies in the very south of the state by the sea. The city's airport has direct flights to Colombo, and (because of the large number of Keralan migrant workers) to the Persian Gulf. The Kaudiyar Palace was the residence of the last reigning Maharaja of Travancore. The ancient palaces of previous rulers are in the fort area.

Kovalam (eight kilometres south of Trivandrum) has a picturesque double cove with clear water and rolling surf, backed by a coast of glistening palms. Most holiday-makers stay here rather than in Trivandrum itself, either in the conventional government resort hotel (to which one of the maharaja's old mansions is attached with luxury suites) or in the numerous small hotels along the beach and the promontory on which the tall lighthouse stands. Here you can go snorkelling and scuba-diving. The small fishing port about one kilometre to the south is an interesting walk. The beach front has small outdoor cafes serving local curries (heavy with coconut) and seafood grilled in tandoori ovens.

Quilon (50 kilometres north of Trivandrum) is an old port that was visited for centuries by Arab, Portuguese and Dutch ships. From here small motorboats run passengers along the backwaters that parallel the coast to Allepey: a continuous palm-fringed chain of lagoons and canals, past quiet villages and sometimes over wide, blue expanses of water.

Cochin, a major port and naval base, is at the northern end of Kerala. It comprises three towns and several islands on inland waterways. You can explore Cochin on foot, cycling or by boat. The Portuguese explorer Vasco da Gama, the first man to reach India from Europe round the Cape of Good Hope, died in Cochin in 1524. He is buried in St Francis' Church. The city has many long-established Christian communities and a few survivors of an ancient local Jewish community, whose synagogue (built in 1568) contains a land grant inscribed on a copper plate thought to have been made by a ruler in the seventh century.

Bangalore is 1,000 metres above sea-level in the centre of Karnataka state. It is known as the "Silicon Plateau" of India, as many Indian and foreign companies operate computer software laboratories here. You can get there by road, rail and air from many corners of the country. Bangalore has a cool climate and is also known as for its yuppie culture — manifested in booming beer pubs, boutiques and sporting facilities.

Mysore (130 kilometres by road from Bangalore) is an older princely capital. The Dusserah festivities (October or November) are marked by a parade of elephants, richly decorated and painted horses, silver coaches and standard bearers. The **Nilgiri Hills**, some 290 kilometres to the south of Mysore city, have several resort towns — Ootacamund (2,130 metres), Coonoor (1,850 metres) and Kotag Kotagiri (2,000 metres). These offer fishing, shooting, hiking and, above all, coolness. The nearest airport is almost 90 kilometres away at Coimbatore, though both road and rail transport (including the famous *Passage to India* mountain-railway) are available from the east and west coasts of South India.

Between Hampi and Bijapur lie the ancient caves of Badami and the temples at Pattadakal and Aihole, some of the oldest Hindu temples in India.

Hyderabad, ruled by Nizams until shortly after independence, is capital of Telugu-speaking Andhra Pradesh state. It is well-connected by road, rail and air. The city proper (founded in 1589) is surrounded by a stone wall with 13 gates, completed in the time of the first Nizam (1724-48). The **Char Minar (Four Minarets) Gate**, where four main roads meet, was built in 1591. The ceremonial **Ashur Khana** Bldg, the hospital, the **Gostha Mahal Palace** and **Mecca Mosque** are also of this early period. **The Salar Jung Museum** contains fine jewellery and precious stones and ivory carvings.

ANDAMAN AND NICOBAR ISLANDS

Tourism to these strategic islands, located at the northern entrance to the Malacca Straits, has only recently been promoted. They abound with fine beaches and reefs for snorkelling. The Shipping Corp. of India runs ferries connecting the capital, Port Blair, with Calcutta (1,255 kilometres away) and Madras (1,190 kilometres). The trip takes three days. Indian Airlines also offers flights from the two cities. The archipelago has about 300 islands, with irregular boat services between them. Negrito tribes inhabit many of the southern Nicobar islands. A permit is needed for a visit.

RESTAURANT SELECTION

Average price for two

BOMBAY

CHINA GARDEN, 123 August Kranti Rd, OM's Corner. Tel: 363 0841, 363 0842, 363 0117. Chinese. US$60.

COPPER CHIMNEY, A.B. Rd, Worli. Tel: 492 4488, 492 4499. Indian. US$50.

GOA PORTUGUESA, Mili Bldg, Kataria Rd, opposite Mahim HPO. Tel: 451633, 454776. Portuguese, Goan. Live music. US$40.

NANKING, Phiroz Bldg, Chatrapati Shivaji Maharaj Rd. Tel: 202 0594. Chinese. US$50.

CALCUTTA

CHUNG WAH, 13A & B, Chittranjan Ave, Tangra. Tel: 277003. Chinese. US$20.

SURUCHI, Elliot Rd. Bengali. US$5.

TRINCA'S, 17B Park St. Tel: 298947, 297825. Indian and Chinese (Ming Room). US$15.

MADRAS

KARAIKUDI CHETTINAD, 84 Dr. Radhakrishna Salai, Mylapore. Tel: 826 9122. South Indian and various seafood. US$30.

RAIN GARDEN, Connemara Hotel, Binny Rd. Tel: 826 0123. South Indian. Cultural performance, US$40.

NEW DELHI

CHOR BIZARRE, Hotel Broadway, Asaf Ali Rd. Tel: 327 3821. Kashmiri. Live music. US$40.

COCONUT GROVE, Ashok Yatri Niwas Hotel, Ashoka Rd. Tel: 371 3052. South Indian. US$15.

CORBETT'S, Claridges Hotel, 12 Aurangzeb Rd. Tel: 301 0211. Indian (Tandoori). Outdoor in "jungle" setting. US$40.

DASAPRAKASH, Ambassador Hotel, Sujan Singh Park. Tel: 469 4966. South Indian Vegetarian. US$8.

FUJIYA, 12-48 Malcha Marg Shopping Centre Chanakyaduri. Tel: 301 6059, 379 3143. Chinese and Japanese US$35.

KARIM'S, Nemat Kada, Nizamuddin West. Tel: 469 8300. Indian Muglai. US$12.

KHYBER, 1514 Kashmir Gate, Old Delhi. Tel: 252 0867. Afghan, Iranian. US$30.

HOTEL GUIDE

AGRA

B: US$100-150

MUGHAL SHERATON, Fatehabad Rd, Taj Ganj. Tel: 361701, Fax: 361730, Tlx: 056 5210. *P, Gym, SatTV. R: I, W, C.*

TAJ VIEW, Fatehabad Rd, Taj Ganj. Tel: 361171-78, Fax: 361179, Tlx: 056 5202. *P. R: I, W, C.*

D: US$50 and below

AGRA ASHOK, 6B Mall Rd. Tel: 361223-32, Tlx: 056 5313. *P, SatTV. R: I, W, C.*

CLARKS SHIRAZ, 54 Taj Rd. Tel: 361421-7, Fax: 361428, Tlx: 056 5211. *R: I, W, C.*

AHMEDABAD

D: US$50 and below

CAMA, Khanpur Rd. Tel: 25281-9, Fax: 25285, Tlx: 0121 6377. *P. R: I, W, C.*

AJMER

D: US$50 and below

MANSINGH PALACE, Vaishali Nagar. Tel: 50855, Tlx: 030 3224. *SatTV. R: I, W, C.*

AMRITSAR

D: US$50 and below

MOHAN INTERNATIONAL, Albert Rd. Tel: 227801-8, Fax: 226520, Tlx: 038 4300. *P, Gym, SatTV. R: I, W, C.*

RITZ, 45 The Mall. Tel: 226606, 226657, Tlx: 038 4242. *P. R: I, W.*

BANGALORE

B: US$100-150

WINDSOR MANOR, 25 Sankey Rd. Tel: 225 9898, Fax: 225 4941, Tlx: 0845 8209. *P, Gym, Biz, Ex, SatTV. R: I, W.*

WEST END, Racecourse Rd. Tel: 225 9281, Fax: 220 0010, Tlx: 0845 2337. *P, SatTV. R: I, W, C.*

C: US$50-100

TAJ RESIDENCY, 41-3 Mahatma Gandhi Rd. Tel: 558 4444, Fax: 558 4748, Tlx: 0845 8367. *P, Gym, Biz, SatTV. R: I, W.*

D: US$50 and below

ASHOK, Kumara Krupa, High Grounds. Tel: 225 9462, 225 9482, Fax: 225 0033, Tlx: 0845 2433. *P, SatTV. R: I, W, C.*

BHOPAL

D: US$50 and below

JEHANNUMA PALACE, 157 Shamla Hill. Tel: 540100, Fax: 540720, Tlx: 070 5343. *Biz, SatTV. R: I, W, C.*

BHUBANESHWAR

C: US$50-100

OBEROI, Naya Palli. Tel: 440890, Fax: 440898, Tlx: 0675 6348. *P, Gym. R: I, W.*

D: US$50 and below

THE KENILWORTH, 86/A-1 Gautam Nagar. Tel: 411723, 411734, Fax: 411561, Tlx: 0675 6343. *P, SatTV. R: I, W, C.*

BIKANER

D: US$50 and below

LALLGARH PALACE. Tel: 61963, Fax: 61263. *R: I, W.*

BODHGAYA

D: US$50 and below

BODHGAYA ASHOK. Tel: 22708, Fax: 22709. *R: I.*

BOMBAY

A: US$150 and above

THE OBEROI, Nariman Point. Tel: 202 5757, Fax: 204 3282, Tlx: 0118 4153-4. *P, Gym, Biz, SatTV. R: I, W.*

TAJ MAHAL, Apollo Bunder. Tel: 202 3366, Fax: 287 2711, Tlx: 011 3837, 011 6175-6, 011 2442. *P, Gym, Biz, SatTV. R: I, W, C.*

TAJ MAHAL INTERCONTINENTAL, Apollo Bunder. Tel: 202 3366, Fax: 282 2711, Tlx: 0118 4153-4. *P, Gym, Biz, SatTV. R: I, W, C.*

OBEROI TOWERS, Nariman Point. Tel: 202 4343, Fax: 204 3282, Tlx: 0118 4153-4. *P, Gym, Biz, SatTV. R: I, W.*

LEELA KEMPINSKI, Sahar. Tel: 836 3636, Fax: 836 0606, 834 1865, Tlx: 0117 9241, 0117 9236. *P, Gym, Biz, Ex, SatTV. R: I, W, C.*

B: US$100-150

CENTAUR, Juhu Beach, Tara Rd. Tel: 611 3040, Fax: 611 6343, Tlx: 0117 8181. *P, Gym, SatTV. R: I, W, C.*

PRESIDENT, Cuffe Parade, Colaba. Tel: 215 0808, Fax: 215 1201, Tlx:

P — Swimming pool **Gym** — Health club **Biz** — Business centre **Ex** — Executive floor
SatTV — Satellite TV **R** — Restaurant **I** — Indian **W** — Western food
C — Chinese food

HOTEL GUIDE

0118 4135. *P, Gym, Biz, SatTV. R: I, W, Thai.*
HOLIDAY INN, Balraj Sahani Rd. Tel: 620 4444, Fax: 620 4452, Tlx: 0117 8411. *P, Gym, Biz, SatTV. R: I, W, C.*
SEA ROCK SHERATON, Land's End, Bandra. Tel: 642 5454, Fax: 640 8046. *P, Gym, Biz, SatTV. R: I, W, C.*

C: US$50-100

CENTAUR, Santa Cruz. Tel: 611 6660, Fax: 611 3535, Tlx: 0117 1171. *P, Gym, SatTV. R: I, W, C.*
RAMADA INN PALM GROVE, Juhu Beach. Tel: 611 2323, Fax: 614 2105, Tlx: 0117 1419. *P, Gym, Biz, SatTV. R: I, W, C.*
AMBASSADOR, Veer Nariman Rd. Tel: 204 1131, Fax: 204 0004, Tlx: 0118 2918. *SatTV. R: I, W, C.*

D: US$50 and below

THE RESORT, Aksa Beach, Malad. Tel: 882 3331, Fax: 882 0738, Tlx: 0117 0191. *P, Gym, SatTV. R: I, W.*
SEA PRINCESS, Juhu Beach. Tel: 611 6080, 611 7600, Fax: 611 3973, Tlx: 0117 8160. *P. R: I, W, C.*

BORODA (VADODARA)

D: US$50 and below

EXPRESS, R.C. Dutt Rd. Tel: 337001-4, Fax: 330980, Tlx: 0175 6311. *SatTV. R: I, W, C.*

CALCUTTA

A: US$150 and above

OBEROI GRAND, Nehru Rd. Tel: 249 2323, Fax: 249 1217, Tlx: 021 5919, 021 5937, 021 5971. *P, Gym, Biz, SatTV. R: I, W, C.*
TAJ BENGAL, Belvedere Rd. Tel: 248 3939, Fax: 248 1766, 248 8875, Tlx: 021 4776, 021 5998. *P, Gym, Biz, SatTV. R: I, W, C.*

C: US$50-100

AIRPORT ASHOK, Dum Dum. Tel: 552911, Fax: 552 9137, Tlx: 021 5296. *P, SatTV. R: I, W.*
PARK, Park St. Tel: 249 7336, Fax: 249 8027, Tlx: 021 5867, 021 5912. *P, Biz, SatTV. R: I, W, C.*

D: US$50 and below

KENILWORTH, Little Russell St. Tel: 242 8394-5, Fax: 242 5136, Tlx: 021 3395. *Biz, SatTV. R: I, W, C.*

CHANDIGARH

D: US$50 and below

PICCADILLY, Himalaya Rd, Sector 22B. Tel: 707571, 705795, Fax: 705692, Tlx: 039 5256. *R: I, W, C.*
CHANDIGARH MOUNTAIN VIEW, Sector 10. Tel: 547268-9, Fax: 547126, Tlx: 039 5337. *R: I, W, C.*

COCHIN

B: US$100-150

MALABAR, Willingdon Island. Tel: 340010, Fax: 69497, Tlx: 0885 6661. *P, Gym. R: I, W, C.*

D: US$50 and below

CASINO, Willingdon Island. Tel: 668221, Fax: 668001, Tlx: 0885 6314. *P. R: I, W.*

DARJEELING

C: US$50-100

WINDEMERE, Observatory Hill. Tel: 2397, 2841, Fax: 2739, Tlx: 0260 1201-2. *R: I, W, C, Tibetan.*

D: US$50 and below

NEW ELGIN, H.D. Lama Rd. Tel: 3314, 3316. *R: I, W, C.*
SINCLAIRS, Gandhi Rd. Tel: 3431-2, Tlx: 0260 1212. *SatTV. R: I, W, C.*

DEHRADUN

D: US$50 and below

PRESIDENT, Astley Hall. Tel: 27082, 28883, Fax: 28210, Tlx: 058 5238. *R: I, W, C.*
MADHUBAN, Rajpus Rd. Tel: 24094-7, Fax: 23181, Tlx: 058 5268. *R: I, W, C.*

GANGTOK

D: US$50 and below

NOR-KHILL, Stadium Rd. Tel: 23186-87. *R: I, W, C.*
TIBET, Stadium Rd. Tel: 22523, 23468, Fax: 2707. *SatTV. R: I, W, C, Tibetan.*

GOA

A: US$150 and above

LEELA BEACH, Mobor Cavelossim, Salcette. Tel: 246363, Fax: 246352, Tlx: 019 6258. *P, Gym, Biz, SatTV. R: I, W, C.*

B: US$100-150

BOGMALO BEACH, Bogmalo. Tel:

P — Swimming pool **R** — Restaurant **Gym** — Health club **I** — Indian **Biz** — Business centre **W** — Western food **SatTV** — Satellite TV **C** — Chinese food

HOTEL GUIDE

513291, Fax: 512510, Tlx: 019 4297. *P, Gym, SatTV. R: I, W, C.*

C: US$50-100

FORT AGUADA BEACH RESORT, Sinqurim. Tel: 7501-7, Fax: 7733, Tlx: 019 4291. *P, Gym, SatTV. R: I, W, C, Thai.*
MAJORDA BEACH RESORT, Majorda, Salcette. Tel: 220025-6, Fax: 220212, Tlx: 019 6234. *P, Gym. R: I, W, C.*
RAMADA RENAISSANCE RESORT, Colva Beach, Salcette. Tel: 245200, Fax: 245335, Tlx: 019 6211. *P, Gym, SatTV. R: I, W, C.*

D: US$50 and below

FIDALGO, June Rd, Panjim. Tel: 226291, Fax: 226299, Tlx: 019 4213. *P, Gym, SatTV. R: I, W, C.*

GULMARG

D: US$50 and below

HIGHLANDS PARK. Tel: 207, 203, 291. *Gym. R: I, W.*

GUWAHATI

D: US$50 and below

BRAHMAPUTRA ASHOK, M.G. Rd. Tel: 41064, Tlx: 0235 2522. *R: I, W, C.*
NANDAN, G.S. Rd. Tel: 40856, Tlx: 0235 2267. *Biz, SatTV. R: I, W, C.*
DYNASTY, S.S. Rd. Tel: 35610-2, Fax: 24813, Tlx: 0235 2362. *SatTV. R: I.*

GWALIOR

C: US$50-100

USHA KIRAN PALACE, Jayendraganj. Tel: 323993, Fax: 321103, Tlx: 078 6274. *R: I, W, C.*

D: US$50 and below

GWALIOR REGENCY, New Bus Stand Rd. Tel: 329516, 328845, Tlx: 0782 1869-70. *P, Gym, SatTV. R: I, W, C.*

HYDERABAD

B: US$100-150

KRISHNA OBEROI, Bangara Hills. Tel: 392323, Fax: 393079, Tlx: 0425 6931. *P, Gym, SatTV. R: I, W, C.*

C: US$50-100

RITZ, Hill Fort Palace. Tel: 233571, Tlx: 0425 6215. *P, SatTV. R: I, W, C.*

D: US$50 and below

GATEWAY, Banjara Hills. Tel: 222222, Fax: 222218, Tlx: 0425 6947. *P. R: I, W, C.*
BHASKAR PALACE, Banjara Hills. Tel: 396141, 396202, Fax: 392712, Tlx: 0425 6182. *Gym, SatTV. R: I, W.*

INDORE

D: US$50 and below

PRESIDENT, R.N.T. Rd. Tel: 433156, 432858, 432860, Fax: 32230. *Gym, Biz, SatTV. R: I, W, C.*

JAIPUR

B: US$100-150

JAI MAHAL PALACE. Tel: 68381, Fax: 65237, Tlx: 0365 2250. *R: I, W, C.*
RAMBAGH PALACE, Bhawani Singh Rd. Tel: 521241, Fax: 521098, Tlx: 0365 2254. *SatTV. R: I, W, C.*

C: US$50-100

RAMGARH LODGE, Jamuva Ramgarh. Tel: 521241, Fax: 521098, Tlx: 0365 2254, 0365 2147. *R: I, W.*

D: US$50 and below

CLARKS AMER, J.L. Nehru Rd. Tel: 550616, 550701, Fax: 550013, Tlx: 036 2276. *P, SatTV. R: I, W, C.*
NARAIN NIWAS PALACE, Kanota Bagh, Narain Singh Rd. Tel: 563448, 561291, Tlx: 0365 2482. *P. R: I, W, C.*

JAISALMER

D: US$50 and below

HERITAGE INN, Sam Rd. Tel: 2769. *R: I, W, C.*
NARAYAN NIWAS PALACE. Tel: 2753, 2408, 2601. *Gym. R: I, W, C.*

JAMMU

D: US$50 and below

JAMMU ASHOK. Tel: 47621-5, Fax: 547110, Tlx: 037 7227. *P. R: I, W.*
ASIA JAMMU-TAWI, Nehru Market. Tel: 535760, 535758-9, Fax: 535756, Tlx: 037 7224. *P, Gym, SatTV. R: I, W, C.*

JODHPUR

C: US$50-100

UMAID BHAWAN PALACE. Tel: 33316, 33516, 33366, Fax: 35373, Tlx: 055 2202. *P, SatTV. R: I, W, C.*
RATANADA POLO PALACE, Resi-

P — Swimming pool **Gym** — Health club **Biz** — Business centre **SatTV** — Satellite TV
R — Restaurant **I** — Indian **W** — Western food **C** — Chinese food

HOTEL GUIDE

dency Rd. Tel: 31910-4, 33359-60, Fax: 31188, Tlx: 055 2233. *P. R: I, W, C.*

D: US$50 and below

AJIT BHAWAN, nr. Circuit House. Tel: 37410, Tlx: 37774. *R: I.*

KHAJURAHO

D: US$50 and below

CHANDELA. Tel: 2054, 2102, Fax: 2095. *P, Gym. R: I, W, C.*
JASS OBEROI, By-pass Rd. Tel: 2085, Fax: 2088, Tlx: 015 0112-02. *P, Gym, SatTV. R: I, W.*

KOVALAM (TRIVANDRUM)

C: US$50-100

ASHOK KOVALAM BEACH RESORT. Tel: 480101, Fax: 481522, Tlx: 0435 6216. *P, Gym, SatTV. R: I, W, C.*

D: US$50 and below

PALMANOVA, Light House Rd. Tel: 494-6, Fax: 446859, Tlx: 043 5270. *R: I, W, C.*
ROCKHOLM, Light House Rd. Tel: 306, 406-7, Fax: 607. *R: I, W, C.*
SEAWEED, Light House Rd. Tel: 391, Fax: 60806, Tlx: 043 5435. *R: I, W, C.*

KULU-MANALI

C: US$50-100

AMBASSADOR RESORT, Sunny Side, Chadiyari. Tel: 2173, 2235, Tlx: 0390 4207. *Gym, SatTV. R: I, W, C.*
SPAN RESORTS, Katrain. Tel: 38, 40. *SatTV. R: I, W, C.*

D: US$50 and below

MANALI RESORTS. Tel: 2274, 2174. *R: I.*
JOHN BANONS. Tel: 2335, 2392, Tlx: 0390 4202. *R: I, W, C.*

LUCKNOW

C: US$50-100

CLARKS AVADH, Mahatmah Gandhi Rd. Tel: 236500-9, 240131-3, Fax: 236507, Tlx: 053 5243. *SatTV. R: I, W, C.*

D: US$50 and below

CARLTON, Shahnajaf Rd. Tel: 244021, 244024, Tlx: 053 5217. *SatTV. R: I, W, C.*

MADRAS

A: US$150 and above

CHOLA SHERATON, Cathedral Rd. Tel: 828 0101, Fax: 827 8779, Tlx: 041 6660. *P, Gym, Biz, Ex, SatTV. R: I, W, C.*
PARK SHERATON, T.T.K. Rd, Alwarpet. Tel: 499 4101, Fax: 499 7201, Tlx: 041 6868, 041 8881. *P, Gym, Biz, SatTV. R: I, W, C.*

C: US$50-100

CONNEMARA, Binny Rd. Tel: 852 0123, Fax: 852 3361, 852 4723, Tlx: 041 8197. *P, SatTV. R: I, W.*
TAJ COROMANDEL, Nungambakkam High Rd. Tel: 827 2827, Fax: 825 7104, Tlx: 041 7194. *P, Gym, SatTV. R: I, W, C.*
TRIDENT, G.S.T. Rd. Tel: 234 4747, Fax: 234 6699, Tlx: 0412 6055, 0412 6069. *SatTV. R: I, W, C, Thai.*
FISHERMAN'S COVE, Covelong Beach, Chingleput. Tel: 44304, Fax: 825 7104, Tlx: 041 7194. *P, SatTV. R: I, W, C.*

D: US$50 and below

AMBASSADOR PALLAVA, Montieth Rd. Tel: 852 8584, Fax: 852 2061, Tlx: 041 7453. *P, Gym, SatTV. R: I, W, C.*
MADRAS INTERNATIONAL, Mount Rd. Tel: 852 1811, Fax: 852 1520, Tlx: 041 7373. *SatTV. R: I, W, C.*

MADURAI

C: US$50-100

TAJ GARDEN RETREAT, Thiruparamkundrum Rd, Pasumali. Tel: 601020, 602300, Fax: 604004, Tlx: 044 5205. *P. R: I, W, C.*

D: US$50 and below

MADURAI ASHOK, Alagarkoil Rd. Tel: 42531, Fax: 42530-1, Tlx: 044 5297. *P, SatTV. R: I, W.*
PANDIAN, Racecourse. Tel: 42470-9, Tlx: 044 5214. *R: I, W, C.*

MANGALORE

D: US$50 and below

MOTI MAHAL, Falnir Rd. Tel: 22211, Tlx: 083 2314. *P, Gym, SatTV. R: I, W, C.*
MANJARUN, Old Port Rd. Tel: 31791, Tlx: 083 2316. *P, SatTV. R: I, W, C.*

MUSSOORIE

D: US$50 and below

SAVOY, The Mall. Tel: 2010, 2620,

P — Swimming pool | **Gym** — Health club | **Biz** — Business centre | **Ex** — Executive floor
SatTV — Satellite TV | **R** — Restaurant | **I** — Indian | **W** — Western food
C — Chinese food

HOTEL GUIDE

Tlx: 058 5302. *R: I, W, C.*
CARLTON'S PLAISANCE, Happy Valley Rd. Tel: 2800. *R: I, W, C.*

MYSORE

C: US$50-100

LALITHA MAHAL PALACE. Tel: 26316, 27650, 27771, Tlx: 084 6217. *P, Gym, SatTV. R: I, W.*

D: US$50 and below

METROPOLE, Jhansilakshmibai Rd. Tel: 20681, 20871, 31916, Tlx: 084 6214. *R: I, W, C.*

NAGPUR

D: US$50 and below

CENTRE POINT, Central Bazaar Rd. Tel: 520910-2, Fax: 523093, Tlx: 071 5584. *P, Biz, SatTV. R: I, W, C.*
JAGSONS, Back Central Ave. Tel: 48611-4, Tlx: 071 5369. *R: I, W, C.*

NAINITAL

D: US$50 and below

SHERVANI HILLTOP INN, Mallital. Tel: 3298, 3128, 3304. *R: I, W, C.*
GRAND, The Mall. Tel: 2406, 2008. *R: I, W.*
ARIF CASTLES, Mallital. Tel: 2801-3, 3231, Tlx: 0570 3201. *Gym, SatTV. R: I, W, C.*

NEW DELHI

A: US$150 and above

HOLIDAY INN CROWNE PLAZA, Barakhamba Rd, Connaught Place. Tel: 332 0101, Fax: 331 5335, 331 6163, Tlx: 0316 1186. *P, Gym, Biz, Ex, SatTV. R: I, W, C, Thai.*
HYATT REGENCY, Ring Rd. Tel: 609911, Fax: 678833, Tlx: 0316 1512. *P, Gym, Biz, Ex, SatTV. R: I, W, C.*
THE OBEROI, Zakir Hussain Rd. Tel: 436 3030, Fax: 436 0484, 436 0758, Tlx: 0316 3222, 0317 4019. *P, Gym, Biz, SatTV. R: I, W, C.*
TAJ MAHAL, Mansingh Rd. Tel: 301 6162, Fax: 301 7299, Tlx: 0316 6874. *P, Gym, Ex, SatTV. R: I, W, C.*
TAJ PALACE INTERCONTINENTAL, Sardar Patel Rd. Tel: 301 0404, Fax: 301 1252, Tlx: 0316 1673. *P, Gym, Biz, SatTV. R: I, W, C.*

B: US$100-150

LE MERIDIEN, Janpath. Tel: 371 0101, Fax: 371 4545, Tlx: 0316 3076. *P, Gym, SatTV. R: I, W, C.*
MAURYA SHERATON, Sardar Patel Rd. Tel: 301 0101, Fax: 301 0908, Tlx: 0316 1447. *P, Gym, Biz, Ex, SatTV. R: I, W, C.*
PARK, Sansad Rd. Tel: 352477, 345043, Fax: 352025, Tlx: 0316 5231. *P, Biz, SatTV. R: I, W, C.*
VASANT CONTINENTAL, Vasant Vihar. Tel: 678800, Fax: 687 3842, Tlx: 0317 2263, 0317 2386. *P, Biz, SatTV. R: I, W, C.*

C: US$50-100

ASHOK, Chanakyapuri. Tel: 600121, 600412, Fax: 687 3216, 687 6378, 687 6060, Tlx: 0318 2063. *P, Gym, Biz, SatTV. R: I, W, C, Japanese.*
CLARIDGES, Aurangzeb Rd. Tel: 301 0211, Fax: 301 0625, Tlx: 0316 5526, 0316 2898. *P, SatTV. R: I, W, C.*
IMPERIAL, Janpath. Tel: 332 5332, Fax: 332 4542, Tlx: 0316 2603. *P, SatTV. R: I, W, C.*

D: US$50 and below

QUTAB, Aurobindo Rd. Tel: 660060, Tlx: 0316 2537. *P, SatTV. R: I, W.*
SAMRAT, Chanakyapuri. Tel: 603030, Tlx: 0317 2122, 0317 2126. *P, SatTV. R: I, W.*
AMBASSADOR, Sujan Singh Park. Tel: 690391, 463 2600, Fax: 463 2252, Tlx: 0317 4045. *SatTV. R: I, W, C.*
DIPLOMAT, Sardar Patel Rd. Tel: 301 0204, Fax: 301 8605, Tlx: 0316 1042. *SatTV. R: I, W, C.*
JANPATH, Janpath. Tel: 332 7083, Fax: 332 7083, Tlx: 0316 1546. *SatTV. R: I, W, C.*
KANISHKA, Ashok Rd. Tel: 332 4242, Fax: 332 4242, Tlx: 0316 2788, 0316 2736. *P, Biz. R: I, W.*
OBEROI MAIDENS, Shyam Nath Rd, Old Delhi. Tel: 252 5464, Fax: 292 9800, Tlx: 0316 6303, 0317 8163. *P, SatTV. R: I, W.*
BROADWAY, Asaf Ali Rd, Old Delhi. Tel: 326 9966, Fax: 326 9966, Tlx: 0316 6299. *SatTV. R: I, W.*
MARINA, Connaught Circus. Tel: 332 8609, Fax: 332 8609, Tlx: 0316 2969. *SatTV. R: I, W, C.*

OOTACAMUND

C: US$50-100

SAVOY, Sylks Rd. Tel: 4142-4, Tlx:

P — Swimming pool; **Gym** — Health club; **Biz** — Business Centre; **Ex** — Executive floor
SatTV — Satellite TV; **R** — Restaurant; **I** — Indian; **W** — Western food
C — Chinese food

HOTEL GUIDE

085 3240. *SatTV. R: I, W, C.*

D: US$50 and below

SOUTHERN STAR, Havelock Rd. Tel: 3601, 3609, Tlx: 085 3249. *SatTV. R: I,W, C.*
LAKE VIEW, West Lake Rd. Tel: 3904, 3580-2, Tlx: 085 3223. *SatTV. R: I, W, C.*

PATNA

D: US$50 and below

MAURYA PATNA, South Gandhi Maidan. Tel: 222061, Tlx: 022352. *P, SatTV. R: I, W, C.*

PONDICHERRY

D: US$50 and below

PONDICHERRY ASHOK, Chinnakalapet. Tel: 852160, Fax: 852140, Tlx: 046 9239. *SatTV. R: I, W.*
SEASIDE GUEST HOUSE, Goubert Ave. Tel: 26494, Tlx: 046 9221. *R: I, W.*

PORT BLAIR

D: US$50 and below

ANDAMAN BEACH RESORT, Corbyn's Cove. Tel: 21462-5, Tlx: 069 5203. *R: I, W, C, Burmese.*
BAY ISLAND, Marine Hill. Tel: 20881, 21389, Fax: 20651, Tlx: 069 5207. *P. R: I, W, C.*

PUNE

D: US$50 and below

BLUE DIAMOND, Koregaon Rd. Tel: 663775, Fax: 666101, Tlx: 0145 7369. *P, Gym, Biz, SatTV. R: I, W, C.*
EXECUTIVE ASHOKA, University Rd. Tel: 57391, 56463, 51101, Tlx: 0145 7565. *Gym, Biz, SatTV. R: I, W, C.*
REGENCY, Dhole Patil Rd. Tel: 669411, Fax: 666675, Tlx: 0145 7609. *R: I, W, C.*

PURI

D: US$50 and below

TOSHALI SANDS, Konark Marine Drive. Tel: 2888, 2999, 2572, Tlx: 067 5395. *P, Gym, SatTV. R: I, W, C.*
HANS COCO PALMS, Swargadwar. Tel: 2638, 3751-2, 3762-3, Fax: 3165, Tlx: 0670 1208. *SatTV. R: I, W, C.*

SHIMLA

C: US$50-100

OBEROI CLARKES, The Mall. Tel: 212991, Fax: 211321, Tlx: 039 1206. *R: I, W, C.*

D: US$50 and below

WOODVILLE PALACE, Raj Bhawan Rd. Tel: 27263. *R: I, W, C.*

SRINAGAR

D: US$50 and below

AHDOO'S, Residency Rd. Tel: 72593, 71984. *R: Kashmiri.*
BROADWAY, Maulana Azad Rd. Tel: 75621-3, Tlx: 037 5212. *P. R: Kashmiri.*

TRIVANDRUM

D: US$50 and below

HORIZON, Aristo Rd. Tel: 66888, Fax: 446859, Tlx: 043 5346. *R: I, W, C.*
LUCIYA CONTINENTAL, East Fort. Tel: 73443, Fax: 73347, Tlx: 043 5330. *Biz, SatTV. R: I, W, C.*

UDAIPUR

B: US$100-150

LAKE PALACE, Pichola Lake. Tel: 527961-73, Fax: 527974, Tlx: 033203. *P. R: I, W, C.*

D: US$50 and below

SHIKARBADI, Goverdhan Vilas. Tel: 583200, 583204, Fax: 584841, Tlx: 033 5227. *P. R: I, W, C.*
SHIV NIWAS PALACE, City Palace. Tel: 528015-6, Fax: 23823, Tlx: 033 5226. *P, Gym. R: I, W.*

VARANASI

C: US$50-100

TAJ GANGES, Nadesar Palace Grounds. Tel: 42481, 42491, Fax: 348067, Tlx: 054 5219. *P, SatTV. R: I, W.*

VISAKHAPATNAM

D: US$50 and below

PARK, Beach Rd. Tel: 54181, Tlx: 049 5230. *P, SatTV. R: I, W, C.*
DOLPHIN, Daba Gardens. Tel: 64810, Fax: 63737, Tlx: 049 5316. *P, Biz, SatTV. R: I, W, C.*

P — Swimming pool
R — Restaurant
Gym — Health club
I — Indian
Biz — Business centre
W — Western food
SatTV — Satellite TV
C — Chinese food

MALDIVES

The Republic of Maldives, an archipelago in the central Indian Ocean, is one of the world's last remaining unspoilt tropical-island paradises — yet easily accessible. Its natural attractions include year-round sunshine and white sandy beaches. The crystal-clear waters offer a spectacular underworld of multicoloured coral reefs teeming with marine life. It is also a haven for sea birds and the clean air makes for great photography.

The republic, which lies about 600 kilometres southwest of India and Sri Lanka, comprises 26 atolls and close to 1,200 islands, of which only 201 are inhabited. They form an 820-kilometre-long chain straddling the equator. The islands are only a few feet above sea level — the highest elevation in the country is about two metres. No wonder the islanders are keenly aware of the threat of global warming and what a higher level of sea would mean for them.

With a population of only 231,000 the Maldives is the smallest nation in South Asia. About 60,000 of its people live on Male, the capital, an island of only 1.77 square kilometres.

Tourism, the leading industry and major foreign-exchange earner, was developed only relatively recently. In 1975, a mere 9,000 visitors were recorded; by 1993 the annual number was up to 241,000. Most of the tourist resorts are located on the Male atoll, within a few hours' ferry ride from Male and the international Hulule airport.

Most working Maldivians are engaged in fishing — either commercial or subsistence fishing. Other economic activities include shipping and coconut farming and fruit and vegetable production. The main exports are marine products and textiles.

Islam is the strength of Maldivian society and no other religion exists, or is permitted, among Maldivian citizens. But while the Muslim faith is taken very seriously, Islam in the Maldives has its own unique character, a delicate blend of tradition and modernity. Women are much freer than in many other Muslim countries.

History

The origins of the Maldivian people are shrouded in mystery, but scholars believe that a Dravidian population from south India inhabited some of the islands as early as the fifth century BC. Perhaps two millennia ago, a second wave of settlers — Aryans from India and Ceylon — came to dominate the islands. Archaeological findings and legends tell that the Maldivian people practised Buddhism before the sultan was converted to Islam by a Moroccan saint in 1153 AD and ordered his people to follow the Muslim faith.

Throughout history the Maldivians have depended for their livelihood on the sea, and most of the people have been involved in one way or another with fishing. Male, the capital and home of the sultan, is the most developed and urban area as a result of its historical role as the government and commercial centre of the country.

The Maldivians have never been conquered or ruled for long by any foreign power, though they had to fight off Portuguese invaders several times in the 16th century, and time and again they battled marauding pirates from southern India. The Maldivians, though never very wealthy or major traders, always participated in the ancient Indian Ocean trading system borne annually by the monsoons. They were known in the trade for their cowrie shells, dried fish, ambergris and tortoiseshell.

In 1887, the Maldives became a protector-

◄ *Sun, sea and lots of fish.*

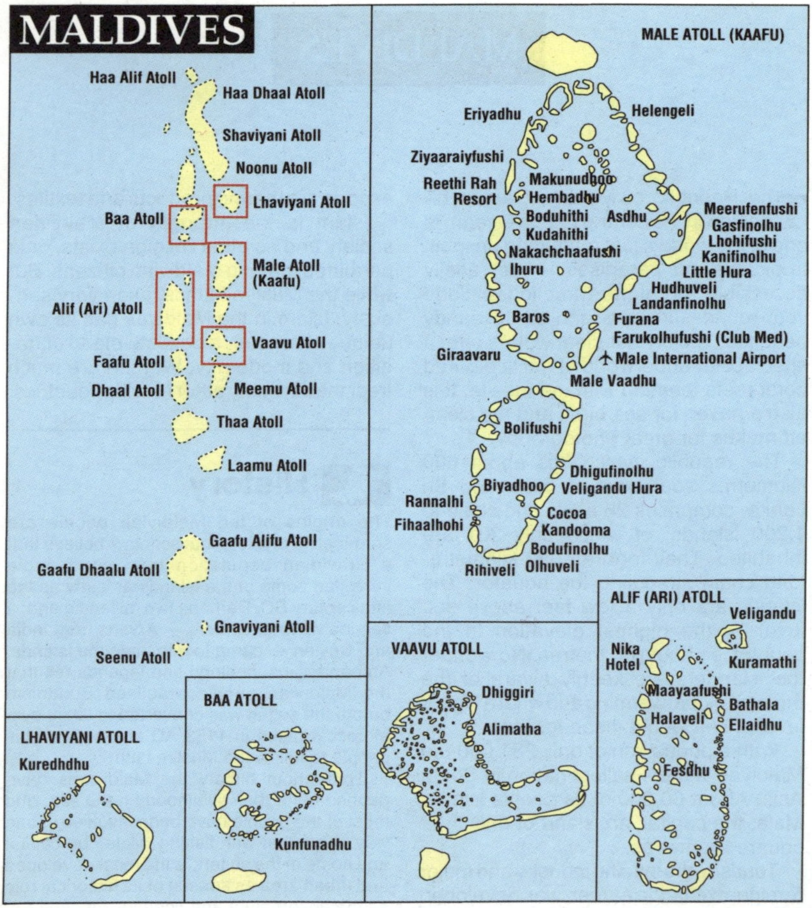

ate of the British (though they did not install a government or representative there) until 1965, when the Maldives regained independence. In 1968 the Maldives became a republic, with an elected president and national assembly. At that time, Ibrahim Nasir was prime minister under the last titular sultan, Mohamed Farhid Didi. Ibrahim Nasir went on to rule as president until 1978. The current president, Maumoon Abdul Gayoom, was elected on November 11, 1978. The Maldives has become both more modern and slightly more democratic under his administration.

In November 1988, a disgruntled Maldivian businessman launched a coup attempt, using Tamil mercenaries from Sri Lanka. The government survived, thanks to the intervention of Indian commandos.

Entry

AIR: Most visitors arrive in the Maldives by air at Hulule International Airport, adjacent to the capital island of Male. The airport was modernized in 1981 to accommodate wide-body aircraft. Work on a new terminal is in progress.

A good number of scheduled and charter flights fly to Hulule from various points in Europe, the Maldives' major tourism market, and Asia. Charter air links have also been established with South Africa. Singapore Airlines offers five flights a week (on Airbus A310 aircraft) and Emirates two a week from Singapore. Air Lanka operates direct flights to the Maldives daily from Colombo. Indian Airlines flies daily from Trivandrum in south India (US$129) and Pakistan International Airlines flies twice a week from Karachi.

Air Maldives, the national airline, was launched with its new partner, Malaysian Helicopter Services, in November 1993. It flies four times a week to Dubai and twice a week to Colombo, Kuala Lumpur and Trivandrum, using an Airbus A300.

There is an airline departure tax of US$10 for each passenger. It would be wise to book your return flight when you are making reservations for the flight over.

Immigration

You will need a valid passport and onward or return air ticket to enter the Maldives, though not a visa; visitors are granted a 30-day visa upon arrival. Visas can be extended for a minimal fee.

Health

If you are coming from, or simply passing through, areas infected with yellow fever, you must have certificates of inoculation. The islands have mosquitoes, but reportedly no malaria. If you are venturing beyond Male or the resort islands, however, you should take anti-malaria pills as a precaution.

Customs

The Maldives has the barest of customs formalities. There is a strict ban, however, on the import of nude pictures, firearms, ammunition, saltpetre, explosives, narcotics, intoxicants (including all types of alcoholic beverages), poisons, dangerous animals, dogs, pigs and statues of idolatry. Tortoiseshell and black coral can now only be exported as ornaments.

Currency

The national currency of the Maldives, the rufiyaa, exchanged at Rf 11.60:US$1 in April 1995. It is divided into 100 larees and comes in denominations of 2, 5, 10, 20, 50, 100 and 500 rufiyaas. The coins are issued in 1, 2, 5, 10, 25 and 50 larees and 1 rufiyaa.

Major currencies can be converted to rufiyaa at banks, resorts, hotels and leading shops. The U.S. dollar is the most common foreign currency. Payments in hotels can be made in most hard currencies in cash, travellers' cheques or credit cards. The most commonly accepted credit cards are American Express, Visa, MasterCard, Diners Club, JCB and Euro Card.

Language

Dhivehi, the national language, is one of the Indo-Aryan family of languages. It is unique to the Maldives, but very similar to Sinhala spoken in Sri Lanka.

Dhivehi is a phonetic language and English transliterations vary, so you will see a variety of spellings for name places. There are a few phrase books in Dhivehi.

Since the Maldives' conversion to Islam in the 12th century, many Arabic words have been brought into the language. A common and appreciated form of greeting is the Arabic "Salaam Alekum."

English is widely spoken in Male and on all the resort islands, as well as in the country's southernmost Addu Atoll, where a British airbase was once located.

Climate

The Maldives has a tropical climate. It is warm throughout the year, but there is always a cooling breeze because the coral islands are so small. Like other Indian Ocean islands, the Maldives has the two seasons of southwest and northeast monsoon. The climate remains much the same throughout the year; daytime temperatures range around 26-31°C. Even during the rougher, stormy southwest monsoon months (between May and October), there are seldom more than a few days of rain at a time and the sun shines periodically even on those days.

Dress

You will only need light, informal clothing in the Maldives. In the early years of tourism, many tourists showed little regard for local customs by wearing hardly any clothing in the capital,

Male. Now, however, there are regulations requiring visitors to wear appropriate clothes so as not to offend the locals. Nudism is strictly prohibited in the Maldives.

If you are on business in Male, and especially if you will be dealing with senior government officials, wear the appropriate dress — a jacket and a tie for men or the equivalent for women.

Business Hours

Most Maldivian workers have only a one-day weekend on Friday, the Muslim day of rest. Schools are closed on Thursdays as well. Banks are the only institutions that are also closed on Saturdays. Banking hours are 9 a.m.-1 p.m., Sunday through Thursday.

Government offices open 7:30 a.m.-1:30 p.m. for most of the year. But during the Islamic fasting month of Ramadan, which is determined according to the lunar calendar, offices seldom get going before 9 a.m.

If you wish to meet government officials, write in advance, or at least first contact the protocol officer in the Ministry of External Affairs. Appointments are usually available from 9 a.m. onwards.

The General Post Office is open 8:15-11:45 a.m. and 1:30-3:30 p.m. six days a week. Postal, telephone and fax services including IDD are available.

Most shops in Male are open 8 a.m.-noon in the mornings, in the afternoons at 3:30-6:30 p.m. and again in the evenings at 8-11 p.m. Even on Fridays many shops are open some time during the day, except 11:30 a.m.-2 p.m. — the time for Friday prayers.

Transport

FROM THE AIRPORT: Most visitors to the Maldives go directly from Hulule airport to one of the resort islands. Each resort provides ferry services at rates anywhere from US$20-200 (return), depending on distance and the type of craft. You can also hire a local fishing vessel, called *dhoanis,* from Hulule airport to Male.

There are inexpensive ferry services between Hulule airport and Male, which run almost hourly, except during meal times (noon-3 p.m. and 5-7 p.m.). You can also arrange to hire diesel launches or speedboats (fares are negotiable, but costly).

AIR: Domestic air services are available on Air Maldives, Air Taxi Service and by helicopter. These can shorten a two-and-a-half-hour ferry journey to about 10 minutes and cost only slightly more than the price of a ferry trip. Hydrofoils and hovercraft also run between the islands.

TRANSPORT IN MALE

The area of the capital is only 1.77 square kilometres, so the most practical way of covering distances is to walk. You can also rent cars, motorcycles and bicycles. Taxis are available, but they do not cruise around town in search of fares.

You can hire them at the taxi stand in front of the Male Government Hospital. Some of them have radio service, and you can phone for those. Rates average around US$1-2, depending on the number of passengers and the amount of baggage.

TRANSPORT INTER-ISLAND

You can make your own arrangements with local boatmen in Male for travel to other islands and atolls. Passenger boats — uncomfortable, but very cheap — run from Male to distant atolls. Dhoanis, the local fishing boats, are another means of getting around, but there are no set rates and sometimes the price may remain in dispute throughout the voyage.

Most resorts will make more expensive arrangements for their guests to charter yachts and other boats for sailing around the islands.

Tours

Each resort offers several similar types of excursion tours. There are half-day excursions to Male and day-trips to nearby uninhabited and inhabited fishing-village islands (these are usually about US$25 per person and include a barbecue picnic). Resorts also offer diving and sailing safaris, aerial excursions by helicopter or seaplane, dawn and dusk fishing trips and moonlight cruises.

Accommodation

Most visitors to the Maldives go for the sun and sea and would not enjoy staying long in Male, which has no beaches and only limited hotel accommodation. Even the few people going to Male on business often stay at one of the nearby resorts and arrange to go into the capital by boat every day. Some resorts such as Kurumba, Bandos, Full Moon, Embudhu and Vaadu are convenient for making daily trips to Male.

Some 47 private agencies operate the 69 resorts outside the capital. The largest of them — Universal (Orchid Magu, Male) — runs Kurumba, Lagoona, Bandos, Nakatchafushi, Baros, Full Moon and Fesdu.

The sea and the sun are the main attractions of any beach resort, and all of them have their quota of underwater life. There is thus little to choose between the resort islands except in terms of service and the range of recreation available — or wanted. All resorts are now required to have fresh water and more than half have hot and cold water and air-conditioning.

The rates at most resorts and guesthouses in the Maldives (though not the business hotels in the capital) are on a full-board basis, though some charge only for bed and breakfast. All feature communal dining rooms with set meals, though some of them have restaurants with *a-la-carte* menus.

Some resorts have swimming pools. Many resorts do not, since they are small islands surrounded by the sea. Some provide TV sets in their guest rooms.

Maldives resort addresses are written simply as: Name of Resort, Republic of Maldives.

Dining

Food quality at the resorts has improved a good deal, though cuisine is not one of the Maldives' major attractions since virtually everything — with the important exceptions of fish, coconuts and some fruit — must be imported. Maldivian cuisine is monotonous — basically fish, usually fresh tuna.

Set meals at the resorts usually consist of Western food, sometimes bland, with one or two Maldivian dishes. *A-la-carte* meals of a higher standard, including Japanese, Chinese and Indian cuisine, are available in the additional restaurants provided in several resorts, which have foreign chefs with the relevant expertise. Some of the more expensive resorts, particularly those that cater to Europeans, have imported European chefs.

Water is the Maldives' main problem and visitors to Male are advised to be extremely careful about drinking it outside the hotels. All the tourist resorts provide rainwater (which is safe) for drinking.

Despite strict local laws against the consumption of alcohol for the local population, liquor is freely available at the resort islands. A Singapore beer costs about US$2 and prices are similar for most spirits. Wine is more expensive, from around US$15 for the cheapest bottle.

Entertainment

Several resorts offer weekly dances with live music by various local rock bands, barbecue nights, disco bars and karaoke rooms. Tourists staying at the other resorts may hire boats to attend dances on other islands. You might see the traditional Maldivian dance *bodu beru*, said to have been brought long ago from East Africa, which is often performed for tourists.

In Male there are three cinemas, which usually show Indian- and English-language films and sometimes video-taped TV shows.

Although the Maldives has one TV station that transmits in colour for a few hours each evening, few resorts provide TV sets in guests' rooms. Some of them place a TV in the common lounge. Transmission ends as early as 11 p.m. Video-films are becoming a more widespread form of entertainment for guests.

Shopping

The Maldives once exported tortoiseshell, shark's fin, ambergris, cowrie shells and lacquerware in the ancient Indian Ocean dhow trade. Now tourists can buy limited quantities of tortoiseshell from the Hawksbill turtle and the shells and stuffed carcasses of other sea turtles. Exports of turtle products have waned dramatically, however, since the government passed a regulation prohibiting the killing or catching of sea turtles and tortoises less than 30 centimetres long. The export of whole turtle shells is banned and now you can buy only smaller items made from them.

The best buys are seashells, specially woven sarongs called *felis* (in wide, black-and-white stripes) and woven grass mats in black, brown and orange designs. Collectors also consider Chinese ceramics here to be good buys. The Palm Store has duty-free goods, and the gift shops have local souvenirs, books and magazines. Some are on Chandhani Magu, the main shopping street.

Sports

Aquatic sports, especially the spectacular diving opportunities, are the chief tourist attractions. Almost all the resorts rent snorkelling and

Away from it all.

scuba equipment and most also have full-time professional diving instructors.

Resorts offer wind-surfing, sailing and water-skiing. Indoor games, such as table-tennis, snooker and chess are also available.

The Maldivians enjoy various sports and hold tournaments throughout the year in Male. The annual sports calendar for these tournaments roughly follows this schedule: January — bicycle races; February — tennis; March — cricket; June — soccer; August — table tennis; September — dhoani racing; October — volleyball; November — swimming; and December — hockey.

Soccer is currently the most popular spectator sport in the capital. Maldivians also play basketball.

Holidays

Most Maldivian holidays are not celebrated publicly in a big way, except for Independence Day, and Republic Day on November 11, when there are usually parades, programmes in the national stadium and fireworks. The other festivals for special Muslim days are family occasions and are observed by private feasting and visiting.

Maldivian holidays:

January 1: New Year's Day. Public holiday.

July 26: Independence Day. Public holiday.

November 11: Republic Day. Public holiday.

The Islamic holidays follow the lunar calendar, so they vary annually. Among those are: Prophet Muhammad's birthday; first of the fasting month of Ramadan; the day marking the end of the fasting month; Haj day commemorating the pilgrimage to Mecca; the 10th day of the last month of the Muslim calendar; the first day of the first month of the Muslim calendar.

PUBLICATIONS

Since you can walk around Male comfortably in a single morning, a map is not really necessary. You can buy large and detailed (but often out-of-date) maps of the Maldives, produced by the British Admiralty, at ship's chandlers in Colombo, Sri Lanka. These maps can be confusing to tourists, since the spelling is not always consistent.

The **Maldives Department of Information** has a number of small booklets describing different aspects of the archipelago. *Maldives, a Nation of Islands* (Media Transasia) is beautifully illustrated and fairly informative, if a little propagandist. You can buy it from the Department of Tourism (Rf 50). *Through Maldives* is another recent publication, but consists mostly of illustrations and is scant on information. *Island World of Maldives* is beautifully illustrated and can be purchased from the **Ministry of Tourism** (Rf 50). The ministry also sells *Journey Through Maldives*, another recent publication, for Rf 200.

DISCOVERING MALDIVES

At first sight, there is not much to distinguish the islands, which are all relatively small (most being less than one square kilometre). But the Maldives can be grouped into four different worlds — Male, the fishing-village islands, the resort islands and the uninhabited islands.

As the former seat of the sultanate, Male has been the administrative, cultural and commercial centre of the country for centuries. Its urban traits and larger population distinguish it from the rest of the nation. Then there are the fishing-village islands, which include all the other inhabited islands of the country. These islands are the rural area of the nation.

The differences between the people of Male and all the other inhabited islands (Male residents refer to the others as "islanders," the Maldivian equivalent of country folk) are as great as between urban and rural people in most other countries. Some of the people on other islands farm and some have specialized occupations such as lacquer-work, mat-weaving, melon-growing, weaving, boat-building and lace-making.

HOTEL GUIDE

Categories are based on peak season (November through April) double room rates. All prices for resorts include full board and they offer snorkelling, scuba-diving and windsurfing facilities amongst other recreational activities. Rates are often reduced up to one third of those quoted here during the low tourist season (May through October). The seasonality of tourist arrivals is narrowing.

MALE ATOLL

HOTELS

B: US$95-175

NASANDHURA PALACE HOTEL, Boduthakurufaanu Magu, Male. Tel: 323380, Fax: 320822. *1.5 km. AC.*

C: US$50-95

HOTEL ALIA, Haveeree Higun, Male. Tel: 322080, Fax: 322197. *1.5 km. AC.*

KAM HOTEL, H. Roanuge, Meheli Goalhi, Male. Tel: 320611, Fax: 320614. *1.5 km.*

RESORTS

A: US$175 and above

BANDOS ISLAND RESORT, H. Jazeera, Boduthakurufaanu Magu, Male. Tel: 327450, 440088, Fax: 321026, 443877. *8 km. AC, H.*

CLUB MED, FARUKOLHUFUSHI, 1 Ibrahim Hassan Didi Magu, Majeedhee Bazaru, Male. Tel: 322976, 444552, Fax: 322850, 441997. *1.5 km. AC.*

COCOA ISLAND (MAKUNUFUSHI), M. Gulisthaanuge, Male. Tel: 322326, 443713, Fax: 322326, 441919. *33 km.*

DHIGUFINOLHU TOURIST RESORT, H. Athireege aage, Lotus Goalhi, Male. Tel: 327058, 443599, Fax: 327058, 443886. *27 km. AC, H.*

FULL MOON BEACH RESORT (FURANA FUSHI), Universal Enterprises Ltd., 38 Orchid Magu, Male. Tel: 323080, 441976, Fax: 320274, 441979. *8 km. AC. H*

GASFINOLHU ISLAND RESORT, Valtur Maldives, Imad's Agency, Chandhani Magu, Male. Tel: 323441, 442078, Fax: 322964, 445941. *22 km. H.*

GIRAAVARU TOURIST RESORT, Phoenix Hotels & Resorts Pvt Ltd., Male. Tel: 323181, 440440, Fax: 325499, 444818. *11 km. AC, H.*

IHURU TOURIST RESORT, Ihuru Investments Pvt Ltd., Ameeru Ahmed Magu, Male. Tel: 326720, 443502, Fax: 326700, 445933. *16 km. AC, H.*

KUDAHITHI TOURIST RESORT, Holiday Club Maldives, H. Maizandhoshuge, Sosun Magu, Male. Tel: 313938, 444613, Fax: 313939, 441992. *27 km. AC, H.*

KURUMBA VILLAGE (VIHAMANA FUSHI), Universal Enterprises Ltd., 38 Orchid Magu, Male. Tel: 322971, 442324, Fax: 322678, 443885. *5 km. AC, H.*

LAGUNA BEACH RESORT (VELASSARU), Universal Enterprises Ltd., 38 Orchid Magu, Male. Tel: 322971, 443042, Fax: 322678, 443041. *11 km. AC, H.*

MAKUNUDU CLUB, Sunland Travel Pvt Ltd., Asrafee Bldg, Male. Tel: 324658, 446464, Fax: 325543, 446565. *36 km.*

OLHUVELI VIEW HOTEL, P.O. Bag 72. Tel: 441957, Fax: 445942. *35 km. AC, H.*

RIHIVELI BEACH RESORT (MAHAANA ELHI HURAA), Jamaal Store, Male. Tel: 322421, 443731, Fax: 322964, 450052. *40 km.*

THULHAAGIRI ISLAND RESORT, H. Jazeera, Boduthakurufaanu Magu, Male. Tel: 322844, 445929, Fax: 321026, 445939. *11 km. AC, H.*

VAADHOO DIVING PARADISE, H. Maarandhooge (Irumatheebai), Male. Tel: 325844, 443976, Fax: 325846, 443397. *9 km. AC, H.*

VABBINFARU (BANYAN TREE), Dhirham Travels & Chandelling, Faamudheyri Magu, Male. Tel: 323369, 443147, Fax: 324752, 443843. *16 km.*

km — Distance from airport **AC** — Air-Conditioned **H** — Hot water

HOTEL GUIDE

B: US$95-175

ASDU SUN ISLAND, H. Shoanary, Boduthakurufaanu Magu, Male. Tel: 322726, 445051, Fax: 324300, 445051. *32 km.*

BAROS HOLIDAY RESORT, Universal Enterprises Ltd., 38 Orchid Magu, Male. Tel: 322971,442672, Fax: 322678, 443497. *14 km. AC, H.*

BIYADHOO ISLAND RESORT, Prabalaji Enterprises Pvt Ltd., H. Maarandhooge, Male. Tel: 324699, 447171, Fax: 327014, 447272. *33 km. AC, H.*

BODUHITHI CORAL ISLE, Holiday Club Maldives, H. Maizandhoshuge, Sosun Magu, Male. Tel: 313938, 442637, Fax: 313939, 442634. *27 km. AC, H.*

EMBUDHU FINOLHU ISLAND RESORT, Taj Maldives Pvt Ltd., 10 Medhuziyaaraiy Magu, Male. Tel: 317530, 444451, Fax: 317530, 445925. *11 km. AC, H.*

EMBUDHU VILLAGE, H. Roanuge, Meheli Goalhi, Male. Tel: 322212, 444776, Fax: 320614, 442673. *11 km.*

FIHALHOHI TOURIST RESORT, Dhirham Travels Ltd., Faamudheyri Magu, Male. Tel: 323369, 442903, Fax: 324752, 443803. *35 km. AC.*

FUN ISLAND RESORT (BODU FINOLHU), Villa Bldg, Ibrahim Hassan Didi Magu, Male. Tel: 324478, 444558, Fax: 322678, 443958. *35 km. AC, H.*

HELENGELI TOURIST VILLAGE, H. Huvadhoo, Male, Tel: 324500, 444615, Fax: 324500, 444615. *43 km.*

HUDHUVELI BEACH RESORT, H. Jazeera, Boduthakurufaanu Magu, Male. Tel: 325529, 443391, Fax: 321026, 443942. *12 km. H.*

KANIFINOLHU TOURIST RESORT, Cyprea Ltd., 25 Boduthakurufaanu Magu, Male. Tel: 322451, 443152, Fax: 323523, 444859. *19 km. AC, H.*

LHOHIFUSHI TOURIST RESORT, Altaf Enterprises, Ibrahim Hassan Didi Magu, Male. Tel: 323378, 441909, Fax: 324783, 441908. *35 km. AC, H.*

LILY BEACH RESORT, Lily Hotels, Chandhani Magu, Male. Tel: 317464, 450013, Fax: 327466, 450646. *84 km.*

LITTLE HURAA CLUB, H. Jazeera, Boduthakurufaanu Magu, Male. Tel: 327450, 445934, Fax: 321026, 444231. *16 km. AC.*

NAKATCHAFUSHI TOURIST RESORT, Universal Enterprises Ltd., 38 Orchid Magu, Male. Tel 322971, 443847, Fax: 322678, 442665. *24 km. AC, H.*

REETHI RAH RESORT (MEDHU FINOLHU), M. Shaazeewin, Fareedhee Magu, Male. Tel: 323758, 441905, Fax: 328842, 441906. *35 km.*

VILLIVARU ISLAND RESORT, Prabalaji Enterprises Pvt Ltd., H. Maarandhooge, Male. Tel: 324699, 447070, Fax: 327014, 447272. *33 km. AC, H.*

C: US$50-95

BOLIFUSHI ISLAND, Gateway Maldives Pte. Ltd., Ameer Ahmed Magu, Male. Tel: 317526, 443517, Fax: 317529, 445924. *16 km. AC.*

ERIYADHU ISLAND RESORT, STO Trade Centre 3 Flr, Male. Tel: 324933, 444487, Fax: 324943, 445926. *40 km.*

HEMBADHOO ISLAND RESORT, Transit Inn, Maaveyo Magu, Male. Tel: 322016, 443884, Fax: 326606, 441948. *32 km. AC.*

KANDOOMA TOURIST RESORT, Kandooma Male Office, Orchid Magu, Male. Tel: 323360, 444452, Fax: 326880, 445948. *28 km. AC.*

MEERU ISLAND RESORT, Champa Trade & Travels, Ahmadhee Bazaar, Male. Tel: 326545, 443157, Fax: 326544, 445946. *38 km. H.*

ZIYAARAIYFUSHI TOURIST RESORT, Phoenix Hotels & Resorts Pvt Ltd., Male. Tel: 323181, 443088, Fax: 325499, 441910. *36 km.*

ARI ATOLL AND OTHERS

A: US$175 and above

ATHURUGAU ISLAND RESORT, Voyages Maldives Pvt Ltd., Fareedhee Magu, Male. Tel: 324435, 450508, Fax: 324435, 450574. *77 km. AC, H.*

GANGEHI ISLAND RESORT, Holiday Club, H. Maizaandhoshuge, Sosun Magu, Male. Tel: 313938, 450505, Fax: 313939, 450506. *76 km. AC, H.*

KUDARAH ISLAND RESORT, Holiday Club Maldives, H. Maizandhoshuge, Sosun Magu, Male. Tel: 313938, 450549, Fax: 313939, 450550. *88 km. AC, H.*

MADOOGALI RESORT, Medhuziyaaraiy Magu, Male. Tel: 317984, 450581, Fax: 317974, 450554. *73 km. AC, H.*

MOOFUSHI ISLAND RESORT, Alia Flat, Handhuvaree Higun, Male. Tel: 326648, 450517, Fax: 326648, 450509. *83 km. AC, H.*

km — Distance from airport **AC** — Air-Conditioned **H** — Hot water

HOTEL GUIDE

NIKA HOTEL (KUDA FOLHUDHOO), P.O. Box 2076, 10 Fareedhee Magu, Male. Tel: 325087, 450516, Fax: 325097, 450577. *73 km. H.*

PALM TREE ISLAND (VELIGANDU HURAA), H. Athireege aage, Lotus Goalhi, Male. Tel: 327058, 443882, Fax: 327058, 440009. *27 km. AC, H.*

TARI VILLAGE (KANU HURAA), Phoenix Hotels & Resorts Pvt Ltd., Male. Tel: 323181, 440012, Fax: 325499, 440013. *16 km. AC, H.*

THUNDUFUSHI ISLAND RESORT, Voyages Maldives Pvt Ltd., Fareedhee Magu, Male. Tel: 324435, 450597, Fax: 324435, 450515. *86 km. AC, H.*

TWIN ISLAND (MAAFUSHIVARU), Universal Enterprises Ltd., 38 Orchid Magu, Male. Tel: 322971, 450596, Fax: 322678, 450524. *84 km. AC, H.*

B: US$95-175

ALIMATHA AQUATIC RESORT, Safari Tours, S.E.K. No. 1, Chandhani Magu, Male. Tel: 323524, 450544, Fax: 322516, 450575. *57 km. AC, H.*

ANGAGA ISLAND RESORT, STO Koshi 9, Ameeni Magu, Male. Tel: 313636, 450520, Fax: 323115, 450520. *91 km. AC, H.*

ARI BEACH RESORT (DHIDHDHOO FINOLHU), 52 Boduthakurufaanu Magu, Male. Tel: 321930, 450513, Fax: 327355, 450512. *91 km. AC.*

AVI ISLAND RESORT (VELIDHOO), G. Lifadhoo, Rukkediya Higun, Male. Tel: 322180, 450595, Fax: 325982, 450595. *69 km.*

DHIGGIRI TOURIST RESORT, Safari Tours, S.E.K. No. 1, Chandhani Magu, Male. Tel: 323524, 450592, Fax: 322516, 450592. *67 km. AC, H.*

ELLAIDHOO TOURIST RESORT, Safari Tours, S.E.K. No. 1, Chandhani Magu, Male. Tel: 323524, 450514, Fax: 322516, 450586. *57 km.*

HALAVELI HOLIDAY VILLAGE, Eastinvest Pvt Ltd., Akiri, Male. Tel: 322719, 450559, Fax: 323463, 450564. *60 km. H.*

HOLIDAY ISLAND (DIFFUSHI), Villa Bldg, Ibrahim Hassan Didi Magu, Male. Tel: 324478, 450011, Fax: 327845, 450022. *92 km.*

KURAMATHI TOURIST RESORT, Universal Enterprises Ltd., 8 Orchid Magu, Male. Tel: 322971, 450540, Fax: 322678, 450556. *52 km. AC, H.*

MACHCHAFUSHI ISLAND RESORT, Ocean View Shop No. 1, Male. Tel: 327849, 450615, Fax: 327277, 450618. *94 km.*

MIRIHI MARINA LUXURY RESORT, 3 Silver Star, Haveeree Higun, Male. Tel: 325448, 450500, Fax: 325448, 450501. *91 km. AC, H.*

RANGALI ISLAND RESORT, Crown Co. Pte. Ltd., P.O. Box 2034, Male. Tel: 322432, 450629, Fax: 324009, 450619. *97 km. AC, H.*

RANVELI BEACH RESORT (VILINGILIVARU), Holiday Club Maldives, H. Maizandhoshuge, Male. Tel: 313938, 450570, Fax: 313939, 450523. *76 km. AC, H.*

VAKARUFALHI ISLAND RESORT, Champa Trade & Travel, Ahmadhee Bazaar, Male. Tel: 321751, 450004, Fax: 314150, 450007. *64 km.*

VELIGANDU ISLAND, Crown Co. Pte. Ltd., P.O. Box 2034, Male. Tel: 322432, 450594, Fax: 324009, 450419. *51 km. AC, H.*

VILAMENDHU RESORT, Vision Maldives, STO Trade Centre, 3 Flr, Male. Tel: 322417, 450637, Fax: 324943, 450639. *84 km.*

C: US$50-95

BATHALA ISLAND RESORT, H. Kinolhas, Abadhahfehi Magu, Male. Tel: 323323, 450587, Fax: 324628, 450558. *57 km. AC.*

FESDU FUN ISLAND, Universal Enterprises Ltd., 38 Orchid Magu, Male. Tel: 322971, 450541, Fax: 322678, 450547. *72 km.*

KUREDHDHOO ISLAND RESORT, Champa Trade & Travel, Ahmadhee Bazaar, Male. Tel: 321751, 230337, Fax: 326544, 230332. *116 km. AC.*

MAAYAFUSHI TOURIST RESORT, H. Luxwood 1, Upstairs, Boduthakurufaanu Magu, Male. Tel: 320097, 450588, Fax: 326658, 450568. *62 km. AC.*

OCEAN REEF CLUB (GAN, SEENU ATOLL), Phoenix Hotels & Resorts Pvt Ltd., Male. Tel: 323181, Fax: 325499. *476 km.*

km — distance from airport **AC** — Air-conditioned **H** — Hot water

NEPAL

Nepal offers unique art, culture and civilization. The pagoda-style architecture found all over the kingdom, the fascinating array of temples honouring various deities and various ethnic groups of the people form a veritable museum. Added to this the almost mystic appearance of the Himalayan mountain ranges in the northern part of the country, and the most hardened traveller finds a trip to Nepal a stimulus to imagination and contemplation.

The kingdom still bears signs of its long isolation, only partially broken in the last half century. The capital, Kathmandu, seemingly floating between the world's tallest mountain, Mt Everest, and the lowland tropical jungles, is very much rural in character. The Nepalese are proud, both as Bhuddhists and as Hindus, because their country was the birthplace of both the Gautama Buddha (at Lumbini, 350 kilometres southwest of Kathmandu) and Sita, the mythological heroine of the great Hindu epic, the Ramayan (at Janakpur 200 kilometres south of the capital).

The other source of their pride is that Nepal did not give way to either the Muslims or the British as did the people of the Indian plains.

Nepal is still a country of thousands of small villages where men and women work hard and long, and where the gods are felt to be as close and as real as the huge mountains which form a dazzling white, jagged barrier to the north.

The country is trying to strike a balance between traditional values and the realities of the modern world. This becomes obvious when one travels or walks around the towns of the Kathmandu valley, where buildings using contemporary materials are replacing the old-style structures noted for their wood-carved windows and other features created by Nepalese craftsmen.

Above all, the Nepalese are a friendly people, perhaps a little shy on first contact with a newcomer but nonetheless willing to go to any lengths to help outsiders feel welcome in their country. If your taxi driver is unable to find the place you want to visit and stops to ask someone to interpret for you, it is odds-on your newfound interpreter will get into the taxi to show the driver the way — all with a great show of smiles and genuine goodwill.

Nepal is a beautiful, gentle country with none of the tensions of Western civilization. Until the early 1950s the country was relatively unknown to the travel industry and this, too, is one of its great attractions. The age of the organized, hyper-efficient group tour has not yet reached Kathmandu on any scale and so there is, as yet, little or no sense of the visitor being an intruder merely collecting another country's stamp in a passport. Instead, the visitor is welcomed as a friend or a guest.

History

The early history of Nepal is veiled in mythology. Its recorded history stretches back to the Lichhavi Dynasty, which ruled from the fifth to 12th centuries AD when it was replaced by the Malla Dynasty. Before the fall of the Mallas in 1768, Nepal split into 46 independent principalities that were constantly at war with each other. Even three principalities in the Kath-

◄ *Swoyambhu stupa in Kathmandu valley.* PHOTO: K.M. SINGH

mandu valley were fighting each other.

The modern history of the country began with the followers of a Rajput ruling family self-exiled from north India for political and religious reasons, pushing eastwards at Riddi in 1494 AD. In the second half of the 16th century they based themselves in the town of Gurkha in central Nepal, from which they now take their name. The Gurkha king, Prithvinarayan (The Unifier), conquered the whole of Nepal in 1768, founding the Shah Dynasty that reigns to this day.

From 1846 to 1950, Nepal was, in effect, ruled by a family of hereditary prime ministers, the Ranas, who pursued a policy of close cooperation with the British power in India. However, the movement against British rule by the Indian Congress had its repercussions among Nepalese intellectuals and politicians, who agitated through the Nepali Congress Party for a more democratic government. This led to a revolution by which the royal line, represented by King Tribhuvan returned to power.

A general election in 1959 resulted in an overwhelming victory for the Congress, but at the end of 1960 King Mahendra, who had succeeded Tribhuvan, dismissed the ministry and imprisoned Congress Prime Minister B.P. Koirala. A system of partyless *Panchayat* (village democracy) government was installed and political parties were not allowed. The Panchayat system was abolished by Mahendra's son and successor, King Birendra, who succeeded to the throne on Mahendra's death in 1972. His action came in April 1990 after eight weeks of violent unrest.

In the general election held one year after the dissolution of the Panchayat system, the Nepali Congress won a comfortable majority with which to form a government under Girija Prasad Koirala. But in mid-term elections in November 1994, the Nepal Communist Party (united Marxist Leninist) gained power. Soon afterwards it appeared to be shifting rapidly to a moderate stance from its former position on the far left of Nepal's political spectrum.

Nepal covers 151,600 square kilometres (after the signing of the Sino-Nepalese joint boundary protocol on November 20, 1979) and has a population of 19.5 million (1994). To the north, in the highest mountains and valleys, dwell the Bhotes (Tibetan-Nepalese in origin), to the west the Gurungs and Magars. The

Brahmins, Kshetris, Tamangs, Gurungs and Newars occupy the central parts and the Kirats, Limbus and Rais the eastern. A majority of the country's population is Hindu, the country being the only Hindu-dominated kingdom in the world. Buddhism, the other important religion, is followed by the Bhotes, Gurungs, Rais and a section of the Newars. But there is a high degree of intermingling between the two faiths. The installation of a multi-party democracy made religious freedom universal, including the freedom to practice Islam and Christianity, but proselytizing continues to be banned by law.

The country is traversed from north to south by four great rivers and split into four main areas: the plains, the foothill jungle (*terai*), the great central trough of hills and valleys and the Inner Himalayas whose peaks range from 6,000 metres to the 8,848 metres of the world's highest peak, Mt Everest.

Along the southern border there are the beginnings of industrial development — textiles, paper, sugar and cement — and this area also has the best network of roads. Some 40% of the country's trade is with India, with exports consisting mostly of food-grains. The famous Gurkha soldiers were for a long time Nepal's largest foreign-currency earners, remitting much of their earnings home, but now tourism, woollen carpets and garment exports earn more.

Entry

AIR: Kathmandu's **Tribhuvan International Airport** is served by nine Asian and European airlines with links to Hong Kong, Bangkok, Singapore, Osaka, Lhasa, Karachi, Dhaka, Colombo, Calcutta, New Delhi, Varanasi, Bombay, Dubai, Frankfurt, Paris, London and Moscow. Thai International flies five times a week from Bangkok. Aeroflot flies once a week from Moscow. There are five flights a week by Biman Bangladesh Airlines from Dhaka and two a week by Pakistan International Airlines from Karachi via Dhaka. Indian Airlines flies daily from New Delhi, Calcutta and Varanasi. Nepal's national carrier, Royal Nepal Airlines Corp. (RNAC), has three flights a week from Hong Kong, five from Bangkok and two from Calcutta. It has daily flights from New Delhi and a weekly flight from Bombay. It also provides twice-weekly connections to Frankfurt and London via Dubai and to Paris once a week via Dubai, Sharjah and Frankfurt. China Southern Airlines flies to Kathmandu from Lhasa once a week (March-October) and Bhutan's Druk Air flies from Paro twice a week.

ROAD: By land there are seven points of entry, but the most common and recommended entry points are Birgunj (near the Raxaul rail head in India), Kakar Bhitta (approached from Siliguri, Darjeeling and Assam) and Sunauli (near Gorakhpur and best approached from New Delhi), plus Nepalgunj, Dhangadhi and Nahendra Nagar in the west. There is also one overland entry point on the Nepal-China border, at Kodari, 114 kilometres east of Kathmandu, linking the capital with Lhasa. There are regular bus services to Kathmandu from these points. The 13-hour journey from Kakar Bhitta costs Rs 250, the eight-hour journey from Birgunj approximately Rs 150 and that from Bhairahwa (close to Sunauli) takes 10 hours and costs about Rs 150. Buses are tolerable but not air-conditioned. There are regular deluxe bus services between Kathmandu and Pokhara (Rs 150) and between the capital and Bhairahawa (Rs 160) operated by **Swiss Deluxe Bus Service**, Sundhara, Kathmandu (Tel: 225871, 227209). Buses to many parts of the country are available at the Central Bus Terminal at Gongabu, near Balaju, Kathmandu's industrial area.

Immigration

Passports and visas are required for all except Indian nationals. A transit visa for 48 hours can be obtained at the airport for US$5 on presentation of an onward air ticket. Visas for 15 days can be obtained from Nepalese diplomatic missions or consulates abroad for a fee of US$15. A month's visa may also be obtained upon arrival at Tribhuvan airport or other entry points by land for US$40, which may be extended at **Central Immigration** at Tridevi Marg (Tel: 418573) for another four weeks at no extra cost. Extensions for up to a second month cost US$1 a day. Travellers who want their visas extended must present a currency declaration form or bank receipts showing that they have converted foreign currency to the equivalent of US$20 per day for the intended period of stay. Extensions beyond three months are granted on the recommendation of the **Home Ministry**.

Note that visas are valid only for Kathmandu, Pokhara, Chitwan and areas linked by highways. For trekking, a special permit is required, also obtainable from Central Immigration or at Pokhara for travelling or trekking in the Mt

Annapurna region. Indian nationals are exempt from visa requirements provided they carry an identity card issued by a city or district magistrate in India.

Health

Yellow fever vaccination is required for those arriving within six days of leaving or transiting an infected area. Inoculations against typhoid, paratyphoid and gamma-globulin shots against hepatitis are recommended. Travellers are advised only to drink boiled or mineral water, served at major hotels. Filtered but unboiled water, served at smaller establishments and restaurants, is unsafe.

Customs

Baggage is spot-checked on arrival. The following personal effects are allowed duty-free entry (provided they are taken out on departure): one pair of binoculars, one perambulator, one camera, 12 rolls of film (officials are fairly flexible on this), one tape-recorder and five tapes, one radio, one musical instrument and one fishing rod and accessories. Photographers can generally bring additional equipment provided it is taken out of Nepal on departure.

Duty-free facilities are available both on arrival and departure from Tribhuvan airport. Items permitted: one carton of cigarettes, 20 cigars, one bottle (limit, 1.15 litres) of alcoholic liquor and two bottles or 12 cans of beer.

Firearms and ammunition, explosives, transmitter-radios, walkie talkies and narcotic drugs cannot be imported. Firearms may be brought in with prior permission of the Foreign Ministry. Permission is needed from the Ministry of Forests to export animal and bird trophies. The export of antiques requires the approval of National Archives, Ram Shah Path; objects more than 100 years old cannot be taken out.

Cars entering the country require a carnet de passage, with which no customs duty is levied for three months. On arrival in Kathmandu, car registration with the police is necessary to obtain a temporary licence and number plate and the vehicle cannot be sold in Nepal.

Currency

Nepalese rupees come in banknotes of 1,000, 500, 100, 50, 10, 5, 2 and 1, and in coins of Rs 5, 2 and 1. A rupee is made up of 100 paisa which come in coins of 50, 25, 10, 5 and 2. The value of foreign currencies against the rupee fluctuates from day to day as the exchange is based on a floating system. Official exchange rates in March 1995 were Rs 49.9:US$1 and Indian Rs 100 to Nepalese Rs 160.

Foreign currency must be exchanged through official banks or authorized hotels. Foreign currency can be imported in reasonable amounts except for Indian rupees, which may be brought in by Indian and Nepali nationals only. Nepalese rupees may not be imported. The U.S. dollar fetches about 8% more on the blackmarket. Most credit cards are accepted at major hotels and luxury shops in Kathmandu.

On entry, visitors are given a currency-exchange declaration form on which all exchange transactions must be entered and stamped by the authorized dealer or bank.

All payments to hotels and travel agents authorized to deal in foreign currency and to RNAC must be made in foreign currency, except for those made by Indian nationals.

On leaving Nepal, up to 10% of converted Nepalese rupees can be changed back into to hard currency at the airport exchange counter on presentation of bank or hotel currency-exchange receipts.

Language

Nepali is the national language and is written in its own distinctive Devanagari script. English is widely spoken and understood in Kathmandu, particularly by those who regularly come into contact with tourists.

Climate

The popular tourist season is from October (13-26°C) to mid-June (19-30°C) Kathmandu is, however, cooler than most cities in Asia during summer and can still be pleasant to visit then; short treks from Kathmandu, sightseeing in the Kathmandu valley and raft trips are all still feasible at this time of year. The only real disadvantage of summer is the monsoon rains, which cloud views of the mountains and make trek trails slushy.

November (7-22.5°C) to February (3-9°C) is winter, when mornings and evenings are especially cold, with night temperatures often dropping to zero. During the day when the sun is out it is warm and pleasant. Late September (18-28°C) to October (13-28°C) is autumn, with warm days and mildly cold nights. March (11°C) to mid-May (15°C) is spring, with weather similar to that of autumn. Late May to mid-September is the warm season, with an average of 35 millimetres of rain from mid-June (19°C) to mid-September. Between mid-December to the end of January the weather is below freezing in the mornings but reaches an average 18°C in the afternoons.

It is severely cold in the mountains between November and February, but otherwise pleasant the rest of the year.

The lowlands are hot for most of the year and pleasant in winter.

Dress

In Kathmandu, light clothing with perhaps a jacket for the evenings is all that is required for the warm months of April (11°C) to September (18°C). For the rest of the year warm clothing is needed, particularly from November to February when a down jacket would serve well. A raincoat and umbrella might help during the monsoon (mid-June to mid-September).

Those going on treks in winter should be prepared for severely cold conditions (-6°C to 15°C) when good-quality warm, windproof jackets and trousers and thermal underwear are necessary. Medium-weight boots with gripping rubber soles that give ankle support are best for walking in the mountains.

Business Hours

Government offices are open 10 a.m.-5 p.m. Sunday through Friday, Saturday being the day of rest in Nepal. Offices close at 4 p.m. in winter. Embassies and international organizations take a two-day weekend; their office hours are 9 a.m.-5:30 p.m. Commercial offices keep the same hours but open on Sunday, and travel agencies are open seven days a week.

Banks keep government office hours, but exchange facilities in some branches are open 8 a.m.-8 p.m.; main banks close exchange facilities at 2 p.m., and at noon on Fridays. Shops generally open around 10 a.m. and close at 8 p.m., some remaining open seven days a week except between mid-November and mid-February.

Doing Business

The communist government elected in 1994 has pursued the same open-market policy as its predecessor, and has also continued the liberal and open trade and industrial policies with adequate tax holidays, capital repatriation and 100% convertibility of the current dollar account which were started in February 1993. All goods except ball bearings, cosmetics and perfumes, oil products, spices and betel nuts can be imported without a licence.

Always make an appointment before calling on Nepalese businessmen or entrepreneurs. The Nepalese tradition on meeting is to say "Namaste," joining both palms above the chest. This will demonstrate politeness and gain the confidence of the person visited. But often handshakes are offered. Business cards are a must while making first contacts and attending receptions. Punctuality demonstrates the seriousness with which business is to be pursued.

Woman are treated with exact equality in business dealings in Nepal.

English speaking has now become a general habit and a mark of elegance. Most businessmen speak English and their medium of correspondence is English. Drinking alcohol is generally accepted, though many Nepalese are teetotallers and vegetarians. Most important civil servants and government officials will offer or accept dinner at leading hotels, but after the first or second meeting they may prefer to entertain at home for a more open dialogue.

Communications

Nepal has excellent telecommunications facilities via Intelsat with an excellent telex, fax and international direct dialling system to 64 countries in Asia, Europe, the Americas and Africa.

There are Subscriber Trunk Dialling (STD) connections between 71 of the 75 districts of Nepal. Mobile phones are currently only available to a limited number of people on a trial basis but should be open to the general public in early 1996.

Transport

Overland transport is difficult in Nepal, though an increasing number of motor roads are being built. At present the main road links are: the Tribhuvan Raj Path, a 200-kilometre road, and the Gorkha Narayanghat via Mugling and Naubise that links Kathmandu to Raxaul at the Indian border; the Arniko Highway (114 kilometres) which links Kathmandu to the Tibetan border at Kodari; the Prithvia Raj Marg (225 kilometres) between Kathmandu and Pokhara (this road also has extensions from Annbu, Khaireni, Gorkha and Mugling to Narayanghat); the 188-kilometre road between Pokhara and Sunauli on the Indian border; and the 1,040-kilometre east-west thoroughfare called the Mahendra Raj Marg, and the extension from Dharan to Dhankuta in the east. A 79-kilometre road linking Pokhara and Baglung opened early in 1994.

Travel by air remains the best means of covering long distances, and aircraft are the only means of access — apart from walking — to most areas in the northern highlands. Apart from RNAC there are three domestic airlines — Everest Air, Nepal Airways and Necon Air — and a helicopter service.

KATHMANDU

FROM THE AIRPORT: Metered taxis are available from the airport and a ride into the city costs Rs 200. Taxis often choose not to use the meter, particularly in the evenings when fares go up to Rs 300. Some hotels provide their own transport, but charges are almost double those of metered taxis. A pre-paid limousine service is also available from **Kathmandu Airport Facilitation Service** (Tel: 470981) at Rs 200 during the day and Rs 300 at night, with pre-paid insurance coverage of Rs 100,000 at no extra charge.

TAXIS: Metered taxis are usually easily available, except when it rains and also after 9 p.m. Best places to find them are in front of larger hotels and in Thamel Durbarmarg and New Rd. Fare is Rs 2.50 for flag-fall and rarely exceeds Rs 90 plus 30% surcharge for a ride within city limits. A 50% surcharge on metered fares is made at night. Not all of them use their meters, in which case bargaining is necessary. One taxi service which does not use bargaining is **Kathmandu Yellow Cabs** (Tel: 414565).

RICKSHAWS: Pedal rickshaws (three-wheelers) are plentiful and are good for distances of a mile or so. Expect to pay about Rs 50-70, subject to bargaining before getting in. Rickshaws are often available late at night at hotel entrances.

BUSES: Buses and minibuses are available to most places within the city and to outlying areas. They are cheap — most fares are Rs 3 or less — but crowded and very slow. Buses for Boudhnath, Patan and the airport leave from Ratna Park. A regular trolleybus service operates between Kathmandu (from Tripureswore) and Bhaktapur, a conch-shell-shaped city of Hindu and Buddhist devotees.

SCOOTERS AND TEMPOS: The former are three-wheeled taxis painted black with yellow tops, have meters and cost about half the fare of a regular taxi. Tempos are the same vehicles, generally painted grey or blue, which operate like buses, packing up to six passengers in the back; these cost Rs 3 or so per person. They go to most places and are found at Rani Pokhari, Ratna Park and near the post office at Sudhara.

HIRE CARS: These can be arranged through travel agencies such as Himalayan Travel and Tours and Shangri-La Tours. Toyota Corollas are available for half-day or extended trips, prices depending on mileage and the quality of the road. All cars are chauffeur-driven at Rs 600 for half a day or Rs 2,000 for a full day from 9 a.m. to 6 p.m.

MOTORCYCLES: These can be hired for Rs 200 an hour or Rs 900 per day from 8 a.m. to 6 p.m.

BICYCLE HIRE: The valley is ideal for cycling, which is cheap at Rs 4 per hour and Rs 40 per day. Mountain bicycles are available at Rs 100 per day. No deposit is required.

UPCOUNTRY TRANSPORT

BUSES: From Kathmandu buses are available to the following destinations: Pokhara (approximate fare Rs 150, but the Swiss Mini Express leaving from Sundhara is available at Rs 150); Kakar Bhitta (Rs 250 — night service only); Sunauli (Rs 150); Birgunj (Rs 150); Narayanghat (Rs 120); Trisuli (Rs 150); Nepalgunj (Rs 250); Gorkha (Rs 140); Janakpur (Rs 200), and Kodari (Rs 140). Mini-buses and Land-Rovers can also be hired for most trips from Pako and Dharmapath.

AIR: RNAC is the biggest domestic carrier with an extensive network served by a fleet of HS748s, DHC6s (Twin Otters) and a Pilatus Porter. Some of the destinations served by RNAC are: Pokhara, Meghauly, Pokhara-Jomsom, Manang, Nepalgunj, Phaplu, Simra, Tumlingta, Jumla and Lukla. There are flights to Jomsom from Pokhara and to Jumla from Nepalgunj. Most flights to the remote mountainous areas do not operate from June to late September. Tourists have to pay Rs 50 airport tax at each point. In addition to flying and driving, walking is the other major means of travel in Nepal.

Tours

Travel agencies operate half-day or day sightseeing tours to the cities of Kathmandu, Patan and Bhaktapur, and other sights in the valley and outside such as Dakshinkali, Pashupatinath, Boudhnath and Swayambhu at Rs 175, Dhulikhel, Changu Narayan and Nagarkot at Rs 250. The cost varies according to the type of vehicle, number of passengers, distance and time involved. A charge of about US$20-30 for a four-hour tour for a car for three, plus guide, would be reasonable. Coach tours would cost US$48 per person, depending on the number of passengers, for a four-hour trip. Some agencies — **Nepal Travel Agency** (Tel: 229013, 413188), for example — operate daily scheduled tours.

TREKKING: Nepal offers arguably the best trekking holidays in the world and every year it attracts more than 60,000-75,000 visitors — mainly from the West — who set out on treks which last from one week to a month. The trekking season extends from late September to May. Travellers need a trek permit and should apply two days in advance at **Central Immigration Office** at Tridevi, enclosing two passport photographs and a fee which can range from US$5 for a month for many areas to an exceptional US$190 a week.

Trekking agents will make all arrangements and provide camping gear, food, guides, porters and other services for a fee of US$50-60 per day per trekker, depending on the size of the group, the length and difficulty of the trek and the quality of the service. Trekkers who want to go on their own must allot several days for preparation, which is generally too troublesome for the first-time visitor. If you want to live in village huts and eat at teahouses along the trail (possible only on a few treks), you can expect to spend about US$10 a day.

RAFTING: This has become very popular with visitors, being a novel way to see the countryside as well as an exciting sport. Rafting agencies offer one to nine days of rafting and camping trips on rivers with scenic stretches and some rousing whitewater rapids. The most popular are the two-to-three-day trips that begin at points on the Kathmandu-Pokhara road and end in the Terai lowlands, often with a two-night stay at one of the wildlife lodges in the Chitwan National Park. Raft trips cost US$60-80 per person per day, inclusive of all gear, food and guides but not transport to the starting point and back from the finishing point. High-quality inflatable rafts — operated by an oarsman or by everyone on board handling paddles — life-jackets and water-proof protection for cameras and personal items are all provided.

WILDLIFE VIEWING: The Chitwan National Park, 120 kilometres south of Kathmandu, has become a permanent attraction for visitors. Several jungle lodges operate in and around the 960-square-kilometre national park, offering comfortable accommodation and high quality service, with wildlife viewing from elephant back, excursions by Land-Rover and on foot, bird-watching, canoeing in dugouts, and cultural tours to nearby Tharu villages.

At the top of the list is the famous Tiger Tops Jungle Lodge, with its Tented Camp and Tharu Village at US$250 per person per night, plus US$140 air transport. Others offering similar activities at more moderate prices include Temple Tiger, Gaida Wildlife, Elephant Camp and its Chitwan Jungle Lodge and the Jungle Safari Camp. Rates range upwards from US$150 for two nights at Jungle Safari.

Besides flying, trekking offers the only means of seeing Nepal's central hills and valleys and all the northern highlands. The main trekking areas are the Everest region, approached via Lukla airstrip (more than 3,000 metres), for visits to Sherpa villages, the monasteries of Thyangboche and Pangboche, the peaks of Kala Pathar (5,045 metres) and Gokyo (5,483 metres) for the best views and the Everest Base Camp; the region north of Pokhara, including Jomsom and the Annapurna Sanctuary and the villages of Ghandrung and Landrung, the Helambu-Langtang and Gosaiklund Lake area, approached via Sundarijal or Trisuli, and the Jumla and Rara area, approached via Jumla airstrip. RNAC operates scheduled flights to all the trek regions; aircraft can also be chartered if a booking is made two-to-six weeks in advance.

TREK PERMIT FEES: Kanchenjunga — US$10 per person per week for the first four weeks; US$20 per person per week for following weeks. Other areas — US$5 per person per week for the first four weeks; US$3 per person per week for following weeks. A trek permit includes a visa extension during the trek.

Newly permitted trek areas in the Kanchenjunga region are: Taplejung, Sekhathum, Gyabla, Ghunsa, Mirginla, Seram, Ramze up to Yalung Glacier, Serman, Torontan, Chitre, Yamphudin, Mamankhe, Khesewa, Bhanjang, Tambawa and Taplejung. Restricted areas in the district of Taplejung are Olangchung, Gola, Lelep and Pabung.

The newly permitted trek areas in the dis-

The Gai Jatra festival. PHOTO: K.M. SINGH

trict of Dolpo are Rimi, Kaigaon, Sharmi, Naku, Kalika, Laha, Lekhu, Pahada, Tripurakot, Suhu, Gufal, Mazfal, Dunai, Raha, Laban and Sahar Tara.

MOUNTAIN FLIGHTS: All four local airlines operate a one-hour mountain scenery flight to the Everest region daily from October to March, weather permitting. The cost is around US$100, plus airport tax. Helicopters and light aircraft may be chartered.

Accommodation

KATHMANDU

Kathmandu has a wide range of hotels from first-class establishments that are about the lowest-priced in the region to budget-class lodges of excellent value. First-class and tourist-class hotels include the **Soaltee Oberoi**, **Yak and Yeti**, **Annapurna**, **Everest**, **Sherpa**, **Malla**, **Shanker**, **Himalaya**, **Shangri-La**, **Summit**, **Narayani**, **Yellow Pagoda**, **Dwarika'd Village Hotel**, **Blue Star**, **Hotel Kathmandu**, **Woodlands** and **Tara Gaon Village**. Good low-cost hotels are the **Evergreen Nook**, **Vajra**, **Kohinoor**, **Blue Star**, **Blue Diamond**, **Kathmandu Guest House**, **International Guest House**, **MM International Central**, **Manaslu** and **Sayapatri Hotel**, **Mansyangdi Hotel Thamel**, **Ambassador**, **Tridevi**, **Puja**, **Gautam**, **Janak** and **Mountain Hotel**.

UPCOUNTRY

Two excellent and unusual hotels upcountry are **Tiger Tops** — in the lowland tropical region 120 kilometres south of Kathmandu — and the **Everest View,** at 4,330 metres in the Everest region. West Nepal Adventures, an affiliate of Tiger Tops runs the **Karnali Tented Camp** in West Nepal. Other tourist-class hotels include **Temple Tiger**, **Gaida Wildlife**, **Elephant Camp** and **Chitwan Jungle Lodge** in the Chitwan National Park, and the **Narayani Safari Hotel**, with swimming pool and tennis court, in Bharatpur.

In Pokhara there is the charming **Fish Tail Lodge**, plus the **New Crystal**, **Hotel Dragon**, **Hotel Mountain Top**, **Lakeside Pokhara** and **Mount Annapurna**. An ambitious project, the **Begnas Lake Resort**, with houseboats and water sports, is also under way. The **Shangri-La** has been added recently. Two recently added properties are the **Dhulikhel Mountain Resort**, 35 kilometres from Kathmandu (ideal for bird-watching, seeing the sun rise and set over Mt Everest and for whitewater rafting), and **Tara Gaon Resort** and **Hotel Space Mountain** in Nagarkot, also 35 kilometres from the capital. Apart from these, smaller hotels with basic facilities are to be found in all places patronized by tourists.

Dining

Nepali food is basically rice, curry and lentils prepared in hot spices, though it is not as rich as Indian cuisine. Newari cuisine, indigenous to the Kathmandu valley, is more exotic with rice-and-meat pancakes and offal and blood fried with spices. Mountain-goat curry and wild fowl are everyone's favourites. Beef, though officially banned, is available in most hotels and restaurants. Fresh fish, shellfish and canned food are imported from Calcutta, the EC and Scandinavia.

Hotel Annapurna has two excellent outlets — the **Arniko Room** for Chinese and **Ghare-Kabab** for Indian meals. At the Soaltee, **Al Fresco** serves the best Italian food in town and **Himalchuli** is good for Indian and Nepali fare. The **Chimney Room** at the Yak and Yeti serves fine Russian and Continental cuisine and exotic local cocktails. Good Indian food can be had at **Kebab Corner** on Kantipath and at **Amber** (owned by the well-known Amber Restaurant in Calcutta). Good Chinese food is served at Hotel Malla's **Mountain City restaurant**, which has two cooks from Sichuan, and **Top in Town Restaurant & Bar**, New Rd, which specializes in Beijing cuisine. The best Japanese food is offered at **Tamura Restaurant** in Thapathali and **Kushi Fuji** on Durbar Marg, **Fuji** on Kantipath, and the **Sakura-Ya Restaurant and Garden** and **Molisyu** in Lazimpat. **Sun Kosi** on Durbar Marg is good for Nepali dishes, while the **Dhulikhel Mountain Resort**, 35 kilometres from Kathmandu, serving Indian and Continental meals, makes for a pleasant evening out and overnight stop. The capital's **Kathmandu Kitchen** and the **Bhansa Ghar** at Kamaladi are good for home-distilled Nepali *raksi* liquor and ethnic Newari dishes.

Only the larger hotels have bars stocked with a wide range of imported drinks. Most restaurants serve only local drinks — Nepali rum, vodka, gin, whisky and beer.

Entertainment

There is no night life to speak of in Kathmandu. Nepali folk-dance and music performances are held every evening at 6 p.m. at the **Everest Cultural Society** at New Himalchuli, which offers an elaborate meal and a cultural show. Other hotels offer cultural shows and some dancing. The **Yak and Yeti**, **Everest**, **Soaltee** and **Annapurna** have casinos open round the clock with roulette, keno, blackjack, pontoon, flush, poker, jackpot machines and a video room for non-gamblers. Transport is provided free after 8 p.m.

Shopping

Craftsmanship is good and relatively inexpensive. Thus Kathmandu offers a wide range of souvenirs or items for use that will interest the visitor. Silverware or wood-carving of pagodas, temple struts, bronze cast deities, windows and woodblocks of traditional design can be bought in the **Patan Industrial Estate** and in **Indrachowk** and **Asan**. Brass and copperware such as water vessels, cooking utensils, butter lamps and candlestick holders — some made for domestic use — make excellent decorative items and are found in the same shopping areas. Images of Hindu and Buddhist deities cast by the "lost-wax" process are available in varying sizes and quality and can be bought in the **Patan Industrial Estate Cottage Industry** department store at New Rd and **Nepal Arts and Handicraft Centre** in Durbar Marg.

Nepali and Tibetan traditional jewellery of silver and old coins, and of turquoise, amber and coral is sold in Thamel, Durbar Marg, Patan and Boudhnath. Precious and semi-precious stones mounted in various designs are best bought in New Rd gem shops and in the shopping arcades of major hotels. Stones include lapis lazuli, moonstone, black-star, agate, garnet, aquamarine, crystal, emerald and sapphire. Other excellent buys are old and new Tibetan carpets, Nepali radi rugs, made of mountain sheep and goats, Nepali and Tibetan *thangka* paintings, rice-paper paraphernalia, lambs-wool *pashmina* shawls, hand-knitted sheep-wool sweaters and jackets, Nepali silk and felt slippers.

The main shopping areas are New Rd or Juddha Sadak, Thamel, Patan Industrial Estate, Asan-Indrachowk, Boudhnath, Durbar Marg and the arcades at major hotels.

Shops especially worth visiting include **Mandala Boutique**, **Blue Star Shopping Centres**, **Mannies Boutique**, **Nepal Traditional Crafts**, the **Print-shop**, **Nepal Arts and Handicrafts Centre** and **Curio Shop** at Durbar Marg. **Nanglo Fair Price Shopping Centre** at Ram Shaa Path and **Selwel** in Tripureswore Marga are also worth a visit.

GEMS AND JEWELLERY

Popular stones available in Nepal are turquoise, lapis lazuli, rubies, garnets, topaz and beryl cats' eyes. The yellow and smoky topaz are available at most of the curio shops in New Rd, Durbar Marga and the shops at the deluxe hotels. Hard bargaining is needed to bring down the prices asked by 25%, and gems should be bought only on the issue of a guarantee certificate and cash receipts.

INTERNATIONAL CREDIT CARDS

Most major credit cards are accepted by major tourist and deluxe hotels and curio shops in Kathmandu.

Sports

Sporting facilities are mainly limited to swimming, tennis, fishing, hiking, cycling, squash and golf. The major hotels have swimming pools and tennis courts (fee Rs 300-400 an hour). **The Royal Golf Club**, near the airport, has a nine-hole golf course and the **Battisputalli Sports Club** has a squash court for members and guests. There are good billiards tables at the **Annapurna** and **Soaltee** hotels. Cycle hire-stands can be found in Asan at Rs 40 a day, at Thamel and at the entrances of smaller hotels. Hang-gliding and ballooning can be arranged through **International Trekkers**, but the most attractive sporting activities remain mountaineering and trekking.

Holidays

Not a week passes without celebration of some festival, whether Hindu or Buddhist, in all or part of the kingdom. Each year most occasions are celebrated on different dates, though birthday celebrations and those commemorating modern political events remain fixed. In addition to the public holidays mentioned (which are the main ones), some other religious festivals are also taken as public holidays.

February-March: Tibetan Lhosar New Year is celebrated at Swayambhu and Baudha Nath on the day of the new moon in February after the Shivaratri celebration in honour of Lord Shiva, a Hindu god, and there is a great fair with religious observance at the Pashupatinath Temple (public holiday).

Democracy Day commemorates the overthrow of the Rana regime in 1951.

February 18: National Democracy Day (public holiday).

Mid-April: Navabarsha (Nepalese New Year — public holiday).

April: Baisakh Purnima (triple anniversary of Lord Buddha — public holiday).

Ghoda Jatra celebrates the defeat of the demon at Tundi Khel; highlights are horse-racing, gymnastics and military acrobatic displays.

May: Rato Machhendra Nath Ratha Jatra is celebrated in the town of Patna with the highlight of the month-long observance being the parading of a large decorated chariot.

August-September: Gai Jatra honours Yama, Lord of Death. Newars who have had a death in the family parade a cow or its effigy to help the passage of souls and stage a carnival festival, and Indra Jatra pays homage to Indra, King of Gods.

September-October: Durga Puja (Desain) lasts 15 days and is one of the great festivals of the year. Houses are decorated and people wear their best clothes to worship at the temples over a week-long public holiday.

There are animal sacrifices and various processions for traditional feasts and enjoyment.

A fortnight later the Festival of Lights is celebrated for three days by both Hindus and Buddhists.

November: Mani Rimdu — Buddhist monks evoke the protector gods with colourful mask dances and chart prayers for prosperity, especially celebrated in Thyangboche and Solukhumbu.

December 28: Birthday of King Birendra (public holiday).

ADDRESSES

Nepal Chamber of Commerce, Head Office, Kantipath, P.O. Box No. 198. Fax: (9771) 229998, Tlx: 2349 NP, Tel: (9771) 213535, 222890.

Federation of Nepalese Chambers of Commerce and Industry, Koteswore, Kathmandu. Tel: (9771) 474051, 475032, Tlx: 2476 NP.

PUBLICATIONS

There are several excellent guide books for the casual visitor to Nepal, among them the *Insight Guide to Nepal* by Apa (Rs 220); *Nepal; Namaste* by Robert Rieffel (Rs 85); *Kathmandu and the Kingdom of Nepal* by Prakash Raj (Rs 87); *Trekking in the Himalayas* by Stan Armington (Rs 72); *Trekking in the Himalayas* by Tomoya Iozawa (Rs 215), and *The Kathmandu-Nepal Handbook* by Uttara Crees and

Children taking part in the Indra Jatra festival. PHOTO: K.M. SINGH

Kesang Tseten (Rs 25).

Monthly publications for tourists — *Enjoy Nepal*, *Nepal Traveller* and *Himalaya Monthly* — are available free at the airport and all leading hotels and travel agencies.

The **Department of Tourism** has also published more than a dozen free brochures for tourists. The department is in Phatan Dhoka (Tel: 523692, Fax: 527852), with branches at Basantpur at New Rd (Tel: 220818), the airport and in various towns on the border.

DISCOVERING NEPAL

THE KATHMANDU VALLEY

The Kathmandu Valley is the most popular place in the kingdom. In addition to the capital city, it contains the ancient towns of Bhadgaon and Patan, mostly built between the sixth and 16th centuries, plus many temples, 217 monuments and scenic spots.

Kathmandu is said to have been founded in 723 and its **Durbar Square** forms the heart of the city. The square (also called the Hanuman-Dhokha) houses an intriguing collection of temples and palaces and boasts some unexpected erotic wood carvings on the walls of its Hindu temples.

Of note in the square: the famous image of Hanuman (the Monkey God), which guards the entrance to the Royal Palace; the Taleju Temple built by Raja Mahendra Malla; the gigantic figure of Kal Bhairab (God of Terror); the Basantapur Durbar; the Coronation Platform; the Hall of Public Audience; the golden statue of Raja Pratap Malla and his four sons, seated on a stone pillar with a lotus capital; the Big Bell and the Big Drum; Sweta Bhairab's Huge Golden mask and numismatic collection. There is a Rs 5 charge for foreigners to enter the Royal Palace.

Near the Durbar Square stands the **House of the Living Goddess (Kumari Devi)**, a picturesque building with heavily carved wooden balconies and latticed windows. You may enter the courtyard and see the window of the goddess and you may even be lucky enough to glimpse the young goddess herself, for she reverts to ordinary human form on reaching puberty. The goddess is taken through the city on a special carriage on the third day of the Indra Jatra Festival, celebrated in September. Photography is not allowed, except during the festival.

Also worth seeing is the old house known as **Kastmandup**, built by Raja Laxmi Narsingha Malla in 1596 with a single tree. The white **Machendra Nath Temple** is an outstanding example of pagoda-style architecture and is situated off Indra Chowk, the central market.

The **Singha Durbar** (now the Central Secretariat Bldg) to be found in the southeast of the city was once the official residence of the Rana prime ministers; it is an outstanding piece of architecture set in wide, fountained gardens. It was damaged by fire in 1973 but has been rebuilt in the same style, yet only to one third of the area of the original building.

To the northwest of the city, about six kilometres away, lies the **Balaju Water Garden**, an 18th-century design of spouting crocodile heads set in pleasant gardens. There is an Olympic-size swimming pool and an aquarium in the park.

On the banks of the Bagmati River, eight kilometres to the east of Kathmandu, is the Hindu golden temple of **Pashupatinath**, 0dedicated to Lord Shiva who is worshipped in the form of a lingam. The temple is the centre of an annual pilgrimage on the day of Shivaratri during February. Only Hindus are allowed inside the temple but visitors can obtain a good view from the east bank of the river.

On a small hill to the northwest of the city, just past the museum, is the Buddhist sanctuary of **Swayambhunath**. The hill itself is a pleasant spot overlooking the valley and the town and is the home of hordes of small monkeys. The history of Swayambhunath is reputed to stretch back to the time of the Buddha himself. The stupa is daily patronized by adherents who walk around the base of the hill, turn prayer wheels, prostrate themselves and burn butter lamps and incense to accumulate merit from such devotional practices. On such occasions as the Buddha's birthday or Tibetan Losar (New Year), Tibetans throng to the stupa, visiting all the important pilgrimage spots, images and resident lamas. They carry ceremonial scarves (*khatag*), butter for the butter-fed lamps and small donations.

At the other end of town lies the other important Buddhist stupa in Kathmandu, **Boudhnath**, possibly one of the world's largest stupas. The place now bustles with a large Tibetan population, busy with carpet manufacture, trade and prayers at the several monasteries belonging to different sects of Tibetan Buddhism.

The fifth-century **Lichhavi Buddhanilkantha** at the base of the **Shivapuri Hill**, nine kilometres north of Kathmandu, is a stone sculpture of Narayan (Vishnu) lying on a bed formed by the coils of the king serpent Sesha Noga.

Sundarijal, 13 kilometres north of Kathmandu, is famous for waterfalls and mountain scenery. It makes a delightful excursion and picnic spot, especially immediately after the monsoon. **Chovar**, six kilometres southwest of Kathmandu, is the site of a gorge where the water drains from the valley (and is said to have been cut by the god Manjushree to drain the lake that supposedly then filled the valley). There is a small pagoda (**Adinath**) at the top of the gorge, offering a good view. The picnic and pilgrimage spots of **Pharping** and **Dakshinkali** are nearby.

Kirtipur, six kilometres west of Kathmandu, is a picturesque Newari village with fifth-century temples, old lanes and houses and weavers dressed in traditional clothing.

Phulchowki, 16 kilometres southeast of Kathmandu and 3,330 metres high, is a noted spot for wild flowers and butterflies. You can go by car some of the way, but it is a three-hour climb on foot to the top of the ridge. The **Nepal Museum**, just beyond the town towards Swayambhunath, possesses a wide range of historical and archaeological objects, including a leather gun allegedly captured in the Tibetan War of 1880.

Patan (Lalitpur), six kilometres southeast of Kathmandu across the river, is an interesting town, full of Buddhist monuments, temples and buildings adorned with elaborate wood-carvings and sculptures. It is said to have been founded in 299 AD. Special places of interest in the town include: the **Hiranya Varma Mahavihar**, a 12th-century gilded temple dedicated to Lokeswore; **Kumbheshore Temple** (to Shiva), which has a natural spring in its courtyard; **Jagat Narayan Temple** (to Vishnu) near the confluence of the Bagmati and Manahara rivers; **Krishna Temple**, which has some interesting descriptive sculpture from the ancient Hindu religious epics; **Durbar Square**, once the centre of rule for the Malla kings and still a fascinating cluster of temples; **Machhendra Nath Temple** (13th century); **Mahaboudha** (14th century), and the **Ashoka Stupa**, one of four such stupas erected at Patan to mark the pilgrimage of the Indian emperor Ashoka in 250 BC to the Kathmandu Valley.

About 20 kilometres south of Patan is **Godavari**, an excellent jungle picnic spot and the lofty temple of **Bajra**, known as Bajra Barahi and likewise set in jungle surroundings.

About 14 kilometres east of Kathmandu is the town of **Bhadgaon** (Bhaktapur), founded by Raja Ananda Malla in 889 AD. Its Durbar Square, the main architectural showplace of

The Annapurna range above Pokhara. PHOTO: SHRIDHAR L. MANANDHAR

the valley, displays the best examples of the ancient building crafts of the Newar people. The town's traditional industries are pottery and weaving.

There are more than a dozen temples devoted to Buddhism and Hinduism. The most notable are the **Batsala Temple**; the **Pashupatinath Temple**, which is a replica of one on the Bagmati River and of interest for its erotic wood-carvings and fine pictures; the **Temple of Bhawani**, guardian goddess of the once-ruling dynasty; the five-storey **Nyatapola Temple** (the finest example of pagoda-style architecture in Nepal), and the huge Bhairab Nath Temple built in 1708-18 by Raja Bhupatindra Malla, whose bronze statue sits on top of a seven-metre pillar in the middle of the square. Facing the Raja's statue is the superb **Golden Gate**, decorated with gods, goddesses and mythical animals.

Five kilometres north of Bhadgaon on a hill is the **Changu Narayan Temple**, the oldest pagoda-style temple in the valley. Some inscriptions found inside the temple have been dated to the late fifth century.

Nagarkot, which lies at 2,715 metres, is one of the most beautiful spots in the valley. It is about 34 kilometres northeast of Kathmandu. It is an ideal spot from which to watch the sun rise over Mt Everest. Motor vehicles can reach the village and from there it is a further 20 minutes to the hilltop, which gives magnificent views of Everest and other Himalayan peaks. The recently opened **Club Himalaya Nagarkot Resort** charges US$80-100 a night, while the **Taragaon Nagarkot Resort** has comfortable rooms for US$25 a single; there is also the budget-class **Everest Cottage**. After taking the bus from Kathmandu, get off just beyond Bhaktapur and hike up to Nagarkot (three hours).

Another excellent spot for mountain views is **Kakani** at an altitude of 2,000 metres, about 28 kilometres northwest of Kathmandu. The road to the town takes you out of the valley on a winding drive along its northern rim. Here you can walk and picnic and view the mountains in the middle distance. There is also a tourist bungalow offering accommodation.

Also within easy range of Kathmandu is the ancient and scenic town of **Dhulikhel**, just 32 kilometres to the east along the Arniko Raj Marg road that leads to the Kodari Pass on the Chinese border. From this town the panorama includes the snowy ranges from Makalu in the east to Manaslu in the west. Just four kilometres beyond is **Dhulikhel Mountain Resort**, well worth a visit for a meal or an overnight stay (approximately US$75 a single).

UPCOUNTRY

Pokhara, 225 kilometres west of Kathmandu, is the second most popular tourist spot in Nepal after Kathmandu. Easily accessible by land

TREKKING AGENCIES GUIDE

(All addresses in Kathmandu unless otherwise stated)

ANNAPURNA MOUNTAINEERING & TREKKING, Durbar Marg, P.O. Box 795. Tel: 222999, Tlx: 2204 YETI NP.

ASIAN TREKKING, Thamel, P.O. Box 3022. Tel: 413732, Tlx: 2276 HOSANG NP.

GLACIER SAFARI TREKS, Bhagwan Bahal, P.O. Box 2238795. Tel: 412116, Fax: 418578, Tlx: 2654 GST.

HIMALAYAN JOURNEYS, Kanti Path, P.O. Box 989. Tel: 226138-9, Fax: 227068, 418182, Tlx: 2344 HJ TRED NP.

INTERNATIONAL TREKKERS, Naxal, P.O. Box 1273. Tel: 418561, 418594, Fax: 221151, Tlx: 2353 INTREX.

IN WILDERNESS TREKKING, Bauda Nath, P.O. Box 3043. Tel/Fax: 470760.

LAMA EXCURSIONS, Durbar Marg, P.O. Box 2485. Tel: 220186, 226706, Fax: 227292, Tlx: 2659 LAMEX.

MOUNTAIN TRAVEL, Lazimpat, P.O. Box 170. Tel: 414508, Fax: 414075, Tlx: 2216 TIGTOP.

NATRAJ TREKKINGS, Kanti Path, P.O. Box 495. Tel: 226644, Fax: 227372, Tlx: 2270 NATRAJ NP.

NEPAL TREKS & NATURAL HISTORY EXPEDITION, Pattisputali, P.O. Box 459. Tel: 472556, Tlx: 2239 KTT NP.

SAGARMATHA TREKKING, Kamal Pokhari, P.O. Box 2236. Tel: 417036, Tlx: 2375 PEACE NP.

SHERPA COOPERATIVE TREKKING, Durbar Marg, P.O. Box 1338. Tel: 224068, Fax: 227983, Tlx: 2558 NEPEX NP.

SNOW LEOPARD TREKKING, Naxal, P.O. Box 1811. Tel: 415784, Fax: 414719, Tlx: 2358 SINGER NP.

SUMMIT NEPAL TREKKING, Kupondole Height, Lalitpur, P.O. Box 1406. Tel: 525408, Fax: 523731, Tlx: 2342 SUMMIT NP.

TRANS HIMALAYAN TREKKING, Durbar Marg, P.O. Box 283. Tel: 224854, Tlx: 2233 THT NP.

(six hours) and air (US$61), Pokhara is at a lower elevation than Kathmandu, thus warmer and pleasant in winter, and it has three beautiful lakes with the background of the Annapurna-Dhaulagiri ranges; most conspicuous is the magnificent **Machhapurchare**, or Fish Tail Mountain. Regarded as the lakeside resort valley of Nepal, it offers a whole range of activities-trekking (being the gateway to Annapurna Sanctuary and Jomsom), cycling, swimming, boating and horse-riding. There are some good hotels — the recently built **Shangri-La** luxury resort, the **Fish Tail, New Crystal, Dragon and Mount Annapurna** and plenty of cheap ones around the **Phewatal** (Lake).

On the **Tribhuvan Rajpath** nearly 2,650 metres up and 80 kilometres southwest of Kathmandu is **Daman**, which commands a good view of Everest and other great peaks. The **Everest Point Hotel** offers rooms at Rs 95 single and Rs 160 double. There is a special tower from which to view the mountain.

Further still to the southwest, some 240 kilometres from the capital, are the **Rapti Valley** and **Chitwan Forest**. Here is the **Royal Chitwan National Park**, the home of the one-horned rhinoceros, elephants, tigers and leopards. **Bharatpur**, the main centre in the Rapti Valley, is connected by road to Kathmandu via Hetaud. From Bharatpur a good road leads to the small but novel bazaar of **Narayangarh**. Nearby is the Narayani River, famous for boating, fishing and crocodile hunting.

Lumbini, the Buddha's birthplace 250 kilometres southwest of Kathmandu, is accessible by the 32-kilometre motorable road from Naubise on the loop line of Indian Railways (via Gorakhpur). Here in Lumbini Gardens are a broken Ashoka pillar (discovered in 1896) with an inscription commemorating a pilgrimage by the great ruler in the 20th year of his reign, the remnants of a monastery and a holy pond and a stone image of the Buddha's mother, Maya Devi. There are also two top-class tourist hotels, the **Lumbini Garden Guest House** and the **Lumbini Hokke Hotel**, plus the comfortable **Maya Devi** (20 rooms).

Biratnagar in the southeast is Nepal's main industrial centre and the site of Kosi River Valley project to provide electricity and irrigation. **Dharan**, 40 kilometres to the north, has some attractive scenic spots. **Dhankuta**, 55 kilometres further east of Dharan, is connected by a modern highway.

The district of **Helambu**, 80 kilometres north-east of Kathmandu (three days on foot), is a region of Sherpa villages; it also has seven monasteries and the famous lake of **Gosainkunda**. **Namche Bazaar**, even further to the east in the **Mahalangoor Himalayas**, is the home of the famous Sherpa mountaineers and gives a superb view of Everest and the neighbouring peaks — **Lhotse, Nuptse** and **Ama Dablam**. One can fly there, but overland by the bridle path it is a 16-day journey for the adventurous. Note that trekking permits are necessary for this type of journey (*see Immigration*). The celebrated monastery of **Thyangboche** is a one-day walk from Namche.

About 96 kilometres west of Kathmandu is **Gorkha**, the old capital of the Gurkha principality, which is noted for the temples of **Gorkhanath** and **Goddess Kalika** and for its scenic spots at Bar Park.

TREKKING IN THE HIMALAYAS

Trekking, besides flying, is the only means of seeing the country's central hills and valleys and all the northern highlands. The main trekking areas are in the Everest region, approached via Lukla airstrip (over 3,000 metres). From here it is possible to visit Sherpa villages, the monasteries of Thyangboche and Pangboche, the peaks of Kala Pathar (5,045 metres) and Gokyo (5,483 metres) for the best views, and the Everest Base Camp; the region north of Pokhara, including Jomsom and the Annapurna Sanctuary and the villages of Ghandrung and Landrung; the Helambu-Langtang and Gosainkund Lake area, approached via Sundarijal or Trisuli, and the Jumla and Rara area, approached via Jumla airstrip. All four domestic airlines operate scheduled flights to all the trek regions.

HOTEL GUIDE

KATHMANDU

A: US$110 and above

SOALTEE HOLIDAY INN CROWNE PLAZA, Tahachal. Tel: (9771) 272555, Fax: 272205, Tlx: 0891 2203 SOALTE NP. *P, Gym, Biz, Ex, SatTV. Casino. R: C, W.*

HOTEL YAK AND YETI, Durbar Marg. Tel: (9771) 413999, Fax: 227782, Tlx: 0891 2237 YAKNYETI KTM NP. *P, Gym, Biz, Ex, SatTV. Casino. R: W.*

THE EVEREST HOTEL, New Baneswor. Tel: (9771) 220657, Fax: 224421, Tlx: 0891 2260 HOTEVS NP. *P, Gym, Biz, Ex, SatTV. Casino. R: C, W.*

HOTEL DE L'ANNAPURNA, Durbar Marg. Tel: (9771) 221711, Fax: 225236, Tlx: 0891 2205 APPU NP. *P, Gym, Biz, Ex, SatTV. Casino. R: C, W.*

HOTEL SHERPA, Durbar Marg. Tel: (9771) 227000, Fax: 222026, Tlx: 0891 2223 SHERPA NP. *P, Gym, Biz, Ex, SatTV. R: W.*

HOTEL SHANGRI-LA, Lazimpat. Tel: (9771) 412999, Fax: 414184, Tlx: 0891 2276 HOSANG NP. *P, Gym, Biz, Ex, SatTV. R: C, W.*

THE MALLA HOTEL, Lekhnath Marg. Tel: (9771) 410968, Fax: 418382, Tlx: 0891 2238 MALLA NP. *P, Gym, Biz, Ex, SatTV. R: C, W.*

HOTEL HIMALAYA, Pulchok. Tel: (9771) 523900, Fax: 523909, Tlx: 0891 2566. *P, Gym, Biz, Ex, SatTV. R: W.*

B: US$90-125

HOTEL SHANKER, Lazimpat. Tel: (9771) 410151, Fax: 412691, Tlx: NP 0891 2230. *Biz, Ex, SatTV. R.*

HOTEL BLUE STAR, Tripureswor. Tel: (9771) 224056, Fax: 226820, Tlx: 0891 2322. *P, Gym, Biz, Ex, SatTV. R: W.*

HOTEL NARAYANI, Pulchok. Tel: (9771) 521442, Fax: 521291, Tlx: 0891 2262. *P, Biz, Ex, SatTV. R: W.*

HOTEL WOODLANDS DYNASTY PLAZA, Durbarmarg. Tel: (9771) 222683, Fax: 225650. *P, Gym. R: W.*

C: US$70 and below

HOTEL YELLOW PAGODA, Jamal. Tel: (9771) 220338, Fax: 228914, Tlx: 0891 2268. *Biz, SatTV. R.*

HOTEL MOUNTAIN, Jamal. Tel: (9771) 224498, Fax: 227736, Tlx: 0891 2780. *Biz, SatTV. R: W.*

HOTEL AMBASSADOR, Lazimpat. Tel: (9771) 414432, Fax: 413641, Tlx: 0891 2321 BASS NP. *Biz, SatTV. R: W.*

MARCOPOLO BUSINESS HOTEL, Kamaladi. Tel: (9771) 415432, Fax: 418832. *Biz, Ex, SatTV. R: C, W.*

KATHMANDU GUEST HOUSE, Thamel. Tel: (9771) 418733, Fax: 417133. *R: W.*

P — Swimming pool | **Gym** — Health club | **Biz** — Business centre | **Ex** — Executive floor
SatTV — Satellite TV | **R** — Restaurant | **C** — Chinese food | **W** — Western food

PAKISTAN

Pakistan comes as something of a surprise. It has magnificent scenery, a long and interesting history and serves as the intermediary between the cultures of the Indian Subcontinent and the Middle East.

Northern Pakistan — Swat, Kaghan, Gilgit, Skardu and Chitral — contains some of the world's most impressive sights, yet it remains relatively unknown. Three great mountain ranges — the Himalayas, the Karakorums and the Hindu Kush — meet in this region. The headwaters of the Indus River, Pakistan's life blood and a key transport link, also rise here.

The other main communications arteries are the north-south trunk railway and the grand trunk road. The railway has dozens of branch lines which form a network that covers virtually the entire country, while the trunk road winds down to the plains from the Khyber Pass. To travel along either allows the visitor to see evidence of the once great civilization that shaped this part of the world and set the cultural tone of Pakistan.

Pakistan is divided by regional and ethnic differences: Punjab in the east, Kashmir and the North-West Frontier Province in the north, Sindh in the south and Baluchistan in the west.

Vast and partly arid, with a population of 110 million over its 796,095 square kilometres, Pakistan depends on one of the most extensive irrigation systems in the world to grow wheat, rice, cotton, sugarcane and maize.

Karachi, with a population of nearly 8 million, is the country's largest city and its economic and financial centre. Lahore, with more than 4 million is the second largest. Other major towns are the capital, Islamabad, and its twin city Rawalpindi, Faisalabad, Hyderabad, and Peshawar, the gateway to Afghanistan.

Access has become easy in recent years with the government's desire to boost tourism as a foreign-exchange earner. Karachi in the south and Islamabad in the north are on international air routes and both cities have plenty of domestic airline connections to every region.

History

The Indus civilization, which dated from about 2,500-1,500 BC, was centred on two main regions — one in the central Indus river system near the remains of the city known now as Harappa, and the other on the southern Indus near the remains of Moenjodaro. This civilization, whose written script has yet to be deciphered, ended abruptly around the middle of the second millennium BC for still unexplained reasons.

Northern Pakistan then became the target of invaders, including Aryans, Persians, Greeks, Scythians, White Huns, Arabs, Turks and Afghans. The country was divided into many, and often hostile, states. It was not until the establishment of the Delhi sultanate by the Muslim Afghan-Turks in 1207 AD that some semblance of a centralized government was restored.

The Mogul dynasty established in 1526 by Emperor Babar ruled much of Pakistan and northern India until the British took over in the 18th century. The Mogul emperors were retained as figureheads until 1857, when the British Empire was proclaimed.

Pakistan became independent of Britain on August 14, 1947, when it was partitioned from former British India. The idea of a separate state for the Muslims of British India was con-

◄ *Punjabi folk-singing group.* PHOTO: TOURISM DEPARTMENT OF PAKISTAN

ceived by the poet-philosopher Sir Mohammad Iqbal in 1930. It was formally adopted by the All-India Muslim League, led by Mohammad Ali Jinnah, generally known in Pakistan as the Quaid-e-Azam (Great Leader), in 1940. Pakistan originally comprised two wings, the one in the west being present-day Pakistan and the former eastern wing being what is now Bangladesh.

Partition led to rioting between Muslims and non-Muslims in Punjab and Bengal, and resulted in the migration of several million people, with most Muslims opting for Pakistan and most Hindus and Sikhs for India.

For its first 11 years Pakistan worked under a parliamentary system, though during that period not a single election was held. As governments rose and fell through palace intrigues, army chief Field Marshal Mohammad Ayub Khan seized power through a coup. He abolished universal franchise, and introduced an indirect system of elections which restricted the right to vote in presidential and parliamentary elections to only 80,000 members of municipal groups.

Discontent with Ayub's dictatorial rule and demands for autonomy in East Pakistan led to riots in 1969 and Ayub's handing over of power to the then army chief Yahya Khan, who declared himself president and annulled Ayub's constitution.

Yahya held the country's first free general elections on December 7, 1970, resulting in a massive victory for the Awami League in East Pakistan and Zulfikar Ali Bhutto's Pakistan People's Party (PPP) in the west. The results emphasized a sharp regional polarization that led to a civil war and later in 1971 to war with India, which supported the breakaway Bangladesh.

Yahya Khan resigned on December 20, 1971 and handed over power in the west to Bhutto. Bhutto framed the country's first unanimous constitution, signed by all the nation's political parties in 1973. After disputed elections in early 1977, the army chief, Gen. Zia-ul Haq, staged a coup and arrested Bhutto and his cabinet. Zia promised to hold elections within 90 days, but when he realized that Bhutto's PPP was poised for victory, he put them off indefinitely. Bhutto was subsequently hanged on a charge of conspiracy to murder dating from 1974.

Zia dismissed the National Assembly in May 1978 and changed his title from Chief Martial Law Administrator to President, He ruled until August 17, 1988, when he died in a never-explained explosion aboard an aircraft. The PPP came to power in general elections in November 1988.

In August 1990 President Ghulam Ishaq Khan dismissed the PPP government, led by Bhutto's daughter, Benazir, for alleged corruption, a charge which was never proved. The Islamic Democratic Alliance won October 1990 elections amid charges of electoral fraud, and Nawaz Sharif became the prime minister. This government lasted until July 1993, when it resigned under pressure, and the PPP — still headed by Benazir Bhutto — was swept back into power through elections in October that year.

Entry

Pakistan is accessible by air, sea and land. Except for some international flights into Islamabad, Lahore, Peshawar and Quetta, virtually all international traffic passing through Pakistan stops at Karachi. British Airways links London with Beijing via the Gulf and Islamabad. There are also flights between New Delhi and Lahore and between Karachi and Bombay. These are operated by Pakistan International Airlines (PIA), Indian Airlines and Air-India.

PIA flights from Islamabad include services to Amsterdam, Athens, Damascus, Frankfurt, Istanbul, London, Moscow, New York, Paris, Beijing and Tashkent.

Overland access is from Iran, Afghanistan, India and China. The route from Iran is from Zahidan via the Pakistani town of Taftan. A weekly train service operates every Saturday from Quetta and every Monday from Zahidan. Entry from Afghanistan through the Khyber Pass near Peshawar or through Chaman near Quetta has been suspended due to security problems in Afghanistan.

There is only one crossing point between Pakistan and India, between Lahore and nearby Amritsar. Visas for this route are only available at the Indian Embassy in Islamabad and the Indian Consulate in Karachi, and in the reverse direction at the Pakistan Embassy in New Delhi. The border is open every day 8:30 a.m.-2:30 p.m. Pakistan standard time, which is 30 minutes behind Indian standard time.

Buses leave Lahore railway station for the border every 15 minutes, and the walk across the frontier between the Pakistani and Indian

PAKISTAN
UZBEKISTAN
TAJIKISTAN
CHINA
TURKMENISTAN
Boundary claimed by India
NWFP
Line of control
AFGHANISTAN
Peshawar
Islamabad
Rawalpindi
Gujrat
PUNJAB
Lahore
IRAN
Chaman
Montgomery
Multan
Quetta
Sutlej R.
Qila Safed
Kalat
Nukundi
Jacobabad
BALUCHISTAN
Sukkur
Khairpur
INDIA
Bela
Indus R.
Gwadar
SINDH
Karachi
Thatta
Railways
Roads
Arabian Sea
km
0
200

bus terminals takes about 10 minutes, with porters carrying the luggage.

Trains for India leave daily at noon, but passengers must be at the station at 9 a.m. at the latest for customs and immigration formalities. The journey is not recommended, as the customs and immigration staff are notorious for extortion. The bribes they sometimes demand can make it cheaper to travel by air.

The route to China is by the Karakorum highway across the world's highest mountain range. The border at the 4,876-metre-high Khunjerab Pass is open daily from May 1 to November 30, but closes for individual travellers on October 31. Valid visas for China and Pakistan are required, and no visas are issued at the border. Transport from the Pakistan side is available at Sost.

Immigration

All foreigners entering Pakistan need visas, except nationals of Fiji, Hong Kong, Iceland, Malaysia, Maldives, Mauritius, Nepal, the Philippines, Romania, Singapore, South Korea, Tanzania, Tobago, Tonga, Trinidad, Uganda, Western Samoa and Zambia. Israelis may not enter Pakistan.

A single-journey entry visa is valid for a stay of up to three months. Multiple-journey visas also are valid for five months at a time. Any number of journeys during the specified period, not exceeding one year, may be allowed on such visas. Foreigners do not need a visa or permission to cross provincial boundaries within Pakistan, but specific permission must be obtained for visits to restricted areas.

However, tourists who are likely to stay for more than 30 days must register at the nearest foreigners' registration office. Failure to do so can lead to prosecution. Nationals of India and Bangladesh, unless otherwise stated in their visas, are required to register with the nearest foreigners' registration office, irrespective of the length of their stay. Unless stated otherwise in their visas, Indians are normally allowed to visit only four towns of their choice specifically mentioned in their visas.

Health

A cholera vaccination certificate is required from all travellers arriving from an infected area. A valid yellow-fever vaccination certificate is demanded from all travellers arriving from any country where yellow fever is endemic. Aids-free certification is required for anyone staying more than a year.

Customs

Visitors can bring in duty free 200 cigarettes or 50 cigars or 220 grams of manufactured tobacco or an assortment of cigarettes and manufactured tobacco not exceeding 220 grams, plus up to 28.5 millilitres of perfume or toilet-water.

One camera with five rolls of film and one standard movie or video camera with two rolls of film/tape and one projector, binoculars, portable typewriter or personal computer, portable tape recorder and radio, portable musical instrument, pram, toys in reasonable quantity, games and sporting equipment (including sporting firearms and cartridges in reasonable quantity) are also allowed duty free. No sporting firearm is released by customs unless an arms licence issued by a competent authority is produced. Personal jewellery not exceeding Rs 1,000 in value, and gifts not exceeding Rs 500 in value may be brought in duty free.

Visitors are prohibited from bringing alcoholic drinks into Pakistan. Non-Muslims, however, may buy liquor from authorized hotels. Liquor permits for buying drinks at designated stores, where prices are far below those charged by the hotels, can be obtained from the **Excise and Taxation Department**.

Currency

The basic unit of currency in Pakistan is the rupee, which is divided into 100 paisa. Coins of 5, 10, 25 and 50 paisa and Rs 1 are in circulation. Currency notes are in the denominations of Rs 1, 2, 5, 10, 50, 500 and 1,000. The Pakistan rupee has a floating exchange rate adjusted against a basket of currencies. The State Bank of Pakistan announces the rates daily. It was Rs 30.85:US$1 in March 1995. Tourists may bring in any amount of foreign currency but not more than Rs 100 in Pakistani currency. Visitors are not allowed to take more than Rs 20 in Pakistani currency out of the country. Unspent local currency can be reconverted without any limit, provided the visitor has vouchers to show conversion of foreign currency into rupees. An application has to be made to the State Bank through an exchange bank to reconvert larger amounts. Visitors are advised not to hold any more rupees than they need to pay for transport, the Rs 370 per head airport tax and other incidentals.

Hotels are forbidden to accept rupees in settlement of visitors' bills, which must be paid in foreign currency. There are also private, government-licensed money-changers. It is not advisable to change money at hotels as they normally offer lower rates than the banks.

Language

Pakistan's national language is Urdu. However, English is used extensively by many in government and business and fairly widely in hotels, railway stations, post offices and large stores. Basic English is taught in all schools and is the medium of instruction for higher education.

Climate

Pakistan experiences extremes in temperature. The areas close to the snow-covered northern mountains are cold. Temperatures on the Baluchistan plateau are high — as they are in the desert regions of Thar in Sindh and Cholistan in Punjab. Along the coast the climate is hot and humid, though modified by sea breezes. In the rest of the country temperatures rise steeply in summer as hot winds blow across the plains during the day. Dust storms and rain showers lower the temperature. Winter on the plains is pleasant, with minimum temperatures of 4°C in January. Although the country lies within the monsoon belt, it is generally arid — except for the southern slopes of the Himalayas and the sub-mountainous tract.

There are well-defined local seasons. Winter runs from December-February, spring from March-April, summer from May-September and autumn from October-November. In summer the temperatures on the plains may be as high as 45°C. June-August is the hottest part of the year. Between July-August the monsoon begins, bringing an average of 38-50 centimetres of rain on the plains and 150-200 centimetres in the lower Himalayan valleys.

Dress

Very light, preferably cotton, clothes are required for summer in the plains. Light woollens are needed in the northern areas in summer and on the plains in winter. In the hills and northern areas winter temperatures may fall to -17°C. Night-time temperatures in winter in the deserts of Thar and Cholistan can drop as low as 1°C.

Business Hours

Government offices work five days a week, and are closed on Fridays and Saturdays. Summer hours (April 15-October 15) are 8:30 a.m.-4:30 p.m., and the winter schedule is 9 a.m.-5 p.m., with a 12:45-1:30 p.m. break in both seasons. General Post Offices in all major towns work normal office hours, with late evening service up to 8 p.m. Telegraph offices are permanently open. Large stores are open 9 a.m.-9 p.m., while smaller stores remain open longer. Restaurants in major towns are usually open until midnight. During the 30 days of the Ramadan fast, observed according to the Muslim lunar calendar, office hours are 8:30 a.m.-1:30 p.m. with no break. All restaurants, except those in hotels, remain closed between dawn and dusk during Ramadan, as Muslims are not allowed to eat in public during that month.

Doing Business

English is the language of commerce and government. Most business contacts are likely to be hospitable and effusive, which is the local tradition. A suit is advisable for business meetings, though a safari suit is acceptable in summer. Pakistan is an Islamic and conservative country, and while women have gradually begun to make their way into business — as well as into politics — male chauvinism remains the norm. Handshakes and the exchange of business cards are appreciated, but do not take initiative in shaking hands with women.

Most business entertaining is done either at home or in the restaurants of leading hotels. Since alcohol is strictly forbidden both by religion and law, it does not figure in social life and no toasts are made at banquets, though speeches are in order. There is no prejudice against smoking. In casual conversations, any discussion of religion is best avoided. Anyone visiting a mosque, even if it is an historical monument, must take off their shoes.

Rip-Offs

It is advisable to use the hotel taxi service or those offered at special counters at all major airports. Although these taxis are slightly more expensive than a regular cab, they remove the risk of misunderstandings over the fare as the meters of street cabs are rigged. Telephone directories in all major towns list taxi services, which all charge uniformly both for distance and time. Check the meter of these special taxis at the beginning and end of each trip to ensure the charge is correct.

Local leather goods, copperware, onyx and carpets are among the best, and cheapest, in the world. But shop around, compare prices and bargain — bargaining is virtually mandatory. Vendors around some of the famous archaeological sites like Taxila and Moenjodaro offer "antiques" which may well have been manufactured the previous week. It is illegal to buy or export genuine artifacts.

Media

All good hotels provide at least one local English-language daily newspaper to their guests. Usually a different newspaper is delivered each morning, as the hotels seek to avoid giving the impression of preferring any one of the local dailies. International newspapers and magazines are normally available at hotel bookshops. Most leading hotels have CNN and/or StarTV satellite or local TV services.

Communications

Pakistan has an efficient telecommunications system with international telephone and fax connections available from most parts of the country. All top hotels provide international telephone and fax links, while the Telecommunications Corp. of Pakistan has centres in all major towns. Mobile telephones are also available, as are card payphones in Islamabad, Karachi and Lahore.

Transport

FROM KARACHI, LAHORE AND ISLAMABAD AIRPORTS: The average taxi fare from Karachi airport into the city is Rs 200, and Rs 150 from Islamabad airport. The fare from Islamabad airport to Rawalpindi is Rs 60 and from Lahore airport into town costs Rs 100. Fares are raised by 10% in the early hours or late at night. Taxis are available round the clock at the airports. Yellow-top taxis cost less, but fares have to be negotiated.

TAXIS: Fares are charged at Rs 5 per kilometre by meter, which is likely to be rigged. Fares are therefore negotiable. Hire cars at the top hotels are relatively more expensive. The yellow-top taxis may be flagged down on the streets.

MOTORIZED RICKSHAWS: For those with steady nerves these offer a cheaper means of travel at Rs 3 per kilometre, though their meters are also suspect.

HORSE-DRAWN CARRIAGES: Two-wheeled (*tongas*) and four-wheeled (Victorias) carriages are available for transport in some city areas. Fares are negotiable before the journey, and work out at about Rs 10 per kilometre. There are point-to-point regular services of tongas which charge a minimum of Rs 2 per person.

BUSES: City bus fares are cheap, though the vehicles are overcrowded during rush hours. Fares for most journeys range between Rs 1-4 for a journey of up to 20 kilometres.

TRANSPORT UPCOUNTRY

BUSES: These operate round the clock on all the main highways but are more frequent in the north from Lahore through Islamabad to Peshawar. Private company buses leave Lahore from Badami Bagh bus-stand every 15 minutes for the six-hour journey to Islamabad/Rawalpindi. **Government Transport Service** (GTS) buses, which are more reliable, leave from opposite the Lahore Railway station. Advance bookings can be made on what are known as luxury buses of the **Punjab Tourism Department**, the GTS and special coaches of private companies. These vehicles are air-conditioned, comfortable and fast. The GTS and Punjab Tourism Department operate luxury bus services on the Lahore-Multan-Bahawalpur and the direct Lahore-Karachi routes.

Northern Areas Transport Corp. buses operate between Rawalpindi's Pirwadhai bus-stand and Gilgit, from where buses leave for Skardu, Hunza and Sost. There is a bus service between Sost and the Chinese border at Pirali. There are also daily minibus services from Rawalpindi's Kashmiri Bazaar bus-stand to Gilgit. Buses also leave Pirwadhai daily for Mingora in Swat, Mansehra on the Karakorum highway, Dir and dozens of other destinations.

TRAINS: An extensive rail network links the main towns. The trunk line runs from Karachi through Rawalpindi to Peshawar, while services are also available from Karachi through Sukkhur and Quetta to the Iranian town of Zahidan. It is essential to reserve seats several days ahead if a visitor wants to travel in a first-class, air-conditioned coach. All sleeping accommodation also needs to be reserved in advance. There are two services a day between Quetta and Lahore, three between Lahore and Peshawar via Rawalpindi and two direct trains a day between Lahore and Rawalpindi.

Pakistan Railways allows a 25% reduction in rail fares to all foreign visitors, except Indian nationals, travelling either in a group or individually provided their stay does not exceed six months. Foreign students are allowed half-fare concessions.

AIR: **Pakistan International Airlines (PIA)** is the sole domestic carrier and operates regular services to all the country's main towns. There are several flights a day between Karachi, Lahore, Islamabad, Multan, Faisalabad and Peshawar. There are also daily flights to Quetta, Hyderabad, Sukkhur, Saidu Sharif in the Swat valley, Moenjodaro, Gwadar, Pasni, Chitral (daily from Peshawar and twice a week from Islamabad), Gilgit, Skardu (both twice daily from Islamabad), Bahawalpur and Muzaffarabad in Azad Kashmir. Services to Gilgit, Skardu, Chitral and Swat are subject to weather restrictions. Airport tax on tickets bought abroad is Rs 20 on domestic flights and Rs 700 on international flights.

Tours

PIA offers a variety of package tours of special interest which include history and archaeology, mountaineering, trekking and trout-fishing. Inquiries can be made at the nearest PIA office or the tours-promotion section of PIA at Karachi airport.

Pakistan Tours Ltd. (PTL), a subsidiary of the government-owned **Pakistan Tourist Development Corp. (PTDC)**, offers sight-seeing tours in and around Karachi, Lahore, Islamabad/Rawalpindi, Peshawar, Quetta, the Swat valley, Gilgit, Hunza, Skardu and Chitral among others. These tours are conducted in air-conditioned coaches, minibuses, cars and jeeps, which can also be hired by tourists on request. Inquiries can be made at tourist information centres in any major town. Mountain-trekking trips are arranged in northern areas between April-October.

Accommodation

Pakistan has long suffered from a lack of good hotel accommodation, which still gives leading hoteliers an opportunity to charge exceptionally high rates. However, the situation is gradually improving as competition increases.

Older, more "atmospheric" hotels, still operating are **the Falettis** in Lahore, **Flashman's** in Rawalpindi, the **Cecil** in Murree and **Dean's** in Peshawar. All rooms normally have adjoining baths. Most of the popular hotels throughout the country are listed in the easily available hotel guides.

In places of historic interest like Taxia, Moenjodaro and Katas, there are motels and resthouses run by the PTDC which offer accommodation that can be booked through PTL. PTDC runs motels and resorts at Hunza, Gilgit, Skardu, Chitral, Naran (Kaghan valley), Balakot (Kaghan), Besham (Karakorum Highway), Miandam and Kalam (Swat valley), Ziarat (near Quetta) and Keenjhar Lake. In Thatta region, north of Karachi there are a number of bungalows at Thatta itself, Makli Hill, Haleji and Keenjhar lakes, Bhambore and Jherruck.

Accommodation in the northern mountain valleys in Swat and Kaghan is available in PTDC motels and small bungalows belonging to various government departments. Temporary membership of some clubs in big towns is possible and, depending upon availability, would provide accommodation for a three-to-four day stay. YMCA and YWCA hostels at Lahore, Karachi, Rawalpindi and Peshawar are available to members of affiliated organizations.

There are a number of good clubs which tourists may use in Karachi, Lahore, Quetta, Islamabad, Rawalpindi, Abbotabad and Peshawar. Most of them have facilities for golf, tennis, squash, cricket and indoor sports. There are also race, boat and flying clubs. Accommodation in public retiring rooms is also available at the major railway stations.

Dining

Pakistani food is unexpectedly varied. What is generally known as Moghul cuisine is popular, highly spiced and complex. Curries are the norm, though they are generally less spicy than in India. *Seekh kebabs* (minced spiced meat grilled on skewers), *shami kebabs* (minced meat and chickpea cakes), *tekka* (barbecued cubes of mutton, beef chicken or fish) and barbecued leg of lamb are local specialities.

Curries come in many combinations of spices known as *masalas*, which are used in beef, mutton, chicken, fish and egg. Lightly

PHOTO: MUZAMMIL PASHA/REUTER

Water-seller at work.

spiced rice dishes with various meats are known as *pullao*. The more highly spiced dish is called *biryani*. Desserts are generally very sweet and often flavoured with saffron, rose water and other floral extracts, plus a generous sprinkling of various nuts. Often edible silver foil decorates the dish. *Kulfi*, a sweet dish similar to ice cream, is widely available with *falooda* sprinkled with rose water. Much of the good food in Pakistan is served in small restaurants in the city bazaars and village markets. Follow your nose and eyes.

While the large tourist hotels' versions of local dishes lack the touch of authenticity, they are the best available source of Western food for conservative palates. Tuesdays and Wednesdays are meatless and only poultry and fish are served in restaurants.

Shopping

Local handicrafts are among the best buys in Pakistan. These include worked gold and silver, brass and copper vessels and ornaments, leather goods, embroidery, cottons, silks, camel-skin lamps, vases and onyx. Pakistan also produces emeralds, though the local cutting leaves much to be desired. Carpets are among the world's best and cheapest.

Digging around in the markets and bazaars, such as Kissa Khwani bazaar in Peshawar, can turn up some interesting and traditional pieces, especially in copper and brassware.

Among the main shopping centres in Lahore are Anarkali Bazaar, Liberty Market in Gulberg, The Mall, Shah Alam Market and the old bazaars inside the walled city.

The cheapest and most interesting places to shop in Karachi include Zaibunnisa St, Abdulah Haroon Rd, Bori Bazaar, M.A. Jinah Rd and the city's many bazaars. As in most other parts of Asia, bargaining is not only acceptable but a pleasant way of getting to know people. Compare prices before buying and drive a hard bargain, for the shopkeeper is doing his best to get the maximum from you.

Sports

Hockey and cricket are the most popular games in Pakistan, but there are plenty of opportunities for golf, with excellent courses at Lahore, Rawalpindi, Islamabad, Bhurban in Murree Hills, Kabal in the Swat valley and Peshawar. There are tennis and squash courts in the main towns.

There are more than 70 kilometres of beaches near Karachi, with another 560 kilometres of largely unspoiled sands running down the Makran coast, making swimming, scuba-diving, sailing and deep sea fishing popular pastimes. Useful Karachi contact numbers for scuba and sailing enthusiasts include: **Karachi Diving and Salvage Agency** (Tel: 224101); **Karachi Yachting Club** (Tel: 232127); and the **Boat Club** (Tel: 552057).

Angling for brown or rainbow trout draws enthusiasts to the Kaghan valley, Swat, Hunza, Baltistan and other areas in the mountains.

Haleji Lake near Karachi is a bird-watchers' paradise. Birds that can be seen include flamingoes, pelicans, herons, ducks, egrets, purple gallinule, jacanas and kingfishers.

The Malam Jabba ski resort is about 45 kilometres from Saidu Sharif, which in turn is served by daily flights from Islamabad and Peshawar. The resort is about 3,000 metres above sea level with temperatures hovering between -5°C and 5°C during the December-March season. The resort has a 52-room hotel and fully equipped family cottages are also available. Skiing equipment is available at the resort. Other outdoor activities include skating and trekking. Inquiries should be directed to either **Ramada Renaissance Worldwide Reservation** system or to the **Malam Jabba Resort**'s Islamabad sales and information office, Tel: (051) 819203, 817656; Fax: (051) 828844; Tlx: 54476 Avari Park.

Some of the highest peaks of the world are in the Karakorum and Himalayan mountain ranges. The world's second-highest peak, K2, is in Pakistan. Nearly 75% of the country's northern areas are covered by the Karakorum ranges, the southern portion of which face Kashmir and the northern portion Ladakh and Xinjiang province of China. The Hindu Kush ranges lie in the centre of the northern areas, touching Chitral and Gilgit. These provide a wide choice for mountaineers, trekkers and lovers of natural beauty and wildlife.

Mountains are divided into open and restricted zones with permits for the open zones now issued within 24 hours. It takes 14 days from the date of application to secure a permit for climbing peaks in the restricted zone. Pakistani liaison officers accompany all mountaineering expeditions. All mountaineering and trekking parties may bring food and equipment with them duty free.

Trekking in Pakistan involves walking at heights of up to 6,000 metres to places where modern transport is either not available or deliberately not used. Anyone trekking above 6,000 metres must have a permit, but no permit is required for trekking in open zones. Trekking permits for restricted zones are issued by the **Government Tourism Division**, 13-T/U College Rd, Commercial Area, Markaz F-7, Islamabad. A list of open and restricted treks and application forms are available at this address.

The PTDC also arranges tours and has marked seven treks, including two medium-class and five strenuous treks, taking six to 30 days at different altitudes and covering various distances. The tours are organized in collaboration with British Airways and local tourist authorities. The PTDC provides all equipment, camping gear, guides and food for trekkers.

Dec. 25 Holidays

Some public holidays change their dates annually according to the Gregorian calendar and others by the Muslim lunar calendar.
January-March: Shabe Barat (public holiday).
March: Eid-ul-Fitr (marks the end of Ramadan).
March 23: Pakistan Day (public holiday).
May 1: May Day (public holiday).
May: Eid-ul-Azha (the Day of Sacrifice).
August: Eid-Milad-un-Nabi (marks the birthday of the Holy Prophet Mohammad).
August 14: Independence Day (public holiday).
September 6: Defence of Pakistan Day.
November 9: Birthday of national poet Mohammad Iqbal (public holiday).
December 25: Christmas and birthday of the founder of the nation (public holiday).
December 31: Bank Holiday (only banks are closed; government offices and businesses stay open).

ADDRESSES

PTDC information centres can be found in the international arrival lounges at Karachi, Lahore, Islamabad and Peshawar airports and at Shafi Chambers and the Metropole Hotel, both on Club Rd in Sadar area of Karachi, Falettis Hotel on Egerton Rd in Lahore, 13-T/U College Rd in the commercial area of Islamabad and Deans Hotel on Islamia Rd in Peshawar. They are also at Thatta, Moenjodaro, Quetta, Taftan, Bahawalpur, Multan, Rawalpindi, Taxila, Abbotabad, Saidu Sharif in Swat Valley, Skardu and Gilgit.

PUBLICATIONS

The PTDC provides free brochures, maps and the Tourist Calendar booklet, which contains much useful general information. Detailed maps can only be brought overseas as they are regarded internally as classified information. Other useful publications available at PTDC information centres include a tourism directory, trekking books and a hotel and restaurant guide.

DISCOVERING PAKISTAN

ISLAMABAD AND RAWALPINDI

The twin cities of Islamabad and Rawalpindi, though under separate administrations, have merged physically over time. They are located in northern Pakistan on the Potohar Plateau. Although Islamabad is the country's capital, because of its recent origin — worked only started on the city in 1961 — it has yet to acquire the patina of a mature settlement. With the completion of administrative building complexes over the past few years, the various government offices and associated agencies have been moving up from the old capital, Karachi.

Rawalpindi, on the other hand, has a long

Dharmajike Stupa, Taxila. PHOTO: TOURISM DEPARTMENT OF PAKISTAN

history. Its location on the grand trunk road running to the west beyond Peshawar and the Khyber Pass, and to the east beyond Lahore to India, has always made it important to traders and soldiers alike. The British used it as a major military base, and it served as the interim capital for some years after independence.

Rawalpindi's old buildings, mosques and bazaars are in complete contrast to the hard-edged impression created by Islamabad's self-assured modernism.

Places of special interest in the immediate Islamabad-Rawalpindi area complex include: the **National Park**, on the outskirts of Rawalpindi; the **Army Museum** on Church Rd, near The Mall in Rawalpindi; **Daman-e-koh** and the **Shakar Parian Hills**, two pleasant picnic spots in Islamabad; the nearby **Institute of Folk Art Heritage**, which has a permanent exhibition of folk art and collection of folk music; and 25 kilometres from Rawalpindi, the **Margala Hills** overlooking Islamabad and the Rawal Lake.

UPCOUNTRY

Taxila, 32 kilometres north of Rawalpindi, was once a satrapy of the Persian Empire. At the time of Alexander the Great's invasion in 325 BC, it was a flourishing city with a renowned university. It later came under the sway of Central Asian and Indian dynasties until sacked by the White Huns in 455 AD.

Today, the remains of Taxila constitute one of the region's most important **archaeological sites**. There are three distinct city sites within about five kilometres of each other: Bhir Mound, the oldest, goes back to the sixth century BC; Sirkap, constructed under Greco-Bactrian rule in the second century BC, comprises a long street with many buildings including an apsidal temple, a shrine of the double-headed eagle (probably of Scythian inspiration), and a large building believed to be a palace from which has been recovered a good deal of Western-influenced Gandhara-style sculpture; and Sirsukh, believed to date from the time of Kanishka (a powerful king of the Kushan dynasty who reigned around 130 AD), though only a section of the fortifications has so far been excavated.

Besides the three cities, there are the remains of Buddhist monasteries and stupas. An interestingly arranged collection of Gandharan art is housed in the nearby museum.

A little more than 160 kilometres northwest of Rawalpindi lies the ancient city of **Peshawar**, the traditional gateway between Central Asia and the Indian Subcontinent. The heart of the city is the **Qissa Khawani Bazaar** (street of the story-tellers), where over the centuries travellers have met and exchanged stories of places and adventures over endless cups of green tea.

The bazaar is no less colourful now than over the ages, with its thronging bearded tribesmen resplendent in their bright robes — Iranis, Uzbeks, Tadjiks, Afridis and Shinwaris. But most of all the city is filled with armed Afghans, fresh from the still-chaotic factional civil strife in their home country. The streets are packed with people and vehicles of all sorts, from brightly decorated long-distance lorries to horse-drawn gigs. One may still enjoy the tea and take a pull on the communal water-cooled pipe, but the conversation inevitably is of politics.

Other fascinating bazaars in Peshawar include the **Bazaar Bater Bazen** (just off the Qissa), named for the bird market that once stood there but which in more recent years has become the centre for shops dealing in brass and copper wares; and **Mochilara** — the shoemakers' bazaar also in the same area — which sells slippers and shoes, especially the beautiful Pathan *chappal*, embroidered in gold, silver or silk.

On the northwest edge of the city, the bastions of the **Bala Hissar Fort** (originally built by the Moghul Emperor Babar in 1519 and reconstructed in its present form by the Sikhs who ruled the Peshawar Valley from 1791-1849) give a magnificent view of the city and surrounding areas. The museum on the grand trunk road in the cantonment area houses a rich collection of objects from the Gandharan period. **Mahabat Khan's mosque**, on the southeast outskirts of the city, comprises the crumbled remains of a huge stupa and monastery built by King Kanishka. Other important archaeological sites in the area are Charsada, 28 kilometres to the northeast, captured by Alexander the Great in 324 BC and long identified as a pre-Kushan capital of the region, and Takht-i-Bahi, some 80 kilometres to the northeast.

Some 16 kilometres from Peshawar along the Khyber Pass road is **Jamrud Fort**, a ragged jumble of towers and loop-holed walls. The Khyber Pass itself begins 18 kilometres west of Peshawar and extends to the Pakistan-Afghan border at Torkham, 55 kilometres from Peshawar.

Northeast of Rawalpindi are the pleasant hill-stations where visitors and residents alike escape the heat of the plains in summer. **Murree**, 64 kilometres from Rawalpindi and 2,380 metres above sea level, is the most popular. Originally developed as a resort for British troops and their families, it has grown into a sizeable town and is well provided with hotels, cafes and theatres.

Further to the north around the town of Nathiagali (2,500 metres) are the small resort villages known collectively as the **Galis**. One can drive to any of them — Khairagali, Chagalagali and Ghora Dhakka-Khanspur — from Murree.

Beyond the Galis, the beautiful **Valley of Kaghan** winds away into the north through the mountains, and even further to the northwest across the upper reaches of the Indus River is the picturesque and rugged region of Swat.

Kaghan Valley is most easily reached by road from Rawalpindi via Hasan Abdal, Haripur, Havelian, Abbottabad and Mansehra to Balakot, the starting point of the valley. Alternatively, a visitor can travel to Havelian by train and go on to the valley by road. Taxis and buses run as far as Balakot, but from there only jeeps or ponies continue further up the valley to such spots as Kaghan and Naran.

There are a number of resthouses throughout the valley. Inquiries concerning reservations should be made at the tourist offices in Rawalpindi and Abbottabad.

Lake Saiful Muluk (altitude 3,390 metres) can be reached by a track leading up from Naran. Up the valley from Naran is the Babusar Pass (4,400 metres and snowbound eight months of the year), which leads into the Gilgit Agency. On clear days **Mount Nanga Parbat** (the naked lady) can be seen reaching up to 8,500 metres; more usually, she is in misty *purdah*.

The **Valley of Swat** runs north from the regional capital, Saidu Sharif. Chinese pilgrims who visited Swat in the fifth to seventh centuries said that almost 1,400 Buddhist monasteries could be found in the region. Many stupas are still there, and together with the widespread ruins confirm the country's great importance not only as a religious centre but as a home of the Greco-Buddhist artistic tradition.

The **Valley of Kafiristan** is about 80 kilometres from Swat. There is no road and a visitor must ride up by donkey along winding paths and across rope bridges to 3,500 metres. The recently completed 640-kilometre, all-weather Indus Valley Rd runs from Swat along the west bank of the Indus River to Gilgit town, capital of the Gilgit Agency which can also be reached daily by air from Rawalpindi.

From Gilgit a visitor can travel to Hunza on

the Karakorum highway, with excellent views of **Mount Rakaposhi** (8,368 metres) and other peaks along the way. A new road runs from Gilgit to Skardu, the principal town of Baltistan, from where **K2** — the world's second-highest peak — and **Mount Godwin-Austen** can be clearly seen.

There are resthouses and a number of small hotels in these regions, but it is advisable to check in Rawalpindi's tourist office for details of their exact location and reservation and whether a permit is required to visit the outlying areas.

Those wishing to get a dramatic taste of Pakistan's northern areas should take a journey along the Karakorum highway. Hacked through the Karakorum Mountain range, it passes through Kohistan, Gilgit and Hunza, connecting Pakistan with China's **Xinjiang** province via the Khunjerab Pass.

The road trip from Islamabad or Rawalpindi up to the Chinese border is among the most dramatic anywhere in the world. Group tours are available from Rawalpindi-Islamabad to Xinjiang between May and October, for which PTL, Flashman's Hotel, Rawalpindi and private tour operators can be contacted.

About 275 kilometres southeast of Rawalpindi, almost on the border with India, lies **Lahore**, Pakistan's City of Gardens. Conquered for Islam by Mahmud of Ghazni in 1021, Lahore enjoyed a golden age during the Moghul Empire from the reign of Humayun (died 1556) to that of Aurangzeb (1707).

It later became the capital of the Sikh empire of Ranjit Singh (1839) and then, with the rest of Punjab, fell under British rule after the second Sikh War in 1849.

Lahore is Pakistan's second-largest city, with a population of nearly 4 million, and its foremost cultural and educational centre. It owes its distinctive personality to the old walled city and to its many fine buildings and gardens.

Within the old city stands **Lahore Fort**, enlarged and restored by the Moghul emperor Akbar (reigned 1555-1605). Notable features include the Diwan-i-Am (Hall of Common Audience) with its Jharoka (balcony) on which the emperor was enthroned, the Shish Mahal (Hall of Mirrors) and the Naulakha, a marble pavilion in the form of a Bengali dwelling. Its northern wall displays magnificent *kashi* tile work, as does the panelling of the walls and minarets of the nearby mosque of Wazir Khan (built in 1634).

Just west of the fort is Aurangzeb's huge **Badshahi Masjid** (mosque). The **Shalimar Gardens**, nine kilometres east of the city and laid out by the Emperor Shah Jahan in 1637, are an outstanding example of Moghul landscaping. In the north of the city is the **tomb of Emperor Jahangir and his wife, Noor Jahan**, the only empress whose name appears on Moghul coins.

The more recent buildings, such as the Punjab University, the railway station and the Supreme Court and High Court buildings, display a blend of Gothic and Moghul styles. In front of the university stands the great gun **Zamzama** immortalized in Rudyard Kipling's *Kim*. On the other side stands the **Lahore Museum**, notable for its collection of Moghul paintings and Gandhara-style sculpture; Kipling's father was curator of the museum from 1875-93.

The town of **Multan**, well south of Lahore, is noted for its carpets, shoes, glazed pottery and enamel work. Of interest in the town are the Old Fort, the Shrine of Raknud-Din and **the tomb of Shams-i-Tabrez**.

Between Lahore and Multan is the town of Sahiwal, 2.5 kilometres away from the significant archaeological site of **Harappa**. Harappa, like Moenjodaro, is one of the great cities of the ancient Indus Valley civilization. There is a museum and a resthouse at the site where visitors with reservations can stay. It is best to visit Harappa in the winter, spring or autumn months when the heat is not a problem.

The **Quetta and Kalat** Division of Baluchistan in the west is a rugged, sparsely populated land, but dotted with fertile valleys and some of Pakistan's finest fruit-growing areas. The town of Quetta, Baluchistan's major city, derives its name from the Pushtu word *kwata* (fort). Its summers are pleasant, the winters severe. It is reached through the Bolan Pass which begins at Mach, the railway emerging into the Quetta plain at Kolpur (1,910 metres), the highest point on the route.

Pishin Valley, 48 kilometres from Quetta, is surrounded by 4,850 hectares of vineyards and orchards that produce a rich harvest of apples, grapes, plums, peaches and apricots. Ziarat (2,480 metres) — also called Kishgi — is a pretty little hill town set amid a large juniper forest 130 kilometres from Quetta. It can be reached by two roads, the Kach and Kuchlak, that link it with the railhead. There are government bungalows and a youth hostel in the town.

Karachi, a hot and dusty city sandwiched

Badshahi Mosque, Lahore. PHOTO: TOURISM DEPARTMENT OF PAKISTAN

between the Arabian Sea and the desert, has little of obvious tourist interest. In early 1995 the government was trying, with some success, to eradicate random terrorism and rampant lawlessness, and until this is done Karachi should be avoided by tourists. It is Pakistan's largest city and serves as the country's principal commercial and industrial centre.

For the visitor with some time to spare, the crowded **Bohri Bazaar** offers a variety of interesting buys and sights: snake charmers, fortune tellers, pavement dentists and musicians operate side by side with vendors of great piles of spices and sellers of cheap plastic toys.

Other places of interest include the grandly Victorian **Frere Hall** set in the pleasant Bagh-e-Jinnah gardens, the **Quaid-e-Azam Mausoleum** (to the Father of the Nation, Quaid-e-Azam-M.A. Jinnah), the President's House and the zoo.

Popular bathing beaches are Sandspit (16 kilometres away), Hawks Bay (18 kilometres), Paradise Point and Baleji. Swimming is enjoyed most of the year with the exception of the monsoon season from about May to August. Keamari, Karachi's harbour, offers boats for those interested in sailing or fishing. *Bunder* boats (outrigger sailing vessels) can be rented very cheaply, complete with crew.

About 22 kilometres east of Karachi on the road to Thatta are the **Chaukandi tombs**, whose decorative motifs in stone are some of the finest such works in the subcontinent. Further on (64 kilometres from Karachi) are the recently excavated ruins of the ancient city of Bhanbore, once a great port.

Thatta, 103 kilometres from Karachi, is famed for its Indo-Muslim architecture. Although these particular monuments go back only to the 16th and 17th centuries, the town has a history reaching back much earlier; it was here that Alexander the Great rested his troops after their long march from the north, and his admiral, Nearchus, assembled his fleet before leading it back to the Persian Gulf.

Once the seat of a number of ruling dynasties of Sindh (as this southern area of Pakistan is known), Thatta stands amid the ruins of its ancient glory. The most notable building is a great mosque of the Moghul Emperor Shah Jahan, which has 93 domes. Its glazed earthenware tiles and painted stucco decorations rank among the finest in the world.

On the Karachi side, Thatta is dominated by the **Makli Hill**, a vast cemetery extending over an area of 1,540 hectares and said to contain some one million graves. Most of the remains date back to the dynasty of the Summas, who ruled Sindh from the mid-14th to the early 16th centuries, though the latest monuments were left by Moghul governors of the region.

Perhaps the most notable feature of these remains is the wealth of geometric and floral designs carved in the stone. The tomb of Jam Nizamuddin, even though partly despoiled, is the richest of all in this respect. The later Arghun and Moghul tombs are distinguished by brick, enamel and glazed tiles of beautiful colour. Thatta blue tiles are still made in the area.

Thatta can be reached from Karachi by road and rail, though the nearest railway station, Jungshahi, is about 20 kilometres from Thatta town; the rest of the journey must be made by road.

Some 192 kilometres northwest of Karachi along the National Highway is the town of **Hyderabad**, with a population of more than 1 million. The city is known for the tombs of the Kalhore and Talpur families who ruled from the mid-18th to the mid-19th centuries, and for its fine embroidery.

There are also **two old forts** worthy of attention, one entirely mud-walled. Close by, Kotri barrage and Ghulam Mohammad barrage supply water through a network of canals to convert the land from desert into fertile fields.

But of all the places of interest in Sindh, the excavated remains of the ancient city of **Moenjodaro** (mound of the dead) are by far the most fascinating. Work on the site was begun by the British in 1922, revealing an elaborate urban complex with buildings made of baked bricks, paved and drained streets and what was probably a system of chutes and receptacles for rubbish disposal. All this originated as early as the middle of the third millennium BC.

Moenjodaro — along with the city of Harappa farther north — is believed to have been a major city of a vigorous civilization that flourished in the Indus Valley from 2500-1500 BC. There is evidence that the city was hit by some form of cataclysm, though what caused it has not been determined. Moenjodaro lies 656 kilometres north of Karachi and can be reached either by road, rail or air.

The sites and local museum can be covered in a single day. Those interested in making a more thorough inspection can stay overnight in the Archaeological Department's bungalow if a reservation has been made through the tourist office in Karachi. Between November and March, when temperatures are moderate, is the best time to visit the area.

RESTAURANT SELECTION

Average price for two

KARACHI

KABANA, Clifton Rd. Tel: (21) 536961. Pakistani, Western. US$15.
HAKKA, Jinnah Rd. Tel: (21) 414208. Pakistani. US$12.
KOREAN JAPANESE, Abdullah Haroon Rd. Tel: (21) 522401. Korean, Japanese. US$15.
KOWLOON, Pechs. Tel: (21) 446259. Chinese. Music. US$15.
MAXMS, Clifton Rd. Tel: (21) 532588. English. Music. US$15.
NEW PREIRA, Daud Pota Rd. Tel: (21) 511439. Arabian. Music. US$15.
SHEKEY'S, Clifton Rd. Tel: (21) 574587. Italian. Music. US$15.

LAHORE

GULBERG KABANA, Gulberg. Tel: (42) 871064. Pakistani. Music. US$15.
HONG KONG, Gulberg-III. Tel: (42) 371980. Chinese. Music. US$15.
KABANA, Davis Rd. Tel: (42) 305489. Pakistani. Music. US$15.
KHAN BABA, Chouburji Chowk. Tel: (42) 213410. Pakistani. Music. US$12.

PESHAWAR

SHIRAZ, University Rd. Tel: (521) 42014. Pakistani, Western. Music. US$15.
USMANIA, University Rd. Tel: (521) 43535. Pakistani. Music. US$15.

RAWALPINDI

JAVED KABANA, Liaqat Bagh. Tel: (51) 74300. Pakistani. Music. US$12.
MEI KONG CHINESE, Haider Rd. Tel: (51) 566577. Chinese. Music. US$15.

ISLAMABAD

OMAR KHAYAM, Blue Area. Tel: (51) 812847. Iranian, Pakistani, English. Music. US$15.
PAPPA SALLIS, Markaz F-7. Tel: (51) 818287. Italian. Music. US$15.
VALENTINE, Blue Area. Tel: (51) 824134. French. Music. US$15.

HOTEL GUIDE

FAISALABAD

A: US$100 and above

FAISALABAD SERENA, Club Rd. Tel: (411) 30972-76, Fax: (411) 30549, Tlx: 43453 SERENA PK. *Gym, Biz, SatTV. R: L, W.*

GILGIT

B: US$50-100

GILGIT SERENA LODGE, Jutial. Tel: 2330-31, Fax: (572) 2525. *SatTV. R: L, W.*

ISLAMABAD

A: US$100 and above

ISLAMABAD MARRIOTT, Aga Khan Rd. Tel: 826121-35, Fax: (51) 820648, Tlx: 57405612 HIISD PK. *P, Gym, Biz, SatTV. R: L, W.*

B: US$50-100

HOLIDAY INN, Civic Centre. Tel: 827311-30, Fax: (51) 820763, Tlx: 5643 IHI PK. *Biz, SatTV. R: L, W.*
THE PRESIDENT, Blue Area. Tel: 819206, 819651-52, Fax: (51) 820457. *Biz, SatTV. R: L, W.*

KARACHI

A: US$100 and above

AVARI TOWERS RAMADA RENAISSANCE, Fatima Jinnah Rd. Tel: 525261-80, Fax: (21) 510310, Tlx: 24400 AVARI PK. *P, Gym, Biz, Ex, SatTV. R: L, W.*
KARACHI MARRIOTT, Abdullah Harroon Rd. Tel: 568 2011-25, 568 0111-25, Fax: (21) 568 1610, Tlx: 25466, 28035 HIK PK. *P, Gym, Biz, Ex, SatTV. R: L, W.*
PEARL CONTINENTAL, Club Rd. Tel: 568 5021-70, Fax: (21) 568 1835, 568 2655, Tlx: 23617 PEARL PK. *P, Gym, Biz, Ex, SatTV. R: L, W.*
SHERATON, Club Rd. Tel: 521021-60, Fax: (21) 512875, Tlx: 25255 ASHER PK. *P, Gym, Biz, Ex, SatTV. R: L, W.*
TAJ MAHAL, Shahrah-e-Faisal. Tel: 520211-20, Fax: (21) 568 3146, Tlx: 24267 TAJ PK. *P, Gym, Biz, SatTV. R: L, W.*

B: US$50-100

METROPOLE, Club Rd. Tel: 512061-70, Fax: (21) 668 4301, Tlx: 24329 MTRO PK. *Biz, SatTV. R: L, W.*

LAHORE

A: US$100 and above

AVARI LAHORE RAMADA RENAISSANCE, Shahrah-e-Quaid-e-Azam. Tel: 365366-86, Fax: (42) 365367, 368694, Tlx: 44678 AVARI PK. *P, Gym, Biz, Ex, SatTV. R: L, W.*
PEARL CONTINENTAL, Shahrah-e-Quaid-e-Azam. Tel: 360210-14, 360140-49, Fax: (42) 362760, Tlx: 44877 44167 PEARL PK. *P, Gym, Biz, Ex, SatTV. R: L, W.*

B: US$50-100

FALETTIS, Egerton Rd. Tel: 363946-55, Tlx: 44469 FLH PK. *Biz. R: L, W.*
SERVICES INTERNATIONAL, Shahrah-e-Quaid-e-Azam. Tel: 870281-87, 877011-12, Fax: (42) 872363, Tlx: 44230 SINTL PK. *P, Biz, SatTV. R: L, W.*
SHALIMAR, Liberty Market, Gulberg. Tel: 870331-33, Fax: (42) 872800. *Biz, SatTV. R: L.*

MURREE

A: US$100 and above

PEARL CONTINENTAL, Bhurban. Tel: 427082, Fax: (593) 427081. *P, Gym, Biz, Ex, SatTV. R: L, W.*

PESHAWAR

A: US$100 and above

PEARL CONTINENTAL, Khyber Rd. Tel: 276361-9, 271091-4, Fax: (521) 276465, Tlx: 52309 52389 PEARL PK. *P, Gym, Biz, Ex, SatTV. R: L, W.*

QUETTA

A: US$100 and above

QUETTA SERENA, Shahrah-e-Zarghoon. Tel: 70071-100, Fax: (81) 70070, Tlx: 78221 SERENA PK. *P, Gym, Biz, Ex, SatTV. R: L, W.*

RAWALPINDI

A: US$100 and above

PEARL CONTINENTAL, The Mall. Tel: 566011-20, Fax: (51) 563927, Tlx: 5735 54063 PEARL PK. *P, Gym, Biz, Ex, SatTV. R: L, W.*

B: US$50-100

FLASHMAN'S, The Mall. Tel: 581480-86, Fax: (51) 563294, Tlx: 5620 FH PK. *P. R: L, W.*
SHALIMAR, Off-The-Mall. Tel: 562901-10, Fax: (51) 566061, Tlx: 5764 SHLMR. *P, Biz, SatTV. R: L, W.*

P — Swimming pool
SatTV — Satellite TV
Gym — Health club
R — Restaurant
Biz — Business centre
L — Local food
Ex — Executive floor
W — Western food

8
7
6

SRI LANKA

The tropical island of Sri Lanka, suspended like a teardrop at the foot of the Indian Subcontinent, is one of the delights of Asia. Rich in natural beauty and ancient and living culture, it offers the visitor a panorama of delights.

These include 11th century cities and statuary, important religious shrines and festivals, reminders of the gracious aspect of the Raj. All these are set amid natural beauty which stretches from the cool tea plantations in the central highlands down to white-sand beaches and beyond to a treasure trove of coral reefs and tropical fish.

The fact that Sri Lanka has lagged behind many Asian countries as a tourist destination in recent years is due largely to the bloody civil unrest which has affected many parts of the island for the past 25 years.

But the government of President Chandrika Bandaranaike Kumaratunga, elected in November 1994, managed to bring about a ceasefire with the separatist Tamil Tigers in their stronghold of Jaffna in the north of the country. This has resulted in hopes of a settlement and much improved security, including the reopening to visitors of the east-coast port of Trincomalee. It has also brought an upswing in tourists — back to the 400,000 mark in 1994 for the first time in more than a decade.

The country now faces the need for more and better facilities if it is to cope with returning demand. Already there are shortages of rooms in the peak months of January, February and March — the European winter seasons — and in July or August during the dazzling world-famous *Esala Perahera* festival in the old hill capital of Kandy.

Sri Lanka boasts an almost perfect tropical climate, with daytime temperatures rarely falling below 27°C and rarely rising above 32°C. The two monsoon rains, which keep the country verdant and productive, fall on the western and southern sides of the island in May to July and on the north and east between December and January.

Measuring 436 kilometres from north to south and 225 kilometres from east to west at its widest, the island is large enough for its diversity but small enough for the visitor to cover during a short trip.

Despite the years of ethnic tension, the visitor will get a friendly welcome from all Sri Lankans, many of whom speak English. The majority of people — some 74% — are Sinhalese. Tamils make up just over 18% of the population and Muslims 7%. About 69% are Buddhist, 15% Hindu, and Muslims and Christians each make up about 7%.

History

The history of Sri Lanka recedes into legend. Some of the earliest references to the island were made in the Indian epic Ramayana, which describes how the hero, Rama, conquered most of the island while rescuing his wife Sita, who had been abducted by Ravana, king of Lanka.

From then on, the history of Sri Lanka revolves around the island's struggle with invaders, most of whom came from neighbouring India and from Europe (starting around the 15th century). All of them left their mark on the contemporary make-up of the nation, its people and their beliefs.

The arrival of the North Indian Prince Vijaya

◄ *Buddhist festival art on show.* PHOTO: HAMISH McDONALD

in Lanka established the Sinhala race here, the first people to develop a permanent agrarian-based industry. Of the original settlements, Anuradhapura grew into a powerful kingdom under the rule of King Pandukabhava and became the governing seat of Lanka for many centuries. In 247 BC the Arahat Mahinda, a disciple of the Lord Buddha and son of Emperor Ashoka of India, visited Anuradhapura with an entourage of monks, effectively opening the doors to the Buddhist philosophy.

The island was partitioned from time to time by the rule of invading forces, but there were also periods when a Sinhala king emerged to defeat invaders and rule all Lanka under one banner. King Parakramabahu, who united the country in 1155, made the country militarily strong and economically prosperous.

Among the European powers that conquered parts of the island were the Portuguese (in the 16th century), the Dutch (in the 17th century) and the British. In 1815 the British succeeded in taking the last Inhala Kingdom on the island at Kandy. They named it Ceylon and ruled until 1948, when it won independence. Since independence, two principal parties have shared power in Sri Lanka — the United National Party and the Sri Lanka Freedom Party — with two other minor parties contesting elections. During this time the electorate brought into power and subsequently removed Sirimavo Bandaranaike, the world's first woman prime minister.

The country experienced its first major disturbance of recent times in 1971, when radical insurgents rose against the government. The revolt caused much damage and loss of life, though the full death toll is unknown.

In July 1983 unprecedented communal violence broke out, mainly directed against Tamils living outside predominantly Tamil areas. This led to demands for a separate Tamil state, backed by a virtual civil war waged by the Liberation Tigers of Tamil Eeelam. At the invitation of President J.R. Jayewardene, India sent a Peacekeeping Force to the island in 1987, but it withdrew at his request two years later after suffering more than 1,500 fatal casualties.

Jayewardene's successor, Ranasinghe Premadasa, was assassinated in May 1993 and Mrs. Chandrika Bandaranaike Kumaratunga — whose father and husband had both been victims of political killings — was elected prime minister and then president in 1994, on a platform including peace with the Tamils, which brought about a ceasefire.

Entry

AIR: Most visitors to Sri Lanka arrive by air at Colombo International Airport at Katunayake, 32 kilometres northwest of the city. About 15 international airlines are operating flights in and out of Colombo. Air Lanka, Sri Lanka's national carrier, handles the bulk of the inbound and outbound traffic. About 90% of the inbound visitors are tourists, while approximately 8% are travelling on business.

SEA: A few visitors still arrive by sea, via the Colombo Harbour, which, since 1977, has developed into one of Asia's finest port services.

The island has two other harbours — at Trincomalee in the northeast and at Galle in the south, both of which function as cargo inlets. The harbour at Trincomalee was naturally formed and is reported to be one of the deepest in the world.

Immigration

Visitors to Sri Lanka must possess a valid passport. You do not need a visa to visit Sri Lanka if you are a citizen of one of the following lands: Britain and its colonies, Australia, Austria, Belgium, Bangladesh, Canada, Denmark, Finland, France, Germany, Indonesia, Ireland, Italy, Japan, Luxembourg, Malaysia, the Netherlands, New Zealand, Norway, Pakistan, Philippines, Singapore, Sweden, Switzerland, Thailand, Yugoslavia, United States, South Korea, Saudi Arabia, Oman, Bahrain, Qatar, United Arab Emirates, Kuwait, Spain and the Maldives. If you fall into the above category, you can stay as a tourist for one month, provided you have onward tickets or can prove you have the means for an onward journey.

When you enter Sri Lanka, you will be required to fill in and turn in an immigration landing card. The immigration officer will detach and retain Part I. You will need to hold on to Part II and surrender it to an immigration officer on departure.

Travellers in transit may arrange to see parts of the island and visit places of interest. Contact information counters at Colombo International Airport for assistance.

Travel within Sri Lanka is unrestricted except that there is no access to the Tamil stronghold in the Jaffna peninsula in the extreme north, and access to Trincomalee by road is limited to daylight hours.

SRI LANKA
km
0
50
Roads
Railways
Airports
INDIA
Palk Strait
Jaffna
Bay of Bengal
Talaimannar
Ferry
Mannar
Gulf of Mannar
Medawachchiya
Trincomalee
Anuradhapura
Wilpattu National Park
Puttalam
Sigiriya
Polonnaruwa
Batticaloa
Matale
Kurunegala
Gal Oya National Park
Kandy
Negombo
Kegalla
Nuwara Eliya
Badulla
Colombo
Dehiwala
Mt Lavinia
Belihul Oya
Pottuvil
Panadura
Haputale
Wellawaya
Ratnapura
Okanda
Kalutara
Beruwala
Ruhunu National Park
Bentota
Tissamaharama
Yala
Hikkaduwa
Hambantota
Galle
Tangalla
Matara

Monks head for evening prayers. PHOTO: ELLEN RUDOLPH

Health

You will need a certificate of inoculation against yellow fever if you are arriving from an infected area.

Customs

You may bring an unlimited amount of foreign currency into Sri Lanka, except for Indian and Pakistani rupees, which are restricted to a maximum of Rs 250 per person.

You must declare on the "D" form the amount of currency you are bringing into the country. Keep this form; you will be required to show it when you leave. You may take out the equivalent of the amount you declare (or goods to the equivalent), but not more, when you leave.

Visitors are allowed to bring in duty free up to 340 grams of tobacco, or 200 cigarettes or 50 cigars, 1.5 litres of spirits and two bottles of wine, 57 millilitres of perfume and 25 millilitres of toilet water. You may also bring in two cameras and portable tape recorder, typewriter and other equipment for personal use.

You may bring in items of high value duty free as long as you declare them and the Collector of Customs is satisfied that you intend to bring them out again when you leave.

Visitors may not take antiques (any item more than 50 years old) out of Sri Lanka. You should check with the Director of National Archives and the Archaeological Commissioner before buying old statues, ornaments, furniture, palm leaf manuscripts and the like.

You may bring out Sri Lanka gems — including sapphires, rubies and cat's-eyes — of any value, as long as you have declared sufficient currency when you entered and can show receipts from the purchases. You may also take out duty free up to three kilograms of Sri Lankan tea.

You will have to pay a departure tax of Rs 500 at the airport when you leave the country.

Currency

The Sri Lankan rupee is the national currency. A rupee consists of 100 cents. Notes are available in denominations of Rs 10, 20, 50, 100, 500 and 1,000. Coins of 10, 25, 50, 100, 200 and 500 cents are in circulation.

As of April 1995, the exchange rate for the Sri Lankan rupee was Rs 48.15:US$1.

The Central Bank of Sri Lanka fixes the daily exchange rate for telegraphic transfers. The rate for travellers' cheques is 5-10% better than the rate for currency.

To get the best rates, exchange your money at banks. Most hotels are authorized money-changers, but they give a poorer rate of exchange. International credit cards are accepted at most hotels, but not at all restaurants, so check when you enter.

Keep all your foreign-exchange vouchers and receipts, from banks or hotels. You will need to show them if you want to reconvert rupees on your way out of Sri Lanka. You may not bring out more than US$25 worth of rupees out of the country.

Language

Sinhala, the mother tongue of 74% of the population, is the most widely spoken language. Both Sinhala and Tamil, which is predominant in the north and east, enjoy the joint status of official languages. English is used as a link language; about half the population speaks English, while many more understand it but are not fluent in conversation. Street signs, shop boards, product names and the like are generally in all three languages.

Climate

Sri Lanka is a tropical island; most of the country's weather hovers around 27°C and rarely rises above 32°C. The central region is hilly and cooler, with average temperatures ranging around 16°C. Temperatures in the mountainous areas of the interior, which rise up to 2,400 metres above sea level, range around 10°C, occasionally dropping to freezing point for a few hours.

The overall climate is generally hot and humid during the day and cooler in the evenings. Early mornings and late afternoons are ideal times for outdoor exercise and sightseeing. The southwest monsoon brings rain to the western, southern and central regions from May to July, while the northeastern monsoon occurs in the north and east in December and January.

Dress

Light cotton-wear is best for coastal areas, while a light jacket or sweater is advisable for the cooler evenings in the hill country. Slacks, sports shirts and shoes (casual dresses and skirts for women) will fit almost any occasion. Coats and ties and business suits or dress are not usually required in restaurants and other places, except for formal functions. For business calls, a shirt and tie are acceptable.

If you intend to spend long hours outdoors, bring a wide-brimmed hat and sunglasses for protection from the sun. When visiting temples and other places of worship, you will be required to remove your shoes and hat and be decently clad; it is a good idea to have a pair of slip-on shoes handy and women should wear a skirt.

All the hotels provide laundry services and all cities and towns advertise such services, but they are much cheaper outside hotels. It may be difficult to find same-day or 24-hour service outside hotels. Inquire at your hotel or ask a taxi driver.

Business Hours

Sri Lanka has a five-day working week, Monday to Friday. Government offices, private businesses, schools and all other services all operate on this schedule.

Most department stores, shops, supermarkets, pharmacies and similar businesses open at 9-10 a.m. Some department stores close at 6 p.m., while supermarkets are open until 9 p.m. There are all-night dispensaries for medicines — ask your hotel or a taxi diver for guidance. Most petrol stations open at 7-8 a.m. and close at 9 p.m., but some stay open round the clock.

Government offices open at 8:30 a.m. and close at 4:30 p.m., while post offices open 8:30 a.m.-5 p.m. daily and on Saturdays at 8:30 a.m.-noon. Banks are open 9 a.m.-1 p.m. on Mondays and 9 a.m.-1:30 p.m Tuesday-Friday.

The General Post Office in Colombo Fort and several privately run post offices are open 24 hours a day, seven days a week, and offer all postal and telecommunication facilities, including international telephone calls, faxes and telexes. Card-operated pay phones in Colombo are cheaper for local and international calls. Phone cards are sold in many places.

Most shops in the cities pull down their shutters by 8 p.m. — and earlier in rural areas. Restaurants are open for lunch and in the evening from 7 p.m. until midnight. Breakfast can be had in many eating houses. Round-the-clock services are available in all the five-star hotels and most of the smaller hotels that cater to tourists.

Sri Lankans also enjoy a variety of public and bank holidays (approximately 30 such days during a year) and tourists are advised to check the local calendar before making important appointments. In keeping with traditional

Buddhist customs, every full-moon day of the lunar calendar is observed as a public holiday.

Doing Business

Most local businessmen and entrepreneurs are educated and have been exposed to the West, so Western ways of doing business are widely accepted. Women are accepted and respected in business circles.

Do not arrive early to a business meeting, since you will only waste your time waiting for others. Promptness counts, but a late arrival of 15 minutes acceptable if an apology is given. Strong handshakes are preferred. Sri Lankans exchange business cards, so do not forget to bring yours. Exchanging gifts during visits is considered a sign of friendship. Foreign liquors, chocolates, ties and books are considered suitable gifts.

Long-sleeved shirts and ties are the norm for men at business meetings. Women should wear a two- or three-piece business outfit. Jackets are necessary for formal calls on VIPs.

Evening cocktails are casual in dress, unless otherwise stated. Buy a typical Sri Lankan shirt and impress your host or hostess. If you are going to a Sri Lankan home, there is no need to remove your shoes when entering. Smoke only if others do or with permission of your host. Sri Lankans toast with a "cheers" and it is acceptable to take more than one drink in the evening.

The conversation at cocktail parties is liable to cover government and politics at some point, so learn at least some basic details about the country and its leaders.

Rip-Offs

Touts are everywhere and you should not be fooled by smart dress and a good command of English. Try to deal only with people who have been recommended by someone reliable. Seek advice from your hotel or local contacts before committing yourself to almost anything — from hiring a taxi to buying lace, crafts or gems.

You have to be prepared to be tough on beggars, who are encountered mostly in Colombo, and also the strangers who attach themselves to you with all sorts of stories from the plausible to the absurd if you walk about in the city.

Beware of snake charmers, who may offer to be photographed and then demand a large fee. The same can happen elsewhere, for instance with the famous stilt fishermen along the southern coast.

In general, be on your guard. There is very little violence against foreigners, and if you get robbed or cheated it will almost certainly be because you were careless or gullible.

If you pay far too much for any goods you buy in Sri Lanka, it will almost certainly be because you failed to bargain down to a fair price. Ask expert opinion and do not give way on a price you believe is right.

Media

There are several English-language newspapers of good standard, both in terms of coverage and presentation. *The Daily News* and *The Island* are the only local English-language morning newspapers available. *The Observer* is the one local, evening English newspaper. There are four Sunday papers: *The Sunday Observer*, *The Sunday Times, The Sunday Leader* and *The Sunday Island*. You can get them all at newsstands and hotels in most places.

You can buy foreign newspapers — *The International Herald Tribune, Asian Wall Street Journal, USA Today, Gulf News* and *The Hindu* — at the **Vijitha Yapa Bookshop** (163A, Galle Rd, Colombo 4, Tel: 583505). You can also buy other foreign news magazines — such as *Time*, *Newsweek, Forbes* and others.

All five-star hotels have CNN on cable. There are five local TV networks. All carry programmes in English, Sinhala and Tamil. These networks also carry CNN and BBC news.

Communications

International Direct Dialling (IDD) services are available from all parts of the island. Privately operated post offices offer reliable telephone and fax services. Two companies in Colombo — **DataNet** and **Electrotech** — provide local and international data transmission services. Contact them through your hotel.

Three cellular mobile telephone companies — **Celtell**, **Mobitel** and **Call Link** — provide reliable service, for overseas calls and local ones limited to a radius of about 50 kilometres from Colombo. Celtell has a convenient counter at the Colombo International Airport, where visiting foreign businessmen can rent a phone upon arrival and return it when leaving.

Should you need to send an urgent telegram, contact the **Central Telegraph Office** (Duke

St, Colombo 1, Tel: 24340, 27167, 27187, 25799).

About 12 international courier services operate in Sri Lanka, providing reliable overseas and local delivery services. Among them are: **Federal Express**, **DHL**, **UPS**, **TNT Skypack** and **Airborne Express**. They are all listed in the local Yellow pages.

Almost all hotels in Colombo provide secretarial services by professional English-speaking secretaries. Contact the business centre of your hotel.

Transport

FROM THE AIRPORT: The distance to downtown Colombo from the International Airport is 32 kilometres, or 45 minutes by road. Approved agents provide a reliable and comfortable taxi service from the airport to Colombo at Rs 800-900. Inquire at airport information counters.

TAXIS: Taxi services are available only in Colombo and a few of the bigger cities. You can order air-conditioned radio taxi cabs in Colombo by calling the agents; see the Yellow Pages for details. Their minimum rate is Rs 28 per kilometre. Taxis may be hailed outside hotels, along the roads or at central locations such as the **Colombo Fort railway station**. Meters in these taxis are often broken, defective or rigged, so try to negotiate a price before your trip begins.

A ride on an auto-rickshaw is a treat and a convenient way of getting about town. The minimum rate is about Rs 25 per kilometre. It is common to bargain for the fare, but do so at the beginning of your journey.

BUSES: Sri Lanka's island-wide bus network, maintained by a combination of semi-government and private companies, is considered one of the most comprehensive and least expensive bus services in the world. Buses are very crowded much of the time and particularly during rush hour. Express bus services operate between major towns. Buses leave every hour for many destinations from the **Central Bus Station** in Colombo's Pettah area. Privately operated minibuses also ply the roads on most of the routes at a slightly higher fare than those of the government buses.

While travelling on public transport, keep your money in a safe place. Pickpockets often operate in buses and trains.

TRAINS: Trains run from the Colombo Fort station to many places of interest. Trains, too, are very crowded during rush hour, but you may reserve seats in advance for long-distance travel to the hill country, the north or down south, via the Colombo Fort station. First-class carriages with air-conditioning, sleeping berths and observation cars also are available. For those willing to meet locals and mingle with the ordinary people, a trip by train can be a pleasant experience. A luxury Hitachi tourist train, a modified steam train (the Viceroy Special) and a luxury rail car run along the southern line. For information on train travel, contact the **Railway Tourist Information Centre** (Fort railway station, Colombo 1, Tel: 435838).

INLAND AIR TRANSPORT: The Sri Lanka Air Force operates commercial flights between Colombo and Jaffna, Trincomalee, Ampara, Batticaloa and Vavuniya. Some air force aircraft and helicopters are listed for charter; their availability may be restricted, however, due to military operations in the north and east. Several private companies offer air travel (helicopters and small aircraft) to any part of the island. These advertise through hotels and travel agents. Rates are negotiable, depending upon the number of passengers. A helicopter shuttle service ferries passengers from the international airport to resorts in the south and to other day-trip destinations.

CAR RENTAL: Cars with drivers — who double as guides — are easily available for a day or for longer trips outside Colombo. Most cars will not be air-conditioned and often are far from new, but the driving standard is good. Rates are around Rs 25 per kilometre, and some companies offer large discounts on return journeys up to 45%. A 100-kilometre journey should only cost about US$50. Take the advice of the hotel travel desk and make sure you negotiate clearly before starting. If you are planning a trip of several days outside Colombo, it is a good idea to agree on one stage only at first. If you like the driver, ask him to pick you up for the second stage. Otherwise hire another one.

Self-drive cars are also available from **Hertz**, **Avis**, **Europcar** and other companies which are listed in the Yellow Pages. Driving is on the left-hand side of the road. Main roads are generally in good condition though some are more pot-holed than others.

Motorcyles are also available and are becoming popular with younger European and Japanese visitors. They can be hired from several companies, including **Gold Wings Pleasure Rides** at 346, Dean's Rd, Colombo 10.

If you are planning to drive yourself, try to

obtain a road map before arriving in Sri Lanka, because they are often scarce in Colombo. One good map, published by the Survey Department, can be obtained, if in stock, from the **Windsor Bookshop**, 372, Galle Rd, Wellawatta, Colombo 6.

Most people you meet while travelling are friendly, speak good or passable English and will be helpful with directions.

For information on driving in Sri Lanka, contact the **Automobile Association of Ceylon**, 40 Sir Macan Markar Mawatha, Galle Face, Colombo 3, Tel: 421528.

Tours

Tours of Colombo city by day and night, boat cruises on the Indian Ocean and guided bus tours to places of interest in the outstations originate from the capital every day. Local travel agents will arrange a tour for you.

Tourists visiting and photographing the ancient monuments must get a ticket from the Cultural Triangle Office, Ministry of Cultural Affairs (221 Bauddhaloka Ave, Colombo 7, Tel: 587912). It is a good idea to buy a single round-trip ticket for one month (US$30 per adult and half that rate per child). This will permit you to view and photograph monuments in all parts of Sri Lanka where photography is permitted without having to pay at each site upon entry.

Accommodation

Sri Lanka offers a very large range of accommodation from international standard hotels in Colombo, Kandy and the more popular beach resorts — the top ones charging as much as US$160 a night — right down to simple guests houses asking as little as US$8 for a double room. All hotel prices are subject to an additional 10% service charge and 5% tax.

Be warned that with the increase in tourist arrivals, thanks to the improved security situation, rooms in the better hotels are becoming scarce in January, February and March and again during the July or August Esala Perahera festival in Kandy.

An invaluable publication for all (except package tourists whose accommodation is arranged) is the *Accommodation Guide* published by the Ceylon Tourist Board, available at Colombo airport or through tourist board or diplomatic offices worldwide. One can write for a copy to **Travel Information Centre**, 78 Steuart Place, Colombo 3, Tel: 437059-60.

All the establishments listed in the Tourist Board guide have been inspected and found suitable for tourists, and this helps keep up the standards of even the simplest establishment.

While Sri Lankans tend to be proudest of their modern hotels, which include the **Ceylon Intercontinental**, the **Lanka Oberoi**, **Colombo Renaissance**, **Taj Samudra**, **Galadari** and **Colombo Hilton**, among the great attractions are many fine survivors from the period of the Raj. Pre-eminent among these is the **Galle Face**, on the Colombo seafront, which has been open since 1864.

Dining

Sri Lankan food is spicy, colourful and a treat for the adventurous palate. Rice and curry are the staples of the local diet. Meals usually consist of a large plate of rice, accompanied by five or six savoury meat, fish and vegetable curries.

Sri Lankan curries consist of a ground chili and coconut milk base, mixed with a variety of fresh spices, cooked well and served hot. Since any food can be prepared with a curry sauce and each curry tastes different, there is an endless diversity.

Restaurants that cater to foreign tourists prepare tamer curries in keeping with the sensitive palates and digestive systems of Westerners. For a true taste of Sri Lanka you must venture out and experience a real rice and curry meal, though you may need a big glass of water, or better still, some ripe bananas, to cool off from the hot spices.

Egg-hoppers and string-hoppers are two typically Lankan dishes you should try. The first is a thin, crisp, bowl-shaped pancake made of rice flour with an egg baked on top. It is eaten with curry or *sambol*. You can also order hoppers without eggs and eat them crisp and hot, straight from the pan, with curry or jam and butter. String-hoppers are nests of thin rice noodles; steamed and lighter than rice, they are popular on dinner and breakfast tables and go well with *kiri-hodi*, a very mild coconut milk gravy. Other tasty and uniquely Lankan foods are *pittu*, *roti*, *kiri-bath* (milk rice), *achchar* (pickled onions and green chilies), breadfruit and a variety of local yams.

Sri Lanka has an abundance of fresh fruit, available at every street corner at reasonable prices. Savour a fresh pineapple, mango or an avocado. There are hundreds of other varieties of exotic fruits, including rambutan, mango-

Colombo street scene. PHOTO: GAVIN GREENWOOD

steen, durian and close to 50 varieties of bananas.

On a hot day, you may want to take part in another pleasant Sri Lankan experience — drinking a king coconut. These orange-coloured coconuts are sold at roadside stands. Drink the sweet coconut water as locals do, by making a hole in the fruit, tilting your head back and placing the hole directly over your mouth.

Wayside restaurants may not be up to standard, though most of them will dish out tasty food at reasonable prices. Local restaurants will not automatically provide cutlery, since the local customs is to eat with the hands, but you can request cutlery if you feel you need it.

Most of the larger cities have restaurants that serve Western meals on request. Colombo has many fine ethnic restaurants, including establishments that specialize in Chinese, German, French, Indian, Moghul, Italian, Japanese, Korean and Mexican cuisines.

All the five-star hotels have restaurants, bars, nightclubs and coffee shops open round the clock. Most bars serve foreign liquor, though it is expensive. Among the locally produced liquors are coconut arrack, rum, gin, brandy and beer. Established restaurants add a 10% service charge to the bill, but most local eateries are so casual they may not even give you a formal bill.

Entertainment

Most big hotels have floor shows and provide excellent music for dancing late into the night. The five-star hotels also offer karaoke. Among the better known and lively night spots are: **the Supper Club** at the Hotel Lanka Oberoi (for an elegant dinner and dancing to band music); **the Colombo 2000** at the Galadari Hotel; the **Blue Elephant** at the Hilton; **My Kind of Place** at the Taj; and the **Little Hut** at Mount Lavinia Hotel. These offer lively crowds and a nice mixture of live and DJ music. Up in the hills, **Hotel Suisse** in Kandy is promoting Country and Western music.

English and Sinhala language plays and Sinhala translations of Western plays are staged frequently in Colombo. Popular theatres are: **The Lionel Wendt Theatre** (Guildford Crescent, Colombo 7); **YMBA** (Borella, Colombo 8); **Tower Hall** (Maraddana, Colombo 10); and **John de Silva Memorial Theatre** (Ananda Coomarawamy Rd, Colombo 7).

In the resort areas, especially during the tourist season, there are organized outdoor cultural performances, which include traditional dances from ancient times.

Colombo has several excellent, air-conditioned cinemas that screen British,

American and Hindi films. Check morning newspapers for current attractions.

Shopping

Gems and precious stones are Sri Lanka's most celebrated products, but shoppers will also find a wide range of exotic and interesting items for sale, including ceramics, batiks, brassware, caneware, leather products and ready-made garments. Most of the bigger hotels have their own shopping arcades, but for the real bargains, you should walk about town.

Galle Rd, which runs along the coastline, is a busy shopping district. There you will find **Unity Plaza**, **Majestic City**, **Lucky Plaza** and the **Galle Face Shopping Arcade** at the Galle Face Hotel. There are several other shopping centres, including **World Market** in Pettah, **Liberty Plaza** (Duplication Rd, Colombo 3) and **Cornels Supermarkets** (in Colombo 4, 5 and 6).

Shoppers will find the following places attractive: **Laksala** (York St, Colombo 1); **Lakmedura** (26 Rotunda Gardens, Colombo 3); **Lakpahana** (Colombo 3); **Dankotuwa Porcelain** (Laklain Showrooms, 293 Galle Rd, Colombo 3); **Lanka Ceramic Showroom** (Galle Rd); **Salu Sala** (Vilasitha Niwasa, Havelock Rd, Colombo 5); **Viskam Nivasa** (Thunmulla Junction, Colombo 5); **Mariposa** (61 Dharmapala Mawatha, Colombo 7); and **Arcadia** (450 Galle Rd, Colombo 3).

Visitors can buy blue sapphires, cat's-eyes, rubies, amethysts and other jewels for personal use and take them out of the country duty free. Keep your receipts to show to customs on departure. There are no limits on the value of the gems you can take out, as long as you can show (by your currency declaration form) that you brought in enough money to cover the purchase.

The reputable private gem dealers in Colombo are listed in the numerous shopping guides issued free of charge by the trade. Legitimate dealers will issue guarantees for stones.

The **State Gem Corp.** guarantees the stones it sells and also tests all outside purchases free of charge at its commercial branch office (York St in the Colombo Fort, Tel: 23075). The corporation also provides valuable information on Sri Lanka's gems at its headquarters (25 Galle Face Terrace, Colombo 3, Tel: 29295).

The Colombo International Airport offers duty-free shopping. Although the range of goods is wide, the prices here are not as low as in Dubai. Purchases must be made in foreign currency. You can buy gold at the airport at a facility run by the Central Bank.

Sports

WATER SPORTS: These are Sri Lanka's major sports attractions, for obvious reasons. All the resort areas offer professional lessons and equipment for yachting, canoeing, deep-sea fishing, diving, snorkelling, skiing, surfing and wind surfing, among others. Serious fishermen should contact the **Ceylon Anglers Club** in Colombo (Tel: 421752). For fishing in inland lakes, contact the **Department of Wildlife Conservation**.

GOLF: There are two excellent 18-hole golf courses in Sri Lanka — one in Colombo and the other in Nuwara Eliya.

OTHER SPORTS: Tennis, squash and fitness programmes are available at the leading hotels. Sri Lanka is a cricket-mad country. On any given day, visitors can watch at most of the city cricket grounds. Rugby is also popular from May to September.

Holidays

Most of Sri Lanka's festivals, which date back many centuries, were born of the religious, superstitious and agricultural traditions that have persisted through the years. All four of the country's major religious traditions — Buddhism, Christianity, Hinduism and Islam — feature prominently in the Sri Lankan holiday calendar. Similarly, all the major communities that inhabit the island — the Sinhalese, Tamils, Muslims and Burghers — are included in national holidays.

Sri Lankans observe the major festivals, as well as the full-moon (*poya*) days, as public holidays. All places of entertainment are closed and no liquor is sold on those days. In most cases, visitors are encouraged to participate in the functions and events that mark the festivities. Here is a brief sample of the festival calendar:

January: *Duruthu Perahera* — this colourful festival, which falls on the full-moon, includes a procession of elephants and lights originating from the Kelaniva Temple in the outskirts of Colombo. Tamils celebrate *Thai Pongal* day during this month.

February 4: Independence Day — Lankans celebrate with parades and cultural shows, mostly in Colombo. *Navam Perahera* (full-moon

Beach hawkers near Colombo. ►

427 recorded species — 242 species of butterflies and many reptiles, including small crocodiles, tortoise and turtles. It is also rich in plant life, of which several endangered species, including Baobab trees and six types of orchids, are protected by law. Production, sale and possession of articles made from wild animals and reptiles or such items as leopard and crocodile skins and elephant tusks, is illegal.

The best place to see wildlife is at the **Ruhuna National Park** at Yala, 300 kilometres southwest of Colombo, and the best times of year are between December and May. Visitors can stay overnight at this and other national parks in bungalows maintained by the Department of Wild Life Conservation. These are rustic buildings catering to the hardy enthusiast and offer only the basics. They are in heavy demand and reservations should be made well in advance with the **Department of Wild Life and Conservation**, 54 Chatham St, Colombo, Tel: 24208.

RESTAURANT SELECTION

Average price for two

ALT HEIDELBERG, 11 Galle Face Court, Colombo 3. Tel: 421577. German. Rs 1,000.
ARI RANG, 16 Abdul Gafoor Mawatha, Colombo 3. Tel: 575186. Chinese. Rs 800.
CALIFORNIA GRILL, Galadari Hotel. Tel: 544544. European. Lunch Rs 1,000, dinner Rs 2,000.
CHESA SWISS, 3 Deal Place, Colombo 3. Tel: 573433. Swiss. Rs 2,000.
DON STANLEY'S 69, Alexandra Place, Colombo 7. Tel: 686486. Rather formal European-style. Rs 1,900.
FLOWER LOUNGE, 18 Bagatelle Rd, Colombo 3. Tel: 582038, 593032. Chinese. Rs 1,300.
FLOWER DRUM, 26 Thurston Rd, Colombo 3. Tel: 574216. Chinese. Rs 1,100.
GABLES, Colombo Hilton. Tel: 544644. European. Rs 3,000.
GINZA HOSHEN, Colombo Hilton. Tel: 544644, ext. 2123. Japanese. Rs 1,800.
GOLDEN DRAGON, Taj Samudra Hotel. Tel: 446622, ext. 2644. Chinese. Rs 1,500.
GREEN CABIN, 453 Galle Rd, Colombo 3. Tel: 591841, 588811. Sri Lankan. Rs 300.
HAKATA, 110 Havelock Rd, Colombo 5. Tel: 501397. Japanese. Rs 1,050.
HAN GOOK GWAN, 25 Havelock Rd, Colombo 5. Tel: 587961. Korean. Rs 950.
IBN BATUTA, Colombo Renaissance. Tel: 544200, ext. 1948. Sri Lankan. Rs 750.
IL PONTA RISTORANTE, Colombo Hilton. Tel: 544644. Italian. Rs 1,500.
JADE GARDENS, 126 Havelock Rd, Colombo 5. Tel: 580678. Chinese. Rs 1,000.
JAPAN DOLL, 32 Sir Mohamed Marcan Markar Mawatha, Colombo 3. Tel: 446589. Japanese. Rs 1,200.
KOLIO, 383 R.A. De Mel Mawatha, Colombo 3. Tel: 574930. Korean, Chinese. Rs 960.
LONDON GRILL, Oberoi Hotel. Tel: 421171. European. Rs 2,500.
LONG FENG, Colombo Renaissance Hotel. Tel: 544200, ext. 1949. Chinese. Rs 1,500.
NAVARATNA, Taj Samudra Hotel. Tel: 446622, ext. 2633. Indian. Rs 1,000.
NOBLESSE, Colombo Renaissance Hotel. Tel: 544200, ext. 1945. European. Rs 1,500.
PALMS SUPPER CLUB, Inter-Continental Hotel. Tel: 421221. European. Rs 1,500.
PALMYRAH RESTAURANT, 328 Galle Rd, Colombo 3. Tel: 573598. Sri Lankan. Rs 1,000.
PEARL SEAFOOD, Inter-Continental Hotel. Tel: 421221. Seafood. Rs 1,750-2,000.
PIZZA HUT, 321A Union Place, Colombo 2. Tel: 334760. Pizzas. Rs 700.
PIZZERIA, Intercontinental Hotel. Tel: 421221. Italian. Rs 650.
THE RENDEZVOUS, Taj Samudra Hotel. Tel: 446622, ext. 2643. French. Rs 1,300.
SAKURA, 14 Rheinland Place, Colombo 3. Tel: 573877. Japanese. Rs 1000.
SANTA FE, 53 Galle Rd, Colombo 3. Tel: 335644. Mexican. Rs 500.
SARAS, 450 Duplication Rd, Colombo 3. Tel: 575226. Indian. Rs 1,000.
SAWASDEE, 237 Galle Rd, Colombo 4. Tel: 508487. Thai. Rs 1,000.
SEA FISH, 15 Sir Chittapalam Gardiner Mawatha, Colombo 2. Tel: 326915. Seafood and Sri Lankan. Rs 750.
SHANTI VIHAR, 3 Havelock Rd, Colombo 5. Tel: 580224. Indian vegetarian. Rs 200.
SPICE MARKET, Galadari Hotel. Tel: 544544. Sri Lankan. Rs 1,250.
VERANDAH RESTAURANT, Galle Face Hotel. Tel: 541010. European. Rs 1,200.

HOTEL GUIDE

COLOMBO

A: US$90 and above

COLOMBO HILTON, Echelon Square, Colombo 1. Tel: 544644, Fax: 544657, Tlx: 22803 HILTON CE. *P, Gym, Biz, Ex, SatTV.*

COLOMBO RENAISSANCE HOTEL, 115 Sir Chittampalam Gardiner Mawatha, Colombo 2. Tel: 544200, Fax: 449184, Tlx: 22386 RAMADA CE. *P, Gym, Biz, Ex, SatTV.*

HOTEL CEYLON INTERCONTINENTAL, 48 Janadipathi Mawatha, Colombo 1. Tel: 421221, Fax: 447326, Tlx: 21188. *P, Gym, Biz, Ex, SatTV.*

HOTEL LANKA OBEROI, 77 Steuart Place, Colombo 3. Tel: 421221, Fax: 447326. *P, Gym, Biz, Ex, SatTV.*

B: US$60-90

AIRPORT GARDEN HOTEL, 238 Colombo Rd, Seeduwa. Tel: 452950, Fax: 452952, Tlx: 22430 AIRGAR CE. *P, Gym, Biz, SatTV.*

GALLE FACE HOTEL, Galle Face Court, Colombo 3. Tel: 541010, Fax: 541072, Tlx: 21281 GFH CE. *P.*

HOLIDAY INN COLOMBO, 30 Sir Mohamed Marcan Markar Mawatha, Colombo 3. Tel: 422001, Fax: 447977, Tlx: 21200 HOLINN CE. *P, Gym, SatTV. Secretarial services.*

GALADARI HOTEL, 64 Lotus Rd, Colombo 1. Tel: 544544, Fax: 449875, Tlx: 22334 GALMER CE. *P, Gym, Biz, Ex, SatTV.*

MT LAVINIA HOTEL, Mt Lavinia. Tel: 715221, Fax: 715228. *P, Gym, SatTV. Secretarial services.*

PEGASUS REEF HOTEL, P.O. Box 2. Wattala. 150 rooms. Tel: 530205. *P, Gym, Biz, SatTV.*

TAJ SAMUDRA HOTEL, 25 Galle Face Centre Rd, Colombo 3. Tel: 446622, Tlx: 21729 TAJLAN CE. *P, Gym, Biz, Ex, SatTV.*

C:US$20-60

GRAND ORIENTAL HOTEL, 2 York St, Colombo 1. Tel: 320391, Fax: 447670, Tlx: 21557 TAPRO CE.

HOTEL GALAXY, 388 Union Place, Colombo 2. 52 rooms. Tel: 696372, Tlx: 22325 GALAXY CE. *P, SatTV.*

HOTEL RENUKA, 328 Galle Rd, Colombo 3. Tel: 573598, Fax: 574137. *P.*

BEACH RESORTS

A: US$90 and above

TRITON HOTEL, Ahungalle. *P, Gym, SatTV. Heliport.*

B: US$60-90

BENTOTA BEACH HOTEL, Bentota. Tel: 0347 5266. *P, Gym. Heliport.*

C: US$20-60

BROWNS BEACH HOTEL, 175 Lewis Place, Negombo. Tel: 031 2031. *P, Gym.*

CORAL GARDENS HOTEL, Hikkaduwa. Tel: 092 3023. *P, Gym.*

HOTEL SINDBAD OF KALUTARA, Tel: 0342 2537. *P, Gym, SatTV.*

ROYAL OCEANIC HOTEL, Ethukala, Negombo. Tel: 031 3098, Fax: 314277. *P, Gym.*

KANDY

C: US$20-60

HOTEL SUISSE, Fax: 32083. *P, SatTV.*

HUNAS FALLS HOTEL, Kandy. Tel: (08) 73402-3. *P.*

QUEENS HOTEL, Kandy. Tel: (08) 33290.

NUWARA ELIYA

C: US$20-60

GRAND HOTEL, Nuwara Eliya. Tel: 052 2881-5.

SIGIRIYA

C: US$20-60

SIGIRIYA VILLAGE, Tel: 066 8216. *P.*

POLONNARUWA

C: US$20-60

ROYAL LOTUS HOTEL, Polonnaruwa. Tel: 027 6316. *P.*

P — Swimming pool **Gym** — Health club **Biz** — Business centre **Ex** — Executive floor
SatTV — Satellite TV

west coast for those prepared to make their own way. There are hundreds of kilometres of road round the eastern coast, with its gentle seas, beautiful beaches and many inlets and bays, but even the *Tourist Board Accommodation Guide* lists no hotels or guesthouses. Beds in private homes can be found, however, by those prepared to ask for them.

Only two hotels have been reopened so far in the once thriving **Trincomalee**, now declared safe from further insurrection, and there is a resort between **Kalkudah** and **Pasekudah**.

HILL COUNTRY

Kandy is the former capital of Sri Lanka and fell to the British with the capture of the last King, Sri Wickrema Rajasinghe, in 1815. Sitting in the central hills 488 metres above sea level, it has a refreshing atmosphere after the heat of the coast. It is a city of temples, and its main attraction is the wonderful golden **Dalada Maligawa** or **Temple of the Tooth**, at the edge of an artificial lake. The 16th century temple houses the **Sacred Tooth Relic** of the Buddha, brought to Sri Lanka in the fourth century AD. Two of the most important other religious buildings are the **Malwatte (Flower Garden) Monastery** and the **Asgiriya Temple**, but there are many more.

Kandy is most famous for the Esala Perahera festival. At the start of each year the temple authorities decide on the dates of the festival, either in July or August according to the moon — and hotels should be booked as soon as possible once the date is known. The brilliant festival, involving music, dancing and torchlight parades of richly decorated elephants, lasts for 10 day and nights, mounting to a rousing climax.

The other world-famous attraction of the hills are the tea plantations, and fascinating tours of tea factories are on offer at every station. The centre of the area is the town of **Nuwara Eliya**, 1,890 metres above sea level. Often shrouded in mist, temperatures here can really plunge and jackets and sweaters are necessary. The old colonial **Grand Hotel** is the usual stop, but even better for a glimpse of the past is the **Hill Club** (which sports an 18-hole golf course), not listed in hotel guides but with a limited number of rooms for passing guests.

Other attractions in the area are the **Nuwara Eliya botanical gardens**, the **Ramboda** and **Bambarakanda Falls**, terraced rice paddy fields and the grassy **Horton Plains**, which are particularly good for birdwatching.

Most rural towns lack hotels or restaurants but there are a number of government-approved resthouses in the hill country which offer simple but clean accommodation and/or meals. Rooms can be reserved through the Travel Bureau of the **Sri Lanka Hotels Corp.**, 63 Janadhipathi Mawatha, Colombo 1.

UPCOUNTRY ANCIENT CITIES

Sri Lanka's most famous ancient ruins at **Anuradhapura** and **Polonnaruwa** each require a long day trip from Colombo or Kandy. Alternatively, since neither of the towns has first-class accommodation, a good solution is to stay at either of the two hotels at **Sigiriya**, which lies between the two ancient sites.

Anuradhapura, some 200 kilometres from Colombo, was the capital of Sri Lanka for more than a thousand years, starting in the fifth century BC. The ruins include the third century BC **Thuparama Dagaba**, the second century BC **Ruvanveliseya** and the **Abhayagiri Dagaba** (the precincts of which are now being excavated in a special United Nations project).

Other wonders include the **Sri Maha Bodhi** (the oldest historically documented tree in the world) and 1,000-year-old irrigation reservoirs.

Polonnaruwa, some 100 kilometres south east of Anuradhapura, became the island's capital in the 11th century AD. The **Terrace of the Tooth Relic** is at the city's centre — where the relic was kept until its later removal to Kandy. In addition to many well-preserved buildings, the town contains the massive carved images of the Buddha at the **Gal Viharaya** — including a 14-metre reclining figure — carved out of the face of a granite cliff.

Other sites — in a rough circle all north of Kandy — include **Dambulla**, **Mihintale**, **Yapahuwa** and **Sigiriya**, famous for its sixth century AD murals of beautiful bare-breasted women.

WILDLIFE

Elephants are seen all over Sri Lanka, but very few of them count as wildlife, since these are the docile Indian variety which, unlike their African cousins, are easily trained and put to work. An elephant carrying a load is a common sight on rural roads.

But there are wild elephants on the island, along with more than 80 species of wild mammals including leopard, sloth, bear, porcupine, ant-eater, civet cat, jackal, mongoose, and many varieties of monkey.

The island boasts an abundance of birds —

Nuwara Eliya temple dancers. PHOTO: ELLEN RUDOLPH

and only six kilometres from the international airport.

The town has many quaint buildings dating back to the Dutch and Portuguese colonial days in the 16th and 17th centuries, swaying palm groves and a lagoon, all of which make it a wonderful subject for the keen photographer.

To the south of the capital is a stretch of 130 kilometres of unspoiled tropical beaches. It is a spectacular and seductive drive along the coast road, through palms — watch for the men on ropes high between some of the trees collecting the fermented *toddy* from their pots — with constant glimpses of the blue sea and white surf. This area is at its best from October to March, with the southwest monsoon bringing rain between May and July.

The first of the resorts you come to is **Kalutara**, followed by **Beruwala**, **Bentota**, **Induruwa**, **Kosgoda** and **Hikkaduwa**, the most popular with young travellers. All have excellent modern beach resorts, and at Hikkaduwa there is the added attraction of the coral reef, rich in tropical fish. Glass-bottomed boats, masks, snorkels and flippers can all be hired. A pamphlet on all the best diving sites round Sri Lanka, which include wrecks on the east coast, can be obtained from the Ceylon Tourist Board.

A short drive to the south of Hikkaduwa is the walled town of **Galle**, dating back to the 16th and 17th centuries and in many respects unchanged since then. With a beautiful natural harbour and spectacular views from the town walls, it lacks a beach or modern hotel, but can easily be reached for a day from one of the nearby resorts and should not be missed. For the more intrepid traveller, there is the remarkable **New Oriental Hotel** in a former Dutch colonial barracks — with plumbing of about the same era — and one of the most beautiful swimming pools in the world. The poll is set in a tumbling tropical garden and can be used and viewed by resident's only. The management here will arrange, on request, fascinating day trips to local fruit and palm plantations.

In **Weligama** bay is a perfect romantic house, built by a French nobleman, perched on what is still know as **Count de Mauny's Isle**. South again and you catch sight of the unique stilt fishermen perched just off the coast — but be prepared to pay them a tip before they will pose for you.

At **Dondra Head**, Sri Lanka's southernmost point, there is nothing but ocean between you and the South Pole. This is where most travellers turn north and inland to the highlands, but those who persevere will find their determination well rewarded.

The **East Coast**, which has the better weather between April and October, is still almost undeveloped for tourists. It offers a different but equally lovely aspect from the

day) in Colombo proceeds along the Beira Lake.
March: Easter is celebrated throughout the country.
April: Sinhala and Tamil New Year — the festive season for most Lankans, a time for visiting relatives, lighting firecrackers, observing auspicious times and giving gifts.
May: May Day (observed in Colombo). *Vesak* — this Buddhist festival of lanterns, which falls on the full-moon, marks the birth, enlightenment and *parinibbhana* (death) of the Lord Buddha.
June: *Poson* — this full-moon day, which commemorates the arrival of Buddhism to the island, is specially celebrated in the ancient capital of Anuradhapura.
June 30: special bank holiday — businesses are closed.
July-August: Esala Perahera in Kandy — the renowned parade of the sacred tooth relic in the hill capital lasts for 10 days. The Hindu Vel festival is celebrated in Colombo. The Kataragama Festival — held at Kataragama (450 kilometres south of Colombo) in homage to the god Skanda.
October-November: Prophet Muhammad's Birthday. Hindus celebrate Deepavali Festival Day.
December: Christmas celebrations and end-of-year parties.

PUBLICATIONS

For tourist information you can buy a copy of *Travel Lanka*, published by the tourist trade, at any tourist information centre. Or pick up a free copy of *Explore Sri Lanka*, a monthly trade magazine, available at the Explore Sri Lanka counter at the Colombo International Airport and at hotels. Both magazines are updated every month and contain comprehensive cuisine guides, shopping guides, information on nightlife and other activities in the country during the month.

Publications by the Ceylon Tourist Board, such as the *Accommodation Guidebook* and *Sri Lanka Official Tourist Handbook* are available at information centres. (The tourist board itself is located at Steuart Place, opposite the Hotel Oberoi, Colombo 3, Tel: 437059-60).

Colombo bookshops offer ample publications on the country's history, traditions, politics, civic life and the economy. Three well-known bookshops in Colombo are **Lake House Book Shop** (100 Sir Chittampalam Gardiner Mawatha, Colombo 2), **K.V.G. de Silva & Sons** (415 Galle Rd, Colombo 4) and **Vijitha Yapa Bookshop**, 376 Galle Rd, Colombo 3.

DISCOVERING SRI LANKA

COLOMBO

All visits to Sri Lanka start in **Colombo**, and the 32-kilometre drive in from the airport to the city centre is not one of the best introductions to any country. Built on the edge of the Indian Ocean, and still the country's major port, Colombo (say it ColUMbo, not ColOMbo) is a sprawling mass of city of 4,000,000, with all the attendant urban problems of pollution, noise and traffic jams.

Despite its open spaces, imposing 19th century government buildings and a few modern towers, Colombo is not one of the most attractive of cities, but is saved by the seafront and nature's other blessing — spectacular sunsets virtually every evening of the year. Most of the modern hotels are built with a view of the sea and the huge open public space along Galle Rd which, late every afternoon, is alive with Sri Lankans taking a stroll under a virtual umbrella of kites flown by a multitude of children.

Although most travellers, especially those on business, prefer these modern hotels, one of the great glories of Colombo, which has to be sampled even if only for tea or dinner, is the **Galle Face Hotel**, now 131 years old. Some may find its vast rooms and creaking lifts — soon to be modernized — not to their taste, but a meal on the verandah, accompanied by no sound but the constant pounding of the surf, is one of the world's great travelling experiences.

Somewhere else not to be missed before leaving the capital is the **Mount Lavinia Hotel**, some seven kilometres south of the city, with its vast terracotta-tiled terrace, seeming to hang over the waves.

Outside the capital, Sri Lanka has a panorama of treasures to offer, and one simply has to decide which to visit first and for how long. There are three basic attractions: The coast, the hill country and the ancient cities. Given a well-planned schedule, a visitor can easily take in all three in as little as two weeks, but three would be better.

THE COAST

If your time is short, the nearest place to visit from Colombo is the old fishing port of **Negombo**, 35 kilometres north of the capital